Microsoft®
BizTalk™
Server 2000

Documented

The official documentation—direct from the
BizTalk Server 2000 development team

PUBLISHED BY
Microsoft Press
A Division of Microsoft Corporation
One Microsoft Way
Redmond, Washington 98052-6399

Library of Congress Cataloging-in-Publication Data
Microsoft BizTalk Server 2000 Documented /Microsoft Corporation.
      p. cm.
   Includes index.
   ISBN 0-7356-1384-2
   1. Client/server computing. 2. Microsoft BizTalk. I. Microsoft Corporation.

  QA76.9.C55 M526   2001
  005.7'13769--dc21
                                       00-069527

Printed and bound in the United States of America.

2 3 4 5 6 7 8 9   QWT   6 5 4 3 2 1

Distributed in Canada by Penguin Books Canada Limited.

A CIP catalogue record for this book is available from the British Library.

Microsoft Press books are available through booksellers and distributors worldwide. For further information about international editions, contact your local Microsoft Corporation office or contact Microsoft Press International directly at fax (425) 936-7329. Visit our Web site at mspress.microsoft.com. Send comments to *mspinput@microsoft.com*.

Acquisitions Editor: Juliana Aldous
Project Editor: Maureen Williams Zimmerman

Part No. X08-03730

Principal Writers:

Morris Brown, Rick DeBroux, Jeff Deveaux, Doug Goodwin, John Hallows,
Syd Phillips, Cynthia Randall, Scot Vidican

Project Lead: Cynthia Randall

Documentation Manager: Eric Hansen

Lead Technical Writers: Sharon Lloyd, Cynthia Randall

Lead Programmer Writer: Scot Vidican

Lead Technical Editor: Jeff Deveaux

Production Lead: Scott Dines

Graphic Arts Lead: Curtis Christman

Technical Editor: Judy Nessen

Desktop Publisher: Cheryl Howlett

Production Specialist: Dave Swift

Graphic Artist: Scott Perrine

Localization: Max Parta

Technical Contributors:

Agarwal, Mukesh; Agrawal, Mahendra K.; Andrews, Anthony D.; Ballard, John D.;
Bhandarkar, Aditya G.; Bhaskara, Udaya K.; Chao, Lucy L.; Chkodrov, Gueorgui B.; Clark,
Wayne A.; Clawson, Dennis O.; Davis, Robert; Dial, Jim; Elien, Jean-Emile; Fong, David T.;
Gadwal, Dinesh; Goli, Naveen K.; Graber, Lee B.; Hall, Stephen C.; Ho, Ivan; Ibrahim,
Mohamed A.; Jason, Richard Z.; Kim, Byung Chan; Klein, Johannes; Kothari, Susmitha H.;
Kumar, Rajiv; Kumar, Vinod; Lake, Thomas R.; Lao, David Q.; LaSalle, Derek N.; Levanoni,
Yosseff; Levy, Marc; Lindberg, Lance E.; Lo, Wei-Lun; Lu, Yao; Luty, Andrew R.; Malhi,
Balinder S.; Marks, Lawrence R; Matsumoto, Scott; McCall, Kevin; McCrady, Donald J.;
Mehta, Bimal K.; Mital, Amit; Mitra, Kanchan; Myerson, Terry J.; Ng, Andrew; Nylin,
Bryan; Paul, Todd L.; Pogrebinsky, Vladimir; Posch, Johann; Putrevu, Suryanarayana V.;
Ramanathan, Anand C.; Sagar, Akash J.; Santa Maria Filho, Ivan; Schwarz, Lidia;
Sedghinasab, Zahra; Shaw, Sun H.; Shukla, Dharma K.; Sipos, Catalin; Sivakumar, A.S.;
Smith, Kevin B.; Sol, Alisson A.S.; Somasekaran, Anandhi; Sripathi Panditharadhya,
Nagalinga Durga Prasad; Sriram, Balasubramanian; Sundberg, Gregory G.; Swamy, Shekhar
N.; Teegan, Hugh A.; Thatte, Satish R.; Thurman, Darren C.; Tipton, Kelly S.; Torta,
Gianluca; Varlet, Laurence; Vedula, Nagender P.; Vedula, Ravi S.; Visintainer, James J.;
Wai, Man-Chun; Warden, Luanne; Wascha, Dave; White, Steve; Woodgate, Scott; Yang,
Wesley S.; Yildirim, Tolga

Contents

Introducing
Microsoft BizTalk Server 2000

A member of the Microsoft® .NET Enterprise Server family of products, Microsoft BizTalk™ Server 2000 unites, in a single product, enterprise application integration (EAI) and business-to-business integration. BizTalk Server 2000 enables developers, IT professionals, and business analysts to easily build dynamic business processes that span applications, platforms, and businesses over the Internet.

In addition to BizTalk Server 2000, Microsoft, with industry partners, has led innovation on enabling technologies that are necessary for Internet-based business solutions, including BizTalk Framework 2.0, which is a platform-independent, Extensible Markup Language (XML) framework for application integration and electronic commerce. BizTalk Framework 2.0 is not a standard, but it builds upon existing standards, such as the Simple Object Access Protocol (SOAP). SOAP is also a key technology in other members of the .NET product line, such as Microsoft Visual Studio® 7.0. BizTalk Framework 2.0 provides the basis for interoperable reliable messaging for BizTalk Server 2000.

For more information about BizTalk Framework 2.0, as well as information about BizTalk Server 2000 product resources such as community services, a large library of schemas, and white papers, go to the Microsoft BizTalk Server 2000 Web site (www.microsoft.com/biztalk).

Getting Started with BizTalk Server 2000

Microsoft BizTalk Server 2000 provides a powerful Web-based development and execution environment that integrates loosely coupled, long-running business processes, both within and between businesses. BizTalk Server can handle transactions that run as long as weeks or months, not just minutes or hours.

BizTalk Server 2000 features include the ability to design and use XLANG schedules; integrate existing applications; define document specifications and specification transformations; and monitor and log run-time activity.

The server provides a standard gateway for sending and receiving documents across the Internet, as well as providing a range of services that ensure data integrity, delivery, security, and support for the BizTalk Framework and other key document formats.

BizTalk Server Features

The following table provides information about BizTalk Server features and how to use them.

Feature	Function
Administration • Server Administration • Programmatic Administration	• Create and manage servers and server groups. • Configure global server group properties, such as the location for the Shared Queue database and the Tracking database. • Configure server settings. • Configure and manage receive functions. • View and manage document queues. • Programmatically access the XLANG Scheduler System Manager, group managers, XLANG schedule instances, and XLANG ports.
Document Tracking • Tracking Documents	• Track the progress of documents processed by Microsoft BizTalk Server 2000. • Search for, display, view, and save complete copies of any interchange or document processed by BizTalk Server 2000. • Create queries to extract essential information from the Tracking database in an easy-to-view format. • Extract, store, and analyze important user-defined data from within documents.
Orchestration Design • Designing BizTalk Orchestrations	• Create drawings that describe business processes, and programmatically implement these drawings within an integrated design environment. • Compile XLANG schedule drawings into XLANG schedules. • Define the flow of data between messages within business processes.
Messaging • Using BizTalk Messaging Manager • Accessing the BizTalk Messaging Configuration Object Model	• Manage the exchange of data locally or remotely using BizTalk Messaging Manager. • Manage the exchange of data programmatically using the BizTalk Messaging Configuration object model. • Create and manage channels, messaging ports, document definitions, envelopes, organizations, and distribution lists.
XML Tools • Creating Specifications • Mapping Data	• Create and manage specifications. • Create records and fields, and set their properties. • Map records and fields from a source specification to records and fields of a destination specification. • Use functoids to implement powerful data-transformation functionality.

BizTalk Services

Microsoft BizTalk Server 2000 provides a complete set of messaging and orchestration services that you can use to automate your business and data-exchange processes.

BizTalk Messaging Services

BizTalk Messaging Services include receiving incoming documents, parsing the documents to determine their specific format, extracting key identifiers and identifying specific processing rules, delivering documents to their respective destinations, and tracking documents. Also included are services for data mapping, receipt generation and correlation, and services to ensure data integrity and security.

Receive functions

BizTalk Server 2000 provides receive functions that enable the server to monitor documents posted at specified locations. BizTalk Server 2000 supports the following receive functions, which are configured by using BizTalk Server Administration:

- File
- Message Queuing

BizTalk Server 2000 also supports the following protocols, which are configured by using ASP pages or a Microsoft Exchange script:

- HTTP (by using an .asp page)
- HTTPS (by using an .asp page)
- SMTP (by using a Microsoft Exchange script)

Transport services

BizTalk Server 2000 provides transport services that enable the transmission of documents to their destinations. BizTalk Server 2000 supports the following transport services:

- HTTP
- HTTPS
- SMTP
- File
- Message Queuing
- Application integration components
- Loopback

Data parsers

BizTalk Server 2000 supports data parsers for a variety of industry document standards, such as ANSI X12, UN/EDIFACT, and valid, well-formed Extensible Markup Language (XML). BizTalk Server 2000 also supports BizTalk Framework 2.0. For more information about BizTalk Framework 2.0, go to the Microsoft BizTalk Server 2000 Web site (www.microsoft.com/biztalk/). Parser support for flat files is also available. You can also register and use your own custom parser components.

Data validation

BizTalk Server 2000 provides data validation by verifying each instance of a document against a specification. If the document does not adhere to the specification rules, the document is placed into a suspended queue for further analysis.

Reliable document delivery

BizTalk Server 2000 provides reliable document delivery by using configurable BizTalk Messaging Services properties. These properties include setting service windows for sending documents, sending or receiving receipts, setting the number of retries, and setting the time between retries. BizTalk Server 2000 supports the use of BizTalk Framework-compliant envelopes, which provide reliable messaging features. For more information about BizTalk Framework 2.0, go to the Microsoft BizTalk Server 2000 Web site (www.microsoft.com/biztalk/). BizTalk Server 2000 also queues documents to a central location. In the event of a server failure, rollover mechanisms enable new servers to take control of documents and process them.

Security

BizTalk Server 2000 supports encryption and digital signatures. Public-key encryption technology is supported for all documents that are transmitted by using BizTalk Server 2000 transport services. BizTalk Server 2000 also supports decryption and signature verification for the documents that it receives.

BizTalk Orchestration Services

BizTalk Orchestration Services include the integration of long-running business processes with the applications that run those business processes. This integration is provided by an executable business-process file called an XLANG schedule. Additional services provide control for running XLANG schedule instances.

A key feature of BizTalk Orchestration Services is the ability to handle complex transactions that run as long as weeks or months, not just minutes or hours. Another important feature is the ability to implement concurrent actions within a single XLANG schedule.

XLANG schedules

An XLANG schedule is a business process implemented by connecting each step in the process to a technology component or service that executes the step. An XLANG schedule is then run by a service called the XLANG Scheduler Engine. The engine controls the instantiation, execution, dehydration, and rehydration of an XLANG schedule, or multiple instances of one or more schedules.

Implementation technologies

Implementation technologies that are supported by BizTalk Orchestration Services include BizTalk Messaging Services, COM components, Message Queuing Services, and Windows Script Components.

XLANG language

XLANG is a language that describes the logical sequencing of business processes, as well as the implementation of the business process by using various technology components or services. The XLANG language is expressed in Extensible Markup Language (XML).

BizTalk Server Application Model

Microsoft BizTalk Server 2000 provides tools and services that enable you to create executable applications for controlling your business processes and the exchange of data between trading partners and applications within your business. For a list of the services provided by BizTalk Server 2000, see the previous section, "BizTalk Services."

Integrating BizTalk Orchestration Services and BizTalk Messaging Services enables you to control the exchange of documents and messages between your trading partners and internal applications by using multiple transport services. It also provides:

- Control over complex, long-running transactions and business processes.

- Reliable delivery of documents and messages.

- Data validation by verifying each document instance against a specification.

- Data mapping by using maps to transform document structure and format.

- Data security and integrity by using encryption and digital signature certificates.

- Receipt generation and correlation support.

BizTalk Server Administration Model

The following table describes the four main areas of administration in Microsoft BizTalk Server 2000 and relevant administrative functions of each area.

Area of administration	Administrative function overview
Server administration	• Configure and manage server groups and servers. • Configure and manage receive functions. • Manage queues.
Application administration	• Configure and manage the COM+ applications that host XLANG schedules. • Configure and manage the default XLANG Scheduler application.
Programmatic administration	• Configure XLANG system managers, XLANG group managers, XLANG schedule instances, and XLANG ports.

Database administration	• Configure, manage, and maintain the following databases:
	  • BizTalk Messaging Management
	  • Orchestration Persistence
	  • Tracking
	  • Shared Queue

Server administration

In BizTalk Server 2000, server administration includes tasks such as managing and configuring server groups, adding, deleting and configuring servers, adding and configuring receive functions, managing the Shared Queue for each server group, and so on. The following table describes the general server administrative tasks and provides descriptive information about each task.

Administrative task	Description
Configure servers and server groups	• Configure the connections for the Tracking and Shared Queue databases. • Configure transport services and parser order. • Configure server settings.
Manage queues	• Delete and resubmit interchanges and documents. • View data and error messages.
Manage receive functions	• Configure receive functions.
Troubleshooting	• Troubleshoot server and document processing problems.

Application administration

Application administration includes configuring and managing the COM+ applications that host XLANG schedules, the default XLANG Scheduler application, and the Orchestration Persistence database that is created when you install BizTalk Server 2000. The following table describes the general application administrative tasks and provides descriptive information about each task.

Administrative task	Description
Manage the default XLANG scheduler application	• Change the default settings for the XLANG Scheduler application.
Manage COM+ applications	• Create COM+ applications to run specific XLANG schedules.

Programmatic administration

The management and administration of servers and applications can be done programmatically. The following table describes the general programmatic administrative tasks and provides descriptive information about each task.

Administrative task	Description
Manage Queues	• View interchange and document data. • Change the BizTalk Messaging Management database. • Read from the Shared Queue database.
Configure and manage the XLANG Scheduler System Manager, group managers, XLANG schedule instances, and XLANG ports	• Start, stop, and retrieve information about the XLANG Scheduler System Manager and group managers. • Stop, suspend, resume, and retrieve information about all the schedules associated with a group.

Database management

In addition to regular database maintenance and administration, such as compressing data files and backing up the database and transaction file logs, you must perform other database-related tasks, such as maintaining connectivity between BizTalk Server and Microsoft SQL Server™, adding, deleting, and restoring databases, configuring new databases, and so on. The following table describes general database administrative tasks and provides descriptive information about each task.

Administrative task	Description
Manage databases	• Configure and/or change the BizTalk Messaging Management database.
	• Create and configure new persistence databases.
	• Restore and/or manually remove the Tracking and Shared Queue databases.
Monitor traffic to the databases	• Configure server settings.

Conventions Used in This Book

The following conventions are used throughout this book.

Convention	Indicates
	Note. Notes provide relevant information about a topic or procedure, but are not essential to the completion of a task.
	Important. Important notes provide information that is essential to the understanding of a topic or the completion of a task.
	Caution. Cautions advise that the failure to take or avoid a specific action could result in the loss of data.
	Shortcut. Shortcuts are available in the tutorial and enable you to save time and effort by using an existing XLANG schedule, a document specification, a map, or a configuration script. By using shortcuts, you can advance to subsequent sections of the tutorial. To use shortcuts, the components must be installed on drive C.
Italic text	Code variables and parameters.
Bold text	Interfaces, methods, objects, properties, and other common programming language elements; most user interface elements; and in procedures, anything that you must click or type explicitly as shown.

In addition to the previously listed conventions, the following Enterprise Edition bars denote the sections of this book that apply to the Enterprise Edition of BizTalk Server 2000. If you are using the Standard Edition of BizTalk Server 2000, information located within these bars does not apply to your installation; however, this information can provide valuable information to help you determine whether and when to upgrade your installation.

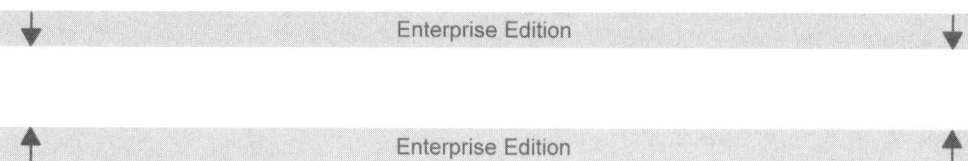

Part 1: Planning for Microsoft BizTalk Server 2000

This part describes how to install Microsoft BizTalk Server 2000 and discusses the hardware and software requirements of the application. In addition, there is information about the security methods used by BizTalk Server to ensure your data transactions are protected. You will also find in-depth information about how to optimize BizTalk Server for your environment, and learn what you need to know to configure various deployment scenarios.

In This Part

- **Installing BizTalk Server 2000.** This chapter provides the information that you need to complete your installation and explains the various options available to help you optimize BizTalk Server to best suit the needs of your organization.

- **Understanding Security.** This chapter describes how BizTalk Server 2000 addresses security by providing several authentication and encryption components that use Microsoft Windows® 2000 security services in addition to Microsoft SQL Server security, which protects the data stored in the databases.

- **Enhancing Performance and Scalability.** This chapter explains the various components of BizTalk Server 2000 and details several methods that you can use to increase the performance of BizTalk Server and create scalable, high-performance solutions.

- **BizTalk Server 2000 Deployment.** This chapter describes deployment configurations, explains why you might decide to implement each configuration, and offers guidelines for building them.

Installing Microsoft BizTalk Server 2000

If you have not yet installed Microsoft BizTalk Server 2000, this chapter provides you with the information that you need to complete your installation. There are several ways to install BizTalk Server. The method that you choose depends on the environment in which you are working. The decisions that you make during setup determine what features and options you can use when you run BizTalk Server 2000.

This chapter guides you through the setup process and discusses the various options available that help you to optimize BizTalk Server to best suit your needs. Specifically, the following installation options are available:

- **Complete Installation.** Enables you to perform a complete installation of BizTalk Server 2000 that includes all BizTalk services and tools.

- **Tools Installation.** Enables you to perform a complete installation of the BizTalk Server 2000 tools, including BizTalk Orchestration Designer, BizTalk Document Tracking, BizTalk Editor, and BizTalk Mapper. The BizTalk Server 2000 parser, serializer, correlation, and run-time binaries are not installed.

- **Custom Installation.** Enables you to perform a custom installation that includes any combination of BizTalk Server 2000 tools and services.

◆ Important

- A comprehensive set of BizTalk Server 2000 documentation is provided with this product. To use the documentation after you install BizTalk Server, click **Start**, point to **Programs**, point to **Microsoft BizTalk Server 2000**, and then click **BizTalk Server Documentation**.

- Prior to installing the software, it is strongly recommended that you review the Microsoft BizTalk Server 2000 Readme file, which contains important, late-breaking information about BizTalk Server 2000. The Readme also contains important information about the French, German, and Japanese versions of the product.

In This Chapter

- Hardware and Software Requirements
- Windows 2000 Prerequisites
- Installing SQL Server 7.0 or SQL Server 2000
- Installing Visio 2000 SR-1A
- Installation Instructions

Hardware and Software Requirements

This section includes information about minimum hardware requirements and configuration options to install Microsoft BizTalk Server 2000. In addition, you will find a list of software requirements.

Minimum Hardware Requirements

The minimum hardware requirements for a basic installation of Microsoft BizTalk Server 2000 include:

- An Intel® Pentium 300 processor.

- 128 megabytes (MB) of RAM.

- A 6-gigabyte (GB) hard disk.

- A CD-ROM drive.

- A network adapter card.

- A VGA or Super VGA monitor.

- A Microsoft Mouse or compatible pointing device.

Recommended Configuration to Optimize Performance for Document Messaging

The following are guidelines to help you achieve optimal performance with BizTalk Server 2000:

- Build a three-computer configuration. In a three-computer configuration, install BizTalk Server 2000 on one computer, install the Tracking database on a second computer, and install the BizTalk Messaging Management and Shared Queue databases on a third computer.

- For a configuration in which a single server is performing all processing and receiving functions, configure two BizTalk Server 2000 servers, one dedicated to processing and the other dedicated to receiving.

- Install the Tracking database on a computer with multiple physical hard disks. The optimal configuration includes four SCSI II hard disks and a SCSI II controller. The first hard disk is dedicated to document-tracking storage. The second hard disk is dedicated to the Microsoft Windows 2000 system page file. The third hard disk is dedicated to the Tracking transaction log. The fourth hard disk is dedicated to the Distributed Transaction Coordinator (DTC) log.

- Create multiple instances of receive functions to monitor multiple receive locations for documents that are to be processed. To balance the load of documents across several computers, locate the receive functions on separate computers. Each monitoring location must be unique and must have a separate receive function. To avoid overloading any individual receive function, the business application that sends documents must evenly distribute the documents to all the monitoring locations.

◈ Important

- For more information about performance enhancements to BizTalk Server, see Chapter 3, "Enhancing Performance and Scalability."

Software Requirements

The following table lists the software that must be installed to run BizTalk Server 2000.

Complete installation	Tools installation	Custom installation
Microsoft Windows 2000 Server, Microsoft Windows 2000 Advanced Server, or Microsoft Windows 2000 Professional with the NTFS file system and Service Pack 1	Microsoft Windows 2000 Server, Microsoft Windows 2000 Advanced Server, or Microsoft Windows 2000 Professional with the NTFS file system and Service Pack 1	Microsoft Windows 2000 Server, Microsoft Windows 2000 Advanced Server, or Microsoft Windows 2000 Professional with the NTFS file system and Service Pack 1
Microsoft Internet Explorer 5 or later	Microsoft Internet Explorer 5 or later	Microsoft Internet Explorer 5 or later
Microsoft Visio® 2000 SR-1A or later (required to use BizTalk Orchestration Designer)	Microsoft Visio 2000 SR-1A or later (required to use BizTalk Orchestration Designer)	Microsoft Visio 2000 SR-1A or later (required to use BizTalk Orchestration Designer)
Microsoft SQL Server 7.0 and SQL Server Service Pack 2 (SP2) or SQL Server 2000		Microsoft SQL Server 7.0 and SQL Server Service Pack 2 (SP2)* or SQL Server 2000
✐ Note	**✐ Note**	**✐ Note**
• BizTalk Messaging Manager will not run unless the World Wide Web Publishing Service is running.	• BizTalk Messaging Manager will not run unless the World Wide Web Publishing Service is running.	• BizTalk Messaging Manager will not run unless the World Wide Web Publishing Service is running.

*Microsoft SQL Server is required for a custom installation only if you install the core BizTalk services. It is not required for a tools installation.

◈ Important

- BizTalk Server 2000 can be installed on Microsoft Windows 2000 Server or Windows 2000 Advanced Server, with the NTFS file system. Microsoft

Internet Explorer 5 (or later) and Microsoft Visio 2000 SR-1 are required. In addition, the computer installed with BizTalk Server 2000 must have read/write access to a server(s) installed with Microsoft SQL Server 7.0 (SP2 or later) or Microsoft SQL Server 2000 under one of the following conditions:

- SQL Server must be installed on the same computer as BizTalk Server 2000.

  –Or–

- The computer that runs BizTalk Server 2000 must have read/write access to a remote computer(s) running SQL Server.

- If you plan to install BizTalk Server 2000 on a computer that has Microsoft Windows 2000 Professional with Service Pack 1, you must install SQL Server 7.0 and SQL Server Service Pack 2 (SP2) or SQL Server 2000 on another computer. Windows 2000 Professional does not support SQL Server 7.0 or SQL Server 2000 installations. When you install the databases for BizTalk Server 2000, you need to specify the name of the computer where you installed SQL Server 7.0 or SQL Server 2000.

Windows 2000 Prerequisites

Microsoft Windows 2000 Server, Microsoft Windows 2000 Advanced Server, and Microsoft Windows 2000 Professional with Service Pack 1 are the recommended platforms for all Microsoft BizTalk Server 2000 installations. Because BizTalk Server 2000 has been thoroughly tested on Windows 2000 with Service Pack 1, this installation guide includes detailed information regarding the necessary configuration of Windows 2000 Server, Windows 2000 Advanced Server, and Windows 2000 Professional in combination with BizTalk Server. After installing Windows 2000 Server, Advanced Server, or Professional with Service Pack 1, you must add a Windows 2000 user account to the Administrators group before you install any software. For more information, see "To add a user account to the Administrators group" later in this chapter. You must also install Message Queuing. For more information, see "To install Message Queuing" later in this chapter. If your installation does not include Service Pack 1, you must install it. For more information, see "To install Windows 2000 Service Pack 1" later in this chapter.

To install Windows 2000 Server, Advanced Server, or Professional with Service Pack 1

If Windows 2000 Server, Advanced Server, or Professional is installed on your computer, be sure that you meet the requirements listed in step 2:

1. Insert the Windows 2000 Server, Advanced Server, or Professional with Service Pack 1 compact disc into the appropriate drive.

   If you do not have a version of Windows 2000 that includes Service Pack 1, first install Windows 2000 and then install Service Pack 1 separately.

2. Run the Windows 2000 Server, Advanced Server, or Professional with Service Pack 1 Setup program and follow the online instructions.

Observe the following requirements:

- Use only alphanumeric characters in the computer name because Microsoft SQL Server supports a limited character set in server computer names.

- Format the partition with the Windows NT® File System (NTFS).

- On the **Windows 2000 Components** page, in the **Components** list, click **Message Queuing Services**. If you are installing Windows 2000 Professional, click **Internet Information Services (IIS)** and click **Next**. On the **Message Queuing Type** page, click **Next**.

- On the **Network Settings** page, click **Typical settings**.

Notes

- After installing Windows 2000 Server, Advanced Server, or Professional with Service Pack 1, you must add a Windows 2000 user account to the Administrators group before you install any software. For more information, see "To add a user account to the Administrators group" later in this chapter.

- If you did not select **Message Queuing Services** on the **Windows 2000 Components** page during setup, you must install it. For more information, see "To install Message Queuing" later in this chapter.

- If you did not select **Internet Information Services (IIS)** on the **Windows 2000 Components** page during setup of Windows 2000 Professional, you must install it. For more information, see "To install Internet Information Services (IIS)" later in this chapter.

- If your installation did not include Service Pack 1, you must install it. For more information, see the following procedure, "To install Windows 2000 Service Pack 1."

- The Windows 2000 Server, Advanced Server, or Professional partition must be converted to the most recent version of NTFS. Setup automatically performs this update if the existing file system is the old version of NTFS. If the existing partition is FAT or FAT32, you are given the option to convert to NTFS. When prompted, choose NTFS.

To install Windows 2000 Service Pack 1

1. Insert the Windows 2000 Service Pack 1 compact disc into the appropriate drive.

   You can also go to the downloads area of the Microsoft Windows 2000 Web site (www.microsoft.com/windows2000/) to download Windows 2000 Service Pack 1 or to order the compact disc.

2. Run the Windows 2000 Service Pack 1 Setup program and follow the online instructions.

To install Message Queuing

1. On the **Start** menu, point to **Settings** and click **Control Panel**.

2. Double-click **Add/Remove Programs**.

   The **Add/Remove Programs** dialog box appears.

3. Click **Add/Remove Windows Components**.

    The Windows Components Wizard opens.

4. In the **Components** list, select the **Message Queuing Services** check box and click **Next**.

5. On the **Message Queuing Type** page, click **Next**.

6. Click **Finish** to close the wizard.

✎ Note

- Accept the default settings when installing the Message Queuing Services component.

To install Internet Information Services (IIS)

1. On the **Start** menu, point to **Settings** and click **Control Panel**.

2. Double-click **Add/Remove Programs**.

    The **Add/Remove Programs** dialog box appears.

3. Click **Add/Remove Windows Components**.

    The Windows Components Wizard opens.

4. In the **Components** list, select the **Internet Information Services (IIS)** check box and click **Next**.

5. Click **Finish** to close the wizard.

To configure IIS settings for BizTalk Server 2000

To avoid problems accessing and saving specifications to the BizTalk Server 2000 repository, you must turn off the **Enable authoring** option in Internet Information Services (IIS):

1. On the **Start** menu, point to **Settings**, click **Control Panel**, double-click **Administrative Tools**, and then double-click **Internet Services Manager**.

2. Click the expand indicator (+) for the local IIS server.

3. Right-click **Default Web Site** and click **Properties**.

    The **Default Web Site Properties** dialog box appears.

4. Click the **Server Extensions** tab and clear the **Enable authoring** check box.

Setting Up User Accounts

If you are installing BizTalk Server 2000 for development purposes only, you can create a standard user account. For more information, see "To add a user account to the Administrators group." If you are installing BizTalk Server 2000 for production purposes, you should create a service account. For more information, see "To create a service account." If you do not create a service account, which is a regular user account with specific properties, BizTalk Server 2000 is automatically configured for the interactive user (the user who is currently logged on during the setup process). If BizTalk Server 2000 is set up with an interactive user, it fails if the specified user logs off from the server.

To add a user account to the Administrators group

1. Log on as Administrator.

2. On the **Start** menu, point to **Settings**, click **Control Panel**, double-click **Administrative Tools**, and then double-click **Computer Management**.

   The **Computer Management** dialog box appears.

3. In the console tree, click the expand indicator (+) for **Local Users and Groups**.

4. Click **Groups** and, in the details pane, double-click **Administrators**.

   The **Administrators Properties** dialog box appears.

5. Click **Add**.

6. In the **Look in** box, click your computer name.

7. In the text box that contains the text <<*Type names separated by semicolons or choose from list>>*, delete the text and type your domain and user name in the following format:

   Domain\user name

8. Click **OK**.

9. If necessary, on the **Enter Network Password** page, complete the following:

   • In the **Connect as** box, type your domain and user name in the following format:

     Domain\user name

   • In the **Password** box, type the password associated with your user name and click **OK**.

   • Click **OK** to close the **Administrators Properties** dialog box.

10. If necessary, restart the computer and log on using your domain user account.

To create a service account

1. Log on as Administrator.

2. On the **Start** menu, point to **Settings**, click **Control Panel**, double-click **Administrative Tools**, and then double-click **Computer Management**.

   The **Computer Management** dialog box appears.

3. In the console tree, click the expand indicator (+) for **System Tools** and click **Local Users and Groups**.

4. Click **Users**, right-click anywhere in the details pane, and then click **New User**.

   The **New User** dialog box appears.

5. In the **User name** box, type a name for the service account; in the **Password** box, type a password; and then type the same password in the **Confirm password** box.

6. Clear the **User must change password at next logon** check box, click **Create**, and then click **Close**.

7. Close the **Computer Management** dialog box.

8. On the **Start** menu, point to **Settings**, click **Control Panel**, double-click **Administrative Tools**, and then double-click **Local Security Policy**.

   The **Local Security Settings** dialog box appears.

9. In the console tree, click the expand indicator (+) for **Local Policies** and click **User Rights Assignment**.

10. In the details pane, double-click **Act as part of the operating system**, click **Add**, click the account name you just created from the list box, click **Add**, and then click **OK** twice.

11. Repeat steps 8 and 9 for the **Log on as a service** policy.

If BizTalk Server 2000 is already installed and using the interactive user account, complete the following steps after you have created a service account:

1. On the **Start** menu, point to **Settings**, click **Control Panel**, double-click **Administrative Tools**, and then double-click **Services**.

2. In the details pane, double-click **BizTalk Messaging Service**.

   The **BizTalk Messaging Service Properties (Local Computer)** dialog box appears.

3. Click the **Log On** tab and click **This account**.

4. Click **Browse**, locate the user account name you created, and double-click it.

5. In the **Password** box, type the same password you previously associated with the user account name; in the **Confirm Password** box, type the password again and click **OK**.

6. A message box appears; click **OK**.

7. Restart the computer.

Installing SQL Server 7.0 or SQL Server 2000

Prior to installing Microsoft BizTalk Server 2000, you must install Microsoft SQL Server 7.0 and SQL Server Service Pack 2 (SP2) or Microsoft SQL Server 2000. When you install BizTalk Server 2000, the installation procedure creates four BizTalk Server 2000 databases (the BizTalk Messaging Management database, the Shared Queue database, the Tracking database, and the Orchestration Persistence database) within SQL Server.

◆ **Important**

- If you plan to install BizTalk Server 2000 on a computer that has Microsoft Windows 2000 Professional with Service Pack 1, you must install SQL Server 7.0 and SQL Server Service Pack 2 (SP2) or SQL Server 2000 on another computer. Windows 2000 Professional does not support SQL Server 7.0 or SQL Server 2000 installations. When you install the databases for BizTalk Server 2000, you need to specify the name of the computer where you installed SQL Server 7.0 or SQL Server 2000.

Before you install SQL Server, verify that your logon account is a member of the Windows 2000 Administrators group on the computer on which you want to install SQL Server. For more information about adding your logon account, see "To add a user account to the Administrators group" earlier in this chapter.

If you install SQL Server 2000, you must specify mixed authentication. By default, when you install SQL Server 2000, the authentication mode is set to Windows 2000 only. BizTalk Server 2000 uses SQL Authentication to access the BizTalk Messaging Management, Shared Queue, and Tracking databases and does not work with this setting. Verify that you have the authentication mode set to mixed before installing BizTalk Server 2000. For more information, see "To set SQL authentication mode for SQL Server 2000" later in this chapter.

If you install SQL Server on a cluster and you plan to install BizTalk Server 2000 on another computer, you must install SQL Server client tools on the computer where BizTalk Server 2000 is installed. A cluster is a collection of servers that act as a single server. For more information, see "To install SQL Server client tools" later in this chapter. When complete, you must use the Client Network Utility to change the default network library from named pipes to TCP/IP. For more information, see "To change the default network library to TCP/IP" later in this chapter.

When you install SQL Server 7.0 or SQL Server 2000, it is important to use the correct collation settings. Collation refers to a set of rules that determines how data is sorted and compared. Character data is sorted using rules that define the correct character sequence, with options for specifying case sensitivity, accent marks, kana character types, and character width. For instance, to store Japanese characters, select case-sensitive sort order to distinguish Japanese-Hiragana from Japanese-Katakana when setting up SQL Server. For more information about collation settings, on the **Start** menu, point to **Programs**, point to **Microsoft SQL Server**, and then click **Books Online**. The topics "Using SQL Collation" and "Windows Collation Sorting Styles" provide additional information.

To install SQL Server 7.0 or 2000

1. Insert the Microsoft SQL Server compact disc into the appropriate drive.

2. Run the SQL Server Setup program and follow the online instructions.

   The setup wizard walks you through the steps necessary to install SQL Server, but you must observe the following requirements:

   - On the **Setup Type** page, click **Typical**.

   - On the **Services Accounts** page, use a domain user account (if connected to a network).

   - When installing SQL Server 2000, specify mixed authentication.

◈ **Important**

- If you install SQL Server 7.0, you must install SQL Service Pack 2 (SP2). You can check to see whether you have SP2 installed by using the Query Analyzer. For more information, see the following procedure, "To check for SQL Server 7.0 Service Pack 2." For more information about installing SQL SP2, see "To install SQL Service Pack 2 for SQL Server 7.0" later in this chapter.

To check for SQL Server 7.0 Service Pack 2

1. On the **Start** menu, point to **Programs**, point to **Microsoft SQL Server 7.0**, and then click **Query Analyzer**.

   The **Connect to SQL Server** dialog box appears.

2. Click **OK**.

   If your server name does not appear in the **SQL Server** list, select it from the list or type it in, and then click **OK**.

3. In the **Query** box, type **SELECT @@VERSION**.

4. On the **Query** menu, click **Execute**.

   The first line of the query return indicates the version of SQL Server that is running. If you have SP2 installed, you should see 7.00.842.

To install SQL Service Pack 2 for SQL Server 7.0

1. Insert the SQL Service Pack 2 compact disc into the appropriate drive.

2. Run the SQL Service Pack 2 Setup program and follow the online instructions.

To install SQL Server client tools

1. Insert the Microsoft SQL Server compact disc into the appropriate drive.

2. Run the SQL Server Setup program and follow the online instructions.

The setup wizard walks you through the steps necessary to install SQL Server, but you must observe the following requirements:

- On the **Installation Selection** page, click **Create a new instance of SQL Server, or install Client Tools**.

- On the **Installation Definition** page, click **Client Tools Only**.

To change the default network library to TCP/IP

1. On the **Start** menu, point to **Programs**, point to **Microsoft SQL Server 7.0** or **Microsoft SQL Server**, and then click **Client Network Utility**.

    The **SQL Server Client Network Utility** dialog box appears.

2. If you have installed Microsoft SQL Server 7.0, on the **General** tab, in the **Default network library** list, click **TCP/IP**.

    -Or-

    If you have installed Microsoft SQL Server 2000, on the **Network Libraries** tab, in the **Network Library** list, click **TCP/IP**.

3. Click **OK**.

To set SQL authentication mode for SQL Server 2000

1. Click **Start**, point to **Programs**, point to **Microsoft SQL Server**, and then click **Enterprise Manager**.

2. Click the expand indicator (+) for **Microsoft SQL Servers** and for **SQL Server Group**.

3. Right-click the name of your server and click **Properties**.

    The **SQL Server Properties** dialog box appears.

4. Click the **Security** tab, click **SQL Server and Windows**, and then click **OK**.

To verify that SQL Server is running

Before installing BizTalk Server 2000, verify that SQL Server is running on your server. This is necessary because BizTalk Server 2000 must create four SQL databases during installation.

1. On the **Start** menu, point to **Programs**, point to **Microsoft SQL Server** (if you installed SQL Server 2000) or **Microsoft SQL Server 7.0** (if you installed SQL Server 7.0), and then click **Service Manager**.

    The **SQL Server Service Manager** dialog box appears.

2. In the **Server** list, verify that the name of the server is the name of your computer.

    If it is not, click the drop-down arrow to view a list of available servers and scroll to locate your server.

3. In the **Services** list, click **MSSQLServer** (for SQL Server 7.0) or **SQL Server** (for SQL Server 2000).

4. Verify that the MSSQLServer or SQL Server service is running.

   The service is running if the **Start/Continue** button in the dialog box is unavailable. Also, at the bottom of the dialog box is a message that states that the service is running. For example, \\<servername>—MSSQLServer—Running.

5. If the service is not running, the **Start/Continue** button is available; click it to start the service.

To avoid unnecessary disk space allocation

1. Click **Start**, point to **Programs**, point to **Microsoft SQL Server 7.0** or **Microsoft SQL Server**, and then click **Enterprise Manager**.

2. Click the expand indicator (+) for **Microsoft SQL Servers**, **SQL Server Group**, **<server name>**, and **Databases**.

3. Right-click the BizTalk Messaging Management database and click **Properties**.

   The BizTalk Messaging Management database properties dialog box appears.

4. Click the **Options** tab.

5. In the **Settings** area, select the **Truncate log on checkpoint** and the **Auto shrink** check boxes and click **OK**.

   ### ✎ Note

   - If you have Microsoft SQL Server 2000 installed, you can only select the **Auto shrink** check box.

6. Repeat steps 3 through 5 for the Tracking and Shared Queue databases.

◆ Important

- You can complete this procedure only if you have BizTalk Server 2000 installed. For more information about installing BizTalk Server 2000, see "Installation Instructions" later in this chapter.

✎ Note

- During setup, the BizTalk Messaging Management database object name defaults to **InterchangeBTM**; the Tracking database object name defaults to **InterchangeDTA**; and the Shared Queue database object name defaults to **InterchangeSQ**. You might have renamed these default database object names during setup.

SQL Server and BizTalk Server 2000 Database Interactions

To avoid unnecessary disk space allocation, use the **Truncate log on checkpoint** and **Auto shrink** features of Microsoft SQL Server. Otherwise, the SQL Server logs can consume large amounts of disk space. For more information, see "To avoid unnecessary disk space allocation" earlier in this chapter.

Installing Visio 2000 SR-1A

Because BizTalk Orchestration Designer is a Microsoft Visio 2000-based user interface, you must have Visio 2000 Service Release 1A installed on your computer prior to using BizTalk Orchestration Designer. BizTalk Orchestration Designer has been tested with Visio 2000 Standard Edition SR-1A, and might work with later versions of Visio.

To install Visio 2000 Standard Edition SR-1A

1. Insert the Visio 2000 Standard Edition SR-1A compact disc (or a later version of Visio 2000 Standard Edition) into the appropriate drive.

2. Run the Visio 2000 Standard Edition SR-1A Setup program and follow the online instructions.

Note

- For more information, see the Microsoft Visio 2000 Standard Edition SR-1A documentation.

Installation Instructions

You can install Microsoft BizTalk Server 2000 using the Installation Wizard (Microsoft BizTalk Server.msi) or using Microsoft Windows Installer (Msiexec.exe). The Installation Wizard is a step-by-step process in which you select options that correspond to specific property values. The Microsoft Windows Installer allows you to specify property values from the command line. You can use this method to install BizTalk Server 2000 silently (without constant interaction or prompts). A silent installation of BizTalk Server 2000 is ideal for test scenarios or as part of a large-scale enterprise deployment. Regardless of which installation you perform, it is recommended that you maintain a record of the following information for later use:

- BizTalk Server group names
- SQL Server names
- User names
- Passwords

- The BizTalk Messaging Management database name

- The Tracking database name

- The Shared Queue database name

- The WebDAV repository URL

⚡ **Important**

- BizTalk Server 2000 requires Microsoft XML Parser version 3.0. This release of BizTalk Server 2000 automatically installs Microsoft XML (MSXML) Parser version 3.0. If you install other versions of the MSXML parser, it might cause unexpected results with BizTalk Server 2000.

📝 **Note**

- During BizTalk Server 2000 installation, the installation program determines the hard-disk space availability of your computer. A complete installation requires approximately 52 megabytes (MB), not including the requirements of the BizTalk Messaging Management database, the Tracking database, the Shared Queue database, and the Orchestration Persistence database. A tools installation requires approximately 30 MB of hard disk space. A custom installation requires approximately 2 to 52 MB of hard disk space, not including database requirements, depending on the services and tools that you install.

Before you run Setup, verify that your logon account is a member of the Windows 2000 Administrators group for the computer on which you are installing BizTalk Server 2000. For more information about joining the Administrators group, see "To add a user account to the Administrators group" earlier in this chapter.

📝 **Note**

- If BizTalk Server was installed using an interactive user, it will not start if a user is not logged on to BizTalk Server 2000. All COM+ packages run under an interactive user account, not the local system account. This means that the service starts only if a user is logged on to BizTalk Server 2000. For example, if a user is not logged on to BizTalk Server 2000 when a client application submits documents to BizTalk Server 2000 remotely, the service does not start. To avoid this situation, create a service account or have the user who starts the service lock the computer and keep the services running in the background. For more information about creating a service account, see "To create a service account" earlier in this chapter.

Complete Installation

You can use the following section to perform a complete installation of BizTalk Server 2000 that includes all BizTalk services, tools, and samples.

To perform a complete installation of BizTalk Server 2000

1. Insert the Microsoft BizTalk Server 2000 Setup compact disc into the appropriate drive.

2. Run the Microsoft BizTalk Server 2000 Setup program and follow the online instructions.

   ◆ **Important**

   - The setup wizard guides you through the steps necessary to install BizTalk Server 2000. You must observe the requirements listed in the following steps.

   - BizTalk Server 2000 requires Microsoft XML Parser version 3.0. This release of BizTalk Server 2000 automatically installs Microsoft XML (MSXML) Parser version 3.0. If you install other versions of the MSXML parser, it might cause unexpected results with BizTalk Server 2000.

3. On the **License Agreement** page, read the license agreement, click **I accept this license agreement**, and then click **Next**.

   ✎ **Note**

   - If you do not accept the license agreement, you cannot continue with the installation.

4. On the **Customer Information** page, type your name in the **User name** box, type the name of your company in the **Organization** box, click either **Anyone who uses this computer (all users)** or **Only for me** if you want to limit access to BizTalk Server 2000, and then click **Next**.

5. On the **Destination Folder** page, click **Next** to install BizTalk Server 2000 to the folder shown on the page, or click **Change** to select another location.

6. On the **Setup Type** page, click **Complete** and click **Next**.

7. On the **Configure BizTalk Server Administrative Access** page, in the **Group name** box, type the group name that you want to use (or accept the default, **BizTalk Server Administrators**).

   To create a group name, adhere to the following group naming restrictions:

   - The group name must be different from any other group or user name on this computer.

   - The group name cannot contain the following characters:

     ` ! @ # $ % ^ & * ( ) + = [ ] { } | \\ ;\" '< > , . ?

   - The group name cannot consist solely of periods (.) or spaces.

- Do not rename this group without also modifying the value of "AdminGroupName" in the Windows registry under HKEY_LOCAL_MACHINE\SOFTWARE\Microsoft\BizTalk Server\1.0\NTGroups. BizTalk Server 2000 relies on this registry key to find the group.

8. In the **Group description** box, type a new description for the group name or accept the default and click **Next**.

9. On the **Microsoft BizTalk Server Service Log On Properties** page, click the default setting, **Local system account**, or click **This account** to limit BizTalk Server 2000 access to a specific user.

   If you select **This account**, type a new user name or accept the default name in the **User name** box and type a valid password in the **Password** box.

   If you do not want BizTalk services to automatically start when setup completes, clear the **Start service after setup completes** check box. BizTalk services will not automatically start, but Orchestration Services will.

   📝 **Notes**

   - BizTalk Server setup grants **Log on as a service** and **Act as part of the operating system** rights to the account specified on the **Microsoft BizTalk Server Service Log On Properties** page.

   - If you select **This account**, specify an account that is in the Windows 2000 Administrators group. To configure certificates for the S/MIME components by using BizTalk Messaging Manager, you must belong to a user account in the Windows 2000 Administrators group, and BizTalk Messaging Services must be running as a local system account or as a user account in the Windows 2000 Administrators group.

10. Click **Next**.

11. On the **Ready to Install the Program** page, click **Install**.

    The BizTalk Server 2000 installation procedure might take several minutes.

12. When the **Welcome to the Microsoft BizTalk Server 2000 Messaging Database Setup Wizard** page appears, click **Next**.

    During BizTalk Server 2000 database setup, you are prompted for logon information (server, database, user name, and password) to configure the BizTalk Messaging Management, Tracking, and Shared Queue databases.

🐦 **Caution**

- Do not change the code, such as stored procedures or triggers, in the BizTalk Messaging Management, Tracking, and Shared Queue databases. Do not access the database directly. Do not directly call the stored procedures. Make all changes to the database by using the methods and properties of the BizTalk Messaging Configuration object model. Making changes to the database directly bypasses many constraints enforced by the BizTalk Messaging Configuration object model and either causes the server to function incorrectly or corrupts the database.

13. On the **Configure a BizTalk Messaging Management Database** page, click either **Create a new BizTalk Messaging Management database** or **Select an existing database** and type a server name and user information in the following text boxes:

- **Server name**

- **User name**

- **Password**

- **Database**

You can choose unique server and database names and type new information or accept the defaults.

◆ **Important**

- If you are installing BizTalk Server 2000 on a computer that has Microsoft Windows 2000 Professional with Service Pack 1, the **Server name** you specify must be the name of the computer where you installed Microsoft SQL Server 7.0 or Microsoft SQL Server 2000.

- If you select **Create a new BizTalk Messaging Management database** and choose an existing database, you should manually delete the contents of the database. For more information about deleting database content, on the **Start** menu, point to **Programs**, point to **Microsoft SQL Server**, and then click **Books Online**. To create a new database with the same name as an existing database on the same server, it is recommended that you manually delete the database content. BizTalk Server setup only verifies if a stored procedure required by the database exists, rather than verifying if all the variables required by the database exist. If a stored procedure exists, BizTalk Server setup does not modify the database. If the stored procedure does not exist, BizTalk Server setup deletes the database. Then it reinitializes the BizTalk Messaging Management database tables. The above-mentioned information is true for the Shared Queue and Tracking databases.

- If you set up more than one BizTalk Server installation and want to centrally manage the BizTalk Messaging Management database, it is highly recommended that you review information about BizTalk Server database interactions. For more information about configuring the database, see "Changing the BizTalk Messaging Management database" in Chapter 11, "Administering Servers and Applications."

14. Click **Next**.

15. On the **Configure a BizTalk Server Group** page, type the name that you want to use as your BizTalk Server group in the **Group name** box, or accept the default (**BizTalk Server Group**) and click **Next**.

    You can also click **Select an existing BizTalk Server group** and select a name from the **Group Name** list.

    🖉 **Note**

    - The group name cannot contain the following characters:

        ` ! @ # $ % ^ & * ( ) + = [ ] { } | \\ ;\" '< > , . ?

16. On the **Configure a Tracking Database** page, repeat the procedure in step 13 and click **Next**.

    ◆ **Important**

    - If you change the default **User name** on the **Configure a Tracking Database** page, the account that you specify must have SA-level permissions. This account is used to create a SQL Server user login. After installing BizTalk Server, change the account user name and password to remove SA-level access to the Tracking database by the BizTalk Server service. For more information, see "To configure connection properties for a server group" in Chapter 11, "Administering Servers and Applications." Or you can change the SA-level permission for the account used during setup. For more information about changing SQL Server account permissions, on the **Start** menu, point to **Programs**, point to **Microsoft SQL Server**, and then click **Books Online**.

17. On the **Configure a Shared Queue Database** page, repeat the procedure in step 13 and click **Next**.

18. On the **Verify BizTalk Server Group** page, verify that the information in the **BizTalk Server group properties** box is correct and click **Next**.

19. On the final page of the Microsoft BizTalk Server 2000 Messaging Database Setup Wizard, click Finish to complete the configuration of the BizTalk Messaging Management, Tracking, and Shared Queue databases.

20. On the **Welcome to the Microsoft BizTalk Server 2000 Orchestration Persistence Database Setup Wizard** page, click **Next** to install the Orchestration Persistence database.

☑ Note

- If you click **Cancel**, BizTalk Server 2000 is installed, but the Orchestration Persistence database and the Data Source Name (DSN) are not installed. You can install the database and the DSN later. For more information, see "To create a new persistence database" and "To configure the default XLANG Scheduler application" in Chapter 11, "Administering Servers and Applications," and "To configure a COM+ application to host XLANG schedules" in Chapter 8, "BizTalk Orchestration Services."

21. On the **Configure a default Orchestration Persistence Database** page, click either **Create a new default Orchestration Persistence database** or **Select an existing database**, choose a server name, and then type database information in the appropriate text boxes, or accept the defaults.

◈ Important

- If you select **Create a new default Orchestration Persistence database** and choose a database with the same name, on the same server, as an existing database, BizTalk Server setup deletes everything in the database. BizTalk Server setup then reinitializes the Orchestration Persistence database tables.

- If you are installing BizTalk Server 2000 on a computer that has Windows 2000 Professional with Service Pack 1, the **Server name** you specify is the name of the computer where you installed SQL Server 7.0 or SQL Server 2000.

☑ Notes

- The Orchestration Persistence database is created based on the current user log-on identity.

- To use SQL Server remotely, you must have the appropriate permissions set for the Orchestration Persistence database. If you have not reconfigured the identity for the XLANG Scheduler Engine, permissions are granted to the interactive user (the user who was logged on during installation of BizTalk Server 2000). If you have reconfigured the identity for the XLANG Scheduler Engine to match a service account you created or another unique user account, you must set permissions to match the reconfigured identity.

22. Click **Finish**.

23. On the final page of the Microsoft BizTalk Server 2000 Setup Wizard, click **View Readme** to read important, late-breaking information about BizTalk Server 2000, and then click **Finish**.

☞ Caution

- Do not change the impersonation level for any COM+ application. By default, it is set to Impersonate. Changing this security property to Anonymous, Identify, or Delegate might cause problems during installation.

◆ **Important**

- To dramatically increase the performance of BizTalk Orchestration Services, in Windows Explorer, browse to \Program Files\Common Files\System\ado and double-click adofre15.reg. In the confirmation dialog box, click **Yes** and then click **OK**. This procedure changes the ADO threading model from "Apartment threaded" to "Both" and might affect other applications that use ADO. Any provider that is not thread safe cannot be used.

📝 **Note**

- BizTalk Messaging Manager will not run unless the World Wide Web Publishing Service is running. For more information about the World Wide Web Publishing Service, see the following procedure, "To start the World Wide Web Publishing Service."

To start the World Wide Web Publishing Service

1. On the **Start** menu, point to **Settings**, click **Control Panel**, double-click **Administrative Tools**, and then double-click **Component Services**.

2. In the console tree, click **Services (Local)**.

3. In the details pane, right-click **World Wide Web Publishing Service** and click **Start**.

Install BizTalk Document Tracking Remotely

When BizTalk Document Tracking is installed from the BizTalk Server 2000 compact disc, a shortcut is created in the program group for BizTalk Server 2000 to access the BizTalk Document Tracking Web application. However, when BizTalk Document Tracking is installed over the Internet, you must manually create a shortcut or a favorite for later access to the Web application. Additionally, to prevent the display of security warning dialog boxes, you must manually configure your browser's settings to trust the Web application.

To configure Internet Explorer security settings

1. Click **Start**, point to **Programs**, and then click **Internet Explorer**.

2. On the **Tools** menu, click **Internet Options**.

   The **Internet Options** dialog box appears.

3. On the **Security** tab, click **Trusted Sites** and click the **Sites** button.

   The **Trusted Sites** dialog box appears.

4. In the **Add this Web site to the zone** box, type the location of the BizTalk Document Tracking server.

   To find the location of the BizTalk Document Tracking server, on the **Start** menu, point to **Programs**, point to **Microsoft BizTalk Server 2000**, and then click **BizTalk Document Tracking**. The location of the BizTalk Document Tracking server appears in the **Address** list.

5. Clear the **Require server verification (https:) for all sites in this zone** check box.

6. Click **Add** and click **OK** twice to close the dialog boxes.

Tools Installation

A Microsoft BizTalk Server 2000 tools installation enables you to install only BizTalk Orchestration Designer, BizTalk Document Tracking, BizTalk Editor, BizTalk Mapper, and BizTalk Server 2000 Help.

To perform a tools installation of BizTalk Server 2000

1. Insert the Microsoft BizTalk Server 2000 Setup compact disc into the appropriate drive and follow the on-screen instructions.

   ### ◈ Important

   - The setup wizard guides you through the steps necessary to install BizTalk Server 2000. Observe the requirements listed in the following steps.

2. On the **License Agreement** page, read the license agreement, click **I accept this license agreement**, and then click **Next**.

   ### ◈ Note

   - If you do not accept the license agreement, you cannot continue with the installation.

3. On the **Customer Information** page, type your name in the **User name** box, type the name of your company in the **Organization** box, click **Anyone who uses this computer (all users)** or **Only for me** if you want to limit access to BizTalk Server 2000, and then click **Next**.

4. On the **Destination Folder** page, click **Next**.

5. On the **Setup Type** page, click **Tools** and click **Next**.

6. On the **Ready to Install the Program** page of the Microsoft BizTalk Server 2000 Setup Wizard, click **Install**.

7. On the final page of the Microsoft BizTalk Server 2000 Setup Wizard, click **View Readme** to read important, late-breaking information about this release of BizTalk Server 2000.

8. Click **Finish** to complete the installation process.

◈ Important

- To dramatically increase the performance of BizTalk Orchestration Services, in Windows Explorer, browse to \Program Files\Common Files\System\ado and double-click adofre15.reg. In the confirmation dialog box, click **Yes** and then click **OK**. This procedure changes the ADO threading model from "Apartment threaded" to "Both" and might affect other applications that use ADO.

☑ **Note**

- To install the BizTalk Server 2000 interchange component on a remote computer, use the Windows 2000 COM Application Export Wizard:

  1. On the **Start** menu, point to **Settings**, click **Control Panel**, double-click **Administrative Tools**, and then double-click **Component Services**.

  2. In the console tree, expand **Component Services**, **Computers**, **My Computer**, and **COM+ Applications**.

  3. Right-click **BizTalk Server Interchange Application** and click **Export**.

     Follow the on-screen instructions to create an .msi file that you can run on a client computer.

Custom Installation

A custom Microsoft BizTalk Server 2000 installation enables you to install all the features of BizTalk Server 2000 or only those features that you want.

☑ **Note**

- If you want to install the server components of BizTalk Server 2000, you must first install Microsoft SQL Server. For more information, see "To install SQL Server 7.0 or 2000" earlier in this chapter.

To perform a custom installation of BizTalk Server 2000

1. Insert the Microsoft BizTalk Server 2000 Setup compact disc into the appropriate drive and follow the on-screen instructions.

   ◆ **Important**

   - The setup wizard guides you through the steps necessary to install BizTalk Server 2000. You must observe the requirements listed in the following steps.

2. On the **License Agreement** page, read the license agreement, click **I accept this license agreement**, and then click **Next**.

   ☑ **Note**

   - If you do not accept the license agreement, you cannot continue with the installation.

3. On the **Customer Information** page, type your name in the **User name** box, type the name of your company in the **Organization** box, click **Anyone who uses this computer (all users)** or **Only for me** if you want to limit access to BizTalk Server 2000, and then click **Next**.

4. On the **Destination Folder** page, click **Next**.

5. On the **Setup Type** page, click **Custom** and click **Next**.

6. On the **Custom Setup** page, follow the on-screen instructions to select the BizTalk Server 2000 components that you want to install.

   To perform a different type of installation, click **Back**. Otherwise, click **Next**. Additional pages appear on which you provide additional information, depending on the installation components that you have selected.

7. On the **Ready to Install the Program** page, click **Install**.

   The BizTalk Server 2000 custom installation procedure might take a few minutes.

8. On the final page of the Microsoft BizTalk Server 2000 Setup Wizard, click **View Readme** to read important, late-breaking information about this release of Microsoft BizTalk Server 2000.

9. Click **Finish** to complete the installation process.

◆ Important

- BizTalk Messaging Manager will not run unless the World Wide Web Publishing Service is running. To start the World Wide Web Publishing Service:

  1. On the **Start** menu, point to **Settings**, click **Control Panel**, double-click **Administrative Tools**, and then double-click **Component Services**.

  2. In the console tree, click **Services (Local)**.

  3. In the details pane, right-click **World Wide Web Publishing Service** and click **Start**.

- To dramatically increase the performance of BizTalk Orchestration Services, in Windows Explorer, browse to \Program Files\Common Files\System\ado and double-click adofre15.reg. In the confirmation dialog box, click **Yes** and then click **OK**. This procedure changes the ADO threading model from "Apartment threaded" to "Both" and might affect other applications that use ADO.

Silent Installation

The Microsoft Windows Installer allows you to specify property values from the command line. This method gives you the ability to install Microsoft BizTalk Server 2000 silently (without constant interaction or prompts). A silent installation of BizTalk Server 2000 is ideal for test scenarios or as part of a large-scale enterprise deployment.

To perform a silent installation of BizTalk Server 2000

1. Click **Start** and click **Run**.

2. In the **Open** box, type **cmd** and click **OK**.

3. Type the following to install BizTalk Server 2000 silently:

```
msiexec /I "\\server\folder\Microsoft BizTalk Server.msi"
/qb /Lv* "C:\Temp\install.log" INSTALLLEVEL=200
ALLUSERS=1
PIDKEY="your 25-character product key (without dashes)"
DSNCONFIG="C:\Temp\BizTalkInstall.ini"
```

❖ **Important**

- You must add the ALLUSERS=1 parameter to complete the installation for all users. This parameter also ensures that the services are able to see the registry settings.

✏ **Notes**

- In the preceding code:

  - /I is the command line to install or configure a product.

  - /qb is the command line to present a basic user interface (progress bar only).

  - /Lv* produces a log file.

  - INSTALLLEVEL=200 installs the server. If you do not specify the INSTALLLEVEL, the value defaults to 100, which is the Tools installation of BizTalk Server 2000.

  - PIDKEY="your 25-character product key (without dashes)" is the product key. For example, PIDKEY=**AB6CDEFGH7IJK8LMN45LLTT34.**

  - DSNCONFIG="C:\Temp\BizTalkInstall.ini" provides installation information to the setup wizard.

You can specify various options at the command line to set properties for a BizTalk Server 2000 installation. Unspecified properties take on the default values. The properties unique to BizTalk Server 2000 are listed in the following table.

Public property	Value	Description
USERNAME (built-in installer property)	\<name\> Default: {LogonUser}	The name of the user performing the installation. **Customer Information** dialog box; **User name** edit box.
COMPANYNAME (built-in installer property)	\<organization\> Default: {LogonCompany}	The organization name for the user performing the installation. **Customer Information** dialog box; **Organization** edit box.
PIDKEY	\<product-id\> Default: ""	The CD-key of the form ###-####### for the product. **Customer Information** dialog box; **Serial number** masked edit box.
INSTALLLEVEL (built-in installer property)	\<install level\> Default: 100	The feature installation level. For BizTalk Server 2000 setup, 100=Client and 200=Server setup type.
INSTALLDIR (built-in installer property)	\<install path\> Default: "{ProgramFiles}\Microsoft BizTalk Server"	The destination folder for the installation.
BTS_GROUP_NAME (Complete installation only)	\<Group Name\> Default: "BTSAdmin"	The name of the BizTalk Server 2000 Windows NT group. **ConfigAdminGroup** dialog box; **Group name** edit box.
BTS_GROUP_DESCRIPTION (Complete installation only)	\<Group Description\> Default: "Members can fully administer Microsoft BizTalk Server"	The description of the BizTalk Server 2000 Windows NT group. **ConfigAdminGroup** dialog box; **Group description** edit box.
BTS_USERNAME (Complete installation only)	\<username\> Default: ""	The logon DOMAIN\name for the BizTalk Server 2000 service. **ConfigServiceLogon** dialog box; **User name** edit box.
BTS_PASSWORD (Complete installation only)	\<password\> Default: ""	The logon password for the BizTalk Server 2000 service. **ConfigServiceLogon** dialog box; **Password** edit box.
BTS_SERVER (Complete and Tools installation)	\<servername\> Default: "localhost"	The name of the BizTalk Server to remotely administer. **ConfigMgmtDesk** dialog box; **Server name** edit box.
BTS_SDK_SERVER (Complete and Tools installation)	\<servername\> Default: ""localhost""	The name of the BizTalk Server to use for DCOM. **ConfigSDK** dialog box; **Server name** edit box.
DSNCONFIG (initialization file)	\<pathname\> Default: ""	The path of the initialization file for the BTSsetupDB.exe and XLANGsetupDB.exe database setup wizards to use.

📝 Notes

- The DSNCONFIG property is required to complete a silent installation of BizTalk Server 2000. The initialization path file listed on the command line is passed to the BTSsetupDB.exe and XLANGsetupDB.exe database setup wizards. Use one of the following command-line values:

  - DSNCONFIG="Full path to .ini file for BTSsetupDB.exe and XLANGsetupDB.exe"

    -Or-

  - BTSSETUPDB.INI="Full path to .ini file for BTSsetupDB.exe" and XLANGSETUPDB.INI="Full path to .ini file for XLANGsetupDB.exe"

- The database setup wizard processes the contents of the initialization file using these rules:

  - All [sections] and keys= are optional; if a key is absent, the default value as shown in the sample initialization file is used.

  - If the GroupName exists in the specified BizTalk Messaging Management database, the [InterchangeDTA] and the [InterchangeSQ] sections are ignored since the group defines the values.

  - Specified databases are created if they do not already exist on the specified server.

- The BizTalk Messaging Management database setup and the Orchestration Persistence database setup are mutually independent.

- Depending on the features you install, setup configures either, neither, or both of the following:

  - BizTalk Messaging Management database—only configured if BizTalk Messaging Services and its associated components are installed.

  - Orchestration Persistence database—only configured if Orchestration Service is installed.

- The following properties are used on the command line:

  - DSNCONFIG—specifies the location of the .ini file to be used by BTSsetupDB.exe and XLANGsetupDB.exe

    -Or-

    BTSSETUPDB.INI—specifies the location of the .ini file to be used by BTSsetupDB.exe

  - XLANGSETUPDB.INI—specifies the location of the .ini file to be used by XLANGsetupDB.exe

Sample initialization file with all [sections], keys=, and default values shown

The following is an example of the format of an .ini file needed to silently install
BizTalk Server 2000. These command-line properties are required to perform a first-time
installation of BizTalk Server 2000 using the Windows Installer.

Example SetupDB.ini

```
;---------------------------------------------------------------------------
; SQL Server connection parameters for BizTalk Messaging Management database
; Required section used by BTSsetupDB.exe only.
; Specify new or existing database.
;
[InterchangeBTM]
Server=localhost
Username=sa
Password=
Database=InterchangeBTM

;---------------------------------------------------------------------------
; Name for BizTalk Server Group
; Required section used by BTSsetupDB.exe only.
; Specify new or existing server group.
;
[Group]
GroupName=BizTalkGroup

;---------------------------------------------------------------------------
; SQL Server connection parameters for BizTalk Tracking database
; Required section used by BTSsetupDB.exe only.
; Optional if existing server group specified.
;
[InterchangeDTA]
Server=localhost
Username=sa
Password=
Database=InterchangeDTA

;---------------------------------------------------------------------------
;
[InterchangeSQ]
Server=localhost
Username=sa
Password=
Database=InterchangeSQ

;---------------------------------------------------------------------------
```

```
; SQL Server connection parameters for Orchestration database
; Required section used by XLANGsetupDB.exe only.
; Specify new or existing Orchestration database.
;
[Orchestration]
Server=localhost
Database=XLANG
```

The following table describes the properties and values of the sample BizTalkDB.ini initialization file.

Property	Value	Description
[InterchangeBTM]	Server=BIZTALK	Log on to this first SQL Server with default user name and password. `Database=BizTalkBTM` Create this BizTalk Messaging Management database if it does not already exist on the server.
[Group]	GroupName=BizTalkServerGroup	The rest of the values are ignored if this group already exists.
[InterchangeDTA]	Server=DTA-SERVER	Log on to this second SQL Server with default user name and password. `Database=BizTalkDTA` Create this Tracking database if it does not already exist on the server.
[InterchangeSQ]	Server=SQ-SERVER	Log on to this third SQL Server with default user name and password. `Database=BizTalkSQ` Create this Shared Queue database if it does not already exist on the server.
[Orchestration]	Server=localhost	Log on to this fourth SQL Server with default user name and password. `Database=Orchestration` Create this XLANG database if it does not already exist on the server.

Command-line options of Microsoft Windows Installer

Microsoft Windows Installer (Msiexec.exe) is the program that interprets packages and installs products. It also sets an error level on return that corresponds to the Microsoft Win32® error codes. The following table describes command-line options for this program that you can use in addition to the properties and values listed previously.

Option	Parameters	Meaning
/I	Package|ProductCode	Installs or configures a product.
/f	[p|o|e|d|c|a|u|m|s|v] Package|ProductCode	Repairs a product. This option ignores any property values entered on the command line. The default argument list for this option is pecms. This option shares the same argument list as the REINSTALLMODE property. p - Reinstall only if file is missing. o - Reinstall if file is missing or if an older version is installed. e - Reinstall if file is missing or an equal or older version is installed. d - Reinstall if file is missing or a different version is installed. c - Reinstall if file is missing or the stored checksum does not match the calculated value. Repairs only files that have msidbFileAttributesChecksum in the Attributes column of the File table. a - Force all files to be reinstalled. u - Rewrite all required user-specific registry entries. m - Rewrite all required computer-specific registry entries. s - Overwrite all existing shortcuts. v - Run from source and recache the local package.
/a	Package	Administrative installation option. Installs a product on the network.
/x	Package|ProductCode	Uninstalls a product.
/j	[u|m]Package or [u|m]Package /t Transform List or [u|m]Package /g LanguageID	Advertises a product. This option ignores any property values entered on the command line. u - Advertise to the current user. m - Advertise to all users of the computer. t - Apply transform to advertised package. g - Language ID.

Option	Parameters	Meaning
/L	[i|w|e|a|r|u|c|m|o|p|v|+|!]Logfile	Specifies the path to a log file; the flags indicate which information to log. i - Status messages w - Nonfatal warnings e - All error messages a - Startup of actions r - Action-specific records u - User requests c - Initial UI parameters m - Out-of-memory or fatal exit information o - Out-of-disk-space messages p - Terminal properties v - Verbose output + - Append to existing file ! - Flush each line to the log "*" - Wildcard; log all information except the v option. To include the v option, specify "/l*v".
/m	filename	Generates a Systems Management Server (SMS) status .mif file. Must be used with the install (-i), remove (-x), administrative installation (-a), or reinstall (-f) option. The Ismif32.dll file is installed as part of SMS and must be on the path. The fields of the status .mif file are filled with the following information: Manufacturer - Author Product - Revision number Version - Subject Locale - Template Serial Number - Not set Installation - Set by Ismif32.dll to "DateTime" InstallStatus - "Success" or "Failed" Description - Error messages in the following order: 1) Error messages generated by installer; 2) Resource from Msi.dll if installation could not commence or user exits; 3) System error message file; 4) Formatted message: "Installer error %i", where %i is the error returned from Msi.dll.
/p	PatchPackage	Applies a patch. To apply a patch to an installed administrative image, you must combine options as follows: /p <PatchPackage> /a <Package>

Option	Parameters	Meaning
/q	n|b|r|f	Sets the user interface level. q, qn - No UI. qb - Basic U. qr - Reduced UI with a modal dialog box displayed at the end of the installation. qf - Full UI with a modal dialog box displayed at the end. qn+ - No UI except for a modal dialog box displayed at the end. qb+ - Basic UI with a modal dialog box displayed at the end. The modal dialog box is not displayed if the user cancels the installation. qb- - Basic UI with no modal dialog boxes. /qb+- is not a supported UI level.
/? or /h		Displays copyright information for the Windows Installer.
/y	module	Calls the system API DllRegisterServer to self-register modules passed in on the command line. For example, msiexec /y my_file.dll. This option is used only for registry information that cannot be added using the registry tables of the .msi file.
/z	module	Calls the system API DllUnRegisterServer to unregister modules passed in on the command line. For example, msiexec /z my_file.dll. This option is used only for registry information that cannot be removed using the registry tables of the .msi file.

Notes

- In the preceding table:

  - The options /i, /x, /f[p\|o\|e\|d\|c\|a\|u\|m\|s\|v], /j[u\|m], /a, /p, /y, and /z should not be used together. The one exception to this rule is that patching an administrative installation requires using both /p and /a.

  - The options /t and /g should be used only with /j.

  - The options /l and /q can be used with /i, /x, /f[p\|o\|e\|d\|c\|a\|u\|m\|s\|v], /j[u\|m], /a, and /p.

Syntax rules for properties and values

Only public properties can be modified using the command line. All property names on the command line are interpreted as uppercase, but the value retains case sensitivity. If you type MyProperty at a command line, the installer overrides the value of MYPROPERTY and not the value of MyProperty in the Property table. To install a product with PROPERTY set to

VALUE, use the following syntax on the command line. You can put the property anywhere except between an option and its argument.

Correct syntax:

```
msiexec /i A:\Example.msi PROPERTY=VALUE
```

Incorrect syntax:

```
msiexec /i PROPERTY=VALUE A:\Example.msi
```

Property values that are literal strings must be enclosed in quotation marks. Include any white spaces in the string between these marks.

```
msiexec /i A:\Example.msi PROPERTY="Embedded White Space"
```

To clear a public property using the command line, set its value to an empty string.

```
msiexec /i A:\Example.msi PROPERTY=""
```

For sections of text set apart by literal quotation marks, enclose the section with a second pair of quotation marks.

```
msiexec /i A:\Example.msi PROPERTY="Embedded ""Quotes"" White Space"
```

The following is an example of a complicated command line.

```
msiexec /i testdb.msi INSTALLLEVEL=3 /l* msi.log COMPANYNAME="Acme ""Widgets"" and
""Gizmos."""
```

The following example illustrates advertisement options. Switches are not case sensitive.

```
msiexec /JM msisample.msi /T transform.mst /G langid /LIME logfile.txt
```

For more information about Microsoft Windows Installer, go to the MSDN® Downloads Web site (msdn.microsoft.com/downloads/).

Removing BizTalk Server 2000

Use the Microsoft Windows 2000 Add/Remove Programs utility to remove Microsoft BizTalk Server 2000.

To remove BizTalk Server 2000

1. On the **Start** menu, point to **Settings** and click **Control Panel**.

2. Click **Add/Remove Programs**.

   The **Add/Remove Programs** dialog box appears.

3. Click **Microsoft BizTalk Server 2000** and click **Remove**.

4. Follow the on-screen instructions and click **Yes** when prompted to remove BizTalk Server 2000.

CHAPTER 2

Understanding Security

Microsoft BizTalk Server 2000 enables businesses to securely exchange data with trading partners. BizTalk Server takes advantage of the security features offered through Microsoft Windows 2000 and Microsoft SQL Server security.

Windows 2000 security features include the following:

- Public-key infrastructure
- Microsoft Component Services
- Microsoft Cryptography API
- Smart Cards
- Kerberos Protocol

Public-key certificate management includes requesting certificates, processing certificates in a certificate-request response, and exchanging certificates with trading partners. These certificates are available for both digital signature and encryption. Exchanging certificates provides a method of securing data with trading partners. However, as a business grows, the process of managing certificates can be time-consuming.

Because BizTalk Server takes advantage of Windows 2000 security features, such as Secure Sockets Layer (SSL), Web pages can be created and used by trading partners to securely exchange data using the Internet. SSL, which is implemented in Internet Information Services (IIS), is a protocol designed to provide privacy between a Web client and a Web server. The protocol begins with a handshake phase that negotiates an encryption algorithm, checks the keys (public and private), and authenticates the server to the client. Once the handshake is complete and application data transmission begins, all data is encrypted using the session keys negotiated during the handshake. Support for open PKI (public-key infrastructure) standards and secure protocols, such as IPSec, L2TP, SSL/TLS, and S/MIME, enables a network to be extended to suppliers and partners quickly, while protecting against impostors, data theft, or malicious hackers.

Component Services, one of Windows 2000 Administrative Tools, offers comprehensive component functionality, such as automatic transaction support for data-integrity protection and simple, but powerful, role-based security.

In This Chapter

- BizTalk Server 2000 Setup and Configuration

- Transport Services

- Security for Applications That Host XLANG Schedule Instances

- Certificates Overview

- Crypto API

- Collaborative Data Objects

BizTalk Server 2000 Setup and Configuration

Trading partner transactions must be secure. Microsoft BizTalk Server 2000 addresses security by providing several authentication and encryption components that leverage Microsoft Windows 2000 security services. In addition to Windows 2000 security, BizTalk Server also takes advantage of Microsoft SQL Server security. To keep data secure in the BizTalk Messaging Management database, BizTalk Server relies primarily on SQL Server login security. However, the default BizTalk Orchestration Persistence database relies on Windows 2000 authentication. When creating a COM+ component that hosts schedule instances and its persistence database, you can choose whether to use SQL Server authentication or Windows 2000 authentication. In addition, the administration console uses the Windows Management Instrumentation (WMI) available in Windows 2000 security.

Logon Properties

Logon properties are the initial layer of security for BizTalk Server 2000. These properties control a user's ability to log on to a specific computer. Logon properties require a user to provide a user name and password prior to accessing resources, such as a file share or message queue. Messages received through HTTP and SMTP also use logon properties to ensure security. For example, an ASP page accessed through HTTP would require a user to enter a user name and password prior to displaying the contents of the Web page.

BizTalk Server uses Internet Information Services (IIS) and ASP pages for its receive functions. ASP pages (actually the code behind the pages) provide a layer of security for BizTalk Server by verifying signatures from Secure Sockets Layer (SSL) and maximizing additional security, such as certificates, through IIS. For more information about IIS security, see Internet Information Services in Windows 2000 Help.

Local Policies

Local Policies, which is part of the Local Security Settings console, determine the security options for a user or service account. Local policies are based on the computer a user is logged on to, and the rights the user has on that particular computer. To set local policies, on the **Start** menu, point to **Settings**, click **Control Panel**, double-click **Administrative Tools**, double-click **Local Security Policy**, and then expand the **Local Policies** folder.

Local policies define the privileges and rights for BizTalk Server 2000 users. Local policies can be used to configure:

- **Audit policy.** Determines which security events are logged into the Security log on the computer (successful attempts, failed attempts, or both). (The Security log is part of Event Viewer.)

- **User rights assignment.** Determines which users or groups have logon or task privileges on the computer.

- **Security options.** Enables or disables security settings for the computer, such as digital signing of data, Administrator and Guest account names, floppy drive and CD ROM access, driver installation, and logon prompts.

Other policies in the Local Security Settings console can be configured to maintain the integrity of your data. For example, Account Policies can be used to configure:

- **Password policy.** For local user accounts, determines settings for passwords such as enforcement, and lifetimes.

- **Account lockout policy.** For local user accounts, determines when and for whom an account will be locked out of the system.

◆ Important

- Local policies, by definition, are local to a computer. When these settings are imported to a Group Policy object in Active Directory, they affect the local security settings of any computer accounts to which that Group Policy object is applied. Therefore, it is important to note the order of precedence for security policies. Security policies associated with Group Policy (Organizational Units) override policies established at the local level. Policies from the domain override locally defined policies. In either case, user account rights might no longer apply if there is a local policy setting that overrides those privileges. This is important because the behavior of Microsoft Windows 2000 can be quite different from the behavior in Microsoft Windows NT. For example, when password policies are configured for the Domain group policy (as they are by default), they affect every computer in that domain. This means that the local account databases (on individual workstations) in the domain have the same password policy as the domain itself.

☑ Note

- Do not set Local Policies for public keys. Public keys provide security protection for BizTalk Server. Public keys are a component of certificates that are used to encrypt and decrypt data. If you add additional policies to a public key, BizTalk Server will not be able to use the associated certificate.

Using a Service Account

A service account is similar to an interactive user account because they both enable a user to access computer and/or network resources. A service account is a regular user account with specific properties that allow it to act as part of the operating system, whereas an interactive user account refers to the user currently logged on during the BizTalk Server 2000 setup process.

If the identity is set to interactive user, the application runs only when a user is logged on. Therefore, if BizTalk Server is set up with an interactive user account, it fails if the specified user logs off from the server. Choosing interactive user identity, though, carries security risks, because the application runs under the identity of the logged-on user without that user's knowledge or consent. For instance, if the application is running on a computer while an administrator is logged on, the application runs under the administrator's identity, potentially making calls as such on behalf of clients.

If the identity is set to a service account, it can act as part of the operating system and allow users to access applications on a server even when the user is not logged on to the computer.

For more information about service accounts, see "To create a service account" in Chapter 1, "Installing BizTalk Server 2000."

Submitting Work Items

Controlling a user's ability to send work items to BizTalk Server 2000 can be accomplished using the BizTalk Server Interchange Application COM+ component. The BizTalk Server Interchange Application COM+ component uses the following security configuration properties:

- Authentication level
- Impersonation level
- Access permissions
- Launch permissions
- Configuration permissions

To control a user's ability to send work items, a role must first be added to the BizTalk Server Interchange Application, which is one of the COM+ applications, and then associate the role with the **Submit** and **SubmitSync** methods.

To add a role to the BizTalk Server Interchange Application

1. On the **Start** menu, point to **Settings**, click **Control Panel**, double-click **Administrative Tools**, and then double-click **Component Services**.

   The Component Services console appears.

2. Expand **Component Services**, **Computers**, **My Computer**, and **COM+ Applications**.

3. Right-click **BizTalk Server Interchange Application** and click **Properties**.

   The **BizTalk Server Interchange Application Properties** dialog box appears.

4. Click the **Advanced** tab and, in the **Permission** area, clear the **Disable changes** check box, click **OK**, and then, in the message dialog box, click **Yes**.

5. Repeat step 3.

6. Click the **Security** tab and, in the **Authorization** area, select the **Enforce access checks for this application** check box.

7. In the **Security level** area, click **Perform access checks at the process and component level. Security property will be included on the object context. The COM+ security call is available**.

8. Click **OK**.

9. In the message dialog box, click **Yes**.

10. Expand **BizTalk Server Interchange Application**.

11. Double-click the **Roles** folder, right-click the folder, point to **New**, and then click **Role**.

   The **Role** dialog box appears.

12. Type a name for the role and click **OK**.

13. In the message dialog box, click **Yes**.

14. Expand the role you just created, double-click the **Users** folder, right-click **Users**, point to **New**, and then click **User**.

15. In the **Select Users or Groups** box, type the full name of the user you want to add.

16. When you have finished adding user accounts to the role, click **OK**.

✎ Note

• For each user account or group assigned to the role, an icon appears in the **Users** folder. The new role membership will be activated when the application is started.

To associate a new role with the Submit and SubmitSync methods

1. On the **Start** menu, point to **Settings**, click **Control Panel**, double-click **Administrative Tools**, and then double-click **Component Services**.

   The Component Services console appears.

2. Expand **Component Services**, **Computers**, **My Computer**, **COM+ Applications**, **BizTalk Server Interchange Application**, **Components**, **BizTalk.Interchange.1**, **Interfaces**, **IInterchange**, and **Methods**.

3. Right-click **Submit** and click **Properties**.

   The **Submit Properties** dialog box appears.

4. Click the **Security** tab.

5. In the **Roles explicitly set for selected item(s)** area, select the check box for the role you just created in the "Add a role to the BizTalk Server Interchange Application" procedure and click **OK**.

6. Right-click **SubmitSync** and click **Properties**.

   The **SubmitSync Properties** dialog box appears.

7. Click the **Security** tab.

8. In the **Roles explicitly set for selected item(s)** area, select the check box for the role you just created in the "Add a role to the BizTalk Server Interchange Application" procedure and click **OK**.

✎ **Note**

- A new role for the BizTalk Server Interchange Application must first be created before the **Submit** and **SubmitSync** methods can be associated with it.

Related Topics

"Administration Privileges" in Chapter 11, "Administering Servers and Applications"

"To shut down the BizTalk Server Interchange Application" in Chapter 11, "Administering Servers and Applications"

Transport Services

Microsoft BizTalk Server 2000 supports a core set of transport services. These transport services enable the server to send documents to organizations or applications whether or not the applications are capable of communicating directly with the server by using a COM interface. BizTalk Server supports the HTTP, HTTPS, and SMTP network protocols and Message Queuing and file access control.

HTTP and HTTPS

HTTPS is used to provide strong authentication when using HTTP to gain access to content on the Web. The most common use of HTTPS is to provide an encrypted connection to an authenticated Web server. When clients attempt to establish an HTTPS connection, typically triggered by browsing to a URL beginning with https://, the client and server jointly negotiate a security protocol to use and then exchange authenticating information.

Microsoft Internet Explorer 5 or later supports common secure communication protocols for HTTP transactions, including the following:

- Transport Layer Security (TLS version 1.0)

- Secure Sockets Layer (SSL versions 2 and 3)

- Private Communications Technology (PCT version 1.0)

Each protocol provides both encryption services (for confidentiality of exchanged data) and authentication services (for mutual identification between clients and servers). SSL support, which is provided through the built-in HTTPS transport service, adds server-to-server authentication and transport layer encryption to an interchange.

BizTalk Server and HTTPS can be used to securely exchange data within an organization or with a trading partner by means of HTTP. The following provides specific details regarding how BizTalk Server 2000 uses HTTP and HTTPS to send and receive data.

Send

The HTTP and HTTPS transport services can be used to secure data that is sent to an application or trading partner. Security for these transport services relies on certificates.

For example, prior to sending data over HTTP, a BizTalk Server administrator sends a copy of the client certificate to a trading partner. The trading partner retains a copy of the certificate in the BizTalk store. In the future, the certificate is used to authenticate the trading partner sending data. A unique certificate manager must be created to send or export a certificate to a trading partner.

Receive

To secure data over HTTP, BizTalk Server uses Microsoft Internet Information Services (IIS) and ASP pages. When using HTTPS to connect to IIS, the client and browser negotiate a common protocol to secure the channel. In cases where the server and client have multiple protocols in common, IIS secures the channel with a supported protocol, such as SSL. To secure data that is received by BizTalk Server over HTTP, the process is identical. The ASP page serves as the gateway for sending data to BizTalk Server. If the data is secure, BizTalk Server receives the data provided the ASP code uses the **Submit** method or the **SubmitSync** method to make a call.

SMTP

SMTP (Simple Mail Transfer Protocol) is a protocol for sending e-mail messages between servers. SMTP is a common protocol for sending mail over the Internet. An e-mail message can be retrieved with an e-mail client using either POP or IMAP. In addition, SMTP is used to send messages from a mail client to a mail server. When configuring an e-mail application, both the POP or IMAP server and the SMTP server must be specified.

SMTP can be used to securely exchange data within an organization or with a trading partner. BizTalk Server 2000 uses SMTP to send and receive data using the following methods:

Send

BizTalk Server implements a transport protocol to send data over SMTP. At a minimum, SMTP requires that data be MIME-encoded. This process enables BizTalk Server to identify where a set of data ends and the next set of data begins. However, MIME-encoding does not provide security. S/MIME is the secure MIME version. Documents encoded using built-in S/MIME encoding components ensure document integrity, authentication of the sending party, and payload encryption. BizTalk Server creates an S/MIME document with the encrypted message as the body of the document. To add this security layer, a certificate must be associated with the MIME-encoded message. MIME encoding can be specified when messaging ports are created in BizTalk Messaging Manager. This is also where certificates are specified.

Receive

To implement security on the receive side of SMTP using Microsoft Exchange Server, an administrator must create a receive account for BizTalk Server. Once the account is set up, trading partners send their public keys to Exchange Server, which authenticates the sender (trading partner). The public key is added to the Exchange Server certificate store.

When Exchange Server receives a message, the **Submit** method sends the data to BizTalk Server. BizTalk Server verifies the certificate against the public key; if they match, BizTalk Server decrypts the data and processes the document.

Message Queuing 2.0

Message Queuing 2.0 supports privacy and security using the following:

- Access control
- Auditing
- Encryption
- Authentication

Message Queuing also takes advantage of the Kerberos V5 security protocol available with Microsoft Windows 2000. In addition, Message Queuing supports 128-bit encryption as well as 40-bit encryption. Message Queuing can also be used to integrate applications, implement a push-style business-event delivery environment between applications, and build reliable applications that work over unreliable but cost-effective networks.

Message Queuing can be used to securely exchange data within an organization and with a trading partner. BizTalk Server 2000 uses Message Queuing to send and receive data using the following methods:

Send

The first layer of security for Message Queuing is a user name and password, which is required by anyone to store data or retrieve data from Message Queuing. In addition, Message Queuing can store data that has a certificate. Users are able to specify a certificate for data stored on a message queue using BizTalk Messaging Manager.

Receive

If an administrator creates logon properties for a message queue, a user name and password must be used to retrieve the data. Creating logon properties forms a fundamental layer of security. If a trading partner has added a certificate to the data, a copy of its private key must be received to decrypt the data before BizTalk Server can process the package.

File

Microsoft Windows 2000 ensures data and system protection by defining discretionary file access control. The Windows NTFS file system, required for BizTalk Server 2000, can prevent users from damaging key system or application files. NTFS also provides robust security for the supporting files in an application.

File storage can be used to securely exchange data within an organization and with a trading partner. File storage can also be used to send and receive data using the following:

Send

The first layer of security for file storage is a user name and password. A user name and password is required by anyone storing or retrieving data from a folder. In addition, folders can store data that has a certificate associated with it. To use this added layer of security, use BizTalk Messaging Manager to create a certificate for the data to be stored in a folder.

Receive

If logon properties for a folder have been applied, a user name and password must be used to retrieve the data. An administrator can also designate access levels (read, delete, and so on) to the file directory for specific users. If a trading partner has added a certificate to the data, a copy of its private key must be received to decrypt the data before BizTalk Server can process the package. Inbound documents can also be digitally signed to ensure that the sending source cannot deny that it sent the document.

Related Topics

"Messaging Port Elements" in Chapter 9, "Configuring BizTalk Messaging Services"

"Set Transport Properties" in Chapter 9, "Configuring BizTalk Messaging Services"

"To add a File receive function" in Chapter 11, "Administering Servers and Applications"

"To add a Message Queuing receive function" in Chapter 11, "Administering Servers and Applications"

"To configure advanced properties for File or Message Queuing receive functions" in Chapter 11, "Administering Servers and Applications"

"To configure a File receive function: General tab" in Chapter 11, "Administering Servers and Applications"

"To configure a File receive function: Services tab" in Chapter 11, "Administering Servers and Applications"

"To configure a Message Queuing receive function: General tab" in Chapter 11, "Administering Servers and Applications"

"To configure a Message Queuing receive function: Services tab" in Chapter 11, "Administering Servers and Applications"

"To select a transport type" in Chapter 9, "Configuring BizTalk Messaging Services"

"To select an encryption certificate" in Chapter 9, "Configuring BizTalk Messaging Services"

Security for Applications That Host XLANG Schedule Instances

After installing BizTalk Orchestration Services, security levels can be set for the following:

- Creating new XLANG schedule instances

- Interacting with existing XLANG schedule instances

- Administrative functions relating to XLANG schedule instances

- Applications hosting XLANG schedule instances

Applications that host XLANG schedule instances rely on role-based security, which is an automatic service provided by COM+. Role-based security enables users to construct and enforce an access control policy for COM+ applications. With a flexible and extensible security configuration model, role-based security offers considerable benefits over enforcing all security within components. There are two default COM+ applications, the XLANG Scheduler and the XLANG Scheduler Persistence Helper, which are automatically created when BizTalk Orchestration Services are installed. The XLANG Scheduler COM+ application has four roles that can be used to ensure the security of schedule instances regardless of the COM+ application in which they execute. The four roles are:

- **XLANG Schedule Creator.** This role allows specified users to create XLANG schedule instances. For instance, if an administrator wants a user to be able to create an XLANG schedule instance, the administrator must add the user to the membership list for this role. Any user who is not listed as a member of this role and attempts to create an XLANG schedule instance will see an error message indicating that access has been denied. In addition, an entry is generated in the event log indicating that access has been denied.

- **XLANG Schedule User.** This role allows specified users to interact with XLANG schedule instances. For instance, if an administrator wants a user to be able to interact with a schedule instance, the administrator must add the user to the membership list for this role. Any user who is not listed as a member of this role and attempts to interact with a schedule instance will see an error message indicating that access has been denied. In addition, an entry is generated in the event log indicating that access has been denied.

- **XLANG Scheduler Administrator.** This role can be used to indicate who has administrative rights to the following tasks:

  - Determining whether a COM+ application is able to act as a host for XLANG schedule instances.

  - Setting the DSN type for a COM+ application that is hosting XLANG schedule instances and setting the state management value for the level of persistence the COM+ application needs to support.

  - Shutting down all XLANG schedule instances.

  - Suspending, resuming, or terminating an XLANG schedule instance.

- **XLANG Scheduler Application.** This role is used by the XLANG Scheduler to interact with any COM+ application that a user creates. Therefore, the role must include the same identity that the COM+ application is using to run.

Best Practices for Securing COM+ Applications

Using roles, an administrator can administratively construct an authorization policy for an application, choosing (down to the method level, if necessary) which users can access which resources. Because all XLANG schedules are hosted in COM+ server applications, access to the installed COM objects can be limited by configuring security properties for various roles.

❖ **Important**

- If security properties are added at the component level, individual components, interfaces, and methods based on the role settings at these levels are also limited. For more information about COM+ security, go to the MSDN Online Library Web site (msdn.microsoft.com/library/default.asp) and browse to the Security in COM+ page.

Recommendations for securing COM+ applications

The following recommendations apply primarily to securing deployed applications:

- **Do not configure a COM+ application as an interactive user.** COM+ applications that use the interactive user identity can be used only if a user is logged on to the computer where the application resides. If no one is logged on, the COM+ application cannot run. In addition, if a user creates a COM+ application using interactive user, it will be more difficult to configure access to its persistence database and other resources. For more information about service accounts, see "Using a Service Account" earlier in this chapter.

- **Reconfigure the identity for XLANG Scheduler.** During setup, the XLANG Scheduler identity is automatically configured as Interactive User. This configuration is suitable for most developers. On production systems, you should change the identity property for the XLANG Scheduler so that the application runs under a unique user account. The identity is used by all messages sent by the XLANG Scheduler.

✍ Note

- When using the client for Microsoft Windows 2000 Terminal Services to initiate an XLANG schedule, the COM+ application hosting the XLANG Scheduler Engine must have its identity set to a valid Windows 2000 user or group name. The identity of the COM+ application is set on the **Identity** page of the properties dialog box for that application. The identity cannot be set to interactive when using the XLANG Scheduler Engine through a session hosted by Terminal Services.

- **Create a new COM+ application with a unique identity for every application that is hosting XLANG schedule instances.** Create a new COM+ application with a unique identity for each business process, such as purchasing, with unique security requirements. This enables individual security levels to be specified for each application. In addition, it safeguards from excessive damage that can be done by unstable application code and makes it easier to audit the operations of individual applications.

- **Install application-specific components into their associated business processes.** This protects data and keeps out applications that do not have access to these components, provided the server application is adequately protected.

✍ Note

- Each COM+ application must contain at least one component. If an application-specific component is not installed, a placeholder component in the application must be created and installed, or the COM+ application will not be available.

- **Change the membership list of the XLANG Scheduler roles from their defaults to provide added security.** When BizTalk Server is installed, the XLANG Scheduler is created and configured with the following roles, shown with their default settings:
  - **XLANG Schedule Creator.** Membership role defaults to Everyone.
  - **XLANG Schedule User.** Membership role defaults to Everyone.
  - **XLANG Scheduler Administrator.** Membership role defaults to Administrators.
  - **XLANG Scheduler Application.** Membership role defaults to Everyone.

Securing the Orchestration Persistence Database

When a COM+ application that hosts XLANG schedule instances is created, a persistence database must be associated with the COM+ application. Therefore, first create a persistence database in Microsoft SQL Server. When creating a database, a user must choose whether to use SQL Server authentication or Microsoft Windows 2000 authentication for security. After creating the database, a user needs to give permission rights to the COM+ application that will be created later to host XLANG schedule instances. Make sure that the COM+ application has permissions to both create tables and create procedures to the persistence database associated with it. The interaction between the BizTalk Orchestration Services and the default BizTalk

Server Orchestration Persistence database is based on the Windows 2000 security model rather than on SQL Server.

Confirming the Sender's Identity

During schedule design, various shapes can be used to describe implementation technologies used to implement a port in a business process. The **COM Component** shape and the **Script Component** shape represent a technology that can be used to implement a port by using a method call for each message that is sent or received. The **Message Queuing** shape represents a technology that is used to implement a port. Message Queuing transport services are used to send or receive messages. When adding one of the three technologies, a user can require that the sender's identity be confirmed prior to receiving messages.

For more information about COM components, Windows Script Components, or Message Queuing security for XLANG schedules, see "To implement a port by using a COM component," "To implement a port by using a Windows Script Component," and "To implement a port by using Message Queuing" in Chapter 8, "BizTalk Orchestration Services."

Related Topics

"Manage the Default XLANG Scheduler Application and Database" in Chapter 11, "Administering Servers and Applications"

"To change the application identity for the default XLANG Scheduler application" in Chapter 11, "Administering Servers and Applications"

"To create a COM+ application to host XLANG schedules" in Chapter 8, "BizTalk Orchestration Services"

"Understanding XLANG Schedules" in Chapter 8, "BizTalk Orchestration Services"

"Using the COM Component Shape" in Chapter 8, "BizTalk Orchestration Services"

"Using the Message Queuing Shape" in Chapter 8, "BizTalk Orchestration Services"

"Using the Script Component Shape" in Chapter 8, "BizTalk Orchestration Services"

Certificates Overview

Digital certificates bind a cryptographic key with one or more attributes of a user. Issued by certification authorities, the certificates protect the Internet by assuring the authenticity of network messages. This technology and its underlying digital signatures are now helping to increase the widespread deployment of electronic commerce on the Internet.

Understanding Certificates

Microsoft BizTalk Server 2000 relies heavily on the security provided by certificates. Through the use of public keys, which encrypt the data, and private keys, which enable the data to be decrypted, BizTalk Server can send data that can be trusted and can ensure that the data it processes is secure. Public Key Policies, which are part of the Microsoft Management Console, enable a user to configure encrypted data recovery agents for Encrypting File System (EFS), domain-wide root certificate authorities, trusted certificate authorities, and so on. Certificates also contain digital signatures, which can be applied to documents and verified on inbound documents using the BizTalk Server native support for digital signatures.

Certificates are used to authenticate and secure exchanges of information on nonsecured networks, such as the Internet. Certificates can be managed for a user, a computer, or a service. The X.509-based Public Key Certificate Server built into Windows 2000 Server lets organizations issue public-key certificates for authentication to their users, without depending on commercial Certification Authority (CA) services.

BizTalk Server supports certificates through BizTalk Messaging Manager. Certificates make it easy to encrypt, decrypt, and digitally sign data. Public-key encryption technology is supported for all documents that are transmitted using BizTalk Server transport services. BizTalk Server also supports decryption and signature verification for the documents that it receives.

MachineKeys versus UserKeys

When obtaining certificates, it is best to use MachineKeys, which are associated with the computer, rather than UserKeys, which are associated with the current, logged on user. If a user, currently logged on to a server, obtains a certificate with UserKeys, only that user can access the certificate because the certificate UserKey contains the user's logon information. Therefore, if users need to access certificates with UserKeys in BizTalk Server, BizTalk Server must be run in the context of that user. To enable any user to log on to BizTalk Server and access keys, certificates must have MachineKeys.

For BizTalk Server to access the Certificates (Local Computer), BizTalk Server must run as LocalSystem or Administrator. Additionally, if UserKeys are used, BizTalk Server must run in the context of that user, who also must be an administrator.

Certificates Needed by BizTalk Server

A certificate server stores certificates for a user and for a computer. Every user has a certificate store, and every computer has its own certificate stores. If a user creates a certificate, Windows 2000 assumes the certificate is for the user. An organization needs to store its certificates in the Personal store located under Certificates (Local Computer) of the Certificates console. However, to provide the proper security, BizTalk Server 2000 needs all trading partner certificates to be stored in the BizTalk store located under Certificates (Local Computer) of the Certificates console.

During design time, when messaging ports and channels are created, a user needs to have all trading partner certificates associated with the BizTalk store, under Certificate (Local Computer) of the Certificates console, rather than with the user. When specifying security, such as encryption or signature verification, for trading partners through BizTalk Messaging Manager, the certificates displayed are the trading partner certificates located in the BizTalk store. BizTalk Messaging Manager displays the certificates located in the Personal store under Certificate (Local Computer) of the Certificates console when specifying security, such as verified decryption and signing, for SSL clients. Where certificates are located is important because at run time, when a user attempts to process documents through BizTalk Server, the computer is acting as the background service, and it is this service that needs to access the certificates.

There are two ways to resolve issues about where certificates are stored:

- If a user has already created certificates, Windows 2000 has stored them in the user store. The certificates must be moved from the user store to the corresponding store under Certificates (Local Computer). This process is done through the certificate manager.

- If a user has created a service account, all the certificates are associated with the computer, rather than with the user.

Certificate management through Windows 2000

BizTalk Server provides certificate management through Microsoft Windows 2000. Tightly integrated within the Windows 2000 security model is IIS 5.0, which includes a certificate server. This lets organizations issue and manage Internet-standard X.509 digital certificates. In addition to key management services in IIS 5.0, the Microsoft certificate server in IIS 5.0 provides customizable services for issuing and managing digital certificates. A certificate server performs a central role in the management of software security systems to enable secure communications across the Internet, corporate intranets, and other nonsecure networks.

To create a certificate manager

1. On the **Start** menu, click **Run** and type **mmc**.

    The **Console1** dialog box appears.

2. On the **Console** menu, click **Add/Remove Snap-in**.

    The **Add/Remove Snap-in** dialog box appears.

3. Click **Add**.

    The **Add Standalone Snap-in** dialog box appears.

4. Click **Certificates** and click **Add**.

    The **Certificates snap-in** dialog box appears.

5. Click **Computer account**, click **Next**, and then click **Finish**.

6. In the **Add Standalone Snap-in** dialog box, click **Certificates** and click **Add**.

    The **Certificates snap-in** dialog box appears.

7. Click **Computer account**, click **Next**, click **Finish**, click **Close**, and then click **OK** to close the dialog boxes.

Certificate Name Restrictions

Microsoft BizTalk Server 2000 does not allow identical names for certificates. If identical names for certificates exist, only one of the certificates can be selected in BizTalk Messaging Manager. For example, if an organization uses two certificates that have the same name and reference, it is impossible for the organization to use both certificates. If the organization uses one of the certificates, the other certificate disappears from the list of available certificates in the **Channel** dialog box.

Related Topics

"To select a certificate for outbound signature" in Chapter 9, "Configuring BizTalk Messaging Services"

"To select a certificate to verify inbound document decryption" in Chapter 9, "Configuring BizTalk Messaging Services"

"To select a certificate to verify inbound document signature" in Chapter 9, "Configuring BizTalk Messaging Services"

"To select an encryption certificate" in Chapter 9, "Configuring BizTalk Messaging Services"

Crypto API

Microsoft BizTalk Server 2000 uses Crypto API to secure data it processes. Recent developments in cryptography have added additional uses, including mechanisms for authenticating users on a network, ensuring the integrity of transmitted information, and preventing users from denying ownership of their transmitted messages.

Any application, message, data, and so on that uses encryption and uses Microsoft-specific encryption, such as Microsoft Windows 2000 for generating certificates, uses Crypto API. BizTalk Server uses Crypto API for receive functions that a user specifies when using a custom-made COM+ component such as a preprocessing component, which enables BizTalk Server to handle unique encryption components.

Collaborative Data Objects

Microsoft BizTalk Server 2000 requires MIME encoding for all its data, whether sending the data or receiving it. Through the use of Collaborative Data Objects (CDOs), which are part of the Windows 2000 environment, data can be encoded and processed by BizTalk Server. For example, before BizTalk Server can send a catalog that contains text and graphics, it first needs the data (graphics) to be changed from binary to string. CDOs encode the text and graphics into a string format so that BizTalk Server can process it.

Enhancing Performance and Scalability

Understanding the various components of BizTalk Server 2000 enables you to create scalable, high-performance solutions. There are several methods, such as identifying potential bottlenecks, addressing latency, and managing databases, that you can use to increase the performance of BizTalk Server. However, the extent to which you can achieve an optimal solution depends on the complexity of your organization's system architecture and your budget requirements.

Optimizing the BizTalk Messaging Management database, the Shared Queue database, the Tracking database, and the Orchestration Persistence database is critical to achieving optimal performance with BizTalk Server. For more information about optimizing the databases, see "Scale Up the Databases" and "Scale Out the Databases" later in this chapter.

In This Chapter

- Scaling BizTalk Server
- Performance Optimization

Scaling BizTalk Server

To optimize performance, it is highly recommended that you distribute key components across multiple servers. The key components of BizTalk Server 2000 include:

- **BizTalk Services.** These services include BizTalk Messaging Services and BizTalk Orchestration Services. For more information, see "BizTalk Services" in Chapter 1, "Introducing Microsoft BizTalk Server 2000."

- **Databases.** These databases include the BizTalk Messaging Management, Tracking, Shared Queue, and Orchestration Persistence databases.

- **Transport services.** The transport services include HTTP, File, SMTP, and Message Queuing. Each component has unique scaling requirements.

BizTalk Server 2000 Enterprise Edition fully utilizes all the processors on any computer on which the server runs. Using all processors enables the server to achieve high scalability and performance by using the complete hardware configuration of the computer.

BizTalk Server 2000 Standard Edition uses only a single processor, irrespective of the hardware on which the server is run. The processor that is used is always the processor that is referenced by a processor affinity mask of 1.

Most aspects of BizTalk Server scaling are unavailable in the standard edition. The performance and scalability information in this chapter applies primarily to the enterprise edition.

Related Topics

"Managing BizTalk Server Databases" in Chapter 11, "Administering Servers and Applications"

"Managing the BizTalk Messaging Management Database" in Chapter 11, "Administering Servers and Applications"

"Persistence" in Chapter 8, "BizTalk Orchestration Services"

"Shared Queue Database" in Chapter 11, "Administering Servers and Applications"

"Tracking Database" in Chapter 11, "Administering Servers and Applications"

Scaling BizTalk Server Vertically

By using multiple processors and significant memory, you can vertically scale (scale up) BizTalk Server 2000. Scaling BizTalk Server vertically requires fewer servers and simplifies site management, but is more costly than scaling a system horizontally or improving software architecture. In addition, once capacity on existing hardware is maximized, you must begin to scale the system horizontally.

Scale Up BizTalk Server

To scale BizTalk Server 2000 vertically, the following are recommended:

- Increase the processor size (such as the Pentium III and its Xeon derivatives with large level II caches).

- Use symmetric multiple processing (SMP) servers that accommodate up to eight CPUs.

- Decrease file I/O and network bottlenecks.

- Run Microsoft Windows 2000 Server on four-way SMP servers.

  ### ✎ Note

  - When running Microsoft Windows 2000 Server on one CPU, adding three additional CPUs improves performance, but it does not increase the processing speed of one CPU by a multiple of four.

Recommended solutions for scaling BizTalk Server vertically

To achieve optimal performance with BizTalk Server, the following are recommended:

- A multiprocessor PIII Xeon MHz processor system (the highest MHz possible for maximum performance), capable of being upgraded to eight CPUs.

- A 1- to 2-MB L2 Processor Cache (increases parsing performance).

- 512 MB of RAM (more if an organization is processing multiple megabyte documents).

- Use multiple 100 Mbps (megabits per second), or greater, network cards connected to 100 MB/s switch ports to increase network I/O throughput.

- Provide multiple disks and controllers for Message Queuing and Distributed Transaction Coordinator (DTC) file and log operations. Write DTC log operations to a central remote server to offload file I/O contention on the local BizTalk Server.

- Use dual-honed network interface cards (NICs) in the BizTalk servers to separate HTTP processes from the Shared Queue and BizTalk Messaging Management databases dedicated to SQL Server processes.

- These recommendations assume that BizTalk Server is running on a dedicated server. If the BizTalk Services are sharing the server with other application services, additional hardware is recommended.

Scale Up the Databases

To vertically scale the databases, you must determine the disk configuration. To determine the disk configuration, you must consider throughput, fail-over, and cost.

The following table identifies the options available and compares each option relative to each other.

RAID level	Cost	Effective disk utilization percentage	Speed	Fault tolerance
0 (Striping)	Low	100	Fast	Low
1 (Mirroring)	High	50	Medium	High
5 (Striping with parity)	Moderate	Effective disk space is the total space of all disks in the array combined minus 1 (for parity)	Slow	Moderate (only because performance degrades with a failed disk)

To achieve optimal performance, it is recommended that you install an efficient caching Redundant Array of Independent Disks (RAID) controller with a fast CPU and a high amount of RAM that is nonvolatile. You can also combine multiple RAID levels to achieve desired performance. For example, RAID 0 provides the best performance but does not provide fault tolerance. RAID 1 provides the best fault tolerance but does not provide the best performance (due to writing data to one disk, as opposed to multiple disks, concurrently). To achieve optimal performance, you can combine RAID 1 and RAID 0 by mirroring a set of striped disks.

Notes

- RAID 5 does not meet or exceed the speed or cost of any other RAID level. RAID 5 provides key advantages, but is slower when writing data to disk than RAID 0 or RAID 1.

- For any strategy, the number of available disk controllers is critical. You can significantly improve overall performance by using one disk per controller. When configuring disks, effectively using disk channels is equally important. Disk channels are disks that share the same controller. These disks can be configured as stand-alone disks, or they can be configured to run as part of an array. For example, if there were 10 disks in a server, 5 disks each in two arrays, and each array is connected to its own controller, there would be 2 disk channels.

Ideally, the BizTalk Messaging Management, Shared Queue, Tracking, and Orchestration Persistence databases should be on separate disk channels. However, if your organization's system environment requires that the databases reside on individual servers, it is important to understand the use of each database when planning for this deployment scenario:

- The BizTalk Messaging Management database contains all the configuration information, such as organizations, server groups, servers, channels, and messaging ports, for BizTalk Server. This information is read and cached in Microsoft SQL Server memory. This database receives the least activity of the four databases and can reside on the same disk channel as one of the other three databases if necessary.

- The Shared Queue database manages the data for all the queues. Every document that uses asynchronous communication is sent to and stored in the Shared Queue database. When BizTalk Server is ready to handle the document, it is removed from the Shared Queue database for processing. Because this database manages all transactions, data is written to and read from the Shared Queue database frequently.

- The Tracking database tracks documents that pass through the server, either individually or in batches. This database stores both the data and its logging information. Therefore, data is often written to the Tracking database, but data is rarely read from the database.

- The Orchestration Persistence database stores the structure of the XLANG schedules, the progress of activated XLANG schedule instances, and messages that are sent or received when an XLANG schedule instance begins or completes a transaction, when the system is shut down, or when the XLANG schedule instance is dehydrated.

Optimization recommendations to vertically scale the databases

Consider the following for optimal performance of BizTalk Server databases:

- A multiprocessor PIII Xeon MHz processor system (the highest MHz possible for maximum performance), capable of being upgraded to eight CPUs.

- 512 MB of RAM (more if an organization is processing multiple megabyte documents).

- Optimize the underlying Microsoft SQL Server databases and logs based on standard database best practices. For more information about SQL Server, on the **Start** menu, point to **Programs**, point to **Microsoft SQL Server**, and then click **Books Online**.

- If you initially plan to complete only a few transactions, you can install the databases on the same disk I/O channel. As more transactions are being processed, add disks and/or controllers to a server and move the databases to these new disk I/O channels. Additionally, an individual database can be moved to a new server. For more information about scaling the databases horizontally, see "Scale Out the Databases" later in this chapter.

To optimize the BizTalk Messaging Management database:

- Install the database on the same disk I/O channel as the Shared Queue database or the Tracking database. The contents of the BizTalk Messaging Management database are read and cached in Microsoft SQL Server memory.

- If an organization processes a high volume of data, consider placing this database on its own disk I/O channel so as not to hinder the performance of the Shared Queue or the Tracking database.

To optimize the Shared Queue database:

- If the CPU capacity exceeds 80 percent, add additional CPUs.

- If disk queue length averages more than 1, or if disk I/O utilization is greater than 100 percent, add additional physical disks.

- Install the database on its own dedicated disk I/O channel.

- Purchase disks with the fastest access times, and controllers with the highest throughput.

- Consider RAID 0 and mirror it to obtain fault tolerance.

To optimize the Tracking database:

- Add more physical disks and additional disk space than currently exists on the Shared Queue database.

- Estimate the average document size for a single transaction. Multiply the document size by the number of times the document will be logged to the Tracking database. This estimate suggests the amount of document storage space required per document in the Tracking database. Multiply the document storage space value by the throughput requirement to determine the amount of space needed before the Tracking database becomes full. Ensure that the Tracking database has adequate space to accommodate logging an average document size.

- Install this database on its own disk I/O channel due to the high volume of data that is written to it. A separate disk I/O channel is particularly important in heavy transaction environments.

Note

- There is a size limit for tracking interchanges and documents, which if exceeded greatly affects the performance of BizTalk Server. For more information about the size limit, see "Interchange and document size limit" in Chapter 11, "Administering Servers and Applications."

To optimize the Orchestration Persistence database:

- Because data is written to and read from this database frequently, the database should have a dedicated disk I/O channel. It is best to purchase disks with the fastest access times, and controllers with the highest throughput, if possible. Consider RAID 0 and mirror it to achieve fault tolerance.

- If the CPU capacity exceeds 80 percent, add more CPUs.

- If the disk queue length averages more than 1, or if disk I/O utilization is greater than 100 percent, add more physical disks.

Scale Up the Transport Services

BizTalk Server 2000 supports four transport services. Each of these transport services can be scaled vertically:

- HTTP
- File
- SMTP
- Message Queuing

HTTP/HTTPS (Scale Up)

Receive

The HTTP/HTTPS receive function sends documents to BizTalk Server 2000 by calling the BizTalk Server **Interchange** object. BizTalk Server does not have a unique HTTP/HTTPS receive function. The HTTP receive function calls a local object. Therefore, no network latency exists to affect performance. However, because the HTTP receive function and BizTalk Server both reside on the same server, the HTTP receive function must perform two functions: transport data and process data.

In high-volume environments, running the HTTP receive function and BizTalk Services on the same server degrades the performance of both. Additionally, if Secure Sockets Layer (SSL, also referred to as HTTPS) is used to receive documents, performance is degraded further due to decryption processing. Depending on the security needs of an organization, data might need to be encrypted using HTTPS. This added level of security might affect the performance of BizTalk Server.

Send

BizTalk Server is a native HTTP/HTTPS client. If a channel is configured to use HTTP/HTTPS as its outbound transport service, BizTalk Server uses HTTP/HTTPS to send data to a trading partner's HTTP/HTTPS server. You cannot move the HTTP/HTTPS outbound transport service to a separate server from the server on which BizTalk Messaging Services resides. If a server is configured to participate in work-item processing and it processes a document that uses an HTTP/HTTPS transport service, this same server sends the document. For more information about work-item processing, see "Scale Up BizTalk Server" later in this chapter.

BizTalk Server functions as an HTTP client, which affects the document-serializing power of the server. If the port is using HTTPS, the performance of the HTTP transport service is greatly affected. SSL accelerator cards cannot be used when acting as an HTTPS client because these cards only enhance HTTPS server performance.

Recommended optimization for HTTP/HTTPS

To optimize performance for HTTP/HTTPS, which enhances the performance of BizTalk Server:

- Configure the inbound HTTP/HTTPS receive service on a separate server than BizTalk Server. If the inbound HTTP/HTTPS receive service cannot be installed on a separate server than BizTalk Server, use a faster CPU or add more CPUs.

- Increase the CPU MHz that is required for BizTalk Server (to accommodate the additional need for sending documents) and add additional CPUs until the desired performance level is achieved.

- Apply best practices when using ASP pages with the receive or send HTTP/HTTPS service. For more information about optimizing ASP pages and Internet Information Services, go to the Internet Information Services Help Web site (localhost/iisHelp) and click Active Server Pages Guide.

File (Scale Up)

Receive

Although performance is high when using a File receive function for business-to-business transactions, a File receive function is not secure for Internet-based transactions and therefore is not widely used. However, for application-to-application transactions within a corporation, a File receive function can provide optimal performance without jeopardizing security. In addition, a File receive function can be used securely with external trading partners provided it is combined with another receive function, such as SMTP or HTTP. The SMTP or HTTP receive function can accept a document from a trading partner (using HTTPS or S/MIME for security) and write the file to an internal file system directory. Then BizTalk Server can use a File receive function to receive the document. This combination of transports might not increase performance, but it will provide greater flexibility and security.

Note

- Using S/MIME significantly degrades the performance of BizTalk Server.

Send

The security and performance issues detailed for a File receive function are also applicable for sending documents using a File transport service.

Recommended optimization for File receive function and File transport service

To optimize performance for the File receive function and File transport service, which enhances the performance of BizTalk Server:

- Use a local file directory rather than a remote file directory to reduce network latency.
- Use disk arrays to achieve high throughput. For more information about disk array speed and redundancy tradeoffs, see "Scale Up the Databases" earlier in this chapter.

SMTP (Scale Up)

Receive

The SMTP receive function is similar to the HTTP receive function for inbound transactions in that there is no native SMTP receive function built into BizTalk Server. An SMTP receive function can receive a document through an event-based mechanism and send the document to BizTalk Server. If an SMTP receive function exists, BizTalk Server accepts the MIME/SMIME-encoded document and prepares it for processing.

Send

The same security and performance issues listed in the inbound S/MIME and outbound HTTP/HTTPS sections apply here. If a channel uses SMTP as a transport service in a messaging port or port, the processing server processes the document and sends it to the receiving application.

◢ Note

- BizTalk Server performance is significantly degraded if a digital certificate is needed to S/MIME-encode the outbound document.

Recommended optimization for SMTP

To optimize performance for SMTP, which enhances the performance of BizTalk Server:

- The performance level achieved depends greatly on the SMTP service that is used for receiving documents. An organization might have an SMTP server that is used to perform this function. However, if an SMTP server is not available and an organization chooses to use Microsoft Exchange Server or another third-party messaging system, the server might need a significant amount of additional hardware to maintain an adequate performance level for BizTalk Server. The SMTP server must be able to invoke an event-based mechanism, which is capable of sending documents to BizTalk Server.

- If an organization chooses to run BizTalk Server on an SMTP server, CPU performance will be impacted. To minimize the impact to performance, use a faster CPU.

- If an organization uses S/MIME, BizTalk Server performance is significantly degraded. To reduce the overall performance impact of S/MIME to BizTalk Server, use faster CPUs.

Message Queuing (Scale Up)

Receive

Message Queuing generally uses a high volume of disk I/O to receive and send messages. Message Queuing is transactional, which is highly recommended to improve fault tolerance. However, it is only transactional on a local server. If Message Queuing is used to improve fault tolerance, an adequate number of disks must be installed on each BizTalk Server to handle the increased disk I/O.

Send

Sending documents by using Message Queuing creates the same security and performance issues as receiving documents by using Message Queuing.

Recommended optimization for Message Queuing

To optimize performance for Message Queuing, which enhances the performance of BizTalk Server:

- Use transactional queues (local queues on BizTalk Server, rather than remote queues, must be used for transactional queues to receive) and a fast disk I/O channel. Local queues do not need to query Microsoft Active Directory™; however, a public message queue must query Active Directory. Therefore, reading data from and writing data to local message queues results in better performance. Nontransactional local queues can be used to achieve better performance. However, nontransactional local queues do not provide the same reliability offered by transactional queues. Additional memory is also required.

☑ Note

- For more information about how to define hardware requirements for Message Queuing, see "Selecting Message Queuing server hardware" in Windows 2000 Server Help.

- The maximum limit for Message Queuing messages is 4 MB. If documents exceed 4 MB, the Message Queuing transport service cannot be used. The Orchestration Persistence database has a 2-MB document size limit.

- Message Queuing is database-intensive if journaling is used. Ensure that the standard rules for optimizing databases are applied when setting up Message Queuing transport services.

- To maximize throughput, separate data and logs and use multiple disks and controllers.

Scaling BizTalk Server Horizontally

A successful BizTalk Server 2000 implementation uses both a vertical and horizontal (scale out) strategy. Scaling vertically minimizes the number of servers required. Scaling horizontally provides the following benefits:

- **Heightened performance.** Performance exceeds what could cost-effectively be accomplished on a single server.

- **Server fault-tolerance.**

- **Separation and optimization of the different components.** Performance of BizTalk services, the databases, and the transport services can be increased.

Scaling hardware horizontally minimizes costs. However, as site management complexity increases, your organization must begin scaling vertically.

Scale Out BizTalk Messaging Services

BizTalk Messaging Services can be scaled horizontally by using server groups. Server groups are collections of individual servers that are centrally managed, configured, and monitored.

For more information about adding and configuring server groups, see "Groups and Servers" in Chapter 11, "Administering Servers and Applications."

Servers that are members of the same server group share the following:

- A Shared Queue database that monitors activity in the BizTalk Server state engine.

- A Tracking database that logs document activity and generates reports.

- A BizTalk Messaging Management database that stores configuration information.

- Receive functions.

- All components that the server requires at run time, such as transport components and application integration components (AICs), as well as data translation, data encryption, and signing.

A BizTalk Server group does not provide a load-balancing mechanism for either receiving inbound documents or for facilitating document submission by using Distributed Component Object Model (DCOM). It does provide multiple-server work processing. Once a document is sent to the Shared Queue database, any server in the group can process, serialize, and send it out. This functionality allows for one server in a group to send a document that another server processes.

An organization can have multiple server groups for the following reasons:

- Group similar transport services (HTTP or File)

- Enhanced security

- Trading partner categorization

You can also use server groups to avoid duplicating organization, channel, and messaging port configurations. Server groups share databases. Configuration information for the organization, group, channel, and messaging port is stored in the BizTalk Messaging Management database. Therefore, two or more BizTalk Server groups can share the same BizTalk Messaging Management database.

Note

- If two or more BizTalk Server groups share the same BizTalk Messaging Management database, each group must have its own Shared Queue, Tracking, and Orchestration Persistence databases, which are shared by all members of the group.

Recommended solutions for scaling BizTalk Server horizontally

To optimize BizTalk Server performance:

Separate transport services and receive functions

By separating transport services and receive functions for BizTalk Server groups, you can achieve higher performance. The level of performance you can achieve depends on the number of documents being processed and the complexity of the data translation. BizTalk

Server provides separate thread pools for receiving and processing data. Separating transport services and receive functions reduces context switching by eliminating the need for the server to alternate between send and receive operations.

All servers process work items by default, which involves picking up work from the Shared Queue database, processing it, and then sending it out using the transport service the channel is configured to use (process outbound work). This process degrades the overall performance of the CPU because context switching must occur. Provided you use two or more servers, you can eliminate this degradation by enabling at least one server to function as a receive service. To configure a server to act as a receive service, you can use BizTalk Server Administration to disable the **Participate in work-item processing** functionality and create a new receive function for the server. For more information about disabling the **Participate in work-item processing** functionality, see "To configure a server in a group" in Chapter 11, "Administering Servers and Applications." For more information about setting up a File receive function, see "To add a File receive function" in Chapter 11, "Administering Servers and Applications." For more information about setting up a Message Queuing receive function, see "To add a Message Queuing receive function" in Chapter 11, "Administering Servers and Applications."

📝 Note

- For Message Queuing, only transacted reads can be done from local queues, so only one server can read from that queue.

BizTalk Server receives documents if one of the following conditions exist:

- A receive function has been configured on the same server as BizTalk Server.

- An SMTP or HTTP process has been configured to call the **Submit** method on the server where BizTalk Server has been installed.

Prioritize parsers

By prioritizing parsers, you can optimize the performance of BizTalk Server. BizTalk Server provides four data parsers:

- XML

- EDIFACT

- X12

- Flat file

When BizTalk Server receives a document, it attempts to parse the document in the order in the previous list. By moving the most commonly used parsers to the top of the list, you can improve the performance of BizTalk Server. For more information about configuring the parser order, see "To configure the parser order for a server group" in Chapter 11, "Administering Servers and Applications."

Because the parser order functionality is a server group setting, it is recommended that you create a separate group for each data type (XML, EDIFACT, X12, flat file) that is processed. Then, specify the appropriate parser priorities set for each group.

Component Load Balancing

Component load balancing (CLB) is a feature of Microsoft Application Center 2000. To use CLB, Application Center 2000 must be installed on the same server as Microsoft BizTalk Server 2000. CLB enables organizations to load-balance the **BizTalk.Interchange.1** component in the COM+ Services manager. CLB is a load-balancing mechanism for COM components. In a BizTalk Server environment, CLB provides the ability for an HTTP transport to use the **Submit** method to call a cluster of servers instead of a single server (to the sending application, using the **Submit** method to call the cluster still appears as a submission to a node). A cluster is a collection of servers that acts as a single server. For example, if you use a cluster of HTTP servers, a single submission can go to any of the three servers. Without CLB, the HTTP transport services must be configured to send to one of the three servers. In the latter scenario, if the server that an HTTP service was configured to send to failed, the HTTP transport service would need to be reconfigured to send to a different server in the BizTalk Server group.

◆ Important

*   Do not replicate the default XLANG Scheduler application or any COM+ applications that host XLANG schedules. If component load balancing is used, these COM+ applications must be installed on each server. You can replicate COM components that are bound to XLANG schedules.

Scale Out the Databases

To horizontally scale the databases, install each database on its own server. In high-volume transaction environments, installing a database on a unique server enables the server's CPU, disk I/O, and memory resources to be allocated to the appropriate database.

Recommended optimization for horizontally scaling the databases

To optimize database performance of BizTalk Server:

*   Install each database on a separate server with 933 MHz, or greater, CPU. Do not install any of the databases on the same server as BizTalk Server 2000.

*   Install any COM+ application that hosts XLANG schedules on its own server with 933 MHz, or greater, CPU.

*   Use multiple 100 Mbps (megabits per second), or greater, network cards connected to 100 mb/s switch ports to increase network I/O throughput.

*   For an organization that is processing a small number of documents, use a database that can be upgraded easily. If processing needs increase, move the Shared Queue database,

Tracking database, and Orchestration Persistence database to their own servers. However, moving the BizTalk Messaging Management database is more difficult. It is highly recommended that the server on which the BizTalk Messaging Management database is stored contain suitable disk space and memory available to cache the configuration as document processing needs increase.

- For the Tracking database, install fast network hardware to compensate for the high volume of uncompressed data that is exchanged between BizTalk Server and the database.

✎ Note

- There is a size limit for tracking interchanges and documents, which if exceeded greatly affects the performance of BizTalk Server. For more information about the size limit, see "Interchange and document size limit" in Chapter 11, "Administering Servers and Applications."

Scale Out the Transport Services

BizTalk Server supports four transport services. Each of these transport services can be scaled horizontally:

- HTTP
- File
- SMTP
- Message Queuing

HTTP/HTTPS (Scale Out)

Receive

The HTTP/HTTPS receive function can be horizontally scaled by using a Web cluster. For example, a trading partner can send a document to one address, but the submission can be routed to any server in the cluster. Web clusters are a feature of the network load-balancing (NLB) service included with Microsoft Windows 2000 Advanced Server. For more information about configuring NLB, see Windows 2000 Advanced Server Help. To improve the performance of BizTalk Server, you can configure a Web cluster to place received documents into a file directory or a message queue, or you can configure it to send documents directly to BizTalk Server through one of the following two methods:

- By statically configuring each server to send documents to a BizTalk Server.

- By configuring each server to send documents to a Web cluster of servers (servers that are members of the same group) by using the Microsoft Application Center 2000 component load-balancing (CLB) functionality.

◆ Important

- Do not replicate the default XLANG Scheduler application or any COM+ applications that host XLANG schedules. If component load balancing is used, these COM+ applications must be installed on each server. You can replicate COM components that are bound to XLANG schedules.

Send

Horizontally scaling the send HTTP/HTTPS transport service is an inherent feature of using multiple servers in a group that are configured to participate in work-item processing. The HTTP/HTTPS send functionality cannot be separated from the BizTalk Server that processes documents because sending functionality is used on every server in the group that is configured to participate in work-item processing.

Recommended optimization for HTTP/HTTPS

To optimize the HTTP/HTTPS transport service, which enhances the performance of BizTalk Server:

- Dedicate the receive HTTP/HTTPS transport to a separate server from the BizTalk services (in high-volume transaction environments). In addition, have the HTTP/HTTPS server send documents to a File or Message Queue receive function, or call the **Submit** method on the BizTalk Server **Interchange** object using DCOM. Dedicating the receive HTTP/HTTPS transport or having the HTTP/HTTPS server send documents to a receive function introduces network latency; however, configuring the HTTP/HTTPS transport server and the BizTalk Server separately enables you to accommodate their unique architectures and optimize each. In addition, by separating these servers, you can maintain optimal performance on the BizTalk Server because it is not affected by the cost of using SSL for encryption/decryption.

- Create a load-balanced cluster of HTTP/HTTPS transport servers. This will further enhance the performance of the receive HTTP/HTTPS transport because it provides horizontal scaling redundancy. For more information about using the network load-balancing service to create a Web cluster, see Windows 2000 Advanced Server Help.

- Forecast how many documents need to be processed by servers in a group configured to participate in work-item processing. Then determine how many channels use messaging ports that require the send HTTP/HTTPS transport. Combine the channels that use the send HTTP/HTTPS transport into a single group. This will allow all servers in the group configured to participate in work-item processing to serialize documents that use any transport.

- Apply best practices when using ASP pages with the receive or send HTTP/HTTPS service. For more information about optimizing ASP pages and Internet Information Services, go to the Internet Information Services Help Web site (localhost/iisHelp) and click Active Server Pages Guide.

- Use Message Queuing or a File transport service on a local system with a receive function, rather than calling the **Submit** method to poll documents into BizTalk Server.

File (Scale Out)

Receive

The File receive function can be separated from the servers or can reside on the server. Although separating the File receive function to a separate server can minimize performance impact to the disk I/O, network latency will impact performance when attempting to retrieve the file.

Send

Scaling horizontally is accomplished with multiple servers in the group processing documents and then sending them to the File transport service. Performance depends on whether BizTalk Server is used as the receive function, or whether BizTalk Server is configured as a separate server as the receive function.

Recommended optimization for a File receive function or File transport service

To optimize a File receive function or File transport service, which will enhance the performance of BizTalk Server:

- Store the File receive function on a separate server from BizTalk Server. This solution, however, does not address the performance impact resulting from network latency, which occurs when attempting to retrieve the file. Storing the File receive function on a separate server from BizTalk Server also reduces the disk I/O impact on the performance of BizTalk Server. Additionally, this separation of servers keeps unknown applications from placing files on BizTalk Server, or making requests, which can maximize server resources and cause poor performance.

- Configure a receive function to run on every server in the group polling the same File receive function to ensure that all servers in the group are retrieving documents for processing. File receive services are configured by default to run on a server within a group. Therefore, if you have five servers in a group and you configure a File receive function to run on one server in the group, when a File receive function is polled at \\receiveserver\receivelocation, only the one server of the five retrieves files for processing. This limits the number of document-processing servers to one for the entire group. The remaining four servers are not capable of retrieving files from the receive function to parse.

- Configure a File receive function on a separate server from BizTalk Server. This keeps unknown applications from retrieving files from BizTalk Server. Because sending files and receiving files are different processes, all servers in the group that are configured to participate in work-item processing send out files. Horizontal scalability is based only on the number of servers in the group that are configured to participate in work-item processing.

SMTP (Scale Out)

Receive

SMTP can receive documents from BizTalk Server, but it cannot send documents to BizTalk Server. To send a document to BizTalk Server, SMTP must be able to invoke an event-based mechanism to poll the received message and send it to a file share or a message queue, or send the document using the BizTalk Server **Interchange** object. The SMTP servers, which are capable of providing these event-based mechanisms (Microsoft Exchange Server or a third-party messaging server), typically use a high volume of hardware resources. Therefore, adding this functionality to a server degrades its ability to process documents.

Send

Lightweight SMTP transport services that do not have event-based mechanisms can be used for sending documents using SMTP. The SMTP transport server sending the document simply acts as a relay agent. The outbound SMTP server is configured at the group level, not at the server level. Therefore, if the SMTP transport exists on one server in a group, the server containing the SMTP transport service uses it to send outbound documents. All other servers in the group use the same server for SMTP outbound.

Recommended optimization for SMTP

To optimize SMTP, which enhances the performance of BizTalk Server:

- Configure the SMTP transport to execute on a separate server from the BizTalk services (for send and receive functionality). In most cases, an organization will have an SMTP server on its network that can be used for send and receive functionality.

Message Queuing (Scale Out)

Receive

You must decide whether to have the Message Queuing receive function on the same server as BizTalk Server, or to install it on a separate server. If you are using a transacted queue, the Message Queuing receive function must reside on the same server. However, if you are not using a transacted queue, the Message Queuing receive function can reside on a separate server. You must decide whether to incur the effects on performance by having the disk I/O on the local BizTalk Server or the network latency of the multiple server communication. In the latter example, the need for disk I/O would still exist, but it would exist only on the remote server instead of the local server. For more information about how to define hardware requirements for the Message Queuing service, see "Selecting Message Queuing server hardware" in Windows 2000 Server Help.

Send

Sending documents by using Message Queuing creates the same security and performance issues as receiving documents by using Message Queuing.

Recommended optimization for Message Queuing

To optimize performance for Message Queuing, which enhances the performance of BizTalk Server:

- Message Queuing is database-intensive if journaling is used. Ensure that the standard rules for optimizing databases are applied when setting up Message Queuing transport services. For example, separate data and logs and use multiple disks and controllers to maximize throughput.

Performance Optimization

To meet your transaction requirements and enhance performance, you must optimize BizTalk Server 2000. In addition to BizTalk Server, you can optimize Microsoft Windows 2000 and database interactions to enhance performance. After configuring your system, test it, and then evaluate the results to determine if your initial configuration can meet your transaction requirements. It is likely that you will need to reconfigure your architecture to achieve optimal performance. After each reconfiguration, test it again and evaluate the results. Once you have achieved your desired results, initiate a maintenance plan, because server performance changes over time, and the quantity and type of transactions that your organization handles might change.

General Performance Recommendations

This section provides general recommendations for optimizing system settings and includes topics for optimizing BizTalk Server 2000 settings to obtain increased performance. For example:

- Optimize Microsoft Windows 2000 settings. Apply best practices, such as not running unnecessary services or protocols, to improve Windows 2000 performance. Many techniques used to optimize Windows 2000 also can be used to optimize BizTalk Server. For more information about optimizing Microsoft Windows 2000 settings, see Best Practices in Windows 2000 Help.

- Maintain fast, reliable network connectivity between transport services, BizTalk services (BizTalk Orchestration Services and BizTalk Messaging Services), and the databases (100 megabits per second or higher Ethernet). To optimize network throughput, use multiple adapters in each server, with a unique switch port for each, with inbound and outbound transactions separated between the network interface cards (NICs). When used in conjunction with Microsoft Windows 2000 NLB or Microsoft Application Center 2000 component load balancing (CLB) (**IInterchange** or **IPipelineComponent**), performance is significantly increased.

✦ Important

- Do not replicate the default XLANG Scheduler application or any COM+ applications that host XLANG schedules. If CLB is used, these COM+ applications must be installed on each server. You can replicate COM components that are bound to XLANG schedules.

Optimizing BizTalk Orchestration Services

Using BizTalk Orchestration Services, you can optimize XLANG schedules and the contents contained within schedules. By understanding how schedules use memory and how the structure of a business-process flow affects performance, you can design schedules that improve the performance of BizTalk Orchestration Services. Implementation technologies that are supported by BizTalk Orchestration Services include BizTalk Messaging Services, COM components, Message Queuing Services, and Windows Script Components. By optimizing these components and services, you can further enhance the performance of BizTalk Orchestration Services.

Optimizing XLANG Schedules

An XLANG schedule can contain a large number of internal business processes. The business processes might include short-lived transactions or long-running transactions. While BizTalk Server does not control the contents of these processes, it does manage the flow of information through these processes within an XLANG schedule. When designing an XLANG schedule, whether it consists of several short-lived transactions or long-running transactions, consider the following:

- An XLANG schedule instance runs in memory each time it is invoked.

- Multiple XLANG schedules can run on the same server.

- Several different XLANG schedules might be running concurrently, with multiple XLANG schedule instances.

The Orchestration Persistence database provides a mechanism, called dehydration, to control the memory that is used by running XLANG schedules. Dehydration occurs if an XLANG schedule instance is waiting for a message, and no other activity is occurring within the XLANG schedule. At this point, the XLANG Scheduler Engine dehydrates the XLANG schedule instance to maximize performance. Dehydrating an XLANG schedule instance consists of persisting all instance-specific states to a database and removing the instance from memory. Only a small portion of the XLANG schedule instance remains in memory within the XLANG Scheduler Engine. When a message arrives at a port for the XLANG schedule instance, the instance is rehydrated. Rehydrating an XLANG schedule instance consists of restoring the instance from the database to memory.

An XLANG schedule instance remains dehydrated until it is either rehydrated or explicitly terminated by an administrator. This enables a business process to run reliably for an extended time period. For more information about configuring hydration settings, see "Dehydration and

Rehydration" in Chapter 8, "BizTalk Orchestration Services." While dehydration and rehydration saves memory, it does affect performance. Because dehydration and rehydration requires that data be read and written to the Orchestration Persistence database, network latency is incurred.

✦ Important

- To dramatically increase the performance of BizTalk Orchestration Services, in Windows Explorer, browse to \Program Files\Common Files\System\ado and double-click adofre15.reg. In the confirmation dialog box, click **Yes** and click **OK**. This procedure changes the ADO threading model from "Apartment threaded" to "Both" and might affect other applications that use ADO.

Optimizing the Contents of XLANG Schedules

An XLANG schedule describes the business process and the binding of that process to implementation technologies. The performance of an XLANG schedule often mirrors the performance level of the actions contained within it. There are a number of relevant issues for optimizing the contents of an XLANG schedule. Some of these issues are specific to an XLANG schedule, while others are applicable to authoring any distributed application:

- **Reset the dehydration value to conserve memory for XLANG schedules.** The default wait time is 0 seconds. You can change this time. Any time less than or equal to 180 seconds causes the XLANG schedule to never dehydrate. Any time greater than 180 seconds causes the XLANG schedule to dehydrate immediately. For more information about wait times and XLANG schedule dehydration, see "Dehydration and Rehydration" and "Synchronous and Asynchronous Communication" in Chapter 8, "BizTalk Orchestration Services."

- **Use persistent components.** Persistent components, such as **IPersistStream** or **IPersistStreamInit**, enable the XLANG Scheduler Engine to dehydrate XLANG schedules flexibly.

- **Run the COM objects on the same server as the Orchestration Persistence database.** This ensures that the XLANG schedule does not incur the network latency.

- **Run COM+ packages in-process to achieve optimal performance.** Although running a COM+ package in-process can affect the stability of the COM+ application (for example, if one component within the application fails, the entire application can fail), it is significantly faster than running the application out-of-process. To avoid this potential instability, be sure to heavily test the components within the application for stability prior to deploying the application to a production environment.

- **Batch work into a single transaction.** Persisting the state of an XLANG schedule instance at the beginning and end of a transaction greatly impacts the computer's resources. However, batching work items in a single transaction greatly reduces this impact to performance. In addition, an XLANG schedule cannot dehydrate in the middle of a Microsoft Distributed Transaction Coordinator (MSDTC) transaction. MSDTC transactions are quick, but they degrade performance. Group multiple actions within a single MSDTC transaction, provided the actions can be completed quickly.

- **Long-running transactions should be accomplished asynchronously and XLANG schedules should be designed to complete COM calls quickly.** Results from asynchronous work can be communicated back to the XLANG schedule instance through message queues, or through COM calls. With COM, the name of a "response" port can be passed in the form of a moniker that will be valid even with computer restarts.

Related Topic

"Moniker Syntax" in Chapter 8, "BizTalk Orchestration Services"

Optimizing BizTalk Messaging Services

To optimize BizTalk Messaging Services:

- Send documents to a server group. BizTalk Server groups are used to distribute work across multiple servers. To send data to BizTalk Server, use the following methods:

  - Configure a receive function (such as Message Queuing or File).

  - Call the **Submit** method on the BizTalk Server **Interchange** object.

  Using receive functions provides better performance than using the **Submit** method to call the **Interchange** object because the receive functions run within BizTalk services and can cache the internal state of objects, whereas the **Submit** method runs out-of-process and has to rebuild its internal state for each call.

  Calling the **Interchange** object for submission rather than using a receive function uses more resources because the **Interchange** object needs to be created outside the BizTalk Server process. However, if the **Interchange** object is used, there are two methods available for sending data to the servers in a group:

  - Statically configure portions of the total submissions to specific servers within the group, although this does not provide much fault tolerance if the server, which has a transport service, is statically mapped to a BizTalk Server that has failed.

  - Use the Microsoft Application Center 2000 component load-balancing (CLB) functionality to improve performance. BizTalk Server groups do not provide load balancing for the submission of documents. In addition to load balancing, CLB provides fault tolerance. For more information about CLB, see "Component Load Balancing" earlier in this chapter.

◆ **Important**

- Do not replicate the default XLANG Scheduler application or any COM+ applications that host XLANG schedules. If component load balancing is used, these COM+ applications must be installed on each server. You can replicate COM components that are bound to XLANG schedules.

Creating and Optimizing Specifications

If the default global tracking settings are used, BizTalk Server 2000 can support a 20-MB XML Unicode format document. For other file types, such as an ANSI flat file, BizTalk Server does not support a 20-MB file size because any file that is not XML has to be converted to XML. The conversion process adds XML tags to the data, thus increasing the size of the document that BizTalk Server needs to process. Other file types must be less than 20 MB to maintain optimal performance by BizTalk Server. The amount of memory required to process a document that has been converted to XML depends on the original structure of the document. If global tracking settings are enabled, XML Unicode format documents that are larger than 20 MB can be processed without greatly impacting BizTalk Server performance.

✏ **Note**

- Exceeding the size limit for tracking interchanges impacts the performance of BizTalk Server. For more information about the size limit, see "Interchange and document size limit" in Chapter 11, "Administering Servers and Applications." Performance is also affected by document logging. For more information about document logging, see "To set document logging properties" in Chapter 9, "Configuring BizTalk Messaging Services."

When designing specifications, you can configure validation rules within a specification. For example, you can specify that a field contain a particular data type (such as a string) or more complex rules (such as requiring a field to be validated against a list of 80 values). The latter requires that the data be checked against 80 values; if it does not conform to one of them, the specification fails validation. Specification validation in BizTalk Server is enabled by default; it affects performance but ensures the validity of the data being sent or received. You can disable validation, which increases performance and might not adversely affect the validity of data, because BizTalk Server has several other mechanisms for validating data. For example, if you have a map that requires certain data types and values and specification validation is disabled, the data successfully passes the parsing phase but fails during the serializing phase when the map is applied. If other mechanisms (such as maps that rely on valid data) are available, specification validation can be disabled to avoid the potential performance degradation caused by the validation process. Alternatively, you might choose to do so because you have agreed to data standards with business partners and have validated these transactions. You might also choose to do so because you have complete control of how the data is sent (such as application-to-application transactions).

The following registry setting can be used to disable validation:

- **NoValidation.** If specification validation is not required (documents are not validated against a specification for settings such as minimum/maximum values, data types, and/or required values), set this to a nonzero value and the data will not be validated. This might help with performance but can result in nonvalid data being sent. Changing the specification validation to a nonzero value might be the right option for servers that are receiving documents for which the organization has control over the structure.

The registry setting is accomplished at the individual server level. When specification validation is on, every document processed by the server is validated against its specification. This performs more slowly than if no specification validation were used.

Recommended solutions for optimizing document size and specifications

To optimize performance of BizTalk Server:

- Do not include more fields and attributes in specifications than necessary. Increased fields and attributes equate to increased memory requirements for BizTalk Server. A larger specification requires a proportional increase in memory. For example, the EDI specifications included with BizTalk Server are compliant with EDI standards. Typically, most organizations that use EDI specifications require approximately ten percent of the entire specification. So if an organization and its trading partner use only ten percent of the entire specification, the unnecessary records and fields can be deleted and the modified specification can be used for transactions.

- If specification validation is enabled, do not specify validation rules in specifications for fields that will contain valid data. For example, if a field contains a number but will be processed only as a string (a phone number, for example), do not specify that it must be numeric. In this situation it is not necessary to specify a data type because the default data type is string. Therefore, the data type field could be left blank. Specifying acceptable values for a field takes longer to validate than a simple data type validation.

Creating and Optimizing Maps

Translating data, as part of a transaction, might reduce the performance of BizTalk Server 2000. Mapping specifications can be CPU-intensive, which can reduce the ability of BizTalk Server to process the overall transaction. The level to which BizTalk Server is affected depends largely on the complexity of the map being used for translation. For example, mapping a field called productID in the source specification to a field called itemID in the destination specification is not as intensive as performing a complex mathematical operation on the data being translated.

Recommended solutions for designing maps

- Use functoids only when needed. Functoids use script, which causes BizTalk Server to load a scripting engine. This might degrade performance as opposed to native XML transformations.

- Use the **Database Lookup** functoid only when needed. BizTalk Server must establish a database connection, query for data, populate a recordset, and close the connection each time this functoid is used. This can degrade performance of BizTalk Server.

- Avoid invoking COM objects within functoid scripts and using custom functoids. Both of these techniques cause BizTalk Server to instantiate an instance of a COM object. This affects the performance of the overall operation. In addition, the performance of instantiating COM objects is affected by the answers to the following questions:

  - Is it in-process or out-of-process?

  - Is the object local or remote?

  - How well is the object written?

  - Is it transactional?

- Analyze each map to determine how to achieve optimal performance. For example, two different techniques can be used to concatenate two source fields together and have the resultant value placed in two different destination fields. The first concatenation technique would be to use one concatenation functoid and map its output to two places. The second concatenation technique would be to use two functoids, each with a single output link to a destination source field. The first technique is slightly more efficient because the script, which runs as part of the functoid, is called only once. Through testing, you can determine which techniques result in the best performance.

Optimizing BizTalk Server Group Properties

In BizTalk Server Administration, you can specify the following properties in the **BizTalk Server Group Properties** dialog box:

- **Messaging Management object cache refresh interval (seconds).** You can set this field to a maximum of 300 seconds. BizTalk Server 2000 caches configurations (such as channels, messaging ports, envelopes, and document definitions) in memory to avoid calling the database each time. If these objects are not regularly changed, set this value to 300 to reduce the number of times data is written to and read from the database. Because BizTalk Server refreshes management objects every five minutes, the service must be restarted for the change to take effect immediately.

- **Disable document tracking.** You can use the **Tracking** tab to enable or disable document tracking. If tracking is not used, disable this field to minimize the number of read/writes to the database for a single transaction. If this field is enabled, BizTalk Server connects to the database and logs data. Do not disable this field unless tracking is not needed. However, it is highly recommended that document tracking remain enabled. For more information about setting tracking properties, see "To configure tracking properties for a server group" in Chapter 11, "Administering Servers and Applications."

🗒 **Note**

- A size limit exists for tracking interchanges. If the size limit is exceeded, the performance of BizTalk Server is affected. For more information about the size limit, see "Interchange and document size limit" in Chapter 11, "Administering Servers and Applications." Performance is also affected by document logging. For more information about document logging, see "To set document logging properties" in Chapter 9, "Configuring BizTalk Messaging Services."

- **Arrange the server call sequence.** You can prioritize BizTalk Server parsers if a group is predominately receiving a particular document type. BizTalk Server has four parsers that it uses to parse data: XML, EDIFACT, X12, and Flat File. When BizTalk Server receives a document, it tries to parse it using these parsers in the order in which they are listed. If an organization primarily receives a particular document type, the order of the parsers should be changed so that the first one matches the type of documents being received.

Optimizing Server Properties

In BizTalk Server Administration, you can set the following properties in the *<Server>* **Properties** dialog box:

- **Create multiple instances of receive functions.** This enables BizTalk Server to poll multiple receive functions for documents that are processed. To balance the load of documents across several computers, locate the receive functions on separate computers. Each polling location must be unique and must have a separate receive function. To avoid overloading any individual receive function, the business application that sends documents must evenly distribute the documents to all the polling locations.

- **Maximum number of receive function threads allowed.** You can specify how many receive function worker threads per processor you want for a receive function. Setting this too low can cause a slowdown in BizTalk Server because it uses I/O completion ports. Setting this too high should not have serious effects, but it might cause performance degradation. You can adjust this number to find the optimal value for your setup. The recommended value for the **Maximum number of receive function threads allowed** is 4.

- **Maximum number of worker threads per processor allowed.** You can specify the number of worker threads per processor for the processing side. By appropriately adjusting the number of worker threads, you can improve performance. In BizTalk Server Administration, right-click a server in the console tree and click **Properties**. Change the default value in the **Maximum number of worker threads per processor allowed** box. The default value is 4. The recommended value is from 10 to 16, depending on the deployment.

Optimizing Registry Settings

You can optimize the registry settings to improve BizTalk Server performance. All keys should be added as DWORD values to \HKEY_LOCAL_MACHINE\SYSTEM\CurrentControlSet\Services\BTSSVC. To improve performance, you can implement the following registry setting adjustments:

- **NoValidation.** Use this registry key to disable specification validation. If specification validation is not required (documents are not validated against a specification for minimum/maximum values, data types, or required values, for example), set this to a nonzero value and the data will not be validated. While this might improve performance, it can result in nonvalid data being sent. This setting would be appropriate for servers that are receiving documents for which the organization controls the structure.

- **ParserRefreshInterval.** By default this is set to 60,000 (60 seconds). This value indicates how often BizTalk Server should check the database to see if a new parser has been added (this is the only group-level property that is refreshed while the server is running). If no new parsers will be added, set this value to 0 and BizTalk Server will not check the database. This value is also used to verify if new parsers have been added to the Tracking database group settings or if the settings have been altered.

- **CacheSize.** Use this registry key to indicate how large the BizTalk Server management object cache is allowed to grow. The default value for this is 20. Therefore, as soon as the BizTalk Server object cache exceeds 20 channels, messaging ports, envelopes, or document definitions, BizTalk Server must delete some items from memory. If a server has a high volume of memory, this value can be set higher (above 20) and BizTalk Server will keep more in memory. This does not affect the refresh interval. BizTalk Server deletes the cached objects and reloads them when they have expired.

- **BatchSize.** Use this value only with the Message Queue receive function. By default BatchSize is set to 20. To improve performance, BizTalk Server reads up to 20 items at a time from the queue and sends all 20 within one transaction. Reducing the number of times data is written to a database greatly improves performance. If a deadlock occurs, and BizTalk Server ends the transaction, it must resubmit the items. BizTalk Server does not lose the documents. Values that exceed 20 have not been tested. Do not set this value to 0.

To improve processing performance

1. Click **Start**, click **Run**, type **regedit**, and then click **OK**.

2. In the **Registry Editor** dialog box, click the expand indicator (+) for the **HKEY_LOCAL_MACHINE** node; expand **SYSTEM**, **CurrentControlSet**, and **Services**, and then click **BTSSvc**.

3. Right-click in the details pane, point to **New**, and then click **DWORD Value**.

4. Type **NoValidation** and press ENTER twice.

    The **Edit DWORD Value** dialog box appears.

5. In the **Value data** box, type any nonzero value, such as 1, and click **OK**.

   The default value is 0 (validation).

6. Right-click in the details pane, point to **New**, and then click **DWORD Value**.

7. Type **ParserRefreshInterval** and press ENTER.

8. Right-click in the details pane, point to **New**, and then click **DWORD Value**.

9. Type **CacheSize** and press ENTER twice.

   The **Edit DWORD Value** dialog box appears.

10. In the **Value data** box, type the number of channels, messaging ports, envelopes, and document definitions that you expect to or do have in memory.

11. Right-click in the details pane, point to **New**, and then click **DWORD Value**.

12. Type **BatchSize** and press ENTER twice.

    The **Edit DWORD Value** dialog box appears.

13. In the **Value data** box, type a value for the number of items you want to process as a batch.

Optimizing Encryption

Using encryption or other security mechanisms might decrease the performance of BizTalk Server. When using encryption, follow these recommendations:

- **Increase CPU clock rating (MHz).** Increasing the number of processors will increase performance.

- **Increase the number of servers.**

- **Use a faster CPU.**

- **Separate BizTalk Server functionality.** For example, send and receive functions can be placed on separate servers. The HTTPS transport service can also be placed on a separate server.

- **Use an existing virtual private network (VPN) if File or Message Queuing is used.** If a VPN is available, data transfer is secure. It is not required to secure BizTalk Server transactions if all data transfer conducted with trading partners is secured through a VPN.

- **Purchase encryption hardware accelerator cards.** Accelerator cards provide dedicated processors that can eliminate the performance impact of encryption and decryption on a server's CPU. Accelerator cards are less expensive than adding multiple CPUs.

Optimizing Communication

BizTalk Server provides both synchronous communication and asynchronous communication integration mechanisms. BizTalk Server 2000 can accept documents through COM integration or through server receive functions (File or Message Queuing).

Typically, when a document is sent to BizTalk Server, it is placed in the Shared Queue database. BizTalk Server polls the database and then processes the document. This process is an asynchronous communication mechanism. It uses the Microsoft SQL Server database as a queue for check-pointing documents that are waiting to be processed. This extra layer of abstraction allows the transport service to send documents to BizTalk Server independent of the transport mechanism used to deliver the documents.

A synchronous communication interchange bypasses all queues and processes all the components required by the messaging port on the calling thread. For synchronous communication protocols, an optional response document is returned, if available. This method is valid only for a single channel match and only for a single messaging port (not distribution lists). If the parameters that are set cause multiple channels to match, a synchronous communication submission returns an error, which indicates that multiple channel matches are not allowed for a synchronous communication submission. This method can be used only for single document interchanges. If the submission contains multiple documents, an error is returned for synchronous submissions, which indicates that multiple document submissions are not allowed. This method does not support groups. Synchronous communication is not scalable. Synchronous communication uses a single thread to process a transaction and cannot be load-balanced with other servers in the group because the entire process must run on the server that sends documents.

The synchronous communication mechanism sends documents directly to BizTalk Server for immediate processing. BizTalk Server blocks the return to the caller of the **IInterchange::SubmitSync** method until processing is completed, whereby a response document is delivered to the caller. This mechanism is available only to the COM-based integration method.

Recommended solutions for optimizing synchronous and asynchronous communication

To optimize performance of BizTalk Server:

- To achieve optimal performance and scalability, asynchronous communication is highly recommended. Asynchronous communication is highly scalable and provides a high level of throughput. Synchronous communication calls provide a near-immediate response to the caller under a high volume of transactions because each **SubmitSync** call runs under a separate thread. However, if there are many calls at once, this leads to many threads running on a single server, thereby degrading the overall performance of BizTalk Server. Microsoft Windows 2000 is designed to context switch between all the threads, thus degrading the overall performance of BizTalk Server. Additionally, the following criteria cause a synchronous communication submission to fail but do not cause an asynchronous communication submission to fail:

  - If the transaction criteria matches more than one channel.

  - If the interchange contains multiple documents.

- Self-routing documents might degrade the performance of BizTalk Server.

Configuring Firewalls

Firewalls help secure internal networks, but they introduce latency and can potentially create a single point of failure. Even if a load-balancing mechanism is used to alleviate the single point of failure, a firewall can reduce a network's performance.

When configuring a BizTalk Server 2000 environment with a firewall, two primary configurations are recommended:

- **Configuration 1.** Install servers on an internal corporate network and some, which communicate to trading partners, on a corporate demilitarized zone (DMZ). A company that wants to host its own Internet services without sacrificing unauthorized access to its private network uses a DMZ. The DMZ is the boundary between the Internet and an internal network's line of defense, usually a combination of firewalls and bastion hosts, which are gateways between inside networks and outside networks. The servers in the DMZ should use local transport services, such as HTTP, Message Queue, or SMTP. In this environment, all inbound and outbound transactions pass through a firewall. The servers in the DMZ send documents through another firewall to Microsoft SQL Server. This configuration allows servers, such as BizTalk Server and HTTP in the DMZ, to communicate with SQL Server through an internal firewall.

- **Configuration 2.** Install the servers on a corporate network. Trading partners exchanging documents through the Internet send their data using SMTP/HTTP servers in the DMZ (first firewall of protection). These servers then send the data to the servers residing on the corporate network through a second firewall.

Both configurations impact performance. To avoid a noticeable degradation in performance, you can construct the firewall to accommodate a typical number of transactions between an organization and its trading partners.

Architecture Design, Review, and Testing

The key components of BizTalk Server 2000 include the BizTalk services, the BizTalk Server databases, and the transport services. Poor configuration of any component can degrade the performance of the entire system.

This section provides comprehensive detail about defining, testing, and refining the architecture of BizTalk Server to optimize performance.

Architectural Design

To accurately determine the number of the documents that can be processed by BizTalk Server 2000, you must first consider if the following are in use:

- Specification validation

- Application integration components

- Transport services

- Encryption

- BizTalk Orchestration Services

- Firewalls

- Maps

You must also consider the size of the documents being processed, as well as the current server configuration.

Performance testing is successful when accomplished with controlled processes. It is important to start with a few variables and then slowly add additional variables. When performance begins to degrade, you can easily identify the cause of degradation.

Related Topics

Chapter 11, "Administering Servers and Applications"

Chapter 8, "BizTalk Orchestration Services"

"Creating Application Integration Components" in Chapter 15, "Creating Custom Components"

Chapter 5, "Creating Specifications"

Chapter 6, "Mapping Data"

Develop Transaction Components

To develop transaction components, you must design transactions and set transaction properties for business processes. For more information about designing transactions and setting transaction properties, see the following sections in Chapter 8, "BizTalk Orchestration Services":

- "Designing Business Processes"

- "Designing Transactions"

- "Transaction Properties for an XLANG Schedule Drawing"

For information about techniques that can help you to determine the most efficient transaction configuration, see "Evaluating the Performance of a Configuration" later in this chapter.

To develop transaction components, you must first determine the transaction types that the components process. In an application-to-application or business-to-business environment, you must determine transaction needs and transaction profiles. For example, you might have a scenario in which a single transaction receives a custom XML purchase order and maps it to a standard EDI purchase order, which is later processed by a custom internal application.

This scenario requires that you create a specification for the XML purchase order and a specification for the EDI purchase order. To create these specifications, use BizTalk Editor, which includes XML and EDI templates. Because the templates include all potential records and fields, you can remove unnecessary records and fields, and then save the templates as the final specifications. During design time, any fields in a specification that require validation decrease the performance of BizTalk Server 2000. For more information about optimizing specifications, see "Creating and Optimizing Specifications" earlier in this chapter.

In addition to creating a specification, you must map data. Because there are a number of ways to translate data in map files (by using XSLT translations, functoids, or a custom script), all of which affect performance, it is important to test different translation methods. Testing one method of data translation over another helps to reduce performance impacts to BizTalk Server as a result of mapping. For more information, see "Creating and Optimizing Maps" earlier in this chapter.

Identify Transports

To determine how to send and receive data, consider if the following are in use:

- Business-to-business transactions

- Application-to-application transactions

- Transport services (send and receive)

- Encryption

- HTTPS or S/MIME

Consider whether different transports are needed based on the type of transactions you are processing. Determine whether unique transports are required for business-to-business and application-to-application transactions or if the same transports can be used for these two types of transactions.

Initial Architecture

To successfully plan an initial architecture, consider the following:

- One server with Microsoft SQL Server and BizTalk Server can be used to process a low volume of transactions.

- Installing BizTalk Server and SQL Server on separate computers can be used for a moderate volume of transactions.

- An existing SMTP transport service can be used to send and receive data. Placing this service on a separate server is recommended for this transport type.

- HTTP, Message Queuing, or File transport services can be used to write data to disk drives on other servers than the local BizTalk Server, which can improve BizTalk Server performance.

An initial architecture should contain as many separate servers as possible. For example, within a company, one person might administer SMTP servers and Message Queuing, whereas another person might handle security policies. The goal of the initial architecture is to determine how many servers are needed and the hardware required by those servers to process the anticipated work. After you determine the required number of servers, test the initial architecture.

Architecture Testing and Analysis

Prior to testing the architecture, define the architectural components, determine the transaction needs and profiles, determine what transaction components need to be developed, and determine the necessary transports. Begin this process by creating a baseline, which requires the following:

- Configure BizTalk Messaging Services, organizations, document definitions, channels, and messaging ports needed to process transactions.

- Configure BizTalk Orchestration Services.

- Install and/or configure any COM+ applications, BizTalk Server channels, databases, or message queues required for XLANG schedules.

Once a baseline has been established, process transactions using BizTalk Server. This test helps to identify factors affecting performance.

Evaluating the Performance of a Configuration

You can use the Microsoft Windows 2000 Performance tool to test the performance of BizTalk Messaging Services.

To use the Performance tool, on the **Start** menu, point to **Programs**, point to **Administrative Tools**, and then click **Performance**. The System Monitor, which is part of the Performance tool, graphically displays counter readings as they change over time. There are, however, different counters that should be monitored depending on the system component being monitored. Numerous white papers are available describing how to monitor performance for Windows 2000, IIS, SQL Server, and the Message Queue; however, the following table lists only some of the primary objects and counters to monitor. In addition, the table contains specific information regarding the objects and counters to monitor to determine BizTalk Messaging Services performance.

Object	Counter	Observation	Component affected
Active Server Pages	Requests queued	There should not be a significant queue except at peak periods.	HTTP transport services that use .asp pages
	Requests/sec	Indicates the volume of ASP requests the HTTP transport services are receiving (if using ASP). If files are posted to an HTTP page, this counter does not provide any pertinent information.	HTTP transport services that use .asp pages
	Request wait time	Close to zero.	HTTP transport services that use .asp pages
Network Segment	Bytes received per second/Bytes sent per second	If this number is close to the capacity of the connection, and processor and memory use are moderate, the connection might affect performance.	All
Process, Inetinfo instance	Private bytes	Monitor this for memory leaks or size approaching maximum available RAM.	HTTP transport service
Memory	Available bytes	Available bytes should not stay below 10 MB consistently. If so, a memory spike would cause paging to disk to start.	All
	Page Faults/sec, Memory: Pages Input/sec, and Memory: Page Reads/sec	If these numbers are low, the server should be responding to requests quickly. If they are high, an increase in the amount of RAM on your server might be needed.	All

Object	Counter	Observation	Component affected
Physical Disk	Disk read/writes/sec	Combined, these two counters should be significantly under the maximum capacity for the disk device. To enable this counter, on the **Start** menu, point to **Programs**, point to **Accessories**, and then click **Command Prompt**. At the command prompt, type **diskperf –y**. Then restart the computer.	SQL Server, Message Queue, and File transport services
	% Disk time	This counter should be well below 100 percent. If it is above this value (and it can go into the 1000 percent range), add more physical disks or move one of the databases to another server.	SQL Server, Message Queue, and File transport services
	Current Disk Queue Length	This counter is the number of requests outstanding on the disk at the time the performance data is collected. This counter should average less than 2 for good performance.	BizTalk Server, SQL Server
SQL Server	I/O transactions/sec	Indicates how much activity the SQL server actually performs.	SQL Server
BizTalk Server	Documents Processed/sec	Indicates how quickly BizTalk Server 2000 is polling documents from its Work queue and sending them.	BizTalk Messaging Services
BizTalk Server	Documents Received/sec	Indicates how quickly BizTalk Server is sending documents to the Work queue. This number reflects only the number of documents BizTalk Server has received (this includes documents that fail parsing), not the number of documents BizTalk Server checkpoints to its Work queue. The number of documents that are checkpointed to the Work queue is essentially equal to the Documents Processed/sec counter.	BizTalk Messaging Services

Object	Counter	Observation	Component affected
BizTalk Server	Synchronous Submissions/sec, Asynchronous Submissions/sec	Indicates how quickly the **Submit** method and/or the **SubmitSync** method calls occur. Because each interchange can contain any number of documents, this counter is not useful for determining documents processed. If pass-through (processing interchanges without parsing them) is being used exclusively, this is the counter you need to monitor to determine inbound performance.	BizTalk Messaging Services
Message Queue	Messages in queue	This number should not get extremely large (over 50K) because it will cause excessive memory use on the Message Queue server and degrade the performance of the entire system.	Message Queue transport service
System	Processor Queue Length	This counter displays the number of threads waiting to be executed in the queue that is shared by all processors on the system. If this counter has a sustained value of two or more threads, the processor is degrading the performance of the entire system.	All
	Context switches/sec	If this is a high number on BizTalk Server, it could be because send and receive functions are running on the same server. If this is the case, consider separating the send and receive functions to separate servers.	All
Processor	%Processor Time	If this counter's value is high, while the network adapter card and disk I/O remain well below capacity, the processor is affecting performance. On a multiprocessor computer, examine this counter to identify any imbalance. Additionally, while peak utilization can be 100 percent, sustained utilization should be below this value. All server elements can be scaled horizontally.	All
Web Service	Get or post requests/sec	Indicates the volume of files being received through the HTTP **get/post** methods.	HTTP transport service

There are no counters specific to the SMTP transport service listed because there are a variety of SMTP transport service products available. Regardless of the SMTP transport service being used, monitor the volume of messages sent to and from BizTalk Server. Monitoring the counters listed in the table enables you to identify performance degradation. Because all the components work together to determine the health of a system, do not make drastic changes to your system configuration based on the poor performance of one.

Data obtained from performance monitoring is also useful for identifying symptoms that can contribute to problems. For example, a high amount of disk activity might indicate that SQL Server is writing a large amount of data to disk, but it might also indicate that the system is often paging to disk. Excessive disk paging typically indicates that memory is too low. In this case, the disk activity is the indicator of a problem, but not the problem.

Improving the Architecture

By identifying areas that affect performance, you can refine the system architecture to achieve optimal results. For example, hardware might need to be upgraded, or different components of BizTalk Server might need to be moved to separate servers. Additionally, you might need to adjust BizTalk Server settings. For more information about adjusting settings, see "Optimizing Server Properties" earlier in this chapter.

Ensure that changes are made methodically. After implementing a change, such as adding CPUs, changing a setting, or separating functionality to separate servers, document the change and then test the new configuration to determine if performance has improved. If the new configuration enhances performance, you can continue to modify the configuration. However, if the new configuration is degrading performance, reconfigure the system to its previous state and analyze the data to determine what might be contributing to the problem.

Maintaining Performance

To maintain performance, create an ongoing maintenance plan to ensure the health and future performance of BizTalk Server. BizTalk Server will most likely process increased numbers of documents over time. Although the initial BizTalk Server architecture might have performed well, if the number of transactions has increased over time, it might not be capable of sustaining the same level of performance unless the system architecture or configuration is modified. Hardware failures, or out-of-memory conditions, also can affect the performance of a system.

Creating a Performance Maintenance Plan

A successful monitoring plan includes:

- **A detailed plan of which counters to monitor.** For example, there are several Windows 2000 System Monitor counters, thresholds to monitor, and possible interpretations of the problems that might be indicated by the thresholds. Additionally, you can also monitor application-level problems such as whether SQL Server queries should return valid data or return hardware problem conditions.

- **Identifying processes for resolving performance issues.** For example, a Windows 2000 event-log message might be written, e-mail notification might be enabled, or a custom program might start a series of events.

- **Defining which performance thresholds generate a notification.** For example, a monitoring tool might be configured to write an event to the Windows 2000 event log if the CPU reaches 90-percent use capacity. However, if the CPU stayed at 90-percent use capacity for more than 5 minutes, an e-mail message might be sent. Defining different actions for different problem-severity levels depends on the monitoring tool that you use.

- **Defining the course of action in response to events published in Windows 2000 event logs.** Windows 2000, BizTalk Server 2000, SQL Server, and native Microsoft transport services such as Message Queuing and HTTP write events to the Windows 2000 event log. This event log contains valuable information that can indicate impending problems on one of the servers in a BizTalk Server system. If addressed early, you can avoid a system failure that would degrade the performance of the overall system. A plan should include the frequency at which the logs are monitored and archived, and include the party responsible for the tasks. A third-party tool can be used to accumulate the logs from multiple servers and write them to a database for consolidated analysis. These tools can also be used to purge the logs from the servers.

- **Determining the required tools for performance monitoring.** The built-in Windows 2000 System Monitor tool examines performance counters and can take action when a predefined condition occurs. For more information about configuring System Monitor alerts, see "Setting up a monitoring configuration" in Windows 2000 Help. Additionally, Microsoft Application Center 2000, as well as a number of other third-party tools, perform this functionality with additional features such as logging to a database and performing application-level tests.

Using Application Center 2000

Microsoft Application Center 2000 contains a tool called Health Monitor. Health Monitor supercedes the functionality of the Windows 2000 event log and system monitor tools. It allows administrators to set up monitors. These monitors include checking TCP/IP, performance monitor counter thresholds, event log errors, and WMI events. Conditions can be configured for these monitors so that when certain criteria are met (for example, when a threshold of 90 percent on a CPU is met or exceeded), an action occurs such as taking a server offline or sending an e-mail message to an administrator. These tools can be used to proactively monitor and maintain the performance of BizTalk Server 2000.

◆ Important

- Do not replicate the default XLANG Scheduler application or any COM+ applications that host XLANG schedules. If component load balancing is used, these COM+ applications must be installed on each server. You can replicate COM components that are bound to XLANG schedules.

Microsoft BizTalk Server 2000 Deployment Considerations

BizTalk Server 2000 provides an application infrastructure that enables businesses to implement remote data interchange with external partners. BizTalk Server 2000 also solves the problem of integrating dissimilar applications across multiple remote and autonomous business units within a business domain. This chapter describes the deployment models and considerations for business-to-business electronic-commerce and enterprise application integration (EAI) implementations. For small businesses, deploying BizTalk Server can be straightforward and relatively trivial, but for large global businesses with a distributed application environment, much care and thought must be taken to design a deployment architecture that reduces the complexity of management while providing a robust and extensible application environment.

This chapter outlines two basic deployment models and six types of deployment considerations:

- **Deployment models.** The deployment models are grouped into two general categories: application integration within a small- to medium-sized organization (SMORG), and application integration within a large organization (LORG). The information in this section will help you determine which deployment model is appropriate for your business environment.

- **Deployment considerations.** This section contains a variety of guidelines that describe the issues you need to consider when you deploy BizTalk Server 2000. The six most important deployment considerations are:

  - **Firewall restrictions and considerations.** Many of the constraints that are placed on the implementation of business-to-business deployments are driven by the need for protection from external attacks. This section describes what you need to consider when you deploy BizTalk Server 2000 behind a firewall.

  - **Load balancing considerations.** This section describes how to increase performance and optimize the use of processing power in a multiple-server deployment.

  - **Building scalable and available Web applications.** This section compares the issues you need to consider when you build Web applications using either the synchronous model or the asynchronous model.

- **Designing BizTalk Server groups.** This section explains the key organizing principle in BizTalk Server Administration.

- **BizTalk Messaging Services.** This section describes some background information, information about best practices, and troubleshooting tips relating to BizTalk Messaging Services.

- **BizTalk Orchestration Services.** This section describes some of the design issues that are specific to BizTalk Orchestration Services that you need to consider for BizTalk Server deployment.

In This Chapter

- Deployment Models
- Deployment Considerations
- Conclusion

Deployment Models

Unlike many competitive products that focus on either external or internal data interchange, BizTalk Server 2000 offers a platform and feature set that solves both the business-to-business and enterprise application integration (EAI) problem set. It can be as difficult to integrate custom-built applications with applications that are purchased as it is to integrate business processes between trading partners. The architecture for integrating applications within a business depends greatly on the size of the business, its structure, and the complexity of the business processes. The following sections focus on two deployment models. The first deployment model is for a simple small- to medium-sized business. The second model is for a more complex, large-scale business.

Small- to Medium-sized Organization Application Integration

Typically, small- to medium-sized organizations (SMORGs) have a centralized Information Technology (IT) group that controls systems and applications. Often, a limited number of systems and applications within these businesses are core to business operations. Point-to-point application integration is a typical deployment architecture in this environment.

In a SMORG environment, you can deploy BizTalk Server as a routing and transformation hub that connects all applications with a single BizTalk Server group to facilitate application integration. Channels, ports, and XLANG schedules are created for the purpose of integrating specific applications. This model for a simple deployment of BizTalk Server is suitable for SMORGs. The same deployment in a LORG environment can quickly become inefficient and unmanageable. In point-to-point application integration, there is a one-to-one relationship between an application on one system and an application on another system. For example, a procurement application on one system might have a point-to-point application integration relationship with an inventory application on another system. Using BizTalk Server, management is centralized and each application is under the control of a single group.

The following illustration shows point-to-point application integration.

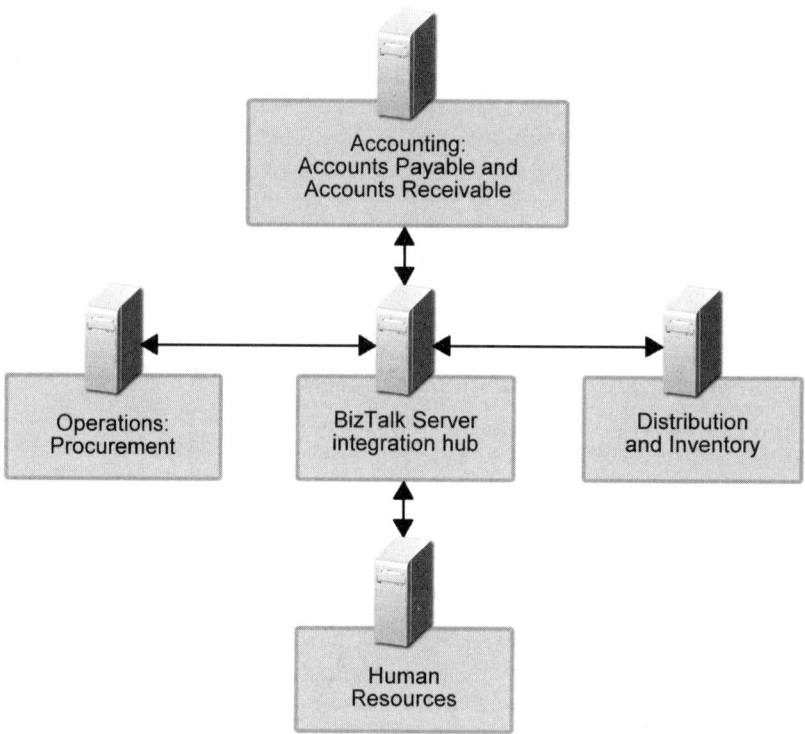

Large Organization Application Integration

Many large businesses do not use a single centrally managed system. Large organizations (LORGs) are typically organized in autonomous, discrete business units that develop, maintain, support, and administer their own systems. There is a need for these business units to share data with applications that are controlled by other business units as well as to communicate with external trading partners. Cross-business-unit integration is the combined burden of the central Information Technology (IT) group and the business unit development staff.

Many LORGs need a more distributed and manageable solution than the simple point-to-point application integration used by SMORGs. Competitive EAI technologies that specifically market to LORGs have adopted a new paradigm for integrating applications, known as Publish and Subscribe, or Pub-Sub. In Pub-Sub–based integration products, the publishers of, and subscribers to, the data are unaware of each other. Data is published by one application and subscribed to by other applications. This paradigm focuses on integrating applications with the data distribution infrastructure of the business domain, instead of integrating applications directly with each other. In this model, applications can be easily plugged into the business network data bus and the applications can participate in the business process flow without creating tightly coupled dependencies between systems. The BizTalk Server distributed integration bus can be deployed to provide Pub-Sub–based integration functionality. The BizTalk Server distributed integration bus is made up of distribution lists that enable a one-to-many data distribution model.

The following illustration shows one-to-many application integration using the BizTalk Server distributed integration bus.

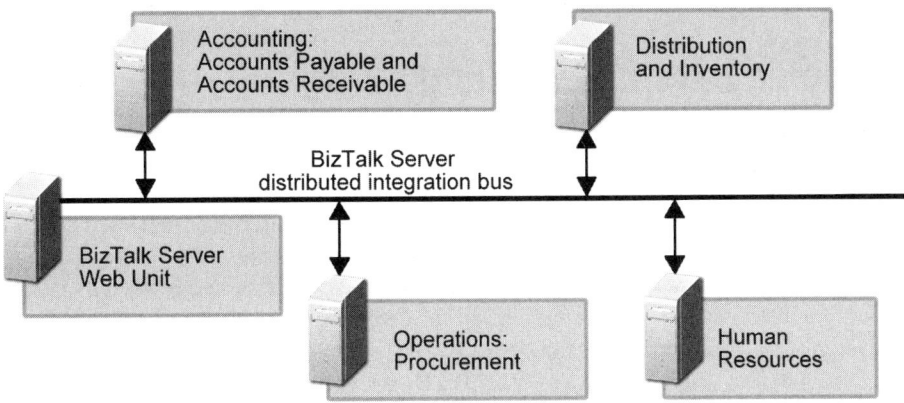

XML Format Integration

Because applications are not bound by interfaces or common data stores but by common or intermediary data formats, the applications can evolve their implementations without affecting the overall process flow of the business. BizTalk Server 2000 provides the basis for implementing content-based routing and an integration platform based on formats of document types, also known as specifications. BizTalk Server is document-type or specification-centric in nature. To achieve a greater level of business integration than most other products, BizTalk Server uses XML. When applications require specific non-XML formats, BizTalk Server provides transformation and serialization features that can deliver data in the native format of the target application or endpoint at the point of integration/transport. The ultimate goal is that the data flowing between applications is in an intermediary XML format and not in a format of any particular or specific application. This goal might not be realized initially and does not hamper the integration.

BizTalk Server Distribution Lists

A key feature of BizTalk Server is the distribution list, which allows one-to-many distribution of data to applications and other BizTalk Server groups. Distribution lists are implemented in BizTalk Messaging Services by first creating a distribution list that contains a set of previously configured messaging ports. Channels for particular types of documents are then added to deliver documents to the distribution list that contains a collection of messaging ports that determines the delivery endpoints of the document. Each messaging port in the distribution list refers to another organization or application.

Loosely Coupled Integration Using a Data Distribution Bus

BizTalk Server distribution lists facilitate the deployment of BizTalk Server-based enterprise application integration (EAI) middleware that interconnects applications and external counter-parties in a *loosely coupled* fashion. In this context, *loosely coupled* is defined as integrating endpoints by using a messaging infrastructure that does not require the sending and receiving endpoints to be preconfigured with specific knowledge of the counter endpoint's existence. Each BizTalk Server group can be configured as a part of a BizTalk Server data distribution bus so that each BizTalk Server group is aware of other BizTalk Server groups that have channels configured to receive and process a particular set of data. In this fashion, BizTalk Server groups can be linked for more efficient distribution of data by using distribution lists. Each BizTalk Server group can represent a subset of all endpoints, whether they are applications or trading partners. Effectively, each BizTalk Server group can serve to model the business unit and departmental system partitioning. For example, BizTalk Server groups used by the accounting department do not need to carry configuration data for subscribing members of other BizTalk Server groups that require copies of the same messages. BizTalk Server inter-group document delivery is a more efficient way to distribute data than using application-to-application integration.

Deployment Considerations

The architecture for deploying EAI, using distributed and discrete application processing, is driven by the necessity to build business domains and boundaries. This section discusses and recommends solutions for these deployment problems. As deployments of BizTalk Server mature, new and updated XLANG schedules must be seamlessly integrated with tools that provide version control of server configurations. In high-performance environments, it is critical that BizTalk Server can be remotely monitored and proactively administered.

The BizTalk Server 2000 deployment areas for you to consider are:

- Firewall restrictions and considerations.
- Load balancing considerations.
- Building scalable and available Web applications.
- Designing BizTalk Server groups.
- BizTalk Messaging Services.
- BizTalk Orchestration Services.

Firewall Restrictions and Considerations

Among the challenges that arise when businesses engage in business-to-business data interchange is the question of how companies can implement robust application solutions while maintaining a secure environment. Protecting systems and data is paramount to most businesses. Web-based application deployment must take into account the dangerous and volatile environment encountered on the Internet, where attacks are anticipated and occur frequently. To protect their domains, many businesses use firewalls that restrict network traffic to the HTTPS and FTP transport protocols. Additionally, firewalls open only a limited number of ports to the Internet (for example, port 80 for HTTP). Also, double firewalls are often used to isolate Web servers from an intranet or from local area networks (LANs). The space between these firewalls is referred to as the demilitarized zone (DMZ). In the past, network groups within businesses have stipulated that data cannot be persisted within the DMZ, and that all traffic from the DMZ to an intranet must be strictly monitored or filtered for textual data, using HTTP as the transport protocol. However, some of these restrictions have recently been relaxed, as new business models require the implementation of Web-based applications running dynamic content. Previously, only static Web content crossed into the DMZ.

HTTP-Only Interactions

Many Web-based applications require synchronous interactions between the client and the server. Although there are concerns about the scalability of this type of application architecture, it is still the predominant scenario that is deployed on the Internet at this time. Synchronous Web-based applications receive a request from a client and return a response to the client using the same request session. This is the model for HTTP Request and HTTP Response. Many clients expect HTTP Response to carry a business level response to the request that they posted. The expectation is that the request waits for the response. The following scenario describes an architecture that complies with this synchronous requirement.

This scenario includes a data farm of Internet Information Services (IIS) servers. The data farm might also include Commerce Servers. These servers receive documents over HTTPS and then submit the documents to a BizTalk Server group for processing. In this scenario, there might be a firewall that allows only HTTP traffic through port 80 between the IIS and Commerce Server data farm and the BizTalk Server group.

To build a configuration based on this scenario, you must adhere to the following requirements:

- The IIS and Commerce Server data farm and the BizTalk Server group must be scaled out independently.

- Communication between the two data farms must be restricted to port 80 and use HTTP exclusively.

- Load balance requests across servers in both data farms must be made independently.

- Optionally, you can design support for synchronous HTTP interactions between Web clients and BizTalk Servers.

To comply with these requirements, it is often not possible to use Distributed Component Object Model (DCOM) calls between the data farms. DCOM calls from the IIS and Commerce Servers in the DMZ to BizTalk Servers would require the opening of arbitrary ports. This is often unacceptable in a business environment.

The following illustration shows a configuration based on the scenario described in this section, using Microsoft Internet Security and Acceleration (ISA) Server as the firewall server.

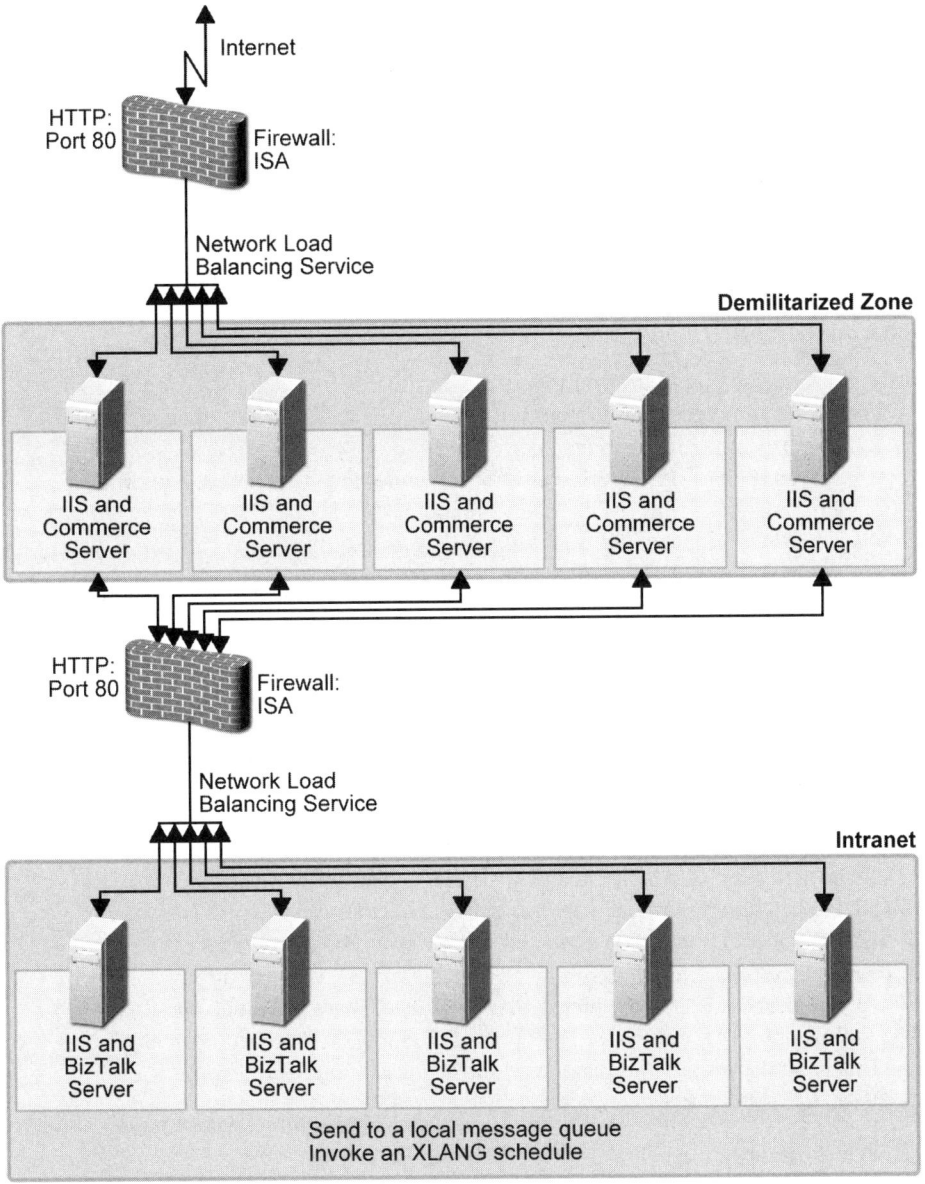

This configuration provides a simple implementation model. The two data farms are loosely coupled and can scale out independently by using HTTP and the Network Load Balancing Service (NLBS) as intermediary load-balancing servers.

Active Server Pages (ASPs) on Commerce Server and IIS servers in the DMZ use the server-optimized MSXML 3.0 HTTP client to forward HTTP Requests with messages to the internal IIS and BizTalk Servers over HTTPS. The MSXML 3.0 HTTP client is multithreaded and reentrant. Optionally, a Microsoft Internet Security and Acceleration server can be used to implement a request-forwarding reverse proxy.

In the synchronous model, ASP pages on the IIS and BizTalk Servers within an intranet call directly into the local BizTalk Servers by using the **SubmitSync** method of the **IInterchange** interface. BizTalk Server returns a response. In the asynchronous model, the ASP page calls the **Submit** method or places the message onto a local message queue, or file share, that a Message Queuing receive function monitors. When asynchronous calls to the BizTalk Server are used, the following occurs:

- BizTalk Messaging Services are optimized to receive documents from a message queue by using a Message Queuing receive function. If the document size is greater than 4 MB in ASCII, or 2 MB in Unicode, the message queue size limit is exceeded. In this case, the document must be submitted to BizTalk Server by using either the **IInterchange** interface (to support transactions), or by using a File receive function.

- ASP pages can quickly save messages in message queues without processing the messages. This reduces the page latency and releases HTTP connections in an expedient manner.

- ASP pages submit documents to BizTalk Server by using receive functions or the **Submit** method on the **IInterchange** interface.

When BizTalk Orchestration Services are used to implement business logic, the document that is passed to the **Submit** method or the **SubmitSync** method of the **IInterchange** interface is processed on the local server by an XLANG schedule instance. You can configure BizTalk Server to activate a new XLANG schedule instance to process the document, or the document can be processed by an activated XLANG schedule instance. For information about configuring BizTalk Orchestration Services, see "BizTalk Orchestration Services" later in this chapter. If new XLANG schedules are to be activated when a specified document type is received, and if there is a high volume of incoming documents of this type, the tightly coupled approach could overwhelm the servers on which XLANG schedules are activated. Newly activated XLANG schedules will compete for resources with the XLANG schedules that are already running. This might affect the throughput and the latency of the overall application. To avoid this problem, use a loosely coupled approach.

Responses and Time-Outs in Long-Running Processes

In this scenario, the Web page is blocking the HTTP Request that is awaiting a response from the stateless component. The stateless component is polling a queue, awaiting a response message that is based on the globally unique identifier (GUID) of the request (also referred to as the message label). When processing on the back end is expeditious to the client, it appears to be synchronous. If there is heavy load, a time-out thread in the stateless object returns an out parameter to the Web page. This out parameter represents the following instruction:

> Processing incomplete, please check back later with the Message GUID to retrieve the response.

At that time, the Web page either redirects the client requests to a **CheckStatus/FetchResponse** page, which simply calls a component to poll the queue, or a script in the client browser handles the response polling. The GUID can be placed in the cookie and used to retrieve the response asynchronously.

Variations of this are possible; for example, using an SQL query to the **CheckStatus/FetchResponse** page from the Web page or component. This is not possible in businesses that require no direct back-end database interaction from Web servers in the firewall. In this situation, Message Queuing can be used for decoupling and throttling requests from responses.

Message Queuing Fan-Out

To enable a firewall to allow Internet access to Message Queuing Services, Message Queuing traffic is delivered through port 1801, which is a reserved Transmission Control Protocol (TCP) port. If port 1801 is open for Message Queuing traffic and if asynchronous communication is used for the interaction between the Web client and the BizTalk Servers, it is recommended that you use Message Queuing to move messages out of the DMZ and into the business domain. Because Message Queuing 2.0 does not support remote transacted reads, a custom message queue fan-out component is required to move messages in a transacted fashion to local queues in the data farm. Assuming that messages have not been placed in the queue by an ASP page on the server running Message Queuing, this custom message queue fan-out component can be developed to pull messages off the queue and send them to local queues on the BizTalk Servers. Load balancing schemes can take advantage of Microsoft Windows Management Instrumentation (WMI) reporting to determine the performance characteristics of each server before forwarding the message to the BizTalk Server with the smallest load.

The following illustration shows a configuration based on the scenario described in this section, using Microsoft Internet Security and Acceleration Server (ISA) as the firewall.

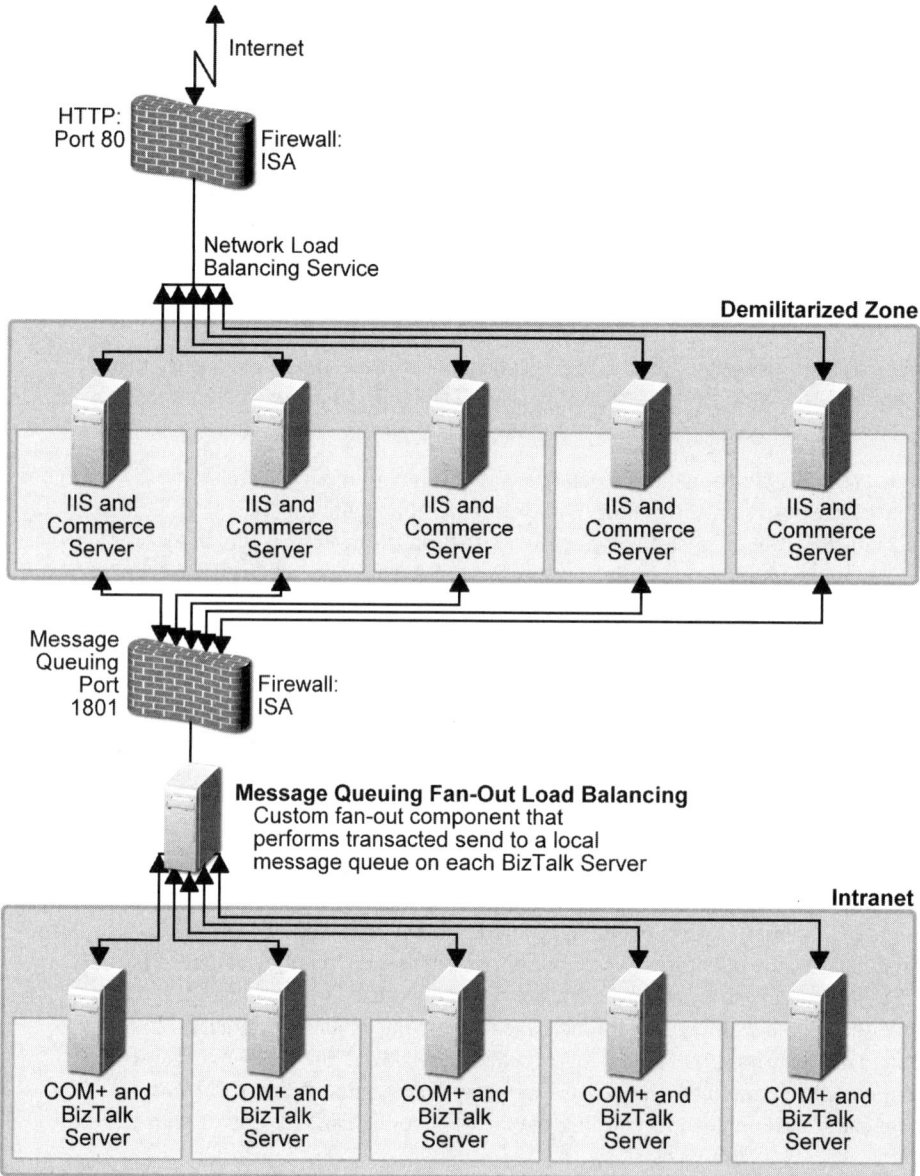

Load Balancing Considerations

To increase performance and optimize the use of processing power in a multiple-server deployment, it is necessary to ensure that new work is submitted to the server that is currently performing the least amount of processing. Load balancing is the process of determining the identity of the server that is currently performing the least amount of processing, and then directing new work to that server.

There are two load-balancing tools you can use in your BizTalk Server deployment:

- COM+ component load balancing
- Windows Network Load Balancing Service

COM+ Component Load Balancing

COM+ component load balancing implements load balancing on the middle tier of a three-tier deployment. In a three-tier deployment, the middle tier provides business services. The deployment model described in this section uses component load balancing to distribute the **Submit** method load across a BizTalk Server data farm where the messages are moved through the DMZ from IIS and Commerce Servers by using Message Queuing. Within a single transaction, a component reads messages from the clustered Message Queuing server, making a Distributed Component Object Model (DCOM) invocation to the **Submit** method on the **IInterchange** interface. Although a synchronous implementation can be used, it is recommended that you use the asynchronous model for component load balancing because of the improvement in scalability that can be achieved with Message Queuing.

The following illustration shows a configuration based on the scenario described in this section, using Microsoft Internet Security and Acceleration (ISA) Server as the firewall server.

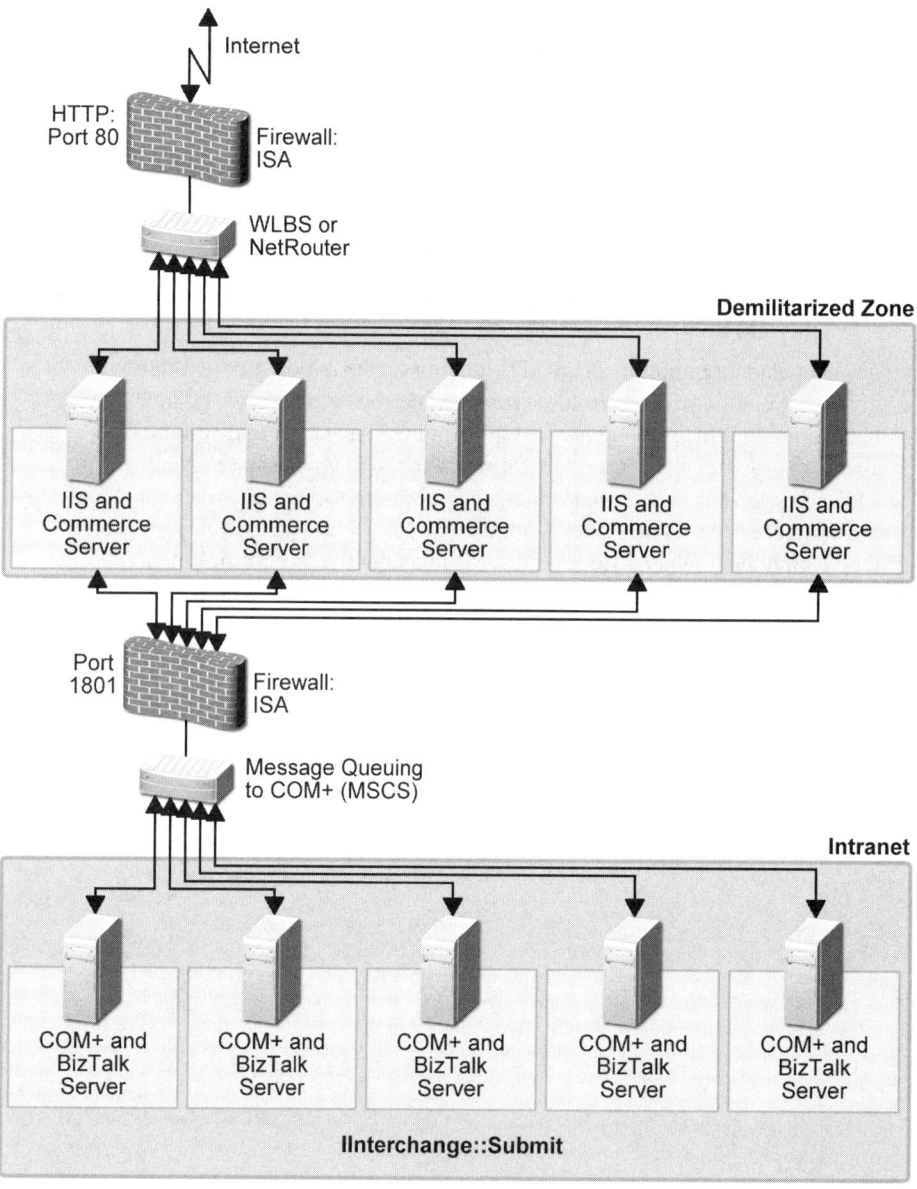

Windows Network Load Balancing Service

Windows Network Load Balancing Service (NLBS), a component of Microsoft Windows 2000 Advanced Server and Windows 2000 Datacenter Server, distributes Internet Protocol (IP) requests across cluster members. NLBS is a software-based load balancer that resides on each cluster member. NLBS can be used to distribute HTTP calls across BizTalk Servers running within an IIS data farm. It is recommended that you separate NLBS traffic from BizTalk Server and Microsoft SQL Server processing traffic by using two network interface cards (NICs) in each NLBS server.

Building Scalable and Available Web Applications

There are two core models you can use to build scalable and available Web applications. These models are:

- A synchronous Web-based model.
- A synchronous façade on an asynchronous back-end processing system.

Synchronous Web-based Model

When using the Component Object Model (COM), the **SubmitSync** method on the **IInterchange** interface is used to make synchronous calls into BizTalk Server. In this way, a response document can be returned to the caller by using a back-end application integration component or by using an XLANG schedule. If the **SubmitSync** method is used, care must be taken to handle time-out and back-end application processing component failures. Using an asynchronous model is a more scalable approach to building application services, but it does not always correspond to many of the current synchronous Web application models. A request-response correlation architecture must be implemented to provide users and client applications with the synchronous façade that either provides an asynchronous **Submit** method invocation or sends a response to a message queue.

Due to the nature of processing Web applications that require a synchronous HTTP interface, there are many scalability issues. Retaining open connections for long periods of time can make the application unavailable for new requests. The design goals for the processing of Web applications requiring a synchronous HTTP interface are:

- To receive and save the request, providing the caller with the acknowledgement and assurance that the request was received and understood.
- To process the request without impacting the ability to receive new requests.
- To return a response to the caller that is correlated to their request. When the scenario requires, return the response on the same HTTP connection stream of the original request.
- To support time-outs of the client requests by providing a subsequent mechanism that retrieves stored (queued) responses.

Synchronous Façade on an Asynchronous Back-end Processing System

Many businesses want the Web-based user experience (or the programmatic experience) to be synchronous, if possible. However, understanding that there are scalability limitations when implementing a front-to-back synchronous solution, these businesses have chosen to place a synchronous façade on an asynchronous, back-end processing application architecture. In this way, these applications can continue to receive requests at high rates regardless of the back-end processing latencies. The back end can then be scaled out independently of the Web server layer.

The Web page that is accessed passes the message to a stateless component. This stateless component invokes a component (that might be pooled) to encapsulate Message Queuing and save the message to a queue. Either the Web page or the stateless component provides a globally unique identifier (GUID) to each request message. If the stateless component provides the GUID, the GUID is returned to the ASP page as an out parameter or placed into the IIS application or session object. In this way, messages can be safely moved from the DMZ through a single port in the last firewall into the business domain. These messages are then read within a Distributed Transaction Coordinator (DTC) transaction from the queue. This is known as a clustered resource. The messages are then sent in a load-balanced fashion to a data farm of processing servers using either COM+ Component Load Balancing or Message Queuing by a multithreaded component or service.

Designing BizTalk Server Groups

A BizTalk Server group is the key organizing principle in BizTalk Server. BizTalk Server groups are collections of individual BizTalk Servers that are centrally managed, configured, and monitored. BizTalk Server uses the following queues to contain incoming and outgoing documents that are in various stages of routing and processing in BizTalk Server:

- Work queue

- Scheduled queue

- Retry queue

- Suspended queue

All servers in a group can be configured the same so they perform the same receiving and processing functions. Or servers can be configured to perform a specific function, such as receive only. The purpose of grouping is to provide redundancy and to increase performance and fault tolerance. This section provides recommendations for structuring a BizTalk Server group.

BizTalk Servers in a group host services that manage document interchange between endpoints and/or applications. These services include messaging components that are used to send and receive documents, and orchestration components that are used to implement business logic and manage state for long-running transactions.

Redundant Server Group Configurations

In a redundant server group configuration, all BizTalk Servers within a group are configured to share the same Shared Queue, Tracking, and BizTalk Messaging Management databases. In this configuration, a document is posted to an ASP page. The ASP page is configured to place documents in a specific message queue that a Message Queuing receive function monitors. The Message Queuing receive function submits the document to BizTalk Server, where it is placed in the Work queue. The first available server picks up the document from the Work queue and completes processing. This solution enables any server in the group to process the document. The following illustration shows the structure of a group of servers.

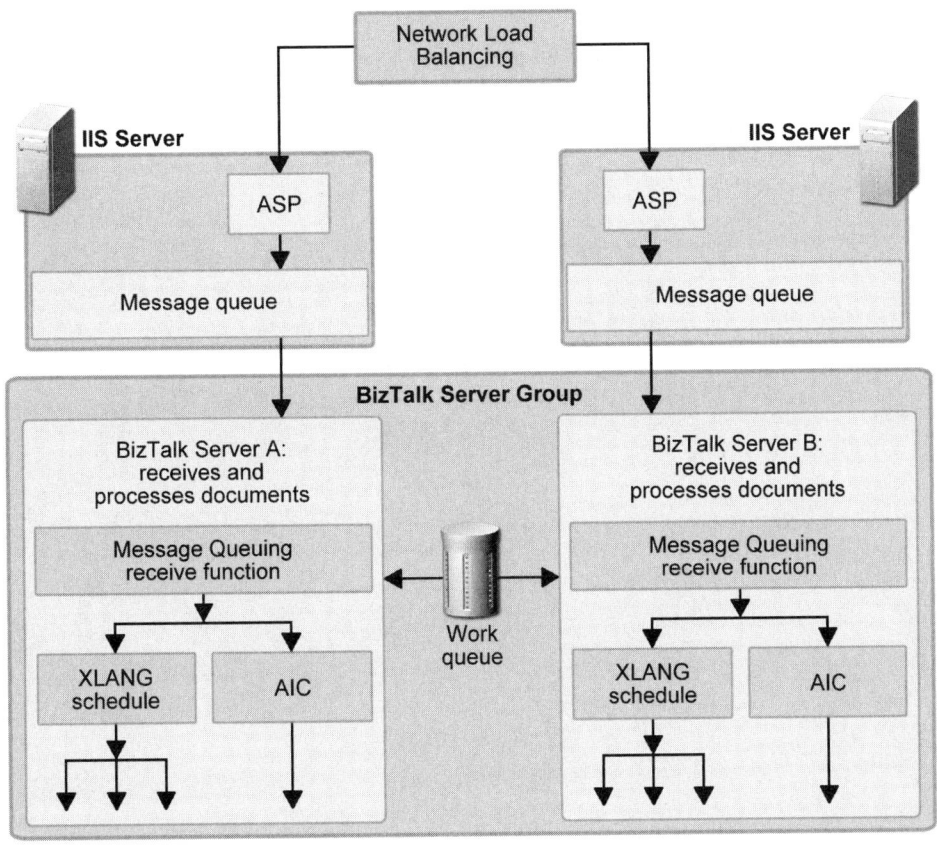

Partitioned or Specialized Server Group Configurations

In this configuration, all servers in the group are configured to share the same Shared Queue, Tracking, and BizTalk Messaging Management databases. However, at least one BizTalk Server is specifically configured to receive documents, usually by using the HTTP transport service. A document arrives in a message queue and is picked up and submitted to BizTalk Server. The BizTalk Server that runs the Message Queuing receive function does not participate in document processing. This results in rapid document submission that helps prevent documents from accumulating in the message queue. BizTalk Servers configured only to receive documents provide the following functionality:

- Decryption, decoding, and digital signature verification.

- Parsing and document validation.

- Submitting the document to the Work queue for processing on successful submissions or into the Suspended queue for faulty submissions.

The other BizTalk Servers in the group are responsible for processing. In this partitioned configuration, the server used to receive documents must be part of a fail-over cluster to provide fault tolerance. This is because the receiving server is neither functionally replicated nor redundant. The following illustration shows the structure of a group of servers for partitioned processing.

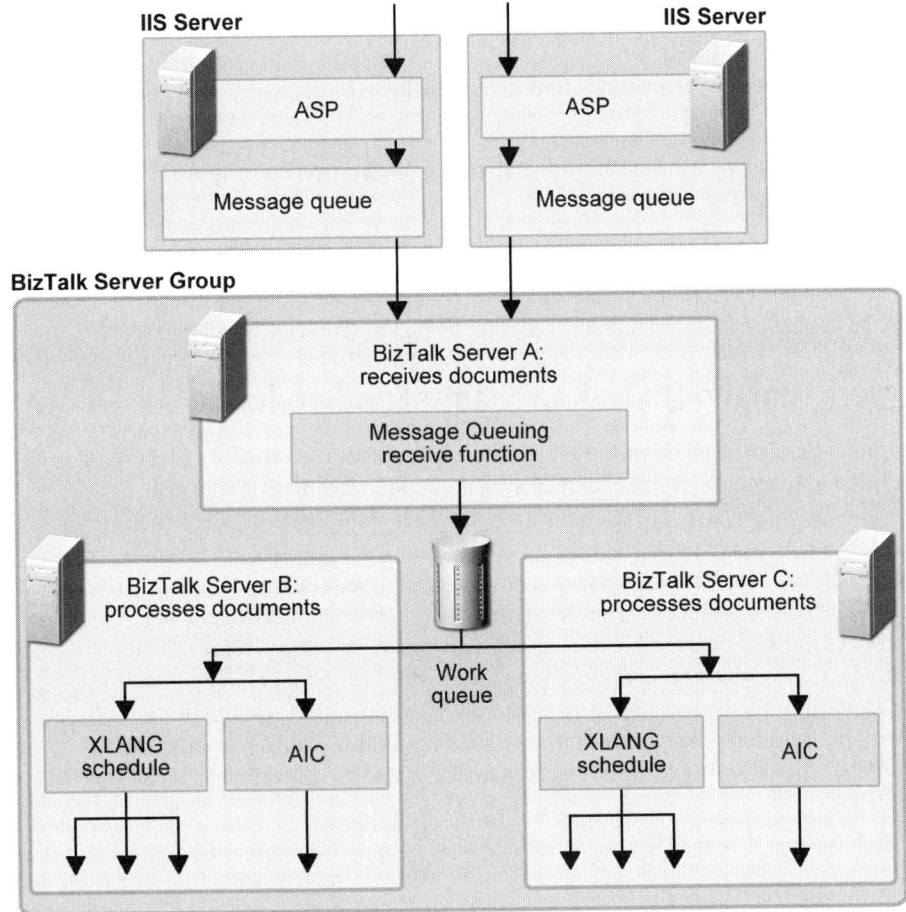

To configure a BizTalk Server to receive documents

1. Open BizTalk Server Administration, expand **Microsoft BizTalk Server 2000**, and expand the server group for the server that you want to configure.

2. Right-click the server that you want to configure and click **Properties.**

   The **Properties** dialog box appears.

3. Clear the **Participate in work-item processing** check box.

To configure a BizTalk Server for document processing

1. Open BizTalk Server Administration, expand Microsoft **BizTalk Server 2000**, and expand the server group for the server that you want to configure.

2. Right-click the server that you want to configure and click **Properties.**

   The **Properties** dialog box appears.

3. Select the **Participate in work-item processing** check box.

4. In the **Maximum number of receive function threads allowed** box, type a value greater than zero.

5. In the **Maximum number of worker threads per processor allowed** box, type the number of worker threads that you want to use.

Note

- The server will not participate in document processing if no receive functions are activated and no applications post documents to it by using the **IInterchange** interface.

BizTalk Servers running BizTalk Orchestration Services

BizTalk Orchestration Services can either run on the same server that runs BizTalk Messaging Services, or BizTalk Orchestration Services can be scaled out on individually dedicated BizTalk Servers. By scaling out BizTalk Orchestration Services on individually dedicated servers, BizTalk Messaging Services do not need to contend for CPU and file I/O resources with BizTalk Orchestration Services. XLANG schedule activation requires server affinity for rehydrated XLANG schedule instances; therefore, BizTalk Servers running BizTalk Orchestration Services must be clustered in an active-passive manner. Active servers and passive servers are part of a redundant configuration that provides a high level of availability. If the server that is performing the processing (the active server) fails, one or more of the passive servers will become active and perform the processing. In this configuration, if the active server fails, the passive server continues executing the XLANG schedule instances from the last known state.

BizTalk Messaging Services

It is highly recommended that you review the information in "BizTalk Services," in "Introducing Microsoft BizTalk Server 2000," before you read the following sections. This content contains background information, information about best practices, and troubleshooting tips relating to BizTalk Messaging Services.

BizTalk Messaging Objects

BizTalk Server uses the following objects to configure the necessary properties to process and transmit submitted work items:

- **Channels.** A set of properties that direct BizTalk Server through the appropriate steps to process documents. Channel properties include a source organization or application, a document definition, a map, and field and document tracking settings.

- **Messaging ports.** A set of properties that specify how an interchange or document is transported to a destination organization or application. Messaging port properties include transport services, destination organization or application, security settings, and envelope settings.

- **Distribution lists.** A group of messaging ports. Use a distribution list to send the same document to more than one trading partner organization or applications. In the BizTalk Messaging Configuration object model, a distribution list is called a port group.

- **Organizations.** The trading partners with which your business exchanges interchanges and documents. An organization can be internal, such as an application of another division of a company. Or an organization can be external, such as a different business.

- **Document definitions.** A set of properties that represents an inbound or outbound document and that might provide a pointer to a specification. A specification defines the document structure, document type, and version. However, a pointer from the document definition to a specification is not required.

- **Envelopes.** A set of properties that can represent the transport information for a document. An envelope associated with an inbound interchange or document provides BizTalk Server with the information that it needs to interpret the submitted document. For example, the envelope can contain a pointer to the document definition. An envelope associated with an outbound interchange or document gives BizTalk Server the information that it needs to create the document. Envelope properties are optional for most file formats.

- **BizTalk Configuration Assistant (BTConfigAssistant).** This tool enables you to view all of the details of a configuration. It also provides a mechanism for easily importing and exporting configurations, and deploying BizTalk Messaging Services to a new server. BTConfigAssistant is in the Messaging Samples folder in the Microsoft BizTalk Server installation drive. Browse to \Program Files\Microsoft BizTalk Server\SDK\Messaging Samples on the installation drive to find this tool. This is only a relative path. Depending on your installation of BizTalk Server 2000, you might have to modify this path.

Custom BizTalk Messaging Components

There are several extensibility options for BizTalk Messaging Services. These include the ability to integrate custom components that implement one or more integration interfaces.

BizTalk Server 2000 Enterprise Edition supports product extensibility that enables more complex document processing. The extensions available in BizTalk Server Enterprise Edition are:

- **Custom parsers.** To enable parsing of formats that are not supported in the native parsers provided by BizTalk Server 2000, the enterprise edition enables you to create custom parser components that conform to a well-defined parser interface. You can configure these components in BizTalk Server to parse documents for the formats that they support.

- **Custom serializers.** To enable serializing of documents into proprietary or other formats that are not supported by the serializers that are provided with BizTalk Server 2000, the enterprise edition enables you to create custom serializer components that conform to a well-defined serializer interface. You can configure these components in BizTalk Server to serialize documents into the formats that they support.

- **Custom preprocessing components.** BizTalk Messaging Services support a preprocessing link to the Message Queuing and File receive functions that enables custom components implementing the **IPreProcess** interface to provide custom processing on the receiving of documents prior to submission to the server.

Application Integration Components

Integrating with BizTalk Messaging Services using the Component Object Model (COM) at the transport layer is possible by implementing one of two sets of interfaces:

- **IPipelineComponent** and **IPipelineComponentAdmin**
- **IBTSAppIntegration**

Any object that implements the interface set (or the single interface) and selects the AIC messaging port transport type will be invoked by BizTalk Messaging Services when a document passes through the messaging port. Registering these AICs with an affinity GUID or within a COM+ application package enables them to appear in BizTalk Messaging Manager.

ASP Property Pages

AICs that implement the **IPipelineComponent** set of interfaces can optionally receive additional configuration data at run time along with the delivery of messages on the **CDictionary** object. The additional run-time data is configured by placing ASP property pages in the directory designated for the property pages (for example, \Program Files\Microsoft BizTalk Server\MessagingManager\pipeline). To select and set the values of these property pages, open BizTalk Messaging Manager and edit the channel. The **Advanced** button in the last dialog box enables you to set the properties for the primary transport.

Tracking Database Maintenance

When document tracking is used, the Tracking database will increase in size. It is necessary to implement SQL replication and purge procedures to move data from the Tracking database to a data warehouse. To maintain the Tracking database, you can use DTA_SampleJobs.sql, a sample SQL Server script that is provided to remove records from the Tracking database. You can find this sample script in the \Program Files\Microsoft BizTalk Server\SDK\Messaging Samples\SQLServerAgentJobs folder. Review the readme included with this sample for more information about how to tailor the script to your specific BizTalk Server deployment.

⌕ Notes

- If you are using SQL Server 7.0 with SP 2, the tables that have image or text columns might not shrink in size, even if you delete rows from those tables in the Tracking database. SQL Server SP 3 helps to alleviate this issue. SP 3 is available at the Microsoft SQL Server Web site (www.microsoft.com/sql/downloads/sp3.htm).

    This issue does not occur in SQL Server 2000.

- If you configure your BizTalk Server deployment to track documents, you might need to change the following SQL Server settings for the Tracking database:
    - **Auto shrink**
    - **Truncate log on checkpoint**
    - **Automatically grow file**

        The **Automatically grow file** option is the recommended configuration option for the Tracking database.

For more information about maintaining the Tracking database, see "Administering Databases" in Chapter 12, "BizTalk Server 2000 Operations."

BizTalk Orchestration Services

It is highly recommended that you review the information in "BizTalk Services," in "Introducing Microsoft BizTalk Server 2000," as well as Chapter 11, "Administering Servers and Applications," before you read the following sections. The Server Administration topics contain detailed information about the configuration of BizTalk Servers running BizTalk Orchestration Services. This section contains background information, information about best practices, and troubleshooting tips relating to BizTalk Orchestration Services.

BizTalk Orchestration .skx and .skv Files

In BizTalk Orchestration Designer, XLANG schedule drawings are saved with the .skv file extension. You can then compile the XLANG schedule drawing into an XLANG schedule, which is an XML-structured file with the .skx file extension. The XLANG Scheduler Engine can then process the .skx file. You will need to implement version control for both .skv files and .skx files using products such as Microsoft Visual SourceSafe®.

Implementation Technologies

BizTalk Orchestration Designer provides four **Implementation** shapes. These shapes are used to describe the implementation technologies that are used to implement a port in a business process. The implementation technologies are:

- **COM components.** This implementation technology enables you to use preexisting components or applications to perform actions within an XLANG schedule. The COM implementation technology is synchronous. There is always a bidirectional flow of messages when an action is performed.

- **Windows Script Components.** This implementation technology enables you to use preexisting components or applications to perform actions within an XLANG schedule, using a Windows Script Component (.wsc) file. The Windows Script Component implementation technology is synchronous. There is always a bidirectional flow of messages when an action is performed.

- **Message Queuing.** This implementation technology enables an XLANG schedule to communicate with another XLANG schedule (or with an application) in a loosely coupled manner by using a message queue.

- **BizTalk Messaging.** This implementation technology enables you to use BizTalk Messaging Services to exchange messages between BizTalk Orchestration Services and BizTalk Messaging Services.

By visually inspecting the *.skv file, you can build an inventory of the required implementation technologies. It is also possible to create a list of specific binding objects programmatically by parsing the *.skx files and extracting binding-specific elements.

The following code shows XLANG binding examples:

COM binding

```
<portBinding tag="0!57">
   <portRef location="LineItemUtil"/>
   <portTranslation>
     <com:interface tag="0!53" iid="55f3c4f3-fb27-4789-a5bd-263bbc4b672a"
     clsid="a8f6910c-bb6b-4edc-a93c-fa104066e858" holdstate="1" />
   </portTranslation>
   </portBinding>
```

Message queue binding

```
<portTranslation>
    <msmq:queue tag="0!41"
    queueName=".\private$\Items_in"/>
</portTranslation>
```

BizTalk Server Run-Time Authentication and Identity

When BizTalk Server is installed, a COM+ application named *XLANG Scheduler* is created on the system. This application can host or execute XLANG schedules. To simplify setup, especially for developers who initially install BizTalk Server, the COM+ application is configured to run as interactive user. However, in the deployment scenario it is strongly recommended that you do not configure COM+ applications that host XLANG schedules to use the interactive user account. Instead, configure COM+ applications that host XLANG schedules to run under a specific user account. This account should be distinct for each host, depending on the types of XLANG schedules that are being executed by the different hosts and depending on the security requirements. Configure access to the persistence database for this account, and configure access to any other required resources.

Configuring BizTalk Orchestration Services

On a computer, multiple COM+ applications can be configured to host XLANG schedules. Hosting the BizTalk Orchestration Services run-time environment in different COM+ applications provides the following benefits:

- **Fault isolation.** An access violation in an in-process component used by an XLANG schedule can cause the BizTalk Scheduler Engine to fail. This is similar to a poorly written in-process Internet Server Application Programming Interface (ISAPI) dynamic-link library (DLL) causing Internet Information Services (IIS) servers to fail. If an access violation in an in-process component used by an XLANG schedule does cause the BizTalk Scheduler Engine to fail, it can affect all of the other hosted XLANG schedules. Therefore, it is recommended that you limit the use of in-process components used by XLANG schedules to those that have been thoroughly tested.

- **Flexible security.** Different COM+ applications can run using different security settings (such as COM+ roles).

To create a new COM+ application that can host the BizTalk Orchestration run-time environment:

- When creating the XLANG host, configure the application to run under a specific user identity (ID); do not use interactive user. Otherwise, you will need to have the system logged on as this user permanently. This is not practical in a business deployment.

- Use unique accounts for each COM+ application, but group them together to simplify access control.

- It is recommended that you group all Access Control Lists (ACLs) in a single Windows 2000 group. This will enable you to use a unique identity for each server application and treat them the same with respect to ACLs on other system resources.

- Configure a Data Source Name (DSN) for the newly created XLANG host. As described in the following section, "Persistence Database Configuration and Maintenance," the DSN can point to a database that is shared by other XLANG hosts within the BizTalk Server group.

For more information, see "Create and Configure an XLANG Schedule Host Application" in Chapter 8, "BizTalk Orchestration Services."

✎ Note

- For Component Services Administration Help, on the **Start** menu, point to **Settings**, click **Control Panel**, double-click **Administrative Tools**, and then double-click **Component Services**. Press **F1** or, on the **Help** menu, click the **Help topics** item.

Persistence Database Configuration and Maintenance

BizTalk Orchestration Services use a Microsoft SQL Server database to manage the state of XLANG schedule instances. A Data Source Name (DSN) must be configured for every instance of an XLANG schedule to ensure that each XLANG schedule instance points to a SQL Server database. As part of the setup process, the DSN is configured for the default XLANG Scheduler Engine. A DSN, pointing to a SQL Server database, must be configured for additional COM+ applications that can host XLANG schedules. Each of the individual BizTalk Servers running BizTalk Orchestration Services can point to different databases, or share a common database. Using multiple SQL Servers introduces additional complexity. It is recommended that you deploy a SQL Server that is dedicated to providing state management for BizTalk Servers running BizTalk Orchestration Services.

For more information about how to configure a DSN for a persistence database, see "Manage XLANG Applications and Databases" in Chapter 11, "Administering Servers and Applications."

The persistence database size must be configured to grow as the XLANG Scheduler Engine persists data about activated XLANG schedule instances. BizTalk Orchestration Services will not remove the information about XLANG schedule instances from the persistence database. This is true even for XLANG schedule instances that have completed. Because the persistence database increases in size with use, it is necessary to implement SQL replication and purge procedures to move data from the persistence database to a data warehouse.

Scripts to purge completed XLANG schedule instances, along with other utilities to manage the persistence database, are not included with BizTalk Server. For information about maintaining the persistence database, go to the Microsoft BizTalk Server Web site (www.microsoft.com/biztalk/).

☞ Caution

- Do not attempt to create your own tool(s) to maintain the persistence database. By creating and using your own tool(s) to maintain the persistence database, you risk deleting important production data or corrupting the persistence database.

Security

XLANG Scheduler, the default COM+ application that is installed by BizTalk Server, defines the security roles that control which users can interact with XLANG hosts in different ways. These security roles apply to all XLANG hosts configured on a server. It is not possible to define unique sets of users for these roles on a per-XLANG host basis. For more information, see "Security for Applications That Host XLANG Schedule Instances" in Chapter 2, "Understanding Security."

Security administration

Security data used to access resources such as message queues and file shares (for example, Domain\Account) must be implemented for the given deployment environment.

Server Affinity of XLANG Schedules

Instances of an XLANG schedule have affinity to the COM+ XLANG application and the server on which they were activated. This implies that the XLANG schedule instances are not automatically rehydrated on a different server if the server on which the XLANG schedule instance has affinity fails. One way to address this issue is to set up servers running BizTalk Server in an active-passive type of fail-over cluster. In this configuration, if the active server fails, the passive server continues executing the XLANG schedule instances from the last known state.

Message Queue Size Limits

A message queue has a storage limit of 4 megabytes (MB) per message that is stored in a message queue and a total limit of 2 gigabytes (GB) for all messages that can be stored in a message queue.

Scalability Issues

There are several reasons why the scalability of activated XLANG schedules might be affected by a particular deployment. The most common reasons are discussed here. Some of these are not related to the deployment architecture, but relate to the design and implementation of the XLANG schedules.

- If Microsoft Visual Basic® components are called in an XLANG schedule, a performance decrease is experienced when there is a large number of outstanding calls. The XLANG Scheduler Engine is configured to execute within a multithreaded apartment, and there is only a limited pool of threads that can be used by the XLANG Scheduler Engine to invoke components that need to execute in single threaded apartments. Because all Visual Basic components are single threaded apartments, calls to these components will block if there are many outstanding concurrent calls. To avoid this problem, use Microsoft Visual C++® to create multithreaded apartment components.

- Low throughput of XLANG schedule instances is often caused by bottlenecks in the database that is used to store the state of XLANG schedules. The problem is amplified when multiple BizTalk Servers are configured to use the same database. Throughput can be improved by configuring BizTalk Orchestration Services to use different databases. For further improvement, the databases can be configured to use different hard disks. Using different Microsoft SQL Servers for some or all of the Orchestration Services is likely to provide even better results.

  Following are two additional methods you can use to reduce the use of the database by the XLANG Scheduler Engine:

  - Review the design of XLANG schedule drawings to minimize the use of the **Transaction** shape.

  - Review the design of XLANG schedule drawings to ensure that the latency on receive actions is set to a value that is less than three minutes. This prevents the dehydration of XLANG schedule instances that contain rapidly occurring receive actions.

- Private message queues are known to perform substantially better than public message queues because they do not require an Active Directory lookup. As described in "Persistence Database Configuration and Maintenance" earlier in this chapter, the persistence database might become a bottleneck.

- Visual Basic components used from COM+ server applications could deadlock and cause XLANG schedule instances to stop responding. This is a known Visual Basic issue. The workaround is to ensure that the components are built with the **Retain in memory** option set (from project properties in the Visual Basic environment).

- Avoid making method calls to components that run for an extended period of time.

- The XLANG Scheduler Engine uses ActiveX® Data Objects (ADO) to save the state of XLANG schedules to the persistence database. By default, ADO installs itself as apartment threaded, which could cause a severe performance slowdown. You can run a batch file that ADO provides (\Program Files\Common Files\System\ado\makfre15.bat) that converts ADO to be "Both threaded."

- When XLANG schedules using transactions are executed under heavy stress (a large number of concurrent XLANG schedule instances), Distributed Transaction Coordinator (DTC) transactions might time out. This might occur because the XLANG Scheduler Engine enrolls in the application's DTC transaction to perform state management. XLANG schedule designers might not realize this and set the time-out to a value that might work well under low-stress situations but that can encounter problems at higher stress levels. Transaction time-out values of less than 60 seconds are not recommended.

- In addition to increasing the transaction time-out, the time-out values for ADO connection and commands might also need to be increased. Executing the following code in a .reg file adds the appropriate registry keys to the registry and also sets the time-out values to 300 seconds (the default is 60 seconds):

```
Windows Registry Editor Version 5.00

[HKEY_LOCAL_MACHINE\SOFTWARE\Microsoft\BizTalk Server\1.0\XLANG Scheduler]
"ADOConnectionTimeout"=dword:0000012c
"ADOCommandTimeout"=dword:0000012c
```

Unfortunately, the error messages in the event log might not be very helpful when time-out problems occur. The following entries are typically seen in the event log:

```
event log:
Error1
The state of the XLANG schedule instance could not be saved to the database. Detailed
information is provided in the following message.
Module name: mymodule
Module ID: {EE8FB9FA-AB64-492A-A127-56A1EFDB2C50}
Instance ID: {6B48FF17-791B-474F-8EE2-AD35FF8E5A30}
Database error(s):
Error Code = 0x8004e007 : You made a method call on a COM+ component that has a
transaction that has already committed or aborted.
XLANG Scheduler Engine Internals Information:
File: d:\bts\private\sked\src\runtime\persistence\persist.cpp
Line: 261
Error 2:
An error was encountered while attempting to persist an XLANG schedule instance. Detailed
information is provided in the following message.
Error source: Field
name: __Correlation__
HRESULT: 0x80040e14
Module name: mymodule
Module ID: {EE8FB9FA-AB64-492A-A127-56A1EFDB2C65}
Instance ID: {6FE02E74-7FE2-401B-93F3-EC208636257B}
Error Code = 0x80040e14 :
```

Shutting Down Applications That Host XLANG Schedules

If you need to bring a BizTalk Server that hosts BizTalk Orchestration Services offline, for example for maintenance purposes, you must perform a controlled shutdown of all XLANG applications to ensure that data associated with XLANG schedules is not lost. A controlled shutdown saves the state for running XLANG schedules to the appropriate persistence database. If you perform a controlled shutdown on the default XLANG Scheduler application, all XLANG schedules are gracefully shut down and preserved. If you perform a controlled shutdown on a COM+ application that you created after installation, only the XLANG schedules associated with that COM+ application are gracefully shut down and preserved. All other XLANG schedules will remain running until you shut down the COM+ application(s) with which they are associated.

To restart the XLANG schedules, you must restart all the schedules at the same time in the default XLANG Scheduler application. You cannot restart applications that are associated with a specific COM+ application.

Message Queuing Dead Letter Queues

Each configured XLANG host creates a dead letter queue that is used to store documents that are rejected. The dead letter queue is a private message queue in the following format: *<xlang hostname>*.deadletter. All XML documents that either fail schema validation or are ill formed (and cannot, therefore, be parsed) are dropped into this queue. Data left in private queues that are created on a per-instance basis for the XLANG schedule is also moved to the dead letter queue before the queues are destroyed.

XLANG Schedule Activation

The BizTalk Messaging implementation technology in BizTalk Orchestration Services uses a private message queue to pass data between BizTalk Orchestration Services and BizTalk Messaging Services. A private queue is created for each port that is bound to BizTalk Messaging Services when an XLANG schedule instance is activated. The private queue is destroyed when the XLANG schedule instance completes. Per-instance queues might become a management problem when there are hundreds of simultaneously active XLANG schedule instances.

To avoid the use of per-instance queues, use a Message Queuing port, instead of a BizTalk Messaging port, to activate an XLANG schedule. To implement this design, no changes are needed in the configuration of the messaging port in BizTalk Messaging Manager. However, if you require correlation to a running instance of an XLANG schedule, you must use per-instance queues.

Updating XLANG Schedules

As newer versions of BizTalk Server become available, you might need to update existing XLANG schedules to run on these newer versions. There are two ways to update an existing XLANG schedule. You can overwrite the original XLANG schedule, or you can add a new XLANG schedule that runs concurrently with the original XLANG schedule.

To overwrite the original XLANG schedule, use BizTalk Orchestration Designer to create a new XLANG schedule drawing and then compile the XLANG schedule drawing as an XLANG schedule that has the same name as the original XLANG schedule. The XLANG schedule drawing is saved as an .skv file. You can then compile the XLANG schedule drawing into an XLANG schedule, which is an XML-structured .skx text file. To update the original XLANG schedule, copy the new .skx file over the original .skx file.

To add a new XLANG schedule that runs concurrently with the original XLANG schedule, use BizTalk Orchestration Designer to create a new XLANG schedule drawing and compile the XLANG schedule drawing as an XLANG schedule with a new name. To ensure that the new XLANG schedule is correctly activated, you must change the XLANG schedule instance activation mechanism to point to the new .skx file instead of pointing to the old .skx file. When you have completed this process, new requests for XLANG schedules create instances of the new XLANG schedule.

Because all XLANG schedules and their components typically work on a per-instance basis, XLANG schedule instances that are in the process of executing the original XLANG schedule continue to run to completion. This includes XLANG schedule instances that have been dehydrated. In this scenario, the execution path continues to follow the original business process, and new requests for XLANG schedules create instances of the new XLANG schedule.

Note

- When an XLANG schedule uses an object with an interface that has changed, you must open the XLANG schedule drawing (the .skv file) in BizTalk Orchestration Designer and compile a new .skx file. This updates the binding information in the .skx file, enabling synchronization with the component's type library.

Conclusion

BizTalk Server 2000 enables you to create solutions for enterprise application integration (EAI) and business-to-business integration with strategic trading partners.
BizTalk Server 2000 enables Information Technology (IT) professionals and business analysts to build dynamic business processes that span applications, platforms, and businesses over the Internet. BizTalk Server 2000 also enables you to:

- Integrate dissimilar applications across multiple remote and autonomous business units within a business domain.

- Implement remote data interchange with external trading partners.

- Maintain security within your business, even as you use the Internet to expand your ability to implement data interchange with trading partners.

- Use existing XLANG schedules with future versions of BizTalk Server, as they become available.

Related Topics

Chapter 12, "BizTalk Server 2000 Operations"

Chapter 14, "Orchestrating Business Processes with BizTalk Server 2000"

Part 2: Creating Specifications and Mapping Data

This part describes how to use BizTalk Editor to create specifications for your organization. In addition, there is information about BizTalk Mapper, which enables you to translate incoming and outgoing data from one specification format to another. You will also find in-depth information about how to use EDI with Microsoft BizTalk Server 2000.

In This Part

- **Creating Specifications.** This chapter provides you with the information that you need to create specifications that are based on industry standards and common schemas, or specifications that are unique to your organization. In addition, you'll find valuable information about importing an instance of a document. You will also learn about the values and properties associated with the records and fields contained within a specification.

- **Mapping Data.** This chapter explains how to create a map between the records and fields of two different specifications. You will learn how to create simple value-copy translations by using links, and complex structural manipulations by using functoids. By combining these elements, you can easily map data between a source specification and a destination specification.

- **Using EDI with BizTalk Server 2000.** This chapter provides a brief history and overview of EDI, and describes the ways BizTalk Server can operate within and enhance an EDI environment. In addition, you'll gain a better understanding of how a small-sized company can use BizTalk Server to exchange electronic business documents with a large-sized company that uses EDI.

Creating Specifications

BizTalk Editor is a tool with which you can create, edit, and manage specifications. BizTalk Editor uses Extensible Markup Language (XML), which provides a common vocabulary to handle overlaps between syntactic, database, and conceptual schemas.

BizTalk Editor creates specifications by interpreting the properties of records and fields that are contained in a file. Specifications represent the structured data as XML, regardless of the original format. In addition, specifications that you create or modify in BizTalk Editor provide common data descriptions that BizTalk Mapper can use to transform data across dissimilar formats. The specifications provide data portability across business processes. A specification created using BizTalk Editor can be based on any of the following:

- Well-formed XML.

- XML-based document templates.

- XML-Data Reduced (XDR) schemas.

- Document type definitions (DTDs).

- ActiveX Data Objects (ADO) recordsets stored as XML.

- Electronic data interchange (EDI) (X12 and EDIFACT).

- Flat files, including delimited and positional files (for example, SAP IDOCs). A flat file can also be both delimited and positional.

- Structured document formats.

In BizTalk Editor you can open a blank specification, which contains no structure, or you can import an existing schema or specification. For example, you can import a DTD, which is a structured file that denotes elements and attributes as well as any constraints on the order, frequency, and content of the elements and attributes. Standard specifications, such as XML, X12, or EDIFACT, can also be used to create new specifications.

When an instance of a document is imported, BizTalk Editor translates the structure of the document and produces a specification that is an XML representation of the document. You can edit any necessary records and fields that appear in the BizTalk Editor specification tree, and then save the structure as a specification. You can import the following file types:

- XDR schemas

- Well-formed XML

- DTDs

Each specification describes the structure of the file, given a specific set of tags. BizTalk Editor also provides several templates that can be used as starting points for creating specifications for common documents, such as purchase orders, invoices, and advance shipping notices.

When BizTalk Server processes documents, the server uses a map, which you create by using BizTalk Mapper, to translate incoming and outgoing data from one specification format to another.

In This Chapter

- Understanding Specifications

- BizTalk Editor Environment

- Records, Fields, and Properties

- Troubleshooting BizTalk Editor

Understanding Specifications

Specifications are BizTalk Server-specific Extensible Markup Language (XML) schemas that are created by BizTalk Editor. You can create specifications that are based on industry standards (such as XML, EDIFACT, or X12) or non-industry standards (such as delimited flat files, positional flat files, delimited and positional flat files, blank specifications, or existing files).

Industry standards

Industry standards provide uniform ways for businesses to exchange data electronically. The use of a common business language enables computers to communicate within an organization or from one business to another. Industry standards specify the format and data content of electronic business transactions. A specification that is based on an industry standard is considered a subset of the standard. To create a specification that meets your needs, you can begin with an industry-standard specification as a baseline and then delete any records and fields you do not need. In addition, you might need to modify properties for the remaining records and fields.

Non-industry standards

In specifications that are based on non-industry standards, you must define the structure of the document in BizTalk Editor. You can use BizTalk Editor for various types of non-industry standards: positional flat files, delimited flat files, or combined positional and delimited flat files.

Note

- On the **Parse** tab, you must set the **Structure** property of the root node to **Delimited** if your flat file is both delimited and positional. Additional record properties are set to either **Delimited** or **Positional**, depending on their attributes.

Blank specifications

A blank specification contains only the root-node element. If you start from a blank specification, you must build the entire specification structure. Rename the root element and then modify the root-element property values you want to change, such as the heading information for the specification. You can then add records and fields and their properties as required for your business processes.

Existing files

You can reuse existing files to take advantage of the investment you have made in developing documents that meet the specific needs of your business. To reuse an existing file, you must first import the file into BizTalk Editor and save it as a specification. Then you must open the saved specification in BizTalk Mapper and map it to whatever format your trading partners require.

Specification Structure

Specifications created by BizTalk Editor are well-formed XML. Specification structures vary depending on the type of file you choose as the basis for building your specification. Regardless of the type, each specification contains the same basic structure. For example, all specifications start with the `<?xml version=""?>` tag and continue with header information such as the name of the file and namespace data. Then the remaining structure is built based on the records and fields contained within your specification and the attributes associated with the records and fields. You can view the underlying code of a specification by opening it in Microsoft Internet Explorer 5 or later.

You can create an XML-Data Reduced (XDR) schema from a specification by using the **Export XDR Schema** command from the **Tools** menu.

To export XDR schemas

1. On the **Tools** menu, click **Export XDR Schema**.

    The **Export XDR schema as** dialog box appears.

2. Browse to the location to which you want to export the XML-Data Reduced (XDR) file.

3. In the **File name** box, type a name for the file.

4. In the **Encoding** list, click either **UTF-8** or **Unicode** and click **Save**.

    If you want to export a specification associated with ASCII characters, in the **Encoding** list, click **UTF-8**. For specifications associated with double-byte characters, in the **Encoding** list, click **UTF-8** or **Unicode**.

Notes

*   You can export new and existing specifications only while they are open in BizTalk Editor.

*   When you export a specification, the unique specification information is removed from the structure, and the resulting structure is saved as a general schema that can be used by other applications.

*   You can create an XSD schema from an XDR schema with a conversion script provided with a complete installation of BizTalk Server.

To convert an XDR schema to an XSD schema

1. Create a folder on your local drive called **Convert**.

2. Copy the contents of **\Program Files\Microsoft BizTalk Server\SDK\Messaging Samples\XSDConverter** to **Convert**.

3. Copy the XDR schema to be converted to **Convert**.

4. Open a command prompt.

5. Change to the **Convert** directory.

6. At the command prompt, type:

```
wscript convert.js xdrfilename.xml xsdfilename.xsd
```

The converted XSD schema, named *xsdfilename.xsd*, appears in the Convert folder.

Note

- If you do not type a file name for the XSD schema, the script gives the XSD schema the name of the original XDR schema with .xsd appended to it. For example, if the XDR schema were named xdrfilename.xml, the converted XSD schema would be named xdrfilename.xml.xsd.

To create a specification based on an empty template

1. On the **File** menu, click **New**.

    The **New Document Specification** dialog box appears.

2. Click **Blank Specification** and click **OK**.

3. Add new records to the root node.

4. Add new records to existing records.

5. Add new fields to the root node.

6. Add new fields to records.

7. Specify properties for records and fields.

8. Save the new specification.

To create a specification based on an existing specification

1. On the **File** menu, click **Open**.

    The **Open Document Specification** dialog box appears.

2. Browse to a folder that contains an existing specification.

3. Click a file from the list and click **Open**.

4. Modify the specification as needed.

5. On the **File** menu, click **Save As**.

    The **Save Document Specification As** dialog box appears.

6. In the **File Name** box, type a name for the specification.

7. In the **Encoding** list, click either **UTF-8** or **Unicode** and click **Save**.

    If you want to create a specification associated with ASCII characters, in the **Encoding** list, click **UTF-8**. For specifications associated with double-byte characters, in the **Encoding** list, click **UTF-8** or **Unicode**.

8. Manage records and fields.

   For more information, see "Records and Their Properties" later in this chapter.

9. Save the new specification.

To open existing specifications from a local drive

1. On the **File** menu, click **Open**.

   The **Open Document Specification** dialog box appears.

2. Browse to the folder that contains the specification that you want to open, click the specification, and then click **Open**.

To open existing specifications from WebDAV

1. On the **File** menu, click **Retrieve From WebDAV**.

   The **Retrieve from WebDAV** dialog box appears.

2. In the **Server** list, type the server name and press ENTER.

   You also can select a server name from the list.

3. Browse to the folder that contains the specification that you want to open, click the specification, and then click **Open**.

Note

- You might experience a delay the first time you connect to a remote WebDAV server during a session.

To validate a specification

1. Open a specification or import a schema.

   For more information, see "To create a specification based on an imported file" later in this chapter.

2. On the **Tools** menu, click **Validate Specification**.

The **Warnings** tab displays warnings indicating any problems that might exist with the specification's structure. You can double-click a warning and the record or field, and the associated property, are displayed in red in the panes above.

Related Topics

"Specify Properties for Records and Fields" later in this chapter

"Code List Values and Descriptions" later in this chapter

"Troubleshooting BizTalk Editor" later in this chapter

Save and Close Specifications

You can quickly save new and existing specifications to your hard disk or to WebDAV, provided you have permission to store the file on the server. Once you have saved the file, you can close it.

To save new specifications

1. On the **File** menu, click **Save As**.

   The **Save Document Specification As** dialog box appears.

2. In the **File Name** box, type a name for the file.

3. In the **Encoding** list, click either **UTF-8** or **Unicode** and click **Save**.

   If you want to save a specification associated with ASCII characters, in the **Encoding** list, click **UTF-8**. For specifications associated with double-byte characters, in the **Encoding** list, click **UTF-8** or **Unicode**.

To save existing specifications

- On the **File** menu, click **Save**.

☑ Note

- When you save a file, BizTalk Editor stores the file on your hard disk. To save a file to WebDAV, you must have permission to store the file on the server.

To store specifications

1. On the **File** menu, click **Store to WebDAV**.

   The **Store to WebDAV** dialog box appears.

2. In the **Server** list, type the server name and press ENTER.

   You also can select a server name from the list.

3. Browse to the folder in which you want to store your specification.

4. In the **File Name** box, type the name of the file.

5. In the **Encoding** list, click either **UTF-8** or **Unicode** and click **Save**.

   If you want to store a specification associated with ASCII characters, in the **Encoding** list, click **UTF-8**. For specifications associated with double-byte characters, in the **Encoding** list, click **UTF-8** or **Unicode**.

◆ Important

- You cannot store files with double-byte character set file names if you have an incorrect locale setting. To correct this problem, see "???.xml appears in the WebDAV dialog box" later in this chapter.

☑ **Notes**

- You might experience a delay the first time you connect to a remote WebDAV server.
- When you store a file to WebDAV, BizTalk Editor stores the file on a server. To save a file to your hard disk, on the **File** menu, click **Save As**.

To close specifications

- On the **File** menu, click **Close**.

Related Topics

"Specify Properties for Records and Fields" later in this chapter

"Troubleshooting BizTalk Editor" later in this chapter

Supporting Standards

Electronic data interchange (EDI) standards, such as EDIFACT and X12, define a great number of the possible segments and elements that make up the file structure needed in business documents. Using BizTalk Editor, you can start with these structures as the basis for your specification and then remove the segments and elements you do not need. The final structure is a subset of the standard that you and your trading partner(s), or someone else in your organization, agree to use for business data exchange.

If you create or move nodes in an EDIFACT or X12 document, it is strongly recommended that you set the document standard to **CUSTOM**. In addition, you should also set the **Delimiter Type** property to make the altered structure compatible with the rest of the document. Note that if you set the document standard from **CUSTOM** back to **EDIFACT** or **X12**, all **Delimiter Type** settings will be lost. For more information about setting the **CUSTOM** property, see "To set reference properties" later in this chapter. For more information about setting the **Delimiter Type** property, see "To set parse properties" later in this chapter.

BizTalk Editor also supports X12 syntax rules, which are relational conditions that exist among two or more data elements for a record. If the specification contains syntax rules, they are enforced during the server run-time process when the specification is validated.

There are five types of rules:

- **All**

  If TXI08 exists then all of the following nodes must exist:
  - TXI03

- **Grouped**

  If any of the following nodes exist, then all must exist:
  - TXI04
  - TXI05

- **Any**

  At least one of the following nodes must exist:
  - TXI02
  - TXI03
  - TXI06

- **One**

  At most one of the following nodes must exist:
  - TXI02
  - TXI03
  - TXI06

- **Any(conditional)**

  If PO413 exists then at least one of the following nodes must exist:
  - PO410
  - PO411
  - PO412

To create a specification based on a standard

1. On the **File** menu, click **New**.

   The **New Document Specification** dialog box appears.

2. Click **XML**, **X12**, or **EDIFACT**, and then click **OK**.

   If you select EDIFACT or X12, you must also select a version. Click the folder for the version that you want and click **OK**.

3. Click the specification type and click **OK**.

4. Delete records, if necessary.

5. Delete fields, if necessary.

6. Clear codes, if necessary.

7. Save the new specification.

Summary List of Included EDI-Based Documents

BizTalk Editor supports all EDI-based documents. The table on the following page lists the standard specifications, versions, and document standards for EDI-based documents available when you create a new specification based on a standard.

Standard	Version	Document standards
X12	• 2040 • 3010 • 3060 • 4010	• 810 • 832 • 846 • 850 • 852 (available in all versions except 2040) • 855 • 856 • 861 • 864 • 867 • 940 (available only with 3060 and 4010 versions) • 944 (available only with 3060 and 4010 versions) • 997
EDIFACT	• D93A • D95A • D95B • D97B • D98A • D98B	• APERAK (available in all versions except D93A) • CONTRL (available only with D98A and D98B versions) • DESADV • INVOIC • INVRPT • ORDERS • ORDRSP • PARTIN • PAYEXT • PRICAT • PRODAT (available only with D97B, D98A, and D98B versions) • RECADV (available only with D97B, D98A, and D98B versions) • SLSRPT
XML	• N/A	• CommonAdvancedShipNotice • CommonInventoryAdvice • CommonInvoice • CommonPartnerProfile • CommonPO • CommonPOAcknowledgment • CommonPriceCatalog • CommonShippingAdvice • CommonShippingOrder • CanonicalReceipt • Simple SOAP Envelope • BTF1 Envelope

Related Topics

"Specify Properties for Records and Fields" later in this chapter

"To set reference properties" later in this chapter

"Understanding Specifications" earlier in this chapter

Supporting Other File Formats

BizTalk Editor is designed to make it easy to create specifications with positional, delimited, and combined positional and delimited file structure. The following sections provide specific details about each of these file structures.

Positional flat files

A positional flat file is made up of fields that are the same fixed length and records that have a common end-of-record terminator. The structure of an incoming file must be represented in the records and fields of the source specification so the positional nature of the incoming file is preserved. Therefore, before defining the document structure of a source specification, obtain a layout of the necessary records and fields.

The following table shows an example of a fixed format.

Name	Address	City	Phone
Xxxxxxxxxx	Aaaaaaaaaa	Cccccccccccccccc	xxx-xxx-xxxx
Yyyyyyyyyy	Bbbbbbbbbb	Ddddddddddddd	xxx-xxx-xxxx

The Name field is fixed at a maximum of 10 characters, the Address field maximum is 10 characters, the City field maximum is 15 characters, and the Phone field maximum is 12 characters. The end-of-record terminator is a carriage return and/or line feed character or characters.

You can use BizTalk Editor to create consecutive records and fields. You can create multiple record types and assign different delimiters for parent records. For structures that contain multiple record types, the specification of the types and record terminators must also be specified in the order in which they appear in the document. Fields must be specified by start position, length, and data type.

♦ Important

- A positional record must always be a child of a delimited record. The delimiter character specified for the parent delimited record must not appear in the data of the child positional record. There is no way to escape the delimiter character of the parent delimited record in the data of the child positional field. For more information about delimiters and escape characters, see "To set parse properties" later in this chapter.

✎ Notes

- On the **Parse** tab, you must set the **Structure** property of the root node to **Delimited** if your flat file is both delimited and positional. Additional record properties are set to either **Delimited** or **Positional**, depending on their attributes.

- If a specification is positional and you change the structure to delimited, the compiled specification includes the original start position and end position specified on the **Reference** tab. However, when BizTalk Server parses a specification, the parser ignores this information and processes the specification as a delimited file.

Delimited flat files

A delimited flat file contains one or more records separated by a delimiter. BizTalk Editor does not read delimiters as part of the data. However, if the delimiter character does appear as data, the data can be formatted so the data and the delimiter are distinguishable. For example, the field in which a delimiter character appears can be enclosed in quotation marks to indicate that the delimiter character is to be treated as data and not as a delimiter.

Using BizTalk Editor, you can select specific fields and the delimiters that are associated with them. You can also specify end-of-record delimiters. To enable the use of delimited flat files, BizTalk Editor supports:

- Structures that consist of multiple groups of records.

- Multiple record types that are defined by record-type tags.

- End-of-record delimiters.

- Wrap and escape characters, to distinguish between field data and delimiter values.

- Field start, length, and type values.

- Field content tags and descriptions.

- The ability to transform flat files into specifications that can be used by BizTalk Mapper.

✎ Note

- On the **Parse** tab, you must set the **Structure** property of the root node to **Delimited** if your flat file is both delimited and positional. Additional record properties are set to either **Delimited** or **Positional**, depending on their attributes.

To create a specification based on a flat file

1. On the **File** menu, click **New**.

   The **New Document Specification** dialog box appears.

2. Click **Blank Specification** and click **OK**.

3. Highlight the root node and click the **Reference** tab.

4. Double-click the Value field in the Standard row.

5. In the **Standard** list, click **CUSTOM**.

6. Press ENTER.

7. Click **Yes** to confirm the change.

8. Add new records to the root node.

9. Add new records to existing records.

10. Add new fields to the root node.

11. Add new fields to records.

12. Specify properties for records and fields.

13. Save the new specification.

✒ Notes

- On the **Parse** tab, you must set the **Structure** property of the root node to **Delimited** if your flat file is both delimited and positional. Additional record properties are set to either **Delimited** or **Positional**, as required.

- Flat files based on the UTF-8 code page are not supported by BizTalk Editor.

Related Topics

"Specify Properties for Records and Fields" later in this chapter

"Understanding Specifications" earlier in this chapter

Invalid XML Name Characters

Unicode characters that range from xF900 to xFFFE are not valid in Extensible Markup Language (XML) names. If you use an invalid Unicode character in an XML name, that character is translated into an escaped numeric entity when you view it in the specification tree. The escaped numeric entity is encoded as _xHHHH_, where HHHH stands for the four-digit hexadecimal Unicode code. For example, the name *Ship To* in a purchase order specification contains a space character, and appears in a specification tree as *Ship_x0020_To*. If you move the mouse pointer over a node that contains an encoded Unicode character, a ToolTip appears that displays the node name with the unencoded Unicode character.

✒ Note

- This occurs when you view a specification tree in BizTalk Editor or in BizTalk Mapper.

Invalid Character Ranges

You can block a character or a range of characters from being output by BizTalk Server. To do this, in BizTalk Editor, open a specification that is to be used as a destination specification. Open the **Invalid Character Ranges** dialog box and enter the characters or the character ranges that you want to prevent being output by BizTalk Server. Whenever BizTalk Server attempts to process a character specified in the **Invalid Character Ranges** dialog box of an output specification, processing stops and an error message appears.

✎ Note

- Character ranges can be blocked only for non-XML documents.

To add invalid character ranges

1. On the **View** menu, click **Invalid Character Map**.

   The **Invalid Character Ranges** dialog box appears.

2. Click the **New Character Range** button ▣.

   The **Enter Invalid Character Range** dialog box appears.

3. Click a value in the **Invalid start range** list and press TAB.

4. Click a value in the **Invalid end range** list and click **OK**.

5. Repeat steps 2 through 4 to add additional invalid character ranges.

◆ Important

- You can set invalid character ranges only for non-XML documents.

- The correct hexadecimal value for a question mark symbol (**?**) is **(0x3f)**. The default setting in the **Invalid start range** list and **Invalid end range** list is **? (0x0)**. Do not use this to represent a question mark symbol. To specify a question mark symbol, select the **? (0x3f)** value from the list.

✎ Notes

- The values that appear in the **Invalid start range** and **Invalid end range** lists are hexadecimal values. If you view the specification as an Extensible Markup Language (XML) source file by using an application such as Microsoft Internet Explorer 5 or later, the values appear as decimal values. For example, if you type a semicolon (;) in the **Invalid start range** and **Invalid end range** boxes, the value that appears is **; (0x3b)**. Viewed by using a browser, this value appears as **59**.

- To enter an invalid character range, you can also highlight the value in the **Invalid start range** list, type a numeric or alphabetic character, and then press TAB to move to the **Invalid end range** list.

To edit invalid character ranges

1. On the **View** menu, click **Invalid Character Map**.

   The **Invalid Character Ranges** dialog box appears.

2. Select the character range that you want to modify and click the **Change Character Range** button ⓐⓑⓘ.

   The **Enter Invalid Character Range** dialog box appears.

3. In the **Invalid start range** list, select a value.

   –Or–

   In the **Invalid end range** list, select a value.

4. Click **OK**.

5. Repeat steps 2 through 4 to modify additional invalid character ranges.

◆ **Important**

- You can set invalid character ranges only for non-XML documents.
- The correct hexadecimal value for a question mark symbol (**?**) is (**0x3f**). The default setting in the **Invalid start range** list and **Invalid end range** list is **?** (**0x0**). Do not use this to represent a question mark symbol. To specify a question mark symbol, click the **?** (**0x3f**) value in the list.

✎ **Notes**

- The values that appear in the **Invalid start range** and **Invalid end range** lists are hexadecimal values. If you view the specification as an XML source file by using an application such as Microsoft Internet Explorer 5 or later, the values appear as decimal values. For example, if you type a semicolon (;) in the **Invalid start range** and **Invalid end range** boxes, the value that appears is **;** (**0x3b**). Viewed by using a browser, this value appears as **59**.
- To enter a character range, you can also highlight the value in the **Invalid start range** list, type a numeric or alphabetic character, and then press TAB to move to the **Invalid end range** list.

To delete invalid character ranges

◆ **Important**

- You can set invalid character ranges only for non-XML documents.

1. On the **View** menu, click **Invalid Character Map**.

   The **Invalid Character Ranges** dialog box appears.

2. Click the character range that you want to delete and click the **Delete Character Range** button ☒.

3. Click **Yes** to confirm the change.

Related Topic

Chapter 6, "Mapping Data"

Manage Document Instances

In BizTalk Editor you can create a document instance based on a specification and you can validate a document instance against a specification.

To create a document instance

1. Open a specification on which you want to base a document instance.

2. On the **Tools** menu, click **Create XML Instance**.

   The **Create Document Instance as** dialog box appears.

3. Browse to the folder in which you want to create a document instance.

4. In the **File Name** box, type a name for the document instance and click **Save**.

   The new document instance is displayed on the **Output** tab.

🖉 Note

- The only format available for creating a document instance is Unicode.

To validate a document instance

1. Open a specification against which you want to validate a document instance.

2. On the **Tools** menu, click **Validate Instance**.

   The **Validate Document Instance** dialog box appears.

3. Browse to the document instance you want to validate and click **Open**.

   When you validate a document instance against a specification based on either the X12 or EDIFACT standard, the **Document Delimiters** dialog box appears. Do one of the following:

   - **X12-based specifications.** Select the delimiters appropriate for the document you want to validate and click **OK**.

   - **EDIFACT-based specifications.** Select the delimiters and the escape character appropriate for the document you want to validate and click **OK**.

The **Warning** tab displays the message "The document instance validation succeeded" if the document instance is validated against the specification. If the document instance is not validated against the specification, the **Warning** tab indicates this and displays errors that indicate why the document instance was not validated. If you validate a non-XML document instance against a non-XML specification, if the document instance is validated you can view an Extensible Markup Language (XML) version of the document on the **Output** tab.

◆ **Important**

- It is strongly recommended that before you use a document instance in a production environment, you validate the instance against its source specification and correct any problems displayed on the **Warnings** tab.

📝 **Notes**

- BizTalk Editor will not validate a document instance that contains multiple documents.

- A document instance that contains a field with a blank attribute value ("") can be validated successfully against a specification regardless of the value that is set for the **Minimum Length** property for that field. For example, if a specification has a field with a **Minimum Length** property value set to 4, and you attempt to validate a document instance that has a corresponding field with a blank attribute value, the validation will not fail because of this mismatch. The reason for this is that the MSXML parser that underlies the validation engine treats an attribute with a blank value as though the attribute is not specified. This issue will be corrected for the next release of BizTalk Server.

- Instance validation does not work properly against electronic data interchange (EDI) instances (both X12 and EDIFACT standards) unless you remove interchange, group, and document envelopes (both headers and trailers). For X12 documents, you must remove the ISA, GS, ST, SE, GE, and IEA segments, and for EDIFACT documents you must remove the UNA (if present), UNB, UNG, UNH, UNT, UNE, and UNZ segments.

- A well-formed XML document instance that contains elements typed as XML-Data Reduced (XDR) data types might not validate against its corresponding specification. To make such a document instance validate against its corresponding specification, ensure that all elements typed as XDR data types have their **Model** properties set to **Open**. For more information about the **Model** property, see "To set declaration properties" later in this chapter.

- Non-XML document instances saved in Unicode will not validate correctly unless you remove the byte order marker at the beginning of the file.

- When validating a document instance against a specification with the standard set to X12, EDIFACT, or CUSTOM, the document instance must have a document structure that conforms to the standard of the specification. For example, you can validate an X12 document instance only against an X12 specification.

- A document instance that contains an "x-schema" schema reference is always validated using that schema reference, regardless of the schema that is loaded in BizTalk Editor.

- An invalid character map is not a criterion of instance validation. For example, if an instance contains data contained within the start range and end range in the **Invalid Character Ranges** dialog box, validation might still succeed.

Importing Files

You can import three types of files into BizTalk Editor: well-formed XML instances, document type definitions (DTDs), and XML-Data Reduced (XDR) schemas. The following sections provide more information about importing files in BizTalk Editor.

◸ Note

- If BizTalk Editor cannot determine which element should be the root node, the **Select Root Element** dialog box appears. Select the element that should be the root node and click **OK**.

After importing a well-formed XML instance, a DTD, or an XDR schema, BizTalk Editor creates a structure that is based on the imported file and displays a set of records and fields. After you save the file in BizTalk Editor, the file becomes a specification. This specification has the appropriate header information, and it adheres to a specified structure.

◆ Important

- The following table explains which XDR files and DTDs can be imported when they contain certain data types, and whether the data type can be imported. The columns represent the data types.

	"entity" and "entities"	"nmtoken" and "nmtokens"	"notation"
XDR	The file cannot be imported.	The file can be imported, but the data types are removed.	The file cannot be imported.
DTD	The file can be imported, but the data types are removed.	The file can be imported, but the data types are removed.	The file can be imported, but the data type is imported as an enumeration type.

- When the last line of a DTD is an entity reference (for example, "%xx"), the DTD cannot be imported into BizTalk Editor. Creating a new line at the end of the DTD that contains an end-of-line character will enable the DTD to be imported into BizTalk Editor.

- If you try to import a file that contains an external reference to another file, the import will not succeed.

- If BizTalk Editor displays warnings related to cyclical references after importing a well-formed Extensible Markup Language (XML) file, it is highly recommended that you fix the warnings and save the specification before continuing.

- When importing well-formed XML or DTDs, BizTalk Editor cannot interpret data type or field length parameters.

To create a specification based on an imported file

1. On the **Tools** menu, click **Import**.

   The **Select Import Module** dialog box appears.

2. Click **Well-Formed XML Instance**, **Document Type Definition**, or **XDR Schema**, and then click **OK**.

   If you are importing an XML-Data Reduced (XDR) file, click **XDR Schema**.

3. In the **Import** dialog box, browse to the folder that contains the file that you want to import, click the file, and then click **Open**.

   BizTalk Editor creates a specification based on the structure of the imported file. You must assign all record and field property values.

4. Add new records to the root node.

5. Add new records to existing records.

6. Add new fields to the root node.

7. Add new fields to records.

8. Specify properties for records and fields.

9. Save the new specification.

◆ Important

- BizTalk Editor does not support the import of document type definitions (DTDs) that contain comments within elements. To import these DTDs successfully, you must edit the affected files to remove any comments within elements.

- If the file that you import has an element that has content, is repeated in the instance data, and has no children, BizTalk Editor creates it as a field, rather than a record, when it imports the structure.

- If BizTalk Editor cannot determine which element should be the root node, it displays the **Select Root Element** dialog box. Select the element that is the root node and click **OK**.

- BizTalk Editor cannot import a DTD and/or an XDR schema that contains a cyclical reference involving the root node. BizTalk Editor can import a well-formed XML document that contains a cyclical reference involving the root node, although it displays a warning indicating that cyclical references cannot involve the root node of a document. For more information, see "Cyclical References" later in this chapter.

- If you import a well-formed XML file that contains a namespace on the root node, the namespace becomes the target namespace and is ignored elsewhere in the specification. For more information about target namespaces, see "To set reference properties" later in this chapter.

- If you import a file that contains an element with mixed content (text information as well as subelements), the text information in that element is ignored on import.

- The following table shows what happens when you try to import XDR files or DTDs that contain certain data types. The columns represent the data types.

	"entity" and "entities"	"nmtoken" and "nmtokens"	"notation"
XDR	The file cannot be imported.	The file can be imported. The data types are removed.	The file cannot be imported.
DTD	The file can be imported. The data types are removed.	The file can be imported. The data types are removed.	The file can be imported. The data type is imported as an enumeration type.

BizTalk Editor Environment

The BizTalk Editor environment consists of menus, toolbar buttons, and three main panes. This environment makes it easy to create new or use existing specifications, work with records and fields, and validate a document instance.

BizTalk Editor User Interface

The BizTalk Editor user interface has three main panes. The left pane displays the specification tree, which is a graphical representation of a specification. The top node in the specification tree is the root node; it is represented by a document icon with horizontal green lines 🗎. Records and fields fall below the root node in the specification hierarchy. Records share the same icon with the root node. Fields are represented by a document icon with vertical blue lines 🗎. You can expand or collapse a node in the specification tree by clicking the plus or minus icon to the left of the node.

The right pane contains six tabs: **Declaration**, **Reference**, **Parse**, **Namespace**, **Dictionary**, and **Code List**. Use these tabs to set property values, namespaces, dictionary properties, and code lists for nodes in a specification. For more information about these tabs, see "Specify Properties for Records and Fields" later in this chapter.

The bottom pane contains two tabs: **Output** and **Warning**. The **Output** tab displays an Extensible Markup Language (XML) document instance created when using the **Create XML Instance** command in BizTalk Editor. For more information about creating an XML document instance from a specification, see "To create a document instance" earlier in this chapter. The **Warning** tab indicates whether an attempt to validate a document instance against a specification was successful, and displays warnings related to an unsuccessful document validation attempt. For more information, see "To validate a document instance" earlier in this chapter.

To expand tree items

- Click the root node or record that you want to expand and, on the **View** menu, click **Expand Tree Items**.

🖉 **Note**

- To expand the entire tree, you must click the root node. If you click a record, you expand only the child records and fields within the record.

To collapse tree items

- Click the root node or record that you want to collapse and, on the **View** menu, click **Collapse Tree Items**.

🖉 **Note**

- To collapse the entire tree, you must click the root node. If you click a record, you collapse only the child records and fields within the record.

To view property values

- On the **View** menu, click one of the following properties:
  - **Declaration**
  - **Reference**
  - **Parse**
  - **Namespace**
  - **Dictionary**
  - **Code List**

To change text sizes

- On the **View** menu, point to **Text Size** and click the size that you want.

To change BizTalk Editor options

1. To view or change options in the **BizTalk Editor Options** dialog box, on the **Tools** menu, click **Options**.

2. On the **General** tab, you can select the **Create a new field as an element** check box.

   For information about this option, see "To create a new field as an element" later in this chapter.

Related Topics

"Specify Properties for Records and Fields" later in this chapter

"To create a document instance" earlier in this chapter

"To create a new field as an element" later in this chapter

"To validate a document instance" earlier in this chapter

BizTalk Editor Menus

BizTalk Editor menus logically group commands together, making it easy to perform a specific task. For example, you can use the commands on the **View** menu to view or to collapse all the records and fields in the specification tree.

The BizTalk Editor menus are as follows:

- **File.** Use this menu to create, open, save, or close a specification.

- **Edit.** Use this menu to cut, copy, paste, insert, rename, or delete records or fields in a specification.

- **View.** Use this menu to select views in the right pane of the user interface, to select views in the bottom pane of the user interface, to select a text size for the BizTalk Editor display, to display the **Invalid Character Ranges** dialog box, to expand or collapse the specification tree, or to highlight the next warning on the **Warnings** tab.

- **Tools.** Use this menu to validate a specification, to validate a document instance against a specification, to create an Extensible Markup Language (XML) document instance from a specification, to import files, to export XML-Data Reduced (XDR) schemas, or to view BizTalk Editor options.

- **Help.** Use this menu to get how-to and conceptual information about using BizTalk Editor.

BizTalk Editor Toolbar Buttons

BizTalk Editor provides a toolbar to complement the menu bar. All of the toolbar buttons display graphic representations of the tasks they perform. They appear in the following order from left to right:

- **New**
- **Open**
- **Save**
- **Retrieve from WebDAV**
- **Store to WebDAV**
- **Cut Specification Node**
- **Copy Specification Node**
- **Paste Specification Node**
- **Delete Specification Node**
- **New Record**
- **New Field**
- **Insert Record**
- **Insert Field**
- **Collapse**
- **Expand**

BizTalk Editor Shortcut Keys

You can use shortcut keys to accomplish tasks in BizTalk Editor. The following table is a quick reference to these shortcut keys.

✎ **Note**

- Functionality that is not included in this list can be obtained by using the numeric keypad to move the mouse pointer with MouseKeys. For more information about MouseKeys in Windows 2000 Server and Advanced Server Help, see "Using the keyboard to move the mouse pointer." For more information about MouseKeys in Windows 2000 Professional Help, see "Move the mouse pointer by using MouseKeys."

Press	To
CTRL+N	Open a new specification.
CTRL+O	Open an existing specification.
CTRL+S	Save a specification.
SHIFT+R	Insert a record.
CTRL+R	Add a new record to a record.
SHIFT+F	Insert a field.
CTRL+F	Add a new field to a record.
DEL	Delete a record or a field.
F4	Highlight the next warning.
F5	Validate a schema.
CTRL+C	Copy an object.
CTRL+X	Cut an object.
CTRL+V	Paste an object.
F6	Move the focus clockwise from pane to pane.
SHIFT+F6	Move the focus counterclockwise from pane to pane.
TAB	Toggle the focus from the tab in the right pane to the data sheet below. In a dialog box, pressing TAB moves the focus through the buttons and fields of the dialog box.
SPACEBAR	Select or clear a check box. The spacebar also acts like a mouse click when the focus is on a button.
F2	Activate edit mode for a highlighted node in the specification tree. Activate edit mode for a highlighted row in the data sheet of the right pane.

Press	To
SHIFT+F2	Activate edit mode for the following fields:
	• The Property column of a highlighted custom annotation row on the **Declaration** or **Reference** tab.
	• The Prefix column of a highlighted custom annotation row on the **Namespace** tab.
	• The Property column of a highlighted custom dictionary row on the **Dictionary** tab.
ALT+ DOWN ARROW	Display the list for an activated list box.
SHIFT++	Add a new custom annotation when the focus is on the namespace data sheet in the right pane.
ENTER	Confirm edits to nodes and values.
ESC	Cancel edits to nodes and values.
F1	View the online Help.
ALT+F4	Exit from the program.
LEFT ARROW	Activate the tab to the left.
RIGHT ARROW	Activate the tab to the right.
Any arrow key	Highlight a folder or a file in the main pane of a dialog box, while the focus is on that pane. This functionality occurs in the **New Document Specification**, the **Store to WebDAV**, and the **Retrieve from WebDAV** dialog boxes. For more information about the **New Document Specification** dialog box, see "Manage Document Instances" earlier in this chapter. For more information about WebDAV, see "To open existing specifications from WebDAV" earlier in this chapter.
The Application key and click **Add** on the shortcut menu	Insert a custom property in a specification. This functionality occurs on the **Declaration**, **Reference**, **Namespace**, and **Dictionary** tabs while a property is highlighted.

Records, Fields, and Properties

BizTalk Editor presents a specification as a tree view of records and fields in a given order. Within this structure, you can create parent-to-child relationships by using records and fields. Records can contain other records or fields, but fields cannot contain other fields or records. A record is always an element, but a field can be either an element or an attribute. The specification tree, which presents the records and fields as nodes, provides you with an easy way to view, create, edit, and delete all the records and fields in a specification. Each node in the specification tree has a set of property definitions, which are represented on six tabs in the main window of BizTalk Editor: **Declaration**, **Reference**, **Parse**, **Namespace**, **Dictionary**, and **Code List**. The data on these tabs is necessary for BizTalk Editor to translate a document from its original format to XML. The information defines the structure of the document, whether the document is positional or delimited, the order and length of the data, and the format of the data.

Records and Their Properties

Depending on the type of specification you are building, you might need to add and/or remove records. After adding records to any specification, you must specify properties. If you remove a record, its properties are also removed, along with all child records and fields.

If your specification is based on X12 or EDIFACT, you can add only the type of records that exist in that standard, but you can remove any or all records. If you are building a specification that is based on a blank specification, you must add records. In some cases, such as when you are building a new specification that is based on an existing specification, you might need to add and remove records.

When you add or insert a record, you can immediately begin typing to rename the record. You can edit the name of an existing record and its properties by selecting the record and editing as appropriate.

If you paste into a specification a record with a name that is the same as an existing record, a number is appended to the end of the name of the record you are pasting.

For information about creating a new instance of an existing record, see "To create a new instance of an existing record" later in this chapter. For information about creating a cyclical reference, see "To create cyclical references" later in this chapter.

To add new records to the root node

1. Click the root node.

2. On the **Edit** menu, click **New Record**.

   A child record is inserted after the last node in the specification tree.

3. Type a name for the record and press ENTER.

🗒 Notes

- For a non-XML file such as a flat file, you can type a **Source Tag Identifier** property to identify the tag in the non-XML source file.

- Sibling records cannot have the same name.

To add new records to existing records

1. Click a record.

2. On the **Edit** menu, click **New Record**.

   A child record is inserted directly after the selected record or after the last child node of the selected record.

3. Type a name for the record and press ENTER.

 Notes

- For a non-XML file such as a flat file, you can type a **Source Tag Identifier** property to identify the tag in the non-XML source file.

- Sibling records cannot have the same name.

To insert records

1. Click a record.

2. On the **Edit** menu, click **Insert Record**.

   A sibling record is inserted directly after the selected record or after the last child node of the selected record.

3. Type a name for the record and press ENTER.

 Note

- Sibling records cannot have the same name.

To move records within a specification

1. Click the root node.

2. On the **View** menu, click **Expand Tree Items**.

3. Click the record that you want to move and drag it to another node in the tree.

   When you release the mouse button, if the mouse pointer is in the upper half of the highlighted node text, the record is inserted above the node as a sibling. If the mouse pointer is in the lower half of the highlighted node text, the record is inserted below the node as a sibling. If the mouse pointer is to the right of highlighted node text, the record is inserted below the highlighted record as a child.

To move records from one specification to another

1. Click the root node in the specification that contains the record that you want to move.

2. On the **View** menu, click **Expand Tree Items**.

3. Click the record that you want to move and, on the **Edit** menu, click **Cut**.

4. Click **Start**, point to **Programs**, point to **Microsoft BizTalk Server 2000**, and then click **BizTalk Editor**.

   You must open a second instance of BizTalk Editor to open a different specification.

5. On the **File** menu, click **Open**.

   The **Open Document Specification** dialog box appears.

6. Browse to the folder that contains the specification to which you want to move the record.

7. Click the file in the list and click **Open**.

8. Click the root node in the specification.

9. On the **View** menu, click **Expand Tree Items**.

10. Click the root node, a record, or a field after which you want to insert the record.

11. On the **Edit** menu, click **Paste**.

✎ Note

- If you move a record that has the same name as an existing record, BizTalk Editor automatically adds a number to the end of the record's name.

To copy records within a specification

1. Click the root node.

2. On the **View** menu, click **Expand Tree Items**.

3. Click the record that you want to copy and, on the **Edit** menu, click **Copy**.

4. Click the node after which you want to insert the record and, on the **Edit** menu, click **Paste**.

   If the selected node is a record, a child record is inserted directly after the selected node. If the selected node is a field, a sibling record is inserted directly after the selected node.

To copy records from one specification to another

1. Click the root node in the specification that contains the record that you want to copy.

2. On the **View** menu, click **Expand Tree Items**.

3. Click the record that you want to copy and, on the **Edit** menu, click **Copy**.

4. Click **Start**, point to **Programs**, point to **Microsoft BizTalk Server 2000**, and then click **BizTalk Editor**.

   You must open a second instance of BizTalk Editor to open a different specification.

5. On the **File** menu, click **Open**.

   The **Open Document Specification** dialog box appears.

6. Browse to the folder that contains the specification to which you want to copy the record.

7. Click the file in the list and click **Open**.

8. Click the root node in the specification in which you want to copy the record.

9. On the **View** menu, click **Expand Tree Items**.

10. Click the root node, record, or field after which you want to insert the record and, on the **Edit** menu, click **Paste**.

If the selected node is a record, a child record is inserted directly after the selected node. If the selected node is a field, a sibling record is inserted directly after the selected node.

✍ Note

- If you copy a record that has the same name as an existing record, BizTalk Editor automatically adds a number to the end of the record's name.

To rename a single record

1. Click the record that you want to rename.

2. On the **Edit** menu, click **Rename**.

3. Type a new name for the record and press ENTER.

To rename all records that have the same name

1. Click any record that has the name that you want to change.

2. On the **Edit** menu, click **Rename All** *record name*.

3. Type a new name for the records.

All records that have the same name are renamed.

✍ Note

- This command is unavailable on the **Edit** menu unless there are at least two records with the same name.

To delete records

1. Click the record that you want to delete.

2. On the **Edit** menu, click **Delete**.

3. Click **Yes** in the confirmation dialog box.

✌ Caution

- When you delete a record, all child records and fields are deleted.

To create a new instance of an existing record

1. Click a node where you want to create a new instance of an existing record.

2. On the **Edit** menu, click **New Record** or **Insert Record**.

✍ Note

- If you selected a field in step 1, **New Record** is unavailable on the **Edit** menu.

3. Name the new record the same name as the existing record and press ENTER.

You have created two instances of the same record.

◆ **Important**

- You cannot name a new record instance the same name as a sibling record.

- If you name a new record the same name as an ancestor record, you create a cyclical reference, not a new instance of the existing record. For more information, see "Cyclical References" later in this chapter.

📝 **Notes**

- If you click **New Record**, the new record instance is inserted as a descendant of the record that you selected.

- If you click **Insert Record**, the new record instance is inserted as a sibling of the record or field that you selected.

- The node structure below instances of a record is identical; if you remove or add a node to one instance of a record, that change is automatically reflected in all other instances of the record. Some properties of record instances are identical, and other properties can be set independently for each instance. For more information about which properties are identical across record instances and which are not, see "Property Scope" later in this chapter.

- You cannot name an existing record the same name as another existing record.

- An alternative way to create a new instance of an existing record is to press the CTRL key and drag an existing record to the right of the node below which you want to insert the new record instance.

Related Topics

"Property Scope" later in this chapter

"Specify Properties for Records and Fields" later in this chapter

"To create cyclical references" later in this chapter

Edit Notes and Syntax Rules for Records

In the **Node Properties** dialog box, you can:

- Read and edit notes for records.
- Read syntax rules for records.

To view the **Node Properties** dialog box, follow these steps:

1. In the specification tree, right-click a record or field and click **Properties**.
   The **Note** tab appears by default.

2. To view syntax rules for a record, click the **Syntax Rules** tab.

📝 **Note**

- Syntax rules apply only to records.

Enter Record Notes

You can use notes to record any information relevant to the record with which they are associated; for example, the purpose of the record or the reason why it was created.

- To record a note, type some text in the **Node Properties** dialog box and click **OK**.

📝 **Notes**

- You cannot add a note to the root node.

- You cannot type unprintable characters in notes.

View Syntax Rules

For information about how to open the **Node Properties** dialog box, see "Edit Notes and Syntax Rules for Records" earlier in this chapter.

Syntax rules provide information about how the specification tree must be organized. Syntax rules are found only in specifications based on the X12 standard.

📝 **Note**

- Syntax rules apply only to records.

Fields and Their Properties

Depending on the type of specification you are building, you might need to add and/or remove records. Fields correspond to electronic data interchange (EDI) elements. After adding fields to any specification, including EDI documents, you must specify property values.

If your specification is based on X12 or EDIFACT, you can add only the type of fields that exist in that standard, but you can remove any or all fields. If you are building a specification that is based on a blank specification, you must add fields. Regardless of the document type, you can change the properties of any field.

When you add or insert a new field in a specification, the **Type** property, located on the **Declaration** tab, is set to **Attribute** by default. You can manually change this value to **Element** for any field. For information about creating new fields with the **Type** property set to **Element** by default, see "To create a new field as an element" later in this chapter.

When you add or insert a field, you can immediately begin typing to rename the field. You can edit the name of an existing field and its properties by selecting the field and editing as appropriate.

If you paste into a specification an element field with a name that is the same as an existing element field, a number is appended to the end of the name of the field you are pasting. If you paste into a specification a field with the same name as an existing sibling field (and both fields have the same **Type** value), a number is appended to the end of the name of the field you are pasting. For more information about **Type** values, see "To set declaration properties" later in this chapter. For information about creating a new instance of an existing element field, see "To create a new instance of an existing element field" later in this chapter.

To add new fields to the root node

1. Click the root node.

2. On the **Edit** menu, click **New Field**.

   A child field is inserted after the last node in the specification tree.

3. Type a name for the field and press ENTER.

 Note

- Sibling fields cannot have the same name unless one field has its **Type** property set to **Attribute** and the other has its **Type** property set to **Element**.

To add new fields to records

1. Click a record.

2. On the **Edit** menu, click **New Field**.

   A child field is inserted directly after the selected record or after the last child node of the selected record.

3. Type a name for the field and press ENTER.

 Note

- Sibling fields cannot have the same name unless one field has its **Type** property set to **Attribute** and the other has its **Type** property set to **Element**.

To insert fields

1. Click the record or field after which you want to insert a field.

2. On the **Edit** menu, click **Insert Field**.

   A sibling field is inserted directly after the selected record or after the last child node of the selected record.

3. Type a name for the field and press ENTER.

 Note

- Sibling fields cannot have the same name unless one field has its **Type** property set to **Attribute** and the other has its **Type** property set to **Element**.

To create a new field as an element

1. On the **Tools** menu, click **Options**.

   The **BizTalk Editor Options** dialog box appears.

2. Select the **Create a new field as an element** check box and click **OK**.

🖉 Notes

- While this check box is cleared, fields are created as attributes. However, if you select the **Create a new field as an element** check box, all new fields are created as elements.

- Sibling fields cannot have the same name unless one field has its **Type** property set to **Attribute** and the other has its **Type** property set to **Element**.

To change fields from attributes to elements

1. Click a field in the specification tree.

2. On the **Declaration** tab, double-click the Value field in the Type row.

   The current setting is **Attribute**.

3. In the **Type** list, click **Element** and press ENTER.

4. Click **Yes** to confirm the change.

🖉 Note

- Sibling fields cannot have the same name unless one field has its **Type** property set to **Attribute** and the other has its **Type** property set to **Element**.

To change fields from elements to attributes

1. Click a field in the specification tree.

2. On the **Declaration** tab, double-click the Value field in the Type row.

   The current setting is **Element**.

3. In the **Type** list, click **Attribute** and press ENTER.

4. Click **Yes** to confirm the change.

🖉 Note

- Sibling fields cannot have the same name unless one field has its **Type** property set to **Attribute** and the other has its **Type** property set to **Element**.

To move fields within a specification

1. Click the root node.

2. On the **View** menu, click **Expand Tree Items**.

3. Click the field that you want to move and drag it to another node in the tree.

When you release the mouse button, if the mouse pointer is in the upper half of the highlighted node text, the field is inserted above the node as a sibling. If the mouse pointer is in the lower half of the highlighted node text, the field is inserted below the node as a sibling. If the mouse pointer is to the right of highlighted node text, the field is inserted below the record as a child.

To move fields from one specification to another

1. Click the root node in the specification that contains the field that you want to move.

2. On the **View** menu, click **Expand Tree Items**.

3. Click the field that you want to move and, on the **Edit** menu, click **Cut**.

4. Click **Start**, point to **Programs**, point to **Microsoft BizTalk Server 2000**, and then click **BizTalk Editor**.

   You must open a second instance of BizTalk Editor to open a different specification.

5. On the **File** menu, click **Open**.

   The **Open Document Specification** dialog box appears.

6. Browse to the folder that contains the specification to which you want to move the record.

7. Click the file in the list and click **Open**.

8. Click the root node in the specification in which you want to move the field.

9. On the **View** menu, click **Expand Tree Items**.

10. Click the root node, a record, or a field after which you want to insert the field.

11. On the **Edit** menu, click **Paste**.

✎ Note

- If you move a field that has the same name as an existing field, BizTalk Editor automatically adds a number to the end of the field's name.

To copy fields within a specification

1. Click the root node.

2. On the **View** menu, click **Expand Tree Items**.

3. Click the field that you want to copy and, on the **Edit** menu, click **Copy**.

4. Click a node after which you want to insert the field and, on the **Edit** menu, click **Paste**.

   If the selected node is a record, a child field is inserted directly after the selected node. If the selected node is a field, a sibling field is inserted directly after the selected node.

To copy fields from one specification to another

1. Click the root node in the specification that contains the field that you want to copy.

2. On the **View** menu, click **Expand Tree Items**.

3. Click the field that you want to copy and, on the **Edit** menu, click **Copy**.

4. Click **Start**, point to **Programs**, point to **Microsoft BizTalk Server 2000**, and then click **BizTalk Editor**.

   You must open a second instance of BizTalk Editor to open a different specification.

5. On the **File** menu, click **Open**.

   The **Open Document Specification** dialog box appears.

6. Browse to the folder that contains the specification to which you want to move the field.

7. Click the file in the list and click **Open**.

8. Click the root node in the specification to which you want to copy the field.

9. On the **View** menu, click **Expand Tree Items**.

10. Click the root node, a record, or a field after which you want to paste the record and, on the **Edit** menu, click **Paste**.

    If the selected node is a record, a child field is inserted directly after the selected node. If the selected node is a field, a sibling field is inserted directly after the selected node.

✎ Note

- If you copy a field that has the same name as an existing field, BizTalk Editor automatically adds a number to the end of the field's name.

To rename a single field

1. Click the field that you want to rename.

2. On the **Edit** menu, click **Rename**.

3. Type a new name for the field and press ENTER.

✎ Note

- Fields that are elements cannot have the same name as an existing record.

To delete fields

1. Click the field that you want to delete.

2. On the **Edit** menu, click **Delete**.

3. Click **Yes** in the confirmation dialog box.

To create a new instance of an existing element field

1. Select a node where you want to create a new instance of an element field.

   ### ✎ Note

   - You can create multiple instances of fields only of type **Element** (on the **Declaration** tab). You cannot create multiple instances of fields of type **Attribute**. If you create two or more attribute fields with the same name, the fields remain completely independent of each other.

2. On the **Edit** menu, click **New Field** or **Insert Field**.

   ### ✏ Note

   - If you selected a field in step 1, **New Field** is unavailable on the **Edit** menu.

3. Name the new field the same name as the existing field and press ENTER.

   You have created two instances of the same field.

◆ Important

- You cannot name a new element field instance the same name as a sibling element field instance.

✏ Notes

- If you click **New Field**, the new field instance is inserted as a descendant of the record that you selected.

- If you click **Insert Field**, the new field instance is inserted as a sibling of the record or field that you selected.

- Some properties of field instances are identical, and other properties can be set independently for each instance. For more information about which properties are identical across field instances and which are not, see "Property Scope" later in this chapter.

- You cannot name an existing field the same name as another existing field, unless one field has its **Type** property set to **Attribute** and the other field has its **Type** property set to **Element**.

- An alternative way to create a new instance of an existing element field is to press the CTRL key and drag an existing element field to the right of the node below which you want to insert the new field instance.

Related Topics

"Cyclical References" later in this chapter

"Property Scope" later in this chapter

"Specify Properties for Records and Fields" later in this chapter

"To set declaration properties" later in this chapter

Edit Notes for Fields

You can use notes to record any information relevant to the field with which they are associated; for example, the purpose of the field or the reason why it was created.

Enter Field Notes

For information about how to open the **Node Properties** dialog box, see "Edit Notes and Syntax Rules for Records" earlier in this chapter.

You can use notes to record any information relevant to the field with which they are associated; for example, the purpose of the field or the reason why it was created.

- To record a note, type some text in the **Node Properties** dialog box and click **OK**.

Note

- You cannot type unprintable characters in notes.

Specify Properties for Records and Fields

BizTalk Editor creates specifications by interpreting the properties of records and fields that are contained in a file.

Declaration Property Settings

This section provides information for setting properties on the **Declaration** tab of BizTalk Editor.

To set declaration properties

1. In the specification tree, click the root node, a record, or a field for which you want to set a property, and then click the **Declaration** tab.

2. Double-click the field in the Value column that is associated with the property that you want to set.

3. Type data in the field or click the down arrow to select from a list of available options.

4. Press ENTER to accept your changes.

The **Declaration** tab contains the properties shown in the tables on the following pages. The properties that you select are set for the root node, a record, or a field, depending on which node you have selected.

Declaration Tab: Root Node Properties

Property	Value
Name	The name of the root node.

> 📝 **Note**
>
> • If you change the **Name** value on the **Declaration** tab, the name of the root node in the specification tree automatically changes to match it. In a newly created specification, changing the **Name** value on the **Declaration** tab also changes the **Specification Name** value on the **Reference** tab. However, since it is possible to have a specification name that is different from the root node name, changing the **Specification Name** value has no effect on the **Name** value or the root node name in the specification tree. Once the **Specification Name** value has been edited, however, changing the **Name** value or the root node name has no effect on the **Specification Name** value.

Property	Value
Description	The description of the specification.
Type	The type of record.
Model	**Closed.** Indicates that the data contained in the document instance and the specification structure match. **Open.** Indicates that the data in the document instance does not totally adhere to the structure of the specification.

> 📝 **Note**
>
> • If this property value is left blank, the default value is **Open**.

Property	Value
Content	**Element Only.** Indicates that the root node can contain only elements. This is the automatic default when the root contains a child record. **Empty.** Indicates that the root node cannot contain subelements. **Text Only.** Indicates that the root node can contain text and not subelements.

> 📝 **Note**
>
> • BizTalk Editor does not support elements that contain mixed content (text information as well as subelements).

Property	Value
Order	Select one of the following values:

• **Many.** Indicates that zero or more of the constituent elements can appear, in any order or combination.

• **One.** Indicates that one and only one of the constituent elements can appear.

• **Sequence.** Indicates that the constituent elements must appear in the order specified.

Declaration Tab: Record Properties

Property	Value
Name	The name of the record.
Description	The description of the record.
Type	The type of record.
Model	**Closed.** Indicates that the data contained in the document instance and the specification structure match. **Open.** Indicates that the data in the document instance and the specification structure do not match. 📝 Note • If this property value is left blank, the default value is **Open**.
Content	**Element Only.** Indicates that the record can contain only elements. This is the automatic default for any record that contains a child record. **Empty.** Indicates that the record cannot contain subelements. **Text Only.** Indicates that the record can contain text and not subelements. 📝 Note • BizTalk Editor does not support elements that contain mixed content (text information as well as subelements).
Order	Select one of the following values: • **Many.** Indicates that zero or more of the constituent elements can appear, in any order or combination. • **One.** Indicates that one and only one of the constituent elements can appear. • **Sequence.** Indicates that the constituent elements must appear in the order specified.
Cycle Count	Type the number of cycles you want to be available below the base record. For more information, see "Cyclical References" later in this chapter. 📝 Note • This property field appears only if you have created a cyclical reference.

Declaration Tab: Field Properties

Property	Value
Name	The name of the field.
Description	The description of the field.
Type	Select one of the following values: • **Element** • **Attribute**
Model	**Closed.** Indicates that the data contained in the document instance and the specification structure match. **Open.** Indicates that the data in the document instance and the specification structure do not match. 📝 **Notes** • If this property value is left blank, the default value is **Open**. • The **Model** property is available only for a field with its **Type** value set to **Element**.
Content	**Text Only.** Indicates that the record can contain text and not subelements. 📝 **Notes** • The **Content** property is available only for a field with its **Type** value set to **Element**. • **Text Only** is the only value available for the **Content** property of a field.
Data Type	A valid data type. For a list and description of all valid data types, see "Summary of Data Type and Data Type Values" later in this chapter. ◆ **Important** • If the **Standard** property value on the **Reference** tab is set to **X12**, **EDIFACT**, or **CUSTOM**, you can assign a **Custom Data Type** value on the **Parse** tab. If you specify a **Custom Data Type** value, the **Data Type** value is automatically changed to match the selection that you specified for the **Custom Data Type** value. If you have already specified a **Custom Data Type** value and then specify a **Data Type** value on the **Declaration** tab, the **Custom Data Type** value is cleared. • In a specification, if you create a field with the **Data Type** property set to **IDREF** or **IDREFS**, you must create another field in that specification with the **Data Type** set to **ID**. • To select a field for tracking or for use in a channel filtering expression in BizTalk Messaging Manager, you must assign a data type to that field in the specification.

Property	Value
Data Type Values	If you select **Enumeration** in the **Data Type** list, the data type values **a b c** appear by default in the **Data Type Values** box. You can replace the default values with custom values separated by spaces.

If you are working with an X12 or EDIFACT document and include codes associated with a particular field, those codes automatically appear in the **Data Type Values** box, and **Enumeration** automatically appears in the **Data Type** box. |
| **Minimum Length** | The minimum number of characters that the field can contain.

☑ **Note**

- The **Minimum Length** property can be set only for fields with the following **Data Type** values: **String**, **Number**, **Binary (base64)**, and **Binary (hex)**. |
| **Maximum Length** | The maximum number of characters that the field can contain.

☑ **Note**

- The **Maximum Length** property can be set only for fields with the following **Data Type** values: **String**, **Number**, **Binary (base64)**, and **Binary (hex)**. |
| **Default Value** | The value that is provided if the incoming document instance does not contain the field. For more information, see "Default Value Integration" later in this chapter.

☑ **Note**

- The **Default Value** property appears only in specifications when the **Standard** property (on the **Reference** tab for the root node) is set to **XML**, and the **Type** property (on the **Declaration** tab for the field) is set to **Attribute**. |

Related Topics

"Cyclical References" later in this chapter

"Default Value Integration" later in this chapter

"To add a channel filtering expressions" in Chapter 9, "Configuring BizTalk Messaging Services"

"To select specification fields in a channel" in Chapter 9, "Configuring BizTalk Messaging Services"

"To select specification fields in a document definition" in Chapter 9, "Configuring BizTalk Messaging Services"

Summary of Data Types and Data Type Values

The following list provides details and examples to help you specify a value for the **Data Type** property on the **Declaration** tab. After you select one of the following options from the **Data Type** list, you might need to specify a value in the **Data Type Values** box.

Data type

Character

Contains a string, one character long.

String

Contains any text.

Number

Contains a number of digits and can have a leading sign, fractional digits, and an exponent. This follows standard English punctuation; for example, 15, 3.14, -123.456E+10.

Integer (int)

Contains a number and can include an optional sign. It cannot contain a fraction or exponent; for example, 1, 58502, -13.

Float

Contains a number, with no limit on digits; it can potentially have a leading sign, fractional digits, or an exponent.

Fixed Point (14.4)

The same as **Number**, but can contain no more than 14 digits to the left of the decimal point and no more than 4 to the right; for example, 12.0044. This data type can be used for currency values.

Boolean

Contains an expression that is evaluated as either **TRUE** (1) or **FALSE** (0).

Date

Contains a date in a subset ISO 8601 format, with no time information; for example, 1988-04-07.

Date Time

Contains a date in a subset of ISO 8601 format, with optional time and no optional zone information. Fractional seconds can be as precise as nanoseconds; for example, 1988-04-07T18:39:09.

Date Time.tz

Contains a date in a subset ISO 8601 format, with optional time and optional zone information. Fractional seconds can be as precise as nanoseconds; for example, 1988-04-07T18:39:09-08:00.

Time

Contains a time in a subset ISO 8601 format, with no date and no time zone information; for example, 08:15:27.

Time.tz

Contains a time in a subset ISO 8601 format, with no date information but with optional time zone information; for example, 08:15:27-05:00.

Byte (i1)

Contains a number and can contain an optional sign, such as a minus (-) sign. It cannot contain a fraction or an exponent; for example, 1, 127, -128.

Word (i2)

Contains a number and can contain an optional sign, such as a minus (-) sign. It cannot contain a fraction or an exponent; for example, 1, 703, -32768.

Integer (i4)

Contains a number and can contain an optional sign, such as a minus (-) sign. It cannot contain a fraction or an exponent; for example, 1, 703, -32768, 148343, -1000000000.

Double Integer (i8)

Contains a number and can contain an optional sign, such as a minus (-) sign. It cannot contain a fraction or an exponent; for example, 1, 703, -32768, 148343, -1000000000.

Unsigned Byte (ui1)

Contains a number. It cannot contain a sign, fraction, or exponent; for example, 1, 255.

Unsigned Word (ui2)

Contains a number. It cannot contain a sign, fraction, or exponent; for example, 1, 255, 65535.

Unsigned Integer (ui4)

Contains a number. It cannot contain a sign, fraction, or exponent; for example, 1, 703, 3000000000.

Double Unsigned Integer (ui8)

Contains a number. It cannot contain a sign, fraction, or exponent; for example, 1, 703, 3000000000.

Real (r4)

Contains a number that has a minimum value of 1.17549435E-38F and a maximum value of 3.40282347E+38F; for example, 3.14285718E+2.

Double Real (r8)

Contains a number that has a minimum value of 2.2250738585072014E308 and a maximum value of 1.7976931348623157E+308; for example, .314159265358979E+1.

Universal Unique Identifier (uuid)

Contains hexadecimal digits representing octets, with optional embedded hyphens that can be ignored; for example, 333C7BC4-460F-11D0-BC04-0080C7055A83.

Uniform Resource Identifier (uri)

Contains a Uniform Resource Identifier (URI).

Binary (base64)

Contains binary encoding of binary text into characters; for example, conversion of a Graphic Interchange Format (GIF) image into a text representation.

Binary (hex)

Contains a binary hexadecimal digit that represents octets; for example, 0x0ffaa.

ID

Specifies the field as the ID.

IDREF

Specifies that the field is referenced to the field containing the ID value.

IDREFS

Specifies that the field holds a list of IDs, each separated by a space.

Enumeration

Assigns an ordinal sequence to a series of values; for example, Monday, Tuesday, Wednesday might be enumerated as 1 2 3.

Note

- The **Fixed Point (14.4)** data type can be used for currency values.

Reference Property Settings

This section provides information for setting properties on the **Reference** tab of BizTalk Editor.

To set reference properties

1. In the specification tree, click the root node, a record, or a field for which you want to set a property, and then click the **Reference** tab.

2. Double-click the field in the Value column that is associated with the property that you want to set.

3. Type data in the Value column field or click the down arrow to select from a list of available options.

The **Reference** tab contains the properties described in the tables on the following pages. The properties that you select are set for the root node, a record, or a field, depending on which node you have selected.

Reference Tab: Root Node Properties

Property	Value
Specification Name	The name of the specification. This name corresponds to the value of the *<Schema>* tag in the specification.
Standard	Select one of the following values: • **XML** for creating a specification based on Extensible Markup Language (XML). • **X12** for creating a specification based on X12. • **EDIFACT** for creating a specification based on EDIFACT. • **CUSTOM** for creating a specification based on flat file, or for creating a custom specification to be parsed with a custom parser.
Standards Version	The standards version, such as X12 version 4010, on which the specification is based.
Document Type	The document type, such as 850, on which the specification is based.
Version	The version number of the document standard on which the specification is based.
Default Record Delimiter	Type or select a character to be used as the delimiter within any node for which the **Delimiter Type** property on the **Parse** tab is set to **Default Record Delimiter.** 🖉 **Note** • This property field displays only if the Standard field on the **Reference** tab (for the root node) is set to **CUSTOM**.
Default Field Delimiter	Type or select a character to be used as the delimiter within any node for which the **Delimiter Type** property on the **Parse** tab is set to **Default Field Delimiter**. 🖉 **Note** • This property field displays only if the Standard field on the **Reference** tab (for the root node) is set to **CUSTOM**.
Default Subfield Delimiter	Type or select a character that will be used as the delimiter within any node for which the **Delimiter Type** property on the **Parse** tab is set to **Default Subfield Delimiter**. 🖉 **Note** • This property field displays only if the Standard field on the **Reference** tab (for the root node) is set to **CUSTOM**.

Property	Value
Default Escape Character	Type or select a character that will be used as the escape character within any node for which the **Escape Type** property on the **Parse** tab is set to **Default Escape Character**.

✎ Note

- This property field displays only if the Standard field on the **Reference** tab (for the root node) is set to **CUSTOM**.

Code Page	Choose one of the following values:

- Arabic (1256)
- Baltic (1257)
- Central-European (1250)
- Cyrillic (1251)
- Greek (1253)
- Hebrew (1255)
- Japanese-Shift-JIS (932)
- Korean (949)
- Little-Endian-UTF16 (1200)
- Simplified-Chinese-GBK (936)
- Thai (874)
- Traditional-Chinese-Big5 (950)
- Turkish (1254)
- Vietnamese (1258)
- Western-European (1252)

✎ Notes

- This property field displays only if the Standard field on the **Reference** tab (for the root node) is set to **CUSTOM**.
- UTF7 (65000) and UTF8 (65001) are not supported by BizTalk Server.
- If the **Code Page** value is left blank, the default value is **Western-European (1252)**.

Property	Value
Receipt	Choose one of the following options:

Choose one of the following options:

- **Yes.** Indicates that the specification is to be used as an inbound receipt document. A correlator component (X12, EDIFACT, or CUSTOM) is expected to correlate the receipt document to the outbound document that it acknowledges (in other words, something previously sent to the sender of the receipt).

- **No.** Indicates that the specification is not to be used as an inbound receipt document.

✎ **Notes**

- If the receipt value is left blank, the default value is **No**.

- For specifications based on the CanonicalReceipt and for specifications to which the CanonicalReceipt is mapped (both are used in the scenario of generating an outbound receipt), the **Receipt** property should be set to **No**.

Envelope Choose one of the following options:

- **Yes.** Indicates that the specification is an interchange specification.

- **No.** Indicates that the specification is not an interchange specification.

Target Namespace If you have a BizTalk Framework instance and have specified a namespace in the instance, you must enter the corresponding namespace used in the instance.

✎ **Note**

- If you use "x-schema" in the target namespace value of an instance, you might cause a test failure when you test the instance in BizTalk Mapper.

Reference Tab: Record Properties

Property	Value
Minimum Occurrences	The minimum number of times a record can occur in its position within the node hierarchy. Possible values are **0** or **1**. 📝 **Note** • If this property value is left blank, the default value is **1**.
Maximum Occurrences	The maximum number of times a record can occur in its position within the node hierarchy. Possible values are **1** and *****. 📝 **Notes** • If you type an asterisk (*****), the record is considered to be a looping record. If this specification is used in BizTalk Mapper, it compiles this record as a loop. If you type **1**, BizTalk Mapper does not consider this record to be a looping record. • If this property value is left blank, the default value is **1**.

Reference Tab: Field Properties

Property	Value
Required	Choose one of the following options: • **Yes.** Indicates that the field is required. • **No.** Indicates that the field is not required. 📝 **Note** • If this property value is left blank, the default value is **No**.
Start Position	A number that indicates the starting position of the field in the record. 📝 **Note** • This property field displays only if the structure of the parent record is positional.
End Position	A number that indicates the ending position of the field in the record. 📝 **Note** • This property field displays only if the structure of the parent record is positional.

Related Topics

"Calculating Field Positions" later in this chapter

"Understanding Receipts" in Chapter 9, "Configuring BizTalk Messaging Services"

Parse Property Settings

This section provides information for setting properties on the **Parse** tab of BizTalk Editor.

To set parse properties

1. In the specification tree, click the root node, a record, or a field for which you want to set a property, and then click the **Parse** tab.

2. Double-click the field in the Value column that is associated with the property that you want to set.

3. Type data in the field or click the down arrow to select from a list of available options.

The **Parse** tab contains the properties described in the tables on the following pages. The available properties depend on the standard (X12, EDIFACT, or CUSTOM) and on the structure property that you use. By default, new specifications based on a blank specification have a standard property of Extensible Markup Language (XML). For each property, enter a value as needed. The properties that you select are set for the root node, a record, or a field, depending on which node you have selected.

Standard: XML

Parse Tab: Root Node, Record, and Field Properties.

These properties do not display.

Standard: X12 or EDIFACT

◆ Important

*   The **Wrap**, **Pad**, **Escape**, and **Delimiter** values for a record and its child fields should be mutually exclusive.

*   It is highly recommended that you ensure that the wrap character is different from the escape character.

Parse Tab: Root Node or Record Properties

Property	Value
Structure	This value automatically defaults to **Delimited** for the root node. 📝 **Note** • If the **Standard** property value is set to **X12** or **EDIFACT** on the **Reference** tab for the root node of a specification, you cannot edit the **Structure** property value on the **Parse** tab for the root node or any record. If you want to edit the **Structure** property value, you must change the standard to **CUSTOM**.
Source Tag Identifier	The name of the source tag identifier. This is the tag name that is used to match the record with the data. 📝 **Notes** • For a non-XML file such as a flat file, you can type a **Source Tag Identifier** property to identify any tag that might exist in the original file. • The **Source Tag Identifier** property is case sensitive.
Field Order	Select one of the following options: • Prefix. A prefix delimiter appears before each component, and each member of a component in a series. For example, where * is the delimiter: *a*a*b*c. • Postfix. A postfix delimiter appears after each component, and each member or a component in a series. For example, where * is the delimiter: a*a*b*c*. • Infix. An infix delimiter appears between components, and members of components in a series. For example, where * is the delimiter: a*a*b*c. This is the inherent field order for all EDI documents. 📝 **Note** • If the **Field Order** value is left blank, the default value is **Prefix**.
Delimiter Type	Select one of the following options to choose a delimiter for the child nodes directly below the current node: • **Default Record Delimiter.** Indicates that the delimiter is the value of the **Default Record Delimiter** property, which is defined in the document instance. • **Default Field Delimiter.** Indicates that the delimiter is the value of the **Default Field Delimiter** property, which is defined in the document instance • **Default Subfield Delimiter.** Indicates that the delimiter is the value of the **Default Subfield Delimiter** property, which is defined in the document instance

Property	Value
Escape Type (Also known as a release character)	Select the following option to indicate that you want an escape character for the child nodes directly below the current node: • **Default Escape Character.** Indicates that the escape character is a value defined in the document instance. An escape character is useful if you have a character in your field data that is also used as the delimiter character for the field's parent node. For example, if your field data is *Browne,Peter,1231,yes* and you have chosen a comma as the delimiter value of the node that contains the field, BizTalk Editor interprets the comma after "Browne" to be a delimiter, even if you intend for it to be part of the field data. A solution for this is to place an escape character directly preceding the delimiter character that you want to include in the field data. For example, if your escape character is specified as a backslash, you can place a backslash directly preceding a delimiter character as in the following example: *Browne\,Peter,1231,yes* BizTalk Editor interprets the comma after the backslash as field data rather than a delimiter character. 📝 **Note** • The **Escape Type** property is not available for X12 specifications.
Append Newline	Select one of the following options: • **Yes.** Indicates that when the serializer reaches the record delimiter, the serializer automatically appends a new line (LF,0x0A). • **No.** Indicates that when the serializer reaches the record delimiter, the serializer continues on the same line for the following record. 📝 **Note** • If the **Append Newline** value is left blank, the default value is **No**.
Skip Carriage Return	Select one of the following options: • **Yes.** Tells the parser to skip the carriage return (CR) value after a delimiter. • **No.** Tells the parser not to skip the CR value after a delimiter. 📝 **Note** • If the **Skip Carriage Return** value is left blank, the default value is **Yes**.

Property	Value
Skip Line Feed	Select one of the following options: • **Yes.** Tells the parser to skip the line feed (LF) value after a delimiter. • **No.** Tells the parser not to skip the LF value after a delimiter. 📝 **Note** • If the **Skip Line Feed** value is left blank, the default value is **Yes**.
Ignore Record Count	Select one of the following options: • **Yes.** Tells the parser or the serializer not to count this record when counting the total number of records in the specification. • **No.** Tells the parser or the serializer to count this record when counting the total number of records in the specification. 📝 **Notes** • When a document instance is submitted to BizTalk Server, if the number of records in the document instance does not match the calculated number of records in the specification, a parsing failure results. For more information, see "Parsing errors" in Chapter 11, "Administering Servers and Applications." • If the **Ignore Record Count** value is left blank, the default value is **Yes**.

Parse Tab: Field Properties

Property	Value
Custom Data Type	Select one of the following options: • **String (AN).** AN is for alphanumeric fields. • **Binary Hexadecimal (B).** B is for binary fields. • **Date (CY).** CY is for four-digit date fields. • **Number (D0-D4).** D0 through D4 (inclusive) are for decimal fields. The single-digit number represents the number of digits to the right of the decimal. • **Date (DT).** DT is for date fields. • **String (ID).** ID is for identification fields. • **Number (N).** N is for integer fields. • **Number (N0-9).** N0 through N9 (inclusive) are for implied decimal fields (the decimal character does not appear in the data). The single-digit number represents the number of digits to the right of the decimal. • **Number (R).** R is for real number fields. • **Number (R0-R9).** R0 through R9 (inclusive) are for real number fields. The single-digit number represents the number of digits to the right of the decimal. • **Time (TM).** TM is for time fields. ◆ **Important** • If you specify a **Custom Data Type** value, the **Data Type** value on the **Declaration** tab is automatically changed to match the selection that you specified for the **Custom Data Type** value. For example, if you change the **Custom Data Type** value on the **Parse** tab to **Date (CY)**, the **Data Type** value on the **Declaration** tab automatically changes to **Date**. If you specify a **Data Type** value on the **Declaration** tab, the **Custom Data Type** value is cleared. 📝 **Notes** • If you specify **Date (DT)**, **Date (CY)**, or **Time (TM)** for the **Custom Data Type** property, you must also set a value for the **Custom Date/Time Format** property. • All of these custom data type values are supported in specifications with the **Standard** property set to **X12**. For specifications with the **Standard** property set to **EDIFACT**, the supported custom data type values are **String (AN)** and **Number (N)**.
Custom Date/Time Format	If you set **Date (DT)**, **Date (CY)**, or **Time (TM)** as the **Custom Data Type** property, click an option in the list. 📝 **Note** • This property field is available only if the **Custom Data Type** is set to **Date (DT)**, **Date (CY)**, or **Time (TM)**.

Property	Value
Justification	Select one of the following options:

Justification — Select one of the following options:

- **Left.** Aligns data to the left in positional files when the data is less than the maximum field length. Also aligns data to the left in delimited files when the amount of data is less than the minimum length requirement.

- **Right.** Aligns data to the right in positional files.

📝 **Note**

- If the **Justification** value is left blank, the default value is **Left**.

Pad Character — Type a character to pad the field. You can choose any character for a pad character, including a space or a zero. For more information, see "Pad Characters" later in this chapter.

Wrap Character — Type a character to enclose field data. This property is useful if you have a character in your field data that is also used as the delimiter value for the field's parent node. For example, if your field data is

Browne,Peter,1231,yes

and you have chosen a comma as the delimiter value of the node that contains the field, BizTalk Editor interprets the comma after "Browne" to be a delimiter, even if you intend for it to be part of the field data. A solution for this is to define a value for the wrap character property and then enclose the field data in the wrap character. For example, you can set the wrap character property to double quotation marks for the first field and then type your field data as in the following example:

"Browne,Peter",1231,yes

The comma between the double quotation marks is interpreted by BizTalk Editor to be field data rather than a delimiter value.

📝 **Notes**

- If your field data includes characters that are also used as the wrap character, you must enclose those characters in another set of wrap characters.

  For example, with the wrap character value set to double quotation marks,

  "Browne,Peter ""Pete"""

  is parsed by BizTalk Editor to appear as

  Browne,Peter "Pete"

- If the field data in an input document instance includes the line feed character followed directly by the carriage return character, the corresponding field data in the output document instance includes only the line feed character, even if both are enclosed in a set of wrap characters.

Property	Value
Minimum Length with Pad Character	The minimum length of a field in an output document instance, including pad characters. For more information about pad characters, see "Pad Characters" later in this chapter.

🖉 **Notes**

- This property is available only if the pad character is set for that field.

- If the **Minimum Length** property on the **Declaration** tab is set for the field, the **Minimum Length with Pad Character** property must be greater than or equal to the value of the **Minimum Length** property. If the **Minimum Length** property is not set, the **Minimum Length with Pad Character** property must be greater than or equal to 1.

Standard: Custom
Structure Property: Delimited

◆ **Important**

- The **Wrap**, **Pad**, **Escape**, and **Delimiter** values for a record and its child fields should be mutually exclusive.

- It is highly recommended that you ensure that the wrap character is different from the escape character.

Parse Tab: Root Node or Record Properties

Property	Value
Structure	Select the following option for the **Root Node** property: • **Delimited.** Indicates that the root node is based on a delimited file structure. Records can be individually based on delimited or positional file structures. Select one of the following options for **Record** properties: • **Delimited.** Indicates that the record is based on a delimited file structure. Descendant records can be individually based on delimited or positional file structures. • **Positional.** Indicates that the record is based on a positional file structure. Positional records cannot have child records. 📝 **Notes** • For a document to be both delimited and positional, the root node must have its **Structure** property set to **Delimited**. You can then set the **Structure** property for individual records to **Positional** or **Delimited**, as necessary. • If you change from one structure to another, a message box appears. Click **Yes** to confirm the structure change. Some new properties might appear, and some existing properties might be removed. • If you right-click the **Structure** property value field of a positional record and click **Clear Property**, BizTalk Editor interprets the structure of the record as delimited. Some new properties might appear, and some existing properties might be removed. • When the **Standard** property for a new document is set to **CUSTOM**, by default the **Structure** property for the root node and all records is blank. If you leave the **Structure** property blank, its value is **Delimited**.
Source Tag Identifier	The name of the source tag identifier. This is the tag name that is used to match the record with the data. 📝 **Notes** • For a non-XML file, such as a flat file, you can type a **Source Tag Identifier** property to identify any tag that might exist in the original file. • The **Source Tag Identifier** property is case sensitive.
Field Order	Select one of the following options: • **Prefix.** A prefix delimiter appears before each component, and each member of a component, in a series. For example, where * is the delimiter: *a*a*b*c. • **Postfix.** A postfix delimiter appears after each component, and each member of a component, in a series. For example, where * is the delimiter: a*a*b*c*. • **Infix.** An infix delimiter appears between components, and members of components, in a series. For example, where * is the delimiter: a*a*b*c. This is the inherent field order for all electronic data interchange (EDI) documents. 📝 **Note** • If the field order value is left blank, the default value is **Prefix**.

Property	Value
Delimiter Type	Select one of the following options to choose a delimiter for the child nodes directly below the current node: • **Character.** Allows you to designate a delimiter value on the **Parse** tab. If you select **Character**, you must specify a delimiter value. • **Default Record Delimiter.** Indicates that the delimiter is the value of the **Default Record Delimiter** property, on the **Reference** tab for the root node. • **Default Field Delimiter.** Indicates that the delimiter is the value of the **Default Field Delimiter** property, on the **Reference** tab for the root node. • **Default Subfield Delimiter.** Indicates that the delimiter is the value of the **Default Subfield Delimiter** property, on the **Reference** tab for the root node.
Delimiter Value	Type or select a character value for the delimiter. To specify a delimiter value, you must first set the **Delimiter Type** to **Character** on the **Parse** tab.
Escape Type (Also known as a release character)	Select one of the following options to choose an escape character for the child nodes directly below the current node: • **Character.** Allows you to designate an escape character value on the Parse tab. If you select Character, you must specify an escape value. • **Default Escape Character.** Indicates that the escape character is the value of the **Default Escape Character** property, on the **Reference** tab for the root node. An escape character is useful if you have a character in your field data that is also used as the delimiter character for the field's parent node. For example, if your field data is *Browne,Peter,1231,yes* and you have chosen a comma as the delimiter value of the node that contains the field, BizTalk Editor interprets the comma after "Browne" to be a delimiter, even if you intend for it to be part of the field data. A solution for this is to place an escape character directly preceding the delimiter character that you want to include in the field data. For example, if your escape character is specified as a backslash, you can place a backslash directly preceding a delimiter character as in the following example: *Browne\,Peter,1231,yes* BizTalk Editor interprets the comma after the backslash as field data rather than a delimiter character.
Escape Value	Type or select a character value for the escape character. To specify an escape character value, you must first set the **Escape Type** to **Character** on the **Parse** tab.

Property	Value
Append Newline	Select one of the following options:

- **Yes.** Indicates that when the serializer reaches the record delimiter, the serializer automatically appends a new line (LF,0x0A).

- **No.** Indicates that when the serializer reaches the record delimiter, the serializer continues on the same line for the following record.

✎ **Note**

- If the **Append Newline** value is left blank, the default value is **No**.

Skip Carriage Return	Select one of the following options:

- **Yes.** Tells the parser to skip the carriage return (CR) value after a delimiter.

- **No.** Tells the parser not to skip the CR value after a delimiter.

✎ **Note**

- If the **Skip Carriage Return** value is left blank, the default value is **Yes**.

Skip Line Feed	Select one of the following options:

- **Yes.** Tells the parser to skip the line feed (LF) value after a delimiter.

- **No.** Tells the parser not to skip the LF value after a delimiter.

✎ **Note**

- If the **Skip Line Feed** value is left blank, the default value is **Yes**.

Ignore Record Count	Select one of the following options:

- **Yes.** Tells the parser or the serializer not to count this record when counting the total number of records in the specification.

- **No.** Tells the parser or the serializer to count this record when counting the total number of records in the specification.

✎ **Notes**

- When a document instance is submitted to BizTalk Server, if the number of records in the document instance does not match the calculated number of records in the specification, a parsing failure results. For more information, see "Parsing errors" in Chapter 11, "Administering Servers and Applications."

- If the **Ignore Record Count** value is left blank, the default value is **Yes**.

Parse Tab: Field Properties

Property	Value
Custom Data Type	Select one of the following options: • **String (AN).** AN is for alphanumeric fields. • **Binary Hexadecimal (B).** B is for binary fields. • **Date (CY).** CY is for four-digit date fields. • **Number (D0-D4).** D0 through D4 (inclusive) are for decimal fields. The single-digit number represents the number of digits to the right of the decimal. • **Date (DT).** DT is for date fields. • **String (ID).** ID is for identification fields. • **Number (N).** N is for integer fields. • **Number (N0-9).** N0 through N9 (inclusive) are for implied decimal fields (the decimal character does not appear in the data). The single-digit number represents the number of digits to the right of the decimal. • **Number (R).** R is for real number fields. • **Number (R0-R9).** R0 through R9 (inclusive) are for real number fields. The single-digit number represents the number of digits to the right of the decimal. • **Time (TM).** TM is for time fields. ◈ **Important** • If you specify a **Custom Data Type** value, the **Data Type** value on the **Declaration** tab is automatically changed to match the selection that you specified for the **Custom Data Type** value. For example, if you change the **Custom Data Type** value on the **Parse** tab to **Date (CY)**, the **Data Type** value on the **Declaration** tab automatically changes to **Date**. If you specify a **Data Type** value on the **Declaration** tab, the **Custom Data Type** value is cleared. ▨ **Note** • If you specify **Date (DT)**, **Date (CY)**, or **Time (TM)** for the **Custom Data Type** property, you must also set a value for the **Custom Date/Time Format** property.
Custom Date/Time Format	If you set **Date (DT)**, **Date (CY)**, or **Time (TM)** as the **Custom Data Type** property, click an option in the list. ▨ **Note** • This property field is available only if the **Custom Data Type** is set to **Date (DT)**, **Date (CY)**, or **Time (TM)**.

Property	Value
Justification	Select one of the following options:

<table>
<tr><td></td><td>• **Left.** Aligns data to the left in positional files when the data is less than the maximum field length. This also aligns data to the left in delimited files when the amount of data is less than the minimum length requirement.</td></tr>
</table>

- **Right.** Aligns data to the right in positional files.

✎ **Note**

- If the **Justification** value is left blank, the default value is **Left**.

Pad Character	Type or select a character to pad the field. You can choose any character for a pad character, including a space or a zero. For more information, see "Pad Characters" later in this chapter.
Wrap Character	Type a character to enclose field data. This property is useful if you have a character in your field data that is also used as the delimiter value for the field's parent node. For example, if your field data is

Browne,Peter,1231,yes

and you have chosen a comma as the delimiter value of the node that contains the field, BizTalk Editor interprets the comma after "Browne" to be a delimiter, even if you intend for it to be part of the field data. The solution to this is to define a value for the wrap character property and then enclose the field data in the wrap character. For example, you can set the wrap character property to double quotation marks for the first field and then type your field data as in the following example:

"Browne,Peter",1231,yes

The comma between the double quotation marks is interpreted by BizTalk Editor to be field data rather than a delimiter value.

✎ **Notes**

- If you have characters in your field data that are also used as the wrap character, you must enclose those characters in another set of wrap characters.

    For example, with the wrap character value set to double quotation marks,

    "Browne,Peter ""Pete"""

    is parsed by BizTalk Editor to appear as

    Browne,Peter "Pete".

- If the field data in an input document instance includes the line feed character followed directly by the carriage return character, the corresponding field data in the output document instance includes only the line feed character, even if both are enclosed in a set of wrap characters.

Property	Value
Minimum Length with Pad Character	The minimum length of a field in an output document instance, including pad characters. For more information, see "Pad Characters" later in this chapter.

✎ **Notes**

- This property can be set for a field only if the pad character is set for that field.

- If the **Minimum Length** property on the **Declaration** tab is set for the field, the **Minimum Length with Pad Character** property must be greater than or equal to the value of the **Minimum Length** property. If the **Minimum Length** property is not set, the **Minimum Length with Pad Character** property must be greater than or equal to 1.

Standard: Custom
Structure Property: Positional

Parse Tab: Root Node Properties or Record Properties

Property	Value
Structure	Select the following option for the **Root Node** property:

- **Positional.** Indicates that the root node is based on a positional file structure.

✎ **Notes**

- A document with a positional root node can have no records.

- If you right-click the **Structure** property value field of a positional root node and click **Clear Property**, BizTalk Editor interprets the structure of the root node as delimited. Some new properties might appear, and some existing properties might be removed.

- When the **Standard** property for a new document is set to **CUSTOM**, by default the **Structure** property for the root node and all records is blank. If you leave the **Structure** property blank, its value is **Delimited**.

| **Source Tag Identifier** | The name of the source tag identifier. This is the tag name that is used to match the record with the data. |

✎ **Notes**

- For a non-XML file, such as a flat file, you can type a **Source Tag Identifier** property to identify any tag that might exist in the original file.

- The **Source Tag Identifier** property is case sensitive.

| **Source Tag Position** | A number that refers to the position of the beginning of the tag in a positional record. |

Property	Value
Append Newline	Select one of the following options:

- **Yes.** Indicates that when the serializer reaches the record delimiter, the serializer automatically appends a new line (LF,0x0A).

- **No.** Indicates that when the serializer reaches the record delimiter, the serializer continues on the same line for the following record.

📝 **Note**

- If the **Append Newline** value is left blank, the default value is **No**.

Property	Value
Skip Carriage Return	Select one of the following options:

- **Yes.** Tells the parser to skip the carriage return (CR) value after a delimiter.

- **No.** Tells the parser not to skip the CR value after a delimiter.

📝 **Note**

- If the **Skip Carriage Return** value is left blank, the default value is **Yes**.

Property	Value
Skip Line Feed	Select one of the following options:

- **Yes.** Tells the parser to skip the line feed (LF) value after a delimiter.

- **No.** Tells the parser not to skip the LF value after a delimiter.

📝 **Note**

- If the **Skip Line Feed** value is left blank, the default value is **Yes**.

Property	Value
Ignore Record Count	Select one of the following options:

- **Yes.** Tells the parser or the serializer not to count this record when counting the total number of records in the specification.

- **No.** Tells the parser or the serializer to count this record when counting the total number of records in the specification.

📝 **Notes**

- When a document instance is submitted to BizTalk Server, if the number of records in the document instance does not match the calculated number of records in the specification, a parsing failure results. For more information, see "Parsing errors" in Chapter 11, "Administering Servers and Applications."

- If the **Ignore Record Count** value is left blank, the default value is **Yes**.

Parse Tab: Field Properties

Property	Value
Custom Data Type	Select one of the following options: • **String (AN).** AN is for alphanumeric fields. • **Binary Hexadecimal (B).** B is for binary fields. • **Date (CY).** CY is for four-digit date fields. • **Number (D0-D4).** D0 through D4 (inclusive) are for decimal fields. The single-digit number represents the number of digits to the right of the decimal. • **Date (DT).** DT is for date fields. • **String (ID).** ID is for identification fields. • **Number (N).** N is for integer fields. • **Number (N0-9).** N0 through N9 (inclusive) are for implied decimal fields (the decimal character does not appear in the data). The single-digit number represents the number of digits to the right of the decimal. • **Number (R).** R is for real number fields. • **Number (R0-R9).** R0 through R9 (inclusive) are for real number fields. The single-digit number represents the number of digits to the right of the decimal. • **Time (TM).** TM is for time fields. ◆ Important • If you specify a **Custom Data Type** value, the **Data Type** value on the **Declaration** tab is automatically changed to match the selection that you specified for the **Custom Data Type** value. For example, if you change the **Custom Data Type** value on the **Parse** tab to **Date (CY)**, the **Data Type** value on the **Declaration** tab automatically changes to **Date**. If you specify a **Data Type** value on the **Declaration** tab, the **Custom Data Type** value is cleared. ✎ Note • If you specify **Date (DT)**, **Date (CY)**, or **Time (TM)** for the **Custom Data Type** property, you must also set a value for the **Custom Date/Time Format** property.
Custom Date/Time Format	If you set **Date (DT)**, **Date (CY)**, or **Time (TM)** as the **Custom Data Type** property, click an option in the list. ✎ Note • This property field is active only if the **Custom Data Type** is set to **Date (DT)**, **Date (CY)**, or **Time (TM)**.

Property	Value
Justification	Select one of the following options:
	• **Left.** Aligns data to the left in positional files when the data is less than the maximum field length. Also aligns data to the left in delimited files when the amount of data is less than the minimum length requirement.
	• **Right.** Aligns data to the right in positional files.
	✒ Note
	• If the **Justification** value is left blank, the default value is **Left**.
Pad Character	Type a character to be used to pad the field. You can choose any character for a pad character, including a space or a zero. For more information, see "Pad Characters" later in this chapter.

Related Topic

"Pad Characters" later in this chapter

Namespace Declarations

Namespaces that are declared in a specification are displayed on the **Namespace** tab of BizTalk Editor. The following table shows the prefixes and namespaces that appear on the **Namespace** tab by default when you open a specification in BizTalk Editor. You cannot edit these prefixes and namespaces.

Prefix	Namespace
(default)	urn:schemas-microsoft-com:xml-data
b	urn:schemas-microsoft-com:BizTalkServer
d	urn:schemas-microsoft-com:datatypes

✒ Note

• The following namespace is not supported by BizTalk Server:

SOAP-ENC="http://schemas.xmlsoap.org/soap/encoding/"

You can declare custom namespaces in a specification by typing a namespace prefix in the Prefix column and a namespace in the Uniform Resource Name column of the **Namespace** tab. BizTalk Editor does not validate the Uniform Resource Name that you enter for a namespace.

You can also add a custom annotation to any record and field. A custom annotation consists of a prefix-name pair and related value. The syntax for a prefix-name pair is shown in the following example:

prefix:name

On either the **Declaration** or **Reference** tab, type a prefix-name pair in the Property column and type a value in the Value column. Property values entered on the **Declaration** tab are global in scope, and property values entered on the **Reference** tab are local in scope. For more information about global and local scope, see "Property Scope" later in this chapter.

To declare namespaces

1. Click any node in the specification tree.
2. Click the **Namespace** tab.
3. Right-click the first blank field in the Prefix column and click **Add**.
4. Type a namespace prefix and press ENTER.
5. Double-click the field directly to the right, in the Uniform Resource Name column.
6. Type a Uniform Resource Name and press ENTER.

Important

- BizTalk Editor does not validate the Uniform Resource Name that you enter for a namespace.

To add custom annotations

1. In the specification tree, click the root node, a record, or a field for which you want to add a custom annotation.

   Note

   - On the **Reference** tab, you cannot add a custom annotation for the root node.
2. Click the **Declaration** tab or the **Reference** tab, depending on where you want to add the custom annotation.
3. Right-click the first blank field in the Property column and click **Add**.

   Edit mode is activated in the Property column.
4. Type a prefix-name pair (separated by a colon) and press ENTER.

   -Or-

   Click one of the custom annotations in the list and press ENTER.
5. Double-click the blank field directly to the right, in the Value column.

6. Type the value of the custom annotation and press ENTER.

◆ Important

- For the specification to compile successfully, the namespace prefix used in step 4 must be declared in the specification.

To edit custom annotations

1. In the specification tree, click the node that contains the custom annotation that you want to edit.

2. Click the tab (**Declaration** or **Reference**) that references the custom annotation that you want to edit.

3. Double-click the Property field of the custom annotation, edit the field, and then press ENTER.

4. Double-click the Value field of the custom annotation, edit the field, and then press ENTER.

To delete custom annotations

1. In the specification tree, click the node that contains the custom annotation that you want to delete.

2. Click the tab (**Declaration** or **Reference**) that references the custom annotation that you want to delete.

3. Right-click the custom annotation and click **Delete**.

4. Click **Yes** to confirm the change.

Related Topics

"Adding SQL Annotations" later in this chapter

"Property Scope" later in this chapter

Preserving Namespaces in Imported Files

You can import three types of files into BizTalk Editor: XML-Data Reduced (XDR) schemas, well-formed XML instances, and document type definitions (DTDs). BizTalk Editor handles existing namespaces and prefix-name pairs differently for each type of document.

Importing an XDR schema

When you import an XDR schema, existing namespaces are handled in the following manner:

- Namespace declarations are preserved as custom namespaces and appear on the **Namespace** tab below the default namespaces.

- Custom namespace prefixes (with the exception of those associated with the **Name** and **Type** properties) are preserved only if the associated namespace is declared.

📝 **Note**

- BizTalk Editor cannot import an XDR schema with a namespace prefix associated with the **Name** or **Type** property.

Importing a well-formed XML instance

When you import a well-formed XML document instance, namespace declarations are removed from the document, and the prefix-name separator symbol is changed from a colon (:) to an underscore (_) so that the original intention of the namespace prefix is not lost. For example:

prefix_name

🔶 **Important**

- If you import a well-formed XML document instance that contains a namespace prefix-name pair, save the imported instance as a specification, and then try to validate the original document instance against the new specification, instance validation fails. In the new specification, delete the node that contains the prefix-name pair. For the parent record of that node (on the **Declaration** tab), select the **Open** value for the **Model** property and save the specification. You can validate the document instance against this specification.

📝 **Note**

- BizTalk Editor cannot import any document that contains a namespace prefix if the associated namespace has not been declared in the document.

Importing a DTD

When you import a DTD that contains a prefix-name pair, the separator symbol is changed from a colon (:) to an underscore (_). This is so that in terms of placement within the overall structure, the original intention of the prefix is not lost even though the prefix notation itself is not supported. For example:

prefix_name

Dictionary Property Settings

This section provides information for setting properties on the **Dictionary** tab of BizTalk Editor.

To set dictionary properties

1. In the specification tree, click the root node, a record, or a field for which you want to specify a property, and then click the **Dictionary** tab.

2. In the Property column, select the check box for the value that you want to associate with the field.

The **Dictionary** tab contains the properties shown in the following tables. Dictionary properties can be set only for specifications with the **Standard** property on the **Reference** tab set to **XML** or **CUSTOM**.

Dictionary Tab: Root Node or Record Properties

Property	Node path
Document Container Node	In an envelope schema, the document node indicates the record that contains the document.

☑ Note

- In a flat file specification (with its **Standard** property on the **Reference** tab set to **CUSTOM**) that is parsed by the BizTalk Server flat file parser, selecting or clearing the **Document Container Node** dictionary property check box has no effect. This dictionary property is made available, however, in case you need to create a custom specification and a custom parser that use the **Document Container Node** dictionary property.

Dictionary Tab: Field Properties

Property	Node path
Document Name	Displays the path to the field of a document instance that contains the document name.
Source Type	Displays the path to the field of a document instance that contains the source type.
Source Value	Displays the path to the field of a document instance that contains the source value.
Destination Type	Displays the path to the field of a document instance that contains the destination type.
Destination Value	Displays the path to the field of a document instance that contains the destination value.

☑ Notes

- When parsing a specification, the parser uses information on the **Dictionary** tab to locate a channel. You can create a channel by using BizTalk Messaging Manager. For more information about channels and BizTalk Messaging Manager, see "Understanding Channels" in Chapter 9, "Configuring BizTalk Messaging Services."

- If you use a specification to define documents that are submitted to an open messaging port, you must select the destination value on the **Dictionary** tab for the field that contains the destination and transport information. The destination information in a document is overwritten if you use submission parameters. For more information about submitting documents, see "Submitting" in Chapter 10, "Submitting Documents."

- You can also set **Dictionary** properties by right-clicking a field in the Property column and clicking **Set Routing Information**.

To add a custom dictionary property

1. In the specification tree, click the field for which you want to add a custom dictionary property.

2. Click the **Dictionary** tab.

3. Double-click the first blank field in the Property column.

4. Type a name for the property and press ENTER.

✎ Notes

- Use a unique name for each custom property that you create.

- The **Standard** property (for the root node) must not be set for X12 or EDIFACT.

To rename a custom dictionary property

1. Click the **Dictionary** tab.

2. Right-click the custom property that you want to rename and click **Rename**.

3. Type a name for the property and press ENTER.

✎ Note

- Use a unique name for each custom property that you create.

To clear a dictionary property

1. In the specification tree, click the node for which you want clear a dictionary property and click the **Dictionary** tab.

2. In the Property column, clear the check box for the value that you want to disassociate from the field.

✎ Notes

- You can also clear a **Dictionary** property value by right-clicking a field in the Property column and clicking **Clear Routing Information**.

- By clearing a dictionary property in a node, you remove the routing information.

To delete a custom dictionary property

1. Click the **Dictionary** tab.

2. Right-click the custom property that you want to delete and click **Delete**.

3. Click **Yes** to confirm the change.

Related Topics

"Submitting" in Chapter 10, "Submitting Documents"

"Understanding Messaging Ports" in Chapter 9, "Configuring BizTalk Messaging Services"

Code List Values and Descriptions

The information contained on the **Code List** tab specifies X12 or EDIFACT code values and their descriptions. The descriptions define the meaning of each code. For example, the code value ST in the Address Qualifier Code field of many standard document specifications means that the information given is for a Ship To address. The codes in the list cannot be modified or deleted. You can only choose whether or not to associate a code with a field.

Only specifications that are based on an X12 or EDIFACT standard have code lists. However, not all fields in a specification that is based on X12 or EDIFACT have codes associated with them. A complete list of available codes for a specific field appears on the **Code List** tab if that field has a code list reference. Codes are valid for a field if the check box in the Value column next to the code is selected. A description of the code appears in the Description column.

You can include or exclude codes associated with a field by selecting or clearing the check boxes in the Value column next to the code listed on the **Code List** tab. Codes are listed by numeric value or alphabetic value, or by a combination of numeric and alphabetic values. The value represents a specific description. You can associate a code value to any field in the specification tree. For example, in the BEG02 field of an X12 850 purchase order, you can select the code OS, which adds an attribute to the BEG02 field that indicates that the field contains special order information.

Code list values and descriptions for the EDI-based specification templates that are provided by BizTalk Server can be found in the Microsoft Access database file at \Program Files\Microsoft BizTalk Server\XML Tools\Databases\CodeLists\CodeListsX12a.mdb. If you create new tables in this database for new specification templates, the format for the table name is *standard_version*. For example, for a D99A EDIFACT specification template, the corresponding table name would be EDIFACT_D99A.

◆ Important

- If you create a new table in the CodeListsX12a.mdb database, do not put invalid Extensible Markup Language (XML) characters (Unicode characters from F900 to FFFE) into the Value column of the table. If you save a specification that contains a field with a selected code list value that is associated with a value in a table with an invalid XML character, you will be unable to open the specification.

If you associate a code with a field, the **Type** value on the **Declaration** tab must be set to **Attribute**.

✍ Note

- Code lists are available only for specifications based on X12 or EDIFACT. For this reason, you might find that if you change the structure of an X12-based or EDIFACT-based specification to CUSTOM, and then change it back again to X12 or EDIFACT, the code list for a particular field might no longer be available on the **Code List** tab. If this happens, save the specification and then reopen it. The code list will reappear on the **Code List** tab for the appropriate field.

To select codes

1. Click a field in a specification tree.

2. Click the **Code List** tab.

3. In the Value column, select the check box next to the code that you want to use.

✍ Notes

- Code lists are available only for specifications based on X12 or EDIFACT. However, not all fields in a specification based on X12 or EDIFACT have codes associated with them. A complete list of available codes for a specific field appears on the **Code List** tab. Codes are associated with a field if the check box in the Value field next to the code is selected. A description of the code appears in the Description field.

- When you associate a code with a field on the **Code List** tab, that association is also shown on the **Declaration** tab. The **Data Type** value on the **Declaration** tab is automatically set to **Enumeration**, and **Data Type Values** shows the code list numbers you selected on the **Code List** tab. If you clear the **Data Type** value on the **Declaration** tab, there will be no codes selected on the **Code List** tab.

- To select a range of codes, select the check box next to a code, press SHIFT, and then select the check box next to a second code. All codes between the first code and the second code are selected.

- Occasionally, duplicate code values appear on the **Code List** tab. These duplicate code values have varying descriptions, depending on the type of document with which the code value is associated. In the context of validating a document instance, it is never necessary to select more than one code value. However, it is possible to inadvertently select more than one code value. The following list summarizes the selection behavior of duplicate code lists:

    - If you select the top code value in a set of duplicate code values, only that code value is selected.

    - If you select any code value other than the top code value in a set of duplicate code values, that code value is selected and the top code value is automatically selected, too.

- The top code value in a set of duplicate code values cannot be cleared while any other code values in the set are selected.

To clear codes

1. Click a field in the specification tree.

2. Click the **Code List** tab.

3. In the Value column, clear the check box that is next to the code that you want to clear.

Notes

- Code lists are available only for specifications based on X12 or EDIFACT. However, not all fields in a specification based on X12 or EDIFACT have codes associated with them. A complete list of available codes for a specific field appears on the **Code List** tab. Codes are associated with a field if the check box in the Value field next to the code is selected. A description of the code appears in the Description field.

- Occasionally, duplicate code values appear on the **Code List** tab. These duplicate code values have varying descriptions, depending on the type of document with which the code value is associated. In the context of validating a document instance, it is never necessary to select more than one code value. However, it is possible to inadvertently select more than one code value. The following list summarizes the selection behavior of duplicate code lists:

  - If you select the top code value in a set of duplicate code values, only that code value is selected.

  - If you select any code value other than the top code value in a set of duplicate code values, that code value is selected and the top code value is automatically selected, too.

  - The top code value in a set of duplicate code values cannot be cleared while any other code values in the set are selected.

To clear a property for any field in the Value column

1. Click the tab that contains the property that you want to clear.

2. Right-click the field in the Value column and click **Clear Property**.

Calculating Field Positions

BizTalk Editor can automatically calculate the start and end positions for all the fields in a positional record. First set a **Data Type** value and a **Maximum Length** value in the **Declaration** tab for each field in the positional record. Then right-click the positional record and, on the shortcut menu, click **Calculate Field Positions**. The start and end positions for the fields in that record are automatically calculated.

The following list explains this feature in greater detail:

- If there are start and end positions specified for the fields in a positional record, all but the start position of the first field are overwritten when you calculate field positions.

- When you calculate field positions, the **Start Position** of the first field of a positional record is set to 1, unless a **Start Position** value was set previously for that field. If a **Start Position** value has already been set for the first field of a positional record, calculations begin from that value.

- Field position calculation takes the **Source Tag Identifier** into account when calculating field positions. For example, consider a positional record with the following properties: the **Source Tag Identifier** is "TAG"; the **Source Tag Position** is 10; there are four fields with **Maximum Length** values of 2, 5, 8, and 6; and there is no **Start Position** value set for the first field. The start and end positions for the four fields are: Field 1 = 1, 2; Field 2 = 3, 7; unused = 8, 9; TAG = 10, 12; Field 3 = 13, 20; and Field 4 = 21, 26. If the **Source Tag Position** had been 1, TAG would have had start and end position values of 1 and 3, and the field count would have started at position 4.

- The field positions of a record are calculated from the first field in the record sequentially to the last field. When calculating field positions, if a field is encountered that does not have a value set for the **Maximum Length** property, the start and end positions for that field and all subsequent fields of the record are not calculated.

- If a sibling record is encountered when calculating field positions, the start and end positions for all fields after the sibling record are not calculated.

- The start and end positions of a field with a **Maximum Length** value of 1 are equal.

- When calculating field positions for a positional record, the positions of fields contained by all descendent records are also calculated. The positions of sibling fields that occur before a record are calculated, but positions of sibling fields that occur after a record are not calculated.

To automatically calculate field positions

1. Select a field in a positional record.

2. Double-click the Value field in the Data Type row.

3. In the **Data Type** list, click a value.

   ✎ Note

   - To specify a **Maximum Length** value (steps 4 and 5), you must select one of the following **Data Type** values: **String**, **Number**, **Binary (base64)**, or **Binary (hex)**.

4. Double-click the Value field in the Maximum Length row.

5. Type a number into the Maximum Length Value field and press ENTER.

6. Repeat steps 1 through 5 for each field in the record.

7. Right-click the record and click **Calculate Field Positions**.

   The following warning appears:

   > This operation will modify the Start Position and End Position properties for the fields in the selected record. Do you want to continue?

8. Click **Yes**.

   The start and end positions are calculated for the fields in the record.

Character Length Limits

There are limits to the number of characters that you can use in names and property values. The following table shows the character limits in BizTalk Editor.

Name or property value	Maximum number of characters
Node name (the name of a root node, a record, or a field)	255
Namespace prefix	64
String property value	1024
LONG property value	11
ULONG property value	10
CHAR property value	1
Electronic data interchange (EDI) format property value (the value of an EDI-specific format property, such as the **Custom Date/Time Format** property value on the **Parse** tab for a field in an EDI-based specification)	15
Target Namespace+Specification name	255

Pad Characters

BizTalk Editor allows you to manage pad characters in delimited documents to ensure that you get the output that you expect. Because every delimited document that is processed by BizTalk Server must be translated into Extensible Markup Language (XML) before mapping takes place, you must make sure that your document specification tells BizTalk Server how to handle pad characters in delimited document instances. For example, you might have a field in a delimited document instance that looks like this:

Green*****

The data content of the field is *Green*, the field is left justified, there are five pad characters to the right of the data content, and the pad character is an asterisk.

If you do not define the pad character for the field in the specification that corresponds to the field in the document instance, BizTalk Server interprets the five asterisks to be part of the data content of the field. To ensure that BizTalk Server correctly handles the pad characters in this field, you need to make sure the properties on the **Parse** tab for this field are set as in the following table.

Property	Value
Justification	Left
Pad Character	*
Minimum Length with Pad Character	Set this property value if you want the length of the field in your output document instance to be greater than or equal to a certain length. BizTalk Server inserts pad characters into the field to achieve the correct minimum field length in the output document instance.

You can use the **Pad Character** property to ensure that pad characters in a field are removed from a document instance submitted to BizTalk Server. The **Minimum Length with Pad Character** property value ensures that BizTalk Server inserts pad characters into a field in the output document instance, if this is desired. The **Justification** property indicates on which side of the field data content the pad characters are removed (from the input document instance) or inserted (into the output document instance). Trailing pad characters are added to or removed from a field that is left justified, and leading pad characters are added to or removed from a field that is right justified. If the **Pad Character** property for a field is not set, no pad characters are added to or removed from that field.

Property Scope

If you have two or more instances of a record in a specification, the values of certain properties for these instances must be identical. In other words, the scope of these properties is global. The scope of certain field properties can also be global, but only if the **Type** property for the field is set to **Element**.

For example, all the properties on the **Declaration** and **Parse** tabs are identical for multiple instances of a record or a field. If you change a declaration or parse property for one instance of a record or a field, that property automatically changes for all other instances of that record or field. The properties on the **Reference** and **Dictionary** tabs are not global in scope, however, so the values for these properties can be set independently for each instance of a record or a field. Code lists apply only to fields, and they are not global in scope.

Notes

- The scope of a field can be global only if the **Type** property is set to **Element**.

- The scope of a field with the **Type** property set to **Attribute** is always local.

- In BizTalk Editor, only **ElementType** declarations are global in scope. If you import a schema into BizTalk Editor that contains **AttributeType** declarations that are global in scope, and then save the schema as a specification, the **AttributeType** declarations are automatically made local in scope within the appropriate **ElementType** declaration or declarations.

Cyclical References

A cyclical reference in a specification occurs when a record is created as a descendant to itself. A cyclical reference can occur only when the **Standard** property value is set to **XML** on the **Reference** tab. BizTalk Editor represents a cyclical reference with an icon ⬚ that appears as a record with a curved arrow through it.

The following illustration shows how a cyclical reference appears in BizTalk Editor.

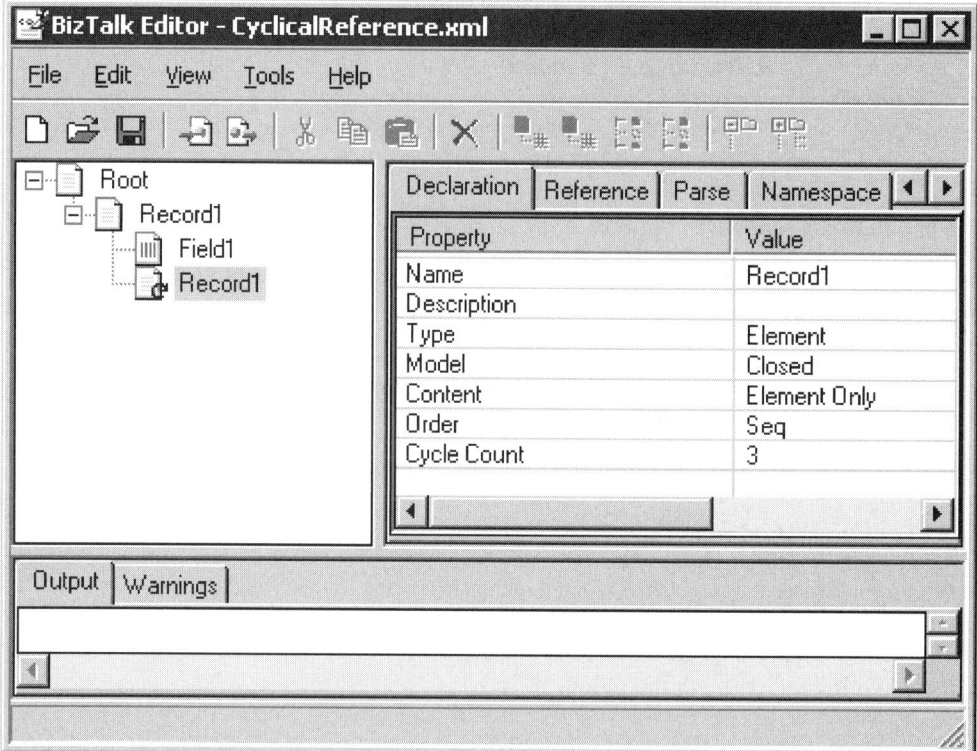

The **Cycle Count** property appears on the **Declaration** tab and applies only to a cyclical node. The default value is 1; the maximum value is 7. The cycle count indicates how many cycles are available below the base record. For example, in the previous illustration there are a total of four levels for Record1: three from the cycle count of 3 and one from the base record. If you open this specification in BizTalk Mapper, all four levels of Record1 appear. A Field1 and Record2 also appear for every Record1. You can connect links to nodes on any level of the cycle.

It is not possible to set dictionary property values for fields that descend from a cyclical node. For example, in the previous illustration, you can set dictionary property values for Root/Record1/Field1, but you cannot set dictionary property values for any of the three Field1 references that cycle below Root/Record1/Record1.

Cyclical references are subject to the following restrictions:

- Nodes on a cycle path (the nodes that occur between the first record and the last record in a cyclical reference) cannot appear anywhere else in the specification.

- Elements on a cycle path cannot be the source or target of any drag-and-drop or cut-and-paste operation.

- Cycles cannot overlap.

- The base record of a cyclical reference cannot be the root node of the specification.

◆ **Important**

- The **Minimum Occurrences** property on the **Reference** tab for the cyclical reference node must be set to **0**. Setting it to **1** causes an infinite loop.

✎ **Note**

- If you import a schema that contains a cyclical reference, BizTalk Editor does not automatically check to ensure that the cyclical reference is valid.

To create cyclical references

1. Select a record below which you want to create a cyclical reference.

   This is the base record.

2. On the **Edit** menu, click **New Record**.

3. Name the new record the same name as the base record and press ENTER.

   A cyclical reference ⌐ is created.

4. On the **Declaration** tab, double-click the Value field in the Cycle Count row.

5. Type a number from 1 to 7 and press ENTER.

◆ **Important**

- The **Minimum Occurrences** property on the **Reference** tab for the cyclical reference node must be set to **0**. Setting it to **1** will cause an infinite loop.

✎ **Note**

- You cannot use cyclic references in non-XML specifications. Make sure that you use an XML-based specification.

Default Value Integration

If a source specification contains a field of type **Attribute**, and an incoming document instance that is based on the source specification does not include that field, you might want the specification to provide a default value for the field. To set the default value for a field in a specification, highlight the field in the specification tree and, on the **Declaration** tab, type a numeric value into the Value field for the **Default Value** property. The **Default Value** property appears only if the **Type** property is set to **Attribute**. If an incoming document instance does not contain the field, the default value for the field is provided. If an incoming document instance contains the field, the default value is ignored.

Adding SQL Annotations

You can specify an SQL annotation for any node in a specification. Specifying an SQL annotation on the **Declaration** tab creates an annotation that is global in scope. The annotation is saved within the **ElementType** or **AttributeType** declaration in the specification. Specifying an SQL annotation on the **Reference** tab creates an annotation that is local in scope. The annotation is saved within the **Element** or **Attribute** reference in the specification.

You can select an SQL annotation in the list that appears when you double-click an empty field in the Property column of either the **Declaration** tab or the **Reference** tab for a node in a specification. Enter a value for the SQL annotation in the corresponding field in the Value column. For all SQL annotations except sql:relationship and sql:xpath-query, the value is ordinary string data. For more information about adding SQL annotations and other custom annotations, see "To add custom annotations" earlier in this chapter.

The following list shows all the possible SQL annotations in BizTalk Editor:

- sql:datatype
- sql:field
- sql:id
- sql:id-prefix
- sql:is-constant
- sql:key-fields
- sql:limit-field
- sql:limit-value
- sql:map-field
- sql:is-mapping-schema
- sql:overflow-field
- sql:relation
- sql:relationship
- sql:target-namespace
- sql:url-encode
- sql:use-cdata
- sql:xpath-query

The value of sql:relationship is one or more name-value pairs, and the name in each name-value pair must be one of four names: **key**, **key-relation**, **foreign-key**, or **foreign-relation**. The value of sql:xpath-query contains two parts: the first part is one or more name-value pairs that comprise an attribute or attributes, and the second part is the content of sql:xpath-query, represented as "content=...". These two parts are separated by the pound character (#).

The following table shows valid examples of the sql:relationship and sql:xpath-query SQL annotations.

SQL annotation	Example values
sql:relationship	key="CustomerID"
sql:relationship	key-relation="Cust"
sql:relationship	foreign-key="CustomerID"
sql:relationship	foreign-relation="Orders"
sql:xpath-query	mapping-schema="Schema.xml" #content=Employees

Notes

- BizTalk Editor does not limit the selection of SQL annotations to only those that are appropriate in the current context. For example, sql:relationship and xpath-query are available on the **Declaration** tab, even though their use must be restricted to the **Reference** tab.

- When you specify an SQL annotation, a namespace with an "sql" prefix and the corresponding Uniform Resource Name (URN) value is automatically declared on the **Namespace** tab.

- When you copy or cut a node with SQL annotations specified on its **Reference** tab and then paste that node to a different location in the specification, the SQL annotations are not present in the new node.

Related Topics

"Namespace Declarations" earlier in this chapter

"To set declaration properties" earlier in this chapter

Troubleshooting BizTalk Editor

This section provides a centralized location for information related to troubleshooting BizTalk Editor. If you are having difficulty with BizTalk Editor, try to find a solution in this section.

Password required when trying to connect to a remote WebDAV server

Cause: User might not have access to the BizTalkServerRepository folder.

Solution: Provide user with access to the BizTalkServerRepository folder. To do this:

1. Click **Start**, point to **Programs**, point to **Administrative Tools**, and then click **Internet Services Manager**.

2. In the console tree, expand the name of the computer.

3. Expand **Default Web Site**.

4. Right-click **BizTalkServerRepository** and click **Properties**.

   The **BizTalkServerRepository Properties** dialog box appears.

5. Click the **Directory Security** tab.

6. In the **Anonymous access and authentication control area**, click **Edit**.

7. Select the **Anonymous Access** check box and click **OK** twice.

Failure to connect to WebDAV or to store files to WebDAV

Cause One: If you attempt to retrieve a map or a specification from WebDAV, or store a map or specification to WebDAV, you might see one of the following messages:

> The file cannot be stored in the WebDAV repository. The server may not be available at this time.

> No key matching the described characteristics could be found within the current range.

> This occurs when the anonymous setting for the user account on the Web server does not have write privileges on the Microsoft Windows 2000 directory that hosts the repository.

Solution: Give user access to the repository. To do this:

1. Click **Start**, point to **Programs**, point to **Accessories**, and then click **Windows Explorer**.

2. Navigate to the location in which you installed Microsoft BizTalk Server 2000.

3. Expand the **Microsoft BizTalk Server** directory, right-click **BizTalkServerRepository**, and then click **Properties**.

   The **BizTalkServerRepository Properties** dialog box appears.

4. Click the **Security** tab.

5. Click **Add** and type the domain name and the user name for the person you want to have permission to the repository in the following format: ***domain name\user name***.

6. Click **OK** twice.

Cause Two: If you attempt to retrieve a map or a specification from WebDAV, or store a map or specification to WebDAV, you might see the following message:

> No BizTalk Server repository was found on http://localhost/BizTalkServerRepository/DocSpecs. Enter another server name to retry the WebDAV connection.

> This occurs when FrontPage Server Extensions are enabled on the Web server.

Solution: Disable FrontPage Server Extensions. If the World Wide Web Publishing service is running, stop and restart this service.

🖉 **Note**

- This problem can occur even if the World Wide Web Publishing Service is not running on the computer hosting the WebDAV repository.

To disable FrontPage Server Extensions

1. Click **Start**, point to **Programs**, point to **Administrative Tools**, and then click **Internet Services Manager**.

2. In the details pane, double-click *<name of the computer>*, right-click **Default Web Site**, and then click **Properties**.

   The **Default Web Site Properties** dialog box appears.

3. On the **Server Extensions** tab, clear the **Enable authoring** check box and click **OK**.

To stop and restart the World Wide Web Publishing Service

1. Click **Start**, point to **Programs**, point to **Administrative Tools**, and then click **Component Services**.

2. In the console tree, click **Services (local)**.

3. In the details pane, right-click **World Wide Web Publishing Service** and click **Stop**.

4. Right-click **World Wide Web Publishing Service** and click **Start**.

???.xml appears in the WebDAV dialog box

Cause: The set of characters that is displayed for your computer is dependent on the locale setting specified in BizTalk Server.

Solution: Specify the same character set for your computer as for the locale setting specified in BizTalk Server. To do this:

1. Click **Start**, point to **Settings**, and then click **Control Panel**.

2. Double-click **Regional Options**.

3. On the **General** tab, in the **Language settings for the system** area, select the check box for the desired language and click **Set Default**.

   The **Select System Locale** dialog box appears.

4. Click the desired locale in the list and click **OK** twice.

   The **Change Regional Options** dialog box appears.

5. Click **Yes** to accept the changes and restart your computer.

🖉 **Note**

- After restarting your computer, the selected language in the **Regional Options** dialog box displays the following information: *Language* **(default)**.

Retrieve from WebDAV dialog box or Store to WebDAV dialog box is empty

Cause: Directory browsing is disabled in the **BizTalkServerRepository Properties** dialog box.

Solution: Enable directory browsing in the **BizTalkServerRepository Properties** dialog box. To do this:

1. Click **Start**, point to **Programs**, point to **Administrative Tools**, and then click **Internet Services Manager**.

2. Expand the computer that you are troubleshooting.

3. Expand **Default Web Site**.

4. Right-click **BizTalkServerRepository** and click **Properties**.

    The **BizTalkServerRepository Properties** dialog box appears.

5. On the **Virtual Directory** tab, select **Directory browsing**.

6. Ensure that **Read** and **Write** are also selected and click **OK**.

Failure to connect to http://localhost

Cause: The **Use a proxy server** check box is selected, but the **Bypass proxy server for local addresses** check box is not selected.

Solution: Keep the **Use a proxy server** setting on, and turn on the **Bypass proxy server for local addresses** setting. To do this:

1. Click **Start**, point to **Programs**, and then click **Internet Explorer**.

2. On the **Tools** menu, click **Internet Options**.

    The **Internet Options** dialog box appears.

3. Click the **Connections** tab and click **LAN Settings**.

    The **Local Area Network (LAN) Setting** dialog box appears.

4. In the **Proxy Server** area, select the **Bypass proxy server for local addresses** check box.

5. Click **OK** twice.

 Note

- This failure will not occur if you connect to **http://<name of the computer>**.

Flat file not completely parsed when submitted to BizTalk Server

Cause: A delimited flat file might have a parsing error when submitted to BizTalk Server if the file has the following characteristics:

- The **Field Order** property for the root node is set to **Prefix** or **Postfix**.

- The name of the root node is a substring of the name of another node in the file.

Solution: Rename the root node so that its name is not a substring of the name of any other node in the specification.

White space not preserved in flat file submitted to BizTalk Server

Cause: When a flat file is submitted to BizTalk Server, white space in fields might be trimmed. This is because by default the underlying MSXML parser does not preserve white space in a field with its **Type** property (on the **Declaration** tab) set to **Element**.

Solution: If it is important to preserve white space in a field contained in a flat file, in BizTalk Editor be sure to set the **Type** property on the **Declaration** tab of the field in the source specification to **Attribute**.

DTD Import Fails

Cause: If you try to import a document type definition (DTD) that contains an external reference to another file, you might see the following message:

Invalid character found in DTD.

Solution: Remove any external references in a DTD before attempting to import it.

Instance validation fails when using the Date or Time field

Cause: While BizTalk Server is processing an incoming document instance, if there is a link from a functoid or source field to a destination node with its **Data Type** property set to **Date**, **Date Time**, **Date Time.tz**, **Time**, or **Time.tz**, instance validation fails if the data coming into the destination node is in any format other than ISO 8601.

Solution: When you link to a field in a destination specification with its **Data Type** property set to **Date**, **Date Time**, **Date Time.tz**, **Time**, or **Time.tz**, make sure the data that links to that field (whether from a functoid or from a node in an incoming document instance) is in ISO 8601 format. The following table shows the correct ISO 8601 format for each of the possible **Data Type** property values.

Data Type property	ISO 8601 format
Date	YYYY-MM-DD (1988-04-07)
Date Time	YYYY-MM-DDTHH:MM:SS (1988-04-07T18:39:09)
Date Time.tz	YYYY-MM-DDTHH:MM:SS-TZH:TZM (1988-04-07T18:39:09-08:00)
Time	HH:MM:SS (08:15:27)
Time.tz	HH:MM:SS-TZH:TZM (08:15:27-05:00)

Mapping Data

Microsoft BizTalk Server 2000 provides tools with which you can define the structure of a document and map data from one format to another. These tools are based on Extensible Markup Language (XML) and standards, and they provide the essential data translation necessary for an application-integration server.

Using BizTalk Mapper, you can create a map between the records and fields of two different specifications. The server uses the map to process and translate data into formats that can be shared within your own organization or with your partner organizations.

In This Chapter

- Mapping Specifications
- BizTalk Mapper User Interface
- Understanding Functiods
- Creating Links
- Editing Link Properties
- Viewing Record, Field, Link, and Functoid Properties
- Mapping Scenarios
- Compiling Maps
- Troubleshooting BizTalk Mapper

Mapping Specifications

A map identifies how data in one format is to be rendered in another format. A map requires two specifications: one is the source, and the other is the destination. Mapping data is a data-translation process in which you define the correspondences between the records and fields in the source specification and the records and fields in the destination specification.

There are two types of mapping: the first is a specific map that is designed to meet the individual needs of one trading partner; the second is a generic map designed to meet the needs of several trading partners. When you map a trading partner's specific record and field requirements, you create a map that is unique and specific to that trading partner only. In generic mapping, you group the requirements of multiple trading partners in one map. Because multiple organizations can be interconnected, and you can use the same map with multiple trading partners, this feature saves you valuable resources and time.

BizTalk Mapper shows a graphical representation of a map that can include simple value-copy translations, referred to as links, and complex structural manipulations, referred to as functoids. By combining these elements, you can easily map data between a source specification and a destination specification.

To create new maps

1. On the **File** menu, click **New**.

   The **Select Source Specification Type** dialog box appears.

2. Double-click one of the following:

   - **Local Files**, and go to step 3.

   - **Templates**, and go to step 4.

   - **WebDAV Files**, and go to step 3.

3. Browse to the folder that contains the source specification that you want to open and go to step 5.

4. Click **EDIFACT**, **X12**, or **XML** and click **OK**.

   If you select EDIFACT or X12, you must also select the version you want to use. Click the folder for the version you want to use, click **OK**, and then go to step 5.

5. Select the source specification and click **Open** or **OK** as appropriate.

   The **Select Destination Specification Type** dialog box appears.

6. Double-click one of the following:

   - **Local Files**, and go to step 7.

   - **Templates**, and go to step 8.

   - **WebDAV Files**, and go to step 7.

7. Browse to the folder that contains the destination specification that you want to open and go to step 9.

8. Click **EDIFACT**, **X12**, or **XML** and click **OK**.

   If you select EDIFACT or X12, you must also select the version you want to use. Click the folder for the version you want to use, click **OK**, and then go to step 9.

9. Select the destination specification and click **Open** or **OK** as appropriate.

✎ Note

- To create a map, you must specify both a source specification and a destination specification.

To replace source specifications

1. On the **Edit** menu, click **Replace Source Specification**.

   If you have not saved your map, you are prompted to save changes to the map source.

   The **Select Source Specification Type** dialog box appears.

2. Double-click one of the following:

   - **Local Files**, and go to step 3.

   - **Templates**, and go to step 4.

   - **WebDAV Files**, and go to step 3.

3. Browse to the folder that contains the source specification and go to step 5.

4. Click **EDIFACT**, **X12**, or **XML** and click **OK**.

   If you select EDIFACT or X12, you must also select the version you want to use. Click the folder for the version you want, click **OK**, and then go to step 5.

5. Select the source specification and click **Open** or **OK** as appropriate.

✎ Notes

- Source test values are preserved when you replace a source specification, provided that the fields associated with these values exist in the new specification. For more information about source test values, see "To test links" later in this chapter.

- The **Warnings** tab lists all warnings related to links that might break as a result of replacing the source specification.

- You also can right-click any record or field in the Source Specification tree and click **Replace Specification**.

To replace destination specifications

1. On the **Edit** menu, click **Replace Destination Specification**.

   If you have not saved your map, you are prompted to save changes to the map source.

   The **Select Destination Specification Type** dialog box appears.

2. Double-click one of the following:

   - **Local Files**, and go to step 3.

   - **Templates**, and go to step 4.

   - **WebDAV Files**, and go to step 3.

3. Browse to the folder that contains the destination specification and go to step 5.

4. Click **EDIFACT**, **X12**, or **XML** and click **OK**.

   If you select EDIFACT or X12, you must also select the version you want to use. Click the folder for the version you want, click **OK**, and then go to step 5.

5. Select the destination specification and click **Open** or **OK** as appropriate.

Notes

- Destination constant values are preserved when you replace a destination specification, provided that the fields associated with these values exist in the new specification. For more information about destination constant values, see "To add constant values" later in this chapter.

- The **Warnings** tab lists all warnings related to links that might break as a result of replacing the destination specification.

- You also can right-click any record or field in the Destination Specification tree and click **Replace Specification**.

To open maps from a local hard drive

1. On the **File** menu, click **Open**.

   The **Open Map Source** dialog box appears.

2. Browse to the folder that contains a map you want to open.

3. Click a map in the list and click **Open**.

To retrieve maps from WebDAV

1. On the **File** menu, click **Retrieve from WebDAV**.

   The **Retrieve from WebDAV** dialog box appears.

2. In the **Server** list, click a server name.

3. Browse to the folder that contains the map you want to retrieve, click the map, and then click **Open**.

📝 Notes

- You might experience a delay the first time you connect to a remote WebDAV server.
- To retrieve a map in WebDAV, you must have permission to retrieve files on the server.

To save new maps

1. On the **File** menu, click **Save As**.

   The **Save Map Source As** dialog box appears.

2. In the **File name** box, type a name for the map.

3. In the **Encoding** list, click either **UTF-8** or **Unicode** and click **Save**.

   If you want to use a specification associated with ASCII characters, click **UTF-8**. For specifications associated with double-byte character sets, click **Unicode**.

📝 Notes

- When you save a map, BizTalk Mapper automatically compiles it. You can view the results of the compiled map on the **Output** tab.
- When you save a map, BizTalk Mapper saves the map on your hard disk. To store a map in WebDAV, you must have permission to store files on the server.

To save existing maps

- On the **File** menu, click **Save**.

📝 Notes

- When you save a map, BizTalk Mapper automatically compiles it. You can view the results of the compiled map on the **Output** tab.
- When you save a map, BizTalk Mapper saves the map on your hard disk. To store a map in WebDAV, you must have permission to store files on the server.

To store maps

1. On the **File** menu, click **Store to WebDAV**.

   The **Store to WebDAV** dialog box appears.

2. In the **Server** list, click a server name.

3. Browse to the folder you want to use to store your map and, in the **File name** box, type the name of the file.

4. In the **Encoding** list, click either **UTF-8** or **Unicode** and click **Save**.

   If you want to use a specification associated with ASCII characters, click **UTF-8**. For specifications associated with double-byte character sets, click **Unicode**.

◆ **Important**

- You cannot store files with double-byte character set (DBCS) file names if your locale setting is incorrect. For more information, see "???.xml appears in the WebDAV dialog box" later in this chapter.

✎ **Notes**

- You might experience a delay the first time you connect to a remote WebDAV server.

- To store a map in WebDAV, you must have permission to store files on the server.

To close maps

- On the **File** menu, click **Close**.

Related Topics

"Testing Maps" later in this chapter

"To add constant values" later in this chapter

"Troubleshooting BizTalk Mapper" later in this chapter

BizTalk Mapper User Interface

The two specifications that are used to create a map appear as tree views in the main window of BizTalk Mapper. The source specification from which the data is mapped is on the left, and the destination specification to which the data is mapped is on the right. The mapping grid between the two specifications graphically displays the structural data transformation between the two specifications. Links and functoids appear in the mapping grid. You can easily move up, down, left, or right in the mapping grid by moving the pointer to the borders of the mapping grid.

You can use the **Grid Preview** dialog box to move quickly from one location in the mapping grid to another. By dragging the green locator bar, you can move up, down, left, or right. A functoid in the mapping grid appears in the preview grid as a red box that is surrounded by a black outline. If there are two or more functoids in the mapping grid, the graphic appears as two red boxes attached to one another, surrounded by a black outline.

Beneath the tree views and mapping grid is the lower pane. This area has four tabs:

- **Properties.** When you select a node in the Source Specification tree or the Destination Specification tree, the **Properties** tab displays the properties and property values for that node.

- **Values.** This tab has two text boxes: **Source test value** and **Destination constant value**. You can select a field and then type a value in the **Source test value** box. This allows you to test maps with actual values assigned to fields. In the **Destination constant value** box, you can specify a value to assign to a field. You cannot create a link from a functoid or from a node in the source specification to a field with a constant value assigned to it.

- **Output.** This tab displays a compiled Extensible Stylesheet Language (XSL) style sheet when you compile a map, and it displays test map output when you test a map.

- **Warnings.** This tab displays compiler warnings after you compile a map.

BizTalk Mapper Menus

BizTalk Mapper menus logically group commands together, making it easy to perform a specific task. For example, you can use the commands on the **View** menu to view all the records and fields in the Source Specification tree or to collapse all the records and fields in the Destination Specification tree.

The BizTalk Mapper menus are as follows:

- **File.** Use this menu to create, open, save, or close a map.

- **Edit.** Use this menu to replace the source or destination specification, or to delete an object in the mapping grid.

- **View.** Use this menu to view the functoid palette, the functoid properties, and the grid preview, as well as to select a text size for the BizTalk Mapper display, to activate tabs in the lower pane, to expand or collapse the specification trees, or to highlight the next warning on the **Warnings** tab.

- **Tools.** Use this menu to compile and test your maps, and to view BizTalk Mapper options.

- **Help.** Use this menu to get how-to and conceptual information about using BizTalk Mapper.

Change BizTalk Mapper Options

In the **BizTalk Mapper Options** dialog box, you can set general options and choose colors for the mapping grid.

- To view the **BizTalk Mapper Options** dialog box, on the **Tools** menu, click **Options**.

  The **General** tab appears by default.

BizTalk Mapper Options: General Tab

The **General** tab provides six options that enable you to customize the behavior of BizTalk Mapper:

- **Warnings for simple linking errors** (selected by default). You receive a warning when you attempt to create a link between nodes whose data types do not match.

- **View compiler links** (selected by default). Compiler links appear on a map after compiling.

- **Clear compiler links after user action** (cleared by default). Compiler links disappear after taking any action in BizTalk Mapper.

- **Allow record content links** (cleared by default). Content links from records to functoids can be created.

  ### ✎ Note

  - Certain functoids have input and/or output that does not use record content and is therefore unaffected by **Allow record content links**. This input and output consists of the logical functoids (output), the **Count** functoid (input), the **Iteration** functoid (input), and the **Looping** functoid (input and output).

- **Allow multiple inputs to destination tree nodes** (cleared by default). Two or more links can be made to a node in the Destination Specification tree.

- **Prompt to save before testing the map** (selected by default). After you click **Test Map** on the **Tools** menu, BizTalk Mapper displays a dialog box that asks if you want to save changes in your map file.

BizTalk Mapper Options: Colors Tab

- The **Colors** tab provides options that enable you to customize the colors on the mapping grid.

BizTalk Mapper Toolbar Buttons

BizTalk Mapper provides a toolbar to complement the menu bar. All of the toolbar buttons display graphical representations of the tasks they perform. They appear in the following order from left to right:

- **New**
- **Open**
- **Save**
- **Retrieve from WebDAV**
- **Store to WebDAV**
- **Delete**
- **Collapse**
- **Expand**
- **View Functoid Palette**
- **Compile Map**
- **Test Map**

BizTalk Mapper Functoid Palette

The functoid palette contains all the functoids available in BizTalk Mapper. A functoid contains code that takes data from a record or field in the source specification, or from another functoid (such as a **Date** functoid), processes the data independently, and then returns a new value that is placed in a record or field in the destination specification. For more information about the functoid palette, see "Understanding Functoids" later in this chapter.

To view links and functoids in the mapping grid

1. Move the cursor into the mapping grid, near the edge, in the direction that you want to scroll.

   The cursor changes from a pointer or pipe (|) to a large arrow.

2. Click and hold the left mouse button to scroll in the direction that the arrow points.

☑ Note

- You can also scroll by clicking in the mapping grid background and then using the arrow keys to scroll in all four directions.

To view links and functoids by using the grid preview

1. On the **View** menu, click **Grid Preview**.

   The **Grid Preview** window opens to display a representation of where the functoids are located on the mapping grid.

2. Drag the green locator bar to a new location on the **Grid Preview** dialog box.

   As you move the green locator bar, links and functoids in the mapping grid also move.

☑ Note

- The grid preview is useful for navigating the mapping grid when you have many functoids spread out over the mapping grid.

Related Topics

"Understanding Functoids" later in this chapter

"Work with the Functoid Palette" later in this chapter

Customizing Your Display

You can customize the look of BizTalk Mapper in several ways. For example, you can change the background mapping grid colors, specify new colors for links and selected objects, change the color of compiler warnings, and modify the size of text. The following items can be customized:

- **Grid foreground.** The dashed lines in the mapping grid.

- **Grid background.** The background color of the mapping grid.

- **Fixed links.** Value-copy links in the mapping grid.

- **Elastic links.** Value-copy links that are dragged from the Source Specification tree to the Destination Specification tree.

- **Partial links.** Links for a field or record whose parent-record node is collapsed.

- **Compiler links.** Compiler directive links, which are automatically created when a link is set from a field in the Source Specification tree to a field in the Destination Specification tree.

These features are available in the **Options** dialog box, which is accessible through the **Tools** menu. You can also make changes to text size from the **View** menu.

To change mapping grid colors

1. On the **Tools** menu, click **Options**.

   The **BizTalk Mapper Options** dialog box appears.

2. Click the **Colors** tab.

3. Click the box next to **Grid foreground**, which represents the dashed lines in the mapping grid, and, in the color palette, select a new color.

   –Or–

   Click the box next to **Grid background**, which represents the background color of the mapping grid, and, in the color palette, select a new color.

4. Click **OK**.

To change the color of links

1. On the **Tools** menu, click **Options**.

   The **BizTalk Mapper Options** dialog box appears.

2. Click the **Colors** tab.

3. Click the box next to one of the following:

   - **Fixed links.** Fixed links are simple value-copy links in the mapping grid.

   - **Elastic links.** Elastic links are simple value-copy links that are dragged from the Source Specification tree to the Destination Specification tree. Once the link is made, the color of the link changes to the predefined fixed links color.

   - **Partial links.** Partial links are links that exist for a field or record whose parent record is collapsed.

   - **Compiler links.** Compiler links are the compiler directive links. They are links that are automatically created when a link is set from a field in the Source Specification tree to a field in the Destination Specification tree and the hierarchy of the two trees does not match.

4. In the color palette, select a new color.

5. Repeat step 3 to change other colors, if necessary.

6. Click **OK**.

To change the color of selected objects

1. On the **Tools** menu, click **Options**.

   The **BizTalk Mapper Options** dialog box appears.

2. Click the **Colors** tab.

3. Click the box next to **Selected objects** and, in the color palette, select a new color.

4. Click **OK**.

To change the color of compiler warnings

1. On the **Tools** menu, click **Options**.

   The **BizTalk Mapper Options** dialog box appears.

2. Click the **Colors** tab.

3. Click the box next to **Compiler warnings** and, in the color palette, select a new color.

4. Click **OK**.

To restore default colors

1. On the **Tools** menu, click **Options**.

   The **BizTalk Mapper Options** dialog box appears.

2. Click the **Colors** tab.

3. Click **Restore Default Colors** and click **OK**.

To change text size

- On the **View** menu, point to **Text Size** and click the size that you want.

To adjust the pane size for the Source Specification tree

1. Place the cursor on the right border of the Source Specification tree pane until the cursor becomes a two-headed arrow.

2. Drag the border to the right to increase the pane size or to the left to decrease the pane size.

Note

- Double-click the border to restore it to its default position.

To adjust the pane size for the Destination Specification tree

1. Place the cursor on the left border of the Destination Specification tree pane until the cursor becomes a two-headed arrow.

2. Drag the border to the left to increase the pane size or to the right to decrease the pane size.

 Note

- Double-click the border to restore it to its default position.

To expand tree items

- Click the root node or a record in the specification tree that you want to expand and, on the **View** menu, click **Expand Tree Items**.

  –Or–

  Right-click the root node or a record in a tree and click **Expand Tree Items**.

To collapse tree items

- Click the root node or a record in the specification tree that you want to collapse and, on the **View** menu, click **Collapse Tree Items**.

 Note

- You also can right-click the root node or a record in a tree and click **Collapse Tree Items**.

To adjust the size of the lower pane

1. Place the cursor on the top border of the lower pane until the cursor becomes a two-headed arrow.

2. Drag the pane upward to increase the pane size or downward to decrease the pane size.

 Note

- Double-click the border to restore it to its default position.

BizTalk Mapper Shortcut Keys

You can use shortcut keys to accomplish tasks in BizTalk Mapper. The following table is a
quick reference to these shortcut keys.

☑ Note

- Functionality that is not included in this list can be obtained by using the numeric keypad
  to move the mouse pointer with MouseKeys. For more information about MouseKeys in
  Windows 2000 Server and Advanced Server Help, see "Using the keyboard to move the
  mouse pointer." For more information about MouseKeys in Windows 2000 Professional
  Help, see "Move the mouse pointer by using MouseKeys."

Press	To
CTRL+N	Open a new specification.
CTRL+O	Open an existing map.
CTRL+S	Save a map.
CTRL+F5	Test a map.
F4	Highlight the next warning.
F5	Compile a map.
DEL	Delete an object in the mapping grid.
F6	Move the focus clockwise from pane to pane.
SHIFT+F6	Move the focus counterclockwise from pane to pane. Pressing SHIFT+F6 after opening the functoid palette moves the focus to the **String** tab, allowing you to use the left and right arrow keys to view the other tabs.
TAB	Move the focus clockwise in the lower pane from the tab to the panes or fields below. In a dialog box, pressing TAB moves the focus through the buttons and fields of the dialog box.
SHIFT+TAB	Move the focus counterclockwise in the lower pane from the tab to the panes or fields below.
SPACEBAR	Select or clear a check box. The spacebar also acts like a mouse click when the focus is on a button.
F1	View online Help.
ALT+F4	Exit from the program.
LEFT ARROW	Activate the tab to the left.
RIGHT ARROW	Activate the tab to the right.
Any arrow key	Highlight a folder or a file in the main pane of a dialog box, while the focus is on that pane. This functionality occurs in the **Store to WebDAV** dialog box and the **Retrieve from WebDAV** dialog box. For more information, see "To retrieve maps from WebDAV" earlier in this chapter.

Understanding Functoids

BizTalk Mapper supports complex structural transformations from records and fields in the Source Specification tree to records and fields in the Destination Specification tree. Functoids perform calculations by using predefined formulas and specific values, called arguments. These calculations are executed based on the designated order of the records and fields. By selecting a functoid from the functoid palette, dragging it to the mapping grid, and linking it to elements in the Source Specification and Destination Specification trees, data can be added together, date or time information can be modified, data can be concatenated, or other operations can be performed. For example, the **Addition** functoid adds values.

The **Functoid Palette** includes the following tabs:

- **String.** These functoids manipulate data strings by using string functions. For example, the **String Find** functoid finds one text string within another text string, and returns the position of the first character of the found string.

- **Mathematical.** These functoids perform calculations by using specific values, called arguments, in a particular order, or structure. For example, the **Addition** functoid adds the values of the designated fields or records.

- **Logical.** These functoids perform specific logical tests. If a logical functoid is connected to a record in the destination specification and returns the value "true", the corresponding record in the output document is generated. If a logical functoid is connected to a record in the destination specification and returns the value "false", the corresponding record in the output document is not generated. The output of a logical functoid can also be accepted as input for other functoids in a map.

- **Date/Time.** These functoids manipulate date and time data or add current date, time, or date and time data to a record or field in the destination specification.

- **Conversion.** These functoids closely match engineering functions such as DEC2HEX, which returns a hexadecimal value given a decimal value. They can also be used to convert a character to its ASCII value or a value to the corresponding ASCII character.

- **Scientific.** These functoids convert a numeric value to a scientific value. For example, the **Cosine** functoid takes a value from a field or record and returns the angle, in radians, for which you want the cosine.

- **Cumulative.** These functoids return the sum, average, or minimum or maximum input of a looping record.

- **Database.** These functoids extract data from a database.

- **Advanced.** This tab has a functoid that can use custom Microsoft Visual Basic script, functoids for value mapping, and functoids for managing and extracting information from record loops.

You can also create your own custom functoids. For a sample of a custom functoid, go to the \Program Files\Microsoft BizTalk Server\SDK\Messaging Samples\SampleFunctoid folder on a computer with a complete installation of BizTalk Server or a custom installation of BizTalk Server that includes Messaging samples.

Work with the Functoid Palette

The functoid palette contains the functoids available in BizTalk Mapper. You can find the functoid that you want in the functoid palette and drag it to the mapping grid. The various types of functoids are organized in tabs. You might need to click the right arrow or left arrow to see tabs that are hidden from view.

To add functoids to the mapping grid

1. On the **Functoid Palette**, click the functoid that you want to add to the map.

2. Drag the functoid to the mapping grid.

To delete functoids

1. Right-click the functoid you want to remove and click **Delete**.

2. Click **Yes** in the confirmation dialog box.

Related Topic

"Creating Links" later in this chapter

String Functoids

String functoids are a collection of functoids that enable you to do a wide variety of string manipulations. The table on the following page describes each type of string functoid and its parameters.

Functoid	Parameters
String Find Returns the position in a string at which another specified string begins.	This functoid requires two input parameters. The first field that you link to the functoid is the string that determines the position of the second string.
String Left Returns a specified number of characters from a text item, starting with the leftmost character.	This functoid requires two input parameters. The first field that you link to the functoid is the string that determines the output string. The second field that you link to the functoid determines the number of characters returned as the output value. The result of the output is a string that is a subset of the first field that you linked to the functoid.
Lowercase Converts a text item to lowercase characters.	This functoid requires one input parameter.
String Right Extracts a specified number of characters from a text item, starting with the rightmost character.	This functoid requires two input parameters. The first field that you link to the functoid is the string that determines the output string. The second field that you link to the functoid determines the number of characters returned as the output value. The result of the output is a string that is a subset of the first field that you linked to the functoid.
String Length Returns, as an integer, the size of an object, exclusive of any pad characters.	This functoid requires one input parameter. The output value indicates the size, in characters, of the data contained in the input field.
String Extract Extracts a string specified by the start and end positions of a super string.	This functoid requires three input parameters, one of which must be a string. The order in which you link the fields to the functoid must adhere to the following criteria: 1. String field 2. Start position field 3. End position field
Concatenate Concatenates a series of input strings.	This functoid can receive multiple input parameters.
String Left Trim Removes leading spaces from a text item.	This functoid requires one input parameter.
String Right Trim Removes trailing spaces from a text item.	This functoid requires one input parameter.
Uppercase Converts a text item to uppercase characters.	This functoid requires one input parameter.

To add string functoids

1. On the **View** menu, click **Functoid Palette**.

2. On the **Functoid Palette**, click the **String** tab.

3. Drag a string functoid from the **Functoid Palette** to the mapping grid.

4. Drag a record or field from the Source Specification tree to the functoid in the mapping grid, and then drag the functoid to a record or field in the Destination Specification tree.

◆ **Important**

- To create a link between a functoid and a record, you must enable the **Allow record content links** property. To do this, on the **Tools** menu, click **Options**. In the **BizTalk Mapper Options** dialog box, on the **General** tab, select the **Allow record content links** check box and click **OK**.

✎ **Note**

- You might need to expand the specification trees to see the records or fields that you want to map. For more information, see "To expand tree items" earlier in this chapter.

Mathematical Functoids

Mathematical functoids are a collection of functoids that enable you to do a wide variety of mathematical operations. The table on the following page describes each type of mathematical functoid and its parameters.

Functoid	Parameters
Absolute Value Returns the absolute value of a number.	This functoid requires one input parameter. The final value is always positive, regardless of the actual input value.
Integer Returns the integer portion of a number.	This functoid requires one input parameter. This functoid removes the decimal point of a number and any digits to the right of the decimal point.
Maximum Value Returns the maximum value from a series of numeric values.	This functoid requires one or more input parameters.
Minimum Value Returns the minimum value from a series of numeric values.	This functoid requires one or more input parameters.
Modulo Returns the remainder after the number is divided by an integer.	This functoid requires two input parameters. This functoid returns the remainder of an integer division. This functoid is useful for determining less-than-load-type calculations, such as shipping quantities.
Round Rounds a number to a specified number of decimal places or to a whole number if no decimal places are specified.	This functoid requires two input parameters. The first input linked to the functoid represents the value; the second input linked to the functoid represents the number of decimal places by which you want the number to be rounded. The functoid rounds up or down based on standard calculating rules.
Square Root Returns the square root of a number.	This functoid requires one input parameter.
Addition Calculates the sum of a series of numbers.	This functoid requires one or more input parameters.
Subtraction Subtracts one number from another number.	This functoid requires one or more input parameters.
Multiplication Multiplies one number by another number.	This functoid requires one or more input parameters.
Division Divides one number by another number.	This functoid requires two input parameters. You can use this functoid with real numbers and integers.

To add mathematical functoids

1. On the **View** menu, click **Functoid Palette**.

2. On the **Functoid Palette**, click the **Mathematical** tab.

3. Drag a mathematical functoid from the **Functoid Palette** to the mapping grid.

4. Drag a record or field from the Source Specification tree to the functoid in the mapping grid, and then drag the functoid to a record or field in the Destination Specification tree.

◆ **Important**

-   To create a link between a functoid and a record, you must enable the **Allow record content links** property. To do this, on the **Tools** menu, click **Options**. In the **BizTalk Mapper Options** dialog box, on the **General** tab, select the **Allow record content links** check box and click **OK**.

✎ **Note**

-   You might need to expand the specification trees to see the records or fields that you want to map. For more information, see "To expand tree items" earlier in this chapter.

Logical Functoids

Logical functoids are a collection of functoids that enable you to do a wide variety of logical operations. The following table describes each type of logical functoid and its parameters.

Functoid	Parameters
> Greater Than Returns "true" if the first parameter is greater than the second parameter.	This functoid requires two input parameters.
>= Greater Than or Equal To Returns "true" if the first parameter is greater than or equal to the second parameter.	This functoid requires two input parameters.
< Less Than Returns "true" if the first parameter is less than the second parameter.	This functoid requires two input parameters.
=< Less Than or Equal To Returns "true" if the first parameter is less than or equal to the second parameter.	This functoid requires two input parameters.
= Equal Returns "true" if the first parameter is equal to the second parameter.	This functoid requires two input parameters.
<> Not Equal Returns "true" if the first parameter is not equal to the second parameter.	This functoid requires two input parameters.
S Logical String Returns "true" if the parameter is a string value.	This functoid requires one input parameter.
Logical Date Returns "true" if the parameter is a date value.	This functoid requires one input parameter.
# Logical Numeric Returns "true" if the parameter is a numeric value.	This functoid requires one input parameter.
Logical OR Returns the logical OR of parameters.	This functoid requires one or more input parameters.
& Logical AND Returns the logical AND of parameters.	This functoid requires one or more input parameters.

To add logical functoids

1. On the **View** menu, click **Functoid Palette**.

2. On the **Functoid Palette**, click the **Logical** tab.

3. Drag a logical functoid from the **Functoid Palette** to the mapping grid.

4. Drag a record or field from the Source Specification tree to the functoid in the mapping grid, and then drag the functoid to a record in the Destination Specification tree.

◆ **Important**

*   To create a link between a functoid and a record, you must enable the **Allow record content links** property. To do this, on the **Tools** menu, click **Options**. In the **BizTalk Mapper Options** dialog box, on the **General** tab, select the **Allow record content links** check box and click **OK**.

🖉 **Notes**

*   Logical functoids are case sensitive when comparing two strings. For example, "Abc" and "abc" are not equal. The exception to this rule is when logical functoids compare strings that represent the Boolean values TRUE and FALSE. For example, "True" and "true" are equal.

*   You might need to expand the specification trees to see the records or fields that you want to map. For more information, see "To expand tree items" earlier in this chapter.

Date and Time Functoids

Date and time functoids are a collection of functoids that enable you to do a wide variety of date and time operations. The following table describes each type of date or time functoid and its parameters.

Functoid	Parameters
🗓 **Add Days** Adds a specified number of days to a date.	This functoid requires two input parameters. The first link must have date information as the input. The second link determines the number of days to add to the date.
🗓 **Date** Returns the current date.	This functoid does not require any input parameters. The output format is YYYY-MM-DD.
🕐 **Time** Returns the current time.	This functoid does not require any input parameters. The output format is HH:MM:SS.
🗓 **Date and Time** Returns the date and time.	This functoid does not require any input parameters. The output format is YYYY-MM-DDTHH:MM:SS.

To add date and time functoids

1. On the **View** menu, click **Functoid Palette**.

2. On the **Functoid Palette**, click the **Date/Time** tab.

3. Drag a date and time functoid from the **Functoid Palette** to the mapping grid.

4. Drag a record or field from the Source Specification tree to the functoid in the mapping grid, and then drag the functoid to a record or field in the Destination Specification tree.

◆ **Important**

- To create a link between a functoid and a record, you must enable the **Allow record content links** property. To do this, on the **Tools** menu, click **Options**. In the **BizTalk Mapper Options** dialog box, on the **General** tab, select the **Allow record content links** check box and click **OK**.

📝 **Notes**

- The **Date**, **Time**, and **Date and Time** functoids require only a link to a field or a record in the Destination Specification tree.

- You might need to expand the specification trees to see the records or fields that you want to map. For more information, see "To expand tree items" earlier in this chapter.

Conversion Functoids

Conversion functoids are a collection of functoids that enable you to do a wide variety of conversions. The following table describes each type of conversion functoid and its parameters.

Functoid	Parameters
ASCII from Character Returns an ASCII value when given a character.	This functoid requires one input parameter. This functoid converts an underlying ASC value code. For example: A=97
Character from ASCII Returns a character when given an ASCII value.	This functoid requires one input parameter. This functoid converts a value to its underlying ASC value code. For example: 98=B
Hexadecimal Returns a hexadecimal value when given a decimal number.	This functoid requires one input parameter. This functoid converts decimal to hexadecimal. For example, 10=A
Octal Returns an octal value when given a decimal number.	This functoid requires one input parameter. This functoid converts decimal to octal. For example: (Octal 0-7), 8=10, and 10=12

To add conversion functoids

1. On the **View** menu, click **Functoid Palette**.

2. On the **Functoid Palette**, click the **Conversion** tab.

   You might need to click the right arrow on the **Functoid Palette** to view the tab.

3. Drag a conversion functoid from the **Functoid Palette** to the mapping grid.

4. Drag a record or field from the Source Specification tree to the functoid in the mapping grid, and then drag the functoid to a record or field in the Destination Specification tree.

◈ Important

- To create a link between a functoid and a record, you must enable the **Allow record content links** property. To do this, on the **Tools** menu, click **Options**. In the **BizTalk Mapper Options** dialog box, on the **General** tab, select the **Allow record content links** check box and click **OK**.

▧ Note

- You might need to expand the specification trees to see the records or fields that you want to map. For more information, see "To expand tree items" earlier in this chapter.

Scientific Functoids

Scientific functoids are a collection of functoids that enable you to do a wide variety of scientific operations. The following table describes each type of scientific functoid and its parameters.

Functoid	Parameters
▦ Arc Tangent Returns the arc tangent of a number.	This functoid requires one input parameter. The input value must be in radians.
▦ Cosine Returns the cosine of a number.	This functoid requires one input parameter. The input value must be in radians.
▦ Sine Returns the sine of a number.	This functoid requires one input parameter. The input value must be in radians.
▦ Tangent Returns the tangent of a number.	This functoid requires one input parameter. The input value must be in radians.
▦ Natural Exponential Function Returns e raised to a specified power.	This functoid requires one input parameter.
▦ Natural Logarithm Returns the logarithm (base e) of a value.	This functoid requires one input parameter.
▦ 10^X Returns 10 raised to a specified power.	This functoid requires one input parameter.
▦ Common Logarithm Returns the logarithm (base 10) of a value.	This functoid requires one input parameter.
▦ X^Y Returns a value raised to a specified power.	This functoid requires two input parameters.
▦ Base-Specified Logarithm Returns the logarithm (base-specified) of a value.	This functoid requires two input parameters.

To add scientific functoids

1. On the **View** menu, click **Functoid Palette**.

2. On the **Functoid Palette**, click the **Scientific** tab.

    You might need to click the right arrow on the **Functoid Palette** to view the tab.

3. Drag a scientific functoid from the **Functoid Palette** to the mapping grid.

4. Drag a record or field from the Source Specification tree to the functoid in the mapping grid, and then drag the functoid to a record or field in the Destination Specification tree.

◆ **Important**

*   To create a link between a functoid and a record, you must enable the **Allow record content links** property. To do this, on the **Tools** menu, click **Options**. In the **BizTalk Mapper Options** dialog box, on the **General** tab, select the **Allow record content links** check box and click **OK**.

🗒 **Note**

*   You might need to expand the specification trees to see the records or fields that you want to map. For more information, see "To expand tree items" earlier in this chapter.

Cumulative Functoids

Cumulative functoids are a collection of functoids that enable you to extract summations, averages, maximum values, and minimum values from particular fields that belong to a parent record. The following table describes each type of cumulative functoid and its parameters.

Functoid	Parameters
Cumulative Sum Sums all values for the connected field by iterating over its parent record.	This functoid requires one input parameter.
Cumulative Average Calculates the average of all values for the connected field by iterating over its parent record.	This functoid requires one input parameter.
Cumulative Minimum Returns the minimum of input spanning over the parent record.	This functoid requires one input parameter.
Cumulative Maximum Returns the maximum of input spanning over the parent record.	This functoid requires one input parameter.
Cumulative String Returns the concatenated string of the string values for the connected field by iterating over its parent record.	This functoid requires one input parameter.

Using Cumulative Functoids

Cumulative functoids operate within the context of the record level in the source specification. Certain records typically occur many times in an input file. For example, in a purchase order, the Item section might occur many times. The Item section might include products, descriptions, prices, and quantities. The following code is an example of a purchase order:

```
<PurchaseOrder>
  <From>Kevin F. Browne</From>
  <To>Bits, Bytes, & Chips</To>
<LineItems>
  <Item>
    <Product>TravelLight 400</Product>
    <Description>laptop computer</Description>
    <Price>2000</Price>
    <Quantity>1</Quantity>
  </Item>
  <Item>
    <Product>TravelTuff Case</Product>
    <Description>laptop computer case</Description>
    <Price>50</Price>
    <Quantity>2</Quantity>
  </Item>
  <Item>
    <Product>ScreenClean</Product>
    <Description>computer monitor cleaner</Description>
    <Price>2</Price>
    <Quantity>100</Quantity>
  </Item>
</LineItems>
</PurchaseOrder>
```

The following illustration shows this purchase order displayed in BizTalk Editor.

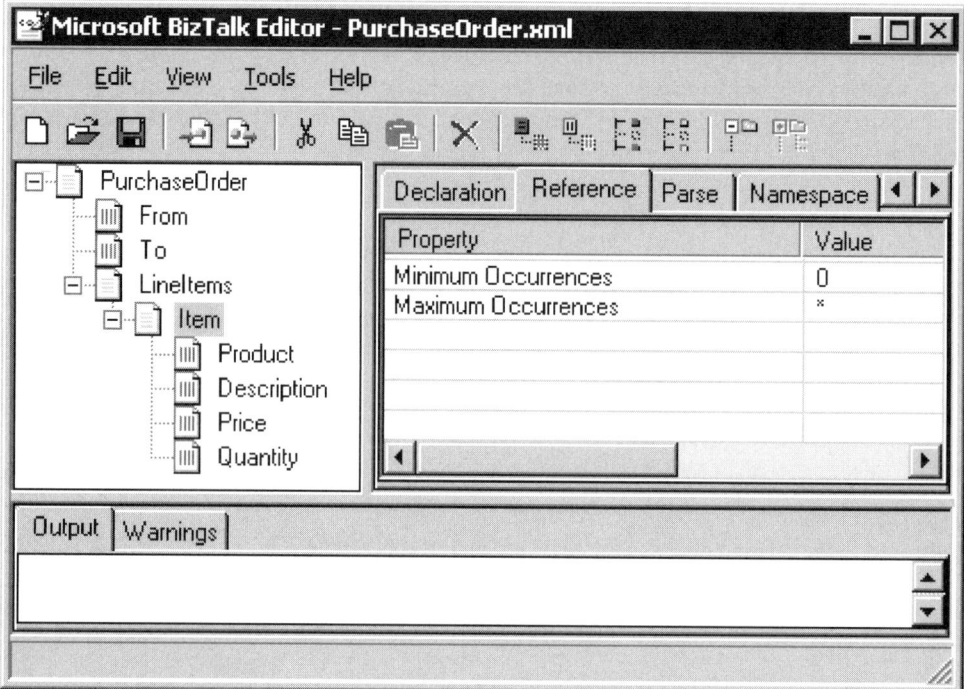

Note that the **Maximum Occurrences** property on the **Reference** tab for the Item record is set at *. This indicates that the item record loops, and BizTalk Mapper compiles this record as a loop.

You might want to find the sum total of all the line items in the purchase order and map the cumulative total into a field in an output document. To do this, you must first calculate the extended price for each item record in the purchase order and then aggregate the individual item record totals as the mapping progresses through all the item records in the purchase order.

The following illustration shows a **Multiplication** functoid and a **Cumulative Sum** functoid used to aggregate item records from an incoming purchase order and output the results in the POTotal field of a TotalsDocument document.

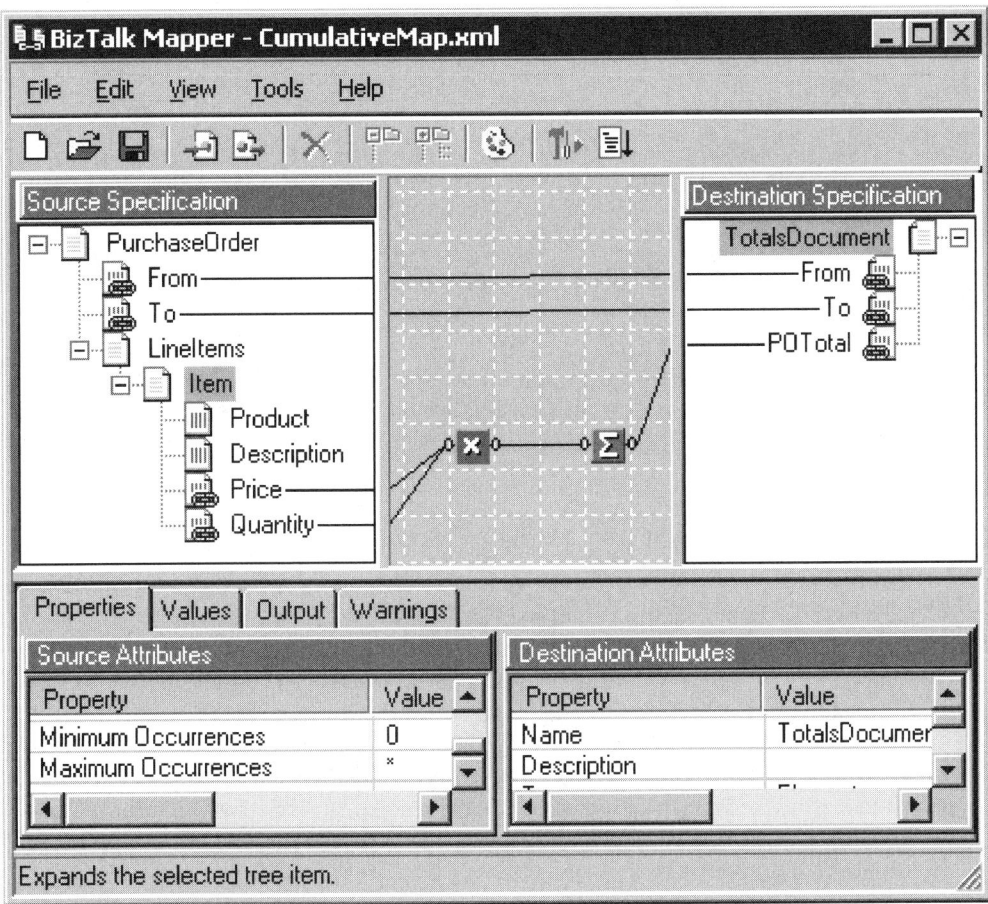

In this example, all the Item records that exist under the LineItems record of an incoming purchase order participate in the cumulative operation. The Price and Quantity fields are sent to a **Multiplication** functoid. The output of the **Multiplication** functoid becomes the input of the **Cumulative Sum** functoid. The output of the **Cumulative Sum** functoid is the accumulated value as the Item records are traversed in the input purchase order. This value is sent to the POTotal field of the TotalsDocument document and is the sum of each of the individual products of price and quantity: $(2000 \times 1)+(50 \times 2)+(2 \times 100)=2300$.

Notes

- The cumulative aggregation of a particular input takes place over the parent record from which the input link originates. This also applies to functoid outputs that are fed as input to a cumulative functoid.

- Cumulative functoids ignore nonnumeric input. For example, an input value of "three" is ignored.

The **Cumulative Average**, **Cumulative Minimum**, and **Cumulative Maximum** functoids behave similarly to the **Cumulative Sum** functoid. The **Cumulative String** functoid behaves differently from the rest of the cumulative functoids in that it concatenates strings rather than aggregating numeric values.

To add cumulative functoids

1. On the **View** menu, click **Functoid Palette**.

2. On the **Functoid Palette**, click the **Cumulative** tab.

   You might need to click the right arrow on the **Functoid Palette** to view the tab.

3. Drag a cumulative functoid from the **Functoid Palette** to the mapping grid.

4. Drag a field (with a parent record that is looping) from the Source Specification tree to the functoid in the mapping grid, and then drag the functoid to a record or field in the Destination Specification tree.

◆ Important

- For information about the context of this procedure, see the previous topic "Using Cumulative Functoids."

- To create a link between a functoid and a record, you must enable the **Allow record content links** property. To do this, on the **Tools** menu, click **Options**. In the **BizTalk Mapper Options** dialog box, on the **General** tab, select the **Allow record content links** check box and click **OK**.

✎ Note

- You might need to expand the specification trees to see the records or fields that you want to map. For more information, see "To expand tree items" earlier in this chapter.

Database Functoids

Database functoids are a collection of functoids that enable you extract information from a database. The following table describes each type of database functoid and its parameters.

Functoid	Parameters
Database Lookup Searches a database for a specific value, retrieves the record that contains the value, and stores it as an ADO record set.	This functoid must have exactly four input parameters.
Value Extractor Returns a value from a specific column in an ADO record set that has been retrieved by the **Database Lookup** functoid.	This functoid must have exactly two input parameters.
Error Return Returns the error string, if any, returned by ODBC when using the **Database Lookup** functoid.	This functoid must have exactly one input parameter.

Using Database Functoids

Database functoids extract data from a database. To understand how database functoids are used, consider a large retail manufacturer with many stores spread over a large geographical area. Each store is designated by a numeric code, and an address list is distributed to all partners. The address list might contain the following structure:

StoreID: 123

Name: A. Datum Corporation

Address: 1234 Main Street

City: Denver, Colorado

PostalCode: 97402

PhoneNumber: 801-555-0179

StoreManager: Anthony Chor

In subsequent transactions, only the numeric code that represents the store is sent in a purchase order. BizTalk Mapper uses that code to extract the address information from a database. The following illustration shows such a scenario.

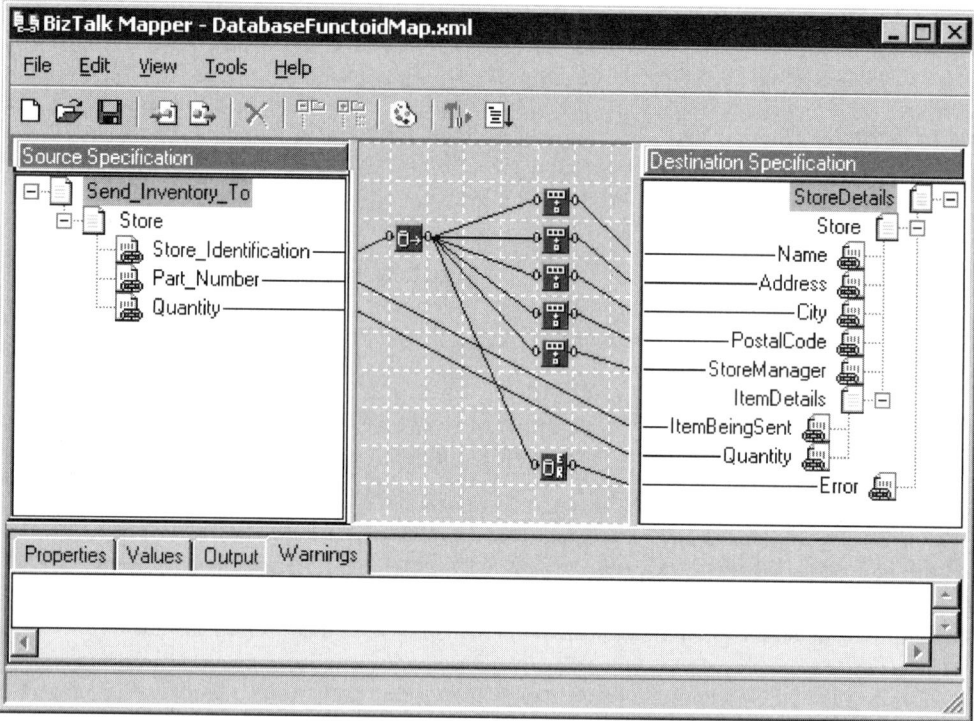

In this illustration, the source specification represents an incoming purchase order, and the destination specification represents an invoice. The **Database Lookup** functoid performs a database lookup to find the appropriate record from the appropriate table. The output of the **Database Lookup** functoid can be connected only to **Value Extractor** functoids. The **Value Extractor** functoids extract the appropriate column name from the lookup record. The **Error Return** functoid outputs a string containing error information if there are errors (such as connection failures) at run time.

The **Database Lookup** functoid requires four input parameters, in the following order:

- The lookup value
- The database connection string
- The table name
- The column name for the lookup value

For information about inserting, deleting, and moving input parameters, see "Input Parameters" later in this chapter.

In the previous example, the first input parameter is taken from the StoreID field of the incoming purchase order, and the remaining three input parameters are constants on the **General** tab of the **Functoid Properties** dialog box for the **Database Lookup** functoid. It is possible to create links from the Source Specification tree to supply values for all four input parameters. For more information about inserting, deleting, and moving input parameters, see "Input Parameters" later in this chapter.

The **Value Extractor** functoid requires the following two input parameters, in the following order:

- A link to the **Database Lookup** functoid

- The column name

The **Error Return** functoid requires exactly one input parameter: a link to the **Database Lookup** functoid.

🖉 Notes

- Some Microsoft SQL Server data types, such as **text**, **ntext**, and **image**, cannot be used as lookup values for the **Database Lookup** functoid.

- If there is more than one record that matches the input parameters of the **Database Lookup** functoid, the **Value Extractor** functoid extracts only the first record in the table.

To add database functoids

1. On the **View** menu, click **Functoid Palette**.

2. On the **Functoid Palette**, click the **Database** tab.

   You might need to click the right arrow on the **Functoid Palette** to view the tab.

3. Drag a database functoid from the **Functoid Palette** to the mapping grid.

◈ Important

- For information about how to use database functoids to extract information from a database, see the previous topic "Using Database Functoids."

- To create a link between a functoid and a record, you must enable the **Allow record content links** property. To do this, on the **Tools** menu, click **Options**. In the **BizTalk Mapper Options** dialog box, on the **General** tab, select the **Allow record content links** check box and click **OK**.

🖉 Note

- You might need to expand the specification trees to see the records or fields that you want to map. For more information, see "To expand tree items" earlier in this chapter.

Advanced Functoids

Advanced functoids are a collection of functoids that enable you to do a wide variety of advanced mapping operations. The following table describes each type of advanced functoid and its parameters.

Functoid	Parameters
S **Scripting** Custom Visual Basic script.	The number of input parameters for this functoid is configurable, based on a custom script.
Record Count Returns a total count of the records found in the instance.	This functoid must have one input parameter.
Index Returns the value of a record or a field at a specified index.	This functoid must have at least two input parameters. The maximum number of input parameters is limited by the number of levels in the specification hierarchy.
Iteration Returns the iteration number (in a loop) of the source record.	This functoid must have one input parameter.
Value Mapping Returns the value of the second parameter if the value of the first parameter is "true".	This functoid must have two input parameters.
Value Mapping (Flattening) Returns the value of the second parameter if the value of the first parameter is "true", and flattens the source document hierarchy.	This functoid must have two input parameters.
Looping Creates multiple output records by iterating over each input record.	This functoid must have at least one input parameter. There is no maximum limit on the number of input parameters.

To add the Scripting functoid

1. On the **View** menu, click **Functoid Palette**.

2. On the **Functoid Palette**, click the **Advanced** tab.

   You might need to click the right arrow on the **Functoid Palette** to view the tab.

3. Drag the **Scripting** functoid **S** to the mapping grid.

4. Double-click the **Scripting** functoid.

   The **Functoid Properties** dialog box appears.

5. Click the **Script** tab, type the script that you want, and then click **OK**.

6. Drag a record or field from the Source Specification tree to the **Scripting** functoid in the mapping grid, and then drag the **Scripting** functoid to the record or field in the Destination Specification tree.

◆ **Important**

- If there are multiple functions within a **Scripting** functoid, the first function is the main or primary function. This function must have parameters set if there are links into the functoid.
- To create a link between a functoid and a record, you must enable the **Allow record content links** property. To do this, on the **Tools** menu, click **Options**. In the **BizTalk Mapper Options** dialog box, on the **General** tab, select the **Allow record content links** check box and click **OK**.

📝 **Note**

- You might need to expand the specification trees to see the records or fields that you want to map. For more information, see "To expand tree items" earlier in this chapter.

Using the Record Count Functoid

The **Record Count** functoid operates within the context of the record level in the source specification. Certain records typically occur many times in an input file. For example, in a purchase order, the Item section might occur many times. The Item section might include products, descriptions, prices, and quantities. The following code is an example of a purchase order:

```
<PurchaseOrder>
  <From>Kevin F. Browne</From>
  <To>Bits, Bytes, & Chips</To>
<LineItems>
  <Item>
    <Product>TravelLight 400</Product>
    <Description>laptop computer</Description>
    <Price>2000</Price>
    <Quantity>1</Quantity>
  </Item>
  <Item>
    <Product>TravelTuff Case</Product>
    <Description>laptop computer case</Description>
    <Price>50</Price>
    <Quantity>2</Quantity>
  </Item>
  <Item>
    <Product>ScreenClean</Product>
    <Description>computer monitor cleaner</Description>
    <Price>2</Price>
    <Quantity>100</Quantity>
  </Item>
</LineItems>
</PurchaseOrder>
```

The following illustration shows this purchase order displayed in BizTalk Editor.

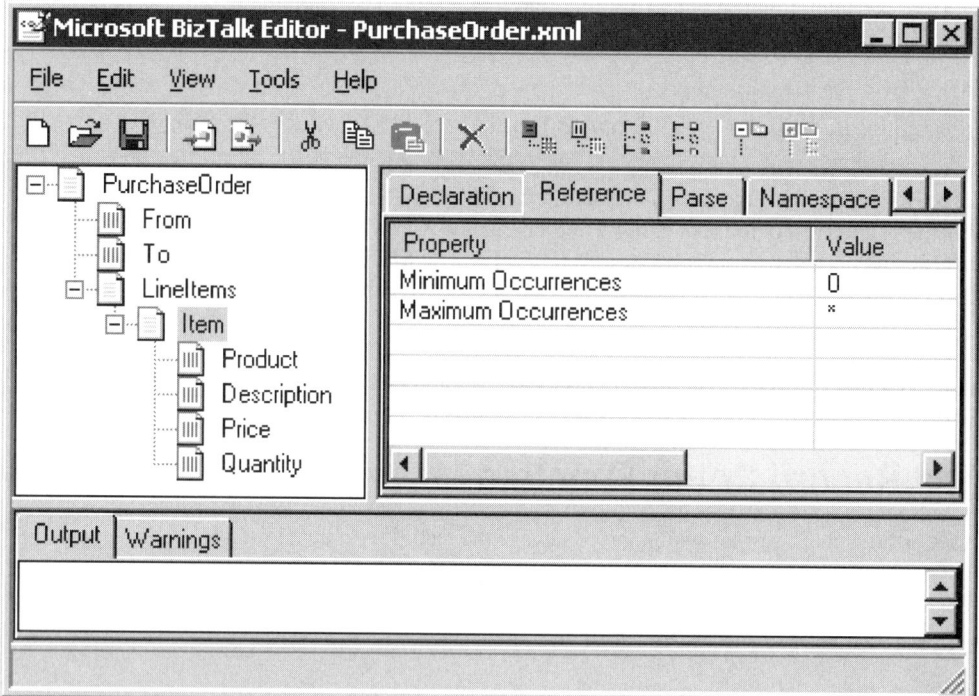

Note that the **Maximum Occurrences** property on the **Reference** tab for the Item record is set at *. This indicates that the Item record loops, and BizTalk Mapper compiles this record as a loop.

You might want to find the total number of line items in the purchase order and map that value into a field in an output document. This scenario is a bit different from the conventional mapping scenario in which content from the source document is mapped to the output document. In this case, the **Record Count** functoid generates the value that is mapped to the output document.

The **Record Count** functoid has one input and one output. The input is a link from a looping record in the source specification. This record appears many times in the original input document. The output of the **Record Count** functoid is a link to a field in the destination specification.

The following illustration shows a **Record Count** functoid that counts the number of items that exist in an incoming purchase order and outputs that value to the Number_Of_Items field in the POReport document.

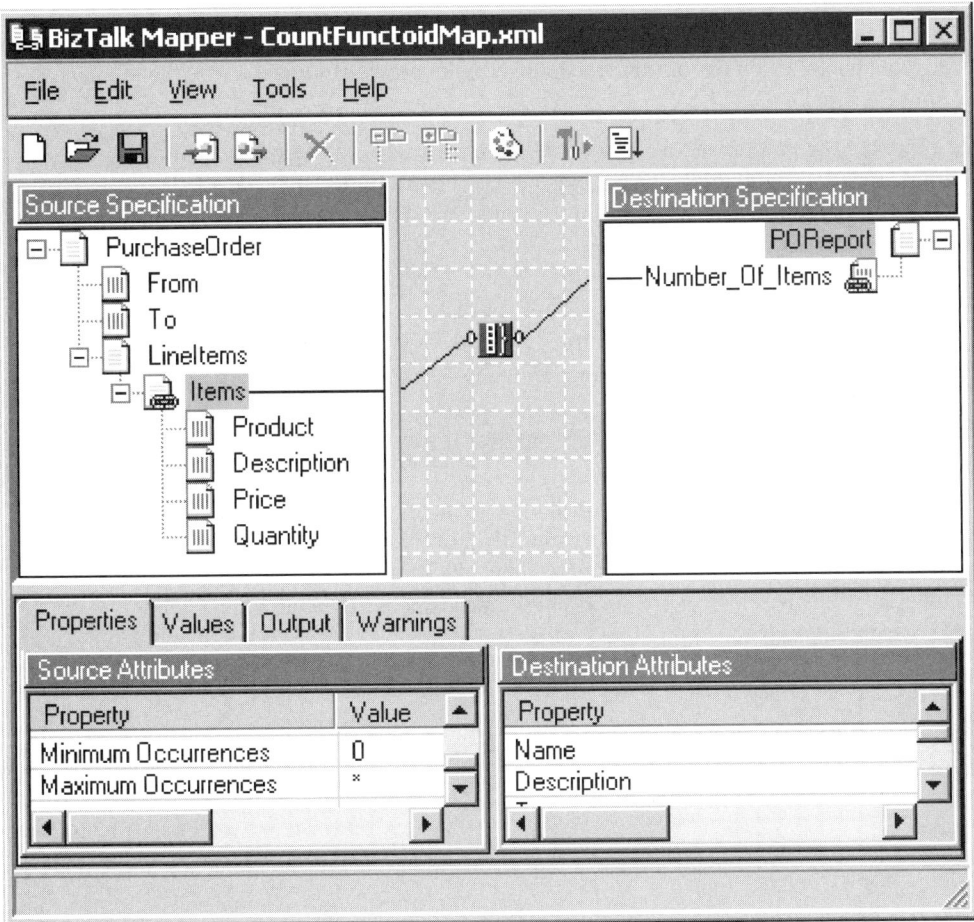

Because, in this example, there were three items in the incoming purchase order, the value of the Number_Of_Items field is 3.

To add the Record Count functoid

1. On the **View** menu, click **Functoid Palette**.

2. On the **Functoid Palette**, click the **Advanced** tab.

    You might need to click the right arrow on the **Functoid Palette** to view the tab.

3. Drag the **Record Count** functoid ▥ from the **Functoid Palette** to the mapping grid.

4. Drag a looping record from the Source Specification tree to the **Record Count** functoid in the mapping grid, and then drag the **Record Count** functoid to a field in the Destination Specification tree.

◆ **Important**

- For information about the context of this procedure, see the previous topic, "Using the Record Count Functoid."

- To create a link between a functoid and a record, you must enable the **Allow record content links** property. To do this, on the **Tools** menu, click **Options**. In the **BizTalk Mapper Options** dialog box, on the **General** tab, select the **Allow record content links** check box and click **OK**.

✎ **Note**

- You might need to expand the specification trees to see the records or fields that you want to map. For more information, see "To expand tree items" earlier in this chapter.

Using the Index Functoid

The **Index** functoid operates within the context of the record level of the source specification. Certain records typically occur many times in an input file. For example, in a weather report, the DailySummary section might occur many times. The DailySummary section might include the temperature, the barometric pressure, and the wind speed. The following code is an example of a weather report:

```
<WeatherReport>
  <DailySummary>
    <Temperature>20</Temperature>
    <Pressure>80</Pressure>
    <WindSpeed>10</WindSpeed>
  </DailySummary>
  <DailySummary>
    <Temperature>23</Temperature>
    <Pressure>78</Pressure>
    <WindSpeed>20</WindSpeed>
  </DailySummary>
  <DailySummary>
    <Temperature>24</Temperature>
    <Pressure>77</Pressure>
    <WindSpeed>16</WindSpeed>
  </DailySummary>
</WeatherReport>
```

The following illustration shows this weather report displayed in BizTalk Editor.

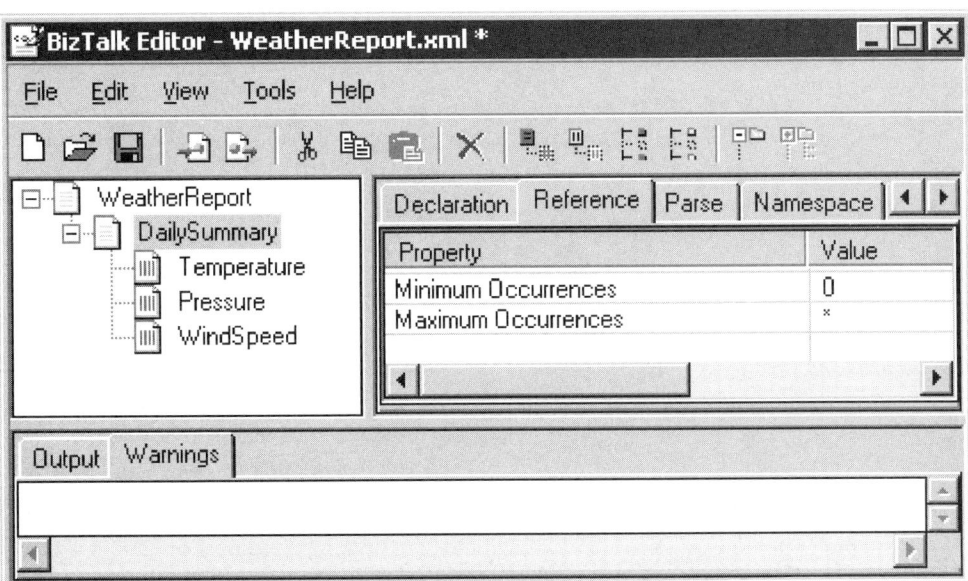

Note that the **Maximum Occurrences** property on the **Reference** tab for the DailySummary record is set at *. This indicates that the DailySummary record loops, and BizTalk Mapper compiles this record as a loop.

You might want to collect weather information for the first two DailySummary records of the weather report. In BizTalk Mapper, each field from the DailySummary record of the incoming source specification can be connected to an **Index** functoid, and each **Index** functoid can specify from which DailySummary record to draw the information: the first and the second. The **Index** functoids can then be connected to the appropriate fields of a destination specification. Note that **Index** functoids operate only between fields that exist below a single parent in the source specification to fields that exist below a single parent in the destination specification.

The following illustration shows **Index** functoids used in this way.

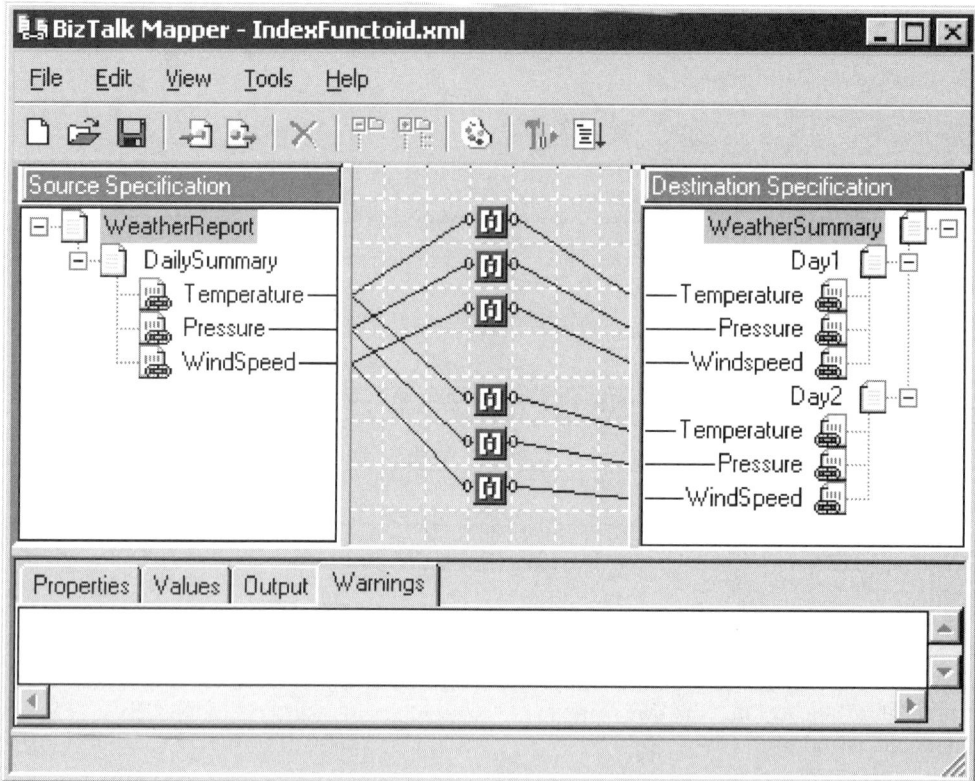

To get the daily summary information for the first day, the top three **Index** functoids must have an index value of 1. To get the daily summary information for the second day, the last three **Index** functoids must have an index value of 2.

Index sequence inputs are set as input parameters on the **General** tab of an **Index** functoid's property sheet. Double-click an **Index** functoid to display its property sheet. The first input parameter identifies the field in the source specification that links into the **Index** functoid. The succeeding input parameter or parameters indicate index values.

The following illustration shows the property sheet for the top **Index** functoid in the previous map.

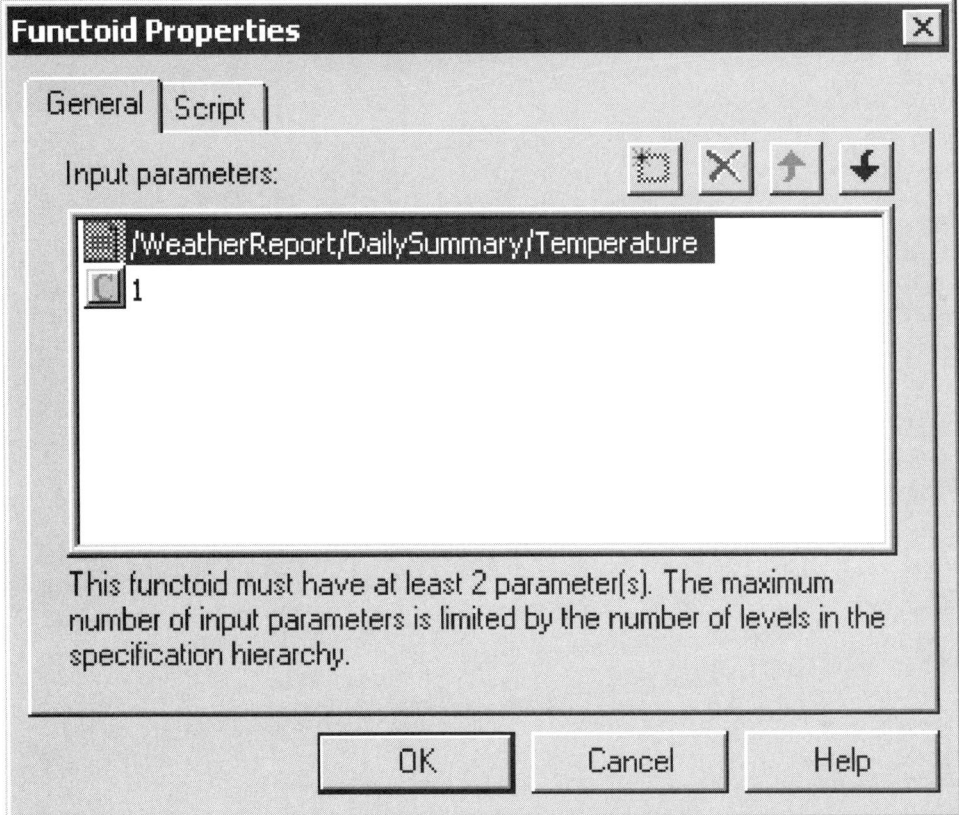

Notes

- An **Index** functoid input parameter assigned any nonnumeric constant value is interpreted by BizTalk Mapper to have a value of 1. For example, in the previous illustration, if the second input parameter were replaced with an input parameter with a value of "anystring", the mapping result would be unchanged.

- Although index sequence input is typically a constant value on the **General** tab of the **Functoid Properties** dialog box, it is possible to use a link from a node in the source specification for the input sequence value. If this link comes from a looping record that is not a parent of the first input parameter, the index sequence input value comes from the first instance of the node in the incoming document.

- The value of the index sequence input is always in relation to the current context in the source document.

If you had multiple weather reports in the same input file, and each weather report had multiple daily summaries, you might need to specify more than one index value. The following code is an example of an input file with multiple weather reports:

```
<WeatherReports>
  <WeatherReport1>
    <DailySummary>
      <Temperature>20</Temperature>
      <Pressure>80</Pressure>
      <WindSpeed>10</WindSpeed>
    </DailySummary>
    <DailySummary>
      <Temperature>23</Temperature>
      <Pressure>78</Pressure>
      <WindSpeed>20</WindSpeed>
    </DailySummary>
  </WeatherReport1>
  <WeatherReport2>
    <DailySummary>
      <Temperature>24</Temperature>
      <Pressure>77</Pressure>
      <WindSpeed>16</WindSpeed>
    </DailySummary>
    <DailySummary>
      <Temperature>22</Temperature>
      <Pressure>79</Pressure>
      <WindSpeed>21</WindSpeed>
    </DailySummary>
  </WeatherReport2>
</WeatherReports>
```

An **Index** functoid with two index values, the first set at 1 and the second set at 2, gets a field value from the first daily summary of the second weather report.

◈ Important

- An **Index** functoid must have as many index values as there are parent nodes from the field level to the first level below the root node. For example, in the multiple weather report sample document, two index values are required. In the single weather report sample document, only one index value is required. Failure to set the required number of index values of an **Index** functoid creates output based on the first node in the source document that matches the first input parameter of the **Index** functoid.

To add the Index functoid

1. On the **View** menu, click **Functoid Palette**.

2. On the **Functoid Palette**, click the **Advanced** tab.

   You might need to click the right arrow on the **Functoid Palette** to view the tab.

3. Drag the **Index** functoid 🔟 from the **Functoid Palette** to the mapping grid.

4. Drag a field (with a parent record that is looping) from the Source Specification tree to the **Index** functoid in the mapping grid, and then drag the **Index** functoid to a field in the Destination Specification tree.

5. Double-click the **Index** functoid to display its property sheet.

6. Click the **Insert New Parameter** button 🔲, type the index value, and then press ENTER.

7. Repeat step 6 as necessary.

8. Click **OK**.

◆ **Important**

*   For information about the context of this procedure, see the previous topic, "Using the Index Functoid."

*   To create a link between a functoid and a record, you must enable the **Allow record content links** property. To do this, on the **Tools** menu, click **Options**. In the **BizTalk Mapper Options** dialog box, on the **General** tab, select the **Allow record content links** check box and click **OK**.

✎ **Note**

*   You might need to expand the specification trees to see the records or fields that you want to map. For more information, see "To expand tree items" earlier in this chapter.

Using the Iteration Functoid

The **Iteration** functoid identifies which sequence number in a looping record is being mapped at any given time. The following illustration shows the **Iteration** functoid used in conjunction with an **Equal** functoid.

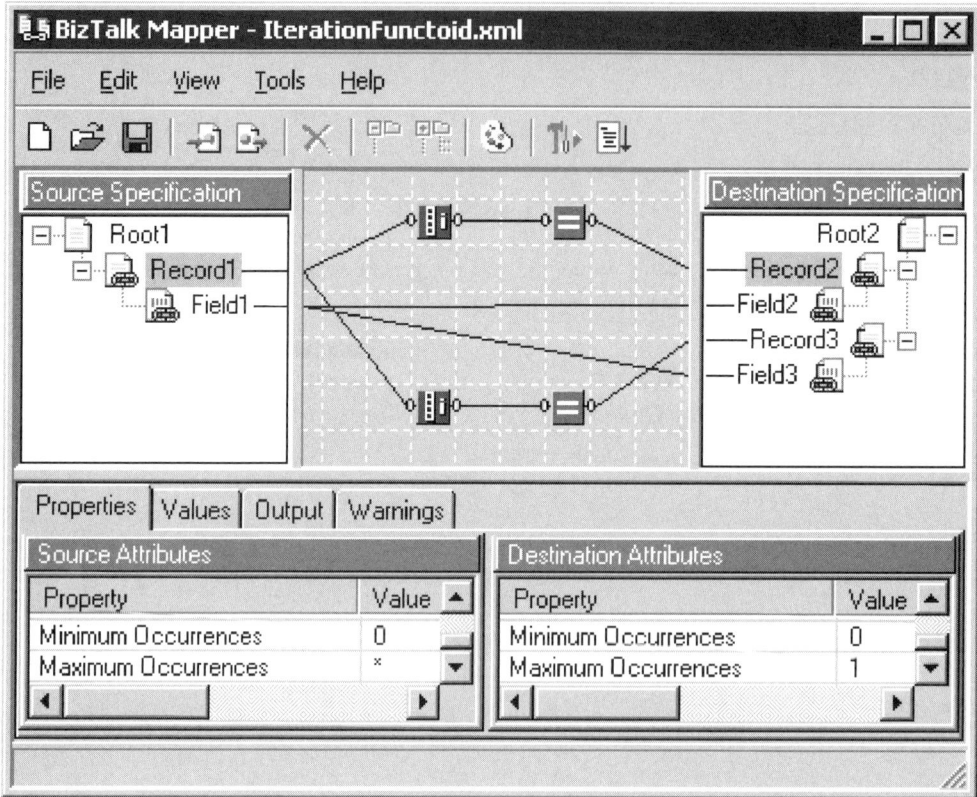

There is a pair of functoids (the **Iteration** functoid and the **Equal** functoid) for each of the two records in the destination specification. The following illustration shows the property sheet for the top **Equal** functoid.

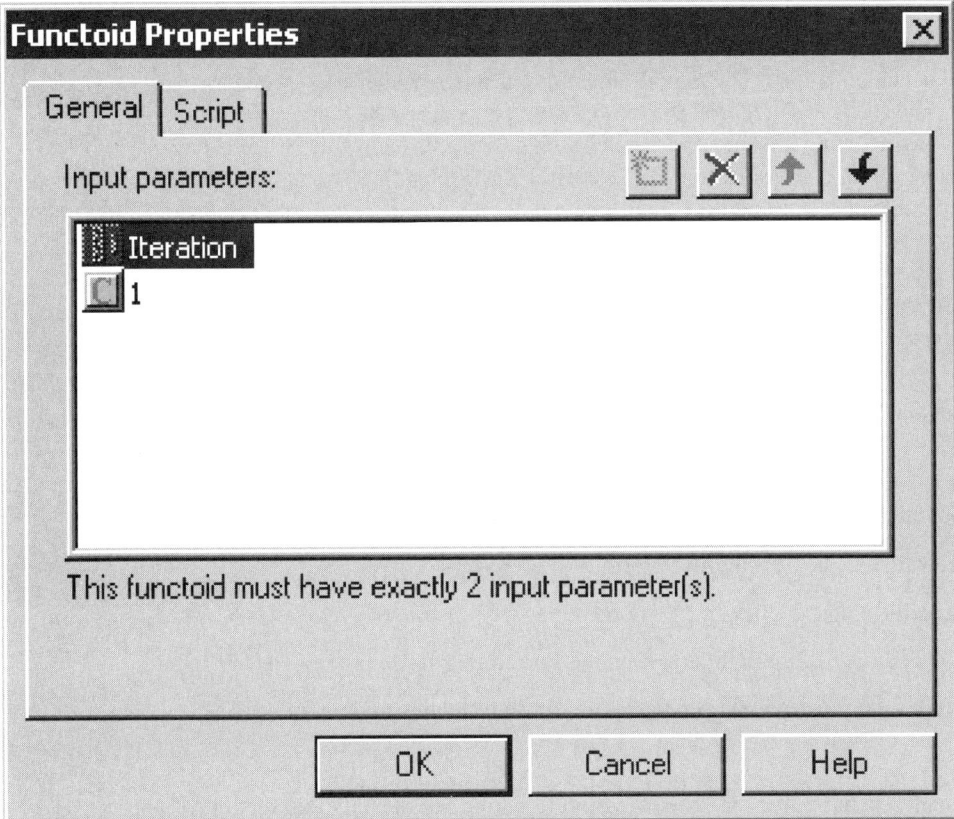

The following code is an example of an incoming document instance that conforms to the structure of the source specification:

```
<Root>
<Record1 Field1="A"/>
<Record1 Field1="B"/>
</Root>
```

As the source specification loops through the incoming document instance, the **Iteration** functoid returns the value 1 while the first record is being mapped and the value 2 while the second record is being mapped. The **Equal** functoid returns the value "true" when its two input parameters are equal. Therefore, the top functoid pair returns the value "true" while the first record of the incoming document instance is being mapped. The value "true" is passed to Record2 of the destination specification, and Record2 is written to the output document. If the second input parameter of the bottom **Equal** functoid has a value of 2, the bottom functoid pair behaves in a manner similar to the top functoid pair. In other words, when the second record of the incoming document instance is mapped, Record3 of the destination specification is written to the output document instance. The following code shows the output document instance:

```
<Root2>
<Record2 Field2="A"/>
<Record3 Field3="B"/>
</Root2>
```

To add the Iteration functoid

1. On the **View** menu, click **Functoid Palette**.

2. On the **Functoid Palette**, click the **Advanced** tab.

   You might need to click the right arrow on the **Functoid Palette** to view the tab.

3. Drag the **Iteration** functoid ![icon] from the **Functoid Palette** to the mapping grid.

◆ **Important**

- For information about how to use the **Iteration** functoid, see the previous section,"Using the Iteration Functoid."

- To create a link between a functoid and a record, you must enable the **Allow record content links** property. To do this, on the **Tools** menu, click **Options**. In the **BizTalk Mapper Options** dialog box, on the **General** tab, select the **Allow record content links** check box and click **OK**.

📝 **Note**

- You might need to expand the specification trees to see the records or fields that you want to map. For more information, see "To expand tree items" earlier in this chapter.

Using the Value Mapping Functoid

The **Value Mapping** functoid 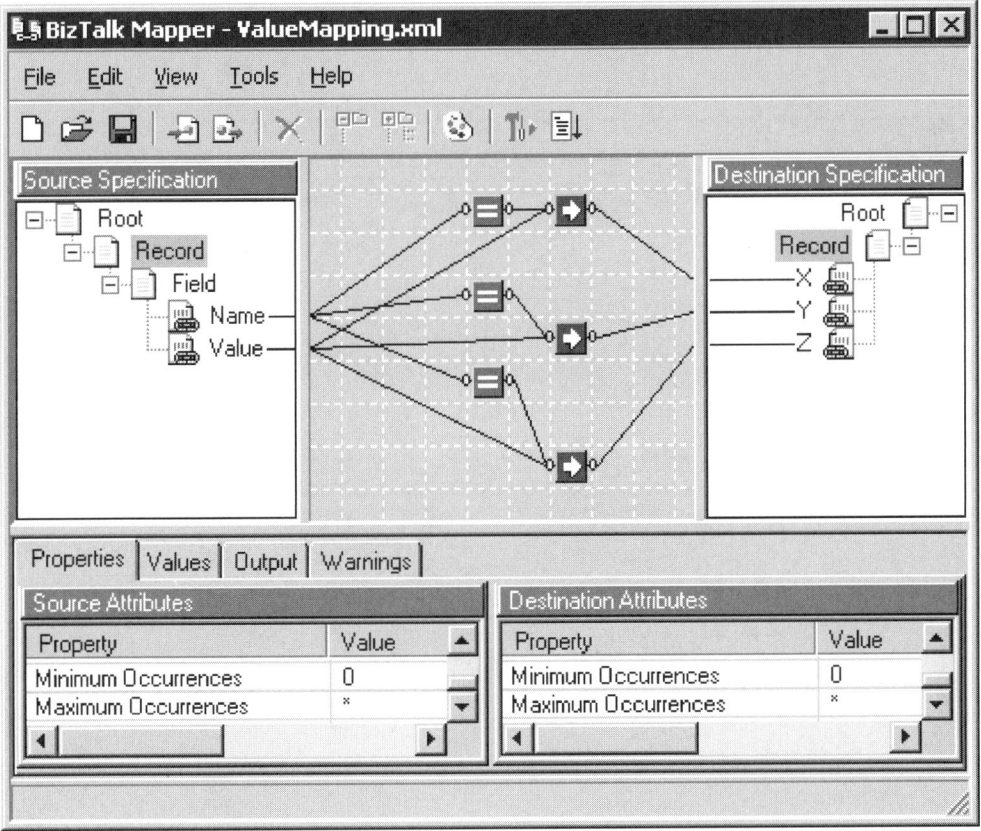 requires two input parameters, and returns the value of the second input parameter if the value of the first parameter is "true". The following illustration shows a map with the **Value Mapping** functoid used in this way.

To complete the map, you must set the input parameters for each functoid. The following illustration shows the property sheet for each of the three **Value Mapping** functoids.

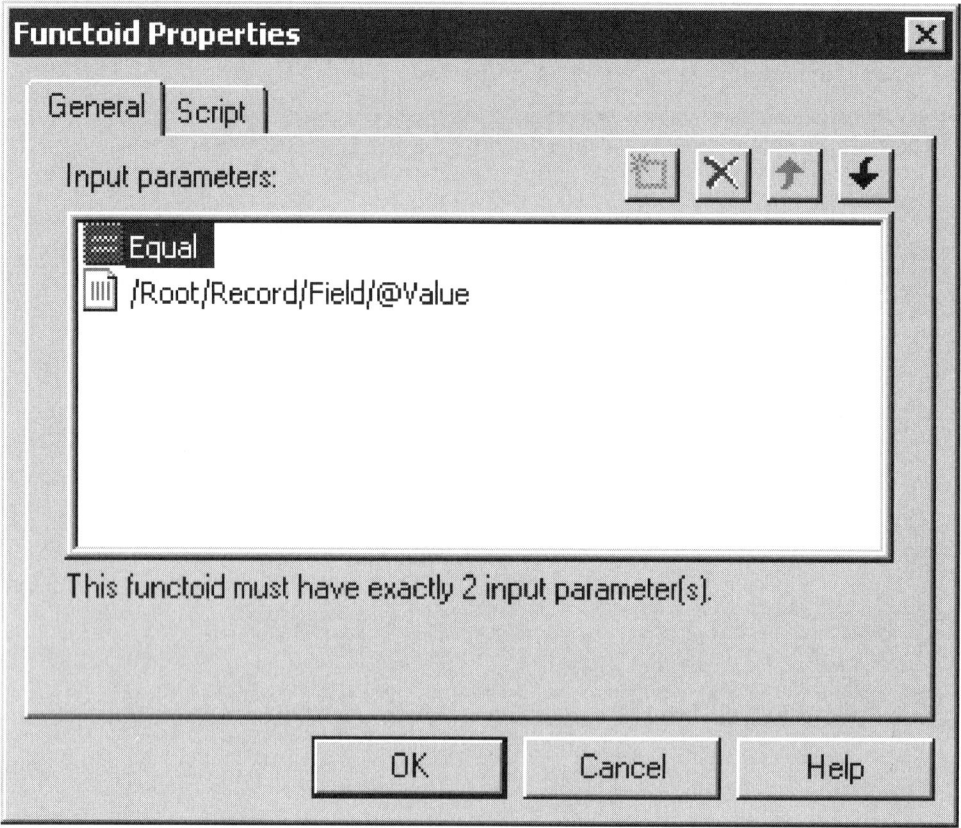

The following illustration shows the property sheet for the top **Equal** functoid.

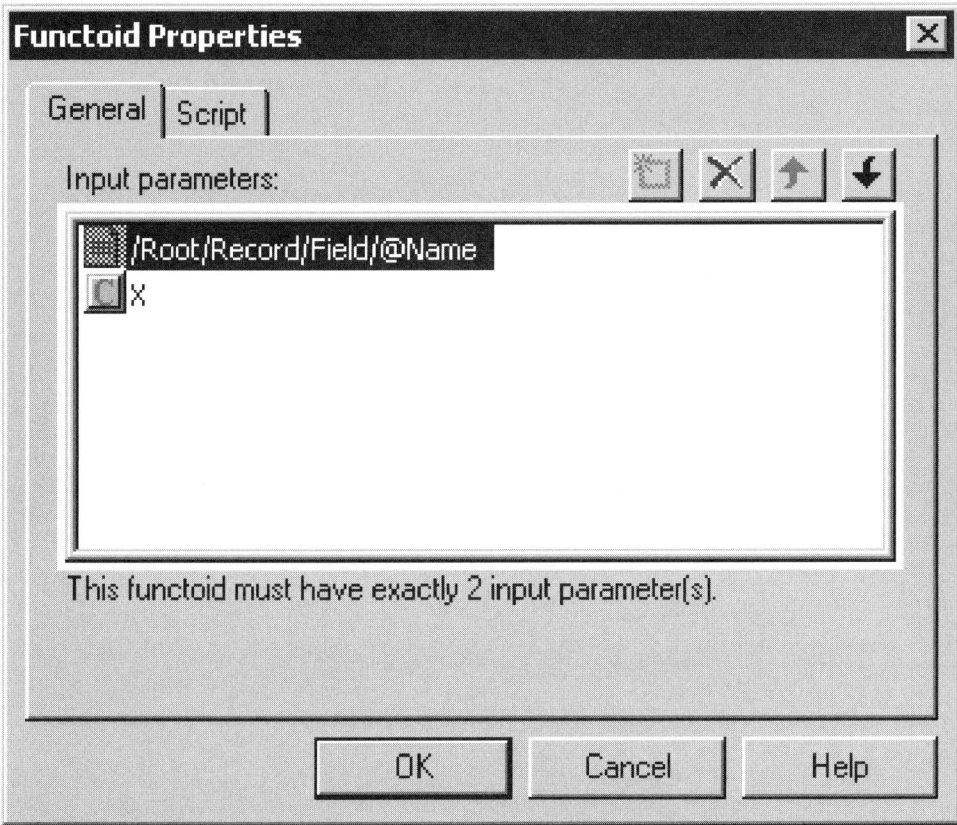

The middle **Equal** functoid property sheet is similar, but its second input parameter has a constant value of **Y**. The bottom **Equal** functoid property sheet is also similar, but its second input parameter has a constant value of **Z**.

You might have a source document instance that contains the following element:

```
<Field Name="X" Value="1"/>
```

A Name value of X makes the top **Equal** functoid of the map return a value of "true". The "true" value returned by the **Equal** functoid makes the **Attribute Value** functoid that it is linked to return a value of 1.

The following code is an example of a document instance that corresponds to the source specification of the map:

```
<Root>
  <Record>
    <Field Name="X" Value="1"/>
    <Field Name="Y" Value="2"/>
    <Field Name="Z" Value="3"/>
  </Record>
  <Record>
    <Field Name="X" Value="4"/>
    <Field Name="Y" Value="5"/>
    <Field Name="Z" Value="6"/>
  </Record>
  <Record>
    <Field Name="X" Value="7"/>
    <Field Name="Y" Value="8"/>
    <Field Name="Z" Value="9"/>
  </Record>
</Root>
```

Using this map and this source document instance, BizTalk Server outputs the following document instance:

```
<Root>
<Record X="1"/>
<Record Y="2"/>
<Record Z="3"/>
<Record X="4"/>
<Record Y="5"/>
<Record Z="6"/>
<Record X="7"/>
<Record Y="8"/>
<Record Z="9"/>
</Root>
```

◆ **Important**

- The **Value Mapping** functoid accepts Boolean input only in the form of the lowercase strings "true" and "false". For example, if a field in an incoming document instance has a value of "True" and is linked directly to the top input parameter of a **Value Mapping** functoid, the value of the second input parameter of the **Value Mapping** functoid is not passed to the output document.

To add the Value Mapping functoid

1. On the **View** menu, click **Functoid Palette**.

2. On the **Functoid Palette**, click the **Advanced** tab.

   You might need to click the right arrow on the **Functoid Palette** to view the tab.

3. Drag the **Value Mapping** functoid ➡ from the **Functoid Palette** to the mapping grid.

◆ **Important**

- For information about how to use the **Value Mapping** functoid, see the previous topic "Using the Value Mapping Functoid."

- To create a link between a functoid and a record, you must enable the **Allow record content links** property. To do this, on the **Tools** menu, click **Options**. In the **BizTalk Mapper Options** dialog box, on the **General** tab, select the **Allow record content links** check box and click **OK**.

✎ **Note**

- You might need to expand the specification trees to see the records or fields that you want to map. For more information, see "To expand tree items" earlier in this chapter.

Using the Value Mapping (Flattening) Functoid

A common scenario for users of Microsoft Commerce Server is to map from a Commerce Server catalog to a flat schema. The **Value Mapping (Flattening)** functoid makes this type of map possible. The following code is an example of a Commerce Server catalog:

```
<Root>
  <Record>
    <Field Name="X" Value="1"/>
    <Field Name="Y" Value="2"/>
    <Field Name="Z" Value="3"/>
  </Record>
  <Record>
    <Field Name="X" Value="4"/>
    <Field Name="Y" Value="5"/>
    <Field Name="Z" Value="6"/>
  </Record>
  <Record>
    <Field Name="X" Value="7"/>
    <Field Name="Y" Value="8"/>
    <Field Name="Z" Value="9"/>
  </Record>
</Root>
```

The following code is an example of a flat schema:

```
<Root>
  <Record X="1" Y="2" Z="3"/>
  <Record X="4" Y="5" Z="6"/>
  <Record X="7" Y="8" Z="9"/>
</Root>
```

In this mapping scenario it is important to maintain the one-to-one correspondence between the three records in the catalog and the three records in the flat schema. The following illustration shows a map that maintains this correspondence.

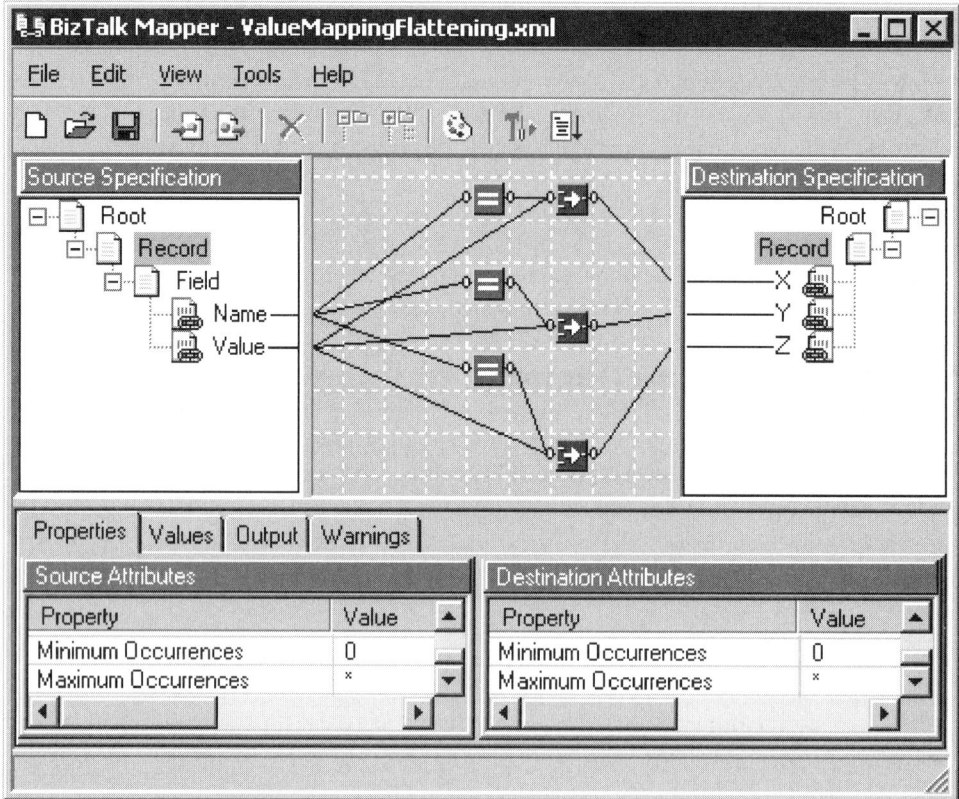

In this map, the source specification represents the structure of the incoming catalog, and the destination specification represents the structure of the outgoing flat schema. There is a pair of functoids (the **Equal** functoid and the **Value Mapping (Flattening)** functoid) for each of the three records.

The following illustration shows the property sheet for each of the three **Value Mapping (Flattening)** functoids.

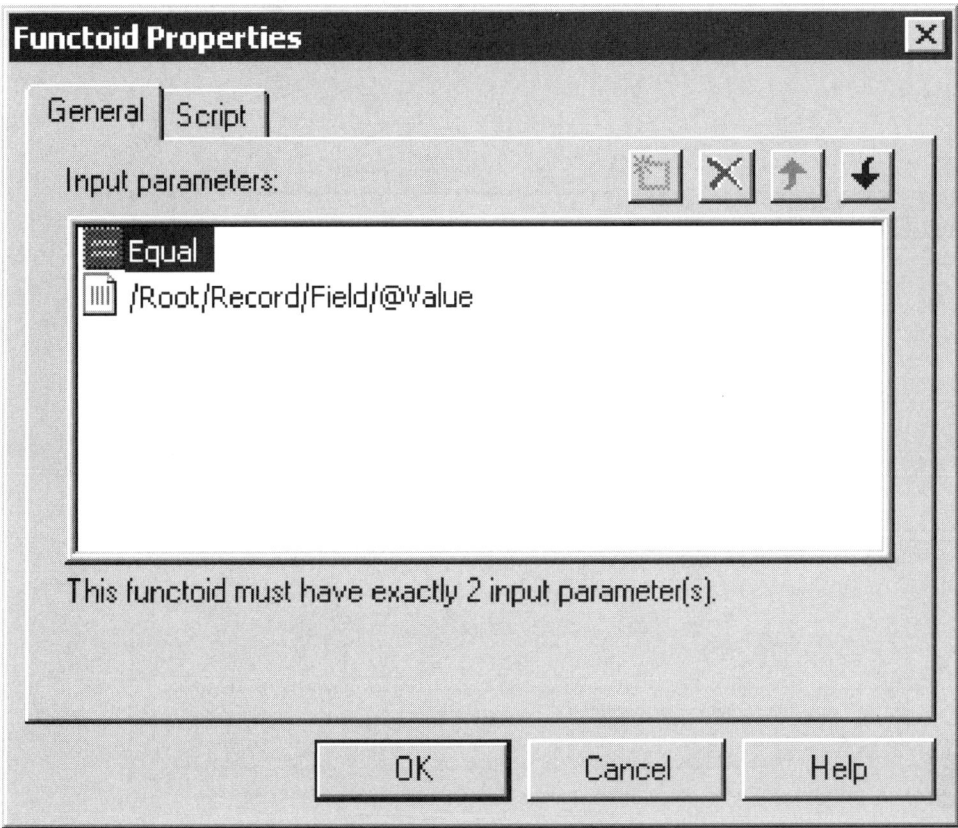

The following illustration shows the property sheet for the top **Equal** functoid.

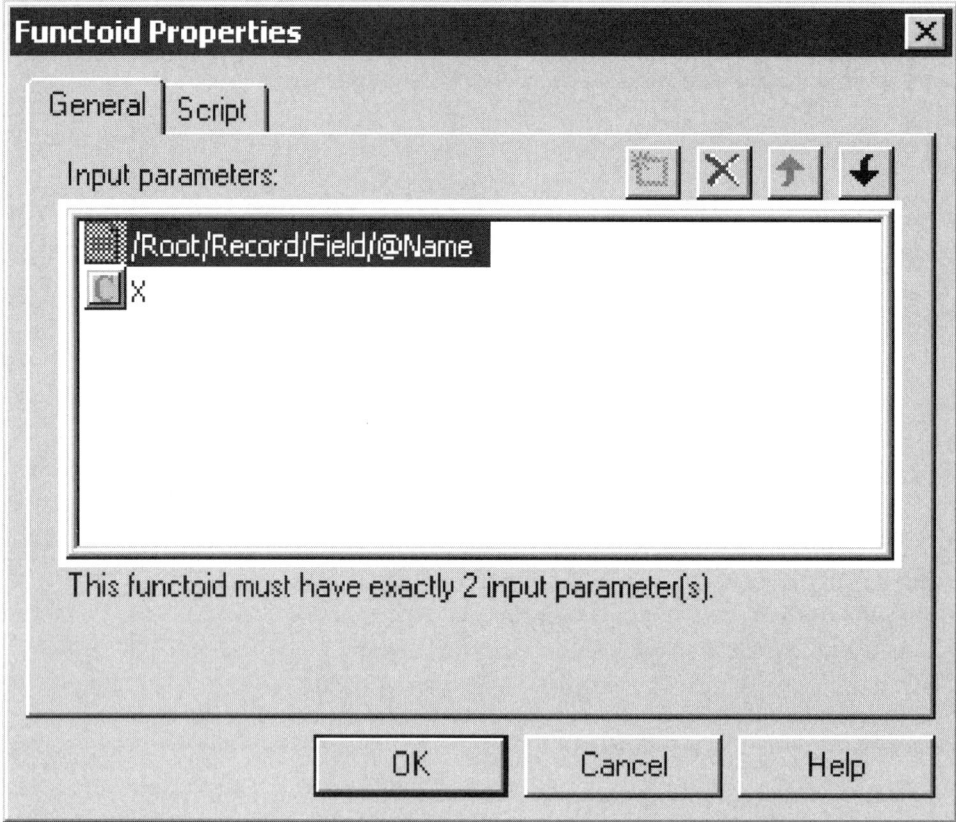

The middle **Equal** functoid property sheet is similar, but its second input parameter has a constant value of **Y**. The bottom **Equal** functoid property sheet is also similar, but its second input parameter has a constant value of **Z**.

The top functoid pair works together to ensure that the value of X is passed from each of the three records in the catalog to each of the three records in the flat schema. The **Value Mapping (Flattening)** functoid returns the value of the second parameter of its property sheet only if the value of the first parameter is "true". For this reason, the top **Value Mapping (Flattening)** functoid returns the value of /Root/Record/Field/@Value only if the **Equal** functoid it is linked to returns a value of "true". The **Equal** functoid to which it is linked returns a value of "true" only for fields in the incoming catalog with Name values of X.

The **Equal** functoid of the middle functoid pair returns a value of "true" only for fields in the incoming specification with Name values of Y, so this pair of functoids ensures that the value of Y is passed from each of the three records in the catalog to each of the three records in the flat schema. The third functoid pair handles the value of Z in a similar manner.

◆ Important

- The **Value Mapping (Flattening)** functoid accepts Boolean input only in the form of the lowercase strings "true" and "false". For example, if a field in an incoming document instance has the value "True" and is linked directly to the top input parameter of a **Value Mapping (Flattening)** functoid, the value of the second input parameter of the **Value Mapping (Flattening)** functoid is not passed to the output document.

☑ Note

- If a record in an incoming catalog document instance has more than one field with an attribute that matches the second input parameter of one of the **Equal** functoids in this mapping scenario, only the last record with this match is mapped to the output document. For example, in the previous example of a Commerce Server catalog, if there were three Field elements in the first Record element that had Name attributes with values of X, only the last Field element would map.

For information about mapping from a flat schema to a Commerce Server catalog (mapping in the opposite direction from the previous mapping scenario), see "Using the Looping functoid" later in this chapter.

To add the Value Mapping (Flattening) functoid

1. On the **View** menu, click **Functoid Palette**.

2. On the **Functoid Palette**, click the **Advanced** tab.

   You might need to click the right arrow on the **Functoid Palette** to view the tab.

3. Drag the **Value Mapping (Flattening)** functoid ⮡ from the **Functoid Palette** to the mapping grid.

◆ Important

- For information about how to use the **Value Mapping (Flattening)** functoid, see the previous topic, "Using the Value Mapping (Flattening) Functoid."

- To create a link between a functoid and a record, you must enable the **Allow record content links** property. To do this, on the **Tools** menu, click **Options**. In the **BizTalk Mapper Options** dialog box, on the **General** tab, select the **Allow record content links** check box and click **OK**.

☑ Note

- You might need to expand the specification trees to see the records or fields that you want to map. For more information, see "To expand tree items" earlier in this chapter.

Using the Looping Functoid

The **Looping** functoid 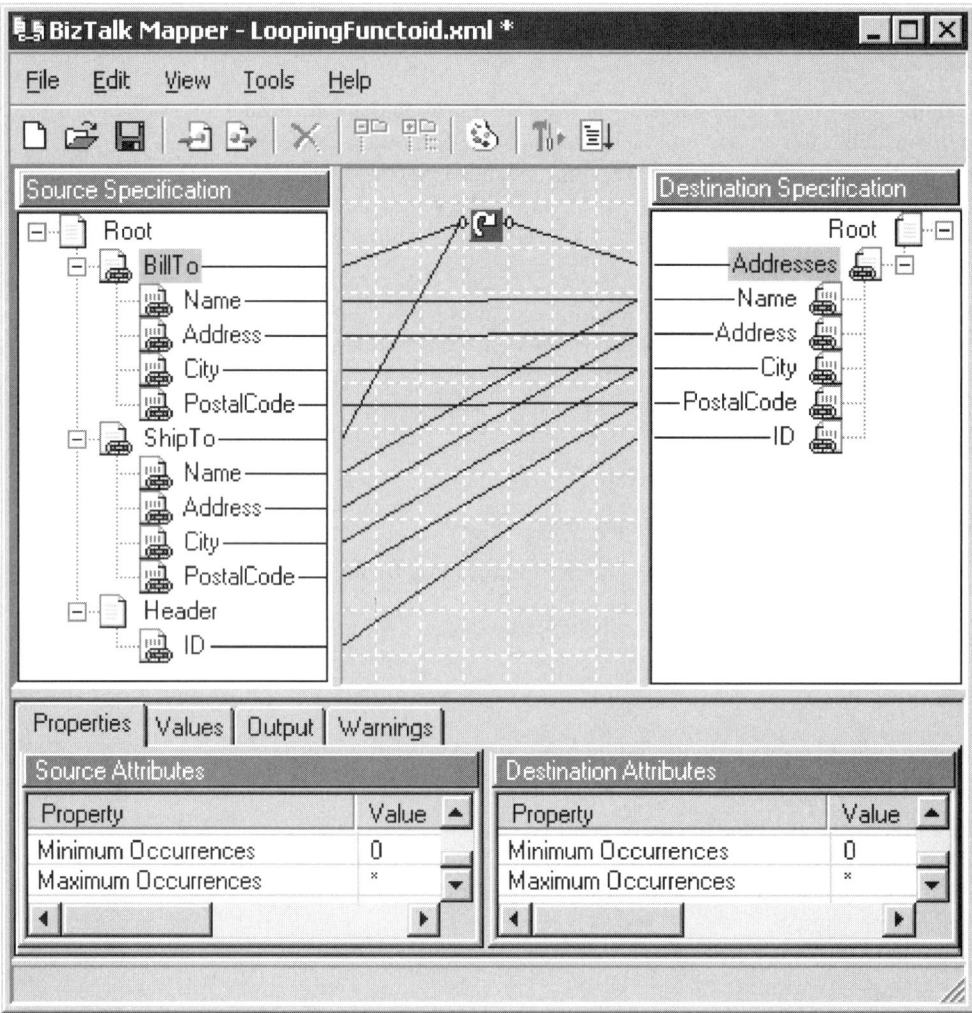 is used to combine multiple records and/or fields in the source specification into a single record in the destination specification. The following illustration shows the **Looping** functoid used in this way.

The BillTo record of the source specification and the Addresses record of the destination specification loop, as indicated by the **Maximum Occurrences** setting of * on the **Source Attributes** and **Destination Attributes** sections of the **Properties** tab. In this example, the ShipTo and Header records of the source specification also loop. If an incoming document instance had three BillTo records and two ShipTo records, the **Looping** functoid would combine these to create five Addresses records in the outgoing document.

The following code is a sample incoming document instance:

```
<Root>
<BillTo Name="Kim Yoshida" Address="345 North 63rd Street"
City="Boston" PostalCode="07458"></BillTo>
<BillTo Name="Michelle Votava" Address="7890 Broadway"
City="Columbus" PostalCode="46290"></BillTo>
<BillTo Name="Tanya Van Dam" Address="1234 Main Street"
City="Denver" PostalCode="97402"></BillTo>
<ShipTo Name="Patricia Esack" Address="456 First Avenue"
City="Miami" PostalCode="81406"></ShipTo>
<ShipTo Name="Peter Kress" Address="567 2nd Avenue"
City="Seattle" PostalCode="98103"></ShipTo>
<Header ID="01"></Header>
<Header ID="02"></Header>
<Header ID="03"></Header>
</Root>
```

This incoming document instance would produce the following outgoing document instance when processed by the map shown in the previous illustration:

```
<Root>
<Addresses Name="Kim Yoshida" Address="345 North 63rd Street"
City="Boston" PostalCode="07458" ID="01" />
<Addresses Name="Michelle Votava" Address="7890 Broadway"
City="Columbus" PostalCode="46290" ID="01" />
<Addresses Name="Tanya Van Dam" Address="1234 Main Street"
City="Denver" PostalCode="97402" ID="01" />
<Addresses Name="Patricia Esack" Address="456 First Avenue"
City="Miami" PostalCode="81406" ID="01" />
<Addresses Name="Peter Kress" Address="567 2nd Avenue"
City="Seattle" PostalCode="98103" ID="01" />
</Root>
```

Notice that in each Addresses record created in the outgoing document instance, the value of the ID field is "01". This is because the Header record is not connected to the **Looping** functoid. The first ID field value of the incoming document instance is passed to each record created in the outgoing document instance.

◈ Important

- Under certain conditions, some functoids might not behave as expected when they are used in a map with a **Looping** functoid. If a functoid meets the following conditions, it does not produce the expected results:

  - The functoid has more than one source specification link.

  - Two or more of the functoid's source specification links are linked to child fields of the **Looping** functoid's input records. The child fields are not siblings.

  - The functoid has a destination specification link that is linked to a child field of the **Looping** functoid's output record.

If you were to add a functoid that met these conditions to the previous map, the functoid might have one source specification link connected to the Name field under the BillTo record, another source specification link connected to the Name field under the ShipTo record, and a destination specification link connected to the Name field under the Addresses record.

Flat schema to Commerce Server catalog

You can use the **Looping** functoid to map a flat schema to a Microsoft Commerce Server catalog. For more information about flat schemas and Commerce Server catalogs, see "Using the Value Mapping (Flattening) Functoid" earlier in this chapter.

The following illustration shows a flat schema mapped to a Commerce Server catalog.

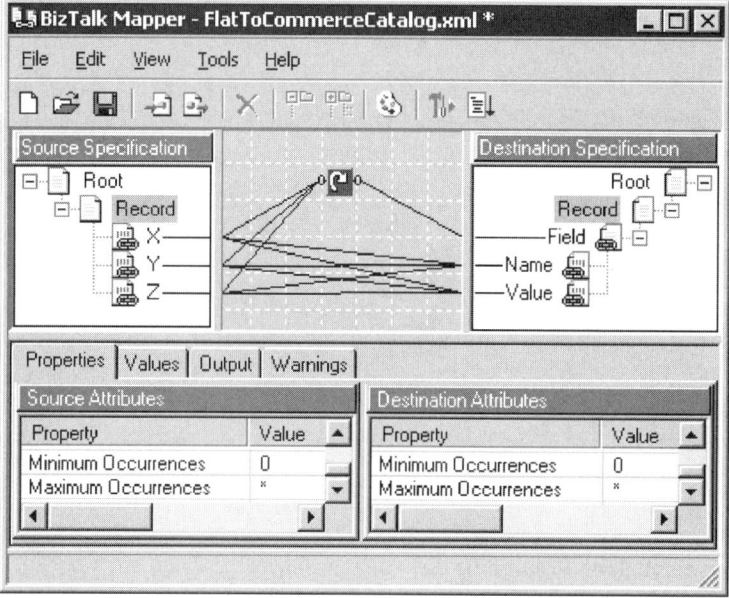

◆ Important

- For this map to work correctly, you must do the following:

  - For each link that connects to the Name field in the destination specification, set the source-specification link properties to copy the name. For more information, see "To select compiler properties for source-specification links" later in this chapter.

    For each link that connects to the Value field in the destination specification, set the source-specification link properties to copy the value. For more information, see "To select compiler properties for source-specification links" later in this chapter.

    For the link that connects the **Looping** functoid to the record named Field in the destination specification, set destination-specification link properties to match links top-down. For more information, see "To select compiler properties for destination-specification links" later in this chapter.

- Ensure that **Allow multiple inputs to destination tree nodes** is selected in the **BizTalk Mapper Options** dialog box. For more information, see "BizTalk Mapper Options: General Tab" earlier in this chapter.

To add the Looping functoid

1. On the **View** menu, click **Functoid Palette**.

2. On the **Functoid Palette**, click the **Advanced** tab.

   You might need to click the right arrow on the **Functoid Palette** to view the tab.

3. Drag the **Looping** functoid ▣ from the **Functoid Palette** to the mapping grid.

◆ **Important**

- For information about how to use the **Looping** functoid, see the previous topic, "Using the Looping Functoid."

- To create a link between a functoid and a record, you must enable the **Allow record content links** property. To do this, on the **Tools** menu, click **Options**. In the **BizTalk Mapper Options** dialog box, on the **General** tab, select the **Allow record content links** check box and click **OK**.

✎ **Note**

- You might need to expand the specification trees to see the records or fields that you want to map. For more information, see "To expand tree items" earlier in this chapter.

Using Cascading Functoids

Cascading functoids enable you to create maps for which you must link fields or records to multiple functoids to produce the necessary output in a field or record in the destination specification. Cascading functoids make it easy to create multiple, consecutive transformations in the mapping grid. Functoids are cascaded when one functoid is linked to another functoid before it is linked to a record or field in the destination specification. For example, you can create cascading functoids in which two concatenated strings are used to produce a third string that is fed into a field in the destination specification. There is no limit to the number of functoids you can cascade together in the mapping grid; however, complex cascading scenarios might result in poor performance.

Edit Functoid Properties

- To view the **Functoid Properties** dialog box, right-click a functoid in the mapping grid and click **Properties**.

Notes

- You also can double-click a functoid to view its properties.

- The **General** tab displays input-parameter information. The **Script** tab displays script information.

For information about how to use this dialog box, see the following topics:

- "Functoid Scripts" later in this chapter

Input Parameters

For information about how to access the **Functoid Properties** dialog box, see the previous topic "Edit Functoid Properties."

Input parameters for many functoids can be added, deleted, and moved up and down on the **General** tab of the **Functoid Properties** dialog box.

Note

- Some functoids have limits on the number of parameters they can have. Information about how many parameters a particular functoid can have can be found beneath the **Input parameters** area on the **General** tab of the **Functoid Properties** dialog box for that functoid.

To insert input parameters

1. Double-click a functoid in the mapping grid.

   The **Functoid Properties** dialog box appears.

2. On the **General** tab, click the **Insert New Parameter** button ▥, type the information for the new parameter, and then press ENTER.

   ### Note

   - If the **Insert New Parameter** button is unavailable, the functoid does not accept or require input parameters.

3. Repeat step 2 to add additional parameters, if necessary.

4. Click **OK**.

Important

- Double quotation marks are not supported within a constant value for an input parameter.

To delete input parameters

1. Double-click a functoid in the mapping grid.

2. On the **General** tab, in the **Input parameters** area, click the input parameter you want to delete.

3. Click the **Delete Selected Parameter** button ⊠ and click **OK**.

To move input parameters

1. Double-click a functoid in the mapping grid.

2. On the **General** tab, in the **Input parameters** area, click the input parameter you want to move.

3. Click the **Move Up Selected Parameter** button ⬆ to move the parameter up, or click the **Move Down Selected Parameter** button ⬇ to move the parameter down, and click **OK**.

To rename input parameters

1. Double-click a functoid in the mapping grid.

2. On the **General** tab, in the **Input parameters** area, right-click the input parameter you want to rename and click **Change Value**.

3. Type a new parameter name and click **OK**.

Functoid Scripts

For information about how to access the **Functoid Properties** dialog box, see "Edit Functoid Properties" earlier in this chapter.

You can view or edit scripts on the **Script** tab of the **Functoid Properties** dialog box.

📝 Note

- You can view the script for any functoid, but you can edit only the script of a **Scripting** functoid.

Creating Links

Links perform the basic function of copying data from the Source Specification tree records and fields to the Destination Specification tree records and fields. BizTalk Mapper supports one-to-one links and one-to-many links. For example, a link can join a single record or field from the Source Specification tree to a single record or field in the Destination Specification tree. A link can also join a single record of a field from the Source Specification tree to multiple records or fields in the Destination Specification tree. Links can also join multiple records or fields from the Source Specification tree to a functoid, which then joins to a single record or field in the Destination Specification tree. Multiple records or fields from the Source Specification tree can join to a single record or field in the Destination Specification tree.

To create links between fields

- Drag a field from the Source Specification tree to a field in the Destination Specification tree.

◆ Important

- The data type of a field in the source specification should match the data type of a field to which it is linked in the destination specification.

✎ Notes

- You cannot link to a node in a destination specification that has a destination constant value associated with it.

- You cannot link to a required field in a destination specification that has a default value associated with it. For more information about making a field required, see "To set reference properties" in Chapter 5, "Creating Specifications." For more information about setting the default value of a field, see "To set declaration properties" in Chapter 5, "Creating Specifications."

- You might need to expand the specification trees to view the fields that you want to map. For more information, see "To expand tree items" earlier in this chapter.

To create links between fields and functoids

- Drag a field from the Source Specification tree or the Destination Specification tree to a functoid in the mapping grid.

    -Or-

    Drag the functoid from the mapping grid to a field in the Source Specification tree or Destination Specification tree.

◆ Important

- A field with a certain data type property in the Destination Specification of a map should not be linked to a functoid that produces output of a different data type.

✎ Notes

- You must first add a functoid to the mapping grid before you can add a link from a field to the functoid. For more information about adding a functoid to the mapping grid, see "Work with the Functoid Palette" earlier in this chapter.

- You cannot link to a node (in a destination specification) that has a destination constant value associated with it.

- You cannot link to a required field (in a destination specification) that has a default value associated with it. For more information about making a field required, see "To set reference properties" in Chapter 5, "Creating Specifications." For more information about setting the default value of a field, see "To set declaration properties" in Chapter 5, "Creating Specifications."

To create links between records and fields

1. On the **Tools** menu, click **Options**.

2. In the **BizTalk Mapper Options** dialog box, select the **Allow record content links** check box and click **OK**.

3. Drag a record from the Source Specification tree to a field in the Destination Specification tree.

   –Or–

   Drag a record from the Destination Specification tree to a field in the Source Specification tree.

Notes

- You cannot link to a node in a destination specification that has a destination constant value associated with it.

- You cannot link to a required field in a destination specification that has a default value associated with it. For more information about making a field required, see "To set reference properties" in Chapter 5, "Creating Specifications." For more information about setting the default value of a field, see "To set declaration properties" in Chapter 5, "Creating Specifications."

- You might need to expand the specification trees to see the records and fields that you want to map. For more information, see "To expand tree items" earlier in this chapter.

To create links between records and functoids

1. On the **Tools** menu, click **Options**.

   The **BizTalk Mapper Options** dialog box appears.

2. Select the **Allow record content links** check box and click **OK**.

3. Drag a record from the Source Specification tree or the Destination Specification tree to a functoid in the mapping grid.

   -Or-

   Drag the functoid from the mapping grid to a record in the Source Specification tree or Destination Specification tree.

Notes

- You must first add a functoid to the mapping grid before you can add a link from a record to the functoid.

- You cannot link to a node in a destination specification that has a destination constant value associated with it. For more information about destination constant values, see "BizTalk Mapper User Interface" earlier in this chapter.

To create links between functoids

- Drag one functoid to another functoid in the mapping grid.

🗹 Note

- Links are processed left to right in the mapping grid. You cannot make a link from one functoid to another functoid directly above or below it.

To allow record content links

1. On the **Tools** menu, click **Options**.

   The **BizTalk Mapper Options** dialog box appears.

2. Select the **Allow record content links** check box and click **OK**.

3. Drag a record from the Source Specification tree to a record in the Destination Specification tree.

To redirect links

1. In the mapping grid, click a link to highlight it.

   The endpoints of the links are highlighted with small blue boxes.

2. Drag either endpoint to the functoid or node to which you want to connect.

   As you drag an endpoint, the pointer becomes a crosshair. If you point to an object to which a link cannot be made, the pointer becomes a circle with a line through it.

◈ Important

- If you have two or more source links connected to a functoid and you redirect one or more of those source links to different nodes in the source specification, the order of the functoid's input parameters might not be preserved. Double-click the functoid to view its input parameters and ensure that they are in the correct order.

To delete links

1. Right-click the link you want to delete and click **Delete**.

2. Click **Yes** in the confirmation dialog box.

Related Topics

"Summary of Data Types and Data Type Values" in Chapter 5, "Creating Specifications"

"To add constant values" later in this chapter

"To set declaration properties" in Chapter 5, "Creating Specifications"

"To set reference properties" in Chapter 5, "Creating Specifications"

"Work with the Functoid Palette" earlier in this chapter

Editing Link Properties

- To view the **Link Properties** dialog box, right-click a link in the mapping grid and click **Properties**.

  The **General** tab appears by default.

🖉 **Note**

- You also can double-click a link to view its properties.

View Link Properties: General Tab

The **General** tab displays information about the source and destination of a link. The **Source** area displays the record path, field path, or functoid name for the link source, depending on whether the link source is a record, a field, or a functoid. The **Destination** area displays the record path, field path, or functoid name for the link destination, depending on whether the link destination is a record, a field, or a functoid.

View Link Properties: Compiler Tab

The **Compiler** tab displays an area for setting compiler properties for source-specification links and an area for setting compiler properties for destination-specification links.

To select compiler properties for source-specification links

1. Right-click a link in the mapping grid that is connected to a node in the source specification and click **Properties**.

2. Click the **Compiler** tab and click one of the following options in the **Source specification links** area:

   - **Copy value (default).** Copies the value of the node in the incoming document instance.

   - **Copy name.** Copies the name of the node in the incoming document instance.

3. Click **OK**.

To select compiler properties for destination-specification links

1. Right-click a link in the mapping grid that is connected to a node in the destination specification and click **Properties**.

2. Click the **Compiler** tab and select one of the following options in the **Destination specification links** area:

   - **Flatten links (default).** This mode means that the source and destination specifications match and that a one-to-one link is created for each record and field.

- **Match links top-down.** This mode matches level to level from the top down.

- **Match links bottom-up.** This mode matches level to level from the bottom up.

3. Click **OK**.

☑ Notes

- If you use a flatten compiler directive, a top-down compiler directive, and a bottom-up compiler directive for links from fields in the source specification to fields in the destination specification that share the same parent record, BizTalk Mapper treats all the links as if they were set to the flatten compiler directive.

- If you use one or more flatten compiler directives and a top-down compiler directive for links from fields in the source specification to fields in the destination specification that share the same parent record, BizTalk Mapper treats all the links as if they were set to the top-down compiler directive.

- If you use one or more flatten compiler directives and a bottom-up compiler directive for links from fields in the source specification to fields in the destination specification that share the same parent record, BizTalk Mapper treats all the links as if they were set to the bottom-up compiler directive.

- If you use one or more top-down compiler directives and one or more bottom-up compiler directives for links from fields in the source specification to fields in the destination specification that share the same parent record, BizTalk Mapper treats all the links as if they were set to the flatten compiler directive.

Related Topics

"Compiling Maps" later in this chapter

"Matching Node-Hierarchy Levels" later in this chapter

Viewing Record, Field, Link, and Functoid Properties

The source specification and destination specification display the records and fields associated with a specification. You can build these specifications using BizTalk Editor, or you can import them into BizTalk Editor as well-formed XML, a document type definition (DTD), or an XDR schema. The source specification appears on the left of the mapping grid, and the destination specification appears on the right of the mapping grid.

Record and field properties and values

The properties and values for records and fields appear on the **Properties** tab, which is located below the main pane. When you select a record or field, the key properties and values from the property tabs of BizTalk Editor appear.

Link and functoid properties

The mapping grid of BizTalk Mapper graphically depicts the structure of the data transformation. Links appear as a single line that connects a record or field in the Source Specification tree to a record or field in the Destination Specification tree. Links are also used to connect a record or field to a functoid. Functoids appear as icons. Properties for links include source and destination data and compiler directive information. Properties for functoids include input parameter and script information.

To view record and field properties

- Click a record or field in either the Source Specification tree or the Destination Specification tree and, on the **View** menu, click **Properties**.

  –Or–

  Click a record or field in either tree and click the **Properties** tab.

Note

- You might need to drag the scroll bar on the **Properties** tab to view a specific property and its associated value.

To view namespaces

You can view the namespaces in a map by viewing the map in Microsoft Internet Explorer 5 or later.

1. Start Internet Explorer and browse to the map file that you want to open.

2. Scroll to the first <schema> tag (directly following the <srctree> tag) to view namespace information for the source specification.

3. Scroll to the second <schema> tag (directly following the <sinktree> tag) to view namespace information for the destination specification.

Related Topics

"Namespace Declarations" in Chapter 5, "Creating Specifications"

"Records, Fields, and Properties" in Chapter 5, "Creating Specifications"

"Understanding Functoids" earlier in this chapter

Mapping Scenarios

BizTalk Server processes a map predictably, according to the way the map is created. The next two sections describe the following mapping scenarios:

- **Loop paths.** A loop path occurs in a map when a field that is contained by a looping record in the source specification is linked to a field that is contained by a looping record in the destination specification.

- **Record and field order.** Records and fields are output according to the way the destination specification is constructed.

Loop Paths

A record in a specification is looping if the **Maximum Occurrences** property on the **Reference** tab for that record is set to *. For more information about the **Maximum Occurrences** property, see "To set reference properties" in Chapter 5, "Creating Specifications."

A loop path occurs in a map when a field contained by a looping record in the source specification is linked to a field contained by a looping record in the destination specification. The following illustration shows two loop paths, one from Root\Record1\Field1 to Root\RecordA\Field1, and the other from Root\Record2\Field2 to \Root\RecordB\Field3.

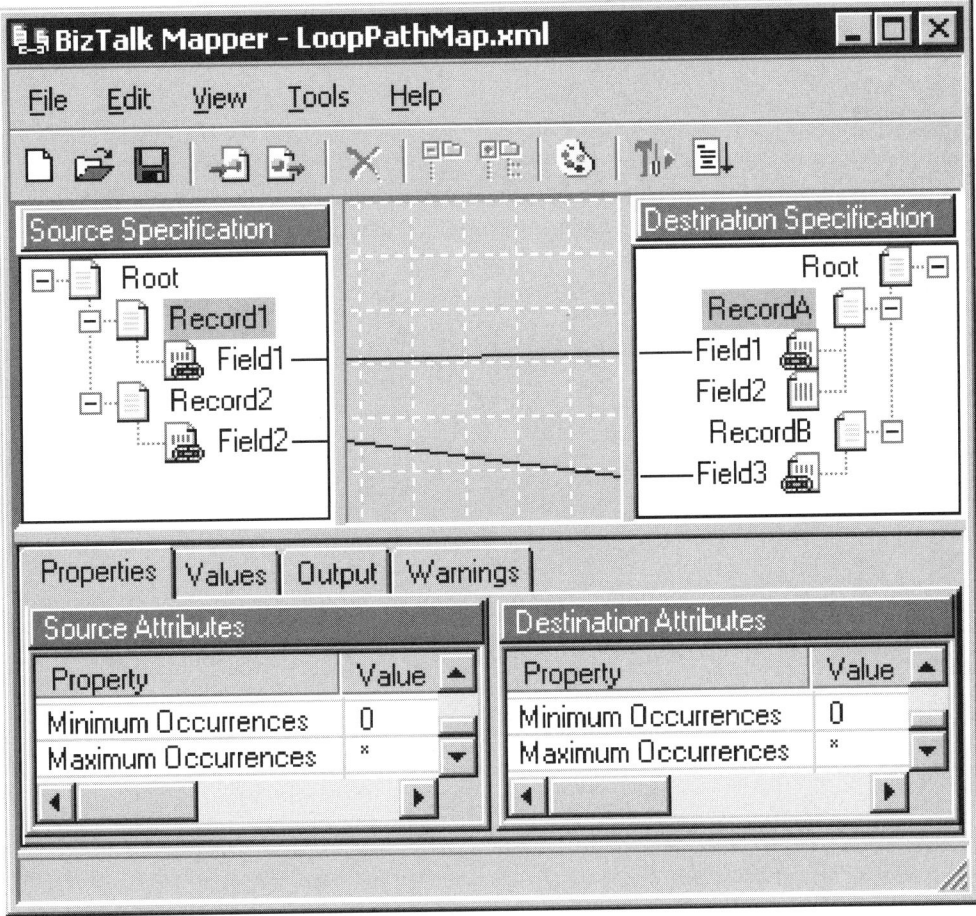

The **Properties** tab shows Record1 and RecordA to be looping. Record2 and RecordB are also looping.

The following code is a sample input document:

```
<Root>
<Record1 Field1=Red>
<Record1 Field1=Green>
<Record1 Field1=Blue>
<Record2 Field2=50>
<Record2 Field2=100>
</Root>
```

Using the previous map, this input document would map to the following output document:

```
<Root>
<RecordA Field1=Red>
<RecordA Field1=Green>
<RecordA Field1=Blue>
<RecordB Field3=50>
<RecordB Field3=100>
</Root>
```

A multiple loop path occurs in a map when fields contained by two or more looping records in the source specification are linked to fields contained by a single looping record in the destination specification.

The following illustration shows an example of a multiple loop path.

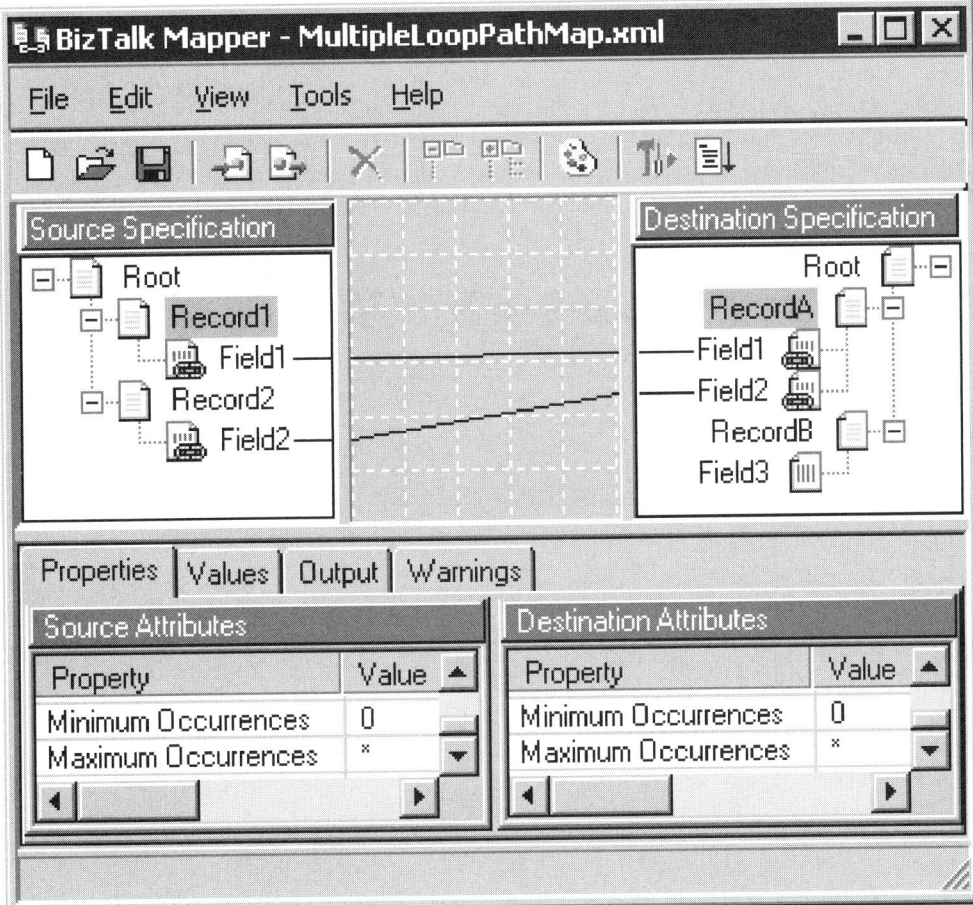

Multiple loop paths are not supported in BizTalk Mapper. If you attempt to compile a map that contains a multiple loop path, the **Warnings** tab indicates that the destination node has multiple source loop paths.

Related Topics

"BizTalk Mapper Options: General Tab" earlier in this chapter

"To set reference properties" in Chapter 5, "Creating Specifications"

"View Link Properties: Compiler Tab" earlier in this chapter

Ordering of Records and Fields

Implied order of output records and fields is not guaranteed in Extensible Stylesheet Language (XSL). This is because BizTalk Mapper generates XSL by walking the destination specification structure and then propagating back through the mapping grid to extract values from the source specification structure. For example, if you want to create an output file that has BillTo Address records listed first, followed by ShipTo Address records, you must ensure that the BillTo Address precedes the ShipTo Address record in the destination specification.

The following illustration shows this structure.

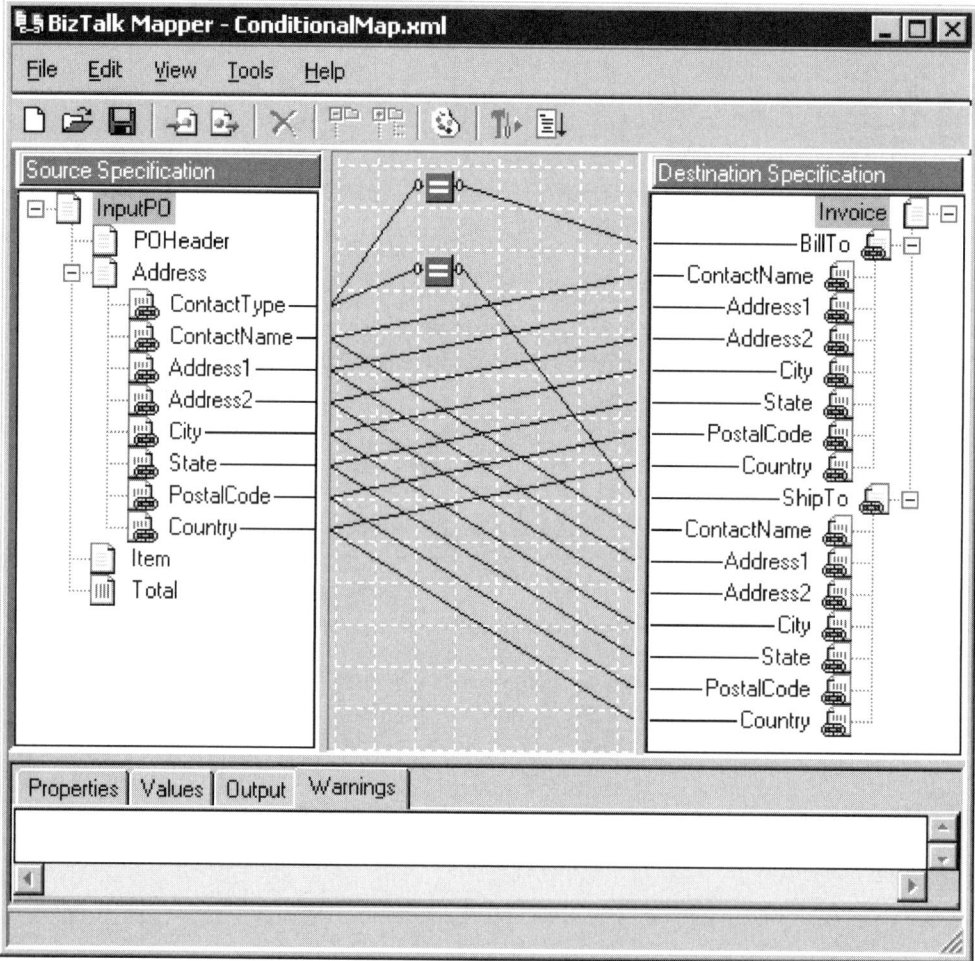

The ContactType field contains two valid codes (BT and ST) that identify the address as either a BillTo address or a ShipTo address. To create the desired output, **Equal** functoids are added to the mapping grid and linked from fields in the source specification to records in the destination specification.

In the map, the first functoid checks for the following condition:

Is ContactType equal to BT?

If this condition is satisfied, an output record, BillToAddresses, is created and the required fields are mapped to it. If the condition is not met, BizTalk Mapper must reiterate all the input address records.

♦ Important

- The order in which records and fields appear in an output document instance is dependent on the order of the records and fields of the corresponding output specification.

Compiling Maps

When you compile maps, a visual representation of the transformations is created by the BizTalk Mapper compiler component. This component also generates the run-time Extensible Stylesheet Language (XSL) style sheet. This process creates a map. Compiling a map enforces the structural rules and transformations that are specified in the mapping grid. Transformations, such as links, are processed in the same order that records and fields appear in the instance of the source structure. For example, when BizTalk Mapper reaches a source record or field that has a link associated with it, BizTalk Mapper compiles the properties of the link. The action might be a simple copy value that populates a record or field in the destination specification, or the action might calculate values from one or more records and fields from the source to one or more records and fields in the destination, based on the properties of a functoid. The execution of each link is independent of the execution of other links.

BizTalk Mapper generates a warning on the **Warnings** tab when the compiler encounters a situation that yields incorrect output. For example, if a functoid that requires one input parameter has no input parameters, BizTalk Mapper generates a warning on the **Warnings** tab when the map is compiled. A map must generate no warnings before it is ready for a production environment.

The compiling process stores all information about the source and destination specifications, including all content and functionality of links and objects. The compiled map is used by BizTalk Server to perform the actual translation of an input instance to an output instance.

To compile maps

- On the **Tools** menu, click **Compile Map**.

🌱 Caution

- BizTalk Mapper generates a warning on the **Warnings** tab when the compiler encounters a situation that yields incorrect results. A map must generate no warnings before it can be considered ready for a production environment.

To resolve warnings and errors after compiling a map

1. Double-click a warning on the **Warnings** tab.

   The link or functoid that relates to the warning or error is highlighted in the mapping grid.

2. Modify the link or functoid as needed.

3. Repeat steps 1 and 2 for each warning.

4. On the **Tools** menu, click **Compile Map**.

To add constant values

1. Select a record or field in the Destination Specification tree and click the **Values** tab.

2. In the **Destination constant value** box, type a value that you want associated with the record or field.

Notes

- You cannot create a link to a record or field that has a constant value associated with it.

- You can only associate a constant value with a record with its **Content** property set to Text Only. For more information about the **Content** property, see "To set declaration properties" in Chapter 5, "Creating Specifications."

Matching Node-Hierarchy Levels

BizTalk Mapper includes compiler directives. Using these directives, you can set the level of matching between the hierarchy of the Source Specification tree and the hierarchy of the Destination Specification tree. When you create a link from one field in the Source Specification tree to a field in the Destination Specification tree, BizTalk Mapper automatically adds compiler links based on the choices you make in the **Destination Specification Links** area on the **Compiler** tab of the **Link Properties** dialog box. For more information, see "To select compiler properties for destination-specification links" earlier in this chapter. The following illustrations show the node-hierarchy level matches that are possible.

- **Flatten link (default mode).** This mode means that the parent record for the link has a one-to-one link to each record in the other tree. In the first case, the source specification is more complex than the destination specification. In the second case, the destination specification is more complex.

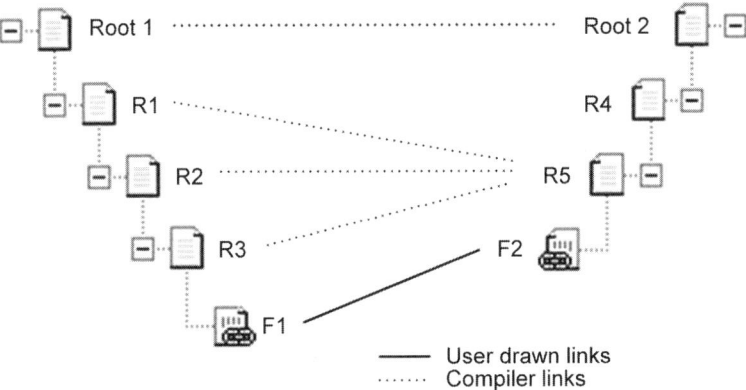

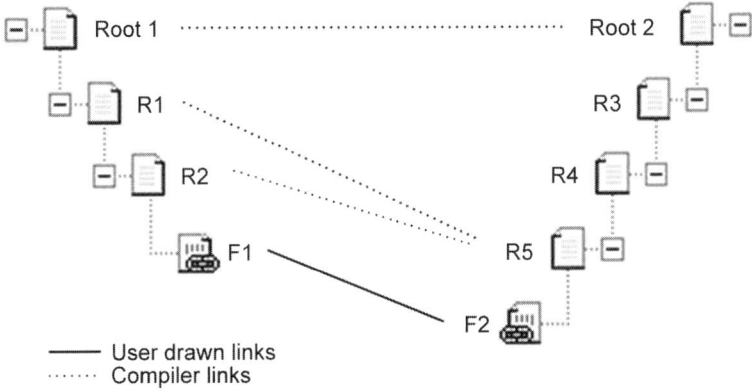

- **Match links top-down.** This mode matches level to level from the top down. In the first case, the source specification is more complex than the destination specification. In the second case, the destination specification is more complex.

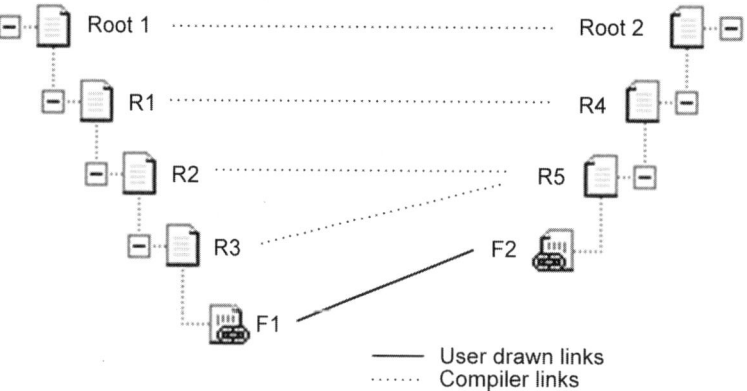

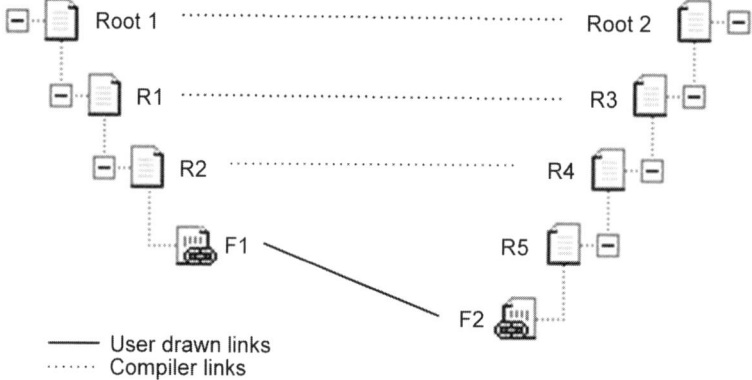

- **Match links bottom-up.** This mode matches level to level from the bottom up. In the first case, the source specification is more complex than the destination specification. In the second case, the destination specification is more complex.

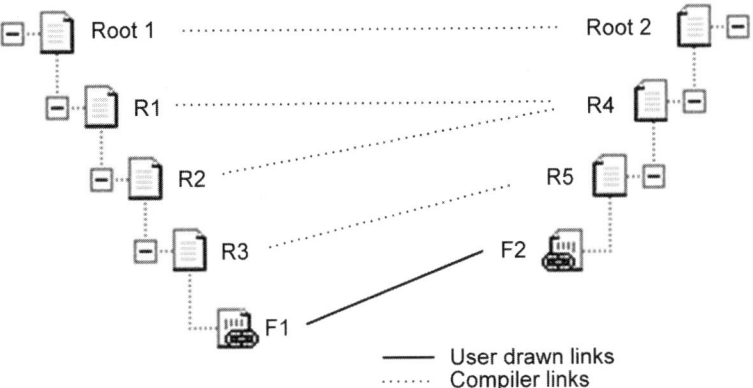

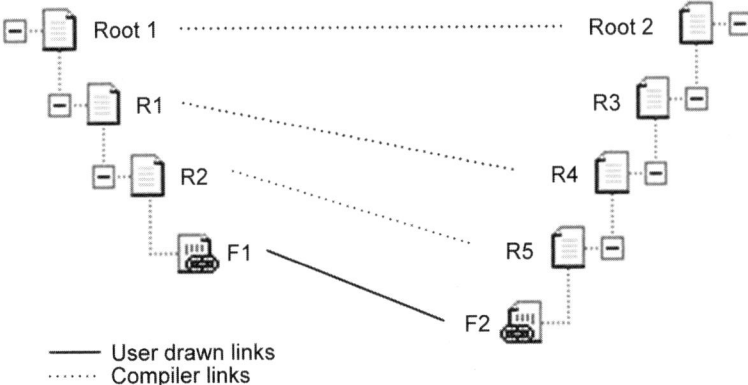

✎ Notes

- If you use a flatten compiler directive, a top-down compiler directive, and a bottom-up compiler directive for links from fields in the source specification to fields in the destination specification that share the same parent record, BizTalk Mapper treats all the links as if they were set to the flatten compiler directive.

- If you use one or more flatten compiler directives and a top-down compiler directive for links from fields in the source specification to fields in the destination specification that share the same parent record, BizTalk Mapper treats all the links as if they were set to the top-down compiler directive.

- If you use one or more flatten compiler directives and a bottom-up compiler directive for links from fields in the source specification to fields in the destination specification that share the same parent record, BizTalk Mapper treats all the links as if they were set to the bottom-up compiler directive.

- If you use one or more top-down compiler directives and one or more bottom-up compiler directives for links from fields in the source specification to fields in the destination specification that share the same parent record, BizTalk Mapper treats all the links as if they were set to the flatten compiler directive.

To save compiled maps

1. On the **File** menu, click **Save Compiled Map As**.

   The **Save Compiled Map As** dialog box appears.

2. In the **File name** box, type a name for the file and click **Save**.

Related Topics

"To set declaration properties" in Chapter 5, "Creating Specifications"

"To store maps" earlier in this chapter

Testing Maps

As you create a map, you can use BizTalk Mapper to verify that the map you designed produces the correct output. The Test Map feature automatically generates a test instance of the source document from the specification. This feature verifies information, such as the number of occurrences of records, data types of fields, and so on, from the specification and generates the test instance. You can specify unique values for any record or field in the **Source test value** box on the **Values** tab and test the results of that data.

When you test a map, BizTalk Mapper automatically compiles it. However, it is best to first compile a map and resolve any warnings or errors prior to testing it. Before the test begins you are prompted to save your file. Saving your file prior to testing it is a precautionary measure to preserve your data in case any problems are accidentally introduced into the map.

After you test a map, the results appear on the **Output** tab. The test data corresponds to the destination specification.

Note

- The BizTalk Mapper map test functionality is limited to testing a map against an automatically generated test document instance. The test document instance is generated by BizTalk Mapper and is based on the source specification. In other words, using BizTalk Mapper you cannot test a map with an actual instance of a business document of your own choosing. However, a sample map test script is included with BizTalk Server that enables you to test a map against a document instance of your choosing. For more information, see \Program Files\Microsoft BizTalk Server\SDK\Messaging Samples\MapTest\Readme.txt.

To test record and field properties that have links

◆ **Important**

- Always compile a map prior to testing it so you can resolve warnings and errors. For more information, see "Compiling Maps" earlier in this chapter.

1. Click a field in the Source Specification tree that is connected to a link.

2. Click the **Values** tab.

3. Type a value in the **Source test value** box.

4. On the **Tools** menu, click **Test Map**.

   ◆ **Important**

   - Before the test begins, you are prompted to save your file. Save your file prior to testing it as a precautionary measure to preserve your data in case any problems are accidentally introduced into the map.

5. Click **Yes** to save the map.

6. Verify the results on the **Output** tab.

📝 **Note**

- If the **Maximum Occurrences** property for a record is an asterisk (*), this indicates that it is a looping record. The incoming document instance that BizTalk Mapper generates to test the map contains two occurrences of the record.

To test links

◆ **Important**

- Always compile a map prior to testing it so you can resolve warnings and errors. For more information, see "Compiling Maps" earlier in this chapter.

1. Click a field in the Source Specification tree that is connected to a link.

2. Click the **Values** tab.

3. Type a value in the **Source test value** box.

4. On the **Tools** menu, click **Test Map**.

   ◆ **Important**

   - Before the test begins, you are prompted to save your file. Save your file prior to testing it as a precautionary measure to preserve your data in case any problems are accidentally introduced into the map.

5. Click **Yes** to save the map.

6. Verify the results on the **Output** tab.

To test functoids

◆ Important

- Always compile a map prior to testing it so you can resolve warnings and errors. For more information, see "Compiling Maps" earlier in this chapter.

1. On the **Tools** menu, click **Test Map**.

   ### ◆ Important

   - Before the test begins, you are prompted to save your file. Save your file prior to testing it as a precautionary measure to preserve your data in case any problems are accidentally introduced into the map.

2. Click **Yes** to save the map.

3. Verify the results on the **Output** tab.

Related Topic

"Compiling Maps" earlier in this chapter

Maps for Integrating BizTalk Services

When you integrate BizTalk Orchestration Services and BizTalk Messaging Services using a non-HTTP transport, you might need to create a map to convert a path name to a format name. For more information, see Chapter 14, "Orchestrating Business Processes with Microsoft BizTalk Server 2000."

Converting a path name to a format name

The following code is an example of a messaging queue path name:

```
private$\sourcechannel2{9e0016bf-be1f-48fe-82de-b27077ab5e73}
```

To convert this path name to a format name, you need to add the following string to the beginning of the path name:

```
queue://Direct=OS:
```

You can easily do this with the **Concatenate** functoid.

The following illustration shows a map that uses the **Concatenate** functoid, which concatenates two or more strings. For more information about the **Concatenate** functoid, see "String Functoids" earlier in this chapter.

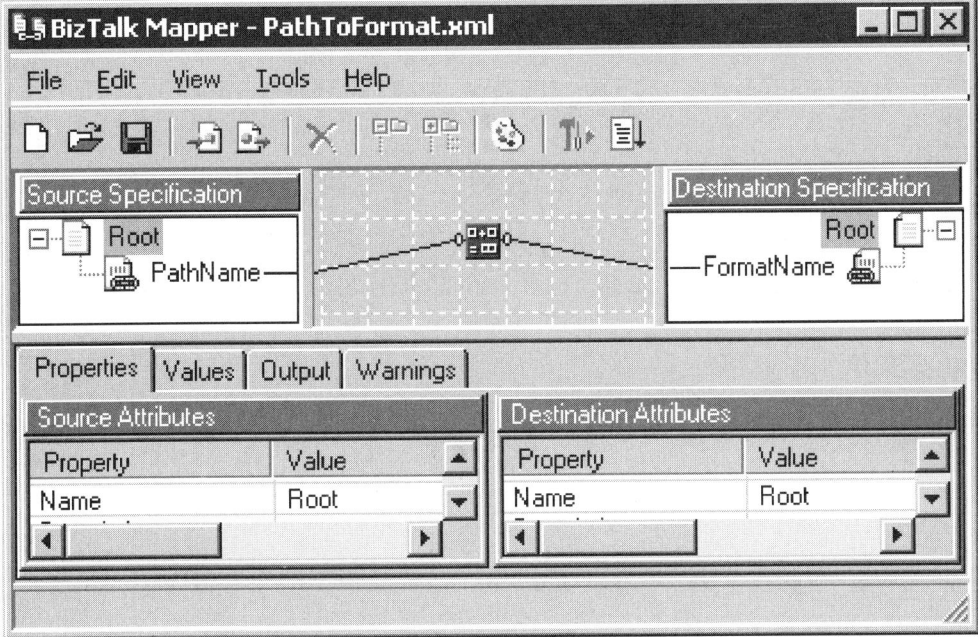

Double-clicking the **Concatenate** functoid displays its properties. The following illustration shows how the properties should look for a **Concatenate** functoid in a map that adds the `queue://Direct=OS:` prefix to the `private$\sourcechannel2{9e0016bf-be1f-48fe-82de-b27077ab5e73}` path name.

For more information, see "Edit Functoid Properties" earlier in this chapter.

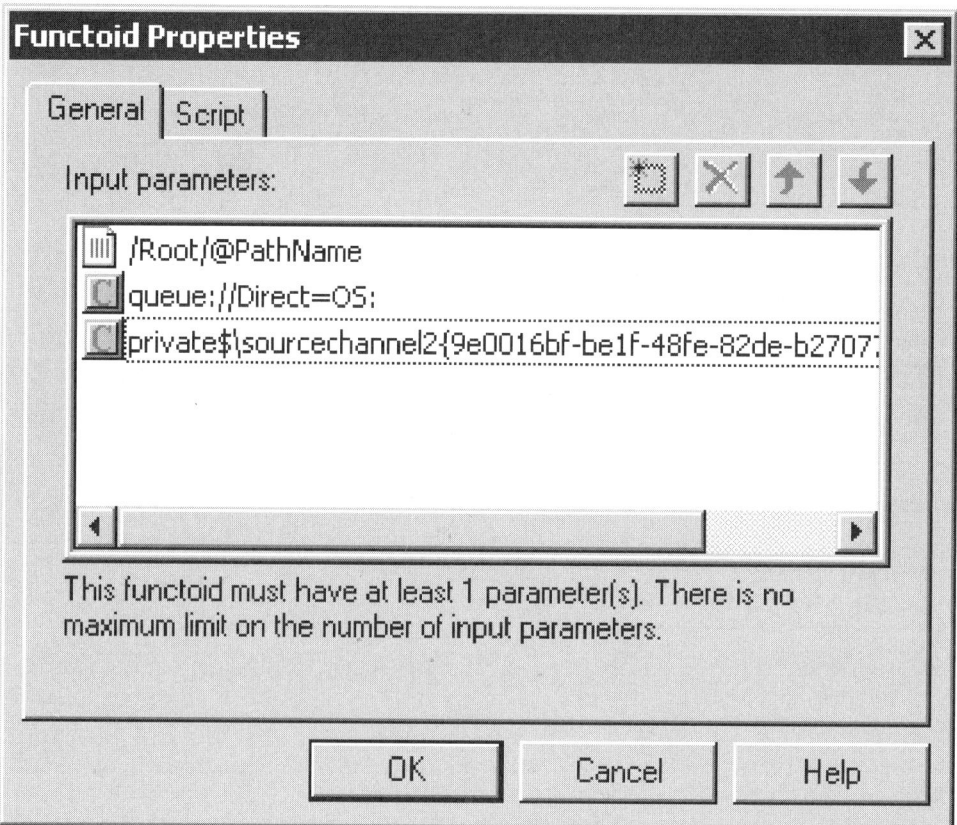

Troubleshooting BizTalk Mapper

This section provides a centralized location for information related to troubleshooting BizTalk Mapper. If you are having difficulty with BizTalk Mapper, try to find a solution in this section.

Password required when trying to connect to a remote WebDAV server

Cause: User might not have access to the BizTalkServerRepository folder.

Solution: Provide user with access to the BizTalkServerRepository folder. To do this:

1. Click **Start**, point to **Programs**, point to **Administrative Tools**, and then click **Internet Services Manager**.

2. In the console tree, expand the name of the computer.

3. Expand **Default Web Site**.

4. Right-click **BizTalkServerRepository** and click **Properties**.

   The **BizTalkServerRepository Properties** dialog box appears.

5. Click the **Directory Security** tab.

6. In the **Anonymous access and authentication control** area, click **Edit**.

7. Select the **Anonymous Access** check box and click **OK** twice.

Failure to connect to WebDAV or to store files to WebDAV

Cause One: If you attempt to retrieve a map or a specification from WebDAV, or store a map or specification to WebDAV, you might see one of the following messages:

   The file cannot be stored in the WebDAV repository. The server may not be available at this time.

   No key matching the described characteristics could be found within the current range.

   This occurs when the anonymous setting for the user account on the Web server does not have write privileges on the Microsoft Windows 2000 directory that hosts the repository.

Solution: Give user access to the repository. To do this:

1. Click **Start**, point to **Programs**, point to **Accessories**, and then click **Windows Explorer**.

2. Navigate to the location in which you installed Microsoft BizTalk Server 2000.

3. Expand the **Microsoft BizTalk Server** directory, right-click **BizTalkServerRepository**, and then click **Properties**.

   The **BizTalkServerRepository Properties** dialog box appears.

4. Click the **Security** tab.

5. Click **Add** and type the domain name and the user name for the person you want to have permission to the repository in the following format: *domain name\user name*.

6. Click **OK** twice.

Cause Two: If you attempt to retrieve a map or a specification from WebDAV, or store a map or specification to WebDAV, you might see the following message:

   No BizTalk Server repository was found on http://localhost/BizTalkServerRepository/DocSpecs. Enter another server name to retry the WebDAV connection.

This occurs when FrontPage Server Extensions are enabled on the Web Server.

Solution: Disable FrontPage Server Extensions. If the World Wide Web Publishing service is running, stop and restart this service.

📝 **Note**

- This problem can occur even if the World Wide Web Publishing Service is not running on the computer hosting the WebDAV repository.

To disable FrontPage Server Extensions

1. Click **Start**, point to **Programs**, point to **Administrative Tools**, and then click **Internet Services Manager.**

2. In the details pane, double-click *<name of the computer>*, right-click **Default Web Site**, and then click **Properties**.

   The **Default Web Site Properties** dialog box appears.

3. On the **Server Extensions** tab, clear the **Enable authoring** check box and click **OK**.

To stop and restart the World Wide Web Publishing Service

1. Click **Start**, point to **Programs**, point to **Administrative Tools**, and then click **Component Services**.

2. In the console tree, click **Services (local)**.

3. In the details pane, right-click **World Wide Web Publishing Service** and click **Stop**.

4. Right-click **World Wide Web Publishing Service** and click **Start**.

???.xml appears in the WebDAV dialog box

Cause: The set of characters that is displayed for your computer is dependent on the locale setting specified in BizTalk Server.

Solution: Specify the same character set for your computer as for the locale setting specified in BizTalk Server. To do this:

1. Click **Start**, point to **Settings**, and then click **Control Panel**.

2. Double-click **Regional Options**.

3. On the **General** tab, in the **Language settings for the system** area, select the check box for the desired language and click **Set Default**.

   The **Select System Locale** dialog box appears.

4. Click the desired locale in the list and click **OK** twice.

   The **Change Regional Options** dialog box appears.

5. Click **Yes** to accept the changes and restart your computer.

✎ Note

- After restarting your computer, the selected language in the **Regional Options** dialog box displays the following information: *Language* (**default**).

BizTalkServerRepositoryMaps folder appears in Retrieve from WebDAV dialog box

Cause: There is a trailing backslash in the **Local Path** box of the **BizTalkServerRepository Properties** dialog box.

Solution: Remove the trailing backslash in the **Local Path** edit box of the **BizTalkServerRepository Properties** dialog box. To do this:

1. On the **Start** menu, point to **Programs**, point to **Administrative Tools**, and then click **Computer Management**.

2. In the Computer Management console, expand **Services and Applications**, expand **Internet Information Services**, and then expand **Default Web Site**.

3. Right-click **BizTalkServerRepository** and click **Properties**.

   The **BizTalkServerRepository Properties** dialog box appears.

4. In the **Local Path** edit box, remove the trailing backslash and click **OK**.

Completing this procedure removes the BizTalkServerRepositoryMaps folder from the **Retrieve from WebDAV** dialog box. This folder is unusable, so it is recommended that you remove it.

Retrieve from WebDAV dialog box or Store to WebDAV dialog box is empty

Cause: Directory browsing is disabled in the **BizTalkServerRepository Properties** dialog box.

Solution: Enable directory browsing in the **BizTalkServerRepository Properties** dialog box. To do this:

1. Click **Start**, point to **Programs**, point to **Administrative Tools**, and then click **Internet Services Manager**.

2. Expand the computer that you are troubleshooting.

3. Expand **Default Web Site**.

4. Right-click **BizTalkServerRepository** and click **Properties**.

   The **BizTalkServerRepository Properties** dialog box appears.

5. On the **Virtual Directory** tab, select **Directory browsing**.

6. Ensure that **Read** and **Write** are also selected and click **OK**.

Failure to connect to http://localhost

Cause: The **Use a proxy server** check box is selected, but the **Bypass proxy server for local addresses** check box is not selected.

Solution: Keep the **Use a proxy server** setting on, and turn on the **Bypass proxy server for local addresses** setting. To do this:

1. Click **Start**, point to **Programs**, and then click **Internet Explorer**.

2. On the **Tools** menu, click **Internet Options**.

   The **Internet Options** dialog box appears.

3. Click the **Connections** tab and click **LAN Settings**.

   The **Local Area Network (LAN) Setting** dialog box appears.

4. In the **Proxy Server** area, select the **Bypass proxy server for local addresses** check box.

5. Click **OK** twice.

✎ Note

- This failure will not occur if you connect to **http://*<name of the computer>***.

Test map fails

Cause: When you test a map, BizTalk Mapper compiles the map before testing it. If a warning occurs during the compile, the test map might not succeed. The following error message appears:

   The Extensible Stylesheet Language (XSL) transformation using the test instance document of the source specification failed.

Solution: Resolve all compiler warnings and then recompile the map. To resolve a compiler warning, complete the following:

1. Double-click the word **Warning** on the **Output** tab.

   This highlights the link or functoid associated with the warning message.

2. Resolve the warning as needed.

To recompile the map:

- On the **Tools** menu, click **Compile Map**.

Using EDI with Microsoft BizTalk Server 2000

Many companies today use electronic data interchange (EDI) to exchange business documents. This chapter discusses how Microsoft BizTalk Server can help both large businesses that are currently using EDI and smaller businesses that do not use EDI but that want to trade with these larger businesses. BizTalk Server can help a company that uses EDI in the following ways:

- **Enabling enterprise application integration (EAI).** BizTalk Server automates the exchange of internal business data.

- **Creating relationships with smaller trading partners.** BizTalk Server provides a cost-effective way to exchange electronic documents with companies that don't use EDI.

- **Facilitating future growth.** BizTalk Server provides a cost-effective way to handle the expansion of a company's messaging and document interchange requirements.

Smaller companies can benefit from BizTalk Server by using it to establish electronic document exchange relationships with larger companies that use both EDI and XML. A smaller company can also streamline its internal business processes by employing the EAI capabilities of BizTalk Server.

The ability of BizTalk Server to translate and transform documents is central to its EAI and document exchange capabilities. This chapter introduces BizTalk Editor and BizTalk Mapper, tools that help to direct the translation and transformation of EDI documents and other electronic documents. BizTalk Editor enables you to create and edit specifications (a BizTalk Server-specific schema). BizTalk Mapper uses specifications to map the structure of one document instance to the structure of another document instance. This chapter compares the relative strengths and weaknesses of BizTalk Server when compared with EDI technology.

In This Chapter

- EDI Overview
- Enhancing an EDI Environment by Using BizTalk Server
- Using BizTalk Server in Smaller Companies
- Translating and Transforming Documents
- Comparing BizTalk Server with EDI Technology
- Conclusion

EDI Overview

Electronic data interchange (EDI) is a set of standards for controlling the exchange of business documents (such as purchase orders and invoices) between computers. Businesses can use EDI to ensure that the documents they exchange are interpreted correctly, regardless of the platforms or internal applications they use. Because EDI enables electronic documents to move from one computer to another without the need for human intervention, it is faster, cheaper, and more accurate than the exchange of paper documents.

Standardization efforts for EDI formats began in the 1960s, led by the transportation industry. The need for a uniform standard that encompassed all industries prompted the creation of the Accredited Standards Committee (ASC) X12, sanctioned by the American National Standards Institute (ANSI), in 1979. The Accredited Standards Committee X12 created the EDI standard commonly referred to as X12, which was used primarily for American domestic trade. Meanwhile, the European community developed its own EDI standard called Guidelines on Trade Data Interchange (GTDI). A new standard that borrowed from both X12 and GTDI, called Electronic Data Interchange for Administration, Commerce, and Transport (EDIFACT), was developed at the United Nations. The International Organization for Standardization (ISO) adopted EDIFACT in 1987. Although in 1992 ASC X12 members approved the adoption of EDIFACT as the universal EDI standard, X12 continues to be a widely used EDI standard in North America.

Although EDI has been around for nearly forty years, it has not triggered an explosion in business-to-business electronic commerce. In fact, the number of businesses trading electronically today compared to those using phone or fax is limited. The reasons for this are numerous and include the following:

- EDI server systems are typically expensive.

- The EDI document format is somewhat cryptic.

- EDI document transport was historically a value-added network (VAN) that incurred both an expensive setup fee and ongoing operational costs.

Enhancing an EDI Environment by Using BizTalk Server

Although many companies have long-term strategies that involve replacing their legacy infrastructure, a company that is heavily invested in EDI might not want to immediately discard its investment and replace it entirely with an XML-based BizTalk Server system. However, BizTalk Server can add a great deal of value to a company that chooses to continue using EDI in the short term. Areas where BizTalk Server can enhance the operations of a company that uses EDI include:

- Enabling enterprise application integration.

- Creating new relationships with smaller trading partners.

- Facilitating future growth.

Enterprise Application Integration

Integrating with business partners is only one of the challenges that face businesses today. Equally important is the integration of internal business applications, such as accounting, inventory, and customer relationship management (CRM) systems.

EDI systems do not typically offer EAI infrastructure, and they support only a limited subset of possible electronic document formats other than EDI. One of the strengths of BizTalk Server is its ability to automate and streamline the flow of a company's business data both internally and externally.

The following illustration shows a simplified representation of how a company that uses EDI might use its EDI server to exchange business documents.

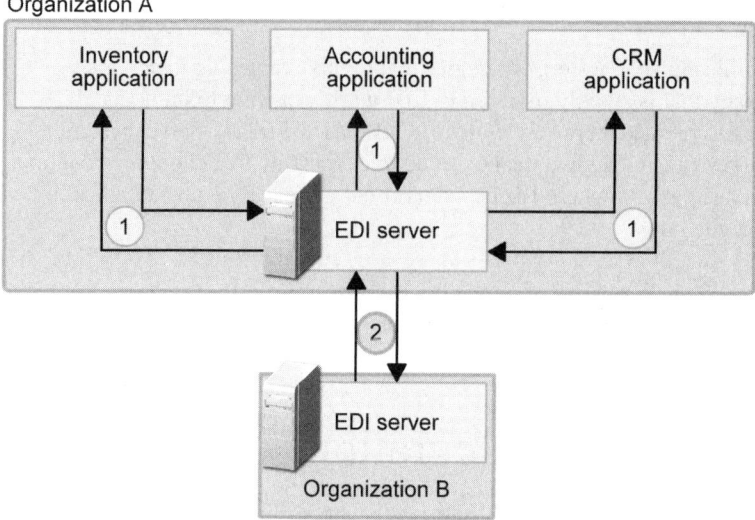

Organization A

Inventory application

Accounting application

CRM application

EDI server

EDI server

Organization B

1 Manual or custom built connections

2 EDI documents over a VAN

Organization A's EDI server sends and receives standard EDI documents to and from Organization B over a VAN. Each transaction over the VAN incurs an expense for Organization A. Organization A's EDI server communicates with its accounting, inventory, and CRM applications either by manual data entry or by custom-built software.

The following illustration shows how a BizTalk Server hub can be added to this system to facilitate the integration of Organization A's internal applications.

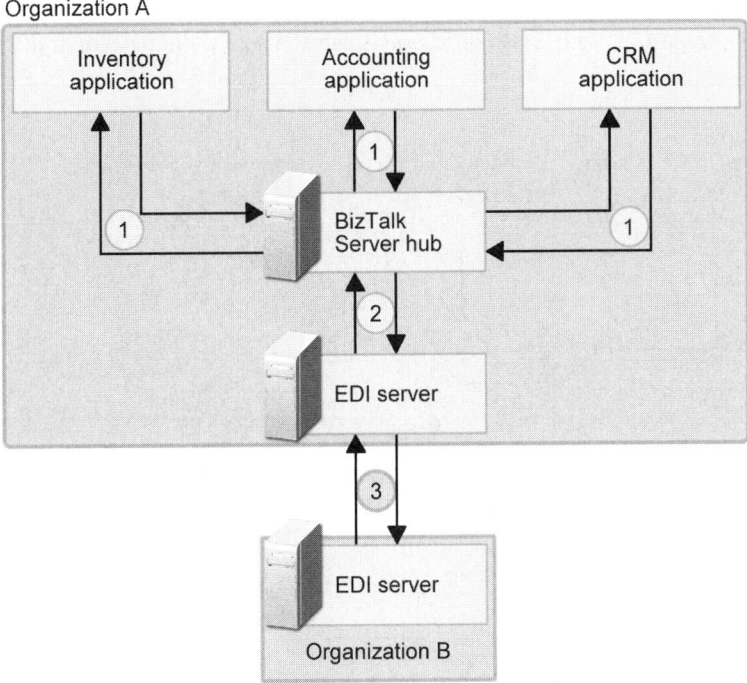

1   Native file formats sent and received by BizTalk Server

2   EDI documents sent and received by BizTalk Server

3   EDI documents over a VAN

In this scenario, BizTalk Server becomes the hub of Organization A's internal data exchange. The BizTalk Server hub provides an accurate and cost-effective way to automatically update the organization's line-of-business applications when a transaction with Organization B occurs. The key to the success of this scenario is the ability of BizTalk Server to be the universal message gateway. BizTalk Server can automatically send data to Organization A's internal applications in XML or flat-file format, or even in custom formats with the introduction of custom parsers and serializers. BizTalk Server uses the TCP/IP communication layer built into Microsoft Windows 2000, which is commonly used for communication between applications in an organization. With BizTalk Server these EAI processes can be put in place at costs far lower than would be possible by paying developers to create custom communications applications. BizTalk Server enables internal data exchange that is far more accurate and efficient than can ever be achieved by manual processes.

New Relationships with Smaller Trading Partners

BizTalk Server makes it easy for a company currently using EDI with trading partners to also exchange documents with smaller trading partners who cannot afford or do not want to use EDI. The following illustration shows how Organization A can add a new trading partner to its existing communications network.

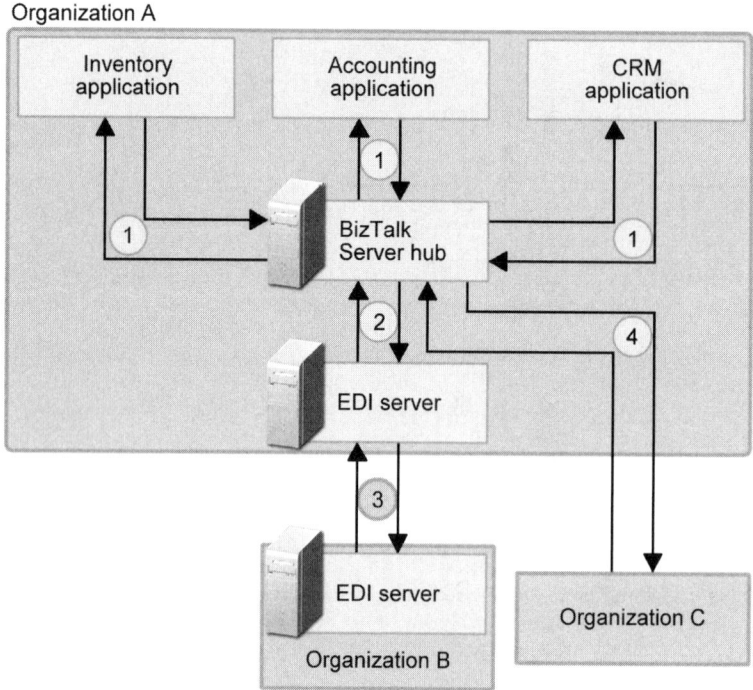

1. Native file formats sent and received by BizTalk Server
2. EDI documents sent and received by BizTalk Server
3. EDI documents over a VAN
4. Native documents through TCP/IP

Organization A's BizTalk Server hub can electronically exchange business documents with Organization C using TCP/IP over the Internet. These documents can be delivered in a format that is easy for Organization C to use, such as XML. In this scenario both Organization A and Organization C enjoy the accuracy and efficiency of the automated exchange of electronic business documents. Neither company needs to incur the high costs of setting up a new EDI relationship or the ongoing expense of a VAN.

Future Growth

Organization A might find that it needs to set up new automated messaging with Organization B beyond what it has implemented with its EDI server. Organization A will find that the least expensive and most direct solution is to use its BizTalk Server hub for exchanging these new messages. In this way it bypasses its EDI server altogether. In time, Organization A might need to make more significant changes in its data-exchange relationship with Organization B. This would be an ideal time for Organization A to forgo its EDI server entirely and replace it with the BizTalk Server hub.

Using BizTalk Server in Smaller Companies

Many smaller companies could benefit from the exchange of electronic business documents with larger companies that use EDI, but they cannot justify the setup and operational costs associated with traditional EDI servers. BizTalk Server provides a cost-effective solution to this problem (and can also be leveraged with trading partners that use XML and other non-EDI formats). BizTalk Server enables a small company to automatically transform its business documents into an electronic format that an EDI server of a larger company can use. The following illustration shows such a relationship.

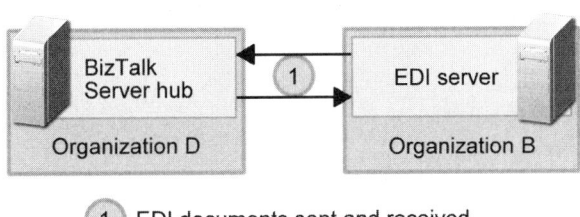

1 EDI documents sent and received by BizTalk Server

Organization D might be so small that it runs its entire business on Microsoft Office, or it might use another business tools suite that can read and write XML documents or provide adapters for BizTalk Server. BizTalk Server can process Organization D's documents and transport them to and from the EDI server of Organization B. Organization D might have BizTalk Server and other business applications installed on a single computer, or it might be a larger company with business applications distributed across several computers. In either case, Organization D's BizTalk Server hub can serve the dual purpose of exchanging EDI documents with Organization B and automatically integrating the flow of internal business data within the company.

Translating and Transforming Documents

A key strength of BizTalk Server is its ability to accept input in a wide variety of document formats, map that input into almost any document structure, and then output the new document structure into a wide variety of document formats. XML is central to the translation and transformation capabilities of BizTalk Server, which is in large part what makes BizTalk Server such a powerful tool for enterprise application integration and business-to-business electronic commerce.

The following illustration and accompanying list show how BizTalk Server internally processes a document.

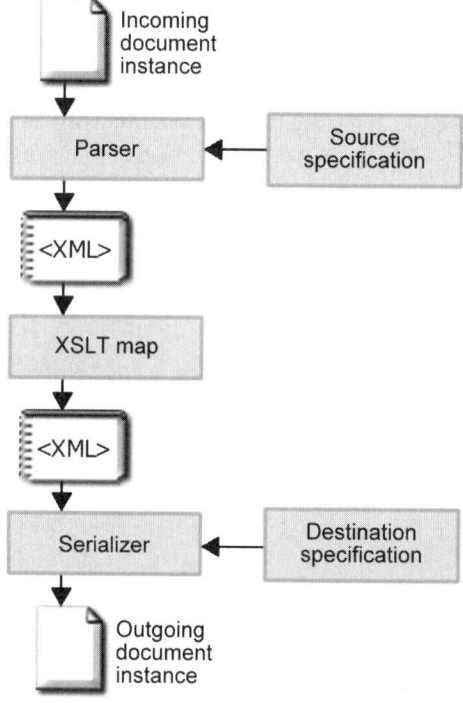

1. The incoming document instance is sent to BizTalk Server.

2. The parser uses the source specification associated with the incoming document instance to translate the incoming document instance to XML (if it is not already in this format). The source specification is created in BizTalk Editor.

3. The XML file is transformed by an XSLT map into another XML file of the desired structure (nodes in the incoming XML file are mapped to nodes in the outgoing XML file). The XSLT map is created in BizTalk Mapper.

4. The serializer uses the destination specification associated with the outgoing document instance to translate the outgoing XML file to the outgoing document instance (if it is not already in this format). The destination specification is created in BizTalk Editor.

5. BizTalk Server outputs the outgoing document instance and transports it to a destination.

The parsers and serializers included with BizTalk Server can translate XML, EDI (X12 and EDIFACT), and flat files (delimited and positional). Parsers and serializers for other formats might be available in the future. For more information, go to the Microsoft BizTalk Server 2000 Web site (www.microsoft.com/biztalk).

If you create your own parsers and serializers, BizTalk Server can translate files of any format. Regardless of the format of an incoming document instance, BizTalk Server translates it to an XML file so that the XSLT map can transform the incoming document structure into the structure necessary for the outgoing document. Even if a BizTalk Server hub inputs and outputs EDI documents, internally these documents are translated to XML. This enables BizTalk Server to take advantage of the power and flexibility of XML when transforming documents from one structure to another.

BizTalk Editor

BizTalk Editor enables you to create the specifications used by BizTalk Server to translate document formats to and from XML, and to create the maps that transform the translated XML files from one structure to another. The following illustration shows an EDI purchase-order specification based on an X12_4010_850 schema displayed in BizTalk Editor. The hierarchical structure of a document is displayed in the left pane of BizTalk Editor, regardless of whether the document format is XML, EDI, or flat-file. The right pane contains tabs that display property settings for the nodes in the document hierarchy.

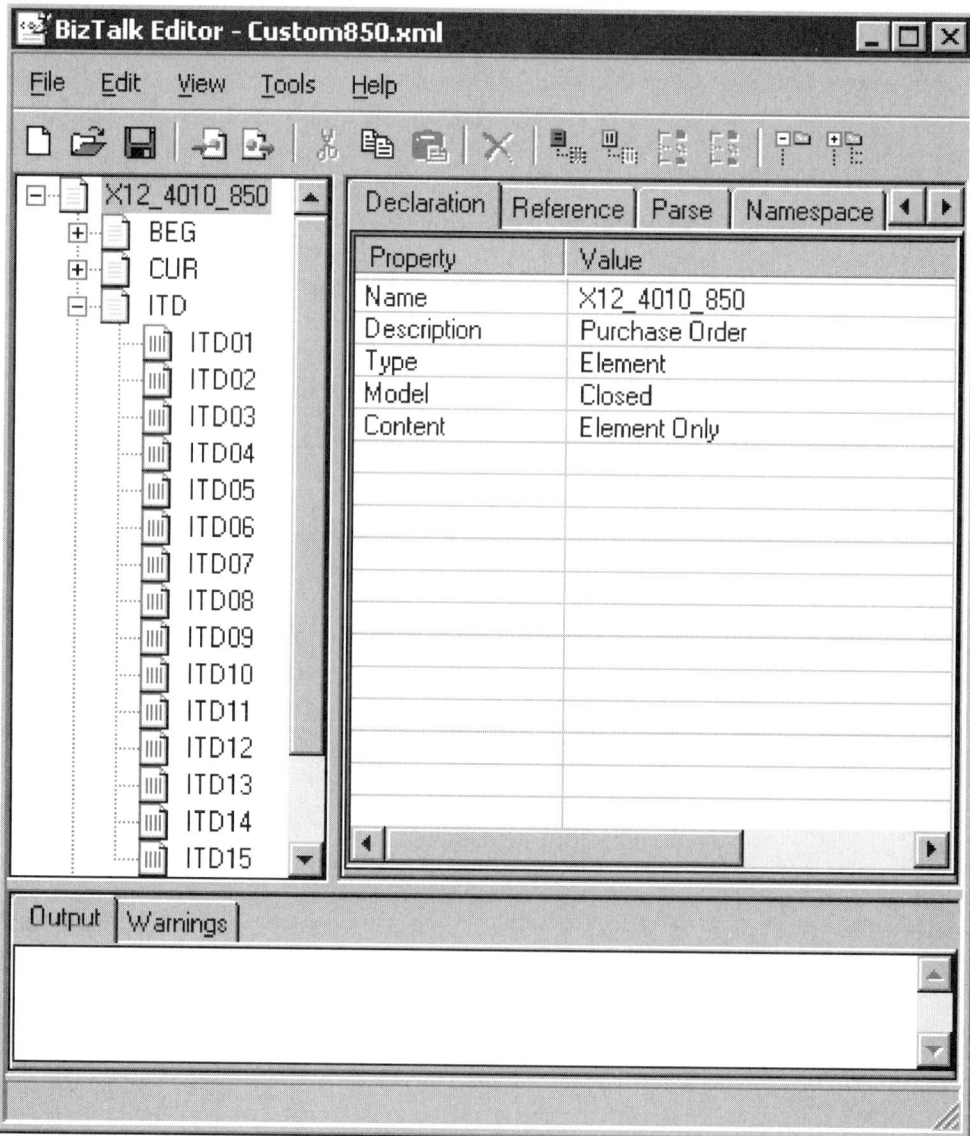

A specification that is based on an industry standard schema, such as the X12_4010_850 schema, is a subset of that standard schema. For example, the specification in the illustration is a subset of the X12_4010_850 schema because the nodes that ordinarily exist between the CUR and ITD nodes have been removed. With BizTalk Editor you can create a new document specification based on a standard X12 or EDIFACT template and remove the nodes that you don't need.

BizTalk Mapper

With no coding, you can use BizTalk Mapper to create XSLT maps that BizTalk Server uses to transform the structure of an incoming document instance to the structure of an outgoing document instance. The source specification in a map is associated with the incoming document, and the destination specification is associated with the outgoing document. The following illustration shows an X12-based purchase-order specification that is mapped to a purchase order specification with a different structure. This map represents the document transformation from the incoming EDI document to the XML format acceptable for the accounting application in Organization A. The display is format independent—in this case the document displayed in the left pane is an EDI file, while the document displayed in the right pane is an XML file.

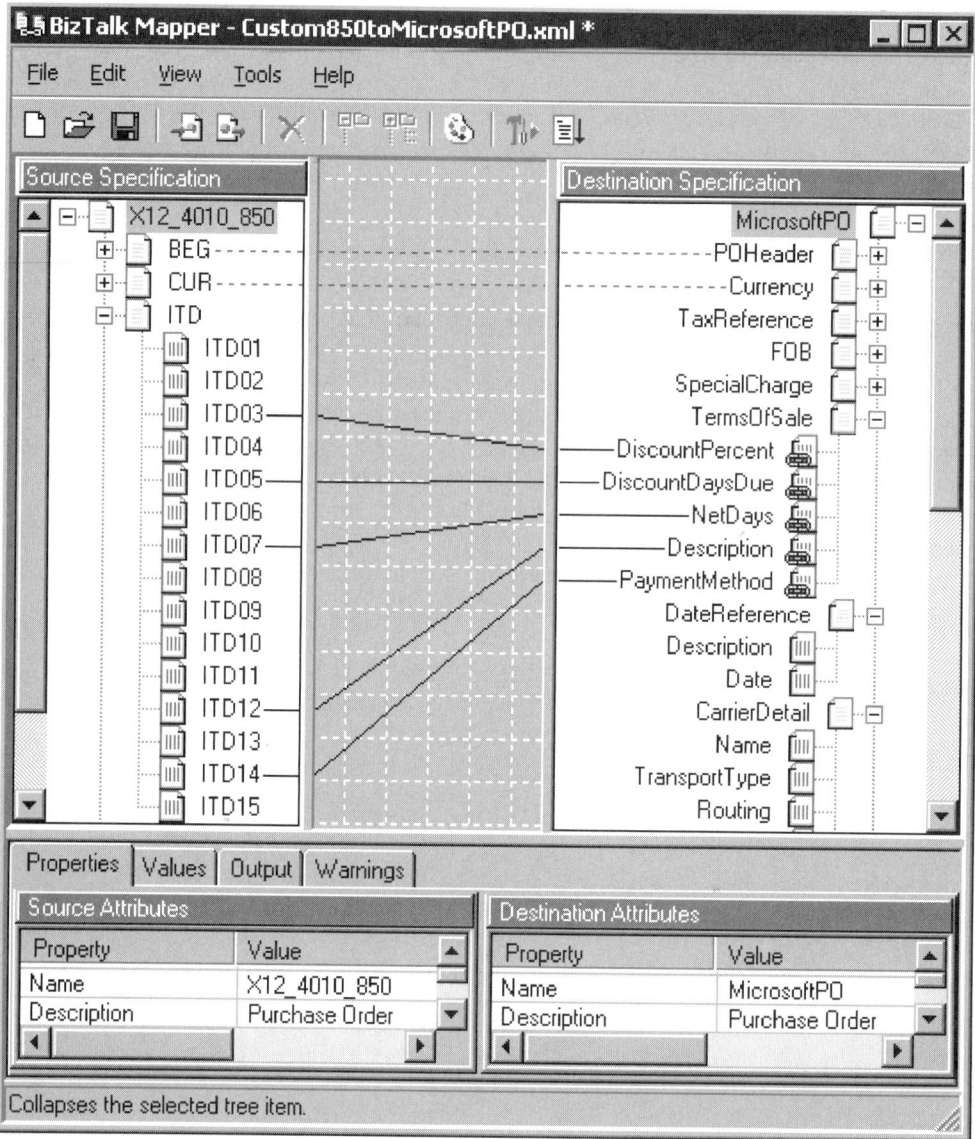

The illustration shows links from five nodes in the source specification to five corresponding nodes in the destination specification. If you viewed this map in BizTalk Mapper, you could see the remainder of the specifications by scrolling and by expanding nodes in the specifications. BizTalk Mapper uses built-in, reusable functions called functoids to enable more complex transformations than the simple links shown here.

BizTalk Mapper has a grid preview function that is useful for navigating to a particular subsection of a complex map, such as might be required when mapping EDI documents.

Comparing BizTalk Server with EDI Technology

As explained earlier in this chapter, BizTalk Server offers functionality and advantages that EDI technology cannot provide. For anyone currently using EDI who is considering deploying BizTalk Server in their business, it is important to understand the strengths and limitations of both EDI and BizTalk Server.

EDI strengths

- **Currently deployed in many businesses.** EDI is a long-established standard, and many large businesses currently use it successfully.

- **Uses agreed-upon standards.** EDI standards are recognized by everyone who uses EDI.

- **Standards are fairly rigid.** Rigid standards require conformity.

EDI limitations

- **High cost.** EDI systems are costly to set up and maintain. Hiring and retaining EDI experts is expensive.

- **Value-added networks (VANs).** Many companies that use EDI use VANs to exchange documents. VANs are expensive to set up and incur costs each time they are used.

- **Document format is not easily human-readable.** It is difficult for a person to read an EDI document.

- **Not well suited for enterprise application integration (EAI).** An EDI server handles connections outside the business. BizTalk Server handles connections both outside the business and within the business.

- **Many industry-specific subvariations of standard documents.** In some industries, such as the automotive and aerospace industries, EDI document standards have been extended for industry-specific purposes. This can cause document translation difficulties between variants of standard EDI documents given the expectation for rigid standards interpretation.

BizTalk Server strengths

- **Uses XML as a foundation.** BizTalk Server uses XML to translate and transform documents regardless of the document format required for input and output. This creates an extremely flexible environment for document exchange both now and in the future. XML as a document format has the following advantages:

  - XML is self-describing and creates documents that are relatively easy for people to read. This makes it easier for a person unfamiliar with a particular BizTalk Server installation to become familiar with it.

  - XML experts are plentiful, and they are less expensive than EDI experts.

  - XML is very flexible and extensible.

- **Easy setup and maintenance.** BizTalk Server systems are easier to set up and maintain than EDI systems.

- **Many schemas available.** There is a large and growing library of schemas available to users of BizTalk Server. For more information about this schema library, go to the Microsoft BizTalk Server 2000 Web site (www.microsoft.com/biztalk).

- **Enterprise application integration.** BizTalk Server handles enterprise application integration, and does it very well. For more information about case studies on BizTalk Server for EAI, go to the Microsoft BizTalk Server 2000 Web site (www.microsoft.com/biztalk).

- **Orchestration capabilities.** In addition to the universal messaging capabilities described in this chapter, BizTalk Server has powerful orchestration capabilities. BizTalk Orchestration enables the user to design and execute long-running, loosely coupled business transactions.

BizTalk Server limitations in its support of EDI

BizTalk Server supports EDI formats and receipting. While many customers have found that this is sufficient for interoperating with EDI-based systems, true EDI servers have functionality that is not available in BizTalk Server at the time of release. Following are limitations in BizTalk Server support of EDI. Included are approaches to using the BizTalk Server extensibility model and consulting to overcome many of these limitations. In a number of cases consultants have already implemented these features for customers, but currently there is no example code available to demonstrate these features. These solutions will add processing time to document throughput.

Outbound batching

- **Limitation.** Although BizTalk Server can process aggregate collections of EDI documents, it cannot produce them.

- **Solution.** Include a predelivery batching routine on the outbound side of BizTalk Server, and a debatching routine on the inbound side of BizTalk Server. This is to accommodate aggregate responses to transmittals batched outside BizTalk Server.

- **Effort Required.** A low to medium level of effort is required to implement a solution.

Segment compound "tags"

- **Limitation.** Currently, the source tag identifier is the only mechanism in BizTalk Server by which instance data is matched to schema-defined structure. BizTalk Server cannot resolve parsing operations when the source tag identifier in the document instance, by itself, is not sufficient for determining a structure match in the schema. An example of this might occur with the HL segments in an X12 856 advanced ship notice, where field data other than the source tag identifier adds hierarchical context to the meaning of the record's tag ("HL" in this case).

- **Solution.** Create new EDI parsers that perform parsing look-ahead logic to consider not only the tag but also the content qualifiers of various EDI segments.

- **Effort Required.** A high level of effort is required to implement a solution.

Envelope creation

- **Limitation.** BizTalk Server cannot populate custom envelopes. Nor can BizTalk Server deviate from the EDI-based envelopes that it provides, in the case where it is necessary to use optional fields on the envelope.

- **Solution.** Develop a predelivery process to add content to envelopes. This might involve having BizTalk Server build an envelope, and then populating the envelope in the add-on process. Alternatively, the add-on process could create and populate the record. In either case, the data could be from the BizTalk Messaging Management database, a private add-on database, or both.

- **Effort Required.** A medium level of effort is required to implement a solution.

Functional acknowledgments

- **Limitation.** There are four limitations in this area:

  - BizTalk Server parsers cannot take advantage of the range of EDI batching or aggregation functionality that an EDI server can. For example, BizTalk Server is unable to reject an entire group based on individual document failure within the group.

  - Detail does not include the field level, so it is often impossible to know, for example, which field failed validation.

- The validation step stops at the first error.

- BizTalk Server provides no notification or other action when receipts become overdue.

- **Solution.** There are no solutions for the first three limitations. To solve the last limitation, you must set up stored procedures as Microsoft SQL Server jobs. The purpose of this is to sweep the tracking database periodically to look for overdue receipts and to perform notification as needed.

- **Effort Required.** A low to medium level of effort is required to implement a solution.

EDI data types

- **Limitation.** When creating a specification in BizTalk Editor, you cannot specify EDI data types for X12 document field contents. This limitation is most significant in custom data types that have to do with explicit or implied decimal placement and the number of digits before and after the decimal.

- **Solution.** There is no solution for this limitation within the context of BizTalk Server.

Envelope mapping

- **Limitation.** BizTalk Server cannot map data from envelopes.

- **Solution.** There is no solution for this limitation within the context of BizTalk Server.

Binary segment content

- **Limitation.** BizTalk Server cannot specify a maximum size for a binary field if that maximum is in excess of 32-bit MAXINT.

- **Solution.** There is no solution for this limitation within the context of BizTalk Server.

Control number enforcement

- **Limitation.** There is no way for BizTalk Server to know when duplicate items are submitted for processing except through the use of the BizTalk Framework.

- **Solution.** Develop a preprocess that scans all data in the tracking database (or in a replicated warehouse of all historic tracking data) to verify the uniqueness of received data prior to submitting it to BizTalk Messaging.

- **Effort Required.** A medium level of effort is required to implement a solution.

Floating segments

- **Limitation.** BizTalk Server does not support floating segments. Segments defined in schemas are fixed to specific locations in the data according to where the schema explicitly places them.

- **Solution.** There is no solution for this limitation within the context of BizTalk Server.

VAN integration

- **Limitation.** There are two limitations in this area:

  - BizTalk Server has no built-in VAN transport components for sending or receiving data.

  - BizTalk Server has no mechanism for entering VAN sender and receiver status reports into a tracking database.

- **Solution.** Develop application integration components (AICs) to serve as the transport mechanism to interact with a VAN. There might also be a need to create tables related to the tracking database that would hold VAN sender and receiver status reports. This is because there is also a foreign key relationship between the new tables and existing tracking tables.

- **Effort Required.** A medium to high level of effort is required to implement a solution.

Envelope data viewing

- **Limitation.** It is not possible to see envelopes in BizTalk Document Tracking, other than by viewing the parent interchange for documents being searched.

- **Solution.** Modify the BizTalk Document Tracking user interface so that the envelopes are optionally displayed with the individual work items.

- **Effort Required.** A high level of effort is required to implement a solution.

Conclusion

BizTalk Server can add value to any company that needs to automate its internal data flow or automate the exchange of business documents with other companies. This includes companies that use EDI as well as companies that don't use EDI but need to do so to build business relationships with EDI-based companies. Although BizTalk Server is not an EDI server, it enables you to use EDI and other formats for business-to-business integration as well as EAI. BizTalk Server provides a very powerful and flexible framework to move your enterprise forward.

Part 3: Understanding BizTalk Orchestration and Messaging Implementation

In this part you'll gain an understanding of the design and implementation functionality of BizTalk Orchestration Services. In addition, you'll learn how to use BizTalk Orchestration Designer to create robust, long-running, loosely coupled business processes that span organizations, platforms, and applications. This part also provides information about configuring BizTalk Messaging Services to manage the exchange of documents between trading partners and applications within your business. In addition, you'll learn how to submit documents to Microsoft BizTalk Server 2000.

In This Part

- **BizTalk Orchestration Services.** This chapter describes how to create XLANG schedule drawings that describe business processes. In addition, you'll learn the steps needed to define the flow of data between messages within business processes. You'll also read about the process for compiling XLANG schedule drawings into XLANG schedules.

- **Configuring BizTalk Messaging Services.** This chapter contains detailed information about how to use BizTalk Messaging Manager, which is a graphical user interface, to configure BizTalk Messaging Services. It also provides step-by-step instructions on how to directly access the BizTalk Messaging Configuration object model to configure BizTalk Messaging Services.

- **Submitting Documents.** This chapter provides detailed conceptual information that is important to understand in order to submit documents to BizTalk Server. It contains procedural information about how to use the **Submit** or **SubmitSync** method of the **IInterchange** interface to send documents to BizTalk Server for processing. You'll also learn how to submit documents to BizTalk Server by using receive functions to accommodate applications that are not capable of invoking methods on COM objects.

BizTalk Orchestration Services

BizTalk Orchestration Services extends the capabilities of established information-exchange technologies. It enables users to create detailed representations of business processes that can be implemented programmatically within an integrated design environment.

In This Chapter

- BizTalk Orchestration Services
- Creating XLANG Schedule Drawings

BizTalk Orchestration Services

Business-process design and implementation have traditionally been performed in two distinct phases: the visual-design phase and the coding phase. The visual-design phase typically consisted of the analysis of an existing business process (such as corporate procurement) and the creation of a workflow diagram or an interaction diagram to describe the process. The coding phase was usually performed separately. In this paradigm, you would build an abstract visual model of a business process and then map the model to an implementation framework.

One of the important features of BizTalk Orchestration is the integration of these previously distinct phases within a unified design environment. This design environment provides a versatile drawing surface and a comprehensive set of implementation tools. BizTalk Orchestration enables you to:

- Create XLANG schedule drawings that describe business processes.

- Implement business processes by connecting specific actions within a drawing to ports that represent locations to which messages are sent, or from which messages are received. Ports are named locations, and messages represent the data sent or received between actions and ports.

- Define the flow of data between messages within business processes.

- Compile XLANG schedule drawings into XLANG schedules. XLANG schedules are executable Extensible Markup Language (XML) representations of the information contained within the drawings.

In addition to the integration of design and implementation functionality, BizTalk Orchestration provides an important additional feature: the ability to create robust, long-running, loosely coupled business processes that span organizations, platforms, and applications. During an asynchronous, loosely coupled, long-running business process, a product that is ordered over the Internet might have to be built from parts that are in inventory. Some of these parts might even be temporarily out of stock. The entire business process might take weeks or months to complete. In contrast, a tightly coupled business process involves the synchronous exchange of messages. For example, when a customer withdraws money from a bank account, the debiting of the account is immediately followed by the delivery of the money.

BizTalk Orchestration enables you to:

- Create a visual representation of long-running business processes.

- Facilitate the exchange of messages by connecting the actions in your visual representation to ports that are implemented by a certain technology.

- Compile the completed drawing into an executable XML representation of the drawing.

- Reliably execute business processes that might take weeks or months to complete.

Understanding Business Processes

Business processes are as important to business management as assembly lines are to manufacturing. Adhering to a well-defined, formalized set of processes can enable any business to increase productivity and lower costs. A business process defines the message exchange protocol between all the distributed participants. To define a business process, you must determine the logical order of actions and the corresponding flow of messages. A business process does not include definitions of the distributed participants who perform these actions.

The sequence of steps in a long-running business process is typically asynchronous. Each step is an action that can be performed by one or more independent, distributed participants. These actions can result in the sending and receiving of messages among the participants, who might or might not be people performing related tasks. A distributed participant might be an automated process that responds to input, or the participant might even be an entirely separate business process. To understand business processes, you must be able to visualize a complex variety of relationships and dependencies. Business process modeling tools, such as workflow diagrams and interaction diagrams, have been developed to visually describe these relationships.

Workflow Diagrams

Workflow is a business-process design technology that automates and improves procedures within organizations. It is a useful technology for delineating the steps that must be taken, the dependencies that must be enforced, and the approvals that must be obtained during the completion of projects. You can use a workflow application to assign tasks to participants, define individual responsibilities, and describe the relationships among the participants. You can also use a workflow application to set time limits for the completion of projects and the achievement of milestones. However, the workflow technology is typically highly centralized. Participants are assigned tasks and given deadlines, but the workflow engine is responsible for routing completed work items from one participant to the next, and enforcing a schedule. In contrast, BizTalk Orchestration is broader in scope. Participants are autonomous and the responsibility for routing a work item from one participant to another is determined by the participants, not by a centralized application.

Interaction Diagrams

An interaction diagram describes the data flow within a business process and the messages that are exchanged. BizTalk Orchestration extends the interaction diagram concept by providing definition and control for decisions, concurrent actions, transactions, and supporting actions that cannot be included in an interaction diagram. Designing a business process by using BizTalk Orchestration results in a compiled, executable business process (an XLANG schedule). In contrast, interaction diagrams are static representations of business processes.

The following illustration shows a typical interaction diagram for an automated procurement system.

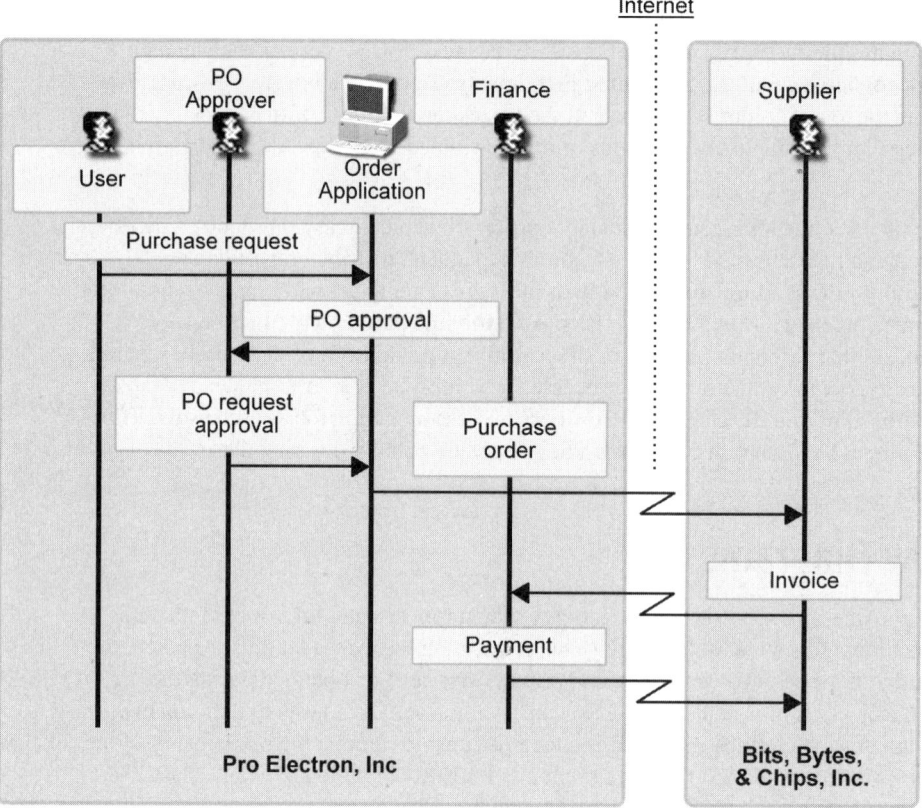

BizTalk Orchestration Designer Environment

BizTalk Orchestration Designer enables you to create XLANG schedule drawings. An XLANG schedule drawing is a representation of a business process. The drawing is saved as an .skv file, which is a customized version of the Microsoft Visio 2000 file format. The XLANG schedule drawing can then be compiled into an XLANG schedule, which is an XML-structured .skx text file that the XLANG Scheduler Engine understands. BizTalk Orchestration Designer enables you to create XLANG schedule drawings that include:

- **A visual description of a business process.** This aspect of an XLANG schedule drawing is similar to a workflow diagram or an interaction diagram.

- **A visual representation of configurable ports.** This is the implementation aspect of an XLANG schedule drawing.

- **A visual representation of the connections between shapes. Flowchart** shapes can be connected to represent process flow in a business process, and actions can be connected to ports to represent the flow of communication in a business process.

- **A visual representation of the flow between specified message fields.** This aspect of an XLANG schedule drawing determines the relationship between a message field on one message and another message field on a different message. By correlating these relationships, you can enable data-sensitive routing.

An XLANG schedule drawing is a representation of the procedures that are performed during a business process. An XLANG schedule drawing can define:

- The message-exchange protocol that trading partners agree to use.

- Actions that are used to send or receive messages that describe the logical sequence in which actions occur.

- The implementation of ports and the actions to which they are linked.

- The data flow between message fields.

Opening and Saving XLANG Schedule Drawings

The procedures in this section provide information about opening and saving XLANG schedules in BizTalk Orchestration Designer.

To create a new XLANG schedule drawing

- In BizTalk Orchestration Designer, on the **File** menu, click **New**.

Notes

- This procedure opens a new XLANG schedule drawing within the design window. The **Business Process** page is the default beginning design page. The **Flowchart** and **Implementation** stencils also open by default when you start a new drawing.

- The file extension for an XLANG schedule drawing is .skv.

To open an existing XLANG schedule drawing

1. In BizTalk Orchestration Designer, on the **File** menu, click **Open**.

   The **Open XLANG Schedule Drawing** dialog box appears.

2. Browse to the XLANG schedule drawing that you want to open, click the drawing, and then click **Open**.

Notes

- The file extension for an XLANG schedule drawing is .skv.

- The file extension for an XLANG schedule is .skx. You cannot open an .skx file within BizTalk Orchestration Designer. To change or update an .skx file, open the source .skv file, make your changes, and then recompile the .skv file into an .skx file.

To save an XLANG schedule drawing

- In BizTalk Orchestration Designer, on the **File** menu, click **Save**.

Notes

- When you save an XLANG schedule drawing, the drawing is saved with the default name *DrawingX*.skv, where *X* is a number that is appended to the drawing name. You can change the name of the file when you save the drawing.

- You can also click **Save As** on the **File** menu. This option opens the **Save XLANG Schedule Drawing As** dialog box. You can:

  - Rename the file to another name.

  - Save the file in a different location.

- The file extension for an XLANG schedule drawing is .skv.

- The file extension for an XLANG schedule is .skx. You cannot open an .skx file within BizTalk Orchestration Designer. To change or update an .skx file, open the source .skv file, make your changes, and then recompile the .skv file into an .skx file.

Design Pages

There are four design pages that are accessible within BizTalk Orchestration Designer. You can use these design pages to create different aspects of your XLANG schedule drawing.

- **Business Process page.** On this page you can use **Flowchart** shapes and **Implementation** shapes to define a business process. For more information about using these shapes, see "Flowchart Shapes" and "Implementation Shapes" later in this chapter.

- **Data page.** On this page you can use **Communication** shapes to control the flow of data between message fields. BizTalk Orchestration Designer provides these shapes automatically. For more information about using these shapes, see "Communication Shapes" later in this chapter.

- **On Failure of *Transaction* page.** On this page you can use **Flowchart** shapes and **Implementation** shapes to design an alternate business process for a failed transaction.

- **Compensation for *Transaction* page.** On this page you can use **Flowchart** shapes and **Implementation** shapes to design an undo process for a committed nested transaction. For more information about transactions, see "Designing Transactions" later in this chapter.

To view the Business Process page

- On the **View** menu, click **Business Process Page**.

Note

- You can also click the **Business Process** tab at the bottom of the design pages.

To view the Data page

- On the **View** menu, click **Data Page**.

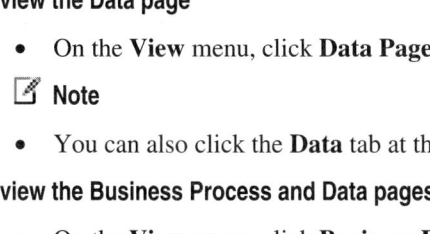 **Note**

- You can also click the **Data** tab at the bottom of the design pages.

To view the Business Process and Data pages

- On the **View** menu, click **Business Process and Data Pages**.

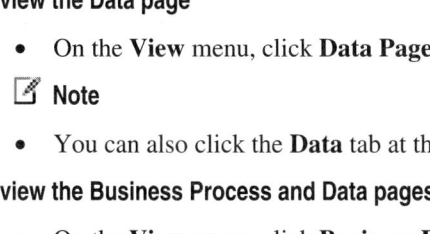 **Note**

- This view option opens two windows for the same XLANG schedule: a Business Process window and a Data window. This functionality is similar to that obtained by using the **New Window** option. For more information about opening multiple windows, see "Using Multiple Windows" later in this chapter.

To view Compensation for Transaction pages

- At the bottom of the design pages, click the **Compensation for *Transaction*** tab for the page that you want to view.

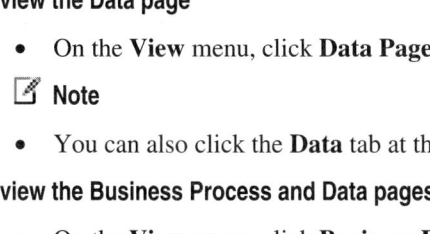 **Notes**

- The parameter *Transaction* in the name of the page is replaced with the name of the transaction with which the error-handling process is associated.

- For information about how to add a **Compensation for *Transaction*** page to an XLANG schedule drawing, see "To enable Compensation error handling" later in this chapter.

To view On Failure of Transaction pages

- At the bottom of the design pages, click the **On Failure of *Transaction*** tab for the page that you want to view.

 Notes

- The parameter *Transaction* in the name of the page is replaced with the name of the transaction with which the error-handling process is associated.

- For information about how to add an **On Failure of *Transaction*** page to an XLANG schedule drawing, see "To enable On Failure error handling" later in this chapter.

To view a page

- Click the tab for the page that you want to view.

 Note

- Tabs for each page are located at the bottom of the design pages.

Flowchart Shapes

BizTalk Orchestration Designer provides eight **Flowchart** shapes that are available on the **Flowchart** stencil. These shapes are used to describe your business process. The eight shapes on the **Flowchart** stencil can be used to describe the structure and meaning of XLANG schedules. XLANG is an XML-based language that describes business-process interactions.

The following table lists and describes the **Flowchart** shapes.

Shape name	Description
Begin 	The **Begin** shape is not available on the **Flowchart** stencil, it cannot be deleted, and you cannot create additional **Begin** shapes. The **Begin** shape represents the start of an XLANG schedule drawing. The **Begin** shape is created automatically on each **Business Process**, **Compensation for** *Transaction*, and **On Failure of** *Transaction* page. The **Begin** shape that appears on the **Business Process** page has configurable properties. The **Begin** shapes that appear on the **Compensation for** *Transaction* page and the **On Failure of** *Transaction* page do not have configurable properties. You cannot enclose a **Begin** shape within a transaction. The business process sequence must flow from the **Begin** shape to the first **Flowchart** shape in your drawing.
Action	The **Action** shape represents a process that receives a message from a port or sends a message to a port. The send or receive action can be synchronous or asynchronous, depending on the component or implementation to which the port is bound.
Decision	The **Decision** shape represents a process that evaluates one or more rules sequentially. This shape has one inbound flow and one or more outbound flows. Each outbound flow is associated with a rule that evaluates to TRUE or FALSE. The first rule that evaluates to TRUE determines which outbound flow is followed in the business process. The sequence of the business process follows the flow from the first rule that evaluates to TRUE. If no rules evaluate to TRUE, the Else flow is followed. The **Decision** shape must contain at least one rule. Each rule must contain a script expression.

Shape name	Description
While ↻	The **While** shape contains one rule and represents a process that can be repeated. If the rule evaluates to TRUE, the flow from the rule is followed to completion and then it repeats. If the rule evaluates to FALSE, the Continue flow is followed. When the business process sequence flows from a rule in a **While** shape, the sequence must conclude in a single **End** shape.
	You can also configure the preservation of state for a while loop. By right-clicking a **While** shape and clicking **Properties**, you can display the **While Properties** dialog box. In the **State persistence** area, you can choose **Yes** to save the messages used in each loop iteration as XLANG schedule state. If the while loop is part of a transaction that fails, an **On Failure of** *Transaction* or **Compensation for** *Transaction* page will be called for each completed loop iteration. If you choose **No**, only messages used in the latest loop iteration will be saved as XLANG schedule state. If the while loop is part of a transaction that fails, an **On Failure of** *Transaction* or **Compensation for** *Transaction* page will be called only once.
	When a business process sequence flows to a **While** shape that is within a nested transaction that fails, the messages and ports that have been created on the **On Failure of** *Transaction* or **Compensation for** *Transaction* page for the nested transaction will not be available to the **On Failure of** *Transaction* page for the outer transaction. Design the On Failure or Compensation code to force the collected messages to flow normally out of the nested transaction.
Fork ✣	The **Fork** shape introduces concurrency into a business process. One flow can enter a fork, and as many as 64 flows can leave a fork. Each flow that leaves a fork is executed concurrently. All business process sequences that flow from a single **Fork** shape must connect to a single **Join** shape or terminate in an **End** shape.
Join ✣	The **Join** shape synchronizes concurrent flows in a business process. As many as 64 flows can enter a **Join** shape, but only one flow leaves a **Join** shape. The logical operators **AND** and **OR** are used to determine how to synchronize the flows. You can set the following **Join** properties:

- **OR.** Enables the first flow that arrives to continue. The other flows continue to execute.

- **AND.** Synchronizes all incoming flows before the outbound flow can continue.

Shape name	Description
Transaction	The **Transaction** shape represents a collection of actions that are either all executed, or else none are. There are three types of transactions: • Short-lived transactions • Long-running transactions • Timed transactions that are long-running Transactions are used to make an application more reliable and to simplify error handling in large applications. The **Transaction** shape is limited to a single path in, and a single path out. The **Transaction** shape cannot contain **End** shapes. Long-running transactions can contain nested transactions; however, short-lived transactions cannot contain nested transactions. Transaction retry attempts are permitted only for short-lived transactions. If you enclose part of your business process within a short-lived **Transaction** shape, you can configure the transaction **Retry count** property. If the short-lived transaction fails, it is retried for the number of times that you have specified. By defining transaction properties, you can make available either the **Compensation for** *Transaction* page (for nested transactions) or the **On Failure of** *Transaction* page. On either page, you can model the error-handling processes that are specific to the transaction. ✎ **Note** • If the borders of an inner **Transaction** shape overlap any of the borders of the outer **Transaction** shape, the inner transaction will not be nested. Do not allow the borders of an inner transaction to overlap the borders of an outer transaction.
End 	The **End** shape represents the completion of one process flow. One drawing can use multiple **End** shapes if the drawing includes **Decision**, **While**, or **Fork** shapes.
Abort	The **Abort** shape terminates execution within a transaction group. This enables either an **On Failure of** *Transaction* or **Compensation for** *Transaction* error-handling page, or else it retries the transaction.

📝 Notes

- For the **Compensation for *Transaction*** and **On Failure of *Transaction*** pages, the parameter *Transaction* is replaced with the name that you give to the associated transaction on the **Business Process** page.

- Shape names must meet certain naming conventions. The following conventions apply to transaction shapes, port shapes, messages, rules, and fields:

  - The name must be a valid XML token name. For more information about XML tokens, go to the W3C Web site (www.w3c.org).

  - The name cannot begin with underscores (__).

  - The name cannot include colons (:).

  - The name length must be less than or equal to 32 characters.

  - Constant names and message names cannot begin with a numeric character.

- Transaction names in single-byte character sets must be less than or equal to 16 characters in length. Transaction names in double-byte character sets must be less than or equal to 8 characters in length.

- Actions are exempt from all naming conventions except the 32-character size limit.

- You cannot name any of the following shapes: **Abort**, **Begin**, **Decision**, **End**, **Fork**, **Join**, and **While**.

To view the Flowchart stencil

- On the **View** menu, point to **Stencils** and click **Flowchart** to toggle the **Flowchart** stencil on or off.

To view Flowchart shapes

- On the **View** menu, click **Flowchart Shapes**.

📝 Notes

- If you use this option, on the design page only **Flowchart** shapes and the connections between them are displayed. This option hides all ports, port messages, implementations, and connections between ports and actions or between ports and implementations.

- This view option cannot be used on the **Data** page.

Implementation Shapes

BizTalk Orchestration Designer provides four **Implementation** shapes that are available on the **Implementation** stencil. These shapes are used to describe the implementation technologies that are used to implement a port in a business process.

The following table lists and describes the **Implementation** shapes.

Shape name	Description
COM Component	The **COM Component** shape represents a technology that can be used to implement a port by using a method call for each message that is sent or received. Drag this shape to the right side of the **Separator** bar to open the COM Component Binding Wizard. For more information about the COM component implementation, see "Using the COM Component Shape" later in this chapter.
Script Component	The **Script Component** shape represents a technology that can be used to implement a port by using a method call for each message that is sent or received. Drag this shape to the right side of the **Separator** bar to open the Script Component Binding Wizard. For more information about the Script Component implementation, see "Using the Script Component Shape" later in this chapter.
Message Queuing	The **Message Queuing** shape represents a technology that can be used to implement a port. Message Queuing Services are used to send or receive messages. Drag this shape to the right side of the **Separator** bar to open the Message Queuing Binding Wizard. For more information about the Message Queuing implementation, see "Using the Message Queuing Shape" later in this chapter.
BizTalk Messaging	The **BizTalk Messaging** shape represents a technology that can be used to implement a port. BizTalk Messaging Services are used to send or receive messages. Drag this shape to the right side of the **Separator** bar to open the BizTalk Messaging Binding Wizard. For more information about the BizTalk Messaging implementation, see "Using the BizTalk Messaging Shape" later in this chapter.

Note

- Shape names must meet certain naming conventions. The following conventions apply to transactions, ports, messages, rules, and fields:

  - The name must be a valid XML token name. For more information about XML tokens, go to the W3C Web site (www.w3c.org).

  - The name cannot begin with underscores (__).

  - The name cannot include colons (:).

  - The name length must be less than or equal to 32 characters.

  - Constant names and message names cannot begin with a numeric character.

To view the Implementation stencil

- On the **View** menu, point to **Stencils** and click **Implementation** to toggle the **Implementation** stencil on or off.

Communication Shapes

BizTalk Orchestration Designer provides several **Communication** shapes that indicate the direction of the flow of data into and out of messages. BizTalk Orchestration Designer provides the **Communication** shapes automatically.

The **Port References**, **Constants**, and **Message** shapes are located on the **Data** page. The **Data** page represents the flow of data between messages used by the XLANG schedule instance while the instance is running. To design the flow of data, you can create connections between the fields within the shapes on the **Data** page.

The following table lists and describes the **Communication** shapes.

Shape name	Description
Port	Ports are named locations where messages are sent or received. Right-click the **Separator** bar and click **Add New Port** to add an unbound port. Or drag an **Implementation** shape to the right side of the **Separator** bar to add a bound port.
	Each port contains messages that correspond to the **Message** shapes that appear on the **Data** page. A message represents the data that is sent or received by an action. The data within a message is separated into a list of fields on the **Data** page.
Port References	The **Port References** message contains a list of all ports that are created on the **Business Process** page. A new reference is added to this list every time a new port is added on the **Business Process** page. The **Port References** message enables you to specify the origin of port locations. The **Port References** message contains one port field for every port in the business process.
Constants	The **Constants** message provides a way to initialize your XLANG schedule with data. To add a constant to the **Constants** message, double-click the **Constants** message, or double-click a field in the **Constants** message to open the **Constants Message Properties** dialog box.
Message	**Message** shapes contain a list of fields with information about the data that is sent or received in the message.

📝 Note

- Shape names must meet certain naming conventions. The following conventions apply to transactions, ports, messages, rules, and fields:

    - The name must be a valid XML token name. For more information about XML tokens, go to the W3C Web site (www.w3c.org).

    - The name cannot begin with underscores (__).

    - The name cannot include colons (:).

    - The name length must be less than or equal to 32 characters.

    - Constant names and message names cannot begin with a numeric character.

Each message that is defined on the **Data** page has additional system fields that the XLANG Scheduler Engine automatically creates and maintains for each message. These fields can be referenced for descriptive information about the message and can be used in script expressions for rules. The following table summarizes system fields that are created automatically.

System field	Description
__Exists__	This field can be used to test for the existence of a message. The existence of a message is determined by whether the message has been received or sent by the XLANG Scheduler Engine. This field is not shown within messages on the **Data** page. It is used only with **Decision** and **While** shapes.
__Sender__	This field contains the identity, if known, of the sender of a message. This field is shown within messages on the **Data** page.
__Status__	This field contains the status returned from a COM method call on a port that is bound to a COM component. This field is shown within the messages on the **Data** page. 📝 **Notes** • This system field is used only with COM component and Script Component implementations. • The status that is returned is always an HRESULT.
Document	This field contains a string containing the message body that is sent or received. It always refers to an XML message. 📝 **Note** • This system field is used only with Message Queuing and BizTalk Messaging implementations.

◈ Important

- Each message that is sent from an XLANG schedule instance must have the source for each field of data defined. To define the source for a field of data, a connection must point to the field from another field in another message.

◪ Note

- The compilation engine used to create an XLANG schedule validates whether a message has all of its input-only fields defined. The schedule will not compile if the input-only fields are partially defined. The arguments to a method can be input, output, or both. The compilation engine ignores the definition requirement for arguments defined as both input and output. If no inbound connections are defined for input-output fields, the schedule will compile, even though there is no definition for the data in the message.

To view Flowchart and Communication shapes

- On the **View** menu, click **Flowchart and Communication Shapes**.

◪ Notes

- If you use this option, on the design page **Flowchart** shapes and the connections between them are displayed. Ports, port messages, and the connections between ports and actions are also displayed. This option hides all implementations, and connections between ports and implementations.

- This view option cannot be used on the **Data** page.

To view Flowchart, Communication, and Implementation shapes

- On the **View** menu, click **Flowchart, Communication, and Implementation Shapes**.

◪ Notes

- All shapes and the connections between them are displayed.

- This view option cannot be used on the **Data** page.

Using Multiple Windows

The procedures in this section provide information about using multiple windows in BizTalk Orchestration Designer.

To open a new window

- On the **Window** menu, click **New Window**.

 Note

- Multiple windows provide additional views of the same XLANG schedule. This enables you to:

  - View different pages of the same XLANG schedule at the same time. For example, you can open views for the **Business Process** page, the **Data** page, and a **Compensation for** *Transaction* page.

  - View different parts of the same page of an XLANG schedule at the same time. For example, in one view you can zoom in to see a specific set of shapes in the XLANG schedule; in another view you can zoom out to see the whole schedule.

To tile windows

- On the **Window** menu, click **Tile**.

 Notes

- Tiling the window views enables you to see several windows at the same time.

- Multiple windows provide additional views of the same XLANG schedule. This enables you to:

  - View different pages of the same XLANG schedule at the same time. For example, you can open views for the **Business Process** page, the **Data** page, and a **Compensation for** *Transaction* page.

  - View different parts of the same page of an XLANG schedule at the same time. For example, in one view you can zoom in to see a specific set of shapes in the XLANG schedule; in another view you can zoom out to see the whole schedule.

To cascade windows

- On the **Window** menu, click **Cascade**.

☑ Notes

- Cascading the window views enables you to bring one window to the front of the screen. You can click the title bars of the other windows to bring them to the front of the screen.

- Multiple windows provide additional views of the same XLANG schedule. This enables you to:

  - View different pages of the same XLANG schedule at the same time. For example, you can open views for the **Business Process** page, the **Data** page, and a **Compensation for *Transaction*** page.

  - View different parts of the same page of an XLANG schedule at the same time. For example, in one view you can zoom in to see a specific set of shapes in the XLANG schedule; in another view you can zoom out to see the whole schedule.

To change the window focus

- On the **Window** menu, click the name of the window to which you want to switch the focus.

☑ Notes

- The name of a window is the name of the XLANG schedule with the name of a design page appended to it (for example, Schedule1.skv:Business Process or Schedule1.skv:Data).

- Multiple windows provide additional views of the same XLANG schedule. This enables you to:

  - View different pages of the same XLANG schedule at the same time. For example, you can open views for the **Business Process** page, the **Data** page, and a **Compensation for *Transaction*** page.

  - View different parts of the same page of an XLANG schedule at the same time. For example, in one view you can zoom in to see a specific set of shapes in the XLANG schedule; in another view you can zoom out to see the whole schedule.

Using Annotations

The procedures in this section provide information about using annotations in BizTalk Orchestration Designer.

To add annotations

1. In BizTalk Orchestration Designer, on the toolbar, click the **Text Tool (A)** button.

2. Use the mouse pointer to drag over the area where you want to create an annotation.

3. Type the annotation.

📝 Notes

- To turn off the Text Tool, on the toolbar, click the **Pointer Tool** (🖈) button.

- Because BizTalk Orchestration Designer uses a custom Microsoft Visio interface, the **Text Tool** button offers two options. The functionality of both buttons is identical:

  - The **Text Tool** (**A**) button

  - The **Text Block Tool** (🖎) button

To edit annotations

1. In BizTalk Orchestration Designer, on the toolbar, click the **Text Tool** (**A**) button.

2. Click the annotation that you want to edit.

3. Edit the annotation.

📝 Notes

- To turn off the Text Tool, on the toolbar, click the **Pointer Tool** (🖈) button.

- Because BizTalk Orchestration Designer uses a custom Microsoft Visio interface, the **Text Tool** button offers two options. The functionality of both buttons is identical:

  - The **Text Tool** (**A**) button

  - The **Text Block Tool** (🖎) button

To format text in annotations

1. In BizTalk Orchestration Designer, on a design page, select one or more annotations that you want to format.

2. On the **Format** menu, click **Text**.

    The **Text** dialog box appears. This dialog box offers several options for the size, font, and appearance of text.

3. Select the options that you want to use and click **OK**.

📝 Notes

- These options are applied to the annotations that you highlight in the XLANG schedule drawing, and to any new annotations that you create.

- You cannot format annotations when the Text Tool is turned on.

- To select an annotation, click it. To select more than one annotation, press and hold the SHIFT key, and then click the annotations that you want to select.

To delete annotations

- In BizTalk Orchestration Designer, on a design page, click the annotation that you want to delete and press DELETE.

✎ **Note**

- You must turn off the Text Tool before you can delete an annotation from the XLANG schedule drawing.

Previewing, Printing, or Resizing XLANG Schedule Drawings

The procedures in this section provide information about previewing, printing, and resizing XLANG schedule drawings in BizTalk Orchestration Designer.

To use Print Preview

- On the **File** menu, click **Print Preview**.

✎ **Note**

- If you change the **Layout Orientation** option from **Landscape** to **Portrait**, you will receive the following message:

  One or more drawing pages are oriented differently from the printed page setup. Click **OK** to print your drawing across multiple pages. To match orientations, change the printed page orientation.

  If you click **OK** and make this change, Print Preview might display the following behavior:

  - When you click **Next Tile** to pan pages forward, and then click **Previous Tile** to pan back to the first page, some shapes might appear in Print Preview as if they are not on the page. This display is harmless. The actual XLANG schedule will print correctly across several pages.

To print an XLANG schedule drawing

1. On the **File** menu, click **Print**.

   The **Print** dialog box appears.

2. Set any options that you want and click **Print**.

To resize an XLANG schedule drawing

1. In BizTalk Orchestration Designer, on the **View** menu, click **Whole Page**.

2. Press and hold CTRL, and then move the mouse pointer to the edge of the page.

   The pointer changes shape to a double arrow at the edge of the page.

3. Click and drag the edge of the page to resize it.

BizTalk Orchestration Designer Shortcut Keys

You can use shortcut keys to accomplish tasks in BizTalk Orchestration Designer. The following table is a quick reference to these shortcut keys.

📝 Note

- Functionality that is not included in this list can be obtained by using the numeric keypad to move the mouse pointer with MouseKeys. For more information about MouseKeys in Windows 2000 Server and Advanced Server Help, see "Using the keyboard to move the mouse pointer." For more information about MouseKeys in Windows 2000 Professional Help, see "Move the mouse pointer by using MouseKeys."

Press	To
ALT or F10	Activate the menu bar.
ALT+F4	Close the active item, or quit the program.
ALT+F7	Cascade windows.
ALT+SPACEBAR	Display the system menu for the active item.
ALT+Underlined letter in a menu name	Display the corresponding menu.
ARROW keys	Move the selected shape in the arrow direction.
CTRL while dragging an item	Copy the selected item.
CTRL+A	Select all.
CTRL+C	Copy the selected item on the design page.
CTRL+F4	Close the active drawing.
CTRL+I	Return the window to its actual size.
CTRL+N	New drawing.
CTRL+O	Open an existing drawing.
CTRL+P	Open the **Print** dialog box.
CTRL+Q	Quit the program.
CTRL+SHIFT with any of the arrow keys	Scroll.
CTRL+SHIFT, then click left mouse key	Zoom in.
CTRL+SHIFT, then click right mouse key	Zoom out.
CTRL+SHIFT+TAB	Toggle tabs of a dialog box in back-to-front order.
CTRL+TAB	Toggle tabs of a dialog box in front-to-back order.
CTRL+V	Paste the selected item on the design page.

Press	To
CTRL+X	Cut the selected item on the design page.
CTRL+Y	Redo.
CTRL+Z	Undo.
DELETE	Delete the selected item on the design page.
ESC	Cancel the current task.
F1	View the online Help.
F11	Launch the text properties dialog box.
F8	Align selected shapes.
LEFT ARROW	When the focus is on a tab in a dialog box, move the focus to the left.
RIGHT ARROW	When the focus is on a tab in a dialog box, move the focus to the right.
SHIFT while dragging an item	Drag the item only in a straight horizontal or vertical direction.
SHIFT+TAB	Move the focus counterclockwise in the lower window from the tab to the windows or fields below.
SPACEBAR	Toggle check boxes.
TAB	Move the focus clockwise in the lower window from the tab to the windows or fields below.
Underlined letter in a command name on an open menu	Carry out the corresponding command.

Understanding XLANG Schedules

The compiled version of an XLANG schedule drawing is an XLANG schedule, and the XLANG Scheduler Engine runs this schedule. The XLANG Scheduler Engine monitors and controls the business process described in the XLANG schedule, based on the actions, rules, and error-handling processes that are defined for the XLANG schedule.

Related Topics

"Designing for XLANG Schedule Instance Management, Persistence, and Data Handling" later in this chapter

"Designing Transactions" later in this chapter

"Handling Exceptions" later in this chapter

Creating XLANG Schedule Drawings

There are five tasks you must perform when you design an XLANG schedule:

- Draw a representation of the business process that the XLANG schedule will run. Use **Flowchart** shapes to describe the flow of the business process on the left side of the design page. Your primary business process is drawn on the **Business Process** page. Alternate processes are drawn on the **Compensation for *Transaction*** and **On Failure of *Transaction*** pages.

- Define rules for the branching decisions and repeated processes that occur within the business process; define concurrent processes; and design the transactions and subordinate transactions required in the business process.

- Create the port implementations that the business process requires. There are four implementation technologies available: COM components, Windows Scripting Components, Message Queuing Services, and BizTalk Messaging Services.

- Define the flow of data between messages. All flow of data between messages is drawn on the **Data** page.

- Draw any necessary business processes for transactions that fail. Alternate business processes are drawn on the **Compensation for *Transaction*** and **On Failure of *Transaction*** pages.

🗹 **Note**

- You can add **Flowchart** and **Implementation** shapes to the **Business Process**, **Compensation for *Transaction***, and **On Failure of *Transaction*** pages. These shapes are not available on the **Data** page.

Designing Business Processes

In BizTalk Orchestration Designer, the left side of the **Business Process** page is the area in which you can design business processes. A **Separator** bar divides the **Business Process** page into a business process design area on the left side and an implementation area on the right side.

Designing Actions

The business process sequence must flow from the **Begin** shape to the first **Flowchart** shape in your XLANG schedule drawing. Typically, the first **Flowchart** shape in your XLANG schedule drawing is an **Action** shape.

There are two configurable properties for a **Begin** shape. In the **Begin Properties** dialog box, you can configure the **Transaction Model** property to determine if **Transaction** shapes are supported within an XLANG schedule instance, or if the XLANG schedule is activated from within a transactional COM component. The first option enables support for **Transaction** shapes; the second option disables support for **Transaction** shapes.

In the **Begin Properties** dialog box, you can also configure the **Transaction Activation** property and the **XLANG identity** property. For more information about transaction activation, see "Designing Transactions" later in this chapter.

XLANG identity is a read-only property. It contains a globally unique identifier (GUID) that is used to correlate a version of the XLANG schedule drawing with the XLANG schedule that is generated by it. The GUID is automatically generated when a new drawing is created, and a new GUID is generated whenever the XLANG schedule drawing is changed.

The only configurable property for an **Action** shape is the name of the action. The name of the action cannot be longer than 32 characters. Action names have no affect on the behavior of the XLANG schedule.

To add shapes

- In BizTalk Orchestration Designer, on the **Flowchart** stencil, click a shape and drag it to the design page.

Notes

- You can add **Flowchart** shapes to the **Business Process**, **Compensation for** *Transaction*, and **On Failure of** *Transaction* pages. **Flowchart** shapes are not available on the **Data** page.

- For information about adding **Implementation** shapes to an XLANG schedule drawing, see "Implementation Shapes" earlier in this chapter.

- You cannot add shapes to the **Data** page. New messages are created automatically on the **Data** page each time an action is connected to a port.

To name shapes

1. In BizTalk Orchestration Designer, on a design page, right-click a shape and click **Properties**.

   The *Shape* **Properties** dialog box appears.

2. In the **Name** box, type a name.

Notes

- The **Name** property of each shape contains a default value that is the name of the shape with a number appended to the name, for example, Action 1. You can replace the default value with a name of your choice.

- You cannot name any of the following shapes: **Abort**, **Begin**, **Decision**, **End**, **Fork**, **Join**, and **While**.

- You can name the following shapes: **Action**, **Transaction**, **Port**, **Message**, and **Rule**.

- Shape names must meet certain naming conventions. The following conventions apply to transactions, ports, messages, rules, and fields:

  - The name must be a valid XML token name. For more information about XML tokens, go to the W3C Web site (www.w3.org).

  - The name cannot begin with underscores (__).

  - The name cannot include colons (:).

  - The name length must be less than or equal to 32 characters.

  - Constant names and message names cannot begin with a numeric character.

- Transaction names in single-byte character sets must be less than or equal to 16 characters in length. Transaction names in double-byte character sets must be less than or equal to 8 characters in length.

- Actions are exempt from all naming conventions except the 32-character size limit.

To delete shapes

- Click the shape that you want to delete and press DELETE.

🖉 Notes

- You can delete a connection between two shapes by clicking the connection and pressing DELETE.

- If a shape has connections to other shapes when you delete the shape, all connections are also deleted.

- Any shapes that are enclosed within a transaction are deleted when you delete the transaction.

- You can delete a BizTalk Messaging or Message Queuing implementation without deleting the ports to which these implementations are connected.

- When you delete a COM component or Windows Script Component implementation, the ports to which they are connected are also deleted.

- You can delete a message by clicking the message that is contained within a port and pressing DELETE. The associated message is deleted on the **Data** page.

  You can also delete messages from the **Data** page. For more information, see "To delete a message" later in this chapter.

- You cannot delete rules by using the delete procedure. For more information about deleting rules, see the following information later in this chapter:

  - "To delete a rule from a decision"

  - "To delete a rule from a while loop"

  - "To delete unused rules"

To delete unused ports and messages

- In BizTalk Orchestration Designer, on the **Tools** menu, click **Delete Unused Ports and Messages**.

☑ **Note**

- This procedure deletes all unused ports, and any messages that the ports contain, from the XLANG schedule drawing. The corresponding messages on the **Data** page are also removed.

Connecting Shapes

The procedures in this section provide information about connecting **Action** and **Port** shapes in BizTalk Orchestration Designer.

To select a shape

- In BizTalk Orchestration designer, on a design page, click the shape that you want to select.

  The shape that you select is surrounded with a green dashed border. Any control handles (✳) available to that shape are enabled.

☑ **Notes**

- Selecting a shape enables you to drag control handles (✳) from that shape to other shapes.

- Selecting a shape enables you to edit available shape properties, and to cut, copy, paste, clear, or duplicate the shape. Not all of these options are available for every shape.

- If you copy an **Action** shape that is connected to a **Port** shape, the copy of that action also has a connection to the same port.

To connect two shapes

1. To connect two shapes, select the first shape.

   The shape that you select is surrounded with a green dashed border. Any control handles (✳) available to that shape are enabled.

2. Drag the appropriate control handle to the connection point (✕) of the second shape.

3. When the connection point is highlighted with a red box (⊠), release the mouse button to set the connection.

☑ **Notes**

- Process flows are connected from the top and bottom connection points and control handles on shapes.

- Communication flows are connected from the right control handle of an **Action** shape to the left connection point of a **Port** shape.

- You also can use the Connector Tool to connect shapes. For more information, see the topic, "To use the Connector Tool," on the following page.

To use the Connector Tool

1. On the toolbar, click the **Connector Tool** (σ⁹) button.

2. Hover over a control handle (✳) that is on the shape from which you want to create a connection.

    The control handle is outlined with a red box to indicate that you can drag it.

3. Press and hold the mouse button to drag the control handle from the shape to a connection point (˟) on the shape to which you want to create the connection.

4. When the connection point on the shape is outlined with a red box (⊠), release the mouse button to establish the connection.

☑ Notes

*   To turn off the Connector Tool, on the toolbar, click the **Pointer Tool** (⬍) button.

*   You can add shapes to a page and perform other operations when the Connector Tool is enabled. However, you might receive an error message. The error message is not valid, and it is harmless. This false error will be corrected in future releases of Microsoft Visio. If you receive this error message, click **OK** and continue. The text of the message is as follows:

    Visio internal error: #-1

    Action 1246: Drop On Page

    First try closing and reopening the file. Next try restarting Visio.

To align shapes along a vertical or horizontal axis

1. In BizTalk Orchestration Designer, on a design page, drag the mouse pointer around the shapes that you want to align along an axis.

2. On the toolbar, click the **Align Shapes** (�⁺) button.

    The **Align Shapes** dialog box appears.

3. In one of the following areas, click the alignment that you want to use:

   - In the **Up/Down alignment** area, click one of the following buttons:

   ⊞ **Horizontal-Top Alignment**

   ⊞ **Horizontal-Center Alignment**

   ⊞ **Horizontal-Bottom Alignment**

   - In the **Left/Right alignment** area, click one of the following:

   ⊞ **Vertical-Left Alignment**

   ⊞ **Vertical-Center Alignment**

   ⊞ **Vertical-Right Alignment**

📝 Notes

- You must select shapes on a design page to enable the **Align Shapes** button.

- It is recommended that you align shapes along one axis only. Aligning shapes along both axes simultaneously might result in shapes being placed on top of each other. Press CTRL+Z to undo any changes that you do not want.

- In the **Align Shapes** dialog box, the **Disable Alignment** (✖) button clears an alignment selection.

- The **Create guide and glue shapes to it** check box is always unavailable.

- You can press and hold the SHIFT key, and then click several shapes to select them.

Related Topic

"Flowchart Shapes" earlier in this chapter

Designing Rules

Rules are Microsoft Visual Basic Scripting Edition (VBScript) expressions that are used by **Decision** and **While** shapes. Rules can include:

- Intrinsic VBScript expressions, such as **Date** and **Time**.

- Expressions that evaluate data within a message field.

- Expressions that can determine whether a message exists.

A rule contains the following properties that define the behavior of the shape:

- **Rule name.** A required property that is displayed on the XLANG schedule drawing within the shape that uses the rule. The rule name uniquely identifies the rule. A single, uniquely named rule can be used in multiple **Decision** and **While** shapes. The width of the **Decision** or **While** shape that uses the rule is determined by the rule with the longest name that is contained within the shape.

- **Rule description.** An optional property. It is a description of the rule.

- **Script expression.** A required VBScript expression that refers to data contained in messages. The expression must evaluate to either TRUE or FALSE.

When you design an XLANG schedule drawing, you create the rules and provide name and rule descriptions. When you add **Implementation** shapes to the drawing, you add script expressions.

✎ Notes

- The **Script expression** property is required only when compiling the XLANG schedule drawing into an XLANG schedule.

- There is a message field called the __Exists__ field that is not shown within messages on the **Data** page. This field can be used to test for the existence of a message. The existence of a message is determined by whether the message has been received or defined by the XLANG Scheduler Engine.

Setting Decision Conditions

The procedures in this section provide information about creating rules that can be used in the **Decision** shape in BizTalk Orchestration Designer.

To add a rule to a decision

1. In BizTalk Orchestration Designer, on a design page, right-click the **Decision** shape for which you want to add a rule and click **Add Rule**.

   The **Add Rule** dialog box appears.

2. Click one of the following options:

   - **Create a new rule**

      Click **OK**. The **Rule Properties** dialog box appears.

      For information about creating rules, see "Creating Rules" later in this chapter.

   - **Add an existing rule**

      In the **Available rules** list, click the rule that you want to add and click **OK**.

      The **Add Rule** dialog box closes, and the rule is added to the decision.

✎ Notes

- The first time you add a rule to an XLANG schedule drawing, clicking **Add Rule** opens the **Rule Properties** dialog box. The **Add Rule** dialog box appears only if you have one or more previously created rules that you can add to a decision. For more information about the **Rule Properties** dialog box, see "Creating Rules" later in this chapter.

- You can also add a rule to a decision by right-clicking a **Decision** shape, clicking **Properties**, and then clicking **Add**.

To edit a rule in a decision

1. In BizTalk Orchestration Designer, on a design page, right-click a **Decision** shape and click **Properties**.

   The **Decision Properties** dialog box appears.

2. Click the rule that you want to edit and click **Edit**.

   The **Rule Properties** dialog box appears.

3. Make the changes that you want and click **OK**.

   For more information about the **Rule Properties** dialog box, see "Creating Rules" later in this chapter.

4. To edit another rule, click the rule and click **Edit**.

   –Or–

   To close the **Decision Properties** dialog box, click **OK**.

✎ Notes

- In the **Decision Properties** dialog box, you can also add a rule by clicking **Add**.

- You can also edit a rule by right-clicking a rule that is contained within a **Decision** shape and clicking **Properties**. This action opens the **Rule Properties** dialog box.

To delete a rule from a decision

1. In BizTalk Orchestration Designer, on a design page, right-click the **Decision** shape for which you want to delete a rule and click **Properties**.

   The **Decision Properties** dialog box appears.

2. Click the rule that you want to delete and click **Delete**.

To determine the evaluation order of rules

1. In BizTalk Orchestration Designer, on a design page, right-click the **Decision** shape and click **Properties**.

   The **Decision Properties** dialog box appears.

2. Click the rule for which you want to change the evaluation order.

3. In the **Order** area, click the **Up** or **Down** arrow to move the rule to change the order in which it appears in the list.

✎ Note

- It is recommended that you order the rules in order of highest priority first. Rules are executed in sequence until a rule evaluates to TRUE. The process flow for the first rule that evaluates to TRUE is followed. If no rules evaluate to TRUE, the Else process flow is followed.

Setting While Loop Conditions

The procedures in this section provide information about creating rules that can be used in the **While** shape in BizTalk Orchestration Designer.

To add a rule to a while loop

1. In BizTalk Orchestration Designer, on a design page, right-click the **While** shape for which you want to add a rule and click **Add Rule**.

   The **Add Rule** dialog box appears.

2. Click one of the following options:
   - **Create a new rule**

     Click **OK**. The **Rule Properties** dialog box appears.

     For information about creating rules, see "Creating Rules" later in this chapter.

   - **Add an existing rule**

     In the **Available rules** list, click the rule that you want to add and click **OK**.

     The **Add Rule** dialog box closes and the rule is added to the while loop.

✎ Notes

- The first time you add a rule to an XLANG schedule drawing, clicking **Add Rule** opens the **Rule Properties** dialog box. The **Add Rule** dialog box appears only if you have one or more previously created rules that you can add to a while loop. For more information about the **Rule Properties** dialog box, see "Creating Rules" later in this chapter.

- You can add only one rule to a while loop.

To edit a rule in a while loop

1. In BizTalk Orchestration Designer, on a design page, right-click the rule that is contained within a **While** shape and click **Properties**.

   The **Rule Properties** dialog box appears.

2. Make the changes that you want and click **OK**.

   For more information about the **Rule Properties** dialog box, see "Creating Rules" later in this chapter.

To delete a rule from a while loop

- In BizTalk Orchestration Designer, on a design page, right-click the **While** shape for which you want to delete a rule and click **Delete Rule**.

To preserve state in a while loop

1. In BizTalk Orchestration Designer, on a design page, right-click a **While** shape and click **Properties**.

   The **While Properties** dialog box appears.

2. In the **State persistence** area, click one of the following options:

   - **Yes**

     The messages used in each loop iteration are saved as XLANG schedule state. If the loop is part of a transaction that fails, an **On Failure of** *Transaction* or **Compensation for** *Transaction* page is called for each completed loop iteration.

   - **No**

     Only messages used in the latest loop iteration are saved as XLANG schedule state. If the loop is part of a transaction that fails, an **On Failure of** *Transaction* or **Compensation for** *Transaction* page is called only once.

Creating Rules

The procedures in this section provide information about creating rules that can be used in the **Decision** and **While** shapes in BizTalk Orchestration Designer.

To create a rule

You can create rules to evaluate conditions within your business process. Rules are used within decisions and while loops in an XLANG schedule. When you add a rule to a **Decision** or **While** shape, the **Rule Properties** dialog box appears.

1. In the **Rule Properties** dialog box, in the **Rule name** box, type a name for the rule.

   This field is required.

2. In the **Rule description** box, you can type a detailed description of the rule.

   This field is optional.

3. Place the cursor in the **Script expression** box to enable the expression assistant.

   You can type the script expression that you want to use, or you can use the expression assistant. For more information about using the expression assistant and creating script expressions, see "To use the expression assistant" later in this chapter.

◆ Important

- Because XML is case sensitive, script expressions must use the same case as messages and their fields.

- You must place the cursor in the **Script expression** box to enable the expression assistant.

✍ Notes

- Shape names must meet certain naming conventions. The following conventions apply to transactions, ports, messages, rules, and fields:

  - The name must be a valid XML token name. For more information about XML tokens, go to the W3C Web site (www.w3.org).

  - The name cannot begin with underscores (__).

  - The name cannot include colons (:).

  - The name length must be less than or equal to 32 characters.

- You cannot name any of the following shapes: **Abort**, **Begin**, **Decision**, **End**, **Fork**, **Join**, and **While**.

- The length of the longest rule name determines the width of the **Decision** or **While** shape in which the rule is used.

- You can add script expressions at any point in the **Script expression** box by placing the cursor at the location where you want to add the expression.

- You cannot create script expressions until you have created the port implementations and the message communications between actions and ports.

- Before you compile the XLANG schedule drawing into an XLANG schedule, you must complete script expressions for all rules in the schedule.

To use the expression assistant

1. In the **Rule Properties** dialog box, in the **Expression assistant** area, click a message in the **Message** list.

2. In the **Expression Assistant** area, click a field in the **Field** list.

3. Click **Insert**.

4. In the **Script expression** box, complete the expression.

   The expression assistant adds only the message and field that you select. To evaluate the script expression, you must provide the condition for the rule. For example:

   PORequest.Total < 500

   You can also combine expressions for more complex conditions. For example:

   PORequest.Total < 500 AND PORequest.Quantity < 20

◆ Important

- Because XML is case sensitive, script expressions must use the same case as messages and their fields.

- You must place the cursor in the **Script expression** box to enable the expression assistant.

- The fields that are available in the **Field** list are based upon the message that you choose in the **Message** list. Only fields contained within that message can be used.

✏ Notes

- The **Message** list contains a list of all messages and constants available on the **Data** page.

- Rules can use the system fields that are provided on the **Data** page. When used within a rule, a system field is always surrounded by brackets. For example:

  Message1.[__Exists__]

  For more information about system fields, see "Data Handling" later in this chapter.

- You can use Microsoft Visual Basic functions such as **Date** and **Time** within rules.

- You can add script expressions at any point in the **Script expression** box by placing the cursor at the location where you want to add the expression.

- Before you compile the XLANG schedule drawing into an XLANG schedule, you must complete script expressions for all rules in the schedule.

To add constants to a rule

You can add constants to script expressions in a rule. To use constants, you must first make constants available.

1. On the **Data** page, add constants to the **Constants** list if no constants are already available.

   For more information about using constants and adding them to the **Constants** list, see "The Constants Message" later in this chapter.

2. In the **Rule Properties** dialog box, in the **Message** list, click **Constants**.

3. In the **Field** list, click the constant that you want to use and click **Insert**.

✏ Note

- All constants in the **Constants** list on the **Data** page are available and can be used in a rule.

To delete unused rules

- On the **Tools** menu, click **Delete Unused Rules**.

✏ Notes

- This procedure deletes any rules that are not used in a decision or a while loop in the XLANG schedule drawing.

- Only rules not currently used within any **While** or **Decision** shape are removed from the XLANG schedule drawing. Any rules that are used in a **While** or **Decision** shape are not deleted, even if these shapes are not currently connected to any other shapes.

Related Topic

"Flowchart Shapes" earlier in this chapter

Designing Concurrency

BizTalk Orchestration Designer supports concurrent actions. The **Fork** and **Join** shapes are used to implement concurrent process flows within an XLANG schedule. You can use the **Fork** shape to create concurrent process flows, and you can use the **Join** shape to synchronize any concurrent process flows that are not terminated by an **End** shape.

Join properties

The **Join** shape has two properties that you can set. These properties represent the following logical operators:

- **AND.** The XLANG schedule waits until all process flows reach the join before it continues to the next action in the business process.

- **OR.** The XLANG schedule waits for the first process flow that reaches the join, and then it continues to the next action in the business process.

  Actions in the other branches of the fork complete their processes; however, the **OR** join does not wait for them to be completed. If the process flow that exits an **OR** join includes an action that requires data flow from a branch that enters the **OR** join and that has not completed its action by the time the action that exits the join is executed, an error occurs.

Valid fork and join process flows

Observe the following guidelines when designing concurrent flows in a business process:

- All forked flows must either terminate with an **End** shape or be synchronized into a single flow by using a **Join** shape.

- Actions within forked flows cannot communicate with each other. For example, an action in one branch cannot send a message to a queue from which an action on another branch is waiting to receive a message.

  ☞ **Caution**

  - If you incorrectly design your XLANG schedule drawing to support communication between actions in different branches, the XLANG schedule instance might fail at run time; however, an error message will not be displayed.

- You cannot use a join to synchronize flows from more than one fork. The **Join** shape can be used only to synchronize flows from a matching fork. There is a one-to-one correspondence between the use of the **Fork** shape and the **Join** shape.

The following illustration shows two forks that are used to create concurrent flows, and a single join that is used in an attempt to synchronize these flows. This connection is not legal. If you attempt this type of connection, you will receive an error message when you compile the XLANG schedule.

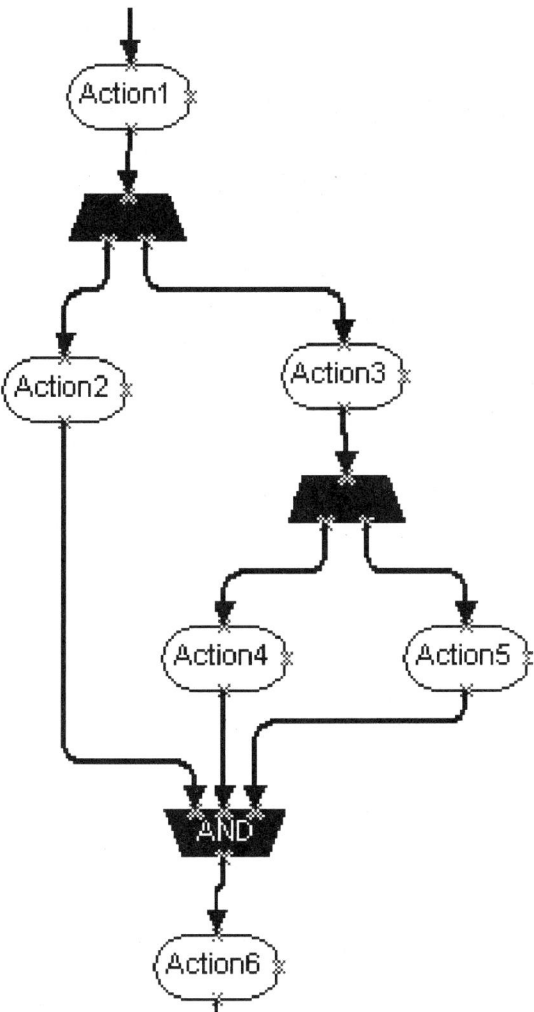

Figure 1. Concurrent flows that use an illegal join.

The following two illustrations provide two examples of legal joins.

In figure 2, two forks are matched with two joins. The second fork and join pair are nested within the first fork and join pair.

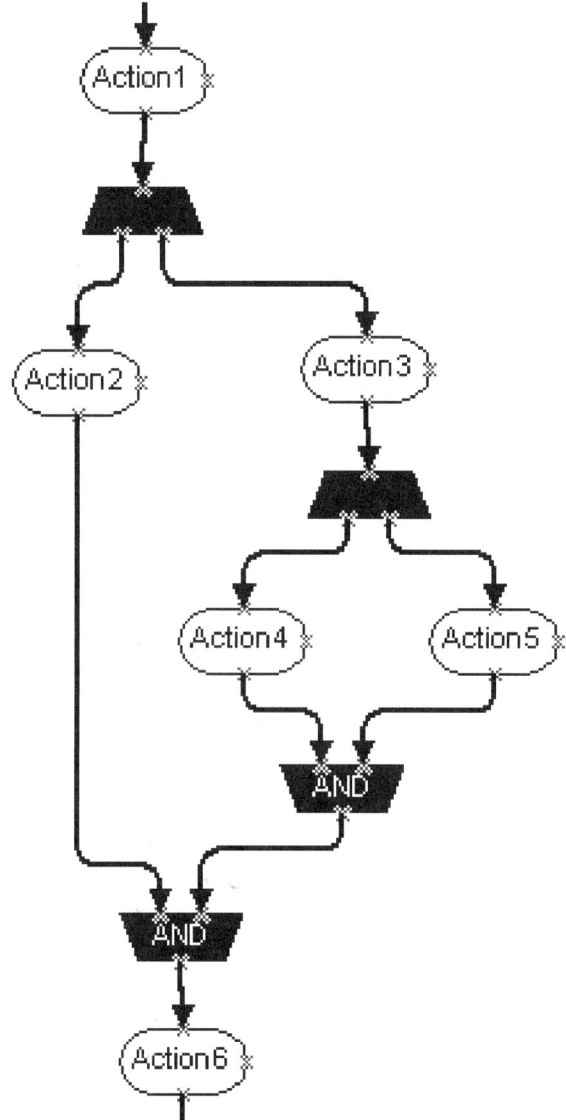

Figure 2. Concurrent flows that use a one-to-one correspondence between the fork and join, and use nested fork-join pairs.

In figure 3, two forks are matched with two joins. The second fork and join pair are nested within the first fork and join pair. Note that even though one concurrent flow within the second fork and join pair is terminated by an **End** shape, the other concurrent flow must still be synchronized by a matching join before its flow can be synchronized with the concurrent flow from the first fork and join pair.

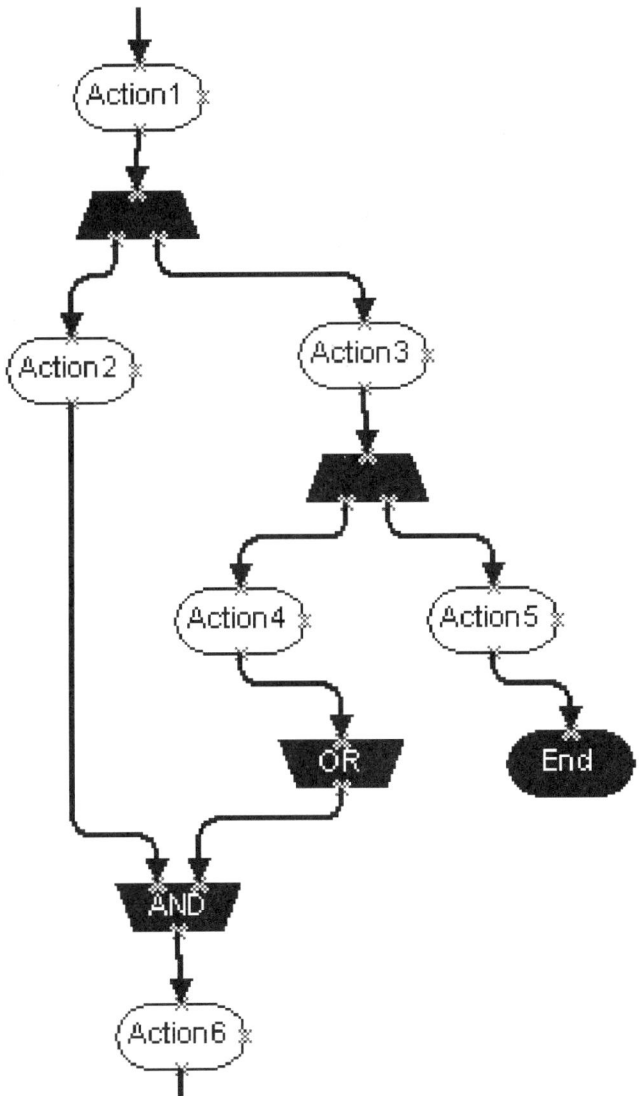

Figure 3. Concurrent flows that use a one-to-one correspondence between the fork and join, and use nested fork-join pairs as well as an End shape to terminate one flow.

- When you synchronize multiple concurrent flows with an **OR** join, each process flow that enters the join can contain only one action. If a flow contains more than one action, the flow is not legal.

The following illustration shows an **OR** join that synchronizes multiple concurrent flows. Each flow contains only one action.

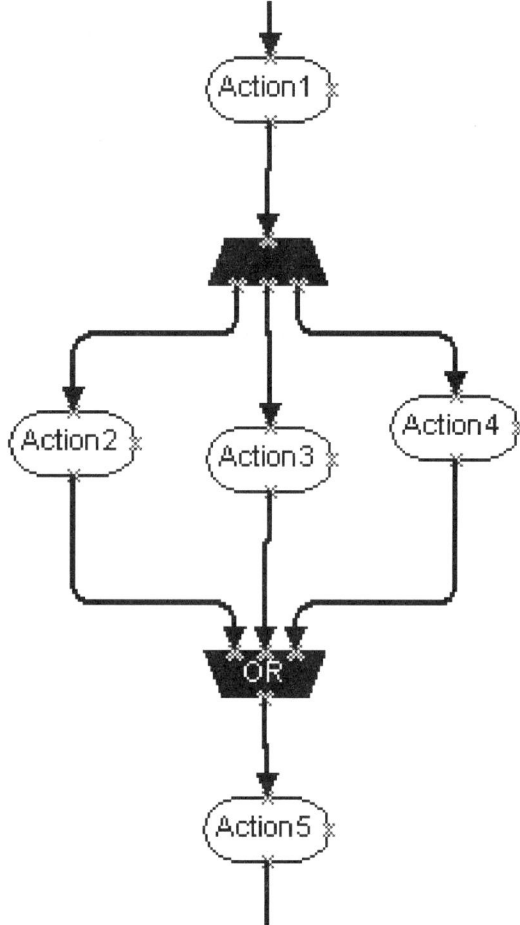

Figure 4. Three concurrent flows that use a one-to-one correspondence between the fork and join, and that are synchronized by an OR join.

To create concurrent flows

1. In BizTalk Orchestration Designer, on a design page, click a **Fork** shape.

2. Connect the bottom control handle (✳) of the **Fork** shape to the top connection point (✕) of a subsequent shape in the flow of the business process.

3. Repeat steps 1 and 2 to create additional concurrent flows.

◈ Important

- For more information about concurrent processes, it is highly recommended that you read "Designing Concurrency" earlier in this chapter.

✎ Notes

- Only one flow can enter a **Fork** shape from the top connection point.

- As many as 64 flows can exit a **Fork** shape to run concurrent processes.

- You must click the **Fork** shape to select it and activate the control handle each time you want to draw an additional flow.

  –Or–

  If you want to create several concurrent flows, you can use the Connector Tool to add the flows quickly. For more information about the Connector Tool, see "To use the Connector Tool" earlier in this chapter.

- You can add **Flowchart** shapes to the **Business Process**, **Compensation for** *Transaction*, and **On Failure of** *Transaction* pages. **Flowchart** shapes are not available on the **Data** page.

To set the Join Type property

1. In BizTalk Orchestration Designer, on a design page, right-click a **Join** shape and click **Properties**.

   The **Join Properties** dialog box appears.

2. In the **Join type** list, click one of the following options:

   - **AND**

   - **OR**

◈ Important

- For more information about concurrent processes, it is highly recommended that you read "Designing Concurrency" earlier in this chapter.

✎ Note

- If you select the **OR** join option, all flows that enter the join can have only one action associated with the flow.

To join concurrent flows

1. In BizTalk Orchestration Designer, on a design page, click a shape in the business process that is running a concurrent process.

2. Connect the bottom control handle (※) of the shape to the top connection point (×) of the **Join** shape.

3. Repeat steps 1 and 2 for all concurrent flows that rejoin this particular join.

◈ Important

- For more information about concurrent processes, it is highly recommended that you read "Designing Concurrency" earlier in this chapter.

◻ Notes

- If you select the **OR** join option, all flows that enter the join can have only one action associated with the flow.

- As many as 64 flows can enter a **Join** shape at the top connection point.

- Only one flow can leave a **Join** shape from the bottom connection point.

- If you want to join several concurrent flows, you can use the Connector Tool to join the flows quickly. For more information about the Connector Tool, see "To use the Connector Tool" earlier in this chapter.

- You can add **Flowchart** shapes to the **Business Process**, **Compensation for** *Transaction*, and **On Failure of** *Transaction* pages. **Flowchart** shapes are not available on the **Data** page.

To end a concurrent flow

1. In BizTalk Orchestration Designer, on a design page, click a shape in the business process that is running a concurrent process.

2. Connect the bottom control handle (※) of the shape to the top connection point (✕) of the **End** shape.

    This concurrent process ends. It does not rejoin other flows in the XLANG schedule.

◈ Important

- For more information about concurrent processes, it is highly recommended that you read "Designing Concurrency" earlier in this chapter.

◻ Note

- You can add **Flowchart** shapes to the **Business Process**, **Compensation for** *Transaction*, and **On Failure of** *Transaction* pages. **Flowchart** shapes are not available on the **Data** page.

Related Topics

"Flowchart Shapes" earlier in this chapter

"To connect two shapes" earlier in this chapter

"To select a shape" earlier in this chapter

"To use the Connector Tool" earlier in this chapter

Designing Transactions

BizTalk Orchestration Designer provides a transactional programming model, including error handling and recovery from failed transactions. You can configure **Transaction** shapes to create two additional types of pages in BizTalk Orchestration Designer: the **On Failure of** *Transaction* page and the **Compensation for** *Transaction* page. These two pages are used to enable business processes to recover from unsuccessful transactions. **On Failure of** *Transaction* and **Compensation for** *Transaction* pages can contain **Transaction** shapes that reference additional **On Failure of** *Transaction* and **Compensation for** *Transaction* pages. The **On Failure of** *Transaction* and **Compensation for** *Transaction* pages can use the same **Port** shapes and **Implementation** shapes that are displayed on the **Business Process** page.

The short-lived transactions that you design within BizTalk Orchestration Designer have the four ACID attributes. ACID is an acronym that is made up of the following properties:

- **Atomicity.** A transaction represents an atomic unit of work. Either all modifications within a transaction are performed, or none of the modifications are performed.

- **Consistency.** When committed, a transaction must preserve the integrity of the data within the system. If a transaction performs a data modification on a database that was internally consistent before the transaction started, the database must still be internally consistent when the transaction is committed. Ensuring this property is largely the responsibility of the application developer.

- **Isolation.** Modifications made by concurrent transactions must be isolated from the modifications made by other concurrent transactions. Isolated transactions that run concurrently perform modifications that preserve internal database consistency exactly as they would if the transactions were run serially.

- **Durability.** After a transaction has committed, all modifications are permanently in place in the system. The modifications persist even if a system failure occurs.

In contrast, long-running transactions sacrifice isolation for the ability to handle operations that require an extended period of time to complete.

Transaction Properties for an XLANG Schedule Drawing

By right-clicking the **Begin** shape on the **Business Process** page and clicking **Properties**, you can display the **Begin Properties** dialog box. In the **Begin Properties** dialog box, you can configure the following properties:

- **Transaction Model.** The default setting for this property is **Include transactions within the schedule**.

  - Choose **Include transactions within the schedule** if you are planning to enclose a collection of grouped actions in a **Transaction** shape within your XLANG schedule drawing. By choosing this option, you disable the **Transaction Activation** property.

- Choose **Treat the XLANG schedule as a COM+ component** if you want a COM+ component to activate your XLANG schedule within its COM+ transactional context. If you choose this option, you will not be able to include transactions within your XLANG schedule drawing, and your use of the **Fork** shape to implement concurrency should be restricted. If you do use the **Fork** shape, all actions containing calls to COM+ components should be restricted to a single outbound branch. This restriction does not apply if the actions in your XLANG schedule drawing contain calls to COM components. Also, all transactional changes should be performed on a single outbound branch.

  By choosing this option, you enable the **Transaction Activation** property.

- **Transaction Activation.** The default setting for this property is **Not Supported**.

  - **Not Supported.** This selection specifies that the XLANG schedule does not support transactions.

  - **Supported.** This selection specifies that the XLANG schedule might participate in a COM+ transaction.

  - **Required.** This selection specifies that the XLANG schedule requires a COM+ transaction.

  - **Requires New.** This selection specifies that the XLANG schedule must participate in a new transaction. If this setting is enabled, the XLANG Scheduler Engine automatically initiates a new transaction that is distinct from the transaction of the caller.

- **XLANG Identity.** For information about the **XLANG identity** property, see "Flowchart Shapes" earlier in this chapter.

To set the transaction model

1. In BizTalk Orchestration Designer, on a design page, right-click the **Begin** shape and click **Properties**.

   The **Begin Properties** dialog box appears.

2. In the **Transaction model** list, click one of the following options:

   - **Include Transactions within the XLANG Schedule**

     This option enables an XLANG schedule to use transactions.

   - **Treat the XLANG Schedule as a COM+ Component**

     This option disables transaction support for an XLANG schedule. A COM component can then activate the XLANG schedule within the context of a COM+ transaction.

Notes

- If you set the **Transaction model** property to **Treat the XLANG Schedule as a COM+ Component**, the **Transaction activation** list is enabled.

- If you set the **Transaction model** property to **Treat the XLANG Schedule as a COM+ Component**, do not add transactions to the XLANG schedule drawing. The XLANG schedule drawing will not compile, and you will receive an error message.

- The **XLANG identity** property is a unique ID that is used to distinguish version instances of an XLANG schedule drawing. This property is read-only and cannot be changed. Every time you update an XLANG schedule drawing, this identity is also updated.

  You can use the **XLANG identity** property to match versions of an XLANG schedule drawing (.skv) with the associated compiled XLANG schedule (.skx).

- The **Begin** shape is available on the **Business Process**, **Compensation for *Transaction***, and **On Failure of *Transaction*** pages. The **Begin** shape is not available on the **Data** page.

To set the transaction activation property

1. In BizTalk Orchestration Designer, on a design page, right-click the **Begin** shape and click **Properties**.

   The **Begin Properties** dialog box appears.

2. In the **Transaction model** list, click **Treat the XLANG Schedule as a COM+ Component**.

   When you enable this option, Component Services treats the XLANG schedule as a COM+ component. This option disables transaction support for an XLANG schedule. A COM component can then activate the XLANG schedule within the context of a COM+ transaction.

3. In the **Transaction activation** list, click one of the following options:

   - **Not Supported**

     The XLANG schedule ignores the transaction on its creator's COM+ object context, if present. None of the schedule's actions are performed within the scope of a transaction.

   - **Supported**

     The XLANG schedule participates in a COM+ transaction if a transaction is present on its creator's COM+ object context.

   - **Required**

     The XLANG schedule must run within the scope of a transaction. If a transaction is not present on the schedule creator's COM+ object context, a transaction is automatically created and used by the XLANG Scheduler Engine.

   - **Requires New**

     The XLANG schedule must run within the scope of a new transaction. The XLANG Scheduler Engine automatically creates a new transaction for the schedule that is distinct from any transaction that might have been present on the creator's COM+ object context.

✎ Notes

- The **XLANG identity** property is a unique ID that is used to distinguish version instances of an XLANG schedule drawing. This property is read-only and cannot be changed. Every time you update an XLANG schedule drawing, this identity is also updated.

  You can use the **XLANG identity** property to match versions of an XLANG schedule drawing (.skv) with the associated compiled XLANG schedule (.skx).

- The **Begin** shape is available on the **Business Process**, **Compensation for** *Transaction*, and **On Failure of** *Transaction* pages. The **Begin** shape is not available on the **Data** page.

Transaction Properties for Specific Transaction Shapes

By right-clicking a **Transaction** shape on the **Business Process** page and clicking **Properties**, you can display the **Transaction Properties** dialog box. In the **Transaction Properties** dialog box, you can configure the following properties:

- **Type.** This property determines the type of transaction that is used for the selected **Transaction** shape. The default setting for this property is **Short-lived, DTC-style**.

  - Choose **Short-lived, DTC-style** if you want the transaction to group a collection of actions that are performed as a single logical unit of work exhibiting the four properties of an ACID transaction. For more information about ACID transactions, see "Designing Transactions" earlier in this chapter. **Short-lived, DTC-style** transactions are shaded gray on the design page. This option is available for nested transactions and stand-alone transactions. You cannot choose this option for an outer transaction that contains a nested transaction.

  - Choose **Long-Running** if you want the transaction to group a collection of actions that send and receive messages over an indefinite period of time. You can also configure a **Long-Running** transaction to group a collection of nested transactions; however, transactions are limited to two levels of nesting. **Long-Running** transactions are shaded yellow on the design page. This option is available for all transactions.

  - Choose **Timed** if you want the **Long-Running** transaction to abort if it has not completed in a specified amount of time. **Timed** transactions are shaded blue on the design page. This option is available for all transactions.

- **Timeout.** This property determines the amount of time (in seconds) that the transaction will be allowed to run before it aborts. This option is available for **Timed** and **Short-lived, DTC-style** transactions.

- **Retry Count.** This property determines the number of times a process within a **Short-lived, DTC-style** transaction will be run if the process within the transaction does not complete. For each retry, the state of the application is reset to the starting point of the process within the transaction.

- **Backoff Time.** This property determines the interval between each attempt to retry the transaction. The backoff time is used with the retry count value to determine how long to wait before the next transaction retry. The backoff value is exponential. A backoff value of 2 seconds results in intervals of 2, 4, 8, 16 seconds, and so on between each retry. The formula is **B******R** (**B** raised to the power of **R**), where **B**=backoff time and **R**=current retry count. If the backoff time of a specific transaction retry attempt is greater than 180 seconds, the XLANG schedule instance will be dehydrated to the persistence database immediately.

- **Isolation Level.** The isolation level determines the degree to which data within concurrent transactions is accessible to each other. This option is available only for **Short-lived, DTC-style** transactions. You should choose:

  - **Serializable** to prevent concurrent transactions from making data modifications until the selected transaction is complete. This is the most restrictive of the four isolation levels.

  - **Read Uncommitted** to allow concurrent transactions to make data modifications before the selected transaction is complete. This is the least restrictive of the four isolation levels.

  - **Read Committed** to prevent the selected transaction from accessing data modifications in concurrent transactions until they are committed. This option is the Microsoft SQL Server default setting.

  - **Repeatable Read** to require read locks until the selected transaction is complete.

- **On Failure.** Click **Add Code**, select the **Enabled** check box, and then click **OK** if you want to enable the **On Failure of** *Transaction* page. You will then be able to use the **On Failure of** *Transaction* page to design an alternate business process to handle the failure of the selected transaction. This option is available for all transactions.

- **Compensation.** Click **Add Code**, select the **Enabled** check box, and then click **OK** if you want to enable the **Compensation for** *Transaction* page. You will then be able to use the **Compensation for** *Transaction* page to design an alternate business process to undo the logical unit of work that was performed in a nested transaction that has already committed. This option is available only for nested transactions.

Note

- Aborting a nested transaction does not automatically cause an abort of the outer transaction. This enables you to design an outer transaction that can recover from the failure of a nested transaction. However, the failure of a nested transaction can cause the failure of an outer transaction if the nested transaction's **On Failure of** *Transaction* page or **Compensation for** *Transaction* page is designed to abort the outer transaction.

To group actions and flows within a transaction

1. In BizTalk Orchestration Designer, on a design page, drag a **Transaction** shape from the **Flowchart** stencil to the left side of the **Separator** bar.

2. Resize the **Transaction** shape to surround the shapes you want enclosed within the transaction.

🗒 Notes

- Any shape or flow within the boundaries of a transaction is considered part of that transaction.

- To select a shape that is within a transaction, click the shape.

- If you delete a transaction that contains shapes within its boundaries, all contained shapes are also deleted.

- Transaction types are denoted by the following colors:

  - **Blue.** This color denotes timed transactions.

  - **Beige.** This color denotes long-running transactions.

  - **Gray.** This color denotes short-lived, DTC-style transactions.

- You can add **Flowchart** shapes to the **Business Process**, **Compensation for** *Transaction*, and **On Failure of** *Transaction* pages. **Flowchart** shapes are not available on the **Data** page.

To design nested transactions

1. In BizTalk Orchestration Designer, on a design page, drag a **Transaction** shape from the **Flowchart** stencil and place it within the boundaries of a current transaction.

2. Resize the **Transaction** shape to surround the shapes you want enclosed within the transaction.

◆ Important

- When you create a nested transaction, certain properties in the outer transaction are disabled:

  - The **Short-lived, DTC-style** transaction type is unavailable.

  - All options in the **Transaction options** area are unavailable.

  - The **Timeout** property is still active, but it cannot be changed after you create a nested transaction unless you change the transaction type to **Timed transaction**.

🗒 Notes

- Any shape or flow within the boundaries of a transaction is considered part of that transaction.

- To select a shape that is within a transaction, click the shape.

- If you delete a transaction that contains shapes within its boundaries, all contained shapes are also deleted.

- Transaction types are denoted by the following colors:

  - **Blue.** This color denotes timed transactions.

  - **Beige.** This color denotes long-running transactions.

  - **Gray.** This color denotes short-lived, DTC-style transactions.

- **Flowchart** shapes that are not fully contained within an inner transaction are considered part of the outer transaction.

- **Flowchart** shapes contained within an outer transaction might be partially hidden from view if an inner transaction partially overlaps them and they are not fully contained within the inner transaction. Select these shapes and reposition them so that they do not overlap.

- You can add **Flowchart** shapes to the **Business Process**, **Compensation for** *Transaction*, and **On Failure of** *Transaction* pages. **Flowchart** shapes are not available on the **Data** page.

To create flows that enter and leave transactions

1. In BizTalk Orchestration Designer, on a design page, click a shape that precedes a transaction in the flow of the business process.

2. Connect the bottom control handle (✳) of the shape to the top connection point (✕) of the **Transaction** shape.

3. Click the **Transaction** shape to select it.

4. Connect the top control handle of the **Transaction** shape to the top connection point of the first shape within the transaction that represents the beginning of the transactional flow.

5. From that shape connect the flow to the next shape within the transaction.

6. Connect all the flows within the transaction, and connect any actions to the ports for which you want to create a communication flow.

7. From the bottom control handle of the last shape within the transaction, connect the flow to the bottom connection point of the **Transaction** shape.

8. Click the **Transaction** shape to select it.

9. Connect the bottom control handle of the **Transaction** shape to the top connection point of the next shape in the flow of the business process that is outside the transaction.

✎ Notes

- To select a shape that is within a transaction, click the shape.

- You can add **Flowchart** shapes to the **Business Process**, **Compensation for** *Transaction*, and **On Failure of** *Transaction* pages. **Flowchart** shapes are not available on the **Data** page.

To name a transaction

1. In BizTalk Orchestration Designer, on a design page, right-click a **Transaction** shape and click **Properties**.

   The **Transaction Properties** dialog box appears.

2. In the **Name** box, type a name for the transaction.

✎ Notes

- Shape names must meet certain naming conventions. The following conventions apply to transactions, ports, messages, rules, and fields:

  - The name must be a valid XML token name. For more information about XML tokens, go to the W3C Web site (www.w3.org).

  - The name cannot begin with underscores (_).

  - The name cannot include colons (:).

  - The name length must be less than or equal to 32 characters.

- Transaction names in single-byte character sets must be less than or equal to 16 characters in length. Transaction names in double-byte character sets must be less than or equal to 8 characters in length.

To set the transaction Type property

1. In BizTalk Orchestration Designer, on a design page, right-click a **Transaction** shape and click **Properties**.

   The **Transaction Properties** dialog box appears.

2. In the **Type** area, click one of the following options:

   - **Timed transaction**

   - **Short-lived, DTC-style**

   - **Long-running**

To set the Timeout property

1. In BizTalk Orchestration Designer, on a design page, right-click a **Transaction** shape and click **Properties**.

   The **Transaction Properties** dialog box appears.

2. In the **Transaction options** area, in the **Timeout** box, enter a time in seconds.

To set the Retry count property

1. In BizTalk Orchestration Designer, on a design page, right-click a **Transaction** shape and click **Properties**.

   The **Transaction Properties** dialog box appears.

2. In the **Transaction options** area, in the **Retry count** box, enter the number of times a transaction can be retried before it is considered to have failed.

To set the Backoff time property

1. In BizTalk Orchestration Designer, on a design page, right-click a **Transaction** shape and click **Properties**.

   The **Transaction Properties** dialog box appears.

2. In the **Transaction options** area, in the **Backoff time** box, enter a time in seconds.

Note

- The **Backoff time** property determines the interval between each attempt to retry the transaction. This option is available only for short-lived, DTC-style transactions. The backoff time is used with the retry count value to determine how long to wait before the next transaction retry. The backoff value is exponential. A backoff value of 2 seconds results in intervals of 2, 4, 8, 16 seconds, and so on between each retry. The formula is **B******R** (**B** raised to the power of **R**), where **B**=backoff time and **R**=current retry count.

To set the Isolation level property

1. In BizTalk Orchestration Designer, on a design page, right-click a **Transaction** shape and click **Properties**.

   The **Transaction Properties** dialog box appears.

2. In the **Transaction options** area, in the **Isolation level** list, click one of the following options:
   - **Serializable**
   - **Read Uncommitted**
   - **Read Committed**
   - **Repeatable Read**

Note

- This property can be set only for short-lived, DTC-style transactions.

Transaction Properties for a Port Implementation

You can configure transaction properties for COM components and Windows Script components on the **Advanced Port Properties** pages of the COM Component Binding Wizard and the Script Component Binding Wizard. The **Advanced Port Properties** page provides an option to abort the current transaction when an error is returned from a method in a component. On the **Advanced Port Properties** page, you can configure the following transactional properties:

- **Transaction support.** The **Transaction support** property specifies the degree to which your component will require, support, or ignore transactions.

- **Disabled.** This selection specifies that the component will ignore COM transaction management.

- **Not Supported.** This selection specifies that the component will not participate in a transaction, or propagate the transactions of other components.

- **Supported.** This selection specifies that if a transaction contains an action that is connected to the port to which the component is bound, the component will be included in the transaction. Otherwise, the component will not have a transaction.

- **Requires New.** This selection specifies that if a transaction contains an action that is connected to the port to which the component is bound, the component will be included in the transaction. If there is no transaction containing an action that is connected to the port to which the component is bound, a new transaction will be created for the component.

- **Requires new.** This selection specifies that a new transaction will always be created for the component.

◆ **Important**

- BizTalk Orchestration Designer relies on the transactional behavior of the implementation technologies that are utilized in an XLANG schedule drawing. It does not provide or impose transactional behavior on a business process if the XLANG schedule drawing contains a **Transaction** shape. If a COM component, Message Queue, or Script component is not transactional, the data manipulated by the XLANG schedule drawing will not be modified in a transactional manner.

✎ **Notes**

- When you set the **Transaction Model** property to treat the XLANG schedule as a COM component, do not use **Transaction** shapes in the XLANG schedule drawing. If you use **Transaction** shapes, and then attempt to compile the XLANG schedule drawing into an XLANG schedule, the compile process will not work. You must remove all **Transaction** shapes from the XLANG schedule drawing before compiling.

- If the use of a COM component occurs in multiple transactions, the COM component must either hold no state or hold state and support persistence.

- If multiple actions communicate with a port bound to a COM or Script component, and these actions can be found within multiple transactions that are not nested within each other, the component instances will be destroyed and instantiated again prior to each new transactional context. If the component holds state and supports persistence, the reactivation will restore the state. If the component holds state and does not support persistence, the state will be lost. If the component was instantiated by another application, the XLANG Scheduler Engine will be able to reactivate the component only if it is persistable. If the component was instantiated by another application and cannot be persisted, the XLANG Scheduler Engine will not be able to instantiate the component again, and the XLANG schedule will fail with an error.

To describe the level of transaction support in a COM component

Transaction support for COM components is set within the COM Component Binding Wizard.

1. Open the COM Component Binding Wizard.

   For more information about this wizard, see "To implement a port by using a COM component" later in this chapter.

2. Follow the instructions in the wizard until you reach the **Advanced Port Properties** page.

3. On the **Advanced Port Properties** page, in the **Transaction support** area, click one of the following options:

   - **Disabled**

     Transaction support for the COM+ component used by this port implementation is disabled.

   - **Not supported**

     The COM+ component used by this port implementation does not support transactions.

   - **Supported**

     The COM+ component used by this port implementation inherits an existing transaction.

   - **Required**

     The COM+ component used by this port implementation can inherit an existing transaction, or use a new transaction.

   - **Requires new**

     The COM+ component used by this port implementation requires that a new transaction be used.

To describe the level of transaction support in a Windows Script Component

Transaction support for Windows Script Components is set within the Script Component Binding Wizard.

1. Open the Script Component Binding Wizard.

   For more information about this wizard, see "To implement a port by using a Windows Script Component" later in this chapter.

2. Follow the instructions in the wizard until you reach the **Advanced Port Properties** page.

3. On the **Advanced Port Properties** page, in the **Transaction support** area, click one of the following options:

- **Disabled**

  Transaction support for the COM+ component used by this port implementation is disabled.

- **Not supported**

  The COM+ component used by this port implementation does not support transactions.

- **Supported**

  The COM+ component used by this port implementation inherits an existing transaction.

- **Required**

  The COM+ component used by this port implementation can inherit an existing transaction, or use a new transaction.

- **Requires new**

  The COM+ component used by this port implementation requires that a new transaction be used.

To describe the transaction support provided by a message queue

Transaction support for message queues is set within the Message Queuing Binding Wizard.

1. Open the Message Queuing Binding Wizard.

   For more information about this wizard, see "To implement a port by using Message Queuing" later in this chapter.

2. Follow the instructions in the wizard until you reach the **Advanced Port Properties** page.

3. On the **Advanced Port Properties** page, in the **Transaction support** area, select or clear the **Transactions are required with this queue** check box.

Long-Running Transactions

Long-running transactions do not support isolation, one of the four ACID attributes described in "Designing Transactions" earlier in this chapter. The data within a long-running transaction is not locked; other processes or applications can modify the data. If your data must be consistent, you should use ACID transactions exclusively. However, because ACID transactions in a long latency environment will cause severe scalability problems, XLANG schedule drawings support long-running transactions. Long-running transactions enable you to avoid having to lock databases for extended periods of time. During a long-running transaction, messages are sent and received over an indefinite period of time. Depending on the requirements of the business process that your XLANG schedule drawing describes, you can enclose an entire business process (with the exception of the **Begin** shape and an **End** shape) within a long-running transaction.

Typically, a long-running transaction will contain several nested short-lived transactions. For example, in a simple wire transfer scenario, a long-running transaction might contain the following actions within a nested short-lived transaction:

- Withdraw money from a bank account.

- Initiate the wire transfer process.

The following illustration shows **Send money**, a short-lived transaction that is nested within a long-running transaction called **Wire transfer**. The nested transaction contains the two actions in the simple wire transfer scenario. When the **Initiate the wire transfer** action has completed, the business process sequence flows out of the nested transaction. When this happens, the nested transaction is committed; the money has been withdrawn from a bank account and sent to a destination. At this point, the business process sequence flows to the **Wait for acknowledgement** action in the outer transaction.

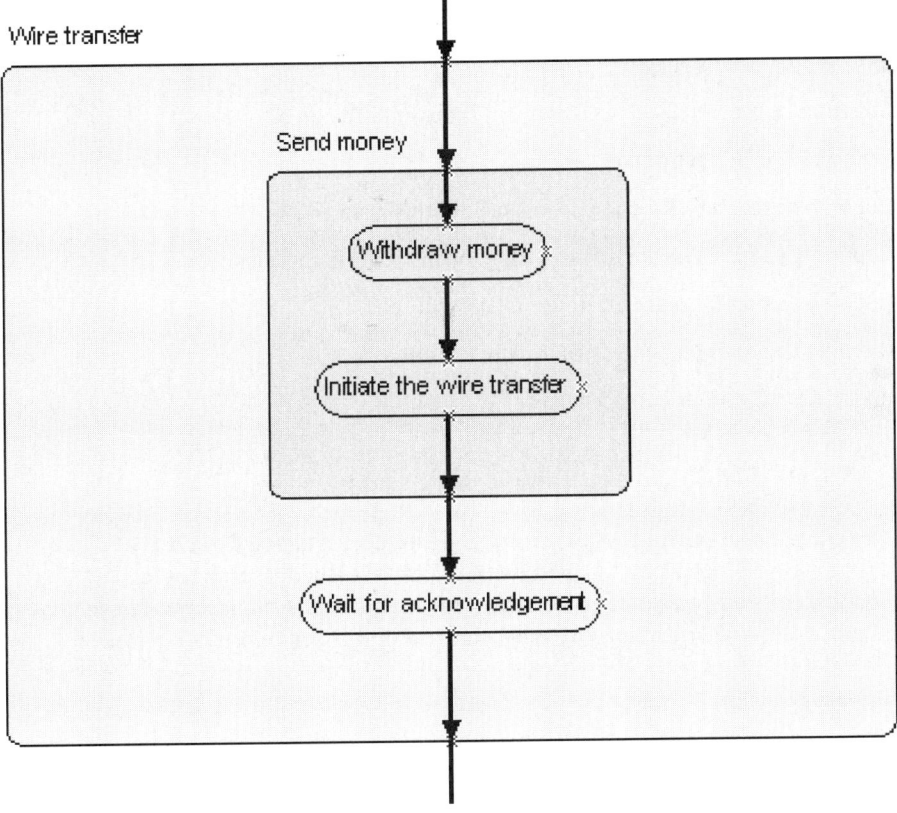

In this scenario, the **Wire transfer** transaction has been configured as a **Timed** transaction. If the sender has not received an acknowledgement of receipt of the money within the specified amount of time, the outer transaction will abort. When this happens, the business process sequence flows to the **Compensation for Send money** page for the nested transaction. Because the nested transaction has already committed, the alternate business process must describe actions that can be performed to credit the sender's account. When the business process described in the **Compensation for Send money** page has been performed, the business process sequence flows to the **On Failure of Wire transfer** page for the outer transaction. This page must contain a business process that describes exception handling for the outer transaction. In this case, the business process might be to send follow-up e-mail to inform the participants of the status of the transfer.

Short-Lived Transactions

A short-lived transaction is a collection of grouped actions that are performed as a single logical unit of work. This logical unit of work exhibits the four properties of an ACID transaction. For more information about ACID transactions, see "Designing Transactions" earlier in this chapter.

Related Topics

"Flowchart Shapes" earlier in this chapter

"To add a bound port to an XLANG schedule drawing" later in this chapter

"To connect two shapes" earlier in this chapter

"To implement a port by using a COM component" later in this chapter

"To implement a port by using a Windows Script Component" later in this chapter

"To implement a port by using Message Queuing" later in this chapter

"To modify port implementation properties" later in this chapter

"To use the Connector Tool" earlier in this chapter

Handling Exceptions

The XLANG Scheduler Engine can trap system errors. BizTalk Orchestration Designer enables you to design XLANG schedules that will react to XLANG schedule errors at run time. If you enclose part of a business process within a **Transaction** shape, you can design an alternate business process that will run if an error is encountered or if a requirement is not met.

System Errors

There are three severity levels for system errors that can occur while the XLANG Scheduler Engine is running. In ascending order of severity, the three levels are:

- Errors that can be trapped within an XLANG schedule.

- Errors that will cause an XLANG schedule instance to terminate.

- Errors that can cause the XLANG Scheduler Engine to fail.

Errors That Can Be Trapped Within an XLANG Schedule

The XLANG Scheduler Engine can trap the following system errors:

- COM errors that cause failure HRESULTs, for example, an Access Denied message from COM that results in a method being called within an XLANG schedule when permission is inadequate. This can apply to COM or Script bindings.

- Transaction aborts that are caused by enlisted services, such as the Distributed Transaction Coordinator (DTC) aborting a transaction because the connection to a database was lost. Another example might be the Message Queuing Service aborting a transaction because the Message Queuing Service is unable to queue a message.

To handle a failure HRESULT using logical branching, the _out message coming from a method call must be tested within a decision rule. The HRESULT value will be stored within the __Status__ field of the _out message.

To handle a failure HRESULT using transaction failure processes, the **Abort transaction if HRESULT indicates failure** property must be set on the last page of the COM Component Binding Wizard or the Script Component Binding Wizard. This property cannot be set unless the action is within a transaction.

◆ Important

- This option determines whether transactions in which the component is used should be aborted when method calls to the component return a failure HRESULT. This option can be set only if the communication action that uses this port is within the process flow of a transaction

Handling a failure in the **Message Queuing** or **BizTalk Messaging** implementation technologies can only be performed with transaction failure processes. To do so, the **Use transactional message queues** property on the last page of the Message Queuing Binding Wizard must be set (this is done automatically for BizTalk Messaging).

✎ Note

- A Message Queuing send action that returns successfully indicates that the message has been successfully placed onto the queue. It does not indicate that the message has been delivered.

To abort a transaction if a COM component returns a failure

Transaction support for COM components is set within the COM Component Binding Wizard.

1. Open the COM Component Binding Wizard.

   For more information about this wizard, see "To implement a port by using a COM component" later in this chapter.

2. Follow the instructions in the wizard until you reach the **Advanced Port Properties** page.

3. On the **Advanced Port Properties** page, in the **Error handling** area, select the **Abort the transaction if the method returns a failure HRESULT** check box.

◆ Important

- This option determines whether transactions in which the component is used should be aborted when method calls to the component return a failure HRESULT.

  This option can be set only if the communication action that uses this port is within the process flow of a transaction.

To abort a transaction if a Windows Script Component returns a failure

Transaction support for Windows Script Components is set within the Script Component Binding Wizard.

1. Open the Script Component Binding Wizard.

    For more information about this wizard, see "To implement a port by using a Windows Script Component" later in this chapter.

2. Follow the instructions in the wizard until you reach the **Advanced Port Properties** page.

3. On the **Advanced Port Properties** page, in the **Error handling** area, select the **Abort the transaction if the method returns a failure HRESULT** check box.

◆ Important

- This option determines whether transactions in which the component is used should be aborted when method calls to the component return a failure HRESULT.

  This option can be set only if the communication action that uses this port is within the process flow of a transaction.

Errors That Will Cause an XLANG Schedule Instance to Terminate

System errors that cause an XLANG schedule instance to fail, but that cannot be trapped within an XLANG schedule, include:

- A scheduled method that is not synchronized with the component that is called.

- A scheduled queue that does not exist.

- A scheduled channel that does not exist.

- Data flow from a message that has not arrived yet.

Errors That Can Cause the XLANG Scheduler Engine to Fail

System errors that cannot be trapped by the XLANG Scheduler Engine can cause the XLANG Scheduler Engine to fail along with all XLANG schedule instances that are running in the same COM+ application. Among these system errors are certain access violations by components that are running within the XLANG Scheduler Engine's process space. The XLANG Scheduler Engine will attempt to trap these errors, but in many cases the XLANG Scheduler Engine will not be able to trap them.

Related Topics

"To add a bound port to an XLANG schedule drawing" later in this chapter

"To implement a port by using a COM component" later in this chapter

"To implement a port by using a Windows Script Component" later in this chapter

"To modify port implementation properties" later in this chapter

"To set the transaction activation property" earlier in this chapter

"To set the transaction model" earlier in this chapter

Application Errors

There are three ways to handle errors that can cause XLANG schedule errors:

- Use logical branching
- Use transactional abort processes
- Use timeouts

Logical Branching

Decisions and rules can be used to branch a process flow on any process page (the **Business Process** page, any **On Failure of** *Transaction* page, or any **Compensation for** *Transaction* page). The following illustration shows a simple test of method execution.

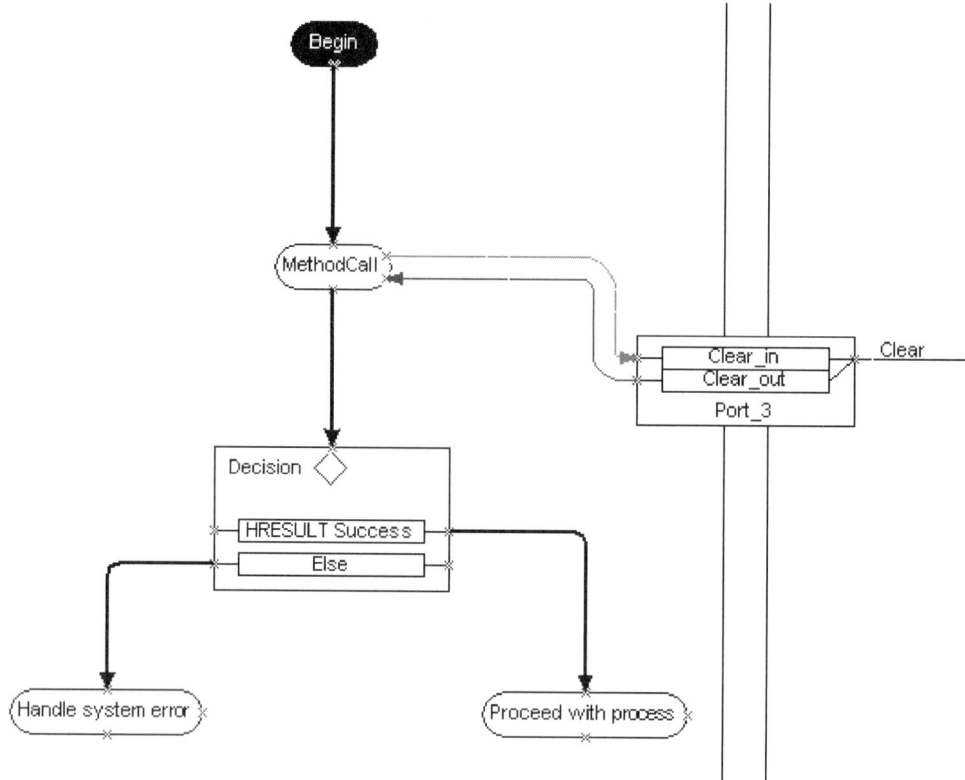

In this example, the Clear_out message has a system field named __Status__. In the **HRESULT Success** rule, the script expression would be **Clear_out.[__Status__] >= *0*,** where a negative HRESULT indicates failure, and 0 or a positive HRESULT indicates success. By using decisions and rules in this way, any data field within any message can be tested (within the VBScript expression of any rule) for exceptions, not exclusively for HRESULTs.

To abort a process flow

1. In BizTalk Orchestration Designer, on the **Flowchart** stencil, click the **Abort** shape and drag it to the design page.

2. Connect the process flow from a logical branch that exits a **Decision** shape to the connection point ($\times$) of the **Abort** shape.

◆ Important

- **Abort** shapes are used to abort a business process in a logical branch. They are used along with decisions.

  The use of the **Abort** shape depends upon the needs of your business process. The rules that are contained within a decision are evaluated until a rule evaluates to TRUE. If a rule evaluates to TRUE, the process flow continues to the next action. If no rules evaluate to TRUE, you might choose to abort the process flow.

The following illustration shows an example of a decision condition where, if the rule evaluates to TRUE, the process flow continues to Action 3. If the rule does not evaluate to TRUE, the process flow is aborted.

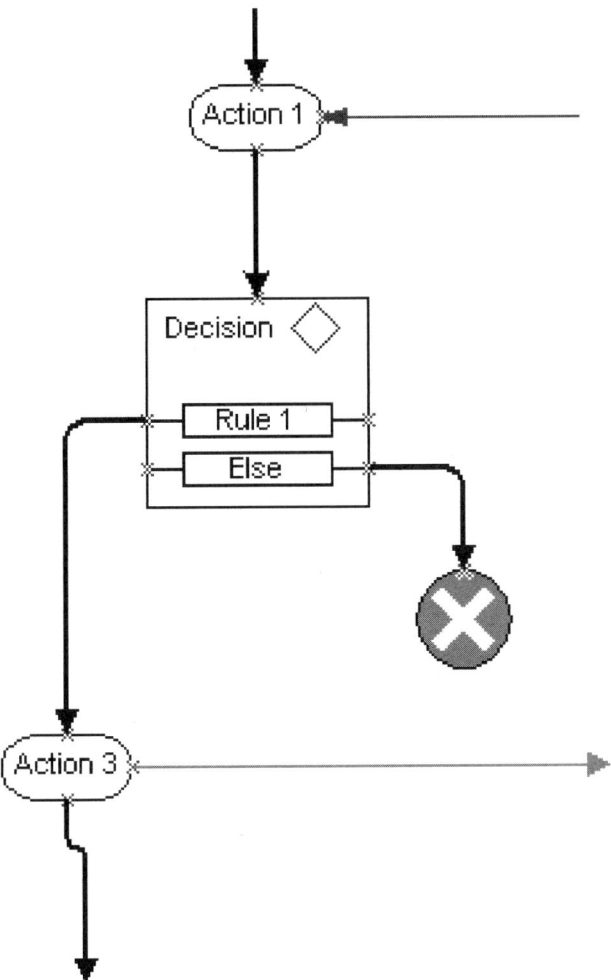

Transactional Abort Processes

In BizTalk Orchestration Designer, you can use transactions to group a collection of actions that are performed as a single logical unit of work and ensure that all of the actions within the group complete, or none of them complete. By grouping business processes within transactions, BizTalk Orchestration Designer can provide the highest level of structure and reliability.

Process flow within a transaction executes normally, until either the transaction completes or an abort event occurs. An abort event can come from one of several places:

- Encountering the **Abort** shape within the process flow.

- An HRESULT failure that is specified to cause an abort in a port binding.

- Any binding technology can, at a system level, introduce a failure event that aborts the transaction. For example, Message Queuing might fail to put a message on a queue.

- The XLANG Scheduler Engine might encounter an error that causes it to abort a transaction within a given instance. For example, there might be a DTC error.

- Pausing a schedule might require all transactions within that schedule to abort.

- A time-out within the transaction properties.

When an abort occurs, a transaction might retry from the beginning, depending on the value set in the **RetryCount** property of the transaction group. If, after a transaction has retried the specified number of times, it continues to fail, the **On Failure of** *Transaction* business process will be called. This **On Failure of** *Transaction* code provides a structured place to handle the failure of a transaction.

The **On Failure of** *Transaction* code does not have to undo any work within the transaction. If the ports are bound to transactional resources, the Distributed Transaction Coordinator will handle the rollback of all enlisted actions within the transaction. Nontransactional resources will not be rolled back. If the transaction is nested within an outer transaction, and if this nested transaction has already committed, the business process sequence will flow to the **Compensation for** *Transaction* business process for the nested transaction. The **Compensation for** *Transaction* business process is described on the **Compensation for** *Transaction* page. This alternate business process must contain actions that can be performed to undo the work within the nested transaction.

When the **Compensation for** *Transaction* or the **On Failure of** *Transaction* code has completed, the business process sequence will flow out of the bottom of the **Transaction** shape on the **Business Process** page. Actions within the business process sequence that occur after a transaction do not receive an explicit indication of whether the transaction completed or aborted. To enable an explicit indication, you can set a flag within a message field on either the **On Failure of** *Transaction* page or the **Compensation for** *Transaction* page.

To enable On Failure error handling

1. In BizTalk Orchestration Designer, on a design page, right-click a **Transaction** shape and click **Properties**.

   The **Transaction Properties** dialog box appears.

2. In the **On failure** area, click **Add Code**.

3. In the **On failure** area, select the **Enabled** check box.

✎ Notes

- Clicking the **Add Code** button creates the **On Failure of *Transaction*** page that is associated with this transaction. The parameter *Transaction* in the name of the page is replaced with the name of the transaction with which the error-handling process is associated.

- Selecting the **Enabled** check box enables the XLANG schedule to run the On Failure code for this transaction. If you do not select this check box, you can still design On Failure processes, but they do not run when the XLANG schedule is run.

To enable Compensation error handling

1. In BizTalk Orchestration Designer, on a design page, right-click an inner **Transaction** shape in a nested transaction group and click **Properties**.

   The **Transaction Properties** dialog box appears.

2. In the **Compensation** area, click **Add Code**.

3. In the **Compensation** area, select the **Enabled** check box.

✎ Notes

- Clicking the **Add Code** button creates the **On Failure of *Transaction*** or **Compensation for *Transaction*** page that is associated with this transaction.

- Selecting the **Enabled** check box enables the XLANG schedule to run the On Failure code or Compensation code for this transaction. If you do not select this check box, you can still design an On Failure or a Compensation process, but it does not run when the XLANG schedule is run.

- The parameter *Transaction* in the name of the page is replaced with the name of the transaction with which the error-handling process is associated.

- Transaction types are denoted by the following colors:
  - **Blue.** This color denotes timed transactions.
  - **Beige.** This color denotes long-running transactions.
  - **Gray.** This color denotes short-lived, DTC-style transactions.

Timeouts

If an action within a transaction does not receive an expected message from a trading partner, the failure is handled as an application error. To test for this error, use timed transactions.

For example, in a simple wire transfer scenario, a timed transaction might contain the following actions within a nested transaction:

- Withdraw money from a bank account.

- Initiate the wire transfer process.

The following illustration shows **Send money**, a nested transaction within a timed transaction called **Wire transfer**. The nested transaction contains the two actions in the simple wire transfer scenario. When the **Initiate the wire transfer** action has completed, the business process sequence flows out of the nested transaction. When this happens, the nested transaction is committed; the money has been withdrawn from a bank account and sent to a destination. At this point, the business process sequence flows to the **Wait for acknowledgement** action in the outer transaction.

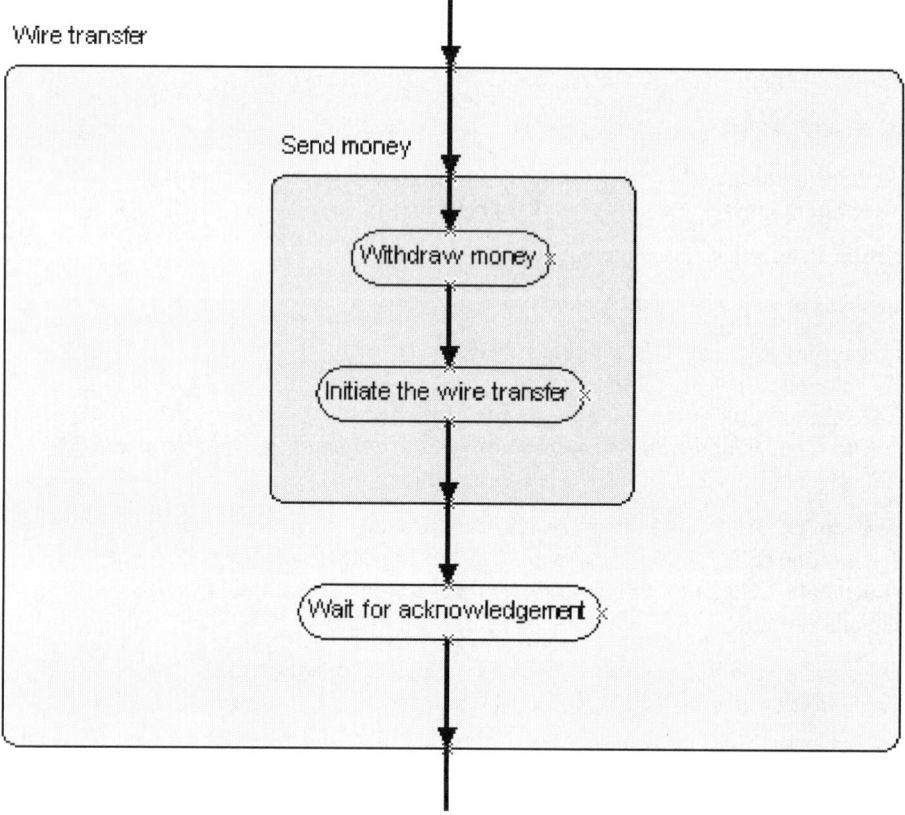

In this scenario, the **Wire transfer** transaction has been configured as a timed transaction. If the sender has not received an acknowledgement of receipt of the money within the specified amount of time, the outer transaction will abort. When this happens, the business process sequence flows to the **Compensation for Send money** page for the nested transaction. Because the nested transaction has already committed, the alternate business process must describe actions that can be performed to credit the sender's account. When the business process described in the **Compensation for Send money** page has been performed, the business process sequence flows to the **On Failure of Wire transfer** page for the outer transaction. This page must contain a business process that describes exception handling for the outer transaction. In this case, the business process might be to send follow-up e-mail to inform the participants of the status of the transfer.

Related Topics

"To design nested transactions" earlier in this chapter

"To group actions and flows within a transaction" earlier in this chapter

Implementing Business Processes

The **Implementation** stencil contains four shapes that correspond to the technologies that can be used to implement a port in a business process. Because every action either sends a message to a port or receives a message from a port, the semantic meaning of sending or receiving messages varies, depending on the specific implementation technology.

Using **Implementation** shapes involves two distinct processes. In the first process, a port is bound to an implementation technology. Conceptually, a port is an abstract location to which a message is sent or from which a message is received. Binding the port to an implementation defines the type of location to which the port is bound. In the second process, an action is connected to the port. This process defines the schema of the message that is sent to or received from the port.

BizTalk Orchestration Designer supports four implementation technologies:

- **COM Components.** This technology enables synchronous communication.
- **Windows Scripting Components.** This technology enables synchronous communication.
- **Message Queuing Services.** This technology enables asynchronous communication.
- **BizTalk Messaging Services.** This technology enables asynchronous communication.

The **Separator** bar divides the design page of BizTalk Orchestration Designer into a business-process design area on the left side and an implementation area on the right side. To open a port binding wizard, drag one of the **Implementation** shapes onto the design page, to the right of the **Separator** bar. You can perform this task on the **Business Process** page, on the **On Failure of** *Transaction* page, and on the **Compensation for** *Transaction* page.

✎ Note

- You cannot configure an envelope in BizTalk Orchestration Designer. Therefore, if you want to submit a flat file to BizTalk Orchestration, use BizTalk Editor to translate the contents of the flat file to XML. You can then submit the XML file to BizTalk Orchestration.

To add an unbound port to an XLANG schedule drawing

- In BizTalk Orchestration Designer, on a design page, right-click the **Separator** bar and click **Add New Port**.

✎ Notes

- You can add a port to the **Business Process**, **Compensation for** *Transaction*, and **On Failure of** *Transaction* pages. Ports are not available on the **Data** page.

- You cannot add shapes to the **Data** page. A port reference is created automatically on the **Data** page each time you create a new port.

- An unbound port can be implemented by using either Message Queuing or BizTalk Messaging. When you add one of those implementations to the page, the implementation wizard provides the option to select any available unbound ports.

To add a bound port to an XLANG schedule drawing

- In BizTalk Orchestration Designer, on a design page, drag an **Implementation** shape from the **Implementation** stencil to the right side of the **Separator** bar and follow the steps in the wizard for that implementation.

Notes

- You can add a port to the **Business Process**, **Compensation for** *Transaction*, and **On Failure of** *Transaction* pages. Ports are not available on the **Data** page.

- You cannot add shapes to the **Data** page. A port reference is created automatically on the **Data** page each time you create a new port.

To modify port implementation properties

1. In BizTalk Orchestration Designer, on a design page, right-click an **Implementation** shape that you want to modify.

2. Click **Properties**.

   The wizard for that **Implementation** shape opens.

3. Follow the steps in the wizard and change any properties that you want to modify.

Notes

- You can modify port implementations on the **Business Process**, **Compensation for** *Transaction*, and **On Failure of** *Transaction* pages. Port implementations are not available on the **Data** page.

- You cannot add shapes to the **Data** page. A port reference is created automatically on the **Data** page each time you create a new port.

- On the first page of the implementation wizard, the **Rename current port** option allows you to rename the port.

Understanding Port Implementations

A port is a named location that uses a specific implementation. In an XLANG schedule, ports facilitate synchronous and asynchronous communications and are used to pass messages into or out of the schedule.

In BizTalk Orchestration Designer, a port is defined by the location to which messages are sent or from which messages are received, and the technology that is used to implement the communication action. Ports are bound on the left side to actions in the business process flow of the XLANG schedule; and they are bound on the right side to an implementation technology that can be used to facilitate the required action. The location is uniquely identified by the name of the port.

The location of a port depends in part on the technology used to implement the port. The following table shows the available port implementations and the location that is associated with each port implementation.

Port implementation	Port location
COM Component	A pointer to an activated instance of an object.
Windows Script Component	A pointer to an activated instance of an object.
Message Queuing	A queue path name to a message queue.
BizTalk Messaging	A channel name for a specific BizTalk Messaging channel.

Ports can be described in two ways:

- **Static ports.** A static port requires all information about the port location and implementation be provided for an XLANG schedule at design time. The designer who creates the XLANG schedule must know the location to which messages are sent or from which messages are received, as well as the technology chosen to implement the communication action.

- **Dynamic ports.** A dynamic port requires that specific location information be provided for an XLANG schedule at run time. The implementation for a dynamic port is chosen at design time, but the location of this port is not known until the XLANG schedule is running. The location for a dynamic port is provided by a message that passes the location information to the reference for the port. This message must arrive at a point in the process flow of the XLANG schedule before the communication that uses this port implementation can be used.

  If you want to use a dynamic port for a communication, and the XLANG schedule has not received a message that contains the reference to the port before the schedule tries to complete the action, an error is generated.

Both static and dynamic ports provide options for synchronous and asynchronous communications, but the port implementations for these communications differ depending on the technology that you use to implement the port.

Any port can be either a static port or a dynamic port; however, all ports cannot implement synchronous and asynchronous communications. If you want to create a synchronous communication action, you must use a COM or Script component port implementation. If you want to create an asynchronous communication action, you must use a Message Queuing or BizTalk Messaging port implementation.

Static and Dynamic Ports

Static and dynamic port behavior varies depending on the type of implementation you use.

Port implementations that use COM or Script components

For a port implementation that uses COM or Script components, the static and dynamic properties represent how a component is instantiated:

- **Static.** For an XLANG schedule that uses a static port, the XLANG Scheduler Engine instantiates the component that is defined for this port implementation.

- **Dynamic.** For an XLANG schedule that uses a dynamic port, the XLANG Scheduler Engine does not instantiate the component. Instead, the XLANG schedule waits for another application to instantiate the component. The object instance must be sent back to the XLANG schedule as a field in a message. On the **Data** page, a connection must be drawn between that message field and the port reference for the port that uses this implementation. The XLANG schedule intercepts both the method request and the method response from the component.

In addition to the **Static** and **Dynamic** options, there is a third choice:

- **No instantiation.** For an XLANG schedule that uses a port with no instantiation, the component is not instantiated, and no code for the method call is executed. Instead, when the XLANG schedule intercepts the method request information, it returns this information as the response. The method call is circumvented.

Port implementations that use Message Queuing

In a port implementation that uses Message Queuing, the static and dynamic properties are represented as static and dynamic queues:

- **Static queue.** A static port uses a static queue that is a known, preexisting queue. You can assign this queue at design time.

  If you use a static queue, you can choose to either use a known queue that never changes, or you can create a new instance of the same queue each time the XLANG schedule is run. The per-instance queue is identified by a unique ID that is appended to the name of the queue.

- **Dynamic queue.** A dynamic port uses a dynamic queue that is unknown at design time. The information for a dynamic queue must be provided at run time within a message field. On the **Data** page you must create a link from a message field to the port reference for this port. When a message arrives that contains the queue name, the XLANG schedule can use the assigned queue. The message that contains the queue name must arrive before the communication that uses this port implementation can be used.

Port implementations that use BizTalk Messaging

In a port implementation that uses BizTalk Messaging, the static and dynamic properties are represented as static and dynamic channels. Dynamic channels can be used only when you are sending messages. Dynamic channels cannot be used to receive messages.

- **Static channel.** A static port uses a static channel that is a known, preexisting channel. You can assign this channel at design time, and it never changes.

- **Dynamic channel.** A dynamic port uses a dynamic channel that is unknown at design time. The information for a dynamic channel must be provided at run time within a message field. On the **Data** page you must create a link from a message field to the port reference for this port. When a message arrives that contains the channel name, the XLANG schedule can use the assigned channel. The message that contains the channel name must arrive before the communication that uses this port implementation can be used.

A port that uses a dynamic channel enables an XLANG schedule to determine which channel to use at run time, rather than requiring that a preexisting channel be defined at design time. This property defines which channel is used when the XLANG schedule passes the message to BizTalk Messaging Services.

The dynamic channel should not be confused with an open channel that is configured in BizTalk Messaging Manager. An open channel enables the source organization to be determined at run time from information within the document or in the parameters submitted with the document. This property defines the source of the documents. For more information about open channels, see "Understanding Channels" in Chapter 9, "Configuring BizTalk Messaging Services."

The message that is passed to a port that uses a dynamic channel could specify either an open channel or a channel that is not open when passing the channel information to BizTalk Messaging Services.

Using the COM Component Shape

The **COM Component** shape enables you to use preexisting components or applications to perform actions within an XLANG schedule. Because COM technology is synchronous, there is always a bidirectional flow of messages when an action is performed. In contrast, the flow of messages for an asynchronous technology is in one direction.

The XLANG Scheduler Engine supports sending or receiving messages by the use of **Action** shapes. When you bind a port to a COM component in BizTalk Orchestration Designer, the port is bound to an interface that is implemented by a COM component that has been registered on your system.

A send action that is connected to the port represents the invocation of a specific method call by the XLANG Scheduler Engine. The *IN* and *IN/OUT* parameters are sent to the port. In return, a message with a schema that is defined by the *IN/OUT* and *OUT* parameters of the method call is received from the port. The method call is supported by the interface that is bound to the port.

A receive action that is connected to the port waits for an external application to make a method call to the port. The *IN* and *IN/OUT* parameters define the schema of the message that is received by the port, and the *IN/OUT* and *OUT* parameters define the schema of the message that is sent from the port.

For every action that is connected to a port and bound to a COM component, two messages are exchanged. The messages identify the method on the interface that is invoked. The schema for the messages correspond to the *IN* and *IN/OUT* parameters (and to the *IN/OUT* and *OUT* parameters) of the method signature. Because the type library for the components is accessible, BizTalk Orchestration Designer can automatically build the schema for these messages without querying the user for this information.

◆ Important

- Use COM components carefully when you implement a long-running business process. If components that hold state are used in an XLANG schedule, it is recommended that you use components that can be saved by using either the **IPersistStream** or **IPersistStreamInit** interface. This ensures that the XLANG schedule can store its state along with the state of the components. XLANG schedules must be able to hold state and run durably over a long period of time. If components that do not hold state are used, a new instance of the component is created every time the XLANG schedule is rehydrated. However, the use of components that do not hold state should not affect the outcome of the schedule.

Binding is the process of specifying the technology that will implement a port. The COM Component Binding Wizard is made up of the following pages:

Welcome to the COM Component Binding Wizard

On the **Welcome to the COM Component Binding Wizard** page, you can create and name a port for which you want to define an implementation.

Static or Dynamic Communication

On the **Static or Dynamic Communication** page, you can define how the component will be instantiated. The following table lists and describes the static and dynamic communication settings.

Static or dynamic communication	Description
Static	Select this option if you can provide the XLANG Scheduler Engine with all the required information to complete the implementation at design time.
Dynamic	Select this option if the XLANG Scheduler Engine requires additional information at run time to complete the implementation.
No instantiation	Select this option to enable the XLANG schedule to receive data by using a method call without activating the component. When you select **No instantiation**, method calls to this component are intercepted, the XLANG Scheduler Engine stores the arguments, and the call returns to the caller. The component is never instantiated.

Class Information

On the **Class Information** page, you can select a class from a list of registered components or from a moniker.

Interface Information

On the **Interface Information** page, you can select the interface that you want to use. This page is displayed only if the selected class contains more than one interface. Visual Basic components always have a single interface.

Method Information

On the **Method Information** page, you can select the methods that you want to use. This page is displayed only if the selected class contains more than one method.

Advanced Port Properties

On the **Advanced Port Properties** page, you can configure security, transaction support, state management support, and error handling.

The state management support properties of the **COM Component** shape include:

- Persisting the state of an XLANG schedule before the start of a transaction, and after the completion of a transaction. This provides durability, ensuring that all committed data modifications are permanently in place in the system. This also enables retries of a transaction if a failure occurs.

- Optimizing instance management by enabling the XLANG Scheduler Engine to dehydrate the XLANG schedule and then rehydrate the schedule when the message it is waiting for arrives.

You can use the **COM Component** shape to request authenticated user information for the messages that are received.

Security area

The following table lists and describes the sender identity confirmation settings.

Sender identity confirmation	Description
Not required	Select this option if you want the XLANG schedule to be able to receive a message without knowing the identity of the sender.
Optional	Select this option if you want the XLANG Scheduler Engine to identify the sender when the component receives a message, if the information is available.
Required	Select this option if you do not want the XLANG Scheduler Engine to receive a message unless it can identify the sender.

Transaction support area

The following table lists and describes the transaction support settings.

Transaction support	Description
Disabled	This is for all non-COM+ components. This option specifies that the component will ignore COM transaction management.
Not Supported	This is only for COM+ components. This option specifies that the component will not participate in a transaction, or propagate the transactions of other components.
Supported	This is only for COM+ components. This option specifies that if a transaction is associated with the port to which the component is bound, the component will be included in the transaction. Otherwise, the component will not have a transaction.
Required	This is only for COM+ components. This option specifies that if a transaction is associated with the port to which the component is bound, the component will be included in the transaction. If there is no transaction associated with the port to which the component is bound, a new transaction will be created for the component.
Requires New	This is only for COM+ components. This specifies that a new transaction will always be created for the component.

State management support area

The following table lists and describes the state management support settings.

State management support	Description
Holds no state	This specifies that the XLANG Scheduler Engine will terminate the component instance when it is dehydrated. If you select this setting, the XLANG Scheduler Engine will create a new component instance, if it is required, when the schedule is rehydrated.
Holds state, but doesn't support persistence	This specifies that the XLANG Scheduler Engine will be required to leave the component instance running. If the system fails while the application is dehydrated, any state that has been held in this component will be lost.
Holds state, and does support persistence	This specifies that the XLANG Scheduler Engine will remove the component instance from memory, and then restore it to memory by calling either **IPersistStream** or **IPersistStreamInit** on the component during dehydration, and then again during rehydration.

Error handling area

In the **Error handling** area, select the **Abort transaction if the method returns a failure HRESULT** check box if you want the XLANG Scheduler Engine to abort the transaction when an error is returned from a method in a component.

🖉 Notes

- When an action communicates with a port bound to a COM component and the specified method does not exist on the component, the XLANG schedule instance will failfast with an event log entry.

- BizTalk Orchestration Designer does not support binding to a COM component method that contains a parameter derived from **IDispatch**. However, BizTalk Orchestration Designer does support binding to COM component methods containing parameters of type **IDispatch**.

- If an application has a reference to a COM component in an XLANG schedule by means of the **IUnknown** interface, that reference will become invalid after the XLANG schedule instance is dehydrated and rehydrated. All persistable COM components will be properly rehydrated to the state they were in at the time of dehydration, but the interfaces will be assigned new addresses. This is expected and normal behavior. If two or more message fields in any single XLANG schedule instance contain pointers to the same COM component, and the schedule is dehydrated, these message fields will contain pointers to a single COM component after rehydration. However, the COM component will not be the same one that existed before dehydration. It will be a newly created COM component that is similar to the COM component that existed before dehydration. If the original COM component is persistable, the new COM component will have the same state that the original COM component had before dehydration.

- Component uniqueness is not maintained across while loops. If one message within a while loop contains a field that has a pointer to a COM component, and a different message outside the while loop contains a field that has a pointer to the same COM component, after dehydration and rehydration these two message fields will no longer have pointers to a single COM component. The two message fields will have pointers to two separate COM components that are similar to the original COM component. If the original COM component is persistable, the two new COM components will hold the same state that the original COM component had before dehydration.

To implement a port by using a COM component

1. In BizTalk Orchestration Designer, on a design page, drag the **COM Component** shape from the **Implementation** stencil to the right side of the **Separator** bar.

   The COM Component Binding Wizard opens.

2. On the **Welcome to the COM Component Binding Wizard** page, type a name for the port that you want to create and click **Next**.

BizTalk Orchestration Designer provides a default port name with a number appended to it for each new port implementation that is added. You can change this name.

3. On the **Static or Dynamic Communication** page, click one of the following options:

- **Static**

  The XLANG Scheduler Engine instantiates this component.

  If you click the **Static** option, the component is automatically destroyed when the XLANG schedule instance ends.

  Click **Next**. Continue to step 4 in this procedure.

- **Dynamic**

  If you select this option, another application instantiates the component. A moniker or a pointer to the object instance must be sent back to the XLANG schedule as a field in a message. On the **Data** page, a connection must be drawn between that message field and the port reference for the port that uses this implementation. For more information about sending a message to a specific port, see "To match a specific message with a specific port" later in this chapter.

  Click **Next**. Continue to step 5 in this procedure.

- **No instantiation**

  Select this option only to receive data. This option specifies that data is passed into an XLANG schedule by using a method; however, none of the code behind the method call is executed. For more information, see "Data Handling" later in this chapter.

  Click **Next**. Continue to step 5 in this procedure.

For more information about static and dynamic communications, see the following information:

- "Static and Dynamic Ports" earlier in this chapter
- "Instance Management" later in this chapter
- "Using the Script Component Shape" later in this chapter

4. On the **Class Information** page, click one of the following options:

- **From a registered component**

  A tree control displays all components registered on your computer. Expand the folder for the class that you want and click the class.

  Click **Next**.

- **From a moniker**

  Type the name of a standard COM moniker to specify the location of the COM component that you want to instantiate. If you use this option, the COM component cannot be used with communications that take place within a transaction in the XLANG schedule.

  Click **Next**.

5. On the **Interface Information** page, click the interface that you want to use and click **Next**.

Notes

- If the COM component has only one interface, this page is skipped.

- If the COM component was created in Microsoft Visual Basic, there is one interface of the same name as each class contained within the component. Each interface name is prefaced with an underscore (_).

6. On the **Method Information** page, select the methods that you want to use and click **Next**.

Notes

- If the COM component has only one method, this page is skipped.

- You must select at least one method.

- You can select several methods, or all of them. The **Check All** and **Uncheck All** buttons enable you to either select or deselect all the methods.

7. On the **Advanced Port Properties** page, in the **Security** area, click one of the following options:

- **Not required**

  No attempt is made to confirm the identity of the sender.

- **Optional**

  The XLANG Scheduler Engine requests the identity of the sender. The XLANG schedule continues to run whether or not the identity is available.

- **Required**

  The XLANG Scheduler Engine requests the identity of the sender. The sender identity is required, and the XLANG schedule ignores the message if the identity is not available.

Note

- If the XLANG schedule rejects an incoming method call when the identity is required but is unavailable, the error code E_ACCESSDENIED is returned to the caller.

8. On the **Advanced Port Properties** page, in the **Transaction support** area, click one of the following options:

- **Disabled**

  Transaction support for the COM+ component used by this port implementation is disabled.

- **Not supported**

  The COM+ component used by this port implementation does not support transactions.

- **Supported**

  The COM+ component used by this port implementation inherits an existing transaction.

- **Required**

  The COM+ component used by this port implementation can inherit an existing transaction or use a new transaction.

- **Requires new**

  The COM+ component used by this port implementation requires that a new transaction be used.

9. On the **Advanced Port Properties** page, in the **State management** area, click one of the following options:

- **Holds no state**

  The component used by this port implementation holds no state across method calls.

- **Holds state, but doesn't support persistence**

  The component used by this port implementation holds state during the lifetime of the component, but the component cannot be persisted.

- **Holds state, and does support persistence**

  The component used by this port implementation holds state that can be saved by using either the **IPersistStream** or **IPersistStreamInit** interface. The use of either **IPersistStream** or **IPersistStreamInit** allows the state of the component to be saved for later instantiations, and the component is recreated using the saved state.

10. On the **Advanced Port Properties** page, in the **Error Handling** area, select or clear the **Abort the transaction if the method returns a failure HRESULT** check box.

◆ Important

- This option determines whether transactions in which the component is used should be aborted when method calls to the component return a failure HRESULT.

  This option can be set only if the communication action that uses this port is within the process flow of a transaction.

11. Click **Finish**.

✎ Notes

- Shape names must meet certain naming conventions. The following conventions apply to transactions, ports, messages, rules, and fields:

  - The name must be a valid XML token name. For more information about XML tokens, go to the W3C Web site (www.w3.org).

- The name cannot begin with underscores (__).

- The name cannot include colons (:).

- The name length must be less than or equal to 32 characters.

- Constant names and message names cannot begin with a numeric character.

- You can add port implementations to the **Business Process**, **Compensation for Transaction**, and **On Failure of** *Transaction* pages. Port implementations are not available on the **Data** page.

- You cannot add shapes to the **Data** page. A port reference is created automatically on the **Data** page each time you create a new port.

- A new port is always created for use with a COM component implementation.

- If you are editing an existing port implementation, on the first page of the implementation wizard, the **Rename current port** option enables you to rename the port.

Using the Script Component Shape

The **Script Component** shape enables you to use a preexisting Windows Script component to perform actions within an XLANG schedule. Because the **Script Component** is synchronous, there is always a bidirectional flow of messages when an action is performed. In contrast, the flow of messages for an asynchronous technology is in one direction.

A send action that is connected to the port represents the invocation of a specific method call by the XLANG Scheduler Engine. The *IN* and *IN/OUT* parameters are sent to the port. In return, a message with a schema that is defined by the *IN/OUT* and *OUT* parameters of the method call is received from the port. The method call is supported by the interface that is bound to the port.

A receive action that is connected to the port waits for an external application to make a method call to the port. The *IN* and *IN/OUT* parameters define the schema of the message that is received by the port, and the *IN/OUT* and *OUT* parameters define the schema of the message that is sent from the port.

For every action that is connected to a port and bound to a Script component, two messages are exchanged. The messages identify the method on the interface that is invoked. The schema for the messages corresponds to the *IN* and *IN/OUT* parameters (and to the *IN/OUT* and *OUT* parameters) of the method signature. Because the type library for the components is accessible, BizTalk Orchestration Designer can automatically build the schema for these messages without querying the user for this information.

The XLANG Scheduler Engine waits until the method returns before continuing the business process. To send a message, the XLANG Scheduler Engine invokes the specified method of a Windows Script component.

To create a new Script component binding, drag the **Script Component** shape from the **Implementation** stencil onto the BizTalk Orchestration design page, to the right of the

Separator bar. To edit an existing Script component, right-click the **Script Component** shape and click **Edit Properties**. Both actions start the Script Component Binding Wizard. Binding is the process of specifying the technology that will implement a port. The Script Component Binding Wizard is made up of the following pages:

Welcome to the Script Component Binding Wizard

On the **Welcome to the Script Component Binding Wizard** page, you can create and name a port for which you want to define an implementation.

Static or Dynamic Communication

On the **Static or Dynamic Communication** page, you can define how the component will be instantiated. The following table lists and describes the static and dynamic communication settings.

Static or dynamic communication	Description
Static	Select this option if you can provide the XLANG Scheduler Engine with all the required information to complete the implementation at design time.
Dynamic	Select this option if the XLANG Scheduler Engine requires additional information at run time to complete the implementation.
No instantiation	Select this option to enable the XLANG schedule to receive data by using a method call without activating the component. When you choose **No instantiation**, method calls to this component are intercepted, the XLANG Scheduler Engine stores the arguments, and the call returns to the caller. The component is never instantiated.

Specify the Script File

On the **Specify the Script File** page, you can type the path to the Windows Script Component (.wsc) file that you want to use.

Component Instantiation Information

On the **Component Instantiation Information** page, you can specify if the XLANG Scheduler Engine will use a moniker or a Prog ID to instantiate the Script component.

Method Information

On the **Method Information** page, you can select the methods that belong to the selected class.

Advanced Port Properties

On the **Advanced Port Properties** page, you can configure security, transaction support, and error handling. You can use the **Script Component** shape to request authenticated user information for the messages that are received.

Security area

The following table lists and describes the sender identity confirmation settings.

Sender identity confirmation	Description
Not required	Select this option if you want the XLANG schedule to be able to receive a message without knowing the identity of the sender.
Optional	Select this option if you want the XLANG Scheduler Engine to identify the sender when the component receives a message, if the information is available.
Required	Select this option if you do not want the XLANG Scheduler Engine to receive a message unless it can identify the sender.

Transaction support area

The following table lists and describes the transaction support settings.

Transaction support	Description
Disabled	This is for all non-COM+ components. This option specifies that the component will ignore COM transaction management.
Not Supported	This is available only if the script is installed as a COM+ component. This specifies that the component will not participate in a transaction, or propagate the transactions of other components.
Supported	This is available only if the script is installed as a COM+ component. This specifies that if a transaction is associated with the port to which the component is bound, the component will be included in the transaction. Otherwise, the component will not have a transaction.
Required	This is available only if the script is installed as a COM+ component. This specifies that if a transaction is associated with the port to which the component is bound, the component will be included in the transaction. If there is no transaction associated with the port to which the component is bound, a new transaction to be created for the component.
Requires New	This is available only if the script is installed as a COM+ component. This specifies that a new transaction will always be created for the component.

Error handling area

In the **Error handling** area, select the **Abort transaction if the method returns a failure HRESULT** check box if you want the XLANG Scheduler Engine to start an abort process when an error is returned from a method in a component. To use **On Failure of** *Transaction* and **Compensation for *Transaction*** pages, this option must be selected for the XLANG Scheduler Engine. If this option is not selected, error-recovery processes that are defined on either page will not be run.

◆ Important

- When you use Windows Script Components, they must adhere to the following rules:
  - Argument declarations must be by reference, not by value.
  - Visual Basic Scripting subroutines are not supported. Only functions are supported.
  - Multiple components cannot be used within a single .wsc file.

◢ Notes

- When an action communicates with a port bound to a Script component and the specified method does not exist within the Script component, the XLANG schedule instance will failfast with an event log entry.

- Script components that have been run by the XLANG Scheduler Engine cannot be modified until both the XLANG Scheduler Engine and the Windows Scripting Host have been shut down.

To implement a port by using a Windows Script Component

1. In BizTalk Orchestration Designer, on a design page, drag the **Script Component** shape from the **Implementation** stencil to the right side of the **Separator** bar.

   The Script Component Binding Wizard opens.

2. On the **Welcome to the Script Component Binding Wizard** page, type a name for the port that you want to create and click **Next**.

   BizTalk Orchestration Designer provides a default port name with a number appended to it for each new port implementation that is added. You can change this name.

3. On the **Static or Dynamic Communication** page, click one of the following options and then click **Next**:

   - **Static**

     The XLANG Scheduler Engine instantiates this component.

     If you click the **Static** option, the component is automatically destroyed when the XLANG schedule instance ends.

   - **Dynamic**

     If you select this option, another application instantiates the component. A moniker or a pointer to the object instance must be sent back to the XLANG schedule as a field in a message. On the **Data** page, a connection must be drawn between that message field and the port reference for the port that uses this implementation. For more information about sending a message to a specific port, see "To match a specific message with a specific port" later in this chapter.

- **No instantiation**

  Select this option only to receive data. This option indicates that data is passed into the XLANG schedule by using a method; however, none of the code behind the method call is executed.

  For more information about static and dynamic communications, see the following information:

  - "Static and Dynamic Ports" earlier in this chapter

  - "Instance Management" later in this chapter

  - "Using the Script Component Shape" later in this chapter

4. On the **Specify the Script File** page, click **Browse**.

   The **Select Script File** dialog box appears.

5. Browse to the location of the .wsc file that you want to use, click the file, and then click **Open**.

6. Click **Next** and continue with one of the following options:

   - If you selected **Static** in step 3, continue to step 7 in this procedure.

   - If you selected **Dynamic** or **No instantiation** in step 3, continue to step 8 in this procedure.

7. On the **Component Instantiation Information** page, click one of the following and then click **Next**:

   - **Use a moniker of the script file**

     The path and file name of the script file is automatically provided as the moniker.

   - **Use the Prog ID "*Prog ID*"**

     The Prog ID is automatically provided, and is extracted from the XML in the Windows Script Component file. This is recommended because the path to the script file is not hard-coded.

8. On the **Method Information** page, select the methods that you want to use and click **Next**.

   📝 **Notes**

   - If the Windows Script Component has only one method, this page is skipped.

   - You must select at least one method.

   - You can select several methods, or all of them. The **Check All** and **Uncheck All** buttons enable you to either select or deselect all the methods.

9. On the **Advanced Port Properties** page, in the **Security** area, click one of the following options:

- **Not required**

  No attempt is made to confirm the identity of the sender.

- **Optional**

  The XLANG Scheduler Engine requests the identity of the sender. The XLANG schedule continues to run whether or not the identity is available.

- **Required**

  The XLANG Scheduler Engine requests the identity of the sender. The sender identity is required, and the XLANG schedule ignores the message if the identity is not available.

Note

- If the XLANG schedule rejects an incoming method call when the identity is required but is unavailable, the error code E_ACCESSDENIED is returned to the caller.

10. On the **Advanced Port Properties** page, in the **Transaction support** area, click one of the following options:

- **Disabled**

  Transaction support for the COM+ component used by this port implementation is disabled.

- **Not supported**

  The COM+ component used by this port implementation does not support transactions.

- **Supported**

  The COM+ component used by this port implementation inherits an existing transaction.

- **Required**

  The COM+ component used by this port implementation can inherit an existing transaction or use a new transaction.

- **Requires new**

  The COM+ component used by this port implementation requires that a new transaction be used.

11. On the **Advanced Port Properties** page, in the **Error Handling** area, select or clear the **Abort the transaction if the method returns a failure HRESULT** check box.

◆ Important

- This option determines whether transactions in which the component is used should be aborted when method calls to the component return a failure HRESULT.

  This option can be set only if the communication action that uses this port is within the process flow of a transaction.

12. Click **Finish**.

◆ Important

- When you use Windows Script Components, they must adhere to the following rules:

  - Argument declarations must be by reference, not by value.

  - Microsoft Visual Basic Scripting subroutines are not supported. Only functions are supported.

  - Multiple components cannot be used within a single .wsc file.

✐ Notes

- Shape names must meet certain naming conventions. The following conventions apply to transactions, ports, messages, rules, and fields:

  - The name must be a valid XML token name. For more information about XML tokens, go to the W3C Web site (www.w3.org).

  - The name cannot begin with underscores (__).

  - The name cannot include colons (:).

  - The name length must be less than or equal to 32 characters.

  - Constant names and message names cannot begin with a numeric character.

- You can add port implementations to the **Business Process**, **Compensation for** *Transaction*, and **On Failure of** *Transaction* pages. Port implementations are not available on the **Data** page.

- You cannot add shapes to the **Data** page. A port reference is created automatically on the **Data** page each time you create a new port.

- A new port is always created for use with a Windows Script Component implementation.

- If you are editing an existing port implementation, on the first page of the implementation wizard, the **Rename current port** option allows you to rename the port.

- Windows Script Component files use the file extension .wsc. For more information about Windows Script Components, go to the Windows Scripting Technologies Web site (msdn.microsoft.com/scripting/default.htm) and browse to the Windows Script Components page.

- Windows Script Components that have been run by the XLANG Scheduler Engine cannot be modified until both the XLANG Scheduler Engine and the Windows Scripting Host are shut down.

Using the Message Queuing Shape

The **Message Queuing** shape enables an XLANG schedule to communicate with another XLANG schedule (or with an application), in a loosely coupled manner, using a queue. To enable communication between XLANG schedules and applications, messages are dropped onto a queue and then read. A single XLANG schedule might use several ports that are bound to the **Message Queuing** shape.

When a port is bound to the **Message Queuing** shape, it is also bound to a message queue. The port can be bound to a named queue or to a per-instance queue. If a port is bound to a per-instance queue, a unique queue is created and used for each instance of this XLANG schedule. Per-instance queues provide a convenient way for an XLANG schedule to have a separate queue for each XLANG schedule instance.

When an action is connected to a port that is bound to a message queue, the following information is used to define the way messages will be represented in the schedule:

- The message that is sent or received by the action must be defined. Because multiple message types can be stored in a queue, the message type helps identify the type of message that should be received by the action. During a **Send** action, the message type is marked on the label property of the message when it is written to the queue.

The **Message Queuing** shape represents the Message Queuing Service that is used to send or receive messages. To receive a message, the XLANG Scheduler Engine requires the name of the queue that is used and the name of the root element of the XML schema that is contained within that message. To send a message, the XLANG Scheduler Engine needs the name of the queue that is used to transmit messages.

If you configure an XLANG schedule instance to use Message Queuing to receive messages, you can use the XML Communication Wizard to specify the destination format as either XML or string.

To create a new Message Queuing binding, drag the **Message Queuing** shape from the **Implementation** stencil onto the BizTalk Orchestration design page, to the right of the **Separator** bar. To edit an existing Message Queuing implementation, right-click the **Message Queuing** shape and click **Edit Properties**. Both actions start the Message Queuing Binding Wizard. Binding is the process of specifying the technology that will implement a port. The Message Queuing Binding Wizard is made up of the following pages:

Welcome to the Message Queuing Binding Wizard

On the **Welcome to the Message Queuing Binding Wizard** page, you can create and name a port for which you want to define an implementation, or you can choose an existing, unbound port.

Static or Dynamic Queue Information

On the **Static or Dynamic Queue Information** page, you can specify if the message queue will be defined at design time or at run time. Choose one of the following options:

- Choose **Static queue** if you can provide queue information at design time.

- Choose **Dynamic queue** if you want the XLANG Scheduler Engine to acquire information from an external source at run time to determine the queue name.

Queue Information

On the **Queue Information** page, you can create a new queue or specify an existing queue. Choose one of the following options:

- Choose **Create a new queue for every instance** if you want the XLANG Scheduler Engine to create a per-instance queue for every XLANG schedule instance.

- Choose **Use a known queue for all instances** if you want the XLANG Scheduler Engine to use a known queue.

Advanced Port Properties

On the **Advanced Port Properties** page, you can configure security and choose whether or not you want to enable transaction support. You can use the **Message Queuing** shape to request authenticated user information for the messages that are received.

Security area

The following table lists and describes the sender identity confirmation settings.

Sender identity confirmation	Description
Not required	Select this option if you want the XLANG schedule to be able to receive a message without knowing the identity of the sender.
Optional	Select this option if you want the XLANG Scheduler Engine to identify the sender when the component receives a message, if the information is available.
Required	Select this option if you do not want the XLANG Scheduler Engine to receive a message unless it can identify the sender.

You can also select or clear the **Use a Windows Group or User Name to control the queue** check box. If you select the check box, enter the name of the user or group that is permitted to write messages to the queue. This option is available only if you are using a static queue.

Transaction support area

In the **Transaction support** area, select the **Transactions are required with this queue** check box to enable transaction support.

Notes

- Currently, the supported name format for queues does not enable remote access to a queue on another computer. Use public queues instead of private queues when an XLANG schedule communicates with an application on a remote computer.

- When an action communicates with a port bound to Message Queuing and the specified queue for the binding does not exist, the XLANG schedule instance will failfast with an event log entry.

- It is important that the XLANG Scheduler Engine be able to determine if a queue is transactional or not. If a queue is in a transactional context and a message is sent to the queue, the XLANG Scheduler Engine must know whether the transaction should be used to communicate with the queue. If the port binding is configured with the **Transactions are required with this queue** check box selected, the XLANG Scheduler Engine will failfast the XLANG schedule if it is determined at run time that the queue is not transactional.

To implement a port by using Message Queuing

1. In BizTalk Orchestration Designer, on a design page, drag the **Message Queuing** shape from the **Implementation** stencil to the right side of the **Separator** bar.

   The Message Queuing Binding Wizard opens.

2. On the **Welcome to the Message Queuing Binding Wizard** page, click one of the following options and click **Next**:

   - **Create a new port**

     BizTalk Orchestration Designer provides a default port name with a number appended to it for each new port implementation that is added. You can change this name.

   - **Existing unbound port**

     In the **Existing unbound port** list, click the port that you want to use.

     Only names for unbound ports appear in the **Existing unbound port** list. An unbound port has no defined implementation.

3. On the **Static or Dynamic Queue Information** page, click one of the following options:

    *   **Static queue**

        A static queue is a known, preexisting queue. This queue must be known at design time.

        Click **Next**. Continue to step 4 in this procedure.

    *   **Dynamic queue**

        If you select this option, on the **Data** page you must create a link from a message field to the port reference for this port.

        The name of the message queue must be provided by another message prior to the communication action that occurs by using this port implementation. For more information about matching a specific message with a specific port, see "To match a specific message with a specific port" later in this chapter.

        Click **Next**. Continue to step 5 in this procedure.

        For more information about static and dynamic queues, see "Static and Dynamic Ports" earlier in this chapter.

4. On the **Queue Information** page, click one of the following options and click **Next**:

    *   **Create a new queue for every instance**

        You must assign the queue a prefix (for example: ".\Private$\PrivateQueuePrefix" or ".\PublicQueuePrefix"). A unique ID is appended to the prefix for each new queue that is created.

        A default queue prefix is provided for you. You can change this default.

        If you want to enable someone to reply to this port, a reference to this port must be sent in a message. To do this, select **Create a new queue for every instance** and enter a root queue name. At run time, the XLANG Scheduler Engine creates a new queue with this root name for every instance, and an instance GUID is appended to the root name for each queue created. This queue is deleted when the instance ends.

        If you do not plan to send out a reference to this port, there is no need for a per-instance queue. You can create a queue that will be used for all instances.

    *   **Use a known queue for all instances**

        Enter the queue name of a known, preexisting queue (for example: ".\private$\queuename").

5. On the **Advanced Port Properties** page, in the **Security** area, click one of the following options:

- **Not required**

  No attempt is made to confirm the identity of the sender. The XLANG schedule always receives the message with a blank __Sender__ field, whether or not the message is authenticated.

- **Optional**

  The XLANG Scheduler Engine sends a request for confirmation of the identity of the sender. The XLANG schedule receives the message, whether or not a message is authenticated. If the message is authenticated, the __Sender__ field contains the Message Queuing message **SenderID** property.

- **Required**

  The XLANG Scheduler Engine sends a request for confirmation of the identity of the sender. Confirmation of the sender identity is required. If the message is authenticated, the XLANG schedule receives the message, and the __Sender__ field contains the Message Queuing message **SenderID** property.

  If the message is not authenticated, an application event-log entry is created, and the message is moved to a new queue that is created and named .\private$*ApplicationName*.DeadLetter.

6. On the **Advanced Port Properties** page, in the **Security** area, select or clear the **Use a Windows Group or User Name to control the queue** check box.

   If you select the check box, enter the name of the user or group that is permitted to write messages to the queue. This option is available only if you are using a static queue.

7. On the **Advanced Port Properties** page, in the **Transaction support** area, select or clear the **Transactions are required with this queue** check box.

8. Click **Finish**.

✐ Notes

- Shape names must meet certain naming conventions. The following conventions apply to transactions, ports, messages, rules, and fields:

  - The name must be a valid XML token name. For more information about XML tokens, go to the W3C Web site (www.w3.org).

  - The name cannot begin with underscores (__).

  - The name cannot include colons (:).

  - The name length must be less than or equal to 32 characters.

  - Constant names and message names cannot begin with a numeric character.

- You can add port implementations to the **Business Process**, **Compensation for Transaction**, and **On Failure of *Transaction*** pages. Port implementations are not available on the **Data** page.

- You cannot add shapes to the **Data** page. A port reference is created automatically on the **Data** page each time you create a new port.

- If you are editing an existing port implementation, on the first page of the implementation wizard, the **Rename current port** option allows you to rename the port.

Using the BizTalk Messaging Shape

The **BizTalk Messaging** shape represents BizTalk Messaging Services that are used to exchange messages between BizTalk Orchestration Services and BizTalk Messaging Services. To receive a message, the XLANG Scheduler Engine requires the HTTP URL address used by the BizTalk Messaging Service to receive documents, the name of the channel, and the message type of the outbound document definition. Receiving documents for XLANG schedule activation only requires the message type of the document definition. To send a message, the XLANG Scheduler Engine requires the name of the channel and the message type of the inbound document definition. For more information about exchanging messages between BizTalk Orchestration Services and BizTalk Messaging Services, see "Maps for Integrating BizTalk Services" in Chapter 6, "Mapping Data."

◆ Important

- If you configure a port to activate a new XLANG schedule when a message arrives, you must observe the following restrictions:

  - Only one port in a schedule can be used to activate the XLANG schedule when the message arrives.

  - Only one action can receive through this port.

  - This one action cannot be in a loop body.

  - You cannot draw a data flow connection from the port reference for this port to any other message in the schedule.

To create a new BizTalk Messaging binding, drag the **BizTalk Messaging** shape from the **Implementation** stencil onto the BizTalk Orchestration design page, to the right of the **Separator** bar. To edit an existing BizTalk Messaging implementation, right-click the **BizTalk Messaging** shape and click **Edit Properties**. Both actions start the BizTalk Messaging Binding Wizard. Binding is the process of specifying the technology that will implement a port. The BizTalk Messaging Binding Wizard is made up of the following pages:

Welcome to the BizTalk Messaging Binding Wizard

On the **Welcome to the BizTalk Messaging Binding Wizard** page, you can create and name a port for which you want to define an implementation, or you can choose an existing, unbound port.

Communication Direction

On the **Communication Direction** page, you can specify if you want to configure the port to send or receive messages.

Static or Dynamic Channel Communication

The **Static or Dynamic Channel Communication** page appears only if you choose **Send** on the **Welcome to the BizTalk Messaging Binding Wizard** page. On the **Static or Dynamic Channel Communication** page, you can specify if you want the XLANG Scheduler Engine to use a static channel that will be defined at design time or a dynamic channel that will be defined at run time.

XLANG Schedule Activation Information

On the **XLANG Schedule Activation Information** page, you can specify if an XLANG schedule instance will be activated on this receive action. If you choose **Yes**, the BizTalk Messaging Binding Wizard finishes. If you choose **No**, the **Channel Information** page appears.

Channel Information

On the **Channel Information** page, you can specify the name of the channel and the HTTP URL address used by the BizTalk Messaging Service to receive documents.

Notes

- When an action communicates with a port bound to BizTalk Messaging and the specified channel for the binding does not exist, the XLANG schedule instance will failfast with an event log entry.

- Including separate send and receive BizTalk Messaging bindings in a single transaction might result in a deadlock condition that will cause the transaction to fail.

- Action events related to messages processed by an XLANG schedule that are either sent to or received from BizTalk Messaging Services can be tracked in the Tracking database. For more information, see "Tracking XLANG Schedule Events in the Tracking Database" in Chapter 13, "Tracking Documents."

To implement a port by using BizTalk Messaging

1. In BizTalk Orchestration Designer, on a design page, drag the **BizTalk Messaging** shape from the **Implementation** stencil to the right side of the **Separator** bar.

    The BizTalk Messaging Binding Wizard opens.

2. On the **Welcome to the BizTalk Messaging Binding Wizard** page, click one of the following options and click **Next**:

    - **Create a new port**

      BizTalk Orchestration Designer provides a default port name with a number appended to it for each new port implementation that is added. You can change this name.

    - **Existing unbound port**

      In the **Existing unbound port** list, click the port that you want to use.

      Only names for unbound ports appear in the **Existing unbound port** list. An unbound port has no defined implementation.

3. On the **Communication Direction** page, click one of the following options:

    - **Send**

      Click **Next**. Continue to step 4 in this procedure.

    - **Receive**

      Click **Next**. Continue to step 5 in this procedure.

    ### 📝 Note

    - If you choose **Receive**, messages can be received by using an HTTP URL destination, or by using BizTalk Messaging Manager to configure a messaging port to instantiate an XLANG schedule, and send messages to a specific port in that schedule. For more information about receiving messages by using an HTTP URL, see "Maps for Integrating BizTalk Services" in Chapter 6, "Mapping Data." For more information about using BizTalk Messaging Manager to configure a messaging port, see "To set destination application properties" in Chapter 9, "Configuring BizTalk Messaging Services."

4. On the **Static or Dynamic Channel Information** page, click one of the following options and then click **Finish**:

    - **Static channel**

      Enter the name of a known, preexisting channel.

    - **Dynamic channel**

      If you select this option, you must configure the port to provide the data that BizTalk Messaging Services needs at run time to identify the correct channel to process the message.

On the **Data** page, you must create a link from a message field of a previously received message to the port reference for this port. The message field must contain a destination address, which BizTalk Messaging Services uses as the destination address for an open messaging port that is associated with that channel. For more information, see "Maps for Integrating BizTalk Services" in Chapter 6, "Mapping Data."

When you establish the communication flow from an action to this port, you use the XML Communication Wizard. On the **Message Type Information** page, in the **Message type** box, you must enter the name of the inbound document definition for the channel. BizTalk Messaging Services uses this data to identify the correct channel to process the message. For more information, see "Identification" in Chapter 9, "Configuring BizTalk Messaging Services."

◆ Important

- There must be at least one channel configured in BizTalk Messaging Services that uses the specified inbound document definition. When an action communicates with a port bound to BizTalk Messaging and the specified channel for the binding does not exist, the XLANG schedule instance will failfast with an event log entry.

- There should be only one channel configured in BizTalk Messaging Services that uses the specified inbound document definition and is configured with **XLANG schedule** as its source. For more information, see "To set source application properties" in Chapter 9, "Configuring BizTalk Messaging Services." That channel also must be associated with an open messaging port. When an action communicates with a port bound to BizTalk Messaging and more than one channel for the binding exists, the XLANG schedule instance will failfast with an event log entry.

5. On the **XLANG Schedule Activation Information** page, click one of the following options:

   - **Yes**

     This port cannot be used in multiple receive actions or within a single receive action within a loop.

     Click **Finish**.

   - **No**

     Click **Next**.

6. On the **Channel Information** page, in the **Channel name** box, type the name of the channel that you want to use. For more information about channels, see "Understanding Channels" and "To search for channels" in Chapter 9, "Configuring BizTalk Messaging Services."

7. On the **Channel Information** page, in the **HTTP URL address where the BizTalk Messaging Service receives documents** box, type the URL address from which BizTalk Server receives documents for this channel.

8. Click **Finish**.

✦ **Important**

- If you configure a port to activate a new XLANG schedule when a message arrives, you must observe the following restrictions:
  - Only one port in a schedule can be used to activate the schedule when the message arrives.
  - Only one action can receive through this port.
  - This one action cannot be in a loop body.
  - You cannot draw a data flow connection from the port reference for this port to any other message in the schedule.

✎ **Notes**

- Shape names must meet certain naming conventions. The following conventions apply to transactions, ports, messages, rules, and fields:
  - The name must be a valid XML token name. For more information about XML tokens, go to the W3C Web site (www.w3.org).
  - The name cannot begin with underscores (__).
  - The name cannot include colons (:).
  - The name length must be less than or equal to 32 characters.
  - Constant names and message names cannot begin with a numeric character.
- You can add port implementations to the **Business Process**, **Compensation for Transaction**, and **On Failure of *Transaction*** pages. Port implementations are not available on the **Data** page.
- You cannot add shapes to the **Data** page. A port reference is created automatically on the **Data** page each time you create a new port.
- If you are editing an existing port implementation, on the first page of the implementation wizard, the **Rename current port** option allows you to rename the port.

Related Topics

Chapter 14, "Orchestrating Business Processes with BizTalk Server 2000"

"Implementation Shapes" earlier in this chapter

"To match a specific message with a specific port" later in this chapter

"To modify port implementation properties" earlier in this chapter

"Understanding Channels" in Chapter 9, "Configuring BizTalk Messaging Services"

"Understanding Port Implementations" earlier in this chapter

Synchronous and Asynchronous Communication

All communication to a COM or Script component implementation is synchronous. If you want to create a communication flow to a port that uses a COM component or Script component implementation, you must use the Method Communication Wizard.

All communication to an unbound port, or to a Message Queuing or BizTalk Messaging implementation, is asynchronous. If you want to create a communication flow to a port that uses a Message Queuing or BizTalk Messaging implementation, or if you want to create a communication flow to an unbound port, you must use the XML Communication Wizard.

The following illustration and text describes what an XLANG schedule does for the four possible communication actions.

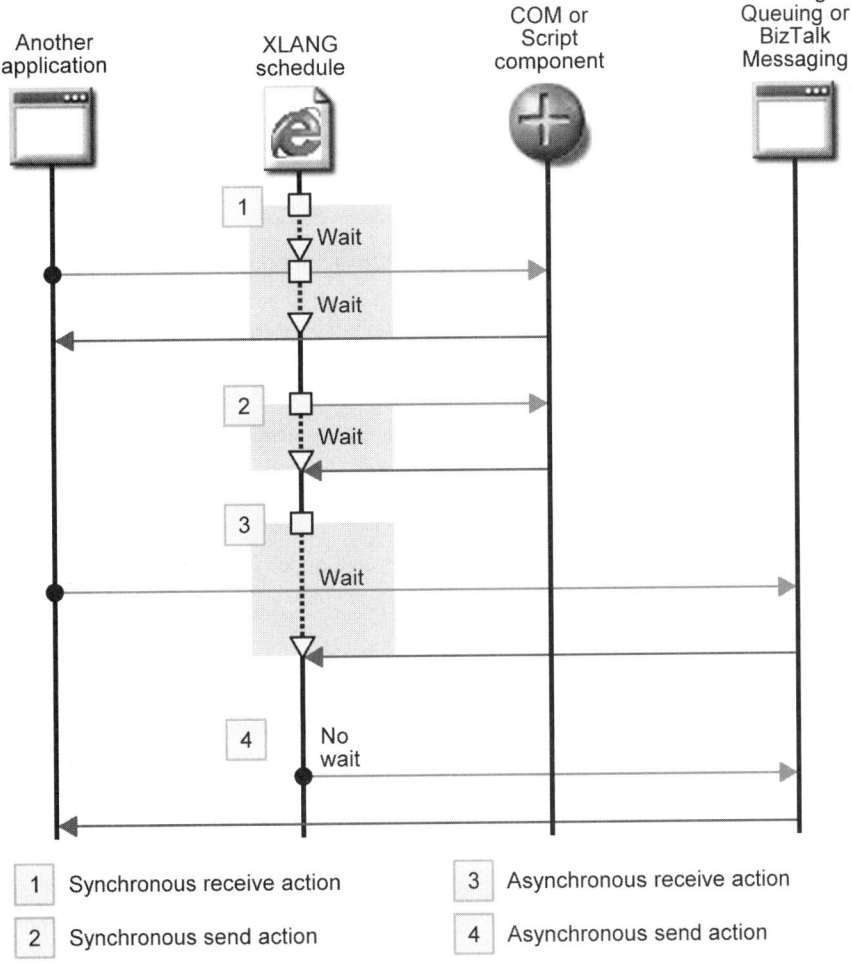

1	Synchronous receive action	3	Asynchronous receive action
2	Synchronous send action	4	Asynchronous send action

1. **Synchronous receive action**

   1. The XLANG schedule waits for another application to send a method request and instantiate a component.

   2. The schedule intercepts the method request.

   3. The schedule waits for the component to return the method response.

   4. The schedule intercepts the method response.

   5. The schedule continues with the next action in the business process flow.

2. **Synchronous send action**

   1. The XLANG schedule initiates the method request and instantiates the component.

   2. The schedule waits for the component to return the method response.

   3. The schedule receives the method response.

   4. The schedule continues with the next action in the business process flow.

3. **Asynchronous receive action**

   1. The XLANG schedule waits for another application to send a message to a messaging queue or to a BizTalk Messaging channel.

   2. The XLANG schedule receives the message from the messaging queue or from the channel.

   3. The schedule continues with the next action in the business process flow.

4. **Asynchronous send action**

   1. The XLANG schedule sends a message to a messaging queue or to a BizTalk Messaging channel.

   2. The schedule continues with the next action in the business process flow.

   3. Another application receives the message from the message queue or BizTalk Messaging channel.

✐ Notes

- A special case exists for the synchronous receive action. If you choose **No instantiation** in the COM Component Binding Wizard or the Script Component Binding Wizard, the component is not instantiated, and no code for the method call is executed. Instead, when the XLANG schedule intercepts the method request information, it returns this information as the response. The method call is circumvented. For more information about static and dynamic ports and the COM Component Binding Wizard and the Script Component Binding Wizard, see the following information earlier in this chapter:

  - "Static and Dynamic Ports"

  - "Implementation Shapes"

- "Using the COM Component Shape"

- "Using the Script Component Shape"

Action events related to messages processed by an XLANG schedule that are either sent to or received from BizTalk Messaging Services can be tracked in the Tracking database. For more information, see "Tracking XLANG Schedule Events in the Tracking Database" in Chapter 13, "Tracking Documents."

To establish the communication flow between an action and a port

1. In BizTalk Orchestration Designer, on a design page, click an **Action** shape to select it.

2. Drag the right control handle (✻) of the **Action** shape to the connection point (✕) of a **Port** shape.

    A communication wizard opens.

3. Continue to one of the following procedures, depending on which type of communication flow you want to create:

    - If you want to create a synchronous communication flow to a port that uses a COM Component or Script Component implementation, use the Method Communication Wizard. Continue to "To send or receive synchronous messages" later in this chapter.

    - If you want to create an asynchronous communication flow to a port that uses a Message Queuing or BizTalk Messaging implementation, or if you want to create an asynchronous communication flow to an unbound port, use the XML Communication Wizard. Continue to "To send or receive asynchronous messages" later in this chapter.

Notes

- You can also use the Connector Tool to connect shapes. For more information, see "To use the Connector Tool" earlier in this chapter.

- You can establish a communication flow between an action and a port on the **Business Process**, **Compensation for** *Transaction*, and **On Failure of** *Transaction* pages. Actions and ports are not available on the **Data** page.

- You cannot add shapes to the **Data** page. New messages are created automatically on the **Data** page each time an action is connected to a port.

To modify the communication flow between an action and a port

1. In BizTalk Orchestration Designer, on a design page, right-click the communication flow that is between an action and a port.

    A communication wizard opens.

2. Follow the steps in the wizard to change any properties that you want to modify.

3. Continue to one of the following procedures, depending on which type of communication flow you want to create:

- If you want to create a synchronous communication flow to a port that uses a COM Component or Script Component implementation, use the Method Communication Wizard. Continue to "To send or receive synchronous messages" later in this chapter.

- If you want to create an asynchronous communication flow to a port that uses a Message Queuing or BizTalk Messaging implementation, or if you want to create an asynchronous communication flow to an unbound port, use the XML Communication Wizard. Continue to "To send or receive asynchronous messages" later in this chapter.

Notes

- You can establish a communication flow between an action and a port on the **Business Process**, **Compensation for** *Transaction*, and **On Failure of** *Transaction* pages. Actions and ports are not available on the **Data** page.

- You cannot add shapes to the **Data** page. New messages are created automatically on the **Data** page each time an action is connected to a port.

Using the Method Communication Wizard

On the **Business Process** page, the **Compensation for** *Transaction* page, and the **On Failure of** *Transaction* page, you can use the Method Communication Wizard to define the flow of messages between an **Action** shape and a **COM Component** shape or a **Script Component** shape. If a message is sent, the XLANG schedule will call the method with the _in message and then wait to receive the _out message from the component. If a message is to be received, the XLANG schedule will wait for another application to send the _in message to the method (by calling a method on the port), and then wait for the _out message from the component to be sent back to the other application.

Notes

- For Visual Basic programmers, **ByVal** parameters appear only in the _in message. All other parameters appear in both the _in message and the _out message.

- For C programmers, **in** parameters appear in the _in message, **out** parameters appear in the _out message, and **in,out** parameters appear in both messages.

- For Visual Basic programmers and C programmers, if a parameter appears in both the _in message and the _out message, the _in message contains the contents of what was sent into the method, and the _out message contains the contents of what was returned by the method.

To start the Method Communication Wizard, drag the right control handle (※) of an **Action** shape to the connection point (✕) on a port bound to a **COM Component** shape or a **Script Component** shape. The Method Communication Wizard is made up of the following pages:

Welcome to the Method Communication Wizard

On the **Welcome to the Method Communication Wizard** page, you can specify whether the XLANG Scheduler Engine will call a method or wait for a method call. If you specify that the

XLANG Scheduler Engine will wait for a method call, you can set a latency value to indicate an amount of time in seconds that the XLANG Scheduler Engine is likely to have to wait before a message arrives. If this value is 180 seconds or less, the XLANG schedule instance will never be dehydrated to the persistence database. If this value is greater than 180 seconds, the XLANG schedule instance will be dehydrated to the persistence database immediately. By default, the latency value is set to zero, indicating that the message is expected to arrive immediately.

If an XLANG schedule instance is rehydrated for any reason other than the arrival of a message for which an action is waiting (and if the XLANG schedule instance then enters a quiescent state), the specified latency value is used to determine whether the XLANG schedule instance will be immediately dehydrated. For example, this can occur when a concurrent branch receives a message for which it was waiting, or when a computer restart causes all XLANG schedule instances to rehydrate. In this situation, the latency value is evaluated from the point when the XLANG schedule instance enters a quiescent state. If the amount of time from the beginning of the XLANG Scheduler Engine's original waiting period (combined with the latency value) is more than 180 seconds from when the XLANG Scheduler Engine entered the quiescent state after rehydration, the XLANG schedule instance will be dehydrated to the persistence database immediately. This point in the XLANG schedule instance can occur long after the XLANG Scheduler Engine begins monitoring the arrival of a message.

Message Information

On the **Message Information** page, you can specify whether a new message or a reference to an existing message should be created. If you specify that a reference to an existing message should be created, you can select from a list of previously created messages that have been sent to or received from methods, and that already have corresponding **Message** shapes. If the message you want to use is not listed, specify that a new message should be created, and define the data flow for the new message.

Message Specification Information

On the **Message Specification Information** page, you can select a message specification for the message you created or referenced on the **Message Information** page.

To send or receive synchronous messages

In BizTalk Orchestration Designer, after you have created a communication flow between an action and a port for a synchronous communication, the Method Communication Wizard opens. For more information about creating a communication flow, see "To establish the communication flow between an action and a port" earlier in this chapter.

1. On the **Welcome to the Method Communication Wizard** page, click one of the following options:

   - **Initiate a synchronous method call**

     The XLANG Scheduler Engine initiates a synchronous method call.

In this case, the XLANG Scheduler Engine sends a method call to a component, waits for a response from the component, and then receives a response.

Click **Next**. Continue to step 3 in this procedure.

- **Wait for a synchronous method call**

  The XLANG Scheduler Engine waits to receive a method call that is initiated by another application.

  In this case, the XLANG Scheduler Engine waits for another application to initiate the method call. This separate application sends a method call to a component; the XLANG Scheduler Engine waits for a response from the component and then returns a response to the application. The XLANG schedule intercepts both the method request and the method response.

  Continue to step 2 in this procedure.

2. On the **Welcome to the Method Communication Wizard** page, to optimize the execution of an XLANG schedule, enter the amount of time (in seconds) that you expect the XLANG Scheduler Engine to wait before a message arrives and click **Next**.

   The default wait time is 0 seconds. You can change this time. Any time less than or equal to 180 seconds causes the XLANG schedule to never dehydrate. Any time greater than 180 seconds causes the XLANG schedule to dehydrate immediately. For more information about wait times and XLANG schedule dehydration, see "Dehydration and Rehydration" later in this chapter and "Using the Method Communication Wizard" earlier in this chapter.

3. On the **Message Information** page, click one of the following options:

   - **Create a new message**

     The name of this message is automatically determined by the method that you select on the next page of this wizard. The data flow for a new message must be connected to other messages on the **Data** page.

     Click **Next**. Continue to step 4 in this procedure.

   - **Add a reference to an existing synchronous message pair**

     A reference to a previously configured message pair is added to this communication flow. These message pairs can be reused only within the same port. They cannot be used by another port implementation.

     Click **Finish**.

4. On the **Message Specification Information** page, in the **Methods** list, click the method that you want to use. You can select only one method in the list.

   Selecting a method defines the messages for this communication flow. The *IN* and *OUT* parameters are automatically determined by the parameter requirements of the method that you choose. Both parameter lists contain the name and data type of the parameter.

For more information about defining the messages used in a communication flow, see the following topic, "Synchronous Communication."

5. Click **Finish**.

Notes

- Shape names must meet certain naming conventions. The following conventions apply to transactions, ports, messages, rules, and fields:

  - The name must be a valid XML token name. For more information about XML tokens, go to the W3C Web site (www.w3.org).

  - The name cannot begin with underscores (_).

  - The name cannot include colons (:).

  - The name length must be less than or equal to 32 characters.

  - Constant names and message names cannot begin with a numeric character.

- The wait time property is not enabled unless you click **Wait for a synchronous method call**.

- The only methods available for use in a synchronous communication are those that were selected for the port implementation. Methods from other port implementations cannot be used, and XML messages from asynchronous communication flows cannot be used. To change the available methods, rerun the appropriate port implementation wizard and select different methods.

- When you create a synchronous communication, a **Message** is created on the **Data** page. The **Message** corresponds to the method and parameters that are used in the communication flow. The **Message** contains all *IN* parameters for the method, and all *OUT* parameters for the method.

  It is possible for a method to contain no parameters; however, the **Message** always contains required system fields. For more information about defining the messages used in a synchronous communication, see the following topic, "Synchronous Communication."

Synchronous Communication

The only methods available for use in synchronous communication are those that were selected for the port implementation. Methods from other port implementations cannot be used, and XML messages from asynchronous communication flows cannot be used. To change the available methods, rerun the appropriate binding wizard and select different methods.

The *IN* and *OUT* parameters are automatically determined by the parameter requirements of the method that you choose. Both parameter lists contain the name and data type of the parameter. In addition to any parameters associated with the method, a message also contains certain required system fields. A synchronous message always contains the following system fields:

- __Sender__

  This system field is a required *IN* parameter for the method used in a synchronous message.

- __Status__

  This system field is a required *OUT* parameter for the method used in a synchronous message.

Synchronous messages

When you create a synchronous communication, a **Message** is created on the **Data** page. The **Message** corresponds to the method and parameters that are used in the communication flow. The **Message** contains all *IN* parameters for the method, and all *OUT* parameters for the method.

It is possible for a method to contain no parameters; however, the **Message** always contains required system fields. The **Message** schema is shown in the following example:

```
Method name_in
__Sender__    string
   parameter 1    Data type 1
   parameter 2    Data type 2
   parameter n    Data type n
Method name_out
__Status__    string
   Parameter 1    Data type 1
   Parameter 2    Data type 2
   Parameter n    Data type n
```

The illustration on the following page shows a synchronous message pair that contains the system fields __Sender__ and __Status__, as well as *IN* and *OUT* parameters for the method call.

Method_in	
Sender	string
Parameter 1	Data type 1
Parameter 2	Data type 2
Parameter 3	Data type 3
Method_out	
Status	Int
Parameter 1	Data type 1
Parameter 2	Data type 2

Using the XML Communication Wizard

On the **Business Process** page, the **Compensation for *Transaction*** page, and the **On Failure of *Transaction*** page, you can use the XML Communication Wizard to define the flow of messages between an **Action** shape and a **Message Queuing** shape, a **BizTalk Messaging** shape, or an unbound port. To start the XML Communication Wizard, drag the right control handle (✳) of an **Action** shape to the connection point (✕) on an unbound port, or on a port bound to a **Message Queuing** shape or a **BizTalk Messaging** shape. The XML Communication Wizard is made up of the following pages:

Welcome to the XML Communication Wizard

On the **Welcome to the XML Communication Wizard** page, you can specify whether the port will send a message to an action or receive a message from an action. If you are creating the communication between an action and a port that has been implemented using the **BizTalk Messaging** shape, the communication direction has already been configured. This occurred when the BizTalk Messaging Binding Wizard was used to create the port binding.

If the port is configured to receive messages, you can set a latency value to indicate an amount of time in seconds that the XLANG Scheduler Engine will wait before a message arrives. If this value is 180 seconds or less, the XLANG schedule instance will never be dehydrated to the persistence database. If this value is greater than 180 seconds, the XLANG schedule instance will be dehydrated to the persistence database immediately. By default, latency is set to zero seconds, indicating that the message is expected to arrive immediately.

If an XLANG schedule instance is rehydrated for any reason other than the arrival of a message for which an action is waiting (and if the XLANG schedule instance then enters a quiescent state), the specified latency value is used to determine whether the XLANG schedule instance will be immediately dehydrated. For example, this can occur when a concurrent branch receives a message for which it was waiting, or when a computer restart causes all XLANG schedule instances to rehydrate. In this situation, the latency value is evaluated from the point when the XLANG schedule instance enters a quiescent state. If the amount of time from the beginning of the XLANG Scheduler Engine's original waiting period (combined with the latency value) is more than 180 seconds from when the XLANG Scheduler Engine entered the quiescent state after rehydration, the XLANG schedule instance will be dehydrated to the persistence database immediately. This point in the XLANG schedule instance can occur long after the XLANG Scheduler Engine begins monitoring the arrival of a message.

Message Information

On the **Message Information** page, you can specify whether a new message or a reference to an existing message should be created. If you specify that a new message should be created, define the data flow for the new message. For more information about data flow, see "Data Handling" later in this chapter. The **Label** property of a message can be used to optimize the performance of a schedule in the following manner:

- If the **Label** property of the message is identical to the **XML root element** that is specified when creating a new **Message** shape, the XLANG Scheduler Engine retrieves the message.

- If the **Label** property does not match the value provided for the **XML root element**, the XLANG Scheduler Engine examines the contents of the message. If the value of the XML root element that is specified when a new **Message** shape is created matches the actual XML root element, the XLANG Scheduler Engine retrieves the message. Otherwise, the XLANG Scheduler Engine leaves the message on the queue and checks the next message.

XML Translation Information

On the **XML Translation Information** page, you can specify whether you want messages sent to or received from the queue as XML formatted data or as text strings. If you specify that you want messages sent as text strings, the XLANG Scheduler Engine's standard XML wrapper will be removed from the messages.

Message Type Information

On the **Message Type Information** page, you can specify a label that the XLANG Scheduler Engine should use to identify messages of the type you define. The text that you enter is used to identify the correct messages to receive from the message queue. If you select the same message type for two different messages, make sure the field names, field types, and XPath queries match exactly. The XLANG Scheduler Engine will report an error if there is an inconsistency between messages of the same message type on the same port. On the **Message**

Type Information page, in the **Message type** box, type a label designation for the message. The XLANG Scheduler Engine will perform the following procedures, based on the information you provide:

- The XLANG Scheduler Engine will attempt to match the message type information with the message label in the queue. When the message type is not matched, the message will be ignored, and the XLANG Scheduler Engine continues looking for new incoming messages that might match. This enables multiple actions to receive multiple message types from a single message queue.

- If the message is in XML format on the queue, the XLANG Scheduler Engine will attempt to match the message type information with the XML root element of the message on the queue.

Message Specification Information

On the **Message Specification Information** page, you can type the path to the message specification (.xml) file that you want to use, or you can browse to it. If the message specification you select is a specification that was created using BizTalk Editor, you will be able to add fields to the data scope of the XLANG Scheduler Engine. You can validate messages against the specification by selecting the **Validate messages against the specification** check box. By clicking **Browse** on the **Message Specification Information** page, you can display the **Browse for Specification** dialog box. You can use the **Browse for Specification** dialog box to find the specification that you want to use.

If you have not selected a specification, you can click **Create** on the **Message Specification Information** page to open BizTalk Editor. If you have already selected a specification, you can click **Edit** on the **Message Specification Information** page to open BizTalk Editor with the selected specification.

By clicking **Add** on the **Message Specification Information** page, you can display the **Field Selection** dialog box. In the **Field Selection** dialog box, in the **Select node** tree, you can expand any nodes that you want, and then click the field that you want to add. In the **Field Selection** dialog box, you can edit the name and the node path for fields you want to add to the message shape for the selected port. The data type fields are displayed, but they cannot be edited.

Notes

- Validation is available only when a message is received. If a message is sent, the validation check box is ignored.

- When you click a field in the **Select node** tree, the field name is automatically added to the **Field name** box.

- When you click a field in the **Select node** tree, the node path to that field is automatically added to the **Node path** box.

- Editing the node path manually is useful when you want to extract specific data from within a field. For example, if the field contains an array, you might want to retrieve just one item from the array and not the entire array. However, it is recommended that you refrain from manually editing the node path for your message specification.

- You cannot select a node to add to the **Message fields** list. You can only select fields. A field also might be referred to as a leaf node. For example, you cannot select the Seller and Address nodes because they contain leaf nodes. The Name and Address fields can be selected because they are fields that do not contain additional nodes.

- While waiting to receive a message from a message queue, some problems (such as invalid XML messages or insufficient authentication) will cause a dead letter queue to be dynamically created. The dead letter queue is specific to a COM+ application. The dead letter queue will be given the name .\private$\\*ApplicationName*.DeadLetter. For example, if a message containing invalid XML arrives on the queue, and you have specified on the **XML Translation Information** page of the XML Communication Wizard that the XLANG Scheduler Engine is expecting XML messages from the queue, any invalid XML messages will be moved to .\private$*ApplicationName*.DeadLetter.

- If you design two different XLANG schedules to receive different messages from the same message queue, it is possible that a message might be processed by the wrong XLANG schedule instance. To avoid this problem, use one message queue for each type of message that is received by an XLANG schedule instance.

To send or receive asynchronous messages

1. On the **Welcome to the XML Communication Wizard** page, choose one of the following options:

   - **Send**

     A message is sent asynchronously.

     Click **Next**. Continue to step 3 in this procedure.

   - **Receive**

     The XLANG Scheduler Engine waits until it receives a message before continuing the XLANG Schedule.

     Continue to step 2 in this procedure.

2. On the **Welcome to the XML Communication Wizard** page, to optimize the execution of an XLANG schedule, enter the amount of time (in seconds) that you expect the XLANG Scheduler Engine to wait before a message arrives and click **Next**.

   The default wait time is 0 seconds. You can change this time. Any time less than or equal to 180 seconds causes the XLANG schedule to never dehydrate. Any time greater than 180 seconds causes the XLANG schedule to dehydrate immediately. For more information about wait times and XLANG schedule dehydration, see "Dehydration and Rehydration" later in this chapter and "Using the XML Communication Wizard" earlier in this chapter.

3. On the **Message Information** page, click one of the following options:

    *   **Create a new message**

        In the **Message name** box, type the name of the message. A default message name with a number appended to it is provided; however, you can change this name.

        The data flow for a new message must be connected to other messages on the **Data** page.

    *   **Add a reference to an existing message**

        A reference to a previously configured message is added to this communication flow.

4. Click **Next** and do one of the following:

    *   If you clicked **Send** on the **Welcome to the XML Communication Wizard** page, continue to step 5 in this procedure.

    *   If you clicked **Receive** on the **Welcome to the XML Communication Wizard** page, continue to step 8 in this procedure.

5. On the **XML Translation Information** page, click one of the following options and click **Next**:

    *   **Send XML messages to the queue**

    *   **Send messages to the queue as a string**

        The XLANG Scheduler Engine must remove the standard XML wrapper from the string.

    Data flow in the XLANG Scheduler Engine is handled by using XML. The engine natively sends XML messages to message queues. The engine can also send a message as a string, from which the engine must remove its standard XML wrapper. The data flow must deliver a message in the correct specification format for this action.

    If you choose to send or receive an XML message as a string, the **Message** shape that is created on the **Data** page for this message contains a field named StringData, and you cannot add specification fields to this message.

6. On the **Message Type Information** page, in the **Message type** box, type a label designation for the message.

    The text that you enter is used to label the message as it is sent to the queue.

7. To continue, do one of the following:

    *   If, on the **XML Translation Information** page, you clicked **Send XML messages to the queue**, click **Next**. Continue to step 10 in this procedure.

    *   If, on the **XML Translation Information** page, you clicked **Send messages to the queue as a string**, click **Finish**.

8. On the **XML Translation Information** page, click one of the following options and click **Next**:

   - **Receive XML messages from the queue**

   - **Receive string messages from the queue**

     The XLANG Scheduler Engine must wrap the string in the engine's standard XML wrapper.

   Data flow in the XLANG Scheduler Engine is handled by using XML. The engine natively receives XML messages from message queues. The engine can also receive a message as a string, which the engine then wraps in XML.

9. On the **Message Type Information** page, in the **Message type** box, type a label designation for the message.

   The text that you enter is used to identify the correct messages to receive from the message queue.

   First, the XLANG Scheduler Engine tries to match the message type information with the message label in the queue.

   Second, if the message is in an XML format on the queue, the XLANG Scheduler Engine tries to match the message type information with the XML root element of the message on the queue.

10. To continue, do one of the following:

    - If, on the **XML Translation Information** page, you clicked **Receive XML messages from the queue**, click **Next**. Continue to step 11 in this procedure.

    - If, on the **XML Translation Information** page, you clicked **Receive string messages from the queue**, click **Finish**.

11. On the **Message Specification Information** page, click **Browse**.

    The **Browse for Specification** dialog box appears.

12. Browse to the specification that you want to use, click it, and then click **Open**.

    On the **Message Specification Information** page, in the **Message specification** box, the file path and file name of the specification that you selected are entered.

    ### Notes

    - If you do not browse for an existing specification, you can click **Create**. This action opens BizTalk Editor, which enables you to select a specification and modify it as needed for use with this message, or create a new specification.

    - If you select a specification by browsing for it, the **Create** button label changes to **Edit**. Click **Edit** to modify the specification that you have selected.

13. On the **Message Specification Information** page, if you want to validate the message against the specification, select the **Validate messages against the specification** check box.

✎ **Note**

- This check box is not enabled unless you select a specification for validation.

14. On the **Message Specification Information** page, if you want to add fields to the **Message fields** list, click **Add**.

◆ **Important**

- If you want to select additional fields for this message specification, you must use a specification that has been created by using BizTalk Editor. You can adapt any standard or schema by first importing it into BizTalk Editor and then saving it as a BizTalk specification. For more information about creating and validating specifications, see Chapter 5, "Creating Specifications."

15. In the **Field Selection** dialog box, in the **Select node** tree, expand any nodes that you want, click the field that you want to add, and then click **OK**.

✎ **Notes**

- When you click a field in the **Select node** tree, the field name is added automatically to the **Field name** box.

- When you click a field in the **Select node** tree, the node path to that field is added automatically to the **Node path** box. This path can be edited manually. For more information, see "Node Path Fields" later in this chapter.

- You cannot select a record node to add to the **Message fields** list. You can select only fields. For more information, see "Node Path Fields" later in this chapter.

- If you want to add several fields to the **Message fields** list, in the **Field Selection** dialog box, you must select a field and click **OK**. On the **Message Specification Information** page, click **Add** and repeat the process to add another field.

16. On the **Message Specification Information** page, if you want to delete fields in the **Message fields** list, click a field in the list and click **Remove**.

✎ **Note**

- You cannot delete any required fields. Required fields appear in the **Message fields** list with a yellow background.

17. Click **Finish**.

Notes

- Shape names must meet certain naming conventions. The following conventions apply to transactions, ports, messages, rules, and fields:

  - The name must be a valid XML token name. For more information about XML tokens, go to the W3C Web site (www.w3.org).

  - The name cannot begin with underscores (__).

  - The name cannot include colons (:).

  - The name length must be less than or equal to 32 characters.

  - Constant names and message names cannot begin with a numeric character.

- The wait time property is not enabled unless you click **Receive**.

- The only messages available for use in an asynchronous communication are XML messages. All XML messages are available for use and can be specified for more than one port. You cannot use any of the synchronous message pairs that are created by using the Method Communication Wizard.

- If you are connecting this communication flow to a port that is implemented by using BizTalk Messaging, the direction of the communication (**Send** or **Receive**) is determined by the port implementation and cannot be set in the XML Communication Wizard. The **Send** or **Receive** option on the first page of the wizard is selected automatically and is unavailable. You must click **Next** and continue to the next page of the wizard to finish the configuration of the communication flow.

- When you create an asynchronous communication, a **Message** is created on the **Data** page. The **Message** corresponds to information sent or received in the communication flow. The **Message** contains required system fields and any additional specification fields that you want. For more information about defining the messages used in an asynchronous messaging communication, see the following topic, "Asynchronous Communication."

Asynchronous Communication

An asynchronous message is put into a message queue or a BizTalk Messaging channel, and the XLANG schedule continues. It does not wait for a response.

The only messages available for use in an asynchronous communication are XML messages. All XML messages are available for use and can be specified for more than one port. You cannot use any of the synchronous message pairs that are created by using the Method Communication Wizard.

Asynchronous messages

When you create an asynchronous communication, a **Message** is created on the **Data** page. The **Message** corresponds to information that is sent or received in the communication flow. The **Message** contains required system fields and any additional specification fields that you want.

The **Message** schema is shown in the following example:

```
Message name
__Sender__   string
Document    string
   Field 1    Data type 1
   Field 2    Data type 2
   Field n    Data type n
```

The following illustration shows a message named Message_1. The system fields __Sender__ and Document are automatically provided and are present in all asynchronous messages. This message also contains two user-selected specification fields.

Message_1	
Sender	string
Document	string
Field 1	Data type 1
Field 2	Data type 2

You can add a specification field by using the **Field Selection** dialog box that is in the XML Communication Wizard. In the **Field Selection** dialog box, you can select a specification field by clicking a node in the **Select node** tree. When you click a node, the node path is added to the **Node path** box. You must select a leaf node. A leaf node is a node with no children. In the following illustration, the node Name is a leaf node; however, the node Address is not a leaf node.

A node path is also known as an XPath. You can use the node path as it is selected, or you can type additional criteria to the path. For example, if you select a node that contains an array, you might want to specify a specific index in the array to retrieve, rather than retrieving the entire array.

☑ Note

* If you choose to send or receive an XML message as a string, the **Message** shape that is created on the **Data** page for this message contains a field named StringData, and you cannot add specification fields to this message.

The following illustration shows the **Field Selection** dialog box.

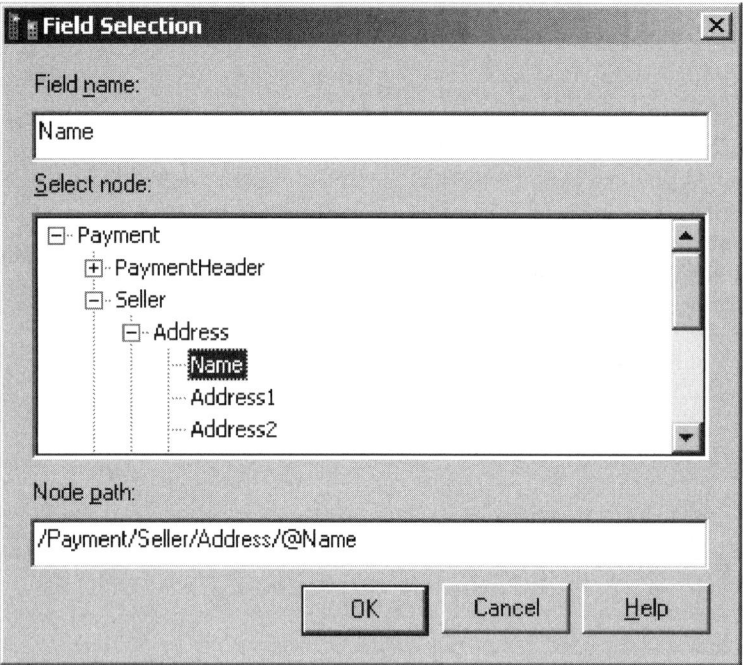

For more information about selecting specification fields and using node paths, see the following topics:

- Chapter 5, "Creating Specifications"
- "Node Path Fields" later in this chapter
- "To send or receive asynchronous messages" earlier in this chapter
- "Using the XML Communication Wizard" earlier in this chapter

Related Topics

Chapter 5, "Creating Specifications"

Chapter 6, "Mapping Data"

"Dehydration and Rehydration" later in this chapter

"Node Path Fields" later in this chapter

"Persistence" later in this chapter

Designing for XLANG Schedule Instance Management, Persistence, and Data Handling

The following sections explain how to manage instances of several running XLANG schedules, how to dehydrate and rehydrate running schedules and save schedule state to a persistence database, and how to handle the flow of data in an XLANG schedule.

Instance Management

To understand how the XLANG Scheduler Engine performs instance management, you must be aware of the distinction between an abstract definition of a business process and multiple running instances of a business process definition. In BizTalk Orchestration Designer, you design a business process definition and save it as an XLANG schedule drawing (an .skv file). After you have created an XLANG schedule drawing, you compile it into an XLANG schedule (an .skx file). After you deploy the XLANG schedule, there are likely to be several instances of the schedule running simultaneously. Each XLANG schedule instance can have a life span that is independent of the life span of any of the other instances. When you design an application to support multiple XLANG schedule instances, you should be aware of the following issues:

- **Activating new instances of XLANG schedules when messages are received.** You can design your application to activate a new XLANG schedule instance by using the COM function **GetObject** every time a message is received. For example, if you use an Active Server Page (ASP) to receive a message containing a purchase order or a customer support request, the ASP must use the COM function **GetObject** to activate an XLANG schedule.

   You can also use the BizTalk Messaging Binding Wizard to create a port binding that can serve as a named location to which messages are sent. BizTalk Server 2000 provides an automated mechanism to activate an instance of an XLANG schedule when a port that is bound to BizTalk Messaging receives a message. On the **XLANG Schedule Activation Information** page of the BizTalk Messaging Binding Wizard, you are prompted to confirm whether the channel has been configured in BizTalk Messaging Services to send a message to this port after the activation of a new instance of this XLANG schedule. To complete this process, you have to run the New Messaging Port Wizard in BizTalk Messaging Manager. On the **Destination Application** page of the New Messaging Port Wizard, specify the name of the port and the name and location of the XLANG schedule.

- **Correlating the exchange of messages to XLANG schedule instances.** Every instance of an XLANG schedule is assigned a globally unique identifier (GUID) by the XLANG Scheduler Engine. Therefore, every port on every running instance of an XLANG schedule can be uniquely addressable. This enables direct communication to specific ports on specific XLANG schedule instances. By enabling direct communication through uniquely addressable port locations, the difficulty of using a single location to distribute messages to instances is avoided. The first message sent by a schedule instance will likely be to a static port (a named location). When the XLANG schedule is activated, this instance sends the locations of its dynamic ports (per-instance, unique locations) to recipients who are responsible for communicating back to the ports. This corresponds to e-mail messages that are sent out with unique reply-to addresses. The following list describes dynamic binding support in each of the BizTalk Server binding technologies:

- On the **Static or Dynamic Communication** page of either the COM Component Binding Wizard or the Script Component Binding Wizard, if you choose **Static**, the XLANG Scheduler Engine will create the XLANG schedule instance of the component. If you choose **Dynamic**, another application must send an interface pointer or moniker (as a field in a message) prior to the instantiation of the component.

  You also have the option of choosing **No instantiation**. For more information about component instantiation, see "Static and Dynamic Ports" earlier in this chapter.

- On the **Static or Dynamic Queue Information** page of the Message Queuing Binding Wizard, if you choose **Static queue** and click **Next**, you will invoke the **Queue Information** page. On this page you can specify the creation of a separate, per-instance queue for every XLANG schedule instance, or you can specify the use of a single queue for all running instances. To enable correlation, you must specify the creation of a separate, per-instance queue for every XLANG schedule instance.

- On the **Static or Dynamic Queue Information** page of the Message Queuing Binding Wizard, if you choose **Dynamic queue**, another application must send the name of the queue (as a field in a message) prior to sending or receiving messages through the port.

- On the **Static or Dynamic Channel Information** page of the BizTalk Messaging Binding Wizard, you can choose to provide a specific channel name, or indicate that port configuration information will be used by BizTalk Messaging Services to identify the correct channel at run time. For more information about message exchange, see "Maps for Integrating BizTalk Services" in Chapter 6, "Mapping Data."

◆ **Important**

- You must make sure that a message correlates to the same XLANG schedule instance that participated in an earlier communication with a trading partner.

- **Scaling the application.** Any XLANG schedule instances that do not need to be in memory should be dehydrated. An XLANG schedule instance might not need to be in memory when an XLANG schedule instance is waiting for the arrival of a message.

▨ **Note**

- All implementation shapes display a shadow to indicate that the location will be bound dynamically and defined at run time.

Persistence

The XLANG Scheduler Engine stores the following information in the persistence database:

- The structure of XLANG schedules.

- The progress of activated XLANG schedule instances.

- Messages that are sent or received while an XLANG schedule instance is running.

The XLANG Scheduler Engine persists information to enable the following scenarios:

- **To enable the dehydration and rehydration of long-running schedules.** The system might fail during a long-running transaction. When the system is running again, the XLANG Scheduler Engine refers to the persistence database to determine where to resume the schedule.

- **To restore the state of a schedule instance when a transaction fails.** The system might fail during a transaction, causing the transaction to abort. The XLANG Scheduler Engine refers to the persistence database to determine where to resume the schedule.

- **To support the debugging and monitoring of running schedules.** Debugging and monitoring tools can query the persistence database to provide information about the progress of schedule instances.

Support for persisting the state of an XLANG schedule before the start of a transaction, and after the completion of a transaction, provides durability, ensuring that all committed modifications are permanently in place in the system. This also enables retries of a transaction if a failure occurs. The state of a running schedule instance is persisted under the following circumstances:

- **At the beginning of a transaction.** When the business process sequence flows to the start of a transaction, the transaction retry count must be updated in the persistence database. This enables the XLANG Scheduler Engine to track the retry count if the system fails during the transaction.

- **At the end of a transaction.** When the business process sequence flows out of a transaction, the schedule state must be updated to enable rollback, if necessary. This update occurs in the context of the transaction to ensure that database persistence is atomic.

Dehydration and Rehydration

If multiple instances of an XLANG schedule are running simultaneously over a long period of time, it can become impractical to allow all of them to remain in memory. The XLANG Scheduler Engine provides a dehydration/rehydration infrastructure to address this problem.

When an XLANG schedule instance is expected to wait for a message for an extended period of time, and no other activity is occurring within the schedule, the XLANG Scheduler Engine can dehydrate the XLANG schedule instance. Dehydrating an XLANG schedule instance consists of persisting all the instance-specific state to the persistence database and removing the instance from memory. When a message arrives at a port address for the dehydrated XLANG schedule instance, the instance is rehydrated. Rehydrating an XLANG schedule instance consists of restoring the instance from the database to memory.

An XLANG schedule instance remains dehydrated until it is either rehydrated or explicitly terminated by an administrator. This enables a business process to run reliably for an extended time period.

The XLANG Scheduler Engine can use a latency setting to determine an amount of time that an action can remain inactive before the XLANG schedule instance is dehydrated to the persistence database. The XLANG Scheduler Engine can use this latency setting to dehydrate the XLANG schedule instance to the persistence database, and then rehydrate it later when the message arrives. However, there are several situations during which the latency setting does not cause a schedule to be dehydrated, including:

- **The schedule instance is not in a quiescent state.** This can occur when actions are being performed on one of the current process flows in the XLANG schedule instance. All process flows in the schedule instance must be in the same state before the XLANG Scheduler Engine will dehydrate the XLANG schedule instance. The latency time for all pending actions must exceed a certain threshold before dehydration is performed.

- **There are pending DTC-style transactions.** The XLANG Scheduler Engine will not dehydrate the schedule when it is running a DTC-style transaction, because DTC-style transactions are typically short-lived.

- **There are live ports in the instance that cannot be persisted.** A live port is a port object or a port that has been implemented and that might be used later in the schedule instance. The lifetime of a port is an important issue during the execution of a schedule instance. Ports are bound to implementation technologies, such as COM interfaces. If the implementation technology that a port is bound to cannot be persisted, and if the implementation technology holds state information that is reused later, the instance cannot be dehydrated and then rehydrated. If the persistence database fails and then runs again later, the state information will be lost and schedule instance execution cannot be resumed from the state of the schedule instance when it was last dehydrated.

When the XLANG Scheduler Engine is shut down, as much information as possible is saved to the persistence database, including all information that is not in a transactional context.

Related Topics

"Using the Method Communication Wizard" earlier in this chapter

"Using the XML Communication Wizard" earlier in this chapter

Data Handling

In XLANG, all data is contained within a set of uniquely named messages. New data enters an XLANG schedule instance when a message is received by an action.

Every XLANG schedule drawing has one **Data** page. On the **Data** page you can describe the data flow within an XLANG schedule. To indicate that data within one message field flows into another message field, draw an arrow from the source message field to the destination message field.

With the exception of the **Constants** message, none of the message fields within the messages on the **Data** page will initially contain a value. The **Constants** message is initialized with the values that are specified on the **Data** page. It is initialized automatically for each new XLANG schedule instance. For more information about using constants, see "The Constants Message" later in this chapter. The values of the other displayed messages are set when each message is sent or received in the XLANG schedule instance. A message can be received by more than one action. Every time a message is received, the values for that message are overwritten. The flow of data into the received message will not be used to set the values for a different received message, even if the message is sent out at another point in the XLANG schedule. Messages that are exclusively sent out rely on the data flow that is displayed on the **Data** page to set their message fields. A schedule will not compile unless all of the fields are specified for all of the messages that have been sent.

When a field on the **Data** page comes from an XPath that points to an optional node in the XML schema, use the following guidelines:

- **For received messages when the optional node exists.** If this message is received, and the optional node exists in the XML document, the XPath field stores the node value.

- **For received messages when the optional node does not exist.** If this message is received, and the optional node does not exist, the XPath field stores a null value. You need to use a **Decision** rule with the Microsoft Visual Basic Scripting Edition (VBScript) expression **IsNull** (Message.Field) on this field to determine if the received message contains the optional node. If you do not test for the existence of a value, and this field provides data flow into another message that is sent, an error occurs when the XLANG Scheduler Engine tries to create the message to be sent.

- **For sent messages when the optional node exists.** If this message (with the XPath node pointing to an optional XML node) is being sent, the XLANG Scheduler Engine relies on data flow to create the message. If the node exists in the Document field of the message, the XLANG Scheduler Engine overwrites it with the value of the XPath.

- **For sent messages when the optional node does not exist.** If this message (with the XPath node pointing to an optional XML node) is being sent, the XLANG Scheduler Engine relies on data flow to create the message. If the node does not exist in the provided Document field, the XLANG Scheduler Engine does not create the node to overwrite. This causes an error.

For messages that will be received from or sent to a message queue, use the following guidelines:

- **For received messages.** If an action will receive a non-XML message from a message queue, you must select **Receive string messages from a queue** on the **XML Translation Information** page of the XML Communication Wizard. In this configuration, the **Message** shape on the **Data** page will display a new StringData field. This StringData field will contain the non-XML message received from the queue. The Document field on the message will contain the StringData field, surrounded by the XLANG Scheduler Engine standard XML wrapper.

- **For sent messages.** If an action will send a non-XML message to a message queue, you must select **Send messages to the queue as a string** on the **XML Translation Information** page of the XML Communication Wizard. In this configuration, the **Message** shape on the **Data** page will display a new StringData field. To complete this configuration, you must create a new constant (containing the XLANG Scheduler Engine standard XML wrapper) in the **Constants** message on the **Data** page. The name of this constant is irrelevant, but the data type must be **string**, and the value of the constant must be **<?xml version="1.0" ?> <StringData> </StringData>**. After you have created this new constant, you must draw a data flow connection from the new constant on the **Constants** message to the Document field in the **Message** shape. You must also draw a data flow connection from the field containing the non-XML string to the new StringData field in the **Message** shape.

Notes

- The direction of data flow is independent of the direction of message flow. Message flow indicates if a message is sent or received.

- If you want to enable the XLANG schedule to receive data by using a method call without instantiating the component, select **No instantiation** on the **Static or Dynamic Communication** page of either the COM Component Binding Wizard or the Script Component Binding Wizard. If you select **No instantiation**, the component is not instantiated, and no code for the method call is executed. Instead, when the XLANG schedule intercepts the method request information, it returns this information as the response. The method call is circumvented.

- If a message is used only within the body of a while loop, the message values are not initialized on every iteration of the loop. If a message is used both inside and outside the body of a while loop, the message values are retained throughout each iteration of the loop. The message values might also be retained before and after the business process sequence flows to the **While** shape.

- If a message that is initialized within the compensation process or the on failure process of a transaction within a while loop, the message values will not be available outside the loop.

- If a field within an XML message (including the constants message) with a data type of **char** provides data flow into a method message field, the field will be converted to an

integer for the method. If the method message field has a data type of **string**, the string will contain the integer value; it will not contain the character. If you encounter this problem, and the source field is part of the constants message, change the data type of the constants field to **string**. If the source field is part of an XML message, you will have to use a component to cast the **char** data type to a **string**.

The Data Page

Every XLANG schedule drawing has a **Data** page. The **Data** page displays:

- One **Message** shape for every message in the XLANG schedule.

- One **Constants** message.

- One **Port References** message containing a port field for each port within the XLANG schedule drawing.

- Diagrammatic connections showing the flow of data between the message fields.

Messages consist of a set of uniquely named fields, each containing one data item of a specific data type. Every message in the XLANG schedule is displayed on the **Data** page as a table. Each table displays the name of the message and a listing of field names and their corresponding data types. System fields that do not require data flow are displayed with a yellow background. User fields, and system fields that do require data flow, are displayed with a white background.

Connections on the **Data** page point from the right side of a source message field to the left side of a destination message field. This connection indicates that the source message field will provide the data for the destination message field. At run time, the XLANG Scheduler Engine will copy the data from the source message field into the destination message field when the destination message has to be created. If the source message has not arrived yet, a run-time error will occur.

🗹 Notes

- The following data types are not supported on the **Data** page:

  - BinHex

  - BinBase64

  - I8

  - UI8

  If you have a node in an XML document of type BinHex, BinBase64, I8, or UI8, and you specify that the node should be brought into the scope of the XLANG Scheduler Engine on the **Data** page, using the XPath to this node, the node will be converted to a string.

- There is a 100-character limit for all field names in XLANG schedules.

To select a message

- In BizTalk Orchestration Designer, on the **Data** page, click the gray header field for the message that you want to select.

    The entire message that you select is surrounded with a green dashed border.

Notes

- You can select the **Constants** list, the **Port References** list, or a **Message**.
- When you select an entire message, you can reposition it on the page by dragging it. Repositioning the messages can clarify the data flows that are drawn between messages.

To select a field within a message

- In BizTalk Orchestration Designer, on the **Data** page, click a field with a message that you want to select.

    The field that you select is surrounded with a green dashed border. Any control handles (✳) available to that field are enabled.

To draw the flow between messages

1. In BizTalk Orchestration Designer, on the **Data** page, click a field within a message to enable its control handles (✳).

2. Drag the control handle to the connection point (✕) of a field in another message to which you want to connect.

3. When the connection point is highlighted with a red box (⊠), release the mouse button to set the connection.

Note

- If you want to create several data flows, you can use the Connector Tool to add the flows quickly. For more information about the Connector Tool, see "To use the Connector Tool" earlier in this chapter.

To delete a message

- In BizTalk Orchestration Designer, on the **Data** page, click the gray header field for the message that you want to delete and press DELETE.

Notes

- You cannot delete the **Port References** list.
- You cannot delete the **Constants** list.
- If you select an individual field within a message and press DELETE, the entire message is deleted, not just the field.

To match a specific message with a specific port

1. Click the field within the **Port References** list that contains the name of the port to which you want to refer.

2. Drag the control handle (✼) from that field to the connection point (✕) of the field in a **Message** in which you want to pass the reference to the port.

◆ **Important**

- For more information about correlating messages and port references, see the following topics earlier in this chapter:

   - "Instance Management"

   - "Data Handling"

   - "Understanding Port Implementations"

The Constants Message

You can use the **Constants** message to initialize an XLANG schedule instance with data. Within the XLANG Scheduler Engine, the **Constants** message performs a unique function; it is neither sent nor received. It is initialized automatically for each new XLANG schedule instance. To add a constant to the **Constants** message, double-click the **Constants** message, or double-click a field in the **Constants** message to open the **Constants Message Properties** dialog box. Click **Add** in the **Constants Message Properties** dialog box to open the **Constant Properties** dialog box. In the **Constant Properties** dialog box, you can name the constant, choose a data type for the constant, and assign a value to the constant.

✑ **Note**

- XML does not handle Windows Locale settings for date formatting. If you want to assign a date in a localized format for a constant, set the constant data type to **string**. If this constant provides data to a field with a **date** data type, the XLANG Scheduler Engine will translate the string to a date, adhering to the localized format.

To add constants

1. In BizTalk Orchestration Designer, on the **Data** page, right-click the **Constants** list and click **Properties**.

   The **Constants Message Properties** dialog box appears.

2. Click **Add**.

   The **Constant Properties** dialog box appears.

3. In the **Name** box, type a name for the constant.

4. In the **Data type** list, click the data type for the constant.

5. In the **Value** box, type the value for the constant.

6. Click **OK**, and then click **OK** again.

☑ Notes

- A default name with a number appended to it is provided for each constant that you create. You can change this name.

- The **Data type description** area provides read-only information about the data type that you select. It might provide a format example for the data type, or a valid range for the value for a data type.

To edit constants

1. In BizTalk Orchestration Designer, on the **Data** page, right-click the **Constants** list and click **Properties**.

    The **Constants Message Properties** dialog box appears.

2. In the **Constants** list, click the constant that you want to edit.

3. Click **Edit**.

    The **Constant Properties** dialog box appears.

4. Edit any constant properties that you want to change and click **OK**.

☑ Notes

- For more detailed information about the properties available in the **Constant Properties** dialog box, see the previous topic, "To add constants."

- A default name with a number appended to it is provided for each constant that you create. You can change this name.

- The **Data type description** area provides read-only information about the data type that you select. It might provide a format example for the data type, or a valid range for the value for a data type.

To delete constants

1. In BizTalk Orchestration Designer, on the **Data** page, right-click the **Constants** list and click **Properties**.

    The **Constants Message Properties** dialog box appears.

2. In the **Constants** list, click the constant that you want to delete.

3. Click **Delete**.

The Port References Message

The **Port References** message contains a list of all ports that are created on the **Business Process** page. A new reference is added to this list every time a new port is added on the **Business Process** page. The **Port References** message enables you to specify the origin of port locations. The **Port References** message contains one port field for every port in the XLANG schedule drawing.

There are scenarios in which ports in an XLANG schedule are not known at design time. This can occur if the destination or origin of messages is determined from the contents of other messages. For example, a business process might describe a situation in which an action must respond to a message with an acknowledgment to the originating trading partner. In this example, the message that is received will typically have a reply-to-address field that contains the originating address of the message. The XLANG schedule must be able to correlate the contents of the reply-to-address field to the destination address of the acknowledgment message. You can use the **Port References** message and an acknowledgment message on the **Data** page to implement this scenario. For more information about message exchange, see "Maps for Integrating BizTalk Services" in Chapter 6, "Mapping Data."

◆ Important

- Actions in different branches of a fork cannot communicate with each other. For example, an action in one branch cannot send a message to a queue from which an action on another branch is waiting to receive a message. If you incorrectly design your XLANG schedule drawing to support communication of any kind between actions in different branches, the XLANG schedule instance might fail at run time; however, an error will not be displayed.

Field Data Types

BizTalk Orchestration Designer displays all data types with their XML data type name. The following table lists the OLE Automation, Visual Basic, and C program equivalents of the displayed XML data type names.

XML UI View	OLE Automation	Visual Basic	C
simple types			
boolean	VT_BOOL	Boolean	VARIANT_BOOL
string	VT_BSTR	String	BSTR
cy	VT_CY	Currency	CURRENCY
date	VT_DATE	Date	DATE
dispatch	VT_DISPATCH	Object	IDispatch
error	VT_ERROR		SCODE
i1	VT_I1		signed char
i2	VT_I2	Integer	SHORT
i4	VT_I4	Long	LONG
int	VT_INT		INT
r4	VT_R4	Single	FLOAT
r8	VT_R8	Double	DOUBLE
ui1	VT_UI1	Byte	BYTE
ui2	VT_UI2		USHORT
ui4	VT_UI4		ULONG
uint	VT_UINT		UINT
unknown	VT_UNKNOWN	Object	IUnknown
variant	VT_VARIANT	Variant	VARIANT

System Fields

Each message can also contain a set of system fields that are automatically created by the XLANG Scheduler Engine.

System field name	When is this system field displayed?	Description
__Status__	When the message is being received from a port bound to a COM or Script binding.	The HRESULT of the method call.
__Sender__	When the message is sent to or received from any port.	When a message is received, this is the SenderID provided by Message Queuing or COM. When this message is sent, the value is NULL.
Document	When the message is sent or received from a port that is bound to Message Queuing or BizTalk Messaging.	A string containing the message body that is sent or received.

Node Path Fields

When a port bound to Message Queuing or BizTalk Messaging receives an XML document, you can bring specific document nodes into the data scope of the XLANG Scheduler Engine. If no specific nodes are selected, the XLANG Scheduler Engine will treat the XML document as an opaque string that is carried within the document system field.

You can bring document nodes into the data scope of the XLANG Scheduler Engine by using the **Message Specification** page in the XML Communication Wizard. When you provide an XML specification, the **Add** and **Remove** buttons are enabled.

Related Topic

"Using the XML Communication Wizard" earlier in this chapter

Compiling and Debugging XLANG Schedules

When you create an XLANG schedule, you will want to compile, run, test, and debug the schedule. BizTalk Orchestration Designer provides features that assist in doing this.

In BizTalk Orchestration Designer, the following options are available:

- Compiling
- Updating method signatures
- Shutting down running instances of XLANG schedules

In addition to these options, there are two tools that you can use to assist in testing and debugging an XLANG schedule:

- **XLANG Event Monitor.** You can use this tool to monitor running XLANG schedule instances. For specific information about using this tool, see the associated Readme.htm file. Both XLANG Event Monitor (XLANGMon.exe) and the Readme installed by the Microsoft BizTalk Server 2000 Setup Wizard are located in the following installation directory: \Program Files\Microsoft BizTalk Server\SDK\XLANG Tools.

- **Windows 2000 Event Viewer.** Windows 2000 Event Viewer can be used to view XLANG schedule errors. For more information, see the following topics:

  - "Handling Server Errors" in Chapter 11, "Administering Servers and Applications"

  - "Monitor Running XLANG Schedules" in Chapter 11, "Administering Servers and Applications"

  - "Using Event Viewer" in Windows 2000 Server Help

Compiling XLANG Schedules

When you have completed an XLANG schedule drawing, you can compile the drawing into an executable XLANG schedule. Before you compile the drawing, make sure the flow of data between messages has been defined on the **Data** page. An XLANG schedule describes the business process and the binding of that process to an implementation technology.

BizTalk Orchestration Designer is designed to provide as much useful information as possible when a problem in your XLANG schedule is discovered during the compilation process. If BizTalk Orchestration Designer encounters an error, it highlights the shape that contains the error, displays an error message, and cancels the compilation of the XLANG schedule.

During compilation, BizTalk Orchestration Designer examines each shape to determine if it is complete and correct. The XLANG Scheduler Engine processes the **Begin** shape on the **Business Process** page first, and then descends recursively through the entire drawing. If the XLANG Scheduler Engine encounters an error, the error typically occurs when the business process flows to a shape in a deeply nested position. To report the error, the XLANG Scheduler Engine constructs an appropriate error message. Then, as the XLANG Scheduler Engine returns up through the stack, each method has an opportunity to concatenate its own error message to the original error message. If none of the methods concatenates an error message to the original error message, the top-level compilation method adds the following generic error message:

Failed to process the XLANG schedule.

The compiled XLANG schedule contains a globally unique identifier (GUID) that matches the **XLANG identity** property of the **Begin** shape. This identification can be used to correlate a version of the XLANG schedule drawing with the XLANG schedule that generated it.

To compile an XLANG schedule drawing into an XLANG schedule

1. In BizTalk Orchestration Designer, on the **File** menu, click **Make XLANG** *DrawingX***.skx**.

   The **Save XLANG Schedule To** dialog box appears.

2. In the **Save in** list, browse to the location where you want to save the XLANG schedule.

3. In the **File name** list, you can rename the file.

4. Click **Save**.

Notes

- When you compile an XLANG schedule drawing into an XLANG schedule, you might receive compiling errors. The error message indicates the possible problem in the drawing, and the affected shape is highlighted with a green, dashed border.

- When you compile an XLANG schedule drawing into an XLANG schedule, the drawing is compiled with the default name *DrawingX*.skx, where *X* is a number that is appended to the schedule name. You can change the name of the file when you compile the drawing.

- The file extension for an XLANG schedule is .skx. An .skx file is an XML file that is written in the XLANG language. You cannot open an .skx file within BizTalk Orchestration Designer. To change or update an .skx file, open the source .skv file, make your changes, and then recompile the .skv file into an .skx file.

- The file extension for an XLANG schedule drawing is .skv.

Related Topics

"Creating and Configuring an XLANG Schedule Host Application" later in this chapter

"Creating an Instantiating Application" later in this chapter

"Manage XLANG Applications and Databases" in Chapter 11, "Administering Servers and Applications"

"Opening and Saving XLANG Schedule Drawings" earlier in this chapter

"Security for Applications That Host XLANG Schedule Instances" in Chapter 2, "Understanding Security"

Debugging XLANG Schedules

XLANG Event Monitor is a tool that you can use to monitor running XLANG schedule instances. For specific information about using XLANG Event Monitor, see the associated Readme.htm file. Both XLANG Event Monitor (XLANGMon.exe) and the readme installed by the Microsoft BizTalk Server 2000 Setup Wizard are located in the following installation directory: \Program Files\Microsoft BizTalk Server\SDK\XLANG Tools.

XLANG Event Monitor includes the following features:

- It displays the XLANG Scheduler Engine working in real time.
- After the initial enumeration of the running schedules, XLANG Event Monitor monitors events. It can be used to suspend and stop running instances.
- It has a multiple-document interface (MDI)-like user interface that enables you to simultaneously view multiple instance traces.
- It can simultaneously monitor selected applications on multiple computers.
- It provides separate recording and viewing filters.

To debug compiled Visual Basic components

There might be situations in which you need to debug components built with Microsoft Visual Basic after they have been compiled.

1. In Visual Basic 6.0, open the Visual Basic project that you want to debug.
2. On the **File** menu, click **Make *<YourProject>*.dll**.

   The **Make Project** dialog box appears.
3. Click **Options**.

   The **Project Properties** dialog box appears.
4. On the **Compile** tab, click **Compile to Native Code**, click **No Optimization**, and then select the **Create Symbolic Debug Info** check box.
5. Click **OK**, and then click **OK** again to compile your project.
6. Open the Visual Basic .dll project.
7. Set the breakpoints that you want to use.
8. On the **Run** menu, click **Start**.

The next time the XLANG schedule calls into your Visual Basic component, the Visual Basic debugger will stop at the breakpoint.

◈ Important

- The Visual Basic .dll must be created with the **Create Symbolic Debug Info** check box selected.

- Ensure that the XLANG Scheduler Engine has not already loaded the .dll. If the .dll has been loaded, you must shut down the engine and retry.

🖉 Note

- For more information about debugging components, or about Component Services and COM+, go to the MSDN Online Library Web site (msdn.microsoft.com/library/default.asp) and browse to Component Services in the Platform SDK.

To refresh method signatures

- In BizTalk Orchestration Designer, on the **Tools** menu, click **Refresh Method Signatures**.

🖉 Notes

- Use this option if you are creating COM+ components at the same time you are creating the XLANG schedule and you change any of the method parameters in any of the available method calls. This refreshes the available method parameters in the XLANG schedule.

- When you compile an XLANG schedule, **Refresh Method Signatures** is run automatically.

To shut down all running XLANG schedules

- In BizTalk Orchestration Designer, on the **Tools** menu, click **Shut Down All Running XLANG Schedule Instances**.

🖉 Note

- When running an XLANG schedule instance, it is not possible to modify COM components used by that XLANG schedule. This option shuts down all running instances of the schedule, unlocking the file containing the component so you can make changes.

Related Topics

"Creating and Configuring an XLANG Schedule Host Application" later in this chapter

"Creating an Instantiating Application" later in this chapter

"Manage XLANG Applications and Databases" in Chapter 11, "Administering Servers and Applications"

"Security for Applications That Host XLANG Schedule Instances" in Chapter 2, "Understanding Security"

"XLANG Schedule Error Messages" in Chapter 11, "Administering Servers and Applications"

Running XLANG Schedules

When installing BizTalk Orchestration Designer, several COM+ applications are installed and configured within Microsoft Windows 2000 Component Services, including the XLANG Scheduler COM+ application. This application hosts a default instance of the XLANG Scheduler Engine. Each new COM+ application created in Component Services has an **XLANG** tab on the properties dialog box. On the **XLANG** tab you can enable the new COM+ application to host the XLANG Scheduler Engine. The specific COM+ application in which a new XLANG schedule will execute can be determined through the moniker syntax used to activate an instance of an XLANG schedule.

The XLANG Scheduler Engine controls the activation, execution, dehydration, and rehydration of running XLANG schedule instances. To activate an XLANG schedule, you can create a small application that passes the moniker of an XLANG schedule to the XLANG Scheduler Engine. The XLANG Scheduler Engine performs the actions within the XLANG schedule and continues the business process sequence until it becomes necessary to dehydrate the XLANG schedule. Dehydrating an XLANG schedule occurs when the XLANG Scheduler Engine expects to wait for more than three minutes to receive a message. When the message arrives, the XLANG Scheduler Engine rehydrates the XLANG schedule instance and continues to perform the actions in the business process sequence until the schedule either completes or the XLANG Scheduler Engine has to wait for another message. To support dehydration, you must have a persistence database configured. The recommended network library is TCP/IP.

To display Microsoft Windows 2000 Component Services information, perform the following procedure:

1. On the **Start** menu, point to **Settings**, click **Control Panel**, double-click **Administrative Tools**, and then double-click **Component Services**.

2. In the console tree, expand **Component Services**, expand **Computers**, expand **My Computer**, and then expand **COM+ Applications**.

The **XLANG** tab on the **Component Services Properties** dialog box displays the following options:

- **This application is a host for XLANG schedule instances.** If enabled, this COM+ application might activate instances of XLANG schedules. To direct the activation of a schedule instance to a particular COM+ application, use a moniker form that includes the name of the application. Check this option when you want the application to serve as a host for the XLANG Scheduler Engine.

- **Persistence.** In this area you can configure Microsoft SQL Server to support the dehydration and rehydration of long-running business processes:

  - **Create DSN** creates the ODBC Data Source Name (DSN) for the COM+ application hosting the XLANG Scheduler Engine. A file DSN stores information about a database connection in a file. The file has the extension .dsn and by default is stored in the $\Program Files\Common Files\ODBC\Data Sources directory. Click the **Create DSN** button to start the DSN Wizard.

  - **Configure DSN** opens the ODBC Data Source Administrator to manage the data source for XLANG schedules in this COM+ application.

  - **Initialize Tables** creates the tables that are needed to support persistence in the SQL Server database you have defined.

  ◈ Important

  - The Data Source Name configured in the **XLANG Scheduler Properties** dialog box must be the same as the name of the COM+ application.

- **Controlled shutdown.** In this area you can select a valid way to shut down the COM+ applications hosting XLANG schedule instances:

  - **All XLANG Applications** shuts down all COM+ applications that are hosting running XLANG schedule instances.

  ▱ Note

  - If you have selected an application other than the default application, **This XLANG Application** will be displayed.

- **Restart dehydrated XLANG applications.** In this area you can manage dehydrated XLANG applications:

  - **All XLANG Applications** rehydrates all COM+ applications that are hosting XLANG schedule instances and, if possible, continues to run them.

◈ Important

- Do not right-click the COM+ application to shut down running instances of an XLANG schedule. This will leave COM components loaded in memory instead of unloading them correctly. Instead, use the **Controlled Shutdown** area of the **XLANG** tab in the properties for the **XLANG Scheduler** COM+ application.

📝 **Note**

- When using the client for Microsoft Windows 2000 Terminal Services to initiate an XLANG schedule, the COM+ application hosting the XLANG Scheduler Engine must have its identity set to a valid Windows 2000 user or group name. The identity of the COM+ application is set on the **Identity** page of the properties dialog box for that application. The identity cannot be set to interactive when using the XLANG Scheduler Engine through a session hosted by Terminal Services.

To run an XLANG schedule

To run an XLANG schedule, you must create a means to activate the XLANG schedule.

There are two primary ways to do this:

- Configure BizTalk Orchestration Services and BizTalk Messaging Services to activate and run XLANG schedules.

  For more information, see the following topics:

  - "Maps for Integrating BizTalk Services" in Chapter 6, "Mapping Data"

  - "To set destination application properties" in Chapter 9, "Configuring BizTalk Messaging Services"

- Programmatically activate the XLANG schedule by creating an instantiation application such as an ASP page.

Related Topics

"Creating and Configuring an XLANG Schedule Host Application" later in this chapter

"Creating an Instantiating Application" later in this chapter

"Manage XLANG Applications and Databases" in Chapter 11, "Administering Servers and Applications"

"Security for Applications That Host XLANG Schedule Instances" in Chapter 2, "Understanding Security"

"To compile an XLANG schedule drawing into an XLANG schedule" earlier in this chapter

Moniker Syntax

Monikers are used to create new XLANG schedule instances or to refer to an existing XLANG schedule instance. In either case, you can refer to a specific port within the schedule instance. Monikers determine which COM+ application will host the XLANG Scheduler Engine.

To create a new instance of an XLANG schedule, a moniker for the XLANG schedule must be passed to the COM+ application. The COM+ application forwards the moniker to the XLANG naming service for resolution and to activate the XLANG schedule instance with an instance of the XLANG Scheduler Engine. The following code sample shows the general syntax for monikers:

```
sked://[HostName][!GroupManager][/FilePath][/PortName]
```

Each segment of the moniker syntax is optional, depending on what type of object you want to instantiate. The following table lists and describes each of the moniker syntax segments.

Moniker syntax segment	Description	Examples
HostName	The host name of the computer running the XLANG Scheduler Engine. This is also referred to as the XLANG system manager. If omitted, localhost is used as the default value. This name is not case sensitive.	sked:// sked://MyServer
GroupManager	The XLANG Scheduler Engine group manager that is used to manage XLANG schedule instances. The name of the group manager is the same as the COM+ application that is designated as an XLANG host. If omitted, XLANG Scheduler is used as the default value. This name is case sensitive and can contain spaces.	sked:/// sked://AnotherServer!/ sked://AnotherServer!MyGroup/
FilePath	The path to an XLANG schedule file (.skx) to be activated. This value is not case sensitive.	sked://host1!MyGrp/C:\basic.skx sked:///C:\basic.skx
PortName	The name of a port that is bound to a COM or Windows Script component on an XLANG schedule. This name is case sensitive.	sked:///C:\basiccom.skx/portA

Moniker syntax can be used to refer to an existing XLANG schedule instance, to start an XLANG schedule, or to establish a communication channel with a particular port on the new XLANG schedule instance.

Monikers that refer to an XLANG schedule instance are created by the XLANG Scheduler Engine and are made available by creating a connection between the **Port References** shape and messages that are sent by the XLANG schedule. The exact form of the port reference depends on which implementation technology the port is bound to and the data type of the target message field. Ports that are bound to Message Queuing or BizTalk Messaging Services can only be connected to fields of data type **String**. The target field contains the name of the queue or messaging endpoint that is bound to the port in the current XLANG schedule instance.

Ports bound to COM components can be connected to fields of data type **String**, **Object**, or **Unknown**. If the target field is of data type **String**, a moniker is created that refers to a port in the current XLANG schedule instance. This moniker is durable. It can be resolved by using the **GetObject** function, and the moniker remains valid after a system restart. If the target field is of data type **Object** or **Unknown**, a COM reference to the port instance is passed to the message shape. If this kind of reference is passed to an external component, it is not valid after a system restart.

The moniker to reference a running XLANG schedule instance can be obtained from the XLANG schedule instance object, as shown in the following Microsoft Visual Basic code:

```
Dim oSchedule as IWFWorkflowInstance
Set oSchedule = GetObject("sked:///C:\temp\myschedule.skx")
dim sMoniker as string
sMoniker = oSchedule.FullyQualifiedName
```

Creating an Instantiating Application

An instantiating application passes a moniker for the completed XLANG schedule file to the XLANG Scheduler Engine by using the COM function **GetObject**. The following Microsoft Visual Basic code shows how to do this:

```
Dim objExecute As object
Dim strURL as string

strURL = "sked:///c:\temp\myschedule.skx"

' This enables the XLANG Scheduler Engine to execute the XLANG schedule.
Set objExecute = GetObject(strURL)
```

If you did not specify a port in the moniker, the **Port** property of the object that is returned by the **GetObject** function enables you to obtain a reference to a port that is bound to a COM component. Similarly, the **FullPortName** property enables you to obtain the full, durable name of a port bound to an implementation technology.

The following code shows how to obtain a proxy to a COM or Script port. This code sample continues from the previous code sample.

```
Dim oPort as Object
Set oPort = objExecute.Port("SchedulePortName")
Call oPort.ComponentMethodName(arg1,arg2,...argN)
```

☑ Note

- If the port is bound to a COM object that does not support a dual interface, the *oPort* variable must be declared with the appropriate class.

Enterprise Edition

Creating and Configuring an XLANG Schedule Host Application

This section contains procedures that explain how to activate and run an XLANG schedule. Although you can use the default XLANG Scheduler application to run XLANG schedules, it is often useful to create a new COM+ application to run schedule instances.

Due to security, deployment, and configuration issues, most COM+ applications that host XLANG schedules must be created when the XLANG schedule is developed. You must take into consideration security and performance needs for the applications and the schedules. You might want to create a new COM+ application to host dedicated instances of running schedules, or you might want to isolate applications that run specific schedule instances from other XLANG schedules that use different applications.

For more information about security and performance issues related to creating XLANG schedules and a COM+ application to host the schedules, see "Security for Applications That Host XLANG Schedule Instances" in Chapter 2, "Understanding Security."

For information about how to manage COM+ applications after they have been created, see "Manage XLANG Applications and Databases" in Chapter 11, "Administering Servers and Applications."

◆ Important

- For Component Services Administration Help, on the **Start** menu, point to **Settings**, click **Control Panel**, double-click **Administrative Tools**, and then double-click **Component Services**. In the console tree, right-click **Component Services** and click **Help**.

- For more information about Component Services and COM+, go to the MSDN Online Library Web site (msdn.microsoft.com/library/default.asp) and browse to Component Services in the Platform SDK.

To create a COM+ application to host XLANG schedules

1. On the **Start** menu, point to **Settings**, click **Control Panel**, double-click **Administrative Tools**, and then double-click **Component Services**.

2. In the console tree, expand **Component Services**, expand **Computers**, expand **My Computer**, and then click **COM+ Applications** to select it.

   You must first select **COM+ Applications** and then right-click it. If you do not select it first, the **New** option is not available.

3. Right-click **COM+ Applications**, point to **New**, and then click **Application**.

   The COM Application Install Wizard opens.

4. On the **Welcome to the COM Application Install Wizard** page, click **Next**.

5. On the **Install or Create a New Application** page, click **Create an empty application**.

6. On the **Create an Empty Application** page, type a name for the application, verify that **Server application** is selected, and then click **Next**.

7. On the **Set Application Identity** page, set the application identity to the appropriate account.

   It is recommended that you create a service account for COM+ applications that host XLANG schedules.

   For more information about security and performance issues related to creating an application identity, see "Security for Applications That Host XLANG Schedule Instances" in Chapter 2, "Understanding Security."

8. Click **Next** and click **Finish**.

9. Right-click the COM+ application that you just created and click **Properties**.

10. On the **XLANG** tab, select the **This application is a host for XLANG schedule instances** check box.

11. To configure the COM+ application, see the following topic, "To configure a COM+ application to host XLANG schedules."

◆ Important

- For Component Services Administration Help, on the **Start** menu, point to **Settings**, click **Control Panel**, double-click **Administrative Tools**, and then double-click **Component Services**. In the console tree, right-click **Component Services** and click **Help**.

- For more information about Component Services and COM+, go to the MSDN Online Library Web site (msdn.microsoft.com/library/default.asp) and browse to Component Services in the Platform SDK.

✎ Note

- When you create a COM+ application to host XLANG schedules, the **Restart dehydrated applications** option is not available. For more information about how to restart dehydrated applications, see "To restart all XLANG applications" in Chapter 11, "Administering Servers and Applications."

To configure a COM+ application to host XLANG schedules

1. On the **Start** menu, point to **Settings**, click **Control Panel**, double-click **Administrative Tools**, and then double-click **Component Services**.

2. In the console tree, expand **Component Services**, expand **Computers**, expand **My Computer**, and then expand **COM+ Applications**.

3. Right-click the COM+ application that you want to configure and click **Properties**.

   The *Application* **Properties** dialog box appears.

   It is highly recommended that you create a service account to manage COM+ applications that host XLANG schedules. If you accepted default settings in the COM Application Install Wizard when you created the COM+ application, you might want to change these settings. For more information, see "To change the application identity for a COM+ application" in Chapter 11, "Administering Servers and Applications."

4. Configure DSN settings for the COM+ application.

   For more information, see "To change the DSN settings for a COM+ application" in Chapter 11, "Administering Servers and Applications."

5. Configure a database for the COM+ application to use.

   You can:

   - Point to an existing database. For more information, see "To change the DSN settings for a COM+ application" in Chapter 11, "Administering Servers and Applications."

     –Or–

   - Create and configure a new database. For more information, see "To create a new persistence database" and "To change the DSN settings for a COM+ application" in Chapter 11, "Administering Servers and Applications."

❦ Caution

- If you create and configure a new database to use with the COM+ application, you must initialize the database tables after you configure the DSN settings for the COM+ application.

  For more information about configuring a DSN and using data sources (ODBC), click **Help** in the **ODBC Data Source Administrator** dialog box.

  To initialize new database tables for the COM+ host application that you configure:

  1. Right-click the COM+ application and click **Properties**.

  2. Click the **XLANG** tab.

  3. Click **Initialize Tables**.

- Do not click **Initialize Tables** if you are configuring a COM+ host application and a DSN for an existing database. This action destroys any data already in the existing database.

📝 Notes

- For Component Services Administration Help, on the **Start** menu, point to **Settings**, click **Control Panel**, double-click **Administrative Tools**, and then double-click **Component Services**. In the console tree, right-click **Component Services** and click **Help**.

- For more information about Component Services and COM+, go to the MSDN Online Library Web site (msdn.microsoft.com/library/default.asp) and browse to Component Services in the Platform SDK.

Related Topics

"Manage Other COM+ Applications That Host XLANG Schedules" in Chapter 11, "Administering Servers and Applications"

"Manage XLANG Applications and Databases" in Chapter 11, "Administering Servers and Applications"

"Security for Applications That Host XLANG Schedule Instances" in Chapter 2, "Understanding Security"

Enterprise Edition

Managing Session State

On the **Advanced Properties** page of the COM Component Binding Wizard, you can select a state management value for the level of persistence that your COM component supports. In the **State management support** area, select one of the following options:

- **Holds no state.** This specifies that the XLANG Scheduler Engine will terminate the component instance when it is dehydrated. If you select this setting, the XLANG Scheduler Engine will create a new component instance, if it is required, when the schedule is rehydrated.

- **Holds state, but doesn't support persistence.** This specifies that the XLANG Scheduler Engine will be required to leave the component instance running. If the system fails while the application is dehydrated, any state that has been held in this component will be lost.

- **Holds state, and does support persistence.** This specifies that the XLANG Scheduler Engine will remove the component instance from memory, and then restore it to memory by calling either **IPersistStream** or **IPersistStreamInit** on the component during dehydration, and then again during rehydration.

Updating XLANG Schedules

There are two ways to update an XLANG schedule. You can overwrite the original XLANG schedule, or you can add a new XLANG schedule that will run concurrently with the original XLANG schedule.

To overwrite the original XLANG schedule, use BizTalk Orchestration Designer to create a new XLANG schedule drawing and then compile the XLANG schedule drawing as an XLANG schedule that has the same name as the original XLANG schedule. The XLANG schedule drawing is saved as an .skv file, which is a customized version of the Microsoft Visio 2000 file format. You can then compile the XLANG schedule drawing into an XLANG schedule, which is an XML-structured .skx text file that the XLANG Scheduler Engine understands. To update the original XLANG schedule, copy the new .skx file over the original .skx file.

To add a new XLANG schedule that will run concurrently with the original XLANG schedule, use BizTalk Orchestration Designer to create a new XLANG schedule drawing and compile the XLANG schedule drawing as an XLANG schedule with a new name. To ensure that the new XLANG schedule will be correctly activated, you must change the XLANG schedule instance activation mechanism to point to the new .skx file instead of pointing to the old .skx file. When you have completed this process, new requests for XLANG schedules will create instances of the new XLANG schedule.

Because all XLANG schedules and their components typically work on a per-instance basis, XLANG schedule instances that are in the process of executing the original schedule will continue to run to completion. This includes XLANG schedule instances that have been persisted because the source code of the original schedule has been saved. In this scenario, the execution path will continue to follow the original business process, and new requests for XLANG schedules will create instances of the new XLANG schedule.

Note

- When an XLANG schedule uses an object with an interface that has changed, load the XLANG schedule drawing (the .skv file) into BizTalk Orchestration Designer and compile a new .skx file. This will update the binding information in the .skx file, enabling synchronization with the component's type library.

CHAPTER 9

Configuring BizTalk Messaging Services

Microsoft BizTalk Server 2000 provides two methods for configuring BizTalk Messaging Services to manage the exchange of documents between trading partners and applications within your business. You can either use BizTalk Messaging Manager, which is a graphical user interface (UI), or directly access the BizTalk Messaging Configuration object model.

In This Chapter

- Using BizTalk Messaging Manager

- Accessing the BizTalk Messaging Configuration Object Model

Using BizTalk Messaging Manager

BizTalk Messaging Manager is a graphical user interface (UI) with which you can manage the exchange of documents by configuring BizTalk Messaging Services. BizTalk Messaging Services can also be configured programmatically. For more information, see "Accessing the BizTalk Messaging Configuration Object Model" later in this chapter.

▼ Caution

- You should use BizTalk Messaging Manager to configure BizTalk Messaging Services prior to processing documents. Accessing and modifying objects that might be in use while BizTalk Server 2000 is processing documents can produce unexpected results.

Documents can be exchanged between trading partners and applications within your business. BizTalk Messaging Manager is available both locally from the computer on which BizTalk Server 2000 is installed and remotely as a client application. This enables system administrators to retain security and central control of the server, while enabling remote users to access BizTalk Messaging Manager.

Microsoft BizTalk Server 2000 Help provides information about how to create and manage channels, messaging ports, document definitions, envelopes, and organizations, as well as how to use distribution lists.

BizTalk Messaging Manager objects

The illustration on the following page shows the relationship between the objects that you can create by using BizTalk Messaging Manager.

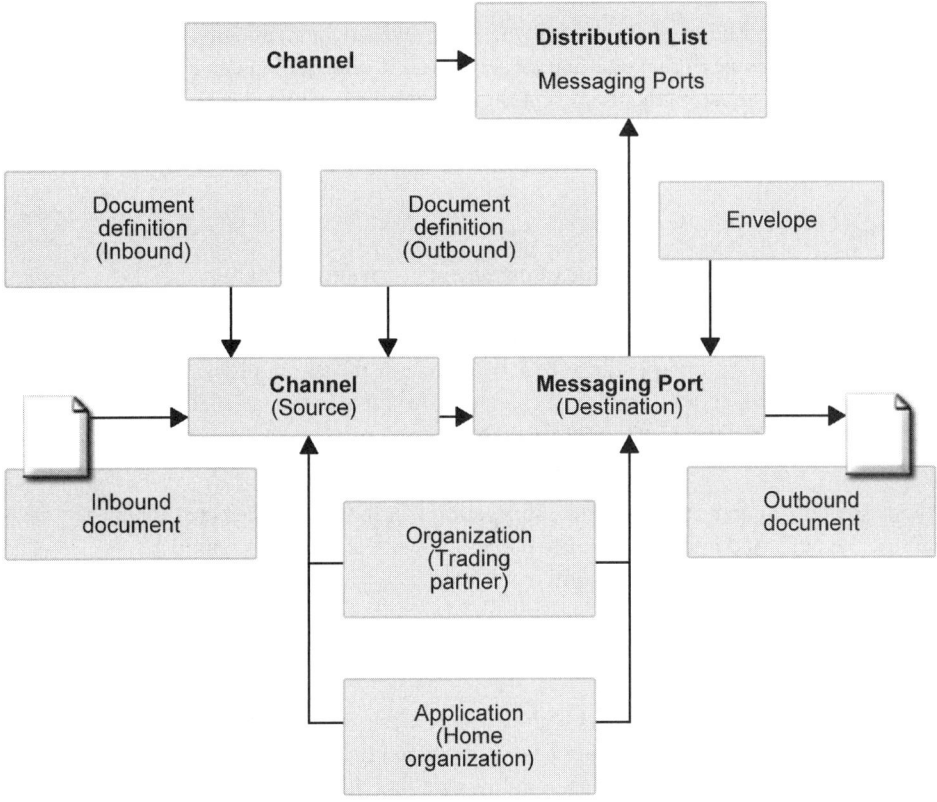

The following summary provides a brief overview of the objects that you can create by using BizTalk Messaging Manager. This summary also further explains the relationship between the objects.

Channels

Channels are the primary objects in BizTalk Messaging Manager. The purpose of all other BizTalk Messaging Manager objects is to either create channels or support the operation of channels. Channels identify the source of documents, which can be an organization, an application within your business, or an XLANG schedule. Channels also identify inbound and outbound documents by using document definitions. For more information, see "Understanding Channels" later in this chapter.

Messaging ports

Messaging ports identify a destination for the documents that are processed by a channel. The destination can be an organization, an application within your business, or an XLANG schedule. A messaging port specifies a destination address to which the documents are sent, how they are transported to that address, and if and how they are secured and enveloped. For more information, see "Understanding Messaging Ports" later in this chapter.

Organizations

Organizations represent other trading partners with which you exchange documents. A special organization type, called the home organization, represents your business. You can create applications for the home organization that represent the internal applications that your business uses. Organizations and applications serve as the source for a channel or the destination for a messaging port. For more information, see "Understanding Organizations" later in this chapter.

Document definitions

A document definition represents a specific type of document that is processed by BizTalk Server 2000. A document definition provides a pointer to a specification. Specifications define the document structure, type, and version. Channels specify an inbound and an outbound document definition to indicate which documents the server processes. A document definition can be used in any number of channels. For more information, see "Understanding Document Definitions" later in this chapter.

Envelopes

Envelopes provide BizTalk Server 2000 with the information that the server needs to either open inbound or create outbound interchanges. Envelopes can be selected from within a messaging port to direct the server in creating outbound interchanges. Envelopes, which are independent of a messaging port, can be used by BizTalk Server 2000 to open inbound interchanges. For more information, see "Understanding Envelopes" later in this chapter.

Distribution lists

Distribution lists are groups of messaging ports with which you can send the same document to a group of different trading partner organizations or internal applications. You must create at least one channel for a distribution list, just as you do for an individual messaging port. For more information, see "Understanding Distribution Lists" later in this chapter.

Notes

- The objects that you can create by using BizTalk Messaging Manager can also be created programmatically by using the BizTalk Messaging Configuration object model. For more information, see "Accessing the BizTalk Messaging Configuration Object Model" later in this chapter

- The objects that you can create by using BizTalk Messaging Manager also use objects that you can create by using other BizTalk Messaging Services user interfaces. Channels use maps, which you can create by using BizTalk Mapper. Document definitions use document specifications, and envelopes use envelope specifications. You can create specifications by using BizTalk Editor.

Configuring BizTalk Messaging Manager Options

This section explains how to modify BizTalk Messaging Manager options. These options include:

- Configuring new messaging ports or channels.

- Managing previously configured messaging ports or channels.

- Setting the search return value.

- Setting the server connection.

- Setting the server time-out value.

📝 Note

- The toolbars in BizTalk Messaging Manager can be repositioned; however, when the application is restarted, the toolbars return to their original positions.

To select a BizTalk Messaging Manager configuration option

1. On the **Start** menu, point to **Programs**, point to **Microsoft BizTalk Server 2000**, and then click **BizTalk Messaging Manager**.

   The **BizTalk Messaging Manager** dialog box appears.

2. In the **Configuration options** area, select one of the following options:

   - If you want to create and configure a new messaging port to an organization, click **Configure a new messaging port to an organization** and click **OK**.

     For more information about creating and configuring a new messaging port to an organization, see "To create messaging ports" later in this chapter.

   - If you want to create and configure a new messaging port to an application, click **Configure a new messaging port to an application** and click **OK**.

     For more information about creating and configuring a new messaging port to an application, see "To create messaging ports" later in this chapter.

   - If you want to manage existing messaging ports, click **Manage previously configured messaging ports** and click **OK**.

     For more information about managing existing messaging ports, see "To edit messaging ports" later in this chapter.

   - If you want to manage existing channels, click **Manage previously configured channels** and click **OK**.

     For more information about creating and configuring existing channels, see "To edit channels" later in this chapter.

📝 **Note**

- If you do not want this dialog box to appear when you open BizTalk Messaging Manager, select the **Don't show this dialog box again** check box. To reset the dialog box to appear, on the **Tools** menu, click **Options** and select the **Show startup dialog box** check box.

To set server connection options

1. In BizTalk Messaging Manager, on the **Tools** menu, click **Options**.

   The **Options** dialog box appears.

2. In the **Maximum number of items to return in a search** box, complete one of the following steps:

   - Type a value for the number of items to be returned in a search.

   - Click the up or down arrow to increase or decrease the value.

3. In the **Name of BizTalk Server to connect to** box, type the name of a server on which BizTalk Server 2000 is installed.

4. In the **Server timeout in seconds** box, complete one of the following steps:

   - Type a value for the number of seconds before the server connection times out.

   - Click the up or down arrow to increase or decrease the value.

5. To have an opening dialog box appear or not appear when BizTalk Messaging Manager starts, select or clear the **Show startup dialog box** check box.

6. After you have set all properties, click **OK**.

📝 **Notes**

- The server to which you connect determines the BizTalk Messaging Management database for which you search, edit, or create new objects by using BizTalk Messaging Manager. The server connection defaults to the last connection that was made. The server that hosts the WebDAV repository that you use to store and retrieve specifications for documents, maps, and envelopes is set independently from within the dialog boxes that you use to select specifications. The WebDAV connection defaults to the last connection that was made.

- The default number of items returned in a search is 500.

- The default number of seconds before the server connection times out is 20.

- The server to which you are currently connected is displayed at the top of the Search pane located on the left side of BizTalk Messaging Manager.

BizTalk Messaging Manager User Interface

The BizTalk Messaging Manager user interface has two main panes.

The left pane displays:

- The name of the server to which BizTalk Messaging Manager is connected.

- A list of objects for which you can search.

- Search criteria that you can use to narrow your search.

You can search for any objects that you create by using BizTalk Messaging Manager. You can choose the type of object for which you want to search by clicking the name in the **Search for other items** area. The search criteria differ according to the object that you select.

The right pane displays:

- The details of the items returned in your most recent search.

The details of the items differ according to the type of object for which you search.

You can sort the items in the search results pane in ascending or descending order by clicking the column headers. You can sort based on only one column at a time.

Notes

- If you have a large number of a particular type of object for which to search, it might take several minutes to return all the items. You can reduce the number of items returned in a search by using search criteria.

- The default number of items returned in a search is 500. You can adjust this number. For more information, see "To set server connection options" earlier in this chapter.

BizTalk Messaging Manager Shortcut Keys

You can use shortcut keys to accomplish tasks in BizTalk Messaging Manager. The following table is a quick reference to these shortcut keys.

Note

- Functionality that is not included in this list can be obtained by using the numeric keypad to move the mouse pointer with MouseKeys. For more information about MouseKeys in Windows 2000 Server and Advanced Server Help, see "Using the keyboard to move the mouse pointer." For more information about MouseKeys in Windows 2000 Professional Help, see "Move the mouse pointer by using MouseKeys."

Press	To
CTRL+A	Select all.
CTRL+C	Copy text.
CTRL+X	Cut text.
CTRL+V	Paste text.
CTRL+Z	Undo text action.
CTRL+R	Create a new messaging port to an organization.
CTRL+SHIFT+R	Create a new messaging port to an application.
CTRL+L	Create a new channel from an organization.
CTRL+SHIFT+L	Create a new channel from an application.
CTRL+T	Create a new distribution list.
CTRL+D	Create a new document definition.
CTRL+G	Create a new organization.
DELETE	Delete the selected item or text.
SHIFT+F10	Display the shortcut menu for the selected item.
SHIFT with any arrow key	Select more than one item in a window or select text.
TAB	In a dialog box, move the focus through the buttons and fields of the dialog box.
SHIFT+TAB	In a dialog box, move the focus through the buttons and fields of the dialog box.
CTRL+TAB	Toggle tabs of a dialog box in front-to-back order.
CTRL+SHIFT+TAB	Toggle tabs of a dialog box in back-to-front order.
SPACEBAR	Select or clear a check box. The spacebar also acts like a mouse click when the focus is on a button.
ALT+SPACEBAR	Display the system menu for the active window.
ALT+Underlined letter in a menu name	Display the corresponding menu.
Underlined letter in a command name on an open menu	Carry out the corresponding command.
ALT+ DOWN ARROW	Display the drop-down list for an activated list box.
ENTER	Carry out the command for the active option or button.

Press	To
ESC	Cancel the current task.
F1	Display online Help.
ALT+F4	Close the active window, or quit the active program.
LEFT ARROW	Move the focus to the tab to the left.
RIGHT ARROW	Move the focus to the tab to the right.
Any arrow key	Highlight a folder or a file in the main window of a dialog box, while the focus is in that window. This functionality occurs in the **Select a Document Specification from the WebDAV Repository**, the **Select an Envelope Specification from the WebDAV Repository**, and the **Select a Map from the WebDAV Repository** dialog boxes. For more information, see "To select a document specification," "To select an envelope specification," and "To select a map" later in this chapter.

Security

To access or create objects by using BizTalk Messaging Manager, you must have a user account in the BizTalk Server Administrators group. The BizTalk Server Administrators group is created when BizTalk Server 2000 is installed. Additional users can be added to this group as necessary. For more information about adding a user account, see "To add users to the BizTalk Server Administrators group" in Chapter 11, "Administering Servers and Applications."

Understanding Channels

A channel is a set of properties that you can use to configure BizTalk Messaging Services to process a document that it receives. Channels can be created for a messaging port or a distribution list. Once a channel has processed a document, the document is transported to the destination specified in the associated messaging port or the messaging ports in the associated distribution list. You can create one or more channels for a messaging port or distribution list.

In a channel, you specify the source of the documents, which can be a source organization or a source application. Before you can designate an application as the source for a channel, you must create an application for the home organization, which represents an actual internal application in your business. You can also designate an XLANG schedule as the source for a channel. You can create an XLANG schedule by using BizTalk Orchestration Designer. For more information, see "BizTalk Orchestration Designer Environent" in Chapter 8, "Biztalk Orchestration Services." For more information about integrating BizTalk Messaging Services with BizTalk Orchestration Services, see Chatper 14, "Orchestrating Business Processes with BizTalk Server 2000."

You can also explicitly declare an open source for a channel, which means that the source must be specified either within the document or in a parameter when the document is submitted. This is referred to as an open channel. For more information, see "Submitting," in Chapter 10, "Submitting Documents."

You also specify an inbound document definition, which represents an incoming document from an internal application or a trading partner organization. And you specify an outbound document definition, which represents a document to be delivered to the specified destination. For more information about document definitions, see "Understanding Document Definitions," later in this chapter.

If the format or structure of an outbound document is different from the format or structure of the inbound document, you must specify a map for the channel. A map transforms the format or structure of the original inbound document into the outbound document format or structure that is required by the destination organization or application. For example, if your accounting application generates purchase orders in a delimited flat-file format but your trading partner requires that purchase orders be in an X12 format, you can use a map to transform the document format. For more information about maps, see Chapter 6, "Mapping Data."

You can create more than one channel for a messaging port or distribution list, each with a different configuration. For example, suppose that you have two internal accounting applications that generate purchase orders in different formats and that you have a trading partner that wants to receive purchase orders from you in still another format. You can create a single messaging port to the trading partner. Then, for that messaging port, you can create a channel from each of the applications. The outbound document definition for both channels would be the same and match the format of your trading partner. However, each channel would have a different map to transform the inbound document formats from the applications. Because you can create different channels connected to a single messaging port, you can send all your purchase orders in the same format.

In addition, you can set other properties within a channel to:

- Designate specification fields to track for the inbound document definition. Any fields that you designate are logged to a Tracking database for each document instance processed using this specific channel, in place of any global tracking fields designated in the document definition. For more information about global tracking fields, see "Tracking Document Data Fields," later in this chapter.

- Create a channel filtering expression, which determines if BizTalk Server 2000 invokes the channel, based on the value of a field or fields within the document being processed.

- Configure receipts. You can request a receipt from the destination for a document that you send, and you can generate a receipt to the source for a document that you receive. For more information about processing receipts, see "Understanding Receipts," later in this chapter.

- Configure security properties. You can specify that the server verify the encryption and signature for an inbound document, or digitally sign the outbound document.

- Specify document logging options. You can store both the inbound and the outbound documents in their native format, in their intermediate XML format, or both.

- Configure advanced properties. You can specify a group control number for documents with EDI formats, set the number and time interval that the server uses to resend documents, and override the transport component and envelope properties for the messaging port or distribution list.

- You can also create receipt channels by using BizTalk Messaging Manager. A receipt channel is a special type of channel that you use to return a receipt to the sender of a document that is received by BizTalk Messaging Services. When you create a channel to process an inbound document that requires a receipt, you can specify the receipt channel that the server should use to process the receipt. Because of this, you should create a messaging port and an associated receipt channel before you create a messaging port and channel to process a document that requires a receipt. For more information about processing receipts, see "Understanding Receipts," later in this chapter.

When BizTalk Server 2000 receives a document, it locates the appropriate channel, which directs the server in how to process the document. The server then locates the messaging port or distribution list associated with the channel. The messaging port directs the server through the sequence of steps necessary to transport the document to the specified destination. If the channel is associated with a distribution list, the server uses the properties of each of the messaging ports in the distribution list to transport the document to the specified destinations.

Channel Elements

Channels consist of the following elements:

Source organization or application

When you create a channel, you designate either an application or an organization as the source for documents. A source application always represents a business application of your home organization. This could be an accounting application, an order-entry system, or a line-of-business application. You can also designate an XLANG schedule as the source for documents. You can create an XLANG schedule by using BizTalk Orchestration Designer. A source organization always represents an external trading partner.

A channel is always created for a messaging port or a distribution list. The destination for the documents that you receive from the source of a channel is designated in the messaging port, or in the messaging ports of the distribution list, for which the channel is created.

Inbound and outbound document definitions

- Document definitions in a channel represent the inbound and outbound documents that are processed by BizTalk Server 2000. A document definition provides a pointer to a specification that defines the document. The specification defines such characteristics as the document structure, type, and version. For more information, see "Understanding Document Definitions," later in this chapter.

When BizTalk Server 2000 receives a document, it locates the appropriate channel to process it. The server uses the specification of the inbound document definition to translate the incoming document into an intermediate XML format. The server maps the inbound document format and structure to the outbound format and structure, if necessary. Then, the server uses the specification of the outbound document to translate the outbound document into the format and structure that the destination application or organization can recognize and use.

Map

The format or structure of an inbound document might be different from the format or structure that is required for the outbound document. If this is the case, a map can be used to transform the format of the inbound document into the format of the outbound document.

For example, if you have an accounting application that generates invoices in a comma-delimited, flat-file format, but your trading partner needs to receive invoices in an X12 format, you can use a map on the channel to transform the format.

A map can also transform the content and structure of a document that uses the same format. For more information, see Chapter 6, "Mapping Data."

Tracking and filtering properties

You can designate specification fields to be logged to a Tracking database for the inbound document definition of a channel. The specification fields that you designate in a channel are logged to a tracking database for each instance of a document processed using this channel. These fields are logged in place of any global tracking fields that are designated in the inbound document definition. Any global tracking fields designated for the outbound document definition are ignored. For more information, see "Tracking Document Data Fields," later in this chapter.

A channel filtering expression provides an additional way to determine which channels are invoked when BizTalk Server 2000 receives a document. In the case of a channel filtering expression, this determination is based upon the value of a specified field or fields within the document instance.

When the server processes a document, the value of each of the specified fields is evaluated against the value of the channel filtering expression. If the expression is found to be true, the channel is invoked. If the expression is found to be false, the channel is not invoked. For example, if the channel filtering expression is created to check for a purchase order total greater than 1000, and the PO Total field in the document is 1500, the channel is invoked.

Document logging properties

BizTalk Server 2000 translates non-XML inbound documents from their original, native format into an intermediate Unicode XML format for processing. BizTalk Server 2000 translates outbound documents from an intermediate Unicode XML format into the required format for the specified destination. You can choose to store the data of each inbound and outbound document in either format or in both.

Valid Channel and Messaging Port Combinations

You can create only certain channel (source) and messaging port (destination) combinations that are valid for use with Microsoft BizTalk Server 2000.

The following valid business scenarios indicate how to configure messaging ports with the correct destination and channels with the correct source designations to correctly route data.

Scenario 1: Trading partner to an internal application

In this scenario, you create a messaging port with an application of the home organization as its destination. You then create a channel for this messaging port with the trading partner organization as its source.

Scenario 2: Internal application to trading partner

In this scenario, you create a messaging port with a trading partner organization as its destination. You then create a channel for this messaging port with an application of the home organization as its source.

Scenario 3: Internal application to internal application

In this scenario, you create a messaging port with an application of the home organization as its destination. You then create a channel for this messaging port with a different application of the home organization as its source.

Scenario 4: Internal application to distribution list

In this scenario, you create a distribution list, which includes a group of existing messaging ports to organizations or applications. You then create a channel for this distribution list with an application of the home organization as its source.

Scenario 5: Internal application to open destination

In this scenario, you create a messaging port that you specify as an open messaging port. You then create a channel for this messaging port with an application of the home organization as its source.

Scenario 6: Open source to internal application

In this scenario, you create a messaging port with an application of the home organization as its destination. You then create a channel for this messaging port that you specify as an open channel.

Note

- A channel that is specified as an open channel cannot be created for a messaging port that is specified as an open messaging port.

Scenario 7: Trading partner through intermediary to trading partner

In this scenario, one trading partner sends documents to another through your BizTalk Server 2000, with your business serving as an intermediary. You create a messaging port with one trading partner organization as its destination. You then create a channel for this messaging port with a different trading partner as its source.

Create and Manage Channels

This section provides task-specific information about how to create and manage channels by using BizTalk Messaging Manager. For more information about channels, see "Understanding Channels" earlier in this chapter.

To create channels

You must create a messaging port or a distribution list before you can create a channel. For more information, see "To create messaging ports" or "To create distribution lists" later in this chapter.

1. In BizTalk Messaging Manager, in the **Search for other items** area, click **Messaging ports** or **Distribution lists** and click **Search Now**.

2. In the **Messaging Port Name** list, click the messaging port for which you want to create a channel.

   –Or–

   In the **Distribution List Name** list, click the distribution list for which you want to create a channel.

3. In BizTalk Messaging Manager, on the **File** menu, point to **New**, point to **Channel**, and then complete one of the following steps:

   • To create a channel from an organization, click **From an Organization**.

   • To create a channel from an application, click **From an Application**.

   The New Channel Wizard opens.

4. On the **General Information** page, set the properties and click **Next**.

   For more information, see "To set general channel-information properties" later in this chapter.

5. Complete one of the following steps:

   • If you are creating a channel from an organization, set the properties on the **Source Organization** page and click **Next**. For more information, see "To set source organization properties" later in this chapter.

   • If you are creating a channel from an application, set the properties on the **Source Application** page and click **Next**. For more information, see "To set source application properties" later in this chapter.

6. On the **Inbound Document** page, set the properties and click **Next**.

    For more information, see "To set inbound document properties" later in this chapter.

7. On the **Outbound Document** page, set the properties and click **Next**.

    For more information, see "To set outbound document properties" later in this chapter.

8. On the **Document Logging** page, set the properties and click **Next**.

    For more information, see "To set document logging properties" later in this chapter.

9. On the **Advanced Configuration** page, set the properties and click **Finish**.

    For more information, see "To set advanced configuration properties" later in this chapter.

10. After you have set all channel properties, on the **Advanced Configuration** page click **Finish** to close the Channel Wizard.

✑ Notes

-   You cannot name a channel using the reserved system name, Reliable Message Acknowledgement Channel.

-   You can use this procedure to create either a standard channel or a receipt channel. The procedures in this section contain notes that explain which channel properties are not available when you are creating a receipt channel.

-   If you create a messaging port and a channel to use for a pass-through submission of data, you can use only the service window and the retry count and interval features of the channel, and the transport features of its associated messaging port. You cannot use the verification of decoding or decryption, filtering, document tracking, or mapping features of the channel.

-   When you save a channel that references a map that is outside your local domain, you might receive an error. If you receive an error, download and configure the WinHTTP proxy utility. To download the utility, go to the MSDN Online Downloads Web site (msdn.microsoft.com/downloads/default.asp) and browse to the WinHTTP Proxy Configuration Utility page, which is located in the XML chapter of the Web Development book.

To search for channels

1. In BizTalk Messaging Manager, in the **Search for other items** area, click **Channels**.

2. To search for all channels, clear all search criteria and click **Search Now**.

3. Do one or more of the following:

    -   To search for channels with a specific name, in the **Search for channels** area, in the **Channel name** box, type the name of the channel that you want to find and click **Search Now**. You can enter an incomplete name and the search returns all possible names that match the incomplete name entry.

- To search for channels from a specific type of source, in the **Source** list, click a source type and click **Search Now**.

- To search for channels associated with a specific messaging port or distribution list, in the **Associated with messaging port or distribution list** box, type the name of a messaging port or distribution list and click **Search Now**. You can enter an incomplete name and the search returns all possible names that match the incomplete name entry.

- To search for channels that use a specific document definition, in the **Using document definition** box, type the name of a document definition and click **Search Now**. You can enter an incomplete name and the search returns all possible names that match the incomplete name entry.

Notes

- You can set more than one search criteria before clicking **Search Now**.

- To clear the search criteria and search results, click **Clear Search**.

- You can also search for channels associated with a specific messaging port or distribution list by right-clicking the messaging port or distribution list and clicking **Find Channels**.

- If you have a large number of objects for which to search, it might take several minutes to return all the objects. You can narrow the objects returned in a search by using selection criteria.

- The default number of items returned in a search is 500. You can adjust this number. For more information, see "To set server connection options" earlier in this chapter.

- You can use the following wildcard characters in the search criteria.

Wildcard character	Description	Example
%	Any string of zero or more characters.	The entry '%open%' finds all names with the word 'open' anywhere in the name.
_ (underscore)	Any single character.	The entry '_ean' finds four-letter names that end with ean (Dean, Sean, and so on).
[ ]	Any single character within the specified range ([a-f]) or set ([abcdef]).	The entry '[C-P]arsen' finds names ending with arsen and beginning with any single character between C and P (Carsen, Larsen, and so on).
[^]	Any single character not within the specified range ([^a-f]) or set ([^abcdef]).	The entry 'de[^s]%' finds all names beginning with de and where the following letter is not s.

To edit channels

1. In BizTalk Messaging Manager, in the **Channel Name** list, click the channel that you want to edit.

   For information about searching for channels, see "To search for channels" earlier in this chapter.

2. On the **File** menu, click **Edit**.

   The Channel Properties Wizard opens.

3. On the **General Information** page, edit the appropriate properties.

   For more information, see "To set general channel-information properties" later in this chapter.

   After editing the properties on any page, you can click **Finish** to close the Channel Properties Wizard or click **Next** to edit additional channel properties.

4. Complete one of the following steps:
   - If you are editing a channel from an organization, edit the appropriate properties on the **Source Organization** page. For more information, see "To set source organization properties" later in this chapter.
   - If you are editing a channel from an application, edit the appropriate properties on the **Source Application** page. For more information, see "To set source application properties" later in this chapter.

5. On the **Inbound Document** page, edit the appropriate properties.

   For more information, see "To set inbound document properties" later in this chapter.

6. On the **Outbound Document** page, edit the appropriate properties.

   For more information, see "To set outbound document properties" later in this chapter.

7. On the **Document Logging** page, edit the appropriate properties.

   For more information, see "To set document logging properties" later in this chapter.

8. On the **Advanced Configuration** page, edit the appropriate properties.

   For more information, see "To set advanced configuration properties" later in this chapter.

🖉 Notes

- You cannot name a channel using the reserved system name, Reliable Message Acknowledgement Channel.

- When you save a channel that references a map that is outside your local domain, you might receive an error. If you receive an error, download and configure the WinHTTP proxy utility. To download the utility, go to the MSDN Online Downloads Web site (msdn.microsoft.com/downloads/default.asp) and browse to the WinHTTP Proxy Configuration Utility page, which is located in the XML chapter of the Web Development book.

To delete channels

1. In BizTalk Messaging Manager, in the **Channel Name** list, click the channel that you want to delete.

   For information about searching for channels, see "To search for channels" earlier in this chapter.

2. On the **File** menu, click **Delete**.

✎ Note

- You cannot delete the receipt channel until all channels that refer to it have been deleted.

To set general channel-information properties

1. On the **General Information** page of the Channel Wizard, in the **Name** box, type the name of the channel.

2. In the **Comments** box, type any comments for the channel.

3. If you want to create a receipt channel, select the **This is a receipt channel** check box.

If you are creating a new channel, click **Next**. For instructions about completing the next step, see "To create channels" earlier in this chapter.

If you are editing an existing channel, click **Next**. For instructions about completing the next step, see "To edit channels" earlier in this chapter. When you have completed your changes, click **Finish**.

✎ Notes

- A receipt channel is a special type of channel that you use to return a receipt to the sender of a document that is received by BizTalk Server 2000. For more information about receipts, see "Understanding Receipts" later in this chapter.

- You cannot create a receipt channel for an open messaging port or a distribution list.

To set source organization properties

1. On the **Source Organization** page of the Channel Wizard, complete one of the following steps:
   - Click **Open source** to create an open channel, which designates that the source is provided either by data within the document or in parameters submitted along with the document, and click **Next**.

     For more information about submitting documents, see "Submitting" in Chapter 10, "Submitting Documents."

   - Click **Organization** to designate a trading partner organization as the source and proceed to step 2.

2. In the **Organization** area, click **Browse**.

   The **Select an Organization** dialog box appears.

3. Click an organization and click **OK**.

   For more information, see "To select a source organization" later in this chapter.

4. If you want to override the default organization identifier for the source organization, click another identifier in the **Organization identifier** list.

5. If you require a receipt from the destination, as specified in the messaging port, select the **Expect receipt** check box and, in the **Receipt interval in minutes** box, type a value or click the up or down arrow to increase or decrease the value.

   The default value is 120 minutes. For more information about receipts, see "Understanding Receipts" later in this chapter.

6. If you want to generate a receipt to the source, select the **Generate receipt** check box, click **Browse**, and then select a receipt channel.

   For more information, see "To select a receipt channel" later in this chapter.

If you are creating a new channel, click **Next**. For instructions about completing the next step, see "To create channels" earlier in this chapter.

If you are editing an existing channel, click **Next**. For instructions about completing the next step, see "To edit channels" earlier in this chapter. If you have completed your changes, click **Finish**.

Notes

- When you select a source organization identifier for use with X12 envelopes, do not select the organization identifier named Organization, or any other identifier that has a qualifier that exceeds 2 characters or a value that exceeds 15 characters.

- When you select a source organization identifier for use with EDIFACT envelopes, do not select the organization identifier named Organization, or any other identifier that has a qualifier that exceeds 4 characters or a value that exceeds 35 characters.

- If you are editing a channel from a specific organization, the **Open Source** option is not available and you cannot change the source organization. If you are editing an open channel, the **Organization** option is not available.

- If you are creating or editing a receipt channel, the **Expect receipt** and **Generate receipt** properties are not available.

To set source application properties

1. On the **Source Application** page of the Channel Wizard, complete one of the following steps:

   - Click **XLANG Schedule** to designate that the source is an XLANG schedule and click **Next**.

     You should not choose this option if you are creating a channel for an open messaging port. For more information about integrating BizTalk Messaging Services with

BizTalk Orchestration Services, see Chapter 14, "Orchestrating Business Processes with BizTalk Server 2000."

- Click **Application** to designate an application of the home organization as the source and proceed to step 2.

2. In the **Name** list, click an application.

3. If you want to override the default organization identifier for the home organization, click another identifier in the **Organization identifier** list.

4. If you want to receive a receipt from the destination, select the **Expect receipt** check box and, in the **Receipt interval in minutes** box, type a value or click the up or down arrow to increase or decrease the value.

   The default value is 120 minutes. For more information about receipts, see "Understanding Receipts" later in this chapter.

5. If you want to generate a receipt to the source, select the **Generate receipt** check box, click **Browse**, and then select a receipt channel.

   For more information, see "To select a receipt channel" later in this chapter.

If you are creating a new channel, click **Next**. For instructions about completing the next step, see "To create channels" earlier in this chapter.

If you are editing an existing channel, click **Next**. For instructions about completing the next step, see "To edit channels" earlier in this chapter. If you have completed your changes, click **Finish**.

✎ Notes

- You can create an XLANG schedule by using BizTalk Orchestration Designer.

- When you are creating or editing a receipt channel, or a channel for which an XLANG schedule is specified as the source, the **Expect receipt** and **Generate receipt** properties are not available.

To set inbound document properties

1. On the **Inbound Document** page of the Channel Wizard, to the right of the **Inbound document definition name** box, click **Browse**.

   The **Select a Document Definition** dialog box appears.

2. Click a document definition and click **OK**.

   For more information, see "To select an inbound document definition" later in this chapter.

3. If you want to verify decryption for the inbound document, select the **Verify decryption certificate on inbound document** check box and, to the right of the **Certificate to verify decryption** box, click **Browse**.

   The **Select Certificate to Verify Decryption** dialog box appears.

4. Select a certificate.

   For more information, see "To select a certificate to verify inbound document decryption" later in this chapter.

5. If you want to verify the digital signature on the inbound document, select the **Verify signature certificate on inbound document** check box and, to the right of the **Certificate to verify signature** box, click **Browse**.

   The **Select Certificate to Verify Signature** dialog box appears.

6. Select a signature certificate.

   For more information, see "To select a certificate to verify inbound document signature" later in this chapter.

7. If you want to track fields in the inbound document, select the **Track inbound document** check box and click **Tracking**.

   The **Tracking for Inbound Document** dialog box appears.

8. Set the tracking properties.

   For more information, see "Set Tracking for Inbound Document Properties" later in this chapter.

9. If you want to create a channel filtering expression for the inbound document, select the **Filter inbound document** check box and click **Filtering**.

   The **Channel Filtering Expressions** dialog box appears.

10. Set the filtering properties.

    For more information, see "Set Channel Filtering Properties," later in this chapter.

If you are creating a new channel, click **Next**. For instructions about completing the next step, see "To create channels" earlier in this chapter.

If you are editing an existing channel, click **Next**. For instructions about completing the next step, see "To edit channels" earlier in this chapter. If you have completed your changes, click **Finish**.

✎ Notes

- When you create a receipt channel, both the inbound and outbound document definitions default to the BizTalk Canonical Receipt and cannot be transformed by using a map. To transform the outbound receipt to a different format, you must create and select in the receipt channel an inbound document definition that refers to the canonical receipt specification in the WebDAV repository. You also must create and select in the receipt channel an outbound document definition that refers to a specification with the format that you want for the outbound receipt, and specify a map in the receipt channel to transform the formats. For more information, see "Understanding Receipts" later in this chapter.

- When you create a receipt channel that uses the default BizTalk Canonical Receipt for the inbound document definition, the tracking and filtering properties are unavailable.

- When you create a channel for an open messaging port, and the destination information is provided in the document, the inbound document definition for that channel must reference a specification that is properly configured. For more information about how to configure a document specification to process documents for an open messaging port, see "To set dictionary properties" in Chapter 5, "Creating Specifications."

To set outbound document properties

1. On the **Outbound Document** page of the Channel Wizard, to the right of the **Outbound document definition name** box, click **Browse**.

   The **Select a Document Definition** dialog box appears.

2. Click a document definition and click **OK**.

   For more information, see "To select an outbound document definition" later in this chapter.

3. If you want to specify a map, select the **Map inbound document to outbound document** check box and, to the right of the **Map reference** box, click **Browse**.

   The **Select a Map from the WebDAV Repository** dialog box appears.

4. Select a map specification.

   For more information, see "To select a map" later in this chapter.

5. If you want to digitally sign the outbound document, select the **Sign outbound document** check box and, to the right of the **Signature certificate** box, click **Browse**.

   If you are creating a channel for a messaging port for which the **Signature** property on the **Security Information** page is set to S/MIME, the **Sign outbound document** check box is automatically selected.

   The **Select a Signature Certificate** dialog box appears.

6. Select a signature certificate.

   For more information, see "To select a certificate for outbound signature" later in this chapter.

If you are creating a new channel, click **Next**. For instructions about completing the next step, see "To create channels" earlier in this chapter.

If you are editing an existing channel, click **Next**. For instructions about completing the next step, see "To edit channels" earlier in this chapter. If you have completed your changes, click **Finish**.

◈ Important

- The format of an envelope that you specify in a messaging port must agree with the format of the document or documents that it contains. The document format is determined by the specification referred to in the outbound document definition of an associated channel. For example, if you choose an envelope with an X12 format for a messaging port, you must select an outbound document definition for the channel that points to an X12 specification.

- When you declare a messaging port as an open messaging port, you should not create channels for the messaging port that have an outbound document definition with an X12 or EDIFACT specification. To build an X12 or EDIFACT envelope, the server must have a source and a destination organization identifier. An open messaging port does not specify a destination organization identifier. In addition, the documents for an open messaging port must have the destination address within the document, but X12 and EDIFACT documents do not contain this information.

- The first time that you open any WebDAV repository dialog box, the WebDAV repository on the local server is selected, even if your BizTalk Messaging Manager is connected to a database on a remote server. If you browse to a WebDAV repository on a remote server, the default changes to that server until you select a new WebDAV repository. The default server for all WebDAV repository dialog boxes is the last server to which a connection was made.

✎ Notes

- When you create a receipt channel, both the inbound and outbound document definitions default to the BizTalk Canonical Receipt and cannot be transformed by using a map. To use a different format for an outbound receipt, you must create and select an inbound document definition that refers to the canonical receipt specification in the WebDAV repository. You also must create an outbound document definition that refers to a specification with the format that you want for the outbound receipt, as well as a map that transforms the format of the receipt. For more information about receipts, see "Understanding Receipts" later in this chapter.

- A map is used to transform the inbound document format into the outbound document format. If the specification reference of the inbound document matches that of the outbound document, no map is required. By default, the **Map inbound document to outbound document** check box is not selected. Maps can be created using BizTalk Mapper. For more information about maps, see Chapter 6, "Mapping Data."

To set document logging properties

1. On the **Document Logging** page of the Channel Wizard, in the **Log inbound document** area, select the appropriate check boxes:

   - **In native format.** Stores inbound documents for the channel in the original format. This is the default setting.

   - **In XML format.** Stores inbound documents for the channel in XML format.

2. In the **Log outbound document** area, select the appropriate check boxes:

- **In native format.** Stores outbound documents for the channel in the original format.

- **In XML format.** Stores outbound documents for the channel in XML format.

If you are creating a new channel, click **Next**. For instructions about completing the next step, see "To create channels" earlier in this chapter.

If you are editing an existing channel, click **Next**. For instructions about completing the next step, see "To edit channels" later in this chapter. If you have completed your changes, click **Finish**.

✎ Notes

- There is a size limit for documents that use logging, which if exceeded will greatly affect the performance of BizTalk Server. For more information about the size limit, see "Interchange and document size limit" in Chapter 11, "Administering Servers and Applications."

- BizTalk Server 2000 translates non-XML inbound documents from their original, native format into an XML format for processing, and outbound documents from an XML format into the required, native format of the destination.

To set advanced configuration properties

1. On the **Advanced Configuration** page of the Channel Wizard, if you are creating a channel for a messaging port that specifies an X12 or EDIFACT envelope format, in the **Group control number** box type a non-zero value.

2. In the **Retry options** area, in the **Number of retries** box, enter the number of times that you want the server to resend the document if a receipt has not been received and, in the **Interval** box, enter the number of minutes between retries.

   For more information about receipts, see "Understanding Receipts" later in this chapter.

3. If you want to override the transport or envelope component settings for a messaging port or distribution list, click **Advanced**.

   - If you are creating or editing a channel for a messaging port, the **Override Messaging Port Defaults** dialog box appears. For more information, see "To override messaging port defaults" later in this chapter.

   - If you are creating or editing a channel for a distribution list, the **Override Distribution List Defaults** dialog box appears. For more information, see "To override distribution list defaults" later in this chapter.

If you are creating a new channel, click **Next**. For instructions about completing the next step, see "To create channels" earlier in this chapter.

If you are editing an existing channel, click **Next**. For instructions about completing the next step, see "To edit channels," earlier in this chapter. If you have completed your changes, click **Finish**.

To select a source organization

1. On the **Source Organization** page of the Channel Wizard, to the right of the **Name** box, click **Browse**.

   The **Select an Organization** dialog box appears.

2. In the **Available organizations** list, click an organization and click **OK**.

To continue setting source organization properties, see "To set source organization properties" earlier in this chapter.

To select a receipt channel

1. On the **Source Application** or **Source Organization** page of the Channel Wizard, select the **Generate receipt** check box and click **Browse**.

   The **Select a Receipt Channel** dialog box appears.

2. In the **Available receipt channels** list, click a receipt channel and click **OK**.

To continue setting source organization properties, see "To set source organization properties" earlier in this chapter.

To continue setting source application properties, see "To set source application properties" earlier in this chapter.

Note

- The **Available receipt channels** list displays only receipt channels that are associated with messaging ports for which the destination is identical to the source for the channel that you are creating. When BizTalk Server 2000 invokes a channel with a receipt channel specified, the server returns a receipt to the original source of that document by using the receipt channel specified. For more information about receipts, see "Understanding Receipts" later in this chapter.

To select an inbound document definition

1. On the **Inbound Document** page of the Channel Wizard, to the right of the **Inbound document definition name** box, click **Browse**.

   The **Select a Document Definition** dialog box appears.

2. In the **Available document definitions** list, click a document definition and click **OK**.

To continue setting inbound document properties, see "To set inbound document properties" earlier in this chapter.

Note

- When you create a receipt channel, both the inbound and outbound document definitions default to the BizTalk Canonical Receipt and cannot be transformed by using a map. To use a different format for an outbound receipt, you must create and select an inbound document definition that refers to the canonical receipt specification in the WebDAV repository. You also must create an outbound document definition that refers to a specification with the format that you want for the outbound receipt, as well as a map that transforms the format of the receipt. For more information about receipts, see "Understanding Receipts" later in this chapter.

To select a certificate to verify inbound document decryption

1. On the **Inbound Document** page of the Channel Wizard, select the **Verify decryption on inbound document** check box and, to the right of the **Certificate to verify decryption** box, click **Browse**.

   The **Select a Certificate to Verify Decryption** dialog box appears.

2. In the **Certificate name** list, click a certificate name and click **OK**.

To continue setting inbound document properties, see "To set inbound document properties" earlier in this chapter.

☑ Notes

- All certificates are stored in the local computer store. To configure certificates for the S/MIME components by using BizTalk Messaging Manager, you must belong to a user account in the Windows 2000 Administrators group, and BizTalk Messaging Services must be running as a local system account or as a user account in the Windows 2000 Administrators group.

- Documents are decrypted when BizTalk Server 2000 receives them so that the server can obtain the data it needs to identify the appropriate channel. The certificate that you specify in the channel verifies that the decryption was done correctly.

- All certificates must be named uniquely. If more than one certificate has the same name, only one of the certificates can be selected. Once one of the certificates is selected, other certificates with the same name no longer appear in the list.

  For more information about certificates, see "Certificates Overview" in Chapter 2, "Understanding Security."

To select a certificate to verify inbound document signature

1. On the **Inbound Document** page of the Channel Wizard, select the **Verify signature on inbound document** check box and, to the right of the **Certificate for signature verification** box, click **Browse**.

   The **Select a Certificate to Verify Signature** dialog box appears.

2. In the **Certificate name** list, click a certificate name and click **OK**.

To continue setting inbound document properties, see "To set inbound document properties" earlier in this chapter.

Notes

- All certificates are stored in the local computer store. To configure certificates for the S/MIME components by using BizTalk Messaging Manager, you must belong to a user account in the Windows 2000 Administrators group, and BizTalk Messaging Services must be running as a local system account or as a user account in the Windows 2000 Administrators group.

- All certificates must be named uniquely. If more than one certificate has the same name, only one of the certificates can be selected. Once one of the certificates is selected, other certificates with the same name no longer appear in the list.

  For more information about certificates, see "Certificates Overview" in Chapter 2, "Understanding Security."

To select an outbound document definition

1. On the **Outbound Document** page of the Channel Wizard, to the right of the **Outbound document definition name** box, click **Browse**.

   The **Select a Document Definition** dialog box appears.

2. In the **Available document definitions** list, click a document definition and click **OK**.

   To continue setting outbound document properties, see "To set outbound document properties" earlier in this chapter.

Note

- When you create a receipt channel, both the inbound and outbound document definitions default to the BizTalk Canonical Receipt and cannot be transformed by using a map. To use a different format for an outbound receipt, you must create and select an inbound document definition that refers to the canonical receipt specification in the WebDAV repository. You also must create an outbound document definition that refers to a specification with the format that you want for the outbound receipt, as well as a map that transforms the format of the receipt. For more information about receipts, see "Understanding Receipts" later in this chapter.

To select a map

1. On the **Outbound Document** page of the Channel Wizard, select the **Map inbound document to outbound document** check box and, to the right of the **Map reference** box, click **Browse**.

   The **Select a Map from the WebDAV Repository** dialog box appears.

2. In the **Server** box, do one of the following if you want to change the server:

   - Click a server in the list.

   - Type the name of a server and press ENTER.

3. Double-click the folder that contains the map that you want, click the map, and then click **Open**.

To continue setting outbound document properties, see "To set outbound document properties" earlier in this chapter.

✦ Important

- The first time that you open any WebDAV repository dialog box, the WebDAV repository on the local server is selected, even if your BizTalk Messaging Manager is connected to a database on a remote server. If you browse to a WebDAV repository on a remote server, the default changes to that server until you select a new WebDAV repository. The default server for all WebDAV repository dialog boxes is the last server to which a connection was made.

📝 Notes

- If you select http://localhost as the server, BizTalk Messaging Manager automatically converts it to the local computer name.

- When you save a channel that references a map that is outside your local domain, you might receive an error. If you receive an error, download and configure the WinHTTP proxy utility. To download the utility, go to the MSDN Online Downloads Web site (msdn.microsoft.com/downloads/default.asp) and browse to the WinHTTP Proxy Configuration Utility page, which is located in the XML chapter of the Web Development book.

To select a certificate for outbound signature

1. On the **Outbound Document** page of the Channel Wizard, select the **Sign outbound document** check box and, to the right of the **Signature certificate** box, click **Browse**.

    The **Select a Signature Certificate** dialog box appears.

2. In the **Certificate name** list, click a certificate name and click **OK**.

To continue setting outbound document properties, see "To set outbound document properties" earlier in this chapter.

📝 Notes

- All certificates are stored in the local computer store. To configure certificates for the S/MIME components by using BizTalk Messaging Manager, you must belong to a user account in the Windows 2000 Administrators group, and BizTalk Messaging Services must be running as a local system account or as a user account in the Windows 2000 Administrators group.

- All certificates must be named uniquely. If more than one certificate has the same name, only one of the certificates can be selected. Once one of the certificates is selected, other certificates with the same name no longer appear in the list.

    For more information about certificates, see "Certificates Overview" in Chapter 2, "Understanding Security."

To override messaging port defaults

1. On the **Advanced Configuration** page of the Channel Wizard, click **Advanced**.

   If you are creating or editing a channel for a messaging port, the **Override Messaging Port Defaults** dialog box appears.

2. On the **Primary Transport** tab, click **Properties**.

   The **BizTalk Component Properties** dialog box appears.

3. Change the transport component properties that you want to override and click **OK**.

4. If the messaging port has an envelope and you want to override its settings, click the **Envelope** tab and click **Properties**.

   The **BizTalk Component Properties** dialog box appears.

5. Change the envelope component properties that you want to override and click **OK**.

To continue setting advanced properties, see "To set advanced configuration properties" earlier in this chapter.

◆ Important

- Overriding the transport and envelope properties for a messaging port is an advanced feature. If you do not thoroughly understand the transport or envelope component properties in these dialog boxes, you should not change them.

- If you specified an envelope with a custom format in the messaging port, you must configure the custom serializer component by using the advanced configuration properties.

◢ Notes

- When you override messaging port properties in a channel, the overrides apply only to that channel.

- You cannot override the transport address that was set in a messaging port.

- The default setting for the HTTP transport component is to use the HTTP proxy server. This is the correct setting to transport data to Web sites outside your business's firewall. To transport data to Web sites that are inside your business's firewall (that is, within your intranet), use this procedure to override the default setting.

- For the HTTPS transport component, use only certificates that are specified for client authentication. Certificates that are specified for all purposes do not appear in the list.

- The default setting for the file transport component is to append files. If you choose the file transport type with its default settings in a messaging port and use antivirus software on the server on which BizTalk Server 2000 is installed, and you send multiple files that have exactly the same name to the same file location, at the same time, BizTalk Server 2000 might stop responding and must be restarted. You can eliminate this problem by changing the default setting for the file transport component from **Append to**

file to **Overwrite file** in the **BizTalk SendLocalFile Properties** dialog box. You also can eliminate this problem by creating a unique file for each document instance processed by using the file path format in the messaging port: file://C:\dir\file%tracking_id%.xml. For more information, see "To specify a transport address" later in this chapter.

- The default setting for the file transport component is to append files. If you choose the file transport type with its default settings and select an envelope with a reliable envelope format in a messaging port, and then send multiple files to the same file location, at the same time, you might have unexpected parsing results. You can eliminate this problem by changing the default setting for the file transport component from **Append to file** to **Overwrite file** in the **BizTalk SendLocalFile Properties** dialog box.

- If the envelope specified in the messaging port has a custom format, and you have created and registered a custom serializer component, you can configure the properties of the custom serializer component by using this procedure.

- The default syntax identifier for an EDIFACT envelope is UNOA (uppercase Latin alphabet). If your data requires a different syntax, select a different syntax identifier by using this procedure.

- If you use EDIFACT release indicators, do not include release indicator characters in your data. Doing so might cause the data to exceed the physical character size limits for fields.

To override distribution list defaults

1. On the **Advanced Configuration** page of the Channel Wizard, click **Advanced**.

   If you are creating or editing a channel for a distribution list, the **Override Distribution List Defaults** dialog box appears.

2. In the **Select Messaging Port** list, select a messaging port that you want to override and click **Override**.

   The **Override Messaging Port Defaults** dialog box appears.

3. Override the transport and envelope component properties for the selected messaging port.

   For more information, see "To override messaging port defaults" earlier in this chapter.

4. When you have changed the messaging ports that you want to override, click **Close**.

To continue setting advanced properties, see "To set advanced configuration properties" earlier in this chapter.

Set Tracking for Inbound Document Properties

The **Tracking for Inbound Document** dialog box lists the specification fields for the inbound document, as well as any global tracking fields selected in the document definition.

If you select any specification fields by using this dialog box, those fields override the global tracking fields for this channel only. For each document instance that is processed, the fields that you select in the channel are logged to the Tracking database, rather than to the global tracking fields.

To select specification fields in a channel

1. On the **Inbound Document** page of the Channel Wizard, select the **Track inbound document** check box and click **Tracking**.

   The **Tracking for Inbound Document** dialog box appears.

2. In the **Specification fields** tree, double-click any record to expand the view.

3. Select a specification field that you want to add to the **Fields to track** list and complete one of the following procedures:

To add the field as	Follow this procedure
Integer	Click **Integer**. You can add two fields as integers.
Real	Click **Real**. You can add two fields as real numbers.
Date	Click **Date**. You can add two fields as dates.
Text	Click **Text**. You can add two fields as text.
Custom	Click **Custom**. You can add unlimited fields as a custom type. The fields are stored as an XML concatenated string with tags for each field.

To continue setting inbound document properties, see "To set inbound document properties" earlier in this chapter.

◆ Important

- If you select any specification fields by using this dialog box, those fields override the global tracking fields for this channel only. For each document instance that is processed, the fields that you select in the channel are logged to the Tracking database, rather than to the global tracking fields.

✎ Notes

- To select a specification field to track as an integer, real, or date data type, the field must have that data type assigned in the specification. For more information about assigning a data type to a specification field, see "To set declaration properties" in Chapter 5, "Creating Specifications."

- Specification fields without a data type assigned in the specification can be tracked only as a text or custom data type.

- If a specification field that you want to track has a character data type, you can track that field only as a custom data type.

- You can select only two specification fields of a specific data type. You can select an unlimited number of fields as a custom data type.

To remove specification fields in a channel

1. On the **Inbound Document** page of the Channel Wizard, select the **Track inbound document** check box and click **Tracking**.

   The **Tracking for Inbound Document** dialog box appears.

2. In the **Fields to track** list, click the specification field or fields that you want to remove and click **Remove**.

To continue setting inbound document properties, see "To set inbound document properties" earlier in this chapter.

✎ Note

- When you remove a field from the list of fields to track, it is removed only from the list in this channel; it is not removed from the specification.

Set Channel Filtering Properties

A channel filtering expression is an XPath expression that can be used to determine if a channel is invoked based upon the value of a specified field or fields within the document. When Microsoft BizTalk Server 2000 processes a document, the value of the specified field or fields in each document is evaluated against the channel filtering expression. If the expression is found to be true, the channel is invoked. If the expression is found to be false, the channel is not invoked.

To add a channel filtering expression

1. On the **Inbound Document** page of the Channel Wizard, select the **Filter inbound document** check box and click **Filtering**.

   The **Channel Filtering Expressions** dialog box appears.

2. In the **Select field** tree, double-click any node to expand the view.

3. Click a specification field that you want to use to create a filtering expression and click **Add**.

   The **Expression Properties** dialog box appears.

4. In the **Operator** list, click an operator.

Operator	Symbol
Equal to (Default)	=
Not equal to	!=
Less than	<
Equal to or less than	<=
Greater than	>
Equal to or greater than	>=

5. In the **Value** box, type a value for the expression and click **OK**.

To continue setting inbound document properties, see "Set inbound document properties," earlier in this chapter.

◆ Important

- A channel filtering expression must be a valid XPath expression. The **Add** button can be used to create a clause that contains a specification field and to insert it into an expression; however, it does not generate the correct syntax needed for a valid XPath expression. For more information about XPath expressions, see "Channel Filtering" later in this chapter; you can also go to the MSDN Online Library Web site (msdn.microsoft.com/library/default.asp) and search on the keyword "XPath."

✎ Notes

- You can type an expression directly into the **Expressions** list.
- To select a specification field for a channel filtering expression, the field must have a data type assigned in the specification. For more information about assigning a data type to a field, see "To set declaration properties" in Chapter 5, "Creating Specifications."
- If the specification field that you are using to create an expression has a Boolean data type, you cannot use the text string "true" or "false" in the expression value. You must use a numerical value instead, "-1" for true and "0" for false.
- If the specification field that you are using to create an expression has a date data type, you must type the value in the following format, including the hyphens: *YYYY-MM-DD*.

To edit a channel filtering expression

1. On the **Inbound Document** page of the Channel Wizard, select the **Filter inbound document** check box and click **Filtering**.

   The **Channel Filtering Expressions** dialog box appears.

2. In the **Expressions** list, edit the expression and click **OK**.

To continue setting inbound document properties, see "To set inbound document properties" earlier in this chapter.

◆ Important

- A channel filtering expression must be a valid XPath expression. For more information about XPath expressions, see "Channel Filtering" later in this chapter; you can also go to the MSDN Online Library Web site (msdn.microsoft.com/library/default.asp) and search on the keyword "XPath."

To remove a channel filtering expression

- On the **Inbound Document** page of the Channel Wizard, clear the **Filter inbound document** check box.

To continue setting inbound document properties, see "To set inbound document properties" earlier in this chapter.

Understanding Messaging Ports

A messaging port is a set of properties that you can use to configure BizTalk Messaging Services to transport documents to a specified destination by using a specified transport service. The documents that a messaging port transports originate from the source that you specify in an associated channel. You can create multiple channels for a single messaging port to send documents from many sources to the same destination.

A messaging port can be configured to send documents to a designated destination organization, an XLANG schedule, or a destination application.

For a messaging port to an organization, you can either designate a specific trading partner as the destination or declare an open destination, which is referred to as an open messaging port. An open messaging port can be used to transport documents only to trading partner organizations. The destination organization information for an open messaging port must be specified either within the document or in a parameter when the document is submitted to BizTalk Server 2000. For more information about submitting documents, see "Submitting" in Chapter 10, "Submitting Documents." For more information about open messaging ports, see "Openness" later in this chapter.

When the address specified for an open messaging port is an SMTP address, the server must have a From address for the home organization. To obtain this address, the server uses the value that is specified for a special organization identifier of the home organization, named Reliable Messaging Acknowledgement SMTP From Address. For more information about how to configure this organization identifier, see "To configure the home organization" later in this chapter.

For a messaging port to an application, you can designate either an XLANG schedule or an application of the home organization as the destination. For more information about the home organization, see "Understanding Organizations" later in this chapter.

A messaging port to an XLANG schedule can be configured to activate a new instance of a specified XLANG schedule, and then deliver the document to a specified messaging port of that schedule. In this case, the specified schedule must contain a messaging port that is bound to BizTalk Messaging. When you specify the schedule, you also name the messaging port. You can also configure a messaging port to deliver a document to a running instance of an XLANG schedule. In this case, the document must contain a queue name to which the document should be delivered and that the targeted schedule is monitoring. For more information about integrating BizTalk Messaging Services with BizTalk Orchestration Services, see Chapter 14, "Orchestrating Business Processes with BizTalk Server 2000."

You also use the messaging port properties to designate a specific address to which documents are delivered, the transport type for getting documents to that location, and how the documents are enveloped and secured prior to transport.

When BizTalk Server 2000 receives a document, it locates the appropriate channel to process it. After the channel processes the document, it points the server to its associated messaging port or distribution list, which directs the server through the sequence of steps necessary to envelope, secure, and transport the document to the specified destination.

Messaging Port Elements

Messaging ports consist of the following elements:

Destination

The destination for a messaging port can be a trading partner organization, an XLANG schedule, or an application of the home organization.

A messaging port to an organization can explicitly designate the destination organization, or a messaging port can be declared as an open messaging port. For open messaging ports, the destination organization is determined at the time the messaging port processes a document. The destination organization information must be specified either in the document or in parameters when the document is submitted. For more information, see "Submitting" in Chapter 10, "Submitting Documents."

A messaging port to an XLANG schedule can be configured in two ways. You can configure a messaging port to activate a new instance of an XLANG schedule by specifying the path to an XLANG schedule. When the messaging port processes a document, it activates this schedule and then delivers the document to a messaging port in that schedule that you also specify in the messaging port properties. Or you can configure the messaging port to deliver documents to an active XLANG schedule. You use this option only when you send a trading partner a message and the trading partner returns a message to a specially configured ASP page using an HTTP transport. For more information, see Chapter 14, "Orchestrating Business Processes with BizTalk Server 2000." You can create an XLANG schedule by using BizTalk Orchestration Designer. For more information, see "BizTalk Orchestration Designer Environent" in Chapter 8, "Biztalk Orchestration Services."

A messaging port can also transport documents to a destination application of the home organization. Before you can designate an application as the destination for a messaging port, you must add the application to the home organization. For more information, see "To add applications" later in this chapter.

Transport properties

The transport properties that you specify for a messaging port determine the transport service used to convey documents to the destination organization or destination application, and the specific address to which the documents are sent.

The transport properties that you set for a messaging port apply to all channels associated with that messaging port. After BizTalk Server 2000 invokes a channel to process documents, the server then refers to the properties of the messaging port that is associated with the channel. The server sends the documents to the address specified in the messaging port, using the transport type specified in the messaging port.

You can also specify a service window, which designates a specific time range within which documents can be transported.

Envelope information

Envelopes are headers and sometimes footers that are used to prefix or encapsulate documents that are transported. An envelope header contains information about the document or documents that it contains and how to route them. An envelope header contains the source organization identifier, destination organization identifier, and information about the type of document or documents that it contains.

BizTalk Server 2000 is capable of receiving and processing interchanges that contain multiple documents and groups of documents. When transporting documents that use an envelope, BizTalk Server 2000 includes each document in a separate interchange.

Envelopes are optional; however, if you choose to use an envelope, the format of an envelope that you specify in a messaging port must agree with the format of the document or documents that it contains. The document format is determined by the specification referred to in the outbound document definition of an associated channel. For example, if you choose an envelope with an X12 format for a messaging port, you must select an outbound document definition for the channel that points to an X12 specification. Conversely, if you select an outbound document definition in a channel, the messaging port that the channel is associated with must have an envelope with a matching format. For example, if you select an outbound document definition that has a specification with an X12 format, you should specify an X12 envelope in the messaging port.

Security properties

The security properties that you designate for a messaging port apply to all channels associated with that messaging port. For example, if you designate Secure Multipurpose Internet Mail Extensions (S/MIME) encryption for a messaging port, all documents processed by channels associated with that messaging port are encrypted using the specified encryption.

If you have documents that need to be secured using a different encryption or that do not need to be encrypted, you need to create a separate messaging port with the appropriate security properties for those documents.

BizTalk Server 2000 supports Multipurpose Internet Mail Extensions (MIME) encoding. The MIME message format standard specifies how to format messages so that client programs can decode and display complex message bodies that can contain rich text, multiple character sets, and binary attachments such as pictures, sounds, spreadsheets, and so on. MIME is a richer and more flexible technology than Uuencode and provides generic and flexible mechanisms for including content within messages. With MIME formatting, you can:

- Specify alternate content encoding mechanisms for each body part.

- Relate groups of multiple content parts within a message.

- Use character sets other than US-ASCII character sets in body parts and message header fields.

- Specify the intended disposition of a content part (for example, inline or attachment).

BizTalk Server 2000 supports Secure Multipurpose Internet Mail Extensions (S/MIME) certificate-based public key encryption.

Encryption can be applied to business data that you send to your trading partners. By using an encryption certificate to secure the data, you can ensure that only the intended recipient can access the information.

To encrypt business data, the source organization must have a copy of the public key for the encryption certificate of the destination organization. The source organization uses this public key certificate to encrypt the business data and then forwards the encrypted data to the destination organization. The destination organization can then use the private key of its encryption certificate to decrypt the business data.

For an open messaging port, the encryption security properties are disabled because the destination organization is unknown.

BizTalk Server 2000 supports Secure Multipurpose Internet Mail Extensions (S/MIME) certificate-based public-key digital signing. For more information about certificates, see "Understanding Certificates" in Chapter 2, "Understanding Security."

Digital signing can be used to ensure the authenticity of the source of data, to ensure that the data has not been modified, and to prevent the source of the data from repudiating the message.

A signature certificate is used to create digital signatures for authenticating data. Signing data does not alter the data, but it generates a digital signature string that is either bundled with the data or transmitted separately.

To digitally sign a document, the data is processed to create a message digest. The source organization's private key is then used to encrypt the message digest to form the digital signature. The data, along with the digital signature, is transmitted to the recipient.

To verify a digital signature, the recipient must have a copy of the public key from the sender's signature certificate. The recipient decrypts the digital signature by using the public key to form a digest and then calculates a message digest independently. The results of the two digests are compared; if they are identical, the information has not been tampered with.

For more information about certificates, see "Certificates Overview" in Chapter 2, "Understanding Security."

Open Messaging Ports

An open messaging port is a messaging port to an organization for which you have not explicitly declared a specific destination organization. An open messaging port cannot have an application as its destination.

For an open messaging port, the destination and transport information must be provided either in the document or in parameters when the document is submitted to Microsoft BizTalk Server 2000. If submission parameters are used, they override any destination and transport information contained in the document. For more information about submitting documents, see "Submitting" in Chapter 10, "Submitting Documents."

When you create a channel for an open messaging port, and the destination information is provided in the document, the inbound document definition for that channel must reference a specification that is properly configured. For more information about how to configure a document specification to process documents for an open messaging port, see "To set dictionary properties" in Chapter 5, "Creating Specifications."

For an open messaging port, the encryption security properties are disabled because the destination organization is unknown. To set the encryption properties, you need to specify a certificate from a specific, known destination organization. An encryption certificate is used to encrypt documents that are transported to the specific destination organization.

You can use an open messaging port to send one or more standardized documents to many different current or future trading partner organizations without creating a messaging port for each destination. All documents share the same envelope, security, and transport properties that are established in the messaging port.

An open messaging port differs from a distribution list in the following ways:

- With an open messaging port, each document from a channel results in only one document being delivered to only one destination. With a distribution list, each document from a channel can result in the document being delivered to multiple destinations.

- With an open messaging port, you do not have to change the properties of the messaging port to send information to a different trading partner organization. With a distribution list, you have to add a messaging port to send information to a different trading partner organization.

◆ **Important**

- When you declare a messaging port as an open messaging port, you should not create channels for the messaging port that have an outbound document definition with an X12 or EDIFACT specification. To build an X12 or EDIFACT envelope, the server must have a source and a destination organization identifier. An open messaging port does not specify a destination organization identifier. In addition, the documents for an open messaging port must have the destination address within the document, but X12 and EDIFACT documents do not contain this information.

Create and Manage Messaging Ports

This section provides task-specific information about how to create and manage messaging ports by using BizTalk Messaging Manager. For more information about messaging ports, see "Understanding Messaging Ports" earlier in this chapter.

To create messaging ports

1. In BizTalk Messaging Manager, on the **File** menu, point to **New**, point to **Messaging Port**, and then complete one of the following steps:
   - To create a messaging port to a trading partner organization, click **To an Organization**.
   - To create a messaging port to an internal application, click **To an Application**.

   The New Messaging Port Wizard opens.

2. On the **General Information** page, set the properties and click **Next**.

   For more information, see "To set general messaging-port information properties" later in this chapter.

3. Complete one of the following steps:
   - If you are creating a messaging port to a specific organization, set the properties on the **Destination Organization** page and click **Next**. For more information, see "To set destination organization properties" later in this chapter.
   - If you are creating an open messaging port, click **Open destination** and click **Next**.

     For an open messaging port, the transport and destination information must be provided either within the document or in a parameter submitted with the document. For more information, see "Submitting" in Chapter 10, "Submitting Documents."
   - If you are creating a messaging port to an application, set the properties on the **Destination Application** page and click **Next**. For more information, see "To set destination application properties" later in this chapter.

4. On the **Envelope Information** page, set the properties and click **Next**.

   For more information, see "To set envelope information properties" later in this chapter.

5. On the **Security Information** page, set the properties.

   For more information, see "To set security information properties" later in this chapter.

6. If you do not want to proceed directly to the Channel Wizard to create a channel, clear the **Create a channel for this messaging port** check box; otherwise, in the **Channel type** list, click one of the following channel types:
   - **From an organization**
   - **From an application**

7. After you have set all messaging port properties, on the **Security Information** page, click **Finish** to close the Messaging Port Wizard.

◆ Important

- When you declare a messaging port as an open messaging port, do not create channels for the messaging port that have an outbound document definition with an X12 or EDIFACT specification. To build an X12 or EDIFACT envelope, the server must have a source and a destination organization identifier. An open messaging port does not specify a destination organization identifier. In addition, the documents for an open messaging port must have the destination address within the document, but X12 and EDIFACT documents do not contain this information.

☑ Notes

- You cannot name a messaging port using the reserved system name, Reliable Message Acknowledgement Port.
- If you create a messaging port and a channel to use for a pass-through submission of data, you can use only the service window and the retry count and interval features of the channel, and the transport features of its associated messaging port. You cannot use the verification of decoding or decryption, filtering, document tracking, or mapping features of the channel.

To search for messaging ports

1. In BizTalk Messaging Manager, in the **Search for other items** area, click **Messaging ports**.

2. Do one or more of the following:
   - To search for all messaging ports, clear all search criteria and click **Search Now**.
   - To search for a messaging port with a specific name, in the **Messaging port name** box, type the name of the messaging port that you want to find and click **Search Now**. You can enter an incomplete name and the search returns all possible names that match the incomplete name entry.
   - To search for messaging ports to a specific type of destination, in the **Destination** list, click a destination type and click **Search Now**.

☑ Notes

- You can set more than one search criteria before clicking **Search Now**.
- If you have a large number of objects for which to search, it might take several minutes to return all the objects. You can narrow the objects returned in a search by using selection criteria.
- The default number of items returned in a search is 500. You can adjust this number. For more information, see "To set server connection options" earlier in this chapter.
- To clear the search criteria and search results, click **Clear Search**.
- You can use the wildcard characters on the following page in the search criteria.

Wildcard character	Description	Example
%	Any string of zero or more characters.	The entry '%open%' finds all names with the word 'open' anywhere in the name.
_ (underscore)	Any single character.	The entry '_ean' finds four-letter names that end with ean (Dean, Sean, and so on).
[ ]	Any single character within the specified range ([a-f]) or set ([abcdef]).	The entry '[C-P]arsen' finds names ending with arsen and beginning with any single character between C and P (Carsen, Larsen, and so on).
[^]	Any single character not within the specified range ([^a-f]) or set ([^abcdef]).	The entry 'de[^s]%' finds all names beginning with de and where the following letter is not s.

To edit messaging ports

1. In BizTalk Messaging Manager, in the **Messaging Port Name** list, click the messaging port that you want to edit.

   For information about searching for messaging ports, see "To search for messaging ports" earlier in this chapter.

2. On the **File** menu, click **Edit**.

   The Messaging Port Properties Wizard opens.

3. On the **General Information** page, edit the appropriate properties.

   For more information, see "To set general messaging-port information properties" later in this chapter.

   After editing the properties on any page, you can click **Finish** to close the Messaging Port Properties Wizard or click **Next** to edit additional messaging port properties.

4. Complete one of the following steps:
   - If you are editing a messaging port to an organization, edit the necessary properties on the **Destination Organization** page and click **Next**. For more information, see "To set destination organization properties" later in this chapter.
   - If you are editing a messaging port to an application, edit the appropriate properties on the **Destination Application** page and click **Next**. For more information, see "To set destination application properties" later in this chapter.

5. On the **Envelope Information** page, edit the appropriate properties and click **Next**.

   For more information, see "To set envelope information properties" later in this chapter.

6. On the **Security Information** page, edit the appropriate properties.

   For more information, see "To set security information properties" later in this chapter.

7. If you do not want to proceed directly to the Channel Wizard to create a channel, clear the **Create a channel for this messaging port** check box; otherwise, in the **Channel type** list, click one of the following channel types:

   - **From an organization**

   - **From an application**

8. After you have edited all appropriate messaging port properties, you can click **Finish** on any page to close the Messaging Port Wizard.

Note

- You cannot name a messaging port using the reserved system name, Reliable Message Acknowledgement Port.

To delete messaging ports

1. In BizTalk Messaging Manager, in the **Messaging Port Name** list, click the messaging port that you want to delete.

   For information about searching for messaging ports, see "To search for messaging ports" earlier in this chapter.

2. On the **File** menu, click **Delete**.

Notes

- If you have created channels for a messaging port, you cannot delete the messaging port until its associated channels have been deleted.

- You can search for channels associated with a messaging port by right-clicking the messaging port and clicking **Find Channels**.

To set general messaging-port information properties

1. On the **General Information** page of the Messaging Port Wizard, in the **Name** box, type the name of the messaging port.

2. In the **Comments** box, type any comments that you want for the messaging port and click **Next**.

If you are creating a new messaging port, click **Next**. For instructions about completing the next step, see "To create messaging ports" earlier in this chapter.

If you are editing an existing messaging port, click **Next**. For instructions about completing the next step, see "To edit messaging ports" earlier in this chapter. If you have completed your changes, click **Finish**.

To set destination organization properties

1. On the **Destination Organization** page of the Messaging Port Wizard, complete one of the following steps:

   - Click **Open destination** to create an open messaging port and click **Next**.

For an open messaging port, the transport and destination information must be provided either within the document or in parameters submitted with the document. For more information, see "Submitting" in Chapter 10, "Submitting Documents."

- Click **Organization** to designate a specific trading partner organization as the destination and then proceed to step 2.

2. In the **Organization** area, click **Browse**.

   The **Select an Organization** dialog box appears.

3. Click an organization and click **OK**.

   For more information, see "To select a destination organization" later in this chapter.

4. In the **Primary transport** area, click **Browse**.

   The **Primary Transport** dialog box appears.

5. Set the primary transport properties.

   For more information, see "Set Transport Properties" later in this chapter.

6. If you want to limit the time when documents can be transported, in the **Primary transport** area, select the **Service window** check box.

   Then, in the **From** and **To** boxes, click the hour and enter a value, or click the up or down arrow to increase or decrease the value.

7. If you want to specify a secondary transport, in the **Backup transport** area, click **Browse**.

   The **Backup Transport** dialog box appears.

8. Set the backup transport properties.

   For more information, see "Set Transport Properties" later in this chapter.

If you are creating a new messaging port, click **Next**. For instructions about completing the next step, see "To create messaging ports" earlier in this chapter.

If you are editing an existing messaging port, click **Next**. For instructions about completing the next step, see "To edit messaging ports" earlier in this chapter. If you have completed your changes, click **Finish**.

◆ Important

- When you declare a messaging port as an open messaging port, do not create channels for the messaging port that have an outbound document definition with an X12 or EDIFACT specification. To build an X12 or EDIFACT envelope, the server must have a source and a destination organization identifier. An open messaging port does not specify a destination organization identifier. In addition, the documents for an open messaging port must have the destination address within the document, but X12 and EDIFACT documents do not contain this information.

✍ Note

- Service window hours are displayed in the coordinated universal time (UTC) format and reflect the time on the server.

To set destination application properties

1. On the **Destination Application** page of the Messaging Port Wizard, complete one of the following steps:

   - Click **New XLANG schedule** to designate a port in a new instance of a specified XLANG schedule as the destination. In the **Schedule moniker** box, type the moniker of the specified schedule or click **Browse** to set the path. Then, in the **Port name** box, type the name of the specific port in this schedule to which the document is sent.

     The syntax for schedule monikers is as follows:

     sked://[localhost][!GroupManager][/FilePath][/PortName]

     You can activate XLANG schedules only on the local computer.

     For more information about monikers, see "Moniker Syntax" in Chapter 8, "BizTalk Orchestration Services."

   - Click **Running XLANG schedule** to designate an active XLANG schedule instance as the destination. Use this option only to transport a message to an active XLANG schedule when a trading partner returns the message to a specially configured ASP page using an HTTP transport. For more information, see Chapter 14, "Orchestrating Business Processes with BizTalk Server 2000."

   - Click **Application** to designate an application of the home organization as the destination, and then click an application in the **Name** list.

2. If you selected an application as the destination, complete steps 3 through 5; otherwise, click **Next**.

3. In the **Primary transport** area, click **Browse**.

   The **Primary Transport** dialog box appears.

4. Set the primary transport properties.

   For more information, see "Set Transport Properties" later in this chapter.

5. If you want to limit the time when documents can be transported, in the **Primary transport** area, select the **Service window** check box.

   Then, in the **From** and **To** boxes, click the hour and enter a value, or click the up or down arrow to increase or decrease the value.

6. If you want to specify a secondary transport, in the **Backup transport** area, click **Browse**.

   The **Backup Transport** dialog box appears.

7. Set the backup transport properties.

   For more information, see "Set Transport Properties" later in this chapter.

If you are creating a new messaging port, click **Next**. For instructions about completing the next step, see "To create messaging ports" earlier in this chapter.

If you are editing an existing messaging port, click **Next**. For instructions about completing the next step, see "To edit messaging ports" earlier in this chapter. If you have completed your changes, click **Finish**.

◆ Important

- If you choose the **New XLANG schedule** option:

  - The port that you name must be bound to BizTalk Messaging in the specified schedule, and that binding must be configured to activate a new schedule instance upon message arrival.

  - You should have only one port in a schedule that is configured to activate a new schedule instance upon message arrival, and it should be the first action in the schedule. For more information, see "To implement a port by using BizTalk Messaging" in Chapter 8, "BizTalk Orchestration Services."

✎ Notes

- If you choose an XLANG schedule as the destination for a messaging port, there is a maximum limit of 2 MB for the documents that you process by using this messaging port.

- BizTalk Orchestration Designer can be used to create XLANG schedules.

- Service window times are displayed in the coordinated universal time (UTC) format and reflect the time on the server.

To set envelope information properties

1. On the **Envelope Information** page of the Messaging Port Wizard, in the **Envelope information** area, select an envelope from the list.

   If you select an envelope that has an X12 or EDIFACT format, the following steps are required. If you select an envelope that has a custom format, the following steps are optional.

   1. Click **Delimiters** and set the delimiter properties.

      For more information, see "Set Envelope Delimiters," later in this chapter.

   2. In the **Interchange control number** box, type an interchange control number.

2. If you want to override the default organization identifier for the destination organization, click another identifier in the **Organization identifier** list.

If you are creating a new messaging port, click **Next**. For instructions about completing the next step, see "To create messaging ports" earlier in this chapter.

If you are editing an existing messaging port, click **Next**. For instructions about completing the next step, see "To edit messaging ports" earlier in this chapter. If you have completed your changes, click **Finish**.

◆ **Important**

- If you choose an envelope with a reliable format, you also must configure the **Reliable messaging reply-to URL** address in the **BizTalk Server Group Properties** dialog box. For more information, see "To configure general properties for a server group" in Chapter 11, "Administering Servers and Applications."

- The format of an envelope that you specify in a messaging port must agree with the format of the document or documents that it contains. The document format is determined by the specification referred to in the outbound document definition of an associated channel. For example, if you choose an envelope with an X12 format for a messaging port, you must select an outbound document definition for the channel that points to an X12 specification.

📝 **Notes**

- When processing envelopes that are compliant with BizTalk Framework 2.0, BizTalk Server 2000 should be considered the endpoint with regard to the expiration time. When BizTalk Framework 2.0–compliant documents are submitted to BizTalk Server 2000, either from an application or a trading partner, the following fields are overwritten if present, or created if absent:

    - In the properties subsection:

      <prop:identity>

      <prop:sentAt>

      <prop:expiresAt>

    - In the receipt information subsection:

      <sendTo>

      <address>

      <sendReceiptBy>

- For a messaging port to an application, the organization identifiers available in the **Organization identifier** list are those of the home organization.

- If you use the Loopback transport type, you cannot choose an envelope with a reliable format.

- When you select a destination organization identifier for use with X12 envelopes, you should not select the organization identifier named Organization, or any other identifier that has a qualifier that exceeds 2 characters or a value that exceeds 15 characters.

- When you select a destination organization identifier for use with EDIFACT envelopes, you should not select the organization identifier named Organization, or any other identifier that has a qualifier that exceeds 4 characters or a value that exceeds 35 characters.

- If you select an envelope with an EDIFACT format, the default syntax identifier is UNOA (uppercase Latin alphabet). If your data requires a different syntax, select a different syntax identifier by overriding the messaging port defaults in the Channel Wizard. For more information, see "To override messaging port defaults" earlier in this chapter.

To set security information properties

1. On the **Security Information** page of the Messaging Port Wizard, in the **Encoding** area, in the **Type** list, click one the following:

    *   **(None).** Specifies no encoding. This is the default setting.

    *   **MIME.** Specifies encoding that uses Multipurpose Internet Mail Extensions.

    *   **Custom.** Specifies encoding that uses a custom encoding component.

    Notes

    *   You can specify a custom encoding component and configure the class identifier (CLSID) only by using the BizTalk Messaging Configuration object model.

    *   If you specify an envelope that uses a reliable format, or an envelope that uses a custom XML format without an envelope specification, and your document has no attachments, your output is not MIME encoded, even if you specify MIME encoding.

2. In the **Encryption** area, in the **Type** list, click one of the following:

    *   **(None).** Specifies no encryption. This is the default setting.

    *   **S/MIME.** Specifies encryption that uses Secure Multipurpose Internet Mail Extensions.

    *   **Custom.** Specifies encoding that uses a custom encryption component.

    Note

    *   You can specify a custom encryption component and configure the class identifier (CLSID) only by using the BizTalk Messaging Configuration object model.

3. If you select S/MIME encryption, in the **Encryption** area, click **Browse**.

    The **Select an Encryption Certificate** dialog box appears.

4. Select an encryption certificate.

    For more information, see "To select an encryption certificate" later in this chapter.

5. In the **Signature** area, in the **Type** list, click one of the following:

    *   **(None).** Specifies no signature. This is the default setting.

    *   **S/MIME.** Specifies a signature that uses Secure Multipurpose Internet Mail Extensions.

    *   **Custom.** Specifies encoding that uses a custom signature component.

Note

- You can specify a custom signature component and configure the class identifier (CLSID) only by using the BizTalk Messaging Configuration object model.

6. If you do not want to proceed directly to the Channel Wizard to create a channel, clear the **Create a channel for this messaging port** check box; otherwise, in the **Channel type** list, click one of the following channel types:

   - **From an organization**

   - **From an application**

If you are creating a new messaging port, click **Next**. For instructions about completing the next step, see "To create messaging ports" earlier in this chapter.

If you are editing an existing messaging port, click **Next**. For instructions about completing the next step, see "To edit messaging ports" earlier in this chapter. If you have completed your changes, click **Finish**.

To select a destination organization

1. On the **Destination Organization** page of the Messaging Port Wizard, click **Organization** and click **Browse**.

   The **Select an Organization** dialog box appears.

2. In the **Available organizations** list, click an organization and click **OK**.

To continue setting destination organization properties, see "To set destination organization properties" earlier in this chapter.

To select an encryption certificate

1. On the **Security Information** page of the Messaging Port Wizard, in the **Encryption** area, in the **Type** list, click **S/MIME** and click **Browse**.

   The **Select an Encryption Certificate** dialog box appears.

2. In the **Certificate name** list, click a certificate name and click **OK**.

To continue setting security properties, see "To set security information properties" earlier in this chapter.

Note

- All certificates must be named uniquely. If more than one certificate has the same name, only one of the certificates can be selected. Once one of the certificates is selected, other certificates with the same name no longer appear in the list.

  For more information about certificates, see "Certificates Overview" in Chapter 2, "Understanding Security."

Set Transport Properties

Transport properties include a transport type. The transport type specifies which transport service Microsoft BizTalk Server 2000 uses to convey documents to the destination designated in the messaging port. Transport properties can also include a specific address to which the data is sent. The address properties vary based on the transport type selected.

To select a transport type

1. On the **Destination Application** or **Destination Organization** page of the Messaging Port Wizard, in the **Primary transport** or **Backup transport** area, click **Browse**.

    The **Primary Transport** or **Backup Transport** dialog box appears.

2. In the **Transport type** list, click one of the following transport types:

    *   **Application Integration Component.** Specifies a transport that uses an application integration component that has been registered with BizTalk Server 2000.

    *   **File.** Specifies a transport that uses the **SendLocalFile** component.

    *   **HTTP.** Specifies a transport that uses the Hypertext Transfer Protocol.

    *   **HTTPS.** Specifies a transport that uses the Secure Hypertext Transfer Protocol.

    *   **Loopback.** Specifies a transport that returns the outbound document of a channel to a business application, component, or XLANG schedule that submitted the inbound document using a synchronous submit call. This transport type is available only for a messaging port that sends documents to an application.

    *   **Message Queuing.** Specifies a transport that uses the Message Queuing service.

    *   **SMTP.** Specifies a transport that uses the Simple Mail Transfer Protocol.

3. Complete one of the following steps:

    *   If you choose the Application Integration Component transport type, see "To select an application integration component," later in this chapter.

    *   If you choose the Loopback transport type, no transport address is required.

    *   If you choose any other transport type, see "To specify a transport address" later in this chapter.

🗒 Notes

*   If you choose the Message Queuing transport type and do not use an envelope, there is a maximum size limit of 2 MB for the documents that you process by using this messaging port.

*   If you choose the Message Queuing transport type and use an envelope, there is a maximum size limit of 4 MB for the documents that you process by using this messaging port.

- Before you can choose the SMTP transport type, you must configure the SMTP host in BizTalk Server Administration. For more information, see "To configure general properties for a server group" in Chapter 11, "Administering Servers and Applications."

- The default setting for the HTTP transport component is to use the HTTP proxy server. This is the correct setting to transport data to Web sites outside your business's firewall. To transport data to Web sites that are inside your business's firewall (that is, within your intranet), override the default setting in the channel. For more information, see "To override messaging port defaults" earlier in this chapter.

- The Loopback transport type can be used to map an inbound document to a different format, envelope or apply security (encoding, encryption, digital signature) to the document, and then synchronously return the outbound document to the caller as the response document.

- If you choose the Loopback transport type, you cannot use an envelope with a reliable format.

To specify a transport address

1. On the **Destination Application** or **Destination Organization** page of the Messaging Port Wizard, in the **Primary transport** or **Backup transport** area, click **Browse**.

   The **Primary Transport** or **Backup Transport** dialog box appears.

2. In the **Transport type** list, click a transport type other than Loopback or Application Integration Component.

3. In the **Address** box, type an address for the destination.

4. If you selected the SMTP transport type, in the **Return e-mail address** box, type an address.

   The server uses this address as the From address in the outbound header and as the destination for return e-mail.

To continue setting destination organization properties, see "To set destination organization properties" earlier in this chapter.

◆ Important

- For the File transport type, the default transport-component setting is to append new files to an existing file in the specified directory.

- If you use the File transport to send multiple files with the same name to the same directory, and the files have different document formats or use different code pages, the data in the appended file will be corrupted.

- If you want to create a new file for each document instance, you must use the following file path format:

```
file://C:\dir\file%tracking_id%.xml
```

📝 Notes

- For all transport types except Message Queuing, a prefix is automatically created for the address. This prefix is required and must not be deleted.

- For the Message Queuing transport type, the following conditions must be met for a valid address:
  - Do not use the queue:// prefix in the address.
  - Use a format name, rather than a path. The following are valid format names:

    DIRECT=Protocol:<*ServerName*>\<*QueueName*>

    PUBLIC=QueueGUID

    PRIVATE=MachineGUID\QueueNumber

    For more information about Message Queuing, go to the MSDN Online Library Web site (msdn.microsoft.com/library/default.asp) and search on the keywords "Message Queuing."

- For the File transport type, the following conditions must be met for a valid address:
  - The file path that you specify must exist. The file path is not created automatically, and you do not receive a warning that it does not exist.
  - You must specify a file name with an extension.

    An example of a valid file path is:

    ```
    file://C:\dir\file.xml
    ```

- For the File transport type, you can include characters and symbols to dynamically modify the file name. The file name created by the server contains any static characters that you type into the **Address** box, along with the value of the symbol. For example, if you type file://C:\Orders\Invoice_%tracking_id%.xml in the **Address** box, the actual file name might appear as C:\Orders\Invoice_{12345678-90AB-CDEF-1234-567890ABCDEF}.

  The following table contains the symbols that you can use with the File transport type.

Symbol	Description	Unique file name
%datetime%	Date and time, in milliseconds, of the file creation. The time is based on Greenwich Mean Time (GMT) rather than local time.	No
%document_name%	Name of the document processed by BizTalk Server.	No
%server%	Host name of the server that processed the document.	No
%tracking_id%	Globally unique tracking number.	Yes
%uid%	Counter that increases over time, represented in milliseconds. This number is reset when the server is restarted.	No

- The default setting for the file transport component is to append files. If you choose the File transport type with its default settings in a messaging port and use antivirus software on the server on which BizTalk Server 2000 is installed, and you send multiple files that have exactly the same name to the same file location, at the same time, BizTalk Server 2000 might stop responding and must be restarted. You can eliminate this problem by changing the default setting for the file transport component from **Append to file** to **Overwrite file** in the **BizTalk SendLocalFile Properties** dialog box. You also can eliminate this problem by creating a unique file for each document instance processed by using the file path format in the messaging port: file://C:\dir\file%tracking_id%.xml. For more information about overriding the append setting for the file transport component in the advanced properties of the channel, see "To override messaging port defaults" earlier in this chapter.

- The default setting for the file transport component is to append files. If you choose the File transport type with its default settings and select an envelope with a reliable format in a messaging port, and then send multiple files to the same file location, at the same time, you might have unexpected parsing results. You can eliminate this problem by changing the default setting for the file transport component from **Append to file** to **Overwrite file** in the **BizTalk SendLocalFile Properties** dialog box. For more information about overriding the append setting for the file transport component in the advanced properties of the channel, see "To override messaging port defaults" earlier in this chapter.

To select an application integration component

1. On the **Destination Application** or **Destination Organization** page of the Messaging Port Wizard, in the **Primary transport** or **Backup transport** area, click **Browse**.

   The **Primary Transport** or **Backup Transport** dialog box appears.

2. In the **Transport type** list, click **Application Integration Component**.

3. To the right of the **Component name** box, click **Browse**.

   The **Select a Component** dialog box appears.

4. In the **Available components** list, click a component and click **OK**.

To continue setting destination organization properties, see "To set destination organization properties" earlier in this chapter.

Note

- An application integration component must be registered with BizTalk Server 2000 before it will be available in the **Available components** list. For more information, see "Registering Application Integration Components" in Chapter 15, "Creating Custom Components."

Set Envelope Delimiters

Delimiter properties specify which characters are used to separate data within an envelope and the documents of an interchange. Delimiters are required only for envelopes that use the X12 and EDIFACT formats. They are optional for envelopes that use a custom format.

Envelope delimiters are set when you select an envelope within a messaging port. The delimiters that are set for a messaging port apply only to that messaging port. Different delimiters can be set for the same envelope when it is used in a different messaging port.

To set X12 delimiters

1. On the **Envelope Information** page of the Messaging Port Wizard, in the **Envelope information** area, select an envelope with an X12 format and click **Delimiters**.

   The **X12 Delimiters** dialog box appears.

2. Enter delimiter values in either the **Character** or **Hexadecimal** box and click **OK**.

The following table describes the X12 delimiters.

Delimiter	Description
Component element separator	Specifies the character that is used to separate components of data within a composite data field. A composite data field is a field that consists of multiple subfields.
Element separator	Specifies the character that is used to separate data fields within a record.
Segment terminator	Specifies the character that is used to indicate the end of a record.

To continue setting destination organization properties, see "To set envelope information properties" earlier in this chapter.

Note

- You can type either one character in the **Character** box or two characters in the **Hexadecimal** box for each delimiter. The **Hexadecimal** box can be used to enter nonprinting character delimiters, such as the ENTER key.

To set EDIFACT delimiters

1. On the **Envelope Information** page of the Messaging Port Wizard, in the **Envelope information** area, select an envelope with an EDIFACT format and click **Delimiters**.

   The **EDIFACT Delimiters** dialog box appears.

2. Enter delimiter values in either the **Character** or **Hexadecimal** box and click **OK**.

The following table describes the EDIFACT delimiters.

Delimiter	Description
Component element separator	Specifies the character that is used to separate components of data within a composite data field. A composite data field is a field that consists of multiple subfields.
Element separator	Specifies the character that is used to separate data fields within a record.
Release indicator	Specifies the character that is used to indicate that the following character should not be evaluated as a delimiter.
Segment terminator	Specifies the character that is used to indicate the end of a record.

✒ Notes

- If you use EDIFACT release indicators, do not include release indicator characters in your data. Doing so might cause the data to exceed the physical character size limits for fields.

- You can type either one character in the **Character** box or two characters in the **Hexadecimal** box for each delimiter. The **Hexadecimal** box can be used to enter nonprinting character delimiters, such as the ENTER key.

- The EDIFACT decimal specification delimiter cannot be used.

To continue setting destination organization properties, see "To set envelope information properties" earlier in this chapter.

To set custom delimiters

1. On the **Envelope Information** page of the Messaging Port Wizard, in the **Envelope information** area, select an envelope with a custom format and click **Delimiters**.

   The **Custom Delimiters** dialog box appears.

2. Enter delimiter values in either the **Character** or **Hexadecimal** box and click **OK**.

The following table describes the custom delimiters.

Delimiter	Description
Subfield	Specifies the character that is used to separate components of data within a multipart data field.
Field	Specifies the character that is used to separate the data fields within a record.
Escape character	Specifies the character that is used to indicate that the following character should not be evaluated as a delimiter.
Record	Specifies the character that is used to indicate the end of a record.

📝 Note

- You can type either one character in the **Character** box or two characters in the **Hexadecimal** box for each delimiter. The **Hexadecimal** box can be used to enter nonprinting character delimiters, such as the ENTER key.

To continue setting destination organization properties, see "To set envelope information properties" earlier in this chapter.

Understanding Organizations

The organizations that you create by using BizTalk Messaging Manager represent the trading partners with which you exchange documents. A special organization type, called the home organization, represents your business.

Home organization

BizTalk Messaging Manager creates the home organization for you automatically. When you configure the home organization, you can rename it to make it easier to identify as your business. There is only one home organization, and you cannot delete it.

You cannot designate the home organization as a source or destination for documents in a messaging port or a channel. Only applications of the home organization can be designated as the source or destination for documents within your business. For example, you might create a messaging port that designates a trading partner organization as the destination for documents that your business sends. Then, when you create a channel for that messaging port, rather than designating your home organization as the source, you would designate a specific internal application within your business where the documents originate. You also can designate one application of the home organization as the source for documents in a channel and another application as the destination in a messaging port.

Applications of the home organization

The applications that you add to the home organization enable you to identify and track the flow of documents between Microsoft BizTalk Server 2000 and actual internal applications within your business. However, simply creating an application and designating it as a source or destination within BizTalk Messaging Manager does not control or enable the flow of documents to or from an actual internal application. To integrate an internal application with BizTalk Server 2000 and direct the flow of documents to or from the application, you need to further configure the server.

There are a number of ways to transport documents from an originating application to BizTalk Server 2000. The configuration needed to integrate an application to transport documents to the server is performed entirely outside BizTalk Messaging Manager. For more information, see "Submitting" in Chapter 10, "Submitting Documents."

To deliver documents from BizTalk Server 2000 to an internal application can require configuration both within and outside BizTalk Messaging Manager. The transport type and address that you specify in a messaging port can determine a specific location to which documents are delivered. An application or a separate component must then be configured to retrieve documents received at that location for the destination application. Or, within the transport properties of a messaging port, you can specify an application integration component that is capable of delivering documents directly to an application. For more information, see "Understanding Messaging Ports" earlier in this chapter.

Trading partner organizations

All other organizations that you create with BizTalk Messaging Manager represent external trading partners or business units of a trading partner. You can create any number of organizations. You can designate a trading partner organization either as a source of documents in a channel or a destination for documents in a messaging port.

You also can designate one trading partner as the source of documents in a channel and another as the destination for the documents in a messaging port. In this case, your business serves as a third-party intermediary between the two trading partners.

As with applications, simply creating an organization and designating it as a source or destination within BizTalk Messaging Manager does not enable the flow of documents to or from that organization. To control and direct the flow of documents between your partner organizations and BizTalk Server 2000, you need to further configure the server.

There are a number of ways for an external trading partner as a source organization to transport documents to your BizTalk Server 2000. The configuration needed to do this is similar to the way that you integrate applications to transport documents to the server, and it is also performed entirely outside BizTalk Messaging Manager. For more information, see "Submitting" in Chapter 10, "Submitting Documents."

To deliver documents from your BizTalk Server 2000 to an external trading partner as a destination organization can require configuration both within and outside BizTalk Messaging Manager. The transport type and address that you specify in a messaging port determine a specific location to which documents are delivered. The destination organization, which must have access to this location, can then configure its own BizTalk Server, one of its internal applications, or a separate component to process the documents received at that location. For more information about configuring messaging ports, see "Understanding Messaging Ports" earlier in this chapter.

📝 Note

- BizTalk Server 2000 Standard Edition supports the creation of five new organizations and five applications within an organization. To create more organizations and applications, you must use BizTalk Server 2000 Enterprise Edition.

Organization Identifiers

Microsoft BizTalk Server 2000 and other trading partners use organization identifiers to uniquely identify organizations. An organization can have more than one organization identifier; however, each identifier must be unique to that organization. For example, a telephone number, a URL, or a DUNS number can each uniquely identify an organization, but no two organizations can use the same telephone number as an organization identifier.

An organization identifier consists of three separate elements: a name, a qualifier, and a value. For example, a business might use a telephone number to uniquely identify itself. In this example, the name of the identifier is "telephone number," the qualifier that identifies the identifier as a telephone number is the number 12, and the value of the actual telephone number is (801-555-1079). Each organization identifier name has a unique qualifier that is used in place of the name to indicate the type of identifier. For example, the standard qualifier for a telephone number identifier is 12. When BizTalk Server 2000 processes documents, only the qualifier and the value are used to identify organizations.

Each organization must have at least one identifier. When you create an organization, BizTalk Messaging Manager creates an identifier with the name Organization. The qualifier for this identifier is OrganizationName, and its value is the name that you give to the organization. This identifier is also set as the default identifier, which means that it is used when no other identifier is specified. You can create additional identifiers and designate any identifier as the default identifier. You cannot delete the OrganizationName identifier or the designated default identifier. The default identifier is used to identify an organization unless you override it by selecting a different identifier in a messaging port or channel.

When BizTalk Server 2000 processes and transports a document, it includes the organization identifiers of the destination organization and the source organization in the envelope header. When BizTalk Server 2000 receives documents, it searches the data for the source organization and the destination organization identifiers. The server then uses the identifiers and the document-definition name to determine which channels to use to process the documents.

Interchanges with an EDI format have restrictions on organization identifiers. When you use an organization identifier for X12 envelopes, you should not use the organization identifier named Organization, or any other identifier that has a qualifier that exceeds 2 characters or a value that exceeds 15 characters. When you use an organization identifier for EDIFACT envelopes, you should not use the organization identifier named Organization, or any other identifier that has a qualifier that exceeds 4 characters or a value that exceeds 35 characters.

Create and Manage Organizations

This section provides task-specific information about how to create and manage organizations by using BizTalk Messaging Manager. For more information about organizations, see "Understanding Organizations" earlier in this chapter.

To configure the home organization

1. In BizTalk Messaging Manager, in the **Search for other items** area, click **Organizations**.

2. In the **Search for organizations** area, select the **Home organization** check box and click **Search Now**.

3. In the **Organization Name** list, double-click **Home Organization**.

   The **Organization Properties** dialog box appears.

4. On the **General** tab, set the general organization properties.

   For more information, see "To set general organization properties" later in this chapter.

5. Click the **Identifiers** tab and set the organization identifier properties.

   For more information, see "Set Organization Identifier Properties" later in this chapter.

6. Click the **Applications** tab and set the application properties.

   For more information, see "Set Application Properties" later in this chapter.

7. After you have set all the necessary home organization properties, click **OK** to close the **Organization Properties** dialog box.

✦ **Important**

- An organization identifier named Reliable Messaging Acknowledgement SMTP From Address is automatically created for the home organization. This identifier cannot be removed. You should not modify the name or qualifier for this identifier, but you can modify the value. The value specified for this identifier is used as the From address when sending reliable messaging receipts that use the SMTP transport protocol. For more information about reliable messaging receipts, see "Processing Receipts Using Reliable Messaging" later in this chapter.

- The value specified for the organization identifier (Reliable Messaging Acknowledgement SMTP From Address) is also used as the From address when the address provided for an open messaging port is an SMTP address. For more information, see "Openness" later in this chapter.

☑ **Notes**

- You can rename the home organization at any time to any name that you want.

- In BizTalk Messaging Manager, you can add applications only to the home organization.

To create organizations

1. In BizTalk Messaging Manager, on the **File** menu, point to **New** and click **Organization**.

   The **New Organization** dialog box appears.

2. On the **General** tab, set the general organization properties.

   For more information, see "To set general organization properties" later in this chapter.

3. Click the **Identifiers** tab and set the organization identifier properties.

   For more information, see "Set Organization Identifier Properties" later in this chapter.

4. After you have set all the necessary properties, click **OK** to close the **New Organization** dialog box.

To search for organizations

1. In BizTalk Messaging Manager, in the **Search for other items** area, click **Organizations**.

2. Do one or more of the following:

   - To search for all organizations, clear all search criteria and click **Search Now**.

   - To search for organizations with a specific name, in the **Search for organizations** area, in the **Organization name** box, type the name of the organization that you want to find and click **Search Now**. You can enter an incomplete name and the search returns all possible names that match the incomplete name entry.

   - To search for the home organization only, select the **Home organization** check box and click **Search Now**.

Notes

- To clear the search criteria and search results, click **Clear Search**.

- If you have a large number of objects for which to search, it might take several minutes to return all the objects. You can narrow the objects returned in a search by using selection criteria.

- The default number of items returned in a search is 500. You can adjust this number. For more information, see "To set server connection options" earlier in this chapter.

- You can use the following wildcard characters in the search criteria.

Wildcard character	Description	Example
%	Any string of zero or more characters.	The entry '%open%' finds all names with the word 'open' anywhere in the name.
_ (underscore)	Any single character.	The entry '_ean' finds four-letter names that end with ean (Dean, Sean, and so on).
[ ]	Any single character within the specified range ([a-f]) or set ([abcdef]).	The entry '[C-P]arsen' finds names ending with arsen and beginning with any single character between C and P (Carsen, Larsen, and so on).
[^]	Any single character not within the specified range ([^a-f]) or set ([^abcdef]).	The entry 'de[^s]%' finds all names beginning with de and where the following letter is not s.

To edit organizations

1. In BizTalk Messaging Manager, in the **Organization Name** list, click the organization that you want to edit.

    For information about searching for organizations, see "To search for organizations" earlier in this chapter.

2. On the **File** menu, click **Edit**.

    The **Organization Properties** dialog box appears.

3. On the **General** tab, edit any properties that you want to change.

    For more information, see "To set general organization properties" later in this chapter.

4. Click the **Identifiers** tab and edit any organization identifier properties that you want to change.

    For more information, see "Set Organization Identifier Properties" later in this chapter.

5. If you are editing the home organization, click the **Applications** tab and edit any application properties that you want to change.

    For more information, see "Set Application Properties" later in this chapter.

6. After you have edited all the properties that you want to change, click **OK** to close the **Organization Properties** dialog box.

◆ **Important**

-   An organization identifier named Reliable Messaging Acknowledgement SMTP From Address is automatically created for the home organization. This identifier cannot be removed. You should not modify the name or qualifier for this identifier, but you can modify the value. The value specified for this identifier is used as the From address when sending reliable messaging receipts that use the SMTP transport protocol. For more information about reliable messaging receipts, see "Processing Receipts Using Reliable Messaging" later in this chapter.

-   The value specified for the organization identifier (Reliable Messaging Acknowledgement SMTP From Address) is also used as the From address when the address provided for an open messaging port is an SMTP address. For more information, see "Openness" later in this chapter.

📝 **Note**

-   In BizTalk Messaging Manager, you can add applications only to the home organization.

To delete organizations

1. In BizTalk Messaging Manager, in the **Organization Name** list, click the organization that you want to delete.

   For more information about searching for organizations, see "To search for organizations" earlier in this chapter.

2. On the **File** menu, click **Delete**.

📝 Notes

- If an organization is used in a messaging port or a channel, you cannot delete it. You must first delete all channels and messaging ports that use the organization.

- You cannot delete the home organization.

To set general organization properties

1. On the **File** menu, point to **New** and click **Organization**, or in the **Organization Name** list, double-click an organization.

   The **Organization** dialog box appears.

2. On the **General** tab, in the **Organization name** box, type a unique name for the organization.

3. In the **Comments** box, type any comments that you want for the organization.

Set Organization Identifier Properties

Organization identifiers are used to uniquely identify organizations. An organization can have more than one organization identifier, but each identifier must be unique for that organization.

When you create a new organization, an organization identifier named Organization is automatically created. The qualifier for this identifier is OrganizationName, and the value is the name that you give the organization. This server uses this organization identifier as the default identifier, unless you create additional identifiers and designate one of them as the default identifier.

To add organization identifiers

1. On the **File** menu, point to **New** and click **Organization**, or in the **Organization Name** list, double-click an organization.

   The **Organization** dialog box appears.

2. Click the **Identifiers** tab and click **Add**.

   The **New Identifier** dialog box appears.

3. In the **Name** area, complete one of the following steps:

   - Click **Standard** and click a name in the list.

- Click **Custom** and type a unique name in the box. Then, in the **Qualifier** box, type a qualifier for the identifier.

4. In the **Value** box, type a value for the identifier.

5. If you want to set this identifier as the default identifier for the organization, select the **Set as default** check box; otherwise, make sure that the check box is cleared.

6. Click **OK** to close the **New Identifier** dialog box.

◆ Important

- An organization identifier named Reliable Messaging Acknowledgement SMTP From Address is automatically created for the home organization. This identifier cannot be removed. You should not modify the name or qualifier for this identifier, but you can modify the value. The value specified for this identifier is used as the From address when sending reliable messaging receipts that use the SMTP transport protocol. For more information, see "Processing Receipts Using Reliable Messaging" later in this chapter.

- The value specified for the organization identifier (Reliable Messaging Acknowledgement SMTP From Address) is also used as the From address when the address provided for an open messaging port is an SMTP address. For more information, see "Openness" later in this chapter.

◢ Notes

- Only one identifier can be designated as the default identifier for an organization. The default identifier is used to identify an organization unless you specify another organization identifier in a channel or messaging port.

- When you create a new organization, an organization identifier named Organization is automatically created. The qualifier for this identifier is OrganizationName, and the value is the name of the organization. You can create additional identifiers, but this identifier cannot be modified or removed.

- If the server encounters an empty qualifier and a non-empty value when processing an inbound document with a format other than EDIFACT, it converts the empty qualifier to OrganizationName.

- If the server encounters an empty qualifier and a non-empty value when processing an inbound document with an EDIFACT format, it converts the empty qualifier to a dash (-). If you want to process an inbound document with an EDIFACT format that has an empty qualifier, or an outbound envelope with an empty qualifier, you must create a custom organization identifier that has a single dash as the qualifier. For an outbound EDIFACT document, the server converts the dash to an empty qualifier.

- When you create an organization identifier for use with EDIFACT envelopes, the qualifier must not exceed 4 characters and the value must not exceed 35 characters.

- When you create an organization identifier for use with X12 envelopes, the qualifier must not exceed 2 characters and the value must not exceed 15 characters.

To edit organization identifiers

1. On the **File** menu, point to **New** and click **Organization**, or in the **Organization Name** list, double-click an organization.

   The **Organization** dialog box appears.

2. Click the **Identifiers** tab.

3. In the **Organization identifiers** list, click the organization identifier that you want to edit and click **Edit**.

   The **Identifier Properties** dialog box appears.

4. In the **Name** area, complete one of the following steps:

   - Click **Standard** and click a name in the list.

   - Click **Custom** and type a unique name in the box. Then, in the **Qualifier** box, type a qualifier for the identifier.

5. In the **Value** box, type a value for the identifier.

6. If you want to set this identifier as the default identifier for the organization, select the **Set as default** check box; otherwise, make sure that the check box is cleared.

7. Click **OK** to close the **Identifier Properties** dialog box.

◆ Important

- An organization identifier named Reliable Messaging Acknowledgement SMTP From Address is automatically created for the home organization. You should not modify the name or qualifier for this identifier, but you can modify the value. This identifier cannot be removed. The value for this identifier is used as the From address when sending reliable messaging receipts that use the SMTP transport protocol. For more information, see "Processing Receipts Using Reliable Messaging" later in this chapter.

- The value specified for the organization identifier (Reliable Messaging Acknowledgement SMTP From Address) is also used as the From address when the address provided for an open messaging port is an SMTP address. For more information, see "Openness" later in this chapter.

✎ Notes

- Only one identifier can be designated as the default identifier for an organization. The default identifier is used to identify an organization unless you specify another organization identifier in a channel or messaging port.

- When you create a new organization, an organization identifier named Organization is automatically created. The qualifier for this identifier is OrganizationName, and the value is the name of the organization. You can create additional identifiers, but this identifier cannot be modified or removed.

- If the server encounters an empty qualifier and a non-empty value when processing an inbound document with a format other than EDIFACT, it converts the empty qualifier to OrganizationName.

- If the server encounters an empty qualifier and a non-empty value when processing an inbound document with an EDIFACT format, it converts the empty qualifier to a dash (-). If you want to process an inbound document with an EDIFACT format that has an empty qualifier, or an outbound envelope with an empty qualifier, you must create a custom organization identifier that has a single dash as the qualifier. For an outbound EDIFACT document, the server converts the dash to an empty qualifier.

- When you create an organization identifier for use with EDIFACT envelopes, the qualifier must not exceed 4 characters and the value must not exceed 35 characters.

- When you create an organization identifier for use with X12 envelopes, the qualifier must not exceed 2 characters and the value must not exceed 15 characters.

To remove organization identifiers

1. On the **File** menu, point to **New** and click **Organization**, or in the **Organization Name** list, double-click an organization.

   The **Organization** dialog box appears.

2. Click the **Identifiers** tab.

3. In the **Organization identifiers** list, click the identifier that you want to remove and click **Remove**.

✎ Notes

- The designated default organization identifier cannot be removed until you have designated another identifier as the default identifier.

- The organization identifier named Organization is automatically created when you create an organization. This organization identifier cannot be removed.

Set Application Properties

In BizTalk Messaging Manager, you can add applications only to the home organization. The applications that you create enable you to identify and track the flow of documents between BizTalk Server 2000 and actual internal applications within your business. You can designate an application of the home organization as a source application in a channel or a destination application in a messaging port.

The home organization can have any number of applications. Each application name must be unique.

To add applications

1. In BizTalk Messaging Manager, in the **Search for other items** area, click **Organizations**.

2. In the **Search for organizations** area, select the **Home organization** check box and click **Search Now**.

3. In the **Organization Name** list, double-click **Home Organization**.

   The **Organization Properties** dialog box appears.

4. On the **Applications** tab, click **Add**.

   The **New Application** dialog box appears.

5. In the **Application name** box, type a unique name for the application and click **OK**.

📝 Note

- In BizTalk Messaging Manager, you can add, edit, and remove applications only for the home organization.

To edit applications

1. In BizTalk Messaging Manager, in the **Search for other items** area, click **Organizations**.

2. In the **Search for organizations** area, select the **Home organization** check box and click **Search Now**.

3. In the **Organization Name** list, double-click **Home Organization**.

   The **Organization Properties** dialog box appears.

4. On the **Applications** tab, in the **Applications** list, click the application that you want to edit and click **Edit**.

   The **Application Properties** dialog box appears.

5. In the **Application name** box, type a unique name for the application and click **OK**.

📝 Note

- In BizTalk Messaging Manager, you can add, edit, and remove applications only for the home organization.

To remove applications

1. In BizTalk Messaging Manager, in the **Search for other items** area, click **Organizations**.

2. In the **Search for organizations** area, select the **Home organization** check box and click **Search Now**.

3. In the **Organization Name** list, double-click **Home Organization**.

   The **Organization Properties** dialog box appears.

4. On the **Applications** tab, in the **Applications** list, click the application that you want to remove and click **Remove**.

📝 Note

- In BizTalk Messaging Manager, you can add, edit, and remove applications only for the home organization.

Understanding Document Definitions

A document definition represents a specific type of document that is processed by Microsoft BizTalk Server 2000. A document definition represents the type of inbound or outbound document in a channel and provides a pointer to a document specification. The document specification defines the document structure, type, and version. The same document specification can be used in any number of document definitions, and the same document definition can be used in any number of channels.

If the format and structure of the inbound and outbound document in a channel are the same, you can use the same specification for both. Otherwise, you must specify a map, which the server uses to transform the format or structure of the inbound document into that of the outbound document.

When BizTalk Server 2000 receives a document, it identifies the appropriate channel or channels that have matching inbound document definitions. The inbound document definition for each channel points to a specification. The server uses the specification to translate a non-XML inbound document from its original format into an intermediate XML format, and to validate the document's structure. The outbound document definition for the channel also points to a specification. The server uses the outbound document specification to validate the data structure of the outbound document. If required, the server also can use the specification to translate the outbound document from an XML format into a format that the destination organization or destination application can recognize and use. The destination is designated in the messaging port with which the channel is associated.

A document specification for a document definition is optional; however, in most cases you should select one. If you do not select a specification:

- The data that you process is not translated into XML on the inbound side or from XML on the outbound side.
- The data is not validated against a specification to ensure that it does not contain errors.
- You cannot transform the structure or format of the data by using a map in a channel.
- You cannot specify global tracking fields or selection criteria.

A document specification is not required if you want to use the document definition in a pass-through submission for data that is not in Unicode XML format. An example would be if you want to send binary data through BizTalk Server 2000 to a destination without transforming the data in any way. In this case, you should not select a document specification for either the inbound or the outbound document definition of the channel that is used for the pass-through submission.

Tracking Document Data Fields

In a document definition, you can designate fields contained within the specification that you want to log to a Tracking database. The fields that you designate in a document definition are tracked for all document instances processed by channels that use the document definition as its inbound document definition. Because these fields are tracked for all channels, they are referred to as global tracking fields.

When you select an inbound document definition for a channel, you can designate specification fields from within the channel to be tracked. The specification fields that you designate in a channel are tracked in place of any global tracking fields for documents that are processed by that specific channel.

The fields that you designate for tracking in a document definition or in a channel are logged to a Tracking database only for the inbound document definition of the channel. Any fields that are designated for tracking in the outbound document definition of the channel are not tracked.

With the tracking data from the documents that are processed, you can analyze information about your operation. For example, an invoice-total field can be tracked for every invoice that you send to your trading partners. You can then determine the total dollar amount for invoices sent to all trading partners for a given period of time, or you can determine the total dollar amount of invoices for each individual trading partner.

Understanding Selection Criteria

Selection criteria are a unique set of name-value pairs that Microsoft BizTalk Server 2000 uses only to process EDI documents. For inbound X12 or EDIFACT documents, the server uses selection criteria to uniquely identify and select a document definition because no document definition name is available within individual EDI documents.

For outbound X12 or EDIFACT documents, selection criteria are used to create the functional group header information in the envelope.

Using Selection Criteria with Inbound Documents

To process inbound documents, BizTalk Server 2000 must have the name of an inbound document definition. The server usually obtains the name of the inbound document definition from either a field within the incoming document or a parameter that is submitted along with the document. For more information, see "Submitting" in Chapter 10, "Submitting Documents."

For X12 and EDIFACT inbound interchanges, the documents can be contained within the functional group or interchange headers. BizTalk Server 2000 processes the documents contained in these groups and interchanges individually. Because the document-related information for each document is contained in the functional group or interchange header, the server cannot obtain a document definition name from within the individual documents. Also, since an interchange can contain multiple groups with different types of documents, a single document definition name cannot be provided as a submission parameter for the server for identifying a document definition.

In such cases, BizTalk Server 2000 is able to extract document-related data from the functional group header (the GS header of an X12 interchange and the UNG header of an EDIFACT interchange) or the interchange header in an EDIFACT interchange without functional groups. By matching the values of this data to the values of selection criteria specified in a document definition, the server can uniquely identify the appropriate document definition.

For BizTalk Server 2000 to match the selection criteria values to the corresponding header elements of an inbound interchange, you must type the selection criteria names exactly as shown in the following tables.

X12 header elements

Name	Requirement	GS element
functional_identifier	Mandatory	GS01
application_sender_code	Mandatory	GS02
application_receiver_code	Mandatory	GS03
standards_version	Mandatory	GS08

EDIFACT header elements

Name	Requirement	UNH element	UNG element
functional_identifier	Mandatory	S009, 0065	0038
application_sender_code	Optional	Not used	S006, 0040
application_receiver_code	Optional	Not used	S007, 0044
standards_version_type	Mandatory	S009, 0052	S008, 0052
standards_version_value	Mandatory	S009, 0054	S008, 0054

Using Selection Criteria with Outbound Documents

To process an outbound X12 or EDIFACT document, BizTalk Server 2000 places each document into a valid envelope of the appropriate format. To create the envelope, the server inserts the value data of the selection criteria into the corresponding fields of the group and message headers. To build the headers, the server uses the selection criteria values contained in the outbound document definition for the channel.

For example, suppose that you create a document definition that has the name-value pair of functional_identifier/ORDERS as one of its selection criteria. If you then use this as the outbound document definition in a channel, the value of the group header field that corresponds with the selection criteria named functional_identifier is set to ORDERS in the envelope header.

For BizTalk Server 2000 to insert selection criteria values to the corresponding header elements, you must type the selection criteria names exactly as shown in the following tables.

X12 header elements

Name	Requirement	GS element
functional_identifier	Mandatory	GS01
application_sender_code	Mandatory	GS02
application_receiver_code	Mandatory	GS03
standards_version	Mandatory	GS08

EDIFACT header elements

Name	Requirement	UNH element	UNG element
functional_identifier	Mandatory	S009, 0065	0038
application_sender_code	Optional	Not used	S006, 0040
application_receiver_code	Optional	Not used	S007, 0044
standards_version_type	Mandatory	S009, 0052	S008, 0052
standards_version_value	Mandatory	S009, 0054	S008, 0054

Create and Manage Document Definitions

This section provides task-specific information about how to create and manage document definitions by using BizTalk Messaging Manager. For more information about document definitions, see "Understanding Document Definitions" earlier in this chapter.

To create document definitions

1. In BizTalk Messaging Manager, on the **File** menu, point to **New** and click **Document Definition**.

    The **New Document Definition** dialog box appears.

2. On the **General** tab, set the general properties.

    For more information, see "To set general document-definition properties" later in this chapter.

3. Click the **Global Tracking** tab and set the tracking properties.

    For more information, see "Set Global Tracking Properties" later in this chapter.

4. Click the **Selection Criteria** tab and set the selection criteria properties.

    For more information, see "Set Selection Criteria Properties" later in this chapter.

5. After you have set all the properties that you want, click **OK** to close the **New Document Definition** dialog box.

✎ Notes

- You cannot name a document definition Reliable Message Acknowledgement Channel or BizTalk Canonical Receipt, which are reserved system names.

- You cannot specify global tracking fields for the document definition unless you select a specification.

- When you select a document definition in a channel, you can override the global tracking fields for that channel by selecting different specification fields to track. For more information, see "To select specification fields in a channel" earlier in this chapter.

- When you save a document definition that references a specification that is outside your local domain, you might receive an error. If you receive an error, download and configure the WinHTTP proxy utility. To download the utility, go to the MSDN Online Downloads Web site (msdn.microsoft.com/downloads/default.asp) and browse to the WinHTTP Proxy Configuration Utility page, which is located in the XML chapter of the Web Development book.

To search for document definitions

1. In BizTalk Messaging Manager, in the **Search for other items** area, click **Document Definitions**.

2. To search for all document definitions, clear all search criteria and click **Search Now**.

   –Or–

   To search for a document definition with a specific name, in the **Search for document definitions** area, in the **Document definition name** box, type the name of the document definition that you want to find and click **Search Now**. You can enter an incomplete name and the search returns all possible names that match the incomplete name entry.

✎ Notes

- To clear the search criteria and search results, click **Clear Search**.

- If you have a large number of objects for which to search, it might take several minutes to return all the objects. You can narrow the objects returned in a search by using selection criteria.

- The default number of items returned in a search is 500. You can adjust this number. For more information, see "To set server connection options" earlier in this chapter.

- You can use the following wildcard characters in the search criteria:

Wildcard character	Description	Example
%	Any string of zero or more characters.	The entry '%open%' finds all names with the word 'open' anywhere in the name.
_ (underscore)	Any single character.	The entry '_ean' finds four-letter names that end with ean (Dean, Sean, and so on).
[ ]	Any single character within the specified range ([a-f]) or set ([abcdef]).	The entry '[C-P]arsen' finds names ending with arsen and beginning with any single character between C and P (Carsen, Larsen, and so on).
[^]	Any single character not within the specified range ([^a-f]) or set ([^abcdef]).	The entry 'de[^s]%' finds all names beginning with de and where the following letter is not s.

To edit document definitions

1. In BizTalk Messaging Manager, in the **Document Definition Name** list, click the document definition that you want to edit.

   For more information about searching for document definitions, see "To search for document definitions" earlier in this chapter.

2. On the **File** menu, click **Edit**.

   The **Document Definition Properties** dialog box appears.

3. On the **General** tab, edit the general properties.

   For more information, see "To set general document-definition properties" later in this chapter.

4. Click the **Global Tracking** tab and edit the tracking properties.

   For more information, see "Set Global Tracking Properties" later in this chapter.

5. Click the **Selection Criteria** tab and edit the selection criteria properties.

   For more information, see "Set Selection Criteria Properties" later in this chapter.

6. After you have edited all the properties that you want to change, click **OK** to close the **Document Definition Properties** dialog box.

Notes

- You cannot name a document definition Reliable Message Acknowledgement Channel or BizTalk Canonical Receipt, which are reserved system names.

- You cannot specify global tracking fields for the document definition unless you select a specification.

- When you save a document definition that references a specification that is outside your local domain, you might receive an error. If you receive an error, download and configure the WinHTTP proxy utility. To download the utility, go to the MSDN Online Downloads Web site (msdn.microsoft.com/downloads/default.asp) and browse to the WinHTTP Proxy Configuration Utility page, which is located in the XML chapter of the Web Development book.

To delete document definitions

1. In BizTalk Messaging Manager, in the **Document Definition Name** list, click the document definition that you want to delete.

   For more information about searching for document definitions, see "To search for document definitions" earlier in this chapter.

2. On the **File** menu, click **Delete**.

Note

- If a document definition is used in a channel, you cannot delete it. You must first delete all channels that use the document definition.

To set general document-definition properties

1. In the **New Document Definition** or **Document Definition Properties** dialog box, click the **General** tab.

2. In the **Document definition name** box, type a unique name for the document definition.

3. Select the **Document specification** check box.

4. Click **Browse** to select a document specification.

   For more information, see "To select a document specification" later in this chapter.

Notes

- A document specification for a document definition is optional. However, if you do not select a specification, you cannot set global tracking fields, and the data processed using the document definition:

  - Is not translated from its native format into XML.

  - Is not validated against a specification.

  - Cannot be transformed into another structure or format by using a map.

- If you are processing data that you do not want to translate, transform, or validate, such as a binary file, you should not select a document specification.

To select a document specification

1. In the **New Document Definition** or **Document Definition Properties** dialog box, click the **General** tab.

2. Select the **Document specification** check box and click **Browse**.

   The **Select a Document Specification from the WebDAV Repository** dialog box appears.

3. In the **Server** box, do one of the following if you want to change the server:

   - Click a server in the list.

   - Type the name of a server and press ENTER.

4. Double-click the folder that contains the specification that you want to open, and double-click the file.

◆ Important

- The first time that you open any WebDAV repository dialog box, the WebDAV repository on the local server is selected, even if BizTalk Messaging Manager is connected to a database on a remote server. If you browse to a WebDAV repository on a remote server, the default changes to that server until you select a new WebDAV repository. The default server for all WebDAV repository dialog boxes is the last server to which a connection was made.

Notes

- If you select http://localhost as the server, BizTalk Messaging Manager automatically converts it to the local computer name.

- If a document definition is used as the inbound document definition in a channel for an open messaging port, and the destination information is provided in the document, the document definition must reference a specification that is properly configured. For more information about how to configure a document specification to process documents for an open messaging port, see "To set dictionary properties" in Chapter 5, "Creating Specifications."

- A document specification is optional; however, in most cases you should select one. If you do not select a specification:

  - The data that you process is not translated into XML on the inbound side or from XML on the outbound side.

  - The data is not validated against a specification to ensure that it does not contain errors.

  - You cannot transform the structure or format of the data by using a map in a channel.

  - You cannot specify global tracking fields for the document definition.

- A document specification is not required if you want to use the document definition in a pass-through submission.

- You might experience some delay the first time that you connect to a WebDAV repository on a remote server.

- When you save a document definition that references a specification that is outside your local domain, you might receive an error. If you receive an error, download and configure the WinHTTP proxy utility. To download the utility, go to the MSDN Online Downloads Web site (msdn.microsoft.com/downloads/default.asp) and browse to the WinHTTP Proxy Configuration Utility page, which is located in the XML chapter of the Web Development book.

Set Global Tracking Properties

On the **Global Tracking** tab, the **Specification fields** list provides a tree view of the specification that you selected for the document definition. You can expand this list to view the fields in the specification and designate a limited number of fields to log to the Tracking database.

When the document definition is selected as the inbound document definition for a channel, these fields are tracked for each instance of a document that is processed by that channel. These fields are referred to as global tracking fields. When you select a document definition in a channel, you have the option of overriding the global tracking fields by selecting different specification fields to track for each document instance processed by that channel only.

To select specification fields in a document definition

1. In the **New Document Definition** or **Document Definition Properties** dialog box, click the **Global Tracking** tab.

2. In the **Specification fields** list, click the expand indicator (+) next to any record, or double-click the record, to expand the view.

3. Select a specification field that you want to add to the **Fields to track** list, and then complete one of the following procedures.

To add the field as	Follow this procedure
Integer	Click **Integer**. You can add two fields as integers.
Real	Click **Real**. You can add two fields as real numbers.
Date	Click **Date**. You can add two fields as dates.
Text	Click **Text**. You can add two fields as text.
Custom	Click **Custom**. You can add unlimited fields as a custom type. The fields are stored as an XML concatenated string with tags for each field.

Notes

- To select a specification field to track as an integer, real, or date data type, the field must have that data type assigned in the specification. For more information about assigning a data type to a specification field, see "To set declaration properties" in Chapter 5, "Creating Specifications."

- Specification fields without a data type assigned in the specification can be tracked only as a text or custom data type.

- If a specification field that you want to track has a character data type, you can only track that field as a custom type.

- When you select a document definition in a channel, you can override the global tracking fields for that channel by selecting different specification fields to track. For more information, see "To select specification fields in a channel" earlier in this chapter.

To remove specification fields from a document definition

1. In the **New Document Definition** or **Document Definition Properties** dialog box, click the **Global Tracking** tab.

2. In the **Fields to track** list, select the specification field or fields that you want to remove and click **Remove**.

Note

- When you remove a field from the list of fields to track, it is removed only from the list in this document definition; it is not removed from the specification.

Set Selection Criteria Properties

Selection criteria are a unique set of name-value pairs that BizTalk Server 2000 only uses to process EDI documents. For inbound X12 or EDIFACT documents, the server uses selection criteria to uniquely identify and select a document definition because no document definition name is available within individual EDI documents.

For outbound X12 or EDIFACT documents, selection criteria are used to create the group header information.

To add selection criteria

1. In the **New Document Definition** or **Document Definition Properties** dialog box, click the **Selection Criteria** tab and click **Add**.

   The **New Name and Value** dialog box appears.

2. In the **Name** box, type a name for the selection criteria.

3. In the **Value** box, type a value for the selection criteria and click **OK**.

◆ **Important**

- For BizTalk Server 2000 to match the selection criteria values to the corresponding header elements of inbound interchanges, and to insert the values into the correct header elements of outbound interchanges, you must type the selection criteria names exactly as shown in the following tables.

X12 header elements

Name	Requirement	GS element
functional_identifier	Mandatory	GS01
application_sender_code	Mandatory	GS02
application_receiver_code	Mandatory	GS03
standards_version	Mandatory	GS08

EDIFACT header elements

Name	Requirement	UNH element	UNG element
functional_identifier	Mandatory	S009, 0065	0038
application_sender_code	Optional	Not used	S006, 0040
application_receiver_code	Optional	Not used	S007, 0044
standards_version_type	Mandatory	S009, 0052	S008, 0052
standards_version_value	Mandatory	S009, 0054	S008, 0054

- For an outbound EDIFACT interchange, a message header (UNH) is always created. If you specify an application_sender_code and an application_receiver_code, a group header (UNG) is also created.

- The set of selection criteria name-value pairs that you use for each document definition must be unique across all document definitions.

To edit selection criteria

1. In the **New Document Definition** or **Document Definition Properties** dialog box, click the **Selection Criteria** tab.

2. In the **Selection criteria** list, click the selection criterion that you want to edit and click **Edit**.

   The **Name and Value Properties** dialog box appears.

3. In the **Name** box, type a name for the selection criteria.

4. In the **Value** box, type a value for the selection criteria and click **OK**.

◆ **Important**

- For BizTalk Server 2000 to match the selection criteria values to the corresponding header elements of inbound interchanges, and to insert the values into the correct header elements of outbound interchanges, you must type the selection criteria names exactly as shown in the following tables.

X12 header elements

Name	Requirement	GS Element
functional_identifier	Mandatory	GS01
application_sender_code	Mandatory	GS02
application_receiver_code	Mandatory	GS03
standards_version	Mandatory	GS08

EDIFACT header elements

Name	Requirement	UNH element	UNG element
functional_identifier	Mandatory	S009, 0065	0038
application_sender_code	Optional	Not used	S006, 0040
application_receiver_code	Optional	Not used	S007, 0044
standards_version_type	Mandatory	S009, 0052	S008, 0052
standards_version_value	Mandatory	S009, 0054	S008, 0054

- For an outbound EDIFACT interchange, a message header (UNH) is always created. If you specify an application_sender_code and an application_receiver_code, a group header (UNG) is also created.

- The set of selection criteria name-value pairs that you use for each document definition must be unique across all document definitions.

To remove selection criteria

1. In the **Document Definition Properties** dialog box, click the **Selection Criteria** tab.

2. In the **Selection criteria** list, click the criterion that you want to remove and click **Remove**.

Related Topics

Chapter 5, "Creating Specifications"

Chapter 6, "Mapping Data"

Understanding Envelopes

An envelope encapsulates electronic business data for transport. An envelope typically consists of header and footer information, or of header information only. The envelope properties that you specify provide Microsoft BizTalk Server 2000 with information that the server needs to either open inbound interchanges or create outbound interchanges. When you create an envelope, you specify an envelope format; for certain types of formats, you also can select an envelope specification.

The envelope formats supported by BizTalk Server 2000 are custom XML, ANSI X12, UN/EDIFACT, flat file (delimited and positional), custom, and reliable. The reliable format processes envelopes that are compliant with BizTalk Framework 2.0. For more information about BizTalk Framework 2.0, go to the Microsoft BizTalk Web site (www.microsoft.com/biztalk/). If you specify a custom envelope format, you must create and register a custom parser component to process inbound envelopes or a custom serializer component to process outbound envelopes. For more information, see "Using the IBizTalkParserComponent Interface" and "Using the IBizTalkSerializerComponent Interface" in Chapter 15, "Creating Custom Components."

To enable BizTalk Server 2000 to process inbound interchanges with a custom XML or flat-file format, you must create envelopes with a matching format. To enable BizTalk Server 2000 to process inbound interchanges with a custom format, you must create and register a custom parser component. BizTalk Server 2000 can process inbound interchanges with ANSI X12, UN/EDIFACT, or reliable formats without using an envelope created by using BizTalk Messaging Manager.

To process outbound documents with any format, you must create an envelope and select it in a messaging port to create an interchange with the required envelope format and header information. BizTalk Server 2000 places only one document in each outbound interchange.

When you select an envelope with an X12 or EDIFACT format in a messaging port, you must also specify delimiters and an interchange control number. These EDI properties apply only to the envelopes selected for use with that messaging port. When you select an envelope with a custom format, delimiters and an interchange control number are optional and depend on the requirements of your custom parser or serializer components. When you create a channel for a messaging port that uses an X12, EDIFACT, or custom envelope, you can specify a functional group control number that applies only to documents processed by that channel and messaging port combination.

The format of an envelope that you select in a messaging port must agree with the format of the outbound document that it contains. The format of the outbound document is determined by the specification referred to in the outbound document definition of a channel. For example, if you choose an envelope with an X12 format for a messaging port, when you create a channel for that messaging port you must select an outbound document definition that points to a specification that also has an X12 format.

If you do not specify an envelope when creating a messaging port, the data is sent in XML format without any header.

Note

- When processing envelopes that are compliant with BizTalk Framework 2.0, BizTalk Server 2000 should be considered the endpoint with regard to the expiration time. When BizTalk Framework 2.0–compliant documents are submitted to BizTalk Server 2000, either from an application or a trading partner, the following fields are overwritten if present, or created if absent:

  - In the properties subsection:

    <prop:identity>

    <prop:sentAt>

    <prop:expiresAt>

  - In the receipt information subsection:

    <sendTo>

    <address>

    <sendReceiptBy>

Using Envelopes for Inbound Processing

Microsoft BizTalk Server 2000 can process an inbound interchange with an X12 or EDIFACT format without using an envelope created by using BizTalk Messaging Manager.

For BizTalk Server 2000 to process an inbound interchange with a flat-file format, you must create an envelope by using BizTalk Messaging Manager. That envelope must point to a specification that the server can use to interpret and open the interchange. The name of the envelope must be provided to the server when the interchange is submitted for processing. For more information, see "Submitting" in Chapter 10, "Submitting Documents."

For BizTalk Server 2000 to process an inbound interchange with a custom XML format, you must create an envelope by using BizTalk Messaging Manager. However, the server is able to locate the custom XML envelope that it needs to interpret and open the interchange without the name of the envelope being provided at submission. You can provide the server with the name of the envelope at submission, but it is not required. For more information, see "Submitting" in Chapter 10, "Submitting Documents."

For BizTalk Server 2000 to process an inbound interchange with a custom format, you must create a custom parser to open the interchange. For more information, see "Using the IBizTalkParserComponent Interface" in Chapter 15, "Creating Custom Components."

The envelopes that you create to process inbound interchanges do not need to be selected in a messaging port to be used by the server. Only envelopes used for processing outbound interchanges need to be selected in a messaging port.

Using Envelopes for Outbound Processing

Messaging ports regulate the outbound flow of data from Microsoft BizTalk Server 2000 to a specified destination. When you create a messaging port, you can select an envelope for the documents that are processed by that messaging port. If you select an envelope, the envelope format must match the format of the documents that the envelope contains. The format of the documents is determined by the specification referred to in the outbound document definition of a channel. Once you create an envelope by using BizTalk Messaging Manager, you can use it in any number of messaging ports.

When BizTalk Server 2000 processes an outbound document, the server uses the properties of the envelope selected in the messaging port to create an interchange by encapsulating or prefixing the document. If you do not specify an envelope for a messaging port, the data is sent in XML format without any header or footer. If you specify a custom XML format, but do not select an envelope specification, the data is sent using the reliable format. The reliable format processes envelopes that are compliant with BizTalk Framework 2.0. For more information about BizTalk Framework 2.0, go to the Microsoft BizTalk Web site (www.microsoft.com/biztalk/).

For BizTalk Server 2000 to process an outbound interchange with a custom format, you must create a custom serializer to create the interchange. For more information, see "Using the IBizTalkSerializerComponent Interface" in Chapter 15, "Creating Custom Components."

When you select an envelope with an X12 or EDIFACT format, you must specify an interchange control number and delimiters. An interchange control number is used to identify and track documents that are processed using the messaging port. The interchange control number is incremented with each use of the envelope and messaging port. Delimiters indicate the characters that are used to separate the records and fields of the envelope and the documents contained in the envelope. For envelopes with a custom format, an interchange control number and delimiters are optional.

◆ Important

- The envelope format for a messaging port must agree with the document type format of the specification that is referred to by the outbound document definition for any associated channel. For example, if you choose an envelope with an X12 format for a messaging port, you must select an outbound document definition for the channel that points to an X12 specification.

Create and Manage Envelopes

This section provides task-specific information about how to create and manage envelopes by using BizTalk Messaging Manager. For more information about envelopes, see "Understanding Envelopes" earlier in this chapter.

To create envelopes

1. In BizTalk Messaging Manager, on the **File** menu, point to **New** and click **Envelope**.

    The **New Envelope** dialog box appears.

2. In the **Envelope name** box, type a unique name for the envelope.

3. In the **Envelope format** list, click one of the following envelope formats:

    - **CUSTOM XML**

      To enable Microsoft BizTalk Server 2000 to process inbound interchanges with a custom XML format, you must create an envelope with a custom XML format and a specification reference. However, when you submit custom XML interchanges, you do not need to specify the envelope name in the submit call parameters. BizTalk Server 2000 is able to locate the appropriate envelope without a name reference.

    - **X12**

      You do not need to create an envelope with an X12 format to enable BizTalk Server 2000 to process inbound interchanges with an X12 format, and you do not need to specify the envelope name in the submit call parameters.

    - **EDIFACT**

      You do not need to create an envelope with an EDIFACT format to enable BizTalk Server 2000 to process inbound interchanges with an EDIFACT format, and you do not need to specify the envelope name in the submit call parameters.

    - **FLATFILE**

      To enable BizTalk Server 2000 to process inbound interchanges with a flat-file format, you must create an envelope with a flat-file format. When you submit inbound flat-file documents, you must specify the envelope name in the submit call parameters. For more information, see "Submitting" in Chapter 10, "Submitting Documents."

    - **CUSTOM**

      To enable BizTalk Server 2000 to process inbound interchanges with a custom format, a format not supported directly by BizTalk Server 2000, you must create a custom parser component. You need to create an envelope only if the custom parser requires one. For more information, see "Using the IBizTalkParserComponent Interface" in Chapter 15, "Creating Custom Components."

      To enable BizTalk Server 2000 to process outbound interchanges with a custom format, you must create an envelope with a custom format and select the envelope in a messaging port. You also must create and register a custom serializer component. For more information, see "Using the IBizTalkSerializerComponent Interface" in Chapter 15, "Creating Custom Components." You can configure the custom serializer in the channel on the **Advanced Configuration** page of the Channel Wizard. For more information, see "To set advanced configuration properties" earlier in this chapter.

- **RELIABLE**

  You do not need to create an envelope with a reliable format to enable BizTalk Server 2000 to process inbound interchanges with a reliable format, and you do not need to specify the envelope name in the submit call parameters.

  The reliable format processes envelopes that are compliant with BizTalk Framework 2.0. For more information about BizTalk Framework 2.0, go to the Microsoft BizTalk Web site (www.microsoft.com/biztalk/).

  If you choose the reliable format, you also must configure the **Reliable messaging reply-to URL** address in the **BizTalk Server Group Properties** dialog box. For more information, see "To configure general properties for a server group" in Chapter 11, "Administering Servers and Applications."

4. If you choose the custom XML, flat-file, or custom format, you can select a specification for the envelope. For more information, see "To select an envelope specification" later in this chapter.

Notes

- To enable BizTalk Server 2000 to process outbound interchanges in any format, you must create an envelope.

- If you choose the custom XML format and you do not select a specification, the envelope format defaults to the reliable format.

- When processing envelopes that are compliant with BizTalk Framework 2.0, BizTalk Server 2000 should be considered the endpoint with regard to the expiration time. When BizTalk Framework 2.0–compliant documents are submitted to BizTalk Server 2000, either from an application or a trading partner, the following fields are overwritten if present, or created if absent:

  - In the properties subsection:

    <prop:identity>

    <prop:sentAt>

    <prop:expiresAt>

  - In the receipt information subsection:

    <sendTo>

    <address>

    <sendReceiptBy>

- If you change the envelope format and you have selected a specification, you also might need to select a different specification.

- When you save an envelope that references a specification that is outside your local domain, you might receive an error. If you receive an error, download and configure the WinHTTP proxy utility. To download the utility, go to the MSDN Online Downloads Web site (msdn.microsoft.com/downloads/default.asp) and browse to the WinHTTP Proxy Configuration Utility page, which is located in the XML chapter of the Web Development book.

To search for envelopes

1. In BizTalk Messaging Manager, in the **Search for other items** area, click **Envelopes**.

2. Do one or more of the following:
    - To search for all envelopes, clear all search criteria and click **Search Now**.
    - To search for an envelope with a specific name, in the **Search for envelopes** area, in the **Envelope name** box, type the name of the envelope that you want to find and click **Search Now**. You can enter an incomplete name and the search returns all possible names that match the incomplete name entry.
    - To search for envelopes of a specific format, in the **Format** list, click a format and click **Search Now**.

📝 Notes

- You can set more than one search criteria before clicking **Search Now**.
- To clear the search criteria and search results, click **Clear Search**.
- If you have a large number of objects for which to search, it might take several minutes to return all the objects. You can narrow the objects returned in a search by using selection criteria.
- The default number of items returned in a search is 500. You can adjust this number. For more information, see "To set server connection options" earlier in this chapter.
- You can use the following wildcard characters in the search criteria:

Wildcard character	Description	Example
%	Any string of zero or more characters.	The entry '%open%' finds all names with the word 'open' anywhere in the name.
_ (underscore)	Any single character.	The entry '_ean' finds four-letter names that end with ean (Dean, Sean, and so on).
[ ]	Any single character within the specified range ([a-f]) or set ([abcdef]).	The entry '[C-P]arsen' finds names ending with arsen and beginning with any single character between C and P (Carsen, Larsen, and so on).
[^]	Any single character not within the specified range ([^a-f]) or set ([^abcdef]).	The entry 'de[^s]%' finds all names beginning with de and where the following letter is not s.

To edit envelopes

1. In BizTalk Messaging Manager, in the **Envelope Name** list, click the envelope that you want to edit.

   For information about searching for envelopes, see "To search for envelopes" earlier in this chapter.

2. On the **File** menu, click **Edit**.

   The **Envelope Properties** dialog box appears.

3. In the **Envelope name** box, type a unique name for the envelope.

4. In the **Envelope format** list, click one of the following envelope formats:

   - **CUSTOM XML**

     To enable BizTalk Server 2000 to process inbound interchanges with a custom XML format, you must create an envelope with a custom XML format and a specification reference. However, when you submit custom XML interchanges, you do not need to specify the envelope name in the submit call parameters. BizTalk Server 2000 is able to locate the appropriate envelope without a name reference.

   - **X12**

     You do not need to create an envelope with an X12 format to enable BizTalk Server 2000 to process inbound interchanges with an X12 format, and you do not need to specify the envelope name in the submit call parameters.

   - **EDIFACT**

     You do not need to create an envelope with an EDIFACT format to enable BizTalk Server 2000 to process inbound interchanges with an EDIFACT format, and you do not need to specify the envelope name in the submit call parameters.

   - **FLATFILE**

     To enable BizTalk Server 2000 to process inbound interchanges with a flat-file format, you must create an envelope with a flat-file format. When you submit inbound flat-file documents, you must specify the envelope name in the submit call parameters. For more information, see "Submitting" in Chapter 10, "Submitting Documents."

   - **CUSTOM**

     To enable BizTalk Server 2000 to process inbound interchanges with a custom format, a format not supported directly by BizTalk Server 2000, you might need to create an envelope. However, you must create a custom parser component to process these interchanges, which might require an envelope. For more information, see "Using the IBizTalkParserComponent Interface" in Chapter 15, "Creating Custom Components."

     To enable BizTalk Server 2000 to process outbound interchanges with a custom format, you must create an envelope with a custom format and select the envelope in a messaging port. You also must create and register a custom serializer component. For more information, see "Using the IBizTalkSerializerComponent Interface" in Chapter 15, "Creating Custom Components." You can configure the custom serializer in the channel on the **Advanced Configuration** page of the Channel Wizard. For more information, see "To set advanced configuration properties" earlier in this chapter.

- **RELIABLE**

    You do not need to create an envelope with a reliable format to enable BizTalk Server 2000 to process inbound interchanges with a reliable format, and you do not need to specify the envelope name in the submit call parameters.

    The reliable format processes envelopes that are compliant with BizTalk Framework 2.0. For more information about BizTalk Framework 2.0, go to the Microsoft BizTalk Web site (www.microsoft.com/biztalk/).

    If you choose the reliable format, you also must configure the **Reliable messaging reply-to URL** address in the **BizTalk Server Group Properties** dialog box. For more information, see "To configure general properties for a server group" in Chapter 11, "Administering Servers and Applications."

5. If you choose the custom XML, flat-file, or custom format, you can select a specification for the envelope. For more information, see "To select an envelope specification" later in this chapter.

✦ Important

- If you create an envelope with the reliable format and select that envelope in a messaging port, you also must configure the **Reliable messaging reply-to URL** address in the **BizTalk Server Group Properties** dialog box. For more information, see "To configure general properties for a server group" in Chapter 11, "Administering Servers and Applications."

✐ Notes

- To enable BizTalk Server 2000 to process outbound interchanges in any format, you must create an envelope.

- If you choose the custom XML format and you do not select a specification, the envelope format defaults to the reliable format.

- When processing envelopes that are compliant with BizTalk Framework 2.0, BizTalk Server 2000 should be considered the endpoint with regard to the expiration time. When BizTalk Framework 2.0–compliant documents are submitted to BizTalk Server 2000, either from an application or a trading partner, the following fields are overwritten if present, or created if absent:

    - In the properties subsection:

        <prop:identity>

        <prop:sentAt>

        <prop:expiresAt>

- In the receipt information subsection:

  <sendTo>

  <address>

  <sendReceiptBy>

- If you change the envelope format and you have selected a specification, you also might need to select a different specification.

- When you save an envelope that references a specification that is outside your local domain, you might receive an error. If you receive an error, download and configure the WinHTTP proxy utility. To download the utility, go to the MSDN Online Downloads Web site (msdn.microsoft.com/downloads/default.asp) and browse to the WinHTTP Proxy Configuration Utility page, which is located in the XML chapter of the Web Development book.

To delete envelopes

1. In BizTalk Messaging Manager, in the **Envelope Name** list, click the envelope that you want to delete.

   For more information about searching for envelopes, see "To search for envelopes" earlier in this chapter.

2. On the **File** menu, click **Delete**.

Note

- If an envelope is used in a messaging port, you cannot delete it. You must first delete all messaging ports that use the envelope.

To select an envelope specification

1. In the **New Envelope** or **Envelope Properties** dialog box, select the **Envelope specification** check box and click **Browse**.

   The **Select an Envelope Specification from the WebDAV Repository** dialog box appears.

2. In the **Server** box, do one of the following if you want to change the server:

   - Click a server in the list.

   - Type the name of a server and press ENTER.

3. Double-click the folder that contains the specification that you want to open, click the specification, and then click **Open**.

◆ **Important**

- The first time that you open any WebDAV repository dialog box, the WebDAV repository on the local server is selected, even if your BizTalk Messaging Manager is connected to a database on a remote server. If you browse to a WebDAV repository on a remote server, the default changes to that server until you select a new WebDAV repository. The default server for all WebDAV repository dialog boxes is the last server to which a connection was made.

📝 **Notes**

- If you select http://localhost as the server, BizTalk Messaging Manager automatically converts it to the local computer name.

- If you choose the custom XML format, you can select a specification for the envelope. If you do not select a specification, the envelope format defaults to the reliable format that complies with BizTalk Framework 2.0. For more information about BizTalk Framework 2.0, go to the Microsoft BizTalk Web site (www.microsoft.com/biztalk/).

- If you choose the flat-file format, you can select a specification for the envelope. You must select a specification if the envelope is used for opening inbound interchanges. A specification is not required if the envelope is used for creating outbound interchanges.

- If you choose a custom format, you can select a specification for the envelope. The custom parser or serializer that you create determines the need for a specification.

  To use the custom format, you also must:

  - Create a custom parser component for opening inbound interchanges with this custom format. For more information, see "Using the IBizTalkParserComponent Interface" in Chapter 15, "Creating Custom Components."

  - Create and configure a custom serializer component for creating outbound interchanges with this custom format. For more information, see "Using the IBizTalkSerializerComponent Interface" in Chapter 15, "Creating Custom Components."

  - Configure the custom serializer component using the messaging port override properties in the Channel Wizard. For more information, see "To override messaging port defaults" earlier in this chapter.

- When you save an envelope that references a specification that is outside your local domain, you might receive an error. If you receive an error, download and configure the WinHTTP proxy utility. To download the utility, go to the MSDN Online Downloads Web site (msdn.microsoft.com/downloads/default.asp) and browse to the WinHTTP Proxy Configuration Utility page, which is located in the XML chapter of the Web Development book.

Understanding Receipts

When exchanging documents with a trading partner, your business processes might require you to receive receipts for the documents that you send, or to generate receipts for documents that a trading partner sends to your business.

BizTalk Messaging Services provides two methods for processing receipts for interchanges. For interchanges that use the X12 or EDIFACT parser, or a custom parser that requires receipts, you can configure BizTalk Messaging Manager to use channel properties to process receipts. For interchanges that use the XML parser, you have the option of using reliable messaging, which processes receipts automatically to guarantee the reliable delivery of data.

Processing Receipts Using Channels

This section explains how you can configure BizTalk Messaging Services to use channel properties to control the processing of receipts. The destination system is configured to generate (send) receipts to the source system. The source system is configured to expect (receive) receipts from the destination system and correlate them with the original interchanges. This configuration applies only if you process interchanges that use the X12 or EDIFACT parser, or a custom parser that requires receipts. For more information about creating custom parsers, see "Using the IBizTalkParserComponent Interface" in Chapter 15, "Creating Custom Components." If you process interchanges that use the XML parser, see "Processing Receipts Using Reliable Messaging," later in this chapter.

If you use a custom parser and want to correlate receipts with the original interchanges, you must create a custom correlation component.

For the source system to receive receipts, the destination system also must be configured to send receipts. Configuring a channel on the source system to expect a receipt is not sufficient to receive receipts.

The illustration on the following page shows the configuration for both the source and destination systems using channel properties for processing receipts.

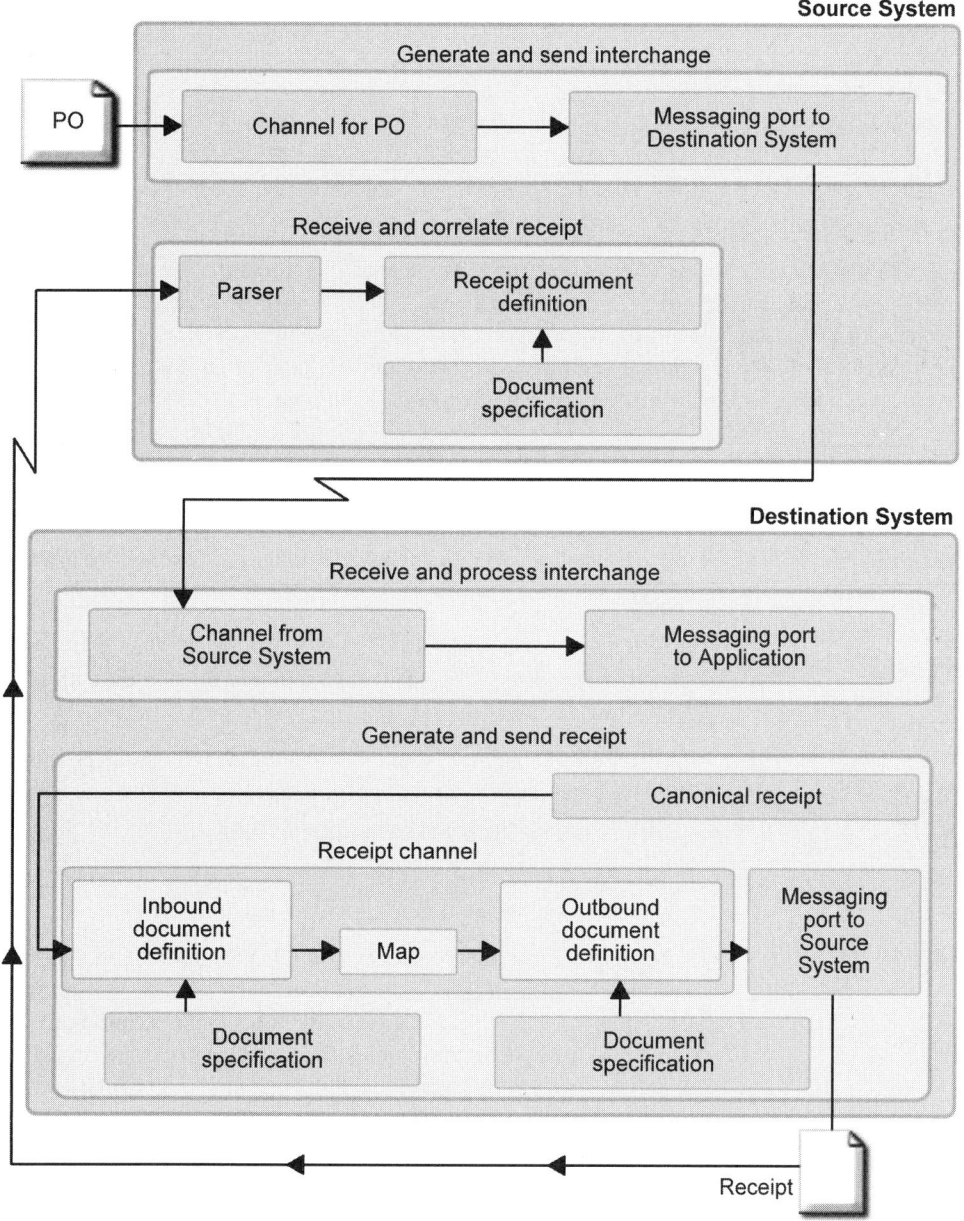

Configuring the Source System for Channel Receipts

This topic explains how to configure BizTalk Messaging Services to send an interchange to a trading partner and to process a receipt by using channel properties.

You must create a channel and a messaging port to process and transport an interchange to the destination system. You do not need to create a channel and messaging port to process the receipt that the destination system returns. However, you must create a document definition that the server uses to validate the receipt when it is returned.

To configure BizTalk Messaging Services to send an interchange to a destination system and to process a receipt by using channel properties, perform the steps in the following table. References are provided for each procedure, and notes are provided to indicate special configuration considerations. Other property settings needed to complete the configuration vary according to your particular business situation and are not specified here.

Step	References and notes
Using BizTalk Editor:	
• Create the specifications for the inbound and outbound document definitions for the original document for the interchange. You also must create a specification for the document definition that the server uses to validate the receipt when it is received.	• See "Understanding Specifications" in Chapter 5, "Creating Specifications." 📝 **Notes** • For the outbound document definition for the channel, you must create a specification that uses the format required by the destination system. For example, X12. When BizTalk Messaging Services on the destination system processes the interchange, and the parser requires receipts, the parser does the following: • Extracts header elements from the interchange. • Generates a canonical receipt. • Inserts the elements into the canonical receipt. For the source system, the specification for the outbound document definition of the channel used to process the interchange also must contain these fields. And, the specification for the document definition to validate the receipt must contain these fields. The source system uses these elements to correlate the receipt with the original interchange. The X12 header elements are: • functional_identifier • standards_version The EDIFACT header elements are: • functional_identifier • standards_version_type • standards_version_value

Step	References and notes
Using BizTalk Messaging Manager:	

Step	References and notes
• Create the inbound and outbound document definitions for creating the channel and a document definition for the receipt.	• See "To create document definitions" earlier in this chapter. ☑ **Notes** • In the document definitions, you must select the specifications that you created previously. For more information, see "To select a document specification" earlier in this chapter. • You also must create a document definition for the receipt.
• Create a messaging port for transporting the receipt to the source system.	• See "To create messaging ports" earlier in this chapter. ☑ **Note** • You must create the messaging port and its associated receipt channel for processing the receipt first. When you create the channel for processing the original interchange, you must specify the receipt channel.
• Create a messaging port for transporting the interchange to the destination system.	• See "To create messaging ports" earlier in this chapter.
• Create a channel to process the original interchange from your trading partner.	• See "To create channels" earlier in this chapter. ☑ **Notes** • On the **Source Application** or **Source Organization** page of the Channel Wizard, select the **Expect receipt** check box. • In the **Expect receipt** area, in the **Receipt interval in minutes** box, set the time that you want to wait to receive the receipt before resending the original interchange. For more information, see "To set source application properties" or "To set source organization properties" earlier in this chapter.

Step	References and notes

Using BizTalk Document Tracking:

- The original interchange is logged to the Tracking database and the receipt status field (nACKStatus) is set to "Pending". The receipt status in the Tracking database subsequently changes to reflect the status of the receipt process.

- See "Understanding Query Results" in Chapter 13, "Tracking Documents."

Submitting receipts on the source system

Receipts are submitted to BizTalk Messaging Services in the same manner as other documents. Once a receipt is submitted, the X12 and EDIFACT parsers can distinguish a receipt from other documents and direct the server to correlate the receipt with the original interchange.

◆ **Important**

- Receipts must be submitted to BizTalk Messaging Services without using any submission parameters.

Configuring the Destination System for Channel Receipts

This topic explains how to configure BizTalk Messaging Services to process an interchange from a trading partner and to generate a receipt by using channel properties. To do this, you must create a channel and a messaging port to process the outbound interchange and transport it to the destination system. You do not need to create a channel or a messaging port to process the receipt that the destination system returns. A parser processes the receipt by using only a document definition.

To configure BizTalk Messaging Services to process an interchange from the source system and to send a receipt by using channel properties, perform the steps in the following table. References are provided for each procedure, and notes are provided to indicate special configuration considerations. Other property settings needed to complete the configuration vary according to your particular business situation and are not specified here.

Step	References and notes
Using BizTalk Editor:	
• Create the specifications for the inbound and outbound document definitions that are used to create the receipt channel.	• See "Understanding Specifications" in Chapter 5, "Creating Specifications."

🖉 **Notes**

• For the inbound document definition of the receipt channel, you use the Canonical Receipt specification. This specification is located in the WebDAV repository.

• For the outbound document definition of the receipt channel, you must create a specification that uses the format required by your business process.

When BizTalk Messaging Services on the destination system processes an inbound interchange, and the parser requires receipts, the parser does the following:

• Extracts group header elements.

• Generates a canonical receipt.

• Inserts the header elements into the canonical receipt.

The outbound document specification for the receipt channel must contain fields for these header elements. The source system uses the header elements to correlate the receipt with the original interchange.

The X12 header elements are:

• functional_identifier

• standards_version

The EDIFACT header elements are:

• functional_identifier

• standards_version_type

• standards_version_value

Step	References and notes
• Create the specifications for the inbound and outbound document definitions that are used to create the channel to process the original interchange from the source system.	• See "Understanding Specifications" in Chapter 5, "Creating Specifications."

Step	References and notes
Using BizTalk Mapper:	
• Create a map for the receipt channel.	• See "To create new maps" in Chapter 6, "Mapping Data." 📝 **Notes** • When you create the receipt channel, you must specify a map. The map is used to transform the canonical receipt into the correct document type for the outbound document. • You can use one of the maps provided with BizTalk Server 2000, if it matches the document type that is required for your business process. You can retrieve these maps from the WebDAV repository. –Or– You can create your own map using the Canonical Receipt specification and a specification that matches the document type required for your business process.
Using BizTalk Messaging Manager:	
• Create the document definitions for the receipt channel and for the channel that you use to process the original interchange.	• See "To create document definitions" earlier in this chapter. 📝 **Notes** • In the document definitions, you must select the specifications that you created previously. For more information, see "To select a document specification" earlier in this chapter. • You also must create the document definitions for the channel that is used to process the original interchange. The configuration for these varies depending on your business process.
• Create a messaging port for transporting the receipt to the source system.	• See "To create messaging ports" earlier in this chapter. 📝 **Note** • You must create the messaging port and its associated receipt channel for processing the receipt before you create those that are used for the original interchange. When you create the channel for processing the original interchange, you must specify the receipt channel.

Step	References and notes
• Create a receipt channel from an application for processing the receipt.	• See "To create channels" earlier in this chapter. 📝 **Notes** • On the **General Information** page of the Channel Wizard, select the **This is a receipt channel** check box. • On the **Source Application** page of the Channel Wizard, in the **Name** list, select an application. You can create an application for the home organization that you use to designate receipts that are generated by the parsers. • On the **Inbound Document** page of the Channel Wizard, click **Browse** and browse to the document definition that you created earlier and that uses the Canonical Receipt specification. • On the **Outbound Document** page of the Channel Wizard, click **Browse** and browse to the document definition that you created earlier and that uses the specification with the document type required for your business process.
• Create a messaging port for transporting the documents contained in the original interchange to their intended destination.	• See "To create messaging ports" earlier in this chapter. 📝 **Note** • This messaging port does not require special configuration for processing receipts.
• Create a channel to process the original interchange from your trading partner.	• See "To create channels" earlier in this chapter. 📝 **Notes** • On the **Source Organization** page of the Channel Wizard, select the **Generate receipt** check box. • In the **Generate receipt** area, click **Browse** and select the receipt channel that you created to process the receipt. For more information, see "To set source organization properties" earlier in this chapter. • On the **Advanced Configuration** page of the Channel Wizard, in the **Retry options** area, you can set the number of retries and the interval. For more information, see "To set advanced configuration properties" earlier in this chapter.

Using BizTalk Document Tracking:

• The original interchange and the receipt are logged to the Tracking database.	• See "Understanding Query Results" in Chapter 13, "Tracking Documents."

Processing Receipts Using Reliable Messaging

This section explains how you can configure BizTalk Messaging Services to send and receive receipts by using reliable messaging envelopes, which create interchanges that are compliant with BizTalk Framework 2.0. Reliable messaging enables receipts to be processed automatically, to ensure the reliable delivery of data. For more information about BizTalk Framework 2.0, go to the Microsoft BizTalk Web site (www.microsoft.com/biztalk/). If you send and receive interchanges that use the X12, EDIFACT, or a custom parser, see "Processing Receipts Using Channels," earlier in this chapter.

By using BizTalk Messaging Manager, you can configure a messaging port to use a reliable envelope format for an outbound interchange. Envelopes that use the reliable messaging format must always include a reply-to URL address in the header. The reply-to address is used by the destination system to send a receipt to the interchange sender system.

Configuring the Source System for Reliable Messaging Receipts

To configure BizTalk Messaging Services to send an interchange to a destination system and to process a receipt by using reliable messaging, perform the steps in the following table. References are provided for each procedure, and notes are provided to indicate special configuration considerations. Other property settings needed to complete the configuration vary according to your particular business situation and are not specified here.

Step	References and notes
Using BizTalk Server Administration:	
• Configure the reliable messaging reply-to address property.	• See "To configure general properties for a server group" in Chapter 11, "Administering Servers and Applications."

☑ **Notes**

- In BizTalk Server Administration, expand **Microsoft BizTalk Server 2000** and click the server group that you want to configure.

- On the **Action** menu, click **Properties**.

- In the **BizTalk Server Group Properties** dialog box, in the **Reliable messaging reply-to URL** box, type the URL that this server group uses to receive reliable messaging delivery receipts.

  When you create an outbound interchange that uses a reliable messaging envelope, the server automatically inserts the **Reliable messaging reply-to URL** into the header of the outbound interchange. The server also places the original interchange into the Retry queue. The server uses the **Retry** options specified in the channel to determine the number of times to resend the original interchange until a receipt has been received.

Using BizTalk Messaging Manager:

Step	References and notes
• Create an envelope that uses the reliable envelope format.	• See "To create envelopes" earlier in this chapter.

☑ **Notes**

- In the **New Envelope** dialog box, in the **Envelope format** list, click **RELIABLE**.

- If you choose the custom XML format and you do not select a specification, the envelope format defaults to the reliable format.

Step	References and notes
• Create a messaging port for transporting the original interchange to the destination system.	• See "To create messaging ports" earlier in this chapter.

☑ **Note**

- On the **Envelope Information** page of the New Messaging Port Wizard, in the **Envelope information** area, select the envelope that you created previously. For more information, see "To set envelope information properties" earlier in this chapter.

Step	References and notes
• Create a channel to process the original interchange.	• See "To create channels" earlier in this chapter. 📝 **Notes** • On the **Source Application** or **Source Organization** page of the Channel Wizard, do not set any receipt properties. • On the **Advanced Configuration** page of the Channel Wizard, in the **Retry options** area, you can set the number of retries and the interval. For more information, see "To set advanced configuration properties" earlier in this chapter.
Using BizTalk Document Tracking:	
• On the source system, the original, outbound interchange is logged to the Tracking database; however, the receipt that is returned is not.	• See "Understanding Query Results" in Chapter 13, "Tracking Documents."

Configuring the Destination System for Reliable Messaging Receipts

When BizTalk Messaging Services for the destination system receives an interchange with a reliable messaging format, it uses a special document definition, channel, and messaging port to process and transport a receipt to the source system. These special system objects are not viewable in BizTalk Messaging Manager, and you cannot create similar objects using the reserved system names.

The server uses the reply-to address that is included in the header of the inbound interchange as the destination address for the receipt.

You do not need to further configure BizTalk Messaging Services for the destination system to return a receipt for an interchange that is sent with a reliable messaging envelope, except when the source system specifies an SMTP address as the reliable messaging reply-to URL address. To send receipts to an SMTP address, your server must be configured to include a From address in the header of the receipt.

When BizTalk Server 2000 is installed, an organization identifier is created for the home organization. This identifier is named Reliable Messaging Acknowledgement SMTP From Address, and it cannot be removed. When sending a reliable messaging receipt to an SMTP address, the server inserts the value that you specify for this organization identifier into the interchange header as the From address.

To configure BizTalk Messaging Services to send a receipt to a source system using an SMTP reliable messaging reply-to address, perform the steps in the following table. References are provided for each procedure, and notes are provided to indicate special configuration considerations. Other property settings needed to complete the configuration vary according to your particular business situation and are not specified here.

Step	References and notes
Using BizTalk Messaging Manager:	
• Configure the Reliable Messaging Acknowledgement SMTP From Address organization identifier of the home organization.	• See "To configure the home organization" earlier in this chapter. ◆ **Important** • Do not modify the name or qualifier for this identifier, but only modify the value. 📝 **Notes** • Open the home organization. • In the **Organization Properties** dialog box, click the **Identifiers** tab. • In the **Organization identifiers** list, click **Reliable Messaging Acknowledgement SMTP From Address** and click **Edit**. • In the **Identifier Properties** dialog box, in the **Value** box, type a value for the identifier. For more information, see "To edit organization identifiers" earlier in this chapter.
• Create a messaging port for transporting the original interchange to its intended destination.	• See "To create messaging ports" earlier in this chapter. 📝 **Note** • This messaging port does not require special configuration.
• Create a channel to process the original interchange.	• See "To create channels" earlier in this chapter. 📝 **Note** • This messaging port does not require special configuration.
Using BizTalk Document Tracking:	
• On the destination system, the inbound interchange is logged to the Tracking database, but the receipt is not.	• See "Understanding Query Results" in Chapter 13, "Tracking Documents."

Understanding Distribution Lists

A distribution list is a group of messaging ports with which you can send the same document to several different trading partner organizations or internal applications.

You can use a distribution list to send the same data to several trading partner organizations or internal applications of your home organization at the same time. For example, you can send the same catalog, price list, or newsletter to several trading partner organizations by submitting the information only once to Microsoft BizTalk Server 2000.

You must first create a messaging port to each of the trading partner organizations or internal applications that you want to receive the data, and then add the messaging ports to a distribution list. Open messaging ports cannot be added to a distribution list. You can create new messaging ports to additional trading partner organizations or internal applications, and then add those messaging ports to an existing distribution list. For more information, see "To create messaging ports" earlier in this chapter.

You must create at least one channel for each distribution list, or else the distribution list is not functional. For more information, see "To create channels" earlier in this chapter.

When BizTalk Server 2000 invokes a channel related to a distribution list, it invokes only the channel that is associated with the distribution list to process the data. None of the channels that are associated with the individual messaging ports in the distribution list are invoked. The server uses the properties of each messaging port successively to transport the data to the destinations specified in the messaging ports.

A distribution list differs from an open messaging port in the following ways:

- With a distribution list, each document from a channel can result in the document being delivered to multiple destinations. With an open messaging port, each document from a channel results in only one document being delivered to only one destination.

- With a distribution list, you have to add a messaging port to send information to a different trading partner organization. With an open messaging port, you do not have to change the properties of the messaging port to send information to a different trading partner organization.

Using Distribution Lists

This section provides task-specific information about how to use distribution lists with BizTalk Messaging Manager.

To create distribution lists

1. In BizTalk Messaging Manager, on the **File** menu, point to **New** and click **Distribution List**.

   The **New Distribution List** dialog box appears.

2. In the **Distribution list name** box, type a unique name for the distribution list.

3. In the **Available messaging ports** list, select the messaging ports that you want to include and click **Add**.

 The selected messaging ports are added to the **Selected messaging ports** list.

4. In the **Selected messaging ports** list, select any messaging ports that you do not want to include and click **Remove**.

5. After you have set all the necessary properties, click **OK** to close the **New Distribution List** dialog box.

Notes

- When you remove a messaging port from a distribution list, it is removed only from the distribution list; it is not removed from the database.

- A distribution list must contain at least one messaging port.

- Open messaging ports cannot be added to a distribution list.

- To be functional, a distribution list requires at least one channel. For more information about channels, see "Create and Manage Channels" earlier in this chapter.

To search for distribution lists

1. In BizTalk Messaging Manager, in the **Search for other items** area, click **Distribution lists**.

2. Do one or more of the following:

   - To search for all distribution lists, clear all search criteria and click **Search Now**.

   - To search for a distribution list with a specific name, in the **Search for distribution lists** area, in the **Distribution list name** box, type the name of the distribution list that you want to find and click **Search Now**. You can enter an incomplete name and the search returns all possible names that match the incomplete name entry.

   - To search for distribution lists that contain a specific messaging port, in the **Containing messaging port** list, type the name of the messaging port and click **Search Now**.

Notes

- To clear the search criteria and search results, click **Clear Search**.

- If you have a large number of objects for which to search, it might take several minutes to return all the objects. You can narrow the objects returned in a search by using selection criteria.

- The default number of items returned in a search is 500. You can adjust this number. For more information, see "To set server connection options" earlier in this chapter.

- You can use the following wildcard characters in the search criteria:

Wildcard character	Description	Example
%	Any string of zero or more characters.	The entry '%open%' finds all names with the word 'open' anywhere in the name.
_ (underscore)	Any single character.	The entry '_ean' finds four-letter names that end with ean (Dean, Sean, and so on).
[ ]	Any single character within the specified range ([a-f]) or set ([abcdef]).	The entry '[C-P]arsen' finds names ending with arsen and beginning with any single character between C and P (Carsen, Larsen, and so on).
[^]	Any single character not within the specified range ([^a-f]) or set ([^abcdef]).	The entry 'de[^s]%' finds all names beginning with de and where the following letter is not s.

To edit distribution lists

1. In BizTalk Messaging Manager, in the **Distribution List Name** list, click the distribution list that you want to edit.

   For information about searching for distribution lists, see "To search for distribution lists" earlier in this chapter.

2. On the **File** menu, click **Edit**.

   The **Distribution List Properties** dialog box appears.

3. In the **Distribution list name** box, type a unique name for the distribution list.

4. In the **Available messaging ports** list, select the messaging ports that you want to include and, to add them to the **Selected messaging ports** list, click **Add**.

5. In the **Selected messaging ports** list, select any messaging ports that you do not want to include and click **Remove**.

6. After you have set all the necessary properties, click **OK** to close the **Distribution List Properties** dialog box.

Notes

- When you remove a messaging port from a distribution list, it is removed only from the distribution list; it is not removed from the database.

- A distribution list must contain at least one messaging port.

- Open messaging ports cannot be added to a distribution list.

To delete distribution lists

1. In BizTalk Messaging Manager, in the **Distribution List Name** list, click the distribution list that you want to delete.

   For more information about searching for distribution lists, see "To search for distribution lists" earlier in this chapter.

2. On the **File** menu, click **Delete**.

Notes

- You cannot delete a distribution list until all channels that are associated with the distribution list have been deleted.

- You can search for channels associated with a distribution list by right-clicking the distribution list and clicking **Find Channels**.

Accessing the BizTalk Messaging Configuration Object Model

This section provides information about how to access the BizTalk Messaging Configuration object model programmatically. It shows how to manage trading partner relationships and set up messaging ports and channels for the exchange of data, using Microsoft BizTalk Server 2000. This section also shows how to create document definitions and envelopes, and how to set organization properties. For examples of code, see Appendix B, "Code Samples."

The BizTalk Messaging Configuration object model can also be configured using the BizTalk Messaging Manager graphical user interface. For more information, see "Using BizTalk Messaging Manager" earlier in this chapter.

BizTalk Messaging Configuration Object Model

The BizTalk Messaging Configuration object model provides an easy way for applications to set up, maintain, and retrieve messaging ports and channels for trading partner relationships and application-to-application integration. The BizTalk Messaging Configuration object model can also create envelopes and document definitions, and set organization properties.

The BizTalk Messaging Configuration object model uses a Structured Query Language (SQL) database to store the port configurations and other relational data. ActiveX Data Objects (ADO) recordsets are returned when querying for lists of object instances (for example, messaging ports, organizations, and so on).

The BizTalk Messaging Configuration object model consists of Component Object Model (COM) objects that expose the configuration data required for Microsoft BizTalk Server 2000 to configure the interchange of structured documents between applications and trading partners. The COM objects represent instances of data in memory that can be stored in the database.

All object properties are read/write, except where noted.

BizTalk Messaging Configuration Objects

The following table shows the objects of the BizTalk Messaging Configuration object model.

Object	Description
BizTalkChannel	Contains the configuration related to the source entity and its binding with a **BizTalkPort** object.
BizTalkConfig	Creates and retrieves other BizTalk Server objects, such as channels, document specifications, and messaging ports.
BizTalkDocument	Identifies and describes the specification of a document.
BizTalkEnvelope	Identifies the envelope format and/or the envelope schema used for documents. Envelopes are required for documents using the X12 or EDIFACT format.
BizTalkOrganization	Identifies the source or destination point for the exchange of electronic data. An organization can represent an external trading partner, your own company, or a business unit of a trading partner or your company. An organization can designate a source application in a channel or a destination application in a port.
BizTalkPort	Defines the destination-related attributes of a document submission.
BizTalkPortGroup	Configures a port group. This is a group of complete **BizTalkPort** objects for sending the same document, such as a catalog, a price list, or a newsletter, to a group of trading partners.

☞ Caution

- Do not access the database directly. Do not directly call the stored procedures. Make all changes to the database by using the methods and properties of the BizTalk Messaging Configuration object model. Making changes to the database directly bypasses many constraints enforced by the BizTalk Messaging Configuration object model and either causes the server to function incorrectly or corrupts the database.

- The BizTalk Messaging Configuration object model should be accessed only at design time. Accessing objects in use while BizTalk Server is processing documents can produce unexpected results.

- BizTalk Server 2000 treats all variables with a **BSTR** data type as NULL-terminated strings. Any data contained in a **BSTR** after the NULL character is ignored. Documents containing embedded NULL characters must be submitted to BizTalk Server using pass-through mode.

Referential Integrity

Referential dependency must be considered when instantiating objects in BizTalk Server 2000. Referential dependency indicates that one object refers to, and is dependent upon, another object. For example, a **BizTalkChannel** object refers to a **BizTalkPort** object.

To maintain referential integrity, an object instance cannot be deleted if it is referred to by another object instance. Referential integrity is maintained when the object referred to exists in the database.

Remove objects in the reverse order from which they are created. If an instance of an object referred to by another instance of an object is removed, a constraint error is returned. Using the example above, a constraint error is returned if a **BizTalkPort** object is removed that is being used by a **BizTalkChannel** object.

The following sequence shows the preferred order for creating objects to maintain the referential integrity of the objects:

1. **BizTalkOrganization**

2. **BizTalkDocument**

3. **BizTalkEnvelope** (if required)

4. **BizTalkPort**
   - The **BizTalkPort** object requires the **BizTalkOrganization** object.
   - The **BizTalkPort** object conditionally uses the **BizTalkEnvelope** object.

5. **BizTalkChannel**
   - The **BizTalkChannel** object requires the **BizTalkPort** object.
   - The **BizTalkChannel** object requires the **BizTalkDocument** object.
   - The **BizTalkChannel** object requires the **BizTalkOrganization** object.
   - The **BizTalkChannel** object conditionally uses the **BizTalkPortGroup** object if the channel is created for port groups.

6. **BizTalkPortGroup** (if used)
   - The **BizTalkPortGroup** object requires the **BizTalkPort** object.

Security

When accessing or creating objects in the BizTalk Messaging Configuration object model, the script or application must be run in the context of a user account in the BizTalk Server Administrators group. The BizTalk Server Administrators group is created when BizTalk Server 2000 is installed. Additional users can be added to this group as necessary. For additional information, see "Add users to the BizTalk Server Administrators group" in Chapter 11, "Administering Servers and Applications."

Channels

The **BizTalkChannel** object contains the configuration information related to the source entity and its binding with a **BizTalkPort** object. When BizTalk Server 2000 receives a document, a specific **BizTalkChannel** object, along with the properties configured in its associated **BizTalkPort** object or an associated **BizTalkPort** object within a **BizTalkPortGroup** object, directs the server through the steps necessary to process that document. Note that multiple channels might be bound to the same **BizTalkPort** object. This represents multiple source entities that exchange documents with the same destination.

The **BizTalkChannel** object identifies the map used for document transformation if the type of the input **BizTalkDocument** object is different from the type of the output **BizTalkDocument** object. It also points to the specification that contains fields for document tracking and selects the type of logging desired.

Identification

BizTalk Server 2000 determines the appropriate **BizTalkChannel** object for processing the input document by one of the following methods:

- The source organization identifier, qualifier, and value, the destination organization identifier, qualifier, and value, and the name of the **BizTalkDocument** object are parameters of the **Submit** or the **SubmitSync** method of the **Interchange** object.

- The source and destination organization identifiers, qualifiers, and values, and the name of the **BizTalkDocument** object are specified in the header fields of the document instance.

- The name of the **BizTalkChannel** object is a parameter of the **Submit** or the **SubmitSync** method call.

When BizTalk Server 2000 receives a document, it first identifies all **BizTalkChannel** objects that support the specified **BizTalkDocument** object. The server then looks up each **BizTalkPort** object and determines if the **SourceOrganization** and **DestinationOrganization** properties identify the source and destination **BizTalkOrganization** objects specified by the organization identifiers in the document or in the parameters of **Submit** when the document is submitted. This includes any open messaging ports that match either the specified source organization or the destination organization.

This identification process can be bypassed by specifying the name of a **BizTalkChannel** object to be used as a parameter of **Submit** or **SubmitSync**.

Document Processing

When BizTalk Server 2000 identifies a **BizTalkChannel** object, the server processes this object, which directs the server in the steps to process the document. To direct the server, the **BizTalkChannel** object follows its own rules and the rules of its associated **BizTalkPort** object.

An input **BizTalkDocument** object is related to an output **BizTalkDocument** object by a **BizTalkChannel** object. The **BizTalkPort** object must be created before an associated **BizTalkChannel** object can be created.

When BizTalk Server 2000 processes a **BizTalkChannel** object, the server calls upon each associated **BizTalkPort** object to provide the document processing rules needed by the server. The rules set by the properties of the **BizTalkChannel** object direct the server in the initial steps of document processing, such as determining which input and output **BizTalkDocument** object to use, which map file to use, and what fields to track. Once a document is in its final output format, the properties of the **BizTalkPort** object direct the server in the steps to prepare and transport the document according to the rules agreed to by the source and destination organizations.

When a document is submitted, the server can identify multiple **BizTalkPort** and **BizTalkChannel** objects that match the source organization, the destination organization, and the specified **BizTalkDocument** object. Therefore, it is possible for one input document to generate multiple output documents. It is also possible for each output document to be transmitted to a different location by using different transport properties in the matching **BizTalkPort** objects, and for each output document instance to include a different subset of data from the original input document by using different map files.

Configuring

A **BizTalkChannel** object consists of the internal document processing data for the specified input and output **BizTalkDocument** objects. To be fully configured, a **BizTalkChannel** object must have one complete **BizTalkPort** object identified by its **Port** property. Input and output **BizTalkDocument** objects must be specified. After the **InputDocument** and **OutputDocument** properties are selected for use in this **BizTalkChannel** object, a **BizTalkPort** object or a **BizTalkPortGroup** object must be selected.

The name of a **BizTalkChannel** object must be unique across the database for all objects of its type.

The following properties are required before a **BizTalkChannel** object can be saved:

- **InputDocument**
- **Port** (or **PortGroup**)
- **OutputDocument**
- **Name**

Once a **BizTalkChannel** object has been created or saved, only the following properties can be changed:

- **Comments**
- **ControlNumberValue**
- **MapReference**
- **Name**
- **TrackFields**

Channel Filtering

Channel filtering enables the user to build a filtering expression to select a **BizTalkChannel** object for processing a document instance. The server uses these expressions to select the correct **BizTalkChannel** object. The **Expression** property contains an XPath expression that evaluates to a Boolean value. If the expression evaluates to true, the channel is used to process the document. Otherwise, the channel is not invoked to process the document.

XPath expressions can be used to obtain the value of a specific element, attribute, or collection of these items within an XML document. Consider the following XML document:

```
<INVOICE>
    <DATE>12/31/2000</DATE>
    <BILLTO>Vigor Airlines</BILLTO>
    <SUMMARY>
        <ITEM PARTNUMBER="10001" QUANTITY="10"/>
        <ITEM PARTNUMBER="20002" QUANTITY="20"/>
        <TOTAL VALUE="550"/>
    </SUMMARY>
</INVOICE>
```

Based on this document, the following XPath expression can be created to ensure that this channel only processes invoices that exceed $500:

```
myChannel.Expression = "/INVOICE/SUMMARY/TOTAL[@VALUE>""500""]"
```

In this example, the channel would process the XML document instance because the total is greater than $500. For more information about XPath expressions, go to the MSDN Online Library Web site (msdn.microsoft.com/library/default.asp) and search for XPath.

Note

- You can use BizTalk Messaging Manager to generate XPath channel filtering expressions. For more information, see "To add a channel filtering expression" earlier in this chapter.

Document Storage

You can choose how to log the activity of a document instance using the **BizTalkLoggingInfo** object. The default is to log the document in its native form.

For document storage, you have the options shown in the table on the following page.

Property	Description
All properties empty	Store no copies of the document.
LogNativeInputDocument	Store input native format (default setting).
LogNativeOutputDocument	Store output native format.
LogXMLInputDocument	Store input XML format.
LogXMLOutputDocument	Store output interim (XML) format.
Any combination of these choices	Store the options as described above.

✐ Note

- There is a size limit for interchanges and documents that use logging, which if exceeded greatly affects the performance of BizTalk Server. For more information about the size limit, see "Interchange and document size limit" in Chapter 11, "Administering Servers and Applications."

Document Tracking

A **BizTalkChannel** object points to the specification that contains fields to track the instance of the document. The designated fields are logged to the Tracking database for each instance of a document that is processed. When you assign an input **BizTalkDocument** object for a **BizTalkChannel** object, you can designate fields to track within the document on this channel.

When BizTalk Server 2000 runs a **BizTalkChannel** object, it uses the input **BizTalkDocument** object to process an input document. The fields that you have designated for tracking are captured and logged for each instance of that document. Any fields designated for tracking in the output **BizTalkDocument** object of the associated **BizTalkChannel** object are ignored. To retrieve the information that is tracked during document processing, use the methods of the **BTSDocTracking** object.

By logging important data from the input documents that are processed, you can track and analyze detailed information about your operation. For example, an invoice-total field can be logged for every invoice that is sent to your trading partners. You can then determine the total dollar amount of invoices sent to all trading partners over time or determine the total dollar amount of invoices to each individual trading partner.

For additional information about document tracking, see "Understanding the Tracking Database Schema" in Chapter 13, "Tracking Documents."

Messaging Ports

Conceptually, a messaging port is a set of rules that trading partner organizations accept for sending documents to one another. It includes information regarding the destination, transport type, security, and envelope. It identifies the source and destination **BizTalkOrganization** objects and the source and destination aliases. It also identifies any applications associated with the organization, if applicable.

A **BizTalkPort** object identifies a specific destination organization unless it is designated as an open messaging port, in which case the destination organization is not specified. For open messaging ports, the **BizTalkPort** object is valid only if the associated document or the parameters on the **Submit** or the **SubmitSync** method of the **Interchange** object contain the destination transport and address information.

The **BizTalkPort** object also identifies delimiter definitions and the EDI interchange control number. Delimiters are used to separate the records and fields of the envelope and the documents within the envelope. An interchange control number is used to identify and track documents that are sent using the envelope. The interchange control number is incremented with each use of the envelope at run time.

A **BizTalkPort** object also identifies the encoding, encryption, and signature type, if required.

✎ Note

- Once a **BizTalkPort** object has been created and saved, the destination organization and the openness associated with the endpoint cannot be changed.

Port Groups

The **BizTalkPortGroup** object configures a group of complete **BizTalkPort** objects for sending the same document to a group of trading partners. For example, you can use this when you want to send a document, such as a catalog, a price list, or a newsletter, that contains identical data to a group of trading partners. One document is sent to a list of partners by calling a single **Submit** method on the **Interchange** object.

There must be at least one **BizTalkPort** object contained by the **BizTalkPortGroup** object. You can add or remove **BizTalkPort** objects to or from a **BizTalkPortGroup** by calling the **AddPort** or the **RemovePort** method.

A **BizTalkPortGroup** object must be associated with at least one **BizTalkChannel** object. After the port group has been created, associate a channel with the port group by using the **PortGroup** property available on the **BizTalkChannel** object. When BizTalk Server 2000 invokes a channel related to a port group, it invokes only the channel that is associated with the port group to process the data. None of the channels that are associated with the individual ports in the port group are invoked. The server uses the properties of each port successively to transport the data to the destinations specified in the ports.

✎ Notes

- Open messaging ports cannot be added to a port group.

- BizTalk Messaging Manager refers to port groups as distribution lists.

Openness

The **Openness** property of the **BizTalkEndPoint** object determines whether the messaging port or channel is open. An open **BizTalkPort** object is a messaging port without a specified destination. An open **BizTalkChannel** object is a channel without a specified source. The missing information for an open messaging port or channel must be supplied by the associated document or by the parameters on the **Submit** or the **SubmitSync** method of the **Interchange** object.

If an open channel is specified using **BIZTALK_OPENNESS_TYPE_EX_SOURCE** or an open messaging port is specified using **BIZTALK_OPENNESS_TYPE_EX_DESTINATION**, the **Type**, **Reference**, and **Store** properties cannot be specified on the **BizTalkEndPoint** object.

Note

- If an open messaging port is used with the SMTP transport type, the value specified for the **BizTalkOrganization** identifier Reliable Messaging Acknowledgement SMTP From Address is used as the From address.

Organizations

BizTalkOrganization objects serve as the source or destination for the exchange of electronic data. An organization can represent an external trading partner, your own company, or a business unit of a trading partner or your company. The home organization can designate a source application in a channel or a destination application in a messaging port.

Applications are properties of the home organization. Applications can be designated as a source application in a **BizTalkChannel** object or as a destination application in a **BizTalkPort** object.

Aliases

An alias is an organization identifier for the **BizTalkOrganization** object. There must always be one and only one default alias for a **BizTalkOrganization** object, but it can have multiple aliases. An alias is autogenerated for each **BizTalkOrganization** object. The default and the autogenerated alias cannot be removed.

For more information, see "To create organizations" earlier in this chapter.

Document Definitions

The **BizTalkDocument** object describes and identifies the document specification used to describe the document sent or received. The document specification defines the structure of a document, as well as any validation rules and descriptions for the individual elements of the document specification. The **BizTalkDocument** object includes the version and type of the specification and, optionally, a reference to the Web Distributed Authoring and Versioning

(WebDAV) location of the specification. For more information about document specifications, see Chapter 5, "Creating Specifications."

✎ Notes

- The document **Content** and **Namespace** properties are not valid until you set the **Reference** property.

- When creating a new **BizTalkDocument** object that uses a namespace that is already registered with BizTalk Server, the new document inherits the **Reference** property of that namespace. The namespace must be unique (case insensitive) for a new **Reference** to be created.

The **BizTalkDocument** object also contains the electronic data interchange (EDI) selection criteria by which BizTalk Server 2000 extracts information from the functional group header of the document to identify this object when the name of the **BizTalkDocument** object is not available.

A **BizTalkDocument** object points to the specification that contains fields to track the instance of the document. The designated fields are logged to the Tracking database for each document that is processed.

Selection criteria

For some EDI input interchanges, documents are contained within functional group envelopes. When BizTalk Server 2000 processes such documents, it cannot obtain the name of the **BizTalkDocument** object from a field within each document. Also, because there are multiple types of documents involved, a single name cannot be specified as a parameter of the **Submit** method of the **Interchange** object. In such cases, the server can locate document-related data within the functional group header (for example, in the GS header of an X12 interchange). By comparing this data to matching selection criteria specified in the **PropertySet** property on the **BizTalkDocument** object, the server can uniquely identify a **BizTalkDocument** object. Once the **BizTalkDocument** object is identified, the server can obtain the name and then identify and instantiate the appropriate **BizTalkChannel** object.

Selection criteria also help BizTalk Server 2000 create the header of the EDI document when it is output.

Global tracking

A **BizTalkDocument** object points to the specification from which fields can be selected for tracking. The designated fields in the input document specification are tracked for each document that is processed using that specification. Any fields designated for tracking in the output document specification are ignored. If a **BizTalkChannel** object that specifies tracking fields is used with an input document specification containing fields designated for tracking, only the fields specified by the channel are used for tracking.

By logging important data from the input documents that are processed, you can track and analyze detailed information about your operation. For example, an invoice-total field can be logged for every invoice that is sent to your trading partners. You can then determine the total dollar amount of invoices sent to all trading partners over time or determine the total dollar amount of invoices to each individual trading partner.

Envelopes

The **BizTalkEnvelope** object consists of two pieces of information:

- The type of envelope is specified in the **Format** property. The document **Type** should match the envelope **Format** for "flatfile", "custom xml", "x12", "edifact", and "reliable" document types.

- The actual envelope file used is specified in the **Reference** property.

Input document envelopes

An envelope is required if the input document **Type** is "flatfile" because the envelope contains information about how to parse the document into XML and which parser should process the document. Input "flatfile" documents without an envelope fail to be processed. For all other input document types, an envelope is optional.

Output document envelopes

Envelopes are used to wrap an output document instance that has been transformed into the native format. The envelope used with an output document is specified on the **BizTalkPort** object. An envelope is required if the output document **Type** is "x12" or "edifact". However, the **Reference** property is ignored for these format types because indicating that the documents are X12 or EDIFACT is sufficient to serialize the document. For output documents with a **Type** of "custom xml", the **Reference** property is used if specified. If the **Reference** property is not specified, "custom xml" documents are submitted for processing in the transformed XML format.

Notes

- Multiple **BizTalkPort** objects can refer to an envelope.

- The envelope **Content** and **Namespace** properties are not valid until you set the **Reference** property.

- When creating a new **BizTalkEnvelope** object that uses a namespace that is already registered with BizTalk Server, the new document inherits the **Reference** property of that namespace. The namespace must be unique (case insensitive) for a new **Reference** to be created.

Object Model Reference for Visual Basic

This section provides reference information about interfaces used by Microsoft BizTalk Server 2000 for programming with Microsoft Visual Basic. Reference information is provided for all interfaces, objects, methods, properties, and enumerations exposed for accessing the BizTalk Messaging Configuration object model. For a complete listing of error messages, see Appendix A, "Error Messages."

IBizTalkBase Object

The **IBizTalkBase** class defines common methods and properties that are implemented by the following objects:

- **BizTalkChannel**
- **BizTalkDocument**
- **BizTalkEnvelope**
- **BizTalkOrganization**
- **BizTalkPort**
- **BizTalkPortGroup**

 Note

The methods and properties of this object are always invoked on the objects listed above, rather than by creating an actual **BizTalkBase** object.

The properties of the **BizTalkBase** object are shown in the following table.

Property	Type	Description
DateModified	**BSTR**	Date and time at which the information in the object was created or last modified. This is a read-only property.
Handle	**long**	Handle to the object. This is a read-only property.
Name	**BSTR**	Name of the object.

The methods of the **BizTalkBase** object are shown in the following table.

Method	Description
Clear	Clears the object in memory. All the member variables of the object in memory are initialized to their default values.
Create	Creates a new object in the database.
Load	Loads a specified object in memory.
LoadByName	Loads a specified object by name in memory.
Remove	Removes the object from the database.
Save	Saves the object in the database.

Requirements

Windows NT/2000: Requires Windows 2000 SP1 or later
Library: Use Microsoft BizTalk Server Configuration Objects 1.0 Type Library
(BizTalkObjectModel.dll)

IBizTalkBase.Clear Method

The **Clear** method clears the object in memory. All member variables of the object in memory are initialized to their default values.

Syntax

object.**Clear**

Parameters

None

Return Values

None

Error Value

If an error is raised, **Err.Number** is set to one of the values documented in Appendix A, "Error Messages."

Applies To

This method is supported by the following objects:

- **BizTalkChannel**
- **BizTalkDocument**
- **BizTalkEnvelope**
- **BizTalkOrganization**
- **BizTalkPort**
- **BizTalkPortGroup**

Requirements

Windows NT/2000: Requires Windows 2000 SP1 or later
Library: Use Microsoft BizTalk Server Configuration Objects 1.0 Type Library
(BizTalkObjectModel.dll)

IBizTalkBase.Create Method

The **Create** method creates a new object in the database.

Syntax

object.**Create**

Parameters

None

Return Values

This method returns a **Long** that contains the handle to the object.

Error Value

If an error is raised, **Err.Number** is set to one of the values documented in Appendix A, "Error Messages."

Applies To

This method is supported by the following objects:

- **BizTalkChannel**
- **BizTalkDocument**
- **BizTalkEnvelope**
- **BizTalkOrganization**
- **BizTalkPortBizTalkPortGroup**

Remarks

The **Name** property must be set before calling this method. **Name** must be unique across the database for each object type. **Create** updates the **DateModified** property.

When creating any object that refers to an XML document specification or map located outside your local domain, you might receive an error. If an error occurs, download and configure the WinHTTP proxy utility. To download this utility, go to the MSDN Online Downloads Web site (msdn.microsoft.com/downloads/default.asp) and browse to the WinHTTP Proxy Configuration Utility page, which is located in the XML chapter of the Web Development book.

Requirements

Windows NT/2000: Requires Windows 2000 SP1 or later
Library: Use Microsoft BizTalk Server Configuration Objects 1.0 Type Library
(BizTalkObjectModel.dll)

IBizTalkBase.DateModified Property

The **DateModified** property contains the date and time at which the information in the object was created or last modified.

Syntax

object.**DateModified**

Parameters

None

Return Values

This property returns a **String** that contains the date modified.

Error Value

If an error is raised, **Err.Number** is set to one of the values documented in Appendix A, "Error Messages."

Applies To

This property is supported by the following objects:

- **BizTalkChannel**
- **BizTalkDocument**
- **BizTalkEnvelope**
- **BizTalkOrganization**
- **BizTalkPort**
- **BizTalkPortGroup**

Remarks

This is a read-only property. The format for the value of this property string is *yyyy-mm-dd hh:mm:ss*. The time is in coordinated universal time (UTC). The server sets this property when the **Create** or the **Save** method is called for the object.

Requirements

Windows NT/2000: Requires Windows 2000 SP1 or later
Library: Use Microsoft BizTalk Server Configuration Objects 1.0 Type Library (BizTalkObjectModel.dll)

IBizTalkBase.Handle Property

The **Handle** property contains the handle to the object.

Syntax

object.**Handle**

Parameters

None

Return Values

This property returns a **Long** that contains the handle to the object.

Error Value

If an error is raised, **Err.Number** is set to one of the values documented in Appendix A, "Error Messages."

Applies To

This property is supported by the following objects:

- **BizTalkChannel**
- **BizTalkDocument**
- **BizTalkEnvelope**
- **BizTalkOrganization**
- **BizTalkPort**
- **BizTalkPortGroup**

Remarks

This is a read-only property.

Requirements

Windows NT/2000: Requires Windows 2000 SP1 or later
Library: Use Microsoft BizTalk Server Configuration Objects 1.0 Type Library
(BizTalkObjectModel.dll)

IBizTalkBase.Load Method

The **Load** method loads an object in memory.

Syntax

object.**Load**(*lBiztalkObjectHandle* **As Long**)

Parameters

lBiztalkObjectHandle
    Long that contains the handle to the object to load.

Return Values

None

Error Value

If an error is raised, **Err.Number** is set to one of the values documented in Appendix A, "Error Messages."

Applies To

This method is supported by the following objects:

- **BizTalkChannel**
- **BizTalkDocument**
- **BizTalkEnvelope**
- **BizTalkOrganization**
- **BizTalkPort**
- **BizTalkPortGroup**

Remarks

Load calls the **Clear** method internally before loading the object.

Requirements

Windows NT/2000: Requires Windows 2000 SP1 or later
Library: Use Microsoft BizTalk Server Configuration Objects 1.0 Type Library
(BizTalkObjectModel.dll)

IBizTalkBase.LoadByName Method

The **LoadByName** method loads an object by name in memory.

Syntax

object.**LoadByName**(*strName* **As String**)

Parameters

strName
   String that contains the name.

Return Values

None

Error Value

If an error is raised, **Err.Number** is set to one of the values documented in Appendix A, "Error Messages."

Applies To

This method is supported by the following objects:

- **BizTalkChannel**
- **BizTalkDocument**
- **BizTalkEnvelope**
- **BizTalkOrganization**
- **BizTalkPort**
- **BizTalkPortGroup**

Remarks

LoadByName calls the **Clear** method internally before loading the object.

Names have a maximum length of 64 characters.

Requirements

Windows NT/2000: Requires Windows 2000 SP1 or later
Library: Use Microsoft BizTalk Server Configuration Objects 1.0 Type Library
(BizTalkObjectModel.dll)

IBizTalkBase.Name Property

The **Name** property contains the name of the object.

Syntax

object.**Name**

Parameters

None

Return Values

This property returns a **String** that contains the name.

Error Value

If an error is raised, **Err.Number** is set to one of the values documented in Appendix A, "Error Messages."

Applies To

This property is supported by the following objects:

- **BizTalkChannel**
- **BizTalkDocument**
- **BizTalkEnvelope**
- **BizTalkOrganization**
- **BizTalkPort**
- **BizTalkPortGroup**

Remarks

The server requires the **Name** property. It must be set before calling the **Create** or the **Save** method for the object. **Name** must be unique across a database for each object type and must be at least one character long. Names have a maximum length of 64 characters.

The following table lists names reserved for use by BizTalk Server.

Name	Object type
Reliable Message Acknowledgement Port	**IBizTalkPort**
Reliable Message Acknowledgement Channel	**IBizTalkChannel**
BizTalk Canonical Receipt	**IBizTalkDocument**
Reliable Messaging Acknowledgement	**IBizTalkDocument**
Reliable Messaging Acknowledgement SMTP From Address	**IBizTalkOrganization** alias
Home Organization	**IBizTalkOrganization**

Requirements

Windows NT/2000: Requires Windows 2000 SP1 or later
Library: Use Microsoft BizTalk Server Configuration Objects 1.0 Type Library
(BizTalkObjectModel.dll)

IBizTalkBase.Remove Method

The **Remove** method removes the object from the database.

Syntax

object.**Remove**

Parameters

None

Return Values

None

Error Value

If an error is raised, **Err.Number** is set to one of the values documented in Appendix A,
"Error Messages."

Applies To

This method is supported by the following objects:

- **BizTalkChannel**
- **BizTalkDocument**
- **BizTalkEnvelope**

- **BizTalkOrganization**
- **BizTalkPort**
- **BizTalkPortGroup**

Remarks

The object cannot be removed if any other object refers to it.

A **BizTalkOrganization** object cannot be removed if it is the default organization. Before it can be removed, the **IsDefault** property must be set to **False**, and another organization must have the **IsDefault** property set to **True**.

Requirements

Windows NT/2000: Requires Windows 2000 SP1 or later
Library: Use Microsoft BizTalk Server Configuration Objects 1.0 Type Library
(BizTalkObjectModel.dll)

IBizTalkBase.Save Method

The **Save** method saves the object in the database.

Syntax

object.**Save**

Parameters

None

Return Values

None

Error Value

If an error is raised, **Err.Number** is set to one of the values documented in Appendix A, "Error Messages."

Applies To

This method is supported by the following objects:

- **BizTalkChannel**
- **BizTalkDocument**
- **BizTalkEnvelope**
- **BizTalkOrganization**
- **BizTalkPort**
- **BizTalkPortGroup**

Remarks

The **Save** method updates the **DateModified** property.

When saving any object that refers to an XML document specification or map located outside your local domain, you might receive an error. If an error occurs, download and configure the WinHTTP proxy utility. To download this utility, go to the MSDN Online Downloads Web site (msdn.microsoft.com/downloads/default.asp) and browse to the WinHTTP Proxy Configuration Utility page, which is located in the XML chapter of the Web Development book.

Requirements

Windows NT/2000: Requires Windows 2000 SP1 or later
Library: Use Microsoft BizTalk Server Configuration Objects 1.0 Type Library (BizTalkObjectModel.dll)

BizTalkCertificateInfo Object

Use this object to configure a certificate associated with a **BizTalkPort** or a **BizTalkChannel** object.

The properties of the **BizTalkCertificateInfo** object are shown in the following table.

Property	Type	Description
Name	**BSTR**	Name of the certificate. This is a read-only property.
Reference	**BSTR**	Reference to the certificate in the certificate store.
Store	**BIZTALK_STORE_TYPE**	Store type of the certificate.
Usage	**BIZTALK_USAGE_TYPE**	Type of use for the certificate. This is a read-only property.

Remarks

This object is automatically created when a **BizTalkPort** or a **BizTalkChannel** object is instantiated with the **CreatePort** or the **CreateChannel** method of the **BizTalkConfig** object.

For output documents, access the **BizTalkCertificateInfo** object by using the **EncryptionCertificateInfo** property of the **BizTalkPort** object. For input documents, access the **BizTalkCertificateInfo** object by using the **SignatureCertificateInfo**, **VerifySignatureCertificateInfo**, or **DecryptionCertificateInfo** property of the **BizTalkChannel** object. To obtain the set of all existing **BizTalkCertificateInfo** objects, use the **Certificates** property of the **BizTalkConfig** object.

⬛ Note

- All certificates are stored in the local computer store. To configure certificates for the S/MIME components, the script or application accessing the object model must be run in the context of a user account in the BizTalk Server Administrators group.

Requirements

Windows NT/2000: Requires Windows 2000 SP1 or later
Library: Use Microsoft BizTalk Server Configuration Objects 1.0 Type Library
(BizTalkObjectModel.dll)

BizTalkCertificateInfo.Name Property

The **Name** property contains the name of the certificate.

Syntax

object.**Name**

Parameters

None

Return Values

This property returns a **String** that contains the name.

Error Value

If an error is raised, **Err.Number** is set to one of the values documented in Appendix A, "Error Messages."

Remarks

This is a read-only property.

Requirements

Windows NT/2000: Requires Windows 2000 SP1 or later
Library: Use Microsoft BizTalk Server Configuration Objects 1.0 Type Library
(BizTalkObjectModel.dll)

BizTalkCertificateInfo.Reference Property

The **Reference** property contains a reference to the certificate in the certificate store.

Syntax

object.**Reference**

Parameters

None

Return Values

This property returns a **String** that contains the certificate reference.

Error Value

If an error is raised, **Err.Number** is set to one of the values documented in Appendix A, "Error Messages."

Remarks

A reference to a certificate should be obtained by using the **Certificates** property on the **BizTalkConfig** object.

Requirements

Windows NT/2000: Requires Windows 2000 SP1 or later
Library: Use Microsoft BizTalk Server Configuration Objects 1.0 Type Library (BizTalkObjectModel.dll)

BizTalkCertificateInfo.Store Property

The **Store** property contains the store type for the certificate.

Syntax

object.**Store**

Parameters

None

Return Values

This property returns an enumeration value. Valid values are from the **BIZTALK_STORE_TYPE** enumeration.

Error Value

If an error is raised, **Err.Number** is set to one of the values documented in Appendix A, "Error Messages."

Remarks

The store, which contains the certificate, is determined by the use of the certificate as follows:

Certificate type	Store
Decryption	MY
Encryption	BIZTALK
Signature	MY
Verify signature	BIZTALK

Requirements

Windows NT/2000: Requires Windows 2000 SP1 or later
Library: Use Microsoft BizTalk Server Configuration Objects 1.0 Type Library (BizTalkObjectModel.dll)

BizTalkCertificateInfo.Usage Property

The **Usage** property contains the type of use for the certificate.

Syntax

object.**Usage**

Parameters

None

Return Values

This property returns an enumeration value. Valid values are from the **BIZTALK_USAGE_TYPE** enumeration.

Error Value

If an error is raised, **Err.Number** is set to one of the values documented in Appendix A, "Error Messages."

Remarks

This is a read-only property.

Requirements

Windows NT/2000: Requires Windows 2000 SP1 or later
Library: Use Microsoft BizTalk Server Configuration Objects 1.0 Type Library
(BizTalkObjectModel.dll)

BizTalkChannel Object

Use the methods and properties of the **BizTalkChannel** object to configure a channel for
processing documents.

The properties of the **BizTalkChannel** object are shown in the following table.

Property	Type	Description
Comments	BSTR	User comments for the object.
ControlNumberValue	BSTR	Value of the group control number.
DateModified	BSTR	Date and time at which the information in the object was created or last modified. This is a read-only property obtained from the **BizTalkBase** object.
DecryptionCertificateInfo	IDispatch	Information about the certificate that decrypts the input document.
ExpectReceiptTimeout	long	Time, in minutes, in which to expect the receipt for the current document before treating the document as expired.
Expression	BSTR	Complete set of equations that filter the selection of the object.
Handle	long	Identifier of the object. This is a read-only property obtained from the **BizTalkBase** object.
InputDocument	long	Handle to the input **BizTalkDocument** object. This is a required property.
IsReceiptChannel	VARIANT_ BOOL	Flag that indicates whether the object is a receipt channel.
LoggingInfo	IDispatch	Information about logging.
MapContent	BSTR	Contents of the map that provide instructions on how the input document in the format used by the source organization is to be rendered in the format used by the destination organization, if different. This is a read-only property.

Property	Type	Description
MapReference	BSTR	Full Web Distributed Authoring and Versioning (WebDAV) URL of the map that provides instructions on how the input document in the format used by the source organization is to be rendered in the format used by the destination organization, if different. This is a required property if the **InputDocument** property is different from the **OutputDocument** property.
Name	BSTR	Name of the object. This is a required property obtained from the **BizTalkBase** object.
OutputDocument	long	Handle to the output **BizTalkDocument** object. This is a required property.
Port	long	Associated **BizTalkPort** object. Either the **Port** or the **PortGroup** property must be specified.
PortGroup	long	Associated **BizTalkPortGroup** object. Either the **Port** or the **PortGroup** property must be specified.
ReceiptChannel	long	Handle to the receipt channel for this object.
RetryCount	long	Number of times to retry submitting a document when there is a failure to connect to the destination.
RetryInterval	long	Interval between attempts to resubmit a document when there is a failure to connect to the destination. This value is specified in minutes.
SignatureCertificateInfo	IDispatch	Information about the certificate that signs the output document.
SourceEndpoint	IDispatch	Information about the source.
TrackFields	IDispatch	Dictionary object that stores additional custom tracking fields used to track interchange data for the **BizTalkDocument** object for the associated **BizTalkChannel** object.
VerifySignatureCertificateInfo	IDispatch	Information about the certificate that verifies the signature of the input document.

The methods of the **BizTalkChannel** object are shown in the following table.

Method	Description
Clear	Clears the object in memory. All member variables of the object in memory are initialized to their default values. This method is obtained from the **BizTalkBase** object.
Create	Creates a new object in the database. This method is obtained from the **BizTalkBase** object.
GetConfigComponent	Reads the CLSID of the component associated with the **BizTalkPort** object.
GetConfigData	Gets the configuration associated with the specified **BizTalkPort** object.
Load	Loads an object in memory. This method is obtained from the **BizTalkBase** object.
LoadByName	Loads an object by name in memory. This method is obtained from the **BizTalkBase** object.
Remove	Removes the object. This method is obtained from the **BizTalkBase** object.
Save	Saves the object to the database. This method is obtained from the **BizTalkBase** object.
SetConfigComponent	Sets the CLSID of the component associated with the **BizTalkPort** object.
SetConfigData	Sets the configuration information for the associated **BizTalkPort** object.

Remarks

A **BizTalkChannel** object requires an associated complete **BizTalkPort** object. One or more **BizTalkChannel** objects can be associated with a **BizTalkPort** object. A **BizTalkChannel** object can be associated with only one input **BizTalkDocument** object and one output **BizTalkDocument** object; however, a **BizTalkDocument** object can be associated with more than one **BizTalkChannel** object.

Requirements

Windows NT/2000: Requires Windows 2000 SP1 or later
Library: Use Microsoft BizTalk Server Configuration Objects 1.0 Type Library
(BizTalkObjectModel.dll)

BizTalkChannel.Comments Property

The **Comments** property contains the user comments for the object.

Syntax

object.**Comments**

Parameters

None

Return Values

This property returns a **String** that contains the comments.

Error Value

If an error is raised, **Err.Number** is set to one of the values documented in Appendix A, "Error Messages."

Requirements

Windows NT/2000: Requires Windows 2000 SP1 or later
Library: Use Microsoft BizTalk Server Configuration Objects 1.0 Type Library (BizTalkObjectModel.dll)

BizTalkChannel.ControlNumberValue Property

The **ControlNumberValue** property contains the value of the group control number.

Syntax

object.**ControlNumberValue**

Parameters

None

Return Values

This method returns a **String** that contains the control number.

Error Value

If an error is raised, **Err.Number** is set to one of the values documented in Appendix A, "Error Messages."

Remarks

The **ControlNumberValue** property must contain a value between 1 and 999999999.

If the **Format** property of the **BizTalkEnvelope** object for the associated **BizTalkPort** object is set to X12, EDIFACT, or Custom, this property is required.

Requirements

Windows NT/2000: Requires Windows 2000 SP1 or later
Library: Use Microsoft BizTalk Server Configuration Objects 1.0 Type Library (BizTalkObjectModel.dll)

BizTalkChannel.DecryptionCertificateInfo Property

The **DecryptionCertificateInfo** property contains information about the certificate that decrypts the input document. This information includes the **Name**, **Reference**, **Store**, and **Usage** properties and is created and stored in memory in the **BizTalkCertificateInfo** object.

Syntax

object.**DecryptionCertificateInfo**

Parameters

None

Return Values

This property returns an **Object** that contains the certificate information.

Error Value

If an error is raised, **Err.Number** is set to one of the values documented in Appendix A, "Error Messages."

Requirements

Windows NT/2000: Requires Windows 2000 SP1 or later
Library: Use Microsoft BizTalk Server Configuration Objects 1.0 Type Library (BizTalkObjectModel.dll)

BizTalkChannel.ExpectReceiptTimeout Property

The **ExpectReceiptTimeout** property contains the value of the time, in minutes, in which to expect the receipt for the current document before treating the document as expired.

Syntax

object.**ExpectReceiptTimeout**

Parameters

None

Return Values

This property returns a **Long** that contains the minutes.

Error Value

If an error is raised, **Err.Number** is set to one of the values documented in Appendix A, "Error Messages."

Requirements

Windows NT/2000: Requires Windows 2000 SP1 or later
Library: Use Microsoft BizTalk Server Configuration Objects 1.0 Type Library
(BizTalkObjectModel.dll)

BizTalkChannel.Expression Property

The **Expression** property contains an expression that filters the selection of the **BizTalkChannel** object. If the expression evaluates to true, the server selects the channel for processing the document.

Syntax

object.**Expression**

Parameters

None

Return Values

This method returns a **String** that contains the expression.

Error Value

If an error is raised, **Err.Number** is set to one of the values documented in Appendix A, "Error Messages."

Remarks

The XPath expression must be based on the input document specification set in the **InputDocument** property.

✎ Note

- If the specification field that you are using to create an expression has a Boolean data type, you cannot use the text strings "true" or "false" as the expression value. You must use a numerical value instead: "-1" for true and "0" for false. For example, to filter a channel so it processes only approved purchase orders, your expression might look like this:

```
Channel1.Expression = "/PORequest/Total[IsApproved = -1]"
```

This sample assumes that the input document specification contains a Total subelement with a Boolean IsApproved field.

Requirements

Windows NT/2000: Requires Windows 2000 SP1 or later
Library: Use Microsoft BizTalk Server Configuration Objects 1.0 Type Library (BizTalkObjectModel.dll)

BizTalkChannel.GetConfigComponent Method

The **GetConfigComponent** method retrieves the CLSID of the component associated with the **BizTalkPort** object.

Syntax

object.**GetConfigComponent**(_
    eConfigType **As BIZTALK_CONFIGDATA_TYPE**, _
    lPortHandle **As Long** _
)

Parameters

eConfigType
    Enumeration value. Valid values are from the **BIZTALK_CONFIGDATA_TYPE** enumeration.

lPortHandle
    Long that contains the handle.

Return Values

This method returns a **String** that contains the CLSID of the component.

Error Value

If an error is raised, **Err.Number** is set to one of the values documented in Appendix A, "Error Messages."

Remarks

If the *eConfigType* parameter is set to **BIZTALK_CONFIGDATA_TYPE_SIGNATURE** and the associated **BizTalkPort** object has both the **EncryptionType** and **SignatureType** properties set to S/MIME, this method returns an empty string ("").

Requirements

Windows NT/2000: Requires Windows 2000 SP1 or later
Library: Use Microsoft BizTalk Server Configuration Objects 1.0 Type Library (BizTalkObjectModel.dll)

BizTalkChannel.GetConfigData Method

The **GetConfigData** method gets the configuration associated with the specified **BizTalkPort** object.

Syntax

object.**GetConfigData**(_
   eConfigType **As BIZTALK_CONFIGDATA_TYPE**, _
   lPortHandle **As Long**, _
   pvarType **As Variant** _
)

Parameters

eConfigType
   [in] Enumeration value. Valid values are from the **BIZTALK_CONFIGDATA_TYPE** enumeration.

lPortHandle
   Long that identifies the handle to the associated **BizTalkPort** object.

pvarType
   Variant that contains the transport type.

Return Values

This method returns a **CDictionary** object that contains the primary transport configuration information.

Error Value

If an error is raised, **Err.Number** is set to one of the values documented in Appendix A, "Error Messages."

Remarks

The **Dictionary** object returned by this method has specific string qualifiers used for EDIFACT and X12. The following tables describe these strings.

EDIFACT

Qualifier string	Description
SerializerEdifact_SenderIntID	Interchange sender internal identification
SerializerEdifact_SenderIntSubID	Interchange sender internal subidentification
SerializerEdifact_RecipientIntID	Interchange recipient internal identification
SerializerEdifact_RecipientIntSubID	Interchange recipient internal subidentification
SerializerEdifact_RecipientRefPwd	Recipient reference/password
SerializerEdifact_RecipientRefPwdQual	Recipient reference/password qualifier
SerializerEdifact_ApplicationRef	Application reference
SerializerEdifact_ProcPriCode	Processing priority code
SerializerEdifact_AckRequest	Acknowledgment request
SerializerEdifact_AgreementID	Interchange agreement identifier
SerializerEdifact_TestInd	Test indicator
SerializerEdifact_UNACtrl	"Send UNA Always" or "Send UNA Only When Required"
SerializerEdifact_SyntaxID	Syntax identifier

X12

Qualifier string	Description
SerializerX12_AuthInfoQual	Authorization information qualifier
SerializerX12_AuthInfo	Authorization information
SerializerX12_SecInfoQual	Security information qualifier
SerializerX12_SecInfo	Security information
SerializerX12_CtrlStdID	Interchange control standards identifier
SerializerX12_CtrlVerNum	Interchange control version number
SerializerX12_AckRequired	Acknowledgment required
SerializerX12_UseInd	Usage indicator

✏ Note

- For more information about the EDIFACT standard, go to the United Nations Economic Commission for Europe Web site (www.unece.org).

- For more information about the X12 standard, go to the Data Interchange Standards Association Web site (www.disa.org).

If you override the transport properties of a **BizTalkPort** object with this method and then change the transport properties in that **BizTalkPort** object, you must call this method again.

If the *eConfigType* parameter is set to **BIZTALK_CONFIGDATA_TYPE_SIGNATURE** and the associated **BizTalkPort** object has both the **EncryptionType** and **SignatureType** properties set to S/MIME, this method returns an empty **Dictionary** object.

Requirements

Windows NT/2000: Requires Windows 2000 SP1 or later
Library: Use Microsoft BizTalk Server Configuration Objects 1.0 Type Library
(BizTalkObjectModel.dll)

BizTalkChannel.InputDocument Property

The **InputDocument** property contains the handle to the **BizTalkDocument** object that describes the input document specification.

Syntax

object.**InputDocument**

Parameters

None

Return Values

This property returns a **Long** that contains the handle to the input **BizTalkDocument** object.

Error Value

If an error is raised, **Err.Number** is set to one of the values documented in Appendix A, "Error Messages."

Remarks

This is a required property.

This property cannot be changed after the **Create** or the **Save** method is called.

Requirements

Windows NT/2000: Requires Windows 2000 SP1 or later
Library: Use Microsoft BizTalk Server Configuration Objects 1.0 Type Library
(BizTalkObjectModel.dll)

BizTalkChannel.IsReceiptChannel Property

The **IsReceiptChannel** property contains a flag that indicates whether the object is a receipt channel.

Syntax

object.**IsReceiptChannel**

Parameters

None

Return Values

This property returns a **Variant** that indicates whether the channel is used as a receipt channel.

Error Value

If an error is raised, **Err.Number** is set to one of the values documented in Appendix A, "Error Messages."

Requirements

Windows NT/2000: Requires Windows 2000 SP1 or later
Library: Use Microsoft BizTalk Server Configuration Objects 1.0 Type Library
(BizTalkObjectModel.dll)

BizTalkChannel.LoggingInfo Property

The **LoggingInfo** property contains information about logging the document. This information includes the **LogNativeInputDocument**, **LogNativeOutputDocument**, **LogXMLInputDocument**, and **LogXMLOutputDocument** properties and is created and stored in memory in the **BizTalkLoggingInfo** object.

Syntax

object.**LoggingInfo**

Parameters

None

Return Values

This property returns an **Object** that contains the logging fields.

Error Value

If an error is raised, **Err.Number** is set to one of the values documented in Appendix A, "Error Messages."

Requirements

Windows NT/2000: Requires Windows 2000 SP1 or later
Library: Use Microsoft BizTalk Server Configuration Objects 1.0 Type Library
(BizTalkObjectModel.dll)

BizTalkChannel.MapContent Property

The **MapContent** property contains the contents of the map that provide instructions on how the input document in the format used by the source organization is to be rendered in the format used by the destination organization, if different.

Syntax

object.**MapContent**

Parameters

None

Return Values

This property returns a **String** that contains the map contents.

Error Value

If an error is raised, **Err.Number** is set to one of the values documented in Appendix A, "Error Messages."

Remarks

This is a read-only property. The **Create** and **Save** methods copy the text of the map specified by the **MapReference** property to this string, if empty.

Once you have created or saved a **BizTalkChannel** object with **MapReference** set to a map, any changes you make to the content of the referenced map are not automatically updated on the referring **BizTalkChannel** object. To update the **BizTalkChannel** object that refers to the revised map, you must save the map, reset the **MapReference** property of the **BizTalkChannel** object to its current value, and then call **Save** on the referring **BizTalkChannel** object.

Requirements

Windows NT/2000: Requires Windows 2000 SP1 or later
Library: Use Microsoft BizTalk Server Configuration Objects 1.0 Type Library
(BizTalkObjectModel.dll)

BizTalkChannel.MapReference Property

The **MapReference** property contains the full Web Distributed Authoring and Versioning
(WebDAV) URL of the map that provides instructions about how the input document in the
format used by the source organization is to be rendered in the format used by the destination
organization, if different.

Syntax

object.**MapReference**

Parameters

None

Return Values

This property returns a **String** that contains the map name.

Error Value

If an error is raised, **Err.Number** is set to one of the values documented in Appendix A,
"Error Messages."

Remarks

This is a required property if the **InputDocument** property refers to a different document
specification than the **OutputDocument** property.

Once you have created or saved a **BizTalkChannel** object with **MapReference** set to a map,
any changes you make to the content of the referenced map are not automatically updated on
the referring **BizTalkChannel** object. To update the **BizTalkChannel** object that refers to the
revised map, you must save the map, reset the **MapReference** property of the
BizTalkChannel object to its current value, and then call **Save** on the referring
BizTalkChannel object.

Requirements

Windows NT/2000: Requires Windows 2000 SP1 or later
Library: Use Microsoft BizTalk Server Configuration Objects 1.0 Type Library
(BizTalkObjectModel.dll)

BizTalkChannel.OutputDocument Property

The **OutputDocument** property contains the handle to the **BizTalkDocument** object that describes the output document specification.

Syntax

object.**OutputDocument**

Parameters

None

Return Values

This property returns a **Long** that contains the handle to the output **BizTalkDocument** object.

Error Value

If an error is raised, **Err.Number** is set to one of the values documented in Appendix A, "Error Messages."

Remarks

This is a required property. This property cannot be changed after the **Create** or the **Save** method is called.

If the **Openness** property of the associated **BizTalkEndPoint** object is set to **BIZTALK_OPENNESS_TYPE_SOURCE**, the **InputDocument** property can identify an input **BizTalkDocument** object that has an X12 or an EDIFACT specification. If it does, however, **OutputDocument** must not identify a **BizTalkDocument** object that has an X12 or an EDIFACT specification.

If the **Openness** property of the associated **BizTalkEndPoint** object is set to **BIZTALK_OPENNESS_TYPE_DESTINATION**, the **OutputDocument** property for this **BizTalkChannel** object must not identify an output **BizTalkDocument** object that has an X12 or an EDIFACT specification.

Requirements

Windows NT/2000: Requires Windows 2000 SP1 or later
Library: Use Microsoft BizTalk Server Configuration Objects 1.0 Type Library (BizTalkObjectModel.dll)

BizTalkChannel.Port Property

The **Port** property contains the handle to the associated **BizTalkPort** object.

Syntax

object.**Port**

Parameters

None

Return Values

This property returns a **Long** that contains the handle to the **BizTalkPort** object.

Error Value

If an error is raised, **Err.Number** is set to one of the values documented in Appendix A, "Error Messages."

Remarks

The following constraints are enforced:

- Either the **Port** or the **PortGroup** property must be specified for a channel.

- This property cannot be changed after the **Create** or the **Save** method is called.

Requirements

Windows NT/2000: Requires Windows 2000 SP1 or later
Library: Use Microsoft BizTalk Server Configuration Objects 1.0 Type Library
(BizTalkObjectModel.dll)

BizTalkChannel.PortGroup Property

The **PortGroup** property contains the handle to the associated **BizTalkPortGroup** object.

Syntax

object.**PortGroup**

Parameters

None

Return Values

This property returns a **Long** that contains the handle to the associated **BizTalkPortGroup** object.

Error Value

If an error is raised, **Err.Number** is set to one of the values documented in Appendix A, "Error Messages."

Remarks

The following constraints are enforced:

- Either the **Port** property or **PortGroup** must be specified for a channel.

- This property cannot be changed after the **Create** or the **Save** method is called.

Requirements

Windows NT/2000: Requires Windows 2000 SP1 or later
Library: Use Microsoft BizTalk Server Configuration Objects 1.0 Type Library (BizTalkObjectModel.dll)

BizTalkChannel.ReceiptChannel Property

The **ReceiptChannel** property contains the handle to the receipt channel for this object.

Syntax

object.**ReceiptChannel**

Parameters

None

Return Values

This property returns a **Long** that contains the handle to the receipt channel.

Error Value

If an error is raised, **Err.Number** is set to one of the values documented in Appendix A, "Error Messages."

Remarks

A **BizTalkChannel** object can specify a receipt channel only if it is not a receipt channel itself. The channel specified as the receipt channel must have the **IsReceiptChannel** property set to TRUE. In addition, the receipt channel must use a messaging port with a **DestinationEndpoint** that is the same as the **SourceEndpoint** on the channel using the receipt channel. This allows the receipt channel to send a receipt to the original source of the document.

Requirements

Windows NT/2000: Requires Windows 2000 SP1 or later
Library: Use Microsoft BizTalk Server Configuration Objects 1.0 Type Library
(BizTalkObjectModel.dll)

BizTalkChannel.RetryCount Property

The **RetryCount** property specifies the number of times to retry submitting a document when a destination connection failure occurs.

Syntax

object.**RetryCount**

Parameters

None

Return Values

This property returns a **Long** that contains the number of retries.

Error Value

If an error is raised, **Err.Number** is set to one of the values documented in Appendix A, "Error Messages."

Remarks

The **RetryCount** property must contain a value between 0 and 999. The default value is 3 retries.

Requirements

Windows NT/2000: Requires Windows 2000 SP1 or later
Library: Use Microsoft BizTalk Server Configuration Objects 1.0 Type Library
(BizTalkObjectModel.dll)

BizTalkChannel.RetryInterval Property

The **RetryInterval** property specifies the amount of time, in minutes, between retry attempts when a destination connection failure occurs during document submission.

Syntax

object.**RetryInterval**

Parameters

None

Return Values

This property returns a **Long** that contains the retry interval, in minutes.

Error Value

If an error is raised, **Err.Number** is set to one of the values documented in Appendix A, "Error Messages."

Remarks

The **RetryInterval** property must contain a value between 1 and 63999. The default value is 5 minutes.

Requirements

Windows NT/2000: Requires Windows 2000 SP1 or later
Library: Use Microsoft BizTalk Server Configuration Objects 1.0 Type Library
(BizTalkObjectModel.dll)

BizTalkChannel.SetConfigComponent Method

The **SetConfigComponent** method sets the CLSID of the component associated with the **BizTalkPort** object.

Syntax

object.**SetConfigComponent**(_
  eConfigType **As BIZTALK_CONFIGDATA_TYPE**, _
  lPortHandle **As Long**, _
  strCLSID **As String** _
)

Parameters

eConfigType
Enumeration value. Valid values are from the **BIZTALK_CONFIGDATA_TYPE** enumeration. The **BIZTALK_CONFIGDATA_TYPE_PRIMARYTRANSPORT** and **BIZTALK_CONFIGDATA_TYPE_SECONDARYTRANSPORT** enumeration values cannot be used with this method.

lPortHandle
Long that contains the handle.

strCLSID
String that contains the CLSID of the component.

Return Values

None

Error Value

If an error is raised, **Err.Number** is set to one of the values documented in Appendix A, "Error Messages."

Requirements

Windows NT/2000: Requires Windows 2000 SP1 or later
Library: Use Microsoft BizTalk Server Configuration Objects 1.0 Type Library (BizTalkObjectModel.dll)

BizTalkChannel.SetConfigData Method

The **SetConfigData** method sets the configuration information for the **BizTalkPort** object.

Syntax

object.**SetConfigData**(_
  eConfigType **As BIZTALK_CONFIGDATA_TYPE**, _
  lConfigDataHandle **As Long**, _
  pConfigDataDisp **As Object** _
)

Parameters

eConfigType
Enumeration value. Valid values are from the **BIZTALK_CONFIGDATA_TYPE** enumeration.

lConfigDataHandle
Long that identifies the handle to the associated **BizTalkPort** object.

pConfigDataDisp
> **CDictionary** object that contains information about the component specified in the *eConfigType* parameter.

Return Values

None

Error Value

If an error is raised, **Err.Number** is set to one of the values documented in Appendix A, "Error Messages."

Remarks

The **Dictionary** object passed to this method has specific string qualifiers used for EDIFACT and X12. For a description of these qualifiers, see "BizTalk Channel.Get Config Data Method" earlier in this chapter.

When using the **BIZTALK_CONFIGDATA_TYPE_PRIMARYTRANSPORT** or **BIZTALK_CONFIGDATA_TYPE_SECONDARYTRANSPORT** enumeration value, the content of the transport dictionary varies according to the transport protocol used. The following tables list the transport dictionary fields for each protocol.

HTTP and HTTPS

Field name	Data type	Required	Description
URL	String	Yes	URL of the document destination.
ContentType	String	No	Value for the Content-Type HTTP/HTTPS property that appears in HTTP headers during transmission. The default value is an empty string ("").
ClientCert	String	No	Reference to the certificate used with SSL connections using HTTPS. The default value is an empty string ("").
ProxyName	String	No	URL of the proxy server used when sending documents outside a firewall.
ProxyPort	Integer	No	Port number used by the proxy server.
UseProxy	Boolean	No	Value that indicates whether the proxy server is used. The default value is **True**.

Local File

Field name	Data type	Required	Description
Filename	String	Yes	Name and path of the file to be created.
CopyMode	Integer	No	Value that indicates how the file should be written. Use a value of 0 for overwrite mode, a value of 1 for append mode, and a value of 2 to create a new file. The default value is append mode (1).
UserName	String	No	Windows NT user name needed to access a file share. The default value is an empty string ("").
Password	String	No	Windows NT user name needed to access a file share. The default value is an empty string ("").

Message Queuing

Field name	Data type	Required	Description
QueueName	String	Yes	Name of the Messaging Queue to which the document is sent.
MessageLabel	String	Yes	Value specified in the message label field on the queue.
Priority	Integer	No	Priority of the message placed in the queue. This must be a value between 0 and 7, where a higher value indicates a higher priority. The default value is 3.
AuthLevel	Integer	No	Value indicating whether the message needs to be authenticated using a digital signature. Use a value of 0 to bypass authentication. A value of 1 indicates that authentication will be used. The default value is 0.
Delivery	Integer	No	Value indicating how a message is delivered to a queue. Use a value of 1 to indicate that the message should be backed up until it is delivered to the queue. A value of 0 indicates that the message is only resident in memory. The default value is 0.

Requirements

Windows NT/2000: Requires Windows 2000 SP1 or later
Library: Use Microsoft BizTalk Server Configuration Objects 1.0 Type Library (BizTalkObjectModel.dll)

BizTalkChannel.SignatureCertificateInfo Property

The **SignatureCertificateInfo** property contains information about the certificate that signs the output document. This information includes the **Name**, **Reference**, **Store**, and **Usage** properties and is created and stored in memory in the **BizTalkCertificateInfo** object.

Syntax

object.**SignatureCertificateInfo**

Parameters

None

Return Values

This property returns a **BizTalkCertificateInfo** object that contains the certificate information.

Error Value

If an error is raised, **Err.Number** is set to one of the values documented in Appendix A, "Error Messages."

Requirements

Windows NT/2000: Requires Windows 2000 SP1 or later
Library: Use Microsoft BizTalk Server Configuration Objects 1.0 Type Library (BizTalkObjectModel.dll)

BizTalkChannel.SourceEndpoint Property

The **SourceEndpoint** property contains information about the source. This information includes the **Alias**, **Application**, and **Organization** properties and is created and stored in memory in the **BizTalkEndPoint** object.

Syntax

object.**SourceEndpoint**

Parameters

None

Return Values

This property returns an **Object** that contains information about the source.

Error Value

If an error is raised, **Err.Number** is set to one of the values documented in Appendix A, "Error Messages."

Requirements

Windows NT/2000: Requires Windows 2000 SP1 or later
Library: Use Microsoft BizTalk Server Configuration Objects 1.0 Type Library (BizTalkObjectModel.dll)

BizTalkChannel.TrackFields Property

The **TrackFields** property identifies the **Dictionary** object that points to the specification that contains fields to track interchange data on input documents for this **BizTalkChannel** object. These tracking fields override the fields set in the **TrackFields** property on the **BizTalkDocument** object.

Syntax

object.**TrackFields**

Parameters

None

Return Values

This property returns a **CDictionary** object that contains the custom tracking fields.

Error Value

If an error is raised, **Err.Number** is set to one of the values documented in Appendix A, "Error Messages."

Remarks

The fields in the **Dictionary** object must contain an XPath value that identifies the field to be tracked in a document. By default, the **Dictionary** object provides eight predefined fields for tracking data in a document. These predefined fields consist of two fields for each of the following data types: integer, real, date, and string. If additional fields are required for tracking, you can use the x_custom_search field in the **Dictionary** object, and set the value to a **SimpleList** object. The **SimpleList** object contains a list of XPath values pointing to the additional tracking fields. XPath values can be added to and deleted from this list using the **Add** and **Delete** methods.

The following table shows the field names in the **Dictionary** object for **TrackFields**.

Field Name	Field type
i_value1	Integer value
i_value2	Integer value
r_value1	Real value
r_value2	Real value
d_value1	Date value
d_value2	Date value
s_value1	String value
s_value2	String value
x_custom_search	A list to return one or more additional data items

For more information about XPath expressions, go to the MSDN Online Library Web site (msdn.microsoft.com/library/default.asp) and search for XPath.

Requirements

Windows NT/2000: Requires Windows 2000 SP1 or later
Library: Use Microsoft BizTalk Server Configuration Objects 1.0 Type Library
(BizTalkObjectModel.dll)

BizTalkChannel.VerifySignatureCertificateInfo Property

The **VerifySignatureCertificateInfo** property contains information about the certificate that verifies the signature of the input document. This information includes the **Name**, **Reference**, **Store**, and **Usage** properties and is created and stored in memory in the **BizTalkCertificateInfo** object.

Syntax

object.**VerifySignatureCertificateInfo**

Parameters

None

Return Values

This property returns a **BizTalkCertificateInfo** object that contains the certificate information.

Error Value

If an error is raised, **Err.Number** is set to one of the values documented in Appendix A, "Error Messages."

Requirements

Windows NT/2000: Requires Windows 2000 SP1 or later
Library: Use Microsoft BizTalk Server Configuration Objects 1.0 Type Library
(BizTalkObjectModel.dll)

BizTalkConfig Object

Use the **BizTalkConfig** object to create channels, document specifications, envelopes, organizations, ports, and port groups.

The properties of the **BizTalkConfig** object are shown in the following table.

Property	Data type	Description
Certificates	**Object**	Returns an ADO recordset that contains all specified certificates. This is a read-only property.
Channels	**Object**	Returns an ADO recordset that contains all **BizTalkChannel** objects. This is a read-only property.
Documents	**Object**	Returns an ADO recordset that contains all **BizTalkDocument** objects. This is a read-only property.
Envelopes	**Object**	Returns an ADO recordset that contains all **BizTalkEnvelope** objects.
Organizations	**Object**	Returns an ADO recordset that contains all **BizTalkOrganization** objects. This is a read-only property.
PortGroups	**Object**	Returns an ADO recordset that contains all **BizTalkPortGroup** objects. This is a read-only property.
Ports	**Object**	Returns an ADO recordset that contains all **BizTalkPort** objects. This is a read-only property.

The methods of the **BizTalkConfig** object are shown in the following table.

Method	Description
CreateChannel	Returns the address of a pointer to a new **BizTalkChannel** object.
CreateDocument	Returns the address of a pointer to a new **BizTalkDocument** object.
CreateEnvelope	Returns the address of a pointer to a new **BizTalkEnvelope** object.
CreateOrganization	Returns the address of a pointer to a new **BizTalkOrganization** object.
CreatePort	Returns the address of a pointer to a new **BizTalkPort** object.
CreatePortGroup	Returns the address of a pointer to a new **BizTalkPortGroup** object.

Remarks

In Microsoft Visual Basic, each object created by using the methods of this class implements
the following common properties and methods from the **IBizTalkBase** class:

- **DateModified**
- **Handle**
- **Name**
- **Clear**
- **Create**
- **Load**
- **LoadByName**
- **Remove**
- **Save**

When **BizTalkPort** and **BizTalkChannel** objects are created, BizTalk Server automatically
creates some associated subobjects. You can access these subobjects by using properties of
the **BizTalkPort** and **BizTalkChannel** objects.

The relationship between objects, their subobjects, and the properties used to obtain the subobjects is shown in the following table.

Subobject	Associated object	Property to set
BizTalkEndPoint	BizTalkPort	DestinationEndpoint
BizTalkEndPoint	BizTalkChannel	SourceEndpoint
BizTalkLoggingInfo	BizTalkChannel	LoggingInfo
BizTalkTransportInfo	BizTalkPort	PrimaryTransport, SecondaryTransport
BizTalkServiceWindowInfo	BizTalkPort	ServiceWindowInfo
BizTalkCertificateInfo	BizTalkPort	EncryptionCertificateInfo
BizTalkCertificateInfo	BizTalkChannel	SignatureCertificateInfo, VerifySignatureCertificateInfo, or DecryptionCertificateInfo

Requirements

Windows NT/2000: Requires Windows 2000 SP1 or later
Library: Use Microsoft BizTalk Server Configuration Objects 1.0 Type Library
(BizTalkObjectModel.dll)

BizTalkConfig.Certificates Property

The **Certificates** property returns an ADO recordset that contains all specified certificates.

Syntax

object.**Certificates**(_
   StoreType **As BIZTALK_STORE_TYPE**, _
   UsageType **As BIZTALK_USAGE_TYPE**, _
   NamePrefix **As String**, _

)

Parameters

StoreType
   Enumeration value. Valid values are from the **BIZTALK_STORE_TYPE** enumeration.

UsageType
   Enumeration value. Valid values are from the **BIZTALK_USAGE_TYPE** enumeration.

NamePrefix

> **String** that contains a prefix used as the selection criteria for certificate names. Any certificate **Name** starting with this value is returned in the recordset. This value is case sensitive.

Return Values

This property returns an **Object** that contains all specified certificates.

Error Value

If an error is raised, **Err.Number** is set to one of the values documented in Appendix A, "Error Messages."

Remarks

This is a read-only property.

Each record in the ADO recordset returned by this property contains information about an existing **BizTalkCertificateInfo** object in the database. The fields in each record contain the following information, listed in order:

- **NameReference**
- **Store**
- **Usage**

Additional information about Microsoft ActiveX Data Objects is available on the MSDN Online Library Web site (msdn.microsoft.com/library/default.asp).

Requirements

Windows NT/2000: Requires Windows 2000 SP1 or later
Library: Use Microsoft BizTalk Server Configuration Objects 1.0 Type Library (BizTalkObjectModel.dll)

BizTalkConfig.Channels Property

The **Channels** property returns an ADO recordset that contains all **BizTalkChannel** objects.

Syntax

object.**Channels**

Parameters

None

Return Values

This property returns an **Object** that contains all **BizTalkChannel** objects.

Error Value

If an error is raised, **Err.Number** is set to one of the values documented in Appendix A, "Error Messages."

Remarks

This is a read-only property.

Each record in the ADO recordset returned by this property contains information about an existing **BizTalkChannel** object in the database. The fields in each record contain the following information, listed in order:

- **Handle**

- **Name**

- **DateModified**

Additional information about Microsoft ActiveX Data Objects is available on the MSDN Online Library Web site (msdn.microsoft.com/library/default.asp).

Requirements

Windows NT/2000: Requires Windows 2000 SP1 or later
Library: Use Microsoft BizTalk Server Configuration Objects 1.0 Type Library (BizTalkObjectModel.dll)

BizTalkConfig.CreateChannel Method

The **CreateChannel** method returns a new **BizTalkChannel** object.

Syntax

object.**CreateChannel**

Parameters

None

Return Values

This method returns a new **BizTalkChannel** object.

Error Value

If an error is raised, **Err.Number** is set to one of the values documented in Appendix A, "Error Messages."

Requirements

Windows NT/2000: Requires Windows 2000 SP1 or later
Library: Use Microsoft BizTalk Server Configuration Objects 1.0 Type Library
(BizTalkObjectModel.dll)

BizTalkConfig.CreateDocument Method

The **CreateDocument** method returns a new **BizTalkDocument** object.

Syntax

object.**CreateDocument**

Parameters

None

Return Values

This method returns a new **BizTalkDocument** object.

Error Value

If an error is raised, **Err.Number** is set to one of the values documented in Appendix A,
"Error Messages."

Requirements

Windows NT/2000: Requires Windows 2000 SP1 or later
Library: Use Microsoft BizTalk Server Configuration Objects 1.0 Type Library
(BizTalkObjectModel.dll)

BizTalkConfig.CreateEnvelope Method

The **CreateEnvelope** method returns a new **BizTalkEnvelope** object.

Syntax

object.**CreateEnvelope**

Parameters

None

Return Values

This method returns a new **BizTalkEnvelope** object.

Error Value

If an error is raised, **Err.Number** is set to one of the values documented in Appendix A, "Error Messages."

Requirements

Windows NT/2000: Requires Windows 2000 SP1 or later
Library: Use Microsoft BizTalk Server Configuration Objects 1.0 Type Library (BizTalkObjectModel.dll)

BizTalkConfig.CreateOrganization Method

The **CreateOrganization** method returns a new **BizTalkOrganization** object.

Syntax

object.**CreateOrganization**

Parameters

None

Return Values

This method returns a new **BizTalkOrganization** object.

Error Value

If an error is raised, **Err.Number** is set to one of the values documented in Appendix A, "Error Messages."

Requirements

Windows NT/2000: Requires Windows 2000 SP1 or later
Library: Use Microsoft BizTalk Server Configuration Objects 1.0 Type Library (BizTalkObjectModel.dll)

BizTalkConfig.CreatePort Method

The **CreatePort** method returns a new **BizTalkPort** object.

Syntax

object.**CreatePort**

Parameters

None

Return Values

This method returns a new **BizTalkPort** object.

Error Value

If an error is raised, **Err.Number** is set to one of the values documented in Appendix A, "Error Messages."

Requirements

Windows NT/2000: Requires Windows 2000 SP1 or later
Library: Use Microsoft BizTalk Server Configuration Objects 1.0 Type Library (BizTalkObjectModel.dll)

BizTalkConfig.CreatePortGroup Method

The **CreatePortGroup** method returns a new **BizTalkPortGroup** object.

Syntax

object.**CreatePortGroup**

Parameters

None

Return Values

This method returns a new **BizTalkPortGroup** object.

Error Value

If an error is raised, **Err.Number** is set to one of the values documented in Appendix A, "Error Messages."

Requirements

Windows NT/2000: Requires Windows 2000 SP1 or later
Library: Use Microsoft BizTalk Server Configuration Objects 1.0 Type Library (BizTalkObjectModel.dll)

BizTalkConfig.Documents Property

The **Documents** property returns an ADO recordset that contains all **BizTalkDocument** objects.

Syntax

object.**Documents**

Parameters

None

Return Values

This property returns an **Object** that contains all **BizTalkDocument** objects.

Error Value

If an error is raised, **Err.Number** is set to one of the values documented in Appendix A, "Error Messages."

Remarks

This is a read-only property.

Each record in the ADO recordset returned by this property contains information about an existing **BizTalkDocument** object in the database. The fields in each record contain the following information, listed in order:

- **Handle**
- **Name**
- **DateModified**

Additional information about Microsoft ActiveX Data Objects is available on the MSDN Online Library Web site (msdn.microsoft.com/library/default.asp).

Requirements

Windows NT/2000: Requires Windows 2000 SP1 or later
Library: Use Microsoft BizTalk Server Configuration Objects 1.0 Type Library (BizTalkObjectModel.dll)

BizTalkConfig.Envelopes Property

The **Envelopes** property returns an ADO recordset that contains all **BizTalkEnvelope** objects.

Syntax

object.**Envelopes**

Parameters

None

Return Values

This property returns an **Object** that contains all **BizTalkEnvelope** objects.

Error Value

If an error is raised, **Err.Number** is set to one of the values documented in Appendix A, "Error Messages."

Remarks

This is a read-only property.

Each record in the ADO recordset returned by this property contains information about an existing **BizTalkEnvelope** object in the database. The fields in each record contain the following information, listed in order:

- **Handle**

- **Name**

- **DateModified**

- **Format**

Additional information about Microsoft ActiveX Data Objects is available on the MSDN Online Library Web site (msdn.microsoft.com/library/default.asp).

Requirements

Windows NT/2000: Requires Windows 2000 SP1 or later
Library: Use Microsoft BizTalk Server Configuration Objects 1.0 Type Library (BizTalkObjectModel.dll)

BizTalkConfig.Organizations Property

The **Organizations** property returns an ADO recordset that contains all **BizTalkOrganization** objects.

Syntax

object.**Organizations**

Parameters

None

Return Values

This property returns an **Object** that contains all **BizTalkOrganization** objects.

Error Value

If an error is raised, **Err.Number** is set to one of the values documented in Appendix A, "Error Messages."

Remarks

This is a read-only property.

Each record in the ADO recordset returned by this property contains information about an existing **BizTalkOrganization** object in the database. The fields in each record contain the following information, listed in order:

- **Handle**

- **Name**

- **DateModified**

- **IsDefault**

Additional information about Microsoft ActiveX Data Objects is available on the MSDN Online Library Web site (msdn.microsoft.com/library/default.asp).

Requirements

Windows NT/2000: Requires Windows 2000 SP1 or later
Library: Use Microsoft BizTalk Server Configuration Objects 1.0 Type Library
(BizTalkObjectModel.dll)

BizTalkConfig.PortGroups Property

The **PortGroups** property returns an ADO recordset that contains all **BizTalkPortGroup** objects.

Syntax

object.**PortGroups**

Parameters

None

Return Values

This property returns an **Object** that contains all **BizTalkPortGroup** objects.

Error Value

If an error is raised, **Err.Number** is set to one of the values documented in Appendix A, "Error Messages."

Remarks

This is a read-only property.

Each record in the ADO recordset returned by this property contains information about an existing **BizTalkPortGroup** object in the database. The fields in each record contain the following information, listed in order:

- **Handle**
- **Name**
- **DateModified**

Additional information about Microsoft ActiveX Data Objects is available on the MSDN Online Library Web site (msdn.microsoft.com/library/default.asp).

Requirements

Windows NT/2000: Requires Windows 2000 SP1 or later
Library: Use Microsoft BizTalk Server Configuration Objects 1.0 Type Library (BizTalkObjectModel.dll)

BizTalkConfig.Ports Property

The **Ports** property returns an ADO recordset that contains all **BizTalkPort** objects.

Syntax

object.**Ports**

Parameters

None

Return Values

This property returns an **Object** that contains all **BizTalkPort** objects.

Error Value

If an error is raised, **Err.Number** is set to one of the values documented in Appendix A, "Error Messages."

Remarks

This is a read-only property.

Each record in the ADO recordset returned by this property contains information about an existing **BizTalkPort** object in the database. The fields in each record contain the following information, listed in order:

- **Handle**
- **Name**
- **DateModified**

Additional information about Microsoft ActiveX Data Objects is available on the MSDN Online Library Web site (msdn.microsoft.com/library/default.asp).

Requirements

Windows NT/2000: Requires Windows 2000 SP1 or later
Library: Use Microsoft BizTalk Server Configuration Objects 1.0 Type Library (BizTalkObjectModel.dll)

BizTalkDocument Object

Use the **BizTalkDocument** object to identify and describe the document specification of a document.

The properties of the **BizTalkDocument** object are shown in the following table.

Property	Type	Description
Content	BSTR	Content of the document specification described by the object. This is a read-only property.
DateModified	BSTR	Date and time at which the information in the object was created or last modified. This is a read-only property obtained from the **BizTalkBase** object.
Handle	long	Handle to the object. This is a read-only property obtained from the **BizTalkBase** object.
Name	BSTR	Name of the object. This is a required property obtained from the **BizTalkBase** object.
NameSpace	BSTR	String that resolves naming conflicts between elements in a document. This is a read-only property.
PropertySet	IDispatch	**Dictionary** object that contains the electronic data interchange (EDI) selection criteria (name/value pairs) by which the server extracts information from the functional group header of the EDI document to identify the object when the document is input. It helps the server create the header of the EDI document when it is output. This is a required property if the document is an EDI document.
Reference	BSTR	Full Web Distributed Authoring and Versioning (WebDAV) URL for the document specification referred to by this **BizTalkDocument** object. This is a required property when the **TrackFields** property is set.
TrackFields	IDispatch	**Dictionary** object that stores the custom fields that Tracking uses to track all documents processed by the server, based on this document instance. The **Reference** property must contain a WebDAV URL when this property is set.
Type	BSTR	Type of document specification. This is a read-only property.
Version	BSTR	Version of the document standard. This is a read-only property.

The methods of the **BizTalkDocument** object are shown in the following table.

Method	Description
Clear	Clears the object in memory. All member variables of the object in memory are initialized to their default values. This method is obtained from the **BizTalkBase** object.
Create	Creates a new object in the database. This method is obtained from the **BizTalkBase** object.
Load	Loads the object in memory. This method is obtained from the **BizTalkBase** object.
LoadByName	Loads the object by name in memory. This method is obtained from the **BizTalkBase** object.
LoadByPropertySet	Loads the document object by its **PropertySet** object.
Remove	Removes the object from the database. This method is obtained from the **BizTalkBase** object.
Save	Saves the object in the database. This method is obtained from the **BizTalkBase** object.

Remarks

Each **BizTalkDocument** object must have at least one associated **BizTalkChannel** object. More than one **BizTalkDocument** object can refer to the same document specification.

Requirements

Windows NT/2000: Requires Windows 2000 SP1 or later
Library: Use Microsoft BizTalk Server Configuration Objects 1.0 Type Library
(BizTalkObjectModel.dll)

BizTalkDocument.Content Property

The **Content** property contains the content of the document specification described by the object.

Syntax

object.**Content**

Parameters

None

Return Values

This property returns a **String** that contains the content.

Error Value

If an error is raised, **Err.Number** is set to one of the values documented in Appendix A, "Error Messages."

Remarks

This is a read-only property.

The **Reference** property is checked when the **Create** or the **Save** method is called. If this string is not empty when **Create** is called, **Content** is set to the contents of the document specification and the **NameSpace** property is changed to the value found in the document specification.

Once you have created or saved an object with **Reference** set to a document specification, any changes you make to the **Content** or **NameSpace** property of the referenced document specification are not automatically updated on the referring object. To update the object that refers to the revised document specification, you must save the document specification, reset the **Reference** property of the object to its current value, and then call **Save** on the referring object.

Requirements

Windows NT/2000: Requires Windows 2000 SP1 or later
Library: Use Microsoft BizTalk Server Configuration Objects 1.0 Type Library
(BizTalkObjectModel.dll)

BizTalkDocument.LoadByPropertySet Method

The **LoadByPropertySet** method loads the document object by its **PropertySet**.

Syntax

object.**LoadByPropertySet**(_
  pPropSetDictionaryDisp **As Object** _
)

Parameters

pPropSetDictionaryDisp
    Object that contains the **PropertySet**.

Return Values

None

Error Value

If an error is raised, **Err.Number** is set to one of the values documented in Appendix A, "Error Messages."

Requirements

Windows NT/2000: Requires Windows 2000 SP1 or later
Library: Use Microsoft BizTalk Server Configuration Objects 1.0 Type Library (BizTalkObjectModel.dll)

BizTalkDocument.NameSpace Property

The **NameSpace** property contains the string that resolves naming conflicts between elements in a document.

Syntax

object.**NameSpace**

Parameters

None

Return Values

This property returns a **String** that contains the namespace.

Error Value

If an error is raised, **Err.Number** is set to one of the values documented in Appendix A, "Error Messages."

Remarks

This is a read-only property. The **Reference** property is checked when the **Create** or the **Save** method is called. If this string is not empty when **Create** is called, **Content** is set to the contents of the document specification and **NameSpace** is changed to the value found in the document specification.

Once you have created or saved an object with **Reference** set to a document specification, any changes you make to the **Content** or **NameSpace** property of the referenced document specification are not automatically updated on the referring object. To update the object that refers to the revised document specification, you must save the document specification, reset the **Reference** property of the object to its current value, and then call **Save** on the referring object.

✒ Note

- When creating a document, the number of characters in the **NameSpace** combined with the number of characters in the specification name cannot exceed 255.

Requirements

Windows NT/2000: Requires Windows 2000 SP1 or later
Library: Use Microsoft BizTalk Server Configuration Objects 1.0 Type Library (BizTalkObjectModel.dll)

BizTalkDocument.PropertySet Property

The **PropertySet** property contains a **Dictionary** object that contains the electronic data interchange (EDI) selection criteria (name/value pairs) by which the server extracts information from the functional group header of the EDI document to identify the object when the document is input. It helps the server create the header of the EDI document when it is output.

Syntax

object.**PropertySet**

Parameters

None

Return Values

This property returns an **Object** that contains the selection criteria.

Error Value

If an error is raised, **Err.Number** is set to one of the values documented in Appendix A, "Error Messages."

Remarks

This is a required property if the document is an EDI document. The **Delimiters** property of the associated **BizTalkPort** object must also be defined.

The following table shows whether names are required in the **Dictionary** object for **PropertySet**.

Selection criteria	X12	EDIFACT
application_sender_code	Yes	Yes
application_receiver_code	Yes	Yes
functional_identifier	Yes	Yes
standards_version	Yes	No
standards_version_type	No	Yes
standards_version_value	No	Yes

Note

- The name/value pairs contained in the **Dictionary** object cannot exceed a total of 450 bytes.

PropertySet can be set only if the **Reference** property is set.

Requirements

Windows NT/2000: Requires Windows 2000 SP1 or later
Library: Use Microsoft BizTalk Server Configuration Objects 1.0 Type Library (BizTalkObjectModel.dll)

BizTalkDocument.Reference Property

The **Reference** property contains the full Web Distributed Authoring and Versioning (WebDAV) URL for the document specification referred to by the object.

Syntax

object.**Reference**

Parameters

None

Return Values

This property returns a **String** that contains the reference.

Error Value

If an error is raised, **Err.Number** is set to one of the values documented in Appendix A, "Error Messages."

Remarks

Reference is checked when the **Create** or the **Save** method is called. If this string is not empty when **Create** is called, **Content** is set to the contents of the document specification and the **NameSpace** property is changed to the value found in the document specification.

Once you have created or saved an object with **Reference** set to a document specification, any changes you make to the **Content** or **NameSpace** property of the referenced document specification are not automatically updated on the referring object. To update the object that refers to the revised document specification, you must save the document specification, reset the **Reference** property of the object to its current value, and then call **Save** on the referring object.

If **Reference** is not set, the **PropertySet** and **TrackFields** properties must not be set.

Requirements

Windows NT/2000: Requires Windows 2000 SP1 or later
Library: Use Microsoft BizTalk Server Configuration Objects 1.0 Type Library (BizTalkObjectModel.dll)

BizTalkDocument.TrackFields Property

The **TrackFields** property identifies the **Dictionary** object that stores the custom fields used to track the document. A **BizTalkDocument** object points to the specification that contains fields to track the document. The designated fields are logged to the Tracking database for each instance of a document that is processed. Tracking fields on the **BizTalkDocument** object are global. The **TrackFields** property on the **BizTalkChannel** object overrides the values specified by this property.

Syntax

object.**TrackFields**

Parameters

None

Return Values

This property returns a **CDictionary** object that contains the custom tracking fields.

Error Value

If an error is raised, **Err.Number** is set to one of the values documented in Appendix A, "Error Messages."

Remarks

TrackFields can be set only if the **Reference** property is set. Tracking fields specified for an output **BizTalkDocument** object are ignored.

The fields in the **Dictionary** object must contain an XPath value that identifies the field to be tracked in a document. By default, the **Dictionary** object provides eight predefined fields for tracking data in a document. These predefined fields consist of two fields for each of the following data types: integer, real, date, and string. If additional fields are required for tracking, you can use the x_custom_search field in the **Dictionary** object and set the value to a **SimpleList** object. The **SimpleList** object contains a list of XPath values pointing to the additional tracking fields. XPath values can be added to and deleted from this list using the **Add** and **Delete** methods.

The following table shows the field names in the **Dictionary** object for **TrackFields**.

Field Name	Field type
i_value1	Integer value
i_value2	Integer value
r_value1	Real value
r_value2	Real value
d_value1	Date value
d_value2	Date value
s_value1	String value
s_value2	String value
x_custom_search	A list to return one or more additional data items

For more information about XPath expressions, go to the MSDN Online Library Web site (msdn.microsoft.com/library/default.asp) and search for XPath.

Requirements

Windows NT/2000: Requires Windows 2000 SP1 or later
Library: Use Microsoft BizTalk Server Configuration Objects 1.0 Type Library (BizTalkObjectModel.dll)

BizTalkDocument.Type Property

The **Type** property contains the type of document specification.

Syntax

object.**Type**

Parameters

None

Return Values

This property returns a **String** that contains the document type.

Error Value

If an error is raised, **Err.Number** is set to one of the values documented in Appendix A, "Error Messages."

Remarks

This is a read-only property. All document instances must have the same document type as the associated envelope. For example, if the **Format** property of the **BizTalkEnvelope** object is set to X12, **Type** must also be X12.

Requirements

Windows NT/2000: Requires Windows 2000 SP1 or later
Library: Use Microsoft BizTalk Server Configuration Objects 1.0 Type Library (BizTalkObjectModel.dll)

BizTalkDocument.Version Property

The **Version** property contains the version of the document standard.

Syntax

object.**Version**

Parameters

None

Return Values

This property returns a **String** that contains the version.

Error Value

If an error is raised, **Err.Number** is set to one of the values documented in Appendix A, "Error Messages."

Remarks

This is a read-only property.

Requirements

Windows NT/2000: Requires Windows 2000 SP1 or later
Library: Use Microsoft BizTalk Server Configuration Objects 1.0 Type Library
(BizTalkObjectModel.dll)

BizTalkEndPoint Object

Use the **BizTalkEndPoint** object to configure source information for a **BizTalkChannel**
object and destination information for a **BizTalkPort** object.

The properties of the **BizTalkEndPoint** object are shown in the following table.

Property	Type	Description
Alias	**long**	Handle to the organization identifier type/value pair for the destination **BizTalkOrganization** object for the associated **BizTalkPort** object.
Application	**long**	Handle to the associated application for the destination **BizTalkOrganization** object for this **BizTalkPort** object.
Openness	**BIZTALK_OPENNESS_TYPE_EX**	Enumeration value that indicates whether the object is open.
Organization	**long**	Handle to the destination **BizTalkOrganization** object for this **BizTalkPort** object. This is a required property for this object to be complete unless the **Openness** property is set to **BIZTALK_OPENNESS_TYPE_EX_ DESTINATION**.

Remarks

The **BizTalkEndPoint** object is automatically created when a **BizTalkPort** object or a
BizTalkChannel object is instantiated with the **CreatePort** or the **CreateChannel** method of
the **BizTalkConfig** object.

For destination endpoints, access the **BizTalkEndPoint** object by using the
DestinationEndpoint property of the **BizTalkPort** object. For source endpoints, access the
BizTalkEndPoint object by using the **SourceEndpoint** property of the
BizTalkChannel object.

Requirements

Windows NT/2000: Requires Windows 2000 SP1 or later
Library: Use Microsoft BizTalk Server Configuration Objects 1.0 Type Library
(BizTalkObjectModel.dll)

BizTalkEndPoint.Alias Property

The **Alias** property contains the handle to the alias.

Syntax

object.**Alias**

Parameters

None

Return Values

This property returns a **Long** that contains the handle to the alias.

Error Value

If an error is raised, **Err.Number** is set to one of the values documented in Appendix A,
"Error Messages."

Requirements

Windows NT/2000: Requires Windows 2000 SP1 or later
Library: Use Microsoft BizTalk Server Configuration Objects 1.0 Type Library
(BizTalkObjectModel.dll)

BizTalkEndPoint.Application Property

The **Application** property contains the handle to the application.

Syntax

object.**Application**

Parameters

None

Return Values

This property returns a **Long** that contains the handle to the application.

Error Value

If an error is raised, **Err.Number** is set to one of the values documented in Appendix A, "Error Messages."

Requirements

Windows NT/2000: Requires Windows 2000 SP1 or later
Library: Use Microsoft BizTalk Server Configuration Objects 1.0 Type Library
(BizTalkObjectModel.dll)

BizTalkEndPoint.Openness Property

The **Openness** property contains an enumeration value that indicates whether the object has an open destination or source, or neither.

Syntax

object.**Openness**

Parameters

None

Return Values

This property returns an enumeration value. Valid values are from the
BIZTALK_OPENNESS_TYPE_EX enumeration.

Error Value

If an error is raised, **Err.Number** is set to one of the values documented in Appendix A, "Error Messages."

Remarks

The **BizTalkPort** object is valid only if the associated document or the parameters on the **Submit** or the **SubmitSync** method of the **IInterchange** interface identify the missing information.

If **Openness** is set to **BIZTALK_OPENNESS_TYPE_EX_SOURCE** for a **BizTalkEndPoint** object associated with a channel, the following constraints apply:

- The **SignatureType** property must not be set.

- The **BizTalkPort** object cannot be included in a port group.

If Openness is set to **BIZTALK_OPENNESS_TYPE_EX_FROMWORKFLOW** on a channel, the associated **BizTalkOrganization** object must be the default organization.

If **Openness** on the object is set to **BIZTALK_OPENNESS_TYPE_EX_DESTINATION** for a **BizTalkEndPoint** object associated with a messaging port, the following constraints apply:

- The **PrimaryTransportType** property must be set to **BIZTALK_TRANSPORT_TYPE_OPENDESTINATION**.

- The **EncryptionType** property must not be set.

- The document or the parameters on **Submit** or **SubmitSync** must specify the destination, transport type, and address.

- The **BizTalkPort** object cannot be included in a port group.

✎ **Note**

- This property cannot be changed on an existing port.

Requirements

Windows NT/2000: Requires Windows 2000 SP1 or later
Library: Use Microsoft BizTalk Server Configuration Objects 1.0 Type Library (BizTalkObjectModel.dll)

BizTalkEndPoint.Organization Property

The **Organization** property contains the handle to the organization.

Syntax

object.**Organization**

Parameters

None

Return Values

This property returns a **Long** that contains the handle to the organization.

Error Value

If an error is raised, **Err.Number** is set to one of the values documented in Appendix A, "Error Messages."

Requirements

Windows NT/2000: Requires Windows 2000 SP1 or later
Library: Use Microsoft BizTalk Server Configuration Objects 1.0 Type Library (BizTalkObjectModel.dll)

BizTalkEnvelope Object

Use the **BizTalkEnvelope** object to configure the envelope format used with documents processed by BizTalk Server. An envelope is the header information for an interchange.

The properties of the **BizTalkEnvelope** object are shown in the following table.

Property	Type	Description
Content	**BSTR**	Contents of the selected envelope format specification. This is a read-only property.
DateModified	**BSTR**	Date and time at which the information in the object was created or last modified. This is a read-only property obtained from the **BizTalkBase** object.
Format	**BSTR**	String that identifies the type of envelope.
Handle	**long**	Handle to the object. This is a read-only property obtained from the **BizTalkBase** object.
Name	**BSTR**	Name of the object. This is a required property obtained from the **BizTalkBase** object.
NameSpace	**BSTR**	String that resolves naming conflicts between elements in an envelope specification. This is a read-only property.
Reference	**BSTR**	Full Web Distributed Authoring and Versioning (WebDAV) URL name of the envelope format specification file. This is a required property if the **Format** property is set to "custom".
Version	**BSTR**	Version of the envelope format specification. This is a read-only property.

The methods of the **BizTalkEnvelope** object are shown in the following table.

Method	Description
Clear	Clears the object in memory. All member variables of the object in memory are initialized to their default values. This method is obtained from the **BizTalkBase** object.
Create	Creates a new object in the database. This method is obtained from the **BizTalkBase** object.
Load	Loads the object in memory. This method is obtained from the **BizTalkBase** object.
LoadByName	Loads the object by name in memory. This method is obtained from the **BizTalkBase** object.
Remove	Removes the object from the database. This method is obtained from the **BizTalkBase** object.
Save	Saves the object in the database. This method is obtained from the **BizTalkBase** object.

Remarks

All document instances in an electronic data interchange (EDI) functional group must have the same format. All document instances must have the same document type as the associated envelope. For example, if **Format** is set to X12, the **Type** property of the **BizTalkDocument** objects for the associated **BizTalkPort** object must also be X12.

If you use an envelope with an EDIFACT format and you want to use a null value for the empty qualifier in the header for the source or the destination, create a custom identifier with a single dash (-) as the qualifier. To do this, use the **CreateAlias** method on the **BizTalkOrganization** object. When an empty qualifier is encountered on an input EDIFACT envelope, the server converts the empty qualifier to a dash. For an output EDIFACT envelope, the server converts the dash to an empty qualifier.

The **BizTalkEnvelope** object is required for input documents if the **Type** property of the **BizTalkDocument** object is set to "flatfile" or "custom xml".

Requirements

Windows NT/2000: Requires Windows 2000 SP1 or later
Library: Use Microsoft BizTalk Server Configuration Objects 1.0 Type Library
(BizTalkObjectModel.dll)

BizTalkEnvelope.Content Property

The **Content** property contains the contents of the selected envelope format specification.

Syntax

object.**Content**

Parameters

None

Return Values

This property returns a **String** that contains the content.

Error Value

If an error is raised, **Err.Number** is set to one of the values documented in Appendix A, "Error Messages."

Remarks

This is a read-only property.

The **Reference** property is checked when the **Create** or the **Save** method is called. If this string is not empty when **Create** is called, **Content** is set to the contents of the envelope specification, and the **NameSpace** property is changed to the value found in the envelope specification.

Once you have created or saved an object with **Reference** set to an envelope specification, any changes you make to the **Content** or **NameSpace** property of the referenced envelope specification are not automatically updated on the referring object. To update the object that refers to the revised envelope specification, you must save the envelope specification, reset the **Reference** property of the object to its current value, and then call **Save** on the referring object.

Requirements

Windows NT/2000: Requires Windows 2000 SP1 or later
Library: Use Microsoft BizTalk Server Configuration Objects 1.0 Type Library
(BizTalkObjectModel.dll)

BizTalkEnvelope.Format Property

The **Format** property contains the string that identifies the type of envelope.

Syntax

object.**Format**

Parameters

None

Return Values

This property returns a **String** that contains the envelope format.

Error Value

If an error is raised, **Err.Number** is set to one of the values documented in Appendix A, "Error Messages."

Remarks

The format value must be one of the following strings:

- x12
- edifact
- custom xml (default)
- custom
- flatfile
- reliable

Note

- Any string other than the ones listed here will cause an error at run time.

If this property is set to "custom", the **Reference** property is required. Also, a custom parser component has to be registered with the server for input documents with this property set to "custom". For more information about custom parser components, see "Using the IBizTalkParserComponent Interface" in Chapter 15, "Creating Custom Components."

All document instances must have the same document type as the associated envelope. For example, if **Format** is set to "x12", the **Type** property of the **BizTalkDocument** objects must also be "x12".

If **Format** is set to "X12," "edifact," or "reliable," the **Reference** property should not be set.

For more information about envelope formats, see "To create envelopes" earlier in this chapter.

Requirements

Windows NT/2000: Requires Windows 2000 SP1 or later
Library: Use Microsoft BizTalk Server Configuration Objects 1.0 Type Library (BizTalkObjectModel.dll)

BizTalkEnvelope.NameSpace Property

The **NameSpace** property contains the string that resolves naming conflicts between elements in an envelope specification.

Syntax

object.**NameSpace**

Parameters

None

Return Values

This property returns a **String** that contains the namespace.

Error Value

If an error is raised, **Err.Number** is set to one of the values documented in Appendix A, "Error Messages."

Remarks

This is a read-only property. The **Reference** property is checked when the **Create** or the **Save** method is called. If this string is not empty when **Create** is called, the **Content** property is set to the contents of the envelope specification, and **NameSpace** is changed to the value found in the envelope specification.

Once you have created or saved an object with **Reference** set to an envelope specification, any changes you make to the **Content** or **NameSpace** property of the referenced envelope specification are not automatically updated on the referring object. To update the object that refers to the revised envelope specification, you must save the envelope specification, reset the **Reference** property of the object to its current value, and then call **Save** on the referring object.

Note

- When creating an envelope, the number of characters in the **NameSpace** property combined with the number of characters in the specification name cannot exceed 255.

Requirements

Windows NT/2000: Requires Windows 2000 SP1 or later
Library: Use Microsoft BizTalk Server Configuration Objects 1.0 Type Library (BizTalkObjectModel.dll)

BizTalkEnvelope.Reference Property

The **Reference** property contains the full Web Distributed Authoring and Versioning (WebDAV) URL of the envelope format specification file.

Syntax

object.**Reference**

Parameters

None

Return Values

This property returns a **String** that contains the reference.

Error Value

If an error is raised, **Err.Number** is set to one of the values documented in Appendix A, "Error Messages."

Remarks

This is a required property if the **Format** property is set to "custom". **Reference** is checked when the **Create** or the **Save** method is called. If this string is not empty when **Create** is called, the **Content** property is set to the contents of the envelope specification, and the **NameSpace** property is changed to the value found in the envelope specification.

Once you have created or saved an object with **Reference** set to an envelope specification, any changes you make to the **Content** or **NameSpace** property of the referenced envelope specification are not automatically updated on the referring object. To update the object that refers to the revised envelope specification, you must save the envelope specification, reset the **Reference** property of the object to its current value, and then call **Save** on the referring object.

Requirements

Windows NT/2000: Requires Windows 2000 SP1 or later
Library: Use Microsoft BizTalk Server Configuration Objects 1.0 Type Library (BizTalkObjectModel.dll)

BizTalkEnvelope.Version Property

The **Version** property contains the version of the envelope format specification.

Syntax

object.**Version**

Parameters

None

Return Values

This property returns a **String** that contains the version.

Error Value

If an error is raised, **Err.Number** is set to one of the values documented in Appendix A, "Error Messages."

Remarks

This is a read-only property.

Requirements

Windows NT/2000: Requires Windows 2000 SP1 or later
Library: Use Microsoft BizTalk Server Configuration Objects 1.0 Type Library (BizTalkObjectModel.dll)

BizTalkLoggingInfo Object

Use the **BizTalkLoggingInfo** object to configure the document-logging information for an associated **BizTalkChannel** object.

The properties of the **BizTalkLoggingInfo** object are shown in the following table.

Property	Type	Description
LogNativeInputDocument	VARIANT_BOOL	Flag that indicates whether the input document instance is saved and logged in its native format.
LogNativeOutputDocument	VARIANT_BOOL	Flag that indicates whether the output document instance is saved and logged in its native format.
LogXMLInputDocument	VARIANT_BOOL	Flag that indicates whether the XML input document is saved and logged.
LogXMLOutputDocument	VARIANT_BOOL	Flag that indicates whether the XML output document is saved and logged.

Remarks

The **BizTalkLoggingInfo** object is automatically created when a **BizTalkChannel** object is instantiated with the **CreateChannel** method of the **BizTalkConfig** object. You can access the **BizTalkLoggingInfo** object by using the **LoggingInfo** property of the **BizTalkChannel** object.

Requirements

Windows NT/2000: Requires Windows 2000 SP1 or later
Library: Use Microsoft BizTalk Server Configuration Objects 1.0 Type Library (BizTalkObjectModel.dll)

BizTalkLoggingInfo.LogNativeInputDocument Property

The **LogNativeInputDocument** property contains a flag that indicates whether the input document instance is saved and logged in its native format.

Syntax

object.**LogNativeInputDocument**

Parameters

None

Return Values

This property returns a **Variant** that contains the flag. A value of **True** indicates that input documents will be saved and logged in their native format. A value of **False** indicates that input documents will not be saved and logged in their native format.

Error Value

If an error is raised, **Err.Number** is set to one of the values documented in Appendix A, "Error Messages."

Requirements

Windows NT/2000: Requires Windows 2000 SP1 or later
Library: Use Microsoft BizTalk Server Configuration Objects 1.0 Type Library
(BizTalkObjectModel.dll)

BizTalkLoggingInfo.LogNativeOutputDocument Property

The **LogNativeOutputDocument** property contains a flag that indicates whether the output document instance is saved and logged in its native format.

Syntax

object.**LogNativeOutputDocument**

Parameters

None

Return Values

This property returns a **Variant** that contains the flag. A value of **True** indicates that output documents will be saved and logged in their native format. A value of **False** indicates that output documents will not be saved and logged in their native format.

Error Value

If an error is raised, **Err.Number** is set to one of the values documented in Appendix A, "Error Messages."

Requirements

Windows NT/2000: Requires Windows 2000 SP1 or later
Library: Use Microsoft BizTalk Server Configuration Objects 1.0 Type Library
(BizTalkObjectModel.dll)

BizTalkLoggingInfo.LogXMLInputDocument Property

The **LogXMLInputDocument** property contains a flag that indicates whether the XML input document instance is saved and logged.

Syntax

object.**LogXMLInputDocument**

Parameters

None

Return Values

This property returns a **Variant** that contains the flag. A value of **True** indicates that input documents will be saved and logged in XML format. A value of **False** indicates that input documents will not be saved and logged in XML format.

Error Value

If an error is raised, **Err.Number** is set to one of the values documented in Appendix A, "Error Messages."

Requirements

Windows NT/2000: Requires Windows 2000 SP1 or later
Library: Use Microsoft BizTalk Server Configuration Objects 1.0 Type Library
(BizTalkObjectModel.dll)

BizTalkLoggingInfo.LogXMLOutputDocument Property

The **LogXMLOutputDocument** property contains a flag that indicates whether the XML output document instance is saved and logged.

Syntax

object.**LogXMLOutputDocument**

Parameters

None

Return Values

This property returns a **Variant** that contains the flag. A value of **True** indicates that output documents will be saved and logged in XML format. A value of **False** indicates that output documents will not be saved and logged in XML format.

Error Value

If an error is raised, **Err.Number** is set to one of the values documented in Appendix A, "Error Messages."

Requirements

Windows NT/2000: Requires Windows 2000 SP1 or later
Library: Use Microsoft BizTalk Server Configuration Objects 1.0 Type Library
(BizTalkObjectModel.dll)

BizTalkOrganization Object

Use the **BizTalkOrganization** object to configure organizations, its organization identifiers (aliases), and the applications within the organization that send and/or receive documents. The application indicates the ultimate source or destination of the document.

The properties of the **BizTalkOrganization** object are shown in the following table.

Property	Type	Description
Aliases	**IDispatch**	ADO recordset of aliases that refer to the object. The alias for an object is the organization identifier type/value pair.
Applications	**IDispatch**	ADO recordset of applications that refer to the object.
Comments	**BSTR**	User comments for the object.
DateModified	**BSTR**	Date and time at which the information in the object was created or last modified. This is a read-only property obtained from the **BizTalkBase** object.
Handle	**long**	Identifier for the object. This is a read-only property obtained from the **BizTalkBase** object.
IsDefault	**VARIANT_BOOL**	Flag that indicates whether the object is the default organization.
Name	**BSTR**	Name of the object. This is a required property obtained from the **BizTalkBase** object.

The methods of the **BizTalkOrganization** object are shown in the following table.

Method	Description
Clear	Clears the object in memory. All member variables of the object in memory are initialized to their default values. This method is obtained from the **BizTalkBase** object.
Create	Creates a new object in the database. This method is obtained from the **BizTalkBase** object.
CreateAlias	Creates an alias for the object. The alias is the organization identifier type/value pair.
CreateApplication	Creates a new application.
GetDefaultAlias	Gets the default alias for the object.
Load	Loads an object in memory. This method is obtained from the **BizTalkBase** object.
LoadAlias	Loads an existing alias for the object in memory.
LoadApplication	Loads an application in memory.
LoadByName	Loads an object by name in memory. This method is obtained from the **BizTalkBase** object.
Remove	Removes the object from the database. This method is obtained from the **BizTalkBase** object.
RemoveAlias	Removes an alias.
RemoveApplication	Removes an application.
Save	Saves the object to the database. This method is obtained from the **BizTalkBase** object.
SaveAlias	Saves this alias.
SaveApplication	Saves this application.

Remarks

A **BizTalkOrganization** object can have more than one application, but each application name must be unique for that object.

Requirements

Windows NT/2000: Requires Windows 2000 SP1 or later
Library: Use Microsoft BizTalk Server Configuration Objects 1.0 Type Library
(BizTalkObjectModel.dll)

BizTalkOrganization.Aliases Property

The **Aliases** property returns an ADO recordset that contains information about all aliases that refer to the object. The alias for an object is the organization qualifier/value pair.

Syntax

object.**Aliases**

Parameters

None

Return Values

This property returns an **Object** that contains all aliases that refer to the object.

Error Value

If an error is raised, **Err.Number** is set to one of the values documented in Appendix A, "Error Messages."

Remarks

BizTalk Messaging Manager refers to aliases as identifiers.

Each record in the ADO recordset returned by this property contains information about the aliases of an existing **BizTalkOrganization** object in the database. The fields in each record contain the following information, listed in order:

- Handle assigned to the alias.

- Name specified in the **CreateAlias** method.

- Boolean specified in the **CreateAlias** method.

- Qualifier specified in the **CreateAlias** method.

- Value specified in the **CreateAlias** method.

Additional information about Microsoft ActiveX Data Objects is available on the MSDN Online Library Web site (msdn.microsoft.com/library/default.asp).

Requirements

Windows NT/2000: Requires Windows 2000 SP1 or later
Library: Use Microsoft BizTalk Server Configuration Objects 1.0 Type Library (BizTalkObjectModel.dll)

BizTalkOrganization.Applications Property

The **Applications** property returns an ADO recordset that contains information about all applications that refer to the **Organization** object.

Syntax

object.**Applications**

Parameters

None

Return Values

This property returns an **Object** that contains all applications that refer to the object.

Error Value

If an error is raised, **Err.Number** is set to one of the values documented in Appendix A, "Error Messages."

Remarks

Each record in the ADO recordset returned by this property contains information about the applications of an existing **BizTalkOrganization** object in the database. The fields in each record contain the following information, listed in order:

- Handle assigned to the application.

- Name specified in the **CreateApplication** method.

Additional information about Microsoft ActiveX Data Objects is available on the MSDN Online Library Web site (msdn.microsoft.com/library/default.asp).

Requirements

Windows NT/2000: Requires Windows 2000 SP1 or later
Library: Use Microsoft BizTalk Server Configuration Objects 1.0 Type Library
(BizTalkObjectModel.dll)

BizTalkOrganization.Comments Property

The **Comments** property contains the user comments for the object.

object.**Comments**

Parameters

None

Return Values

This property returns a **String** that contains the comments.

Error Value

If an error is raised, **Err.Number** is set to one of the values documented in Appendix A, "Error Messages."

Requirements

Windows NT/2000: Requires Windows 2000 SP1 or later
Library: Use Microsoft BizTalk Server Configuration Objects 1.0 Type Library (BizTalkObjectModel.dll)

BizTalkOrganization.CreateAlias Method

The **CreateAlias** method creates a new alias for this **Organization** object. The alias for an object is the organization identifier that contains a name and a qualifier/value pair.

Syntax

object.**CreateAlias**(_
    strName **As String**, _
    bDefault **As Boolean**, _
    strQualifier **As String**, _
    strValue **As String** _
)

Parameters

strName
    String that contains the name of the alias.

bDefault
    Boolean that contains the flag. This default alias overrides the previous default alias when set to **True**. If no alias is specified as the default, one is assigned when the **Create** method is called.

strQualifier
    String that contains the qualifier. This parameter cannot be set to "group".

strValue
    String that contains the value.

Return Values

None

Error Value

If an error is raised, **Err.Number** is set to one of the values documented in Appendix A, "Error Messages."

Remarks

More than one alias can be created for a **BizTalkOrganization** object. The organization alias must contain a name that is unique for the specified **BizTalkOrganization** object, and a qualifier/value pair that is unique across all **BizTalkOrganization** objects. One of these aliases must be specified as the default alias for the object.

The server automatically creates an alias named *Organization* with a default identifier of *OrganizationName* and the value set to the organization's name for new organizations. If the organization name is changed, the value is automatically updated with the new name. This alias cannot be removed.

📝 Note

- When using envelopes with an EDIFACT format and you want to use a null value for the empty qualifier in the header for the source or the destination, create a custom identifier with a single dash (-) as the qualifier.

Requirements

Windows NT/2000: Requires Windows 2000 SP1 or later
Library: Use Microsoft BizTalk Server Configuration Objects 1.0 Type Library (BizTalkObjectModel.dll)

BizTalkOrganization.CreateApplication Method

The **CreateApplication** method creates a new application.

Syntax

object.**CreateApplication**(_
  strName **As String** _
)

Parameters

strName
  String that contains the name of the application.

Return Values

None

Error Value

If an error is raised, **Err.Number** is set to one of the values documented in Appendix A, "Error Messages."

Remarks

If a **BizTalkOrganization** object is associated with more than one application, each application name must be unique.

📝 Notes

- BizTalk Messaging Manager refers to the default organization as the home organization.

- BizTalk Messaging Manager allows applications to be created for the home organization only. The BizTalk Messaging Configuration object model does not enforce this restriction. Therefore, if you create an application for an organization other than the default (home) organization, you cannot modify it using BizTalk Messaging Manager.

Requirements

Windows NT/2000: Requires Windows 2000 SP1 or later
Library: Use Microsoft BizTalk Server Configuration Objects 1.0 Type Library (BizTalkObjectModel.dll)

BizTalkOrganization.GetDefaultAlias Method

The **GetDefaultAlias** method returns the handle to the default alias for the object. The default alias for an object is the default organization identifier type/value pair.

Syntax

object.**GetDefaultAlias**

Parameters

None

Return Values

This method returns a **Long** that contains the handle.

Error Value

If an error is raised, **Err.Number** is set to one of the values documented in Appendix A, "Error Messages."

Requirements

Windows NT/2000: Requires Windows 2000 SP1 or later
Library: Use Microsoft BizTalk Server Configuration Objects 1.0 Type Library
(BizTalkObjectModel.dll)

BizTalkOrganization.IsDefault Property

The **IsDefault** property contains the flag that indicates whether the object is the default organization.

Syntax

object.**IsDefault**

Parameters

None

Return Values

This property returns a **Boolean** that contains the flag. If **True**, this organization is the default organization.

Error Value

If an error is raised, **Err.Number** is set to one of the values documented in Appendix A, "Error Messages."

Remarks

This is a read-only property. There must be one and only one default organization at any time.

Note

- BizTalk Messaging Manager refers to the default organization as the home organization.

Requirements

Windows NT/2000: Requires Windows 2000 SP1 or later
Library: Use Microsoft BizTalk Server Configuration Objects 1.0 Type Library
(BizTalkObjectModel.dll)

BizTalkOrganization.LoadAlias Method

The **LoadAlias** method loads an associated alias for the object in memory. The alias for an object is the organization qualifier/value pair.

Syntax

object.**LoadAlias**(_
   lAliasHandle **As Long**, _
   pvarName **As Variant**, _
   pvarDefault **As Variant**, _
   pvarQualifier **As Variant**, _
   pvarValue **As Variant** _
)

Parameters

lAliasHandle
   Long that contains the handle to the alias.

pvarName
   Variant that contains the name of the organization identifier.

pvarDefault
   Variant that contains the default flag.

pvarQualifier
   Variant that contains the qualifier of the organization identifier.

pvarValue
   Variant that contains the value of the organization identifier.

Return Values

None

Error Value

If an error is raised, **Err.Number** is set to one of the values documented in Appendix A, "Error Messages."

Remarks

The values used with the parameters of this method can be obtained from the **Aliases** property.

Requirements

Windows NT/2000: Requires Windows 2000 SP1 or later
Library: Use Microsoft BizTalk Server Configuration Objects 1.0 Type Library
(BizTalkObjectModel.dll)

BizTalkOrganization.LoadApplication Method

The **LoadApplication** method loads an associated application for the object in memory.

Syntax

object.**LoadApplication**(_
  lApplicationHandle **As Long**, _
  pvarName **As Variant** _
)

Parameters

lApplicationHandle
  Long that contains the application handle.

pvarName
  Variant that contains the name of the application.

Return Values

None

Error Value

If an error is raised, **Err.Number** is set to one of the values documented in Appendix A,
"Error Messages."

Remarks

The values used with the parameters of this method can be obtained from the **Applications**
property.

Requirements

Windows NT/2000: Requires Windows 2000 SP1 or later
Library: Use Microsoft BizTalk Server Configuration Objects 1.0 Type Library
(BizTalkObjectModel.dll)

BizTalkOrganization.RemoveAlias Method

The **RemoveAlias** method removes an alias. The alias for an object is the organization identifier type/value pair.

Syntax

object.**RemoveAlias**(_
  lAliasHandle **As Long** _
)

Parameters

lAliasHandle
  Long that contains the handle to the alias.

Return Values

None

Error Value

If an error is raised, **Err.Number** is set to one of the values documented in Appendix A, "Error Messages."

Remarks

This record cannot be removed if any of the following conditions apply:

• A **BizTalkPort** or a **BizTalkChannel** object refers to it.

• It has been designated the default organization identifier.

• This alias was autogenerated.

The alias handle can be obtained from the **Aliases** property.

Requirements

Windows NT/2000: Requires Windows 2000 SP1 or later
Library: Use Microsoft BizTalk Server Configuration Objects 1.0 Type Library (BizTalkObjectModel.dll)

BizTalkOrganization.RemoveApplication Method

The **RemoveApplication** method removes an application from the default organization.

Syntax

object.**RemoveApplication**(_
  lApplicationHandle **As Long** _
)

Parameters

lApplicationHandle
  Long that contains the handle.

Return Values

None

Error Value

If an error is raised, **Err.Number** is set to one of the values documented in Appendix A, "Error Messages."

Remarks

This record cannot be removed if a **BizTalkPort** or a **BizTalkChannel** object refers to it.

The application handle can be obtained from the **Applications** property.

Requirements

Windows NT/2000: Requires Windows 2000 SP1 or later
Library: Use Microsoft BizTalk Server Configuration Objects 1.0 Type Library
(BizTalkObjectModel.dll)

BizTalkOrganization.SaveAlias Method

The **SaveAlias** method saves an alias for the object. The alias for an object is the organization identifier type/value pair.

Syntax

object.**SaveAlias**(_
   lAliasHandle **As Long**, _
   strName **As String**, _
   bDefault **As Boolean**, _
   strQualifier **As String**, _
   strValue **As String** _
)

Parameters

lAliasHandle
   Long that contains the handle to the alias.

strName
   String that contains the name of the organization identifier. This parameter cannot be changed if this alias was autogenerated.

bDefault
   Boolean that contains the default flag. A value of **True** indicates that this is the default alias for the organization. A value of **False** indicates that this is not the default alias for the organization.

strQualifier
   String that contains the qualifier of the organization identifier. This parameter cannot be changed if this alias was autogenerated. This parameter cannot be set to "group".

strValue
   String that contains the value of the organization identifier. This parameter cannot be changed if this alias was autogenerated.

Return Values

None

Error Value

If an error is raised, **Err.Number** is set to one of the values documented in Appendix A, "Error Messages."

Requirements

Windows NT/2000: Requires Windows 2000 SP1 or later
Library: Use Microsoft BizTalk Server Configuration Objects 1.0 Type Library
(BizTalkObjectModel.dll)

BizTalkOrganization.SaveApplication Method

The **SaveApplication** method saves this application for the default organization object.

Syntax

object.**SaveApplication**(_
  lApplicationHandle **As Long**, _
  strName **As String** _
)

Parameters

lApplicationHandle
  Long that contains the handle to the application.

strName
  String that contains the name of the application.

Return Values

None

Error Value

If an error is raised, **Err.Number** is set to one of the values documented in Appendix A,
"Error Messages."

Requirements

Windows NT/2000: Requires Windows 2000 SP1 or later
Library: Use Microsoft BizTalk Server Configuration Objects 1.0 Type Library
(BizTalkObjectModel.dll)

BizTalkPort Object

The **BizTalkPort** object configures a one-way transfer of a document between organizations
and applications. It identifies the source organization and/or application, the destination
organization and/or application, the primary transport type, and, if selected, the associated
envelope for transmission.

The properties of the **BizTalkPort** object are shown in the following table.

Property	Type	Description
Channels	IDispatch	ADO recordset that contains information about all **BizTalkChannel** objects that refer to the object. This is a read-only property.
Comments	BSTR	User comments for the **Port** object.
ControlNumberValue	BSTR	Value of the interchange control number. This is a required property if the **Format** property of the associated **BizTalkEnvelope** object is set to "x12", "edifact", or "custom". This constraint is not enforced for this release, but the server fails if it is not adhered to.
DateModified	BSTR	Date and time at which the information in the object was created or last modified. This is a read-only property obtained from the **BizTalkBase** object.
Delimiters	IDispatch	Dictionary object that contains all delimiters used in the document specification. This is a required property if the **Format** property of the associated **BizTalkEnvelope** object is set to "x12", "edifact", or "custom".
DestinationEndpoint	IDispatch	Information about the destination.
EncodingType	BIZTALK_ENCODING_TYPE	Enumeration value that indicates the type of document encoding.
EncryptionCertificateInfo	IDispatch	Information about the certificate that encrypts the document.
EncryptionType	BIZTALK_ENCRYPTION_TYPE	Enumeration value that indicates the type of document encryption.
Envelope	long	Handle to the **BizTalkEnvelope** object associated with this **BizTalkPort** object.
Handle	long	Handle to the object. This is a read-only property obtained from the **BizTalkBase** object.
Name	BSTR	Name of the object. This is a required property obtained from the **BizTalkBase** object.

Property	Type	Description
PrimaryTransport	**IDispatch**	Primary transport component information.
SecondaryTransport	**IDispatch**	Secondary transport component information.
ServiceWindowInfo	**IDispatch**	Service window information.
SignatureType	**BIZTALK_SIGNATURE_TYPE**	Enumeration value that indicates the type of digital signing and verification.

The methods of the **BizTalkPort** object are shown in the following table.

Method	Description
Clear	Clears the object in memory. All the member variables of the object in memory are initialized to their default values. This method is obtained from the **BizTalkBase** object.
Create	Creates a new object in the database. This method is obtained from the **BizTalkBase** object.
Load	Loads the object in memory. This method is obtained from the **BizTalkBase** object
LoadByName	Loads the object by name in memory. This method is obtained from the **BizTalkBase** object.
Remove	Removes the object from the database. This method is obtained from the **BizTalkBase** object.
Save	Saves the object in the database. This method is obtained from the **BizTalkBase** object.

Requirements

Windows NT/2000: Requires Windows 2000 SP1 or later
Library: Use Microsoft BizTalk Server Configuration Objects 1.0 Type Library
(BizTalkObjectModel.dll)

BizTalkPort.Channels Property

The **Channels** property contains an ADO recordset that contains information about all
BizTalkChannel objects that refer to the object.

Syntax

object.**Channels**

Parameters

None

Return Values

This property returns an **Object** that contains the **BizTalkChannel** objects that refer to the object.

Error Value

If an error is raised, **Err.Number** is set to one of the values documented in Error Messages.

Remarks

This is a read-only property.

Each record in the ADO recordset returned by this property contains information about the **BizTalkChannel** objects in the database that are associated with this **BizTalkPort** object. The fields in each record contain the following information, listed in order:

- **Handle**

- **Name**

- A unique channel identifier, in GUID format.

Additional information about Microsoft ActiveX Data Objects is available on the MSDN Online Library Web site (msdn.microsoft.com/library/default.asp).

Requirements

Windows NT/2000: Requires Windows 2000 SP1 or later
Library: Use Microsoft BizTalk Server Configuration Objects 1.0 Type Library
(BizTalkObjectModel.dll)

BizTalkPort.Comments Property

The **Comments** property contains the user comments for the **Port** object.

Syntax

object.**Comments**

Parameters

None

Return Values

This property returns a **String** that contains the comments.

Error Value

If an error is raised, **Err.Number** is set to one of the values documented in Error Messages.

Requirements

Windows NT/2000: Requires Windows 2000 SP1 or later
Library: Use Microsoft BizTalk Server Configuration Objects 1.0 Type Library
(BizTalkObjectModel.dll)

BizTalkPort.ControlNumberValue Property

The **ControlNumberValue** property contains the value of the interchange control number.

Syntax

object.**ControlNumberValue**

Parameters

None

Return Values

This property returns a **String** that contains the interchange control number.

Error Value

If an error is raised, **Err.Number** is set to one of the values documented in Appendix A,
"Error Messages."

Remarks

The **ControlNumberValue** property must contain a value between 1 and 999999999.

Requirements

Windows NT/2000: Requires Windows 2000 SP1 or later
Library: Use Microsoft BizTalk Server Configuration Objects 1.0 Type Library
(BizTalkObjectModel.dll)

BizTalkPort.Delimiters Property

The **Delimiters** property contains a **Dictionary** object that contains all delimiters used in the
document specification. **Delimiters** specifies which characters to use to separate data within
the envelope and the documents that are sent using this envelope.

Syntax

object.**Delimiters**

Parameters

None

Return Values

This property returns an **Object** that contains the delimiters.

Error Value

If an error is raised, **Err.Number** is set to one of the values documented in Appendix A, "Error Messages."

Remarks

This is a required property for the object to be complete if the **Format** property of the associated **BizTalkEnvelope** object is set to "x12", "edifact", or "custom". The **PropertySet** property of the associated **BizTalkDocument** object must also be defined. The following table shows which names are required for the delimiters of the **Dictionary** object for various formats.

Delimiter	X12	EDIFACT
Record_delim	Yes	Yes
Field_delim	Yes	Yes
Subfield_delim	Yes	Yes
Escape_char	No	Yes

Requirements

Windows NT/2000: Requires Windows 2000 SP1 or later
Library: Use Microsoft BizTalk Server Configuration Objects 1.0 Type Library (BizTalkObjectModel.dll)

BizTalkPort.DestinationEndpoint Property

The **DestinationEndpoint** property contains information about the destination. This information includes the **Alias**, **Application**, and **Organization** properties and is created and stored in memory in the **BizTalkEndPoint** object.

Syntax

object.**DestinationEndpoint**

Parameters

None

Return Values

This property returns an **Object** that contains information about the destination.

Error Value

If an error is raised, **Err.Number** is set to one of the values documented in Appendix A, "Error Messages."

Remarks

Once a **BizTalkPort** object has been created, the destination **BizTalkOrganization** object cannot be changed.

Requirements

Windows NT/2000: Requires Windows 2000 SP1 or later
Library: Use Microsoft BizTalk Server Configuration Objects 1.0 Type Library (BizTalkObjectModel.dll)

BizTalkPort.EncodingType Property

The **EncodingType** property contains the enumeration value that indicates the type of document encoding.

Syntax

object.**EncodingType**

Parameters

None

Return Values

This property returns an enumeration value. Valid values are from the **BIZTALK_ENCODING_TYPE** enumeration.

Error Value

If an error is raised, **Err.Number** is set to one of the values documented in Appendix A, "Error Messages."

Remarks

The Clear method sets **EncodingType** to **BIZTALK_ENCODING_TYPE_NONE**.

Requirements

Windows NT/2000: Requires Windows 2000 SP1 or later
Library: Use Microsoft BizTalk Server Configuration Objects 1.0 Type Library
(BizTalkObjectModel.dll)

BizTalkPort.EncryptionCertificateInfo Property

The **EncryptionCertificateInfo** property contains information about the certificate that
encrypts the document. This information includes the **Name**, **Reference**, **Store**, and **Usage**
properties and is created and stored in memory in the **BizTalkCertificateInfo** object.

Syntax

object.**EncryptionCertificateInfo**

Parameters

None

Return Values

This property returns an **Object** that contains the certificate information.

Error Value

If an error is raised, **Err.Number** is set to one of the values documented in Appendix A,
"Error Messages."

Requirements

Windows NT/2000: Requires Windows 2000 SP1 or later
Library: Use Microsoft BizTalk Server Configuration Objects 1.0 Type Library
(BizTalkObjectModel.dll)

BizTalkPort.EncryptionType Property

The **EncryptionType** property contains the enumeration value that indicates the type of
document encryption.

Syntax

object.**EncryptionType**

Parameters

None

Return Values

This property returns an enumeration value. Valid values are from the **BIZTALK_ENCRYPTION_TYPE** enumeration.

Error Value

If an error is raised, **Err.Number** is set to one of the values documented in Appendix A, "Error Messages."

Remarks

The **Clear** method sets **EncryptionType** to **BIZTALK_ENCRYPTION_TYPE_NONE**.

If **EncryptionType** is set to **BIZTALK_ENCRYPTION_TYPE_SMIME**, the **EncryptionCertificateInfo** property must be set.

For open messaging ports, **EncryptionType** must be set to **BIZTALK_ENCRYPTION_TYPE_NONE**.

Requirements

Windows NT/2000: Requires Windows 2000 SP1 or later
Library: Use Microsoft BizTalk Server Configuration Objects 1.0 Type Library (BizTalkObjectModel.dll)

BizTalkPort.Envelope Property

The **Envelope** property contains the handle to the associated **BizTalkEnvelope** object.

Syntax

object.**Envelope**

Parameters

None

Return Values

This property returns a **Long** that contains the handle to the object.

Error Value

If an error is raised, **Err.Number** is set to one of the values documented in Appendix A, "Error Messages."

Requirements

Windows NT/2000: Requires Windows 2000 SP1 or later
Library: Use Microsoft BizTalk Server Configuration Objects 1.0 Type Library
(BizTalkObjectModel.dll)

BizTalkPort.PrimaryTransport Property

The **PrimaryTransport** property contains the primary transport component information,
including the **Address**, **Parameter**, and **Type** properties of the **BizTalkTransportInfo**
object.

Syntax

object.**PrimaryTransport**

Parameters

None

Return Values

This property returns an **Object** that contains the primary transport component information.

Error Value

If an error is raised, **Err.Number** is set to one of the values documented in Appendix A,
"Error Messages."

Remarks

This is a required property for the object.

The following constraints are enforced:

- If the **Openness** property of the associated **BizTalkEndPoint** object is set to
  BIZTALK_OPENNESS_TYPE_EX_DESTINATION, the **Address** property cannot be
  set, and **PrimaryTransport** must be set to
  BIZTALK_TRANSPORT_TYPE_OPENDESTINATION. The
  BizTalkServiceWindowInfo object cannot be used with open destination ports.

- Once a **BizTalkPort** object has been created, the **Openness** property of the associated
  BizTalkEndPoint object cannot be changed.

- The **Openness** property cannot be set to
  BIZTALK_OPENNESS_TYPE_EX_SOURCE or
  BIZTALK_OPENNESS_TYPE_EX_FROMWORKFLOW.

- When using a **Type** property of **BIZTALK_TRANSPORT_TYPE_LOOPBACK**, the
  primary and secondary transport **Address** property cannot be set, and the
  BizTalkServiceWindowInfo object cannot be used.

Requirements

Windows NT/2000: Requires Windows 2000 SP1 or later
Library: Use Microsoft BizTalk Server Configuration Objects 1.0 Type Library
(BizTalkObjectModel.dll)

BizTalkPort.SecondaryTransport Property

The **SecondaryTransport** property contains the secondary transport component information, including the **Address**, **Parameter**, and **Type** properties, and is created and stored in memory in the **BizTalkTransportInfo** object.

Syntax

object.**SecondaryTransport**

Parameters

None

Return Values

This method returns an **Object** that contains the secondary transport component information.

Error Value

If an error is raised, **Err.Number** is set to one of the values documented in Appendix A, "Error Messages."

Remarks

This is a required property for the object to be complete.

The following constraints are enforced:

- If the **Openness** property of the associated **BizTalkEndPoint** object is set to **BIZTALK_OPENNESS_TYPE_EX_DESTINATION**, the **Address** property cannot be set, and **SecondaryTransport** must be set to **BIZTALK_TRANSPORT_TYPE_OPENDESTINATION**.

- Once a **BizTalkPort** object has been created, the **Openness** property of the associated **BizTalkEndPoint** object cannot be changed.

- The **Openness** property cannot be set to **BIZTALK_OPENNESS_TYPE_EX_SOURCE** or **BIZTALK_OPENNESS_TYPE_EX_FROMWORKFLOW**.

- The **Type** property cannot be set to **BIZTALK_TRANSPORT_TYPE_LOOPBACK**.

Requirements

Windows NT/2000: Requires Windows 2000 SP1 or later
Library: Use Microsoft BizTalk Server Configuration Objects 1.0 Type Library
(BizTalkObjectModel.dll)

BizTalkPort.ServiceWindowInfo Property

The **ServiceWindowInfo** property contains information about the service window. This
information includes the **FromTime**, **IsEnabled**, and **ToTime** properties and is created and
stored in memory in the **BizTalkServiceWindowInfo** object.

Syntax

object.**ServiceWindowInfo**

Parameters

None

Return Values

This method returns an **Object** that contains information about the service window.

Error Value

If an error is raised, **Err.Number** is set to one of the values documented in Appendix A,
"Error Messages."

Remarks

If this property is used, the **BizTalkServiceWindowInfo** object must specify a valid time
range by using the **FromTime** and **ToTime** properties.

Requirements

Windows NT/2000: Requires Windows 2000 SP1 or later
Library: Use Microsoft BizTalk Server Configuration Objects 1.0 Type Library
(BizTalkObjectModel.dll)

BizTalkPort.SignatureType Property

The **SignatureType** property contains the enumeration value that indicates the type of digital
signing and verification.

Syntax

object.**SignatureType**

Parameters

None

Return Values

This property returns an enumeration value. Valid values are from the **BIZTALK_SIGNATURE_TYPE** enumeration.

Error Value

If an error is raised, **Err.Number** is set to one of the values documented in Appendix A, "Error Messages."

Remarks

The **Clear** method sets **SignatureType** to **BIZTALK_SIGNATURE_TYPE_NONE**.

BizTalkPort objects associated with open channels cannot have a **SignatureType**.

If the **SignatureType** on a **BizTalkPort** object is changed from **BIZTALK_SIGNATURE_TYPE_NONE** to **BIZTALK_SIGNATURE_TYPE_SMIME**, all channels associated with this **BizTalkPort** object must have already been saved with a **SignatureCertificateInfo** object. Also, if a **BizTalkChannel** contains a **SignatureCertificateInfo** object and the **SignatureType** of the **BizTalkPort** is set to **BIZTALK_SIGNATURE_TYPE_NONE**, the signature will be ignored.

Requirements

Windows NT/2000: Requires Windows 2000 SP1 or later
Library: Use Microsoft BizTalk Server Configuration Objects 1.0 Type Library (BizTalkObjectModel.dll)

BizTalkPortGroup Object

Use the **BizTalkPortGroup** object to configure port groups that are used to distribute the same document to many organizations.

The properties of the **BizTalkPortGroup** object are shown in the following table.

Property	Type	Description
Channels	**IDispatch**	ADO recordset that contains information about all **BizTalkChannel** objects that refer to this object.
DateModified	**BSTR**	Date and time at which the information in the object was created or last modified. This is a read-only property obtained from the **BizTalkBase** object.
Handle	**long**	Handle to the object. This is a read-only property obtained from the **BizTalkBase** object.
Name	**BSTR**	Name of the object. This is a required property obtained from the **BizTalkBase** object.
Ports	**IDispatch**	ADO recordset that contains information about all **BizTalkPort** objects that refer to this object.

The methods of the **BizTalkPortGroup** object are shown in the following table.

Method	Description
AddPort	Adds a **BizTalkPort** object to this port group. There must be at least one **BizTalkPort** object in the port group.
Clear	Clears the object in memory. All member variables of the object in memory are initialized to their default values. This method is obtained from the **BizTalkBase** object.
Create	Creates a new object in the database. This method is obtained from the **BizTalkBase** object.
Load	Loads the object in memory. This method is obtained from the **BizTalkBase** object.
LoadByName	Loads the object by name in memory. This method is obtained from the **BizTalkBase** object.
Remove	Removes the **BizTalkPortGroup** object from the database. This method is obtained from the **BizTalkBase** object.
RemovePort	Removes a **BizTalkPort** object from the port group. There must be at least one **BizTalkPort** object in the port group.
Save	Saves the object in the database. This method is obtained from the **BizTalkBase** object.

Remarks

There must always be at least one **BizTalkPort** object and one **BizTalkChannel** object associated with a **BizTalkPortGroup** object. The **BizTalkChannel** object is associated with the **BizTalkPortGroup** object, not the **BizTalkPort** object within the group. Each

BizTalkPort object within the group has another **BizTalkChannel** object or objects associated with it, but these are ignored when the port group channel is invoked.

Requirements

Windows NT/2000: Requires Windows 2000 SP1 or later
Library: Use Microsoft BizTalk Server Configuration Objects 1.0 Type Library
(BizTalkObjectModel.dll)

BizTalkPortGroup.AddPort Method

The **AddPort** method adds a **BizTalkPort** object to this port group.

Syntax

object.**AddPort**(_
   lPortHandle **As Long** _
)

Parameters

lPortHandle
   Long that contains the handle to the object.

Return Values

None

Error Value

If an error is raised, **Err.Number** is set to one of the values documented in Appendix A, "Error Messages."

Remarks

The following constraints apply to this method:

- There must be at least one **BizTalkPort** in this **BizTalkPortGroup** object.

- The **Openness** property of the associated **BizTalkEndPoint** object to be added must be set to **BIZTALK_OPENNESS_TYPE_NOTOPEN**.

- The port group specified by this object cannot contain any duplicate **BizTalkPort** objects.

Requirements

Windows NT/2000: Requires Windows 2000 SP1 or later
Library: Use Microsoft BizTalk Server Configuration Objects 1.0 Type Library
(BizTalkObjectModel.dll)

BizTalkPortGroup.Channels Property

The **Channels** property contains an ADO recordset that contains information about all **BizTalkChannel** objects that refer to the object.

Syntax

object.**Channels**

Parameters

None

Return Values

This property returns an **Object** that contains all **BizTalkChannel** objects that refer to the object.

Error Value

If an error is raised, **Err.Number** is set to one of the values documented in Appendix A, "Error Messages."

Remarks

Each record in the ADO recordset returned by this property contains information about the **BizTalkChannel** objects in the database that are associated with this **BizTalkPortGroup** object. The fields in each record contain the following information, listed in order:

* Handle

* Name

Additional information about Microsoft ActiveX Data Objects is available on the MSDN Online Library Web site (msdn.microsoft.com/library/default.asp).

Requirements

Windows NT/2000: Requires Windows 2000 SP1 or later
Library: Use Microsoft BizTalk Server Configuration Objects 1.0 Type Library (BizTalkObjectModel.dll)

BizTalkPortGroup.Ports Property

The **Ports** property contains an ADO recordset that contains information about all **BizTalkPort** objects that refer to the object.

Syntax

object.**Ports**

Parameters

None

Return Values

This property returns an **Object** that contains all **BizTalkPort** objects that refer to the object.

Error Value

If an error is raised, **Err.Number** is set to one of the values documented in Appendix A, "Error Messages."

Remarks

Each record in the ADO recordset returned by this property contains information about the **BizTalkPort** objects in the database that are associated with this **BizTalkPortGroup** object. The fields in each record contain the following information, listed in order:

- Handle
- Name

Additional information about Microsoft ActiveX Data Objects is available on the MSDN Online Library Web site (msdn.microsoft.com/library/default.asp).

Requirements

Windows NT/2000: Requires Windows 2000 SP1 or later
Library: Use Microsoft BizTalk Server Configuration Objects 1.0 Type Library (BizTalkObjectModel.dll)

BizTalkPortGroup.RemovePort Method

The **RemovePort** method removes a **BizTalkPort** object from this port group.

Syntax

object.**RemovePort**(_
   lPortHandle **As Long** _
)

Parameters

lPortHandle
Long that contains the handle to the object to remove.

Return Values

None

Error Value

If an error is raised, **Err.Number** is set to one of the values documented in Appendix A, "Error Messages."

Remarks

The last **BizTalkPort** object associated with the object cannot be removed. A **BizTalkPort** object cannot be removed if a **BizTalkChannel** object refers to it.

Requirements

Windows NT/2000: Requires Windows 2000 SP1 or later
Library: Use Microsoft BizTalk Server Configuration Objects 1.0 Type Library (BizTalkObjectModel.dll)

BizTalkServiceWindowInfo Object

Use the **BizTalkServiceWindowInfo** object to configure the service window for an associated **BizTalkPort** object. The service window indicates a valid time range for transmitting documents.

The properties of the **BizTalkServiceWindowInfo** object are shown in the following table.

Property	Type	Description
FromTime	**BSTR**	Earliest time that the interchange can be transmitted.
IsEnabled	**VARIANT_BOOL**	Flag that indicates whether the service window is enabled.
ToTime	**BSTR**	Latest time that the interchange can be transmitted.

Remarks

The **BizTalkServiceWindowInfo** object is automatically created when a **BizTalkPort** object is instantiated with the **CreatePort** method of the **BizTalkConfig** object. Access the properties of the **BizTalkServiceWindowInfo** object by using the **ServiceWindowInfo** property of the **BizTalkPort** object.

Requirements

Windows NT/2000: Requires Windows 2000 SP1 or later
Library: Use Microsoft BizTalk Server Configuration Objects 1.0 Type Library
(BizTalkObjectModel.dll)

BizTalkServiceWindowInfo.FromTime Property

The **FromTime** property indicates the earliest hour of any day that the interchange can be
transmitted.

Syntax

object.**FromTime**

Parameters

None

Return Values

This property returns a **String** that contains the earliest time that the interchange can be
transmitted.

Error Value

If an error is raised, **Err.Number** is set to one of the values documented in Appendix A,
"Error Messages."

Remarks

The **FromTime** property must contain an integer value between 0 and 23. Fractional values
and minutes cannot be specified.

Requirements

Windows NT/2000: Requires Windows 2000 SP1 or later
Library: Use Microsoft BizTalk Server Configuration Objects 1.0 Type Library
(BizTalkObjectModel.dll)

BizTalkServiceWindowInfo.IsEnabled Property

The **IsEnabled** property indicates whether a service window is enabled.

Syntax

object.**IsEnabled**

Parameters

None

Return Values

This property returns a **String** that indicates whether a service window is enabled. A value of **True** indicates that the service window is enabled. A value of **False** indicates that the service window is not enabled.

Error Value

If an error is raised, **Err.Number** is set to one of the values documented in Appendix A, "Error Messages."

Requirements

Windows NT/2000: Requires Windows 2000 SP1 or later
Library: Use Microsoft BizTalk Server Configuration Objects 1.0 Type Library (BizTalkObjectModel.dll)

BizTalkServiceWindowInfo.ToTime Property

The **ToTime** property contains the latest hour of any day that the interchange can be transmitted.

Syntax

object.**ToTime**

Parameters

None

Return Values

This property returns a **String** that contains the latest time that the interchange can be transmitted.

Error Value

If an error is raised, **Err.Number** is set to one of the values documented in Appendix A, "Error Messages."

Remarks

The **ToTime** property must contain an integer value between 0 and 23. Fractional values and minutes cannot be specified.

Requirements

Windows NT/2000: Requires Windows 2000 SP1 or later
Library: Use Microsoft BizTalk Server Configuration Objects 1.0 Type Library
(BizTalkObjectModel.dll)

BizTalkTransportInfo Object

Use the **BizTalkTransportInfo** object to configure the transport service for an associated
BizTalkPort object.

The properties of the **BizTalkTransportInfo** object are shown in the following table.

Property	Type	Description
Address	**BSTR**	Destination address of the primary transport component.
Parameter	**BSTR**	Required return e-mail address for the associated source **BizTalkOrganization** object if the **Type** property is **BIZTALK_TRANSPORT_TYPE_SMTP**.
Type	**BIZTALK_TRANSPORT_TYPE**	Enumeration value that indicates the type of transport component to be used for the primary transport.

Remarks

The **BizTalkTransportInfo** object is automatically created when a **BizTalkPort** object is
instantiated with the **CreatePort** method of the **BizTalkConfig** object. Access the
BizTalkTransportInfo object by using the **PrimaryTransport** or **SecondaryTransport**
property of the **BizTalkPort** object.

Requirements

Windows NT/2000: Requires Windows 2000 SP1 or later
Library: Use Microsoft BizTalk Server Configuration Objects 1.0 Type Library
(BizTalkObjectModel.dll)

BizTalkTransportInfo.Address Property

The **Address** property contains the destination address.

Syntax

object.**Address**

Parameters

None

Return Values

This property returns a **String** that contains the address.

Error Value

If an error is raised, **Err.Number** is set to one of the values documented in Appendix A, "Error Messages."

Remarks

If the **Openness** property of the associated **BizTalkEndPoint** object is set to **BIZTALK_OPENNESS_TYPE_DESTINATION**, **Address** cannot be set, and the **Type** property must be set to **BIZTALK_TRANSPORT_TYPE_OPENDESTINATION**.

Address must have one of the following prefixes, according to the **Type** property.

Transport type	Prefix	Example Address value
APPINTEGRATION	Not applicable	{11111111-1111-1111-1111-111111111111}
FILE	file://	file://C:\Test\MyFile.xml
HTTP	http://	http://www.vigorair-18.com/repository/bts.asp
HTTPS	https://	https://www.vigorair-18.com/secure/btss.asp
LOOPBACK	Not applicable	Not applicable
MSMQ	Not applicable	DIRECT=OS:.\private$\myqueue
NONE	Not applicable	Not applicable
OPENDESTINATION	Not applicable	Not applicable
ORCHESTRATIONACTIVATION	Not applicable	C:\XLANG\Schedules\mysched.skx
SMTP	mailto:	mailto:patricia@vigorair-18.com

Notes

- The queue:// prefix must be used with an open messaging port when a Message Queue is specified as the destination address. For open messaging ports, the address is specified either in the document instance or as a parameter when submitting the document. For more information, see Chapter 10, "Submitting Documents."

- When using the Orchestration Activation Component transport type, the **Address** property must contain the full path of the XLANG schedule on the local computer. The file:// prefix cannot be used when specifying the path of the XLANG schedule (.skx) file.

- When using the HTTP or HTTPS transport types, BizTalk Server sends the data using a proxy server by default. This is the correct setting to transport data to computers outside your company's firewall. However, when sending data within your company's intranet, you can bypass the use of a proxy server. To do this, you must set the UseProxy field to **False** in the transport dictionary. For more information, see "BizTalkChannel.SetConfigData Method" earlier in this chapter.

When using the file:// transport type, you can include symbols to modify the file name. The file name created by the server contains any static characters you specified in the **Address** property, along with the actual value of the symbol. For example, if the **Address** property is set to "file://C:\Orders\Invoice_%tracking_id%.xml", the actual file name would use a format similar to: C:\Orders\Invoice_{12345678-90AB-CDEF-1234-567890ABCDEF}. The following table contains the symbols that can be used with the file:// transport type.

Symbol	Description	Unique file name
%datetime%	Date and time, in milliseconds, of the file creation. The time is based on Greenwich Mean Time (GMT) rather than local time.	No
%document_name%	Name of the document processed by BizTalk Server.	No
%server%	Host name of the server that processed the document.	No
%tracking_id%	Globally unique tracking number.	Yes
%uid%	Counter that increases over time, represented in milliseconds. This number is reset when the server is rebooted.	No

When sending reliable messaging receipts that use the SMTP transport protocol, the value specified in the identifier named Reliable Messaging Acknowledgement SMTP From Address is used as the From address. This identifier is automatically created for the default **BizTalkOrganization** object. This identifier cannot be removed. You should not modify the name or qualifier for this identifier, but you can modify the value. For more information, see "Processing Receipts Using Reliable Messaging" earlier in this chapter.

Requirements

Windows NT/2000: Requires Windows 2000 SP1 or later
Library: Use Microsoft BizTalk Server Configuration Objects 1.0 Type Library (BizTalkObjectModel.dll)

BizTalkTransportInfo.Parameter Property

The **Parameter** property contains the required return e-mail address of the associated source **BizTalkOrganization** object if the **Type** property is set to **BIZTALK_TRANSPORT_TYPE_SMTP**.

Syntax

object.**Parameter**

Parameters

None

Return Values

This property returns a **String** that contains the address.

Error Value

If an error is raised, **Err.Number** is set to one of the values documented in Appendix A, "Error Messages."

Requirements

Windows NT/2000: Requires Windows 2000 SP1 or later
Library: Use Microsoft BizTalk Server Configuration Objects 1.0 Type Library (BizTalkObjectModel.dll)

BizTalkTransportInfo.Type Property

The **Type** property contains the enumeration value that indicates the type of transport component.

Syntax

object.**Type**

Parameters

None

Return Values

This property returns an enumeration value. Valid values are from the **BIZTALK_TRANSPORT_TYPE** enumeration.

Error Value

If an error is raised, **Err.Number** is set to one of the values documented in Appendix A, "Error Messages."

Remarks

The following constraints are enforced:

- If the **Openness** property of the associated **BizTalkEndPoint** object is set to **BIZTALK_OPENNESS_TYPE_DESTINATION**, the **Address** property cannot be set, and **Type** must be set to **BIZTALK_TRANSPORT_TYPE_OPENDESTINATION**.

When using the Message Queuing transport type (**BIZTALK_TRANSPORT_TYPE_MSMQ**), the following restrictions apply:

- When using an envelope, the maximum size of a document submitted to BizTalk Server is 4 MB.

- When an envelope is not used, the maximum size of a document submitted to BizTalk Server is 2 MB.

- When using **BIZTALK_TRANSPORT_TYPE_SMTP**, the **Parameter** property must be set to the reply-to SMTP address.

- The transport **Type** of **BIZTALK_TRANSPORT_TYPE_ORCHESTRATIONACTIVATION** is supported only when the **Openness** property of the associated **BizTalkEndPoint** object is set to **BIZTALK_OPENNESS_TYPE_TOWORKFLOW**.

When using the Orchestration activation component type (**BIZTALK_TRANSPORT_TYPE_ORCHESTRATIONACTIVATION**), the maximum size of a document sent to the port on the XLANG schedule is 2 MB.

Requirements

Windows NT/2000: Requires Windows 2000 SP1 or later
Library: Use Microsoft BizTalk Server Configuration Objects 1.0 Type Library (BizTalkObjectModel.dll)

CDictionary Object

The **Dictionary** object is a collection object that supports the creation, storage, and retrieval of name/value pairs in memory. This object is used by several methods in the BizTalk Messaging Configuration object model.

In Microsoft Visual Basic, the **CDictionary** class defines the methods and properties of a **Dictionary** object.

The properties of the **Dictionary** object are shown in the following table.

Property	Type	Description
Count	**long**	Number of entries in the **Dictionary** object. This is a read-only property.
NewEnum	**IUnknown**	Returns the **IUnknown** interface pointer for the **Dictionary** object. The caller can use this interface pointer to call **QueryInterface** for the enumerator for this object. This is a read-only property.
Prefix	**BSTR**	Filter that excludes all entries with a specific prefix when the contents of the **Dictionary** object are saved.
Value	**VARIANT**	Value associated with an entry name.

The methods of the **Dictionary** object are shown in the following table.

Method	Description
GetMultiple	Returns the values of multiple entries from the **Dictionary** object.
PutMultiple	Adds specified entries to the **Dictionary** object or changes them.

Remarks

A **Dictionary** object is designed to be a general-purpose collection. Therefore, it can be used for anything that is supported by its internal structure. Every value in a **Dictionary** object is a **Variant**. This means that a **Dictionary** object can be created that consists of almost any kind of value (including other **Dictionary** objects).

Requirements

Windows NT/2000: Requires Windows 2000 SP1 or later
Library: Use Microsoft Commerce 2000 Core Components Type Library (MscsCore.dll)

CDictionary.Count Property

The **Count** property returns the number of elements in the **Dictionary** object.

Syntax

object.**Count**

Parameters

None

Return Values

This property returns a **Long** that contains the count.

Error Value

If an error is raised, **Err.Number** is set to one of the values documented in Appendix A, "Error Messages."

Remarks

This property is read-only.

Requirements

Windows NT/2000: Requires Windows 2000 SP1 or later
Library: Use Microsoft Commerce 2000 Core Components Type Library (MscsCore.dll)

CDictionary.GetMultiple Method

The **GetMultiple** method returns multiple entries from the **Dictionary** object.

Syntax

object.**GetMultiple**(_
  cb **As Long**, _
  rgolestr **As String**, _
  rgvar **As Variant** _
)

Parameters

cb

    Long that specifies the number of values to retrieve.

rgolestr

    Array of string values that identifies the **CDictionary** object entries for which the values should be retrieved.

rgvar

    Array of **Variant**s. When **GetMultiple** returns, this array contains the values associated with the **CDictionary** object entries identified by the *rgolestr* array.

Return Values

None

Error Value

If an error is raised, **Err.Number** is set to one of the values documented in Appendix A, "Error Messages."

Remarks

If you call **PutMultiple** or **GetMultiple** from Microsoft Visual Basic Scripting Edition (VBScript), these methods fail because they require data types that VBScript does not support.

Requirements

Windows NT/2000: Requires Windows 2000 SP1 or later
Library: Use Microsoft Commerce 2000 Core Components Type Library (MscsCore.dll)

CDictionary.Prefix Property

The **Prefix** property contains a filter that excludes entries with a specific prefix when the contents of the **Dictionary** object are saved.

Syntax

object.**Prefix**

Parameters

None

Return Values

This property returns a **String** that contains the prefix.

Error Value

If an error is raised, **Err.Number** is set to one of the values documented in Appendix A, "Error Messages."

Remarks

Any name/value pair with a name beginning with the specified prefix is not saved to the database. The prefix default is an underscore (_). Therefore, any keywords that begin with an underscore are not saved unless the prefix is changed.

Requirements

Windows NT/2000: Requires Windows 2000 SP1 or later
Library: Use Microsoft Commerce 2000 Core Components Type Library (MscsCore.dll)

CDictionary.PutMultiple Method

The **PutMultiple** method adds specified entries to the **Dictionary** object or changes them.

Syntax

*object***.PutMultiple**(_
   cb **As Long,** _
   rgolestr **As String,** _
   rgvar **As Variant** _
)

Parameters

cb
> **Long** that identifies the number of elements in the *rgolestr* and *rgvar* arrays.

rgolestr
> Array of **String**s that contains the names to add to the **CDictionary** object.

rgvar
> Array of **Variant**s that contains the values to add to the **CDictionary** object.

Return Values

None

Error Value

If an error is raised, **Err.Number** is set to one of the values documented in Appendix A, "Error Messages."

Remarks

A one-to-one mapping exists between the elements of the *rgolestr* and *rgvar* arrays. This means that *rgolestr*[*n*] is added to the **Dictionary** object and is initialized to *rgvar*[*n*]. If the element specified by *rgolestr*[*n*] is already in the **Dictionary** object, the value associated with the element is overwritten with the value stored in *rgvar*[*n*].

If you call **PutMultiple** or **GetMultiple** from Microsoft Visual Basic Scripting Edition (VBScript), these methods fail because they require data types that VBScript does not support.

Requirements

Windows NT/2000: Requires Windows 2000 SP1 or later
Library: Use Microsoft Commerce 2000 Core Components Type Library (MscsCore.dll)

CDictionary.Value Property

The **Value** property returns or sets the value associated with an entry name.

Syntax

object.**Value(** _
   bstrName **As String** _
)

Parameters

bstrName
   String that contains the name.

Return Values

This property optionally returns a **Variant** that contains the value.

Error Value

If an error is raised, **Err.Number** is set to one of the values documented in Appendix A, "Error Messages."

Remarks

The value of a **Dictionary** object can be read or written to without explicitly using the **Value** method by treating the named entry as a property of the **Dictionary** object.

Requirements

Windows NT/2000: Requires Windows 2000 SP1 or later
Library: Use Microsoft Commerce 2000 Core Components Type Library (MscsCore.dll)

CSimpleList Object

Use the **SimpleList** object to create an array of variants that supports enumeration.

In Microsoft Visual Basic, the **CSimpleList** class defines the methods and properties of a **SimpleList** object.

The properties of the **SimpleList** object are shown in the following table.

Property	Type	Description
Count	**long**	Number of elements in the **SimpleList** object. This is a read-only property.
Item	**VARIANT**	Container for an element of the **SimpleList** object.

The methods of the **SimpleList** object are shown in the following table.

Method	Description
Add	Adds the specified item to the **SimpleList** object.
Delete	Deletes the specified item from the **SimpleList** object.

Requirements

Windows NT/2000: Requires Windows 2000 SP1 or later
Library: Use Microsoft Commerce 2000 Core Components Type Library (MscsCore.dll)

CSimpleList.Add Method

The **Add** method adds the specified item to the **SimpleList** object.

Syntax

object.**Add**(_
    pVar **As Variant** _
)

Parameters

pVar
    Variant to add to the **CSimpleList** object.

Return Values

None

Error Value

If an error is raised, **Err.Number** is set to one of the values documented in Appendix A, "Error Messages."

Requirements

Windows NT/2000: Requires Windows 2000 SP1 or later
Library: Use Microsoft Commerce 2000 Core Components Type Library (MscsCore.dll)

CSimpleList.Count Property

The **Count** property returns the number of elements in the **SimpleList** object.

Syntax

object.**Count**

Parameters

None

Return Values

This property returns a **Long** that contains the number of items in the **CSimpleList** object.

Error Value

If an error is raised, **Err.Number** is set to one of the values documented in Appendix A, "Error Messages."

Remarks

This property is read-only.

Requirements

Windows NT/2000: Requires Windows 2000 SP1 or later
Library: Use Microsoft Commerce 2000 Core Components Type Library (MscsCore.dll)

CSimpleList.Delete Method

The **Delete** method deletes the specified item from the **SimpleList** object.

Syntax

object.**Delete(** _
    Index **As Long** _
)

Parameters

Index
    Long that contains the index value of the item to delete.

Return Values

None

Error Value

If an error is raised, **Err.Number** is set to one of the values documented in Appendix A, "Error Messages."

Requirements

Windows NT/2000: Requires Windows 2000 SP1 or later
Library: Use Microsoft Commerce 2000 Core Components Type Library (MscsCore.dll)

CSimpleList.Item Property

The **Item** property is a read/write **Variant** that contains an element of the **SimpleList** object. An initialized **Variant** is stored at a specified array index. If an item is already stored at the specified index, that item is overwritten by the put method.

Syntax

object.**Item**(_
   Index **As Long**_
)

Parameters

Index
   Long that contains the index of the item.

Return Values

This property returns a **Variant** that contains the new item.

Error Value

If an error is raised, **Err.Number** is set to one of the values documented in Appendix A, "Error Messages."

Remarks

When putting a value, use the **putref_Item** method if you are setting an object reference; use the **put_Item** method if you are setting a scalar value.

Requirements

Windows NT/2000: Requires Windows 2000 SP1 or later
Library: Use Microsoft Commerce 2000 Core Components Type Library (MscsCore.dll)

Object Model Reference for C++

This section provides reference information about interfaces used by Microsoft BizTalk Server 2000 for programming with Microsoft Visual C++. Reference information is provided for all interfaces, objects, methods, properties, and enumerations exposed for accessing the BizTalk Messaging Configuration object model. For a complete listing of error messages, see Appendix A, "Error Messages."

IBizTalkBase Interface

The **IBizTalkBase** interface defines common methods and properties that are inherited by the following objects.

- **BizTalkChannel**
- **BizTalkDocument**
- **BizTalkEnvelope**
- **BizTalkOrganization**
- **BizTalkPort**
- **BizTalkPortGroup**

 Note

The methods and properties of this object are always invoked on the objects listed above, rather than by creating an actual **BizTalkBase** object.

The properties of the **BizTalkBase** object are shown in the following table.

Property	Type	Description
DateModified	**BSTR**	Date and time at which the information in the object was created or last modified. This is a read-only property.
Handle	**long**	Handle to the object. This is a read-only property.
Name	**BSTR**	Name of the object.

The methods of the **BizTalkBase** object are shown in the following table.

Method	Description
Clear	Clears the object in memory. All the member variables of the object in memory are initialized to their default values.
Create	Creates a new object in the database.
Load	Loads a specified object in memory.
LoadByName	Loads a specified object by name in memory.
Remove	Removes the object from the database.
Save	Saves the object in the database.

Requirements

Windows NT/2000: Requires Windows 2000 SP1 or later
Header: Include BizTalkObjectModel.h

IBizTalkBase::Clear Method

The **Clear** method clears the object in memory. All member variables of the object in memory are initialized to their default values.

Syntax

HRESULT Clear;

Parameters

None

Return Values

For a list of all error messages returned by BizTalk Server, see Appendix A, "Error Messages."

Applies To

This method is supported by the following objects:

- **BizTalkChannel**
- **BizTalkDocument**
- **BizTalkEnvelope**
- **BizTalkOrganization**
- **BizTalkPort**
- **BizTalkPortGroup**

Requirements

Windows NT/2000: Requires Windows 2000 SP1 or later
Header: Include BizTalkObjectModel.h

IBizTalkBase::Create Method

The **Create** method creates a new object in the database.

Syntax

HRESULT Create(
   long* *plBiztalkObjectHandle*
);

Parameters

plBiztalkObjectHandle
   [out, retval] Pointer to a **long** that contains the handle to the object.

Return Values

For a list of all error messages returned by BizTalk Server, see Appendix A, "Error Messages."

Applies To

This method is supported by the following objects:

- **BizTalkChannel**
- **BizTalkDocument**
- **BizTalkEnvelope**
- **BizTalkOrganization**
- **BizTalkPort**
- **BizTalkPortGroup**

Remarks

The **Name** property must be set before calling this method. **Name** must be unique across the database for each object type. **Create** updates the **DateModified** property.

When creating any object that refers to an XML document specification or map located outside your local domain, you might receive an error. If an error occurs, download and configure the WinHTTP proxy utility. To download this utility, go to the MSDN Online Downloads Web site (msdn.microsoft.com/downloads/default.asp) and browse to the WinHTTP Proxy Configuration Utility page, which is located in the XML chapter of the Web Development book.

Requirements

Windows NT/2000: Requires Windows 2000 SP1 or later
Header: Include BizTalkObjectModel.h

IBizTalkBase::DateModified Property

The **DateModified** property contains the date and time at which the information in the object was created or last modified.

Syntax

Get method:

HRESULT get_DateModified(
   BSTR* *pstrModified*
);

Parameters

pstrModified
   [out, retval] Pointer to a **BSTR** that contains the date modified.

Return Values

For a list of all error messages returned by BizTalk Server, see Appendix A, "Error Messages."

Applies To

This property is supported by the following objects:

- **BizTalkChannel**
- **BizTalkDocument**
- **BizTalkEnvelope**
- **BizTalkOrganization**
- **BizTalkPort**
- **BizTalkPortGroup**

Remarks

This is a read-only property. The format for the *pstrModified* string is *yyyy-mm-dd hh:mm:ss*. The time is in coordinated universal time (UTC). The server sets this property when the **Create** or the **Save** method is called for the object.

Requirements

Windows NT/2000: Requires Windows 2000 SP1 or later
Header: Include BizTalkObjectModel.h

IBizTalkBase::Handle Property

The **Handle** property contains the handle to the object.

Syntax

Get method:

HRESULT get_Handle(
    long* *plBiztalkObjectHandle*
);

Parameters

plBiztalkObjectHandle
    [out, retval] Pointer to a **long** that contains the handle to the object.

Return Values

For a list of all error messages returned by BizTalk Server, see Appendix A, "Error Messages."

Applies To

This property is supported by the following objects:

- **BizTalkChannel**
- **BizTalkDocument**
- **BizTalkEnvelope**
- **BizTalkOrganization**
- **BizTalkPort**
- **BizTalkPortGroup**

Remarks

This is a read-only property.

Requirements

Windows NT/2000: Requires Windows 2000 SP1 or later
Header: Include BizTalkObjectModel.h

IBizTalkBase::Load Method

The **Load** method loads an object in memory.

Syntax

HRESULT Load(
    long *lBiztalkObjectHandle*
);

Parameters

lBiztalkObjectHandle
    [in] **Long** that contains the handle to the object to load.

Return Values

For a list of all error messages returned by BizTalk Server, see Appendix A, "Error Messages."

Applies To

This method is supported by the following objects:

- **BizTalkChannel**
- **BizTalkDocument**
- **BizTalkEnvelope**

- **BizTalkOrganization**
- **BizTalkPort**
- **BizTalkPortGroup**

Remarks

Load calls the **Clear** method internally before loading the object.

Requirements

Windows NT/2000: Requires Windows 2000 SP1 or later
Header: Include BizTalkObjectModel.h

IBizTalkBase::LoadByName Method

The **LoadByName** method loads an object by name in memory.

Syntax

HRESULT LoadByName(
   BSTR *strName*
);

Parameters

strName
   [in] **BSTR** that contains the name.

Return Values

For a list of all error messages returned by BizTalk Server, see Appendix A, "Error Messages."

Applies To

This method is supported by the following objects:

- **BizTalkChannel**
- **BizTalkDocument**
- **BizTalkEnvelope**
- **BizTalkOrganization**
- **BizTalkPort**
- **BizTalkPortGroup**

Remarks

LoadByName calls the **Clear** method internally before loading the object.

Names have a maximum length of 64 characters.

Requirements

Windows NT/2000: Requires Windows 2000 SP1 or later
Header: Include BizTalkObjectModel.h

IBizTalkBase::Name Property

The **Name** property contains the name of the object.

Syntax

Get method:

HRESULT get_Name(
   BSTR* *pstrName*
);

Put method:

HRESULT put_Name(
   BSTR *strName*
);

Parameters

Get method:

pstrName
   [out, retval] Pointer to a **BSTR** that contains the name of the object.

Put method:

strName
   [in] **BSTR** that contains the name of the object.

Return Values

For a list of all error messages returned by BizTalk Server, see Appendix A, "Error Messages."

Applies To

This property is supported by the following objects:

- **BizTalkChannel**
- **BizTalkDocument**

- **BizTalkEnvelope**
- **BizTalkOrganization**
- **BizTalkPort**
- **BizTalkPortGroup**

Remarks

The server requires the **Name** property. It must be set before calling the **Create** or the **Save** method for the object. **Name** must be unique across a database for each object type and must be at least one character long. Names have a maximum length of 64 characters.

The following table lists names reserved for use by BizTalk Server.

Name	Object type
Reliable Message Acknowledgement Port	**IBizTalkPort**
Reliable Message Acknowledgement Channel	**IBizTalkChannel**
BizTalk Canonical Receipt	**IBizTalkDocument**
Reliable Messaging Acknowledgement	**IBizTalkDocument**
Reliable Messaging Acknowledgement SMTP From Address	**IBizTalkOrganization** alias
Home Organization	**IBizTalkOrganization**

Requirements

Windows NT/2000: Requires Windows 2000 SP1 or later
Header: Include BizTalkObjectModel.h

IBizTalkBase::Remove Method

The **Remove** method removes the object from the database.

Syntax

HRESULT Remove;

Parameters

None

Return Values

For a list of all error messages returned by BizTalk Server, see Appendix A, "Error Messages."

Applies To

This method is supported by the following objects:

- **BizTalkChannel**
- **BizTalkDocument**
- **BizTalkEnvelope**
- **BizTalkOrganization**
- **BizTalkPort**
- **BizTalkPortGroup**

Remarks

The object cannot be removed if any other object refers to it.

A **BizTalkOrganization** object cannot be removed if it is the default organization. Before it can be removed, the **IsDefault** property must be set to **False**, and another organization must have the **IsDefault** property set to **True**.

Requirements

Windows NT/2000: Requires Windows 2000 SP1 or later
Header: Include BizTalkObjectModel.h

IBizTalkBase::Save Method

The **Save** method saves the object in the database.

Syntax

HRESULT Save;

Parameters

None

Return Values

For a list of all error messages returned by BizTalk Server, see Appendix A, "Error Messages."

Applies To

This method is supported by the following objects:

- **BizTalkChannel**
- **BizTalkDocument**
- **BizTalkEnvelope**
- **BizTalkOrganization**
- **BizTalkPort**
- **BizTalkPortGroup**

Remarks

The **Save** method updates the **DateModified** property.

When saving any object that refers to an XML document specification or map located outside your local domain, you might receive an error. If an error occurs, download and configure the WinHTTP proxy utility. To download this utility, go to the MSDN Online Downloads Web site (msdn.microsoft.com/downloads/default.asp) and browse to the WinHTTP Proxy Configuration Utility page, which is located in the XML chapter of the Web Development book.

Requirements

Windows NT/2000: Requires Windows 2000 SP1 or later
Header: Include BizTalkObjectModel.h

IBizTalkCertificateInfo Interface

Use this object to configure a certificate associated with a **BizTalkPort** or a **BizTalkChannel** object.

In C++, use the **IBizTalkCertificateInfo** interface to access the methods of the **BizTalkCertificateInfo** object.

The properties of the **BizTalkCertificateInfo** object are shown in the following table.

Property	Type	Description
Name	**BSTR**	Name of the certificate. This is a read-only property.
Reference	**BSTR**	Reference to the certificate in the certificate store.
Store	**BIZTALK_STORE_TYPE**	Store type of the certificate.
Usage	**BIZTALK_USAGE_TYPE**	Type of use for the certificate. This is a read-only property.

Remarks

This object is automatically created when a **BizTalkPort** or a **BizTalkChannel** object is instantiated with the **CreatePort** or the **CreateChannel** method of the **BizTalkConfig** object.

For output documents, access the **BizTalkCertificateInfo** object by using the **EncryptionCertificateInfo** property of the **BizTalkPort** object. For input documents, access the **BizTalkCertificateInfo** object by using the **SignatureCertificateInfo**, **VerifySignatureCertificateInfo**, or **DecryptionCertificateInfo** property of the **BizTalkChannel** object. To obtain the set of all existing **BizTalkCertificateInfo** objects, use the **Certificates** property of the **BizTalkConfig** object.

Note

- All certificates are stored in the local computer store. To configure certificates for the S/MIME components, the script or application accessing the object model must be run in the context of a user account in the BizTalk Server Administrators group.

Requirements

Windows NT/2000: Requires Windows 2000 SP1 or later
Header: Include BizTalkObjectModel.h

IBizTalkCertificateInfo::Name Property

The **Name** property contains the name of the certificate.

Syntax

Get method:

HRESULT get_Name(
  BSTR* *pstrName*
);

Parameters

pstrName
   [out, retval] Pointer to a **BSTR** that contains the name.

Return Values

For a list of all error messages returned by BizTalk Server, see Appendix A, "Error Messages."

Remarks

This is a read-only property.

Requirements

Windows NT/2000: Requires Windows 2000 SP1 or later
Header: Include BizTalkObjectModel.h

IBizTalkCertificateInfo::Reference Property

The **Reference** property contains a reference to the certificate in the certificate store.

Syntax

Get method:

HRESULT get_Reference(
  BSTR* *pstrReference*
);

Put method:

HRESULT put_Reference(
  BSTR *strReference*
);

Parameters

Get method:

pstrReference
  [out, retval] Pointer to a **BSTR** that contains the certificate reference.

Put method:

strReference
  [in] **BSTR** that contains the certificate reference.

Return Values

For a list of all error messages returned by BizTalk Server, see Appendix A, "Error Messages."

✎ Note

- In addition to the HRESULT values listed on the error messages page, the put method returns CryptoAPI errors. Additional information about CryptoAPI is available on the MSDN Online Library Web site (msdn.microsoft.com/library/default.asp).

Remarks

A reference to a certificate should be obtained by using the **Certificates** property on the **BizTalkConfig** object.

Requirements

Windows NT/2000: Requires Windows 2000 SP1 or later
Header: Include BizTalkObjectModel.h

IBizTalkCertificateInfo::Store Property

The **Store** property contains the store type for the certificate.

Syntax

Get method:

HRESULT get_Store(
  BIZTALK_STORE_TYPE* *pStoreType*
);

Put method:

HRESULT put_Store(
  BIZTALK_STORE_TYPE *eStoreType*
);

Parameters

Get method:

pStoreType
  [out, retval] Pointer to an enumeration value that contains the certificate store type. Valid values are from the **BIZTALK_STORE_TYPE** enumeration.

Put method:

eStoreType
  [in] Enumeration value that contains the certificate store type. Valid values are from the **BIZTALK_STORE_TYPE** enumeration.

Return Values

For a list of all error messages returned by BizTalk Server, see Appendix A, "Error Messages."

Remarks

The store, which contains the certificate, is determined by the use of the certificate as follows:

Certificate type	Store
Decryption	MY
Encryption	BIZTALK
Signature	MY
Verify signature	BIZTALK

Requirements

Windows NT/2000: Requires Windows 2000 SP1 or later
Header: Include BizTalkObjectModel.h

IBizTalkCertificateInfo::Usage Property

The **Usage** property contains the type of use for the certificate.

Syntax

Get method:

HRESULT get_Usage(
   BIZTALK_USAGE_TYPE* *pUsageType*
);

Parameters

pUsageType
   [out, retval] Pointer to an enumeration value. Valid values are from the
   BIZTALK_USAGE_TYPE enumeration.

Return Values

For a list of all error messages returned by BizTalk Server, see Appendix A, "Error
Messages."

Remarks

This is a read-only property.

Requirements

Windows NT/2000: Requires Windows 2000 SP1 or later
Header: Include BizTalkObjectModel.h

IBizTalkChannel Interface

Use the methods and properties of the **BizTalkChannel** object to configure a channel for processing documents.

In C++, use the **IBizTalkChannel** interface to access the methods of the **BizTalkChannel** object.

The properties of the **BizTalkChannel** object are shown in the following table.

Property	Type	Description
Comments	BSTR	User comments for the object.
ControlNumberValue	BSTR	Value of the group control number.
DateModified	BSTR	Date and time at which the information in the object was created or last modified. This is a read-only property obtained from the **BizTalkBase** object.
DecryptionCertificateInfo	IDispatch	Information about the certificate that decrypts the input document.
ExpectReceiptTimeout	long	Time, in minutes, in which to expect the receipt for the current document before treating the document as expired.
Expression	BSTR	Complete set of equations that filter the selection of the object.
Handle	long	Identifier of the object. This is a read-only property obtained from the **BizTalkBase** object.
InputDocument	long	Handle to the input **BizTalkDocument** object. This is a required property.
IsReceiptChannel	VARIANT_BOOL	Flag that indicates whether the object is a receipt channel.
LoggingInfo	IDispatch	Information about logging.
MapContent	BSTR	Contents of the map that provide instructions on how the input document in the format used by the source organization is to be rendered in the format used by the destination organization, if different. This is a read-only property.

Property	Type	Description
MapReference	**BSTR**	Full Web Distributed Authoring and Versioning (WebDAV) URL of the map that provides instructions on how the input document in the format used by the source organization is to be rendered in the format used by the destination organization, if different. This is a required property if the **InputDocument** property is different from the **OutputDocument** property.
Name	**BSTR**	Name of the object. This is a required property obtained from the **BizTalkBase** object.
OutputDocument	**long**	Handle to the output **BizTalkDocument** object. This is a required property.
Port	**long**	Associated **BizTalkPort** object. Either the **Port** or the **PortGroup** property must be specified.
PortGroup	**long**	Associated **BizTalkPortGroup** object. Either the **Port** or the **PortGroup** property must be specified.
ReceiptChannel	**long**	Handle to the receipt channel for this object.
RetryCount	**long**	Number of times to retry submitting a document when there is a failure to connect to the destination.
RetryInterval	**long**	Interval between attempts to resubmit a document when there is a failure to connect to the destination. This value is specified in minutes.
SignatureCertificateInfo	**IDispatch**	Information about the certificate that signs the output document.
SourceEndpoint	**IDispatch**	Information about the source.
TrackFields	**IDispatch**	Dictionary object that stores additional custom tracking fields used to track interchange data for the **BizTalkDocument** object for the associated **BizTalkChannel** object.
VerifySignatureCertificateInfo	**IDispatch**	Information about the certificate that verifies the signature of the input document.

The methods of the **BizTalkChannel** object are shown in the following table.

Method	Description
Clear	Clears the object in memory. All member variables of the object in memory are initialized to their default values. This method is obtained from the **BizTalkBase** object.
Create	Creates a new object in the database. This method is obtained from the **BizTalkBase** object.
GetConfigComponent	Reads the CLSID of the component associated with the **BizTalkPort** object.
GetConfigData	Gets the configuration associated with the specified **BizTalkPort** object.
Load	Loads an object in memory. This method is obtained from the **BizTalkBase** object.
LoadByName	Loads an object by name in memory. This method is obtained from the **BizTalkBase** object.
Remove	Removes the object. This method is obtained from the **BizTalkBase** object.
Save	Saves the object to the database. This method is obtained from the **BizTalkBase** object.
SetConfigComponent	Sets the CLSID of the component associated with the **BizTalkPort** object.
SetConfigData	Sets the configuration information for the associated **BizTalkPort** object.

Remarks

A **BizTalkChannel** object requires an associated complete **BizTalkPort** object. One or more **BizTalkChannel** objects can be associated with a **BizTalkPort** object. A **BizTalkChannel** object can be associated with only one input **BizTalkDocument** object and one output **BizTalkDocument** object; however, a **BizTalkDocument** object can be associated with more than one **BizTalkChannel** object.

Requirements

Windows NT/2000: Requires Windows 2000 SP1 or later
Header: Include BizTalkObjectModel.h

IBizTalkChannel::Comments Property

The **Comments** property contains the user comments for the object.

Syntax

Get method:

HRESULT get_Comments(
 BSTR* *pstrComments*
);

Put method:

HRESULT put_Comments(
 BSTR *strComments*
);

Parameters

Get method:

pstrComments
 [out, retval] Pointer to a **BSTR** that contains the comments.

Put method:

strComments
 [in] **BSTR** that contains the comments.

Return Values

For a list of all error messages returned by BizTalk Server, see Appendix A, "Error Messages."

Requirements

Windows NT/2000: Requires Windows 2000 SP1 or later
Header: Include BizTalkObjectModel.h

IBizTalkChannel::ControlNumberValue Property

The **ControlNumberValue** property contains the value of the group control number.

Syntax

Get method:

HRESULT get_ControlNumberValue(
   BSTR* *pstrControlNumberValue*
);

Put method:

HRESULT put_ControlNumberValue(
   BSTR *strControlNumberValue*
);

Parameters

Get method:

pstrControlNumberValue
   [out, retval] Pointer to a **BSTR** that contains the control number.

Put method:

strControlNumberValue
   [in] **BSTR** that contains the control number.

Return Values

For a list of all error messages returned by BizTalk Server, see Appendix A, "Error Messages."

Remarks

The **ControlNumberValue** property must contain a value between 1 and 999999999.

If the **Format** property of the **BizTalkEnvelope** object for the associated **BizTalkPort** object is set to X12, EDIFACT, or Custom, this property is required.

Requirements

Windows NT/2000: Requires Windows 2000 SP1 or later
Header: Include BizTalkObjectModel.h

IBizTalkChannel::DecryptionCertificateInfo Property

The **DecryptionCertificateInfo** property contains information about the certificate that decrypts the input document. This information includes the **Name**, **Reference**, **Store**, and **Usage** properties and is created and stored in memory in the **BizTalkCertificateInfo** object.

Syntax

Get method:

HRESULT get_DecryptionCertificateInfo(
    IDispatch** *ppDecryptionCertificateInfoDisp*
);

Putref method:

HRESULT putref_DecryptionCertificateInfo(
    IDispatch* *pDecryptionCertificateInfoDisp*
);

Parameters

Get method:

ppDecryptionCertificateInfoDisp
    [out, retval] Address of a pointer to an **IDispatch** interface that contains the certificate information.

Putref method:

pDecryptionCertificateInfoDisp
    [in] Pointer to an **IDispatch** interface that contains the certificate information.

Return Values

For a list of all error messages returned by BizTalk Server, see Appendix A, "Error Messages."

Requirements

Windows NT/2000: Requires Windows 2000 SP1 or later
Header: Include BizTalkObjectModel.h

IBizTalkChannel::ExpectReceiptTimeout Property

The **ExpectReceiptTimeout** property contains the value of the time, in minutes, in which to expect the receipt for the current document before treating the document as expired.

Syntax

Get method:

HRESULT get_ExpectReceiptTimeout(
   long* *plMinutes*
);

Put method:

HRESULT put_ExpectReceiptTimeout(
   long *lMinutes*
);

Parameters

Get method:

plMinutes
   [out, retval] Pointer to a **long** that contains the minutes.

Put method:

lMinutes
   [in] **Long** that contains the minutes.

Return Values

For a list of all error messages returned by BizTalk Server, see Appendix A, "Error Messages."

Requirements

Windows NT/2000: Requires Windows 2000 SP1 or later
Header: Include BizTalkObjectModel.h
Library: Use Microsoft BizTalk Server Configuration Objects 1.0 Type Library (BizTalkObjectModel.dll)

IBizTalkChannel::Expression Property

The **Expression** property contains an expression that filters the selection of the **BizTalkChannel** object. If the expression evaluates to true, the server selects the channel for processing the document.

Syntax

Get method:

HRESULT get_Expression(
  BSTR* *pstrExpression*
);

Put method:

HRESULT put_Expression(
  BSTR *strExpression*
);

Parameters

Get method:

pstrExpression

  [out, retval] Pointer to a **BSTR** that contains the XPath expression.

Put method:

strExpression

  [in] **BSTR** that contains the XPath expression.

Return Values

For a list of all error messages returned by BizTalk Server, see Appendix A, "Error Messages."

Remarks

The XPath expression must be based on the input document specification set in the **InputDocument** property.

☑ Note

- If the specification field that you are using to create an expression has a Boolean data type, you cannot use the text strings "true" or "false" as the expression value. You must use a numerical value instead: "-1" for true and "0" for false. For example, to filter a channel so it processes only approved purchase orders, your expression might look like this:

```
Channel1.Expression = "/PORequest/Total[IsApproved = -1]"
```

This sample assumes that the input document specification contains a Total subelement with a Boolean IsApproved field.

Requirements

Windows NT/2000: Requires Windows 2000 SP1 or later
Header: Include BizTalkObjectModel.h

IBizTalkChannel::GetConfigComponent Method

The **GetConfigComponent** method retrieves the CLSID of the component associated with the **BizTalkPort** object.

Syntax

HRESULT GetConfigComponent(
   BIZTALK_CONFIGDATA_TYPE *eConfigType*,
   long *lPortHandle*,
   BSTR* *pstrCLSID*
);

Parameters

eConfigType
   [in] Enumeration value. Valid values are from the **BIZTALK_CONFIGDATA_TYPE** enumeration.

lPortHandle
   [in] **Long** that contains the handle to the **BizTalkPort** object.

pstrCLSID
   [out, retval] Pointer to a **BSTR** that contains the CLSID of the component.

Return Values

For a list of all error messages returned by BizTalk Server, see Appendix A, "Error Messages."

Note

In addition to the HRESULT values listed on the error messages page, this method returns OLEDB provider errors. Additional information about OLEDB is available on the MSDN Online Library Web site (msdn.microsoft.com/library/default.asp).

Remarks

If the *eConfigType* parameter is set to **BIZTALK_CONFIGDATA_TYPE_SIGNATURE** and the associated **BizTalkPort** object has both the **EncryptionType** and **SignatureType** properties set to S/MIME, this method returns an empty string ("").

Requirements

Windows NT/2000: Requires Windows 2000 SP1 or later
Header: Include BizTalkObjectModel.h

IBizTalkChannel::GetConfigData Method

The **GetConfigData** method gets the configuration associated with the specified **BizTalkPort**
object.

Syntax

HRESULT GetConfigData(
    BIZTALK_CONFIGDATA_TYPE *eConfigType,*
    long *lPortHandle,*
    VARIANT* *pvarType,*
    VARIANT* *pvarDictionary*
);

Parameters

eConfigType
    [in] Enumeration value. Valid values are from the **BIZTALK_CONFIGDATA_TYPE**
    enumeration.

lPortHandle
    [in] **Long** that identifies the handle to the associated **BizTalkPort** object.

pvarType
    [in, out] Pointer to a **VARIANT** that contains the transport type.

pvarDictionary
    [in, out] Pointer to a **VARIANT** that contains a pointer to the **IDictionary** interface of an
    object that contains the primary transport configuration information.

Return Values

For a list of all error messages returned by BizTalk Server, see Appendix A, "Error
Messages."

Note

In addition to the HRESULT values listed on the error messages page, this method returns
OLEDB provider errors. Additional information about OLEDB is available on the MSDN
Online Library Web site (msdn.microsoft.com/library/default.asp).

Remarks

The **Dictionary** object returned by this method has specific string qualifiers used for
EDIFACT and X12. The following tables describe these strings.

EDIFACT

Qualifier string	Description
SerializerEdifact_SenderIntID	Interchange sender internal identification
SerializerEdifact_SenderIntSubID	Interchange sender internal subidentification
SerializerEdifact_RecipientIntID	Interchange recipient internal identification
SerializerEdifact_RecipientIntSubID	Interchange recipient internal subidentification
SerializerEdifact_RecipientRefPwd	Recipient reference/password
SerializerEdifact_RecipientRefPwdQual	Recipient reference/password qualifier
SerializerEdifact_ApplicationRef	Application reference
SerializerEdifact_ProcPriCode	Processing priority code
SerializerEdifact_AckRequest	Acknowledgment request
SerializerEdifact_AgreementID	Interchange agreement identifier
SerializerEdifact_TestInd	Test indicator
SerializerEdifact_UNACtrl	"Send UNA Always" or "Send UNA Only When Required"
SerializerEdifact_SyntaxID	Syntax identifier

X12

Qualifier string	Description
SerializerX12_AuthInfoQual	Authorization information qualifier
SerializerX12_AuthInfo	Authorization information
SerializerX12_SecInfoQual	Security information qualifier
SerializerX12_SecInfo	Security information
SerializerX12_CtrlStdID	Interchange control standards identifier
SerializerX12_CtrlVerNum	Interchange control version number
SerializerX12_AckRequired	Acknowledgment required
SerializerX12_UseInd	Usage indicator

✎ Notes

- For more information about the EDIFACT standard, go to the United Nations Economic Commission for Europe Web site (www.unece.org).

- For more information about the X12 standard, go to the Data Interchange Standards Association Web site (www.disa.org).

If you override the transport properties of a **BizTalkPort** object with this method and then change the transport properties in that **BizTalkPort** object, you must call this method again.

If the *eConfigType* parameter is set to **BIZTALK_CONFIGDATA_TYPE_SIGNATURE** and the associated **BizTalkPort** object has both the **EncryptionType** and **SignatureType** properties set to S/MIME, this method returns an empty **Dictionary** object.

Requirements

Windows NT/2000: Requires Windows 2000 SP1 or later
Header: Include BizTalkObjectModel.h

IBizTalkChannel::InputDocument Property

The **InputDocument** property contains the handle to the **BizTalkDocument** object that describes the input document specification.

Syntax

Get method:

HRESULT get_InputDocument(
  long* *plInDocHandle*
);

Put method:

HRESULT put_InputDocument(
  long *lInDocHandle*
);

Parameters

Get method:

plInDocHandle
  [out, retval] Pointer to a **long** that contains the handle to the input **BizTalkDocument** object.

Put method:

lInDocHandle
  [in] **Long** that contains the handle to the input **BizTalkDocument** object.

Return Values

For a list of all error messages returned by BizTalk Server, see Appendix A, "Error Messages."

Remarks

This is a required property.

This property cannot be changed after the **Create** or the **Save** method is called.

Requirements

Windows NT/2000: Requires Windows 2000 SP1 or later
Header: Include BizTalkObjectModel.h

IBizTalkChannel::IsReceiptChannel Property

The **IsReceiptChannel** property contains a flag that indicates whether the object is a receipt channel.

Syntax

Get method:

HRESULT get_IsReceiptChannel(
  VARIANT_BOOL* *pbIsReceiptChannel*
);

Put method:

HRESULT put_IsReceiptChannel(
  VARIANT_BOOL *bIsReceiptChannel*
);

Parameters

Get method:

pbIsReceiptChannel
   [out, retval] Pointer to a **VARIANT_BOOL** that contains the flag. A value of
   VARIANT_TRUE indicates that this channel is used as a receipt channel. A value of
   VARIANT_FALSE indicates that this channel is not used as a receipt channel.

Put method:

bIsReceiptChannel
   [in] **VARIANT_BOOL** that contains the flag. A value of VARIANT_TRUE indicates
   that this channel is used as a receipt channel. A value of VARIANT_FALSE indicates that
   this channel is not used as a receipt channel.

Return Values

For a list of all error messages returned by BizTalk Server, see Appendix A,
"Error Messages."

Requirements

Windows NT/2000: Requires Windows 2000 SP1 or later
Header: Include BizTalkObjectModel.h

BizTalkChannel::LoggingInfo Property

The **LoggingInfo** property contains information about logging the document. This information includes the **LogNativeInputDocument**, **LogNativeOutputDocument**, **LogXMLInputDocument**, and **LogXMLOutputDocument** properties and is created and stored in memory in the **BizTalkLoggingInfo** object.

Syntax

Get method:

HRESULT get_LoggingInfo(
    IDispatch** *ppLoggingInfoDisp*
);

Putref method:

HRESULT putref_LoggingInfo(
    IDispatch* *pLoggingInfoDisp*
);

Parameters

Get method:

ppLoggingInfoDisp
    [out, retval] Address of a pointer to an **IDispatch** interface that contains the logging fields.

Putref method:

pLoggingInfoDisp
    [in] Pointer to an **IDispatch** interface that contains the logging fields.

Return Values

For a list of all error messages returned by BizTalk Server, see Appendix A, "Error Messages."

Requirements

Windows NT/2000: Requires Windows 2000 SP1 or later
Header: Include BizTalkObjectModel.h

IBizTalkChannel::MapContent Property

The **MapContent** property contains the contents of the map that provide instructions on how the input document in the format used by the source organization is to be rendered in the format used by the destination organization, if different.

Syntax

Get method:

HRESULT get_MapContent(
  BSTR* *pstrMapContent*
);

Parameters

pstrMapContent
    [in] **BSTR** that contains the map contents.

Return Values

For a list of all error messages returned by BizTalk Server, see Appendix A, "Error Messages."

Remarks

This is a read-only property. The **Create** and **Save** methods copy the text of the map specified by the **MapReference** property to this string, if empty.

Once you have created or saved a **BizTalkChannel** object with **MapReference** set to a map, any changes you make to the content of the referenced map are not automatically updated on the referring **BizTalkChannel** object. To update the **BizTalkChannel** object that refers to the revised map, you must save the map, reset the **MapReference** property of the **BizTalkChannel** object to its current value, and then call **Save** on the referring **BizTalkChannel** object.

Requirements

Windows NT/2000: Requires Windows 2000 SP1 or later
Header: Include BizTalkObjectModel.h

IBizTalkChannel::MapReference Property

The **MapReference** property contains the full Web Distributed Authoring and Versioning (WebDAV) URL of the map that provides instructions about how the input document in the format used by the source organization is to be rendered in the format used by the destination organization, if different.

Syntax

Get method:

HRESULT get_MapReference(
    BSTR* *pstrReference*
);

Put method:

HRESULT put_MapReference(
    BSTR *strReference*
);

Parameters

Get method:

pstrReference
    [out, retval] Pointer to a **BSTR** that contains the map name.

Put method:

strReference
    [in] **BSTR** that contains the map name.

Return Values

For a list of all error messages returned by BizTalk Server, see Appendix A, "Error Messages."

Remarks

This is a required property if the **InputDocument** property refers to a different document specification than the **OutputDocument** property.

Once you have created or saved a **BizTalkChannel** object with **MapReference** set to a map, any changes you make to the content of the referenced map are not automatically updated on the referring **BizTalkChannel** object. To update the **BizTalkChannel** object that refers to the revised map, you must save the map, reset the **MapReference** property of the **BizTalkChannel** object to its current value, and then call **Save** on the referring **BizTalkChannel** object.

Requirements

Windows NT/2000: Requires Windows 2000 SP1 or later
Header: Include BizTalkObjectModel.h

IBizTalkChannel::OutputDocument Property

The **OutputDocument** property contains the handle to the **BizTalkDocument** object that describes the output document specification.

Syntax

Get method:

HRESULT get_OutputDocument(
  long* *plOutDocHandle*
);

Put method:

HRESULT put_OutputDocument(
  long *lOutDocHandle*
);

Parameters

Get method:

plOutDocHandle
  [out, retval] Pointer to a **long** that contains the handle to the output **BizTalkDocument** object.

Put method:

lOutDocHandle
  [in] **Long** that contains the handle to the output **BizTalkDocument** object.

Return Values

For a list of all error messages returned by BizTalk Server, see Appendix A, "Error Messages."

Remarks

This is a required property. This property cannot be changed after the **Create** or the **Save** method is called.

If the **Openness** property of the associated **BizTalkEndPoint** object is set to **BIZTALK_OPENNESS_TYPE_SOURCE**, the **InputDocument** property can identify an input **BizTalkDocument** object that has an X12 or an EDIFACT specification. If it does, however, **OutputDocument** must not identify a **BizTalkDocument** object that has an X12 or an EDIFACT specification.

If the **Openness** property of the associated **BizTalkEndPoint** object is set to **BIZTALK_OPENNESS_TYPE_DESTINATION**, the **OutputDocument** property for this **BizTalkChannel** object must not identify an output **BizTalkDocument** object that has an X12 or an EDIFACT specification.

Requirements

Windows NT/2000: Requires Windows 2000 SP1 or later
Header: Include BizTalkObjectModel.h

IBizTalkChannel::Port Property

The **Port** property contains the handle to the associated **BizTalkPort** object.

Syntax

Get method:

HRESULT get_Port(
    long* *plPortHandle*
);

Put method:

HRESULT put_Port(
    long *lPortHandle*
);

Parameters

Get method:

plPortHandle
    [out, retval] Pointer to a **long** that contains the handle to the **BizTalkPort** object.

Put method:

lPortHandle
    [in] **Long** that contains the handle to the **BizTalkPort** object.

Return Values

For a list of all error messages returned by BizTalk Server, see Appendix A, "Error Messages."

Remarks

The following constraints are enforced:

*   Either the **Port** or the **PortGroup** property must be specified for a channel.

*   This property cannot be changed after the **Create** or the **Save** method is called.

Requirements

Windows NT/2000: Requires Windows 2000 SP1 or later
Header: Include BizTalkObjectModel.h

IBizTalkChannel::PortGroup Property

The **PortGroup** property contains the handle to the associated **BizTalkPortGroup** object.

Syntax

Get method:

HRESULT get_PortGroup(
    long* *plPortGroupHandle*
);

Put method:

HRESULT put_PortGroup(
    long *lPortGroupHandle*
);

Parameters

Get method:

plPortGroupHandle
    [out, retval] Pointer to a **long** that contains the handle to the associated
    BizTalkPortGroup object.

Put method:

lPortGroupHandle
    [in] **Long** that contains the handle to the associated **BizTalkPortGroup** object.

Return Values

For a list of all error messages returned by BizTalk Server, see Appendix A,
"Error Messages."

Remarks

The following constraints are enforced:

- Either the **Port** property or **PortGroup** must be specified for a channel.

- This property cannot be changed after the **Create** or the **Save** method is called.

Requirements

Windows NT/2000: Requires Windows 2000 SP1 or later
Header: Include BizTalkObjectModel.h

IBizTalkChannel::ReceiptChannel Property

The **ReceiptChannel** property contains the handle to the receipt channel for this object.

Syntax

Get method:

HRESULT get_ReceiptChannel(
   long* *plReceiptChannelHandle*
);

Put method:

HRESULT put_ReceiptChannel(
   long *lReceiptChannelHandle*
);

Parameters

Get method:

plReceiptChannelHandle
   [out, retval] Pointer to a **long** that contains the handle.

Put method:

lReceiptChannelHandle
   [in] **Long** that contains the handle.

Return Values

For a list of all error messages returned by BizTalk Server, see Appendix A, "Error Messages."

Remarks

A **BizTalkChannel** object can specify a receipt channel only if it is not a receipt channel itself. The channel specified as the receipt channel must have the **IsReceiptChannel** property set to VARIANT_TRUE. In addition, the receipt channel must use a messaging port with a **DestinationEndpoint** that is the same as the **SourceEndpoint** on the channel using the receipt channel. This allows the receipt channel to send a receipt to the original source of the document.

Requirements

Windows NT/2000: Requires Windows 2000 SP1 or later
Header: Include BizTalkObjectModel.h

IBizTalkChannel::RetryCount Property

The **RetryCount** property specifies the number of times to retry submitting a document when a destination connection failure occurs.

Syntax

Get method:

HRESULT get_RetryCount(
    long* *plCount*
);

Put method:

HRESULT put_RetryCount(
    long *lCount*
);

Parameters

Get method:

plCount
    [out, retval] Pointer to a **long** that contains the number of retries.

Put method:

lCount
    [in] **Long** that contains the number of retries.

Return Values

For a list of all error messages returned by BizTalk Server, see Appendix A, "Error Messages."

Remarks

The **RetryCount** property must contain a value between 0 and 999. The default value is 3 retries.

Requirements

Windows NT/2000: Requires Windows 2000 SP1 or later
Header: Include BizTalkObjectModel.h

IBizTalkChannel::RetryInterval Property

The **RetryInterval** property specifies the amount of time, in minutes, between retry attempts when a destination connection failure occurs during document submission.

Syntax

Get method:

HRESULT get_RetryInterval(
   long* *pInterval*
);

Put method:

HRESULT put_RetryInterval(
   long *lInterval*
);

Parameters

Get method:

pInterval
   [out, retval] Pointer to a **long** that contains the retry interval, in minutes.

Put method:

lInterval
   [in] **Long** that contains the retry interval, in minutes.

Return Values

For a list of all error messages returned by BizTalk Server, see Appendix A, "Error Messages."

Remarks

The **RetryInterval** property must contain a value between 1 and 63999. The default value is 5 minutes.

Requirements

Windows NT/2000: Requires Windows 2000 SP1 or later
Header: Include BizTalkObjectModel.h

IBizTalkChannel::SetConfigComponent Method

The **SetConfigComponent** method sets the CLSID of the component associated with the **BizTalkPort** object.

Syntax

HRESULT SetConfigComponent(
  BIZTALK_CONFIGDATA_TYPE *eConfigType*,
  long *lPortHandle*,
  BSTR *strCLSID*
);

Parameters

eConfigType
  [in] Enumeration value. Valid values are from the **BIZTALK_CONFIGDATA_TYPE** enumeration. The **BIZTALK_CONFIGDATA_TYPE_PRIMARYTRANSPORT** and **BIZTALK_CONFIGDATA_TYPE_SECONDARYTRANSPORT** enumeration values cannot be used with this method.

lPortHandle
  [in] **Long** that contains the handle.

strCLSID
  [in] **BSTR** that contains the CLSID of the component.

Return Values

For a list of all error messages returned by BizTalk Server, see Appendix A, "Error Messages."

Requirements

Windows NT/2000: Requires Windows 2000 SP1 or later
Header: Include BizTalkObjectModel.h

IBizTalkChannel::SetConfigData Method

The **SetConfigData** method sets the configuration information for the **BizTalkPort** object.

Syntax

HRESULT SetConfigData(
  BIZTALK_CONFIGDATA_TYPE *eConfigType*,
  long *lConfigDataHandle*,
  IDispatch* *pConfigDataDisp*
);

Parameters

eConfigType
   [in] Enumeration value. Valid values are from the **BIZTALK_CONFIGDATA_TYPE** enumeration.

lConfigDataHandle
   [in] **Long** that identifies the handle to the associated **BizTalkPort** object.

pConfigDataDisp
   [in] Pointer to the **IDictionary** interface of an object that contains information about the component specified in the *eConfigType* parameter.

Return Values

For a list of all error messages returned by BizTalk Server, see Appendix A, "Error Messages."

Remarks

The **Dictionary** object passed to this method has specific string qualifiers used for EDIFACT and X12. For a description of these qualifiers, see the "IBizTalk Channel::Get Config Data Method" earlier in this chapter.

When using the **BIZTALK_CONFIGDATA_TYPE_PRIMARYTRANSPORT** or **BIZTALK_CONFIGDATA_TYPE_SECONDARYTRANSPORT** enumeration value, the content of the transport dictionary varies according to the transport protocol used. The following tables list the transport dictionary fields for each protocol.

HTTP and HTTPS

Field name	Data type	Required	Description
URL	String	Yes	URL of the document destination.
ContentType	String	No	Value for the Content-Type HTTP/HTTPS property that appears in HTTP headers during transmission. The default value is an empty string ("").
ClientCert	String	No	Reference to the certificate used with SSL connections using HTTPS. The default value is an empty string ("").
ProxyName	String	No	URL of the proxy server used when sending documents outside a firewall.
ProxyPort	Integer	No	Port number used by the proxy server.
UseProxy	Boolean	No	Value that indicates whether the proxy server is used. The default value is True.

Local File

Field name	Data type	Required	Description
Filename	String	Yes	Name and path of the file to be created.
CopyMode	Integer	No	Value that indicates how the file should be written. Use a value of 0 for overwrite mode, a value of 1 for append mode, and a value of 2 to create a new file. The default value is append mode (1).
UserName	String	No	Windows NT user name needed to access a file share. The default value is an empty string ("").
Password	String	No	Windows NT user name needed to access a file share. The default value is an empty string ("").

Message Queuing

Field name	Data type	Required	Description
QueueName	String	Yes	Name of the Messaging Queue to which the document is sent.
MessageLabel	String	Yes	Value specified in the message label field on the queue.
Priority	Integer	No	Priority of the message placed in the queue. This must be a value between 0 and 7, where a higher value indicates a higher priority. The default value is 3
AuthLevel	Integer	No	Value indicating whether the message needs to be authenticated using a digital signature. Use a value of 0 to bypass authentication. A value of 1 indicates that authentication will be used. The default value is 0.
Delivery	Integer	No	Value indicating how a message is delivered to a queue. Use a value of 1 to indicate that the message should be backed up until it is delivered to the queue. A value of 0 indicates that the message is only resident in memory. The default value is 0.

Requirements

Windows NT/2000: Requires Windows 2000 SP1 or later
Header: Include BizTalkObjectModel.h

IBizTalkChannel::SignatureCertificateInfo Property

The **SignatureCertificateInfo** property contains information about the certificate that signs the output document. This information includes the **Name**, **Reference**, **Store**, and **Usage** properties and is created and stored in memory in the **BizTalkCertificateInfo** object.

Syntax

Get method:

HRESULT get_SignatureCertificateInfo(
    IDispatch** *ppSignatureCertificateInfoDisp*
);

Putref method:

HRESULT putref_SignatureCertificateInfo(
    IDispatch* *pSignatureCertificateInfoDisp*
);

Parameters

Get method:

ppSignatureCertificateInfoDisp
    [out, retval] Address of a pointer to an **IDispatch** interface that contains the certificate information.

Putref method:

pSignatureCertificateInfoDisp
    [in] Pointer to an **IDispatch** interface that contains the certificate information.

Return Values

For a list of all error messages returned by BizTalk Server, see Appendix A, "Error Messages."

Requirements

Windows NT/2000: Requires Windows 2000 SP1 or later
Header: Include BizTalkObjectModel.h

IBizTalkChannel::SourceEndpoint Property

The **SourceEndpoint** property contains information about the source. This information includes the **Alias**, **Application**, and **Organization** properties and is created and stored in memory in the **BizTalkEndPoint** object.

Syntax

Get method:

HRESULT get_SourceEndpoint(
   IDispatch** *ppSrcEndpointDisp*
);

Putref method:

HRESULT putref_SourceEndpoint(
   IDispatch* *pSrcEndpointDisp*
);

Parameters

Get method:

ppSrcEndpointDisp
   [out, retval] Address of a pointer to an **IDispatch** interface that contains information about the source.

Putref method:

pSrcEndpointDisp
   [in] Pointer to an **IDispatch** interface that contains information about the source.

Return Values

For a list of all error messages returned by BizTalk Server, see Appendix A, "Error Messages."

Requirements

Windows NT/2000: Requires Windows 2000 SP1 or later
Header: Include BizTalkObjectModel.h

IBizTalkChannel::TrackFields Property

The **TrackFields** property identifies the **Dictionary** object that points to the specification that contains fields to track interchange data on input documents for this **BizTalkChannel** object. These tracking fields override the fields set in the **TrackFields** property on the **BizTalkDocument** object.

Syntax

Get method:

HRESULT get_TrackFields(
    IDispatch* *ppTrackFieldsDisp*
);

Putref method:

HRESULT putref_TrackFields(
    IDispatch* *pTrackFieldsDisp*
);

Parameters

Get method:

ppTrackFieldsDisp
    [out, retval] Address of a pointer to the **IDictionary** interface of an object that contains the custom tracking fields.

Putref method:

pTrackFieldsDisp
    [in] Pointer to the **IDictionary** interface of an object that contains the custom tracking fields.

Return Values

For a list of all error messages returned by BizTalk Server, see Appendix A, "Error Messages."

Remarks

The fields in the **Dictionary** object must contain an XPath value that identifies the field to be tracked in a document. By default, the **Dictionary** object provides eight predefined fields for tracking data in a document. These predefined fields consist of two fields for each of the following data types: integer, real, date, and string. If additional fields are required for tracking, you can use the x_custom_search field in the **Dictionary** object, and set the value to a **SimpleList** object. The **SimpleList** object contains a list of XPath values pointing to the additional tracking fields. XPath values can be added to and deleted from this list using the **Add** and **Delete** methods.

The following table shows the field names in the **Dictionary** object for **TrackFields**.

Field Name	Field type
i_value1	Integer value
i_value2	Integer value
r_value1	Real value
r_value2	Real value
d_value1	Date value
d_value2	Date value
s_value1	String value
s_value2	String value
x_custom_search	A list to return one or more additional data items

For more information about XPath expressions, go to the MSDN Online Library Web site (msdn.microsoft.com/library/default.asp) and search for XPath.

Requirements

Windows NT/2000: Requires Windows 2000 SP1 or later
Header: Include BizTalkObjectModel.h

IBizTalkChannel::VerifySignatureCertificateInfo Property

The **VerifySignatureCertificateInfo** property contains information about the certificate that verifies the signature of the input document. This information includes the **Name**, **Reference**, **Store**, and **Usage** properties and is created and stored in memory in the **BizTalkCertificateInfo** object.

Syntax

Get method:

HRESULT get_VerifySignatureCertificateInfo(
    IDispatch** *ppVerifySignatureCertificateInfoDisp*
);

Putref method:

HRESULT putref_VerifySignatureCertificateInfo(
    IDispatch* *pVerifySignatureCertificateInfoDisp*
);

Parameters

Get method:

ppVerifySignatureCertificateInfoDisp
[out, retval] Address of a pointer to an **IDispatch** interface that contains the certificate information.

Put method:

pVerifySignatureCertificateInfoDisp
[in] Pointer to an **IDispatch** interface that contains the certificate information.

Return Values

For a list of all error messages returned by BizTalk Server, see Appendix A, "Error Messages."

Requirements

Windows NT/2000: Requires Windows 2000 SP1 or later
Header: Include BizTalkObjectModel.h

IBizTalkConfig Interface

Use the **BizTalkConfig** object to create channels, document specifications, envelopes, organizations, ports, and port groups.

In C++, use the **IBizTalkConfig** interface to access the methods of the **BizTalkConfig** object.

The properties of the **BizTalkConfig** object are shown in the following table.

Property	Data type	Description
Certificates	**Object**	Returns an ADO recordset that contains all specified certificates. This is a read-only property.
Channels	**Object**	Returns an ADO recordset that contains all **BizTalkChannel** objects. This is a read-only property.
Documents	**Object**	Returns an ADO recordset that contains all **BizTalkDocument** objects. This is a read-only property.
Envelopes	**Object**	Returns an ADO recordset that contains all **BizTalkEnvelope** objects.
Organizations	**Object**	Returns an ADO recordset that contains all **BizTalkOrganization** objects. This is a read-only property.
PortGroups	**Object**	Returns an ADO recordset that contains all **BizTalkPortGroup** objects. This is a read-only property.
Ports	**Object**	Returns an ADO recordset that contains all **BizTalkPort** objects. This is a read-only property.

The methods of the **BizTalkConfig** object are shown in the following table.

Method	Description
CreateChannel	Returns the address of a pointer to a new **BizTalkChannel** object.
CreateDocument	Returns the address of a pointer to a new **BizTalkDocument** object.
CreateEnvelope	Returns the address of a pointer to a new **BizTalkEnvelope** object.
CreateOrganization	Returns the address of a pointer to a new **BizTalkOrganization** object.
CreatePort	Returns the address of a pointer to a new **BizTalkPort** object.
CreatePortGroup	Returns the address of a pointer to a new **BizTalkPortGroup** object.

Remarks

In C++, each object created by using one of the methods of this interface inherits the following common methods from the **IBizTalkBase** interface:

- **DateModified**
- **Handle**
- **Name**
- **Clear**
- **Create**
- **Load**
- **LoadByName**
- **Remove**
- **Save**

When **BizTalkPort** and **BizTalkChannel** objects are created, BizTalk Server automatically creates some associated subobjects. You can access these subobjects by using properties of the **BizTalkPort** and **BizTalkChannel** objects.

The relationship between objects, their subobjects, and the properties used to obtain the subobjects is shown in the following table.

Subobject	Associated object	Property to set
BizTalkEndPoint	BizTalkPort	DestinationEndpoint
BizTalkEndPoint	BizTalkChannel	SourceEndpoint
BizTalkLoggingInfo	BizTalkChannel	LoggingInfo
BizTalkTransportInfo	BizTalkPort	PrimaryTransport, SecondaryTransport
BizTalkServiceWindowInfo	BizTalkPort	ServiceWindowInfo
BizTalkCertificateInfo	BizTalkPort	EncryptionCertificateInfo
BizTalkCertificateInfo	BizTalkChannel	SignatureCertificateInfo, VerifySignatureCertificateInfo, or DecryptionCertificateInfo

Requirements

Windows NT/2000: Requires Windows 2000 SP1 or later
Header: Include BizTalkObjectModel.h

IBizTalkConfig::Certificates Property

The **Certificates** property returns an ADO recordset that contains all specified certificates.

Syntax

Get method:

HRESULT get_Certificates(
    BIZTALK_STORE_TYPE *StoreType*,
    BIZTALK_USAGE_TYPE *UsageType,*
    BSTR *NamePrefix*,
    IDispatch** *ppCertsDisp*
);

Parameters

StoreType
    [in] Enumeration value. Valid values are from the **BIZTALK_STORE_TYPE** enumeration.

UsageType
    [in] Enumeration value. Valid values are from the **BIZTALK_USAGE_TYPE** enumeration.

NamePrefix

[in] **BSTR** that contains a prefix used as the selection criteria for certificate names. Any certificate **Name** starting with this value is returned in the recordset. This value is case sensitive.

ppCertsDisp

[out, retval] Address of a pointer to an **IDispatch** interface that contains all specified certificates.

Return Values

For a list of all error messages returned by BizTalk Server, see Appendix A, "Error Messages."

✎ Note

- In addition to the HRESULT values listed on the error messages page, this method returns OLEDB provider errors. Additional information about OLEDB is available on the MSDN Online Library Web site (msdn.microsoft.com/library/default.asp).

Remarks

This is a read-only property.

Each record in the ADO recordset returned by this property contains information about an existing **BizTalkCertificateInfo** object in the database. The fields in each record contain the following information, listed in order:

- **NameReference**

- **Store**

- **Usage**

Additional information about Microsoft ActiveX Data Objects is available on th MSDN Online Library Web site (msdn.microsoft.com/library/default.asp).

Requirements

Windows NT/2000: Requires Windows 2000 SP1 or later
Header: Include BizTalkObjectModel.h

IBizTalkConfig::Channels Property

The **Channels** property returns an ADO recordset that contains all **BizTalkChannel** objects.

Syntax

Get method:

HRESULT Channels(
   IDispatch** *ppChannelsDisp*
);

Parameters

ppChannelsDisp
   [out, retval] Address of a pointer to an **IDispatch** interface that contains all **BizTalkChannel** objects.

Return Values

For a list of all error messages returned by BizTalk Server, see Appendix A, "Error Messages."

Note

- In addition to the HRESULT values listed on the error messages page, this method returns OLEDB provider errors. Additional information about OLEDB is available on the MSDN Online Library Web site (msdn.microsoft.com/library/default.asp).

Remarks

This is a read-only property.

Each record in the ADO recordset returned by this property contains information about an existing **BizTalkChannel** object in the database. The fields in each record contain the following information, listed in order:

- **Handle**
- **Name**
- **DateModified**

Additional information about Microsoft ActiveX Data Objects is available on the MSDN Online Library Web site (msdn.microsoft.com/library/default.asp).

Requirements

Windows NT/2000: Requires Windows 2000 SP1 or later
Header: Include BizTalkObjectModel.h

IBizTalkConfig::CreateChannel Method

The **CreateChannel** method returns the address of a pointer to a new **BizTalkChannel** object.

Syntax

HRESULT CreateChannel(
    IDispatch** *ppChannelDisp*
);

Parameters

ppChannelDisp
    [out, retval] Address of a pointer to an **IDispatch** interface that contains a new **BizTalkChannel** object.

Return Values

For a list of all error messages returned by BizTalk Server, see Appendix A, "Error Messages."

Requirements

Windows NT/2000: Requires Windows 2000 SP1 or later
Header: Include BizTalkObjectModel.h

IBizTalkConfig::CreateDocument Method

The **CreateDocument** method returns the address of a pointer to a new **BizTalkDocument** object.

Syntax

HRESULT CreateDocument(
    IDispatch** *ppDocumentDisp*
);

Parameters

ppDocumentDisp
    [out, retval] Address of a pointer to an **IDispatch** interface that contains a new **BizTalkDocument** object.

Return Values

For a list of all error messages returned by BizTalk Server, see Appendix A, "Error Messages."

Requirements

Windows NT/2000: Requires Windows 2000 SP1 or later
Header: Include BizTalkObjectModel.h

IBizTalkConfig::CreateEnvelope Method

The **CreateEnvelope** method returns the address of a pointer to a new **BizTalkEnvelope** object.

Syntax

HRESULT CreateEnvelope(
   IDispatch** *ppEnvelopeDisp*
);

Parameters

ppEnvelopeDisp
   [out, retval] Address of a pointer to an **IDispatch** interface that contains a new **BizTalkEnvelope** object.

Return Values

For a list of all error messages returned by BizTalk Server, see Appendix A, "Error Messages."

Requirements

Windows NT/2000: Requires Windows 2000 SP1 or later
Header: Include BizTalkObjectModel.h

IBizTalkConfig::CreateOrganization Method

The **CreateOrganization** method returns the address of a pointer to a new **BizTalkOrganization** object.

Syntax

HRESULT CreateOrganization(
   IDispatch** *ppOrganizationDisp*
);

Parameters

ppOrganizationDisp
   [out, retval] Address of a pointer to an **IDispatch** interface that contains a new **BizTalkOrganization** object.

Return Values

For a list of all error messages returned by BizTalk Server, see Appendix A, "Error Messages."

Requirements

Windows NT/2000: Requires Windows 2000 SP1 or later
Header: Include BizTalkObjectModel.h

IBizTalkConfig::CreatePort Method

The **CreatePort** method returns the address of a pointer to a new **BizTalkPort** object.

Syntax

HRESULT CreatePort(
   IDispatch** *ppPortDisp*
);

Parameters

ppPortDisp
   [out, retval] Address of a pointer to an **IDispatch** interface that contains a new
   BizTalkPort object.

Return Values

For a list of all error messages returned by BizTalk Server, see Appendix A, "Error Messages."

Requirements

Windows NT/2000: Requires Windows 2000 SP1 or later
Header: Include BizTalkObjectModel.h

IBizTalkConfig::CreatePortGroup Method

The **CreatePortGroup** method returns the address of a pointer to a new **BizTalkPortGroup** object.

Syntax

HRESULT CreatePortGroup(
   IDispatch** *ppPortGroupDisp*
);

Parameters

ppPortGroupDisp
> [out, retval] Address of a pointer to an **IDispatch** interface that contains a new **BizTalkPortGroup** object.

Return Values

For a list of all error messages returned by BizTalk Server, see Appendix A, "Error Messages."

Requirements

Windows NT/2000: Requires Windows 2000 SP1 or later
Header: Include BizTalkObjectModel.h

IBizTalkConfig::Documents Property

The **Documents** property returns an ADO recordset that contains all **BizTalkDocument** objects.

Syntax

Get method:

HRESULT Documents(
   IDispatch** *ppDocumentsDisp*
);

Parameters

ppDocumentsDisp
> [out, retval] Address of a pointer to an **IDispatch** interface that contains all **BizTalkDocument** objects.

Return Values

For a list of all error messages returned by BizTalk Server, see Appendix A, "Error Messages."

☑ Note

* In addition to the HRESULT values listed on the error messages page, this method returns OLEDB provider errors. Additional information about OLEDB is available on the MSDN Online Library Web site (msdn.microsoft.com/library/default.asp).

Remarks

This is a read-only property.

Each record in the ADO recordset returned by this property contains information about an existing **BizTalkDocument** object in the database. The fields in each record contain the following information, listed in order:

- **Handle**

- **Name**

- **DateModified**

Additional information about Microsoft ActiveX Data Objects is available on the MSDN Online Library Web site (msdn.microsoft.com/library/default.asp).

Requirements

Windows NT/2000: Requires Windows 2000 SP1 or later
Header: Include BizTalkObjectModel.h

IBizTalkConfig::Envelopes Property

The **Envelopes** property returns an ADO recordset that contains all **BizTalkEnvelope** objects.

Syntax

Get method:

HRESULT Envelopes(
   IDispatch** *ppEnvelopesDisp*
);

Parameters

ppEnvelopesDisp
   [out, retval] Address of a pointer to an **IDispatch** interface that contains all **BizTalkEnvelope** objects.

Return Values

For a list of all error messages returned by BizTalk Server, see Appendix A, "Error Messages."

🗐 Note

- In addition to the HRESULT values listed on the error messages page, this method returns OLEDB provider errors. Additional information about OLEDB is available on the MSDN Online Library Web site (msdn.microsoft.com/library/default.asp).

Remarks

This is a read-only property.

Each record in the ADO recordset returned by this property contains information about an existing **BizTalkEnvelope** object in the database. The fields in each record contain the following information, listed in order:

- **Handle**

- **Name**

- **DateModified**

- **Format**

Additional information about Microsoft ActiveX Data Objects is available on the MSDN Online Library Web site (msdn.microsoft.com/library/default.asp).

Requirements

Windows NT/2000: Requires Windows 2000 SP1 or later
Header: Include BizTalkObjectModel.h

IBizTalkConfig::Organizations Property

The **Organizations** property returns an ADO recordset that contains all **BizTalkOrganization** objects.

Syntax

Get method:

HRESULT Organizations(
    IDispatch** *ppOrganizationsDisp*
);

Parameters

ppOrganizationsDisp
    [out, retval] Address of a pointer to an **IDispatch** interface that contains all **BizTalkOrganization** objects.

Return Values

For a list of all error messages returned by BizTalk Server, see Appendix A, "Error Messages."

🖉 Note

- In addition to the HRESULT values listed on the error messages page, this method returns OLEDB provider errors. Additional information about OLEDB is available on the MSDN Online Library Web site (msdn.microsoft.com/library/default.asp).

Remarks

This is a read-only property.

Each record in the ADO recordset returned by this property contains information about an existing **BizTalkOrganization** object in the database. The fields in each record contain the following information, listed in order:

- **Handle**

- **Name**

- **DateModified**

- **IsDefault**

Additional information about Microsoft ActiveX Data Objects is available on the MSDN Online Library Web site (msdn.microsoft.com/library/default.asp).

Requirements

Windows NT/2000: Requires Windows 2000 SP1 or later
Header: Include BizTalkObjectModel.h

IBizTalkConfig::PortGroups Property

The **PortGroups** property returns an ADO recordset that contains all **BizTalkPortGroup** objects.

Syntax

HRESULT PortGroups(
    IDispatch** *ppPortGroupsDisp*
);

Parameters

ppPortGroupsDisp
    [out, retval] Address of a pointer to an **IDispatch** interface that contains all **BizTalkPortGroup** objects.

Return Values

For a list of all error messages returned by BizTalk Server, see Appendix A, "Error Messages."

🗒 Note

- In addition to the HRESULT values listed on the error messages page, this method returns OLEDB provider errors. Additional information about OLEDB is available on the MSDN Online Library Web site (msdn.microsoft.com/library/default.asp).

Remarks

This is a read-only property.

Each record in the ADO recordset returned by this property contains information about an existing **BizTalkPortGroup** object in the database. The fields in each record contain the following information, listed in order:

- **Handle**
- **Name**
- **DateModified**

Additional information about Microsoft ActiveX Data Objects is available on the MSDN Online Library Web site (msdn.microsoft.com/library/default.asp).

Requirements

Windows NT/2000: Requires Windows 2000 SP1 or later
Header: Include BizTalkObjectModel.h

IBizTalkConfig::Ports Property

The **Ports** property returns an ADO recordset that contains all **BizTalkPort** objects.

Syntax

Get method:

HRESULT Ports(
  IDispatch** *ppPortsDisp*
);

Parameters

ppPortsDisp
  [out, retval] Address of a pointer to an **IDispatch** interface that contains all **BizTalkPort** objects.

Return Values

For a list of all error messages returned by BizTalk Server, see Appendix A, "Error Messages."

Note

- In addition to the HRESULT values listed on the error messages page, this method returns OLEDB provider errors. Additional information about OLEDB is available on the MSDN Online Library Web site (msdn.microsoft.com/library/default.asp).

Remarks

This is a read-only property.

Each record in the ADO recordset returned by this property contains information about an existing **BizTalkPort** object in the database. The fields in each record contain the following information, listed in order:

- **Handle**

- **Name**

- **DateModified**

Additional information about Microsoft ActiveX Data Objects is available on the MSDN Online Library Web site (msdn.microsoft.com/library/default.asp).

Requirements

Windows NT/2000: Requires Windows 2000 SP1 or later
Header: Include BizTalkObjectModel.h

IBizTalkDocument Interface

Use the **BizTalkDocument** object to identify and describe the document specification of a document.

In C++, use the **IBizTalkDocument** interface to access the methods of the **BizTalkDocument** object.

The properties of the **BizTalkDocument** object are shown in the following table.

Property	Type	Description
Content	**BSTR**	Content of the document specification described by the object. This is a read-only property.
DateModified	**BSTR**	Date and time at which the information in the object was created or last modified. This is a read-only property obtained from the **BizTalkBase** object.
Handle	**long**	Handle to the object. This is a read-only property obtained from the **BizTalkBase** object.
Name	**BSTR**	Name of the object. This is a required property obtained from the **BizTalkBase** object.
NameSpace	**BSTR**	String that resolves naming conflicts between elements in a document. This is a read-only property.
PropertySet	**IDispatch**	**Dictionary** object that contains the electronic data interchange (EDI) selection criteria (name/value pairs) by which the server extracts information from the functional group header of the EDI document to identify the object when the document is input. It helps the server create the header of the EDI document when it is output. This is a required property if the document is an EDI document.
Reference	**BSTR**	Full Web Distributed Authoring and Versioning (WebDAV) URL for the document specification referred to by this **BizTalkDocument** object. This is a required property when the **TrackFields** property is set.
TrackFields	**IDispatch**	**Dictionary** object that stores the custom fields that Tracking uses to track all documents processed by the server, based on this document instance. The **Reference** property must contain a WebDAV URL when this property is set.
Type	**BSTR**	Type of document specification. This is a read-only property.
Version	**BSTR**	Version of the document standard. This is a read-only property.

The methods of the **BizTalkDocument** object are shown in the following table.

Method	Description
Clear	Clears the object in memory. All member variables of the object in memory are initialized to their default values. This method is obtained from the **BizTalkBase** object.
Create	Creates a new object in the database. This method is obtained from the **BizTalkBase** object.
Load	Loads the object in memory. This method is obtained from the **BizTalkBase** object.
LoadByName	Loads the object by name in memory. This method is obtained from the **BizTalkBase** object.
LoadByPropertySet	Loads the document object by its **PropertySet** object.
Remove	Removes the object from the database. This method is obtained from the **BizTalkBase** object.
Save	Saves the object in the database. This method is obtained from the **BizTalkBase** object.

Remarks

Each **BizTalkDocument** object must have at least one associated **BizTalkChannel** object. More than one **BizTalkDocument** object can refer to the same document specification.

Requirements

Windows NT/2000: Requires Windows 2000 SP1 or later
Header: Include BizTalkObjectModel.h

IBizTalkDocument::Content Property

The **Content** property contains the content of the document specification described by the object.

Syntax

Get method:

HRESULT get_Content(
  BSTR* *pstrContent*
);

Parameters

pstrContent
    [out, retval] Pointer to a **BSTR** that contains the content.

Return Values

For a list of all error messages returned by BizTalk Server, see Appendix A, "Error Messages."

Remarks

This is a read-only property.

The **Reference** property is checked when the **Create** or the **Save** method is called. If this string is not empty when **Create** is called, **Content** is set to the contents of the document specification and the **NameSpace** property is changed to the value found in the document specification.

Once you have created or saved an object with **Reference** set to a document specification, any changes you make to the **Content** or **NameSpace** property of the referenced document specification are not automatically updated on the referring object. To update the object that refers to the revised document specification, you must save the document specification, reset the **Reference** property of the object to its current value, and then call **Save** on the referring object.

Requirements

Windows NT/2000: Requires Windows 2000 SP1 or later
Header: Include BizTalkObjectModel.h

IBizTalkDocument::LoadByPropertySet Method

The **LoadByPropertySet** method loads the document object by its **PropertySet**.

Syntax

HRESULT LoadByPropertySet(
    IDispatch** *pPropSetDictionaryDisp*
);

Parameters

pPropSetDictionaryDisp
    [in] Address of a pointer to an **IDispatch** interface that contains the **PropertySet**.

Return Values

For a list of all error messages returned by BizTalk Server, see Appendix A, "Error Messages."

Requirements

Windows NT/2000: Requires Windows 2000 SP1 or later
Header: Include BizTalkObjectModel.h

IBizTalkDocument::NameSpace Property

The **NameSpace** property contains the string that resolves naming conflicts between elements in a document.

Syntax

Get method:

HRESULT get_NameSpace(
    BSTR* *pstrNameSpace*
);

Parameters

pstrNameSpace
    [out, retval] Pointer to a **BSTR** that contains the namespace.

Return Values

For a list of all error messages returned by BizTalk Server, see Appendix A, "Error Messages."

Remarks

This is a read-only property. The **Reference** property is checked when the **Create** or the **Save** method is called. If this string is not empty when **Create** is called, **Content** is set to the contents of the document specification and **NameSpace** is changed to the value found in the document specification.

Once you have created or saved an object with **Reference** set to a document specification, any changes you make to the **Content** or **NameSpace** property of the referenced document specification are not automatically updated on the referring object. To update the object that refers to the revised document specification, you must save the document specification, reset the **Reference** property of the object to its current value, and then call **Save** on the referring object.

Note

- When creating a document, the number of characters in the **NameSpace** combined with the number of characters in the specification name cannot exceed 255.

Requirements

Windows NT/2000: Requires Windows 2000 SP1 or later
Header: Include BizTalkObjectModel.h

IBizTalkDocument::PropertySet Property

The **PropertySet** property contains a **Dictionary** object that contains the electronic data interchange (EDI) selection criteria (name/value pairs) by which the server extracts information from the functional group header of the EDI document to identify the object when the document is input. It helps the server create the header of the EDI document when it is output.

Syntax

Get method:

HRESULT get_PropertySet(
   IDispatch* *ppPropSetDisp*
);

Putref method:

HRESULT putref_PropertySet(
   IDispatch* *pPropSetDisp*
);

Parameters

Get method:

ppPropSetDisp
   [out, retval] Address of a pointer to an **IDispatch** interface that contains the selection criteria.

Putref method

pPropSetDisp
   [in] Pointer to an **IDispatch** interface that contains the selection criteria.

Return Values

For a list of all error messages returned by BizTalk Server, see Appendix A, "Error Messages."

Remarks

This is a required property if the document is an EDI document. The **Delimiters** property of the associated **BizTalkPort** object must also be defined.

The following table shows whether names are required in the **Dictionary** object for
PropertySet.

Selection criteria	X12	EDIFACT
application_sender_code	Yes	Yes
application_receiver_code	Yes	Yes
functional_identifier	Yes	Yes
standards_version	Yes	No
standards_version_type	No	Yes
standards_version_value	No	Yes

Note

- The name/value pairs contained in the **Dictionary** object cannot exceed a total of 450 bytes.

PropertySet can be set only if the **Reference** property is set.

Requirements

Windows NT/2000: Requires Windows 2000 SP1 or later
Header: Include BizTalkObjectModel.h

IBizTalkDocument::Reference Property

The **Reference** property contains the full Web Distributed Authoring and Versioning
(WebDAV) URL for the document specification referred to by the object.

Syntax

Get method:

HRESULT get_Reference(
  BSTR* *pstrReference*
);

Put method:

HRESULT put_Reference(
  BSTR *strReference*
);

Parameters

Get method:

pstrReference
  [out, retval] Pointer to a **BSTR** that contains the reference.

Put method:

strReference
  [in] **BSTR** that contains the reference.

Return Values

For a list of all error messages returned by BizTalk Server, see Appendix A, "Error Messages."

Remarks

Reference is checked when the **Create** or the **Save** method is called. If this string is not empty when **Create** is called, **Content** is set to the contents of the document specification and the **NameSpace** property is changed to the value found in the document specification.

Once you have created or saved an object with **Reference** set to a document specification, any changes you make to the **Content** or **NameSpace** property of the referenced document specification are not automatically updated on the referring object. To update the object that refers to the revised document specification, you must save the document specification, reset the **Reference** property of the object to its current value, and then call **Save** on the referring object.

If **Reference** is not set, the **PropertySet** and **TrackFields** properties must not be set.

Requirements

Windows NT/2000: Requires Windows 2000 SP1 or later
Header: Include BizTalkObjectModel.h

IBizTalkDocument::TrackFields Property

The **TrackFields** property identifies the **Dictionary** object that stores the custom fields used to track the document. A **BizTalkDocument** object points to the specification that contains fields to track the document. The designated fields are logged to the Tracking database for each instance of a document that is processed. Tracking fields on the **BizTalkDocument** object are global. The **TrackFields** property on the **BizTalkChannel** object overrides the values specified by this property.

Syntax

Get method:

HRESULT get_TrackFields(
    IDispatch** *ppTrackFieldsDisp*
);

Putref method:

HRESULT putref_TrackFields(
    IDispatch* *pTrackFieldsDisp*
);

Parameters

Get method:

ppTrackFieldsDisp
    [out, retval] Address of a pointer to the **IDictionary** interface of the object that contains the custom tracking fields.

Putref method:

pTrackFieldsDisp
    [in] Pointer to the **IDictionary** interface of the object that contains the custom tracking fields.

Return Values

For a list of all error messages returned by BizTalk Server, see Appendix A, "Error Messages."

Remarks

TrackFields can be set only if the **Reference** property is set. Tracking fields specified for an output **BizTalkDocument** object are ignored.

The fields in the **Dictionary** object must contain an XPath value that identifies the field to be tracked in a document. By default, the **Dictionary** object provides eight predefined fields for tracking data in a document. These predefined fields consist of two fields for each of the following data types: integer, real, date, and string. If additional fields are required for tracking, you can use the x_custom_search field in the **Dictionary** object and set the value to a **SimpleList** object. The **SimpleList** object contains a list of XPath values pointing to the additional tracking fields. XPath values can be added to and deleted from this list using the **Add** and **Delete** methods.

The table on the following page shows the field names in the **Dictionary** object for **TrackFields**.

Field Name	Field type
i_value1	Integer value
i_value2	Integer value
r_value1	Real value
r_value2	Real value
d_value1	Date value
d_value2	Date value
s_value1	String value
s_value2	String value
x_custom_search	A list to return one or more additional data items

For more information about XPath expressions, go to the MSDN Online Library Web site (msdn.microsoft.com/library/default.asp) and search for XPath.

Requirements

Windows NT/2000: Requires Windows 2000 SP1 or later
Header: Include BizTalkObjectModel.h

IBizTalkDocument::Type Property

The **Type** property contains the type of document specification.

Syntax

HRESULT get_Type(
   BSTR* *pstrType*
);

Parameters

pstrType
   [out, retval] Pointer to a **BSTR** that contains the document type.

Return Values

For a list of all error messages returned by BizTalk Server, see Appendix A, "Error Messages."

Remarks

This is a read-only property. All document instances must have the same document type as the associated envelope. For example, if the **Format** property of the **BizTalkEnvelope** object is set to X12, **Type** must also be X12.

Requirements

Windows NT/2000: Requires Windows 2000 SP1 or later
Header: Include BizTalkObjectModel.h

IBizTalkDocument::Version Property

The **Version** property contains the version of the document standard.

Syntax

HRESULT get_Version(
    BSTR* *pstrVersion*
);

Parameters

pstrVersion
    [out, retval] Pointer to a **BSTR** that contains the version.

Return Values

For a list of all error messages returned by BizTalk Server, see Appendix A, "Error Messages."

Remarks

This is a read-only property.

Requirements

Windows NT/2000: Requires Windows 2000 SP1 or later
Header: Include BizTalkObjectModel.h

IBizTalkEndPoint Interface

Use the **BizTalkEndPoint** object to configure source information for a **BizTalkChannel** object and destination information for a **BizTalkPort** object.

In C++, use the **IBizTalkEndPoint** interface to access the methods of the **BizTalkEndPoint** object.

The properties of the **BizTalkEndPoint** object are shown in the table on the following page.

Property	Type	Description
Alias	long	Handle to the organization identifier type/value pair for the destination **BizTalkOrganization** object for the associated **BizTalkPort** object.
Application	long	Handle to the associated application for the destination **BizTalkOrganization** object for this **BizTalkPort** object.
Openness	BIZTALK_OPENNESS_TYPE_EX	Enumeration value that indicates whether the object is open.
Organization	long	Handle to the destination **BizTalkOrganization** object for this **BizTalkPort** object. This is a required property for this object to be complete unless the **Openness** property is set to **BIZTALK_OPENNESS_TYPE_EX_DESTINATION**.

Remarks

The **BizTalkEndPoint** object is automatically created when a **BizTalkPort** object or a **BizTalkChannel** object is instantiated with the **CreatePort** or the **CreateChannel** method of the **BizTalkConfig** object.

For destination endpoints, access the **BizTalkEndPoint** object by using the **DestinationEndpoint** property of the **BizTalkPort** object. For source endpoints, access the **BizTalkEndPoint** object by using the **SourceEndpoint** property of the **BizTalkChannel** object.

Requirements

Windows NT/2000: Requires Windows 2000 SP1 or later
Header: Include BizTalkObjectModel.h

IBizTalkEndPoint::Alias Property

The **Alias** property contains the handle to the alias.

Syntax

Get method:

HRESULT get_Alias(
  long* *plAliasHandle*
);

Put method:

HRESULT put_Alias(
    long *lAliasHandle*
);

Parameters

Get method:

plAliasHandle
    [out, retval] Pointer to a **long** that contains the handle to the alias.

Put method:

lAliasHandle
    [in] **Long** that contains the handle to the alias.

Return Values

For a list of all error messages returned by BizTalk Server, see Appendix A, "Error Messages."

Requirements

Windows NT/2000: Requires Windows 2000 SP1 or later
Header: Include BizTalkObjectModel.h

IBizTalkEndPoint::Application Property

The **Application** property contains the handle to the application.

Syntax

Get method:

HRESULT get_Application(
    long* *plAppHandle*
);

Put method:

HRESULT put_Application(
    long *lAppHandle*
);

Parameters

Get method:

plAppHandle
    [out, retval] Pointer to a **long** that contains the handle to the application.

Put method:

lAppHandle
[in] **Long** that contains the handle to the application.

Return Values

For a list of all error messages returned by BizTalk Server, see Appendix A, "Error Messages."

Requirements

Windows NT/2000: Requires Windows 2000 SP1 or later
Header: Include BizTalkObjectModel.h

IBizTalkEndPoint::Openness Property

The **Openness** property contains an enumeration value that indicates whether the object has an open destination or source, or neither.

Syntax

Get method:

HRESULT get_Openness(
  BIZTALK_OPENNESS_TYPE_EX* *pOpennessType*
);

Put method:

HRESULT put_Openness(
  BIZTALK_OPENNESS_TYPE_EX *OpennessType*
);

Parameters

Get method:

pOpennessType
[out, retval] Pointer to an enumeration value. Valid values are from the **BIZTALK_OPENNESS_TYPE_EX** enumeration.

Put Method:

OpennessType
[in] Enumeration value. Valid values are from the **BIZTALK_OPENNESS_TYPE_EX** enumeration.

Return Values

For a list of all error messages returned by BizTalk Server, see Appendix A, "Error Messages."

Remarks

The **BizTalkPort** object is valid only if the associated document or the parameters on the **Submit** or the **SubmitSync** method of the **IInterchange** interface identify the missing information.

If **Openness** is set to **BIZTALK_OPENNESS_TYPE_EX_SOURCE** for a **BizTalkEndPoint** object associated with a channel, the following constraints apply:

- The **SignatureType** property must not be set.

- The **BizTalkPort** object cannot be included in a port group.

If **Openness** is set to **BIZTALK_OPENNESS_TYPE_EX_FROMWORKFLOW** on a channel, the associated **BizTalkOrganization** object must be the default organization.

If **Openness** on the object is set to **BIZTALK_OPENNESS_TYPE_EX_DESTINATION** for a **BizTalkEndPoint** object associated with a messaging port, the following constraints apply:

- The **PrimaryTransportType** property must be set to **BIZTALK_TRANSPORT_TYPE_OPENDESTINATION**.

- The **EncryptionType** property must not be set.

- The document or the parameters on **Submit** or **SubmitSync** must specify the destination, transport type, and address.

- The **BizTalkPort** object cannot be included in a port group.

Note

- This property cannot be changed on an existing port.

Requirements

Windows NT/2000: Requires Windows 2000 SP1 or later
Header: Include BizTalkObjectModel.h

IBizTalkEndPoint::Organization Property

The **Organization** property contains the handle to the organization.

Syntax

Get method:

HRESULT get_Organization(
  long* *plOrganizationHandle*
);

Put method:

HRESULT put_Organization(
  long *lOrganizationHandle*
);

Parameters

Get method:

plOrganizationHandle
  [out, retval] Pointer to a **long** that contains the handle to the organization.

Put method:

lOrganizationHandle
  [in] **Long** that contains the handle to the organization.

Return Values

For a list of all error messages returned by BizTalk Server, see Appendix A, "Error Messages."

Requirements

Windows NT/2000: Requires Windows 2000 SP1 or later
Header: Include BizTalkObjectModel.h

IBizTalkEnvelope Interface

Use the **BizTalkEnvelope** object to configure the envelope format used with documents processed by BizTalk Server. An envelope is the header information for an interchange.

In C++, use the **IBizTalkEnvelope** interface to access the methods of the **BizTalkEnvelope** object.

The properties of the **BizTalkEnvelope** object are shown in the following table.

Property	Type	Description
Content	BSTR	Contents of the selected envelope format specification. This is a read-only property.
DateModified	BSTR	Date and time at which the information in the object was created or last modified. This is a read-only property obtained from the **BizTalkBase** object.
Format	BSTR	String that identifies the type of envelope.
Handle	long	Handle to the object. This is a read-only property obtained from the **BizTalkBase** object.
Name	BSTR	Name of the object. This is a required property obtained from the **BizTalkBase** object.
NameSpace	BSTR	String that resolves naming conflicts between elements in an envelope specification. This is a read-only property.
Reference	BSTR	Full Web Distributed Authoring and Versioning (WebDAV) URL name of the envelope format specification file. This is a required property if the Format property is set to "custom".
Version	BSTR	Version of the envelope format specification. This is a read-only property.

The methods of the **BizTalkEnvelope** object are shown in the following table.

Method	Description
Clear	Clears the object in memory. All member variables of the object in memory are initialized to their default values. This method is obtained from the **BizTalkBase** object.
Create	Creates a new object in the database. This method is obtained from the **BizTalkBase** object.
Load	Loads the object in memory. This method is obtained from the **BizTalkBase** object.
LoadByName	Loads the object by name in memory. This method is obtained from the **BizTalkBase** object.
Remove	Removes the object from the database. This method is obtained from the **BizTalkBase** object.
Save	Saves the object in the database. This method is obtained from the **BizTalkBase** object.

Remarks

All document instances in an electronic data interchange (EDI) functional group must have the same format. All document instances must have the same document type as the associated envelope. For example, if **Format** is set to X12, the **Type** property of the **BizTalkDocument** objects for the associated **BizTalkPort** object must also be X12.

If you use an envelope with an EDIFACT format and you want to use a null value for the empty qualifier in the header for the source or the destination, create a custom identifier with a single dash (-) as the qualifier. To do this, use the **CreateAlias** method on the **BizTalkOrganization** object. When an empty qualifier is encountered on an input EDIFACT envelope, the server converts the empty qualifier to a dash. For an output EDIFACT envelope, the server converts the dash to an empty qualifier.

The **BizTalkEnvelope** object is required for input documents if the **Type** property of the **BizTalkDocument** object is set to "flatfile" or "custom xml".

Requirements

Windows NT/2000: Requires Windows 2000 SP1 or later
Header: Include BizTalkObjectModel.h

IBizTalkEnvelope::Content Property

The **Content** property contains the contents of the selected envelope format specification.

Syntax

HRESULT get_Content(
    BSTR* *pstrContent*
);

Parameters

pstrContent
    [out, retval] Pointer to a **BSTR** that contains the content.

Return Values

For a list of all error messages returned by BizTalk Server, see Appendix A, "Error Messages."

Remarks

This is a read-only property.

The **Reference** property is checked when the **Create** or the **Save** method is called. If this string is not empty when **Create** is called, **Content** is set to the contents of the envelope specification, and the **NameSpace** property is changed to the value found in the envelope specification.

Once you have created or saved an object with **Reference** set to an envelope specification, any changes you make to the **Content** or **NameSpace** property of the referenced envelope specification are not automatically updated on the referring object. To update the object that refers to the revised envelope specification, you must save the envelope specification, reset the **Reference** property of the object to its current value, and then call **Save** on the referring object.

Requirements

Windows NT/2000: Requires Windows 2000 SP1 or later
Header: Include BizTalkObjectModel.h

IBizTalkEnvelope::Format Property

The **Format** property contains the string that identifies the type of envelope.

Syntax

Get method:

HRESULT get_Format(
    BSTR* *pstrFormat*
);

Put method:

HRESULT put_Format(
    BSTR *Format*
);

Parameters

Get method:

pstrFormat
    [out, retval] Pointer to a **BSTR** that contains the envelope format.

Put method:

Format
    [in] **BSTR** that contains the envelope format. The **BSTR** must be one of the values listed in the Remarks section.

Return Values

For a list of all error messages returned by BizTalk Server, see Appendix A, "Error Messages."

Remarks

The format value must be one of the following strings:

- x12
- edifact
- custom xml (default)
- custom
- flatfile
- reliable

Note

- Any string other than the ones listed here will cause an error at run time.

If this property is set to "custom", the **Reference** property is required. Also, a custom parser component has to be registered with the server for input documents with this property set to "custom". For more information about custom parser components, see "Using the IBizTalkParserComponent Interface" in Chapter 15, "Creating Custom Components."

All document instances must have the same document type as the associated envelope. For example, if **Format** is set to "x12", the **Type** property of the **BizTalkDocument** objects must also be "x12".

If **Format** is set to X12, edifact, or reliable, the **Reference** property should not be set.

For more information about envelope formats, see "To create envelopes" earlier in this chapter.

Requirements

Windows NT/2000: Requires Windows 2000 SP1 or later
Header: Include BizTalkObjectModel.h

IBizTalkEnvelope::NameSpace Property

The **NameSpace** property contains the string that resolves naming conflicts between elements in an envelope specification.

Syntax

Get method:

HRESULT get_NameSpace(
   BSTR* *pstrNameSpace*
);

Parameters

pstrNameSpace
    [out, retval] Pointer to a **BSTR** that contains the namespace.

Return Values

For a list of all error messages returned by BizTalk Server, see Appendix A, "Error Messages."

Error Value

If an error is raised, **Err.Number** is set to one of the values documented in Appendix A, "Error Messages."

Remarks

This is a read-only property. The **Reference** property is checked when the **Create** or the **Save** method is called. If this string is not empty when **Create** is called, the **Content** property is set to the contents of the envelope specification, and **NameSpace** is changed to the value found in the envelope specification.

Once you have created or saved an object with **Reference** set to an envelope specification, any changes you make to the **Content** or **NameSpace** property of the referenced envelope specification are not automatically updated on the referring object. To update the object that refers to the revised envelope specification, you must save the envelope specification, reset the **Reference** property of the object to its current value, and then call **Save** on the referring object.

Note

- When creating an envelope, the number of characters in the **NameSpace** property combined with the number of characters in the specification name cannot exceed 255.

Requirements

Windows NT/2000: Requires Windows 2000 SP1 or later
Header: Include BizTalkObjectModel.h

IBizTalkEnvelope::Reference Property

The **Reference** property contains the full Web Distributed Authoring and Versioning (WebDAV) URL of the envelope format specification file.

Syntax

Get method:

HRESULT get_Reference(
  BSTR* *pReference*
);

Put method:

HRESULT put_Reference(
  BSTR *Reference*
);

Parameters

Get method:

pReference
  [out, retval] Pointer to a **BSTR** that contains the reference.

Put method:

Reference
  [in] **BSTR** that contains the reference.

Return Values

For a list of all error messages returned by BizTalk Server, see Appendix A, "Error Messages."

Remarks

This is a required property if the **Format** property is set to "custom". **Reference** is checked when the **Create** or the **Save** method is called. If this string is not empty when **Create** is called, the **Content** property is set to the contents of the envelope specification, and the **NameSpace** property is changed to the value found in the envelope specification.

Once you have created or saved an object with **Reference** set to an envelope specification, any changes you make to the **Content** or **NameSpace** property of the referenced envelope specification are not automatically updated on the referring object. To update the object that refers to the revised envelope specification, you must save the envelope specification, reset the **Reference** property of the object to its current value, and then call **Save** on the referring object.

Requirements

Windows NT/2000: Requires Windows 2000 SP1 or later
Header: Include BizTalkObjectModel.h

IBizTalkEnvelope::Version Property

The **Version** property contains the version of the envelope format specification.

Syntax

Get method:

HRESULT get_Version(
   BSTR* *pstrVersion*
);

Parameters

pstrVersion
   [out, retval] Pointer to a **BSTR** that contains the version.

Return Values

For a list of all error messages returned by BizTalk Server, see Appendix A, "Error Messages."

Remarks

This is a read-only property.

Requirements

Windows NT/2000: Requires Windows 2000 SP1 or later
Header: Include BizTalkObjectModel.h

IBizTalkLoggingInfo Interface

Use the **BizTalkLoggingInfo** object to configure the document-logging information for an associated **BizTalkChannel** object.

In C++, use the **IBizTalkLoggingInfo** interface to access the methods of the **BizTalkLoggingInfo** object.

The properties of the **IBizTalkLoggingInfo** interface are shown in the following table.

Property	Type	Description
LogNativeInputDocument	**VARIANT_BOOL**	Flag that indicates whether the input document instance is saved and logged in its native format.
LogNativeOutputDocument	**VARIANT_BOOL**	Flag that indicates whether the output document instance is saved and logged in its native format.
LogXMLInputDocument	**VARIANT_BOOL**	Flag that indicates whether the XML input document is saved and logged.
LogXMLOutputDocument	**VARIANT_BOOL**	Flag that indicates whether the XML output document is saved and logged.

Remarks

The **BizTalkLoggingInfo** object is automatically created when a **BizTalkChannel** object is instantiated with the **CreateChannel** method of the **BizTalkConfig** object. You can access the **BizTalkLoggingInfo** object by using the **LoggingInfo** property of the **BizTalkChannel** object.

Requirements

Windows NT/2000: Requires Windows 2000 SP1 or later
Header: Include BizTalkObjectModel.h

IBizTalkLoggingInfo::LogNativeInputDocument Property

The **LogNativeInputDocument** property contains a flag that indicates whether the input document instance is saved and logged in its native format.

Syntax

Get method:

HRESULT get_LogNativeInputDocument(
  VARIANT_BOOL* *pbLogNativeInDoc*
);

Put method:

HRESULT put_LogNativeInputDocument(
  VARIANT_BOOL *bLogNativeInDoc*
);

Parameters

Get method:

pbLogNativeInDoc

> [out, retval] Pointer to a **VARIANT_BOOL** type that contains the flag. A value of **VARIANT_TRUE** indicates that input documents will be saved and logged in their native format. A value of **VARIANT_FALSE** indicates that input documents will not be saved and logged in their native format.

Put method:

bLogNativeInDoc

> [in] **VARIANT_BOOL** type that contains the flag. A value of **VARIANT_TRUE** indicates that documents will be saved and logged in their native format. A value of **VARIANT_FALSE** indicates that documents will not be saved and logged in their native format.

Return Values

For a list of all error messages returned by BizTalk Server, see Appendix A, "Error Messages."

Requirements

Windows NT/2000: Requires Windows 2000 SP1 or later
Header: Include BizTalkObjectModel.h

IBizTalkLoggingInfo::LogNativeOutputDocument Property

The **LogNativeOutputDocument** property contains a flag that indicates whether the output document instance is saved and logged in its native format.

Syntax

Get method:

HRESULT get_LogNativeOutputDocument(
   VARIANT_BOOL* *pbLogNativeOutDoc*
);

Put method:

HRESULT put_LogNativeOutputDocument(
   VARIANT_BOOL *bLogNativeOutDoc*
);

Parameters

Get method:

pbLogNativeOutDoc

> [out, retval] Pointer to a **VARIANT_BOOL** type that contains the flag. A value of **VARIANT_TRUE** indicates that output documents will be saved and logged in their native format. A value of **VARIANT_FALSE** indicates that output documents will not be saved and logged in their native format.

Put method:

bLogNativeOutDoc

> [in] **VARIANT_BOOL** type that contains the flag. A value of **VARIANT_TRUE** indicates that output documents will be saved and logged in their native format. A value of **VARIANT_FALSE** indicates that output documents will not be saved and logged in their native format.

Return Values

For a list of all error messages returned by BizTalk Server, see Appendix A, "Error Messages."

Requirements

Windows NT/2000: Requires Windows 2000 SP1 or later
Header: Include BizTalkObjectModel.h

IBizTalkLoggingInfo::LogXMLInputDocument Property

The **LogXMLInputDocument** property contains a flag that indicates whether the XML input document instance is saved and logged.

Syntax

Get method:

HRESULT get_LogXMLInputDocument(
  VARIANT_BOOL* *pbLogXMLInDoc*
);

Put method:

HRESULT put_LogXMLInputDocument(
  VARIANT_BOOL *bLogXMLInDoc*
);

Get method:

pbLogXMLInDoc

> [out, retval] Pointer to a **VARIANT_BOOL** type that contains the flag. A value of
> **VARIANT_TRUE** indicates that input documents will be saved and logged in XML
> format. A value of **VARIANT_FALSE** indicates that input documents will not be saved
> and logged in XML format.

Put method:

bLogXMLInDoc

> [in] **VARIANT_BOOL** type that contains the flag. A value of **VARIANT_TRUE**
> indicates that input documents will be saved and logged in XML format. A value of
> **VARIANT_FALSE** indicates that input documents will not be saved and logged in XML
> format.

Return Values

For a list of all error messages returned by BizTalk Server, see Appendix A, "Error
Messages."

Requirements

Windows NT/2000: Requires Windows 2000 SP1 or later
Header: Include BizTalkObjectModel.h

IBizTalkLoggingInfo::LogXMLOutputDocument Property

The **LogXMLOutputDocument** property contains a flag that indicates whether the XML
output document instance is saved and logged.

Syntax

Get method:

HRESULT get_LogXMLOutputDocument(
   VARIANT_BOOL* *pbLogXMLOutDoc*
);

Put method:

HRESULT put_LogXMLOutputDocument(
   VARIANT_BOOL *bLogXMLOutDoc*
);

Get method:

pbLogXMLOutDoc

[out, retval] Pointer to a **VARIANT_BOOL** type that contains the flag. A value of **VARIANT_TRUE** indicates that output documents will be saved and logged in XML format. A value of **VARIANT_FALSE** indicates that output documents will not be saved and logged in XML format.

Put method:

bLogXMLOutDoc

[in] When putting the property, a **VARIANT_BOOL** type that contains the flag. A value of **VARIANT_TRUE** indicates that output documents will be saved and logged in XML format. A value of **VARIANT_FALSE** indicates that output documents will not be saved and logged in XML format.

Return Values

For a list of all error messages returned by BizTalk Server, see Appendix A, "Error Messages."

Requirements

Windows NT/2000: Requires Windows 2000 SP1 or later
Header: Include BizTalkObjectModel.h

IBizTalkOrganization Interface

Use the **BizTalkOrganization** object to configure organizations, its organization identifiers (aliases), and the applications within the organization that send and/or receive documents. The application indicates the ultimate source or destination of the document.

In C++, use the **IBizTalkOrganization** interface to access the methods of the **BizTalkOrganization** object.

The properties of the **BizTalkOrganization** object are shown in the table on the following page.

Property	Type	Description
Aliases	**IDispatch**	ADO recordset of aliases that refer to the object. The alias for an object is the organization identifier type/value pair.
Applications	**IDispatch**	ADO recordset of applications that refer to the object.
Comments	**BSTR**	User comments for the object.
DateModified	**BSTR**	Date and time at which the information in the object was created or last modified. This is a read-only property obtained from the **BizTalkBase** object.
Handle	**long**	Identifier for the object. This is a read-only property obtained from the **BizTalkBase** object.
IsDefault	**VARIANT_BOOL**	Flag that indicates whether the object is the default organization.
Name	**BSTR**	Name of the object. This is a required property obtained from the **BizTalkBase** object.

The methods of the **BizTalkOrganization** object are shown in the following table.

Method	Description
Clear	Clears the object in memory. All member variables of the object in memory are initialized to their default values. This method is obtained from the **BizTalkBase** object.
Create	Creates a new object in the database. This method is obtained from the **BizTalkBase** object.
CreateAlias	Creates an alias for the object. The alias is the organization identifier type/value pair.
CreateApplication	Creates a new application.
GetDefaultAlias	Gets the default alias for the object.
Load	Loads an object in memory. This method is obtained from the **BizTalkBase** object.
LoadAlias	Loads an existing alias for the object in memory.
LoadApplication	Loads an application in memory.
LoadByName	Loads an object by name in memory. This method is obtained from the **BizTalkBase** object.
Remove	Removes the object from the database. This method is obtained from the **BizTalkBase** object.
RemoveAlias	Removes an alias.
RemoveApplication	Removes an application.
Save	Saves the object to the database. This method is obtained from the **BizTalkBase** object.
SaveAlias	Saves this alias.
SaveApplication	Saves this application.

Remarks

A **BizTalkOrganization** object can have more than one application, but each application name must be unique for that object.

Requirements

Windows NT/2000: Requires Windows 2000 SP1 or later
Header: Include BizTalkObjectModel.h

IBizTalkOrganization::Aliases Property

The **Aliases** property returns an ADO recordset that contains information about all aliases that refer to the object. The alias for an object is the organization qualifier/value pair.

Syntax

Get method:

HRESULT get_Aliases(
    IDispatch** *ppAliasesDisp*
);

Parameters

ppAliasesDisp
    [out, retval] Address of a pointer to an **IDispatch** interface that contains all aliases that refer to the object.

Return Values

For a list of all error messages returned by BizTalk Server, see Appendix A, "Error Messages."

Remarks

BizTalk Messaging Manager refers to aliases as identifiers.

Each record in the ADO recordset returned by this property contains information about the aliases of an existing **BizTalkOrganization** object in the database. The fields in each record contain the following information, listed in order:

- Handle assigned to the alias.
- Name specified in the **CreateAlias** method.
- Boolean specified in the **CreateAlias** method.
- Qualifier specified in the **CreateAlias** method.
- Value specified in the **CreateAlias** method.

Additional information about Microsoft ActiveX Data Objects is available on the MSDN Online Library Web site (msdn.microsoft.com/library/default.asp).

Requirements

Windows NT/2000: Requires Windows 2000 SP1 or later
Header: Include BizTalkObjectModel.h

IBizTalkOrganization::Applications Property

The **Applications** property returns an ADO recordset that contains information about all applications that refer to the **Organization** object.

Syntax

Get method:

HRESULT get_Applications(
   IDispatch** *ppApplicationsDisp*
);

Parameters

ppApplicationsDisp
   [out, retval] Address of a pointer to an **IDispatch** interface that contains all applications that refer to the object.

Return Values

For a list of all error messages returned by BizTalk Server, see Appendix A, "Error Messages."

Note

- In addition to the HRESULT values listed on the error messages page, this method returns OLEDB provider errors. Additional information about OLEDB is available on the MSDN Online Library Web site (msdn.microsoft.com/library/default.asp).

Remarks

Each record in the ADO recordset returned by this property contains information about the applications of an existing **BizTalkOrganization** object in the database. The fields in each record contain the following information, listed in order:

- Handle assigned to the application.

- Name specified in the **CreateApplication** method.

Additional information about Microsoft ActiveX Data Objects is available on the MSDN Online Library Web site (msdn.microsoft.com/library/default.asp).

Requirements

Windows NT/2000: Requires Windows 2000 SP1 or later
Header: Include BizTalkObjectModel.h

IBizTalkOrganization::Comments Property

The **Comments** property contains the user comments for the object.

Syntax

Get method:

HRESULT get_Comments(
 BSTR* *pstrComments*
);

Put method:

HRESULT put_Comments(
 BSTR *strComments*
);

Parameters

Get method:

pstrComments
 [out, retval] Pointer to a **BSTR** that contains the comments.

Put method:

strComments
 [in] When putting the property, a **BSTR** that contains the comments.

Return Values

For a list of all error messages returned by BizTalk Server, see Appendix A, "Error Messages."

Requirements

Windows NT/2000: Requires Windows 2000 SP1 or later
Header: Include BizTalkObjectModel.h

IBizTalkOrganization::CreateAlias Method

The **CreateAlias** method creates a new alias for this **Organization** object. The alias for an object is the organization identifier that contains a name and a qualifier/value pair.

Syntax

HRESULT CreateAlias(
    BSTR *strName*,
    VARIANT_BOOL *bDefault*,
    BSTR *strQualifier*,
    BSTR *strValue*
);

Parameters

strName
> [in] **BSTR** that contains the name of the alias.

bDefault
> [in] **VARIANT_BOOL** type that contains the flag. This default alias overrides the previous default alias when set to **VARIANT_TRUE**. A value of **VARIANT_FALSE** indicates that this alias should not override the previous default alias. If no alias is specified as the default, one is assigned when the **Create** method is called.

strQualifier
> [in] **BSTR** that contains the qualifier. This parameter cannot be set to "group".

strValue
> [in] **BSTR** that contains the value.

Return Values

For a list of all error messages returned by BizTalk Server, see Appendix A, "Error Messages."

Remarks

More than one alias can be created for a **BizTalkOrganization** object. The organization alias must contain a name that is unique for the specified **BizTalkOrganization** object, and a qualifier/value pair that is unique across all **BizTalkOrganization** objects. One of these aliases must be specified as the default alias for the object.

The server automatically creates an alias named *Organization* with a default identifier of *OrganizationName* and the value set to the organization's name for new organizations. If the organization name is changed, the value is automatically updated with the new name. This alias cannot be removed.

Note

- When using envelopes with an EDIFACT format and you want to use a null value for the empty qualifier in the header for the source or the destination, create a custom identifier with a single dash (-) as the qualifier.

Requirements

Windows NT/2000: Requires Windows 2000 SP1 or later
Header: Include BizTalkObjectModel.h

IBizTalkOrganization::CreateApplication Method

The **CreateApplication** method creates a new application.

Syntax

HRESULT CreateApplication(
    BSTR *strName*
);

Parameters

strName
    [in] **BSTR** that contains the name of the application.

Return Values

For a list of all error messages returned by BizTalk Server, see Appendix A, "Error Messages."

Remarks

If a **BizTalkOrganization** object is associated with more than one application, each application name must be unique.

Notes

- BizTalk Messaging Manager refers to the default organization as the home organization.

- BizTalk Messaging Manager allows applications to be created for the home organization only. The BizTalk Messaging Configuration object model does not enforce this restriction. Therefore, if you create an application for an organization other than the default (home) organization, you cannot modify it using BizTalk Messaging Manager.

Requirements

Windows NT/2000: Requires Windows 2000 SP1 or later
Header: Include BizTalkObjectModel.h

IBizTalkOrganization::GetDefaultAlias Method

The **GetDefaultAlias** method returns the handle to the default alias for the object. The default alias for an object is the default organization identifier type/value pair.

Syntax

HRESULT GetDefaultAlias(
  long* *plAliasHandle*
);

Parameters

plAliasHandle
   [out, retval] Pointer to a **long** that contains the handle.

Return Values

For a list of all error messages returned by BizTalk Server, see Appendix A, "Error Messages."

Requirements

Windows NT/2000: Requires Windows 2000 SP1 or later
Header: Include BizTalkObjectModel.h

IBizTalkOrganization::IsDefault Property

The **IsDefault** property contains the flag that indicates whether the object is the default organization.

Syntax

Get method:

HRESULT get_IsDefault(
  VARIANT_BOOL* *pbIsDefault*
);

Parameters

Get method:

pbIsDefault
   [out, retval] Pointer to a **VARIANT_BOOL** type that indicates whether this organization is the default organization. A value of **VARIANT_TRUE** indicates that this organization is the default organization. A value of **VARIANT_FALSE** indicates that this organization is not the default organization.

Return Values

For a list of all error messages returned by BizTalk Server, see Appendix A, "Error Messages."

Remarks

This is a read-only property. There must be one and only one default organization at any time.

📝 Note

- BizTalk Messaging Manager refers to the default organization as the home organization.

Requirements

Windows NT/2000: Requires Windows 2000 SP1 or later
Header: Include BizTalkObjectModel.h

IBizTalkOrganization::LoadAlias Method

The **LoadAlias** method loads an associated alias for the object in memory. The alias for an object is the organization qualifier/value pair.

Syntax

HRESULT LoadAlias(
  long *lAliasHandle,*
  VARIANT* *pvarName,*
  VARIANT* *pvarDefault,*
  VARIANT* *pvarQualifier,*
  VARIANT* *pvarValue*
);

Parameters

lAliasHandle
  [in] **Long** that contains the handle to the alias.

pvarName
  [in, out] Pointer to a **VARIANT** that contains the name of the organization identifier.

pvarDefault
  [in, out] Pointer to a **VARIANT** that contains the default flag.

pvarQualifier
  [in, out] Pointer to a **VARIANT** that contains the qualifier of the organization identifier.

pvarValue
  [in, out] Pointer to a **VARIANT** that contains the value of the organization identifier.

Return Values

For a list of all error messages returned by BizTalk Server, see Appendix A, "Error Messages."

Remarks

The values used with the parameters of this method can be obtained from the **Aliases** property.

Requirements

Windows NT/2000: Requires Windows 2000 SP1 or later
Header: Include BizTalkObjectModel.h

IBizTalkOrganization::LoadApplication Method

The **LoadApplication** method loads an associated application for the object in memory.

Syntax

HRESULT LoadApplication(
   long *lApplicationHandle*,
   VARIANT* *pvarName*
);

Parameters

lApplicationHandle
   [in] **Long** that contains the application handle.

pvarName
   [in, out] Pointer to a **VARIANT** that contains the name of the application.

Return Values

For a list of all error messages returned by BizTalk Server, see Appendix A, "Error Messages."

Remarks

The values used with the parameters of this method can be obtained from the **Applications** property.

Requirements

Windows NT/2000: Requires Windows 2000 SP1 or later
Header: Include BizTalkObjectModel.h

IBizTalkOrganization::RemoveAlias Method

The **RemoveAlias** method removes an alias. The alias for an object is the organization identifier type/value pair.

Syntax

HRESULT RemoveAlias(
   long *lAliasHandle*
);

Parameters

lAliasHandle
   [in] **Long** that contains the handle to the alias.

Return Values

For a list of all error messages returned by BizTalk Server, see Appendix A, "Error Messages."

Remarks

This record cannot be removed if any of the following conditions apply:

- A **BizTalkPort** or a **BizTalkChannel** object refers to it.
- It has been designated the default organization identifier.
- This alias was autogenerated.

The alias handle can be obtained from the **Aliases** property.

Requirements

Windows NT/2000: Requires Windows 2000 SP1 or later
Header: Include BizTalkObjectModel.h

IBizTalkOrganization::RemoveApplication Method

The **RemoveApplication** method removes an application from the default organization.

Syntax

HRESULT RemoveApplication(
   long *lApplicationHandle*
);

Parameters

lApplicationHandle
> [in] **Long** that contains the handle.

Return Values

For a list of all error messages returned by BizTalk Server, see Appendix A, "Error Messages."

Remarks

This record cannot be removed if a **BizTalkPort** or a **BizTalkChannel** object refers to it.

The application handle can be obtained from the **Applications** property.

Requirements

Windows NT/2000: Requires Windows 2000 SP1 or later
Header: Include BizTalkObjectModel.h

IBizTalkOrganization::SaveAlias Method

The **SaveAlias** method saves an alias for the object. The alias for an object is the organization identifier type/value pair.

Syntax

HRESULT SaveAlias(
> **long** *lAliasHandle,*
> **BSTR** *strName,*
> **VARIANT_BOOL** *bDefault,*
> **BSTR** *strQualifier,*
> **BSTR** *strValue*
);

Parameters

lAliasHandle
> [in] **Long** that contains the handle to the alias.

strName
> [in] **BSTR** that contains the name of the organization identifier. This parameter cannot be changed if this alias was autogenerated.

bDefault
> [in] **VARIANT_BOOL** type that contains the default flag. A value of **VARIANT_TRUE** indicates that this is the default alias for the organization. A value of **VARIANT_FALSE** indicates that this is not the default alias for the organization.

strQualifier
> [in] **BSTR** that contains the qualifier of the organization identifier. This parameter cannot be changed if this alias was autogenerated. This parameter cannot be set to "group".

strValue
> [in] **BSTR** that contains the value of the organization identifier. This parameter cannot be changed if this alias was autogenerated.

Return Values

For a list of all error messages returned by BizTalk Server, see Appendix A, "Error Messages."

Requirements

Windows NT/2000: Requires Windows 2000 SP1 or later
Header: Include BizTalkObjectModel.h

IBizTalkOrganization::SaveApplication Method

The **SaveApplication** method saves this application for the default organization object.

Syntax

HRESULT SaveApplication(
    long *lApplicationHandle*,
    BSTR *strName*
);

Parameters

lApplicationHandle
> [in] **Long** that contains the handle to the application.

strName
> [in] **BSTR** that contains the name of the application.

Return Values

For a list of all error messages returned by BizTalk Server, see Appendix A, "Error Messages."

Requirements

Windows NT/2000: Requires Windows 2000 SP1 or later
Header: Include BizTalkObjectModel.h

IBizTalkPort Interface

The **BizTalkPort** object configures a one-way transfer of a document between organizations and applications. It identifies the source organization and/or application, the destination organization and/or application, the primary transport type, and, if selected, the associated envelope for transmission.

In C++, use the **IBizTalkPort** interface to access the methods of the **BizTalkPort** object.

The properties of the **BizTalkPort** object are shown in the table on the following page.

Property	Type	Description
Channels	IDispatch	ADO recordset that contains information about all **BizTalkChannel** objects that refer to the object. This is a read-only property.
Comments	BSTR	User comments for the **Port** object.
ControlNumberValue	BSTR	Value of the interchange control number. This is a required property if the **Format** property of the associated **BizTalkEnvelope** object is set to "x12", "edifact", or "custom". This constraint is not enforced for this release, but the server fails if it is not adhered to.
DateModified	BSTR	Date and time at which the information in the object was created or last modified. This is a read-only property obtained from the **BizTalkBase** object.
Delimiters	IDispatch	Dictionary object that contains all delimiters used in the document specification. This is a required property if the **Format** property of the associated **BizTalkEnvelope** object is set to "x12", "edifact", or "custom".
DestinationEndpoint	IDispatch	Information about the destination.
EncodingType	BIZTALK_ ENCODING_ TYPE	Enumeration value that indicates the type of document encoding.
EncryptionCertificateInfo	IDispatch	Information about the certificate that encrypts the document.
EncryptionType	BIZTALK_ ENCRYPTION_ TYPE	Enumeration value that indicates the type of document encryption.
Envelope	long	Handle to the **BizTalkEnvelope** object associated with this **BizTalkPort** object.
Handle	long	Handle to the object. This is a read-only property obtained from the **BizTalkBase** object.
Name	BSTR	Name of the object. This is a required property obtained from the **BizTalkBase** object.
PrimaryTransport	IDispatch	Primary transport component information.
SecondaryTransport	IDispatch	Secondary transport component information.
ServiceWindowInfo	IDispatch	Service window information.
SignatureType	BIZTALK_ SIGNATURE_ TYPE	Enumeration value that indicates the type of digital signing and verification.

The methods of the **BizTalkPort** object are shown in the following table.

Method	Description
Clear	Clears the object in memory. All the member variables of the object in memory are initialized to their default values. This method is obtained from the **BizTalkBase** object.
Create	Creates a new object in the database. This method is obtained from the **BizTalkBase** object.
Load	Loads the object in memory. This method is obtained from the **BizTalkBase** object.
LoadByName	Loads the object by name in memory. This method is obtained from the **BizTalkBase** object.
Remove	Removes the object from the database. This method is obtained from the **BizTalkBase** object.
Save	Saves the object in the database. This method is obtained from the **BizTalkBase** object.

Requirements

Windows NT/2000: Requires Windows 2000 SP1 or later
Header: Include BizTalkObjectModel.h

IBizTalkPort::Channels Property

The **Channels** property contains an ADO recordset that contains information about all **BizTalkChannel** objects that refer to the object.

Syntax

Get method:

HRESULT get_Channels(
    IDispatch** *ppChannelsDisp*
);

Parameters

ppChannelsDisp
    [out, retval] Address of a pointer to an **IDispatch** interface that contains the **BizTalkChannel** objects that refer to the object.

Return Values

For a list of all error messages returned by BizTalk Server, see Appendix A, "Error Messages."

Remarks

This is a read-only property.

Each record in the ADO recordset returned by this property contains information about the **BizTalkChannel** objects in the database that are associated with this **BizTalkPort** object. The fields in each record contain the following information, listed in order:

- Handle
- Name
- A unique channel identifier, in GUID format.

Additional information about Microsoft ActiveX Data Objects is available on the MSDN Online Library Web site (msdn.microsoft.com/library/default.asp).

Requirements

Windows NT/2000: Requires Windows 2000 SP1 or later
Header: Include BizTalkObjectModel.h

IBizTalkPort::Comments Property

The **Comments** property contains the user comments for the **Port** object.

Syntax

Get method:

HRESULT get_Comments(
   BSTR* *pstrComments*
);

Put method:

HRESULT put_Comments(
   BSTR *strComments*
);

Parameters

Get method:

pstrComments
   [out, retval] Pointer to a **BSTR** that contains the comments.

Put method:

strComments
   [in] **BSTR** that contains the comments.

Return Values

For a list of all error messages returned by BizTalk Server, see Appendix A, "Error Messages."

Requirements

Windows NT/2000: Requires Windows 2000 SP1 or later
Header: Include BizTalkObjectModel.h

IBizTalkPort::ControlNumberValue Property

The **ControlNumberValue** property contains the value of the interchange control number.

Syntax

HRESULT get_ControlNumberValue(
   BSTR* *pstrControlNumberValue*
);

Put method:

HRESULT put_ControlNumberValue(
   BSTR *strControlNumberValue*
);

Parameters

Get method:

pstrControlNumberValue
   [out, retval] Pointer to a **BSTR** that contains the interchange control number.

Put method:

strControlNumberValue
   [in] **BSTR** that contains the interchange control number.

Return Values

For a list of all error messages returned by BizTalk Server, see Appendix A, "Error Messages."

Remarks

The **ControlNumberValue** property must contain a value between 1 and 999999999.

Requirements

Windows NT/2000: Requires Windows 2000 SP1 or later
Header: Include BizTalkObjectModel.h

IBizTalkPort::Delimiters Property

The **Delimiters** property contains a **Dictionary** object that contains all delimiters used in the document specification. **Delimiters** specifies which characters to use to separate data within the envelope and the documents that are sent using this envelope.

Syntax

Get method:

HRESULT get_Delimiters(
    IDispatch** *ppDelimitersDisp*
);

Putref method:

HRESULT putref_Delimiters(
    IDispatch* *pDelimitersDisp*
);

Parameters

Get method:

ppDelimitersDisp
    [out, retval] Address of a pointer to an **IDispatch** interface that contains the delimiters.

Putref method:

pDelimitersDisp
    [in] Pointer to an **IDispatch** interface that contains the delimiters.

Return Values

For a list of all error messages returned by BizTalk Server, see Appendix A, "Error Messages."

Remarks

This is a required property for the object to be complete if the **Format** property of the associated **BizTalkEnvelope** object is set to "x12", "edifact", or "custom". The **PropertySet** property of the associated **BizTalkDocument** object must also be defined. The following table shows which names are required for the delimiters of the **Dictionary** object for various formats.

Delimiter	X12	EDIFACT
Record_delim	Yes	Yes
Field_delim	Yes	Yes
Subfield_delim	Yes	Yes
Escape_char	No	Yes

Requirements

Windows NT/2000: Requires Windows 2000 SP1 or later
Header: Include BizTalkObjectModel.h

IBizTalkPort::DestinationEndpoint Property

The **DestinationEndpoint** property contains information about the destination. This information includes the **Alias**, **Application**, and **Organization** properties and is created and stored in memory in the **BizTalkEndPoint** object.

Syntax

Get method:

HRESULT get_DestinationEndpoint(
    IDispatch** *ppDestEndpointDisp*
);

Putref method:

HRESULT putref_DestinationEndpoint(
    IDispatch* *pDestEndpointDisp*
);

Parameters

Get method:

ppDestEndpointDisp
    [out, retval] Address of a pointer to an **IDispatch** interface that contains information about the destination.

Putref method:

pDestEndpointDisp
    [in] Pointer to an **IDispatch** interface that contains information about the destination.

Return Values

For a list of all error messages returned by BizTalk Server, see Appendix A, "Error Messages."

Remarks

Once a **BizTalkPort** object has been created, the destination **BizTalkOrganization** object cannot be changed.

Requirements

Windows NT/2000: Requires Windows 2000 SP1 or later
Header: Include BizTalkObjectModel.h

IBizTalkPort::EncodingType Property

The **EncodingType** property contains the enumeration value that indicates the type of document encoding.

Syntax

Get method:

HRESULT get_EncodingType(
    BIZTALK_ENCODING_TYPE* *pEncodingType*
);

Put method:

HRESULT put_EncodingType(
    BIZTALK_ENCODING_TYPE *EncodingType*
);

Parameters

Get method:

pEncodingType
    [out, retval] Pointer to an enumeration value. Valid values are from the
    BIZTALK_ENCODING_TYPE enumeration.

Put method:

EncodingType
    [in] When putting the property, an enumeration value. Valid values are from the
    BIZTALK_ENCODING_TYPE enumeration.

Return Values

For a list of all error messages returned by BizTalk Server, see Appendix A, "Error Messages."

Remarks

The **Clear** method sets **EncodingType** to **BIZTALK_ENCODING_TYPE_NONE**.

Requirements

Windows NT/2000: Requires Windows 2000 SP1 or later
Header: Include BizTalkObjectModel.h

IBizTalkPort::EncryptionCertificateInfo

The **EncryptionCertificateInfo** property contains information about the certificate that encrypts the document. This information includes the **Name**, **Reference**, **Store**, and **Usage** properties and is created and stored in memory in the **BizTalkCertificateInfo** object.

Syntax

Get method:

HRESULT get_EncryptionCertificateInfo(
   IDispatch** *ppEncryptionCertificateInfoDisp*
);

Putref method:

HRESULT putref_EncryptionCertificateInfo(
   IDispatch* *pEncryptionCertificateInfoDisp*
);

Parameters

Get method:

ppEncryptionCertificateInfoDisp
   [out, retval] Address of a pointer to an **IDispatch** interface that contains the certificate information.

Putref method:

pEncryptionCertificateInfoDisp
   [in] Pointer to an **IDispatch** interface that contains the certificate information.

Return Values

For a list of all error messages returned by BizTalk Server, see Appendix A, "Error Messages."

Requirements

Windows NT/2000: Requires Windows 2000 SP1 or later
Header: Include BizTalkObjectModel.h

IBizTalkPort::EncryptionType Property

The **EncryptionType** property contains the enumeration value that indicates the type of document encryption.

Syntax

Get method:

HRESULT get_EncryptionType(
   BIZTALK_ENCRYPTION_TYPE* *pEncryptionType*
);

Put method:

HRESULT put_EncryptionType(
   BIZTALK_ENCRYPTION_TYPE *EncryptionType*
);

Parameters

Get method:

pEncryptionType
   [out, retval] Pointer to an enumeration value. Valid values are from the
   BIZTALK_ENCRYPTION_TYPE enumeration.

Put method:

EncryptionType
   [in] Enumeration value. Valid values are from the **BIZTALK_ENCRYPTION_TYPE**
   enumeration.

Return Values

For a list of all error messages returned by BizTalk Server, see Appendix A, "Error Messages."

Remarks

The **Clear** method sets **EncryptionType** to **BIZTALK_ENCRYPTION_TYPE_NONE**.

If the **EncryptionType** is set to **BIZTALK_ENCRYPTION_TYPE_SMIME**, the **EncryptionCertificateInfo** property must be set.

For open messaging ports, **EncryptionType** must be set to **BIZTALK_ENCRYPTION_TYPE_NONE**.

Requirements

Windows NT/2000: Requires Windows 2000 SP1 or later
Header: Include BizTalkObjectModel.h

IBizTalkPort::Envelope Property

The **Envelope** property contains the handle to the associated **BizTalkEnvelope** object.

Syntax

Get method:

HRESULT get_Envelope(
  long* *plEnvelopeHandle*
);

Put method:

HRESULT put_Envelope(
  long *lEnvelopeHandle*
);

Parameters

Get method:

plEnvelopeHandle
  [out, retval] Pointer to a **long** that contains the handle to the object.

Put method:

lEnvelopeHandle
  [in] **Long** that contains the handle to the object.

Return Values

For a list of all error messages returned by BizTalk Server, see Appendix A, "Error Messages."

Requirements

Windows NT/2000: Requires Windows 2000 SP1 or later
Header: Include BizTalkObjectModel.h

IBizTalkPort::PrimaryTransport Property

The **PrimaryTransport** property contains the primary transport component information, including the **Address**, **Parameter**, and **Type** properties of the **BizTalkTransportInfo** object.

Syntax

Get method:

HRESULT get_PrimaryTransport(
 IDispatch** *ppTransportInfoDisp*
);

Putref method:

HRESULT putref_PrimaryTransport(
 IDispatch* *pTransportInfoDisp*
);

Parameters

Get method:

ppTransportInfoDisp
 [out, retval] Address of a pointer to an **IDispatch** interface that contains the primary transport component information.

Putref method:

pTransportInfoDisp
 [in] Pointer to an **IDispatch** interface that contains the primary transport component information.

Return Values

For a list of all error messages returned by BizTalk Server, see Appendix A, "Error Messages."

Remarks

This is a required property for the object.

The following constraints are enforced:

- If the **Openness** property of the associated **BizTalkEndPoint** object is set to **BIZTALK_OPENNESS_TYPE_EX_DESTINATION**, the **Address** property cannot be set, and **PrimaryTransport** must be set to **BIZTALK_TRANSPORT_TYPE_OPENDESTINATION**. The **BizTalkServiceWindowInfo** object cannot be used with open destination ports.

- Once a **BizTalkPort** object has been created, the **Openness** property of the associated **BizTalkEndPoint** object cannot be changed.

- The **Openness** property cannot be set to **BIZTALK_OPENNESS_TYPE_EX_SOURCE** or **BIZTALK_OPENNESS_TYPE_EX_FROMWORKFLOW**.

- When using a **Type** of **BIZTALK_TRANSPORT_TYPE_LOOPBACK**, the primary and secondary transport **Address** property cannot be set, and the **BizTalkServiceWindowInfo** object cannot be used.

Requirements

Windows NT/2000: Requires Windows 2000 SP1 or later
Header: Include BizTalkObjectModel.h

IBizTalkPort::SecondaryTransport Property

The **SecondaryTransport** property contains the secondary transport component information, including the **Address**, **Parameter**, and **Type** properties, and is created and stored in memory in the **BizTalkTransportInfo** object.

Syntax

Get method:

HRESULT get_SecondaryTransport(
   IDispatch** *ppTransportInfoDisp*
);

Putref method:

HRESULT putref_SecondaryTransport(
   IDispatch* *pTransportInfoDisp*
);

Parameters

Get method:

ppTransportInfoDisp
   [out, retval] Address of a pointer to an **IDispatch** interface that contains the secondary transport component information.

Putref method:

pTransportInfoDisp
   [in] Pointer to an **IDispatch** interface that contains the secondary transport component information.

Return Values

For a list of all error messages returned by BizTalk Server, see Appendix A, "Error Messages."

Remarks

This is a required property for the object to be complete.

The following constraints are enforced:

- If the **Openness** property of the associated **BizTalkEndPoint** object is set to **BIZTALK_OPENNESS_TYPE_EX_DESTINATION**, the **Address** property cannot be set, and **SecondaryTransport** must be set to **BIZTALK_TRANSPORT_TYPE_OPENDESTINATION**.

- Once a **BizTalkPort** object has been created, the **Openness** property of the associated **BizTalkEndPoint** object cannot be changed.

- The **Openness** property cannot be set to **BIZTALK_OPENNESS_TYPE_EX_SOURCE** or **BIZTALK_OPENNESS_TYPE_EX_FROMWORKFLOW**.

- The **Type** property cannot be set to **BIZTALK_TRANSPORT_TYPE_LOOPBACK**.

Requirements

Windows NT/2000: Requires Windows 2000 SP1 or later
Header: Include BizTalkObjectModel.h

IBizTalkPort::ServiceWindowInfo Property

The **ServiceWindowInfo** property contains information about the service window. This information includes the **FromTime**, **IsEnabled**, and **ToTime** properties and is created and stored in memory in the **BizTalkServiceWindowInfo** object.

Syntax

Get method:

HRESULT get_ServiceWindowInfo(
   IDispatch** *ppServiceWindowInfoDisp*
);

Putref method:

HRESULT putref_ServiceWindowInfo(
   IDispatch* *pServiceWindowInfoDisp*
);

Parameters

Get method:

ppServiceWindowInfoDisp
> [out, retval] Address of a pointer to an **IDispatch** interface that contains the service window.

Putref method:

pServiceWindowInfoDisp
> [in] Pointer to an **IDispatch** interface that contains the service window.

Return Values

For a list of all error messages returned by BizTalk Server, see Appendix A, "Error Messages."

Remarks

If this property is used, the **BizTalkServiceWindowInfo** object must specify a valid time range by using the **FromTime** and **ToTime** properties.

Requirements

Windows NT/2000: Requires Windows 2000 SP1 or later
Header: Include BizTalkObjectModel.h

IBizTalkPort::SignatureType Property

The **SignatureType** property contains the enumeration value that indicates the type of digital signing and verification.

Syntax

Get method:

HRESULT get_SignatureType(
 BIZTALK_SIGNATURE_TYPE* *pSignatureType*
);

Put method:

HRESULT put_SignatureType(
 BIZTALK_SIGNATURE_TYPE *SignatureType*
);

Parameters

Get method:

pSignatureType
> [out, retval] Pointer to an enumeration value. Valid values are from the
> **BIZTALK_SIGNATURE_TYPE** enumeration.

Put method:

SignatureType
> [in] Enumeration value. Valid values are from the **BIZTALK_SIGNATURE_TYPE**
> enumeration.

Return Values

For a list of all error messages returned by BizTalk Server, see Appendix A, "Error
Messages."

Remarks

The **Clear** method sets **SignatureType** to **BIZTALK_SIGNATURE_TYPE_NONE**.

BizTalkPort objects associated with open channels cannot have a **SignatureType**.

If the **SignatureType** on a **BizTalkPort** object is changed from
BIZTALK_SIGNATURE_TYPE_NONE to **BIZTALK_SIGNATURE_TYPE_SMIME**,
all channels associated with this **BizTalkPort** object must have already been saved with a
SignatureCertificateInfo object. Also, if a **BizTalkChannel** object contains a
SignatureCertificateInfo object and the **SignatureType** of **BizTalkPort** is set to
BIZTALK_SIGNATURE_TYPE_NONE, the signature will be ignored.

Requirements

Windows NT/2000: Requires Windows 2000 SP1 or later
Header: Include BizTalkObjectModel.h

IBizTalkPortGroup Interface

Use the **BizTalkPortGroup** object to configure port groups that are used to distribute the
same document to many organizations.

In C++, use the **IBizTalkPortGroup** interface to access the methods of the
BizTalkPortGroup object.

The properties of the **BizTalkPortGroup** object are shown in the following table.

Property	Type	Description
Channels	**IDispatch**	ADO recordset that contains information about all **BizTalkChannel** objects that refer to this object.
DateModified	**BSTR**	Date and time at which the information in the object was created or last modified. This is a read-only property obtained from the **BizTalkBase** object.
Handle	**long**	Handle to the object. This is a read-only property obtained from the **BizTalkBase** object.
Name	**BSTR**	Name of the object. This is a required property obtained from the **BizTalkBase** object.
Ports	**IDispatch**	ADO recordset that contains information about all **BizTalkPort** objects that refer to this object.

The methods of the **BizTalkPortGroup** object are shown in the following table.

Method	Description
AddPort	Adds a **BizTalkPort** object to this port group. There must be at least one **BizTalkPort** object in the port group.
Clear	Clears the object in memory. All member variables of the object in memory are initialized to their default values. This method is obtained from the **BizTalkBase** object.
Create	Creates a new object in the database. This method is obtained from the **BizTalkBase** object.
Load	Loads the object in memory. This method is obtained from the **BizTalkBase** object.
LoadByName	Loads the object by name in memory. This method is obtained from the **BizTalkBase** object.
Remove	Removes the **BizTalkPortGroup** object from the database. This method is obtained from the **BizTalkBase** object.
RemovePort	Removes a **BizTalkPort** object from the port group. There must be at least one **BizTalkPort** object in the port group.
Save	Saves the object in the database. This method is obtained from the **BizTalkBase** object.

Remarks

There must always be at least one **BizTalkPort** object and one **BizTalkChannel** object associated with a **BizTalkPortGroup** object. The **BizTalkChannel** object is associated with the **BizTalkPortGroup** object, not the **BizTalkPort** object within the group. Each **BizTalkPort** object within the group has another **BizTalkChannel** object or objects associated with it, but these are ignored when the port group channel is invoked.

Requirements

Windows NT/2000: Requires Windows 2000 SP1 or later
Header: Include BizTalkObjectModel.h

IBizTalkPortGroup::AddPort Method

The **AddPort** method adds a **BizTalkPort** object to this port group.

Syntax

HRESULT AddPort(
    long *lPortHandle*
);

Parameters

lPortHandle
    [in] **Long** that contains the handle to the object.

Return Values

For a list of all error messages returned by BizTalk Server, see Appendix A, "Error Messages."

Remarks

The following constraints apply to this method:

- There must be at least one **BizTalkPort** in this **BizTalkPortGroup** object.

- The **Openness** property of the associated **BizTalkEndPoint** object to be added must be set to **BIZTALK_OPENNESS_TYPE_NOTOPEN**.

- The port group specified by this object cannot contain any duplicate **BizTalkPort** objects.

Requirements

Windows NT/2000: Requires Windows 2000 SP1 or later
Header: Include BizTalkObjectModel.h

IBizTalkPortGroup::Channels Property

The **Channels** property contains an ADO recordset that contains information about all **BizTalkChannel** objects that refer to the object.

Syntax

Get method:

HRESULT get_Channels(
   IDispatch** *ppChannelsDisp*
);

Parameters

ppChannelsDisp
   [out, retval] Address of a pointer to an **IDispatch** interface that contains an ADO recordset that contains all **BizTalkChannel** objects that refer to the object.

Return Values

For a list of all error messages returned by BizTalk Server, see Appendix A, "Error Messages."

☑ Note

- In addition to the HRESULT values listed on the error messages page, this method returns OLEDB provider errors. Additional information about OLEDB is available on the MSDN Online Library Web site (msdn.microsoft.com/library/default.asp).

Remarks

Each record in the ADO recordset returned by this property contains information about the **BizTalkChannel** objects in the database that are associated with this **BizTalkPortGroup** object. The fields in each record contain the following information, listed in order:

- Handle

- Name

Additional information about Microsoft ActiveX Data Objects is available on the MSDN Online Library Web site (msdn.microsoft.com/library/default.asp).

Requirements

Windows NT/2000: Requires Windows 2000 SP1 or later
Header: Include BizTalkObjectModel.h

IBizTalkPortGroup::Ports Property

The **Ports** property contains an ADO recordset that contains information about all
BizTalkPort objects that refer to the object.

Syntax

Get method:

HRESULT Ports(
  IDispatch** *ppPortsDisp*
);

Parameters

ppPortsDisp
  [out, retval] Address of a pointer to an **IDispatch** interface that contains an ADO
  recordset that contains all **BizTalkPort** objects that refer to the object.

Return Values

For a list of all error messages returned by BizTalk Server, see Appendix A, "Error
Messages."

✎ Note

- In addition to the HRESULT values listed on the error messages page, this method returns
  OLEDB provider errors. Additional information about OLEDB is available on the MSDN
  Online Library Web site (msdn.microsoft.com/library/default.asp).

Remarks

Each record in the ADO recordset returned by this property contains information about the
BizTalkPort objects in the database that are associated with this **BizTalkPortGroup** object.
The fields in each record contain the following information, listed in order:

- Handle

- Name

Additional information about Microsoft ActiveX Data Objects is available on the MSDN
Online Library Web site (msdn.microsoft.com/library/default.asp).

Requirements

Windows NT/2000: Requires Windows 2000 SP1 or later
Header: Include BizTalkObjectModel.h

IBizTalkPortGroup::RemovePort Method

The **RemovePort** method removes a **BizTalkPort** object from this port group.

Syntax

HRESULT RemovePort(
  long *lPortHandle*
);

Parameters

lPortHandle
  [in] **Long** that contains the handle to the object to remove.

Return Values

For a list of all error messages returned by BizTalk Server, see Appendix A, "Error Messages."

✎ Note

- In addition to the HRESULT values listed on the error messages page, this method returns OLEDB provider errors. Additional information about OLEDB is available on the MSDN Online Library Web site (msdn.microsoft.com/library/default.asp).

Remarks

The last **BizTalkPort** object associated with the object cannot be removed. A **BizTalkPort** object cannot be removed if a **BizTalkChannel** object refers to it.

Requirements

Windows NT/2000: Requires Windows 2000 SP1 or later
Header: Include BizTalkObjectModel.h

IBizTalkServiceWindowInfo Interface

Use the **BizTalkServiceWindowInfo** object to configure the service window for an associated **BizTalkPort** object. The service window indicates a valid time range for transmitting documents.

In C++, use the **IBizTalkServiceWindowInfo** interface to access the methods of the **BizTalkServiceWindowInfo** object.

The properties of the **BizTalkServiceWindowInfo** object are shown in the following table.

Property	Type	Description
FromTime	BSTR	Earliest time that the interchange can be transmitted.
IsEnabled	VARIANT_BOOL	Flag that indicates whether the service window is enabled.
ToTime	BSTR	Latest time that the interchange can be transmitted.

Remarks

The **BizTalkServiceWindowInfo** object is automatically created when a **BizTalkPort** object is instantiated with the **CreatePort** method of the **BizTalkConfig** object. Access the properties of the **BizTalkServiceWindowInfo** object by using the **ServiceWindowInfo** property of the **BizTalkPort** object.

Requirements

Windows NT/2000: Requires Windows 2000 SP1 or later
Header: Include BizTalkObjectModel.h

IBizTalkServiceWindowInfo::FromTime Property

The **FromTime** property indicates the earliest hour of any day that the interchange can be transmitted.

Syntax

Get method:

HRESULT get_FromTime(
   BSTR* *pstrFromTime*
);

Put method:

HRESULT put_FromTime(
   BSTR *strFromTime*
);

Parameters

Get method:

pstrFromTime
> [out, retval] Pointer to a **BSTR** that contains the earliest time that the interchange can be transmitted.

Put method:

strFromTime
> [in] **BSTR** that contains the earliest time that the interchange can be transmitted.

Return Values

For a list of all error messages returned by BizTalk Server, see Appendix A, "Error Messages."

Remarks

The **FromTime** property must contain an integer value between 0 and 23. Fractional values and minutes cannot be specified.

Requirements

Windows NT/2000: Requires Windows 2000 SP1 or later
Header: Include BizTalkObjectModel.h

IBizTalkServiceWindowInfo::IsEnabled Property

The **IsEnabled** property indicates whether a service window is enabled.

Syntax

Get method:

HRESULT get_IsEnabled(
  VARIANT_BOOL* *pbIsEnabled*
);

Put method:

HRESULT put_IsEnabled(
  VARIANT_BOOL *bIsEnabled*
);

Parameters

Get method:

pbIsEnabled

[out, retval] Pointer to a **VARIANT_BOOL** type that indicates whether a service window is enabled. A value of **VARIANT_TRUE** indicates that the service window is enabled. A value of **VARIANT_FALSE** indicates that the service window is not enabled.

Put method:

bIsEnabled

[in] **VARIANT_BOOL** type that indicates whether a service window is enabled. A value of **VARIANT_TRUE** indicates that the service window is enabled. A value of **VARIANT_FALSE** indicates that the service window is not enabled.

Return Values

For a list of all error messages returned by BizTalk Server, see Appendix A, "Error Messages."

Requirements

Windows NT/2000: Requires Windows 2000 SP1 or later
Header: Include BizTalkObjectModel.h

IBizTalkServiceWindowInfo::ToTime Property

The **ToTime** property contains the latest hour of any day that the interchange can be transmitted.

Syntax

Get method:

HRESULT get_ToTime(
  BSTR* *pstrToTime*
);

Put method:

HRESULT put_ToTime(
  BSTR *strToTime*
);

Parameters

Get method:

pstrToTime
> [out, retval] Pointer to a **BSTR** that contains the latest time that the interchange can be transmitted.

Put method:

strToTime
> [in] **BSTR** that contains the latest time that the interchange can be transmitted.

Return Values

For a list of all error messages returned by BizTalk Server, see Appendix A, "Error Messages."

Remarks

The **ToTime** property must contain an integer value between 0 and 23. Fractional values and minutes cannot be specified.

Requirements

Windows NT/2000: Requires Windows 2000 SP1 or later
Header: Include BizTalkObjectModel.h

IBizTalkTransportInfo Interface

Use the **BizTalkTransportInfo** object to configure the transport service for an associated **BizTalkPort** object.

In C++, use the **IBizTalkTransportInfo** interface to access methods of the **BizTalkTransportInfo** object.

The properties of the **BizTalkTransportInfo** object are shown in the following table.

Property	Type	Description
Address	BSTR	Destination address of the primary transport component.
Parameter	BSTR	Required return e-mail address for the associated source **BizTalkOrganization** object if the **Type** property is **BIZTALK_TRANSPORT_TYPE_SMTP**.
Type	BIZTALK_TRANSPORT_ TYPE	Enumeration value that indicates the type of transport component to be used for the primary transport.

Remarks

The **BizTalkTransportInfo** object is automatically created when a **BizTalkPort** object is instantiated with the **CreatePort** method of the **BizTalkConfig** object. Access the **BizTalkTransportInfo** object by using the **PrimaryTransport** or **SecondaryTransport** property of the **BizTalkPort** object.

Requirements

Windows NT/2000: Requires Windows 2000 SP1 or later
Header: Include BizTalkObjectModel.h

IBizTalkTransportInfo::Address Property

The **Address** property contains the destination address.

Syntax

Get method:

HRESULT get_Address(
   BSTR* *pstrTransportAddress*
);

Put method:

HRESULT put_Address(
   BSTR *strTransportAddress*
);

Parameters

Get method:

pstrTransportAddress
   [out, retval] Pointer to a **BSTR** that contains the address.

Put method:

strTransportAddress
   [in] **BSTR** that contains the address.

Return Values

For a list of all error messages returned by BizTalk Server, see Appendix A, "Error Messages."

Remarks

If the **Openness** property of the associated **BizTalkEndPoint** object is set to **BIZTALK_OPENNESS_TYPE_DESTINATION**, **Address** cannot be set, and the **Type** property must be set to **BIZTALK_TRANSPORT_TYPE_OPENDESTINATION**.

Address must have one of the following prefixes, according to the **Type** property.

Transport type	Prefix	Example Address value
APPINTEGRATION	Not applicable	{11111111-1111-1111-1111-111111111111}
FILE	file://	file://C:\Test\MyFile.xml
HTTP	http://	http://www.vigorair-18.com/repository/bts.asp
HTTPS	https://	https://www.vigorair-18.com/secure/btss.asp
LOOPBACK	Not applicable	Not applicable
MSMQ	Not applicable	DIRECT=OS:.\private$\myqueue
NONE	Not applicable	Not applicable
OPENDESTINATION	Not applicable	Not applicable
ORCHESTRATIONACTIVATION	Not applicable	C:\XLANG\Schedules\mysched.skx
SMTP	mailto:	mailto:patricia@vigorair-18.com

Notes

- The queue:// prefix must be used with an open messaging port when a Message Queue is specified as the destination address. For open messaging ports, the address is specified either in the document instance or as a parameter when submitting the document. For more information, see Chapter 10, "Submitting Documents."

- When using the Orchestration Activation Component transport type, the **Address** property must contain the full path of the XLANG schedule on the local computer. The file:// prefix cannot be used when specifying the path of the XLANG schedule (.skx) file.

- When using the HTTP or HTTPS transport types, BizTalk Server sends the data using a proxy server by default. This is the correct setting to transport data to computers outside your company's firewall. However, when sending data within your company's intranet, you can bypass the use of a proxy server. To do this, you must set the UseProxy field to False in the transport dictionary. For more information, see "IBizTalkChannel::SetConfigData Method" earlier in this chapter.

When using the file:// transport type, you can include symbols to modify the file name. The file name created by the server contains any static characters you specified in the **Address** property, along with the actual value of the symbol. For example, if the **Address** property is set to "file://C:\Orders\Invoice_%tracking_id%.xml", the actual file name would use a format similar to: C:\Orders\Invoice_{12345678-90AB-CDEF-1234-567890ABCDEF}. The following table contains the symbols that can be used with the file:// transport type.

Symbol	Description	Unique file name
%datetime%	Date and time, in milliseconds, of the file creation. The time is based on Greenwich Mean Time (GMT) rather than local time.	No
%document_name%	Name of the document processed by BizTalk Server.	No
%server%	Host name of the server that processed the document.	No
%tracking_id%	Globally unique tracking number.	Yes
%uid%	Counter that increases over time, represented in milliseconds. This number is reset when the server is rebooted.	No

When sending reliable messaging receipts that use the SMTP transport protocol, the value specified in the identifier named Reliable Messaging Acknowledgement SMTP From Address is used as the From address. This identifier is automatically created for the default **BizTalkOrganization** object. This identifier cannot be removed. You should not modify the name or qualifier for this identifier, but you can modify the value. For more information, see "Processing Receipts Using Reliable Messaging" earlier in this chapter.

Requirements

Windows NT/2000: Requires Windows 2000 SP1 or later
Header: Include BizTalkObjectModel.h

IBizTalkTransportInfo::Parameter Property

The **Parameter** property contains the required return e-mail address of the associated source **BizTalkOrganization** object if the **Type** property is set to **BIZTALK_TRANSPORT_TYPE_SMTP**.

Syntax

Get method:

HRESULT get_Parameter(
    BSTR* *pstrPrimaryTransportParameter*
);

Put method:

HRESULT put_Parameter(
    BSTR *strPrimaryTransportParameter*
);

Parameters

Get method:

pstrPrimaryTransportParameter
> [out, retval] Pointer to a **BSTR** that contains the address.

Put method:

strPrimaryTransportParameter
> [in] **BSTR** that contains the address.

Return Values

For a list of all error messages returned by BizTalk Server, see Appendix A, "Error Messages."

Requirements

Windows NT/2000: Requires Windows 2000 SP1 or later
Header: Include BizTalkObjectModel.h

IBizTalkTransportInfo::Type Property

The **Type** property contains the enumeration value that indicates the type of transport component.

Syntax

Get method:

HRESULT get_Type(
  BIZTALK_TRANSPORT_TYPE* *pTransportType*
);

Put method:

HRESULT put_Type(
  BIZTALK_TRANSPORT_TYPE *TransportType*
);

Parameters

Get method:

pTransportType
> [out, retval] Pointer to an enumeration value. Valid values are from the
> **BIZTALK_TRANSPORT_TYPE** enumeration.

Put method:

TransportType

> [in] Enumeration value. Valid values are from the **BIZTALK_TRANSPORT_TYPE** enumeration.

Return Values

For a list of all error messages returned by BizTalk Server, see Appendix A, "Error Messages."

Remarks

The following constraints are enforced:

- If the **Openness** property of the associated **BizTalkEndPoint** object is set to **BIZTALK_OPENNESS_TYPE_DESTINATION**, the **Address** property cannot be set, and **Type** must be set to **BIZTALK_TRANSPORT_TYPE_OPENDESTINATION**.

When using the Message Queuing transport type (**BIZTALK_TRANSPORT_TYPE_MSMQ**), the following restrictions apply:

- When using an envelope, the maximum size of a document submitted to BizTalk Server is 4 MB.

- When an envelope is not used, the maximum size of a document submitted to BizTalk Server is 2 MB.

- When using **BIZTALK_TRANSPORT_TYPE_SMTP**, the **Parameter** property must be set to the reply-to SMTP address.

- The transport **Type** of **BIZTALK_TRANSPORT_TYPE_ORCHESTRATIONACTIVATION** is supported only when the **Openness** property of the associated **BizTalkEndPoint** object is set to **BIZTALK_OPENNESS_TYPE_TOWORKFLOW**.

When using the Orchestration activation component type (**BIZTALK_TRANSPORT_TYPE_ORCHESTRATIONACTIVATION**), the maximum size of a document sent to the port on the XLANG schedule is 2 MB.

Requirements

Windows NT/2000: Requires Windows 2000 SP1 or later
Header: Include BizTalkObjectModel.h

IDictionary Interface

The **Dictionary** object is a collection object that supports the creation, storage, and retrieval of name/value pairs in memory. This object is used by several methods in the BizTalk Messaging Configuration object model.

In C++, use the **IDictionary** interface to access the methods of the **Dictionary** object.

The properties of the **Dictionary** object are shown in the following table.

Property	Type	Description
Count	long	Number of entries in the **Dictionary** object. This is a read-only property.
NewEnum	IUnknown	Returns the **IUnknown** interface pointer for the **Dictionary** object. The caller can use this interface pointer to call **QueryInterface** for the enumerator for this object. This is a read-only property.
Prefix	BSTR	Filter that excludes all entries with a specific prefix when the contents of the **Dictionary** object are saved.
Value	VARIANT	Value associated with an entry name.

The methods of the **Dictionary** object are shown in the following table.

Method	Description
GetMultiple	Returns the values of multiple entries from the **Dictionary** object.
PutMultiple	Adds specified entries to the **Dictionary** object or changes them.

Remarks

A **Dictionary** object is designed to be a general-purpose collection. Therefore, it can be used for anything that is supported by its internal structure. Every value in a **Dictionary** object is a **Variant**. This means that a **Dictionary** object can be created that consists of almost any kind of value (including other **Dictionary** objects).

Requirements

Windows NT/2000: Requires Windows 2000 SP1 or later
Header: Include commerce.h

IDictionary::Count Property

The **Count** property returns the number of elements in the **Dictionary** object.

Syntax

HRESULT get_Count(
  long* *Count*
);

Parameters

Count
    [out, retval] **Long** used to return the count.

Return Values

For a list of all error messages returned by BizTalk Server, see Appendix A, "Error Messages."

Remarks

This property is read-only.

Requirements

Windows NT/2000: Requires Windows 2000 SP1 or later
Header: Include commerce.h

IDictionary::GetMultiple Method

The **GetMultiple** method returns multiple entries from the **Dictionary** object.

Syntax

HRESULT GetMultiple(
  long *cb*,
  const LPOLESTR *rgolestr[]*,
  VARIANT *rgvar[]*
);

Parameters

cb
> [in] **Long** that specifies the number of values to retrieve.

rgolestr
> [in, size_is(cb)] Array of string values that identifies the **Dictionary** object entries for which the values should be retrieved.

rgvar
> [out, size_is(cb)] Array of **VARIANT**s. When **GetMultiple** returns, this array contains the values associated with the **Dictionary** object entries identified by the *rgolestr[ ]* array.

Return Values

For a list of all error messages returned by BizTalk Server, see Appendix A, "Error Messages."

Requirements

Windows NT/2000: Requires Windows 2000 SP1 or later
Header: Include commerce.h

IDictionary::NewEnum Property

The **NewEnum** property retrieves an **Enumerator** object that implements the **IEnumVariant** interface of the **Dictionary** object.

Syntax

Get method:

HRESULT get_NewEnum(
  IUnknown** *_NewEnum*
);

Parameters

_NewEnum
> [out, retval] Address of a pointer to an **IUnknown** interface for an object that implements the **IEnumVariant** of this collection. You can call **QueryInterface** through the returned pointer to retrieve a pointer to the **IEnumVariant** for this object. To retrieve the values associated with these elements, you can retrieve the elements in turn, using the **Next** method of the **IEnumVariant** interface, and call the **Value** method on those elements.

Return Values

For a list of all error messages returned by BizTalk Server, see Appendix A, "Error Messages."

Remarks

This property is read-only.

Requirements

Windows NT/2000: Requires Windows 2000 SP1 or later
Header: Include commerce.h

IDictionary::Prefix Property

The **Prefix** property contains a filter that excludes entries with a specific prefix when the contents of the **Dictionary** object are saved.

Syntax

Get method:

HRESULT get_Prefix(
  BSTR * *Prefix*
);

Put method:

HRESULT put_Prefix(
  BSTR *Prefix*
);

Parameters

Get method:

Prefix
  [out, retval] Pointer to a **BSTR** that contains the prefix.

Put method:

Prefix
  [in] **BSTR** that contains the prefix.

Return Values

For a list of all error messages returned by BizTalk Server, see Appendix A, "Error Messages."

Remarks

Any name/value pair with a name beginning with the specified prefix is not saved to the database. The prefix default is an underscore (_). Therefore, any keywords that begin with an underscore are not saved unless the prefix is changed.

Requirements

Windows NT/2000: Requires Windows 2000 SP1 or later
Header: Include commerce.h

IDictionary::PutMultiple Method

The **PutMultiple** method adds specified entries to the **Dictionary** object or changes them.

Syntax

HRESULT PutMultiple(
   long *cb*,
   const LPOLESTR *rgolestr[]*,
   const VARIANT *rgvar[]*
);

Parameters

cb

   [in] **Long** that identifies the number of elements in the *rgolestr* and *rgvar* arrays.

rgolestr

   [in, size_is(cb)] Array of strings that contains the names to add to the **Dictionary** object.

rgvar

   [in, size_is(cb)] Array of **VARIANT**s that contains the values to add to the **Dictionary** object.

Return Values

For a list of all error messages returned by BizTalk Server, see Appendix A, "Error Messages."

Remarks

A one-to-one mapping exists between the elements of the *rgolestr* and *rgvar* arrays. This means that *rgolestr*[*n*] is added to the **Dictionary** object and is initialized to *rgvar*[*n*]. If the element specified by *rgolestr*[*n*] is already in the **Dictionary** object, the value associated with the element is overwritten with the value stored in *rgvar*[*n*].

Requirements

Windows NT/2000: Requires Windows 2000 SP1 or later
Header: Include commerce.h

IDictionary::Value Property

The **Value** property returns or sets the value associated with an entry name.

Syntax

Get method:

HRESULT get_Value(
    BSTR *bstrName*,
    VARIANT* *Value*
);

Put method:

HRESULT put_Value(
    BSTR *bstrName*,
    VARIANT *Value*
);

Parameters

Get method:

bstrName
    [in] **BSTR** that contains the name.

Value
    [out, retval] Pointer to a **VARIANT** used to return the value.

Put method:

bstrName
    [in] **BSTR** that contains the name.

Value
    [in] When putting the property, a **VARIANT** that contains the value.

Return Values

For a list of all error messages returned by BizTalk Server, see Appendix A, "Error Messages."

Remarks

The value of a **Dictionary** object can be read or written to without explicitly using the **Value** method by treating the named entry as a property of the **Dictionary** object.

Requirements

Windows NT/2000: Requires Windows 2000 SP1 or later
Header: Include commerce.h

ISimpleList Interface

Use the **SimpleList** object to create an array of variants that supports enumeration.

In C++, use the **ISimpleList** interface to access methods of the **SimpleList** object.

The properties of the **SimpleList** object are shown in the following table.

Property	Type	Description
Count	long	Number of elements in the **SimpleList** object. This is a read-only property.
Item	VARIANT	Container for an element of the **SimpleList** object.

The methods of the **SimpleList** object are shown in the following table.

Method	Description
Add	Adds the specified item to the **SimpleList** object.
Delete	Deletes the specified item from the **SimpleList** object.

Requirements

Windows NT/2000: Requires Windows 2000 SP1 or later
Header: Include commerce.h

ISimpleList::Add Method

The **Add** method adds the specified item to the **SimpleList** object.

Syntax

HRESULT Add(
  VARIANT* *pVar*
);

Parameters

pVar
  [in] Pointer to the **VARIANT** to add to the **SimpleList** object.

Return Values

For a list of all error messages returned by BizTalk Server, see Appendix A, "Error Messages."

Requirements

Windows NT/2000: Requires Windows 2000 SP1 or later
Header: Include commerce.h

ISimpleList::Count Property

The **Count** property returns the number of elements in the **SimpleList** object.

Syntax

Get method:

HRESULT get_Count(
   long* *Count*
);

Parameters

Count
   [out, retval] Pointer to a **long** used to return the number of items in the **SimpleList** object.

Return Values

For a list of all error messages returned by BizTalk Server, see Appendix A, "Error Messages."

Remarks

This property is read-only.

Requirements

Windows NT/2000: Requires Windows 2000 SP1 or later
Header: Include commerce.h

ISimpleList::Delete Method

The **Delete** method deletes the specified item from the **SimpleList** object.

Syntax

HRESULT Delete(
   long *Index*
);

Parameters

Index
   [in] **Long** that contains the index value of the item to delete.

Return Values

For a list of all error messages returned by BizTalk Server, see Appendix A, "Error Messages."

Requirements

Windows NT/2000: Requires Windows 2000 SP1 or later
Header: Include commerce.h

ISimpleList::Item Property

The **Item** property is a read/write **Variant** that contains an element of the **SimpleList** object. An initialized **Variant** is stored at a specified array index. If an item is already stored at the specified index, that item is overwritten by the put method.

Syntax

Get method:

HRESULT get_Item(
   long *Index,*
   VARIANT* *Item*
);

Put method:

HRESULT put_Item(
   long *Index,*
   VARIANT *Item*
);

Putref method:

HRESULT putref_Item(
   long *Index,*
   VARIANT *Item*
);

Parameters

Get method:

Index
   [in] **Long** that contains the index of the item.

Item
   [out, retval] Pointer to a **VARIANT** used to return the item.

Put and Putref methods:

Index
   [in] **Long** that contains the index of the item.

Item
   [in] **VARIANT** that contains the new item.

Return Values

For a list of all error messages returned by BizTalk Server, see Appendix A, "Error Messages."

Remarks

When putting a value, use the **putref_Item** method if you are setting an object reference; use the **put_Item** method if you are setting a scalar value.

Requirements

Windows NT/2000: Requires Windows 2000 SP1 or later
Header: Include commerce.h

Object Model Enumerations

The enumerations in this section provide the descriptions and possible values of properties and parameters in the BizTalk Messaging Configuration object model. These values are applicable when using either the Microsoft Visual Basic or Visual C++ programming language.

BIZTALK_ENCODING_TYPE

The **BIZTALK_ENCODING_TYPE** enumeration has one of the following values:

Name	Value	Description
BIZTALK_ENCODING_TYPE_NONE	1	Specifies that encoding is not used.
BIZTALK_ENCODING_TYPE_MIME	2	Specifies Multipurpose Internet Mail Extensions (MIME) encoding.
BIZTALK_ENCODING_TYPE_CUSTOM	3	Specifies custom encoding.

BIZTALK_ENCRYPTION_TYPE

The **BIZTALK_ENCRYPTION_TYPE** enumeration has one of the following values:

Name	Value	Description
BIZTALK_ENCRYPTION_TYPE_NONE	1	Specifies that encryption is not used.
BIZTALK_ENCRYPTION_TYPE_CUSTOM	2	Specifies custom encryption.
BIZTALK_ENCRYPTION_TYPE_SMIME	4	Specifies Secure Multipurpose Internet Mail Extensions (S/MIME) encryption.

BIZTALK_OPENNESS_TYPE

The **BIZTALK_OPENNESS_TYPE** enumeration has one of the following values:

Name	Value	Description
BIZTALK_OPENNESS_TYPE_NOTOPEN	1	Specifies that this instance of the object is not open.
BIZTALK_OPENNESS_TYPE_SOURCE	2	Specifies that the source organization of this instance of the object is open.
BIZTALK_OPENNESS_TYPE_DESTINATION	4	Specifies that the destination organization of this instance of the object is open.

BIZTALK_OPENNESS_TYPE_EX

The **BIZTALK_OPENNESS_TYPE_EX** enumeration has one of the following values:

Name	Value	Description
BIZTALK_OPENNESS_TYPE_EX_NOTOPEN	1	Specifies that this instance of the object is not open.
BIZTALK_OPENNESS_TYPE_EX_SOURCE	2	Specifies that the source organization of this instance of the object is open.
BIZTALK_OPENNESS_TYPE_EX_ DESTINATION	4	Specifies that the destination organization of this instance of the object is open.
BIZTALK_OPENNESS_TYPE_EX_ FROMWORKFLOW	8	Specifies that BizTalk Server is receiving a document from an XLANG schedule instance.
BIZTALK_OPENNESS_TYPE_EX_ TOWORKFLOW	16	Specifies that BizTalk Server is sending a document to an XLANG schedule instance.

BIZTALK_SIGNATURE_TYPE

The **BIZTALK_SIGNATURE_TYPE** enumeration has one of the following values:

Name	Value	Description
BIZTALK_SIGNATURE_TYPE_NONE	1	Specifies that there is no signature.
BIZTALK_SIGNATURE_TYPE_CUSTOM	2	Specifies the custom signature of the document.
BIZTALK_SIGNATURE_TYPE_SMIME	4	Specifies the S/MIME signature of the document.

BIZTALK_STORE_TYPE

The **BIZTALK_STORE_TYPE** enumeration has one of the following values:

Name	Value	Description
BIZTALK_STORE_TYPE_MY	1	Specifies that the certificate store is type MY. This store contains certificates authorized only by your organization.
BIZTALK_STORE_TYPE_BIZTALK	2	Specifies that the certificate is stored in the dedicated BizTalk Server 2000 store.

BIZTALK_TRANSPORT_TYPE

The **BIZTALK_TRANSPORT_TYPE** enumeration has one of the following values:

Name	Value	Description
BIZTALK_TRANSPORT_TYPE_NONE	1	Specifies that this instance of the object does not select a transport component.
BIZTALK_TRANSPORT_TYPE_HTTP	4	Specifies that this instance of the object selects a Hypertext Transport Protocol (HTTP) transport component.
BIZTALK_TRANSPORT_TYPE_SMTP	8	Specifies that this instance of the object selects a Simple Mail Transfer Protocol (SMTP) transport component.
BIZTALK_TRANSPORT_TYPE_ APPINTEGRATION	32	Specifies that this instance of the object selects an application integration component (AIC) transport component.
BIZTALK_TRANSPORT_TYPE_MSMQ	128	Specifies that this instance of the object selects a Microsoft Message Queuing transport component.
BIZTALK_TRANSPORT_TYPE_FILE	256	Specifies that this instance of the object selects a file as a transport component.
BIZTALK_TRANSPORT_TYPE_HTTPS	1024	Specifies that this instance of the object selects a Secure Hypertext Transfer Protocol (HTTPS) transport component.
BIZTALK_TRANSPORT_TYPE_ OPENDESTINATION	2048	Specifies that the messaging port is an open destination.
BIZTALK_TRANSPORT_TYPE_LOOPBACK	4096	Specifies that the document submitted to the server with the **SubmitSync** method will be processed and then returned back as the response document of the method.
BIZTALK_TRANSPORT_TYPE_ ORCHESTRATIONACTIVATION	8192	Specifies that the **Address** property contains the path of an XLANG schedule to be executed.

BIZTALK_USAGE_TYPE

The **BIZTALK_USAGE_TYPE** enumeration has one of the following values:

Name	Value	Description
BIZTALK_USAGE_TYPE_ENCRYPTION	1	Specifies that this is an encryption certificate.
BIZTALK_USAGE_TYPE_SIGNATURE	2	Specifies that this is a signature certificate.
BIZTALK_USAGE_TYPE_BOTH	4	Specifies that this certificate is used for both encryption and signature.

BIZTALK_CONFIGDATA_TYPE

The **BIZTALK_CONFIGDATA_TYPE** enumeration has one of the following values:

Name	Value	Description
BIZTALK_CONFIGDATA_TYPE_PRIMARYTRANSPORT	0	Configures the primary transport on the messaging port.
BIZTALK_CONFIGDATA_TYPE_SECONDARYTRANSPORT	1	Configures the secondary transport on the messaging port.
BIZTALK_CONFIGDATA_TYPE_ENCRYPTION	2	Configures the encryption certificate on the messaging port.
BIZTALK_CONFIGDATA_TYPE_ENCODING	3	Configures the encoding type on the messaging port.
BIZTALK_CONFIGDATA_TYPE_SIGNATURE	4	Configures the signature verification on the messaging port.
BIZTALK_CONFIGDATA_TYPE_SERIALIZER	5	Configures the serializer on the messaging port.

Submitting Documents

This chapter provides detailed conceptual information that is important to understand in order to submit documents to Microsoft BizTalk Server 2000.

In This Chapter

- Submitting
- Accessing the Suspended queue
- Routing
- Preprocessing Documents in a Receive Function
- Steps for Submitting a Document by Using COM Interfaces
- Submitting Documents Reference for Visual Basic
- Submitting Documents Reference for C++
- Interchange Enumeration

Submitting

All documents must be sent to Microsoft BizTalk Server 2000 by using the **Submit** or **SubmitSync** method of the **IInterchange** interface in order to be processed. If an application is Microsoft Windows–based and is capable of invoking methods on COM objects, it can submit a document directly. The business application calls the **Submit** or **SubmitSync** method of the **IInterchange** interface, passing in the document or the file path of the document as a string supplied as a parameter. This is the simplest approach because no additional configuration is necessary. However, this method requires that the business application be designed to support direct calls to BizTalk Server 2000.

If the application is not capable of invoking methods on COM objects, receive functions can be used to submit documents to BizTalk Server. Receive functions enable applications to post documents or interchanges to specific locations that BizTalk Server 2000 is monitoring. These locations are defined according to the specific receive function. Each receive function uses event-based monitoring to recognize the presence of a document or interchange. Once the data is received by the function, it submits the data to BizTalk Server 2000. For example, a File receive function can be configured to submit a document to BizTalk Server 2000 when the business application can save a document as a file but cannot submit it directly.

The receive functions are configured to continuously monitor a specific directory or queue for a file to appear and then be submitted to BizTalk Server 2000. HTTP and SMTP protocols are configured outside BizTalk Server 2000. You must create script pages for these transport services.

Notes

- There is a size limit for interchanges and documents that use logging, which, if exceeded, greatly affects the performance of BizTalk Server. For more information about the size limit, see "Interchange and document size limit" in Chapter 11, "Administering Servers and Applications."

- A script or application that uses the **IInterchange** interface to submit documents to BizTalk Server can be run in any user account.

- When processing envelopes that are compliant with BizTalk Framework 2.0, BizTalk Server 2000 should be considered the endpoint with regard to the expiration time. When BizTalk Framework 2.0-compliant documents are submitted to BizTalk Server 2000, either from an application or a trading partner, the following fields are overwritten if present, or created if absent:

  - In the properties subsection:

    <prop:identity>

    <prop:sentAt>

    <prop:expiresAt>

- In the receipt information subsection:

    <sendTo>

    <address>

    <sendReceiptBy>

For examples of code, see Appendix B, "Code Samples."

Sending documents to BizTalk Server 2000 asynchronously

Applications that submit documents asynchronously to BizTalk Server 2000 call **Submit**. Receive functions also call **Submit**. **Submit** returns after sending the document. No response document is returned, since the protocol does not support it.

Submit accepts only a string buffer or a file path as the document or interchange. BizTalk Server 2000 supports UNC and local file path formats.

Sending documents to BizTalk Server 2000 synchronously

Applications that submit documents synchronously to BizTalk Server 2000 call **SubmitSync**.

A synchronous interchange bypasses all queues and executes all the components required by the messaging port on the calling thread. For synchronous protocols, an optional response document is returned to the user, if available. This method is valid only for a single channel match. If the parameters set cause multiple channels to match, synchronous submission returns an error indicating that multiple channel matches are not allowed for synchronous submission. This method can be used only for single document interchanges. If the submission contains multiple documents, synchronous submission returns an error indicating that multiple document submissions are not allowed. This method does not support port groups.

SubmitSync accepts only a string buffer or a file path as the document or interchange. BizTalk Server 2000 supports UNC and local file path formats.

Error handling with the Submit and SubmitSync methods

When an error occurs when submitting interchanges or documents to BizTalk Server 2000, an event log entry is created and/or an error is returned to the caller, depending on which method is called and the nature of the failure. Documents submitted can end up in the Suspended queue due to a number of possible conditions. The following table describes what happens when one or more of the documents or interchanges submitted are placed in the Suspended queue due to an error during submission.

Method called	Error returned to caller	Event log entry
Submit	Document failure error	For every document that fails in processing
SubmitSync	Document failure error	None

To submit a document from a remote client

A document can be submitted to Microsoft BizTalk Server 2000 from a remote client running an application that uses the **IInterchange** interface. To accomplish this, follow these steps:

1. Using a computer that has Microsoft BizTalk Server 2000 installed, on the **Start** menu, point to **Programs**, point to **Administrative Tools**, and then click **Component Services**.

2. In the Tree pane, expand **Component Services**, expand **Computers**, expand **My Computer**, expand **COM+ Applications**, and then click **BizTalk Server Interchange Application**.

3. On the **Action** menu, click **Export**.

   The Welcome to the COM Application Export Wizard opens.

4. On the **Welcome to the COM Application Export Wizard** page, click **Next**.

5. On the **Application Export Information** page, type the name of an export installation package to be created.

6. In the **Export as** area, click the **Application proxy** option, click **Next** and then click **Finish** to close the wizard.

The COM Application Export Wizard creates a Windows Installer Package file with an .msi extension and its associated Cabinet file with a .cab extension. Copy these files to the remote client and run the Windows Installer Package file. Now the remote client can run applications that use the **IInterchange** interface.

📝 Notes

- The remote client must be running Microsoft Windows 2000.

- The computer used to create the installation package acts as an "interchange server" for the remote client that is submitting documents. Therefore, all documents submitted on the remote client are routed through that server.

- You can also create a remote client during the BizTalk Server 2000 installation.

Accessing the Suspended Queue

The Suspended queue contains work items that have failed processing for a variety of reasons, including parsing errors, serialization errors, failed transmissions, or the inability to find a channel configuration. You can retrieve or delete items from the queue using the interfaces provided.

📝 Note

- When accessing or deleting items in the Suspended queue, the script or application must be run in the context of a user account in the BizTalk Server Administrators group. The BizTalk Server Administrators group is created when BizTalk Server 2000 is installed. Additional users can be added to this group as necessary.

Retrieving items from the Suspended queue

To retrieve items from the Suspended queue, applications call the **CheckSuspendedQueue** method of the **IInterchange** interface.

CheckSuspendedQueue retrieves a list of items in the Suspended queue that meets the search criteria specified by the parameters of the method. This returns a list of handles that can subsequently be used to call the **DeleteFromSuspendedQueue** or the **GetSuspendedQueueItemDetails** method of the **IInterchange** interface.

Getting item details from the Suspended queue

CheckSuspendedQueue returns a list of handles to items in the Suspended queue. To process these items, you must get the item details associated with each item in the Suspended queue by using **GetSuspendedQueueItemDetails**.

GetSuspendedQueueItemDetails retrieves the details about an item in the Suspended queue. If this method does not return individual details about this item (because the item has been removed between the time **CheckSuspendedQueue** was called and the call to this method, for example), each parameter that cannot be determined is returned.

Removing items from the Suspended queue

To remove items from the Suspended queue, applications call **DeleteFromSuspendedQueue**.

DeleteFromSuspendedQueue removes a list of items from the Suspended queue that meets the search criteria specified by the parameters of the method.

Routing

To process a document, Microsoft BizTalk Server 2000 must load the rules that govern how the incoming document instance is to be processed. These rules are known as the channel. A specific **BizTalkChannel** object is associated with a **BizTalkPort** object and connects two organizations.

To find the channel to process the received document, the server must have the source organization, the destination organization, and the document definition. The server can obtain this information by one of the following methods:

- This information can be found in the content of the document itself from the data contained in the routing fields (self-routing documents).

- This information can be explicitly declared in the parameter list of the **Submit** method of the **IInterchange** interface (call-based routing).

- This information can be explicitly declared in the properties of a custom receive function. For more information about receive functions, see "Understanding Receive Functions and Document Routing" in Chapter 11, "Administering Servers and Applications."

- You can choose to specify the channel to use when calling **Submit**. This causes the server to bypass the channel selection process.

Once the server has this information, it searches for the messaging port/channel pair that matches these routing criteria. If more than one channel matches, each of the channels is processed, possibly resulting in multiple output documents.

Call-based routing

In call-based routing, the source organization identifier (*SourceID*), the destination organization identifier (*DestID*), and the name of the document definition (*DocName*) are specified as parameters of **Submit**. If *SourceQualifier* and *DestQualifier* are not specified, they default to *OrganizationName* and refer to the name of the organization in the database. If a BizTalk Framework 2.0–compliant document is submitted and a qualifier is not found during parsing, the qualifier defaults to BizTalk. If the *Openness* flag is set to OpenDest, the *DestID* is used as the destination address. If *SourceID*, *DestID*, or *DocName* is left blank, the missing information must be provided by the routing information contained within the document. If one of these parameters/fields is not in **Submit** or in the document, the document goes to the Suspended queue.

✎ Note

- Note that the queue:// prefix must be used with an open messaging port when a Message Queue is specified as the destination address.

Self-routing documents

Self-routing documents have the source organization identifier (SourceID field), the destination organization identifier (DestID field), and the name of the document definition (DocName field) defined in the routing tags defined by the document specification, which are contained within the <SelectionFields> tag. If *SourceQualifier* and *DestQualifier* are not specified, they default to *OrganizationName* and refer to the name of the organization in the database. If a BizTalk Framework 2.0–compliant document is submitted and a qualifier is not found during parsing, the qualifier defaults to BizTalk. The BizTalk Framework specification also defines the routing tags for BizTalk Framework–compliant messages. These tags are defined as the <to> and <from> tags under the <route> tag, which is contained in the <header> tag under the root <biztalk> tag. The first tag under the <body> tag determines the document type. For more information, see the *BizTalk Framework 2.0 Independent Document Messaging Specification* on the Microsoft BizTalk Server Web site (www.microsoft.com/biztalk). For X12 or EDIFACT routing, the locations of the routing fields are hard-coded and are not specified in a document specification.

Preprocessing Documents in a Receive Function

Documents can be submitted to BizTalk Server 2000 for processing by using a receive function. Using this mechanism, other applications can send their output files to a specified directory or message queue. BizTalk Server continually monitors the specified location at regular intervals and processes the files or messages placed in that location. BizTalk Server provides interfaces that enable you to create custom preprocessing components. These components process the file or message picked up by the receive function prior to submitting the data to BizTalk Server for processing.

A custom preprocessor component is required to implement the category identifier (CATID) CATID_BIZTALK_CUSTOM_PROCESS in the registry. This enables the BizTalk Server Administration user interface, or administration console, to recognize the custom preprocessor and display it in the **Preprocessor** list, where it can be selected.

For additional information, C++ programmers should see "IBTSCustomProcess Interface" and "IBTSCustomProcessContext Interface" later in this chapter.

For additional information, Microsoft Visual Basic programmers should see "IBTSCustomProcess Object" and "IBTSCustomProcessContext Object" later in this chapter.

Related Topics

"BizTalk Server Administration User Interface" in Chapter 11, "Administering Servers and Applications"

"Receive Functions" in Chapter 11, "Administering Servers and Applications"

Steps for Submitting a Document by Using COM Interfaces

Use the following steps as a guideline when submitting documents to BizTalk Server with the **IInterchange** interface:

1. Determine whether the source organization, destination organization, and document definition name are in the parameters of the **Submit** or the **SubmitSync** method of the **IInterchange** interface or are included in the document; it might be a combination of the two.

    - This information can be explicitly declared in the parameter list of **Submit** or **SubmitSync** (call-based routing).

        One or more of these parameters can be left blank and the missing information can be provided by the routing information contained within the document.

    - This information can be found in the content of the document itself from the data in the routing fields (self-routing documents).

    - The user can choose to explicitly call out the specific channel to use when calling **Submit**. This causes the server to bypass channel selection.

    - This information can be explicitly declared in the properties of a custom receive function.

2. Decide whether to submit asynchronously or synchronously.

    - Call **Submit**, passing in the document or the file path of the document as a string supplied as a parameter. BizTalk Server 2000 supports URL, UNC, and drive: format for the file path.

        Submit accepts only a string variable as the document or interchange.

    - Call **SubmitSync**, passing in the document or the file path of the document as a string supplied as a parameter. A response document is returned to the user, if available.

        ### ☑ Note

        This method is valid only for a single channel match. In addition, it can be used only for single-document interchanges.

3. Decide whether to call some of the Suspended queue methods. (This is optional and can be implemented in the same application or a different application.)

    - Call the **CheckSuspendedQueue** method of the **IInterchange** interface.

    - Retrieve items from the Suspended queue.

✎ **Note**

This returns a list of handles that can subsequently be used to call the **DeleteFromSuspendedQueue** or the **GetSuspendedQueueItemDetails** method of the **IInterchange** interface.

- Call **GetSuspendedQueueItemDetails**.

  Retrieve the details about a particular item in the Suspended queue.

- Call **DeleteFromSuspendedQueue**.

  Remove items from the Suspended queue.

To read the tracking database

The purpose of the tracking interface, **IBizTalkTrackData**, is to facilitate programmatic access to the tracking information of Microsoft BizTalk Server 2000. This complements the **IInterchange** interface so that returns from **IInterchange** calls can be fed to these **IBizTalkTrackData** methods to access data about the activity of documents submitted to BizTalk Server 2000.

There can be a one-to-one or a one-to-many relationship between input and output documents. In a normal document flow, one document is submitted to the server, is tracked and possibly transformed, and one document results as output from the server. However, the messaging port can be configured so that one document submitted can result in many documents as output to several destinations:

1. Get the *SubmissionHandle* return from the **Submit** method of the **IInterchange** interface.

2. Call the **GetInterchanges** method, using the *SubmissionHandle* return as the input. This method returns a list of interchanges contained in that submission, including all the data from the Tracking database. Because transport-specific information (delivery times, receipt flags, and so on) appears in the interchange data, you can look here to confirm or check status on delivery, for example.

3. Call the **GetInDocDetails** method, using the *SubmissionHandle* return as the input. This method returns a list of the documents that were included in that submission. You can look here to find information about an input document (for example, was a specific document valid, how many bytes was it, and so on).

4. Call the **GetOutDocDetails** method, using the *SubmissionHandle* return as the input. This method returns a list of the documents that were generated as a result of the submission. You can look here to find information about an output document (for example, looking for PO #123456 out of a submission made earlier today).

Submitting Documents Reference for Visual Basic

This section provides reference information about interfaces used by Microsoft BizTalk Server 2000 for programming with Microsoft Visual Basic. For a complete listing of error messages, see Appendix A, "Error Message."

BTSDocTracking Object

Use this object to facilitate programmatic access to the tracking information of Microsoft BizTalk Server 2000. This object complements the **Interchange** object so that returns from **Interchange** methods can be passed to these methods for reading tracking data about the documents submitted to BizTalk Server 2000.

The methods of the **BizTalkTrackData** object are shown in the following table.

Method	Description
GetInDocDetails	Returns an ADO recordset that contains a list of the documents that were included in the *SubmissionHandle* return from the **Submit** method of the **IInterchange** interface. This method returns specific information for an input document.
GetInterchanges	Returns an ADO recordset that contains a list of interchanges contained in the *SubmissionHandle* return from the **Submit** method of the **IInterchange** interface, including all the data from the Tracking database. Transport-specific information, such as delivery times and receipt flags, appears in the Tracking database; you can check there to confirm or check status on delivery, for example.
GetOutDocDetails	Returns an ADO recordset that contains a list of the documents that were generated when the **Submit** method of the **IInterchange** interface was called. This method returns specific information for an output document, for example, PO #123456 from a **Submit** call made earlier today.

Requirements

Windows NT/2000: Requires Windows 2000 SP1 or later
Library: Use Microsoft BizTalk Server Doc Tracking 1.0 Type Library (CISDTA.dll)

BTSDocTracking.GetInDocDetails Method

The **GetInDocDetails** method returns an ADO recordset that contains a list of the documents that were included in the *SubmissionHandle* return from the **Submit** method of the **IInterchange** interface. This method returns specific information for an input document.

Syntax

object.**GetInDocDetails**(_
    bstrSubmissionID **As String** _
)

Parameters

bstrSubmissionID
    String that contains the *SubmissionHandle* string returned by **Submit** for this document
    instance.

Return Values

This method returns an **Object** that contains a list of the documents that were included in
the submission.

Error Value

If an error is raised, **Err.Number** is set to one of the values documented in Appendix A,
"Error Messages."

Requirements

Windows NT/2000: Requires Windows 2000 SP1 or later
Library: Use Microsoft BizTalk Server Doc Tracking 1.0 Type Library (CISDTA.dll)

BTSDocTracking.GetInterchanges Method

The **GetInterchanges** method returns an ADO recordset that contains a list of interchanges
contained in the *SubmissionHandle* return from the **Submit** method of the **IInterchange**
interface, including all the data from the Tracking database. Because transport-specific
information, such as delivery times and receipt flags, appears in the Tracking database, you
can check there to confirm or check status on delivery, for example.

Syntax

object.**GetInterchanges**(_
    bstrSubmissionID **As String**, _
)

Parameters

bstrSubmissionID
    String that contains the *SubmissionHandle* string returned by **Submit** for this
    document instance.

Return Values

This method optionally returns an **Object** that contains a list of interchanges contained in this submission, including all the data from the Tracking database.

Error Value

If an error is raised, **Err.Number** is set to one of the values documented in Appendix A, "Error Messages."

Requirements

Windows NT/2000: Requires Windows 2000 SP1 or later
Library: Use Microsoft BizTalk Server Doc Tracking 1.0 Type Library (CISDTA.dll)

BTSDocTracking.GetOutDocDetails Method

The **GetOutDocDetails** method returns an ADO recordset that contains a list of the documents that were generated as a result of the **Submit** method of the **IInterchange** interface. This method returns specific information for an output document, for example, PO #123456 from a **Submit** call made earlier today.

Syntax

object.**GetOutDocDetails**(_
   bstrSubmissionID **As String** _
)

Parameters

bstrSubmissionID
   String that contains the *SubmissionHandle* string returned by **Submit** for this document instance.

Return Values

This method returns an **Object** that contains a list of the documents that were generated as a result of the submission.

Error Value

If an error is raised, **Err.Number** is set to one of the values documented in Appendix A, "Error Messages."

Requirements

Windows NT/2000: Requires Windows 2000 SP1 or later
Library: Use Microsoft BizTalk Server Doc Tracking 1.0 Type Library (CISDTA.dll)

IBTSCustomProcess Object

Implement **IBTSCustomProcess** to create a custom preprocessor for BizTalk Server receive functions.

The methods of **IBTSCustomProcess** are shown in the following table.

Method	Description
Execute	Performs the custom processing of the data prior to sending the data to BizTalk Server for processing.
SetContext	Retrieves context information associated with the data being processed.

Remarks

For information about custom preprocessors, see "Preprocessing Documents in a Receive Function" earlier in this chapter.

Requirements

Windows NT/2000: Requires Windows 2000 SP1 or later
Library: Use Microsoft BizTalk Server Application Interface Components 1.0 Type Library (btscomplib.tlb)

IBTSCustomProcess.Execute Method

The **Execute** method performs the custom processing on data obtained from a receive function.

Syntax

object.**Execute**(_
   vDataIn **As Variant**, _
   nCodePageIn **As Long**, _
   bIsFilePath **As Boolean**, _
   nCodePageOut **As Variant,** _
   vDataOut **As Variant** _
)

Parameters

vDataIn
   VARIANT that contains the input data read by the receive function. If the data is read from a File receive function, this parameter contains the file path. For File receive functions, the *bIsFilePath* parameter must be set to **True**.

nCodePageIn
> **Long** that contains the code page of the input data. The code page indicates the character set and keyboard layout used on a computer.

bIsFilePath
> **VARIANT_BOOL** flag that indicates the type of input data. A value of **True** indicates that the *vDataIn* parameter contains a file path. A value of **False** indicates that the *vDataIn* parameter contains data from a message queue.

nCodePageOut
> **VARIANT** that contains the code page of the output data. The code page indicates the character set and keyboard layout used on a computer.

vDataOut
> **VARIANT** that contains the output data. The data in this parameter is sent to BizTalk Server for processing.

Return Values

None

Error Value

If an error is raised, **Err.Number** is set to one of the values documented in Appendix A, "Error Messages."

Remarks

If BizTalk Server fails to create the custom preprocessor component, or if the **Execute** method returns an error or invalid data, the document being processed is placed in the Suspended queue.

Requirements

Windows NT/2000: Requires Windows 2000 SP1 or later
Library: Use Microsoft BizTalk Server Application Interface Components 1.0 Type Library (btscomplib.tlb)

IBTSCustomProcess.SetContext Method

The **SetContext** method retrieves information associated with a document submitted to BizTalk Server.

Syntax

object.**SetContext**(_
  pCtx **As IBTSCustomProcessContext** _
)

Parameters

pCtx
   IBTSCustomProcessContext that contains information associated with the document
   being processed by BizTalk Server.

Return Values

None

Error Value

If an error is raised, **Err.Number** is set to one of the values documented in Appendix A,
"Error Messages."

Remarks

For additional information about the custom process context object, see the following section,
"IBTSCustomProcessContext Object."

Requirements

Windows NT/2000: Requires Windows 2000 SP1 or later
Library: Use Microsoft BizTalk Server Application Interface Components 1.0 Type Library
(btscomplib.tlb)

IBTSCustomProcessContext Object

Use this object to retrieve information associated with data being processed by using a custom
preprocessor component.

The properties of the **BTSCustomProcessContext** object are shown in the following table.

Property	Type	Description
ChannelName	**BSTR**	Name of the channel.
DestID	**BSTR**	Value of the destination organization qualifier.
DestQualifier	**BSTR**	Qualifier type of the destination organization.
DocName	**BSTR**	Name of the document.
EnvelopeName	**BSTR**	Name of the envelope used with the document.
Openness	long	Value that indicates if the messaging port is open.
PassThrough	long	Value that indicates whether pass-through submission mode is being used.
SourceID	**BSTR**	Value of the source organization qualifier.
SourceQualifier	**BSTR**	Qualifier type of the source organization.

Remarks

This object can be obtained by calling the **SetContext** method on the **IBTSCustomProcess** object. For information about custom preprocessors, see "Preprocessing Documents in a Receive Function" earlier in this chapter.

Requirements

Windows NT/2000: Requires Windows 2000 SP1 or later
Library: Use Microsoft BizTalk Server Application Interface Components 1.0 Type Library (btscomplib.tlb)

IBTSCustomProcessContext.ChannelName Property

The **ChannelName** property returns the name of the channel used for processing the current document.

Syntax

object.**ChannelName**

Parameters

None

Return Values

This property returns a **String** that contains the channel name.

Error Value

If an error is raised, **Err.Number** is set to one of the values documented in Appendix A, "Error Messages."

Remarks

This is a read-only property.

Requirements

Windows NT/2000: Requires Windows 2000 SP1 or later
Library: Use Microsoft BizTalk Server Application Interface Components 1.0 Type Library (btscomplib.tlb)

IBTSCustomProcessContext.DestID Property

The **DestID** property returns the value of the destination organization qualifier.

Syntax

object.**DestID**

Parameters

None

Return Values

This property returns a **String** that contains the value of the destination organization qualifier.

Error Value

If an error is raised, **Err.Number** is set to one of the values documented in Appendix A, "Error Messages."

Remarks

This is a read-only property.

Requirements

Windows NT/2000: Requires Windows 2000 SP1 or later
Library: Use Microsoft BizTalk Server Application Interface Components 1.0 Type Library (btscomplib.tlb)

IBTSCustomProcessContext.DestQualifier Property

The **DestQualifier** property returns the destination organization qualifier type.

Syntax

object.**DestQualifier**

Parameters

None

Return Values

This property returns a **String** that contains the destination organization qualifier type.

Error Value

If an error is raised, **Err.Number** is set to one of the values documented in Appendix A, "Error Messages."

Remarks

This is a read-only property.

Requirements

Windows NT/2000: Requires Windows 2000 SP1 or later
Library: Use Microsoft BizTalk Server Application Interface Components 1.0 Type Library (btscomplib.tlb)

IBTSCustomProcessContext.DocName Property

The **DocName** property returns the name of the document definition used by the current document.

Syntax

object.**DocName**

Parameters

None

Return Values

This property returns a **String** that contains the document definition name.

Error Value

If an error is raised, **Err.Number** is set to one of the values documented in Appendix A, "Error Messages."

Remarks

This is a read-only property.

Requirements

Windows NT/2000: Requires Windows 2000 SP1 or later
Library: Use Microsoft BizTalk Server Application Interface Components 1.0 Type Library (btscomplib.tlb)

IBTSCustomProcessContext.EnvelopeName Property

The **EnvelopeName** property returns the name of the envelope used with the current document.

Syntax

object.**EnvelopeName**

Parameters

None

Return Values

This property returns a **String** that contains the envelope with the current document.

Error Value

If an error is raised, **Err.Number** is set to one of the values documented in Appendix A, "Error Messages."

Remarks

This is a read-only property.

Requirements

Windows NT/2000: Requires Windows 2000 SP1 or later
Library: Use Microsoft BizTalk Server Application Interface Components 1.0 Type Library (btscomplib.tlb)

IBTSCustomProcessContext.Openness Property

The **Openness** property returns the openness associated with the messaging port.

Syntax

object.**Openness**

Parameters

None

Return Values

This property returns a **Long** that indicates openness on the messaging port. The **Long** returned in this property represents a value in the BIZTALK_OPENNESS_TYPE enumeration.

Error Value

If an error is raised, **Err.Number** is set to one of the values documented in Appendix A, "Error Messages."

Remarks

This is a read-only property.

Requirements

Windows NT/2000: Requires Windows 2000 SP1 or later
Library: Use Microsoft BizTalk Server Application Interface Components 1.0 Type Library (btscomplib.tlb)

IBTSCustomProcessContext.PassThrough Property

The **PassThrough** property indicates whether the document uses pass-through submission mode.

Syntax

object.**PassThrough**

Parameters

None

Return Values

This property returns a **Long** that indicates whether the document uses pass-through submission mode. A value of 0 indicates that pass-through submission mode is not used. A nonzero value indicates that pass-through submission mode is used with the current document.

Error Value

If an error is raised, **Err.Number** is set to one of the values documented in Appendix A, "Error Messages."

Remarks

This is a read-only property.

Requirements

Windows NT/2000: Requires Windows 2000 SP1 or later
Library: Use Microsoft BizTalk Server Application Interface Components 1.0 Type Library (btscomplib.tlb)

IBTSCustomProcessContext.SourceID Property

The **SourceID** property returns the value of the source organization qualifier.

Syntax

object.**SourceID**

Parameters

None

Return Values

This property returns a **String** that contains the value of the source organization qualifier.

Error Value

If an error is raised, **Err.Number** is set to one of the values documented in Appendix A, "Error Messages."

Remarks

This is a read-only property.

Requirements

Windows NT/2000: Requires Windows 2000 SP1 or later
Library: Use Microsoft BizTalk Server Application Interface Components 1.0 Type Library (btscomplib.tlb)

IBTSCustomProcessContext.SourceQualifier Property

The **SourceQualifier** property returns the source organization qualifier type.

Syntax

object.**SourceQualifier**

Parameters

None

Return Values

This property returns a **String** that contains the source organization qualifier type.

Error Value

If an error is raised, **Err.Number** is set to one of the values documented in Appendix A, "Error Messages."

Remarks

This is a read-only property.

Requirements

Windows NT/2000: Requires Windows 2000 SP1 or later
Library: Use Microsoft BizTalk Server Application Interface Components 1.0 Type Library (btscomplib.tlb)

Interchange Object

Use this object to exchange documents between applications and BizTalk Server 2000 directly or through a receive function

The methods of the **Interchange** object are shown in the following table.

Method	Description
CheckSuspendedQueue	Checks the Suspended queue and returns a list of handles to documents or interchanges in the queue that match the request criteria.
DeleteFromSuspendedQueue	Deletes all specified documents from the Suspended queue.
GetSuspendedQueueItemDetails	Returns details of a document in the Suspended queue.
Submit	Submits an interchange to BizTalk Server 2000 for asynchronous processing. This method accepts only a string variable as the document or interchange. This means that applications cannot submit other objects, such as DOM objects, **CDictionary** objects, ADO objects, or any other data type or object type.
SubmitSync	Submits an interchange to BizTalk Server 2000 for synchronous transmission. This method returns a response if one is provided. This method accepts only a string variable for the document or interchange. This means that applications cannot submit other objects, such as DOM objects, **CDictionary** objects, ADO objects, or any other data type or object type.

Remarks

Using parameters with **Submit** and **SubmitSync** overrides certain fields in the header of a self-routing document.

Requirements

Windows NT/2000: Requires Windows 2000 SP1 or later
Library: (cisapi.tlb)

Interchange.CheckSuspendedQueue Method

The **CheckSuspendedQueue** method checks the Suspended queue and returns a list of documents that match the request criteria.

Syntax

object.**CheckSuspendedQueue(** _
   DocName **As String,** _
   SourceName **As String,** _
   DestName **As String** _
)

Parameters

DocName
> **String** that contains the name of the **BizTalkDocument** object. This parameter narrows the search for items in the Suspended queue. If this parameter is omitted, this method matches all **BizTalkDocument** objects. This is an optional parameter.

SourceName
> **String** that contains the name of the source **BizTalkOrganization** object. This parameter narrows the search criteria for items in the Suspended queue. If this parameter is omitted, this method matches all **BizTalkOrganization** objects. This is an optional parameter.

DestName
> **String** that contains the name of the destination **BizTalkOrganization** object. This parameter narrows the search criteria for items in the Suspended queue. If this parameter is omitted, this method matches all **BizTalkOrganization** objects. This is an optional parameter.

Return Values

This method returns a **Variant** that contains a list of handles to all documents in the Suspended queue.

Error Value

If an error is raised, **Err.Number** is set to one of the values documented in Appendix A, "Error Messages."

Remarks

The returned items are not deleted from the queue. To delete items from the Suspended queue, use the **DeleteFromSuspendedQueue** method.

Requirements

Windows NT/2000: Requires Windows 2000 SP1 or later
Library: (cisapi.tlb)

Interchange.DeleteFromSuspendedQueue Method

The **DeleteFromSuspendedQueue** method deletes all specified documents from the Suspended queue.

Syntax

object.**DeleteFromSuspendedQueue(** _
   DocumentHandleList **As Variant** _
)

Parameters

DocumentHandleList
   Variant that contains a full list of handles or a subset for documents to be deleted from the Suspended queue.

Return Values

None

Error Value

If an error is raised, **Err.Number** is set to one of the values documented in Appendix A, "Error Messages."

Requirements

Windows NT/2000: Requires Windows 2000 SP1 or later
Library: (cisapi.tlb)

Interchange.GetSuspendedQueueItemDetails Method

The **GetSuspendedQueueItemDetails** method uses the list of handles returned by the **CheckSuspendedQueue** method to get information about a single entry in the Suspended queue.

Syntax

object.**GetSuspendedQueueItemDetails**(_
    ItemHandle **As String**, _
    SourceName **As Variant**, _
    DestName **As Variant**, _
    DocName **As Variant**, _
    ReasonCode **As Variant**, _
    ItemData **As Variant** _
)

Parameters

ItemHandle
    String that contains the handle to an item in the Suspended queue.

SourceName
    Variant that contains the name of the source **BizTalkOrganization** object. The value of this output parameter is set by calling this method.

DestName
    Variant that contains the name of the destination **BizTalkOrganization** object. The value of this output parameter is set by calling this method.

DocName
    Variant that contains the name of the associated **BizTalkDocument** object. The value of this output parameter is set by calling this method.

ReasonCode
    Variant that contains the reason a document or interchange has been placed in the Suspended queue. For more information about this value, see "CISReasonToQueue" later in this chapter. The value of this output parameter is set by calling this method.

ItemData
    Variant that contains the document instance or interchange. The value of this output parameter is set by calling this method.

Return Values

None

Error Value

If an error is raised, **Err.Number** is set to one of the values documented in Appendix A, "Error Messages."

Requirements

Windows NT/2000: Requires Windows 2000 SP1 or later
Library: (cisapi.tlb)

Interchange.Submit Method

The **Submit** method sends a document to BizTalk Server 2000 for asynchronous processing. BizTalk Server 2000 places the document in a queue until the next available server can process it.

Syntax

object.**Submit**(_
    lOpenness **As BIZTALK_OPENNESS_TYPE**, _
    Document **As String**, _
    DocName **As String**, _
    SourceQualifier **As String**, _
    SourceID **As String**, _
    DestQualifier **As String**, _
    DestID **As String**, _
    ChannelName **As String**, _
    FilePath **As String**, _
    EnvelopeName **As String**, _
    PassThrough **As Long** _
)

Parameters

lOpenness

Enumeration value that indicates whether associated **BizTalkPort** objects can be open. Valid values are from the **BIZTALK_OPENNESS_TYPE** enumeration.

Document

String that contains the document instance submitted. This parameter accepts only a string buffer as the document or interchange. This means that applications cannot submit other objects, such as DOM objects, **CDictionary** objects, ADO objects, or any other data type or object type. Either the *Document* parameter or the *FilePath* parameter must be specified. Do not specify both. This is an optional parameter.

DocName

String that contains the name of the **BizTalkDocument** object associated with the instance of the document being submitted. If the *lOpenness* parameter is set to **BIZTALK_OPENNESS_TYPE_SOURCE**, you can select an input **BizTalkDocument** object that has an X12 or EDIFACT specification. If you do, however, the output **BizTalkDocument** must not have an X12 or EDIFACT specification. If *lOpenness* is set to **BIZTALK_OPENNESS_TYPE_DESTINATION**, the **BizTalkDocument** object must not have an X12 or EDIFACT specification. The *DocName* parameter cannot be used if the *PassThrough* parameter is set to **True**. This is an optional parameter.

SourceQualifier
> **String** that contains the qualifier of the source organization. This indicates how the *SourceID* parameter is to be interpreted. Valid values come from the organization identifier qualifiers that are created when the user creates an alias for an organization. Common qualifiers include the DUNS number, telephone number, and BizTalk. You must specify a *SourceID*. The default qualifier for all new organizations is *OrganizationName* and refers to the name of the organization in the database. If a BizTalk Framework 2.0–compliant document is submitted and a qualifier is not found during parsing, the qualifier defaults to BizTalk. The *SourceQualifier* parameter cannot be used if the *PassThrough* parameter is set to **True**. This is an optional parameter.

SourceID
> **String** that contains the value of the qualifier of the source organization. For example, if the *SourceQualifier* parameter is Telephone, this value is the telephone number. If the *Openness* flag is set to OpenSrc, *SourceID* is interpreted as the source organization name. The *SourceID* parameter cannot be used if the *PassThrough* parameter is set to **True**. This is an optional parameter.

DestQualifier
> **String** that contains the qualifier of the destination organization. This indicates how the *DestID* parameter is to be interpreted. Valid values come from the organization identifier qualifiers that are created when the user creates an alias for an organization. Common qualifiers include the DUNS number, telephone number, and BizTalk. You must specify a *DestID*. The default qualifier for all new organizations is *OrganizationName* and refers to the name of the organization in the database. If a BizTalk Framework 2.0–compliant document is submitted and a qualifier is not found during parsing, the qualifier defaults to BizTalk. The *DestQualifier* parameter cannot be used if the *PassThrough* parameter is set to **True**. This is an optional parameter.

DestID
> **String** that contains the value of the qualifier of the destination organization. For example, if the *DestQualifier* parameter is Telephone, this value is the telephone number. If the *Openness* flag is set to OpenDest, *DestID* is used as the destination address. Note that the queue:// prefix must be used with an open messaging port when a Message Queue is specified as the destination address. The *DestID* parameter cannot be used if the *PassThrough* parameter is set to **True**. This is an optional parameter.

ChannelName
> **String** that contains the name of the **BizTalkChannel** object that is executed for this document. This bypasses the normal processing in which the parser tries to determine which messaging port/channel pair to execute, based on routing information in the parameters or in the document. This is an optional parameter unless the *PassThrough* parameter is set to **True**.

FilePath
> **String** that specifies a fully qualified path that contains the document to be submitted, rather than submitting the document directly as a string. BizTalk Server 2000 supports

URL, UNC, and drive: format only. If the document is submitted as a file that is pointed to by the *FilePath* parameter, the call returns successfully after BizTalk Server 2000 has successfully copied the file to the Work queue. It is safe to delete the file from the specified path as soon as this method returns successfully. When a document is submitted to the server, using *FilePath* to specify the data, **Submit** can take 30 seconds or longer if the location of the file resides on a remote server that is unavailable, if the UNC path is invalid, or if the SQL server is down. Either the *Document* parameter or the *FilePath* parameter must be specified. Do not specify both. The *FilePath* parameter cannot be used if the *PassThrough* parameter is set to **True** and a map is specified. This is an optional parameter.

EnvelopeName

String that contains the name of the envelope specification to use to break the interchange into documents. When an envelope name is provided as an argument, the envelope must have a valid interchange specification. This requirement is enforced for envelopes created for Custom XML format also. When submitting a flat file to BizTalk Server 2000, you must create an envelope for this flat file and specify the name of the envelope in *EnvelopeName*. This is an optional parameter.

PassThrough

Long that indicates how the server processes the document. When this parameter is **True**, no decryption, decoding, or signature verification is performed on the document. When set to **False**, the document is decrypted and decoded, and the signature is verified. When using pass-through submission mode (**True**), the **BIZTALK_OPENNESS_TYPE** value must be set to **BIZTALK_OPENNESS_TYPE_NOTOPEN** and the *ChannelName* parameter must be specified. In addition, the *DocName*, *SourceQualifier*, *SourceID*, *DestQualifier*, and *DestID* parameters cannot be specified with pass-through submission mode. Pass-through submission mode should be used to prevent data corruption when exchanging binary files, or when only the server transport and global tracking features are being used.

Return Values

This method returns a **String** that contains a unique identifier for the submitted document or interchange. This handle can be used to query the Tracking database for the status of the interchange or document submitted. If more than one document is submitted (an interchange), a single handle is returned, yet the Tracking database can access the status of all child documents related to this interchange identifier.

Error Value

If an error is raised, **Err.Number** is set to one of the values documented in Appendix A, "Error Messages."

Requirements

Windows NT/2000: Requires Windows 2000 SP1 or later
Library: (cisapi.tlb)

Interchange.SubmitSync Method

The **SubmitSync** method sends an interchange or document to BizTalk Server 2000 for synchronous processing. An optional response document is returned to the caller.

Syntax

object.**SubmitSync**(_
   lOpenness **As BIZTALK_OPENNESS_TYPE,** _
   Document **As String,** _
   DocName **As String,** _
   SourceQualifier **As String,** _
   SourceID **As String,** _
   DestQualifier **As String,** _
   DestID **As String,** _
   ChannelName **As String,** _
   FilePath **As String,** _
   EnvelopeName **As String,** _
   PassThrough **As Long,** _
   SubmissionHandle **As Variant,** _
   ResponseDocument **As Variant** _
)

Parameters

lOpenness
> Enumeration value that indicates whether associated **BizTalkPort** objects can be open. Valid values are from the **BIZTALK_OPENNESS_TYPE** enumeration.

Document
> **String** that contains the document instance submitted. This parameter accepts only a string buffer as the document or interchange. This means that applications cannot submit other objects, such as DOM objects, **CDictionary** objects, ADO objects, or any other data type or object type. Either the *Document* parameter or the *FilePath* parameter must be specified. Do not specify both. This is an optional parameter.

DocName
> **String** that contains the name of the **BizTalkDocument** object associated with the instance of the document submitted. If the *lOpenness* parameter is set to **BIZTALK_OPENNESS_TYPE_SOURCE**, you can select an input **BizTalkDocument** object that has an X12 or EDIFACT specification. If you do, however, the output **BizTalkDocument** must not have an X12 or EDIFACT specification. If *lOpenness* is set to **BIZTALK_OPENNESS_TYPE_DESTINATION**, the **BizTalkDocument** object must not have an X12 or EDIFACT specification. The *DocName* parameter cannot be used if the *PassThrough* parameter is set to **True**. This is an optional parameter.

SourceQualifier

> **String** that contains the qualifier of the source organization. This indicates how the *SourceID* parameter is to be interpreted. Valid values come from the organization identifier qualifiers that are created when the user creates an alias for an organization. Common qualifiers include the DUNS number, telephone number, and BizTalk. You must specify a *SourceID*. The default qualifier for all new organizations is *OrganizationName* and refers to the name of the organization in the database. If a BizTalk Framework 2.0–compliant document is submitted and a qualifier is not found during parsing, the qualifier defaults to BizTalk. The *SourceQualifier* parameter cannot be used if the *PassThrough* parameter is set to **True**. This is an optional parameter.

SourceID

> **String** that contains the value of the qualifier of the source organization. For example, if the *SourceQualifier* parameter is Telephone, this value is the telephone number. If the *Openness* flag is set to OpenSrc, *SourceID* is interpreted as the source organization name. The *SourceID* parameter cannot be used if the *PassThrough* parameter is set to **True**. This is an optional parameter.

DestQualifier

> **String** that contains the qualifier of the destination organization. This indicates how the *DestID* parameter is to be interpreted. Valid values come from the organization identifier qualifiers that are created when the user creates an alias for an organization. Common qualifiers include the DUNS number, telephone number, and BizTalk. You must specify a *DestID*. The default qualifier for all new organizations is *OrganizationName* and refers to the name of the organization in the database. If a BizTalk Framework 2.0–compliant document is submitted and a qualifier is not found during parsing, the qualifier defaults to BizTalk. The *DestQualifier* parameter cannot be used if the *PassThrough* parameter is set to **True**. This is an optional parameter.

DestID

> **String** that contains the value of the qualifier of the destination organization. For example, if the *DestQualifier* parameter is Telephone, this value is the telephone number. If the *Openness* flag is set to OpenDest, *DestID* is used as the destination address. Note that the queue:// prefix must be used with an open messaging port when a Message Queue is specified as the destination address. The *DestID* parameter cannot be used if the *PassThrough* parameter is set to **True**. This is an optional parameter.

ChannelName

> **String** that contains the name of the **BizTalkChannel** object that is executed for this document. This bypasses the normal processing in which the parser tries to determine which messaging port/channel pair to execute, based on routing information in the parameters or in the document. This is an optional parameter unless the *PassThrough* parameter is set to **True**.

FilePath

> **String** that specifies a fully qualified path that contains the document to be submitted, rather than submitting the document directly as a string. BizTalk Server 2000 supports

URL, UNC, and drive: format only. Either the *Document* parameter or the *FilePath* parameter must be specified. Do not specify both. The *FilePath* parameter cannot be used if the *PassThrough* parameter is set to **True** and a map is specified. This is an optional parameter.

EnvelopeName

String that contains the name of the envelope specification to use to break the interchange into documents. When an envelope name is provided in this parameter, the envelope must have a valid interchange specification. This requirement is enforced for envelopes created for Custom XML format also. This is an optional parameter.

PassThrough

Long that indicates how the server processes the document. When this parameter is **True**, no decryption, decoding, or signature verification is performed on the document. When set to **False**, the document is decrypted and decoded, and the signature is verified. When using pass-through submission mode (**True**), the **BIZTALK_OPENNESS_TYPE** value must be set to **BIZTALK_OPENNESS_TYPE_NOTOPEN** and the *ChannelName* parameter must be specified. In addition, the *DocName*, *SourceQualifier*, *SourceID*, *DestQualifier*, and *DestID* parameters cannot be specified with pass-through submission mode. Pass-through submission mode should be used to prevent data corruption when exchanging binary files, or when only the server transport and global tracking features are being used.

SubmissionHandle

Variant that contains a unique identifier for the submitted document or interchange. This handle can be used to query the Tracking database for the status of the interchange or document submitted. If more than one document is submitted (an interchange), a single handle is returned, yet the Tracking database can access the status of all child documents related to this interchange identifier.

ResponseDocument

Variant that contains the optional response document.

Return Values

None

Error Value

If an error is raised, **Err.Number** is set to one of the values documented in Appendix A, "Error Messages."

Remarks

SubmitSync returns an optional response document when provided. If no response is returned, the call returns successfully, but with no response and with an HRESULT value of S_FALSE. If the destination is another BizTalk Server, an ASP page must be used to return a response.

A synchronous interchange bypasses all queues and executes all the components required by the messaging port on the calling thread. For synchronous protocols (HTTP and AIC), an optional response document is returned to the user, if available. This method is valid only for a single channel match. If the parameters set cause multiple channels to match, synchronous submission returns an error indicating that multiple channel matches are not allowed for synchronous submission. This method can be used only for single document interchanges. If the submission contains multiple documents, synchronous submission returns an error indicating that multiple document submissions are not allowed. This method does not support port groups.

Requirements

Windows NT/2000: Requires Windows 2000 SP1 or later
Library: (cisapi.tlb)

Submitting Documents Reference for C++

This section provides reference information about interfaces used by Microsoft BizTalk Server 2000 for programming with Microsoft Visual C++. For a complete listing of error messages, see Appendix A, "Error Messsages."

IBizTalkTrackData Interface

Use this object to facilitate programmatic access to the tracking information of Microsoft BizTalk Server 2000. This object complements the **Interchange** object so that returns from **Interchange** methods can be passed to these methods for reading tracking data about the documents submitted to BizTalk Server 2000.

In C++, use the **IBizTalkTrackData** interface to access the methods of the **BizTalkTrackData** object.

The methods of the **BizTalkTrackData** object are shown in the following table.

Method	Description
GetInDocDetails	Returns an ADO recordset that contains a list of the documents that were included in the *SubmissionHandle* return from the **Submit** method of the **IInterchange** interface. This method returns specific information for an input document.
GetInterchanges	Returns an ADO recordset that contains a list of interchanges contained in the *SubmissionHandle* return from the **Submit** method of the **IInterchange** interface, including all the data from the Tracking database. Transport-specific information, such as delivery times and receipt flags, appears in the Tracking database; you can check there to confirm or check status on delivery, for example.
GetOutDocDetails	Returns an ADO recordset that contains a list of the documents that were generated when the **Submit** method of the **IInterchange** interface was called. This method returns specific information for an output document, for example, PO #123456 from a **Submit** call made earlier today.

Requirements

Windows NT/2000: Requires Windows 2000 SP1 or later
Header: Include BTSDocTracking.h

IBizTalkTrackData::GetInDocDetails Method

The **GetInDocDetails** method returns an ADO recordset that contains a list of the documents that were included in the *SubmissionHandle* return from the **Submit** method of the **IInterchange** interface. This method returns specific information for an input document.

Syntax

HRESULT GetInDocDetails(
    BSTR *bstrSubmissionID*,
    IDispatch** *ppdispResult*

);

Parameters

bstrSubmissionID
    [in] **BSTR** that contains the *SubmissionHandle* string returned by **Submit** for this document instance.

ppdispResult
    [out, retval] Address of a pointer to an **IDispatch** interface that contains a list of the documents that were included in the submission.

Return Values

For a list of all error messages returned by BizTalk Server, see Appendix A, "Error Messages."

Requirements

Windows NT/2000: Requires Windows 2000 SP1 or later
Header: Include BTSDocTracking.h

IBizTalkTrackData::GetInterchanges Method

The **GetInterchanges** method returns an ADO recordset that contains a list of interchanges contained in the *SubmissionHandle* return from the **Submit** method of the **IInterchange** interface, including all the data from the Tracking database. Because transport-specific information, such as delivery times and receipt flags, appears in the Tracking database, you can check there to confirm or check status on delivery, for example.

Syntax

HRESULT GetInterchanges(
  BSTR *bstrSubmissionID*,
  IDispatch** *ppdispResult*
);

Parameters

bstrSubmissionID
  [in] **BSTR** that contains the *SubmissionHandle* string returned by **Submit** for this document instance.

ppdispResult
  [out, retval] Address of a pointer to an **IDispatch** interface that contains a list of interchanges contained in this submission, including all the data from the Tracking database.

Return Values

For a list of all error messages returned by BizTalk Server, see Appendix A, "Error Messages."

Requirements

Windows NT/2000: Requires Windows 2000 SP1 or later
Header: Include BTSDocTracking.h

IBizTalkTrackData::GetOutDocDetails Method

The **GetOutDocDetails** method returns an ADO recordset that contains a list of the documents that were generated as a result of the **Submit** method of the **IInterchange** interface. This method returns specific information for an output document, for example, PO #123456 from a **Submit** call made earlier today.

Syntax

HRESULT GetOutDocDetails(
    BSTR *bstrSubmissionID*,
    IDispatch** *ppdispResult*
);

Parameters

bstrSubmissionID
    [in] **BSTR** that contains the *SubmissionHandle* string returned by **Submit** for this document instance.

ppdispResult
    [out, retval] Address of a pointer to an **IDispatch** interface that contains a list of the documents that were generated as a result of the submission.

Return Values

For a list of all error messages returned by BizTalk Server, see Appendix A, "Error Messages."

Requirements

Windows NT/2000: Requires Windows 2000 SP1 or later
Header: Include BTSDocTracking.h

IBTSCustomProcess Interface

Implement **IBTSCustomProcess** to create a custom preprocessor for BizTalk Server receive functions.

The methods of **IBTSCustomProcess** are shown in the following table.

Method	Description
Execute	Performs the custom processing of the data prior to sending the data to BizTalk Server for processing.
SetContext	Retrieves context information associated with the data being processed.

Remarks

For information about custom preprocessors, see "Preprocessing Documents in a Receive Function" earlier in this chapter.

Requirements

Windows NT/2000: Requires Windows 2000 SP1 or later
Header: Include btsaic.h

IBTSCustomProcess::Execute Method

The **Execute** method performs the custom processing on data obtained from a receive function.

Syntax

HRESULT Execute(
  VARIANT *vDataIn,*
  long *nCodePageIn,*
  VARIANT_BOOL *bIsFilePath,*
  VARIANT* *nCodePageOut,*
  VARIANT* *vDataOut*
);

Parameters

vDataIn
  [in] **VARIANT** that contains the input data read by the receive function. For data read from a message queue, the data can be either an array or a **BSTR**. If the data is read from a File receive function, this parameter contains the file path. For File receive functions, the *bIsFilePath* parameter is set to **VARIANT_TRUE**.

nCodePageIn
  [in] **Long** that contains the code page of the input data. The code page indicates the character set and keyboard layout used on a computer.

bIsFilePath
  [in] **VARIANT_BOOL** flag that indicates the type of input data. A value of **VARIANT_TRUE** indicates that the *vDataIn* parameter contains a file path. A value of **VARIANT_FALSE** indicates that the *vDataIn* parameter contains data from a message queue.

nCodePageOut
  [out] Pointer to a **VARIANT** that contains the code page of the output data. The code page indicates the character set and keyboard layout used on a computer.

vDataOut

> [out] Pointer to a **VARIANT** that contains the output data. For File receive functions, this will be a **BSTR**. The data in this parameter is sent to BizTalk Server for processing.

Return Values

For a list of all error messages returned by BizTalk Server, see Appendix A, "Error Messages."

Remarks

If BizTalk Server fails to create the custom preprocessor component, or if the **Execute** method returns an error or invalid data, the document being processed is placed in the Suspended queue.

Requirements

Windows NT/2000: Requires Windows 2000 SP1 or later
Header: Include btsaic.h

IBTSCustomProcess::SetContext Method

The **SetContext** method retrieves information associated with a document submitted to BizTalk Server.

Syntax

HRESULT SetContext(
    IBTSCustomProcessContext* *pCtx*
);

Parameters

pCtx

> [in] **IBTSCustomProcessContext** that contains information associated with the document being processed by BizTalk Server.

Return Values

For a list of all error messages returned by BizTalk Server, see Appendix A, "Error Messages."

Remarks

For additional information about the custom process context object, see the following section, "IBTSCustomProcessContext Interface."

Requirements

Windows NT/2000: Requires Windows 2000 SP1 or later
Header: Include btsaic.h

IBTSCustomProcessContext Interface

Use this object to retrieve information associated with data being processed by using a custom preprocessor component.

In C++, use the **IBTSCustomProcessContext** interface to access the methods of the **BTSCustomProcessContext** object.

The properties of the **BTSCustomProcessContext** object are shown in the following table.

Property	Type	Description
ChannelName	**BSTR**	Name of the channel.
DestID	**BSTR**	Value of the destination organization qualifier.
DestQualifier	**BSTR**	Qualifier type of the destination organization.
DocName	**BSTR**	Name of the document.
EnvelopeName	**BSTR**	Name of the envelope used with the document.
Openness	**long**	Value that indicates if the messaging port is open.
PassThrough	**long**	Value that indicates whether pass-through submission mode is being used.
SourceID	**BSTR**	Value of the source organization qualifier.
SourceQualifier	**BSTR**	Qualifier type of the source organization.

Remarks

This object can be obtained by calling the **SetContext** method on the **IBTSCustomProcess** object. For information about custom preprocessors, see "Preprocessing Documents in a Receive Function" earlier in this chapter.

Requirements

Windows NT/2000: Requires Windows 2000 SP1 or later
Header: Include btsaic.h

IBTSCustomProcessContext::ChannelName Property

The **ChannelName** property returns the name of the channel used for processing the current document.

Syntax

Get method:

HRESULT get_ChannelName(
   BSTR* *bstrPipelineName*
);

Parameters

bstrPipelineName
   [out, retval] Pointer to a **BSTR** that contains the name of the channel used for processing the current document.

Return Values

For a list of all error messages returned by BizTalk Server, see Appendix A, "Error Messages."

Remarks

This is a read-only property.

Requirements

Windows NT/2000: Requires Windows 2000 SP1 or later
Header: Include btsaic.h

IBTSCustomProcessContext::DestID Property

The **DestID** property returns the value of the destination organization qualifier.

Syntax

Get method:

HRESULT get_DestID(
   BSTR* *bstrDestID*
);

Parameters

bstrDestID
> [out, retval] Pointer to a **BSTR** that contains the value of the destination organization qualifier.

Return Values

For a list of all error messages returned by BizTalk Server, see Appendix A, "Error Messages."

Remarks

This is a read-only property.

Requirements

Windows NT/2000: Requires Windows 2000 SP1 or later
Header: Include btsaic.h

IBTSCustomProcessContext::DestQualifier Property

The **DestQualifier** property returns the destination organization qualifier type.

Syntax

Get method:

HRESULT get_DestQualifier(
    BSTR* *bstrDestQualifier*
);

Parameters

bstrDestQualifier
> [out, retval] Pointer to a **BSTR** that contains the destination organization qualifier type.

Return Values

For a list of all error messages returned by BizTalk Server, see Appendix A, "Error Messages."

Remarks

This is a read-only property.

Requirements

Windows NT/2000: Requires Windows 2000 SP1 or later
Header: Include btsaic.h

IBTSCustomProcessContext::DocName Property

The **DocName** property returns the name of the document definition used by the current document.

Syntax

Get method:

HRESULT get_DocName(
   BSTR* *bstrDocName*
);

Parameters

bstrDocName
   [out, retval] Pointer to a **BSTR** that contains the document definition name.

Return Values

For a list of all error messages returned by BizTalk Server, see Appendix A, "Error Messages."

Remarks

This is a read-only property.

Requirements

Windows NT/2000: Requires Windows 2000 SP1 or later
Header: Include btsaic.h

IBTSCustomProcessContext::EnvelopeName Property

The **EnvelopeName** property returns the name of the envelope used with the current document.

Syntax

Get method:

HRESULT get_EnvelopeName(
   BSTR* *bstrEnvelopeName*
);

Parameters

bstrEnvelopeName
> [out, retval] Pointer to a **BSTR** that contains the envelope name.

Return Values

For a list of all error messages returned by BizTalk Server, see Appendix A, "Error Messages."

Remarks

This is a read-only property.

Requirements

Windows NT/2000: Requires Windows 2000 SP1 or later
Header: Include btsaic.h

IBTSCustomProcessContext::Openness Property

The **Openness** property returns the openness associated with the messaging port.

Syntax

Get method:

HRESULT get_Openness(
  long* *lOpenness*
);

Parameters

lOpenness
> [out, retval] Pointer to a **long** that indicates openness on the messaging port. The **long** returned in this parameter represents a value in the **BIZTALK_OPENNESS_TYPE** enumeration.

Return Values

For a list of all error messages returned by BizTalk Server, see Appendix A, "Error Messages."

Remarks

This is a read-only property.

Requirements

Windows NT/2000: Requires Windows 2000 SP1 or later
Header: Include btsaic.h

IBTSCustomProcessContext::PassThrough Property

The **PassThrough** property indicates whether the document uses pass-through submission mode.

Syntax

Get method:

HRESULT get_PassThrough(
   long* *fPassThrough*
);

Parameters

fPassThrough
   [out, retval] Pointer to a **long** that indicates whether the document uses pass-through submission mode. A value of 0 indicates that pass-through submission mode is not used. A nonzero value indicates that pass-through submission mode is used with the current document.

Return Values

For a list of all error messages returned by BizTalk Server, see Appendix A, "Error Messages."

Remarks

This is a read-only property.

Requirements

Windows NT/2000: Requires Windows 2000 SP1 or later
Header: Include btsaic.h

IBTSCustomProcessContext::SourceID Property

The **SourceID** property returns the value of the source organization qualifier.

Syntax

Get method:

HRESULT get_SourceID(
   BSTR* *bstrSourceID*
);

Parameters

bstrSourceID
   [out, retval] Pointer to a **BSTR** that contains the value of the source organization qualifier.

Return Values

For a list of all error messages returned by BizTalk Server, see Appendix A, "Error Messages."

Remarks

This is a read-only property.

Requirements

Windows NT/2000: Requires Windows 2000 SP1 or later
Header: Include btsaic.h

IBTSCustomProcessContext::SourceQualifier Property

The **SourceQualifier** property returns the source organization qualifier type.

Syntax

Get method:

HRESULT get_SourceQualifier(
   BSTR* *bstrSourceQualifier*
);

Parameters

bstrSourceQualifier
   [out, retval] Pointer to a **BSTR** that contains the source organization qualifier type.

Return Values

For a list of all error messages returned by BizTalk Server, see Appendix A, "Error Messages."

Remarks

This is a read-only property.

Requirements

Windows NT/2000: Requires Windows 2000 SP1 or later
Header: Include btsaic.h

IInterchange Interface

Use this object to exchange documents between applications and BizTalk Server 2000 directly or through a receive function

In C++, use the **IInterchange** interface to access the methods of the **Interchange** object.

The methods of the **Interchange** object are shown in the following table.

Method	Description
CheckSuspendedQueue	Checks the Suspended queue and returns a list of handles to documents or interchanges in the queue that match the request criteria.
DeleteFromSuspendedQueue	Deletes all specified documents from the Suspended queue.
GetSuspendedQueueItemDetails	Returns details of a document in the Suspended queue.
Submit	Submits an interchange to BizTalk Server 2000 for asynchronous processing. This method accepts only a string variable as the document or interchange. This means that applications cannot submit other objects, such as DOM objects, **CDictionary** objects, ADO objects, or any other data type or object type.
SubmitSync	Submits an interchange to BizTalk Server 2000 for synchronous transmission. This method returns a response if one is provided. This method accepts only a string variable for the document or interchange. This means that applications cannot submit other objects, such as DOM objects, **CDictionary** objects, ADO objects, or any other data type or object type.

Remarks

Using parameters with **Submit** and **SubmitSync** overrides certain fields in the header of a self-routing document.

Requirements

Windows NT/2000: Requires Windows 2000 SP1 or later
Header: Include cisapi.h

IInterchange::CheckSuspendedQueue Method

The **CheckSuspendedQueue** method checks the Suspended queue and returns a list of documents that match the request criteria.

Syntax

HRESULT CheckSuspendedQueue(
    BSTR *DocName*,
    BSTR *SourceName*,
    BSTR *DestName*,
    VARIANT* *DocumentHandleList*
);

Parameters

DocName
> [in] **BSTR** that contains the name of the **BizTalkDocument** object. This parameter narrows the search for items in the Suspended queue. If this parameter is omitted, this method matches all **BizTalkDocument** objects. This is an optional parameter.

SourceName
> [in] **BSTR** that contains the name of the source **BizTalkOrganization** object. This parameter narrows the search criteria for items in the Suspended queue. If this parameter is omitted, this method matches all **BizTalkOrganization** objects. This is an optional parameter.

DestName
> [in] **BSTR** that contains the name of the destination **BizTalkOrganization** object. This parameter narrows the search criteria for items in the Suspended queue. If this parameter is omitted, this method matches all **BizTalkOrganization** objects. This is an optional parameter.

DocumentHandleList
> [out] Pointer to a **VARIANT** that contains a list of handles to all documents in the Suspended queue.

Return Values

For a list of all error messages returned by BizTalk Server, see Appendix A, "Error Messages."

Remarks

The returned items are not deleted from the queue. To delete items from the Suspended queue, use the **DeleteFromSuspendedQueue** method.

Requirements

Windows NT/2000: Requires Windows 2000 SP1 or later
Header: Include cisapi.h

IInterchange::DeleteFromSuspendedQueue Method

The **DeleteFromSuspendedQueue** method deletes all specified documents from the Suspended queue.

Syntax

HRESULT DeleteFromSuspendedQueue(
   VARIANT* *DocumentHandleList*
);

Parameters

DocumentHandleList
   [in] Pointer to a **VARIANT** that contains a full list of handles or a subset for documents to be deleted from the Suspended queue.

Return Values

For a list of all error messages returned by BizTalk Server, see Appendix A, "Error Messages."

Requirements

Windows NT/2000: Requires Windows 2000 SP1 or later
Header: Include cisapi.h

IInterchange::GetSuspendedQueueItemDetails Method

The **GetSuspendedQueueItemDetails** method uses the list of handles returned by the **CheckSuspendedQueue** method to get information about a single entry in the Suspended queue.

Syntax

HRESULT GetSuspendedQueueItemDetails(
    BSTR *ItemHandle,*
    VARIANT* *SourceName,*
    VARIANT* *DestName,*
    VARIANT* *DocName,*
    VARIANT* *ReasonCode,*
    VARIANT* *ItemData*
);

Parameters

ItemHandle
    [in] **BSTR** that contains the handle to an item in the Suspended queue.

SourceName
    [out] Pointer to the **VARIANT** that contains the name of the source **BizTalkOrganization** object.

DestName
    [out] Pointer to the **VARIANT** that contains the name of the destination **BizTalkOrganization** object.

DocName
    [out] Pointer to the **VARIANT** that contains the name of the **BizTalkDocument** object.

ReasonCode
    [out] Pointer to the **VARIANT** that contains the reason a document or interchange has been placed in the Suspended queue. For more information about this value, see "CISReasonToQueue" later in this chapter.

ItemData
    [out] Pointer to the **VARIANT** that contains the document instance or interchange.

Return Values

For a list of all error messages returned by BizTalk Server, see Appendix A, "Error Messages."

Requirements

Windows NT/2000: Requires Windows 2000 SP1 or later
Header: Include cisapi.h

IInterchange::Submit Method

The **Submit** method sends a document to BizTalk Server 2000 for asynchronous processing. BizTalk Server 2000 places the document in a queue until the next available server can process it.

Syntax

HRESULT Submit(
  BIZTALK_OPENNESS_TYPE *lOpenness,*
  BSTR *Document,*
  BSTR *DocName,*
  BSTR *SourceQualifier,*
  BSTR *SourceID,*
  BSTR *DestQualifier,*
  BSTR *DestID,*
  BSTR *ChannelName,*
  BSTR *FilePath,*
  BSTR *EnvelopeName,*
  long *PassThrough,*
  BSTR* *SubmissionHandle*
);

Parameters

lOpenness
  [in] Enumeration value that indicates whether associated **BizTalkPort** objects can be open. Valid values are from the **BIZTALK_OPENNESS_TYPE** enumeration.

Document
  [in] **BSTR** that contains the document instance submitted. This parameter accepts only a string buffer as the document or interchange. This means that applications cannot submit other objects, such as DOM objects, **CDictionary** objects, ADO objects, or any other data type or object type. Either the *Document* parameter or the *FilePath* parameter must be specified. Do not specify both. This is an optional parameter.

DocName
  [in] **BSTR** that contains the name of the **BizTalkDocument** object associated with the instance of the document being submitted. If the *lOpenness* parameter is set to **BIZTALK_OPENNESS_TYPE_SOURCE**, you can select an input **BizTalkDocument** object that has an X12 or EDIFACT specification. If you do, however, the output **BizTalkDocument** must not have an X12 or EDIFACT specification. If *lOpenness* is set

to **BIZTALK_OPENNESS_TYPE_DESTINATION**, the **BizTalkDocument** object must not have an X12 or EDIFACT specification. The *DocName* parameter cannot be used if the *PassThrough* parameter is set to TRUE. This is an optional parameter.

SourceQualifier

[in] **BSTR** that contains the qualifier of the source organization. This indicates how the *SourceID* parameter is to be interpreted. Valid values come from the organization identifier qualifiers that are created when the user creates an alias for an organization. Common qualifiers include the DUNS number, telephone number, and BizTalk. You must specify a *SourceID*. The default qualifier for all new organizations is *OrganizationName* and refers to the name of the organization in the database. If a BizTalk Framework 2.0–compliant document is submitted and a qualifier is not found during parsing, the qualifier defaults to BizTalk. The *SourceQualifier* parameter cannot be used if the *PassThrough* parameter is set to TRUE. This is an optional parameter.

SourceID

[in] **BSTR** that contains the value of the qualifier of the source organization. For example, if the *SourceQualifier* parameter is Telephone, this value is the telephone number. If the *Openness* flag is set to OpenSrc, *SourceID* is interpreted as the source organization name. The *SourceID* parameter cannot be used if the *PassThrough* parameter is set to TRUE. This is an optional parameter.

DestQualifier

[in] **BSTR** that contains the qualifier of the destination organization. This indicates how the *DestID* parameter is to be interpreted. Valid values come from the organization identifier qualifiers that are created when the user creates an alias for an organization. Common qualifiers include the DUNS number, telephone number, and BizTalk. You must specify a *DestID*. The default qualifier for all new organizations is *OrganizationName* and refers to the name of the organization in the database. If a BizTalk Framework 2.0–compliant document is submitted and a qualifier is not found during parsing, the qualifier defaults to BizTalk. The *DestQualifier* parameter cannot be used if the *PassThrough* parameter is set to TRUE. This is an optional parameter.

DestID

[in] **BSTR** that contains the value of the qualifier of the destination organization. For example, if the *DestQualifier* parameter is Telephone, this value is the telephone number. If the *Openness* flag is set to OpenDest, *DestID* is used as the destination address. Note that the queue:// prefix must be used with an open messaging port when a Message Queue is specified as the destination address. The *DestID* parameter cannot be used if the *PassThrough* parameter is set to TRUE. This is an optional parameter.

ChannelName

[in] **BSTR** that contains the name of the **BizTalkChannel** object that is executed for this document. This bypasses the normal processing in which the parser tries to determine which messaging port/channel pair to execute, based on routing information in the parameters or in the document. This is an optional parameter unless the *PassThrough* parameter is set to TRUE.

FilePath

[in] **BSTR** that specifies a fully qualified path that contains the document to be submitted, rather than submitting the document directly as a string. BizTalk Server 2000 supports URL, UNC, and drive: format only. If the document is submitted as a file that is pointed to by the *FilePath* parameter, the call returns successfully after BizTalk Server 2000 has successfully copied the file to the Work queue. It is safe to delete the file from the specified path as soon as this method returns successfully. When a document is submitted to the server, using *FilePath* to specify the data, **Submit** can take 30 seconds or longer if the location of the file resides on a remote server that is unavailable, if the UNC path is invalid, or if the SQL server is down. Either the *Document* parameter or the *FilePath* parameter must be specified. Do not specify both. The *FilePath* parameter cannot be used if the *PassThrough* parameter is set to TRUE and a map is specified. This is an optional parameter.

EnvelopeName

[in] **BSTR** that contains the name of the envelope specification to use to break the interchange into documents. When an envelope name is provided in this parameter, the envelope must have a valid interchange specification. This requirement is enforced for envelopes created for Custom XML format also. When submitting a flat file to BizTalk Server 2000, you must create an envelope for this flat file and specify the name of the envelope in *EnvelopeName*. This is an optional parameter.

PassThrough

[in] **Long** that indicates how the server processes the document. When this parameter is set to TRUE, no decryption, decoding, or signature verification is performed on the document. When set to FALSE, the document is decrypted and decoded, and the signature is verified. When using pass-through submission mode (TRUE), the **BIZTALK_OPENNESS_TYPE** value must be set to **BIZTALK_OPENNESS_TYPE_NOTOPEN** and the *ChannelName* parameter must be specified. In addition, the *DocName*, *SourceQualifier*, *SourceID*, *DestQualifier*, and *DestID* parameters cannot be specified with pass-through submission mode. Pass-through submission mode should be used to prevent data corruption when exchanging binary files, or when only the server transport and global tracking features are being used.

SubmissionHandle

[out, retval] Pointer to a **BSTR** that contains a unique identifier for the submitted document or interchange. This handle can be used to query the Tracking database for the status of the interchange or document submitted. If more than one document is submitted (an interchange), a single handle is returned, yet the Tracking database enables the user to get the status of all child documents related to this interchange identifier.

Return Values

For a list of all error messages returned by BizTalk Server, see Appendix A, "Error Messages."

Requirements

Windows NT/2000: Requires Windows 2000 SP1 or later
Header: Include cisapi.h

IInterchange::SubmitSync Method

The **SubmitSync** method sends an interchange or document to BizTalk Server 2000 for synchronous processing. An optional response document is returned to the caller.

Syntax

HRESULT SubmitSync(
    BIZTALK_OPENNESS_TYPE *lOpenness,*
    BSTR *Document,*
    BSTR *DocName,*
    BSTR *SourceQualifier,*
    BSTR *SourceID,*
    BSTR *DestQualifier,*
    BSTR *DestID,*
    BSTR *ChannelName,*
    BSTR *FilePath,*
    BSTR *EnvelopeName,*
    long *PassThrough,*
    VARIANT* *SubmissionHandle,*
    VARIANT* *ResponseDocument*
);

Parameters

lOpenness
    [in] Enumeration value that indicates whether associated **BizTalkPort** objects can be open. Valid values are from the **BIZTALK_OPENNESS_TYPE** enumeration.

Document
    [in] **BSTR** that contains the document instance submitted. This parameter accepts only a string buffer as the document or interchange. This means that applications cannot submit other objects, such as DOM objects, **CDictionary** objects, ADO objects, or any other data type or object type. Either the *Document* parameter or the *FilePath* parameter must be specified. Do not specify both. This is an optional parameter.

DocName

> [in] **BSTR** that contains the name of the **BizTalkDocument** object associated with the instance of the document submitted. If the *lOpenness* parameter is set to **BIZTALK_OPENNESS_TYPE_SOURCE**, you can select an input **BizTalkDocument** object that has an X12 or EDIFACT specification. If you do, however, the output **BizTalkDocument** must not have an X12 or EDIFACT specification. If *lOpenness* is set to **BIZTALK_OPENNESS_TYPE_DESTINATION**, the **BizTalkDocument** object must not have an X12 or EDIFACT specification. The *DocName* parameter cannot be used if the *PassThrough* parameter is set to TRUE. This is an optional parameter.

SourceQualifier

> [in] **BSTR** that contains the qualifier of the source organization. This indicates how the *SourceID* parameter is to be interpreted. Valid values come from the organization identifier qualifiers that are created when the user creates an alias for an organization. Common qualifiers include the DUNS number, telephone number, and BizTalk. You must specify a *SourceID*. The default qualifier for all new organizations is *OrganizationName* and refers to the name of the organization in the database. If a BizTalk Framework 2.0–compliant document is submitted and a qualifier is not found during parsing, the qualifier defaults to BizTalk. The *SourceQualifier* parameter cannot be used if the *PassThrough* parameter is set to TRUE. This is an optional parameter.

SourceID

> [in] **BSTR** that contains the value of the qualifier of the source organization. For example, if the *SourceQualifier* parameter is Telephone, this value is the telephone number. If the *Openness* flag is set to OpenSrc, *SourceID* is interpreted as the source organization name. The *SourceID* parameter cannot be used if the *PassThrough* parameter is set to TRUE. This is an optional parameter.

DestQualifier

> [in] **BSTR** that contains the qualifier of the destination organization. This indicates how the *DestID* parameter is to be interpreted. Valid values come from the organization identifier qualifiers that are created when the user creates an alias for an organization. Common qualifiers include the DUNS number, telephone number, and BizTalk. You must specify a *DestID* parameter. The default qualifier for all new organizations is *OrganizationName* and refers to the name of the organization in the database. If a BizTalk Framework 2.0–compliant document is submitted and a qualifier is not found during parsing, the qualifier defaults to BizTalk. The *DestQualifier* parameter cannot be used if the *PassThrough* parameter is set to TRUE. This is an optional parameter.

DestID

> [in] **BSTR** that contains the value of the qualifier of the destination organization. For example, if the *DestQualifier* parameter is Telephone, this value is the telephone number. If the *Openness* flag is set to OpenDest, *DestID* is used as the destination address. Note that the queue:// prefix must be used with an open messaging port when a Message Queue is specified as the destination address. The *DestID* parameter cannot be used if the *PassThrough* parameter is set to TRUE. This is an optional parameter.

ChannelName

[in] **BSTR** that contains the name of the **BizTalkChannel** object that is executed for this document. This bypasses the normal processing in which the parser tries to determine which messaging port/channel pair to execute, based on routing information in the parameters or in the document. This is an optional parameter unless the *PassThrough* parameter is set to TRUE.

FilePath

[in] **BSTR** that specifies a fully qualified path that contains the document to be submitted, rather than submitting the document directly as a string. BizTalk Server 2000 supports URL, UNC, and drive: format only. Either the *Document* parameter or the *FilePath* parameter must be specified. Do not specify both. The *FilePath* parameter cannot be used if the *PassThrough* parameter is set to TRUE and a map is specified. This is an optional parameter.

EnvelopeName

[in] **BSTR** that contains the name of the envelope specification to use to break the interchange into documents. When an envelope name is provided in this parameter, the envelope must have a valid interchange specification. This requirement is enforced for envelopes created for Custom XML format also. This is an optional parameter.

PassThrough

[in] **Long** that indicates how the server processes the document. When this parameter is set to TRUE, no decryption, decoding, or signature verification is performed on the document. When set to FALSE, the document is decrypted and decoded, and the signature is verified. When using pass-through submission mode (TRUE), the **BIZTALK_OPENNESS_TYPE** value must be set to **BIZTALK_OPENNESS_TYPE_NOTOPEN** and the *ChannelName* parameter must be specified. In addition, the *DocName*, *SourceQualifier*, *SourceID*, *DestQualifier*, and *DestID* parameters cannot be specified with pass-through submission mode. Pass-through submission mode should be used to prevent data corruption when exchanging binary files, or when only the server transport and global tracking features are being used.

SubmissionHandle

[out] Pointer to a **BSTR** that contains a unique identifier for the submitted document or interchange. This handle can be used to query the Tracking database for the status of the interchange or document submitted. If more than one document is submitted (an interchange), a single handle is returned, yet the Tracking database can access the status of all child documents related to this interchange identifier.

ResponseDocument

[out] Pointer to a **VARIANT** that contains the optional response document.

Return Values

For a list of all error messages returned by BizTalk Server, see Appendix A, "Error Messages."

Remarks

SubmitSync returns an optional response document when provided. If no response is returned, the call returns successfully, but with no response and with an HRESULT value of S_FALSE. If the destination is another BizTalk Server, an ASP page must be used to return a response.

A synchronous interchange bypasses all queues and executes all the components required by the messaging port on the calling thread. For synchronous protocols (HTTP and AIC), an optional response document is returned to the user, if available. This method is valid only for a single channel match. If the parameters set cause multiple channels to match, synchronous submission returns an error indicating that multiple channel matches are not allowed for synchronous submission. This method can be used only for single document interchanges. If the submission contains multiple documents, synchronous submission returns an error indicating that multiple document submissions are not allowed. This method does not support port groups.

Requirements

Windows NT/2000: Requires Windows 2000 SP1 or later
Header: Include cisapi.h

Related Topics

"Document Definitions" in Chapter 9, "Configuring BizTalk Messaging Services"

"Document Tracking" in Chapter 9, "Configuring BizTalk Messaging Services"

"Openness" in Chapter 9, "Configuring BizTalk Messaging Services"

"Understanding the Tracking Database Schema" in Chapter 13, "Tracking Documents"

Interchange Enumerations

This section provides reference information about enumerations used by Microsoft BizTalk Server 2000 for programming with Microsoft Visual Basic and Microsoft Visual C++.

CISReasonToQueue

The **CISReasonToQueue** enumeration values are defined in the cisapi.h header file, located on the BizTalk Server installation drive in the \Program Files\Microsoft BizTalk Server\SDK\Include folder.

The **CISReasonToQueue** enumeration has one of the following values:

Name	Value	Description
noReason	0	Not supported for this release.
rtdlqParserFailure	1	Specifies that the instance of the document was placed in the queue because of failure of the parser.
rtdlqParserDocFailure	2	Specifies that the instance of the document was placed in the queue because the business document was invalid.
rtdlqDocValidation	3	Specifies that the document was placed in the queue because document validation failed.
rtdlqChannelSelectFailure	4	Specifies that the instance of the document was placed in the queue because of failure in selecting the correct **BizTalkChannel** object.
rtdlqInvalidMap	5	Specifies that the instance of the document was placed in the queue because the map referred to by the **BizTalkChannel** object was formatted incorrectly.
rtdlqFieldTrackingFailure	6	Specifies that the instance of the document was placed in the queue because the server was unable to track the requested fields within the document.
rtdlqMappingFailure	7	Specifies that the instance of the document was placed in the queue because of failure of transformation.
rtdlqSerializerFailure	8	Specifies that the instance of the document was placed in the queue because the server could not convert this document to its native format.
rtdlqEncodingFailure	9	Specifies that the instance of the document was placed in the queue because the server was unable to encode this interchange.
rtdlqSigningFailure	10	Specifies that the instance of the document was placed in the queue because the server was unable to sign this interchange.

Name	Value	Description
rtdlqEncryptionFailure	11	Specifies that the instance of the document was placed in the queue because the server was unable to encrypt this interchange.
rtdlqTransmissionFailure	12	Specifies that the instance of the document was placed in the queue because the server was unable to deliver this document.
rtdlqUserMove	13	Specifies that the administrator moved this instance of the document to the queue.
rtdlqTimeout	14	Specifies that the instance of the document was placed in the queue because a time-out occurred.
rtdlqCustomCompFailure	15	Specifies that the instance of the document was placed in the queue because of failure of a custom component.
unkReason	16	Specifies that this item was marked as "In process" by an inactive server. On restart of this server, this item was automatically moved to the Suspended queue. There was probably a catastrophic failure on the original server. Contact the system administrator for more information.
rtdlqNoChannel	17	Specifies that the instance of the document was placed in the queue because the **BizTalkChannel** object was deleted.
rtdlqMissingChannel	18	Specifies that the instance of the document was placed in the queue because the **BizTalkChannel** object specified by the **Submit** method of the **IInterchange** interface was not found.
rtdlqInvalidChannel	19	Specifies that the instance of the document was placed in the queue because the **BizTalkChannel** object specified by the **Submit** method of the **IInterchange** interface specifies an open **BizTalkPort** object. This is not permitted.
rtdlqOutOfMemory	20	Specifies that your computer has run out of memory. Rebooting is recommended.
rtdlqBTFRecReqExpired	21	Specifies that the document was placed in the queue because the BTF timestamp **receiptRequiredBy** expired.
rtdlqBTFExpiresAtExpired	22	Specifies that the document was placed in the queue because the BTF timestamp **expiresAt** expired.
rtdlqCorrelationFailure	23	Specifies that the document receipt failed.

Part 4: Administering Servers and Tracking Documents

This part explains how to effectively administer servers and XLANG-related applications. It also describes important concepts and common administrative issues of which system administrators must be aware. In addition, you'll learn about BizTalk Document Tracking, which is a stand-alone Web application that you can use to view the progress of documents processed by Microsoft BizTalk Server 2000.

In This Part

- **Administering Servers and Applications.** This chapter describes how to centrally configure and manage servers in multiple groups, configure and manage receive functions, manage the Shared Queue database, and manage the COM+ applications that host XLANG schedules.

- **BizTalk Server 2000 Operations.** This chapter outlines the administrative tasks a system administrator must perform to keep an installation of Microsoft BizTalk Server 2000 running on a continual basis.

- **Tracking Documents.** This chapter provides step-by-step instructions about how to create queries and advanced queries to extract essential information from the Tracking database in an easy-to-view format. You'll also learn how to configure BizTalk Document Tracking to display interchange and document records individually or in batches.

CHAPTER 11

Administering Servers and Applications

This chapter covers how to administer servers and XLANG-related applications. Topics covered in this section include centrally configuring and managing servers in multiple groups, configuring and managing receive functions, managing the Shared Queue, and managing the COM+ applications that host XLANG schedules.

In This Chapter

- BizTalk Server Administration User Interface

- Managing BizTalk Server Databases

- Groups and Servers

- Administration Privileges

- Handling Server Errors

- Receive Functions

- Using Queues

- Manage XLANG Applications and Databases

- Administering XLANG Schedules

- Troubleshooting BizTalk Server Administration

BizTalk Server Administration User Interface

BizTalk Server Administration—also called the administration console—is a Microsoft Management Console (MMC) snap-in that provides a visual representation of the BizTalk Server components that a system administrator can manage. The left side of the administration console is called the console tree and consists of folders and subfolders that represent different items, such as server groups. The right side of the administration console is called the details pane and contains information about the item that is selected in the console tree.

Graphically, Microsoft BizTalk Server 2000 is displayed as a subitem of the Console Root on the left side of the administration console. Each server group configured in BizTalk Server is displayed in a separate subfolder and consists of the queues and receive functions for that group, as well as the names of servers in the group. Expand any item in the console tree to display additional details about the item in the details pane of the administration console. You can right-click any item to configure it, or to create new items.

To open BizTalk Server Administration

- On the **Start** menu, point to **Programs**, point to **Microsoft BizTalk Server 2000**, and then click **BizTalk Server Administration**.

To add users to the BizTalk Server Administrators group

To add users to the BizTalk Server Administrators group, you must be a member of the Windows 2000 Administrators group. For more information about adding users to the Windows 2000 Administrators group, see "To add a user account to the Administrators group" in Chapter 1, "Installing BizTalk Server 2000."

1. On the **Start** menu, point to **Settings**, click **Control Panel**, double-click **Administrative Tools**, and then double-click **Computer Management**.

2. Expand **System Tools**, expand **Local Users and Groups**, and then click the **Groups** folder.

    The folder contents appear in the details pane.

3. In the details pane, click **BizTalk Server Administrators**.

4. On the **Action** menu, point to **All Tasks** and click **Add to Group**.

    The **BizTalk Server Administrators Properties** dialog box appears.

5. Click **Add**.

6. In the **Look in** list, click your domain or computer name.

7. In the list that contains the users and computers associated with the domain or computer you selected in step 6, click the user account to add, click **Add**, and then click **OK**.

8. Click **OK** to close the **BizTalk Server Administrators Properties** dialog box.

✍ Notes

- This procedure is based on the assumption that the BizTalk Server Administrators group name is **BizTalk Server Administrators**.

- If necessary, log off and log on using your user account.

To refresh the administration console

1. In BizTalk Server Administration, expand **Microsoft BizTalk Server 2000** and expand the items in the console tree until you locate the item that you want to refresh.

   You might need to expand **Server Groups**, **Queues**, **Receive Functions**, and **Servers** to find the item you want to refresh.

2. Click the item you want to refresh.

3. On the **Action** menu, click **Refresh**.

✍ Notes

- In BizTalk Server Administration, you can refresh the status of the following items:

    - The Microsoft BizTalk Server 2000 node

    - Server groups

    - Servers

    - Queues

    - Receive functions

- You can perform this procedure on any item in the console tree. When you refresh the administration console at the root, all items in the administration console are refreshed. When you refresh a server group, only the items in that group are refreshed.

- There is no automatic refresh cycle for the administration console. Perform this procedure to view the current status of server groups, servers, receive functions, the number of items in a queue, and so on.

Related Topics

"Groups and Servers" later in this chapter

"Receive Functions" later in this chapter

"Using Queues" later in this chapter

"Administration Privileges" later in this chapter

WMI Overview

Windows Management Instrumentation (WMI) is a data-management layer that is included in Microsoft Windows 2000. Microsoft BizTalk Server 2000 uses the WMI layer to encapsulate administrative functions. When you use BizTalk Server Administration to change group, server, and queue settings, the new values are stored in the BizTalk Messaging Management database through the BizTalk Server WMI provider. In BizTalk Server 2000, this WMI provider uses a Microsoft SQL Server database to store administrative objects. WMI supports a uniform scripting application programming interface (API) that gives applications and scripts access to the WMI provider on a local computer or a remote computer.

Notes

- WMI has a restriction on syntax and valid characters for a WMI object path. The following are invalid characters:

  ` ! @ # $ % ^ & * ( ) + = [ ] { } | \\ ;\" '< > , . ?

  Do not use any of these characters when you create a server group name.

- All timestamps are created by using the local time on Microsoft SQL Server. However, the WMI provider refers to all timestamps in coordinated universal time (UTC). The administration console then converts the timestamps back to local time for display.

- To access the WMI database layer programmatically, you can use the InterchangeProvSchema.mof file found in the \Program Files\Microsoft BizTalk Server\Setup folder. This file contains the WMI classes corresponding to the Administration objects. For more information about WMI Application Programming, go to the MSDN Online Library Web site (msdn.microsoft.com/library/default.asp) and search for WMI Application Programming.

BizTalk Server Administration Shortcut Keys

You can use shortcut keys to accomplish tasks in BizTalk Server Administration. The following table is a quick reference to the Microsoft Management Console shortcut keys.

Note

- Functionality that is not included in this list can be obtained by using the numeric keypad to move the mouse pointer with MouseKeys. For more information about MouseKeys in Windows 2000 Server and Advanced Server Help, see "Using the keyboard to move the mouse pointer." For more information about MouseKeys in Windows 2000 Professional Help, see "Move the mouse pointer by using MouseKeys."

Press	To
F5	Refresh BizTalk Server Administration.
	This shortcut key refreshes the current item highlighted in the console tree.
ALT+F4	Close BizTalk Server Administration.
ALT+MINUS SIGN	Display the window menu for the active console window.
SHIFT+F10	Display the **Action** menu for the selected item.
ALT+A	Display the **Action** menu for the selected item.
ALT+V	Display the **View** menu.
F1	View online Help for the selected item.
ALT+ENTER	Display the properties dialog box, if any, for the selected item.

Administration Cache

When you start BizTalk Server, all items, such as server groups, server group properties, receive functions, connections to the Shared Queue and Tracking databases, and so on, in BizTalk Server Administration are stored in the administration cache. All items in the cache are refreshed every 50 seconds except for the server database connections and server properties. This means that if you change the general properties for a server group, such as the SMTP host or the reliable messaging reply-to URL, the changes are picked up within 50 seconds. However, if you change any server properties, such as the **Maximum number of worker threads per processor allowed**, you must stop and restart the server on which you changed the configuration so the change can be stored in the cache. Or, if you change a connection to the BizTalk Messaging Management, Tracking, or Shared Queue database, you must stop and restart the servers in the group and shut down the BizTalk Server Interchange Application.

Managing BizTalk Server Databases

The three databases associated with BizTalk Messaging Services are:

- BizTalk Messaging Management database
- Tracking database
- Shared Queue database

The BizTalk Messaging Management database stores information for all server configurations, including group and server settings, and receive functions. The configuration of these administration objects is handled through BizTalk Server Administration or programmatically. The BizTalk Messaging Management database also stores all messaging configuration information for channels, messaging ports, and other messaging objects.

Although messaging configuration information is stored in this database, the configuration of the objects is handled either by using BizTalk Messaging Manager or programmatically by using the BizTalk Messaging Configuration object model. For more information about configuring channels, messaging ports, and so on, see "Using BizTalk Messaging Manager" or "Object Model Reference" in Chapter 9, "Configuring BizTalk Messaging Services."

The Tracking database keeps a log of all interchanges, documents, and receipts that are processed by BizTalk Server. For more information about the Tracking database, see "Tracking Database" later in this chapter. To configure tracking settings, see "To configure tracking properties for a server group" later in this chapter.

The Shared Queue database holds documents while they are being processed or waiting to be processed. Documents are later removed after they have been processed. For more information about the Shared Queue database, see "Shared Queue Database" later in this chapter.

Managing the BizTalk Messaging Management Database

For most business implementations, there is one central BizTalk Messaging Management database that is used to configure multiple server groups, servers, channels, messaging ports, and so on. One exception to this guideline is businesses that are third-party vendors. Third-party vendors might need a separate BizTalk Messaging Management database for every customer based on each customer's particular business needs. However, in all other cases, it is strongly recommended that you use a central BizTalk Messaging Management database for all your BizTalk server groups.

From time to time, it might be necessary to remove servers from the central BizTalk Messaging Management database. For example, the server on which your BizTalk Messaging Management database resides might need maintenance. In this case, you must point all server groups to a replicated BizTalk Messaging Management database to keep your BizTalk Server enterprise running. It also might be necessary to move servers between one or more BizTalk Messaging Management databases. For example, if you are a third-party vendor with three customers, A, B, and C, and the business from customer A decreased while the business from customers B and C increased, you can move the servers that were associated with customer A's BizTalk Messaging Management database to the databases associated with customers B and C.

Changing the BizTalk Messaging Management Database

There are two ways to configure the BizTalk Messaging Management database:

- Use the configuration options available during installation.

- Use BizTalk Server Administration to change the server in the **Microsoft BizTalk Server 2000** node.

If you want to centrally manage all your BizTalk servers from a single server, during installation configure all servers to point to a central BizTalk Messaging Management database. If you do this, anytime you open BizTalk Server Administration on any one of those BizTalk servers, the servers listed in the **Microsoft BizTalk Server 2000** node point to the same BizTalk Messaging Management database and can be centrally managed. Once a collection of server groups point to a central BizTalk Messaging Management database, you typically do not need to change to a different BizTalk Messaging Management database. An exception to this is when you need to bring that database offline for maintenance. In this situation, use BizTalk Server Administration to point all server groups in the **Microsoft BizTalk Server 2000** node to a replication of the original central database. Do not temporarily point server groups to a different central BizTalk Messaging Management database that has other server groups associated with it. If you do, it might be difficult to return to your original BizTalk Messaging Management database configuration.

To configure the BizTalk Messaging Management database

1. In BizTalk Server Administration, click **Microsoft BizTalk Server 2000**.

2. On the **Action** menu, click **Properties**.

   The **Microsoft BizTalk Server 2000 Properties** dialog box appears.

3. On the **General** tab, you can change the following properties:

   - **SQL database name.** Type the name of the BizTalk Messaging Management database that you want all server groups to use.

   - **SQL Server name.** Type the name of the server that stores the Microsoft SQL Server database on which the BizTalk Messaging Management database is stored.

   - **User name.** You can change the SQL Server logon user name that is used to connect to the server on which the BizTalk Messaging Management database is stored.

   - **Password.** You can change the SQL Server logon password that is used to connect to the server on which the BizTalk Messaging Management database is stored.

4. Click **OK**.

☝ Caution

- Use this procedure if you need to bring the BizTalk Messaging Management database offline for maintenance. However, you must point to a replicated database, not a different BizTalk Messaging Management database that has other server groups associated with it.

✎ Notes

- When you change either the BizTalk Messaging Management database or point the server groups to a different Microsoft SQL Server, you must complete the following steps:

  1. Stop all servers in the **Microsoft BizTalk Server 2000** node. For more information, see "To stop a server in a group" later in this chapter.

  2. Shut down the BizTalk Server Interchange Application. For more information, see "To shut down the BizTalk Server Interchange Application" later in this chapter.

  3. Restart all servers in the **Microsoft BizTalk Server 2000** node. For more information, see "To start a server in a group" later in this chapter.

  When you change the BizTalk Messaging Management database or point the server groups to a different Microsoft SQL Server, all BizTalk servers in the central BizTalk Messaging Management database are updated with the new information.

- If you change the BizTalk Messaging Management database of your existing server and then add your existing server to a new group, you might encounter problems when you submit a document to your existing server. To avoid potential problems, stop all servers in the **Microsoft BizTalk Server 2000** node, shut down the BizTalk Server Interchange Application, and then restart all the servers in the **Microsoft BizTalk Server 2000** node. For more information about how to stop a server, see "To stop a server in a group" later in this chapter. For more information about shutting down the BizTalk Server Interchange Application, see "To shut down the BizTalk Server Interchange Application" later in this chapter. For more information about how to restart servers, see "To start a server in a group" later in this chapter.

To change the BizTalk Messaging Management database for a server

1. In BizTalk Server Administration, expand **Microsoft BizTalk Server 2000**, expand the server group that contains the server for which you want to change the BizTalk Messaging Management database, and then click the server.

2. On the **Action** menu, click **Stop**.

3. On the **Action** menu, click **Delete**.

   The **User Action Confirmation** dialog box appears.

4. Click **Yes**.

5. Close BizTalk Server Administration.

6. On the **Start** menu, point to **Programs**, point to **Accessories**, and then click **Windows Explorer**.

7. Browse to **\Program Files\Microsoft BizTalk Server\Setup**.

8. Click **BTSsetupDB.exe**.

9. On the **File** menu, click **Open**.

   The Microsoft BizTalk Server 2000 Database Setup Wizard opens.

10. On the **Welcome to the Microsoft BizTalk Server 2000 Messaging Database Setup Wizard** page, click **Next**.

11. On the **Configure a BizTalk Messaging Management Database** page, click **Create a new BizTalk Messaging Management database**.

   –Or–

   Click **Select an existing database**.

12. In the **Server name** box, click the name of the server where the new or existing BizTalk Messaging Management database is located.

13. In the **User name** and **Password** boxes, type a valid user name and password to access the SQL server, if required.

14. In the **Database** box, type the name of the new or existing BizTalk Messaging Management database.

15. Click **Next**.

16. On the **Configure a BizTalk Server Group** page, click **Create a new BizTalk Server group**. In the **Group name** box, type the name of the new group and click **Next**.

   –Or–

   Click **Select an existing BizTalk Server group**. In the **Group name** list, click the name of the existing group and click **Next**.

   You can select an existing BizTalk Server group only if you selected an existing database in step 11.

17. If necessary, click **Create a new Tracking database** and click **Next**.

   –Or–

   Click **Select an existing database**. In the **Server name** list, click a server. In the **User name** and **Password** boxes, type a valid Microsoft SQL Server user name and password, if required. In the **Database** box, type the name of the database. Click **Next**.

18. If necessary, click **Create a new Shared Queue database** and click **Next**.

   –Or–

   Click **Select an existing database**. In the **Server name** list, click a server. In the **User name** and **Password** boxes, type a valid SQL Server user name and password, if required. In the **Database** box, type the name of the database. Click **Next**.

19. On the **Verify BizTalk Server Group** page, verify the information you entered and click **Next**.

20. On the **Completing the Microsoft BizTalk Server 2000 Messaging Database Setup Wizard** page, click **Finish**.

21. Open BizTalk Server Administration.

22. Expand **Microsoft BizTalk Server 2000**, expand the server group that contains the server for which you just changed the BizTalk Messaging Management database, and then click the server.

23. On the **Action** menu, click **Start**.

◆ Important

- Use this procedure to associate a server with a different BizTalk Messaging Management database. For more information about moving servers between BizTalk Messaging Management databases, see "Moving Servers between BizTalk Messaging Management Databases" later in this chapter. For more information about changing the BizTalk Messaging Management database for server groups, see "Changing the BizTalk Messaging Management database" earlier in this chapter.

Removing Servers from the BizTalk Messaging Management Database

If you remove all BizTalk servers from your central BizTalk Messaging Management database, the contents of the database remain intact. Likewise, if you have more than one central BizTalk Messaging Management database in your system and you remove all BizTalk Servers from a central BizTalk Messaging Management database, the contents of the database remain intact. You can add new servers to the central BizTalk Messaging Management database by running the BizTalk Server 2000 Database Setup Wizard and selecting an existing database on the **Configure a BizTalk Messaging Management Database** page. For more information about adding or changing the BizTalk Messaging Management database for a server, see "To change the BizTalk Messaging Management database for a server" earlier in this chapter.

Moving Servers between BizTalk Messaging Management Databases

If you are planning to temporarily move a BizTalk server from one central BizTalk Messaging Management database to another, at least one other BizTalk server must remain in place in one of the server groups within the original central database. This enables you to easily restore the BizTalk server to the original central database. Otherwise, to add a new BizTalk server to the central database, you must run the BizTalk Server Database Setup Wizard and select an existing database on the **Configure a BizTalk Messaging Management**

Database page. For more information about adding or changing the BizTalk Messaging Management database for a server, see "To change the BizTalk Messaging Management database for a server" earlier in this chapter.

Moving Remote Servers between BizTalk Messaging Management Databases

If you try to add a remote server to a BizTalk Messaging Management database, and that server was originally in a different central BizTalk Messaging Management database, the following error message appears in the Windows Event Log:

> A new instance of the WMI class "**MicrosoftBizTalkServer_Server**" cannot be created in the BizTalk Server WMI provider. The *<servername>* server may already belong to a different BizTalk Server installation.

This error means that an attempt was made to add a remote server that was originally in a different central database. For more information, see "Error when moving a remote server to a different BizTalk Messaging Management database" later in this chapter. If this procedure was performed within BizTalk Server Administration, the administration console tries to determine if the remote server also belongs to a group in the remote central database. The administration console queries the remote server's Windows Management Instrumentation (WMI) provider to make this determination. For more information on WMI, see "WMI Overview" earlier in this chapter. If the server does belong to a server group in the other central database, an error message from the administration console appears and explains that you cannot add a remote server that already belongs to a group in a different central database.

Managing BizTalk Server Group Databases

Each server group uses two databases, the Shared Queue database and the Tracking database. The Shared Queue database holds all documents and interchanges that are submitted to BizTalk Server 2000 for processing and transmission. The Tracking database tracks and stores incoming and outgoing interchanges for auditing, reconciliation, and dispute-resolution purposes.

To help you organize the logical configuration of your servers and groups, it is important to create unique names for the Shared Queue and Tracking databases that are associated with each server group. For example, if you have two server groups, one called Group1 and one called Group2, label the databases for the first group SharedQueue1 and Tracking1, and label the databases for the second group SharedQueue2 and Tracking2.

Note

- The BizTalk Messaging Management database is a different database than the Shared Queue and Tracking databases. This database is used to store information about the configuration of multiple groups and servers, as well as to store information about the configuration of BizTalk Messaging Services. It does not handle document and interchange transmissions or track document and interchange activities.

Shared Queue Database

All servers in a server group share a single Shared Queue database. All documents and interchanges that are submitted to the servers in a group are stored in the Shared Queue database until they are processed by BizTalk Server. For more information on queues, see "Using Queues" later in this chapter.

The Shared Queue database is graphically represented in BizTalk Server Administration as a series of queues that provide information about the progress of an interchange or document in BizTalk Server. Interchanges and documents are in one of the following queues while they are processed by BizTalk Server:

- **Work queue.** A list of interchanges and documents that are currently being processed by BizTalk Server.

- **Scheduled queue.** A list of interchanges and documents that have been processed by BizTalk Server and are waiting for transmission according to the service window. For more information about the service window, Microsoft Visual Basic programmers should see "BizTalkPort.ServiceWindowInfo Property" in Chapter 9, "Configuring BizTalk Messaging Services." For more information about the service window, C++ programmers should see "IBizTalkPort::ServiceWindowInfo Property" in Chapter 9, "Configuring BizTalk Messaging Services."

- **Retry queue.** A list of interchanges and documents that are being resubmitted, as well as reliable messages that are awaiting receipts.

- **Suspended queue.** A list of interchanges and documents that failed processing for a variety of reasons, including parsing errors, serialization errors, or transmission errors, or that lack a correct channel configuration.

To configure connection properties for a server group

1. In BizTalk Server Administration, expand **Microsoft BizTalk Server 2000** and click the server group that you want to configure.

2. On the **Action** menu, click **Properties**.

   The **BizTalk Server Group Properties** dialog box appears.

3. Click the **Connection** tab.

4. In the **Tracking database** area:

   - In the **Tracking database name** box, type the name of the Tracking database that you want this server group to use.

   - In the **Tracking SQL Server name** box, type the name of the SQL server that stores the Tracking database that you want this server group to use.

   - In the **User name** and **Password** boxes, type the Microsoft SQL Server logon user name and password that are used to connect to the server on which the Tracking database is stored.

5. In the **Shared Queue database** area:

   • In the **Shared Queue database name** box, type the name of the Shared Queue database that you want this server group to use.

   • In the **Shared Queue SQL Server name** box, type the name of the SQL server that stores the Shared Queue database that you want this server group to use.

   • In the **User name** and **Password** boxes, type the SQL Server logon user name and password that are used to connect to the server on which the Shared Queue database is stored.

6. Click **OK**.

Notes

• If you change information in the **Tracking database** or **Shared Queue database** area, you must complete the following steps:

   1. Stop all servers in the **Microsoft BizTalk Server 2000** node. For more information, see "To stop a server in a group" later in this chapter.

   2. Shut down the BizTalk Server Interchange Application. For more information, see "To shut down the BizTalk Server Interchange Application" later in this chapter.

   3. Restart all servers in the **Microsoft BizTalk Server 2000** node. For more information, see "To start a server in a group" later in this chapter.

• If you change any values in the **Tracking database** area, you must update the connection string in the Connection.vb file with the new Tracking database information. You can find Connection.vb in the \Program Files\Microsoft BizTalk Server\BizTalkTracking\VBScripts folder. The **Initial Catalog** property in the connection string contains the name of the Tracking database. Update this property to update the Tracking database name. The connection string in the Connection.vb file is:

```
Const g_ConnectionString = "Provider=SQLOLEDB.1;
Persist Security Info=False;User ID=dta_ui_login;
Password=;Initial Catalog=<databasename>;
Data Source=<servername>;Connect Timeout=15"
```

To manually restore the Shared Queue database

1. On the **Start** menu, point to **Programs**, point to **Microsoft SQL Server**, and then click **Enterprise Manager**.

2. Expand **Microsoft SQL Servers**, expand **SQL Server Group**, and then expand the server on which you want to restore the database.

3. Click **Databases**.

4. On the **Action** menu, click **New Database**.

   The **Database Properties** dialog box appears.

5. On the **General** tab, in the **Name** box, type a name for the Shared Queue database and click **OK**.

6. On the **Start** menu, point to **Programs**, point to **Microsoft SQL Server**, and then click **Query Analyzer**.

   The **Connect to SQL Server** dialog box appears.

7. Click **OK**.

8. If you have Microsoft SQL Server 7.0 installed, in the Query window, in the **DB** list, click the name of the new Shared Queue database.

   –Or–

   If you have Microsoft SQL Server 2000 installed, on the **Objects** tab, click the name of the new Shared Queue database.

9. Click the **Load SQL Script** ☞ button.

10. Browse to **\Program Files\Microsoft BizTalk Server\Setup**.

11. Click **BTS_Core_Schema.sql** and click **Open**.

12. Click the **Execute Query** button.

13. Click the **Load SQL Script** button.

14. Verify that you are in the folder **\Program Files\Microsoft BizTalk Server\Setup**.

15. Click **BTS_Core_Logic.sql** and click **Open**.

16. Click the **Execute Query** button.

17. Close SQL Query Analyzer and SQL Server Enterprise Manager.

❦ Caution

- When you manually restore the Shared Queue database, you lose all data. If you need to keep this data, back up the data before you restore the Shared Queue database.

✎ Note

- Use this procedure if the Shared Queue database becomes corrupted or damaged.

Related Topics

"Available Receive Functions" later in the chapter

"Groups and Servers" later in this chapter

Tracking Database

All servers in a server group share a single Tracking database that stores all information related to interchange and document activity in BizTalk Server. The Tracking database is used to track the status of an interchange or document as it moves through the server. For example, if you want to verify whether an order was sent to a trading partner, you can query the Tracking database. This database can also be used to verify that interchanges and documents are successfully sent or received by BizTalk Server, or it can provide information for reports such as transmission times or receipt responses.

Defining document tracking and logging parameters for the Tracking database

In BizTalk Server Administration, you can select whether interchanges and documents are tracked. For more information about how to configure tracking settings for a server group, see "To configure tracking properties for a server group" later in this chapter. For more information about document tracking, see "Using BizTalk Document Tracking" in Chapter 13, "Tracking Documents." If you enable tracking, the following options are available:

- **Log incoming interchange.** With this setting, you can specify that documents received by BizTalk Server are stored in the Tracking database. Stored incoming documents provide an activity record for dispute resolution. This is selected by default.

- **Log outgoing interchange.** With this setting, you can specify that documents sent by BizTalk Server are stored in the Tracking database. This is selected by default.

- **Log the original MIME-encoded message.** With this setting, you can specify that MIME-encoded documents are stored in the Tracking database in their original message format before they are decoded. This is not selected by default.

To configure tracking properties for a server group

1. In BizTalk Server Administration, expand **Microsoft BizTalk Server 2000** and click the server group that you want to configure.

2. On the **Action** menu, click **Properties**.

   The **BizTalk Server Group Properties** dialog box appears.

3. Click the **Tracking** tab.

4. Select the **Enable document tracking** check box and any of the following options that you want to use:
   - Select the **Log incoming interchange** check box to log incoming interchanges.
   - Select the **Log outgoing interchange** check box to log outgoing interchanges.
   - Select the **Log the original MIME-encoded message** check box to log MIME-encoded messages.

5. Click **OK**.

❦ Caution

- You can disable document tracking by clearing the **Enable document tracking** check box. However, you will lose important BizTalk Server 2000 functionality if you do this. For more information about tracking, see "Understanding Tracking Settings for a Server Group" in Chapter 13, "Tracking Documents."

📝 **Note**

- If the **Enable document tracking** check box is not selected, the **Log incoming interchange**, **Log outgoing interchange**, and **Log the original MIME-encoded message** check boxes are unavailable.

To manually restore the Tracking database

1. On the **Start** menu, point to **Programs**, point to **Microsoft SQL Server**, and then click **Enterprise Manager**.

2. Expand **Microsoft SQL Servers**, expand **SQL Server Group**, and then expand the server on which you want to restore the database.

3. Click **Databases**.

4. On the **Action** menu, click **New Database**.

   The **Database Properties** dialog box appears.

5. On the **General** tab, in the **Name** box, type a name for the Tracking database and click **OK**.

6. On the **Start** menu, point to **Programs**, point to **Microsoft SQL Server**, and then click **Query Analyzer**.

   The **Connect to SQL Server** dialog box appears.

7. Click **OK**.

8. If you have Microsoft SQL Server 7.0 installed, in the Query window, in the **DB** list, click the name of the new Tracking database.

   –Or–

   If you have Microsoft SQL Server 2000 installed, on the **Objects** tab, click the name of the new Tracking database.

9. Click the **Load SQL Script** 📂 button.

10. Browse to **\Program Files\Microsoft BizTalk Server\Setup**.

11. Click **BTS_Tracking_Schema.sql** and click **Open**.

12. Click the **Execute Query** button.

13. Click the **Load SQL Script** button.

14. Verify that you are in the folder **\Program Files\Microsoft BizTalk Server\Setup**.

15. Click **BTS_Reporting.sql** and click **Open**.

16. Click the **Execute Query** button.

17. Click the **Load SQL Script** button.

18. Verify that you are in the folder **\Program Files\Microsoft BizTalk Server\Setup**.

19. Click **BTS_Tracking_Logic.sql** and click **Open**.

20. Click the **Execute Query** button.

21. Click the **Load SQL Script** button.

22. Verify that you are in the folder **\Program Files\Microsoft BizTalk Server\Setup**.

23. Click **BTS_WorkflowEvents.sql** and click **Open**.

24. Click the **Execute Query** button.

25. Click the **Load SQL Script** button.

26. Verify that you are in the folder **\Program Files\Microsoft BizTalk Server\Setup**.

27. Click **BTS_WorkflowSchema.sql** and click **Open**.

28. Click the **Execute Query** button.

29. Close SQL Query Analyzer and SQL Server Enterprise Manager.

Caution

- When you manually restore the Tracking database, you lose all data. If you need to keep this data, back up the data before you restore the Tracking database.

Note

- Use this procedure if the Tracking database becomes corrupted or damaged.

To shut down the BizTalk Server Interchange Application

1. On the **Start** menu, point to **Settings**, click **Control Panel**, double-click **Administrative Tools**, and then double-click **Component Services**.

2. Expand **Component Services**, expand **Computers**, expand **My Computer**, and then expand **COM+ Applications**.

3. Click **BizTalk Server Interchange Application**.

4. On the **Action** menu, click **Shut down**.

Note

- You can shut down the BizTalk Server Interchange Application from a remote server. If you do this, expand the *<remotecomputername>* instead of **My Computer** in step 2.

To remove the Tracking and Shared Queue databases

1. On the **Start** menu, point to **Programs**, point to **Microsoft SQL Server**, and then click **Enterprise Manager**.

2. Expand **Microsoft SQL Servers**, expand **SQL Server Group**, and then expand the individual server that contains the databases that you want to delete.

3. Expand the **Databases** folder and click the database that you want to delete.

4. On the **Action** menu, click **Delete.**

   The **Delete Database** dialog box appears.

5. Click **Yes**.

✎ Note

- The default name for the Tracking database is InterchangeDTA. The default name for the Shared Queue database is InterchangeSQ.

Related Topics

"Administration Cache" in the following section

"Groups and Servers" in the following section

"To open Component Services" later in this chapter

Groups and Servers

In a data-exchange environment that supports the processing of a large number of documents, multiple servers and databases might be required. Businesses must have a way to centralize and manage document exchange.

Microsoft BizTalk Server 2000 centralizes document exchange by assembling servers into groups and managing and configuring these server groups by using BizTalk Server Administration.

BizTalk Server Groups

A server group is the key organizing principle in BizTalk Server Administration. Server groups are collections of individual servers that are centrally managed, configured, and monitored.

Servers in a BizTalk server group have in common:

- A Shared Queue database that persists all documents until they are successfully processed.

- A Tracking database that is used to log document and interchange activity and to run reports.

- Receive functions. For more information about receive functions, see "Receive Functions" later in this chapter.

- All components that the server requires when processing documents and interchanges, such as transport components, application integration components (AICs), and so on.

A central BizTalk Messaging Management database manages multiple groups and servers. Thus, they share the same configuration information. This configuration information specifies the document-processing logic for the servers. For more information about the relationship between groups and servers, see "Relationship between Groups and Servers" later in this chapter. Specify the same BizTalk Messaging Management database for each server installation so that you can remotely administer each server and group from the administration console. Also, if you are setting up multiple server groups for scalability and improved performance, use only one central BizTalk Messaging Management database. Otherwise, these servers cannot share the same BizTalk Messaging Management configuration.

To add a server group

1. In BizTalk Server Administration, click **Microsoft BizTalk Server 2000**.

2. On the **Action** menu, point to **New** and click **Group**.

   The **New Group** dialog box appears.

3. In the **Group name** box, type the name of the new server group.

4. In the **Tracking database** area:

   - In the **Tracking database name** box, type the name of the Tracking database for this server group.

   - In the **Tracking SQL Server name** box, type the name of the server on which the Tracking database for this server group is stored.

   - In the **User name** and **Password** boxes, type the Microsoft SQL Server logon user name and password that are used to connect to the server on which the Tracking database is stored.

     User name is a required field. **Password** is an optional field. Leave this field blank if a password is not required to connect to the server.

5. In the **Shared Queue database** area:

   - In the **Shared Queue database name** box, type the name of the Shared Queue database for this server group.

   - In the **Shared Queue SQL Server name** box, type the name of the server on which the Shared Queue database for this server group is stored.

   - In the **User name** and **Password** boxes, type the SQL Server logon user name and password that are used to connect to the server on which the Shared Queue database is stored.

     User name is a required field. **Password** is an optional field. Leave this field blank if a password is not required to connect to the server.

6. Click **OK**.

◆ **Important**

- Do not use any of the following characters in the name of the server group:

  ` ! @ # $ % ^ & * ( ) + = [ ] { } | \\ ;\ " ' < > , . ?

  For more information about invalid characters, see "WMI Overview" earlier in this chapter.

✎ **Note**

- This procedure creates a server group. To configure the server group with additional settings, see the following procedure, "To configure general properties for a server group."

To configure general properties for a server group

1. In BizTalk Server Administration, expand **Microsoft BizTalk Server 2000** and click the server group you want to configure.

2. On the **Action** menu, click **Properties**.

   The **BizTalk Server Group Properties** dialog box appears.

3. In the **SMTP host** box, type the Simple Mail Transfer Protocol (SMTP) host name that this server group uses.

   This field is optional. Use this configuration if you use BizTalk Server to send documents to a trading partner or to an internal application by using SMTP.

4. In the **Reliable messaging reply-to URL** box, type the URL this server group uses to receive reliable messaging delivery receipts by using one of the following supported protocols: File, Message Queuing, HTTP, HTTP/S, or SMTP.

For the following transport	Use this prefix
File	file://
Message Queuing	queue://Direct=OS:*\<servername>\<queuename>*
Hyper Text Transport Protocol (http)	http://
Hyper Text Transport Protocol Secure (https)	https://
SMTP	mailto:

   If you specify Message Queuing, you must use a format name. In addition, queue:// must precede the format name. For more information about format names, see "Available Receive Functions" later in this chapter.

5. In the **Messaging Management object cache refresh interval (seconds)** list, click the number of seconds between cache updates for the server group.

   By default, the server updates this cache every 50 seconds.

6. In the **Proxy server** area, select the **Use a proxy server** check box if you want to configure BizTalk Server to connect to the Internet through a proxy server.

    Enter the address and port of the proxy server that you want to use.

7. Click **OK**.

8. Perform the following steps only if you made any changes in the **Proxy server** area:

    *   Stop each server in the group for which you configured the general properties. For more information about stopping a server, see "To stop a server in a group" later in this chapter.

    *   Start each server in the group for which you configured the general properties. For more information about starting a server, see "To start a server in a group" later in this chapter.

◆ Important

*   The **SMTP host** field is optional. However, you must configure this field if you plan to use SMTP as a transport service in BizTalk Messaging Manager. For example, you cannot choose SMTP as primary or backup transport in BizTalk Messaging Manager unless you have the SMTP host configured here.

✎ Notes

*   Reliable messaging in BizTalk Server is BizTalk Framework 2.0-compliant. For more information about reliable messaging and BizTalk Framework 2.0, go to the Microsoft Web site (www.microsoft.com/biztalk/) and search for BizTalk Framework 2.0.

*   When you configure the **Reliable messaging reply-to URL**, use an active server page (ASP) or message queue with a receive function monitoring it. If you do not want to configure your own ASP page initially, use the ReceiveStandard.asp file shipped with BizTalk Server. You can find this sample ASP page in \Program Files\Microsoft BizTalk Server\SDK\Messaging Samples\Receive Scripts. This page is designed to take posts and submit them to BizTalk Server. For more information about implementing a secure site, go to the MSDN Online Library Web site (msdn.microsoft.com/library/default.asp) and search for the article "Implementing a Secure Site with ASP."

*   If you specify the URL to include *localhost* in the **Reliable messaging reply-to URL** box, the receive function will not work properly. Do not specify *localhost* in this field.

*   The response to an HTTP post is expected to be text. If the response requires binary data, encode the binary data using MIME or UUEncode.

To configure the parser order for a server group

1. In BizTalk Server Administration, expand **Microsoft BizTalk Server 2000** and click the server group for which you want to configure the parser order.

2. On the **Action** menu, click **Properties**.

    The **BizTalk Server Group Properties** dialog box appears.

3. Click the **Parsers** tab.

   The parsers are listed in the **Arrange the server call sequence** box in the following order:

   - BizTalk.ParserXML.1
   - BizTalk.ParserEdifact.1
   - BizTalk.ParserX12.1
   - BizTalk.ParserFFile.1

   You can improve BizTalk Server performance by moving the most commonly used parsers closer to the top of the list.

4. In the **Arrange the server call sequence** box, click the parser that you want to move and click either the up or down arrow to move the selected parser higher or lower in the server call sequence.

5. When the parsers are arranged in the order you want, click **OK**.

 Note

- The **Refresh** button picks up new parsers registered in the local registry. If you want a new parser to appear in the **Arrange the server call sequence** box, you must click the **Refresh** button on the server on which the parser is registered.

To delete a server group

1. In BizTalk Server Administration, expand **Microsoft BizTalk Server 2000** and expand the server group that you want to delete.

2. Click a server in the server group that you want to delete.

3. On the **Action** menu, click **Stop**.

   Repeat steps 2 and 3 for each server in the group until you have stopped all servers in the group.

4. Click the server group.

5. On the **Action** menu, click **Delete**.

   The **User Action Confirmation** dialog box appears.

6. Click **Yes**.

 Notes

- You cannot delete a server group that contains one or more running servers. To stop the servers and delete the server group, you must have Windows 2000 Administrator privileges for all the servers in the group.

- The Tracking and Shared Queue databases associated with the server group remain in Microsoft SQL Server even after you delete the group. To remove the Tracking and Shared Queue databases, you must manually delete them. For more information about how to delete these databases, see "To remove the Tracking and Shared Queue databases" earlier in this chapter.

Related Topics

"Administration Cache" earlier in this chapter

"Available Receive Functions" later in this chapter

"Managing the BizTalk Messaging Management Database" earlier in this chapter

"Shared Queue Database" earlier in this chapter

"To remove the Tracking and Shared Queue databases" earlier in this chapter

"To start a server in a group" later in this chapter

"To stop a server in a group" later in this chapter

"Tracking Database" earlier in this chapter

"Using the IBizTalkParserComponent Interface" in Chapter 15, "Creating Custom Components"

"WMI Overview" earlier in this chapter

Relationship between Groups and Servers

Each installation of BizTalk Server 2000 must have at least one server group. The relationship between groups and servers is defined by the following:

- An individual server can belong to only one server group.

- All servers in a group use the same Shared Queue and receive functions.

- All servers in a group share the same components, such as transport components, application integration components (AICs), and so on, to process interchanges and documents.

The following illustration shows the relationship between server groups in BizTalk Server 2000. Servers 1-6 are installed with Microsoft BizTalk Server 2000. Servers A-D are installed with Microsoft SQL Server and are dedicated to database management. Although servers A-D are dedicated to either the Tracking or the Shared Queue database, the BizTalk Messaging Management database can reside on one of these servers because it is relatively small and is not processor intensive. It is strongly recommended that your Shared Queue and Tracking databases reside on two separate servers dedicated to database management, and that you use a single central BizTalk Messaging Management database for all server groups.

Logical configuration of groups and servers

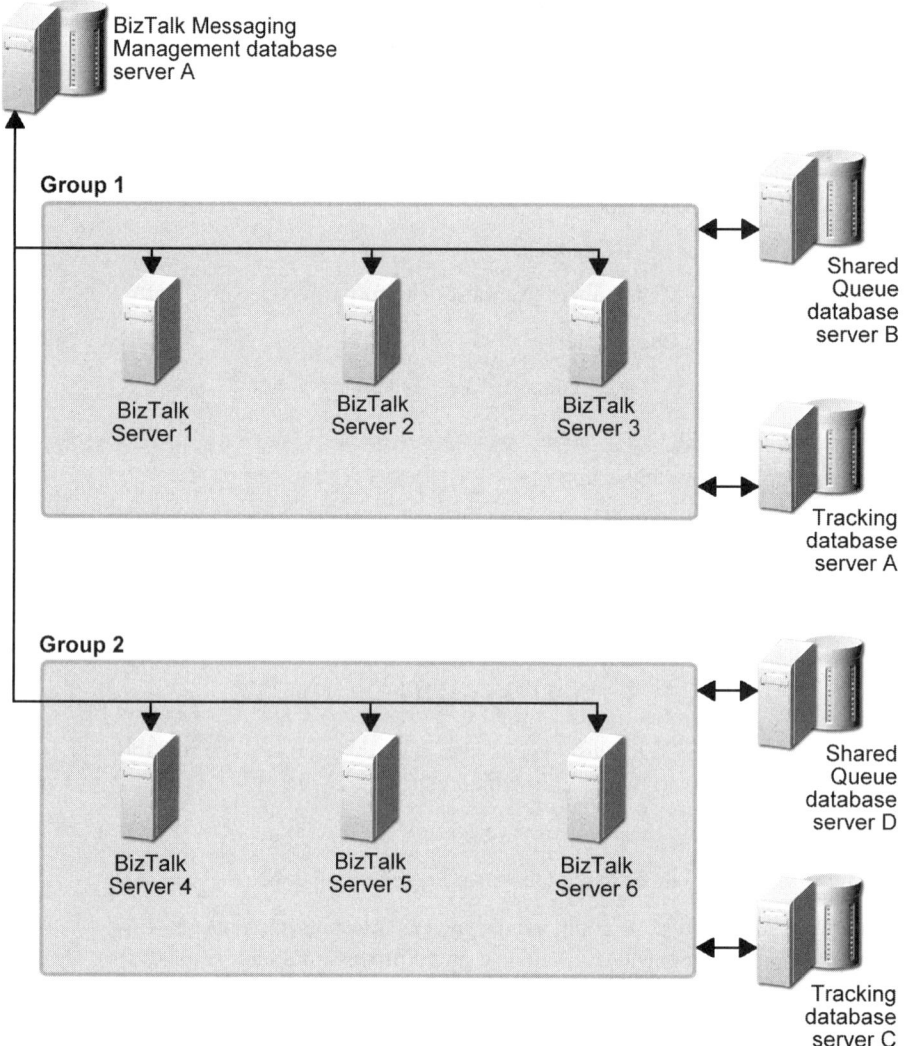

To add a server to a group

1. In BizTalk Server Administration, expand **Microsoft BizTalk Server 2000** and click the server group to which you want to add a server.

2. On the **Action** menu, point to **New** and click **Server**.

   The **Add a BizTalk Server** dialog box appears.

3. In the **BizTalk Server name** box, type the name of an existing server on which you have a complete installation of BizTalk Server 2000.

4. Click **OK**.

Note

- To view the global properties for the server group to which you added the server, right-click the group and click **Properties**.

To delete a server from a group

1. In BizTalk Server Administration, expand **Microsoft BizTalk Server 2000**, expand the server group that contains the server that you want to delete, and then click the server.

2. On the **Action** menu, click **Stop**.

   The server finishes processing all current interchanges and documents.

3. On the **Action** menu, click **Delete**.

   The **User Action Confirmation** dialog box appears.

4. Click **Yes**.

Note

- You cannot delete a server from a server group if a receive function(s) points to it to process documents. You can edit the receive function(s) to point to other servers, or you can delete the receive function(s) if it no longer can be used.

To configure a server in a group

1. In BizTalk Server Administration, expand **Microsoft BizTalk Server 2000**, expand the server group that contains the server that you want to configure, and then click the server.

2. On the **Action** menu, click **Stop**.

   You cannot change server configuration settings while the server is running.

3. On the **Action** menu, click **Properties**.

   The *<Computername>* **Properties** dialog box appears.

4. In the **Maximum number of receive function threads allowed** box, type a number in the range from 1 through 128.

   The default value is 4. For more information about how to configure this option, see "Understanding Server Properties" later in this chapter.

5. If you want the server to process items in the Work queue, select the **Participate in work-item processing** check box.

   When this check box is selected, the server processes documents in the Work queue. Clear this check box if you do not want the server to process documents in the Work queue. For more information about how to configure this option, see "Understanding Server Properties" later in this chapter.

6. In the **Maximum number of worker threads per processor allowed** box, type a number in the range from 1 through 128.

   The default value is 4. For more information about how to configure this option, see "Understanding Server Properties" later in this chapter.

7. In the **Time between BizTalk Server Scheduler calls (milliseconds)** box, type a number in the range from 1 through 4,294,967,295.

   The default value is 200. For more information about how to configure this option, see "Understanding Server Properties" later in this chapter.

8. Click **OK**.

9. Right-click the server you configured and click **Start**.

📝 **Note**

- If the **Participate in work-item processing** check box is not selected, the **Maximum number of worker threads per processor allowed** and **Time between BizTalk Server Scheduler calls (milliseconds)** check boxes are unavailable.

Related Topic

"To free interchanges from a server" later in this chapter

Group Status States

BizTalk Server Administration enumerates server groups and specifies whether each group can connect to the Tracking and/or the Shared Queue database. When you click **Microsoft BizTalk Server 2000**, the group states appear under the status bar in the details pane. The group states are:

- **Connected.** Specifies that the group is connected to the Tracking and Shared Queue databases.

- **Tracking connection failed.** Specifies that the group is not connected to the Tracking database.

- **Shared Queue connection failed.** Specifies that the group is not connected to the Shared Queue database.

- **Tracking and Shared Queue connections failed.** Specifies that the group is not connected to the Tracking and Shared Queue databases.

BizTalk Servers

A server in a server group hosts the appropriate BizTalk Messaging Services functionality—such as data translation, encryption, digital signing, and document tracking—to manage document exchange between other servers and applications that are external to the BizTalk server group. Each server queues and dequeues incoming and outgoing documents to the Shared Queue database, calling the appropriate Component Object Model (COM) methods to transform, serialize, sign, encrypt or decrypt, and transport documents. For applications that do not use the BizTalk Server COM interfaces, BizTalk Server 2000 uses receive functions to receive data.

Depending on your business needs, you can configure all servers in a group exactly the same. This allows you to add and remove servers in a group easily. Or you can configure some servers in a group to be dedicated to receiving documents. For more information, see "BizTalk Server Groups" and "Relationship between Groups and Servers" earlier in this chapter.

Understanding Server Properties

When you configure a server in a group, you must balance maximizing throughput and server performance. For more information about configuring a server in a group, see "To configure a server in a group" earlier in this chapter. Your business needs, server capacity, and network bandwidth are some of the factors that influence how you configure server properties. It is highly recommended that you experiment with different combinations in a test setting that simulates your production environment to determine what works best for your installation.

Maximum number of receive function threads allowed

The maximum number of receive function threads is set on a per-processor basis. The range for this option is 1 through 128. Adjust this number to optimize the performance of the receive functions that are running on the server. In most cases, increasing the number of receive function threads increases the throughput of the receive functions on the server.

Participate in work-item processing

When the **Participate in work-item processing** check box is selected, the server processes documents in the Work queue. When this check box is cleared, the server does not process any documents in the Work queue. There are two situations in which you might want to turn off this option. The first situation is if you receive messages from a message queue. Currently, Message Queuing supports only local transactional reads. This means that your queues must be on a server installed with Microsoft BizTalk Server 2000 and that you can configure only one server in a group to read from those queues. To allow the server where the message queue resides to receive as fast as possible, clear the **Participate in work-item processing** check box.

The second situation in which you might want to turn off this option is when you want to maximize performance for BizTalk Server clusters. For example, you might want to dedicate one of the servers in the BizTalk Server group to handle administration tasks.

Maximum number of worker threads per processor allowed

The maximum number of worker threads is set on a per-processor basis. The range for this option is 1 through 128. A low setting could cause a bottleneck in BizTalk Server in a high traffic situation. A high setting might not have detrimental effects, but it could cause performance degradation.

The **Maximum number of worker threads per processor allowed** and the **Time between BizTalk Server Scheduler calls** settings are two factors that influence how much traffic there is to the Microsoft SQL Server databases. You can limit the traffic to the SQL databases by setting the number low for **Maximum number of worker threads per processor allowed** and higher for **Time between BizTalk Server Scheduler calls**. Likewise, you can increase the traffic to the databases by increasing the number for the maximum number of worker threads and decreasing the settings for the time between scheduler calls.

⬚ Note

- Clear the **Participate in work-item processing** check box if you do not want to process any work items on this server. Do not set the **Maximum number of worker threads per processor allowed** option to zero.

Time between BizTalk Server Scheduler calls (milliseconds)

The range for the **Time between BizTalk Server Scheduler calls** area is 1 through 4,294,967,295. There is a thread that polls for available items in the Work queue. The **Time between BizTalk Server Scheduler calls** controls how often the thread polls the Work queue. If you do not receive a lot of data, keep this number high. If you receive a lot of data, you might want to decrease this number.

To start a server in a group

1. In BizTalk Server Administration, expand **Microsoft BizTalk Server 2000**, expand the server group that contains the server that you want to start, and then click the server.

2. On the **Action** menu, click **Start**.

⬚ Notes

- Starting a server in a server group means starting the BizTalk Messaging Service on the server. After the BizTalk Messaging Service is running, the server can receive, transmit, process, and track documents that are queued to the Microsoft SQL Server databases.

- The **Start** option is available only if the server is stopped. If the server is running, the command is unavailable.

To stop a server in a group

1. In BizTalk Server Administration, expand **Microsoft BizTalk Server 2000**, expand the server group that contains the server that you want to stop, and then click the server.

2. On the **Action** menu, click **Stop**.

📝 Notes

- Stopping a server in a server group means stopping the BizTalk Messaging Service on the server. After the BizTalk Messaging Service is stopped, the server cannot receive, transmit, process, or track documents that are queued to the Microsoft SQL Server databases.

- If you want to redistribute interchanges associated with a server that you have stopped, see the following procedure "To free interchanges from a server."

To free interchanges from a server

This procedure is used to free interchanges from a server so that the interchanges can be redistributed to other servers in the group if the original server is stopped or taken offline.

1. In BizTalk Server Administration, expand **Microsoft BizTalk Server 2000**, expand the server group that contains the server on which you want to free interchanges, and then click the server.

2. On the **Action** menu, click **Stop**.

3. On the **Action** menu, point to **All Tasks** and click **Free Interchanges**.

Related Topic

"Administration Cache" earlier in this chapter

Server States

BizTalk Server Administration enumerates the servers in a server group and returns the list of servers. BizTalk Server Administration can return the following states for servers under the status bar in the details pane:

- **Running.** Specifies that the server is running.

- **Access denied.** Specifies that you do not have Windows 2000 Administrator privileges on a server.

- **Error.** Specifies if a server registered with a server group has had BizTalk Server 2000 removed.

- **Stopped.** Specifies if an administrator has stopped a server.

- **Unknown.** Specifies if a server registered with a server group is unavailable for an unknown reason. When this occurs, it is likely that you have lost connectivity with the server.

Administration Privileges

To view BizTalk Server Administration, you must be a member of the BizTalk Server Administrators group. If you are logged on as a non-BizTalk Server Administrator, you cannot view items inside the Microsoft BizTalk Server 2000 folder. If you are a member of the BizTalk Server Administrators group, but you are not a member of the Microsoft Windows 2000 Administrators group, you can perform only the following tasks:

- Add and remove server groups

- View and modify group properties

- Manage all queues and their entries

- Add and remove receive functions

- View and modify receive function properties

Additionally, if you are administering a server group that contains three servers, for example, Server_1, Server_2, and Server_3, you must have Windows 2000 Administrator privileges on all three servers. If the Windows 2000 Administrator privileges have been changed on Server_1, and you no longer have administrator privileges, the administration console returns a list of all three servers associated with the group and lists the state of each server. The state of Server_1 is returned as Access Denied.

If you are a member of both the BizTalk Server Administrators group and the Windows 2000 Administrators group, you can perform the following additional tasks:

- Add servers to and remove servers from a server group

- View and modify server properties

- View server status

- Free interchanges on a server

During setup, the user who runs the BizTalk Server installation is added to the BizTalk Server Administrators group. You can add other users to the BizTalk Server Administrators group. For more information, see "To add users to the BizTalk Server Administrators group" earlier in this chapter.

Handling Server Errors

You can configure error handling in BizTalk Server 2000 at the server level through Windows 2000 Event Viewer, which is included in BizTalk Server Administration. The Windows 2000 Event Viewer appears in the console tree of the administration console.

Logging events

The Windows 2000 Event Viewer creates a log that contains information about hardware, software, and system problems. From the administration console, you can customize the Event Viewer to show application and XLANG Scheduler errors that are specific to BizTalk Server 2000, which makes troubleshooting for BizTalk Server efficient.

For more information about Event Viewer in Windows 2000 Server Help, in the Event Viewer chapter, see "Using Event Viewer."

Note

- All application errors related to BizTalk Server 2000 are defined as BizTalk Server or XLANG Scheduler errors.

To configure Event Viewer for BizTalk Server errors

1. In BizTalk Server Administration, expand **Event Viewer**.

2. Click **Application**.

3. On the **Action** menu, click **Properties**.

   The **Application Properties** dialog box appears.

4. Click the **Filter** tab.

5. In the **Event source** list, click one of the following:

   - **BizTalk Server.** This option filters the event sources for error messages that are related to BizTalk Messaging Services.

   - **XLANG Scheduler.** This option filters the event sources for error messages that are related to BizTalk Orchestration Services.

6. Click **OK** to close the **Application Properties** dialog box.

To view application-related errors in Event Viewer

1. In BizTalk Server Administration, expand **Event Viewer**.

2. Click **Application**.

   Application error messages are listed in the details pane.

3. Click a message in the details pane.

4. On the **Action** menu, click **Properties**.

Note

- This procedure assumes you configured Event Viewer to display only BizTalk Server and XLANG Scheduler errors. For more information about how to display BizTalk Server and XLANG Scheduler errors, see the previous procedure, "To configure Event Viewer for BizTalk Server errors."

Receive Functions

If you need to receive documents from a receive location and submit them to BizTalk Server, you can configure submit calls programmatically. For more information about submit calls, see "Submitting" in Chapter 10, "Submitting Documents." Or you can configure receive functions to process the data. For example, if you need to receive documents from a business organization or application that cannot communicate directly to BizTalk Server through a COM interface, you can use a receive function to submit the documents to BizTalk Server.

Or, if you need to receive from a message queue, you can use a receive function to submit the document to BizTalk Server. BizTalk Server 2000 supports two types of receive functions: File and Message Queuing.

You can create a generic receive function for BizTalk Server 2000 in the administration console in which you define the receive function name, document definition, and so on. For more information about advanced properties for receive functions, see "Understanding Receive Function Advanced Properties" later in this chapter.

The following illustration shows the relationship between the sending business application, the file system, and a generic BizTalk Server receive function.

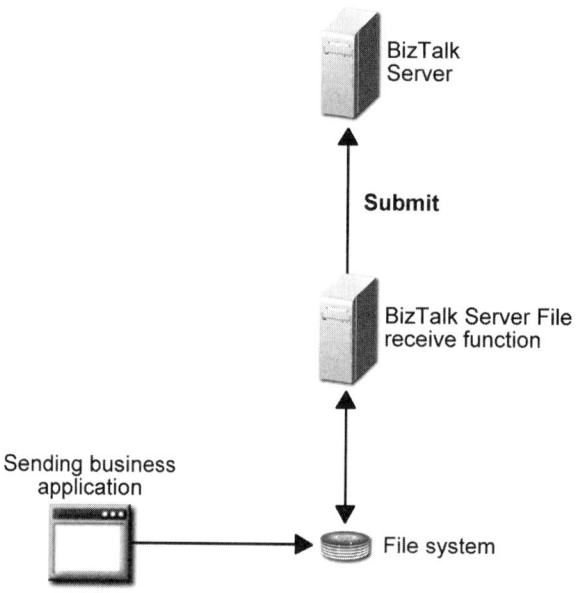

Available Receive Functions

Two types of receive functions are available in BizTalk Server: File and Message Queuing. Your business practices determine which type of receive function you use and when.

File receive function

A File receive function is activated when there is activity in the directory that the receive function monitors. To use a File receive function, you must be able to modify the directory. The File receive function removes the files from the directory and submits them to BizTalk Server 2000.

Message Queuing receive function

A Message Queuing receive function is activated based on activity in a message queue. This receive function extracts the interchange or document from the queue and submits it to BizTalk Server 2000.

When you define the polling location for the message queue, use a format name instead of a path. BizTalk Server is designed to work with raw Message Queuing application programming interfaces (APIs), and the API calls work only with the format name property. Use the following format name when you configure a Message Queuing receive function:

- **Direct=OS:**<*servername*>\<*queuename*>

📝 **Note**

- For more information about Message Queuing and format name, go to the MSDN Online Library Web site (msdn.microsoft.com/library/default.asp) and browse to the Platform SDK, Getting Started, Contents of the Platform SDK, Message Queuing Services page.

To add a File receive function

1. In BizTalk Server Administration, expand **Microsoft BizTalk Server 2000** and expand the server group to which you want to add the File receive function.

2. Click **Receive Functions**.

3. On the **Action** menu, point to **New** and click **File Receive Function**.

   The **Add a File Receive Function** dialog box appears.

4. In the **Name** box, type the name of the File receive function.

5. In the **Comment** box, add a brief description (optional).

6. In the **Server on which the receive function will run** list, click the name of a server in the group.

7. In the **File types to poll for** box, type the extension of the files that BizTalk Server receives.

   The file type extension must be written in the following syntax:

   *.ext

   For example: **.xml

8. In the **Polling location** box, type either the logical path or the universal naming convention (UNC) path to the directory this receive function uses as the file receiving location.

9. In the **Preprocessor** list, click the name of the custom preprocessor.

   Leave this blank if you are not using a custom preprocessor.

925

10. In the **User name** and **Password** boxes, type a valid user name and password to connect to the file receive location (optional).

    This is required only when the receive location is protected and a valid user name and password are required to connect to the server.

11. To customize the receive function for non-self-routing documents, or to specify openness or pass-through options, click **Advanced**.

    For more information about advanced options, see "To configure advanced properties for File or Message Queuing receive functions" later in this chapter.

☑ Notes

- This procedure creates a File receive function with the default settings. To configure the File receive function with additional settings, see the following procedure, "To configure a File receive function: General tab."

- If you want to poll for more than one file type, use any standard wildcard format.

  For example: *.* or *.x?l

- If you configure one or more File receive functions to monitor the same directory, use three-letter file extensions. If you use file extensions of more than three letters, verify that the first three letters are unique.

  For example: *.xml, *.1xml, *.12xml

- File receive functions cannot process read-only files.

- Verify that each receive function that you create has a unique name. You cannot assign identical names to receive functions.

To configure a File receive function: General tab

1. In BizTalk Server Administration, expand **Microsoft BizTalk Server 2000**, expand the server group for which you want to configure a File receive function, and then expand **Receive Functions**.

2. Click the File receive function that you want to configure.

3. On the **Action** menu, click **Properties**.

   The **Properties** dialog box appears.

4. In the **Comment** box, add a brief description (optional).

5. In the **Security** area, in the **User name** and **Password** boxes, type a valid user name and password to connect to this receive function.

   This is required only when the receive location is protected and a valid user name and password are required to connect to the server.

6. If you want to temporarily shut down the functionality of this receive function, select the **Disable receive function** check box and click **Yes** to confirm your choice.

Note

- File receive functions cannot process read-only files.

To configure a File receive function: Services tab

1. In BizTalk Server Administration, expand **Microsoft BizTalk Server 2000**, expand the server group for which you want to configure a File receive function, and then expand **Receive Functions**.

2. Click the File receive function that you want to configure.

3. On the **Action** menu, click **Properties**.

   The **Properties** dialog box appears.

4. Click the **Services** tab.

5. In the **Server on which the receive function will run** list, click the server name.

6. In the **Polling location** box, type either the logical path or the universal naming convention (UNC) path to the directory this receive function uses as the file receive location.

7. In the **File types to poll for** box, type the extension of the files that BizTalk Server receives.

   The file type extension must be written in the following syntax:

   .ext

   For example: *.doc

8. In the **Preprocessor** list, click the name of the custom preprocessor.

   Leave this blank if you are not using a custom preprocessor.

9. Click **OK**.

Notes

- If you want to receive multiple file types, use any standard wildcard format.

  For example: *.*

- If you configure one or more File receive functions to monitor the same directory, use three-letter file extensions. If you use file extensions of more than three letters, verify that the first three letters are unique.

  For example: *.xml, *.1xml, *.12xml

- File receive functions cannot process read-only files.

To add a Message Queuing receive function

1. In BizTalk Server Administration, expand **Microsoft BizTalk Server 2000** and expand the server group for which you want to add a Message Queuing receive function.

2. Click **Receive Functions**.

3. On the **Action** menu, point to **New** and click **Message Queuing Receive Function**.
   The **Add a Message Queuing Receive Function** dialog box appears.

4. In the **Name** box, type the name of the Message Queuing receive function.

5. In the **Comment** box, add a brief description (optional).

6. In the **Server on which the receive function will run** list, click the name of a server in the group.

7. In the **Polling location** box, type the server and Message Queuing names that this receive function uses as the receive location.
   For example:
   Direct=OS:<*servername*>\<*queuename*>
   Select the processing server on which the queue resides. Transactional messaging is supported only by local queues.

8. In the **Preprocessor** list, click the custom preprocessor.
   Leave this blank if you are not using a custom preprocessor.

9. In the **User name** and **Password** boxes, type a valid user name and password to connect to Message Queuing.
   This is required only when the receive location is not on the server processing interchanges and documents.

10. To customize the receive function for non-self-routing documents, or to specify openness or pass-through options, click **Advanced**.
    For more information about advanced options, see "To configure advanced properties for File or Message Queuing receive functions" later in this chapter.

◆ Important

- Do not prefix the <*servername*>\<*queuename*> with queue:// in the **Polling location** box. This is different from the general properties for a server group for which you use queue://. For more information about Message Queuing syntax, see "Available Receive Functions" earlier in this chapter. For more information about properties for a server group, see "To configure general properties for a server group" earlier in this chapter.

✎ Notes

- For more information about custom preprocessing, see "Custom Preprocessors" later in this chapter.

- A Message Queuing receive function will not work unless the user name and password supplied to the server on which BizTalk Server is running has read permission on the queue.

- To ensure reliability, you must use transactional queues. If you use nontransactional queues, messages might be lost. For more information about transactional queues, go to the MSDN Online Library Web site (msdn.microsoft.com/library/default.asp) and search on the keywords "Message Queuing."

- Verify that each receive function that you create has a unique name. You cannot assign identical names to receive functions.

To configure a Message Queuing receive function: General tab

1. In BizTalk Server Administration, expand **Microsoft BizTalk Server 2000**, expand the server group for which you want to configure a Message Queuing receive function, and then expand **Receive Functions.**

2. Click the Message Queuing receive function that you want to configure.

3. On the **Action** menu, click **Properties**.

   The **Properties** dialog box appears.

4. In the **Comment** box, add a brief description (optional).

5. In the **Security** area, in the **User name** and **Password** boxes, type a valid user name and password to connect to the Message Queue.

   This is required only when the receive location is not on the processing server.

6. If you want to temporarily shut down the functionality of this receive function, select the **Disable receive function** check box and click **Yes** to confirm your choice.

To configure a Message Queuing receive function: Services tab

1. In BizTalk Server Administration, expand **Microsoft BizTalk Server 2000**, expand the server group for which you want to configure a Message Queuing receive function, and then expand **Receive Functions**.

2. Click the Message Queuing receive function that you want to configure.

3. On the **Action** menu, click **Properties**.

   The **Properties** dialog box appears.

4. Click the **Services** tab.

5. In the **Server on which the receive function will run** list, click the server name.

6. In the **Polling location** box, type the server and Message Queuing names that this receive function uses as the receive location.

   For example:

   Direct=OS:<*servername*>\<*queuename*>

7. In the **Preprocessor** list, click the custom preprocessor.

   Leave this option blank if you are not using a custom preprocessor.

8. Click **OK**.

◆ **Important**

- Do not prefix the *<servername>\<queuename>* with queue:// in the **Polling location** box. This is different from the general properties for a server group for which you use queue://. For more information about Message Queuing syntax, see "Available Receive Functions" earlier in this chapter. For more information about server group properties, see "To configure general properties for a server group" earlier in this chapter.

📝 **Note**

- For more information about custom preprocessing, see the following topic, "Custom Preprocessors."

Custom Preprocessors

If you have documents that need to be processed before they are submitted to BizTalk Server, you can create a custom preprocessor and configure the receive function to call the preprocessor. For information about creating a custom preprocessor, Microsoft Visual Basic programmers should see "IBTSCustomProcess Object" in Chapter 10, "Submitting Documents." For information about creating a custom preprocessor, C++ programmers should see "IBTSCustomProcess Object" in Chapter 10, "Submitting Documents."

If you send compressed data and need to decompress it before submitting it to BizTalk Server for processing, configure the receive function to call the custom preprocessor to decompress the data. For more information, see "Preprocessing Documents in a Receive Function" in Chapter 10, "Submitting Documents."

Multiple Instances of Receive Function Types

There can be multiple instances of a receive function. For example, if multiple business applications use a File receive function to submit documents and interchanges to BizTalk Server 2000, you can configure either a single instance or multiple instances of the File receive function.

📝 **Note**

- Verify that each of the receive functions that you create has a unique name. You cannot assign identical names to receive functions.

Understanding Receive Functions and Document Routing

When you configure a receive function, determine whether the documents received by the receive function are self-routing or non-self-routing. Self-routing documents contain all the necessary routing information; non-self-routing documents lack some or all routing information.

Self-routing documents

Self-routing documents have all routing information—the source organization identifier, the destination organization identifier, and the document definition—defined in the routing tags that are defined by the document specification or hard-coded in the document, as in the case of X12 and EDIFACT. Any document for which you can create a specification in BizTalk Editor can be configured as a self-routing document. Common types of self-routing documents are XML, X12, and EDIFACT. You do not need to configure any advanced properties in the receive function if a document is self-routing, unless you want to override the data provided in the document.

If the source or destination organization qualifiers or the document definition is missing from the document, it is placed in the Suspended queue. Additionally, if you do not specify a source or destination organization qualifier, BizTalk Server uses the default value of *Organization Name* as the organization qualifier and refers to the name of the organization stored in the BizTalk Messaging Management database.

Non-self-routing documents

Non-self-routing documents are missing all or some of the necessary routing information. When you configure the receive function, the following information must be defined on the **Advanced** tab of the receive function **Properties** dialog box or in the document to be supplied to the receive function:

- Source organization identifier, destination organization identifier, and document definition

  –Or–

- Channel

When you submit a document, BizTalk Server locates a channel to process the document. This can happen in two ways: either by supplying a channel name in the receive function or by supplying the source and destination organization identifiers and the document definition. These three properties help BizTalk Server locate the correct channel. Therefore, if you select a channel, the document definition and source and destination information options are unavailable because the channel supplies all the information that is needed to route the document.

Common types of non-self-routing documents are documents that come from multiple sources (open source) or are going to multiple destinations (open destination).

Configuring a receive function to manage documents from multiple sources

You can configure a single receive function that handles non-self-routing documents to receive a specific type of document from multiple sources. This is an open source scenario. The location of the source organization, the destination organization, and the document-definition information must be in the document or in parameters submitted along with the document. For example, if you plan to receive purchase orders from multiple customers, but want them all sent to the same destination application, set the document definition and destination organization identifier properties in the receive function. When BizTalk Server parses the document, it locates the supplier organization identifier, combines this information with the parameters in the receive function, finds the correct channel, and then processes the document.

Understanding Receive Function Advanced Properties

You can use advanced properties to configure special types of receive functions based on your business practices.

For example, you can define receive functions to submit:

- Documents that have the **Open source** or **Open destination** property set.

- Documents that have the **Pass-through** property set.

- Documents that specify a channel name.

- Other types of non-self-routing documents.

Define the Openness property in a document

The following options define the openness of a document:

- **Not open.** Specifies that the source and destination are both explicitly declared in the receive function or the document instance.

- **Open Destination.** Specifies that the destination information is not explicitly declared in the messaging port. The destination is dynamically specified in the document instance or a submission parameter. You must configure the document definition and the source-organization identifier properties in the receive function or in the document instance in order for BizTalk Server to locate the correct channel.

- **Open Source.** Specifies that the source information is not explicitly declared in the channel. Instead, the source is dynamically specified in the document instance. You must configure the document definition and destination-organization identifier properties in the receive function or in the document instance in order for BizTalk Server to locate the correct channel.

Configure receive functions with pass-through

A receive function configured with pass-through bypasses the parsing, decryption, signature verification, transformation, and decoding functions of BizTalk Server. Choose this option when you are sending binary large object data or other interchanges that do not require parsing, decryption, and decoding. If you configure a receive function with **Submit with a pass-through flag** set, you must specify a channel. Otherwise, BizTalk Server cannot process the document.

Envelope name

If you expect to receive an inbound interchange in a flat file, specify the envelope format in the receive function. The envelope points to a specification that tells BizTalk Server how to open and interpret the interchange. If you plan to receive multiple flat files in a single interchange, the individual flat files must be separated with a delimiter that is postfix or prefix. Infix is not supported. This must be set at the root node of the envelope specification and the document specification when you configure parse properties. For more information about setting parse properties for a flat file, see "To set parse properties" in Chapter 5, "Creating Specifications" and browse to the "Standard: Custom, Structure Property: Delimited" table.

Channel name

Each interchange or document that is submitted to BizTalk Server requires a set of rules for how it is to be processed. The channel contains all the information that the server needs to process the interchange or document. All interchanges and documents that are processed by BizTalk Server must go through a channel. A channel is located in one of two ways. First, when an interchange or document is submitted, BizTalk Server parses the document for the source and destination identifiers and the document definition. If this information is not in the document instance, BizTalk Server then looks at the receive function. Once the source and destination identifiers and the document definition are discovered, BizTalk Server determines which channels have the same document definition, source, and organization identifiers as the received document. When BizTalk Server finds a channel match, the document instance is processed.

The second way channels are located is when they are specified in the receive function. In this case the channel lookup is bypassed and the received document is processed faster.

Document definition, source organization, and destination organization identifiers

You can configure the document definition, source organization identifier, and/or the destination organization identifier when you receive non-self-routing documents. The routing information that is included in the document that you receive determines which of these properties you define in the receive function. For example, if you receive multiple document types from the same source organization and you always send those documents to the same destination, you can configure the source and destination organization identifiers in the receive function and dynamically define the document definition in the document instance.

To configure advanced properties for File or Message Queuing receive functions

1. In BizTalk Server Administration, expand **Microsoft BizTalk Server 2000**, expand the server group for which you want to configure a receive function, expand **Receive Functions**, and then click the receive function that you want to configure

2. On the **Action** menu, click **Properties**.

   The **Properties** dialog box appears.

3. Click the **Advanced** tab.

4. In the **Openness** list, you can select:

   - **Not open.** Click this option when the source and destination are both explicitly declared in the receive function or in the document instance, and BizTalk Server does not have to parse the document for this information.

   - **Open Destination.** Click this option when the destination information is not explicitly declared in the messaging port. The destination is dynamically specified in the document instance or a submission parameter.

   - **Open Source.** Click this option when the source information is not explicitly declared in the channel. The source is dynamically specified in the document instance or a submission parameter.

5. If you want to bypass all processing, such as decoding, decryption, signature verification, parsing, and so on, and only transport an interchange, select the **Submit with a pass-through flag** check box.

   You must select a channel if you select the **Submit with a pass-through flag** check box.

6. In the **Envelope name** list, click the name of an envelope definition.

   Choose an envelope if you plan to receive flat files. Otherwise, leave this blank.

7. In the **Channel name** list, click the name of a channel.

8. In the **Document definition name** list, click the name of a document definition.

9. In the **Source and destination** area, in the **Source selected** area, click **Browse**.

   The **Select Source** dialog box appears.

10. In the **Organization qualifier** list, click the type of source organization qualifier.

11. In the **Organization identifier value** list, click the source-organization identifier value and click **OK**.

12. In the **Source and destination** area, in the **Destination selected** area, click **Browse**.

    The **Select Destination** dialog box appears.

13. In the **Organization qualifier** list, click the type of destination organization qualifier.

    If you send documents to a distribution list, in the **Organization qualifier** list, you must choose **GROUP**.

14. In the **Organization identifier value** list, click the destination-organization identifier value and click **OK**.

15. Click **OK**.

◆ Important

- Before you can assign any of the objects in the following list as advanced properties of a receive function, you must create them. These objects are either created in BizTalk Messaging Manager or they are created programmatically and stored in the BizTalk Messaging Management database.
  - Envelopes
  - Channels
  - Document definitions
  - Source qualifiers
  - Source-organization identifier values
  - Destination qualifiers
  - Destination-organization identifier values

☑ Notes

- If you click **Open Source** or **Open Destination** in the **Openness** list, the **Submit with a pass-through flag** check box is unavailable.

- If you want to send a document to a distribution list, you must select **GROUP** in the **Organization qualifier** list in the **Select Destination** dialog box.

- All the advanced receive-function properties are optional and can be left blank. For more information about submitting documents, see "Routing" in Chapter 10, "Submitting Documents," or "Understanding Receive Functions and Document Routing" earlier in this chapter.

- If the **Submit with a pass-through flag** check box is enabled, only the **Channel** list is available.

- A pass-through submission bypasses the parsing, decryption, and decoding functions of BizTalk Server 2000. For more information about submitting documents with the pass-through flag set, see "Understanding Receive Function Advanced Properties" earlier in this chapter. For more information about submitting, see "Submitting" in Chapter 10, "Submitting Documents."

To delete a receive function

1. In BizTalk Server Administration, expand **Microsoft BizTalk Server 2000**, expand the server group in which you want to delete a receive function, and then expand **Receive Functions**.

2. Click the receive function that you want to delete.

3. On the **Action** menu, click **Delete**.

   The **User Action Confirmation** dialog box appears.

4. Click **Yes**.

Using Queues

Microsoft BizTalk Server 2000 provides shared queue management capabilities in BizTalk Server Administration. BizTalk Server Administrators can move documents from any other queue to the Suspended queue. From the Suspended queue, documents can be deleted, resubmitted, or viewed, depending on the processing state of the document. BizTalk Server Administrators can sort and display error messages for documents in the Suspended queue.

The following queues are used to contain incoming and outgoing documents that are in various stages of routing and processing in BizTalk Server:

- Work queue

- Scheduled queue

- Retry queue

- Suspended queue

📝 **Note**

- Interchanges and documents appear in BizTalk Server Administration in the order of "first in, first out." That is, the oldest items in a queue appear first and the newest items appear last. Additionally, up to 15,000 interchanges and/or documents appear in a queue at a time. If there are more than 15,000 actual items in a queue, you must remove or resubmit current items in the queue so that newer items can be displayed. The queue count in the console tree—the number next to the queue in parentheses—represents how many actual items there are in the queue. You can resubmit or delete documents to remove them from a queue.

Work Queue

The Work queue contains documents that are currently being processed by BizTalk Server. Transactions in the Work queue do not remain in the queue very long because they are processed upon arrival. BizTalk Server Administrators can select any document in this queue and move it to the Suspended queue. For more information about moving documents to the Suspended queue, see "To move documents to the Suspended queue" later in this chapter.

Scheduled Queue

The Scheduled queue contains work items that have been processed by BizTalk Server and are waiting for transmission based on the service window. BizTalk Server Administrators can select any document in this queue and move it to the Suspended queue. For more information about moving documents to the Suspended queue, see "To move documents to the Suspended queue" later in this chapter.

For more information about the service window, Microsoft Visual Basic programmers should see "BizTalkServiceWindowInfo Object" in Chapter 9, "Configuring BizTalk Messaging Services."

For more information about the service window, C++ programmers should see "IBizTalkServiceWindowInfo Interface" in Chapter 9, "Configuring BizTalk Messaging Services."

Retry Queue

The Retry queue contains documents that are being resubmitted for delivery and documents that are waiting for reliable messaging receipts. You cannot tell the difference between the two types of transmissions. By default, failed transmissions are retried every five minutes for a maximum of three tries before they are moved to the Suspended queue. These numbers can be changed through BizTalk Messaging Manager or programmatically. For more information about changing the number of retries, see "To set advanced configuration properties" in Chapter 9, "Configuring BizTalk Messaging Services."

For more information about changing these numbers programmatically, Microsoft Visual Basic programmers should see "BizTalkChannel.RetryCount Property" and "BizTalkChannel.RetryInterval Property" in Chapter 9, "Configuring BizTalk Messaging Services."

For more information about changing these numbers programmatically, C++ programmers should see "IBizTalkChannel::RetryCount Property" and "IBizTalkChannel::RetryInterval Property" in Chapter 9, "Configuring BizTalk Messaging Services."

BizTalk Server Administrators can select any document in this queue and move it to the Suspended queue. For more information about moving documents to the Suspended queue, see "To move documents to the Suspended queue" later in this chapter.

Suspended Queue

The Suspended queue contains work items that have failed processing for a variety of reasons, including parsing errors, serialization errors, failed transmissions, or the inability to find a channel configuration. BizTalk Administrators can right-click any document in this queue to choose any of the following options:

- **View Error Description.** Enables BizTalk Administrators to view error descriptions that indicate why the document was sent to the Suspended queue.

- **View Interchange.** Enables BizTalk Administrators to view the contents of an interchange that has failed processing for a variety of reasons, including parsing errors or failed transmissions. **View Interchange** appears for the following states:

  - Initial
  - Custom component

- Parsing
- Encoding
- Signing
- Encrypting
- Transmitting

- **View Document.** Enables BizTalk Administrators to view the contents of a document that has failed processing for a variety of reasons, including serialization errors or the inability to find a channel. **View Document** appears for the following states:

  - Document validation

  - Channel selection

  - Field tracking

  - Mapping

  - Correlating

  - Serializing

- **Delete.** Enables BizTalk Administrators to completely remove an entry from the Suspended queue. This action is not recoverable. After a document has been deleted from the Suspended queue, you cannot retrieve it.

- **Resubmit.** Enables BizTalk Administrators to resubmit interchanges and documents to BizTalk Server for processing.

Suspended queue states

Interchanges and documents are placed in the Suspended queue for a variety of reasons. The following table explains the Suspended queue states, their associated error messages, and what action you might take in response.

Suspended queue state value	Error message	Error description and possible action
Channel Selection or **Transmitting**	Unexpected Error	There was an unexpected internal server failure. Resubmit the document.
Channel Selection or **Transmitting**	Unknown	The interchange or document was marked as "in process" by an inactive server. When the server was restarted, this item was automatically moved to the Suspended queue. There was probably a failure on the original server. Contact the system administrator for more information. When the problem is corrected, resubmit the document or interchange.
Channel Selection or **Transmitting**	Out of Memory	The computer on which BizTalk Server is running ran out of memory. Restart the server and resubmit all interchanges and documents in the Suspended queue.
Parsing	Parsing Failure	BizTalk Server was unable to parse the data. View the contents of the interchange to determine why BizTalk Server was unable to parse it. Resubmit the interchange using **IInterchange** or a receive function. For more information, see "An interchange or document appears as binary data in the Suspended queue" or "Parsing errors" later in this chapter.
Parsing	Missing Data	The information extracted from the incoming data did not contain enough information to locate a channel. View the interchange and find which data is missing. Resubmit the interchange using **IInterchange** or a receive function. For more information, see "An interchange or document appears as binary data in the Suspended queue" or "Parsing errors" later in this chapter.
Parsing	"expiresAt" Expired	The BizTalk Framework timestamp "expiresAt" expired. This document is no longer valid. For more information, see "An interchange or document appears as binary data in the Suspended queue" later in this chapter.

Suspended queue state value	Error message	Error description and possible action
Channel Selection	No Channels Found	BizTalk Server was unable to find any channels that matched this document.
		Create a channel for the document, or correct the document and then resubmit it.
Channel Selection	Channel Removed	The channel associated with this document was deleted after the document reached the Work queue.
		Reconfigure the channel, or configure the document for a different channel and resubmit the document.
		–Or–
		Do not submit the document and delete it from the Suspended queue.
Channel Selection	Channel Missing	The channel specified by the receive function or submit call could not be found.
		Configure a channel or reconfigure the document and resubmit it.
Channel Selection	Channel Not Valid	The channel specified by the submit call was an open channel. Open channels are not valid for pass-through submit calls.
		Change the channel and resubmit the document.
Mapping	Mapping Failure	The map referenced by the channel is formatted incorrectly.
		Delete the document from the Suspended queue, correct the map, and submit the document as though it were new.
Serializing	Serializing Failure	BizTalk Server could not convert the document to its native format.
		Resubmit the document.
Encoding	Encoding Failure	BizTalk Server could not encode this interchange.
		Resubmit the interchange.
Signing	Signing Failure	BizTalk Server could not sign this interchange.
		The certificate might have expired. See the Certificates Microsoft Management Console snap-in for details. For more information about how to view the Certificates snap-in in Windows 2000 Help, in the Manage Certificates chapter, see "Add the Certificates snap-in to the MMC console."

Suspended queue state value	Error message	Error description and possible action
Encrypting	Encryption Failure	BizTalk Server could not encrypt this interchange.
		The certificate might have expired. See the Certificates Microsoft Management Console snap-in for details. For more information about how to view the Certificates snap-in in Windows 2000 Help, in the Manage Certificates chapter, see "Add the Certificates snap-in to the MMC console."
Transmitting	Transmission Failure	BizTalk Server could not deliver the interchange.
		Check the transport address in the channel. Correct the problem and resubmit the interchange.
Transmitting	Timeout Failure	BizTalk Server was unable to complete processing of this interchange before timing out. This could be because the transmission took too long.
		If you are using an unreliable transport, check to see if this interchange has been sent before you attempt to resubmit the interchange.
Transmitting	User Move	A BizTalk Server Administrator has moved this document to the Suspended queue.
		Resubmit the interchange.
Transmitting	Timestamp Expired	The BizTalk Framework timestamp "receiptRequiredBy" expired. This document is no longer valid.
Document Validation	Document Not Valid	The validation of the document against its specification failed.
		Look for the error in the Event Log for more information. Correct the schema and resubmit the document.
Field Tracking	Field Tracking Failure	BizTalk Server could not track the requested fields within the document.
		View the document to verify that the fields that you want tracked are present, or change the channel configuration for field tracking. Then resubmit the document.
Custom Component	Custom Component Failure	A custom component has failed.
		Troubleshoot the custom component or custom preprocessor and submit the interchange.
Correlating	Correlation Failure	There was a failure correlating this receipt.

☑ **Notes**

- In addition to checking the error messages in the Suspended queue, you can also check the Event Log for more information. For more information about the Event Log, see "Handling Server Errors" earlier in this chapter.

- Not all documents in the Suspended queue can be resubmitted. In some situations, you must delete the document and submit it again from the original application or organization.

To move documents to the Suspended queue

1. In BizTalk Server Administration, expand **Microsoft BizTalk Server 2000**, expand the group that contains the document that you want to move, and then expand **Queues**.

2. Expand the queue that contains the document that you want to move and click the document.

3. On the **Action** menu, point to **All Tasks** and click **Move to Suspended Queue**.

To view error descriptions

1. In BizTalk Server Administration, expand **Microsoft BizTalk Server 2000**, expand the group that contains the document that you want to view, expand **Queues**, and then click **Suspended Queue**.

2. In the details pane, click the document that you want to view.

3. On the **Action** menu, click **View Error Description**.

To view interchanges

1. In BizTalk Server Administration, expand **Microsoft BizTalk Server 2000**, expand the group that contains the interchange that you want to view, expand **Queues**, and then click **Suspended Queue**.

2. In the details pane, click the interchange that you want to view.

3. On the **Action** menu, click **View Interchange**.

   The **Document Content** dialog box appears.

☑ **Notes**

- If you try to view a large interchange, the data might be truncated. You can view up to 4 MB of data in the **Document Content** dialog box.

- If BizTalk Server could not parse the interchange, you might see binary data in the **Document Content** dialog box. For more information about parser errors, see "Parsing errors" later in this chapter.

- **View Interchange** is an available menu option for the following Suspended queue states:

  - Custom Component

  - Parsing

  - Encoding

  - Signing

  - Encrypting

  - Transmitting

- **View Interchange** and **View Document** never appear on the **Action** menu at the same time.

To view documents

1. In BizTalk Server Administration, expand **Microsoft BizTalk Server 2000**, expand the group that contains the document that you want to view, expand **Queues**, and then click **Suspended Queue**.

2. In the details pane, click the document that you want to view.

3. On the **Action** menu, click **View Document**.

   The **Document Content** dialog box appears.

Notes

- If you try to view a large document, the data might be truncated. You can view up to 4 MB of data in the **Document Content** dialog box.

- **View Document** is an available menu option for the following Suspended queue states:

  - Document Validation

  - Channel Selection

  - Mapping

  - Correlating

  - Serializing

- **View Interchange** and **View Document** never appear on the **Action** menu at the same time.

To resubmit documents

1. In BizTalk Server Administration, expand **Microsoft BizTalk Server 2000**, expand the group that contains the document that you want to resubmit, expand **Queues**, and then click **Suspended Queue**.

2. In the details pane, click the document that you want to resubmit.

3. On the **Action** menu, point to **All Tasks** and click **Resubmit**.

✎ Notes

- This procedure can also be used to retransmit documents.

- Not all documents in the Suspended queue can be resubmitted. In some situations, you must delete the document and submit it again from the original application or organization. For more information about documents in the Suspended queue, see "Suspended Queue" earlier in this chapter.

To delete documents

1. In BizTalk Server Administration, expand **Microsoft BizTalk Server 2000**, expand the group that contains the document that you want to delete, expand **Queues**, and then click **Suspended Queue**.

2. In the details pane, click the document that you want to delete.

3. On the **Action** menu, click **Delete**.

   The **User Action Confirmation** dialog box appears.

4. Click **Yes**.

Related Topic

"An interchange or document appears as binary data in the Suspended queue" later in this chapter

Manage XLANG Applications and Databases

This section provides information about how to manage COM+ applications that host XLANG schedules. It also includes information about managing the default XLANG Scheduler application and Orchestration Persistence database that are created when you install BizTalk Server 2000.

BizTalk Server 2000 provides a COM+ application called the XLANG Persistence Helper, which is used by all COM+ applications that host XLANG schedule instances. You should not change the configuration of the XLANG Persistence Helper in any way after setup completes.

✎ Notes

- For more information about Microsoft SQL Server, on the **Start** menu, point to **Programs**, point to **Microsoft SQL Server**, and then click **Books Online**.

- For Component Services Administration Help, on the **Start** menu, point to **Settings**, click **Control Panel**, double-click **Administrative Tools**, and then double-click **Component Services**. In the console tree, right-click **Component Services** and click **Help**.

- For more information about Component Services and COM+, go to the MSDN Online Library Web site (msdn.microsoft.com/library/default.asp) and browse to Component Services in the Platform SDK.

To open Component Services

- On the **Start** menu, point to **Settings**, click **Control Panel**, double-click **Administrative Tools**, and then double-click **Component Services**.

Manage the Default XLANG Scheduler Application and Database

The default XLANG Scheduler application and Orchestration Persistence database are created during the installation of BizTalk Server 2000. On production systems or systems running Microsoft Terminal Server, you need to change the default settings for this application and database. You can also create new COM+ applications to host XLANG schedule instances and new persistence databases to store XLANG schedule state information.

For information about creating a new COM+ application to host XLANG schedule instances, see "To create a COM+ application to host XLANG schedules" in Chapter 8, "BizTalk Orchestration Services."

For more information about security and performance issues related to changing the default settings for the default XLANG Scheduler application, see "Security for Applications That Host XLANG Schedule Instances" in Chapter 2, "Understanding Security."

Notes

- For more information about Microsoft SQL Server, on the **Start** menu, point to **Programs**, point to **Microsoft SQL Server**, and then click **Books Online**.

- For Component Services Administration Help, on the **Start** menu, point to **Settings**, click **Control Panel**, double-click **Administrative Tools**, and then double-click **Component Services**. In the console tree, right-click **Component Services** and click **Help**.

- For more information about Component Services and COM+, go to the MSDN Online Library Web site (msdn.microsoft.com/library/default.asp) and browse to Component Services in the Platform SDK.

To configure the default XLANG Scheduler application

1. On the **Start** menu, point to **Settings**, click **Control Panel**, double-click **Administrative Tools**, and then double-click **Component Services**.

2. In the console tree, expand **Component Services**, expand **Computers**, expand **My Computer**, and then expand **COM+ Applications**.

3. Click **XLANG Scheduler**.

4. On the **Action** menu, click **Properties**.

5. It is highly recommended that you change the application identity of the default XLANG Scheduler application, particularly on production systems or systems running Microsoft Terminal Server. For more information, see "To change the application identity for the default XLANG Scheduler application" later in this chapter.

6. It is highly recommended that you change the default database settings for the Orchestration Persistence database. For more information, see "To change the settings for the default Orchestration Persistence database" later in this chapter.

Notes

- The data source name (DSN) and the COM+ application must be the same. For example, if the COM+ application hosting the XLANG Scheduler Engine is called XLANG Scheduler, the DSN must also be called XLANG Scheduler.

- For Component Services Administration Help, on the **Start** menu, point to **Settings**, click **Control Panel**, double-click **Administrative Tools**, and then double-click **Component Services**. In the console tree, right-click **Component Services** and click **Help**.

- For more information about Component Services and COM+, go to the MSDN Online Library Web site (msdn.microsoft.com/library/default.asp) and browse to Component Services in the Platform SDK.

To change the application identity for the default XLANG Scheduler application

It is recommended that you change the default interactive user account for the default XLANG Scheduler application to a service account.

For more information about security and performance issues related to changing the default settings for the default XLANG Scheduler application, see "Security for Applications That Host XLANG Schedule Instances" in Chapter 2, "Understanding Security."

1. On the **Start** menu, point to **Settings**, click **Control Panel**, double-click **Administrative Tools**, and then double-click **Component Services**.

2. In the console tree, expand **Component Services**, expand **Computers**, expand **My Computer**, and then expand **COM+ Applications**.

3. Click **XLANG Scheduler**.

4. On the **Action** menu, click **Properties**.

   The **XLANG Scheduler Properties** dialog box appears.

5. On the **Advanced** tab, in the **Permission** area, clear the **Disable changes** check box and click **OK**.

   The following message appears:

   The applications were created by one or more external products. Are you certain the changes you are about to make are supported by these products?

6. Click **Yes**.

   The **XLANG Scheduler Properties** dialog box closes.

7. Click **XLANG Scheduler**.

8. On the **Action** menu, click **Properties**.

   The **XLANG Scheduler Properties** dialog box appears.

9. On the **Identity** tab, in the **Account** area, click **This user**.

10. Type the information for the account that you want to use.

11. Click **OK**.

    The following message appears:

    The applications were created by one or more external products. Are you certain the changes you are about to make are supported by these products?

12. Click **Yes**.

✐ Notes

- For Component Services Administration Help, on the **Start** menu, point to **Settings**, click **Control Panel**, double-click **Administrative Tools**, and then double-click **Component Services**. In the console tree, right-click **Component Services** and click **Help**.

- For more information about Component Services and COM+, go to the MSDN Online Library Web site (msdn.microsoft.com/library/default.asp) and browse to Component Services in the Platform SDK.

To change the settings for the default Orchestration Persistence database

When you install BizTalk Server 2000, the Orchestration Persistence database is set up and configured with default settings. You can change these default settings to a configuration that is suitable for the system you are running.

1. On the **Start** menu, point to **Programs**, point to **Microsoft SQL Server**, and then click **Enterprise Manager**.

2. Expand **Microsoft SQL Servers**, expand **SQL Server Group**, expand the server that contains the default database, and then expand **Databases**.

3. Click the **XLANG** database.

4. On the **Action** menu, click **Properties**.

   The **XLANG Properties** dialog box appears.

5. There are six tabs on which you can set various database properties:

   - **General**

   - **Data Files**

- **Transaction Log**

- **Filegroups**

- **Options**

- **Permissions**

For more information about SQL Server, on the **Start** menu, point to **Programs**, point to **Microsoft SQL Server**, and then click **Books Online**.

◈ Important

- This procedure assumes that you set up the default database with the name XLANG.

✎ Notes

- The primary database and transaction log files are created by using the database name as the prefix; for example, *XLANGdb*_Data.mdf and *XLANGdb*_Log.ldf. The primary file contains the system tables for the database.

- The maximum database size is determined by the amount of disk space available and the licensing limits for the version of Microsoft SQL Server that you are using.

- The object name of the default Orchestration Persistence database is XLANG. You can change this name during the installation process.

To shut down all XLANG applications

1. On the **Start** menu, point to **Settings**, click **Control Panel**, double-click **Administrative Tools**, and then double-click **Component Services**.

2. In the console tree, expand **Component Services**, expand **Computers**, expand **My Computer**, and then expand **COM+ Applications**.

3. Click **XLANG Scheduler**.

4. On the **Action** menu, click **Properties**.

   The **XLANG Scheduler Properties** dialog box appears.

5. On the **XLANG** tab, in the **Controlled shutdown** area, click **All XLANG Applications**.

▼ Caution

- You must follow this procedure to execute a controlled shutdown for all COM+ applications. Doing this saves the state for all running XLANG schedules to the persistence database. For more information, see "Persistence" in Chapter 8, "BizTalk Orchestration Services."

- Do not right-click a COM+ application and click **Shut down**. One of the following might occur:

  - If running XLANG schedules are fully transactional, an uncontrolled shutdown causes any executing transactions to abort.

- If running XLANG schedules are not fully transactional, data that is in process in the schedule is lost.

◆ Important

- You cannot restart dehydrated XLANG schedules if the data source name (DSN) is not available or if it is incorrectly configured. For more information about configuring a DSN for the default XLANG Scheduler application, see "To configure the default XLANG Scheduler application" earlier in this chapter.

◻ Notes

- For Component Services Administration Help, on the **Start** menu, point to **Settings**, click **Control Panel**, double-click **Administrative Tools**, and then double-click **Component Services**. In the console tree, right-click **Component Services** and click **Help**.

- For more information about Component Services and COM+, go to the MSDN Online Library Web site msdn.microsoft.com/library/default.asp) and browse to Component Services in the Platform SDK.

To restart all XLANG applications

1. On the **Start** menu, point to **Settings**, click **Control Panel**, double-click **Administrative Tools**, and then double-click **Component Services**.

2. In the console tree, expand **Component Services**, expand **Computers**, expand **My Computer**, and then expand **COM+ Applications**.

3. Click **XLANG Scheduler**.

4. On the **Action** menu, click **Properties**.

   The **XLANG Scheduler Properties** dialog box appears.

5. On the **XLANG** tab, in the **Restart dehydrated XLANG applications** area, click **All XLANG Applications**.

◆ Important

- You cannot restart dehydrated XLANG schedules if the data source name (DSN) is not available or if it is incorrectly configured. For more information about configuring a DSN for the default XLANG Scheduler application, see "To configure the default XLANG Scheduler application" earlier in this chapter.

- When you restart dehydrated applications, this process starts the rehydration of the dehydrated schedules asynchronously. The rehydration process is not immediate. Use XLANG Event Monitor to determine when the rehydration process is complete. For more information about the XLANG Event Monitor tool, see the Readme.htm file associated with the tool. Both XLANG Event Monitor (XLANGMon.exe) and the readme installed by the Microsoft BizTalk Server 2000 Setup Wizard are located in the following installation directory: \Program Files\Microsoft BizTalk Server\SDK\XLANG Tools.

Notes

- For Component Services Administration Help, on the **Start** menu, point to **Settings**, click **Control Panel**, double-click **Administrative Tools**, and then double-click **Component Services**. In the console tree, right-click **Component Services** and click **Help**.

- For more information about Component Services and COM+, go to the MSDN Online Library Web site (msdn.microsoft.com/library/default.asp) and browse to Component Services in the Platform SDK.

Related Topics

"Creating an Instantiating Application" in Chapter 8, "BizTalk Orchestration Services"

"Running XLANG Schedules" in Chapter 8, "BizTalk Orchestration Services"

"To change the DSN settings for a COM+ application" later in this chapter

"To create a new persistence database" later in this chapter

"To run an XLANG schedule" in Chapter 8, "BizTalk Orchestration Services"

"To shut down a COM+ application that hosts XLANG schedules" later in this chapter

Manage Other COM+ Applications That Host XLANG Schedules

Most COM+ applications that host XLANG schedules must be created when the XLANG schedule is developed. You must take into consideration security and performance needs for the applications and the schedules, and you might want to create specific COM+ applications to run specific schedules. For more information, see "Running XLANG Schedules" and "To run an XLANG schedule" in Chapter 8, "BizTalk Orchestration Services."

Notes

- For more information about Microsoft SQL Server, on the **Start** menu, point to **Programs**, point to **Microsoft SQL Server**, and then click **Books Online**.

- For Component Services Administration Help, on the **Start** menu, point to **Settings**, click **Control Panel**, double-click **Administrative Tools**, and then double-click **Component Services**. In the console tree, right-click **Component Services** and click **Help**.

- For more information about Component Services and COM+, go to the MSDN Online Library Web site (msdn.microsoft.com/library/default.asp) and browse to Component Services in the Platform SDK.

To create a new persistence database

1. On the **Start** menu, point to **Programs**, point to **Microsoft SQL Server**, and then click **Enterprise Manager**.

2. Expand **Microsoft SQL Servers**, expand **SQL Server Group**, expand the server for which you want to add a new database, and then expand **Database**.

3. Click **Databases**.

4. On the **Action** menu, click **New Database**.

   The **Database Properties** dialog box appears.

5. On the **General** tab, in the **Name** box, type a name for the new database and click **OK**.

   This action creates a new database with the default values set. You can change the default values. For more information about SQL Server, on the **Start** menu, point to **Programs**, point to **Microsoft SQL Server**, and then click **Books Online**.

Notes

- The primary database and transaction log files are created by using the database name as the prefix; for example, *XLANGdb*_Data.mdf and *XLANGdb*_Log.ldf. The primary file contains the system tables for the database.

- The maximum database size is determined by the amount of disk space available and the licensing limits for the version of Microsoft SQL Server that you are using.

To change the application identity for a COM+ application

1. On the **Start** menu, point to **Settings**, click **Control Panel**, double-click **Administrative Tools**, and then double-click **Component Services**.

2. In the console tree, expand **Component Services**, expand **Computers**, expand **My Computer**, and then expand **COM+ Applications**.

3. Click the COM+ application for which you want to change the identity and, on the **Action** menu, click **Properties**.

   The COM+ application's **Properties** dialog box appears.

4. On the **Advanced** tab, in the **Permission** area, verify that the **Disable changes** check box is cleared and click **OK**.

   The **Properties** dialog box closes.

5. Right-click the COM+ application again and click **Properties**.

   The COM+ application's **Properties** dialog box appears

6. On the **Identity** tab, in the **Account** area, click **This user**.

7. Type the information for the account that you want to use.

8. Click **OK**.

   The following message appears:

   The applications were created by one or more external products. Are you certain the changes you are about to make are supported by these products?

9. Click **Yes**.

✍ Notes

- For more information about security and performance issues and the application identity settings for a COM+ application that hosts XLANG schedules, see "Security for Applications That Host XLANG Schedule Instances" in Chapter 2, "Understanding Security."

- For Component Services Administration Help, on the **Start** menu, point to **Settings**, click **Control Panel**, double-click **Administrative Tools**, double-click **Component Services**, and then click **Help**.

- For more information about Component Services and COM+, go to the MSDN Online Library Web site (msdn.microsoft.com/library/default.asp) and browse to Component Services in the Platform SDK.

To change the DSN settings for a COM+ application

1. On the **Start** menu, point to **Settings**, click **Control Panel**, double-click **Administrative Tools**, and then double-click **Component Services**.

2. In the console tree, expand **Component Services**, expand **Computers**, expand **My Computer**, and then expand **COM+ Applications**.

3. Click the COM+ application for which you want to change data source name (DSN) settings.

4. On the **Action** menu, click **Properties**.

   The COM+ application's **Properties** dialog box appears

5. On the **XLANG** tab, click **Configure DSN**.

   The **ODBC Data Source Administrator** dialog box appears.

6. Change any settings that you want to change.

☞ Caution

- After you change DSN settings, on the **XLANG** tab, do not click **Initialize Tables**. This action destroys any data already in the existing database.

◆ Important

- The DSN and the COM+ application must use the same name. For example, if the COM+ application is called XLANG Scheduler, the DSN must also be called XLANG Scheduler.

- For more information about configuring a DSN and using data sources (ODBC), click **Help** in the **ODBC Data Source Administrator** dialog box.

✍ Notes

- For Component Services Administration Help, on the **Start** menu, point to **Settings**, click **Control Panel**, double-click **Administrative Tools**, double-click **Component Services**, and then click **Help**.

- For more information about Component Services and COM+, go to the MSDN Online Library Web site (msdn.microsoft.com/library/default.asp) and browse to Component Services in the Platform SDK.

To shut down a COM+ application that hosts XLANG schedules

1. On the **Start** menu, point to **Settings**, click **Control Panel**, double-click **Administrative Tools**, and then double-click **Component Services**.

2. In the console tree, expand **Component Services**, expand **Computers**, expand **My Computer**, and then expand **COM+ Applications**.

3. Click the COM+ application that hosts XLANG schedules that you want to shut down.

4. On the **Action** menu, click **Properties**.

   The COM+ application's **Properties** dialog box appears

5. On the **XLANG** tab, in the **Controlled shutdown** area, click **This XLANG Application**.

☝ Caution

- You must follow this procedure to execute a controlled shutdown for all COM+ applications. Doing this saves the state for all running XLANG schedules to the persistence database. For more information, see "Persistence" in Chapter 8, "BizTalk Orchestration Services."

- Do not right-click a COM+ application and click **Shut down**. One of the following might occur:

  - If running XLANG schedules are fully transactional, an uncontrolled shutdown triggers all On Failure and Compensation error-handling processes.

  - If running XLANG schedules are not fully transactional, data that is in process in the schedule is lost.

◈ Important

- You cannot restart dehydrated XLANG schedules if the data source name (DSN) is not available or it is incorrectly configured. For more information about configuring a DSN for a COM+ application that hosts XLANG schedules, see "To configure a COM+ application to host XLANG schedules" in Chapter 8, "BizTalk Orchestration Services."

▨ Notes

- When you create a COM+ application to host XLANG schedules, the **Restart dehydrated applications** option is not available. For more information about how to restart dehydrated applications, see "To restart all XLANG applications" earlier in this chapter.

- For Component Services Administration Help, on the **Start** menu, point to **Settings**, click **Control Panel**, double-click **Administrative Tools**, and then double-click **Component Services**. In the console tree, right-click **Component Services** and click **Help**.

- For more information about Component Services and COM+, go to the MSDN Online Library Web site (msdn.microsoft.com/library/dcfault.asp) and browsc to Component Services in the Platform SDK.

Related Topics

"Running XLANG Schedules" in Chapter 8, "BizTalk Orchestration Services"

"Security for Applications That Host XLANG Schedule Instances" in Chapter 2, "Understanding Security"

"To change the settings for the default Orchestration Persistence database" earlier in this chapter

"To configure a COM+ application to host XLANG schedules" in Chapter 8, "BizTalk Orchestration Services"

"To configure the default XLANG Scheduler application" earlier in this chapter

"To restart all XLANG applications" earlier in this chapter

"To run an XLANG schedule" in Chapter 8, "BizTalk Orchestration Services"

"To shut down all XLANG applications" earlier in this chapter

Monitor Running XLANG Schedules

You can monitor running XLANG schedules by using either XLANG Event Monitor or Windows 2000 Event Viewer.

- **XLANG Event Monitor.** When the XLANG Scheduler Engine executes XLANG schedules, it generates various kinds of events, showing the progress of the schedule instances. You can use XLANG Event Monitor to monitor XLANG schedule events and see the progress of the schedule instances. You can monitor the default XLANG Scheduler application or you can monitor the custom COM+ applications that you create to host XLANG schedules. XLANG Event Monitor can subscribe to all events published by the host applications on any number of local or distributed computers. XLANG Event Monitor can also store these events to a file for later analysis.

  For specific information about using XLANG Event Monitor, see the Readme.htm file associated with the tool. Both XLANG Event Monitor (XLANGMon.exe) and the readme installed by the Microsoft BizTalk Server 2000 Setup Wizard are located in the following installation directory: \Program Files\Microsoft BizTalk Server\SDK\XLANG Tools.

- **Windows 2000 Event Viewer.** Windows 2000 Event Viewer publishes event messages related to XLANG schedules. For more information about using Event Viewer to view error messages, see the following references:

  - For information about configuring Event Viewer to filter for XLANG schedule error messages, see "To configure Event Viewer for BizTalk Server errors" earlier in this chapter.

  - For general information about Event Viewer, in Windows 2000 Server Help, in the Event Viewer chapter, see "Using Event Viewer."

XLANG Schedule Error Messages

The error messages in the following table are returned when a running XLANG schedule generates the error. These messages can be viewed in Windows 2000 Event Viewer.

Message name	Value	Description
ID_CAT_UNKNOWN	0x1	SVC%0
ID_CAT_NAMESVC	0x2	NameSvc%0
ID_CAT_ENGINE	0x3	Engine%0
ID_CAT_SYSMGR	0x4	SystemMgr%0
ID_CAT_GRPMGR	0x5	GroupMgr%0
ID_CAT_WFSVCMGR	0x6	WFSvcMgr%0
ID_CAT_OBJECTMODEL	0x7	WFObjectModel%0
ID_CAT_BINDING	0x8	WFBinding%0
ID_CAT_COM_LAST	0x9	<>%0
IDS_I_MTSTOCOM_LAUNCH_FINISHED	0x1000	An unauthorized client attempted to create a new instance of an XLANG schedule. The remainder of the moniker string and the identity of the client are shown in the following message. The client's security identifier (SID) is included as binary data: %1%0
ID_W_NOT_USER	0x2001	An unauthorized client attempted to gain access to an existing instance of an XLANG schedule. The remainder of the moniker string identifying the instance and the identity of the client are shown in the following message. The client's security identifier (SID) is included as binary data: %1%0
IDS_E_COMSVCS_INTERNAL_ERROR	0x3000	The XLANG Scheduler Engine has detected an inconsistency in its internal state. Please contact Microsoft Product Support Services to report this error: %1%0
IDS_COMSVCS_RESOURCE_ERROR	0x3001	The XLANG Scheduler Engine has detected the absence of a critical resource and has caused the process that hosted it to end: %1%0
IDS_COMSVCS_INTERNAL_ERROR_ASSERT	0x3002	COM+ internal error. Please contact Microsoft Product Support Services to report this error. Assertion failure: %1%0

Message name	Value	Description
ID_E_USER_EXCEPTION	0x3003	The system has called a scheduled component and that component has failed and generated an exception. This indicates a problem with the scheduled component. Notify the developer of this component that a failure has occurred and provide the following information: %1%2%0
ID_INITIALIZE_FOR_DTC	0x3004	The XLANG Scheduler Engine was unable to initialize for transactions that are required to support transactional components. Make sure that MS DTC is running: %1%0
ID_E_CANT_CREATE_COMPONENT	0x3005	The XLANG Scheduler Engine was unable to create a user component that is required by the running XLANG schedule. Detailed information is provided in the following message. %1%0
ID_E_PROGID_NOT_FOUND	0x3006	The XLANG Scheduler Engine was unable to convert the Programmatic ID in the following message to a COM class ID: %1%0
ID_E_CANT_CREATE_INTERCEPTOR	0x3007	The XLANG Scheduler Engine was unable to create an interceptor object for the interface ID shown in the following message. Probable causes for this are 1) the interface isn't registered properly; 2) no type library is provided for the interface; or 3) the file that contains the interface type information can't be loaded. The port name associated with this interceptor is: %1%0
ID_E_INTF_NOT_SUPPORTED	0x3008	The XLANG Scheduler Engine detected an inconsistency between the port implementation and the COM components to which it refers. A component listed in the port implementation has failed to support the expected interface. The class ID of the component and the IID that it failed to support are shown in the following message. The port name associated with this component is: %1%0
ID_E_UNKNOWN_METHOD	0x3009	The XLANG Scheduler Engine received a call to a method that was not specified in the port implementation for this XLANG schedule. The IID and method number are shown in the following message. The name of the port on which the call arrived is: %1%0

Message name	Value	Description
ID_E_UNKNOWN_IDISPATCH_METHOD	0x300A	The XLANG Scheduler Engine received a call through the **IDispatch::Invoke()** interface to a method that no longer exists. The dispatch ID for the method is shown in the following message. The name of the port on which the call arrived is: %1%0
ID_E_NAMED_PARAMS	0x300B	The XLANG Scheduler Engine received a call through the **IDispatch::Invoke()** interface to a method that contains named arguments. Use positional arguments instead. The dispatch ID for the method is shown in the following message. The name of the port on which the call arrived is: %1%0
ID_E_BAD_INVOKE_PARAMS	0x300C	The XLANG Scheduler Engine received a call through the **IDispatch::Invoke()** interface to a method with an incorrect number of parameters. The IID and the dispatch ID for the method are shown in the following message. The name of the port on which the call arrived is: %1%0
ID_E_BAD_RETURN_POINTER	0x300D	The XLANG Scheduler Engine received an incorrect Out parameter through the **IDispatch::Invoke()** interface from a method. The reference returned was either not valid (NULL or a bad pointer) or does not support the expected interface. The expected dispatch ID is shown in the following message. The name of the message containing the bad port reference is: %1%0
ID_E_ACCESS_CHECK_FAILURE	0x300E	The XLANG Scheduler Engine was not able to authorize the client's moniker resolution request. Access is denied.%0
ID_E_BAD_INVOKE	0x300F	The **IDispatch::Invoke()** interface call to a method failed. The dispatch ID for the method is shown in the following message. The name of the port on which the call was attempted is: %1%0
ID_E_INVOKED_METHOD	0x3010	The invoked method, whose dispatch ID is shown in the following message, reported an error. The name of the port on which the call was attempted is: %1%0

Message name	Value	Description
ID_E_CANT_GET_TYPEINFO	0x3011	The component whose port name and COM CLSID are shown in the following message was unable to supply required type information to the XLANG Scheduler Engine.%1%0
ID_E_CANT_INVOKE_METHOD	0x3012	The XLANG Scheduler Engine was unable to deliver a method call to the object associated with the port name shown in the following message. The interface and method name that are invoked are also shown.%1%0
ID_E_CANT_GET_CLASSINFO	0x3013	The component whose port name and COM CLSID are shown in the following message was unable to supply required type information to the XLANG Scheduler Engine through the **IProvideClassInfo::GetClassInfo** interface.%1%0
ID_E_SCRIPT_ERROR	0x3014	A scripted decision rule in an XLANG schedule instance could not be executed. The error returned by the script engine is shown in the following message. The script's source code and information about the schedule instance in which the error occurred is also provided.%1%0
ID_E_SCRIPT_ERROR_NOINFO	0x3015	A scripted decision rule in an XLANG schedule instance has failed. Detailed information regarding the error could not be obtained due to an internal error. The error code is shown in the following message.%1%0
ID_E_SCRIPT_BADCONV	0x3016	A scripted decision rule in an XLANG schedule instance referred to a message field whose type was incompatible with the VBScript Engine. The XLANG Scheduler Engine attempted to convert the field to a compatible type but was unable to do so. The information in the following message shows the script rule, message, and field involved, as well as the original field variant type and the type to which a conversion was attempted. The field's VARIANT data structure is attached to this log entry as binary data.%1%0

Message name	Value	Description
ID_E_SCRIPT_BADARRAY	0x3017	A scripted decision rule in an XLANG schedule instance referred to a message field containing an array type that is incompatible with the VB script engine. Only variant arrays are supported by Visual Basic Scripting. The information in the following message shows the script rule, message, and field involved. The field's VARIANT data structure is attached to this log entry as binary data.%1%0
ID_E_SCRIPT_BADEXPR	0x3018	A scripted decision rule in an XLANG schedule instance contained an expression that did not return a Boolean result. The information in the following message shows the script rule and expression involved. The VARIANT data structure returned by the expression is attached to this log entry as binary data.%1%0
ID_E_SCHEDULE_NOT_RUNNING	0x3019	The XLANG Scheduler Engine received a call to an object associated with a port in an XLANG schedule instance that is not running. The name of the port on which the call arrived is: %1%0
ID_E_INTERNAL_EXCEPTION	0x301A	A COM+ internal exception occurred. Contact Microsoft Product Support Services to report this error, and provide them with the information in the following message.%1%2%0
ID_E_BAD_DATAFLOW_NOMESSAGE	0x301B	There is a problem with the data-flow specification. A message that is indicated as a source of data does not currently exist while this XLANG schedule is running. Detailed information is provided in the following message.%1%0
ID_E_BAD_ARGUMENTVALUE	0x301C	One of the fields that is used as a parameter for a COM method call has a bad value type in it. This is most likely caused by incorrect or missing data flow. Detailed information is provided in the following message.%1%0
ID_E_DEEP_VARIANT_NESTING	0x301D	One of the fields that is used as a parameter for a COM method call has more than one nesting level of VARIANTs. The IID and the method's dispatch ID are shown in the following message. The name of the port on which the call arrived is: %1%0

Message name	Value	Description
ID_E_BAD_MAPPORTVALUE	0x301E	A field carrying a mapped port is not valid. Detailed information is provided in the following message.%1%0
ID_E_BAD_CALLPARAMNUMBER	0x301F	An incorrect number of parameters are being passed into a call. Detailed information is provided in the following message.%1%0
ID_E_EXECUTINGCALLEDSCHEDULE	0x3020	The XLANG schedule cannot be executed as a top-level schedule. Context parameters must be passed to it. Detailed information is provided in the following message.%1%0
ID_E_CANT_GET_SUPPORTERRORINFO	0x3021	The component whose port name and COM CLSID are shown in the following message was unable to return success from an interface that it claimed to support to the XLANG Scheduler Engine via ISupportErrorInfo::InterfaceSupportsErrorInfo. %1%0
ID_E_PERSIST_FAILURE	0x3022	The state of the schedule instance could not be saved to the database. Detailed information is provided in the following message.%1%0
ID_E_TRANSACTION_COMMIT_FAILURE	0x3023	The system failed to commit a transactional context. Detailed information is provided in the following message.%1%0
ID_E_TRANSACTION_ABORTED	0x3024	The system aborted a transactional context. Detailed information is provided in the following message.%1%0
ID_E_TRANSACTION_ABORT_FAILURE	0x3025	The system failed to abort a transactional context. The state of this transaction is not known. Detailed information is provided in the following message.%1%0
ID_E_PENDINGREHYDRATIONERROR	0x3026	The rehydration application encountered an error and is shutting down. Some of the rehydration requests will fail due to this shutdown. Restart the XLANG Scheduler Engine service. Detailed information is provided in the following message.%1%0

Message name	Value	Description
ID_E_REHYDRATIONONSTARTUPERROR	0x3027	One or more XLANG schedules could not be rehydrated because of a system error. There might be problems reading the database or problems with the data that was read. Detailed information is provided in the following message.%1%0
ID_E_REHYDRATIONERROR	0x3028	An error was encountered while rehydrating an XLANG schedule. There might be a problem reading the database, or there might be a problem with the information stored. It is probable that the XLANG schedule was not dehydrated properly. Detailed information is provided in the following message.%1%0
ID_E_FOUNDINITIALIZEDTHREAD	0x3029	The XLANG Scheduler Engine service encountered a critical thread-management error while processing an XLANG schedule. The schedule might fail to continue processing. Contact your technical support.%1%0
ID_E_CALLONCOMPLETEDSCHEDULE	0x302A	The XLANG Scheduler Engine service received a call on a completed XLANG schedule instance. The schedule instance has already been removed from memory. The IID for the interface is shown in the following message.%1%0
IDS_MSG_TIMEBOMB_EXPIRED	0x302B	Thank you for evaluating Microsoft BizTalk Server 2000. The period for this evaluation version has ended. Please contact Microsoft or your software reseller to obtain a licensed version of Microsoft BizTalk Server 2000.%0
ID_E_FIELDPORTPERSISTENCEERROR	0x302C	An error was encountered while attempting to persist an XLANG schedule instance. Detailed information is provided in the following message.%1%0
ID_E_FIELDPORTREHYDRATIONERROR	0x302D	An error was encountered while attempting to restore a particular sub-component of an XLANG schedule instance from the database. Detailed information is provided in the following message.%1%0

Message name	Value	Description
ID_E_SCHEDULEDONE	0x3030	The XLANG Scheduler Engine encountered an error while marking the XLANG schedule instance as done. Either the database could not be updated or another error was encountered in the final stage. Detailed information is provided in the following message.%1%0
ID_E_COMPONENT_INCOMPATIBLE_TXN	0x3031	The XLANG Scheduler Engine encountered an error while attempting to instantiate a component. Either the component was previously enrolled in a different transaction, or the component was previously not enrolled in a transaction and the current instantiation requires a transaction. Detailed information is provided in the following message.%1%0
ID_E_SUSPEND_FAILURE	0x3032	The XLANG schedule instance could not be suspended. Detailed information is provided in the following message.%1%0
ID_E_INITNEW	0x3033	The XLANG Scheduler Engine received an error when doing **IPersistStreamInit::InitNew**. The class ID of the component and the error code are shown in the following message. The port name associated with this component is: %1%0
ID_E_POSSIBLEBYOTISSUE	0x3034	The component you requested could not be created. One possible reason for this is that you have configured the BYOT component inside a COM+ application on this machine. This setting is incompatible with the XLANG Scheduler service. The port name associated with this component is: %1%0
ID_E_FIELDPROCESSINGERROR	0x3035	The field value provided was not valid. Detailed information is provided in the following message.%1%0
ID_E_NO_OBJECT	0x3036	The XLANG schedule could not be instantiated. Detailed information is provided in the following message.%1%0
ID_E_STARTUP_FAILED	0x3037	One or more of the XLANG Group Managers failed to start up with the following error: %1%0

Message name	Value	Description
ID_E_NON_SCRIPT_BADEXPR	0x3038	An XLANG schedule instance has a rule comparing fields for data types that are not permitted. Detailed information is provided in the following message.%1%0
E_BTW_PERSIST_REACHEDEOF	0x3039	The recordset cannot return this row, because the end-of-file (EOF) has been reached.%1%0
ID_E_BAD_DATAFLOW_EMPTYFIELD	0x3040	There is a problem with the data-flow specification. A field indicated as a source of data is empty. This may be because it could not be persisted earlier. Detailed information is provided in the following message.%1%0
ID_E_CANT_OPEN_DEADLETTER_ QUEUE	0x3041	The XLANG Scheduler Engine was unable to create or open the XLANG dead-letter queue for its host COM+ application. The name of the failing COM+ application is: %1%0
ID_E_CANT_XFER_TO_DEADLETTER_ QUEUE	0x3042	The XLANG Scheduler Engine was unable to transfer an invalid message to the XLANG dead-letter queue for its host COM+ application. The name of the failing COM+ application is: %1%0
ID_E_CANT_LOADMODULE	0x3043	The XLANG Scheduler engine was unable to load a required module. This may have been due to compilation/semantic errors with the module. Detailed information is available in the following message: %1%0
ID_E_USER_DATA_EXCEPTION	0x3044	A value that was received from the client has caused an exception to be raised. This can be caused by incorrectly allocating memory for the data, by a reference counting mismatch, or other data corruption. The most likely source of the problem is in the client code. Detailed information is available in the following message: %1%2%0
E_BTW_INTERNAL_ERROR	0x4001	An internal error has occurred. %1%0
E_EXPORT_FAILED	0x4002	The XLANG schedule could not be processed.%0
E_BTW_UNKNOWN_SHAPE	0x4003	The compiler does not understand the shape. This shape is an unknown shape.%0
E_BTW_INCOMPLETE_FLOW	0x4004	The flow is incomplete because a connector is missing.%0

Message name	Value	Description
E_BTW_INCOMPLETE_FLOW_LEFT	0x4005	The flow is incomplete. The shape must have a flow connected to the left connector.%0
E_BTW_INCOMPLETE_FLOW_RIGHT	0x4006	The flow is incomplete. The shape must have a flow connected to the right connector.%0
E_BTW_INCOMPLETE_FLOW_LATERAL	0x4007	The flow is incomplete. The shape is not attached to anything on the side.%0
E_BTW_INCOMPLETE_FLOW_TOP	0x4008	The flow is incomplete. The shape must have a flow connected to the top connector.%0
E_BTW_INCOMPLETE_FLOW_BOTTOM	0x4009	The flow is incomplete. The shape must have a flow connected from the bottom connector.%0
E_BTW_INCOMPLETE_FLOW_ANYLINE	0x400A	The flow is incomplete. Not connected to any shape.%0
E_BTW_MIRRORLIST_INCONSISTENT	0x400B	Mirror shapes are not found in the **On Failure** or **Compensation** page. Retry after replacing the shape with a new one.%0
E_BTW_BEGIN_INSIDE_TRANSACTION	0x4010	The **Begin** shape must not be enclosed within a transaction.%0
E_BTW_END_MULTIPLE_LOOP	0x4020	Only one **End** shape can be used in the loop branch.%0
E_BTW_END_IN_TRANSACTION	0x4021	The **End** shape cannot be used in the context.%0
E_BTW_SYNCACTION_NO_PAIR	0x4030	Binding to a COM port requires actions to appear in pairs.%0
E_BTW_INCOMPLETE_FLOW_BINDING	0x4031	No binding for this action or port.%0
E_BTW_FIELD_TYPE_NOT_SUPPORTED	0x4040	Type (variant type=%1) is not supported.%0
E_BTW_ROLE_NOT_SUPPORTED	0x4050	Contracts (XLANG Schedules with Roles) cannot be compiled.%0
E_BTW_EMPTY_TRANSACTION	0x4060	The transaction contains no valid shapes.%0
E_BTW_TRANSACTION_NOT_PERMITTED	0x4061	**Transaction** shapes are not permitted when the XLANG schedule is treated as a COM+ component. Remove the transaction or edit the properties of the **Begin** shape to change the transaction model.%0

Message name	Value	Description
E_BTW_TRANSACTION_BOUNDARIES_ CROSSED	0x4062	You cannot connect a flow from outside a transaction to a shape within a transaction without first connecting the flow to the transaction. Draw your flow to the top connection point of a transaction to connect it to the transaction. Then, click the transaction to highlight it. Draw another flow from the transaction connection point to the first shape within the transaction. To draw a flow that leaves the transaction, you must first connect the flow to the connection point at the bottom of the transaction. Then, click the transaction to highlight it. Draw another flow from the bottom connection point to the next shape in the business process.%0
E_BTW_TRANSACTION_TERMINATED_ PREMATURELY	0x4063	At least one path within the transaction should flow out of the transaction.%0
E_BTW_NO_RULES_FOR_SWITCH	0x4070	**Decision** shapes must contain at least one rule.%0
E_BTW_CANNOT_WAIT_ON_ALL_ SWITCH_BRANCHES	0x40A0	Cannot wait on "all" branches from the decision.%0
E_BTW_NO_BRANCH_FOUND	0x40A1	The join cannot find the corresponding fork or decision.%0
E_BTW_JOIN_MISMATCH	0x40A2	Only a single join may be used with a given fork or decision.%0
E_BTW_JOIN_SHARED	0x40A3	The same join cannot be used for flows coming from different forks or decisions.%0
E_BTW_CANNOT_WAIT_ON_SOME_ SWITCH_BRANCHES	0x40A4	Not all paths from the decision come to the join.%0
E_BTW_CANNOT_WAIT_ANY_ON_ FORK_BRANCHES	0x40A5	Cannot wait "Or". The branches contain process forms that might never finish, resulting in hung schedules.%0
E_BTW_DATAFLOW_DISALLOWED_ ON_BTM_PORT	0x40C0	This port cannot be used in multiple receive actions or within a single receive action in a loop.%0
E_BTW_MESSAGE_TECH_NOT_FOUND	0x4110	The message is not bound to any port.%0
E_BTW_MESSAGE_TYPE_MISMATCH	0x4111	The message was used with conflicting types "%1" and "%2".%0

Message name	Value	Description
E_BTW_MISSING_TECHNOLOGY	0x4120	The list of available methods for this communication flow has changed. Re-run the Method Communication Wizard to select a different method and update this communication flow.%0
E_BTW_MISSING_PORT_DATAFLOW	0x41A0	The settings for this port indicate that it is created externally to the XLANG Scheduler Engine. You must designate the source of this port reference by drawing a connection from the appropriate message field.%0
E_BTW_CIRCULAR_DATAFLOW	0x41A1	There appears to be a circular path in the data-flow path for this XLANG schedule.%0
E_BTW_LOOP_NORULE	0x41D0	A rule has not been defined.%0
E_BTW_LOOP_BODY_EXITS_ TRANSACTION	0x41D1	The body of the loop cannot exit the enclosing transaction.%0
E_BTW_LOOP_BODY_END_MISSING	0x41D2	The end of the body of the loop is not found.%0
E_BTW_ABORT_NOT_IN_TXN	0x41E0	**Abort** shapes must be associated with an enclosing transaction.%0
E_BTW_ABORT_CONTEXT_INVALID_ SCOPE	0x41E1	**Abort** shapes can refer to current or parent contexts only.%0
E_BTW_END_MULTIPLE_ABORT	0x41E2	Multiple **End** shapes are not allowed on the **On Failure** page.%0
E_BTW_COMPILER_FAILED	0x5000	Compile failed on "%1".%0
E_BTW_PARSE_FAILED	0x5001	Parse failed.%0
E_BTW_FIXUP_FAILED	0x5002	Fixup failed.%0
E_BTW_VALIDATION_FAILED	0x5003	Validation failed.%0
E_BTW_NODE_FAILURE	0x5004	at node "%1" (%2!d!,%3!d!).%0
E_BTW_STACK_TOO_MANY_ITEMS	0x5005	Too many items were found on the stack.%0
E_BTW_STACK_UNEXPECTED_NODE	0x5006	An unexpected node was found.%0
E_BTW_XMLQUERY_RETURNED_ ZERO_NODES	0x5007	The XML Query returned zero nodes.%0
E_BTW_XMLQUERY_RETURNED _MULTIPLE_NODES	0x5008	The XML Query returned multiple nodes.%1%0
E_BTW_XMLQUERY_MISSING_ ATTRIBUTE	0x5009	Required attribute "%1" is missing its value.%0

Message name	Value	Description
E_BTW_LOAD_MODULE_FAILED	0x500A	Failed to load module "%1".%0
E_BTW_XML_LOAD_FAILED	0x500B	The XML-DOM returned an error at "%1!d!, %2!d!".%0
E_BTW_ERROR_LOADING_PACKAGE	0x500C	0x%1!X! error occurred while trying to load the following URL: "%2".%0
E_BTW_NAMED_LIST_HAS_DUPLICATE_ENTRIES	0x500D	The list has duplicate entries with the name "%1".%0
E_BTW_REQUIRED_ELEMENT_MISSING	0x500E	Required element "%1" is missing.%0
E_BTW_ELEMENT_MISSING_VALUE	0x5100	The element value is missing.%0
E_BTW_REFERENCE_RESOLVE_FAILED	0x5110	Unable to resolve "%1" with location value "%2".%0
E_BTW_CONTEXTREF_INVALID_REFERENCE	0x5120	Returning to or "releasing" from an independent (non-enclosing) context is not permitted.%0
E_BTW_CONTEXTREF_SELF_REFERENCE	0x5121	Return or Release referring to a context from within that context is not permitted.%0
E_BTW_ASYNC_ACTION_COM_NOT_ALLOWED	0x5400	An asynchronous action must refer to a non-COM port.%0
E_BTW_CONNECTION_PORT_HAS_TECH_BINDING	0x5490	The port "%1" used in a connection cannot have technology binding.%0
E_BTW_CONNECTION_PORT_REUSED	0x5491	The port "%1" used in a connection has been used before in the XLANG schedule.%0
E_BTW_TRANSACTIONS_NESTED	0x54B0	When transactions are nested, the outer transaction must be long-running.%0
E_BTW_TRANSACTIONS_NESTED_RETRY	0x54B1	When transactions are nested, the outer transaction cannot have retry count.%0
E_BTW_MESSAGE_HAS_NO_DECL	0x5520	Message "%1" has no associated declaration.%0
E_BTW_MESSAGE_HAS_UNSATISFIED_DATA_DEPENDENCIES	0x5521	Message "%1" has unsatisfied data dependencies on "%2". The dependencies are either not getting created in the flow or are potentially expected on a port in which the "No instantiation" option has been selected.%0
E_BTW_PORT_HAS_NO_BINDING	0x5570	Port "%1" has no associated binding.%0

Message name	Value	Description
E_BTW_PORT_HAS_UNSATISFIED_DATA_DEPENDENCIES	0x5571	Port "%1" has unsatisfied data dependencies on messages "%2". The dependencies are either not being created in the flow or are potentially expected on a port in which the "No instantiation" option has been selected.%0
E_BTW_RULE_HAS_NO_BINDING	0x55B0	Rule "%1" has no associated binding.%0
E_BTW_SCHEDULE_SUSPENDED	0x55E0	The XLANG schedule has been suspended.%0
E_BTW_SCHEDULE_STOPPED	0x55E1	The XLANG schedule has been stopped.%0
E_BTW_PERSIST_FAILED	0x55E2	The state of the XLANG schedule instance could not be saved to the database.%0
E_BTW_SUSPEND_FAILED	0x55E3	The XLANG schedule could not be suspended.%0
E_XLANG_SHUTTINGDOWN	0x55E4	The XLANG application is shutting down.%0
E_BTW_MISSING_MESSAGE_BINDING_ON_PORT	0x5730	The action uses port "%1" whose binding does not define the binding for message "%2".%0
E_BTW_MISSING_INCOMING_PORTREF	0x5731	The message used by this receive action contains a field (%1) that is connected to a port reference (%2) but the dataflow connections do not indicate that the port reference should be received.%0
E_BTW_SOURCE_PORT_HAS_NOINVOCATION	0x5740	The send action refers to port "%1", in which the "No instantiation" option has been selected.%0
E_BTW_MISSING_OUTGOING_PORTREF	0x5741	The message used by this source action contains a field (%1) that is connected to a port reference (%2) but the dataflow connections do not indicate that the port reference should be sent.%0
E_BTW_TASK_LIMIT	0x5750	The task has "%1!d!" actions. The current limit is "%2!d!".%0
E_BTW_SYNC_DIFFERENT_PORTS	0x5760	Synchronous action pair refers to different ports: "%1" and "%2".%0
E_BTW_SYNC_SAME_MESSAGE	0x5761	Synchronous action pair refers to the same message: "%1".%0
E_BTW_SYNC_ONLY_COM_ALLOWED	0x5762	Synchronous action pair must refer to COM port only.%0
E_BTW_SYNC_SECOND_MESSAGE_MUST_BE_OUT_FOR_FIRST_MESSAGE	0x5763	In a synchronous action pair the message in the second action must be the out message for the message in the first action.%0

Message name	Value	Description
E_BTW_INVALID_DELAY_TIME	0x5770	The delay time (%1!d!) is not valid. The delay time cannot be a negative number.%0
E_BTW_CALL_MESSAGE_SCHEMA_NAME_MISMATCH	0x5800	The message specification name "%1" for the message "%2" in the calling XLANG schedule does not match the specification name "%3" in the called XLANG schedule.%0
E_BTW_CALL_MESSAGE_SCHEMA_REPRESENTATION_MISMATCH	0x5801	The message specification representation for message "%1" in the calling XLANG schedule does not match the specification representation in the called XLANG schedule.%0
E_BTW_ASSIGNMENT_PORT_HAS_TECH_BINDING	0x5830	Port "%1" used in an assignment in a cut form cannot have technology binding.%0
E_BTW_PARTITION_LIMIT	0x5850	The partition has "%1!d!" process(es). The current limit is "%2!d!".%0
E_BTW_MESSAGE_USED_IN_PARALLEL	0x5851	Parallel actions or processes use the same message "%1".%0
E_BTW_PORT_USED_IN_PARALLEL	0x5852	Parallel actions or processes use the same port "%1".%0
E_BTW_INVALID_RETRY_COUNT	0x5A30	The retry count "%1!d!" is not valid. The retry count cannot be negative.%0
E_BTW_INVALID_BACKOFF_VALUE	0x5A31	The back-off value "%1!d!" is not valid. The back-off value cannot be negative.%0
E_BTW_INVALID_TIMEOUT_VALUE	0x5A32	The timeout value "%1!d!" is not valid. The timeout value cannot be negative.%0
E_BTW_FIELD_RESERVED_NAME	0x5A50	%1 is a reserved field name.%0
E_BTW_ELEMENT_TYPE_NOT_DEFINED	0x5A51	The element type "%1" is not defined.%0
E_BTW_ELEMENT_TYPE_INCOMPLETE	0x5A70	The element type definition is incomplete. Provide either subelements or dt:type.%0
E_BTW_MULTIPLE_PORTS	0x5A90	Distinct ports "%1" and "%2" are used on the same field.%0
E_XLANG_INVALID_COMPARE_TYPE	0x5A91	Comparison of this data type is not permitted.%0
E_BTW_FIELD_NOT_MATCHING_SCHEMA_ELEMENT	0x5A92	FieldBinding for "%1" does not have a matching element in the schema at position "%2!d!".%0

Message name	Value	Description
E_BTW_FIELD_HAS_AMBIGUOUS_DATAFLOW	0x5A93	A message field cannot have both a data flow from another message field and a reference to a port. One of the data flows must be removed.%0
E_BTW_PORT_TARGET_INVALID	0x5A94	The type of this field is inappropriate for use as a port reference. Ports bound to a COM component can be communicated as object references or strings. Ports bound to Message Queuing may only be transferred as strings. Internal ports can be communicated only as object references.%0
E_BTW_FIELD_TARGET_INVALID	0x5A95	The target field "%1", which is of variant type "%2", cannot get data from source field "%3", which is of variant type "%4".%0
E_BTW_INITIALIZED_MESSAGEFIELD_INVALID_OVERWRITE	0x5A96	The data in field "%1" of an initialized message "%2" cannot be overwritten with data from another message or port in the binding specification.%0
E_BTW_DATAFLOW_INCOMPLETE	0x5AB1	A source action accepting [in] parameters must have the corresponding fields populated by data flow (that is, "from").%0
E_BTW_DATAFLOW_FROM_SYSTEM_FIELD	0x5AB2	Port cannot be initialized from a system field.%0
E_BTW_DATAFLOW_FROM_CONSTANT_FIELD	0x5AB3	Port cannot be initialized from a constant message field.%0
E_BTW_MISSING_SCRIPT_EXPRESSION	0x5AC0	No script expression was supplied for the rule.%0
E_BTW_BAD_SCRIPT_EXPRESSION	0x5AC1	%1 %2 at character position %3!d! in "%4".%0
E_BTW_MAP_INVALID_BINDING	0x5AE0	The binding for message "%1" must contain a reference for mapped port "%2".%0
E_BTW_MESSAGE_BINDING_SCHEMA_MISMATCH	0x5AE1	There is a mismatch between the binding and schema for the message "%1".%0
E_BTW_MESSAGEDECL_INIT_DATA_UNAVAILABLE	0x5B00	Unable to obtain initialization data for field "%1".%0
E_BTW_LATENCY_INVALID_VALUE	0x5B20	The Latency property value must be a non-negative integer that is less than the maximum long integer "%1!d!".%0
E_BTW_PORT_LATENCY_ON_INTERNAL	0x5B21	Cannot specify latency on an internal port.%0

Message name	Value	Description
E_BTW_MESSAGE_TECHNOLOGY_MISMATCH	0x5BB0	There is a mismatch between the port "%1" technology "%2" and the message "%3" technology "%4".%0
E_BTW_FIELD_TECHNOLOGY_MISMATCH	0x5BC0	There is a mismatch between the message "%1" technology "%2" and the field "%3" technology "%4".%0
E_BTW_COM_PORT_NOT_CREATABLE	0x5C10	If a COM port can be invoked, it must have a CLSID, a ProgID, or a moniker.%0
E_BTW_AUTORETURN_COM_PORT_MUST_BE_USED_INSIDE_CONTEXT	0x5C11	The port "%1", which is configured to abort a transaction if a method returns a failure HRESULT, can only be used inside a transaction.%0
E_BTW_COM_PORT_GENERAL_ACCESS_FAILURE	0x5C12	A COM port can be invoked. Please refer to the Windows 2000 documentation.%1%0
E_BTW_COM_PARAMETERS_LIMIT	0x5C20	The method has "%1!d!" parameter(s). The current limit is "%2!d!".%0
E_BTW_COM_NO_MATCHING_RETURN	0x5C21	The COM method has no matching Return.%0
E_BTW_COM_NO_MATCHING_METHOD	0x5C22	The COM Return has no matching method.%0
E_BTW_INVALID_SLOT_NUMBER	0x5C23	The slot number "%1!d!" is not valid. Slot numbers cannot be less than the following value: SLOT_NONE(-1).%0
E_BTW_INVALID_INVOKE_KIND	0x5C24	The invokeKind value "%1!d!" is not valid. Acceptable values are: 1,2,3,4 and 8.%0
E_BTW_PROXY_DISCONNECTED	0x5C25	The proxy has been disconnected.%0
E_BTW_COM_DISPATCH_SLOT_SPECIFIED	0x5C26	A slot number cannot be specified for the dispatch interface.%0
E_BTW_COM_SPECIFY_DISPID_OR_SLOT	0x5C27	Valid values for dispid or slot must be specified.%0
E_BTW_COM_INVALID_BYREF_FOR_RETURN_MESSAGES	0x5C30	Byref should be "1" since "%1" is a <com:return> message.%0
E_BTW_COM_INVALID_NESTED_VARIANTS	0x5C31	More than one level of nesting for variants is not permitted.%0
E_BTW_COM_FIELD_INDEX_MUST_BE_NON_NEGATIVE	0x5C32	The index "%1!d!" for the field is not valid. The index must be a non-negative integer.%0
E_BTW_COM_FIELD_INDEX_REPEATED	0x5C33	The index "%1!d!" for the field has been used before on another field in the message.%0

Message name	Value	Description
E_BTW_COM_FIELD_INDEX_NOT_CONTIGUOUS	0x5C34	For synchronous action pair messages "%1" and "%2", the index "%3!d!" for a field is not valid. The field indices for these messages must form a contiguous block of non-negative numbers that start with zero.%0
E_BTW_MSMQ_NO_MQRT_DLL	0x5D00	The Message Queue DLL, MQRT.DLL, cannot be loaded.%0
E_BTW_MSMQ_CREATECHANNEL	0x5D01	MQBinder: CreateChannel failed for: %1.%0
E_BTW_MSMQ_NOT_CONFIGERED_PROPERLY	0x5D02	The Message Queuing Service is not configured properly. A queue object could not be opened %1.%0
E_BTW_MSMQ_NO_CERTIFICATE_AVAILABLE	0x5D03	The Message Queuing Service is not able to obtain a certificate.%1%0
E_BTW_MSMQ_NO_WELLKNOWN_QUEUE_NAME	0x5D04	A message cannot be sent to a known queue because the queue is not named in the XLANG schedule. You must provide a queue name in the XLANG schedule.%1%0
E_BTW_MSMQ_INVALID_FIELD_TYPE	0x5D05	The field type specified for message "%1" field "%2" is not valid.%0
E_BTW_MSMQ_PORT_NOT_BOUND	0x5D06	The Message Queuing port is not bound.%1%0
E_BTW_MSMQ_QUEUE_NOT_TRANSACTIONAL	0x5D10	The queue does not have the correct transactional properties.%1%0
E_BTW_MSMQ_OPEN_ACCESSDENIED	0x5D11	A Message Queuing access denied error occurred when opening the queue. Compare the accessRole specified for the queue in the XLANG schedule with the rights associated to the current user.%1%0
E_BTW_MSMQ_OPEN_GENERALFAILURE	0x5D12	A Message Queuing failure occurred when opening the queue. Refer to the Message Queuing Service documentation in Windows 2000 to look up the error code and diagnose as appropriate.%1%0
E_BTW_MSMQ_PORT_NOT_CREATABLE	0x5D13	A port that is implemented by using a message queue must have a queue name.%0
E_BTW_MSMQ_GENERAL_QUEUE_ACCESS_FAILURE	0x5D14	A Message Queuing failure occurred when accessing the queue. Refer to the Message Queuing Service documentation in Windows 2000 to look up the error code and diagnose as appropriate.%1%0

Message name	Value	Description
E_BTW_MSMQ_INVALID_MESSAGE_VT_TYPE	0x5D20	The Message Queuing message is of unknown format.%1%0
E_BTW_MSMQ_MESSAGE_UNKNOWN_MESSAGETYPE	0x5D21	The Message Queuing message is of unknown message type. The message type could not be obtained from the message.%1%0
E_BTW_MSMQ_MESSAGE_UNAUTHENTICATED	0x5D22	The Message Queuing message is not authenticated but the port only accepts authenticated messages.%1%0
E_BTW_MSMQ_MESSAGE_INCORRECT_AUTHENTICATE_LEVEL	0x5D23	The Message Queuing message is not authenticated at the requested level.%1%0
E_BTW_MSMQ_MESSAGE_INVALID_MESSAGE	0x5D24	The Message Queuing message has a message body that is not valid.%1%0
E_BTW_MSMQ_MESSAGE_NOT_SEND	0x5D25	The Message Queuing message could not be sent.%1%0
E_BTW_MSMQ_MESSAGE_SCHEMAVALIDATION_FAILED	0x5D26	The Message Queuing message was not successfully validated against the schema that was provided. Check the schema and the schema path.%1%0
E_BTW_MSMQ_COULD_NOT_CREATE_MQMESSAGE	0x5D27	The message instance could not be converted to a Message Queuing message. %1%0
E_BTW_MSMQ_NO_TRUSTRELATIONSHIP_FOR_USER	0x5D28	The trust relationship for the provided user could not be established.%1%0
E_BTW_MSMQ_MESSAGE_EMPY_MESSAGE	0x5D29	The Message Queuing message has an empty message body.%1%0
E_BTW_MSMQ_MESSAGE_ONLY_ONE_EMPTY_XPATH_ALLOWED	0x5D2A	The Message Queuing message can have only one field with an empty node path (XPath).%0
E_BTW_MSMQ_MESSAGE_ONE_EMPTY_XPATH_NEEDED	0x5D2B	The Message Queuing message must have one field with an empty node path (XPath).%0
E_BTW_MSMQ_MESSAGE_INVALID_MESSAGEBODY	0x5D2C	The Message Queuing message has a message body that is not valid.%1%0
E_BTW_MSMQ_MESSAGE_INVALID_MESSAGESTRING	0x5D2D	The Message Queuing message has an invalid string for the message body.%1%0
E_BTW_MSMQ_MESSAGE_UNKNOWN_MESSAGE	0x5D2E	The Message Queuing message is an invalid or unknown message and was moved to the dead-letter queue.%1%0

Message name	Value	Description
E_BTW_MSMQ_MESSAGE_TYPE_CONFLICTING_SCHEMA	0x5D2F	The Message Queuing messages "%1" and "%2", which are of type "%3" on port "%4", have conflicting specification representations. This could be because the name, type, or XPath query does not match for one of the fields in the two representations.%0
E_BTW_MSMQ_DOCUMENT_FIELD_TYPE_NOT_STRING	0x5D30	A Message Queuing message's field "%1", that has an empty node path (XPath), must be a string data type.%0
E_BTW_MSMQ_DOCUMENT_FIELD_CANNOT_CONVERT_TO_STRING	0x5D31	A Message Queuing message's field could not be converted to a string.%1%0
E_BTW_MSMQ_DOCUMENT_FIELD_CONVERTION_FAILURE	0x5D32	The Message Queuing message's field could not be converted.%1%0
E_BTW_CANT_DISPOSE_MESSAGE	0x6001	The XLANG schedule instance was bound to a queue that received a message that is not valid. The XLANG Scheduler Engine was unable to transfer this message to the dead-letter queue, so the schedule instance has been terminated.%0

Administering XLANG Schedules

The interfaces in this section provide access to XLANG Scheduler System Managers, XLANG group managers, XLANG schedule instances, and XLANG ports.

The XLANG Scheduler System Manager provides moniker resolution and maintains a collection of group managers. A group manager runs in every COM+ application that has been designated as an XLANG schedule host, and maintains a collection of XLANG schedule instances. An XLANG schedule instance represents a running XLANG schedule that can be queried for information, such as the schedule's completion status. For XLANG schedules with a COM-bound port, a proxy object can be used to obtain a reference to the interface specified in the port binding.

✍ Note

- Only one XLANG Scheduler System Manager can exist on each computer.

The following illustration shows the relationship between these interfaces and the corresponding monikers.

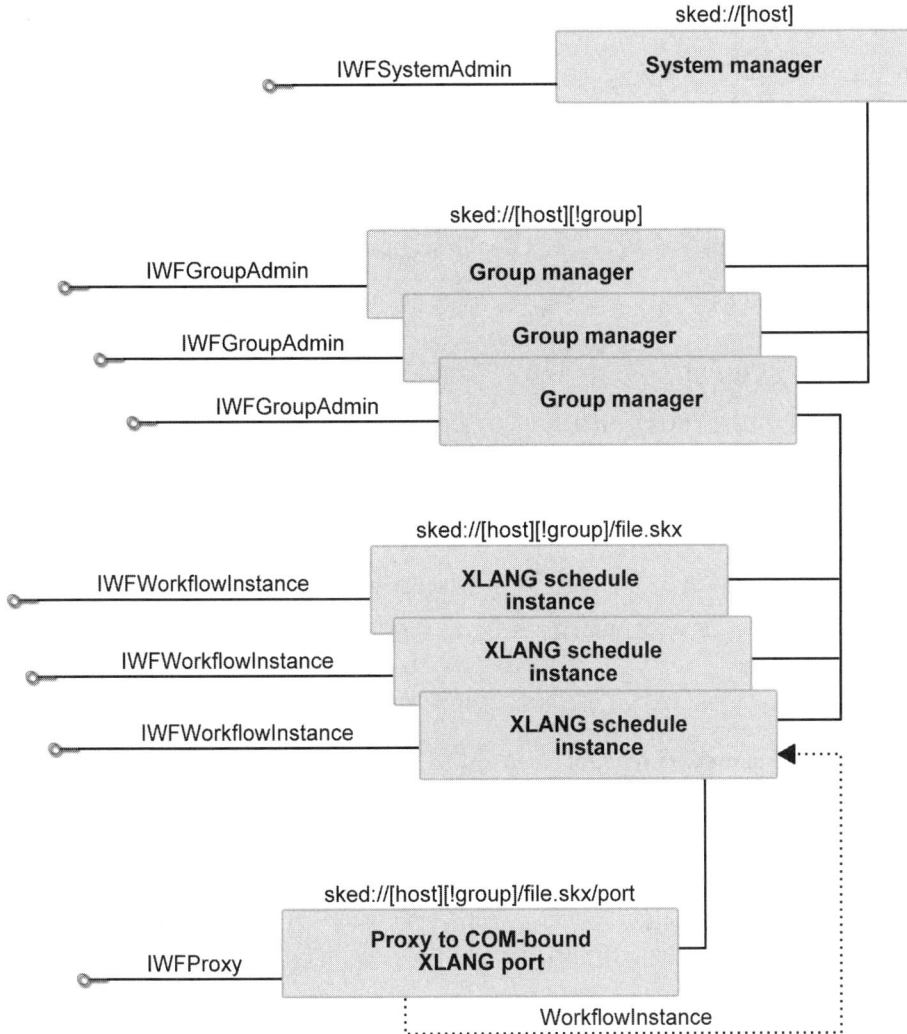

XLANG Schedule Reference for Visual Basic

IWFGroupAdmin Object

The **IWFGroupAdmin** object allows a client application to control running instances of an XLANG schedule. Use this object to stop, suspend, resume, and retrieve information about all the schedule instances associated with a group manager.

The properties of the **IWFGroupAdmin** object are shown in the following table.

Property	Type	Description
Count	long	The number of running schedule instances associated with this group manager.
FullyQualifiedName	BSTR	The moniker of this group manager.
InstanceIsResident	VARIANT_BOOL	A value that indicates whether the specified schedule instance is currently resident in memory.
InstanceIsSuspended	VARIANT_BOOL	A value that indicates whether the specified schedule instance is currently in a suspended state.
Name	BSTR	The name of this group manager.
UseFileDSN	VARIANT_BOOL	A value that indicates whether a data source name (DSN) file is used for dehydrating the schedule instances.

The methods of the **IWFGroupAdmin** object are shown in the following table.

Method	Description
ResumeInstance	Resumes the execution of a schedule in a suspended state.
Shutdown	Dehydrates all running schedule instances, and stops the group manager.
Startup	Starts all the dehydrated schedule instances for the current group manager.
SuspendInstance	Pauses execution of the schedule instance.
TerminateInstance	Stops execution of the schedule instance.

Remarks

To obtain a reference to an **IWFGroupAdmin** object, you can invoke the COM **GetObject** function using a moniker. The following Microsoft Visual Basic code sample shows how to obtain a reference to the default XLANG Scheduler Group Manager on the local computer.

```
Dim oGM As IWFGroupAdmin
Set oGM = GetObject("sked://!XLANG Scheduler")
```

To obtain a reference to other group managers, replace "XLANG Scheduler" with the name of the COM+ application that has been designated as an XLANG Scheduler Engine host or group manager. You can determine whether a COM+ application is a group manager by using the **IsWorkflowHost** method on the **IWFSystemAdmin** interface.

You can also obtain a reference to all group managers associated with the XLANG Scheduler System Manager through the collection of **IWFGroupAdmin** objects contained by the **SysMgr** object. The following Microsoft Visual Basic code displays the fully qualified name of each group manager.

```
Dim oSM As SysMgr
Dim oGM As IWFGroupAdmin
Set oSM = GetObject("sked://")
For Each oGM In oSM
    MsgBox ("Group Manager: " + oGM.FullyQualifiedName)
Next
```

The **IWFGroupAdmin** object also enumerates a collection of the **IWFWorkflowInstance** objects that represent currently running schedule instances for this group manager.

You can determine the XLANG Scheduler System Manager associated with any group manager by following these steps:

1. Retrieve the **FullyQualifiedName** property of the **IWFGroupAdmin** object.

2. Parse the XLANG Scheduler System Manager name out of the moniker string returned.

    This is the portion between the sked:// prefix and the exclamation point (!).

3. Obtain a reference to the **SysMgr** object using a moniker created with the XLANG Scheduler System Manager name from step 2.

For additional information about monikers, see "Moniker Syntax" in Chapter 8, "BizTalk Orchestration Services."

Notes

*   When using C++, the COM **CoGetObject** function is used in place of **GetObject**.

*   When using C++, the **IWFSystemAdmin** object is used in place of the **SysMgr** object.

Requirements

Windows NT/2000: Requires Windows 2000 SP1 or later
Library: Use XLANG Scheduler Runtime Type Library (SkedCore.dll)

IWFGroupAdmin.Count Property

The **Count** property contains the number of running XLANG schedule instances associated with this group manager.

Syntax

object.**Count**

Parameters

None

Return Values

This property returns a **Long** that contains the number of running schedule instances associated with this group manager.

Error Value

If an error is raised, **Err.Number** is set to one of the values documented in "XLANG Schedule Error Messages" earlier in this chapter, or is set to one of the values documented in Appendix A, "Error Messages."

Remarks

This is a read-only property.

Requirements

Windows NT/2000: Requires Windows 2000 SP1 or later
Library: Use XLANG Scheduler Runtime Type Library (SkedCore.dll)

IWFGroupAdmin.FullyQualifiedName Property

The **FullyQualifiedName** property contains the moniker of this group manager.

Syntax

object.**FullyQualifiedName**

Parameters

None

Return Values

This property returns a **String** that contains the moniker of this group manager.

Error Value

If an error is raised, **Err.Number** is set to one of the values documented in "XLANG Schedule Error Messages" earlier in this chapter, or is set to one of the values documented in Appendix A, "Error Messages."

Remarks

This is a read-only property.

Although a group manager can be instantiated through a local moniker, this property always includes the full Domain Name Services (DNS) style system name. For example, suppose the default XLANG Scheduler Group Manager, named *XLANG Scheduler*, is running on a computer named *MyMachine* in the domain *vigorair-18.com*. The **FullyQualifiedName** property would contain a value of *sked://MyMachine.vigorair-18.com!XLANG Scheduler*.

Requirements

Windows NT/2000: Requires Windows 2000 SP1 or later
Library: Use XLANG Scheduler Runtime Type Library (SkedCore.dll)

IWFGroupAdmin.InstanceIsResident Property

The **InstanceIsResident** property contains a value that indicates whether the specified XLANG schedule instance is currently resident in memory.

Syntax

object.**InstanceIsResident**(_
   varInstanceId **As String** _
)

Parameters

varInstanceId
   String that contains the globally unique identifier (GUID) assigned to the schedule instance.

Return Values

This property returns a **Boolean** set to **True** if the specified schedule instance is currently resident in memory. If the specified schedule is currently dehydrated, this property is set to **False**.

Error Value

If an error is raised, **Err.Number** is set to one of the values documented in "XLANG Schedule Error Messages" earlier in this chapter, or is set to one of the values documented in Appendix A, "Error Messages."

Remarks

This is a read-only property.

Requirements

Windows NT/2000: Requires Windows 2000 SP1 or later
Library: Use XLANG Scheduler Runtime Type Library (SkedCore.dll)

IWFGroupAdmin.InstanceIsSuspended Property

The **InstanceIsSuspended** property contains a value that indicates whether the specified XLANG schedule instance is currently in a suspended state.

Syntax

object.**InstanceIsSuspended(** _
   varInstanceId **As String** _
)

Parameters

varInstanceId
   String that contains the globally unique identifier (GUID) assigned to the schedule instance.

Return Values

This property returns a **Boolean** set to **True** if the specified schedule instance is currently in a suspended state. If the specified schedule is not suspended, this property is set to **False**.

Error Value

If an error is raised, **Err.Number** is set to one of the values documented in "XLANG Schedule Error Messages" earlier in this chapter, or is set to one of the values documented in Appendix A, "Error Messages."

Remarks

This is a read-only property.

This property should be checked prior to calling the **ResumeInstance** method.

Requirements

Windows NT/2000: Requires Windows 2000 SP1 or later
Library: Use XLANG Scheduler Runtime Type Library (SkedCore.dll)

IWFGroupAdmin.Name Property

The **Name** property contains the name of this group manager.

Syntax

object.**Name**

Parameters

None

Return Values

This property returns a **String** that contains the name of this group manager.

Error Value

If an error is raised, **Err.Number** is set to one of the values documented in "XLANG Schedule Error Messages" earlier in this chapter, or is set to one of the values documented in Appendix A, "Error Messages."

Remarks

This is a read-only property.

This property is the same as the name of the hosting COM+ application.

Requirements

Windows NT/2000: Requires Windows 2000 SP1 or later
Library: Use XLANG Scheduler Runtime Type Library (SkedCore.dll)

IWFGroupAdmin.ResumeInstance Method

The **ResumeInstance** method starts the XLANG schedule instance executing from a suspended state.

Syntax

object.**ResumeInstance(** _
    bInstanceId **As String** _
)

Parameters

bInstanceId
    String that contains the globally unique identifier (GUID) assigned to the schedule instance to be resumed.

Return Values

None

Error Value

If an error is raised, **Err.Number** is set to one of the values documented in "XLANG Schedule Error Messages" earlier in this chapter, or is set to one of the values documented in Appendix A, "Error Messages."

Remarks

The schedule instance can be paused with the **SuspendInstance** method. Prior to calling the **ResumeInstance** method, the **InstanceIsSuspended** property should be checked.

Requirements

Windows NT/2000: Requires Windows 2000 SP1 or later
Library: Use XLANG Scheduler Runtime Type Library (SkedCore.dll)

IWFGroupAdmin.Shutdown Method

The **Shutdown** method stops the group manager and dehydrates all running XLANG schedule instances.

Syntax

object.**Shutdown**

Parameters

None

Return Values

None

Error Value

If an error is raised, **Err.Number** is set to one of the values documented in "XLANG Schedule Error Messages" earlier in this chapter, or is set to one of the values documented in Appendix A, "Error Messages."

Remarks

Prior to stopping the group manager, all running schedule instances associated with this group manager are dehydrated to the database specified in the data source name (DSN) file, and requests for activation of any new schedule instances are refused until shutdown is completed.

Any component that is bound in an XLANG schedule should not invoke this method to stop the group manager, as this can produce unexpected results.

Requirements

Windows NT/2000: Requires Windows 2000 SP1 or later
Library: Use XLANG Scheduler Runtime Type Library (SkedCore.dll)

IWFGroupAdmin.Startup Method

The **Startup** method starts all the previously running dehydrated XLANG schedule instances associated with this group manager.

Syntax

object.**Startup**

Parameters

None

Return Values

None

Error Value

If an error is raised, **Err.Number** is set to one of the values documented in "XLANG Schedule Error Messages" earlier in this chapter, or is set to one of the values documented in Appendix A, "Error Messages."

Remarks

The XLANG Scheduler System Manager normally calls this method. Users should not call this method directly.

Requirements

Windows NT/2000: Requires Windows 2000 SP1 or later
Library: Use XLANG Scheduler Runtime Type Library (SkedCore.dll)

IWFGroupAdmin.SuspendInstance Method

The **SuspendInstance** method pauses the running XLANG schedule instance in its current state.

Syntax

object.**SuspendInstance**(_
    bInstanceId **As String** _
)

Parameters

bInstanceId

> **String** that contains the globally unique identifier (GUID) assigned to the schedule instance to be suspended.

Return Values

None

Error Value

If an error is raised, **Err.Number** is set to one of the values documented in "XLANG Schedule Error Messages" earlier in this chapter, or is set to one of the values documented in Appendix A, "Error Messages."

Remarks

The schedule instance can be restarted with the **ResumeInstance** method.

This method might block if actions with COM-bound ports are waiting for a method to complete, or if a short-lived transaction is currently in progress.

Requirements

Windows NT/2000: Requires Windows 2000 SP1 or later
Library: Use XLANG Scheduler Runtime Type Library (SkedCore.dll)

IWFGroupAdmin.TerminateInstance Method

The **TerminateInstance** method stops a running XLANG schedule instance.

Syntax

object.**TerminateInstance(** _
　 bInstanceId **As String** _
)

Parameters

bInstanceId

> **String** that contains the globally unique identifier (GUID) assigned to the schedule instance to be stopped.

Return Values

None

Error Value

If an error is raised, **Err.Number** is set to one of the values documented in "XLANG Schedule Error Messages" earlier in this chapter, or is set to one of the values documented in Appendix A, "Error Messages."

Remarks

A terminated schedule instance can never be restarted or resumed.

This method might block if actions with COM-bound ports are waiting for a method to complete, or if a short-lived transaction is currently in progress.

Requirements

Windows NT/2000: Requires Windows 2000 SP1 or later
Library: Use XLANG Scheduler Runtime Type Library (SkedCore.dll)

IWFGroupAdmin.UseFileDSN Property

The **UseFileDSN** property contains a value that indicates whether a data source name (DSN) file is used for dehydrating the XLANG schedule instances.

Syntax

object.**UseFileDSN**

Parameters

None

Return Values

This property returns a **Boolean** set to **True** if the group manager uses a DSN file for dehydrating schedule instances. If a DSN file is not used, **False** is returned.

Error Value

If an error is raised, **Err.Number** is set to one of the values documented in "XLANG Schedule Error Messages" earlier in this chapter, or is set to one of the values documented in Appendix A, "Error Messages."

Remarks

This is a read-only property.

The value of this property is set when the group manager process is launched. The DSN setting in the COM+ catalog is changed either on the **XLANG** tab of the **XLANG Scheduler Properties** dialog box or by setting the **UseFileDSN** property on the **IWFSystemAdmin** object. If the DSN value is changed while the group manager is running, the value of this property is not dynamically updated. The new value is not reflected until the next time the group manager is launched. Updates to this property require the caller to be in the XLANG Administrator role and are not normally performed by user code.

Requirements

Windows NT/2000: Requires Windows 2000 SP1 or later
Library: Use XLANG Scheduler Runtime Type Library (SkedCore.dll)

IWFProxy Object

The **IWFProxy** object contains information about ports in an XLANG schedule instance that is bound to a COM component. Use this object to obtain a schedule instance. If this object is used on a non-COM port binding, an error is returned.

The properties of the **IWFProxy** object are shown in the following table.

Property	Type	Description
FullyQualifiedName	**BSTR**	The fully qualified name of a COM-bound port.
WorkflowInstance	**IWFWorkflowInstance**	The current schedule instance.

Remarks

A reference to this interface can be obtained from:

- The **Port** property available on the **IWFWorkflowInstance** interface.
- An XLANG schedule moniker that specifies the port name.

The following Microsoft Visual Basic code sample shows how to activate an XLANG schedule on the local computer by using a moniker, and obtain a reference to the named port on that XLANG schedule instance.

```
Dim oPort As Object
Set oPort = GetObject("sked:///C:\schedules\test.skx/PortA")
```

At this point, the *oPort* variable contains a reference to the COM object bound in *PortA* of the schedule instance.

For additional information about monikers, see "Moniker Syntax" in Chapter 8, "BizTalk Orchestration Services."

Notes

- When using C++, the COM **CoGetObject** function is used in place of **GetObject**.

Requirements

Windows NT/2000: Requires Windows 2000 SP1 or later
Library: Use XLANG Scheduler Runtime Type Library (SkedCore.dll)

IWFProxy.FullyQualifiedName Property

The **FullyQualifiedName** property contains the moniker of the port instance to which this proxy is bound.

Syntax

object.**FullyQualifiedName**

Parameters

None

Return Values

This property returns a **String** that contains the moniker of the port.

Error Value

If an error is raised, **Err.Number** is set to one of the values documented in "XLANG Schedule Error Messages" earlier in this chapter, or is set to one of the values documented in Appendix A, "Error Messages."

Remarks

This is a read-only property.

The moniker retrieved with this property can be used with the COM **GetObject** function to obtain a reference to the XLANG schedule instance. This moniker is valid as long as the schedule instance is running. If the schedule instance is dehydrated and rehydrated for any reason, such as rebooting the system, the moniker remains valid. Once the schedule instance completes, or ends by using the **TerminateInstance** method, the moniker can no longer be used.

Requirements

Windows NT/2000: Requires Windows 2000 SP1 or later
Library: Use XLANG Scheduler Runtime Type Library (SkedCore.dll)

IWFProxy.WorkflowInstance Property

The **WorkflowInstance** property contains a reference to the current XLANG schedule instance.

Syntax

object.**WorkflowInstance**

Parameters

None

Return Values

This property returns an **Object** that contains the current schedule instance.

Error Value

If an error is raised, **Err.Number** is set to one of the values documented in "XLANG Schedule Error Messages" earlier in this chapter, or is set to one of the values documented in Appendix A, "Error Messages."

Remarks

This is a read-only property.

Requirements

Windows NT/2000: Requires Windows 2000 SP1 or later
Library: Use XLANG Scheduler Runtime Type Library (SkedCore.dll)

SysMgr Object

The **SysMgr** object provides a client application with system-wide administrative control over the XLANG Scheduler Engine. Use this object to start, stop, and retrieve information about the group managers.

The properties of the **SysMgr** object are shown in the following table.

Property	Type	Description
Count	**long**	Contains the number of group managers associated with this XLANG Scheduler System Manager.
FullyQualifiedName	**BSTR**	Contains the fully qualified DNS-style name of the XLANG Scheduler System Manager.
IsWorkflowHost	**VARIANT_BOOL**	Checks whether the COM+ server application is an XLANG Scheduler Engine host.
Item	**BSTR**	Returns a reference to the named schedule group.
UseFileDSN	**VARIANT_BOOL**	Indicates whether a data source name (DSN) file is used for dehydrating the XLANG schedule instances.

The methods of the **SysMgr** object are shown in the following table.

Method	Description
ShutdownAll	Shuts down all group managers.
ShutdownApp	Shuts down a specific group manager.
Startup	Starts all group managers.
TestAdminStatus	Checks a caller for XLANG Scheduler Engine administrator access.

Remarks

To obtain a reference to this object, you can invoke the COM **GetObject** function using a moniker. The following Microsoft Visual Basic code sample shows how to obtain a reference to the XLANG Scheduler System Manager on the local computer.

```
Dim oSM As SysMgr
Set oSM = GetObject("sked://")
```

This object also enumerates a collection of the **IWFGroupAdmin** objects that represent the group managers associated with this XLANG Scheduler System Manager.

For additional information about monikers, see "Moniker Syntax" in Chapter 8, "BizTalk Orchestration Services."

Notes

- When using C++, the COM **CoGetObject** function is used in place of **GetObject**.

Requirements

Windows NT/2000: Requires Windows 2000 SP1 or later
Library: Use XLANG Scheduler - System Manager (SKEDSMGR.dll)

SysMgr.Count Property

The **Count** property contains the number of running group managers.

Syntax

object.**Count**

Parameters

None

Return Values

This property returns a **Long** that contains the number of running group managers.

Error Value

If an error is raised, **Err.Number** is set to one of the values documented in "XLANG Schedule Error Messages" earlier in this chapter, or is set to one of the values documented in Appendix A, "Error Messages."

Remarks

This is a read-only property.

Requirements

Windows NT/2000: Requires Windows 2000 SP1 or later
Library: Use XLANG Scheduler - System Manager (SKEDSMGR.dll)

SysMgr.FullyQualifiedName Property

The **FullyQualifiedName** property contains the moniker of this XLANG Scheduler System Manager.

Syntax

object.**FullyQualifiedName**

Parameters

None

Return Values

This property returns a **String** that contains the moniker of this group manager.

Error Value

If an error is raised, **Err.Number** is set to one of the values documented in "XLANG Schedule Error Messages" earlier in this chapter, or is set to one of the values documented in Appendix A, "Error Messages."

Remarks

This is a read-only property.

Although an XLANG Scheduler System Manager can be instantiated through a local moniker, this property always includes the full Domain Name Services (DNS) style system name. For example, suppose the XLANG Scheduler System Manager is running on a computer named *MyMachine* in the domain *vigorair-18.com*. The **FullyQualifiedName** property would contain a value of *sked://MyMachine.vigorair-18.com*.

Requirements

Windows NT/2000: Requires Windows 2000 SP1 or later
Library: Use XLANG Scheduler - System Manager (SKEDSMGR.dll)

SysMgr.IsWorkflowHost Property

The **IsWorkflowHost** property controls whether the named COM+ server application is an XLANG Scheduler Engine host.

Syntax

object.**IsWorkflowHost**(_
  varAppName **As String** _
)

Parameters

varAppName
  String that contains the COM+ server application name.

Return Values

This property returns a **Boolean** that indicates whether the COM+ server application is hosting the XLANG Scheduler Engine.

Error Value

If an error is raised, **Err.Number** is set to one of the values documented in "XLANG Schedule Error Messages" earlier in this chapter, or is set to one of the values documented in Appendix A, "Error Messages."

Remarks

This property cannot be set on the XLANG Scheduler Engine application, or on any COM+ application marked as read-only.

Requirements

Windows NT/2000: Requires Windows 2000 SP1 or later
Library: Use XLANG Scheduler - System Manager (SKEDSMGR.dll)

SysMgr.Item Property

The **Item** property returns a reference to one of the running group managers.

Syntax

object.**Item**(_
   strGrpMgrName **As String** _
)

Parameters

strGrpMgrName
   String that contains the group name corresponding to the hosting COM+ server
   application name. Group names are case sensitive and can contain spaces.

Return Values

This property returns a group manager **Object**.

Error Value

If an error is raised, **Err.Number** is set to one of the values documented in "XLANG
Schedule Error Messages" earlier in this chapter, or is set to one of the values documented in
Appendix A, "Error Messages."

Remarks

This is a read-only property.

Requirements

Windows NT/2000: Requires Windows 2000 SP1 or later
Library: Use XLANG Scheduler - System Manager (SKEDSMGR.dll)

SysMgr.ShutdownAll Method

The **ShutdownAll** method stops the group managers and terminates their associated COM+
applications.

Syntax

object.**ShutdownAll**

Parameters

None

Return Values

None

Error Value

If an error is raised, **Err.Number** is set to one of the values documented in "XLANG Schedule Error Messages" earlier in this chapter, or is set to one of the values documented in Appendix A, "Error Messages."

Remarks

When the **ShutdownAll** method is called, new schedule activations are disabled and the shutdown notice is propagated to all running group managers. Once this method has completed, all group managers are stopped and the system can be safely rebooted.

Requirements

Windows NT/2000: Requires Windows 2000 SP1 or later
Library: Use XLANG Scheduler - System Manager (SKEDSMGR.dll)

SysMgr.ShutdownApp Method

The **ShutdownApp** method stops a specific group manager application and terminates the associated COM+ application.

Syntax

object.**ShutdownApp(** _
  varAppName **As String** _
)

Parameters

varAppName
  String that contains the COM+ server application name to be stopped.

Return Values

None

Error Value

If an error is raised, **Err.Number** is set to one of the values documented in "XLANG Schedule Error Messages" earlier in this chapter, or is set to one of the values documented in Appendix A, "Error Messages."

Remarks

When the **ShutdownApp** method is called, new schedule activations on the named application are disabled and all running XLANG schedule instances associated with that application are stopped. If this method is called on the default XLANG Scheduler Group Manager, all group managers are shut down. Calling this method on the default XLANG Scheduler Group Manager is equivalent to calling the **ShutdownAll** method.

✐ Note

- The COM+ application name of the default XLANG Scheduler Group Manager is XLANG Scheduler.

Requirements

Windows NT/2000: Requires Windows 2000 SP1 or later
Library: Use XLANG Scheduler - System Manager (SKEDSMGR.dll)

SysMgr.StartUp Method

The **StartUp** method starts the group managers.

Syntax

object.**StartUp**

Parameters

None

Return Values

None

Error Value

If an error is raised, **Err.Number** is set to one of the values documented in "XLANG Schedule Error Messages" earlier in this chapter, or is set to one of the values documented in Appendix A, "Error Messages."

Remarks

When this method is invoked, rehydration is initiated for all group managers and, subsequently, all XLANG schedules. This method is asynchronous, and it can complete before all group managers and schedules are running.

Requirements

Windows NT/2000: Requires Windows 2000 SP1 or later
Library: Use XLANG Scheduler - System Manager (SKEDSMGR.dll)

SysMgr.TestAdminStatus Method

The **TestAdminStatus** method determines whether a caller on the **IWFGroupAdmin** objcct is an XLANG Scheduler Engine administrator.

Syntax

object.**TestAdminStatus**

Parameters

None

Return Values

None

Error Value

If an error is raised, **Err.Number** is set to one of the values documented in "XLANG Schedule Error Messages" earlier in this chapter, or is set to one of the values documented in Appendix A, "Error Messages."

Remarks

This method is intended for internal use by the group managers.

Requirements

Windows NT/2000: Requires Windows 2000 SP1 or later
Library: Use XLANG Scheduler - System Manager (SKEDSMGR.dll)

SysMgr.UseFileDSN Property

The **UseFileDSN** property contains a value that indicates whether a COM+ server application uses a data source name (DSN) file for dehydrating the XLANG schedule instances.

Syntax

object.**UseFileDSN(_**
    varAppName **As String _**
)

Parameters

varAppName
    String that contains the COM+ server application name.

Return Values

This property returns a **Boolean** set to **True** if the COM+ server application uses a DSN file for dehydrating schedule instances. If a DSN file is not used, **False** is returned.

Error Value

If an error is raised, **Err.Number** is set to one of the values documented in "XLANG Schedule Error Messages" earlier in this chapter, or is set to one of the values documented in Appendix A, "Error Messages."

Remarks

If this property is changed while any group manager is running, the value of this property is not dynamically updated in the group managers. Therefore, the **UseFileDSN** property value exposed by the **IWFGroupAdmin** object contains an incorrect value. The updated value is not reflected until the next time the group manager is launched.

Requirements

Windows NT/2000: Requires Windows 2000 SP1 or later
Library: Use XLANG Scheduler - System Manager (SKEDSMGR.dll)

IWFWorkflowInstance Object

The **IWFWorkflowInstance** object allows a client application to navigate the ports of an XLANG schedule instance, check the completion status, and determine whether the schedule instance completed successfully. Use this object to gather information about a specific, running schedule instance.

The properties of the **IWFWorkflowInstance** object are shown in the following table.

Property	Type	Description
CompletionStatus	**long**	A value that indicates the success or failure of the schedule instance.
FullPortName	**BSTR**	The full name of a port in a form usable by the associated technology.
FullyQualifiedName	**BSTR**	The fully qualified name of this schedule instance.
InstanceId	**BSTR**	The unique identifier associated with this schedule instance.
IsCompleted	**VARIANT_BOOL**	A value that indicates whether the schedule instance completed.
ModuleId	**BSTR**	The unique identifier of the XML module that contains the schedule and binding information.
ModuleName	**BSTR**	The name of the XML module that contains the schedule and binding information.
ParentInstanceID	**BSTR**	The unique identifier of the parent schedule instance.
Port	**IUnknown**	A reference to the named port. This is applicable only to COM-based port bindings.

The method of the **IWFWorkflowInstance** object is shown in the following table.

Method	Description
WaitForCompletion	Blocks until the schedule instance completes.

Remarks

A reference to this object can be obtained from:

- The **WorkflowInstance** property available on the **IWFProxy** object.

- The collection of **IWFWorkflowInstance** objects returned by the **IWFGroupAdmin** object.

- An XLANG schedule moniker.

The following Microsoft Visual Basic code sample shows how to instantiate an XLANG schedule on the local computer and obtain a reference to that schedule instance.

```
Dim oWFI As IWFWorkflowInstance
Set oWFI = GetObject("sked:///C:\schedules\test.skx")
```

To obtain a reference to all currently running schedule instances in a group manager, you can access the collection of **IWFWorkflowInstance** objects contained by the **IWFGroupAdmin** object. The following Microsoft Visual Basic code displays the fully qualified name of each schedule instance running in the default XLANG Scheduler Group Manager.

```
Dim oGM As IWFGroupAdmin
Dim oWFI As IWFWorkflowInstance
Set oGM = GetObject("sked://!XLANG Scheduler")
For Each oWFI In oGM
    MsgBox ("XLANG Schedule: " + oWFI.FullyQualifiedName)
Next
```

When using multiple group managers, you can determine the group manager associated with any schedule instance by following these steps:

1. Retrieve the **FullyQualifiedName** property of the **IWFWorkflowInstance** object.

2. Parse the group manager name out of the moniker string returned.

   This is the portion that begins with an exclamation point (!) and ends with a slash (/).

3. Obtain a reference to the **IWFGroupAdmin** object using a moniker created with the group manager name from step 2.

For additional information about monikers, see "Moniker Syntax" in Chapter 8, "BizTalk Orchestration Services."

Notes

- When using C++, the COM **CoGetObject** function is used in place of **GetObject**.

- When accessing this object in Microsoft Visual Basic, you must declare your object variable with the appropriate type information rather than using the **Object** type. For example:

```
Dim myInstance As IWFWorkflowInstance
```

Requirements

Windows NT/2000: Requires Windows 2000 SP1 or later
Library: Use XLANG Scheduler Runtime Type Library (SkedCore.dll)

IWFWorkflowInstance.CompletionStatus Property

The **CompletionStatus** property indicates the final completion status of the XLANG schedule instance.

Syntax

object.**CompletionStatus**

Parameters

None

Return Values

This property returns a **Long** that contains the completion status.

Error Value

If an error is raised, **Err.Number** is set to one of the values documented in "XLANG Schedule Error Messages" earlier in this chapter, or is set to one of the values documented in Appendix A, "Error Messages."

Remarks

This is a read-only property.

Requirements

Windows NT/2000: Requires Windows 2000 SP1 or later
Library: Use XLANG Scheduler Runtime Type Library (SkedCore.dll)

IWFWorkflowInstance.FullPortName Property

The **FullPortName** property contains the full name of the specified port.

Syntax

object.**FullPortName**(_
   varParam **As String** _
)

Parameters

varParam
   String that contains the name of the port to be retrieved.

Return Values

This property returns a **String** that contains the full port name.

Error Value

If an error is raised, **Err.Number** is set to one of the values documented in "XLANG Schedule Error Messages" earlier in this chapter, or is set to one of the values documented in Appendix A, "Error Messages."

Remarks

This is a read-only property.

The full port name is returned in a form that is usable by the associated binding technology. For example, a port that is bound to a COM component returns a fully qualified moniker as the name of the port. For a port that is bound to Microsoft Message Queuing, this method returns the full path of the queue.

Requirements

Windows NT/2000: Requires Windows 2000 SP1 or later
Library: Use XLANG Scheduler Runtime Type Library (SkedCore.dll)

IWFWorkflowInstance.FullyQualifiedName Property

The **FullyQualifiedName** property contains the moniker of the XLANG schedule instance.

Syntax

object.**FullyQualifiedName**

Parameters

None

Return Values

This property returns a **String** that contains the moniker of the schedule instance.

Error Value

If an error is raised, **Err.Number** is set to one of the values documented in "XLANG Schedule Error Messages" earlier in this chapter, or is set to one of the values documented in Appendix A, "Error Messages."

Remarks

This is a read-only property.

Requirements

Windows NT/2000: Requires Windows 2000 SP1 or later
Library: Use XLANG Scheduler Runtime Type Library (SkedCore.dll)

IWFWorkflowInstance.InstanceId Property

The **InstanceId** property contains the globally unique identifier (GUID) assigned to the current XLANG schedule instance.

Syntax

object.**InstanceId**

Parameters

None

Return Values

This property returns a **String** that contains the GUID of the schedule instance.

Error Value

If an error is raised, **Err.Number** is set to one of the values documented in "XLANG Schedule Error Messages" earlier in this chapter, or is set to one of the values documented in Appendix A, "Error Messages."

Remarks

This is a read-only property.

Requirements

Windows NT/2000: Requires Windows 2000 SP1 or later
Library: Use XLANG Scheduler Runtime Type Library (SkedCore.dll)

IWFWorkflowInstance.IsCompleted Property

The **IsCompleted** property indicates whether the XLANG schedule instance has finished executing.

Syntax

object.**IsCompleted**

Parameters

None

Return Values

This property returns a **Boolean** that, if **True**, indicates the schedule instance has finished executing. If **False**, the schedule instance is still executing.

Error Value

If an error is raised, **Err.Number** is set to one of the values documented in "XLANG Schedule Error Messages" earlier in this chapter, or is set to one of the values documented in Appendix A, "Error Messages."

Remarks

This is a read-only property.

Requirements

Windows NT/2000: Requires Windows 2000 SP1 or later
Library: Use XLANG Scheduler Runtime Type Library (SkedCore.dll)

IWFWorkflowInstance.ModuleId Property

The **ModuleId** property contains the globally unique identifier (GUID) of the XLANG module associated with the current XLANG schedule instance.

Syntax

object.**ModuleId**

Parameters

None

Return Values

This property returns a **String** that contains the GUID of the XLANG module associated with the current schedule instance.

Error Value

If an error is raised, **Err.Number** is set to one of the values documented in "XLANG Schedule Error Messages" earlier in this chapter, or is set to one of the values documented in Appendix A, "Error Messages."

Remarks

This is a read-only property.

Requirements

Windows NT/2000: Requires Windows 2000 SP1 or later
Library: Use XLANG Scheduler Runtime Type Library (SkedCore.dll)

IWFWorkflowInstance.ModuleName Property

The **ModuleName** property contains the name of the XLANG module associated with the current XLANG schedule instance.

Syntax

object.**ModuleName**

Parameters

None

Return Values

This property returns a **String** that contains the name of the XLANG module associated with the current schedule instance.

Error Value

If an error is raised, **Err.Number** is set to one of the values documented in "XLANG Schedule Error Messages" earlier in this chapter, or is set to one of the values documented in Appendix A, "Error Messages."

Remarks

This is a read-only property.

The module name is defined in the XLANG schedule (.skx) file.

Requirements

Windows NT/2000: Requires Windows 2000 SP1 or later
Library: Use XLANG Scheduler Runtime Type Library (SkedCore.dll)

IWFWorkflowInstance.ParentInstanceID Property

The **ParentInstanceID** property contains the globally unique identifier (GUID) assigned to the parent XLANG schedule instance of the current schedule instance.

Syntax

object.**ParentInstanceID**

Parameters

None

Return Values

This property returns a **String** that contains the GUID of the parent schedule instance of the current schedule instance.

Error Value

If an error is raised, **Err.Number** is set to one of the values documented in "XLANG Schedule Error Messages" earlier in this chapter, or is set to one of the values documented in Appendix A, "Error Messages."

Remarks

This is a read-only property.

The property returns a NULL value if no parent schedule instance exists.

Requirements

Windows NT/2000: Requires Windows 2000 SP1 or later
Library: Use XLANG Scheduler Runtime Type Library (SkedCore.dll)

IWFWorkflowInstance.Port Property

The **Port** property contains a reference to a COM-bound port.

Syntax

object.**Port**(_
   varParam **As String** _
)

Parameters

varParam
   String that contains the name of the port to which to obtain a reference.

Return Values

This property returns an **Object** that contains the specified port.

Error Value

If an error is raised, **Err.Number** is set to one of the values documented in "XLANG Schedule Error Messages" earlier in this chapter, or is set to one of the values documented in Appendix A, "Error Messages."

Remarks

This is a read-only property.

The MK_E_NOOBJECT error code is returned if the moniker or port name passed in the *varParam* parameter is incorrect.

When using Microsoft Visual Basic, the variable used for the port reference returned by using this property should be declared as a specific class or as a **Variant**. You can't obtain the port reference if you declare the variable as an **Object** since the port actually returns an **IUnknown** reference.

Requirements

Windows NT/2000: Requires Windows 2000 SP1 or later
Library: Use XLANG Scheduler Runtime Type Library (SkedCore.dll)

IWFWorkflowInstance.WaitForCompletion Method

The **WaitForCompletion** method waits until the current XLANG schedule instance completes executing.

Syntax

object.**WaitForCompletion**

Parameters

None

Return Values

None

Error Value

If an error is raised, **Err.Number** is set to one of the values documented in "XLANG Schedule Error Messages" earlier in this chapter, or is set to one of the values documented in Appendix A, "Error Messages."

Requirements

Windows NT/2000: Requires Windows 2000 SP1 or later
Library: Use XLANG Scheduler Runtime Type Library (SkedCore.dll)

XLANG Schedule Reference for C++

IWFGroupAdmin Interface

The **IWFGroupAdmin** interface allows a client application to control running instances of an XLANG schedule. Use this interface to stop, suspend, resume, and retrieve information about all the schedule instances associated with a group manager.

The **IWFGroupAdmin** interface defines the following properties.

Property	Type	Description
Count	**long**	The number of running schedule instances associated with this group manager.
FullyQualifiedName	**BSTR**	The moniker of this group manager.
InstanceIsResident	**VARIANT_BOOL**	A value that indicates whether the specified schedule instance is currently resident in memory.
InstanceIsSuspended	**VARIANT_BOOL**	A value that indicates whether the specified schedule instance is currently in a suspended state.
Name	**BSTR**	The name of this group manager.
UseFileDSN	**VARIANT_BOOL**	A value that indicates whether a data source name (DSN) file is used for dehydrating the schedule instances.

The **IWFGroupAdmin** interface defines the following methods.

Method	Description
ResumeInstance	Resumes the execution of a schedule in a suspended state.
Shutdown	Dehydrates all running schedule instances, and stops the group manager.
Startup	Starts all the dehydrated schedule instances for the current group manager.
SuspendInstance	Pauses execution of the schedule instance.
TerminateInstance	Stops execution of the schedule instance.

Remarks

For additional information about using this interface, see "IWFGroupAdmin Object" earlier in this chapter.

Requirements

Windows NT/2000: Requires Windows 2000 SP1 or later
Header: Include SkedCore.h

IWFGroupAdmin::Count Property

The **Count** property contains the number of running XLANG schedule instances associated with this group manager.

Syntax

Get method:

HRESULT get_Count(
  long* *lCount*
);

Parameters

Get method:

lCount
    [out, retval] Pointer to a **long** that contains the number of running schedule instances associated with this group manager.

Return Values

For a list of error messages returned by the XLANG Scheduler Engine, see "XLANG Schedule Error Messages" earlier in this chapter, or Appendix A, "Error Messages."

Remarks

This is a read-only property.

Requirements

Windows NT/2000: Requires Windows 2000 SP1 or later
Header: Include SkedCore.h

IWFGroupAdmin::FullyQualifiedName Property

The **FullyQualifiedName** property contains the moniker of this group manager.

Syntax

Get method:

HRESULT get_FullyQualifiedName(
  BSTR* *varFullyQualifiedName*
);

Parameters

Get method:

varFullyQualifiedName
    [out, retval] Pointer to a **BSTR** that contains the moniker of this group manager.

Return Values

For a list of error messages returned by the XLANG Scheduler Engine, see "XLANG Schedule Error Messages" earlier in this chapter, or Appendix A, "Error Messages."

Remarks

This is a read-only property.

Although a group manager can be instantiated through a local moniker, this property always includes the full Domain Name Services (DNS) style system name. For example, suppose the default XLANG Scheduler Group Manager, named *XLANG Scheduler*, is running on a computer named *MyMachine* in the domain *vigorair-18.com*. The **FullyQualifiedName** property would contain a value of *sked://MyMachine.vigorair-18.com!XLANG Scheduler*.

Requirements

Windows NT/2000: Requires Windows 2000 SP1 or later
Header: Include SkedCore.h

IWFGroupAdmin::InstanceIsResident Property

The **InstanceIsResident** property contains a value that indicates whether the specified XLANG schedule instance is currently resident in memory.

Syntax

Get method:

HRESULT get_InstanceIsResident(
    BSTR *varInstanceId*,
    VARIANT_BOOL* *pvarIsResident*
);

Parameters

Get method:

varInstanceId
    [in] **BSTR** that contains the globally unique identifier (GUID) assigned to the schedule instance.

pvarIsResident
    [out, retval] Pointer to a **VARIANT_BOOL** set to **VARIANT_TRUE** if the specified schedule instance is currently resident in memory. If the specified schedule instance is currently dehydrated, this parameter is set to **VARIANT_FALSE**.

Return Values

For a list of error messages returned by the XLANG Scheduler Engine, see "XLANG Schedule Error Messages" earlier in this chapter, or Appendix A, "Error Messages."

Remarks

This is a read-only property.

Requirements

Windows NT/2000: Requires Windows 2000 SP1 or later
Header: Include SkedCore.h

IWFGroupAdmin::InstanceIsSuspended Property

The **InstanceIsSuspended** property contains a value that indicates whether the specified XLANG schedule instance is currently in a suspended state.

Syntax

Get method:

HRESULT get_InstanceIsSuspended(
    BSTR *varInstanceId*,
    VARIANT_BOOL* *pvarIsSuspended*
);

Parameters

Get method:

varInstanceId
    [in] **BSTR** that contains the globally unique identifier (GUID) assigned to the schedule instance.

pvarIsSuspended
    [out, retval] Pointer to a **VARIANT_BOOL** set to **VARIANT_TRUE** if the specified schedule instance is currently in a suspended state. If the specified schedule instance is not suspended, this parameter is set to **VARIANT_FALSE**.

Return Values

For a list of error messages returned by the XLANG Scheduler Engine, see "XLANG Schedule Error Messages" earlier in this chapter, or Appendix A, "Error Messages."

Remarks

This is a read-only property.

This property should be checked prior to calling the **ResumeInstance** method.

Requirements

Windows NT/2000: Requires Windows 2000 SP1 or later
Header: Include SkedCore.h

IWFGroupAdmin::Name Property

The **Name** property contains the name of this group manager.

Syntax

Get method:

HRESULT get_Name(
    BSTR* *varName*
);

Parameters

Get method:

varName
    [out, retval] Pointer to a **BSTR** that contains the name of this group manager.

Return Values

For a list of error messages returned by the XLANG Scheduler Engine, see "XLANG Schedule Error Messages" earlier in this chapter, or Appendix A, "Error Messages."

Remarks

This is a read-only property.

This property is the same as the name of the hosting COM+ application.

Requirements

Windows NT/2000: Requires Windows 2000 SP1 or later
Header: Include SkedCore.h

IWFGroupAdmin::ResumeInstance Method

The **ResumeInstance** method starts the XLANG schedule instance executing from a suspended state.

Syntax

HRESULT ResumeInstance(
    BSTR *bInstanceId*
);

Parameters

bInstanceId

   [in] **BSTR** that contains the globally unique identifier (GUID) assigned to the schedule instance to be resumed.

Return Values

For a list of error messages returned by the XLANG Scheduler Engine, see "XLANG Schedule Error Messages" earlier in this chapter, or Appendix A, "Error Messages."

Remarks

The schedule instance can be paused with the **SuspendInstance** method. Prior to calling the **ResumeInstance** method, the **InstanceIsSuspended** property should be checked.

Requirements

Windows NT/2000: Requires Windows 2000 SP1 or later
Header: Include SkedCore.h

IWFGroupAdmin::Shutdown Method

The **Shutdown** method stops the group manager and dehydrates all running XLANG schedule instances.

Syntax

HRESULT Shutdown;

Parameters

None

Return Values

For a list of error messages returned by the XLANG Scheduler Engine, see "XLANG Schedule Error Messages" earlier in this chapter, or Appendix A, "Error Messages."

Remarks

Prior to stopping the group manager, all running schedule instances associated with this group manager are dehydrated to the database specified in the Data Source Name (DSN) file, and requests for activation of any new schedule instances are refused until shutdown is completed.

Any component that is bound in an XLANG schedule should not invoke this method to stop the group manager, as this can produce unexpected results.

Requirements

Windows NT/2000: Requires Windows 2000 SP1 or later
Header: Include SkedCore.h

IWFGroupAdmin::Startup Method

The **Startup** method starts all the previously running dehydrated XLANG schedule instances associated with this group manager.

Syntax

HRESULT Startup;

Parameters

None

Return Values

For a list of error messages returned by the XLANG Scheduler Engine, see "XLANG Schedule Error Messages" earlier in this chapter, or Appendix A, "Error Messages."

Remarks

The XLANG Scheduler System Manager normally calls this method. Users should not call this method directly.

Requirements

Windows NT/2000: Requires Windows 2000 SP1 or later
Header: Include SkedCore.h

IWFGroupAdmin::SuspendInstance Method

The **SuspendInstance** method pauses the running XLANG schedule instance in its current state.

Syntax

HRESULT SuspendInstance(
    BSTR *bInstanceId*
);

Parameters

bInstanceId
    [in] **BSTR** that contains the globally unique identifier (GUID) assigned to the schedule instance to be suspended.

Return Values

For a list of error messages returned by the XLANG Scheduler Engine, see "XLANG Schedule Error Messages" earlier in this chapter, or Appendix A, "Error Messages."

Remarks

The schedule instance can be restarted with the **ResumeInstance** method.

This method might block if actions with COM-bound ports are waiting for a method to complete, or if a short-lived transaction is currently in progress.

Requirements

Windows NT/2000: Requires Windows 2000 SP1 or later
Header: Include SkedCore.h

IWFGroupAdmin::TerminateInstance Method

The **TerminateInstance** method stops a running XLANG schedule instance.

Syntax

HRESULT TerminateInstance(
    BSTR *bInstanceId*
);

Parameters

bInstanceId
    [in] **BSTR** that contains the globally unique identifier (GUID) assigned to the schedule instance to be stopped.

Return Values

For a list of error messages returned by the XLANG Scheduler Engine, see "XLANG Schedule Error Messages" earlier in this chapter, or Appendix A, "Error Messages."

Remarks

A terminated schedule instance can never be restarted or resumed.

This method might block if actions with COM-bound ports are waiting for a method to complete, or if a short-lived transaction is currently in progress.

Requirements

Windows NT/2000: Requires Windows 2000 SP1 or later
Header: Include SkedCore.h

IWFGroupAdmin::UseFileDSN Property

The **UseFileDSN** property contains a value that indicates whether a data source name (DSN) file is used for dehydrating the XLANG schedule instances.

Syntax

Get method:

HRESULT get_UseFileDSN(
  VARIANT_BOOL* *pfUseFileDSN*
);

Parameters

Get method:

pfUseFileDSN

> [out, retval] Pointer to a **VARIANT_BOOL** set to **VARIANT_TRUE** if the group manager uses a DSN file for dehydrating schedule instances. If a DSN file is not used, this parameter is set to **VARIANT_FALSE**.

Return Values

For a list of error messages returned by the XLANG Scheduler Engine, see "XLANG Schedule Error Messages" earlier in this chapter, or Appendix A, "Error Messages."

Remarks

This is a read-only property.

The value of this property is set when the group manager process is launched. The DSN setting in the COM+ catalog is changed either on the **XLANG** tab of the **XLANG Scheduler Properties** dialog box or by setting the **UseFileDSN** property on the **IWFSystemAdmin** interface. If the DSN value is changed while the group manager is running, the value of this property is not dynamically updated. The new value is not reflected until the next time the group manager is launched. Updates to this property require the caller to be in the XLANG Administrator role and are not normally performed by user code.

Requirements

Windows NT/2000: Requires Windows 2000 SP1 or later
Header: Include SkedCore.h

IWFProxy Interface

The **IWFProxy** interface contains information about ports in an XLANG schedule instance that is bound to a COM component. Use this interface to obtain a schedule instance. If this interface is used on a non-COM port binding, an error is returned.

The **IWFProxy** interface defines the following properties.

Property	Type	Description
FullyQualifiedName	BSTR	The fully qualified name of a COM-bound port.
WorkflowInstance	**IWFWorkflowInstance**	The current schedule instance.

Remarks

A reference to this interface can be obtained from:

- The **Port** property available on the **IWFWorkflowInstance** interface.

- An XLANG schedule moniker that specifies the port name.

For additional information about using this interface, see "IWFProxy Object" earlier in this chapter.

Requirements

Windows NT/2000: Requires Windows 2000 SP1 or later
Header: Include SkedCore.h

IWFProxy::FullyQualifiedName Property

The **FullyQualifiedName** property contains the moniker of the port instance to which this proxy is bound.

Syntax

Get method:

HRESULT get_FullyQualifiedName(
    BSTR* *varFullyQualifiedName*
);

Parameters

Get method:

varFullyQualifiedName
    [out, retval] Pointer to a **BSTR** that contains the moniker of the port.

Return Values

For a list of error messages returned by the XLANG Scheduler Engine, see "XLANG Schedule Error Messages" earlier in this chapter, or Appendix A, "Error Messages."

Remarks

This is a read-only property.

The moniker retrieved with this property can be used with the COM **GetObject** function to obtain a reference to the XLANG schedule instance. This moniker is valid as long as the schedule instance is running. If the schedule instance is dehydrated and rehydrated for any reason, such as rebooting the system, the moniker remains valid. Once the schedule instance completes, or ends by using the **TerminateInstance** method, the moniker can no longer be used.

Requirements

Windows NT/2000: Requires Windows 2000 SP1 or later
Header: Include SkedCore.h

IWFProxy::WorkflowInstance Property

The **WorkflowInstance** property contains a reference to the current XLANG schedule instance.

Syntax

Get method:

HRESULT get_WorkflowInstance(
   IWFWorkflowInstance* *varScheduleInst*
);

Parameters

Get method:

varScheduleInst
   [out, retval] Address of a pointer to an **IWFWorkflowInstance** interface that contains the current schedule instance.

Return Values

For a list of error messages returned by the XLANG Scheduler Engine, see "XLANG Schedule Error Messages" earlier in this chapter, or Appendix A, "Error Messages."

Remarks

This is a read-only property.

Requirements

Windows NT/2000: Requires Windows 2000 SP1 or later
Header: Include SkedCore.h

IWFSystemAdmin Interface

The **IWFSystemAdmin** interface provides a client application with system-wide administrative control over the XLANG Scheduler Engine. Use this interface to start, stop, and retrieve information about the group managers.

The **IWFSystemAdmin** interface defines the following properties.

Property	Type	Description
Count	long	Contains the number of group managers associated with this XLANG Scheduler System Manager.
FullyQualifiedName	BSTR	Contains the fully qualified DNS-style name of the XLANG Scheduler System Manager.
IsWorkflowHost	VARIANT_BOOL	Checks whether the COM+ server application is an XLANG Scheduler Engine host.
Item	BSTR	Returns a reference to the named schedule group.
UseFileDSN	VARIANT_BOOL	Indicates whether a data source name (DSN) file is used for dehydrating the XLANG schedule instances.

The **IWFSystemAdmin** interface defines the following methods.

Method	Description
ShutdownAll	Shuts down all group managers.
ShutdownApp	Shuts down a specific group manager.
Startup	Starts all group managers.
TestAdminStatus	Checks a caller for XLANG Scheduler Engine administrator access.

Remarks

For additional information about using this interface, see "SysMgr Object" earlier in this chapter.

Requirements

Windows NT/2000: Requires Windows 2000 SP1 or later
Header: Include SysMgr.h

IWFSystemAdmin::Count Property

The **Count** property contains the number of running group managers.

Syntax

Get method:

HRESULT get_Count(
  long* *lCount*
);

Parameters

Get method:

lCount
    [out, retval] Pointer to a **long** that contains the number of running group managers.

Return Values

For a list of error messages returned by the XLANG Scheduler Engine, see "XLANG Schedule Error Messages" earlier in this chapter, or Appendix A, "Error Messages."

Remarks

This is a read-only property.

Requirements

Windows NT/2000: Requires Windows 2000 SP1 or later
Header: Include SysMgr.h

IWFSystemAdmin::FullyQualifiedName Property

The **FullyQualifiedName** property contains the moniker of this XLANG Scheduler System Manager.

Syntax

Get method:

HRESULT get_FullyQualifiedName(
  BSTR* *varFullyQualifiedName*
);

Parameters

Get method:

varFullyQualifiedName
> [out, retval] Pointer to a **BSTR** that contains the moniker of this XLANG Scheduler System Manager.

Return Values

For a list of error messages returned by the XLANG Scheduler Engine, see "XLANG Schedule Error Messages" earlier in this chapter, or Appendix A, "Error Messages."

Remarks

This is a read-only property.

Although an XLANG Scheduler System Manager can be instantiated through a local moniker, this property always includes the full Domain Name Services (DNS) style system name. For example, suppose the XLANG Scheduler System Manager is running on a computer named *MyMachine* in the domain *vigorair-18.com*. The **FullyQualifiedName** property would contain a value of *sked://MyMachine.vigorair-18.com*.

Requirements

Windows NT/2000: Requires Windows 2000 SP1 or later
Header: Include SysMgr.h

IWFSystemAdmin::IsWorkflowHost Property

The **IsWorkflowHost** property controls whether the named COM+ server application is an XLANG Scheduler Engine host.

Syntax

Get method:

HRESULT get_IsWorkflowHost(
  BSTR *varAppName*,
  VARIANT_BOOL* *pIsWorkflowHost*
);

Put method:

HRESULT put_IsWorkflowHost(
  BSTR *varAppName*,
  VARIANT_BOOL *varIsWorkflowHost*
);

Parameters

Get method:

varAppName
> [in] **BSTR** that contains the COM+ server application name.

pIsWorkflowHost
> [out, retval] Pointer to a **VARIANT_BOOL** that indicates whether the COM+ server application is hosting the XLANG Scheduler Engine.

Put method:

varAppName
> [in] **BSTR** that contains the COM+ server application name.

varIsWorkflowHost
> [out, retval] **VARIANT_BOOL** that indicates whether the COM+ server application is hosting the XLANG Scheduler Engine.

Return Values

For a list of error messages returned by the XLANG Scheduler Engine, see "XLANG Schedule Error Messages" earlier in this chapter, or Appendix A, "Error Messages."

Remarks

This property cannot be set on the XLANG Scheduler Engine application, or on any COM+ application marked as read-only.

Requirements

Windows NT/2000: Requires Windows 2000 SP1 or later
Header: Include SysMgr.h

IWFSystemAdmin::Item Property

The **Item** property returns a reference to one of the running group managers.

Syntax

Get method:

HRESULT get_Item(
  BSTR *strGrpMgrName,*
  IUnknown** *ppItem*
);

Parameters

Get method:

strGrpMgrName
> [in] **BSTR** that contains the group name corresponding to the hosting COM+ server application name. Group names are case sensitive and can contain spaces.

ppItem
> [out, retval] Address of a pointer to an **IUnknown** interface that refers to a group manager.

Return Values

For a list of error messages returned by the XLANG Scheduler Engine, see "XLANG Schedule Error Messages" earlier in this chapter, or Appendix A, "Error Messages."

Remarks

This is a read-only property.

Requirements

Windows NT/2000: Requires Windows 2000 SP1 or later
Header: Include SysMgr.h

IWFSystemAdmin::ShutdownAll Method

The **ShutdownAll** method stops the group managers and terminates their associated COM+ applications.

Syntax

HRESULT ShutdownAll;

Parameters

None

Return Values

For a list of error messages returned by the XLANG Scheduler Engine, see "XLANG Schedule Error Messages" earlier in this chapter, or Appendix A, "Error Messages."

Remarks

When the **ShutdownAll** method is called, new schedule activations are disabled and the shutdown notice is propagated to all running group managers. Once this method has completed, all group managers are stopped and the system can be safely rebooted.

Requirements

Windows NT/2000: Requires Windows 2000 SP1 or later
Header: Include SysMgr.h

IWFSystemAdmin::ShutdownApp Method

The **ShutdownApp** method stops a specific group manager application and terminates the associated COM+ application.

Syntax

HRESULT ShutdownApp(
    BSTR *varAppName*
);

Parameters

varAppName
    [in] **BSTR** that contains the COM+ server application name to be stopped.

Return Values

For a list of error messages returned by the XLANG Scheduler Engine, see "XLANG Schedule Error Messages" earlier in this chapter, or Appendix A, "Error Messages."

Remarks

When the **ShutdownApp** method is called, new schedule activations on the named application are disabled and all running XLANG schedule instances associated with that application are stopped. If this method is called on the default XLANG Scheduler Group Manager, all group managers are shut down. Calling this method on the default XLANG Scheduler Group Manager is equivalent to calling the **ShutdownAll** method.

Note

*   The COM+ application name of the default XLANG Scheduler Group Manager is XLANG Scheduler.

Requirements

Windows NT/2000: Requires Windows 2000 SP1 or later
Header: Include SysMgr.h

IWFSystemAdmin::StartUp Method

The **StartUp** method starts the group managers.

Syntax

HRESULT StartUp;

Parameters

None

Return Values

For a list of error messages returned by the XLANG Scheduler Engine, see "XLANG Schedule Error Messages" earlier in this chapter, or Appendix A, "Error Messages."

Remarks

When this method is invoked, rehydration is initiated for all group managers and, subsequently, all XLANG schedules. This method is asynchronous, and it can complete before all group managers and schedules are running.

Requirements

Windows NT/2000: Requires Windows 2000 SP1 or later
Header: Include SysMgr.h

IWFSystemAdmin::TestAdminStatus Method

The **TestAdminStatus** method determines whether a caller on the **IWFGroupAdmin** interface is an XLANG Scheduler Engine administrator.

Syntax

HRESULT TestAdminStatus;

Parameters

None

Return Values

For a list of error messages returned by the XLANG Scheduler Engine, see "XLANG Schedule Error Messages" earlier in this chapter, or Appendix A, "Error Messages."

Remarks

This method is intended for internal use by the group managers.

Requirements

Windows NT/2000: Requires Windows 2000 SP1 or later
Header: Include SysMgr.h

IWFSystemAdmin::UseFileDSN Property

The **UseFileDSN** property contains a value that indicates whether a COM+ server application uses a data source name (DSN) file for dehydrating the XLANG schedule instances.

Syntax

Get method:

HRESULT get_UseFileDSN(
  BSTR *varAppName*,
  VARIANT_BOOL* *pfUseFileDSN*
);

Put method:

HRESULT put_UseFileDSN(
  BSTR *varAppName*,
  VARIANT_BOOL* *varUseFileDSN*
);

Parameters

Get method:

varAppName
  [in] **BSTR** that contains the COM+ server application name.

pfUseFileDSN
  [out, retval] Pointer to a **VARIANT_BOOL** set to **VARIANT_TRUE** if the COM+ server application uses a DSN file for dehydrating schedule instances. If a DSN file is not used, this parameter is set to **VARIANT_FALSE**.

Put method:

varAppName
  [in] **BSTR** that contains the COM+ server application name.

varUseFileDSN
  [out, retval] **VARIANT_BOOL** that indicates whether the COM+ server application uses a DSN file for dehydrating schedule instances. If a DSN file is not used, this parameter is set to **VARIANT_FALSE**.

Return Values

For a list of error messages returned by the XLANG Scheduler Engine, see "XLANG Schedule Error Messages" earlier in this chapter, or Appendix A, "Error Messages."

Remarks

If this property is changed while any group manager is running, the value of this property is not dynamically updated in the group managers. Therefore, the **UseFileDSN** property value exposed by the **IWFGroupAdmin** interface contains an incorrect value. The updated value is not reflected until the next time the group manager is launched.

Requirements

Windows NT/2000: Requires Windows 2000 SP1 or later
Header: Include SysMgr.h

IWFWorkflowInstance Interface

The **IWFWorkflowInstance** interface enables a client application to navigate the ports of an XLANG schedule instance, check the completion status, and determine whether the schedule instance completed successfully. Use this interface to gather information about a specific, running schedule instance.

The **IWFWorkflowInstance** interface defines the following properties.

Property	Type	Description
CompletionStatus	**long**	A value that indicates the success or failure of the schedule instance.
FullPortName	**BSTR**	The full name of a port in a form usable by the associated technology.
FullyQualifiedName	**BSTR**	The fully qualified name of this schedule instance.
InstanceId	**BSTR**	The unique identifier associated with this schedule instance.
IsCompleted	**VARIANT_BOOL**	A value that indicates whether the schedule instance completed.
ModuleId	**BSTR**	The unique identifier of the XML module that contains the schedule and binding information.
ModuleName	**BSTR**	The name of the XML module that contains the schedule and binding information.
ParentInstanceID	**BSTR**	The unique identifier of the parent schedule instance.
Port	**IUnknown**	A reference to the named port. This is applicable only to COM-based port bindings.

The **IWFWorkflowInstance** interface defines the following method.

Method	Description
WaitForCompletion	Blocks until the schedule instance completes.

Remarks

A reference to this interface can be obtained from:

- The **WorkflowInstance** property available on the **IWFProxy** interface.

- The collection of **IWFWorkflowInstance** objects returned by the **IWFGroupAdmin** object.

- An XLANG schedule moniker.

For additional information about using this interface, see "IWFWorkflowInstance Object" earlier in this chapter.

Requirements

Windows NT/2000: Requires Windows 2000 SP1 or later
Header: Include SkedCore.h

IWFWorkflowInstance::CompletionStatus Property

The **CompletionStatus** property indicates the final completion status of the XLANG schedule instance.

Syntax

Get method:

HRESULT get_CompletionStatus(
   long* *varCompletionStatus*
);

Parameters

Get method:

varCompletionStatus
   [out, retval] Pointer to a **long** that contains the completion status of the schedule instance. A value of 0 indicates success.

Return Values

For a list of error messages returned by the XLANG Scheduler Engine, see "XLANG Schedule Error Messages" earlier in this chapter, or Appendix A, "Error Messages."

✎ Note

- A return value of S_OK does not indicate that the processes or applications associated with the schedule instance completed successfully. It indicates only that the schedule instance was completely processed by the XLANG Scheduler Engine, without errors.

Remarks

This is a read-only property.

Requirements

Windows NT/2000: Requires Windows 2000 SP1 or later
Header: Include SkedCore.h

IWFWorkflowInstance::FullPortName Property

The **FullPortName** property contains the full name of the specified port.

Syntax

Get method:

HRESULT get_FullPortName(
    BSTR *varParam,*
    BSTR* *varFullPortName*
);

Parameters

Get method:

varParam
    [in] **BSTR** that contains the name of the port to be retrieved.

varFullPortName
    [out, retval] Pointer to a **BSTR** that contains the full port name.

Return Values

For a list of error messages returned by the XLANG Scheduler Engine, see "XLANG Schedule Error Messages" earlier in this chapter, or Appendix A, "Error Messages."

Remarks

This is a read-only property.

The full port name is returned in a form that is usable by the associated binding technology. For example, a port that is bound to a COM component returns a fully qualified moniker as the name of the port. For a port that is bound to Microsoft Message Queuing, this method returns the full path of the queue.

Requirements

Windows NT/2000: Requires Windows 2000 SP1 or later
Header: Include SkedCore.h

IWFWorkflowInstance::FullyQualifiedName Property

The **FullyQualifiedName** property contains the moniker of the XLANG schedule instance.

Syntax

Get method:

HRESULT get_FullyQualifiedName(
  BSTR* *varFullyQualifiedName*
);

Parameters

Get method:

varFullyQualifiedName
    [out, retval] Pointer to a **BSTR** that contains the moniker of the schedule instance.

Return Values

For a list of error messages returned by the XLANG Scheduler Engine, see "XLANG Schedule Error Messages" earlier in this chapter, or Appendix A, "Error Messages."

Remarks

This is a read-only property.

Requirements

Windows NT/2000: Requires Windows 2000 SP1 or later
Header: Include SkedCore.h

IWFWorkflowInstance::InstanceId Property

The **InstanceId** property contains the globally unique identifier (GUID) assigned to the current XLANG schedule instance.

Syntax

Get method:

HRESULT get_InstanceId(
  BSTR* *varInstanceId*
);

Parameters

Get method:

varInstanceId
> [out, retval] Pointer to a **BSTR** that contains the GUID of the schedule instance.

Return Values

For a list of error messages returned by the XLANG Scheduler Engine, see "XLANG Schedule Error Messages" earlier in this chapter, or Appendix A, "Error Messages."

Remarks

This is a read-only property.

Requirements

Windows NT/2000: Requires Windows 2000 SP1 or later
Header: Include SkedCore.h

IWFWorkflowInstance::IsCompleted Property

The **IsCompleted** property indicates whether the XLANG schedule instance has finished executing.

Syntax

Get method:

HRESULT get_IsCompleted(
  VARIANT_BOOL* *varIsCompleted*
);

Parameters

Get method:

varIsCompleted
> [out, retval] Pointer to a **VARIANT_BOOL** that, if **VARIANT_TRUE**, indicates the schedule instance has finished executing. If **VARIANT_FALSE**, the schedule instance is still executing.

Return Values

For a list of error messages returned by the XLANG Scheduler Engine, see "XLANG Schedule Error Messages" earlier in this chapter, or Appendix A, "Error Messages."

Remarks

This is a read-only property.

Requirements

Windows NT/2000: Requires Windows 2000 SP1 or later
Header: Include SkedCore.h

IWFWorkflowInstance::ModuleId Property

The **ModuleId** property contains the globally unique identifier (GUID) of the XLANG module associated with the current XLANG schedule instance.

Syntax

Get method:

HRESULT get_ModuleId(
 BSTR* *varModuleId*
);

Parameters

Get method:

varModuleId
   [out, retval] Pointer to a **BSTR** that contains the GUID of the XLANG module associated with the current schedule instance.

Return Values

For a list of error messages returned by the XLANG Scheduler Engine, see "XLANG Schedule Error Messages" earlier in this chapter, or Appendix A, "Error Messages."

Remarks

This is a read-only property.

Requirements

Windows NT/2000: Requires Windows 2000 SP1 or later
Header: Include SkedCore.h

IWFWorkflowInstance::ModuleName Property

The **ModuleName** property contains the name of the XLANG module associated with the current XLANG schedule instance.

Syntax

Get method:

HRESULT get_ModuleName(
  BSTR* *varModuleName*
);

Parameters

Get method:

varModuleName
  [out, retval] Pointer to a **BSTR** that contains the name of the XLANG module associated
  with the current schedule instance.

Return Values

For a list of error messages returned by the XLANG Scheduler Engine, see "XLANG
Schedule Error Messages" earlier in this chapter, or Appendix A, "Error Messages."

Remarks

This is a read-only property.

The module name is defined in the XLANG schedule (.skx) file.

Requirements

Windows NT/2000: Requires Windows 2000 SP1 or later
Header: Include SkedCore.h

IWFWorkflowInstance::ParentInstanceID Property

The **ParentInstanceID** property contains the globally unique identifier (GUID) assigned to
the parent XLANG schedule instance of the current schedule instance.

Syntax

Get method:

HRESULT get_ParentInstanceID(
  BSTR* *varParentInstanceID*
);

Parameters

Get method:

varParentInstanceID
> [out, retval] Pointer to a **BSTR** that contains the GUID of the parent schedule instance of the current schedule instance.

Return Values

For a list of error messages returned by the XLANG Scheduler Engine, see "XLANG Schedule Error Messages" earlier in this chapter, or Appendix A, "Error Messages."

Remarks

This is a read-only property.

The property returns a NULL value if no parent schedule instance exists.

Requirements

Windows NT/2000: Requires Windows 2000 SP1 or later
Header: Include SkedCore.h

IWFWorkflowInstance::Port Property

The **Port** property contains a reference to a COM-bound port.

Syntax

Get method:

HRESULT get_Port(
   BSTR *varParam,*
   IUnknown** *varPort*
);

Parameters

Get method:

varParam
> [in] **BSTR** that contains the name of the port to which to obtain a reference.

varPort
> [out, retval] Address of a pointer to an **IUnknown** interface that contains a reference to a port in the current XLANG schedule instance.

Return Values

For a list of error messages returned by the XLANG Scheduler Engine, see "XLANG Schedule Error Messages" earlier in this chapter, or Appendix A, "Error Messages."

Remarks

This is a read-only property.

The MK_E_NOOBJECT error code is returned if the moniker or port name passed in the *varParam* parameter is incorrect.

When using Microsoft Visual Basic, the variable used for the port reference returned by using this property should be declared as a specific class or as a **Variant**. You can't obtain the port reference if you declare the variable as an **Object** since the port actually returns an **IUnknown** reference.

Requirements

Windows NT/2000: Requires Windows 2000 SP1 or later
Header: Include SkedCore.h

IWFWorkflowInstance::WaitForCompletion Method

The **WaitForCompletion** method waits until the current XLANG schedule instance completes executing.

Syntax

HRESULT WaitForCompletion;

Parameters

None

Return Values

For a list of error messages returned by the XLANG Scheduler Engine, see "XLANG Schedule Error Messages" earlier in this chapter, or Appendix A, "Error Messages."

Requirements

Windows NT/2000: Requires Windows 2000 SP1 or later
Header: Include SkedCore.h

Troubleshooting BizTalk Server Administration

This section provides a centralized location for information related to troubleshooting BizTalk Server Administration. If you receive error messages, try to find a solution in this section.

Supplemental information related to troubleshooting BizTalk Server Administration is included in Appendix C, "Release Notes."

✎ Notes

- You can also check the error messages in the Suspended queue for more troubleshooting information. For more information about the Suspended queue, error messages, and possible actions, see "Suspended Queue" earlier in this chapter.

- You can also check the Event Log for detailed information, such as error and warning messages. For more information about the Event Log, see "Handling Server Errors" earlier in this chapter.

Error getting all groups from a database

Cause: The BizTalk Messaging Management database is offline if you receive the following message:

> Instances of Microsoft BizTalkServer_Group cannot be enumerated: The connection to the BizTalk Messaging Management database could not be opened.

Solution: Find out why the server is offline and retry the connection when it is back online. For example, you could receive this message if the server that hosts the BizTalk Messaging Management database is offline for maintenance.

Interchange and document size limit

The maximum supported size limit for a document submitted to BizTalk Server is 20 MB. The maximum supported size limit for an interchange submitted to BizTalk Server is 20 MB.

If you plan to receive interchanges in XML Unicode format that are larger than 20 MB, it is advisable to turn off global tracking settings. If you plan to receive ANSI flat-file interchanges that are larger than 7-10 MB in size, it is advisable to turn off global tracking settings. For more information about configuring tracking settings for a server group, see "To configure tracking properties for a server group" earlier in this chapter.

Similarly, if you plan to receive document instances in XML Unicode format that are greater than 20 MB, it is advisable to turn off document logging settings in BizTalk Messaging Manager. Or, if you plan to receive ANSI flat files that are larger than 7-10 MB, it is advisable to turn off document logging settings in BizTalk Messaging Manager. For more information about storing copies of specific document instances, see "To set document logging properties" in Chapter 9, "Configuring BizTalk Messaging Services."

Transaction time-out discrepancy between Component Services and BizTalk Server 2000

There is a file time-out discrepancy between Component Services and BizTalk Server 2000. When sending a file that exceeds the default transaction time-out value of 60 seconds through BizTalk Server 2000, BizTalk Server 2000 records the transaction as sent, and the receiving server receives the file without errors. Component Services records the transaction as aborted. Transactions cannot be rolled back.

BizTalk Messaging Service does not start

Cause: The BizTalk Messaging Service does not start if BizTalk Server cannot connect to the SQL server that stores the BizTalk Messaging Management database. All COM+ packages run under an interactive user account, not the local system account. The service starts only if a user is logged on to BizTalk Server. For example, if a client application submits documents to BizTalk Server remotely and no user is logged on to the server running BizTalk Server 2000, the service does not start.

Solution: Verify the BizTalk Server connection to the BizTalk Messaging Management database. Verify that Microsoft SQL Server is running properly. You might need to create a service account under which to run BizTalk Server. For more information about creating a service account in Windows 2000 Help, in the Services chapter, see "Select a user account that a service will use to log on."

Slowed performance when deleting a large quantity of documents from the Suspended queue

Cause: You might experience slow performance when you delete a large quantity of documents from the Suspended queue.

Solution: If you need to delete all documents from the Suspended queue, you might want to use PurgeBizTalkSuspendedQueue.vbs, a sample Microsoft Visual Basic script that is provided for this purpose. After BizTalk Server 2000 installation, you can find this script in the \Program Files\Microsoft BizTalk Server\SDK\Messaging Samples\Miscellaneous folder.

❦ Caution

- Do not use this script unless you want to permanently delete the entire contents of the Suspended queue for the specified BizTalk Server group.

Output validation failure

Cause One: The data type of a field in the source specification does not match the data type of the field to which it is linked in the destination specification. This failure is logged to the Event Viewer.

Solution: Correct the data type in either the source or destination specification. For more information about source and destination specifications, see "Understanding Specifications" in Chapter 5, "Creating Specifications."

Cause Two: A functoid is linked to a field in the destination specification, and the field data type property is not a string.

Solution: In the destination specification, change the field data type to **String**. Submit the document to BizTalk Server for processing. For more information about data types, see "To set declaration properties" in Chapter 5, "Creating Specifications."

Cause Three: In the destination specification, a field is assigned a constant value that uses a different data type than the data type already assigned to the field.

Solution: In the destination specification, change the data type associated with the field. Submit the document to BizTalk Server for processing. For more information about data types, see "To set declaration properties" in Chapter 5, "Creating Specifications."

Cause Four: Release indicators are included in EDIFACT data. The release characters are included in the logical character count when validating the maximum physical character limit for a field. This failure is logged to the Event Viewer.

Solution: Do not use release indicators in EDIFACT data. BizTalk Server automatically inserts release indicators in outbound data when needed.

Server does not return all documents in a flat-file interchange

Cause: One of the documents in the interchange does not meet the document specification. For example, one of the documents is missing a required field.

Solution: Locate the document that does not meet the specification, fix it, and resubmit the interchange. Although an error is returned for the document that does not meet the specification, BizTalk Server cannot process all the documents in the interchange. The flat-file structure is an open format and is not designed to implement redundancy checking.

Class identifier appears in the Preprocessor list

Cause: The custom preprocessor is no longer registered.

Solution: Check the Event Log to confirm that the custom preprocessor is no longer registered. Then register the custom preprocessor again or choose another preprocessor from the list.

Related Topics

"Custom Preprocessors" earlier in this chapter

"Preprocessing Documents in a Receive Function" in Chapter 10, "Submitting Documents"

"To configure a File receive function: Services tab" earlier in this chapter

An interchange or document appears as binary data in the Suspended queue

Cause One: BizTalk Server could not parse the interchange or document.

Solution: Delete the document from the Suspended queue. Verify that the incoming interchange or document is in a format that BizTalk Server can process (XML, X12, EDIFACT, or flat file). Submit it to BizTalk Server from the original organization or application again.

If BizTalk Server cannot parse a document, it appears as binary data in the Suspended queue because BizTalk Server does not have enough information to read and process the document correctly. For more information about parsing errors, see "Parsing errors" later in this chapter.

Cause Two: BizTalk Server was able to parse the interchange or document, but the data content was not valid. The timestamp "expiresAt" expired and the document is no longer valid. This failure occurs in BizTalk Framework documents that use the expiredAt field.

Solution: Delete the document from the Suspended queue. This document is no longer valid. Investigate why the document is no longer valid.

Cause Three: BizTalk Server could not parse the document because the schema for the document is incorrect. If you receive a flat file and the code page for the document specification is set to UTF-8, BizTalk Server cannot parse the document because UTF-8 is not supported.

Solution: If you receive a flat file, check to see if the document specification is correct. If the code page for the document specification is set to UTF-8, BizTalk Server cannot process the document. Delete the document from the Suspended queue. For more information, see "To set reference properties" in Chapter 5, "Creating Specifications."

Related Topic

"Suspended Queue" earlier in this chapter

BizTalk Server stopped processing documents

Cause One: BizTalk Server cannot continue processing documents if the connection to any of the three databases—BizTalk Messaging Management, Tracking, or Shared Queue—is lost or if those databases are otherwise inaccessible. This might occur if Microsoft SQL Server is shut down or paused from Enterprise Manager. If BizTalk Server 2000 encounters this error, the BizTalk Messaging Service shuts down gracefully to properly preserve the state of processing and integrity at the moment of failure. An error is logged to the Event Viewer with a full description of the error causing the service to shut down.

Solution: System administrators can use this error for notification that BizTalk Server is offline through pager notification or status delivery through e-mail. Upon such notification the administrator must manually restart the BizTalk Messaging Service through the Services Microsoft Management Console snap-in, and then check the Event Log again to determine whether the error is still present. If it is, the administrator must confirm that SQL Server services are available to BizTalk Server.

Cause Two: If you have antivirus software on the server on which BizTalk Server 2000 is installed, the default setting in a messaging port might be incorrect.

Solution: The default setting for the file transport component is to append files. If you choose the file transport type with its default settings in a messaging port and use antivirus software on the server on which BizTalk Server 2000 is installed, and you send multiple files that have exactly the same name to the same file location, at the same time, BizTalk Server 2000 might stop responding and must be restarted. You can eliminate this problem by changing the default setting for the file transport component in the **BizTalk SendLocalFile Properties** dialog box from **Append to file** to **Overwrite file**. You also can eliminate this problem by creating a unique file for each document instance processed by using the file path format in the messaging port: file://C:\dir\file%tracking_id%.xml. For more information, see "To specify a transport address" in Chapter 9, "Configuring BizTalk Messaging Services." If you need to restart the server, see "To start a server in a group" earlier in this chapter.

Receive function does not delete the document

Cause: The retry interval might be set below the processing capability for the number of documents generated.

Solution: Double the retry interval and resubmit the documents to BizTalk Server. For more information about configuring the retry interval, see "To set advanced configuration properties" in Chapter 9, "Configuring BizTalk Messaging Services."

Unable to connect to an SQL server installed on a clustered machine

Cause: When Microsoft SQL Server is installed on a cluster, SQL Server can support only clients that connect using TCP/IP.

Solution: Install SQL Server client tools and change the default network library to TCP/IP. For more information about installing SQL Server client tools, see "To install SQL Server client tools" in Chapter 1, "Installing BizTalk Server 2000." For more information about changing the default network library, see "To change the default network library to TCP/IP" in Chapter 1, "Installing BizTalk Server 2000."

Receive functions stopped processing documents

Cause: A single remote server cannot support more than 50 receive functions at the same time.

Solution: For more information about supporting multiple receive functions, go to the Microsoft Product Support Services Web site (search.support.microsoft.com/kb/c.asp) and search the Knowledge Base for the following article:

- "IIS Runs Out of Work Items and Causes RPC Failures When Connecting to a Remote UNC Path" (Article number Q221790).

For additional information, see the following Knowledge Base articles:

- "Local System Account and Null Sessions in Windows NT" (Article number Q132679).

- "Service Running As System Account Fails Accessing Network" (Article number Q124184).

- "PRB: Access Denied When Opening a Named Pipe from a Service" (Article number Q126645).

- "FindFirstChangeNotification May Not Notify All Processes on File Changes" (Article number Q188321).

Error when moving a remote server to a different BizTalk Messaging Management database

Cause: The server might belong to another BizTalk Messaging Management database.

Solution: If you try to add a remote server to a BizTalk Messaging Management database, and that server was originally in a different central BizTalk Messaging Management database, the following error message appears in the Windows Event Log:

> A new instance of the WMI class **"MicrosoftBizTalkServer_Server"** cannot be created in the BizTalk Server WMI provider. The *<servername>* server may already belong to a different BizTalk Server installation.

This error means that an attempt was made to add a remote server that was originally in a different central database. If this procedure was performed within BizTalk Server Administration, the administration console tries to determine if the remote server also belongs to a group in the remote central database. The administration console queries the remote server's Windows Management Instrumentation (WMI) provider to make this determination. If the server does belong to a group in the other central database, an error message from the administration console appears and explains that you cannot add a remote server that already belongs to a group in a different central database.

Related Topic

"WMI Overview" earlier in this chapter

Parsing errors

Cause One: If you are sending reliable messages, the default settings in a port might be incorrect.

Solution: The default setting for the file transport component is to append files. If you choose the file transport type with its default settings and select an envelope with a reliable envelope format in a messaging port, and then send multiple files to the same file location, at the same time, you might have unexpected parsing results. You can eliminate this problem by changing the default setting for the file transport component from **Append to file** to **Overwrite file** in the **BizTalk SendLocalFile Properties** dialog box. For more information about changing the default settings in a port, see "To override messaging port defaults" in Chapter 9, "Configuring BizTalk Messaging Services."

Other Causes: BizTalk Server cannot parse a document for a variety of reasons. Some common reasons are:

- The interchange or document is in a format that BizTalk Server cannot understand.

- The schema for the document is incorrect.

- A flat-file interchange has the wrong or invalid schema.

- A flat-file interchange contains invalid characters.

- A flat-file interchange is missing characters.

- A flat-file interchange is missing delimiters.

- A BizTalk Framework 2.0 document has an invalid alias listed in the port or channel.

- The document container node is missing in a custom XML header.

- An attribute is missing in a custom XML document.

- An EDI document specification does not match the envelope.

Solution: View the interchange or document data to determine why BizTalk Server could not parse the interchange or document. To view the interchange or document data, you can:

- View the first 512 bytes of the interchange or document data. For more information about how to view interchange and document data, see "To view interchanges" or "To view documents" earlier in this chapter.

- View the interchange data in the interchange record in BizTalk Document Tracking. For more information about how to view interchanges in BizTalk Document tracking, see "To search by date for interchange and document information," "To search by organization for interchange and document information," "To search by document type for interchange and document information," or "To search for interchange and document information by combining query parameters" in Chapter 13, "Tracking Documents."

- Use the Windows Management Instrumentation (WMI) layer to view the interchange data. For more information about WMI Application Programming, go to the MSDN Online Library Web site (msdn.microsoft.com/library/default.asp) and search for WMI Application Programming.

Once you determine why BizTalk Server could not parse the document, correct the problem and resubmit the interchange or document using **IInterchange** or a receive function.

Related Topic

"Suspended Queue" earlier in this chapter

Microsoft BizTalk Server 2000 Operations

Organizations that deploy a business-to-business e-commerce solution must keep the deployment functioning 24 hours a day, 7 days a week. Indeed it has become increasingly more common for enterprise application integration to have a similar up-time requirement. This chapter outlines the administrative tasks a system administrator must perform to keep an installation of Microsoft BizTalk Server 2000 running on a continual basis. Also discussed are important concepts and common administrative issues about which system administrators must be aware.

The eight major areas of administration and management related to BizTalk Server 2000 are:

- **Server administration.** You can use BizTalk Server Administration to manage server groups and adjust server properties for maximum performance.

- **Database administration.** You can use scripts and tools to maintain the following four types of databases associated with BizTalk Server: BizTalk Messaging Management, Tracking, Shared Queue, and Orchestration Persistence.

- **Messaging objects administration.** You can use BizTalk Messaging Manager or the BizTalk Messaging Configuration object model to update messaging objects, such as channels and messaging ports. You can also use BizTalk Messaging Manager or the BizTalk Messaging Configuration object model to facilitate the processing and transmission of interchanges and documents.

- **Receive function and parser administration.** You can use BizTalk Server Administration to manage receive functions and parsers.

- **Application administration.** You can use Component Services to manage the default XLANG Scheduler application, or to add and configure additional COM+ applications that host XLANG schedules.

- **Tracking interchanges and documents.** You can use BizTalk Server Administration to change the tracking settings for a server group. Additional tracking settings can be set by using BizTalk Messaging Manager or the BizTalk Messaging Configuration object model. Tracking results can be viewed by using BizTalk Document Tracking.

- **Monitoring a BizTalk Server deployment.** You can use System Monitor, Windows 2000 Event Viewer, and XLANG Event Monitor to monitor BizTalk Server.

- **Troubleshooting.** You can use BizTalk Server Administration to view the Suspended queue for processing and transmission errors. You can use Event Monitor to troubleshoot server errors, BizTalk Server application errors, XLANG Scheduler errors, and other COM+ application errors.

In addition to the administrative tasks associated with managing a BizTalk Server installation, all system administrators must be aware of the following concepts and administrative issues:

- **BizTalk Messaging Services.** How to submit interchanges and documents to BizTalk Server and how the appropriate properties must be configured to process and transmit submitted interchanges and documents.

- **BizTalk Orchestration Services.** The difference between XLANG schedule drawings and XLANG schedules and how XLANG schedules work.

- **Tracking overview.** How interchanges, documents, and action events related to messages processed by XLANG schedules are tracked in the Tracking database and viewed in BizTalk Document Tracking. After BizTalk Server is implemented, settings might need to be reconfigured to accommodate changes in business processes.

- **Transport services.** Common implementation and maintenance issues for a variety of transport services that should be considered when administering a BizTalk Server 2000 installation.

- **Security.** The security features that BizTalk Server uses and the configuration changes that might be necessary when managing a BizTalk Server 2000 installation.

In This Chapter

- BizTalk Messaging Services Concepts
- BizTalk Orchestration Services Concepts
- Administering BizTalk Server
- Administering Transport Services
- Tracking Interchanges and Documents
- Security Issues
- Monitoring a BizTalk Server 2000 Deployment
- Troubleshooting BizTalk Server
- Conclusion

BizTalk Messaging Services Concepts

BizTalk Messaging Services are services included in Microsoft BizTalk Server 2000 that enable you to send, receive, parse, and track interchanges and documents from other organizations or applications. In addition, BizTalk Messaging Services include the ability to generate receipts for certain file formats, correlate and map data, verify the integrity of documents, and provide secure methods for exchanging documents with trading partners and applications.

To implement BizTalk Messaging Services, BizTalk Server uses messaging objects, receive functions, COM methods, parsers, and a Microsoft SQL Server database (version 7.0 with SP2 or SQL Server 2000). Messaging objects, such as channels and messaging ports, are used to configure the necessary properties to process and transmit interchanges and documents submitted to BizTalk Server. Receive functions and in some cases the **Submit** and **SubmitSync** methods are used to submit incoming documents to BizTalk Server for processing. Once a document is submitted, the appropriate parser parses it and, if necessary, converts it to XML. Finally, the Tracking database stores interchange and document records for incoming and outgoing interchanges and documents that are processed by BizTalk Server.

Messaging Objects

BizTalk Server uses the following messaging objects to configure the necessary properties to process and transmit submitted work items:

- **Channels.** A set of properties that directs BizTalk Server through the appropriate steps to process documents. Channel properties include a source organization or application, a document definition, a map, and field and document tracking settings.

- **Messaging ports.** A set of properties that specifies how an interchange or document is transported to a destination organization or application. Messaging port properties include transport services, destination organization or application, security settings, and envelope settings.

- **Distribution lists.** A group of messaging ports. Use a distribution list to send the same document to more than one trading partner organization or application. In the BizTalk Messaging Configuration object model, a distribution list is called a port group.

- **Organizations.** The trading partners with which your business exchanges interchanges and documents. An organization can be internal, such as an application in another division of your company. Or an organization can be external, such as a different business.

- **Document definitions.** A set of properties that represents an inbound or outbound document and that might provide a pointer to a specification. A specification defines the document structure, document type, and version. However, a pointer from the document definition to a specification is not required.

- **Envelopes.** A set of properties that can represent the transport information for a document. An envelope associated with an inbound interchange or document provides BizTalk Server with the information that it needs to interpret the submitted document. For example, the envelope can contain a pointer to the document definition. An envelope associated with an outbound interchange or document gives BizTalk Server the information that it needs to create the document. Envelope properties are optional for most file formats.

Submitting Interchanges and Documents

Interchanges and documents must be submitted to BizTalk Server by using receive functions or the **Submit** or **SubmitSync** method of the **IInterchange** interface. Once an interchange or document is submitted, the appropriate parser in BizTalk Server parses it, unless the interchange or document is submitted with the pass-through flag enabled. BizTalk Server does not parse interchanges and documents submitted with the pass-through flag enabled.

Using Receive Functions

It is recommended that you use receive functions to submit interchanges and documents to BizTalk Server. Receive functions can take advantage of caching, thus optimizing the performance of BizTalk Server. BizTalk Server supports two types of receive functions: File and Message Queuing.

Receive functions are event-based. This means that a receive function waits for an event in a specified folder or message queue. When an interchange or document is placed in the folder or message queue, the receive function immediately picks up the interchange or document and submits it to BizTalk Server for processing. If the interchange or document is large and it takes more than a few seconds to write the interchange or document to the folder or message queue, the receive function locks the file and goes into a polling mode until the interchange or document is completely copied to the receive location. Once the interchange or document is completely copied, the receive function submits it to BizTalk Server for processing and deletes the document from the message queue or the file system.

Using the Submit and SubmitSync methods

You can use the **Submit** and **SubmitSync** methods if the application that submits interchanges and documents to BizTalk Server meets the following criteria:

- The application is a Microsoft Windows-based application.

- The application is capable of invoking methods on COM objects.

- The application can be designed to support direct calls to BizTalk Server 2000.

Again, it is recommended that you use receive functions to submit interchanges and documents to BizTalk Server. Use the **Submit** or **SubmitSync** method only if you cannot use a receive function.

Parsers

Once an interchange or document is submitted to BizTalk Server, it is parsed. If the document is in a non-XML format, such as EDI or flat file, the parser converts the submitted interchange or document into an intermediary XML format for processing. Four specialty parsers are included with BizTalk Server to parse the following document type formats: XML, X12, EDIFACT, and flat file.

Tracking Overview

Included in BizTalk Server 2000 is the capability to track:

- Metadata for interchanges, such as source and destination organization, time the interchange or document was processed, and so on.

- Whole copies of documents in their native or XML format.

- Specific fields.

- Custom fields.

- Action events related to messages processed by XLANG schedules.

For more information about tracking documents and interchanges, see "Tracking Interchanges and Documents" later in this chapter.

Security Overview

To facilitate the exchange of secure information between trading partners, BizTalk Server 2000 uses security features offered through Microsoft Windows 2000 and Microsoft SQL Server. Some of the security features used by BizTalk Server 2000 are included in the following list:

- **Authentication.** Authentication verifies the identity of a user who is logging on to a computer.

- **Public key infrastructure.** Public key infrastructure is a set of policies and procedures used to securely exchange information between trading partners. Elements of public key infrastructure include a public key, a private key, Certification Authorities, and digital signing.

  For more information about planning your public key infrastructure by using Secure Sockets Layer (SSL) and Secure Multipurpose Internet Mail Extensions (S/MIME), go to the Microsoft TechNet Web site (www.microsoft.com/TechNet/) and search for "Public Key Infrastructure."

- **Digital signatures.** Digital signatures are a guarantee that a document has not been altered after the digital signature was added. Digital certificates are used to ensure that the sender is not an impersonator.

- **Multipurpose Internet Mail Extensions (MIME).** MIME is a standard encoding method used to transmit data through Internet e-mail. When data is sent, it is encoded. When data is received, it is decoded. The file header includes the information that the recipient needs to decode the information.

  For more information about MIME, go to the MSDN Online Library Web site (msdn.microsoft.com/library/default.asp) and search for "About Simple Internet (RFC 822) Messages."

- **Secure/Multipurpose Internet Mail Extensions (S/MIME).** S/MIME is the secure version of MIME. Before data is sent, it is encrypted to guarantee secure transmission.

- **Secure Sockets Layer (SSL).** Secure Sockets Layer uses a randomly generated private key that can be used only for that session. At the beginning of a session, the server sends the public key to the browser. The browser randomly generates a private key and sends it back to the server.

  For more information about SSL, go to the MSDN Online Library Web site (msdn.microsoft.com/library/default.asp) and search for "Using Schannel CSPs."

In addition to the security features listed here, BizTalk Server 2000 uses logon properties, local policies, service accounts, control of a user's ability to send interchanges and documents to BizTalk Server 2000, and certificates to enhance security. These issues are described in "Security Issues" later in this chapter.

BizTalk Orchestration Services Concepts

BizTalk Orchestration Services are composed of tools and services included in BizTalk Server that enable you to design, compile, and run XLANG schedules. Typically, a business analyst and a developer are involved in designing and compiling XLANG schedules. The system administrator manages the deployment and operation of XLANG schedules. Additionally, the system administrator might create custom COM+ applications to host XLANG schedules and create persistence databases to store dehydrated XLANG schedule states.

There are eight concepts related to understanding and running XLANG schedules. They are:

- **XLANG language.** An XML-based language that describes the logical sequencing of business processes. The XLANG language also describes the implementation of the business process by using various application services.

- **XLANG schedule drawing.** A representation of all the different steps in a business process. For example, if an employee requests a new computer, an XLANG schedule can be used to show the flow of information from the initial request from the employee, to the acceptance or denial of the request, to the purchase of the computer—if the request is accepted—to the generation of the invoice and the payment of the invoice. The XLANG schedule drawing includes the protocol that trading partners agree to use to exchange data and the flow of data between message fields. A completed drawing can be compiled and run as an XLANG schedule. An XLANG schedule drawing is saved with the file extension .skv.

- **XLANG schedule.** Specific business processes expressed in the XLANG language. An XLANG schedule is saved with the file extension .skx.

- **XLANG schedule instance.** A particular occurrence of an XLANG schedule. The XLANG Scheduler Engine can run a single instance, or multiple instances, of an XLANG schedule. Different instances of the same XLANG schedule contain different messages, but all instances follow the same business-process rules.

- **XLANG identity.** A globally unique identifier that is used to distinguish version instances of an XLANG schedule drawing. This property is read-only and cannot be changed by users. Each time an XLANG schedule drawing is updated, the identity is also updated. The XLANG identity can be used to correlate an XLANG schedule with the specific version of an XLANG schedule drawing from which the schedule was compiled.

- **XLANG schedule state.** The information contained in an XLANG schedule instance. This information includes:

  - Messages that have been sent or received by that instance.

  - Any COM objects used by that instance that contain state information and are able to preserve state information.

  - The progress of that instance toward the completion of the business process.

- **XLANG Scheduler.** The default COM+ application that is installed when you install BizTalk Server 2000. This application is used to host running instances of XLANG schedules.

- **XLANG Scheduler Engine.** A service that runs XLANG schedule instances and controls the activation, execution, dehydration, and rehydration of an XLANG schedule.

Dehydration and Rehydration

When an instance of an XLANG schedule is running, it is processed in memory. Because XLANG schedules are designed to support long-running, loosely coupled, executable business processes, it can become impractical to have thousands of XLANG schedule instances continuously running over a long period of time because it would be a poor use of resources. In addition, if an XLANG schedule runs only in memory, data is lost or possibly corrupted if the server on which the XLANG schedule is running fails. In these situations, the XLANG Scheduler Engine infrastructure dehydrates or rehydrates XLANG schedule instances.

An XLANG schedule is dehydrated when an XLANG schedule instance is waiting for a message and no other activity is occurring in the schedule instance. Dehydration means that the instance-specific state information is stored in the appropriate persistence database and the XLANG schedule no longer resides in memory.

An XLANG schedule is rehydrated when the message for which the XLANG schedule instance is waiting arrives. At this time the XLANG schedule instance is rehydrated, the instance-specific state information is removed from the persistence database, and the schedule instance resides in memory again.

An XLANG schedule instance remains dehydrated until it is either rehydrated or explicitly terminated by an administrator. This enables a business process to run reliably for an extended time period.

Administering BizTalk Server

The following five areas of administration are related to maintaining BizTalk Server in a state of continuous operation:

- **Administering servers.** Administrative tasks include managing server groups and servers.

- **Administering databases.** Administrative tasks include maintaining the four types of databases associated with BizTalk Server.

- **Administering messaging objects.** Administrative tasks include managing messaging objects such as channels, messaging ports, and envelopes.

- **Administering receive functions and parsers.** Administrative tasks include managing receive functions and changing the parser order.

- **Administering applications.** Administrative tasks include managing the default XLANG Scheduler, creating and managing COM+ applications to host new XLANG schedules, and managing application identities.

Administering Servers

Some of the most common tasks related to server administration include:

- Adding and managing server groups.

- Adding and managing servers installed with BizTalk Server 2000.

- Managing interchanges and documents in the Shared Queue database.

Use BizTalk Server Administration to perform these server administration tasks. Or perform many of these tasks programmatically by using the Windows Management Instrumentation (WMI) layer.

Managing Server Groups

Server groups are the basic organizing principle for server administration in BizTalk Server 2000. Servers are organized into groups to increase performance and provide a level of redundancy and fault tolerance. Server groups have eight properties that can be configured to manage the servers within the group. There are many reasons why you might need to modify one or more of these properties after the initial deployment of BizTalk Server. For example, you might need to associate a server group with a new and/or replicated Tracking or Shared Queue database, or you might need to update the SMTP host that a server group uses.

Server group properties can be modified in BizTalk Server Administration in the *<Server Group Name>* **Properties** dialog box. The following table lists some of the common configuration updates and which property you must modify to implement the update.

If you need to do this	Modify this server group property	On this tab
Change the SMTP host that a server group uses.	**SMTP Host**	**General**
Change the URL the server group uses to receive reliable messaging receipts.	**Reliable messaging reply-to URL**	**General**
Modify how often the Messaging Management object cache is refreshed.	**Messaging Management object cache interval**	**General**
Add and/or change the proxy server that the server group uses.	**Proxy server**	**General**
Change the Tracking database that the server group uses.	**Tracking database**	**Connection**
Change the Shared Queue database that the server group uses.	**Shared Queue database**	**Connection**
Turn on or off tracking settings.	**Enable document tracking**	**Tracking**
Turn on or off the ability to log incoming interchanges.	**Log incoming interchange**	**Tracking**
Turn on or off the ability to log outgoing interchanges.	**Log outgoing interchange**	**Tracking**
Turn on or off the ability to log original MIME-encoded messages.	**Log the original MIME-encoded message**	**Tracking**
Change the parser order or refresh the parser list from the registry.	**Arrange the server call sequence**	**Parser**

Managing Servers

There are two situations that require you to change server properties:

- Adding a server to a group
- Changing the balance between throughput and performance for one or more servers in one or more groups

Servers in a server group are configured to balance server performance and maximum throughput. If your business needs change, you might need to adjust the server settings that were configured when BizTalk Server was installed. For example, you might be required to process more documents more quickly. Or you might need to configure a server in a group to receive only interchanges and documents. When you adjust server properties, experiment with various combinations in a test environment before you change the server properties on your production BizTalk Servers.

You can change server properties in BizTalk Server Administration in the *<Server name>* **Properties** dialog box. The following list describes each of the server properties and the implications of changing the settings:

- **Maximum number of receive function threads allowed.** Specifies the maximum number of receive function threads on a per-processor basis. Increasing this number increases the throughput of the receive functions on the server. In general, if a BizTalk Server is receiving and processing documents or just processing documents, set this property to 1. However, if a BizTalk Server is configured to receive only, set this property to 4 to optimize throughput.

- **Participate in work-item processing.** Specifies whether the server is processing interchanges and documents. If the **Participate in work-item processing** check box is selected, the server processes interchanges and documents in the Work queue. If this check box is cleared, the server does not process any interchanges or documents in the Work queue.

  If you need to configure a server so it receives only documents, clear the **Participate in work-item processing** check box. Or if you need to dedicate a server in one of the server groups to administration, clear the check box for this option on that server.

- **Maximum number of worker threads per processor allowed.** Specifies the maximum number of worker threads on a per-processor basis. A low setting might cause a bottleneck if your BizTalk Server installation processes a high volume of documents and interchanges. Increase the setting to relieve the bottleneck. However, if the setting is too high, performance degradation might occur. In general, setting this property to 14 or 16 provides the best throughput.

- **Time between BizTalk Server Scheduler calls.** Specifies the range for time between BizTalk Server Scheduler calls. A thread polls the Work queue for interchanges and documents that need to be processed. This option controls how often that thread polls the Work queue. If the amount of data that you receive increases, you might need to lower this number. If the amount of data that you receive decreases, you might need to increase this setting.

The **Maximum number of worker threads per processor allowed** and the **Time between BizTalk Server Scheduler calls** settings are two factors that influence how often the Shared Queue database is accessed by BizTalk Server. If the amount of data that you receive and process has changed since you installed BizTalk Server 2000, you might need to adjust these settings. For example, if you need to limit how often the Shared Queue database is accessed, set the number lower for **Maximum number of worker threads per processor allowed** and higher for **Time between BizTalk Server Scheduler calls**. Similarly, if you need to increase the volume to the databases, increase the number for the maximum number of worker threads and decrease the setting for the time between scheduler calls. Again, test the new configurations in a simulated environment before you implement the changes on your production BizTalk Servers.

Managing Queues

When an interchange or document is submitted to BizTalk Server 2000, it is stored in the Shared Queue database until it is completely processed. The Shared Queue SQL Server database is graphically represented in BizTalk Server Administration as the **Queues** item in each server group. The **Queues** item, also called the Shared Queue, contains four subitems that represent the four queues of the Shared Queue. They are the Work, Scheduled, Retry, and Suspended queues. By accessing these queues, you can determine what stage of processing the interchange or document is in. For example, you can determine if a document has been processed and is waiting for transmission or if an interchange or document failed processing.

Managing the Work queue

The Work queue contains interchanges and documents that are currently in process. Unless you are continually processing a large number of documents, this queue usually is empty. Interchanges and documents placed in this queue are processed upon arrival, and they are not in the queue for very long.

Any item in the Work queue can be moved to the Suspended queue. Move interchanges and documents to the Suspended queue only if you want to prevent them from being processed. Once an interchange or document is moved to the Suspended queue, it can be deleted, resubmitted, or retransmitted to the Work queue to complete processing.

Managing the Scheduled queue

The Scheduled queue contains interchanges and documents that have been processed by BizTalk Server and are waiting for transmission based on the service window. Like the Work queue, any item in the Scheduled queue can be moved to the Suspended queue.

Managing the Retry queue

The Retry queue contains interchanges and documents to be resubmitted for delivery and documents that are waiting for reliable messaging receipts. You cannot tell the difference between the two types of transmissions. By default, failed transmissions are retried every five minutes for a maximum of three tries before they are moved to the Suspended queue. If your business process requires that you change this default setting, you can change the number of retries available and the interval in the appropriate channel in BizTalk Messaging Manager. Or you can change the interval number of retries programmatically by using the **RetryCount** and **RetryInterval** properties of the BizTalk Messaging Configuration object model.

Managing the Suspended queue

The Suspended queue stores and displays interchanges and documents that have failed processing for reasons such as parsing errors, serialization errors, missing channels, and so on. Most interchanges or documents in this queue can be deleted, resubmitted, or retransmitted to BizTalk Server for processing. Interchanges and documents that failed parsing cannot be resubmitted or retransmitted. You must delete these documents and submit them to BizTalk Server again from the original application or organization. In addition, the Suspended queue is a source of information to help you troubleshoot BizTalk Server errors and processing problems. For more information about troubleshooting, see "Troubleshooting BizTalk Server" later in this chapter.

Accessing and viewing the Shared Queue

You can access the Shared Queue by viewing the **Queues** item in each server group in BizTalk Server Administration. You can also access the Shared Queue by using the Windows Management Instrumentation (WMI) layer. Interchanges and documents appear in each of the queues in the order of "first in, first out." That is, the oldest items in the Work, Retry, Scheduled, or Suspended queue appear first and the newest items appear last. Additionally, up to 15,000 interchanges and/or documents appear in a queue at a time. In BizTalk Server Administration, the queue count in the console tree—the number in parentheses next to each queue—represents how many actual items are in that particular queue. If there are more than 15,000 actual items in a queue, remove or resubmit current items in the queue so that newer items can be displayed. For example, if there are 16,000 items in the Retry queue, you must move at least 1,000 items from the Retry queue to the Suspended queue to view the newest 1,000 items in the Retry queue. From the Suspended queue, you can resubmit or delete the interchanges or documents that were in the Retry queue.

Refreshing BizTalk Server Administration

There is no automatic refresh cycle for BizTalk Server Administration. If you want to view the current status of server groups, servers, receive functions, the number of items in a queue, and so on, you must refresh BizTalk Server Administration. You can perform this procedure on any item in the console tree or on an individual item. For example, when you refresh the **Microsoft BizTalk Server Administration** item, all items in BizTalk Server Administration are refreshed. When you refresh a server group, only the items in that server group are refreshed.

Administering Databases

The second aspect of administration that relates to BizTalk Server is database administration. The following four types of Microsoft SQL Server databases are associated with BizTalk Server 2000:

- **BizTalk Messaging Management database.** This database stores information for all server and messaging configuration. Server configuration information includes server group and server settings, and receive functions. Messaging configuration includes channels, messaging ports, document definitions, organizations, and so on.

- **Tracking database.** This database stores all interchanges, documents, and receipts that are processed by BizTalk Server if tracking settings for a server group, channel, and/or document definition are turned on.

- **Shared Queue database.** This database holds documents while they are being processed or waiting to be processed. Documents are removed from this database after they have been processed.

- **Orchestration Persistence database.** This database stores the XLANG schedule state when an XLANG schedule is dehydrated.

BizTalk Server 2000 stores the four types of databases it uses in SQL Server, so a majority of the administrative tasks associated with managing the databases are associated with managing SQL Server. Because there is a large amount of information published about SQL Server administration, this chapter will not repeat that information with the exception of the following topics:

- Database replication

- SQL Server settings

- Database administration issues

For more information about administering SQL Server, see the Microsoft SQL Server Web site (www.microsoft.com/sql).

Database Replication

A general administrative task that can be performed with databases is replication. It is recommended that you replicate and provide a backup facility for the four types of databases associated with BizTalk Server. You can make duplicate copies of your data, move those copies to different locations, and synchronize the data automatically. This ensures that all copies have the same data values. Replication can be implemented between databases on the same server, or on different servers that are connected by a local area network (LAN).

SQL Server Settings

After you deploy BizTalk Server 2000, you might need to change the following settings associated with your SQL Server databases:

- **Auto shrink**

- **Truncate log on checkpoint**

- **Automatically grow file**

You can change the **Auto shrink** and **Truncate log on checkpoint** settings in SQL Server Enterprise Manager in the **<*Database Name*> Properties** dialog box on the **Options** tab. You can change the **Automatically grow file** setting in SQL Server Enterprise Manager in the **<*Database Name*> Properties** dialog box on the **Settings** tab.

The **Auto shrink** and **Truncate log on checkpoint** settings control disk space allocation. If you want to avoid unnecessary disk space allocation, enable the **Auto shrink** and **Truncate log on checkpoint** options in SQL Server. The **Truncate log** option is available only in SQL Server 7.0.

The **Automatically grow file** setting enables the four types of SQL Server databases associated with BizTalk Server to grow in size if necessary. When SQL Server is installed, the **Automatically grow file** setting is enabled by default. Keep this setting enabled under the following conditions:

- If you want SQL Server to handle low database space conditions automatically.

- If SQL Server is the only application using disk space and when ample disk space exists to grow databases.

- If you want to use disk Quota Alerts to alert you that a database is nearing its capacity limits. This enables you to prevent a BizTalk Server from failing because one of the databases it uses reaches capacity.

Although it is recommended that you leave the **Automatically grow file** setting enabled, you might need to turn this setting off in the following situations:

- If you must have control over how much space SQL Server uses.

- If SQL Server shares the same disk with other applications and those applications must have disk space available at all times.

- If you want BizTalk Server or other processes to stop when SQL Server is out of space. This allows clean-up processes to run, and BizTalk Server can be restarted when the clean-up process is complete.

Database Administration Issues

Of the four types of databases associated with BizTalk Server, two require special maintenance attention: the Tracking and Orchestration Persistence databases. These two types of databases can grow in size quickly and require regular maintenance.

Maintaining the Tracking database

If you configured all tracking options for a server group in BizTalk Server Administration and if you configured any channels or document definitions to track specific fields, your Tracking database will grow in size very quickly. To maintain the Tracking database, you can use DTA_SampleJobs.sql, a sample SQL Server script that is provided to remove records from the Tracking database. This script removes copies of the intermediary XML records stored in the dta_debug_doc table if the number of records in the table is greater than 25,000. This script also monitors the dta_outdoc_details table for records that are expecting receipts, but the waiting period has elapsed. You can find this sample script in the \Program Files\Microsoft BizTalk Server\SDK\Messaging Samples\SQLServerAgentJobs folder. Review the readme included with this sample for more information about how to tailor the script to your specific BizTalk Server deployment.

✎ Note

- If you are using SQL Server 7.0 with SP2, the tables that have image or text columns might not shrink in size, even if you delete rows from those tables in the Tracking database. SQL Server SP3 helps to alleviate this issue. SP3 is available at the Microsoft SQL Server Web site (www.microsoft.com/sql/downloads/sp3.htm).

  This issue does not occur in SQL Server 2000.

Replicating the Tracking database

It is recommended that your database maintenance plan include automatic replication of the Tracking database. If the Tracking database grows too large, BizTalk Server performance is greatly affected. You can use the SQL Server Enterprise Manager console to set up replication and to set up jobs to remove transactions from the database based on criteria that you specify.

☞ Caution

- Do not change the code, such as stored procedures or triggers, in the Tracking database. Do not access the Tracking database directly. Do not directly call the stored procedures or add triggers. Making changes to the Tracking database in this way might cause BizTalk Server to function incorrectly, cause the loss of data, or corrupt the Tracking database.

Maintaining the Orchestration Persistence database

Scripts to clean up old XLANG schedule instances along with other utilities to manage the persistence database used by BizTalk Orchestration Services are not included with BizTalk Server. However, this issue will be corrected in a future release. For information about maintaining the persistence database, white papers, and the most recent updates on the availability of such scripts, go to the Microsoft BizTalk Server Web site (www.microsoft.com/biztalk/).

❦ Caution

- Do not attempt to create your own tool(s) to maintain the Orchestration Persistence database(s). If you access the Orchestration Persistence database in this way, you could delete important production data or corrupt the Orchestration Persistence database.

Administering Messaging Objects

You can use BizTalk Messaging Manager or the BizTalk Messaging Configuration object model to configure additional messaging objects or to update and manage current messaging objects. For example, you might need to update the URL for the HTTP transport service in a messaging port. Or you might want to change the fields that you track in a channel or document definition.

The following table lists some of the messaging object properties that a system administrator might need to update or reconfigure.

If you need to do this	Configure this property	On this messaging object
Update or reconfigure a transport service.	**Primary transport, Backup transport**	Messaging ports or distribution lists (port groups)
Change where an interchange or document is sent.	**Open destination, Organization, New XLANG schedule, Running XLANG schedule, Application**	Messaging port or distribution list (port group)
Change the envelope for an interchange or document instance for a specific trading partner.	**Envelope information**	Messaging port or distribution list (port group)
Change or update an envelope format.	**Envelope format**	Envelope
Set the option so an interchange or document generates a receipt when it is received from a trading partner.	**Generate receipt**	Channel
Set the option for an interchange or document to expect a receipt when it is sent to a trading partner.	**Expect receipt**	Channel
Change from whom an interchange or document is expected.	**XLANG schedule, Application, Open source, Organization**	Channel
Change the name of an organization.	**Organization name**	Organization
Change fields that are tracked.	**Fields to track**	Channel or document definition
Change the name of a document definition.	**Document definition name**	Document definition

Administering Receive Functions and Parsers

In addition to messaging objects, receive functions and parsers must also be managed in BizTalk Server 2000. You can use BizTalk Server Administration to manage receive functions and parsers.

Receive Function Administration Issues

For many different reasons, you might need to delete a server from a server group. For example, you might need to replace a server with a new one. Or you might need to move a server from one group to another to provide better load balancing in the new server group. If you plan to delete a server from a server group, you must first complete one of the following tasks:

- Reconfigure all receive functions that point to the server that you want to delete to point to a different server in the server group.

- Delete the receive functions that point to the server you want to delete if they can no longer be used.

You are prevented from deleting a server from a server group if one or more receive functions point to it.

Parser Administration Issues

If you receive files in formats other than XML, X12, EDIFACT, or flat file, you must create your own parser and register it on the appropriate BizTalk Server. If you create a custom parser, it appears at the bottom of the parser list after the parser is registered and the list is refreshed. This list can only be refreshed locally. That is, if you registered the custom parser on BizTalk Server A, you must refresh the parser list on BizTalk Server A. You cannot refresh the parser list from a remote computer.

When BizTalk Server is installed, parsers appear in the parser list in the following order:

- BizTalk.ParserXML.1

- BizTalk.ParserEdifact.1

- BizTalk.ParserX12.1

- BizTalk.ParserFFile.1.

Again, if you add any custom parsers, they appear at the end of this list unless you change the parser order. To maximize BizTalk Server performance, for the document format that you receive most frequently, put the corresponding parser at the top of the list. For example, if you receive mostly flat files, change the parser order so that the flat-file parser is at the top of the list.

Administering Applications

The focus of application administration is managing the COM+ applications that host XLANG schedules. When BizTalk Server is installed, two COM+ applications are installed that you must administer:

- **The default XLANG Scheduler application.** This application hosts the default instance of the XLANG Scheduler Engine.

- **The BizTalk Server Interchange Application.** This application hosts the roles that limit who can send interchanges and documents to BizTalk Server.

Tasks related to application administration include:

- Changing the configuration of the default XLANG Scheduler application.
- Adding new COM+ applications.
- Changing the application identity.
- Changing the default Orchestration Persistence database settings and configuring settings for new persistence databases.
- Adding new persistence databases.
- Changing data source name (DSN) settings.
- Performing a controlled shutdown of XLANG schedules.
- Restarting XLANG schedules.

Managing XLANG Scheduler and Other COM+ Applications

The default XLANG Scheduler application and Orchestration Persistence database are created during the installation of BizTalk Server 2000. If all your security and application processes are exactly the same, the default XLANG Scheduler application could host all of your XLANG schedules. Since this business scenario is unlikely, you will probably need to create new COM+ applications to host XLANG schedules or you might need to modify the default XLANG Scheduler application. How and when you create new COM+ applications depends on security issues and application processes. For example, you might want to isolate applications that run specific schedule instances. To do this, you need to create a COM+ application for each application that you want to isolate. Or, if you have specific security requirements for some applications or XLANG schedules, you will need to create a COM+ application for those XLANG schedules.

Each new COM+ application that you create has an **XLANG** tab in the properties dialog box for that COM+ application. On the **XLANG** tab, you can enable the new COM+ application to host instances of the XLANG Scheduler Engine. The specific COM+ application in which a new XLANG schedule runs is determined by the moniker syntax used to activate an instance of an XLANG schedule.

Changing the Application Identity

When you create a COM+ application, it is recommended that you change the application identity from an interactive user account to a service account. With an interactive user account, if a user is not logged on, the application will not run. However, if you change the interactive account to a service account, a specific user does not have to be logged on all the time, thus compromising security. A service account is an account with specific properties that allow the account to act as part of the operating system. Therefore, a specific user, or any user at all, does not have to be logged on for the application to process messages.

Managing Orchestration Persistence Database Settings

You could use the default Orchestration Persistence database to store all dehydrated XLANG schedules. However, this configuration would cause the persistence database to grow in size quickly. It is recommended that you create new persistence databases as appropriate for your business needs and processes. If you have many XLANG schedules that dehydrate often, you will need more persistence databases than if you have a few XLANG schedules that dehydrate infrequently.

In addition, if you associate a COM+ application with a new or existing persistence database, you must change the data source name (DSN) for that COM+ application. The DSN connects the COM+ application to the correct persistence database. If you change the persistence database, you must change the DSN for the COM+ application.

Shutting Down and Restarting XLANG Applications

If you need to bring a BizTalk Server that hosts BizTalk Orchestration Services offline, for example for maintenance purposes, you must perform a controlled shutdown of all XLANG applications so that data associated with XLANG schedules is not lost. A controlled shutdown saves the state for running XLANG schedules to the appropriate persistence database. If you perform a controlled shutdown on the default XLANG Scheduler application, all XLANG schedules are gracefully shut down and the XLANG schedule instance data is preserved. If you perform a controlled shutdown on a COM+ application that you created after installation, only the XLANG schedules associated with that COM+ application are gracefully shut down and preserved. All other XLANG schedules remain running until you shut down the COM+ application(s) with which they are associated.

To restart the XLANG schedules, you must restart all the schedules at the same time in the default XLANG Scheduler application. You cannot restart applications that are associated with a specific COM+ application.

☞ Caution

- If you want to perform a controlled shutdown, do not right-click a COM+ application and choose **Shut down**. Additionally, do not use the **Shut down** item on the **Action** menu.

These procedures perform an uncontrolled shutdown. If you perform an uncontrolled shutdown, one of the following might occur:

- If running XLANG schedules are fully transactional, executing transactions might abort.

- If running XLANG schedules are not fully transactional, data that is in process in the schedule is lost.

- If an XLANG schedule has not been persisted, there will be data loss and the XLANG schedule will not automatically restart.

  Instead, go to BizTalk Server 2000 Help and follow the "Shut down all XLANG applications" procedure.

- Do not shut down Windows without performing a controlled shutdown of all XLANG applications.

Administering Transport Services

BizTalk Server 2000 supports the following transport services:

- HTTP

- HTTPS

- SMTP

- File

- Message Queuing

- Application integration components (AICs)

- Loopback

The type of transport that is used depends on the business process and the type of data that is exchanged. For example, the File transport service is often used with internal applications or with legacy systems. Message queuing is used to exchange messages and documents between BizTalk Orchestration Services and BizTalk Messaging Services. HTTP is often used to exchange documents with trading partners.

Each transport service requires special considerations to keep the system running smoothly. This topic discusses some of the issues you might encounter with some of the transport services.

When managing your BizTalk Server deployment, here are some things to keep in mind about some of the transport services.

HTTP and HTTPS

- **Proxy servers and firewalls.** If you do not properly configure TCP ports or if you use nonstandard ports, BizTalk Server might have problems connecting to the HTTP server. In both cases, BizTalk Server will not specify that the improperly configured TCP ports or the nonstandard ports are the issue. However, an "unable to connect" error will appear in the Event Log.

- **User name and password changes.** HTTPS can be configured to require a user to log on. However, if the user name and password change, BizTalk Server might be unable to access the Active Server Pages (ASP). In this case, the failure shows up as a random HTTP error.

  For more information about configuring user names and passwords with HTTPS, see "Advanced Configuration of Channel Properties" later in this chapter.

- **Secure Sockets Layer port.** Determine if the server is using the standard Secure Sockets Layer (SSL) port. If you do not use the standard SSL port, port 443, you must know what port should be used and modify the HTTP URL accordingly.

- **Client certificates.** If you decide to implement client certificates, ensure that you determine if the issuer of the client certificate is a trusted Certificate Authority (CA). You might encounter situations where an HTTP client receives a certificate from a valid issuing Certificate Authority, but the HTTP server might not have knowledge of the Certificate Authority. In this situation, the HTTP server might not accept the client certificate when the client attempts a connection with the HTTP server. If you or your trading partners require client certificate authentication over HTTP, you must agree upon the Certificate Authority. For example, if you send a client certificate to a trading partner, you must also send them a link to where they can download the Certificate Authority's certificate.

  Likewise, all your trading partners must inform you as to who their Certificate Authority is. Additionally, they must provide you with a link to their Certificate Authority's certificate.

Message Queuing

Because transactional receives are limited to local computers and BizTalk Server does not forward messages, you can configure the Message Queuing server to forward messages. For more information about Message Queuing, go to the MSDN Online Library Web site (msdn.microsoft.com/library/default.asp) and search for "Message Queuing."

Note

- Transactional message queues are recommended, but not required. However, it is recommended that you use transactional message queues to ensure that no data is lost when documents are submitted from a message queue to BizTalk Server.

SMTP

A common issue that you might encounter when using SMTP as a transport service is the recognition of the e-mail address to which the application is sending an interchange or document. For example, the SMTP address might not be known or the server that houses the address might not be known. In these situations, verify that the e-mail address is correct.

When BizTalk Server sends an interchange or document to a trading partner or internal application using SMTP as a transport service, it does not send the mail directly to the Internet or intranet. Instead, BizTalk Server uses an SMTP server to forward the mail message to its final destination. If the SMTP server is offline, the interchange or document will not be delivered. Administrators must check the SMTP server to verify that it is running and routing e-mail correctly.

Some SMTP servers require a From address before they forward an e-mail message. In this situation, the messaging port must be configured with the correct return e-mail alias to accommodate the return SMTP address.

Tracking Interchanges and Documents

When BizTalk Server is installed, the ability to track metadata for interchanges is automatically activated. However, the capability to store whole copies of documents or specific or custom fields, or to track action events related to messages processed by XLANG schedules, must be configured separately. This section provides an overview of the available tracking settings in BizTalk Server 2000 and when you might need to configure and/or adjust those settings.

Tracking Settings for a Server Group

When BizTalk Server 2000 is installed, or when you add a new server group, the following tracking options for a server group are enabled by default:

- **Enable document tracking**
- **Log incoming interchange**
- **Log outgoing interchange**

These settings allow BizTalk Server to store the metadata for interchanges and documents to the Tracking database. The metadata for interchanges and documents includes source organization information, destination organization information, document type, date and time the interchange was processed by BizTalk Server, document count, error information, and control ID.

This tracking setting applies to a server group and is configured in BizTalk Server Administration.

Tracking Settings in Channels and Document Definitions

The ability to store whole copies of documents or to store standard and/or custom fields is not automatically enabled. These options are configured in the appropriate channel or document definition. If channels and document definitions were not configured to track documents or standard and/or custom fields as part of the initial BizTalk Server deployment, be judicious about configuring these settings. Configure tracking settings in BizTalk Messaging Manager only if you need to:

- Store complete copies of incoming and outgoing document instances.

- Track specific fields.

- Track custom fields.

If you turn all the tracking settings on in a channel and/or document, you will store redundant data. This will cause the Tracking database to grow quickly in size. If the Tracking database gets too large and if you do not regularly maintain it, the performance of BizTalk Server 2000 will be negatively impacted.

Tracking XLANG Schedule Action Events

Messages processed by an XLANG schedule can be exchanged between BizTalk Messaging Services and BizTalk Orchestration Services. The ability to track the action events related to these messages is not automatically enabled. If tracking XLANG schedule events was not configured as part of your BizTalk Server deployment, you can enable the sample application, WorkFlowAuditClient.exe, to track action events related to messages processed by XLANG schedules. You must complete the following three steps to enable this feature:

1. Register the sample dynamic-link library (DLL) file, WorkFlowAudit.dll.

   You can find this sample file in the \Program Files\Microsoft BizTalk Server\SDK\XLANG Samples\WorkFlowAudit\bin folder.

2. Run the WorkFlowAuditClient.exe application to activate WorkFlowAudit.dll.

   You can find this sample application in the \Program Files\Microsoft BizTalk Server\SDK\XLANG Samples\WorkFlowAuditClient folder.

   For additional information, you can view the documentation (Readme.txt) found in the \Program Files\Microsoft BizTalk Server\SDK\XLANG Samples\WorkFlowAudit\Docs folder.

3. Click the **Start** button in the WorkFlowAuditClient application to initiate the logging of action events related to an XLANG schedule in the Tracking database.

Tracking Issues

If you need to change the tracking settings configured with your deployment of BizTalk Server, this section discusses some of the implications involved:

- **Tracking settings.** Administrative issues include determining when you need to track metadata for interchanges and documents, whole copies of documents, specific fields, and custom fields.

- **Balancing tracking settings.** Administrative issues include adjusting the settings in BizTalk Server Administration, BizTalk Messaging Manager, or the BizTalk Messaging Configuration object model.

- **When to turn off tracking settings.** Administrative issues include determining if and when you need to turn off tracking settings.

- **Tracking action events related to messages processed by XLANG schedules.** Administrative issues include starting the application that enables the Tracking database to store action events related to messages processed by XLANG schedules.

- **Tracking database schema overview.** Administrative issues include accessing the Tracking database if you need to present data stored in the Tracking database in a different format—for example, when using a reporting tool such as Crystal Reports.

Types of Tracking Settings

If your business needs require that you keep a copy of interchanges in their original format for nonrepudiation and commerce law concerns, make sure that the tracking settings for each server group are enabled. If you want to create an audit trail for internal purposes, or if you want easy access to data on a per-document basis, configure tracking settings in channels and/or document definitions using the BizTalk Messaging Configuration object model or BizTalk Messaging Manager.

Note

- If you use a preprocessor, be sure to provide a mechanism to preserve the interchange document before it is preprocessed. Interchanges and documents are not stored in the Tracking database until they are submitted to BizTalk Server for processing. Preprocessing occurs before an interchange or document is submitted to BizTalk Server. Therefore the interchange or document is not stored in the Tracking database before it is preprocessed.

Balancing Tracking Settings

You can configure tracking settings for a server group and in channels and/or document definitions. However, enabling all these tracking settings will cause your Tracking database to grow quickly in size. In addition to affecting the performance of BizTalk Server, you will store redundant data.

When to Turn Off Tracking Settings

There are two common situations in which you might need to turn off tracking settings for a server group and/or in a channel and/or document definition. They are:

- You plan to receive interchanges or documents that are larger than the equivalent of 20 MB of Unicode XML.

- You have absolutely no need to track interchanges and documents processed by BizTalk Server.

If you plan to receive interchanges or documents in XML Unicode format that are larger than 20 MB, it is advisable to turn off tracking settings for the server group that will receive the interchange. If you plan to receive ANSI flat-file interchanges that are larger than 7 to 10 MB in size, it is advisable to turn off tracking settings for the server group that will receive the interchange.

Similarly, if you plan to receive document instances in XML Unicode format that are greater than 20 MB, it is advisable to turn off document logging settings in BizTalk Messaging Manager. Or, if you plan to receive ANSI flat files that are larger than 7 to 10 MB, it is advisable to turn off document logging settings in BizTalk Messaging Manager.

If you have absolutely no need to track interchanges and documents that you send and receive, you can turn off all tracking settings. However, you must understand the implications of doing this. First, if tracking settings for a server group are disabled, tracking settings configured in channels and/or document definitions are also disabled. Second, no interchanges or documents are tracked in the Tracking database. This means that once a document leaves the Shared Queue, there is no way to trace it. If you need to trace an interchange or document for troubleshooting purposes, your task will be more difficult. Therefore, you must be very careful about disabling tracking settings for a server group(s).

Tracking Action Events Related to Messages Processed by XLANG Schedules

If you completed the three steps necessary to track action events related to messages processed by XLANG schedules, but no action events appear in the BizTalk Document Tracking user interface, the WorkFlowAuditClient application might have been stopped. Records are logged in the dta_wf_EventData and dta_wf_WorkFlowEvent tables only if the WorkFlowAuditClient application is started. To start the WorkFlowAuditClient application, you must complete the three steps listed in the topic "Tracking XLANG Schedule Action Events" earlier in this chapter. If the WorkFlowAuditClient application is stopped, no records are logged in the dta_wf_EventData and dta_wf_WorkFlowEvent tables.

Tracking Database Schema Overview

BizTalk Document Tracking is a stand-alone Web application included with BizTalk Server 2000 for the purpose of creating queries on the Tracking database to view interchange and document records. Most of the data that is stored in the Tracking database is available through BizTalk Document Tracking. However, it might be necessary for you to query the Tracking database directly. For example, you might want to create your own user interface or use Crystal Reports to create a custom report from the Tracking database.

In these situations, you will need to access the Tracking database tables directly. This section provides a general overview of the Tracking database schema. For more detailed information, see "Understanding the Tracking Database Schema" in Chapter 13, "Tracking Documents."

All servers in a server group share a single Tracking database. If tracking settings are enabled for the server group, the Tracking database stores metadata related to interchange and document activity in BizTalk Server. If tracking settings are enabled in a channel and/or document definition used by the server group, the Tracking database can also store:

- Whole copies of documents.
- Specific fields.
- Custom fields.

The Tracking database consists of three main tables and six secondary tables. The three main tables in the Tracking database are:

- **dta_interchange_details.** Contains one record for each document submitted to BizTalk Server.
- **dta_outdoc_details.** Contains one record for each document generated by BizTalk Server.
- **dta_indoc_details.** Contains one record for each interchange processed by BizTalk Server.

The secondary tables are:

- **dta_group_details.** Provides extensibility components (parser, serializer, and receipt correlator) for document formats that employ like-kind document groups (for example, X12 or EDIFACT) within an interchange.
- **dta_interchange_data.** Contains one row for every interchange submitted to or sent by BizTalk Server. This table also stores any response documents returned to the **IInterchange::SubmitSync** method.
- **dta_document_data.** Contains one record for every document submitted to or sent by BizTalk Server.
- **dta_debugdoc_data.** Contains one row for every inDoc or outDoc item that is configured (on the messaging channel object) to record its interim XML format.

- **dta_routing_details.** Functions as a mirror of messaging ports for the purpose of eliminating a cross-database dependency on the BizTalk Messaging Management database.

- **dta_custom_field_names.** Contains a row for each distinct capture-field node name and data type pair encountered by BizTalk Server.

- **dta_MIME_data.** Contains one row for every MIME-encoded interchange submitted to BizTalk Server.

The following illustration shows the overall database schema of the Tracking database. For clarity, only the table names are listed. The lines that connect the tables demonstrate how the tables are connected through foreign key fields and the relationship between the tables.

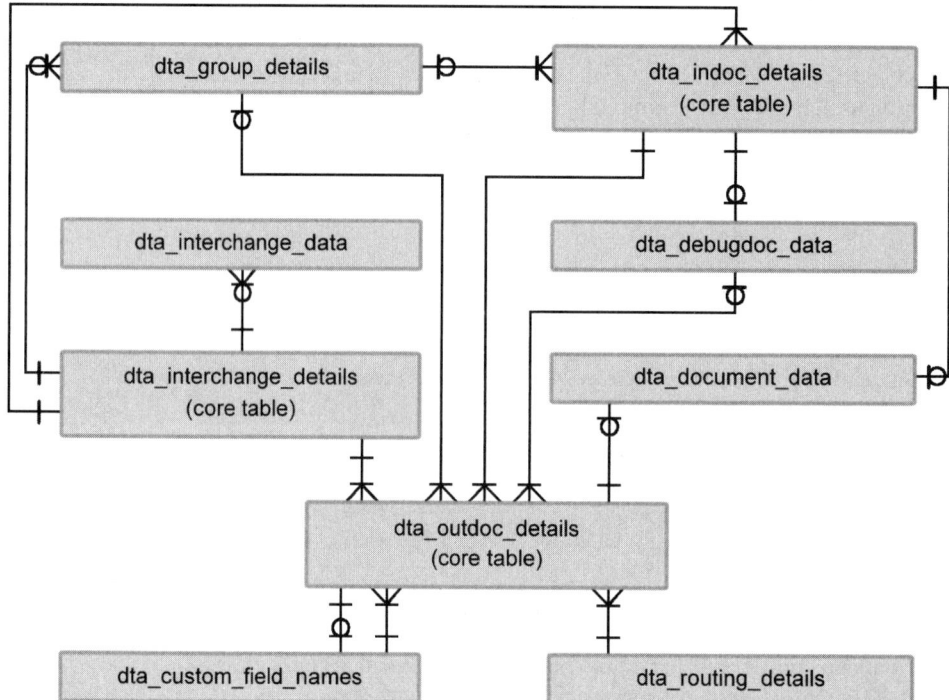

The following table explains what the different links between the tables represent.

This link	Represents this relationship
+⊀	One-to-many relationship
⊅⊀	None or one-to-many relationship
+⊲⊀	One-to-none or one-to-many relationship
++	One-to-one relationship
+⊲	One-to-none or one-to-one relationship

☙ Caution

- Do not change the code, such as stored procedures or triggers, in the Tracking database. Do not access the Tracking database directly. Do not directly call the stored procedures or add triggers. Making changes to the Tracking database in this way might cause BizTalk Server to function incorrectly, cause the loss of data, or corrupt the Tracking database.

✎ Note

- If you need to access the Tracking database, for example to use a reporting tool such as Crystal Reports, access a replicated copy of the Tracking database.

Related Tables

There are thirteen additional tables that are a part of the Tracking database. These tables are not included in the illustration because they support the secondary tables or store binary large object data. The related tables are:

- **dta_ack_status_values.** Stores the receipt status values.

- **dta_blobtype_values.** Stores the binary large object types.

- **dta_data_level_values.** Stores the data level values used in BizTalk Server.

- **dta_direction_values.** Stores the direction of the interchange.

- **dta_error_message.** Stores the error messages used in BizTalk Document Tracking.

- **dta_group_correlation_keys.** Stores the group correlation keys.

- **dta_interchange_correlation_keys.** Stores the interchange correlation keys.

- **dta_transport_type_values.** Stores the transport type values.

- **dta_ui_codepage_charset.** Stores the system code pages for character encoded data.

- **dta_ui_user_queries.** Stores the advanced queries that individual users create and save.

- **dta_validity_values.** Stores the validity values.

- **dta_wf_EventData.** Contains one record for each property logged in relation to a monitored COM+ event fired by an XLANG schedule. Sets of multiple rows in this table share a common parent in the dta_wf_WorkFlowEvent table. Records are logged only if WorkFlowAudit.dll is activated. For more information about activating WorkFlowAudit.dll, see "Tracking XLANG Schedule Action Events" earlier in this chapter.

- **dta_wf_WorkFlowEvent.** Contains one record for each monitored COM+ event fired by an XLANG schedule. Records are logged only if WorkFlowAudit.dll is activated. For more information about activating WorkFlowAudit.dll, see "Tracking XLANG Schedule Action Events" earlier in this chapter.

Security Issues

After the initial installation of BizTalk Server, you might need to change the following security settings:

- Logon properties and local policies

- Service accounts

- Roles in the BizTalk Server Interchange Application

Logon Properties and Local Policies

Logon properties control a user's ability to access specific computers or data, such as a page on a Web site. If users provide the correct user name and password, they gain access to resources. If they do not provide the correct user name and password, they are denied access.

Local policies are based on the computer a user is logged on to and provide the second layer of security. The local policies on a computer control policies such as user rights assignment, audit policy, and passwords.

For more information about settings for logon properties and local policies, see "BizTalk Server 2000 Setup and Configuration" in Chapter 2, "Understanding Security."

Service Accounts

It is recommended that BizTalk Server 2000 be run under service accounts rather than interactive user accounts. With interactive user accounts, a user must be logged on for the application to run. For example, if BizTalk Server is set up to run under an interactive user account, and if that particular user is not logged on, BizTalk Server will not process any documents.

When BizTalk Server is installed, the account identity is automatically configured to run under a service account. However, the default XLANG Scheduler application, any new COM+ applications that you create, and the BizTalk Server Interchange Application default to an interactive user account. There are several potential problems with using an interactive user account. First, if the user logs off, the application stops running. Second, if a malicious hacker obtains the user's user name and password, the hacker could do a lot of damage. Third, if an application is running on a computer while an administrator is logged on, the application runs under the administrator's identity and could make calls on behalf of the client using the administrator's rights. To prevent this, it is recommended that you create a service account and use the service account to run BizTalk Server.

For more information about settings for service accounts, in BizTalk Server 2000 Help, see "To create a service account" in Chapter 1, "Installing BizTalk Server 2000."

Control a User's Ability to Submit Documents

Controlling a user's ability to submit interchanges and documents to BizTalk Server provides yet another layer of security. The following properties for the BizTalk Server Interchange Application are configured to control who can send interchanges and documents:

- Authentication level

- Impersonation level

- Access permissions

- Launch permissions

- Configuration permissions

Using Certificates

If your deployment of BizTalk Server includes using certificates, it is recommended that you associate all certificates with a computer instead of with a specific user. This means that when you issue a certificate, you must do one of the following:

- If you created a service account, log on using the service account you created.

- Specify that you want the certificate associated with the computer and not with a specific user when you issue the certificate.

If you associate a certificate with a specific user, BizTalk Server must be configured to run with the credentials of that specific user. Additionally, if you have certificates associated with multiple users, the administration tasks can increase significantly. However, if a certificate is associated with the computer, any valid user can be logged on and the validity of the certificate is not affected.

If your business process requires that you associate certificates with specific users, you must store the certificates in the **Certificates (Local Computer)** item in the Certificates snap-in. BizTalk Server does not check the user store for certificates. In addition, if a user's password changes and that user is associated with a certificate, you must update the following two applications:

- BizTalk Server Interchange Application

- BizTalk Messaging Service

For more information about certificates and BizTalk Server, see "Certificates Overview" in Chapter 2, "Understanding Security." Or go to the MSDN Online Library Web site (msdn.microsoft.com/library/default.asp) and search for "Certificate services and components."

Advanced Configuration of Channel Properties

When you create or edit a channel, you can configure the channel to override the messaging port properties, if necessary. This allows you to send interchanges and documents to password-protected folders, message queues, ASP pages, and so on. User names and passwords can be associated with a channel and messaging port combination for the following transport services:

- File

- HTTP and HTTPS

- SMTP

- Messaging Queuing

To associate a user name and password with a channel and messaging port combination, on the **Advanced Configuration** page of the Channel Wizard, click the **Advanced** button. Verify that the **Primary Transport** tab is selected and then click **Properties**. Type a valid user name and password. If necessary, you can change other relevant information such as the name of the message queue location or the From address if you are using SMTP.

Monitoring a
BizTalk Server 2000 Deployment

Three tools are available to monitor and test the performance of BizTalk Messaging Services. They are:

- **System Monitor.** A part of the Performance tool provided with Microsoft Windows 2000. Use this tool to collect and review real-time data about memory, disk, processor, and so on.

- **Windows 2000 Event Viewer.** Included in BizTalk Server Administration. Use this tool to view BizTalk Server and XLANG Scheduler errors.

- **XLANG Event Monitor.** A tool provided with BizTalk Server 2000 that allows you to monitor XLANG schedule events and the progress of XLANG schedules.

This section describes each of these tools and provides an overview of how to use them to monitor your deployment of BizTalk Server 2000.

System Monitor

You can use System Monitor, a part of the Performance tool included with Windows 2000, to graphically display counter readings that you specify as they change over time. To access System Monitor, perform the following step:

- On the **Start** menu, point to **Settings**, click **Control Panel**, double-click **Administrative Tools**, and then double-click **Performance**.

System Monitor is an item in the Performance tool console. What you monitor and how depends on your specific deployment of BizTalk Server 2000. However, you want to choose counters that monitor objects relevant to your installation and that indicate how well a specific component is working and/or is affected. For example, you might choose the Disk read/writes/sec counter to monitor the Physical Disk object. The information that you collect regarding the Disk read/writes/sec counter gives you insight about how SQL Server and the Message Queuing and File transport services are performing.

For more information about specific counters to use to monitor BizTalk Messaging Services, see "Evaluating the Performance of a Configuration" in Chapter 3, "Enhancing Performance and Scalability."

Windows 2000 Event Viewer

Event Viewer is the second component of the monitoring plan. Use Event Viewer to assist you in troubleshooting server and document processing problems. You can find Event Viewer in BizTalk Server Administration.

You can configure Event Viewer to display all information about security, application, and system problems. Or you can configure Event Viewer to display only BizTalk Server application and XLANG Scheduler errors.

XLANG Event Monitor

When the XLANG Scheduler Engine executes XLANG schedules, it generates many types of events, showing the progress of the schedule instances. BizTalk Server 2000 provides a tool that you can use to monitor XLANG schedule events and to see the progress of the schedule instances. You can monitor the default XLANG Scheduler application, or you can monitor the custom COM+ applications that you create to host XLANG schedules. XLANG Event Monitor can subscribe to all events published by the host applications on local or remote computers. XLANG Event Monitor can also store these events to a file for future analysis.

XLANG Event Monitor has the capability to receive events from all XLANG schedule host applications on the local computer or from XLANG schedule host applications on one or more remote computers. When XLANG Event monitor is installed, the default behavior is to receive events from the XLANG schedule host applications on the local computer. If you want to include events from XLANG schedule hosts on remote computers, you must update the event sources by clicking the **EventSources** option on the **Recording** menu to include remote computers.

If you want to use XLANG Event Monitor, you must install it separately. You can find the XLANG Event Monitor application in the \Program Files\Microsoft BizTalk Server\SDK\XLANG Tools folder. Review the readme located in the same folder for more information about how to use XLANG Event Monitor.

Troubleshooting BizTalk Server

Three major tools are available to aid you in troubleshooting BizTalk Server 2000: Event Viewer, the Suspended queue, and XLANG Event Monitor.

Troubleshooting Using Windows 2000 Event Viewer

You can configure error handling in BizTalk Server 2000 at the server level through Event Viewer. Event Viewer creates a log that contains information about hardware, software, and system problems. From BizTalk Server Administration, you can customize the Event Viewer to show application and XLANG Scheduler errors that are specific to BizTalk Server 2000, which makes troubleshooting for BizTalk Server efficient.

Troubleshooting Using the Suspended Queue

The following options are available from the Suspended queue to aid you in the troubleshooting process:

- **View Error Description.** Enables system administrators to view error descriptions that indicate why the document was sent to the Suspended queue.

- **View Interchange.** Enables system administrators to view the contents of an interchange that has failed processing for a variety of reasons, including parsing errors or failed transmissions.

- **View Document.** Enables system administrators to view the contents of a document that has failed processing for a variety of reasons, including serialization errors or the inability to find a channel.

Once you have determined the reason BizTalk Server could not process the interchange or document, the following options are available in the Suspended queue to help you resolve the situation:

- **Delete.** Enables system administrators to completely remove an entry from the Suspended queue. This action is not recoverable. After a document has been deleted from the Suspended queue, you cannot retrieve it.

- **Resubmit.** Enables system administrators to resubmit most interchanges and documents to BizTalk Server for processing. You cannot resubmit or retransmit interchanges or documents that failed parsing. You must delete those interchanges and documents and submit them to BizTalk Server again from the original organization or application. **Resubmit** can also be used to retransmit documents in the Suspended queue. When an interchange or document is resubmitted, it is processed from the point of failure. When a document is retransmitted, it is processed as though it was submitted to BizTalk Server for the first time.

Troubleshooting Using XLANG Event Monitor

You can use XLANG Event Monitor to aid in troubleshooting BizTalk Server. XLANG Event Monitor can help you identify the following states of XLANG schedules:

- Running
- Successfully completed
- Completed with errors
- Dehydrated
- Suspended

You can also use XLANG Event Monitor to examine events that are published for an instance. Combine the event information with the XLANG schedule state information and the Event Viewer error messages to get a clearer picture of the issue you are troubleshooting.

Conclusion

Understanding the eight major areas of administration related to BizTalk Server and understanding the concepts behind how BizTalk Messaging Services and BizTalk Orchestration Services work can help system administrators manage and configure BizTalk Server to boost performance for their particular installations. Understanding these concepts also helps the system administrator troubleshoot more effectively.

Related Topics

Chapter 4, "BizTalk Server 2000 Deployment Considerations"

Chapter 14, "Orchestrating Business Processes with BizTalk Server 2000"

CHAPTER 13

Tracking Documents

BizTalk Document Tracking is a stand-alone Web application that you can use to view the progress of documents processed by Microsoft BizTalk Server 2000. You can create queries or advanced queries to extract essential information from the Tracking database in an easy-to-view format. For example, in BizTalk Document Tracking you can view captured information about the document source and destination, the document name and document type, and relevant date and time parameters. Or you can create queries that display standard and custom-search fields so you can analyze your business practices. For example, a Purchase Order Total field can be stored for every purchase order sent to suppliers. You can then use this data to analyze and report the monetary volume of purchases to one or several suppliers over a period of time.

In addition, you can configure BizTalk Document Tracking to display interchange and document records individually or in batches. You can also use BizTalk Document Tracking to display, view, and save complete copies of the incoming and outgoing document instances for future reference.

❖ **Important**

- Because BizTalk Document Tracking is accessed as a Web application by using Microsoft Internet Explorer, Microsoft BizTalk Server 2000 Help is accessed differently and Help functionality is somewhat restricted. The **Table of Contents**, **Index**, **Search**, and **Favorites** tabs are not available. You can access all topics through links from the opening page, and through Related Topics links as well as the browser's **Back** button.

  If you want to search for a specific Help topic, or if you want to access information about other features and services of BizTalk Server 2000, on the **Start** menu, point to **Programs**, point to **Microsoft BizTalk Server 2000**, and then click **BizTalk Server Documentation**. For Help to be available from the **Start** menu, BizTalk Server 2000 must be installed on your computer.

- Because BizTalk Document Tracking uses Microsoft ActiveX Controls, an ActiveX control download dialog box might appear during selections or query submissions. If this happens, click **Yes** to continue.

📝 Note

- A dialog box with the following message might appear during selection or query submission:

   This page accesses data on another domain. Do you want to allow this?

   To avoid this message in Internet Explorer, you can add a secure Web site to the Trusted site zones on the Security tab of the Internet Options dialog box.

   To manually configure your browser's settings to trust this Web application, add the Web application to the list of trusted sites in Internet Explorer. For more information about adding the Web application to the list of trusted sites, see "To configure Internet Explorer security settings" in Chapter 1, "Installing BizTalk Server 2000."

In This Chapter

- Using BizTalk Document Tracking

- Understanding the Tracking Database Schema

- BizTalk Document Tracking User Interface

- Understanding How to Find Interchanges and Associated Documents

- Understanding Query Results

- Troubleshooting BizTalk Document Tracking

Using BizTalk Document Tracking

You can use BizTalk Document Tracking to do the following:

- Track interchanges and associated documents processed by Microsoft BizTalk Server 2000.

- Fulfill legal and/or standards requirements to keep copies of all electronic business transactions.

- Answer customer questions quickly and easily. For example, if a customer asks "When did we send trading partner A an invoice?", you can locate the date, time, and whether they returned a receipt.

- Aid in troubleshooting.

- Help resolve disputes.

Documents can be tracked either in batches or as single transactions. BizTalk Document Tracking automatically stores metadata associated with an interchange, such as source and destination information, document type, and date and time parameters. Metadata is stored automatically; however, additional fields, such as Purchase Order Date or Purchase Order Total, are captured only if you configure the BizTalk Messaging Configuration object model or BizTalk Messaging Manager to capture this information. For more information about configuring selected fields to be tracked, see "Set Tracking for Inbound Document Properties" in Chapter 9, "Configuring BizTalk Messaging Services."

All tracking information—either the metadata or the fields that you configured to be tracked—is stored in the Tracking database that you configured during installation or when you configured a server group. Through the BizTalk Document Tracking user interface (UI), you can access the data stored in the Tracking database associated with a particular server group. While not all the information that is stored in the Tracking database is available through the user interface, the metadata and the fields that you configured to be tracked are readily available. For example, if you need to track when purchasing application C sent a purchase order to trading partner D and if and when trading partner D responded to the purchase order, this can be accomplished by using BizTalk Document Tracking.

☑ Note

- Reliable messaging receipts are not displayed in the BizTalk Document Tracking user interface.

To add users to BizTalk Server Report Users group

To view the BizTalk Document Tracking user interface and to save Advanced Query expressions, you must be a member of the BizTalk Server Report Users group.

1. On the **Start** menu, point to **Settings**, click **Control Panel**, double-click **Administrative Tools**, and then double-click **Computer Management**.

2. Expand **System Tools**, expand **Local Users and Groups**, and then click the **Groups** folder.

3. In the details pane, click **BizTalk Server Report Users**.

4. On the **Action** menu, point to **All Tasks** and click **Add to Group**.

   The **BizTalk Server Report Users Properties** dialog box appears.

5. Click **Add**.

6. In the **Look in** list, click your domain or computer name.

7. In the list that contains the users and computers associated with the domain or computer you selected in step 6, click the user account to add, click **Add**, and then click **OK**.

8. Click **OK** to close the **BizTalk Server Report Users Properties** dialog box.

To open BizTalk Document Tracking for the first time

If you open BizTalk Document Tracking for the first time and if you do not have Windows Common Controls and the BizTalk Document Tracking control installed on your computer, you are prompted to install the components. If you have the components installed on your computer, see the following procedure, "To open BizTalk Document Tracking."

1. On the **Start** menu, point to **Programs**, point to **Microsoft BizTalk Server 2000**, and then click **BizTalk Document Tracking**.

   The **Web Page Dialog** dialog box appears to prompt you to install the following components:

   • Windows Common Controls

   • BizTalk Document Tracking Installation Control

2. Click **Continue** to install the Windows Common Controls.

   The **Security Warning** dialog box appears.

3. Click **Yes** to install the BizTalk Document Tracking Installation Control.

Note

• A dialog box with the following message might appear during selection or query submission:

   This page accesses data on another domain. Do you want to allow this?

   To avoid this message in Internet Explorer, you can add a secure Web site to the Trusted site zones on the Security tab of the Internet Options dialog box.

To manually configure your browser's settings to trust this Web application, add the Web application to the list of trusted sites in Internet Explorer. For more information about adding the Web application to the list of trusted sites, see "To configure Internet Explorer security settings" in Chapter 1, "Installing BizTalk Server 2000."

To open BizTalk Document Tracking

- On the **Start** menu, point to **Programs**, point to **Microsoft BizTalk Server 2000**, and then click **BizTalk Document Tracking**.

  —Or—

  If you created a favorite in Microsoft Internet Explorer, you can open BizTalk Document Tracking from Internet Explorer.

✒ Note

- A dialog box with the following message might appear during selection or query submission:

  This page accesses data on another domain. Do you want to allow this?

  To avoid this message in Internet Explorer, you can add a secure Web site to the Trusted site zones on the Security tab of the Internet Options dialog box.

  To manually configure your browser's settings to trust this Web application, add the Web application to the list of trusted sites in Internet Explorer. For more information about adding the Web application to the list of trusted sites, see "To configure Internet Explorer security settings" in Chapter 1, "Installing BizTalk Server 2000."

Understanding Tracking Settings for a Server Group

Tracking settings for a server group determine whether tracking of interchanges is enabled or disabled. This global tracking setting is configured in BizTalk Server Administration. For more information about configuring tracking settings for a server group, see "To configure tracking properties for a server group" in Chapter 11, "Administering Servers and Applications." If the **Enable document tracking** option is selected, you can configure BizTalk Server to log incoming interchanges, log outgoing interchanges, and/or log the original MIME-encoded messages.

When you install Microsoft BizTalk Server 2000, document tracking is automatically enabled, the log incoming interchange and log outgoing interchange options are selected, and the metadata for interchanges is tracked, such as:

- Source organization information
- Destination organization information
- Document type
- Date and time the interchange was processed by BizTalk Server
- Document count
- Error information
- Control ID

In addition to tracking interchanges, you can also configure BizTalk Server to track specific fields, such as Purchase Order Total or Invoice Total. For more information about tracking specific fields, see "Understanding Tracking Settings in BizTalk Messaging Manager" later in this chapter. If you need to keep a copy of interchanges in their original format for nonrepudiation and commerce law concerns, use the global tracking settings. If you want to create an audit trail for internal purposes, or if you want easy access to data on a per-document basis, configure tracking settings in the BizTalk Messaging Configuration object model or in BizTalk Messaging Manager. You can configure tracking settings in the BizTalk Messaging Configuration object model or in BizTalk Messaging Manager and BizTalk Server Administration; however, this can cause your Tracking database to grow quickly in size and you will store duplicate data.

Disabling BizTalk Document Tracking settings

If you have absolutely no need to track documents, you can disable BizTalk Document Tracking. However, if you disable document tracking, you lose important functionality. For example, if document tracking is disabled, you cannot:

- Track interchanges and associated documents as they pass through BizTalk Server 2000.

- Fulfill legal and/or standards requirements to keep copies of all electronic business transactions.

- Answer customer questions quickly and easily. For example, if a customer asks "When did we send trading partner A an invoice?", you cannot locate the date, time, and whether they returned a receipt.

- Aid in troubleshooting.

- Help resolve disputes.

To enable or disable document tracking, or to change global tracking settings, use BizTalk Server Administration. For more information about configuring tracking settings for a server group, see "To configure tracking properties for a server group" in Chapter 11, "Administering Servers and Applications."

Notes

- To open BizTalk Server Administration, on the **Start** menu, point to **Programs**, point to **Microsoft BizTalk Server 2000**, and then click **BizTalk Server Administration**.

- There is a size limit for tracking interchanges and documents. For more information about the size limit, see "Interchange and document size limit" in Chapter 11, "Administering Servers and Applications."

Related Topics

"Set Tracking for Inbound Document Properties" in Chapter 9, "Configuring BizTalk Messaging Services"

"To configure Internet Explorer security settings" in Chapter 1, "Installing BizTalk Server 2000"

"To configure tracking properties for a server group" in Chapter 11, "Administering Servers and Applications"

"Tracking Database" in Chapter 11, "Administering Servers and Applications"

Understanding Tracking Settings in BizTalk Messaging Manager

Configure tracking settings in BizTalk Messaging Manager if you need to:

- Store complete copies of incoming and outgoing document instances.

- Configure specific fields, such as Purchase Order Total or Purchase Order Date, to be captured.

Unlike tracking properties for a server group, tracking specific fields or storing copies of document instances is not automatically enabled. You must configure these options when you configure the appropriate channel(s) and/or document definition(s) in BizTalk Messaging Manager.

For more information about storing copies of incoming or outgoing document instances, see "To set document logging properties" in Chapter 9, "Configuring BizTalk Messaging Services." For more information about tracking specific fields, see "To select specification fields in a channel" in Chapter 9, "Configuring BizTalk Messaging Services."

✎ Notes

- To open BizTalk Messaging Manager, on the **Start** menu, point to **Programs**, point to **Microsoft BizTalk Server 2000**, and then click **BizTalk Messaging Manager**.

- There is size limit for tracking and storing documents. For more information about the size limit, see "Interchange and document size limit" in Chapter 11, "Administering Servers and Applications."

Understanding the Tracking Database Schema

All servers in a server group share a single Tracking database that stores all information related to interchange and document activity in BizTalk Server. The Tracking database is used to track the status of an interchange or document as it moves through the server. The three main tables in the Tracking database are:

- dta_indoc_details
- dta_outdoc_details
- dta_interchange_details

The supporting tables are:

- dta_document_data
- dta_debugdoc_data
- dta_interchange_data
- dta_routing_details
- dta_group_details
- dta_custom_field_names
- dta_MIME_data

The following illustration shows the overall database schema of the Tracking database. For clarity, only the table names are listed in the illustration. The lines that connect the tables demonstrate how the tables are connected through foreign key fields. These key fields and their relationships to other tables are described in detail in the topics "Metadata Core Table Structure" and "Structure of Secondary Tables" later in this chapter.

Tracking database schema

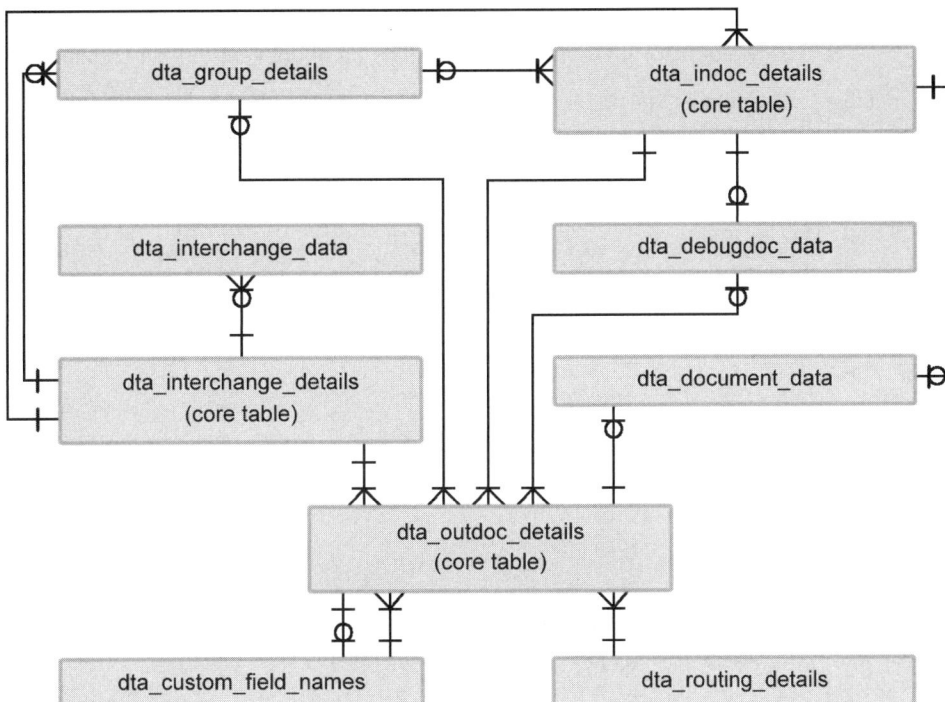

Metadata Core Tables

The core tables store the metadata for interchanges processed by BizTalk Server. Metadata includes source and destination organization information, document type, date and time the interchange was processed, document count, error information, control identification, and so on.

The following three tables form the metadata core of the Tracking database:

- dta_indoc_details
- dta_outdoc_details
- dta_interchange_details

The following table describes the function of each core table.

Table name	Description
dta_indoc_details	Contains one record for each document submitted to BizTalk Server.
dta_outdoc_details	Contains one record for each document generated by BizTalk Server. One document submitted to BizTalk Server could result in one or more documents generated and delivered to a set of respective destinations due to multiple channel matching and port groups. Separation of in and out documents into two tables allows physical representation of this one-to-many relationship.
dta_interchange_details	Contains one record for each interchange processed by BizTalk Server. A direction flag on this table distinguishes submissions from transmissions.

Secondary Tables

The seven secondary tables that support the metadata core tables are:

- dta_document_data
- dta_debugdoc_data
- dta_interchange_data
- dta_routing_details
- dta_group_details
- dta_custom_field_names
- dta_MIME_data

These tables store supporting information, such as document data, routing information, custom search information, and so on. The following table describes the function of each table.

Table name	Description
dta_document_data	Contains one record for every document submitted to or sent by BizTalk Server.
dta_debugdoc_data	Contains one row for every inDoc or outDoc item that is configured (on the messaging channel object) to record its interim XML format.
dta_interchange_data	Contains one row for every interchange submitted to or sent by BizTalk Server. This table also stores any response documents returned to the **IInterchange::SubmitSync** calling application.
dta_routing_details	Functions as a mirror of messaging ports for the purpose of eliminating a cross-database dependency on the BizTalk Messaging Management database. Specifically, it is necessary to track source and destination information relating to documents handled. This information, which comes from the BizTalk Messaging Management database, is repeated here as new permutations are encountered.
dta_group_details	Provides extensibility components (parser, serializer, and receipt correlator) for document formats that employ like-kind document groups (for example, X12 or EDIFACT) within an interchange. This table contains one row for each group parsed or serialized by these components.
dta_custom_field_names	Contains a row for each distinct capture-field node name and data type pair encountered by BizTalk Server. This table is a cross-reference for the dta_outdoc_details table, which uses a foreign key into this table for its capture field names. The dta_indoc_details table is connected to this set of field names indirectly by the existence of a foreign key pointed from the dta_outdoc_details table to its parent in the dta_indoc_details table.
dta_MIME_data	Contains one row for every MIME-encoded interchange submitted to BizTalk Server. This table provides a way for tracking MIME data that contains attachments.

Metadata Core Table Structure

The metadata core tables are linked as described in this section and store the metadata for all interchanges processed by BizTalk Server, if tracking settings are configured. For more information about configuring tracking settings for a server group, see "Understanding Tracking Settings for a Server Group" earlier in this chapter.

dta_indoc_details

This table has a one-to-many relationship with the following table:

- dta_outdoc_details

This table has a many-to-one relationship with the following tables:

- dta_group_details
- dta_interchange_details
- dta_error_message
- dta_validity_values

This table has a one-to-one relationship with the following tables:

- dta_debugdoc_data
- dta_document_data

The dta_indoc_details table contains one row per document submitted to BizTalk Server. The following table describes the fields in the dta_indoc_details table.

Field name	Description
nInDocKey	Primary key unique record identifier.
nDocumentDataKey	Foreign key to the dta_document_data table.
nDebugDocDataKey	Foreign key to the dta_debugdoc_data table for the XML form of the received document, even if the received document is XML.
nGroupKey	Foreign key to the dta_group_details table.
nInterchangeKey	Foreign key to the dta_interchange_details table.
uidTrackingGUID	Master tracking key value based on a globally unique identifier (GUID).
dtProcessedTimeStamp	Time the record was created.
nvcSyntax	Code for document syntax (XML, X12, EDIFACT, HL7, and so on). In the case of unrecognized syntax due to parsing failure or pass-through submission, this field has a value of "UNKNOWN".
nvcVersion	Version of the syntax.
nvcRelease	Release of the version.
nvcDocType	Document type or transaction set identifier.
nvcControlID	Unique control number for electronic data interchange (EDI) documents and functional groups.
nlsValid	Code that indicates validation results. Possible values are 0 (invalid), 1 (valid), or 2 (pass-through).
nError	Code that indicates the occurrence of an error. This is the foreign key to dta_error_message, the table that contains the descriptions of the error messages.

dta_outdoc_details

This table has a many-to-one relationship with the following tables:

- dta_indoc_details
- dta_interchange_details
- dta_group_details
- dta_debugdoc_data
- dta_routing_details
- dta_error_message
- dta_ack_status
- dta_data_level_values
- dta_validity_values

This table has a one-to-one relationship with the following table:

- dta_document_data

This table has a many-to-many relationship with the following tables:

- dta_custom_field_names
- dta_ack_status_values

The dta_outdoc_details table contains one row per document sent by BizTalk Server. The following table describes the fields in the dta_outdoc_details table.

Field name	Description
nOutDocKey	Primary key unique record identifier.
nInDocKey	Foreign key to the dta_indoc_details parent record.
nDocumentDataKey	Foreign key to the dta_document_data table.
nDebugDocDataKey	Foreign key to the dta_debugDoc_data table for the XML form of the outgoing document, even if the outgoing document is XML. When an outbound document is sent to a port group, only one copy of the dta_debugDoc_data record is stored, and all resulting dta_outdoc_details records point to it.
nGroupKey	Foreign key to the dta_group_details table.
nInterchangeKey	Foreign key to the dta_interchange_details table.
uidTrackingGUID	Master tracking key value based on a globally unique identifier (GUID).
dtProcessedTimeStamp	Time the record was created.
nvcSyntax	Code for document syntax (XML, X12, EDIFACT, HL7, and so on). In the case of unrecognized syntax due to parsing failure or pass-through submission, this field has a value of "UNKNOWN".
nvcVersion	Version of the syntax.
nvcRelease	Release of the version.
nvcDocType	Document type or transaction set identifier.
nvcControlID	Unique control number for EDI documents and functional groups.
nlsValid	Code that indicates validation results. Possible values are 0 (invalid), 1 (valid), or 2 (pass-through).
nError	Code that indicates the occurrence of an error. This is a foreign key to dta_error_message, the table that contains the error message descriptions.
nAckStatus	Code for the status of the receipt. This is a foreign key to dta_ack_status_values, the table that contains the receipt status descriptions.
nRoutingKey	Foreign key to the dta_routing_details table.

Field name	Description
nReceiptFlag	Flag that indicates to which table a receipt is associated. Possible values are 1 (interchange), 2 (group), 4 (indoc), or 8 (outdoc). For more information about receipts, see "How Receipts Are Logged" later in this chapter.
nReceiptKey	Unique number that identifies the receipt. For more information about receipts, see "How Receipts Are Logged" later in this chapter.
ntReceiptDueBy	Receipt deadline timestamp, computed to be the processing timestamp.
nRealName1	Foreign key to the dta_custom_field_names table.
rlRealValue1	Real capture field 1. This field must be an 8-byte real value.
nRealName2	Foreign key to the dta_custom_field_names table.
rlRealValue2	Real capture field 2. This field must be an 8-byte real value.
nIntName1	Foreign key to the dta_custom_field_names table.
nIntValue1	Integer capture field 1.
nIntName2	Foreign key to the dta_custom_field_names table.
nIntValue2	Integer capture field 2.
nDateName1	Foreign key to the dta_custom_field_names table.
dtDateValue1	Date capture field 1.
nDateName2	Foreign key to the dta_custom_field_names table.
dtDateValue2	Date capture field 2.
nStrName1	Foreign key to the dta_custom_field_names table.
nvcStrValue1	String capture field 1.
nStrName2	Foreign key to the dta_custom_field_names table.
nvcStrValue2	String capture field 2.
nvcCustomSearch	Binary large object for concatenated string capture as XML.

dta_interchange_details

This table has a one-to-many relationship with the following tables:

- dta_indoc_details
- dta_outdoc_details
- dta_group_details
- dta_interchange_data

This table has a many-to-one relationship with the following tables:

- dta_direction_values
- dta_error_message
- dta_transport_type_values

The dta_interchange_details table contains one row per interchange processed by BizTalk Server. The following table describes the fields in the dta_interchange_details table.

Field name	Description
nInterchangeKey	Primary key unique record identifier.
nInterchangeDataKey	Foreign key to the dta_interchange_data table.
nResponseDocDataKey	Foreign key to the dta_document_data table for the response document returned by the recipient of an outbound transport.
uidInterchangeGUID	Globally unique identifier (GUID) for the interchange.
uidSubmissionGUID	Globally unique identifier (GUID) for the parent submission. Note that this holds the correlation identifier (correlationID) provided from or to BizTalk Orchestration Services. This field is empty if the record is for an inbound interchange that does not come from BizTalk Orchestration Services. For inbound interchanges, this field is populated only if the interchange comes from BizTalk Orchestration Services. For outbound interchanges, this field is always populated.
dtProcessedTimeStamp	Time the record was created.
nvcSyntax	Code for document syntax (XML, X12, EDIFACT, HL7, and so on). In the case of unrecognized syntax due to parsing failure or pass-through submission, this field has a value of "UNKNOWN".
nvcVersion	Version of the syntax.
nvcControlID	Unique control number for electronic data interchange (EDI) interchanges or an identifier for BizTalk reliable messages.
nDirection	Flag indicating whether the interchange is incoming or outgoing. Possible values are 0 (outbound) or 1 (inbound). This is a foreign key to dta_direction_values, the table that contains the direction values.
dtTimeSent	Timestamp for a successful transmission.
nError	Code that indicates the occurrence of an error. This is a foreign key to dta_error_message, the table that contains the error message descriptions.
nTestMode	Test or production indicator. This field is reserved and is not used.
nvcSrcAliasQualifer	Sender qualifier value extracted from the submitted or transmitted interchange.

Field name	Description
nvcSrcAliasId	Sender identifier value extracted from the submitted or transmitted interchange.
nvcSrcAppName	Interchange level identifier for the source application extracted from the submitted or transmitted interchange.
nvcDestAliasQualifier	Recipient qualifier extracted from the submitted or transmitted interchange.
nvcDestAliasID	Recipient identifier value extracted from the submitted or transmitted interchange.
nvcDestAppName	Interchange level identifier for the destination application extracted from the submitted or transmitted interchange.
nAckStatus	Code for the status of the receipt. This is a foreign key to dta_ack_status_values, the table that contains the receipt status descriptions.
nvcSMTPMessageID	SMTP transport message identifier (for EDIINT). This field is reserved and is not used.
nDocumentsAccepted	Number of documents accepted in the interchange.
nDocumentsRejected	Number of documents rejected in the interchange.
nTransportType	Transmission protocol indicator code. This is a foreign key to the dta_transport_type_values table.
nvcTransportAddress	Address of the transport target.
nvcServerName	Server that processed the interchange.
nNumberOfBytes	Size of the interchange, in bytes. This field represents what is tracked in the related dta_interchange_data record and can be different than what is actually transmitted. The size can be increased by additional envelope processing and data format conversion during transmission.
nNumOfTransmitAttempts	Transmission attempt counter.

Structure of Secondary Tables

The secondary tables store the supporting data for the core tables in the Tracking database. For example, the secondary tables store information such as:

- Custom-field search data

- Routing information

- Interchange data

- Document data

dta_document_data

This table has a one-to-one relationship with the following tables:

- dta_indoc_details

- dta_outdoc_details

The dta_document_data table is the central repository for document storage. The following table describes the fields in the dta_document_data table.

Field name	Description
nDocumentDataKey	Primary key unique record identifier.
nCodePage	System code page (for example, 1200-Unicode, 65001-UTF-8, and so on) for the character-encoded stored data. This field has a value of -1 if BizTalk Server does not have any code page information about the data. In this case, the value of the nBLOBType field might provide information about how to interpret the data.
nBLOBType	Flag that indicates the type of data stored in the imgDocumentData field. Possible values are 0 (Unknown) or 1 (XMLDOM Loadable). XMLDOM Loadable indicates that the data can be loaded into and manipulated by the MSXML DOMDocument object. This field is a foreign key to the dta_blobtype_values table.
imgDocumentData	Storage of a document, as a binary large object.
nNumberOfBytes	Size of the document, in bytes.
nNumberOfRecords	Records or segments comprised in the document.

dta_debugdoc_data

This table has a one-to-one relationship with the following table:

- dta_indoc_details

This table has a one-to-many relationship with the following table:

- dta_outdoc_details

This table is a central repository for debug document storage. The following table describes the fields in the dta_debugDoc_data table.

Field name	Description
nDebugDocDataKey	Primary key unique record identifier.
ntxtDocumentData	Storage of the document, as a binary large object. This is always in Unicode.
nNumberOfBytes	Size of the document, in bytes.
dtProcessedTimeStamp	Time that the record was created. This is used by the purge job sample located in \Program Files\Microsoft BizTalk Server\SDK\Messaging Samples\SQLServerAgentJobs\DTA_SampleJobs.sql in the BizTalk Server installation directory.

dta_interchange_data

This table has a many-to-one relationship with the following table:

- dta_interchange_details

The dta_interchange_data table is a central repository for interchange storage and contains one record for each interchange processed by the system. For interchanges submitted to BizTalk Server only, the nlsFile field indicates whether the stored data originally came from the file system. If the flag is set, the nvcOriginalFileName field is a universal naming convention (UNC) path to the file system location where the data originated. The imgInterchangeData field holds the data submitted, regardless of its origination.

Field name	Description
nInterchangeDataKey	Primary key unique record identifier.
nCodePage	System code page (for example, 1200-Unicode, 65001-UTF-8, and so on) for the character-encoded stored data. This has a value of -1 if BizTalk Server does not have any code page information about the data, or if the data is tracked as a result of a pass-through submission. In this case, the value of the nBLOBType field might provide information about how to interpret the data.
nlsFile	Flag indicating file-based data submission. Possible values are 0 (non-file-based) or 1 (file-based).
nvcOriginalFileName	Universal naming convention (UNC) path to the file, if the nlsFile field has a value of 1.
nBLOBType	Flag that indicates the type of data stored in the imgDocumentData field. Possible values are 0 (Unknown) or 1 (XMLDOM Loadable). XMLDOM Loadable indicates that the data can be loaded into and manipulated by the MSXML DOMDocument object. This field is a foreign key to the dta_blobtype_values table.
imgInterchangeData	Storage of the interchange, as binary large object.

dta_group_details

This table has a one-to-many relationship with the following tables:

- dta_indoc_details

- dta_outdoc_details

This table has a many-to-one relationship with the following tables:

- dta_interchange_details

- dta_direction_values

The dta_group_details table creates one row per group processed by extensibility components for electronic data interchange (EDI). The following table describes the fields in the dta_group_details table.

Field name	Description
nGroupKey	Primary key unique record identifier.
nInterchangeKey	Foreign key to the dta_interchange_details table.
dtProcessedTimeStamp	Time the record was created.
nvcSyntax	Code for document syntax (XML, X12, EDIFACT, HL7, and so on). In the case of unrecognized syntax due to parsing failure or pass-through submission, this field has a value of "UNKNOWN".
nvcVersion	Version of the standard.
nvcRelease	Release of the version.
nvcFunctionalGroupID	Code for the type of documents in the group.
nvcControlID	Unique control number for electronic data interchange (EDI) documents and functional groups.
nvcSrcAppName	Group level identifier for the source application.
nvcDestAppName	Group level identifier for the destination application.
nAckStatus	Code for the status of the receipt. This is a foreign key to dta_ack_status_values, the table that contains the receipt status descriptions.
nDirection	Flag that indicates whether the group was incoming or outgoing. Possible values are 0 (outbound) or 1 (inbound). This is a foreign key to the dta_direction_values table.
nDocumentsAccepted	Transactions accepted in the group.
nDocumentsRejected	Transactions rejected in the group.
nNumberOfBytes	Size of the interchange, in bytes.

dta_routing_details

This table has a one-to-many relationship with the following table:

- dta_outdoc_details

The dta_routing_details table contains one row per distinct source or destination information set. Two documents might have identical routing field values at the organization or application level. In this case, these documents are differentiated by document type or some other lower-level filter. When this happens, the dta_routing_details table contains rows that are identical except for a difference in their respective parent messaging ports. This link to the parent messaging port is used to facilitate a connection between the BizTalk Messaging Manager user interface functionality and tracking. The following table describes the fields in the dta_routing_details table.

Field name	Description
nRoutingKey	Primary key unique record identifier.
nvcSrcOrgName	Source organization name, as specified on the parent channel object.
nvcSrcAppName	Source application name, as specified on the parent channel object.
nvcDestOrgName	Destination organization name, as specified on the parent messaging port object.
nvcDestAppName	Destination application name, as specified on the parent messaging port object.
nvcDistributionName	Distribution list name.
uidChannelGUID	Unique key for the parent channel based on a globally unique identifier (GUID). This is used as a channel correlation key into the BizTalk Messaging Management database.
uidPortGUID	Unique key for the parent port based on a globally unique identifier (GUID). This is a port correlation key into the BizTalk Messaging Management database.

dta_custom_field_names

This table has a many-to-one relationship with the following table:

- dta_outdoc_details

The dta_custom_field_names table contains one row per distinct node name and data type pair captured. The following table describes the fields in the dta_custom_field_names table.

Field name	Description
nNameKey	Primary key unique record identifier.
nvcName	Text of the node name, for example, /CommonPO/Total/@POTotal.
nDataType	Data type contained in the node named.

dta_MIME_data

The dta_MIME_data table stores the incoming MIME data processed by BizTalk Server. This provides a way to track MIME data that contains attachments. The following table describes the fields in the dta_MIME_data table.

Field name	Description
nMIMEDataKey	Primary key unique record identifier.
uidSubmissionGUID	Globally unique identifier (GUID) for the parent submission.
nCodePage	System code page for character-encoded stored data in the imgMIMEData field. For MIME data, the value is 1252 (ASCII) or 1200 (Unicode).
imgMIMEData	Storage of the document as a binary large object.

Related Tables

There are 13 additional tables in the Tracking database that support the core tables or the supporting tables. These tables store information such as group and interchange correlation keys, receipt status values, data level values, and so on. The following table describes each table and its functionality.

Table name	Function
dta_ack_status_values	Stores the receipt status values. Possible values are None, Pending, Overdue, Accepted, Accepted with errors, and Rejected.
dta_blobtype_values	Stores the binary large object types. Possible values are Unknown and XMLDOM Loadable.
dta_data_level_values	Stores the data level values used in BizTalk Server. Possible values are Interchange, Group, Incoming Document, and Outgoing Document.
dta_direction_values	Stores the direction of the interchange. Possible values are incoming and outgoing.
dta_error_message	Stores the error messages used in BizTalk Document Tracking. Possible values are no error, a custom component could not be called, the interchange could not be parsed, the specified channel does not exist, the interchange could not be serialized, the interchange could not be encoded, the interchange could not be signed, the interchange could not be encrypted, the transmission attempt failed (a retry is pending), the last transmission attempt failed, the document could not be parsed, the document could not be validated, a valid channel could not be found, the document could not be parsed, the document could not be validated, a valid channel could not be found, the document could not be mapped, a valid messaging port could not be found, and the document could not be serialized.

Table name	Function
dta_group_correlation_keys	Stores the group correlation keys. The values are dynamically generated for identifying possible group candidates during receipt correlation.
dta_interchange_correlation_keys	Stores the interchange correlation keys. The values are unique and dynamically generated for identifying possible group candidates during receipt correlation.
dta_transport_type_values	Stores the transport type values. Possible values are None, HTTP, SMTP, DCOM, App Integration, Message Queuing, File, HTTPS, Open Destination, Loopback, and Orchestration Activation.
dta_ui_codepage_charset	Stores the system code pages for character encoded data.
dta_ui_user_queries	Stores the advanced queries that individual users create and save.
dta_validity_values	Stores the validity values. Possible values are Not valid, Valid, and Pass-through. A value of Pass-through indicates that the document was not parsed and validity does not apply. For more information about pass-through, see "Understanding Receive Function Advanced Properties" in Chapter 11, "Administering Servers and Applications."
dta_wf_EventData	Contains one record for each property logged in relation to a monitored COM+ event fired by an XLANG schedule. Sets of multiple rows in this table share a common parent in the dta_wf_WorkFlowEvent table.
dta_wf_WorkFlowEvent	Contains one record for each monitored COM+ event fired by an XLANG schedule.

How Interchanges and Documents Are Logged

Different processing scenarios, such as open source, open destination, and pass-through, are logged differently in the Tracking database. The six common processing scenarios are Not open, Open source, Open destination, Loopback, Pass-through, and Expect receipt and Generate receipt (Expect receipt and Generate receipt are considered one scenario). The Expect receipt and Generate receipt processing scenarios are described in the following section, "How Receipts Are Logged." The remaining processing scenarios are outlined in the following table.

Processing scenario	Description
Not open	Occurs when the source and destination are both explicitly declared in the receive function, the document instance, the **Submit** method, or the **SubmitSync** method.
Open source	Occurs when the source information is not explicitly declared in the channel. The channel must be marked as open source, and the submit call or the receive function must specify source openness.
Open destination	Occurs when the destination information is not explicitly declared in the messaging port. The destination is dynamically specified in the document instance, the **Submit** method, or the **SubmitSync** method. The port must be marked as open destination, and the submit call or the receive function must indicate destination openness.
Loopback	Occurs when loopback is the specified transport in a channel. Loopback returns the outbound document of a channel to a business application, component, or XLANG schedule that submitted the inbound document using the **SubmitSync** method. This transport type is available only for a messaging port that connects to an application and is available only through the **SubmitSync** method.
Pass-through	Occurs when you select the **Submit with a pass-through** option in the receive function or configure the **Pass-through** property in the **Submit** or the **SubmitSync** method. BizTalk Server does not process the document. This means that the document is not parsed, signed, decrypted, verified, and so on. The document is transported only by BizTalk Server.

The following table outlines what outgoing records are logged in the Tracking database.

Processing scenario	dta_interchange_details (outgoing)	dta_outdoc_details	Response document
Not open	X	X	X
Open source	X	X	X
Open destination	X	X	X
Loopback	X	X	
Pass-through	X	X	X

Notes

- Response documents are generated only when you use the following transports: HTTP, HTTPS, or AIC. In addition, the recipient address must post return data.

- For the pass-through scenario, the record logged in the dta_outdoc_details table is an empty record. The nlsValid field has a value of 2 to designate that this record is associated with a pass-through document, and the nSyntax field has a value of "UNKNOWN". Because BizTalk Server does not process the document, BizTalk Server cannot populate most of the fields in this table with relevant data.

The following table outlines what incoming records are logged in the Tracking database.

Processing scenario	dta_interchange_details (incoming)	dta_indoc_details	Response document
Not open	X	X	X
Open source	X	X	X
Open destination	X	X	X
Loopback	X	X	
Pass-through	X	X	X

Notes

- Response documents are generated only when you use the following transports: HTTP, HTTPS, or AIC. In addition, the recipient address must post return data.

- For the pass-through scenario, the record logged in the dta_indoc_details table is an empty record. The nlsValid field has a value of 2 to designate that this record is associated with a pass-through document, and the nSyntax field has a value of "UNKNOWN". Because BizTalk Server does not process the document, BizTalk Server cannot populate most of the fields in this table with relevant data.

How Receipts Are Logged

The following illustration shows the receipt flow in BizTalk Server.

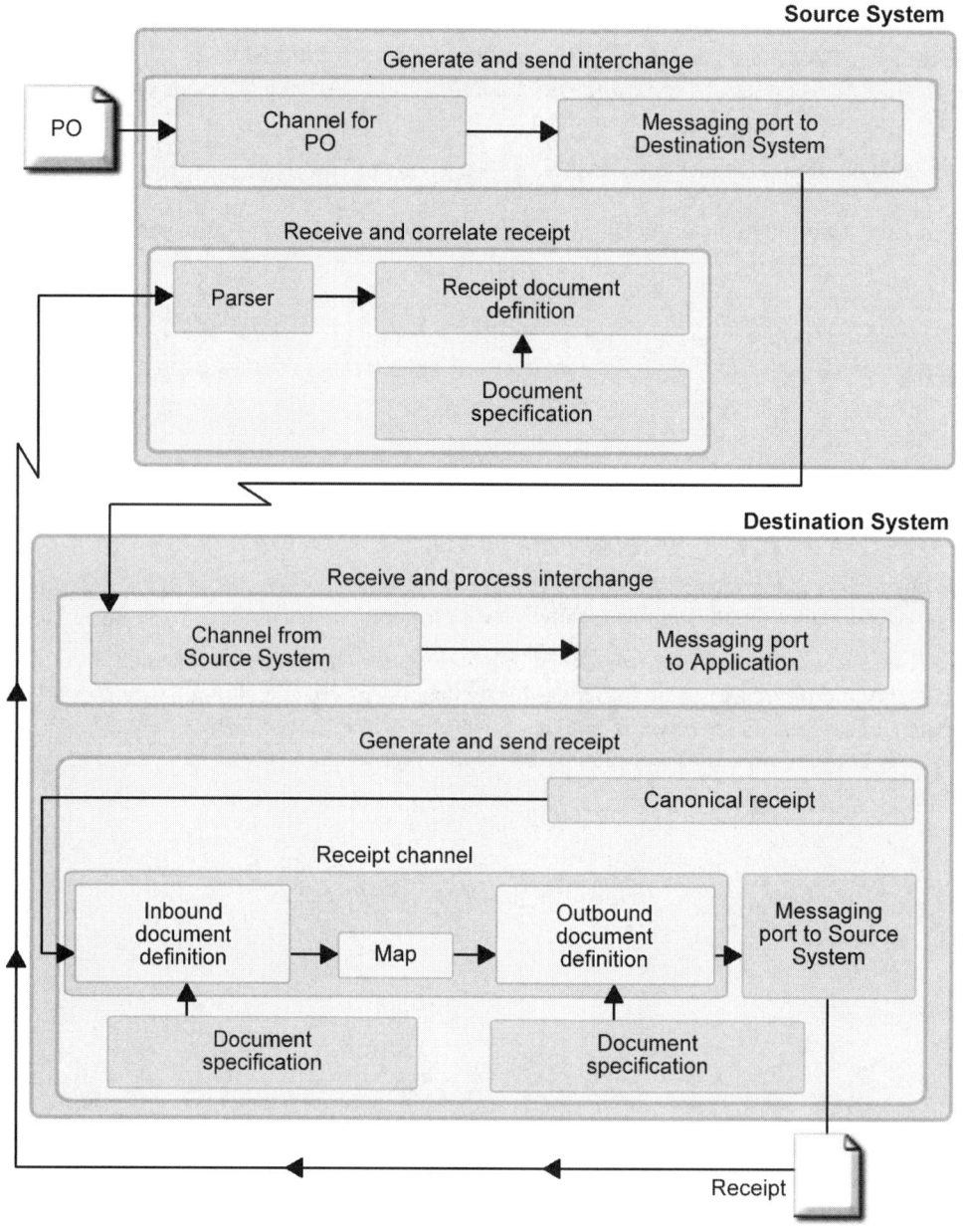

In this scenario:

- The source system and the destination system use Microsoft BizTalk Server 2000.

- The source system is sending a purchase order to the destination system, and the source system expects a receipt from the destination system for the purchase order.

- Both systems are configured to expect and generate receipts.

When the purchase order is processed by the source system and sent to the destination system, a record is logged in the dta_outdoc_details table. The following table shows what the fields relevant to receipts in that record might look like.

Field name	Sample value	Description
nOutDocKey	1	Is a unique number that identifies the record.
nAckStatus	1	Indicates that a receipt for the document is pending.
nReceiptFlag		Is not populated at this time.
nReceiptKey		Is not populated at this time.

When the destination system receives and processes the purchase order, a record is logged in the dta_indoc_details table and two records are logged in the dta_outdoc_details table. The record in the dta_indoc_details table tracks information relevant to the purchase order. The first record in the dta_outdoc_details table tracks information relevant to the purchase order and the second record tracks information relevant to the receipt for the purchase order.

The following table shows what the fields relevant to the purchase order in the record in the dta_indoc_details table might look like.

Field name	Sample value	Description
nInDocKey	1	Is a unique number that identifies the record.
nDocType	CommonPO	Identifies the type of document received.

The first record logged in the dta_outdoc_details table pertains to the purchase order processed by BizTalk Server. The following table shows what the fields relevant to receipts in that record might look like.

Field name	Sample value	Description
nOutDocKey	10	Is a unique number that identifies the record.
nInDocKey	1	Links the record to the parent record in the dta_indoc_details table.

The second record logged in the dta_outdoc_details table pertains to the receipt that is generated by the purchase order. The following table shows what the fields relevant to receipts in that record might look like.

Field name	Sample value	Description
nOutDocKey	2	Is a unique number that identifies the record.
nInDocKey	1	Links the record to the parent record in the dta_indoc_details table.
nAckStatus	0	Indicates that the receipt does not expect a receipt in return.
nReceiptFlag	4	Indicates that the receipt is associated with a record in the dta_indoc_details table.
nReceiptKey	1	Is a unique number that identifies the receipt record.

When the source system receives the receipt generated by the destination system and a record is logged in the dta_indoc_details table, the original record logged in the dta_outdoc_details table is updated. The following table shows what the fields that pertain to receipts in the record in the dta_indoc_details table might look like.

Field name	Sample value	Description
nInDocKey	9	Is a unique number that identifies the record.
nDocType	997	Identifies the type of document received.

The following table shows what the fields that pertain to receipts in the updated record in the dta_outdoc_details table might look like.

Field name	Sample value	Description
nOutDocKey	1	Is a unique number that identifies the record.
nAckStatus	3	Indicates that a receipt was received.
nReceiptFlag	4	Indicates that the receipt is associated with a record in the dta_indoc_details table.
nReceiptKey	9	Is a unique number that identifies the receipt record.

How Routing Information Is Logged

The routing information logged in the Tracking database varies depending on whether the document is incoming or outgoing and how BizTalk Server processed the data. For inbound interchanges, when BizTalk Server receives a document, it views the document instance for routing information. Then, BizTalk Server checks the receive function or the routing parameters specified in **IInterchange::Submit**. If routing information is provided in the receive function or **IInterchange::Submit**, those parameters are used to route the document instance. However, the routing information supplied in the document instance is logged in the dta_routing_details table in the Tracking database.

For outbound interchanges, the source and destination routing information always comes from the channel, and this information is logged in the dta_routing_details table.

This affects what information is shown in the BizTalk Document Tracking user interface for alias information. It does not affect how interchanges submitted to and transmitted from BizTalk Server are related as a single data flow instance.

Tracking XLANG Schedule Events in the Tracking Database

Action events related to messages processed by an XLANG schedule that are exchanged between BizTalk Messaging Services and BizTalk Orchestration Services can be tracked in the appropriate tables in the Tracking database. The action events can be viewed by using BizTalk Document Tracking. However, tracking and viewing action events related to messages processed by an XLANG schedule is not automatically enabled when you install BizTalk Server 2000. To enable this feature, you must complete the following steps:

1. Register the sample dynamic-link library (DLL) file, WorkFlowAudit.dll.

    You can find this sample file in the \Program Files\Microsoft BizTalk Server\SDK\XLANG Samples\WorkFlowAudit\bin folder.

2. Run the WorkFlowAuditClient.exe application, to activate WorkFlowAudit.dll.

    You can find this sample application in the \Program Files\Microsoft BizTalk Server\SDK\XLANG Samples\WorkFlowAuditClient folder.

    For additional information, you can view the documentation (Readme.txt) found in the \Program Files\Microsoft BizTalk Server\SDK\XLANG Samples\WorkFlowAudit\Docs folder.

3. Click the **Start** button in the WorkFlowAuditClient application to initiate the logging of action events related to an XLANG schedule in the Tracking database.

◆ Important

*   Records are logged in the dta_wf_EventData and dta_wf_WorkFlowEvent tables only if the WorkFlowAuditClient application is started. To start the WorkFlowAuditClient application, you must complete the three steps listed in this topic. If WorkFlowAuditClient is stopped, no records are logged in the dta_wf_EventData and dta_wf_WorkFlowEvent tables.

After you complete these steps, records are logged in the dta_wf_EventData and dta_wf_WorkFlowEvent tables for messages that are exchanged between BizTalk Orchestration Services and BizTalk Messaging Services. The value logged in the nvcName field in the dta_wf_EventData table serves as a link between the dta_wf_EventData and dta_wf_WorkFlowEvent tables and the dta_interchange_details table, a core table in the Tracking database. For more information about the core tables, see "Metadata Core Table Structure" earlier in this chapter.

Messages sent from BizTalk Orchestration Services to BizTalk Messaging Services

All messages that are sent from BizTalk Orchestration Services to BizTalk Messaging Services by using the BizTalk Messaging port implementation in BizTalk Orchestration Designer are identified by a globally unique identifier (GUID) called the correlation identifier (correlationID). When a message is submitted from BizTalk Orchestration Services to BizTalk Messaging Services, the correlationID is logged in the uidSubmissionGUID field in the dta_interchange_details table. In addition, records are logged in the dta_wf_EventData and dta_wf_WorkFlowEvent tables. This enables you to use BizTalk Document Tracking to view the action events related to messages processed by an XLANG schedule.

Documents sent from BizTalk Messaging Services to BizTalk Orchestration Services

All documents that are submitted to BizTalk Messaging Services are identified by a globally unique identifier called the submission handle (SubmissionHandle). For more information about the submission handle, see "IInterchange::Submit Method" in Chapter 10, "Submitting Documents." When the document is sent from BizTalk Messaging Services to BizTalk Orchestration Services, the submission handle is recorded in the uidSubmissionGUID field in the dta_interchange_details table. In addition, when a document is sent from BizTalk Messaging Services to BizTalk Orchestration Services , the following two events occur:

- The submission handle is inserted into the **correlationID** property of the document that is sent to BizTalk Orchestration Services.

- Records are logged in the dta_wf_EventData and dta_wf_WorkFlowEvent tables. Because the document is sent from BizTalk Messaging Services, the submission handle is logged as the correlationID in the nvcName field in the dta_wf_EventData table.

Viewing action events

To use BizTalk Document Tracking to view action events related to messages processed by an XLANG schedule, you must create a query in BizTalk Document Tracking and then click the XLANG schedule icon. For more information about how to create queries and view XLANG schedule events, see "Understanding Queries" later in this chapter.

The dta_wf_EventData table

The following table contains one record for each property logged in relation to a monitored COM+ event that is generated by an XLANG schedule. Sets of multiple rows in this table share a common parent in the dta_wf_WorkFlowEvent table.

Field name	Description
nEventDataId	Integer key field that is incremented automatically.
nWorkFlowEventId	Foreign key to the parent event record in dta_wf_EventData.
nvcName	Correlation identifier (correlationID).
nvcValue	Any value. This is usually based on a globally unique identifier (GUID).

The dta_wf_WorkFlowEvent table

The following table is the parent table to dta_wf_EventData and contains one record for each monitored COM+ event that is generated by an XLANG schedule.

Field name	Description
nWorkFlowEventId	Integer key field that is incremented automatically.
nvcEventId	Type of event.
nvcEventName	Name of the event.
nProcessId	Process identifier for the originating event.
nvcApplicationId	XLANG schedule identifier.
nvcInstanceId	Identifier for the particular instance of the schedule.
nEventTime	Coordinated universal time (UTC) of the event as seconds elapsed since midnight, January 1, 1970.
nEventSubTime	Microseconds added to the **ITime** argument for time to a microsecond solution.
nEventTick	Value of the high-resolution performance counter when the event originated.
nvcServerName	Server on which the event was detected.
dtDateEntered	Date of the event.

Related Topics

Chapter 14, "Integrating BizTalk Messaging and Orchestration Services"

"IInterchange::Submit Method" in Chapter 10, "Submitting Documents"

"Interchange and document size limit" in Chapter 11, "Administering Servers and Applications"

"To select specification fields in a channel" in Chapter 9, "Configure BizTalk Messaging Services"

"To set document logging properties" in Chapter 9, "Configure BizTalk Messaging Services"

"Understanding Integrated XLANG Schedule Status for an Interchange" later in this chapter

"Understanding Tracking Settings for a Server Group" earlier in this chapter

BizTalk Document Tracking User Interface

BizTalk Document Tracking is a stand-alone Web application that you can use to view interchanges and documents that you configured to be tracked in Microsoft BizTalk Server. The main page contains six areas:

- **Date Range**
- **Source Selection**
- **Destination Selection**
- **Advanced Query**
- **Sort Control**
- **Document Type Selection**

You can configure query parameters in the **Date Range**, **Source Selection**, **Destination Selection**, and **Document Type Selection** areas.

The lower-left side of the page contains the **Advanced Query** and **Sort Control** areas. Configure parameters in the **Advanced Query** area to find specific information or custom-search fields. Configure options in the **Sort Control** area to specify the sort order on the **Query Results** page.

When you click the **Query** button on the main page, the **Query Results** page appears. If any records in the Tracking database match your query parameters, interchange records appear in a list. The following table lists and describes the icons that are available on the **Query Results** page.

Click this icon	To
	Access the interchange or document instance data. If you click the data icon in the interchange record, the interchange data appears. If you click the data icon in the document instance record, the document data appears.
	Expand the interchange record to view the document instance record.
	Collapse the interchange record to hide the document instance record.
	View the XLANG schedule status related to an interchange.
	View a new **Query Results** page to view the receipt contents. For more information about receipt results, see "Understanding Receipt Results" later in this chapter.
	View the custom-search data.

BizTalk Document Tracking Shortcut Keys

You can use shortcut keys to accomplish tasks in BizTalk Document Tracking. The following table is a quick reference to the shortcut keys available on the main page.

✎ Note

- Functionality that is not included in this list can be obtained by using the numeric keypad to move the mouse pointer with MouseKeys. For more information about MouseKeys in Windows 2000 Server Help, see "Using the keyboard to move the mouse pointer." In Windows 2000 Professional Help, see "To move the mouse pointer by using MouseKeys."

Press	To
ALT+N	Open the **Advanced Query Builder** page.
ALT+B	Open the **Advanced Queries** dialog box.
ALT+C	Clear the advanced query from the current query session.
ALT+S	Select all organizations and applications in the **Source Selection** list.
ALT+R	Clear the **Source Selection** list.
ALT+E	Select all organizations and applications in the **Destination Selection** list.
ALT+A	Clear the **Destination Selection** list.
ALT+W	Show all document types in the **Document Type Selection** list.
ALT+T	Select all document types in the **Document Type Selection** list.
ALT+L	Clear the **Document Type Selection** list.
ALT+Q	Open the **Query Results** page.
ALT+O	Close BizTalk Document Tracking.
ALT+H	View online Help.
ALT+Underlined letter or number of a field name	Move the focus to that particular field. For example, ALT+1 moves the focus to **Sort order 1**.

The following table lists and describes the shortcut keys available on the **Query Results** page. To open the **Query Results** page, on the main page press ALT+Q.

Press	To
ALT+C	Close the **Query Results** page.
ALT+H	View online Help.
SPACEBAR	Open or close an icon. You must use the TAB key to place the focus on the icon that you want to open or close. For example, if you want to expand an interchange record, press TAB until the focus is on the expand icon for the selected interchange record. Then press SPACEBAR.

The following table lists and describes the shortcut keys available on the **Advanced Query Builder** page. To open the **Advanced Query Builder** page, on the main page press ALT+N.

Press	To
ALT+N	Add a condition to the advanced query expression.
ALT+E	Edit a condition.
ALT+R	Remove a condition from an advanced query expression.
ALT+S	Save the expression.
ALT+O	Limit the use of the expression to the current query session.
ALT+C	Close the **Advanced Query Builder** page.
ALT+H	View online Help.
ALT+Underlined letter of a field name	Move the focus to that particular field. For example, ALT+V moves the focus to the Value field.

☑ Note

- If you move the focus to the **Query** area and there is more than one condition in the **Query** area, use the UP and DOWN arrow keys to select the desired condition.

The following table lists and describes the shortcut keys available on the **Advanced Queries** page. To open the **Advanced Queries** page, on the main page press ALT+B.

Press	To
ALT+E	Edit an existing expression.
ALT+N	Open the **Advanced Query Builder** page.
ALT+D	Delete an expression.
ALT+O	Add the expression to the current query.
ALT+C	Close the **Advanced Queries** dialog box without saving your changes.
ALT+H	View online Help.

Understanding How to Find Interchanges and Associated Documents

You can use BizTalk Document Tracking to view all interchanges and documents using the query parameters that you specify. To maximize your search results and to minimize load on the server, it is important to understand queries and how to use them. For example, if you create a query with very few parameters defined, the query might return thousands of interchange records. This places a high demand on your time and on the server's processing capabilities. This situation is compounded if more than one person is querying the database at the same time.

There are two levels of queries in BizTalk Server: queries and advanced queries. Queries include the most common criteria that are used to narrow query results. Advanced queries allow you to further define query results by using expressions to search for specific data.

Understanding Queries

The three standard query parameters included in BizTalk Document Tracking are date range and time zone, source and destination identifiers, and document type. You can find interchange and document records by defining one or more of these criteria in a query. For example, you can search for all document types in a specified date range. Or you can find interchanges and documents that are a certain document type and that match selected source and destination organizations.

Date range and time zone

The date and time listed in BizTalk Document Tracking is the time that the document was processed by BizTalk Server. If you do not specify a date range for the query, the default date range is the previous seven business days. Unlike the **Source Selection**, **Destination Selection**, and **Document Type Selection** lists, you cannot leave the date range blank to search for documents for any date and time. You must always specify a date and time range in BizTalk Document Tracking.

You can also specify whether you want the date and time to display in local time or in coordinated universal time (UTC). Most often, you probably want to view interchanges and documents using local time. However, if you are working with someone who is in a different time zone and you need to create common criteria for defining when a document was sent or received, use coordinated universal time.

Source and destination organization

You can search for interchanges and documents based on the source organization, the destination organization, or both. In addition, when you create a query you can filter for documents from one or more organizations or all organizations. You can also search for interchanges and documents that originate in an application associated with an organization. For example, if source organization A has a spreadsheet application that sends information to a database application in destination organization B, you can determine when the information was sent and received.

Document type

You can search for interchanges and documents that have a specific document type, such as a purchase order or an invoice. In a query, you can combine document type criteria with source and destination qualifiers to find interchanges and documents sent and received between you and your trading partners. This type of query can help you analyze the business relationship between you and your trading partners.

Sort control

There are six sort controls that determine in what order the columns on the **Query Results** page are sorted. The default sort order of a query is as follows:

- **Source organization name.** The name of the source organization for the document.

- **Source application name.** The name of the application in which the document originated.

- **Destination organization name.** The name of the destination organization for the document.

- **Destination application name.** The name of the application to which the document is being sent.

- **Document type.** The type of the document.

- **Time processed.** The time at which the document was processed by BizTalk Server.

You can also use queries to locate, view, and save interchange and document instance records and associated data using standard search criteria, such as document type or source organization.

✍ Notes

- When you select your query parameters, be as specific as possible. This reduces load on the server and the amount of time it takes to return your query results.

- A dialog box with the following message might appear during selection or query submission:

   This page accesses data on another domain. Do you want to allow this?

   To avoid this message in Internet Explorer, you can add a secure Web site to the Trusted site zones on the Security tab of the Internet Options dialog box.

To manually configure your browser's settings to trust this Web application, add the Web application to the list of trusted sites in Internet Explorer. For more information about adding the Web application to the list of trusted sites, see "To configure Internet Explorer security settings" in Chapter 1, "Installing BizTalk Server 2000."

To search by date for interchange and document information

1. In BizTalk Document Tracking, in the **Date Range** area, in the **Display dates in** list, click **Local Time** or **UTC** to specify the time zone of the display dates.

2. In the **From date** list, type the beginning date for the period that you want to track, or click the arrow to display a calendar from which you can select a date.

   To change the time, type the beginning time in the list next to the **From date** list, or click the up or down arrow.

3. In the **To date** list, type the end date for the period that you want to track, or click the arrow to display a calendar from which you can select a date.

   To change the time, type the end time in the list next to the **To date** list, or click the up or down arrow.

4. Click the **Query** button.

   The **Query Results** page appears.

5. To view interchange data, locate the interchange record that contains the data you want to view and, in the Data column, click a Data icon.

   The **View Interchange Data** page appears.

6. To view the XLANG schedule status for an interchange, in the Schedule column, click a Schedule icon.

   The **View Schedule Summary** page appears.

7. To view a document instance record associated with an interchange, click the expand indicator icon (+) next to the interchange that contains the document instance record you want to view.

8. To view the data associated with a document instance, in the Data field, click the Data icon.

   The **View Document Instance Data** page appears.

9. To view the data in its native format or XML format, click **View native format** or **View XML format**.

10. To view the receipt data associated with a document instance, in the Receipt field, click the Receipt icon.

    A new **Query Results** page appears.

11. Click the expand indicator icon (+) next to the interchange and then click the Data icon in the data field.

12. To view the custom-search field data for a document instance, locate the document for which you want to view the custom-search field data, use the horizontal scroll bar to display the Custom Search field, and then click the Custom Search icon.

The **View Custom Search Field** page appears.

☑ Notes

- The value you select in the **Display dates in** list controls the search times and the display results. For example, if you select **UTC** in the **Display dates in** list and you specify 0800 in the time field, you search for all data processed on or after 0800 hours in coordinated universal time (UTC). This is not the same as 0800 Local Time.

- The default date setting is seven days prior to the current date.

- The display dates are the BizTalk Server–generated timestamps on the metadata for the document instances and interchanges. They are not dates for the actual document content. To locate documents based on the actual document date, create an **Advanced Query** expression. For more information about advanced queries, see "To build advanced queries" later in this chapter.

- If you specify only a date range in a query, BizTalk Document Tracking searches for all source and destination organizations and all document types. This single search parameter is not recommended. For best results, always create a query with very specific parameters to limit the number of interchange records returned on the **Query Results** page.

- The XLANG schedule status is the last detected event, processed start time, processed end time, and so on.

To search by organization for interchange and document information

1. In BizTalk Document Tracking, in the **Source Selection** list, click the organization(s) for which you want to view interchanges and documents. To select an application that is associated with a source organization, click the expand indicator icon (+) next to the organization and click the application(s) you want. To select all source organizations, click **Select All**.

   —Or—

   In BizTalk Document Tracking, in the **Destination Selection** list, click the organization(s) for which you want to view interchanges and documents. To select an application that is associated with a destination organization, click the expand indicator icon (+) next to the organization and click the application(s) you want. To select all destination organizations, click **Select All**.

   You can choose organizations and applications in the **Source Selection** and **Destination Selection** lists for the same query.

2. Click the **Query** button.

   The **Query Results** page appears. Any interchanges that match your query criteria are listed here.

3. To view interchange data, locate the interchange record that contains the data you want to view and, in the Data column, click the Data icon.

   The **View Interchange Data** page appears.

4. To view the XLANG schedule status for an interchange, in the Schedule column, click a Schedule icon.

   The **View Schedule Summary** page appears.

5. To view a document instance record associated with an interchange, click the expand indicator icon (+) next to the interchange that contains the document instance records you want to view.

6. To view the data associated with a document instance, in the Data field, click the Data icon.

   The **View Document Instance Data** page appears.

7. To view the data in its native format or XML format, click **View native format** or **View XML format**.

8. To view the receipt data associated with a document instance, in the Receipt field, click the Receipt icon.

   A new **Query Results** page appears.

9. Click the expand indicator icon (+) next to the interchange and, in the Data field, click the Data icon.

10. To view the custom-search field data for a document instance, locate the document for which you want to view the custom-search field data, use the horizontal scroll bar to display the Custom Search field, and then click the Custom Search icon.

    The **View Custom Search Field** page appears.

Notes

- If you do not select specific source and destination organizations, the query returns interchange and document records for all source and destination organizations. The options **Clear All** and **Select All** generate the same results on the **Query Results** page. For best results, always create a query with very specific parameters to limit the number of interchange records generated on the **Query Results** page.

- The XLANG schedule status is the last detected event, processed start time, processed end time, and so on.

To search by document type for interchange and document information

1. In BizTalk Document Tracking, in the **Document Type Selection** area, click **Show Documents**.

2. In the **Document Type Selection** list, click the document type(s) that you want to find.

   To select all document types, click **Select All**.

3. Click the **Query** button.

   The **Query Results** page appears.

4. To view interchange data, locate the interchange record that contains the data you want to view and, in the Data column, click a Data icon.

   The **View Interchange Data** page appears.

5. To view the XLANG schedule status for an interchange, in the Schedule column, click a Schedule icon.

   The **View Schedule Summary** page appears.

6. To view a document instance record associated with an interchange, click the expand indicator icon (+) next to the interchange that contains the document instance records you want to view.

7. To view the data associated with a document instance, in the Data field, click the Data icon.

   The **View Document Instance Data** page appears.

8. To view the data in its native format or XML format, click **View native format** or **View XML format**.

9. To view the receipt data associated with a document instance, in the Receipt field, click the Receipt icon.

   A new **Query Results** page appears.

10. Click the expand indicator icon (+) next to the interchange and, in the Data field, click the Data icon.

11. To view the custom-search field data for a document instance, locate the document for which you want to view the custom-search field data, use the horizontal scroll bar to display the Custom Search field, and then click the Custom Search icon.

    The **View Custom Search Field** page appears.

✎ Notes

- If you do not select one or more document types to narrow your search, the query returns all document types in the list. For best results, always create a query with very specific parameters to limit the number of interchange records generated on the **Query Results** page.

- The XLANG schedule status is the last detected event, processed start time, processed end time, and so on.

To search for interchange and document information by combining query parameters

1. In BizTalk Document Tracking, you can combine any of the following query parameters in a single query session to find and view interchange and document instance records and associated data:

    - **Source selection.** For more information about creating queries using the source selection parameter, see "To search by organization for interchange and document information" earlier in this chapter.

    - **Destination selection.** For more information about creating queries using the destination selection parameter, see "To search by organization for interchange and document information" earlier in this chapter.

    - **Document type.** For more information about creating queries using the document type parameter, see "To search by document type for interchange and document information" earlier in this chapter.

    - **Date and time.** For more information about creating queries using date and time parameters, see "To search by date for interchange and document information" earlier in this chapter.

2. Click the **Query** button.

To clear search criteria for organizations and document types

- In BizTalk Document Tracking, click **Clear All** beneath the **Source Selection**, the **Destination Selection**, or the **Document Type Selection** list.

Note

- When you click **Clear All**, BizTalk Document Tracking returns to the default search for all source and destination organizations and for all document types. For best results, always create a query with very specific parameters to limit the number of interchange records returned on the **Query Results** page.

To customize the Query Results page

1. In BizTalk Document Tracking, in the **Sort Control** area, select the **Group related interchanges** check box.

    This step configures the **Query Results** page to display incoming interchanges grouped with associated outgoing interchanges. Clear this check box if you do not want to view incoming interchanges with associated outgoing interchanges.

2. In the **Sort Control** area, in the **Sort order 1** list, click the first sort order option that you want to use.

    Repeat this step for each sort order list to configure the sort order of your documents on the **Query Results** page.

Each **Sort order** list contains the following options:

- **Source Organization Name**
- **Source Application Name**
- **Destination Organization Name**
- **Destination Application Name**
- **Document Type**
- **Time Processed**

To view search parameters for the Query Results page

1. Define parameters for a query and click the **Query** button.

   The **Query Results** page appears.

   For more information about how to create queries or advanced queries, see:

   - "To search by date for interchange and document information" earlier in this chapter
   - "To search by organization for interchange and document information" earlier in this chapter
   - "To search by document type for interchange and document information" earlier in this chapter
   - "To build advanced queries" later in this chapter

2. On the **Search Parameters** bar, click the Show icon.

   The following search parameters and associated values are listed in the **Search Parameters** area:

   - Date Range
   - Time Zone
   - Expression Name
   - Sort Order
   - Source Selection
   - Destination Selection
   - Document Type Selection

Related Topics

"Understanding Advanced Queries" in the next section

"Understanding Query Results" later in this chapter

Understanding Advanced Queries

If you find that a query returns too many interchange and document records, you can refine your search by implementing query expressions. In the **Advanced Queries** dialog box, you can create a new query expression in the **Advanced Query Builder** or browse through a list of query expressions that you previously saved. The expressions are SQL statements formed by the creation of conditional clauses that you add to the query. You have the following options to help you create an advanced query:

- **Source selection.** A list of the fields on which you want to search. In BizTalk Messaging Manager, if you configured a channel or document definition to track a custom field(s), the field(s) appears in the **Source Selection** list. If you have not configured BizTalk Messaging Manager to track any fields, only "<Custom Search>" appears in the **Source Selection** list. For more information about tracking specific fields, see "To set document logging properties" and "To select specification fields in a channel" in Chapter 9, "Configuring BizTalk Messaging Services."

- **Operators.** A list of the available operators (such as >, <, =, **contains**, or **does not contain**).

- **Value.** You can type a value in this box to indicate the boundary value for the advanced query.

- **AND/OR.** A list that contains the grouping operators (**AND** and **OR**) that are used to combine search conditions.

- **Query.** A list of the queries you created.

- **Logical grouping.** A description of the combined search conditions that you created by using the **AND** and **OR** grouping operators. When you add clauses to a query, information about grouping operators appears in the **Logical grouping** box. For example, the **Logical grouping** box might display the following:

  1 **AND** 2 **AND** (3 **OR** 4)

  In this example, conditions 1 and 2 apply, and either condition 3 or 4 is combined with conditions 1 and 2.

✎ Note

- You can have more than one query with the same name.

- If you need to locate specific data, such as a document instance with a specific purchase order number, you can use an advanced query to locate the information.

To build advanced queries

1. In BizTalk Document Tracking, in the **Advanced Query** area, click **New**.

   The **Advanced Query Builder** page appears.

2. In the **Source selection** list, click an option to specify your source selection criteria.

   This is the name of the captured field for which you are searching.

3. In the **Operators** list, click an operator.

4. In the **Value** box, type a value.

5. In the **AND/OR** list, click either **AND** or **OR** to combine or compare this condition with another condition.

   This step is optional.

6. Click **Done**.

7. Repeat steps 2 through 6 until you add all conditions you want.

8. Perform one of the following procedures:

   - Click **OK** to limit the use of this expression to the current query session.

   - Click **Save** to save the expression for future query sessions. In the **BizTalk Document Tracking** dialog box, type the expression name in the **Enter the expression name** box (limit the expression name to 50 characters) and click **OK**.

📝 Notes

- The collection of one or more conditions in an advanced query is called an expression.

- If you have the focus on the **Source Selection** list and you click a button, you might need to click the button a second time to activate it.

- In BizTalk Messaging Manager, if you configured a channel or document definition to track a custom field(s), the field(s) appears in the **Source Selection** list. If you have not configured BizTalk Messaging Manager to track any fields, only "<Custom Search>" appears in the **Source Selection** list. For more information about tracking specific fields, see "To set document logging properties" and "To select specification fields in a channel" in Chapter 9, "Configuring BizTalk Messaging Services."

To locate existing advanced queries

1. In BizTalk Document Tracking, in the **Advanced Query** area, click **Browse**.

   The **Advanced Queries** dialog box appears.

2. Select an existing query and click **OK**.

📝 Note

- If you have the focus on the **Source Selection** list and you click a button, you might need to click the button a second time to activate it.

To edit existing advanced queries

1. In BizTalk Document Tracking, in the **Advanced Query** area, click **Browse**.

   The **Advanced Queries** dialog box appears.

2. Select an existing query to edit and click **Edit**.

   The **Advanced Query Builder** dialog box appears.

3. Perform one or more of the following procedures:

- Click **New** to add an additional condition, specify conditions for each of the four fields, and then click **Done**.

- Click an existing condition, click **Edit**, modify any of the four fields, and then click **Done**.

- Select an existing condition and click **Remove**.

4. Click **Save**.

   The **Advanced Queries** dialog box appears.

5. Select the query you just edited and click **OK**.

✎ Note

- If you have the focus on the **Source Selection** list and you click a button, you might need to click the button a second time to activate it.

To clear existing advanced queries from a query

- In BizTalk Document Tracking, in the **Advanced Query** area, click **Clear** to remove the current expression from the **Expression name** box.

✎ Note

- If you click the **Refresh** button in Internet Explorer, the advanced query is not cleared from the **Expression name** box.

To delete existing advanced queries

1. In BizTalk Document Tracking, in the **Advanced Query** area, click **Browse**.

   The **Advanced Queries** dialog box appears.

2. Select a query and click **Delete**.

3. Close the **Advanced Queries** dialog box when you are finished.

✎ Note

- If you have the focus on the **Source Selection** list and you click a button, you might need to click the button a second time to activate it.

Understanding Query Results

Query results are organized on the **Query Results** page in two levels, interchange records and document records. The highest level of organization is interchange records. An interchange record represents an interchange submitted to or transmitted from BizTalk Server 2000. Interchange records are the parent records for document instance records and thus help to organize the document instance records in a meaningful way. For more information about what fields are included in an interchange record, see "Understanding Interchange Record Results" later in this chapter. Graphically, interchange records appear as rows of data fields with an expand indicator icon at the left end of each row.

If you click the expand indicator icon, the document instance record(s) appears. Graphically, the document instance record(s) also appears as a row of data fields. Usually, there is one document instance record per interchange record. However, if multiple document types are sent in a single interchange, there is a document record for each document type sent in the interchange. For more information about what fields are included in a document instance record, see "Understanding Document-Instance Record Results" later in this chapter.

Tracking Database Schema Basics

To understand what appears on the **Query Results** page, it is important to have a basic understanding of the Tracking database schema. There are three core tables in the Tracking database that store the metadata (such as source and destination organization identifiers, date, time, and document type) for every interchange and document processed by BizTalk Server. The database tables are:

- dta_interchange_details
- dta_indoc_details
- dta_outdoc_details

dta_interchange_details

The dta_interchange_details table stores all the relevant data for interchanges and is the parent table of the dta_indoc_details table and the dta_outdoc_details table. One record is stored in the table for each interchange processed by BizTalk Server. The fields in interchange records on the **Query Results** page are populated with data from this table. A field in this table designates whether the interchange is incoming or outgoing. For example, if you receive an interchange, it is represented on the **Query Results** page as an incoming interchange record. If you send an interchange, it is represented on the **Query Results** page as an outgoing interchange record. For more information about the dta_interchange_details table, see "Metadata Core Tables" or "Metadata Core Table Structure" earlier in this chapter.

dta_indoc_details

The dta_indoc_details table stores all data for every document submitted to BizTalk Server. This table is linked to the dta_interchange_details table through a primary key. The fields in document instance records associated with incoming interchange records on the **Query Results** page are populated with data from this table. For example, if you send a document and you want to view the tracking information for that document on the **Query Results** page, you must first locate the appropriate outgoing interchange record. Then, expand the record and the document instance record appears. That document instance record is associated with the dta_indoc_details table and displays the data in the fields you configured to be tracked. For more information about the dta_indoc_details table, see "Metadata Core Tables" or "Metadata Core Table Structure" earlier in this chapter.

dta_outdoc_details

The dta_outdoc_details table stores all data for every document generated by BizTalk Server. There might be multiple records in the dta_outdoc_details table for every record in the dta_indoc_details table because multiple documents can be generated from a single submission. For example, a document submitted to BizTalk Server might be sent to a distribution list of 10 ports. In this case, a single record is logged in the dta_indoc_details table and 10 records are logged in the dta_outdoc_details table. Thus, one outgoing interchange record with an associated document instance record appears on the **Query Results** page. The fields in the document instance record are populated with data from the dta_outdoc_details table. For more information about the dta_outdoc_details table, see "Metadata Core Tables" or "Metadata Core Table Structure" earlier in this chapter.

Understanding Interchange Record Results

Based on the query parameters that you specify, one or more interchange records are returned if matches for your query criteria are found. An interchange record represents an interchange submitted to or transmitted from Microsoft BizTalk Server 2000.

An interchange contains the information shown in the following table.

Interchange column heading	Description
Data	Provides a link to view the interchange data in its native format.
Schedule	Provides a link to the XLANG schedule status information for the individual interchange, if it is available. If there is no XLANG schedule status information associated with the interchange, the following message appears:

There is no XLANG schedule information available for this interchange. |
| Direction | Specifies whether the interchange is submitted to BizTalk Server (incoming) or sent from BizTalk Server (outgoing). |
| Error | Specifies if there are any errors associated with the document. Possible error messages are:

- no error
- calling a custom component failed
- parsing of the interchange failed
- specified channel does not exist
- serialization of the interchange failed
- encoding of the interchange failed
- signing of the interchange failed
- encryption of the interchange failed
- transmission attempt failed (with retry pending)
- the last transmission attempt failed
- parsing of the document failed
- validation of the document failed
- unable to find a valid channel
- mapping of the document failed
- unable to find a valid port
- serialization of the document failed |
Source Organization	Specifies the name of the source organization.
Source Application	Specifies the application from which the document originated.
Destination Organization	Specifies the name of the destination organization.
Destination Application	Specifies the destination application for the document.
Document Type	Specifies the type of the document. If there is more than one document type in an interchange, "<Multiple>" appears in this field.
Document Count	Specifies the number of documents in the interchange.

Interchange column heading	Description
Control ID	Specifies a unique control number for electronic data interchanges (EDI) or an identifier for BizTalk reliable messages.
Receipt Status	Specifies the receipt status. Possible values for receipt status are none, pending, overdue, accepted, accepted with errors, or rejected.
Time Processed	Indicates the time at which the interchange was processed. The time is set when the document tracking records are created. Once the field is set, it is not updated.
Time Sent	Specifies the time at which the interchange was sent if the transmission was successful. If the transmission is not successful, it is null. For inbound transmissions, this field is always null.
Source ID Qualifier	Specifies the type of source organization qualifier. This is the qualifier that BizTalk Server uses internally.
Source Identifier	Specifies the source organization identifier value. This is the source identifier as denoted in the data and is used to route the document. This is different from Source ID Qualifier. For more information about routing, see "How Routing Information Is Logged" earlier in this chapter.
Destination ID Qualifier	Specifies the type of destination organization qualifier.
Destination Identifier	Specifies the destination organization identifier value. For more information about routing, see "How Routing Information Is Logged" earlier in this chapter.

Understanding Document-Instance Record Results

Document instance records in an interchange appear as a row of fields that describe the document information.

The document-instance record results contain the information shown in the following table.

Document column heading	Description
Data	Provides a link to view the data that is contained in the document instance in its native and XML format.
Tracking ID	Indicates a tracking key based on a globally unique identifier (GUID).
Document type	Specifies the type of document. If there are multiple documents in an interchange, this field specifies the document type. There is never more than one document type in this field. Additional document types appear as separate document instance records.
Compliance	Indicates whether the document is valid. Possible values for compliance are valid or invalid.
Error	Specifies whether there are any errors associated with the document. Possible error messages are: <ul><li>no error</li><li>calling a custom component failed</li><li>specified channel does not exist</li><li>transmission attempt failed (with retry pending)</li><li>the last transmission attempt failed</li><li>parsing of the document failed</li><li>validation of the document failed</li><li>unable to find a valid channel</li><li>mapping of the document failed</li><li>unable to find a valid port</li><li>serialization of the document failed</li></ul>
Receipt	Provides a link to the receipt information.

The following fields apply only to outgoing documents.

Document column heading	Description
Receipt Status	Specifies the receipt status. Possible values for receipt status are none, pending, overdue, accepted, accepted with errors, or rejected.
Real 1, Real 2	Specifies data that has been captured from the document content as a real number. There are two fields than can contain real numbers.
Integer 1, Integer 2	Specifies data that has been captured from the document content as an integer value. There are two fields that can contain integers.
Date 1, Date 2	Specifies data that has been captured from the document content as a date value. There are two fields that can contain dates.
String 1, String 2	Specifies data that has been captured from the document content as a string value. There are two fields that can contain strings.
Custom Search	Indicates additional data that has been captured as a string value. The limit for this field is 2 GB.

📝 Notes

- To configure what information you want tracked in outgoing documents, see "To select specification fields in a document definition" or "To select specification fields in a channel" in Chapter 9, "Configuring BizTalk Messaging Services."

- If you configure fields (such as integers, reals, strings, dates, or custom fields) in the document definition as optional, if you configure those fields to be tracked, and if these fields are not included in the submitted document instance, the fields do not appear in the query results. BizTalk Document Tracking does not generate an error or warning message to let you know that data is missing from optional fields.

- In a document instance, a 1 is tracked as a -1 if the following conditions are met:

  - The data type is set to Boolean when you set declaration properties for a particular field in BizTalk Editor.

  - The field is selected to be tracked as an integer in the BizTalk Messaging Configuration object model or in BizTalk Messaging Manager.

Understanding Receipt Results

The following illustration shows the receipt flow in BizTalk Document Tracking. In the illustration, Document 1 is first processed by BizTalk Server A and is flagged to expect a receipt (Document 1, Expect receipt flag set). Next, BizTalk Server B picks up the document through a receive function (Document 1, Generate receipt flag set), processes the document, and generates a receipt [Receipt for Document 1 (outgoing)]. BizTalk Server A then receives the receipt [Receipt for Document 1 (incoming)].

Receipt flow

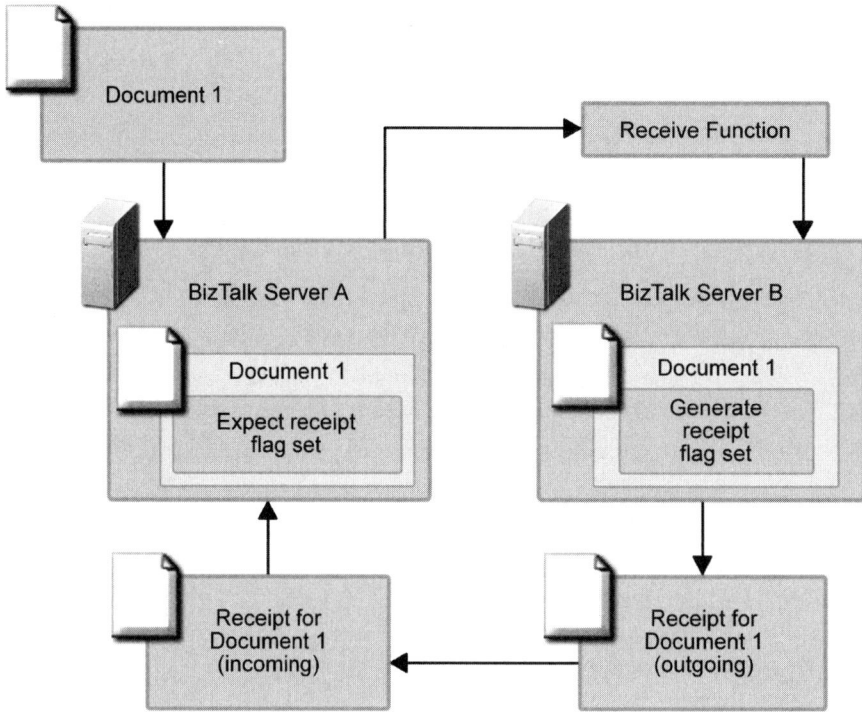

When you view the receipt for *Document 1, Expect receipt flag set*, you first locate the appropriate interchange record on the **Query Results** page that corresponds to *Document 1, Expect receipt flag set*. Click the Receipt icon in the receipt field. This opens a new **Query Results** page that contains the interchange record that BizTalk Server A generated when it processed *Document 1, Expect receipt flag set*. Click the Data icon in the Data column. The data displayed is the actual contents of the receipt. In the illustration above, this last step corresponds to *Receipt for Document 1 (incoming)*.

When you view the receipt for *Document 1, Generate receipt flag set*, you must first locate the appropriate interchange record on the **Query Results** page that corresponds to *Document 1, Generate receipt flag set*. Click the Receipt icon in the receipt field. This opens a new **Query Results** page that contains the interchange record that BizTalk Server B generated when it processed *Document 1, Generate receipt flag set*. Expand the interchange record to view the document instance details, and then click the Data icon in the Data field. The data displayed is the actual contents of the receipt. In the illustration, this last step corresponds to *Receipt for Document 1 (outgoing)*.

🗒 Notes

- Sending and receiving receipts works only with parsers that can process receipts. For information about receipts, see "Understanding Receipts" in Chapter 9, "Configuring BizTalk Messaging Services."

- Reliable messaging receipts are not displayed in the BizTalk Document Tracking user interface.

Understanding Results for Failed Transmissions

When a transmission fails, the failure is logged in the Tracking database. However, not all errors that are logged in the Tracking database appear in the BizTalk Document Tracking user interface. Errors appear in the user interface only if a record was logged in the dta_outdoc_details table. For more information about the core tables, see "Tracking Database Schema Basics" or "Metadata Core Tables" earlier in this chapter.

The following table outlines possible error messages and whether records get logged into the various core tables in the Tracking database.

Error message	Records logged	Comments
No error.	dta_indoc_details dta_interchange_details (incoming) dta_interchange_details (outgoing) dta_outdoc_details	The appropriate fields are logged in the three core tables.
A custom component could not be called.		This error message appears only if you have a custom preprocessor associated with a receive function. No records are logged in the Tracking database.
The interchange could not be parsed.	dta_interchange_details (incoming)	The interchange and the data are logged if there is a parsing error.
The specified channel does not exist.	dta_indoc_details dta_interchange_details (incoming)	
The interchange could not be serialized.	dta_indoc_details dta_interchange_details (incoming) dta_interchange_details (outgoing) dta_outdoc_details	An empty record is logged in the dta_interchange_details (outgoing) table. If the interchange is resubmitted and it succeeds, the record is updated.
The interchange could not be encoded.	dta_indoc_details dta_interchange_details (incoming) dta_interchange_details (outgoing) dta_outdoc_details	

Error message	Records logged	Comments
The interchange could not be signed.	dta_indoc_details dta_interchange_details (incoming) dta_interchange_details (outgoing) dta_outdoc_details	
The interchange could not be encrypted.	dta_indoc_details dta_interchange_details (incoming) dta_interchange_details (outgoing) dta_outdoc_details	
The transmission attempt failed (a retry is pending).	dta_indoc_details dta_interchange_details (incoming) dta_interchange_details (outgoing) dta_outdoc_details	
The last transmission attempt failed.	dta_indoc_details dta_interchange_details (incoming) dta_interchange_details (outgoing) dta_outdoc_details	
The document could not be parsed.	dta_indoc_details dta_interchange_details (incoming)	
The document could not be validated.	dta_indoc_details dta_interchange_details (incoming)	
A valid channel could not be found.	dta_indoc_details dta_interchange_details (incoming)	
The document could not be mapped.	dta_indoc_details dta_interchange_details (incoming) dta_interchange_details (outgoing) dta_outdoc_details	The record in the dta_outdoc_details table records the logging error, and an empty record is logged in the dta_interchange_details (outgoing) table.
A valid messaging port could not be found.	dta_indoc_details dta_interchange_details (incoming) dta_interchange_details (outgoing) dta_outdoc_details	The record in the dta_outdoc_details table records a NoPort error, and an empty record is logged in the dta_interchange_details (outgoing) table.
The document could not be serialized.	dta_indoc_details dta_interchange_details (incoming) dta_interchange_details (outgoing) dta_outdoc_details	Records in the dta_indoc_details and dta_outdoc_details tables contain the serialization error.

Understanding Integrated XLANG Schedule Status for an Interchange

You can track the status of related XLANG schedules in BizTalk Document Tracking. Actions in schedules on a server can be monitored and stored in the appropriate tables in the Tracking database with an identifier that correlates them to specific message instances. Storage schema in the Tracking database and correlation are part of Microsoft BizTalk Server 2000, but event subscription functionality is not implemented when you install BizTalk Server 2000. However, a sample for performing tracking integration is provided. After you install BizTalk Server 2000, you can find the source code for this sample in the \Program Files\Microsoft BizTalk Server\SDK\XLANG Samples\WorkFlowAudit folder. Additionally, the bin subfolder contains the dynamic-link library (WorkFlowAudit.dll), and the Docs subfolder contains the documentation (Readme.txt) for this sample. There is a sample client application located in \Program Files\Microsoft BizTalk Server\SDK\XLANG Samples\WorkFlowAuditClient.

Save Interchange, Document, and Custom Search Data

If you configured BizTalk Messaging Manager, the BizTalk Messaging Configuration object model, and/or BizTalk Server Administration to store incoming and outgoing interchanges and their documents, you can save interchanges, document data, and custom-field search data so you can view them offline. This helps you to troubleshoot certain situations or analyze your business practices.

To save interchange data

1. Define parameters for a query and click the **Query** button.

   The **Query Results** page appears.

   For more information about how to create queries or advanced queries, see the following earlier in this chapter:

   - "To search by date for interchange and document information"

   - "To search by organization for interchange and document information"

   - "To search by document type for interchange and document information"

   - "To build advanced queries"

2. Locate the interchange record that contains the interchange data you want to save and, in the Data field, click the Data icon.

   The **View Interchange Data** page appears.

3. Click **Save As**.

4. In the **File name** box, type a name for the file and click **Save**.

To save document instance data

1. Define parameters for a query and click the **Query** button.

    The **Query Results** page appears.

    For more information about how to create queries or advanced queries, see the following earlier in this chapter:
    - "To search by date for interchange and document information"
    - "To search by organization for interchange and document information"
    - "To search by document type for interchange and document information"
    - "To build advanced queries"

2. Locate the interchange record that contains the document instance data you want to save and click the expand indicator icon (+) to the left of the interchange.

3. In the Data field, click the Data icon.

    The **View Document Data** page appears.

4. Click **Save As**.

5. In the **File name** box, type a name and an extension (either the .xml file extension or the native file extension of the document) for the file and click **Save**.

To save custom-field search data

1. Define parameters for a query and click the **Query** button.

    The **Query Results** page appears.

    For more information about how to create queries or advanced queries, see the following earlier in this chapter:
    - "To search by date for interchange and document information"
    - "To search by organization for interchange and document information"
    - "To search by document type for interchange and document information"
    - "To build advanced queries"

2. Click the expand indicator icon (+) to the left of the interchange record that contains the document you want to view.

3. Use the horizontal scroll bar to display the Custom Search field for the document you want to view and click the Custom Search icon.

    The **View Custom Search Field** page appears.

4. Click **Save As**.

5. In the **File name** box, type a name for the file and click **Save**.

Related Topics

"Configure tracking properties for a server group" in Chapter 11, "Administering Servers and Applications"

"Suspended queue" in Chapter 11, "Administering Servers and Applications"

"To select specification fields in a channel" in Chapter 9, "Configuring BizTalk Messaging Services"

"To select specification fields in a document definition" in Chapter 9, "Configuring BizTalk Messaging Services"

Troubleshooting BizTalk Document Tracking

This section provides a centralized location for information related to troubleshooting BizTalk Document Tracking. If you receive error messages, try to find a solution in this section.

Problem displaying BizTalk Document Tracking user interface

Cause: Microsoft Office Web Components are not installed.

Solution: Install Microsoft Office Web Components.

1. Click **Start**, point to **Settings**, and then click **Control Panel**.

2. Double-click **Add/Remove Programs**.

   The **Add/Remove Programs** dialog box appears.

3. Click **Microsoft Office 2000 SR-1 Premium**.

4. Click **Change**.

5. Click **Add or Remove Features**.

6. Click the expand indicator (+) next to **Office Tools**.

7. Click **Office Web Components** and click the option appropriate for your installation.

8. Click **Update Now**.

Interchanges and documents are not stored

Cause: Tracking is turned off in BizTalk Server Administration.

Solution: Turn on tracking in BizTalk Server Administration.

1. Click **Start**, point to **Programs**, point to **Microsoft BizTalk Server 2000**, and then click **BizTalk Server Administration**.

2. Expand **Microsoft BizTalk Server 2000** and click the server group for which documents are not being stored.

3. On the **Action** menu, click **Properties**.

   The **BizTalk Server Group Properties** dialog box appears.

4. Click the **Tracking** tab.

5. Select the **Enable document tracking** check box.

6. Select one or more of the following options:

   - **Log incoming interchange**

   - **Log outgoing interchange**

   - **Log the original MIME-encoded message**

7. Click **OK**.

Related Topic

"To configure tracking properties for a server group" in Chapter 11, "Administering Servers and Applications"

Nothing is displayed in the query results

Cause one: The date and time range is incorrect.

Solution: Check that the date and time range is correct. For example, if you sent a document in the past 5 minutes and the time range is set to look for documents in the past 10 minutes or greater, your document will not appear in the query results.

Cause two: The data might have been removed from the database.

Solution: Contact your Database Administrator for more information.

Related Topic

"To search by date for interchange and document information" earlier in this chapter

Tracking fields are not displayed in the query results

Cause: BizTalk Server could not convert the data or there is an arithmetic overflow error.

Solution: Look for the following error message in the Event Log:

<<path and file name>>: The following tracking field for submission *<<globally unique identifier>>* could not be logged:

Tracking field: *<<name of field>>*

Specification field name: *<<name of specification field>>*/DTADataTypeTest/String/@_String

Actual value: *<<actual value of field>>*

Check and correct the tracking field settings in the document or channel configuration.

Related Topics

"To select specification fields in a channel" in Chapter 9, "Configuring BizTalk Messaging Services"

"To set document logging properties" in Chapter 9, "Configuring BizTalk Messaging Services"

Too many search arguments

Cause: You specified too many options in the **Source Selection** and/or **Destination Selection** list.

Solution: Make your query as specific as possible. Reduce the number of options selected in the **Source Selection** and/or **Destination Selection** list and click **Query**.

Related Topic

"Understanding Queries" earlier in this chapter

Part 5: Integrating Applications and Extending Microsoft BizTalk Server 2000

This part details what you need to know to use BizTalk Orchestration Services and BizTalk Messaging Services in a business-to-business scenario. In addition, there is information to help you create custom components to extend the functionality of Microsoft BizTalk Server 2000.

In This Part

- **Orchestrating Business Processes with BizTalk Server 2000.** This chapter introduces the concepts involved to use the two primary layers within BizTalk Server 2000—BizTalk Messaging Services and BizTalk Orchestration Services—in a concerted manner.

- **Creating Custom Components.** This chapter provides information about how to create custom components and extend Microsoft BizTalk Server 2000 to integrate line-of-business applications and add features such as encryption and decryption or digital signature.

Orchestrating Business Processes with Microsoft BizTalk Server 2000

The problem of business-process integration—for example, between two trading partners—is often approached initially by understanding the external interfaces that each system exposes, and the message formats and specifications used to transfer messages. Typically, quality of services issues, such as security, message encoding, and reliable delivery, must also be addressed. BizTalk Messaging Services meets all these needs.

However, addressing, sending, and receiving messages are not enough to provide a total solution for business-process integration: How is the original message created? How is a message received, processed, and responded to? In all but the simplest cases, these are business processes. A business process determines the logical order of actions and the corresponding flow of messages, and it defines the message-exchange protocol between the distributed participants. Most business processes today are created using custom code. As a result, businesses are often constrained from rapidly changing their business-process implementations to reflect the evolving business needs in today's fast-paced environment. BizTalk Orchestration Services solves this problem by removing the custom coding aspect of creating business processes, resulting in an environment that can be changed quickly.

The goal of this chapter is to introduce the concepts involved in integrating the two primary layers within Microsoft BizTalk Server 2000: BizTalk Messaging Services and BizTalk Orchestration Services. This chapter also explains how you can integrate the services to:

- Start a new business process (an XLANG schedule) in response to a message.

- Return a message to a running business process (an XLANG schedule).

A common scenario for integrating the two services is the correlation of messages within a single running XLANG schedule instance, that is, to have an XLANG schedule instance send a message to an internal application or a trading partner, and to expect a message in return. An example is sending a purchase order and expecting a purchase order acknowledgement in return.

This chapter also explains how BizTalk Server 2000 fits within the traditional n-tier architecture. From the n-tier architecture perspective, the top layer of BizTalk Server 2000 is BizTalk Orchestration Services, which enables you to manage your business processes. BizTalk Messaging Services provides a supporting layer, which enables you to integrate with your business applications and trading partners, and provides data mapping, security, and enveloping.

In This Chapter

- BizTalk Server 2000 Overview
- BizTalk Server and N-Tier Architecture
- Using BizTalk Orchestration Services
- Using BizTalk Messaging Services
- Integrating BizTalk Orchestration Services and BizTalk Messaging Services
- Integrating BizTalk Services Reference

BizTalk Server 2000 Overview

BizTalk Server 2000 unites, in a single product, enterprise application integration (EAI), business-to-business integration, and the advanced BizTalk Orchestration technology to enable developers, IT professionals, and business analysts to easily build dynamic business processes that span applications, platforms, and businesses over the Internet.

BizTalk Server 2000 provides a powerful Web-based development and execution environment that integrates loosely coupled, long-running business processes, both within and between businesses. BizTalk Server can handle transactions that run as long as weeks or months, not just minutes or hours.

While BizTalk Server includes a broad set of tools and services, the two principal services and the focus of this chapter are BizTalk Orchestration Services and BizTalk Messaging Services.

BizTalk Orchestration Services represents the top layer of BizTalk Server 2000. It is used to design business processes that manage the overall business logic. Business processes are as important to business management as assembly lines are to manufacturing. Adhering to a well-defined, formalized set of processes can enable any business to increase productivity and lower costs. To define a business process, you must determine the logical order of actions and the corresponding flow of messages. A business process does not include definitions of the distributed participants who perform these actions.

BizTalk Messaging Services provides an underlying support layer for BizTalk Orchestration Services. It is used to send and receive messages between trading partners, and between business applications and XLANG schedules within your business. This enables you to integrate trading partners and existing applications into comprehensive business processes that are managed by BizTalk Orchestration Services.

Differentiating Ports and Messaging Ports

An important distinction for understanding BizTalk Server 2000 is the difference between a port, which is used in BizTalk Orchestration Services, and a messaging port, which is used in BizTalk Messaging Services. Even though they sound similar, ports and messaging ports perform entirely different functions.

A port is used in BizTalk Orchestration Services and is a named location in an XLANG schedule that implements a specific technology to send or receive messages. For example, a port can implement BizTalk Messaging or COM technology to send or receive messages. A port can facilitate either synchronous or asynchronous communications, and is used to pass messages into or out of an XLANG schedule.

A messaging port is used in BizTalk Messaging Services and is a set of properties that directs BizTalk Server 2000 to transport messages to a specified destination. Messaging ports can also direct BizTalk Server 2000 to secure and envelope messages, if necessary. A messaging port defines only the destination for messages and must be associated with a channel, which defines the source of messages. A channel directs BizTalk Server 2000 in the steps required to process the messages prior to passing them to a messaging port for transport to a destination.

In BizTalk Orchestration Services, a port that implements the BizTalk Messaging technology can be configured either to send messages to or receive messages from BizTalk Messaging Services. A port that sends messages to BizTalk Messaging Services does so by sending them to a channel. The channel can be specified at design time or can be determined dynamically at run time. A port that receives messages from BizTalk Messaging Services receives them from a messaging port.

In BizTalk Messaging Services, a messaging port can be configured to transport a message to a port in an XLANG schedule in BizTalk Orchestration Services. The XLANG schedule and port can be specified at design time or, in the case of the HTTP correlation scenario described later in this chapter, can be determined at run time based on parameters submitted with the message.

BizTalk Server and N-Tier Architecture

In traditional n-tier architecture there are at least three major layers: the presentation layer, the business logic layer, and the data storage layer. The business logic layer consists of:

- **Business logic components.** Interfaces that are usually implemented with COM+ services and perform business transactions.

- **Data access components.** Components that communicate with the data storage layer by sending and receiving messages, such as SQL dynamic Insert or Select statements.

The following illustration shows the presentation layer of n-tier architecture and the new layer that BizTalk Messaging Services creates.

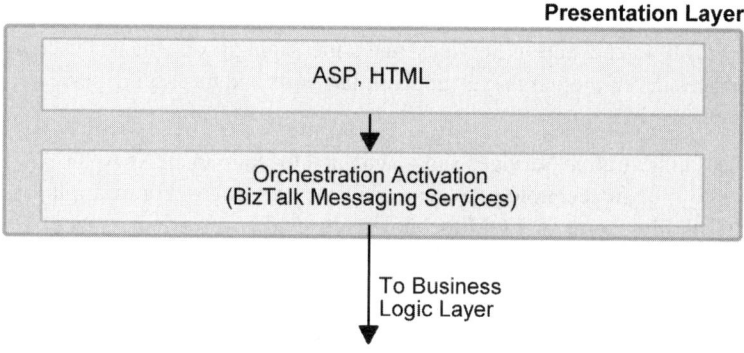

BizTalk Server 2000 does not play a direct role in the presentation layer. However, it can provide an interface between the presentation and business logic layers; for example, between an ASP page on a commerce Web site and a new BizTalk Orchestration layer. In this role, BizTalk Messaging Services provides a layer that can instantiate an XLANG schedule, which manages a business process, in response to the receipt of a message.

BizTalk Orchestration Services supports and extends the n-tier architecture used by Microsoft .NET and Web application programming. With BizTalk Orchestration Services, the business logic layer is maintained in a central location that services and can be accessed by any number of remote clients. Furthermore, BizTalk Orchestration Services extends the business logic layer by providing a common layer over the business logic components and the data access components.

The illustration on the following page shows the business logic and data storage layers of the n-tier architecture, and the ways that BizTalk Server extends and supports that architecture.

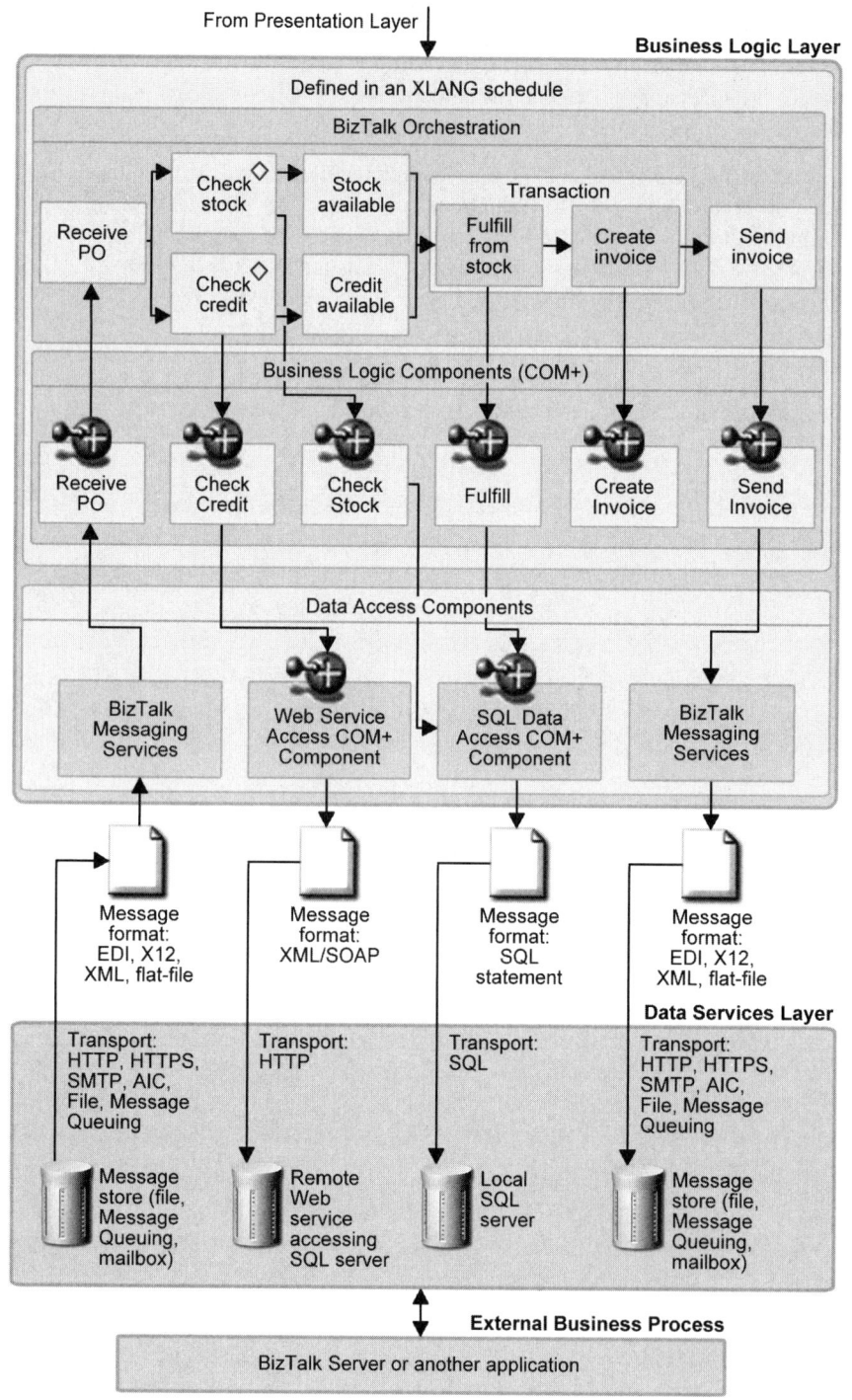

BizTalk Server 2000 extends and supports the n-tier architecture in two ways:

- It extends the n-tier architecture by creating a new layer (BizTalk Orchestration Services) above the business logic layer. BizTalk Orchestration Services supports the n-tier architecture by enabling you to assemble your business logic components into a business process that you can change rapidly to reflect the ever-changing business environment. By abstracting the functional control of the business process away from the middle of the business logic layer, you can avoid the use of custom code to create and manage your business process implementations.

- It supports the n-tier architecture by acting as a data access component (BizTalk Messaging Services) in the business logic layer. Data access components provide the technical infrastructure to send messages to and receive messages from the data storage layer. BizTalk Messaging Services provides you with the ability to send and receive messages, such as invoices and purchase orders, to and from data sources. BizTalk Messaging supports a variety of transports to do this, such as TCP/IP (HTTP/SMTP) and File transports. The data sources can include file systems, mailboxes in Microsoft Exchange servers, ASP pages, and message queues. Much like an SQL Insert statement, messages are sent to a data source, such as a purchase order to a file system. And, much like an SQL Select statement, messages are received from a data source, such as receiving an invoice from a trading partner.

Using BizTalk Orchestration Services

BizTalk Orchestration Services is ideally suited for developing business processes. Business-process design and implementation have traditionally been performed in two distinct phases: the visual-design phase and the coding phase. The visual-design phase typically consisted of the analysis of an existing business process (such as corporate procurement) and the creation of a workflow diagram or an interaction diagram to describe the process. The coding phase was usually performed separately. In this paradigm, you would build an abstract visual model of a business process and then map the model to an implementation framework.

One of the important features of BizTalk Orchestration Services is the integration of these previously distinct phases within a unified design environment. This design environment provides a versatile drawing surface and a comprehensive set of implementation tools. BizTalk Orchestration Services enables you to:

- Create XLANG schedule drawings that describe business processes.

- Implement business processes by connecting specific actions within a drawing to ports that represent locations to which messages are sent or from which messages are received. Ports are named locations, and messages represent the data sent or received between actions and ports.

- Define the flow of data between messages within business processes.

- Compile XLANG schedule drawings into XLANG schedules. XLANG schedules are executable Extensible Markup Language (XML) representations of the information contained within the drawings.

In addition to the integration of design and implementation functionality, BizTalk Orchestration Services provides another important feature: the ability to create and manage robust, long-running, loosely coupled business processes that span organizations, platforms, and applications. During an asynchronous, loosely coupled, long-running business process, a product that is ordered over the Internet might have to be built from parts that are in inventory. Some of these parts might even be temporarily out of stock. The entire business process might take weeks or months to complete. In contrast, a tightly coupled business process involves the synchronous exchange of messages. For example, when a customer withdraws money from a bank account, the debiting of the account is immediately followed by the delivery of the money.

By providing an integrated, graphical modeling environment, BizTalk Orchestration Services provides the following important benefits:

- When business processes change, the implementation can be quickly and easily redefined.

- Concurrent processes can be easily designed, implemented, and maintained.

- Transactions (long-running, short-lived, and nested) can be easily structured and maintained.

One of the key strengths of BizTalk Orchestration Services is to manage and maintain the state of long-running transactions. If you already have a means for controlling state, you should migrate that entire process into BizTalk Orchestration Services. Controlling state in multiple places is not recommended.

BizTalk Orchestration Services is also designed to manage business processes that might need to be altered quickly or often. In the past, developers have created COM+ components that controlled the business processes, and more traditional COM+ components that did the work. BizTalk Orchestration Services enables you to replace the business-process-control components with XLANG schedules. However, it is not recommended that you use BizTalk Orchestration Services to define processes at the work level. Instead, use your existing traditional COM+ components. The value of BizTalk Orchestration Services diminishes if it is used to control small portions of a larger business process. Ideally, it is recommended that you migrate your entire business processes to BizTalk Orchestration Services.

BizTalk Orchestration Services is a business-process-automation tool. It is not intended to be a complete workflow replacement. In particular, it is not intended to define role-based, hierarchical escalation in person-to-person processes. If your business processes contain role-based aspects that are escalated in a no-response situation, implement these processes by using Microsoft Exchange workflows, which can be integrated with BizTalk Orchestration Services.

If you need to apply encryption, digital signatures, mapping, or tracking to message contents, use BizTalk Messaging Services.

Using BizTalk Messaging Services

BizTalk Messaging Services is ideally suited for sending and receiving messages between other trading partners using Internet protocols, and between applications and XLANG schedules within your business.

Additionally, the features of BizTalk Messaging Services enable you to:

- Parse and validate inbound messages.

- Track inbound and outbound messages.

- Generate and correlate receipts.

- Use maps to change the structure and format of data.

- Ensure data integrity and security.

BizTalk Messaging Services can be configured either by using BizTalk Messaging Manager, a graphical user interface (UI), or programmatically by using the BizTalk Messaging Configuration object model.

BizTalk Messaging Services is designed to support the receipt of messages that then flow into a business process, or to send messages that flow out of a business process. BizTalk Orchestration is designed to manage business processes. Therefore, the two services are designed to work together, with BizTalk Messaging Services providing a receipt and delivery support layer for BizTalk Orchestration Services.

BizTalk Orchestration Services also can use BizTalk Messaging Services to integrate one business process with another by sending or receiving messages between the two business processes.

To send or receive messages between two business processes, you must:

- Use BizTalk Orchestration Services to create an XLANG schedule that sends a message and an XLANG schedule that receives it.

- Use BizTalk Messaging Services to create a messaging port. This messaging port must be configured to instantiate a new instance of the receiving XLANG schedule and deliver a message to a specified port in that schedule.

- Use BizTalk Messaging Services to create a channel for the messaging port that you created. This channel must be configured to receive a message from the sending XLANG schedule.

If you want to deliver a message to a business process, send the message to BizTalk Orchestration Services. Do not create monolithic application integration components to act as business-process components. This defeats one of the design goals of BizTalk Server, which is to abstract the business process from its implementation.

Integrating BizTalk Orchestration Services and BizTalk Messaging Services

By integrating BizTalk Orchestration Services and BizTalk Messaging Services, you can manage the exchange of messages between your trading partners and internal applications using multiple transport services, as well as the flow of those messages in broader business processes.

Integrating the two services also provides:

- Control over complex, long-running transactions and business processes.

- Reliable delivery of messages.

- Data validation by verifying each message instance against a specification.

- Data mapping by using maps to transform message structure and format.

- Data security and integrity by using encryption and digital signature certificates.

- Support for receipt generation and correlation.

When sending messages to an XLANG schedule by using BizTalk Messaging Services, there are two ways that you can integrate BizTalk Messaging Services with BizTalk Orchestration Services:

- Start a new business process (an XLANG schedule) in response to a message.

- Return a message to a running business process (an XLANG schedule).

Starting a New Business Process in Response to a Message

To configure BizTalk Messaging Services and BizTalk Orchestration Services to start a new business process:

- Use BizTalk Orchestration Designer to create an XLANG schedule. In the schedule, add a receiving port that uses a BizTalk Messaging implementation. In the BizTalk Messaging Binding Wizard, when you configure options on the **XLANG Schedule Activation Information** page, select the **Yes** option.

  When the port is properly configured, the graphic on the design page displays the word "Activate." This means that a new instance of the XLANG schedule is activated when a message is delivered to this port.

- Use BizTalk Messaging Manager to create a messaging port to an application. In the New Messaging Port Wizard, when you configure options on the **Destination Application** page, select the **New XLANG schedule** option, browse to the directory path of the XLANG schedule file (.skx) that you created, and then type the name of the orchestration port that you added to the schedule.

  After creating the messaging port, use BizTalk Messaging Manager to create a channel for the messaging port. A channel defines the source of the messages.

Returning a Message to a Running Business Process

To have a message returned to a running business process (XLANG schedule instance) in response to a message that is sent, you must store information in the outgoing message. This information is used to deliver a return message to the same XLANG schedule instance. The process of the same XLANG schedule instance sending a message and receiving a return message is referred to as message correlation.

The specific steps for configuring BizTalk Server 2000 to perform message correlation differ depending on whether you receive the return message by using an HTTP transport or by using a non-HTTP transport, such as SMTP.

The recommended configuration for integrating the two services to perform message correlation is to use an HTTP transport for the return message, and to use an ASP page that contains a specific script to receive the return message.

The following illustration shows the flow of messages involved in correlating a return message with the outgoing message in the same running XLANG schedule instance.

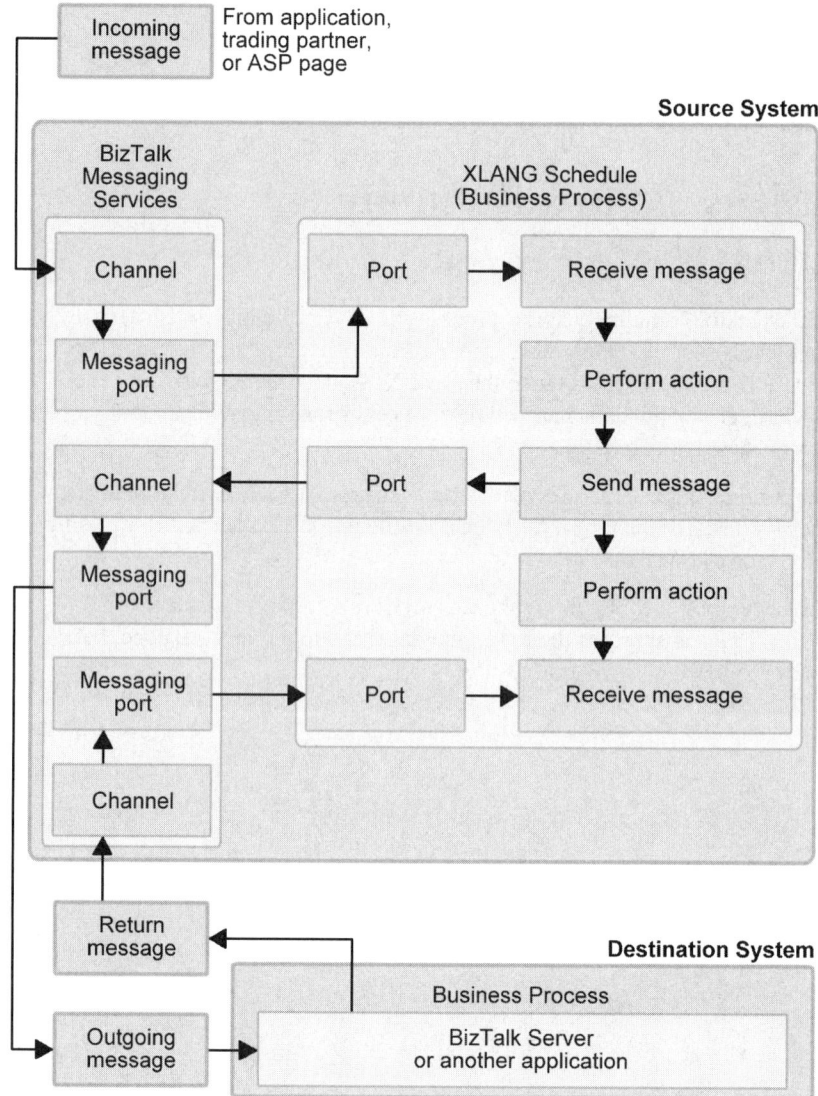

In a message correlation scenario, an XLANG schedule instance on the source system receives an incoming message and, as a result, initiates an outgoing message. The outgoing message is sent to a destination system, such as a trading partner. The destination system then responds by sending a return message. When the source system receives the return message, it then correlates that return message with the outgoing message by delivering it to the same XLANG schedule instance that manages the related business process and that is expecting the return message. An example of a common business process where you might use message correlation is receiving an order, sending a purchase order, and then waiting to receive a purchase order acknowledgment before continuing to the next step in the process. Since BizTalk Messaging Services manages the delivery and receipt of messages with trading partners, and BizTalk Orchestration Services manages the XLANG schedule instances that manage the business process, there is a need to closely integrate the two services.

There is also a need to closely coordinate with the trading partner that maintains the destination system. The source system must communicate the following information to the destination system in some manner:

- The structure and format of return messages as defined by a specification.

- The reply-to address where return messages should be sent.

- If using a non-HTTP transport, the queue path information that the trading partner must insert into a return message. The source system uses the queue path information to direct the return message to the appropriate XLANG schedule instance.

- The specific location of the reply-to address or queue path data field within the specification of the outgoing message.

Using an HTTP Transport

This section describes how to integrate BizTalk Orchestration Services and BizTalk Messaging Services on the source system to use an HTTP transport to exchange and correlate messages. The primary focus of this chapter is to describe how to integrate the services on the source system. The destination system configuration is also discussed, but in less detail.

The key concept for the HTTP transport scenario is an HTTP URL return address that is generated by the source system at run time and is then used by the destination system to send a return message. This address does not need to be known by the destination system at design time, and it does most of the work of message correlation on the source system automatically.

In this scenario the source system is configured to:

- Initiate and send a message that contains an HTTP URL reply-to address of an ASP page on the Web site of the source system.

- Receive a return message sent by the destination system in response to the outgoing message.

- Process the return message and deliver it to a per-instance queue that is monitored by the same XLANG schedule instance that initiated the outgoing message.

When the destination system receives the outgoing message, it uses the reply-to address that it contains to send a return message. The reply-to address directs the return message to an ASP page on the Web site of the source system, and it also contains a query string. When the source system receives the return message, the ASP page contains script that parses the query string of the address and uses the information as parameters to submit the return message to

BizTalk Messaging Services on the source system. BizTalk Messaging Services then uses the submission parameters to deliver the return message to a per-instance queue that is monitored by the same instance of the XLANG schedule that initiated the outgoing message.

The reply-to address for this configuration is generated automatically at run time based on the port properties that are specified at design time.

The reply-to address is comprised of the following elements:

- The address of an ASP page on the Web site of the source system, to which the destination system sends a return message.

- A query string that contains the following information:

  - The name of the channel that BizTalk Messaging Services on the source system uses to process a return message from the destination system.

  - The fully qualified path of a per-instance queue of the XLANG schedule instance that initiated the outgoing message. A messaging port for BizTalk Messaging Services uses this queue path as the destination for the return message.

The following is an example of an HTTP URL reply-to address that might be generated by an XLANG schedule:

http://hostname/receiveresponse.asp?channel=ChannelForReply&qpath=hostname.domai n.corp.vigorair-18.com\private$\ChannelForReply{9e0016bf-be1f-48fe-82de-b27077ab5e73}

The reply-to address is inserted into the outgoing message at run time, based on the configuration of the **Data** page at design time. The per-instance queue is also created at run time and is named by using the channel name specified in the port properties at design time and a globally unique identifier (GUID).

Configuring the source system to send a message by using HTTP

The steps in this section describe how to integrate BizTalk Orchestration Services and BizTalk Messaging Services on the source system to initiate a message that contains a reply-to address and send the message to the destination system of a trading partner. The steps that follow are abbreviated for the purposes of this section. For more detailed information about completing each step, see "Configuring the Source System to Use an HTTP Transport" later in this chapter.

Using BizTalk Editor

- Create the specifications that include a reply-to address field.

  The reply-to address field can be added at any level of the specification; however, the location must be agreed upon with the trading partner. The trading partner must know where to locate the reply-to address information, which is necessary for sending a return message.

Using BizTalk Messaging Manager

- Create a messaging port to deliver the outgoing message to the destination system of the trading partner.

  The address for the destination system must be agreed upon with the trading partner. For this scenario, the destination transport address is assumed to be another ASP page, this one on the Web site of the destination system. Therefore, an HTTP transport would be used when configuring the messaging port.

- Create a channel for the messaging port that you created.

  In BizTalk Messaging Services, a channel specifies the source of messages to be processed and is always associated with a messaging port that specifies the destination of the messages. In this scenario, the channel specifies an XLANG schedule as its source, but it does not explicitly state which XLANG schedule. Using BizTalk Orchestration Designer, you can configure a port in which you identify this channel. At run time, the port in the XLANG schedule sends a message to the specified channel in BizTalk Messaging Services.

Using BizTalk Orchestration Designer

- Implement a port in an XLANG schedule to send a message to the channel in BizTalk Messaging Services that you created.

  When you configure this port, you also must select the specification for the message that you created and add the reply-to address field of that specification to the port configuration. This makes the reply-to address field available on the **Data** page of the XLANG schedule.

- Establish the communication flow between an **Action** shape and the port that you created.

  This **Action** shape initiates the outgoing message and is connected to the port that sends it to BizTalk Messaging Services.

- Implement a port to receive a return message from BizTalk Messaging Services.

  To generate the reply-to address that is inserted into the outgoing message at run time, BizTalk Orchestration Services must have the port reference of the port that receives the return messages. Therefore, you must configure the receiving port as a part of the configuration for sending the outgoing message. When properly configured, the port reference for the receiving port will be the URL HTTP reply-to address, complete with the query string. The port reference is inserted into the reply-to address field of the message by using the **Data** page.

  When configuring the receiving port, you must specify a channel name. The channel name provided in this port is the name of the channel that BizTalk Messaging Services uses to process a return message sent by the destination system in response to the outgoing message.

  BizTalk Orchestration Designer also uses the channel name that you specify and a globally unique identifier (GUID) to name and create the query string path for a per-instance queue for the XLANG schedule. BizTalk Messaging Services later uses this path to transport the return message to this queue. Because the path is fully qualified, the return message is delivered to the appropriate port in the correct XLANG schedule instance.

You also must specify the URL address of the ASP page to which the destination system of the trading partner should send a return message. This information is used to generate the HTTP URL portion of the reply-to address.

- Establish the communication flow between an **Action** shape and the port.

The **Action** shape receives the return message and the business process continues.

- Use the **Data** page to establish the data flow to pass the port reference data into the reply-to address field of the message.

On the **Data** page of the XLANG schedule, connect the port reference field for the port that receives the return message to the reply-to address field of the outgoing message. This causes the port reference data for the receiving port, which is the HTTP URL, to be passed into the reply-to address field of the outgoing message at run time.

Configuring the source system to correlate a return message by using HTTP

The steps in this section describe how to integrate BizTalk Orchestration Services and BizTalk Messaging Services to correlate a return message received from a trading partner with the outgoing message. When a return message is received, it is submitted to BizTalk Messaging Services, which processes and delivers it to the same XLANG schedule instance that initiated the outgoing message. The following steps are abbreviated for the purposes of this section. For more detailed information about completing each step, see "Configuring the Source System to Use an HTTP Transport" later in this chapter.

Using BizTalk Messaging Manager

- Create a messaging port to deliver the return message to the running XLANG schedule instance that initiated the outgoing message.

This messaging port specifies an XLANG schedule as its destination, but it does not explicitly state which XLANG schedule. When the ASP page receives a return message, it submits the message to BizTalk Messaging Services using an open-destination submission. An open-destination submission requires that the destination information be provided either in the message or as a submission parameter. The ASP page uses the per-instance queue path from the query string of the reply-to address as the destination submission parameter. Once the channel has processed the return message, it is passed to the messaging port. The messaging port uses the per-instance queue path information to transport the message to the correct port on the running XLANG schedule instance.

- Create a channel for the messaging port that you created.

The name of this channel must match exactly the channel name that you used when you configured the XLANG schedule port to receive the return message. When the ASP page receives a return message, it uses the channel name from the query string of the reply-to address as the channel name submission parameter. If the names are not exactly the same, BizTalk Messaging Services cannot locate the channel and the submission fails.

Using BizTalk Orchestration Designer

- The receiving port and **Action** shape in the XLANG schedule were already configured as a requirement to send the outgoing message.

Using the ASP page

- You can use the sample ASP page provided with BizTalk Server 2000 to receive a return message, or you can use your own ASP page that contains the same script.

  To use the sample ASP page, browse to \Program Files\Microsoft BizTalk Server\SDK\Messaging Samples\ReceiveScripts on the BizTalk Server installation drive to locate the ReceiveResponse.asp sample. Place this file in the appropriate directory for the Web site of the source system. To use your own ASP page, you can copy the script from the sample ASP page or write a similar script that meets your business process needs.

  When the ASP page receives a return message, it submits the message to BizTalk Messaging Services by using the information contained in the query string of the return address as submission parameters, as described earlier in this section.

Configuring the destination system by using HTTP

The business process on the destination system can be configured in a variety of ways to receive and process the outgoing (from the source) message and to send a return message. For example, it can use an ASP page that contains script similar to the ASP page on the source system. Or, if the destination system also is a BizTalk Server, BizTalk Orchestration Services and BizTalk Messaging Services can be integrated on that system to accomplish this. For detailed information about integrating BizTalk Server 2000 services for the destination system, see "Configuring the Destination System to Use an HTTP Transport" later in this chapter.

Regardless of its configuration, the destination system must perform the following tasks:

- Extract the reply-to address contained within the outgoing message.

- Generate a return message to the source organization.

- Send the return message to the reply-to address, which is an HTTP URL.

Using a Non-HTTP Transport

This section describes how to integrate BizTalk Orchestration Services and BizTalk Messaging Services on the source system to use a non-HTTP transport to exchange and correlate messages. The primary focus of this section is to describe how to integrate the services on the source system. The destination system configuration is also discussed, but in less detail. The most common scenario for a non-HTTP transport to perform correlation is to use the SMTP transport to transport a return message.

In this scenario the source system is configured to:

- Initiate and send a message that contains the path of a well-known queue for an XLANG schedule on the source system.

- Modify the format of the queue path prior to sending the message to the destination system.

- Receive a return message, which also contains the queue path, from the destination system in response to the outgoing message.

- Process the return message and use the queue path it contains to deliver it to the well-known queue that is monitored by the same XLANG schedule instance that initiated the outgoing message.

When the destination system receives the outgoing message, that system must be configured to extract the queue path information from the outgoing message and place it into a field of the return message. The location of the queue path field in the outgoing message, and in the return message, do not have to be the same, but they both must be agreed upon between the source and destination systems. The destination system sends the return message to an agreed-upon address of the source system. For this scenario, it is assumed that the SMTP transport is used to transport a return message to the source system.

When the source system receives the return message, that system must be configured to submit the message to BizTalk Messaging Services using an open-destination submission. An open-destination submission requires that the destination information for a message be provided either in the message or as a submission parameter. In this scenario, BizTalk Messaging Services uses the queue path field in the return message as the destination submission parameter.

For BizTalk Messaging Services on the source system to recognize the queue path field as the destination information, the specification for the return message must explicitly designate that field as such. This field can be so designated by using BizTalk Editor, as described in greater detail in the following steps. This specification then must be referenced by the inbound document definition of the channel you use to process the return message. BizTalk Messaging Services then uses the queue path as the destination address to deliver the return message to the designated queue. The XLANG schedule instance that initiated the outgoing message monitors this queue and retrieves the message from there.

The queue path for this configuration is generated automatically at run time based on the port properties that are specified at design time, and is inserted into the outgoing message at run time, based on the **Data** page configuration at design time.

Configuring the source system to send a message by using a non-HTTP transport

The steps in this section describe how to integrate BizTalk Orchestration Services and BizTalk Messaging Services on the source system to initiate a message that contains a queue path and send it to the destination system of a trading partner. The following steps are abbreviated for the purposes of this section. For more detailed information about completing each step, see "Configuring the Source System to Use a Non-HTTP Transport" later in this chapter.

Using BizTalk Editor

- Create the specifications that include a queue path field.

  The queue path field can be added at any level of the specification; however, the location must be agreed upon with the trading partner. The trading partner must know where to locate the queue path information, so that the information can be extracted from the outgoing message and inserted into a return message.

  For the channel that processes a return message on the source system, the specification for the inbound document definition must designate the queue path field as the destination value in the dictionary properties. For more information, see "To set dictionary properties" in Chapter 5, "Creating Specifications."

  When the return message is received and submitted to BizTalk Messaging Services, this queue path field is recognized as the destination for the message. This process is described later in this section.

Using BizTalk Mapper

- Create a map to use in the channel that processes the outgoing message.

  The syntax for the queue path that the XLANG schedule generates must be changed from a path name to a format name and have the queue:// prefix added. This is required so that BizTalk Messaging Services can use the queue path for the destination information in the return message. For the HTTP transport scenario, the script in the sample ASP page makes this change in the query string information after the return message is received. For the non-HTTP transport scenario, the change must be made before sending the outgoing message. To do this you must use a **Concatenate** functoid in a map. For more information, see "Maps for Integrating BizTalk Services" in Chapter 6, "Mapping Data."

Using BizTalk Messaging Manager

- Create a messaging port to deliver the outgoing message to the destination system of the trading partner.

  This messaging port is configured to transport the outgoing message to the destination system of the trading partner. The address of the destination system must be agreed upon with the trading partner and known at design time.

- Create a channel for the messaging port that you created.

  This channel receives the outgoing message from the XLANG schedule, processes it, and then passes it to the messaging port to be transported to the destination. In BizTalk Messaging Services, a channel specifies the source of messages. In this scenario, the channel specifies an XLANG schedule as its source, but it does not explicitly state which XLANG schedule. In the step immediately following, you configure a port in the XLANG schedule, in which you identify this channel. At run time, the port sends the outgoing message to the specified channel in BizTalk Messaging Services.

Using BizTalk Orchestration Designer

- Implement a port in an XLANG schedule to send a message to the channel that you created.

  In BizTalk Orchestration Services, ports are used to send or receive messages. This port is configured to send the outgoing message to BizTalk Messaging Services. When you configure this port, you also must select the message specification that you created in an earlier step and add the queue path field of that specification to the port. This makes the queue path field available for further configuration on the **Data** page of the XLANG schedule.

- Establish the communication flow between an **Action** shape and the port.

  The **Action** shape represents the step in the business process that initiates the outgoing message. The shape is connected to a port, which sends the message to BizTalk Messaging Services.

- Implement a port to receive a return message from BizTalk Messaging Services by using a well-known message queue.

  To generate the queue path address that is inserted in the outgoing message at run time, BizTalk Orchestration Services must have the port reference for the port that will receive the return message. Therefore, you must configure the receiving port as a part of the configuration for sending the outgoing message. When properly configured, the port reference for the receiving port will be the queue path. The port reference is inserted into the queue path field of the message by configuring the **Data** page.

  This port functions differently than the receiving port in the HTTP transport scenario. This port receives the return message by way of a message queue, rather than directly from BizTalk Messaging Services. Therefore, you use a **Message Queuing** shape to implement this port, rather than a **BizTalk Messaging** shape. This port uses a static queue that is a well-known, preexisting queue that you assign at design time.

- Use the **Data** page of BizTalk Orchestration Designer to establish the data flow to pass the port reference data into the queue path field of the message.

  On the **Data** page of the XLANG schedule, you connect the port reference field for the port that receives the return message to the queue path field of the outgoing message. This causes the port reference data for the receiving port, which is the queue path, to be passed into the queue path field of the outgoing message at run time.

Configuring the source system to correlate a return message by using a non-HTTP transport

The steps in this section describe how to integrate BizTalk Orchestration Services and BizTalk Messaging Services to correlate a return message received from a trading partner with the outgoing message. When a return message is received, it is submitted to BizTalk Messaging Services, which processes and delivers it to the same XLANG schedule instance that sent the outgoing message. The following steps are abbreviated for the purposes of this section. For more detailed information about completing each step, see "Configuring the Source System to Use a Non-HTTP Transport" later in this chapter.

Using BizTalk Messaging Manager

- Create an open messaging port to deliver the return message to the running XLANG schedule instance that initiated the outgoing message.

  The open messaging port specifies a message queue transport, but it does not explicitly state which message queue is the destination. When the return message is received using the SMTP transport, a Microsoft Exchange script submits the message to BizTalk Messaging Services using an open-destination submission. An open-destination submission requires that the destination information be provided either in the message or as a submission parameter. In this submission, the destination information is provided as a field in the message. The messaging port uses the queue path field as the destination information for transporting the return message. The same running XLANG schedule instance that initiated the outgoing message monitors this queue, and retrieves the return message from it.

- Create a channel for the messaging port that you created.

  The name of this channel does not have to match exactly the channel name that you used when you configured the XLANG schedule port to receive the return message.

Using BizTalk Orchestration Designer

- The receiving port and **Action** shape in the XLANG schedule were already configured as a requirement to send the outgoing message. This channel name does need to be specified in the Microsoft Exchange script that submits the return message to BizTalk Messaging Services.

Using a Microsoft Exchange script

- For the Microsoft Exchange script that you use to submit the return message, you can use a sample script provided with BizTalk Server 2000 or use a similar script of your own.

  To use the sample script, browse to \Program Files\Microsoft BizTalk Server\SDK\Messaging Samples\ReceiveScripts\Exchange Server 2000 or Exchange Server 5.5 on the BizTalk Server installation drive. To install the script, follow the instructions provided in the Readme file. To use your own Microsoft Exchange script, you can copy the script from the sample and modify it as needed, or you can write a similar script that meets your business process needs.

When the return message is received by the source system, the Microsoft Exchange script submits it to BizTalk Messaging Services using an open-destination submission. An open-destination submission requires that the destination information be provided either in the message or as a submission parameter. In this scenario, the destination information is contained within the queue path field of the return message. The specification referred to by the inbound document definition of the channel identifies the queue path field as the destination value. For more information about submission parameters, see "Submitting" in Chapter 10, "Submitting Documents." Once the channel has processed the return message, it passes the message to the open messaging port. The messaging port uses the queue path information to transport the return message to the correct queue. The XLANG schedule that initiated the outgoing message monitors this queue, and it retrieves the return message.

Configuring the destination system by using a non-HTTP transport

The destination system can be configured in a variety of ways to process the outgoing (from the source) message and send a return message. If the destination system also is a BizTalk Server, BizTalk Orchestration Services and BizTalk Messaging Services can be integrated on that system to accomplish this. For detailed information about integrating BizTalk Server 2000 services for the destination system, see "Configuring the Destination System to Use a Non-HTTP Transport" later in this chapter.

Regardless of its configuration, the destination system must perform the following tasks:

- Extract the queue path information contained within the outgoing message.

- Generate a return message to the source organization, and insert the queue path information into a field of the return message.

- Send the return message to an agreed-upon address of the source system, which for this scenario is an SMTP address.

Related Topics

Chapter 4, "Microsoft BizTalk Server 2000 Deployment Considerations"

Chapter 12, "Microsoft BizTalk Server 2000 Operations"

Integrating BizTalk Services Reference

Integrating BizTalk Orchestration Services and BizTalk Messaging Services enables you to control the exchange of documents and messages between your trading partners and internal applications using multiple transport services. It also provides:

- Control over complex, long-running transactions and business processes.

- Reliable delivery of documents and messages.

- Data validation by verifying each document instance against a specification.

- Data mapping by using maps to transform document structure and format.

- Data security and integrity by using encryption and digital signature certificates.

- Support for receipt generation and correlation.

While there are many ways to integrate BizTalk Orchestration Services and BizTalk Messaging Services, this section presents a common scenario.

In this scenario, you configure an XLANG schedule instance on the source system to initiate and send a message to a destination system of a trading partner, wait to receive a return message from that partner, and then deliver that return message to the same XLANG schedule instance that sent the initial message. One example of a common business process where you might apply this configuration is for sending a purchase order and waiting to receive a purchase order receipt before continuing the process.

The topics in this section explain the configuration steps required for exchanging messages between your business and a trading partner by using an HTTP transport and a non-HTTP transport. However, you can use a similar configuration to control the exchange of messages between applications within your business.

Because BizTalk Server 2000 can serve either as the source system, which sends the initial message, or the destination system, which sends the return message, this section provides the configuration steps required for both. This also allows you to see the entire configuration that is required.

For samples of XLANG schedules that reflect these configurations and other related files, browse to the \Program Files\Microsoft BizTalk Server\SDK\XLANG Samples\Integrating BizTalk Services folder.

✎ Notes

- The term messaging port, which is used in BizTalk Messaging Services, and the term port, which is used in BizTalk Orchestration Services, have entirely different meanings:

  - A messaging port is a set of properties that directs BizTalk Messaging Services to transport documents to a specified destination by using a specified transport service.

- A port is a named location that uses a specific implementation. In an XLANG schedule, ports facilitate synchronous and asynchronous communications and are used to pass messages into or out of the schedule.

- Action events related to messages processed by an XLANG schedule that are either sent to or received from BizTalk Messaging Services can be tracked in the Tracking database. For more information, see "Tracking XLANG schedule events in the Tracking database" in Chapter 13, "Tracking Documents."

Related Topics

"BizTalk Services" in "Introducing Microsoft BizTalk Server 2000"

"Instance Management" in Chapter 8, "Configuring BizTalk Orchestration Services"

Using an HTTP Transport

This section explains how to integrate and configure BizTalk Orchestration Services and BizTalk Messaging Services for both the source system and destination system so that:

- The source system generates and sends a message to the destination system of a trading partner by using a specific XLANG schedule instance.

- The destination system sends a return message by using an HTTP transport.

- The source system receives the return message and routes it to the same XLANG schedule instance that generated and sent the initial message.

To configure both systems so that the destination system can use a non-HTTP transport to send return messages, see "Using a Non-HTTP Transport" later in this chapter.

Configuring the Source System to Use an HTTP Transport

The steps in this topic explain how to configure the source system to generate and send a message that contains an HTTP URL reply-to address. The destination system of the trading partner uses the reply-to address contained in the initial message to send a return message to an ASP page on the Web site of the source system by using an HTTP transport. If you want to configure the source system so that the destination system can use a non-HTTP transport to send return messages, see "Configuring the Source System to Use a Non-HTTP Transport" later in this chapter. The configuration steps required for using a secure HTTPS transport are discussed later in this topic.

The HTTP URL that is used as the reply-to address in this configuration is generated by the XLANG schedule based on data from the port properties. It is comprised of the following elements:

- The address of an ASP page on the Web site of the source system to which a return message is sent.

- A query string that contains the name of the channel in BizTalk Messaging Services for the source system that is used to process the return message, and a fully qualified path of a per-instance queue that the XLANG schedule instance creates and to which the return message is delivered.

The following is an example of an HTTP URL reply-to address:

http://hostname/receiveresponse.asp?channel=ChannelForReply&qpath=hostname.do main.corp.vigorair-18.com\private$\ChannelForReply{9e0016bf-be1f-48fe-82de-b27077ab5e73}

When the ASP page on the source system receives the return message, it contains script that performs the following steps:

- Extracts the channel name and queue path information from the query string.

- Converts the queue path from a path name to a format name, and inserts a queue:// prefix, which is required by BizTalk Messaging Services.

- Submits the return message to BizTalk Messaging Services for the source system using the channel name and queue path information as submission parameters. For more information about submitting documents, see "Submitting" in Chapter 10, "Submitting Documents."

BizTalk Messaging Services for the source system uses the specified channel to process the return message and uses the associated messaging port, which uses the queue path to transport the return message to the same running XLANG schedule instance that generated the initial message.

For this source system configuration to work correctly, the destination system of the trading partner also must be correctly configured. For information about configuring the destination system, see "Configuring the Destination System to Use an HTTP Transport" later in this chapter.

To configure the source system to use an HTTP transport, complete the steps in the following table. References are provided for each procedure, and notes are provided to indicate special configuration considerations. Other property settings needed to complete the configuration vary according to your particular business situation and are not specified here.

Step	References and notes

Using BizTalk Editor:

- Create the specifications that are needed for the inbound and outbound document definitions of the channel that will process the initial message.

- "Manage Document Instances" in Chapter 5, "Creating Specifications"

  ☑ **Note**

  - You must add a field in each of these specifications for the reply-to address. This field can be added at any level; however, the location must be agreed upon with the trading partner and match the specifications on the destination system of your trading partner. For more information, see "Records, Fields, and Properties" in Chapter 5, "Creating Specifications."

- Create the specifications that are needed for the inbound and outbound document definitions of the channel that will process the return message.

- "Manage Document Instances" in Chapter 5, "Creating Specifications"

  ☑ **Note**

  - These specifications do not require special configuration.

Using BizTalk Messaging Manager:

- Create an organization to represent the trading partner and the destination system.

- "To create organizations" in Chapter 9, "Configuring BizTalk Messaging Services"

  ☑ **Note**

  - This organization does not require special configuration.

- Create the document definitions needed to create the channel that you use to process the initial message.

- "To create document definitions" in Chapter 9, "Configuring BizTalk Messaging Services"

  ☑ **Note**

  - In the document definitions, select the specifications that have the reply-to field. For more information, see "To select a document specification" in Chapter 9, "Configuring BizTalk Messaging Services."

- Create the document definitions needed to create the channel that you use to process the return message.

- "To create document definitions" in Chapter 9, "Configuring BizTalk Messaging Services"

  ☑ **Note**

  - These document definitions do not require special configuration.

Step	References and notes
• Create a messaging port to an organization to transport the initial message to the destination system.	• "To create messaging ports" in Chapter 9, "Configuring BizTalk Messaging Services" 📝 **Note** • This messaging port cannot be an open messaging port.

• Create a channel from an application to process the outbound message from the XLANG schedule.	• "To create channels" in Chapter 9, "Configuring BizTalk Messaging Services"
	
	📝 **Notes**
	
	  • On the **Source Application** page of the Channel Wizard, click **XLANG schedule**. For more information, see "To set source application properties" in Chapter 9, "Configuring BizTalk Messaging Services."
	
	  • Make a note of the channel name and the inbound document definition name. These names are used to configure BizTalk Orchestration Services.

• Create a messaging port to an application to transport the return message to the active XLANG schedule instance that generated the outbound message.	• "To create messaging ports" in Chapter 9, "Configuring BizTalk Messaging Services" 📝 **Note** • On the **Destination Application** page of the Messaging Port Wizard, click **Running XLANG schedule**. For more information, see "To set destination application properties" in Chapter 9, "Configuring BizTalk Messaging Services."
• Create a channel from an organization to process the return message from the destination system.	• "To create channels" in Chapter 9, "Configuring BizTalk Messaging Services" 📝 **Note** • Make a note of the channel name and the outbound document definition name that you use. These names are used to configure BizTalk Orchestration Services.

Step	References and notes
Using BizTalk Orchestration Designer:	
• Use a **BizTalk Messaging** shape to implement a port to send the initial message.	• "To implement a port by using BizTalk Messaging" in Chapter 8, "Configuring BizTalk Orchestration Services" 📝 **Note** • On the **Static or Dynamic Channel Information** page of the BizTalk Messaging Binding Wizard, click **Static channel** and, in the **Enter the name of a known, pre-existing channel** box, type the name of the channel in BizTalk Messaging Manager that you use to process the initial message.
• Establish the communication flow between an **Action** shape and the port that sends the initial message.	• "To send or receive asynchronous messages" in Chapter 8, "Configuring BizTalk Orchestration Services" 📝 **Notes** • On the **Message Information** page of the XML Communication Wizard, click **Create a new message** and, in the **Message name** box, type a name for the message. You can use any name; however, using the name of the inbound document definition for the channel makes it more apparent which message you are sending. • On the **Message Type Information** page, in the **Message type** box, type the name of the inbound document definition for the channel that you use to process the message. • On the **Message Specification Information** page, click **Browse** and browse to the specification that you use for the inbound document definition of the channel that you use to process the initial message. • On the **Message Specification Information** page, in the **Message fields** area, click **Add** and add the field in the specification that was created to contain the reply-to address in the initial message.

Step	References and notes
• Use a **BizTalk Messaging** shape to implement a port where you receive a return message.	• "To implement a port by using BizTalk Messaging" in Chapter 8, "Configuring BizTalk Orchestration Services" 🖉 **Notes** • On the **XLANG Schedule Activation Information** page of the BizTalk Messaging Binding Wizard, click **No**. • On the **Channel Information** page, in the **Channel name** box, type the name of the channel in BizTalk Messaging Manager that you use to process the return message. BizTalk Orchestration Designer uses the channel name and a GUID to create and name a per-instance queue to which the return message is delivered. • On the **Channel Information** page, in the **HTTP URL address where the BizTalk Messaging Service receives documents** box, type the address of the ASP page where the trading partner can send a return message. BizTalk Orchestration Designer uses the address and the channel name that you entered previously to create an HTTP URL address with a query string that includes the channel name and the queue path of the per-instance queue.
• Establish the communication flow between an **Action** shape and the port where you receive a return message.	• "To send or receive asynchronous messages" in Chapter 8, "Configuring BizTalk Orchestration Services" 🖉 **Notes** • On the **Message Information** page of the XML Communication Wizard, click **Create a new message** and, in the **Message name** box, type a name for the message. You can use any name; however, using the name of the outbound document definition for the channel makes it more apparent which message you are receiving. • On the **Message Type Information** page, in the **Message type** box, type the name of the outbound document definition for the channel that you use to process the return message. All messages delivered from BizTalk Messaging Services to an XLANG schedule instance are sent to a message queue. The message label given to these messages is the name of the outbound document definition of the channel.

Step	References and notes
• Establish the data flow for passing the port reference data to the reply-to address field.	• "To draw the flow between messages" in Chapter 8, "Configuring BizTalk Orchestration Services"

Notes

- Click the **Data** tab.

- On the **Data** page, in the **Port References** message, click the port reference for the port that will receive the return message. Then drag its control handle to the connection point of the reply-to address field in the initial message.

  This passes the port reference data into the reply-to address field of the outbound initial message. The port reference is an HTTP URL address of an ASP page, which includes a query string with a channel name and the queue path of the per-instance queue for the port.

Using the ASP page:

- You can use the sample ASP page that is provided with BizTalk Server 2000, or configure an ASP page that uses the same script as the sample page.

Notes

- To use the sample ASP page, browse to \Program Files\Microsoft BizTalk Server\SDK\Messaging Samples\ReceiveScripts on the installation drive to locate the ReceiveResponse.asp sample. Place this file in the appropriate directory for the Web site of the source system.

- When the sample ASP page receives a return message, its script extracts the channel name and queue path from the query string in the address of the HTTP header. The ASP page also converts the queue path from a path name to a format name and inserts a queue:// prefix. The page then uses this data as parameters to submit the return message to BizTalk Messaging Services for the source system. For more information about submitting documents, see "Submitting" in Chapter 10, "Submitting Documents."

Using a secure HTTPS transport

If your business process requires a secure transport for exchanging messages with a trading partner, you must use an HTTPS transport.

The only change that you need to make in the source system configuration to use an HTTPS transport is to modify the URL address for the port where you receive the return message.

When you implement the port that receives the return message, the URL that you enter for the reply-to address must use an HTTPS prefix, rather than an HTTP prefix.

The following is an example of a reply-to address that uses HTTPS:

https://hostname/receiveresponse.asp?channel=ChannelForReply&qpath=hostname.do
main.corp.vigorair-18.com\private$\ChannelForReply{9e0016bf-be1f-48fe-82de-
b27077ab5e73}

The destination system does not require any additional configuration changes.

Configuring the Destination System to Use an HTTP Transport

The steps in this section explain how to configure the destination system to receive a message that contains an HTTP URL reply-to address and send a return message to the source system by using an HTTP transport. If you want to configure the destination system to use a non-HTTP transport to send return messages, see "Configuring the Destination System to Use a Non-HTTP Transport" later in this chapter. The configuration considerations for using a secure HTTP/S transport are discussed later in this section.

When BizTalk Messaging Services for the destination system receives the initial message, it is configured to activate a new instance of a specified XLANG schedule and send the message to a specified port in that XLANG schedule instance.

The XLANG schedule is configured to pass the reply-to address data that is contained in a field of the initial message to the port reference field for the port that is used to send the return message. The XLANG schedule then submits the return message to BizTalk Messaging Services using the dynamic channel option.

For the dynamic channel option, specific port data is passed as submission parameters when the message is submitted to BizTalk Messaging Services. The port reference data, in this case the reply-to address, is passed as the destination identifier parameter, and the **Message type** for the port is passed as the document definition name parameter. For more information about submission parameters, see "Submitting" in Chapter 10, "Submitting Documents." The submission parameters enable BizTalk Messaging Services to identify a specific channel to process the return message. For more information, see "Identification" in Chapter 9, "Configuring BizTalk Messaging Services."

When you use the dynamic channel option, the channel in BizTalk Messaging Services must be associated with an open messaging port. The open messaging port transports the return message to the source system of the trading partner by using the reply-to address, which is passed as the destination identifier parameter. Because this is the HTTP URL of an ASP page on the source system, the HTTP transport is used. For more information about open messaging ports, see "Open Messaging Ports" in Chapter 9, "Configuring BizTalk Messaging Services."

For this destination system configuration to work correctly, the source system of the trading partner also must be correctly configured. For information about configuring the source system, see "Configuring the Source System to Use an HTTP Transport" earlier in this chapter.

To configure the destination system to use an HTTP transport, complete the steps in the following table. References are provided for each procedure, and notes are provided to indicate special configuration considerations. Other property settings needed to complete the configuration vary according to your particular business situation and are not specified here.

Step	References and notes
Using BizTalk Editor:	
• Create the specifications for the inbound and outbound document definitions of the channel that you use to process the initial message.	• "Manage Document Instances" in Chapter 5, "Creating Specifications" 🗹 **Note** • You must add a field in each of these specifications for the reply-to address. This field can be added at any level; however, the location must be agreed upon with the trading partner and match the specifications on the source system of your trading partner. For more information, see "Records, Fields, and Properties" in Chapter 5, "Creating Specifications."
• Create the specifications that are needed for the inbound and outbound document definitions of the channel that will process the return message.	• "Manage Document Instances" in Chapter 5, "Creating Specifications" 🗹 **Note** • These specifications do not require special configuration.
Using BizTalk Messaging Manager:	
• Create an organization to represent the trading partner with the source system.	• "To create organizations" in Chapter 9, "Configuring BizTalk Messaging Services" 🗹 **Note** • This organization does not require special configuration.
• Create the document definitions needed for creating a channel to process the initial message and a channel to process the return message.	• "To create document definitions" in Chapter 9, "Configuring BizTalk Messaging Services" 🗹 **Note** • In the document definitions, select the previously created specifications. For more information, see "To select a document specification" in Chapter 9, "Configuring BizTalk Messaging Services."

Step	References and notes
• Create a messaging port to an application to activate a new XLANG schedule instance, and transport the initial message to a port in that XLANG schedule instance.	• "To create messaging ports" in Chapter 9, "Configuring BizTalk Messaging Services" 🖉 **Notes** • On the **Destination Application** page of the Messaging Port Wizard, click **New XLANG schedule**. • In the **Schedule moniker** box, type the moniker of the specified schedule or click **Browse** to set the path. • In the **Port name** box, type the name of the specific port in this schedule to which the document is sent. For more information, see "To set destination application properties" in Chapter 9, "Configuring BizTalk Messaging Services."
• Create a channel from an organization to process the initial message from the trading partner.	• "To create channels" in Chapter 9, "Configuring BizTalk Messaging Services" 🖉 **Note** • Make a note of the channel name and the outbound document definition name that you use. These names are used to configure BizTalk Orchestration Services.
• Create an open messaging port to an organization to transport the return message to the source system.	• "To create messaging ports" in Chapter 9, "Configuring BizTalk Messaging Services" 🖉 **Note** • On the **Destination Organization** page of the Messaging Port Wizard, click **Open destination**. For more information, see "To set destination organization properties" in Chapter 9, "Configuring BizTalk Messaging Services." An open messaging port requires that the destination information be contained in the document or provided by submission parameters. When the XLANG schedule submits the return message to BizTalk Messaging Services, it passes the reply-to address data, which was contained in the initial message, as the destination identifier submission parameter.
• Create a channel from an application to process the return message from the XLANG schedule.	• "To create channels" in Chapter 9, "Configuring BizTalk Messaging Services" 🖉 **Note** • On the **Source Application** page of the Channel Wizard, click **XLANG schedule**. For more information, see "To set source application properties" in Chapter 9, "Configuring BizTalk Messaging Services."

1171

Step	References and notes

Using BizTalk Orchestration Designer:

- Use a **BizTalk Messaging** shape to implement a port to receive the initial message.

  - "To implement a port by using BizTalk Messaging" in Chapter 8, "Configuring BizTalk Orchestration Services"

    📝 **Notes**

    - On the **Communication Direction** page of the BizTalk Messaging Binding Wizard, click **Receive**.

    - On the **XLANG Schedule Activation Information** page of the BizTalk Messaging Binding Wizard, click **Yes**.

    ◆ **Important**

    - Choosing **Yes** configures the port to activate a new schedule instance when a message arrives. For important information about using this option, see the topic referenced for this step.

- Establish the communication flow between an **Action** shape and the port that receives the initial message.

  - "To send or receive asynchronous messages" in Chapter 8, "Configuring BizTalk Orchestration Services"

    📝 **Notes**

    - On the **Message Information** page of the XML Communication Wizard, click **Create a new message** and, in the **Message name** box, type a name for the message.

      You can use any name; however, using the name of the outbound document definition for the channel makes it more apparent which message you are sending.

    - On the **Message Type Information** page, in the **Message type** box, type the name of the outbound document definition for the channel that you use to process the return message.

      All messages passed from BizTalk Messaging to an XLANG schedule use a message queue. The label for these messages is the name of the outbound document definition of the channel.

Step	References and notes
• Use a **BizTalk Messaging** shape to implement a port to send the return message with a dynamic channel.	• "To implement a port by using BizTalk Messaging" in Chapter 8, "Configuring BizTalk Orchestration Services" 📝 **Notes** • On the **Static or Dynamic Channel Information** page of the BizTalk Messaging Binding Wizard, click **Dynamic channel**. • When you create a port that uses a dynamic channel, the channel that BizTalk Messaging Services uses to process the message is determined by port data passed as submission parameters. This is described later in this table.
• Establish the communication flow between an **Action** shape and the port that is used to send the return message.	• "To Send or receive asynchronous messages" in Chapter 8, "Configuring BizTalk Orchestration Services" 📝 **Notes** • On the **Message Information** page of the XML Communication Wizard, click **Create a new message** and, in the **Message name** box, type a name for the message. You can use any name; however, using the name of the inbound document definition for the channel makes it more apparent which message you are sending. • On the **Message Type Information** page, in the **Message type** box, type the name of the inbound document definition for the channel that you use to process the message. The inbound document definition data is passed as a submission parameter to BizTalk Messaging Services. This is described later in this table.

Step	References and notes
• Establish the data flow to pass the reply-to address field to the port reference of the port that sends the return message.	• "To draw the flow between messages" in Chapter 8, "Configuring BizTalk Orchestration Services"

📝 **Notes**

• Click the **Data** tab.

• On the **Data** page, in the initial message, click the reply-to address field. Then drag its control handle to the left connection point of the port reference in the **Port References** message for the port that is used to send the return message.

◆ **Important**

• You must connect the reply-to address field to the left connection point of the port reference. A left connection point on a port reference is available only when a port is configured to use a dynamic channel to send messages.

For a port that uses a dynamic channel, the data for the port reference must be passed from a field in a previously received message.

In this scenario, the reply-to address data from the initial message is passed to the port reference field for the port that is used to send the return message. The reply-to address is the HTTP URL to where the return message is sent.

When a port that uses a dynamic channel passes a message to BizTalk Messaging Services, the port reference data is passed as the destination identifier parameter and the message type data is passed as the document definition parameter. The parameters enable BizTalk Messaging Services to identify which channel to invoke to process the message. For more information, see "Identification" in Chapter 9, "Configuring BizTalk Messaging Services," and "Submitting" in Chapter 10, "Submitting Documents."

When a port is configured to use a dynamic channel, the destination information is passed as a parameter in an open destination submission. Therefore, any channel that is invoked by a port that uses a dynamic channel must be associated with an open messaging port. |

Using a secure HTTPS transport

Because the messaging port that you use to transport return messages is an open messaging port, you cannot use an encryption certificate to encrypt documents.

If your business process requires a secure transport for exchanging messages with a trading partner, the source system must include an HTTPS URL as the reply-to address in the initial messages that are sent to you, rather than an HTTP URL.

For more information, see "Configuring the Source System to Use an HTTP Transport" earlier in this chapter.

Using a Non-HTTP Transport

This section explains how to integrate and configure BizTalk Orchestration Services and BizTalk Messaging Services for both the source system and destination system so that:

- The source system generates and sends a message to the destination system of a trading partner by using a specific XLANG schedule instance.

- The destination system receives the initial message, activates an XLANG schedule instance that generates a return message, and then sends the return message to the source system using a non-HTTP transport.

To configure both systems so that the destination system can use an HTTP transport to send return messages, see "Using an HTTP Transport" earlier in this chapter.

Configuring the Source System to Use a Non-HTTP Transport

The steps in this section explain how to configure the source system to generate and send a message that contains the path of a static queue. The destination system of the trading partner is configured to pass the queue path contained in the message into a field of a return message, and send it to the source system by using a non-HTTP transport. If you want to configure the source system so that the destination system can use an HTTP transport to send return messages, see "Configuring the Source System to Use an HTTP Transport" earlier in this chapter.

When the source system receives the return message, it submits the message to BizTalk Messaging Services. BizTalk Messaging Services transports the return message to the queue that is specified by the queue path contained in the document field. This queue is monitored by the same XLANG schedule instance that generated the initial message, and the schedule retrieves the return message from that queue.

For this source system configuration to work correctly, the destination system of the trading partner also must be correctly configured. For information about configuring the destination system, see "Configuring the Destination System to Use a Non-HTTP Transport" later in this chapter.

To configure the source system to use a non-HTTP transport, complete the steps in the following table. References are provided for each procedure, and notes are provided to indicate special configuration considerations. Other property settings needed to complete the configuration vary according to your particular business situation and are not specified here.

Step	References and notes
Using BizTalk Editor:	
• Create the specifications for the inbound and outbound document definitions of the channel that you use to process the initial message.	• "Manage Document Instances" in Chapter 5, "Creating Specifications" 📝 **Note** • You must add a field in each of these specifications for the queue path. This field can be added at any level; however, the location must be agreed upon with the trading partner and match the specifications on the destination system of your trading partner. For more information, see "Records, Fields, and Properties" in Chapter 5, "Creating Specifications."
• Create the specifications for the inbound and outbound document definitions of the channel that you use to process the return message.	• "Manage Document Instances" in Chapter 5, "Creating Specifications" 📝 **Notes** • You must add a field to the inbound specification for the queue path. This field can be added at any level; however, the location must be agreed upon with the trading partner and match the specifications on the destination system of your trading partner. For more information, see "Records, Fields, and Properties" in Chapter 5, "Creating Specifications." • The queue path field in the inbound specification must be set as the destination value in the dictionary properties. For more information, see "To set dictionary properties" in Chapter 5, "Creating Specifications." When the return message is received and submitted to BizTalk Messaging Services on the source system, the queue path field is recognized and treated as the destination identifier parameter. For more information, see "Submitting" in Chapter 10, "Submitting Documents." The messaging port transports the return message to the queue specified by this queue path. The XLANG schedule monitors this queue and retrieves the return message.

Step	References and notes
Using BizTalk Mapper:	
• Create a map to be used in the channel that processes the initial message.	• "To create new maps" in Chapter 6, "Mapping Data"

◆ **Important**

• The syntax for the queue path name that the XLANG schedule generates must be changed from a path name to a format name and have the queue:// prefix added. For the HTTP transport scenario, the script in the ASP page makes this change. To make this change for the non-HTTP transport scenario, you must use a **Concatenate** functoid in a map. For more information, see "Maps for Integrating BizTalk Services" in Chapter 6, "Mapping Data."

Step	References and notes
Using BizTalk Messaging Manager:	
• Create an organization to represent the trading partner with the destination system.	• "To create organizations" in Chapter 9, "Configuring BizTalk Messaging Services"

📝 **Note**

• This organization does not require special configuration.

Step	References and notes
• Create the document definitions needed to create a channel to process the initial message and a channel to process the return message.	• "To create document definitions" in Chapter 9, "Configuring BizTalk Messaging Services"

📝 **Note**

• In the document definitions, select the previously created specifications. For more information, see "To select a document specification" in Chapter 9, "Configuring BizTalk Messaging Services."

Step	References and notes
• Create a messaging port to an organization to transport the initial message to the destination system.	• "To create messaging ports" in Chapter 9, "Configuring BizTalk Messaging Services"

📝 **Note**

• This messaging port does not require special configuration.

Step	References and notes
• Create a channel from an application to process the initial message from the XLANG schedule.	• "To create channels" in Chapter 9, "Configuring BizTalk Messaging Services" 🖾 **Notes** • On the **Source Application** page of the Channel Wizard, click **XLANG schedule**. For more information, see "To set source application properties" in Chapter 9, "Configuring BizTalk Messaging Services." • On the **Outbound Document** page, select the **Map inbound document to outbound document** check box and, to the right of the **Map reference** box, click **Browse**. Then browse to the map that you created previously and click **Open**. • Make a note of the channel name and the inbound document definition name that you use. These names are used to configure BizTalk Orchestration Services.
• Create an open messaging port to an organization to transport the return message to the active XLANG schedule instance that generated the initial message.	• "To create messaging ports" in Chapter 9, "Configuring BizTalk Messaging Services" 🖾 **Notes** • On the **Destination Organization** page of the Messaging Port Wizard, click **Open destination**. For more information, see "To set destination organization properties" in Chapter 9, "Configuring BizTalk Messaging Services." • For this scenario, you create a messaging port to an organization, even though you send the return message to an application or an XLANG schedule. This allows you to use an open messaging port to submit the return message using the queue path information as a submission parameter. For more information, see "Submitting" in Chapter 10, "Submitting Documents." The open messaging port transports the return message to the static queue that is specified in the queue path, where the XLANG schedule is configured to retrieve it.

Step	References and notes
• Create a channel from an organization to process the return message from the destination system.	• "To create channels" in Chapter 9, "Configuring BizTalk Messaging Services"

Using BizTalk Orchestration Designer:

• Use a **BizTalk Messaging** shape to implement a port to send the initial message.	• "To implement a port by using BizTalk Messaging" in Chapter 8, "Configuring BizTalk Orchestration Services"

For the first row, the References and notes cell also contains:

📝 **Notes**

• The inbound document definition for this channel must use the document definition that uses the previously created specification in which you designated the queue path field as the destination value in the dictionary properties.

• Make a note of the channel name and the inbound document definition name that you use. These names are used to configure BizTalk Orchestration Services.

For the BizTalk Messaging shape row, the References and notes cell also contains:

📝 **Note**

• On the **Static or Dynamic Channel Information** page of the BizTalk Messaging Binding Wizard, click **Static channel** and, in the **Enter the name of a known, pre-existing channel** box, type the name of the channel in BizTalk Messaging Manager that you use to process the initial message.

• Establish the communication flow between an **Action** shape and the port that sends the initial message.	• "To send or receive asynchronous messages" in Chapter 8, "Configuring BizTalk Orchestration Services"

For the last row, the References and notes cell also contains:

📝 **Notes**

• On the **Message Information** page of the XML Communication Wizard, click **Create a new message** and, in the **Message name** box, type a name for the message.

You can use any name; however, using the name of the inbound document definition for the channel makes it more apparent which message you are sending.

• On the **Message Type Information** page, in the **Message type** box, type the name of the inbound document definition for the channel that you use to process the message.

• On the **Message Specification Information** page, click **Browse** and browse to the specification that you use for the inbound document definition of the channel for the initial message.

• On the **Message Specification Information** page, in the **Message fields** area, click **Add** and add the field in the specification that was created to contain the queue path.

1179

Step	References and notes
• Use a **Message Queuing** shape to implement a port where you receive a return message.	• "To implement a port by using Message Queuing" in Chapter 8, "Configuring BizTalk Orchestration Services"

Notes

- In this scenario, you use a Message Queuing port binding, even though you are receiving a message from BizTalk Messaging Services.

- On the **Static or Dynamic Queue Information** page of the Message Queuing Binding Wizard, click **Static queue**.

- On the **Queue Information** page, click **Use a known queue for all instances** and, in the **Enter the queue name** box, type the name of the static queue that you use to process the return message.

| • Establish the communication flow between an **Action** shape and the port where you receive a return message. | • "To send or receive asynchronous messages" in Chapter 8, "Configuring BizTalk Orchestration Services" |

Notes

- On the **Welcome to the XML Communication Wizard** page of the XML Communication Wizard, click **Receive**.

- On the **Message Information** page, click **Create a new message** and, in the **Message name** box, type a name for the message.

  You can use any name; however, using the name of the outbound document definition for the channel makes it more apparent which message you are receiving.

- On the **Message Type Information** page, in the **Message type** box, type the name of the outbound document definition for the channel that you use to process the return message.

  All messages passed from BizTalk Messaging to an XLANG schedule use a message queue. The label for these messages is the name of the outbound document definition of the channel.

Step	References and notes
• Establish the data flow from the receiving port reference to the queue path field.	• "To draw the flow between messages" in Chapter 8, "Configuring BizTalk Orchestration Services"

✎ **Notes**

• Click the **Data** tab.

• On the **Data** page, in the **Port References** message, click the field for the port that receives the return message. Then drag its control handle to the connection point of the queue path field in the initial message.

This inserts the port reference data into the queue path field of the initial message. The port reference is the queue path of the static queue for the port that you use to receive a return message.

Configuring the Destination System to Use a Non-HTTP Transport

The steps in this section explain how to configure the destination system to receive a message that contains a queue path and to send a return message that contains the same queue path to the source system by using a non-HTTP transport. If you want to configure the destination system to use an HTTP transport to send return messages, see "Configuring the Destination System to Use an HTTP Transport" earlier in this chapter.

When BizTalk Messaging Services for the destination system receives the initial message, it is configured to activate a new instance of a specified XLANG schedule and pass the message to a specified port in that XLANG schedule instance.

The XLANG schedule is configured to pass the data contained in the queue path field of the initial message into a matching field of the return message, and then submit the return message to a channel in BizTalk Messaging Services.

BizTalk Messaging Services uses the specified channel to process the return message and pass it to a messaging port. This messaging port is configured to transport the return message to an address that is agreed upon with the trading partner with the source system. This messaging port cannot be an open messaging port.

For this destination system configuration to work correctly, the source system of the trading partner also must be correctly configured. For information about configuring the source system, see "Configuring the Source System to Use a Non-HTTP Transport" earlier in this chapter.

To configure the destination system to use a non-HTTP transport, complete the steps in the following table. References are provided for each procedure, and notes are provided to indicate special configuration considerations. Other property settings needed to complete the configuration vary according to your particular business situation and are not specified here.

Step	References and notes

Using BizTalk Editor:

- Create the specifications for the inbound and outbound document definitions of the channel that you use to process the initial message.

- "Manage Document Instances" in Chapter 5, "Creating Specifications"

  Note

  - You must add a field in each of these specifications for the queue path. This field can be added at any level; however, the location must be agreed upon with the trading partner and match the specifications on the source system of your trading partner. For more information, see "Records, Fields, and Properties" in Chapter 5, "Creating Specifications."

- Create the specifications for the inbound and outbound document definitions of the channel that you use to process the return message.

- "Manage Document Instances" in Chapter 5, "Creating Specifications"

  Note

  - You must add a field in each of these specifications for the queue path. This field can be added at any level; however, the location must be agreed upon with the trading partner and match the specifications on the source system of your trading partner. For more information, see "Records, Fields, and Properties" in Chapter 5, "Creating Specifications."

Using BizTalk Messaging Manager:

- Create an organization to represent the trading partner with the source system.

- "To create organizations" in Chapter 9, "Configuring BizTalk Messaging Services"

  Note

  - This organization does not require special configuration.

- Create the document definitions needed for creating a channel to process the initial message.

- "To create document definitions" in Chapter 9, "Configuring BizTalk Messaging Services"

  Note

  - In the document definitions, select the previously created specifications. For more information, see "To select a document specification" in Chapter 9, "Configuring BizTalk Messaging Services."

Step	References and notes
• Create the document definitions needed for creating a channel to process the return message.	• "To create document definitions" in Chapter 9, "Configuring BizTalk Messaging Services" ✎ **Note** • In the document definitions, select the previously created specifications. For more information, see "To select a document specification" in Chapter 9, "Configuring BizTalk Messaging Services."
• Create a messaging port to an application to activate a new XLANG schedule instance, and transport the initial message to a port in that XLANG schedule instance.	• "To create messaging ports" in Chapter 9, "Configuring BizTalk Messaging Services" ✎ **Notes** • On the **Destination Application** page of the Messaging Port Wizard, click **New XLANG schedule**. • In the **Schedule moniker** box, type the moniker of the specified schedule or click **Browse** to set the path. • In the **Port name** box, type the name of the specific port in this schedule to which the document is sent. For more information, see "To set destination application properties" in Chapter 9, "Configuring BizTalk Messaging Services." To complete this step, you need the path of an XLANG schedule and the name of the port in that schedule to which the initial message is delivered. Therefore, you must first create the XLANG schedule and configure its port, as described later in this table.
• Create a channel from an organization to process the initial message from the trading partner.	• "To create channels" in Chapter 9, "Configuring BizTalk Messaging Services" ✎ **Note** • Make a note of the channel name and the outbound document definition name that you use. These names are used to configure BizTalk Orchestration Services.

Step	References and notes
• Create a messaging port to an organization to transport the return message to the source system.	• "To create messaging ports" in Chapter 9, "Configuring BizTalk Messaging Services" 📝 **Notes** • On the **Destination Organization** page of the Messaging Port Wizard, click **Organization**. To the right of the **Name** box, click **Browse**. • In the **Select an Organization** dialog box, select the organization that you created previously to represent the trading partner with the source system. For more information, see "To select a destination organization" in Chapter 9, "Configuring BizTalk Messaging Services." • On the **Destination Organization** page of the Messaging Port Wizard, in the **Primary Transport** area, click **Browse**. • In the **Primary Transport** dialog box, in the **Transport type** list, select the transport type and, in the **Address** box, type an address. The transport type and address must be agreed upon with the trading partner and match the specifications on the source system of your trading partner. • You cannot use an open messaging port to send the return message.
• Create a channel from an application to process the return message from the XLANG schedule.	• "To create channels" in Chapter 9, "Configuring BizTalk Messaging Services" 📝 **Notes** • On the **Source Application** page of the Channel Wizard, click **XLANG schedule**. For more information, see "To set source application properties" in Chapter 9, "Configuring BizTalk Messaging Services." • Make a note of the channel name and the inbound document definition name that you use. These names are used to configure BizTalk Orchestration Services.

Step	References and notes

Using BizTalk Orchestration Designer:

- Use a **BizTalk Messaging** shape to implement a port to receive the initial message.

- "To implement a port by using BizTalk Messaging" in Chapter 8, "Configuring BizTalk Orchestration Services"

  ◆ **Important**
  - Choosing **Yes** configures the port to activate a new schedule instance when a message arrives. For important information about using this option, see the topic referenced for this step.
  Make a note of the name that you give to this port and the location to which you save the compiled XLANG schedule. You need this information to configure a messaging port in BizTalk Messaging Services, as described previously in this table.

  🗒 **Notes**
  - On the **Communication Direction** page of the BizTalk Messaging Binding Wizard, click **Receive**.
  - On the **XLANG Schedule Activation Information** page of the BizTalk Messaging Binding Wizard, click **Yes**.

- Establish the communication flow between an **Action** shape and the port that receives the initial message.

- "To send or receive asynchronous messages" in Chapter 8, "Configuring BizTalk Orchestration Services"

  🗒 **Notes**
  - On the **Message Information** page of the XML Communication Wizard, click **Create a new message** and, in the **Message name** box, type a name for the message.
  You can use any name; however, using the name of the outbound document definition for the channel makes it more apparent which message you are sending.
  - On the **Message Type Information** page, in the **Message type** box, type the name of the outbound document definition for the channel that you use to process the return message.
  All messages passed from BizTalk Messaging to an XLANG schedule use a message queue. The label for these messages is the name of the outbound document definition of the channel.
  - On the **Message Specification Information** page, click **Browse** and browse to the specification that you use for the outbound document definition of the channel for the initial message.
  - In the **Message fields** area, click **Add** and add the field in the specification that was created to contain the queue path address for the initial message.

Step	References and notes
• Use a **BizTalk Messaging** shape to implement a port to send the return message.	• "To implement a port by using BizTalk Messaging" in Chapter 8, "Configuring BizTalk Orchestration Services" 📝 **Notes** • On the **Static or Dynamic Channel Information** page of the BizTalk Messaging Binding Wizard, click **Static channel** and, in the **Enter the name of a known, pre-existing channel** box, type the name of the channel in BizTalk Messaging Manager that you use to process the return message. • Because this port uses a static channel, an open destination submission call to BizTalk Messaging is not made. Therefore, the channel that is specified cannot be associated with an open messaging port.
• Establish the communication flow between an **Action** shape and the port that sends the return message.	• "To send or receive asynchronous messages" in Chapter 8, "Configuring BizTalk Orchestration Services" 📝 **Notes** • On the **Message Information** page of the XML Communication Wizard, click **Create a new message** and, in the **Message name** box, type a name for the message. You can use any name; however, using the name of the inbound document definition for the channel makes it more apparent which message you are sending. • On the **Message Type Information** page, in the **Message type** box, type the name of the inbound document definition for the channel that you use to process the message. • On the **Message Specification Information** page, click **Browse** and browse to the specification that you use for the inbound document definition of the channel that you use to process the return message. • In the **Message fields** area, click **Add** and add the field in the specification that was created to contain the queue path address for the return message.
• Establish the data flow for the queue path field in the initial message to the queue path field in the return message.	• "To draw the flow between messages" in Chapter 8, "Configuring BizTalk Orchestration Services" 📝 **Notes** • Click the **Data** tab. • On the **Data** page, click the queue path field in the initial message. Then drag its control handle to the connection point of the queue path field in the return message. This passes the queue path data from the initial message into the return message.

Creating Custom Components

The information contained in this chapter applies only to BizTalk Server 2000 Enterprise Edition and Developer Edition. This chapter provides information about how to create custom components and extend Microsoft BizTalk Server 2000 to integrate line-of-business applications and add features such as encryption and decryption or digital signature.

In This Chapter

- Creating Application Integration Components

- Using the IBizTalkParserComponent Interface

- Using the IBizTalkSerializerComponent Interface

- Supporting the Tracking Database with Parser and Serializer Components

- Creating Receipt Correlator Components

- Creating Custom Components Reference for Visual Basic

- Creating Custom Components Reference for C++

- Custom Component Enumerations

Creating Application Integration Components

When creating an application integration component (AIC), you can implement either the pipeline model using the **IPipelineComponent** interface or the lightweight model using the **IBTSAppIntegration** interface.

Application integration components are COM objects that the BizTalk Server state engine calls to deliver data to an application. If a messaging port is configured in BizTalk Server 2000 to include the use of an AIC for application integration, this component is automatically instantiated and passed the requisite data. The component then determines how to handle communicating this data back to the application. This can be done using private API calls, invoking other COM objects, using database writes, and so on.

By default, AICs run in the LocalSystem account. If another security context is required, set it as part of the implementation of the AIC. However, if an AIC is installed as a COM+ application, an administrator can configure security of the AIC by using the Component Services console.

Pipeline Application Integration Components

One approach for application integration with BizTalk Server 2000 is the creation of a pipeline component. This is the same model used in Microsoft Site Server Commerce Edition 3.0 for application integration with the Commerce Interchange pipeline (CIP) and the Order Processing pipeline (OPP). BizTalk Server 2000 supports this method so that pipeline components written for application integration for CIP and OPP are compatible. This is also a useful technique when the component requires configuration properties.

The primary entry point for a pipeline component is the **Execute** method of the **IPipelineComponent** interface. This is the method that BizTalk Server 2000 calls to transfer control and to pass the data to the component. It is in the implementation of this method that the component does its work.

To create pipeline components

Use the following steps to create a pipeline component:

1. Create an Active Template Library wizard–generated Inproc server project.

2. Add a simple COM object.

3. Go to the Projectname.idl file and remove the dual or custom interface generated by the wizard in step 2.

4. Verify that the resulting IDL file looks like the code examples that follow. You might choose to implement your own set of interfaces from the ones defined in Pipecomp.idl.

```
// SimplePipeComponent.idl : IDL source for SimplePipeComponent.dll
//
import "oaidl.idl";
import "ocidl.idl";
import "pipecomp.idl";

[
    uuid(D26A52F6-63A0-42B1-8C88-3C71C66BB189),
    version(1.0),
    helpstring("SimplePipeComponent 1.0 Type Library")
]
library SIMPLEPIPECOMPONENTLib
{
    importlib("stdole32.tlb");
    importlib("stdole2.tlb");
    [
        uuid(E66CAF06-18D8-4C70-9D39-5ED9756C21AD),
        helpstring("MySimplePipelineComponent Class")
    ]
    coclass MySimplePipelineComponent
    {
        [default] interface IPipelineComponentAdmin;
        interface IPipelineComponent;
        interface IPipelineComponentDescription;
    };
};
```

5. One of the implementations of MySimplePipelineComponent [coclass] is defined in the header file as follows:

```
// MySimplePipelineComponent.h : Declaration of the
// CMySimplePipelineComponent

#ifndef __MYSIMPLEPIPELINECOMPONENT_H_
#define __MYSIMPLEPIPELINECOMPONENT_H_

#include "resource.h"       // main symbols

//////////////////////////////////////////////////////////////////////
// CMySimplePipelineComponent
class ATL_NO_VTABLE CMySimplePipelineComponent :
    public CComObjectRootEx<CComSingleThreadModel>,
    public CComCoClass<CMySimplePipelineComponent, &CLSID_MySimplePipelineComponent>,
    public ISupportErrorInfo,
    public IDispatchImpl<IPipelineComponentAdmin, &IID_IPipelineComponentAdmin,
&LIBID_SIMPLEPIPECOMPONENTLib>,
    public IDispatchImpl<IPipelineComponent, &IID_IPipelineComponent,
&LIBID_SIMPLEPIPECOMPONENTLib>,
```

```
        public IDispatchImpl<IPipelineComponentDescription,
&IID_IPipelineComponentDescription, &LIBID_SIMPLEPIPECOMPONENTLib>
{
public:
    CMySimplePipelineComponent()
    {
    }

DECLARE_REGISTRY_RESOURCEID(IDR_MYSIMPLEPIPELINECOMPONENT)

DECLARE_PROTECT_FINAL_CONSTRUCT()

BEGIN_COM_MAP(CMySimplePipelineComponent)
    COM_INTERFACE_ENTRY2(IDispatch,IPipelineComponentAdmin)
    COM_INTERFACE_ENTRY(IPipelineComponentAdmin)
    COM_INTERFACE_ENTRY(IPipelineComponent)
    COM_INTERFACE_ENTRY(IPipelineComponentDescription)
    COM_INTERFACE_ENTRY(ISupportErrorInfo)
END_COM_MAP()

// ISupportsErrorInfo
    STDMETHOD(InterfaceSupportsErrorInfo)(REFIID riid);

public://IPipelineComponentAdmin
    STDMETHODIMP GetConfigData(IDispatch** ppDict );
    STDMETHODIMP SetConfigData(IDispatch* pDict );

public://IPipelineComponent
    STDMETHODIMP Execute(IDispatch*  pdispObject,IDispatch*  pdispContext,LONG
lFlags,LONG* plErrorLevel);
    STDMETHODIMP EnableDesign(BOOL fEnable);
public: //IPipelineComponentDescription
    STDMETHODIMP ValuesRead(VARIANT* pvar);
    STDMETHODIMP ValuesWritten(VARIANT* pvar);
    STDMETHODIMP ContextValuesRead(VARIANT* pvar);

};

#endif //__MYSIMPLEPIPELINECOMPONENT_H_
```

To use the SAP R/3 AIC

To use the Systems, Applications, and Products in Data Processing (SAP) AIC, do the following:

Install the DCOM connector

1. Download the SAP Remote Function Call SDK (www.sap.com/bapi).

    *   Go to the COM section and click the DCOM Component Connector.

    *   Follow the instructions from the File Download wizard.

2. Run the image, and unzip it to add the Rfcsdk subdirectories to the client computer.

3. Install the DCOM connector.

4. Follow the installation instructions from the \Rfcsdk\Ccwww subdirectory Install page.

5. Once the connector is installed, create a destination, entering information for the following:

- Destination name

- Application server

- Server number

- Client

- Language

- User

- Password

Enter the destination name in BizTalk Messaging Manager

This is the destination name chosen during SAP DCOM connector configuration. For more information, see "To select a destination organization" in Chapter 9, "Configuring BizTalk Messaging Services."

Create a COM+ server package

1. Create a COM+ server package.

2. Mark it as Transactions Not Supported.

3. Add AICOMP.dll to this package.

Lightweight Application Integration Components

BizTalk Server 2000 supports an additional model for application developers who want a lighter-weight model for application integration, one that does not support a design-time user interface or configuration properties. This model requires a single interface that contains a single method as an entry point. The component is implemented, and the document is passed to it through the **ProcessMessage** method of the **IBTSAppIntegration** interface.

IBTSAppIntegration is for applications that do not need properties for their component and need only an entry point for receiving a document. This is a simpler approach to application integration than pipeline components. BizTalk Server 2000 queries for this interface first. If it does not find this interface implemented, it queries for the pipeline component interfaces.

Registering Application Integration Components

To use an application integration component (AIC) in BizTalk Server 2000, the component must be registered with the category IDs for all pipeline components and for the specific type of pipeline component, in this case application integration.

Register the AIC as an out-of-process component to provide better isolation. An AIC can be registered as an in-process (inproc) component to increase its performance. However, an inproc component that fails to respond during an error condition might cause BizTalk Server to fail. Therefore, an AIC should be thoroughly tested before registering it as an inproc component.

☑ Notes

- An out-of-process component registered as a COM+ application must be configured to run in an identity other than the interactive user.

- The application integration component must be registered by a user in the BizTalk Server Administrators group. The BizTalk Server Administrators group is created when BizTalk Server 2000 is installed. Additional users can be added to this group as necessary.

For more information about Component Services and COM+, go to the MSDN Online Library Web site (msdn.microsoft.com/library/default.asp) and browse to Component Services in the Platform SDK.

Assigning affinity

Each application integration component (AIC) must be associated with two category IDs. One category ID marks the component as a BizTalk Server component. A component so marked appears in a list of components in the BizTalk Server administration console. The second category ID indicates the type or purpose of the component. This second association is called affinity. Only those components whose affinity is registered as application integration components appear in lists of such components.

To register affinity for an AIC created with Microsoft Visual C++ using ATL, include the following code in your header file:

```
#include "bts_sdk_guids.h"
// Implement the Component and AIC Category IDs (CATID)
BEGIN_CATEGORY_MAP(AIC_ClassName)
    IMPLEMENTED_CATEGORY(CATID_BIZTALK_COMPONENT)
    IMPLEMENTED_CATEGORY(CATID_BIZTALK_AIC)
END_CATEGORY_MAP()
```

To register affinity for an AIC created with Microsoft Visual Basic:

1. After registering your component using Regsvr32.exe, search the registry for the CLSID of your AIC under the following key:

   HKEY_CLASSES_ROOT\CLSID

2. Expand the **Implemented Categories** key of your AIC.

3. Add two new keys with the following names:

    HKEY_CLASSES_ROOT\CLSID*AIC_CLSID*\Implemented Categories\{5C6C30E7-C66D-40e3-889D-08C5C3099E52}

    HKEY_CLASSES_ROOT\CLSID*AIC_CLSID*\Implemented Categories\{BD193E1D-D7DC-4b7c-B9D2-92AE0344C836}

These GUIDs can be found in bts_sdk_guids.h in the \Program Files\Microsoft BizTalk Server\SDK\Include folder. The first key shown in step 3 above identifies the AIC as a BizTalk Server component (CATID_BIZTALK_COMPONENT). The second key shown in step 3 above identifies the component as an AIC (CATID_BIZTALK_AIC).

Testing affinity

To test affinity, use BizTalk Messaging Manager to create a port that uses the AIC. For more information, see "To select an application integration component" in Chapter 9, "Configuring BizTalk Messaging Services."

Using the IBizTalkParserComponent Interface

The parser has two responsibilities:

*   Convert the documents to XML for later processing.

*   Get the parameters necessary to select the channel (these are the source qualifier, source identifier, destination qualifier, destination identifier, and document definition name). These returned fields are combined with the parameters of the **Submit** method of the **IInterchange** interface to select the channels necessary to process the documents.

This interface gets information from the component for one interchange. If the incoming data stream represents multiple interchanges, the server selects the component at every interchange boundary. This simplifies construction of a component because it deals with only one interchange at a time. There is one component instance per thread. No single object needs to be safe for multiple threads. This interface is supported only in C++.

If the **ProbeInterchangeFormat** method of the **IBizTalkParserComponent** interface returns an error in the middle of the document list, it blocks the server from detecting more document types, even if they could be handled by a custom parser that follows the failed parser, if there are two or more custom parsers on a server. If the first custom parser fails, any document that follows is not parsed, even if the other custom parser could handle it, because the server ends the entire parsing operation at the time of the failure.

Sequence for Calling Methods of the IBizTalkParserComponent Interface

The following tables show a possible sequence for calling the methods, based on the sample interchange.

If you have an interchange with two groups, with two documents in the first group and one in the second, the methods are called in the following sequence.

Method	Return
ProbeInterchangeFormat	Non-empty format string
GetInterchangeDetails	N/A
GroupsExist	TRUE
GetGroupDetails	N/A
GetNextDocument	The *LastDoc* parameter is set to FALSE.
GetNativeDocumentOffsets	N/A
GetNextDocument	The *LastDoc* parameter is set to TRUE.
GetNativeDocumentOffsets	N/A
GetGroupSize	The *LastGroup* parameter is set to FALSE.
GetGroupDetails	N/A
GetNextDocument	The *LastDoc* parameter is set to TRUE.
GetNativeDocumentOffsets	N/A
GetGroupSize	The *LastGroup* parameter is set to TRUE.

If you have an interchange with two documents, the methods are called in the following sequence.

Method	Return
ProbeInterchangeFormat	Non-empty format string
GetInterchangeDetails	N/A
GroupsExist	FALSE
GetNextDocument	The *LastDoc* parameter is set to FALSE.
GetNativeDocumentOffsets	N/A
GetNextDocument	The *LastDoc* parameter is set to TRUE.
GetNativeDocumentOffsets	N/A

Using the IBizTalkSerializer Component Interface

The serializer converts the document from XML back to its native format. This interface is intended to work on a single interchange and is designed to get information from the component for one interchange. This simplifies the construction of this component because it has to deal with only one interchange at a time. There is only one instance per thread. No single object needs to be safe for multiple threads. This interface is supported only in C++.

Sequence for Calling Methods of the IBizTalkSerializerComponent Interface

The following tables show the possible sequence of calling the methods of the **IBizTalkSerializerComponent** interface, based on the following sample interchanges.

If you have an interchange with one document, the methods are called in the following sequence.

Method	Return
Init	The *numdocs* parameter is set to 1.
AddDocument	The *docHandle* parameter is set to 0.
GetInterchangeInfo	The *numGroups* parameter is set to 0.
GetDocInfo	The *docHandle* parameter is set to 0.

If you have an interchange with one group, with one document in the group, the methods are called in the following sequence.

Method	Return
Init	The *numdocs* parameter is set to 1.
AddDocument	The *docHandle* parameter is set to 0.
GetInterchangeInfo	The *numGroups* parameter is set to 1.
GetGroupInfo	The *numdocs* parameter is set to 1.
GetDocInfo	The *docHandle* parameter is set to 0.

If you have an interchange with two groups, with two documents in the first group and one in the second, the methods are called in the following sequence (this assumes support of batching).

Method	Return
Init	The *numdocs* parameter is set to 3.
AddDocument	The *handle* parameter is set to 0.
AddDocument	The *handle* parameter is set to 1.
AddDocument	The *handle* parameter is set to 2.
GetInterchangeInfo	The *numGroups* parameter is set to 2.
GetGroupInfo	The *numdocs* parameter is set to 2.
GetDocInfo	The *handle* parameter is set to 1.
GetDocInfo	The *handle* parameter is set to 0.
GetGroupInfo	The *numdocs* parameter is set to 1.
GetDocInfo	The *handle* parameter is set to 2.

Supporting the Tracking Database with Parser and Serializer Components

When creating a custom parser or serializer, you might want your component to support the BizTalk Server Tracking database. To accomplish this, the component must use the **IDictionary** interface to add key/value pairs into the database.

Interchange table

The following table contains the list of keys that can be used to support the Tracking database from the interchange level with a custom component. The table used in the database is dta_interchange_details.

Dictionary key	Inbound or Outbound	Column logged in Tracking database	Description
Src_ID_Type	Both	*nvcSrcAliasQualifier	The qualifier for the source organization. This value can come from a parameter supplied in a **Submit** call or from a receive function in the BizTalk Server Administration user interface. A parser can overwrite this value to manipulate the routing information used for channel selection.
Src_ID_Value	Both	*nvcSrcAliasId	The value of the qualifier of the source organization. This value can come from a parameter supplied in a **Submit** call or from a receive function in the BizTalk Server Administration user interface. A parser can overwrite this value to manipulate the routing information used for channel selection.
In_Src_ID_App	Inbound	nvcSrcAppName	The interchange level identifier for the source application of an EDI interchange. When the parser sets the value with this dictionary key, the value is logged on the inbound interchange in the Tracking database.
Dest_ID_Type	Both	*nvcDestAliasQualifier	The qualifier for the destination organization. This value can come from a parameter supplied in a **Submit** call or from a receive function in the BizTalk Server Administration user interface. A parser can overwrite this value to manipulate the routing information used for channel selection.
Dest_ID_Value	Both	*nvcDestAliasId	The value of the qualifier of the destination organization. This value can come from a parameter supplied in a **Submit** call or from a receive function in the BizTalk Server Administration user interface. A parser can overwrite this value to manipulate the routing information used for channel selection.

Dictionary key	Inbound or Outbound	Column logged in Tracking database	Description
In_Dest_ID_App	Inbound	nvcDestAppName	The interchange level identifier for the destination application of an EDI interchange. When the parser sets the value with this dictionary key, the value is logged on the inbound interchange in the Tracking database.
interchange_id	Inbound	nvcControlID	The unique control number used to identify an EDI interchange instance between trading partners. When the parser sets the value with this dictionary key, the value is logged on the inbound interchange in the Tracking database.
interchange_version	Inbound	nvcVersion	The version of an EDI interchange. When the parser sets the value with this dictionary key, the value is logged on the inbound interchange in the Tracking database.
Out_Src_ID_App	Outbound	*nvcSrcAppName	The interchange level identifier for the source application of an EDI interchange. When the serializer sets the value with this dictionary key, the value is logged on the outbound interchange in the Tracking database.
Out_Dest_ID_App	Outbound	*nvcDestAppName	The interchange level identifier for the destination application of an EDI interchange. When the serializer sets the value with this dictionary key, the value is logged on the outbound interchange in the Tracking database.
out_interchange_id	Outbound	*nvcControlID	The unique control number used to identify an EDI interchange instance between trading partners. The serializer usually generates this unique value. When the serializer sets the value with this dictionary key, the value is logged on the outbound interchange in the Tracking database.
out_interchange_ version	Outbound	*nvcVersion	The version of the EDI standard. When the serializer sets the value with this dictionary key, the value is logged on the outbound interchange in the Tracking database.

✎ Note

- The columns of the dta_interchange_details table marked with an asterisk (*) are used for receipt correlation.

Group table

The following table contains the list of keys that can be used to support the Tracking database from the group level with a custom component. The table used in the database is dta_group_details. This table applies to both inbound and outbound documents.

Dictionary key	Column logged in Tracking database	Description
group_id	*nvcControlID	The unique control number of a group instance within an EDI interchange. Both the parser and the serializer can set the value with this key. The value is logged on the inbound and the outbound group, respectively, in the Tracking database. For outbound document processing, the serializer usually generates this value.
functional_identifier	*nvcFunctionalGroupID	The code for the type of documents in an EDI group. Both the parser and the serializer can set the value with this key. The value is logged on the inbound and the outbound group, respectively, in the Tracking database. In the serializer, this value can be read from the document's **PropertySet**.
application_sender_code	*nvcSrcAppName	The group level identifier for the source application in an EDI group. Both the parser and the serializer can set the value with this key. The value is logged on the inbound and the outbound group, respectively, in the Tracking database. In the serializer, this value can be read from the document's **PropertySet**.
application_receiver_code	*nvcDestAppName	The group level identifier for the destination application in an EDI group. Both the parser and the serializer can set the value with this key. The value is logged on the inbound and the outbound group, respectively, in the Tracking database. In the serializer, this value can be read from the document's **PropertySet**.
standards_version	*nvcVersion	The version of the EDI standard. Both the parser and the serializer can set the value with this key. The value is logged on the inbound and the outbound group, respectively, in the Tracking database.
standards_release	*nvcRelease	The release of the version of the EDI standard. Both the parser and the serializer can set the value with this key. The value is logged on the inbound and the outbound group, respectively, in the Tracking database.

✎ Note

The columns of the dta_group_details table marked with an asterisk (*) are used for receipt correlation.

Inbound document table

The following table contains the list of keys that can be used to support the Tracking database from the document level with a custom component. The table used in the database is dta_indoc_details. This table applies to inbound documents only.

Dictionary key	Column logged in Tracking database	Description
doc_id	nvcControlID	The unique control number of an EDI document instance. When the parser sets the value with this dictionary key, the value is logged on the inbound document in the Tracking database.
standards_version	nvcVersion	The version of the EDI standard. When the parser sets the value with this dictionary key, the value is logged on the inbound document in the Tracking database.
standards_release	nvcRelease	The release of the version of the EDI standard. When the parser sets the value with this dictionary key, the value is logged on the inbound document in the Tracking database.
doc_type	nvcDocType	The document type or transaction set identifier. When the parser sets the value with this dictionary key, the value is logged on the inbound document in the Tracking database.

Outbound document table

The following table contains the list of keys that can be used to support the Tracking database from the document level with a custom component. The table used in the database is dta_outdoc_details. This table applies to outbound documents only.

Dictionary key	Column logged in Tracking database	Description
out_doc_doc_id	nvcControlID	The unique control number of an EDI document instance. When the serializer sets the value with this dictionary key, the value is logged on the outbound document in the Tracking database.
out_doc_syntax	nvcSyntax	The code for document syntax, such as XML, X12, EDIFACT, H7, and so on. When the serializer sets the value with this dictionary key, the value is logged on the outbound document in the Tracking database.
out_doc_standards_version	nvcVersion	The version of the EDI standard. When the serializer sets the value with this dictionary key, the value is logged on the outbound document in the Tracking database. In the serializer, this value can be read from the document's **PropertySet**.
out_doc_standards_release	nvcRelease	The release of the version of the EDI standard. When the serializer sets the value with this dictionary key, the value is logged on the outbound document in the Tracking database. In the serializer, this value can be read from the document's **PropertySet**.
out_doc_doc_type	nvcDocType	The document type or transaction set identifier. When the serializer sets the value with this dictionary key, the value is logged on the outbound document in the Tracking database.
Tracking_ID	uidTrackingGUID	The tracking identifier of the document for which a receipt is generated.

☑ Note

• The Tracking_ID key is used when calling the **AckDocument** method.

Interchange and document tables

The following table contains the list of keys that can be used to support the Tracking database from the interchange and document level with a custom component. The table used in the database for interchange data is dta_interchange_data. The table used in the database for document data is dta_document_data.

Dictionary key	Inbound or Outbound	Column logged in Tracking database	Description
in_codepage	Inbound	nCodePage	The system code page value with which interchange or document data is encoded. When the parser sets the value with this dictionary key, the value is logged in the data record related to the inbound interchange or document in the Tracking database.
out_codepage	Outbound	nCodePage	The system code page value with which interchange or document data is encoded. When the serializer sets the value with this dictionary key, the value is logged in the data record related to the outbound interchange or document in the Tracking database.

Creating Receipt Correlator Components

Receipt correlator components can be implemented to correlate documents, groups of documents, and interchanges with their receipts. To use a receipt correlator, you must implement a custom parser using the **IBizTalkParserComponent** interface. This is required because the server can obtain only the **progID** of the receipt correlator to be used by calling the **GetNextDocument** method on the **IBizTalkParserComponent** interface.

In addition, with BizTalk Server on the receiver side where the receipt is being generated, the parser component is responsible for putting the receipt status, as well as sufficient information, on the receipt (a Canonical Receipt to begin with, but it can be mapped into other receipt document schemas, such as AK997 in EDI) to allow the correlator component on the sender side to uniquely identify the original outbound interchange, group, or document record. For an XML document, using the GUID is usually sufficient. But for EDI interchanges, since GUID cannot be used (there is no placeholder for any GUID in an EDI interchange), a combination of EDI-specific fields is needed for this unique identifier. For example, the default X12 correlator component uses a combination of the following fields for this purpose: version, release, functional group ID, control ID, source application name, and destination application name.

Whenever the server receives a receipt as an inbound document, the parser component's responsibility is to detect the inbound document as being a receipt, to extract all relevant information needed for correlation, and to place the receipt onto the transport dictionary. Upon returning from the **GetNextDocument** method call, the parser should set the *DocIsReceipt* parameter to TRUE and the *CorrelationCompProgID* parameter to the **progID** of the corresponding correlator component.

The server calls the **Correlate** method on the **IBizTalkCorrelation** interface, and passes in a pointer to the **IBizTalkAcknowledge** object and the transport dictionary containing the receipt as the working data. Then the receipt correlator's implementation of the **Correlate** method extracts all relevant information about the document, document group, or interchange that should have been set by the parser component from the transport dictionary. Using this information, the **Correlate** method then calls **AckDocument**, **AckGroup**, or **AckInterchange** on the **IBizTalkAcknowledge** interface and sets the **DTA_ACK_STATUS** value for that document, group, or interchange.

Note that the server does not immediately call **IBizTalkCorrelation**. The receipt document and the correlation **progID** are stored to the database for later correlation. When the document is picked up for processing, the correlation component is created and invoked with the transport dictionary that was given by the parser component and a pointer to **IBizTalkAcknowledge**.

Related Topics

"Understanding Receipts" in Chapter 9, "Configuring BizTalk Messaging Services"

"Understanding the Tracking Database Schema" in Chapter 13, "Tracking Documents"

Creating Custom Components Reference for Visual Basic

This section provides reference information about components and interfaces used by Microsoft BizTalk Server 2000 for Microsoft Visual Basic programming. Reference information is provided for all interfaces exposed for extending BizTalk Server 2000.

IBizTalkAcknowledge Object

Use this object to process receipts sent to the server.

The methods of the **BizTalkAcknowledge** object are shown in the following table.

Method	Description
AckDocument	Processes receipts received for documents.
AckGroup	Processes receipts received for document groups.
AckInterchange	Processes receipts received for document interchanges.

Requirements

Windows NT/2000: Requires Windows 2000 SP1 or later
Library: Use Microsoft BizTalk Server Doc Tracking 1.0 Type Library (CISDTA.dll)

IBizTalkAcknowledge.AckDocument Method

The **AckDocument** method processes receipts for documents.

Syntax

object.**AckDocument(** _
    bstrSyntax **As String,** _
    bstrTrackingId **As String,** _
    enumAckStatus **As DTA_ACK_STATUS** _
)

Parameters

bstrSyntax
   String that contains the syntax of the outbound document to be acknowledged, for
   example, X12 or EDIFACT.

bstrTrackingId
   String that contains the unique tracking identifier of the document. This value is a
   globally unique identifier (GUID). This value can be obtained from the Tracking_ID field
   in the dta_outdoc_details table. For more information, see "Supporting the Tracking
   Database with Parser and Serializer Components" earlier in this chapter.

enumAckStatus
   Enumeration value that indicates the receipt status. Valid values are from the
   DTA_ACK_STATUS enumeration.

Return Values

None

Error Value

If an error is raised, **Err.Number** is set to one of the values documented in Appendix A, "Error Messages."

Remarks

This method is called only for receipts on individual documents. If the receipt must be mapped, a document definition that points to the CanonicalReceipt.xml file (available in the WebDAV repository) must be created for the receipt.

Requirements

Windows NT/2000: Requires Windows 2000 SP1 or later
Library: Use Microsoft BizTalk Server Doc Tracking 1.0 Type Library (CISDTA.dll)

IBizTalkAcknowledge.AckGroup Method

The **AckGroup** method processes receipts for document groups.

Syntax

object.**AckGroup**(_
   bstrSyntax **As String**, _
   bstrVersion **As String**, _
   bstrRelease **As String**, _
   bstrFunctionalGroupId **As String**, _
   bstrControlId **As String**, _
   bstrSrcAppName **As String**, _
   bstrDestAppName **As String**, _
   enumAckStatus **As DTA_ACK_STATUS** _
)

Parameters

bstrSyntax
   String that contains the syntax of the outbound document to be acknowledged, for example, X12 or EDIFACT. You must use the exact strings for the following syntax types:

- X12

- EDIFACT

- Custom XML

bstrVersion
  String that contains the version of the syntax, used primarily for EDI.

bstrRelease
  String that contains the release of the version of the syntax, used primarily for EDI.

bstrFunctionalGroupId
  String that contains the code for the type of documents in a group, used primarily for EDI.

bstrControlId
  String that contains the unique identifier for the control number, used primarily for EDI.

bstrSrcAppName
  String that contains the name of the source application.

bstrDestAppName
  String that contains the name of the destination application.

enumAckStatus
  Enumeration value that indicates the receipt status. Valid values are from the **DTA_ACK_STATUS** enumeration.

Return Values

None

Error Value

If an error is raised, **Err.Number** is set to one of the values documented in Appendix A, "Error Messages."

Remarks

This method is called only for receipts on document groups.

Requirements

Windows NT/2000: Requires Windows 2000 SP1 or later
Library: Use Microsoft BizTalk Server Doc Tracking 1.0 Type Library (CISDTA.dll)

IBizTalkAcknowledge.AckInterchange Method

The **AckInterchange** method processes receipts for document interchanges.

Syntax

object.**AckInterchange**(_
  bstrSyntax **As String**, _
  bstrInterchangeId **As String**, _
  bstrVersion **As String**, _
  bstrControlId **As String**, _

bstrSrcAliasQualifier **As String,** _
bstrSrcAliasId **As String,** _
bstrSrcAppName **As String,** _
bstrDestAliasQualifier **As String,** _
bstrDestAliasId **As String,** _
bstrDestAppName **As String,** _
enumAckStatus **As DTA_ACK_STATUS** _
)

Parameters

bstrSyntax
String that contains the syntax of the outbound document to be acknowledged, for example, X12 or EDIFACT. You must use the exact strings for the following syntax types:

- X12

- EDIFACT

- Custom XML

bstrInterchangeId
String that contains the unique tracking identifier of the interchange. This value is a globally unique identifier (GUID).

bstrVersion
String that contains the version of the syntax, used primarily for EDI.

bstrControlId
String that contains the unique identifier for the control number, used primarily for EDI.

bstrSrcAliasQualifier
String that contains the qualifier of the source organization. This value indicates how the *bstrSrcAliasId* parameter is to be interpreted. Valid values come from the organization identifier qualifiers that are created when the user creates an alias for an organization. Common qualifiers include the DUNS number, telephone number, and BizTalk. The default qualifier for all new organizations is *Organization Name* and refers to the name of the organization in the database. If a BizTalk Framework 2.0–compliant document is submitted and a qualifier is not found during parsing, the qualifier defaults to *BizTalk*.

bstrSrcAliasId
String that contains the value of the qualifier of the source organization. For example, if the *bstrSrcAliasQualifier* parameter is Telephone, this value is the telephone number.

bstrSrcAppName
String that contains the name of the source application.

bstrDestAliasQualifier
String that contains the qualifier of the source organization. This value indicates how the *bstrDestAliasId* parameter is to be interpreted. Valid values come from the organization

identifier qualifiers that are created when the user creates an alias for an organization. Common qualifiers include the DUNS number, telephone number, and BizTalk. The default qualifier for all new organizations is *Organization Name* and refers to the name of the organization in the database. If a BizTalk Framework 2.0–compliant document is submitted and a qualifier is not found during parsing, the qualifier defaults to *BizTalk*.

bstrDestAliasId

String that contains the value of the qualifier of the source organization. For example, if the *bstrDestAliasQualifier* parameter is Telephone, this value is the telephone number.

bstrDestAppName

String that contains the name of the destination application.

enumAckStatus

Enumeration value that indicates the receipt status. Valid values are from the **DTA_ACK_STATUS** enumeration.

Return Values

None

Error Value

If an error is raised, **Err.Number** is set to one of the values documented in Appendix A, "Error Messages."

Remarks

This method is called only for receipts on document interchanges.

Requirements

Windows NT/2000: Requires Windows 2000 SP1 or later
Library: Use Microsoft BizTalk Server Doc Tracking 1.0 Type Library (CISDTA.dll)

CannedFunctoid Object

In Microsoft Visual Basic, implement the **CannedFunctoid** object to create custom mapping functions. The **CannedFunctoid** object defines the generic protocol for calling custom functions used by the mapping tool.

This object must register its class identifier (CLSID) under a well-known category identifier (CATID) of the function objects enumerated by the mapping tool. The CATID is {2560F3BF-DB47-11D2-B3AE-00C04F72D6C1}. Each custom object can support multiple functions and can contain icons and names for each supported function.

Function identifiers from 0 to 1000 are reserved for built-in functions in BizTalk Mapper. User-defined functions (custom functions) should use function identifiers 1001 and higher.

The properties of the **CannedFunctoid** object are shown in the following table.

Property	Description
FunctionsCount	Returns the number of functions implemented by the functoid.
Version	Returns the version of the functoid.

The methods of the **CannedFunctoid** object are shown in the following table.

Method	Description
GetFunctionParameter	Retrieves the connection-type bit flags for the specified parameter.
GetFunctionDescripter	Retrieves information about a specific functoid.
GetScriptBuffer	Retrieves the script code used to implement the functoid.

Requirements

Windows NT/2000: Requires Windows 2000 SP1 or later
Library: Use Microsoft BizTalk Server Canned Functoids 1.0 Type Library
(CannedFunctoid.dll)

CannedFunctoid.FunctionsCount Property

The **FunctionsCount** property returns the number of functions implemented by the functoid.

Syntax

object.**FunctionsCount**

Parameters

None

Return Values

This property returns a **Long** that contains the number of functions implemented by the functoid.

Error Value

If an error is raised, **Err.Number** is set to one of the values documented in Appendix A, "Error Messages."

Remarks

This is a read-only property.

Requirements

Windows NT/2000: Requires Windows 2000 SP1 or later
Library: Use Microsoft BizTalk Server Canned Functoids 1.0 Type Library
(CannedFunctoid.dll)

CannedFunctoid.GetFunctionDescripter Method

The **GetFunctionDescripter** method retrieves information about a specific functoid.

Syntax

object.**GetFunctionDescripter(** _
    lIndex **As Long,** _
    pFuncCategory **As FUNC_CATEGORY,** _
    pScriptCategory **As SCRIPT_CATEGORY,** _
    pFuncType **As FUNC_TYPE,** _
    pbstrName **As String,** _
    pbstrToolTip **As String,** _
    plBitmapID **As Long,** _
    plParmCount **As Long** _
)

Parameters

lIndex
    Long that specifies the index number of the function.

pFuncCategory
    Value that contains the **FUNC_CATEGORY** bit flags for this function.

pScriptCategory
    Value that contains the **SCRIPT_CATEGORY** bit flags for this function. This value
    must be set to **SCRIPT_CATEGORY_VBSCRIPT** for this release.

pFuncType
    Value that contains the **FUNC_TYPE** bit flags for this function.

pbstrName
    String that contains the function name.

pbstrToolTip
    String that contains the ToolTip that appears when the mouse pointer is paused over the
    custom functoid icon in the mapping tool.

plBitmapID
    Long that contains the bitmap identifier of the bitmap used for the custom functoid icon
    displayed in the mapping tool.

plParmCount
    Long that contains the number of parameters implemented by the function.

Return Values

This method returns a **Long** that contains the function identifier.

Error Value

If an error is raised, **Err.Number** is set to one of the values documented in Appendix A, "Error Messages."

Requirements

Windows NT/2000: Requires Windows 2000 SP1 or later
Library: Use Microsoft BizTalk Server Canned Functoids 1.0 Type Library (CannedFunctoid.dll)

CannedFunctoid.GetFunctionParameter Method

The **GetFunctionParameter** method retrieves the connection-type bit flags for the specified parameter.

Syntax

object.**GetFunctionParameter**(_
  funcId **As FUNCID**, _
  lParameter **As Long** _
)

Parameters

funcId
  Long that contains the function identifier.

lParameter
  Long that contains the function parameter number. For output parameters, a value of -1 is used.

Return Values

This method returns a **Long** that contains the **CONNECTION_TYPE** bit flags for the specified parameter.

Error Value

If an error is raised, **Err.Number** is set to one of the values documented in Appendix A, "Error Messages."

Remarks

This is a read-only property.

Requirements

Windows NT/2000: Requires Windows 2000 SP1 or later
Library: Use Microsoft BizTalk Server Canned Functoids 1.0 Type Library
(CannedFunctoid.dll)

CannedFunctoid.GetScriptBuffer Method

The **GetScriptBuffer** method retrieves the script code used to implement the functoid.

Syntax

object.**GetScriptBuffer(** _
  cFuncId **As FUNCID,** _
  lInputParameters **As Long** _
)

Parameters

cFuncId
  Long that contains the function identifier.

lInputParameters
  Long that indicates the number of connected input parameters for the specified function.

Return Values

This method returns a **String** that contains the script code used to implement the function.

Error Value

If an error is raised, **Err.Number** is set to one of the values documented in Appendix A, "Error Messages."

Remarks

This is a read-only property.

Requirements

Windows NT/2000: Requires Windows 2000 SP1 or later
Library: Use Microsoft BizTalk Server Canned Functoids 1.0 Type Library
(CannedFunctoid.dll)

CannedFunctoid.Version Property

The **Version** property returns the version of the functoid.

Syntax

object.**Version**

Parameters

None

Return Values

This property returns a **Long** that contains the custom functoid version.

Error Value

If an error is raised, **Err.Number** is set to one of the values documented in Appendix A, "Error Messages."

Remarks

This is a read-only property.

If the custom functoid is modified in any way, the author should update the version number.

Requirements

Windows NT/2000: Requires Windows 2000 SP1 or later
Library: Use Microsoft BizTalk Server Canned Functoids 1.0 Type Library
(CannedFunctoid.dll)

IBTSAppIntegration Object

Use this object to create an entry point for receiving a document.

The method of the **BTSAppIntegration** object is shown in the following table.

Method	Description
ProcessMessage	Processes the document.

Remarks

Application integration components must be properly registered so that they are recognized by BizTalk Server 2000. Application integration components register with the category ID **CATID_BIZTALK_AIC**. The CATIDs are defined in the bts_sdk_guids.h file. For more information, see "Registering Application Integration Components" earlier in this chapter.

Requirements

Windows NT/2000: Requires Windows 2000 SP1 or later
Library: Use Microsoft BizTalk Server Application Interface Components 1.0 Type Library
(btscomplib.tlb)

IBTSAppIntegration.ProcessMessage Method

The **ProcessMessage** method processes a document and returns a response document, if
available. This method is called at run time when the server is sending a document to the
component.

Syntax

object.**ProcessMessage(_**
    bstrDocument **As String _**
)

Parameters

bstrDocument
    String that contains the document.

Return Values

String that contains the response document.

Error Value

If an error is raised, **Err.Number** is set to one of the values documented in Appendix A,
"Error Messages."

Remarks

Components can return a response string to pass back a text-based response to an application,
using the **SubmitSync** method of the **IInterchange** interface to send documents.

Components must raise an error if a problem with processing occurs so that the document can
be retransmitted or sent to the Suspended queue. If no error is returned, the server assumes
that the component successfully processed the data.

Requirements

Windows NT/2000: Requires Windows 2000 SP1 or later
Library: Use Microsoft BizTalk Server Application Interface Components 1.0 Type Library
(btscomplib.tlb)

IPipelineComponent Object

Use this object to create custom pipeline components that can run in BizTalk Server 2000 to extend its functionality.

The methods of the **PipelineComponent** object are shown in the following table.

Method	Description
EnableDesign	Configures the component for execution in one of two modes: design mode or execution mode.
Execute	Executes the operation expected of the component, given the transport **Dictionary** object and other configuration settings.

Remarks

Application integration components must be properly registered so that they are recognized by BizTalk Server 2000. Application integration components register with the category ID **CATID_BIZTALK_AIC**. The CATIDs are defined in the bts_sdk_guids.h file. For more information, see "Registering Application Integration Components" earlier in this chapter.

Requirements

Windows NT/2000: Requires Windows 2000 SP1 or later
Library: Use Microsoft Commerce 2000 Default Pipeline Components Type Library (pipecomplib.tlb)

IPipelineComponent.EnableDesign Method

The **EnableDesign** method configures the component for execution in one of two modes: design mode or execution mode.

Syntax

object.**EnableDesign(** _
    fEnable **As Boolean** _
)

Parameters

fEnable
    Boolean that indicates the mode of the component. A value of **True** specifies that the component runs in design mode. A value of **False** (default) specifies execution mode.

Return Values

None.

Error Value

If an error is raised, **Err.Number** is set to one of the values documented in Appendix A, "Error Messages."

Remarks

The pipeline component runs in execution mode by default.

This method is called when the **Override messaging port defaults** page is opened in the Channel Wizard's **Advanced Configuration** page. It is also called when the property page is closed and the *fEnable* parameter is set to **True**. Design mode is not enabled unless this method has been called with the *fEnable* parameter set to **True**.

Design-only fields are returned only when the *fEnable* parameter is set to **True**. Otherwise, the **Dictionary** object passed to the server contains unnecessary information.

Requirements

Windows NT/2000: Requires Windows 2000 SP1 or later
Library: Use Microsoft Commerce 2000 Default Pipeline Components Type Library (pipecomplib.tlb)

IPipelineComponent.Execute Method

The **Execute** method executes the operation expected of the component, given the transport **Dictionary** object and other configuration settings. Microsoft BizTalk Server 2000 calls this method, passing in the transport **Dictionary** object. The component can read these **Dictionary** object values, perform the necessary functions, and optionally write new values back to the transport **Dictionary** object for further processing.

Syntax

object.**Execute**(_
  pDispOrder **As Object**, _
  pDispContext **As Object**, _
  lFlags **As Long** _
)

Parameters

pDispOrder
  Object that contains the transport **CDictionary** object.

pDispContext
  Not supported for this release.

lFlags
  Reserved.

Return Values

This method returns a **Long** that contains the error level.

Error Value

If an error is raised, **Err.Number** is set to one of the values documented in Appendix A, "Error Messages."

Remarks

For a component designed to run in BizTalk Server 2000, the first parameter is a **Transport Dictionary** object. The **Transport Dictionary** values can be read by the component for processing. The string values supplied by the server for all application integration components (AICs) are as follows:

- Src_ID_Type: The type of identifier used for the source organization.

- Src_ID_Value: The value of the source organization identifier.

- Dest_ID_Type: The type of identifier used for the destination organization.

- Dest_ID_Value: The value of the destination organization identifier.

- Document_Name: The name of the input document definition.

- Tracking_ID: A key value that is based on the globally unique identifier (GUID) and used for tracking.

For a component that runs in a Commerce Server order-processing pipeline, the first parameter contains the **OrderForm** object.

This method is called at run time when the server is sending a document to the component. This method is called immediately after the **SetConfigData** method of the **IPipelineComponentAdmin** interface. The document is passed in the first parameter as a dictionary within the working_data field of the **Dictionary** object. Components can add the *ResponseField* key to the **Dictionary** object to pass back a text-based response to an application, using the **SubmitSync** method of the **IInterchange** interface.

The component must raise an error if a problem with processing occurs so that the server can retry transmission later and, after all retries, send the document to the Suspended queue. If no error is returned, the server assumes that the component successfully processed the data.

Requirements

Windows NT/2000: Requires Windows 2000 SP1 or later
Library: Use Microsoft Commerce 2000 Default Pipeline Components Type Library (pipecomplib.tlb)

IPipelineComponentAdmin Object

Use this object between the component and the component user interface.

The methods of the **PipelineComponentAdmin** object are shown in the following table.

Method	Description
GetConfigData	Returns a **Dictionary** object that contains the configuration data for the component for the user interface to display these values.
SetConfigData	Sets the configuration settings for a component, using the contents of a **Dictionary** object.

Remarks

Application integration components must be properly registered so that BizTalk Server 2000 can recognize that they belong to BizTalk Server 2000. Application integration components register themselves with the category ID **CATID_BIZTALK_AIC**. The CATIDs are defined in the bts_sdk_guids.h file. For more information, see "Registering Application Integration Components" earlier in this chapter.

Requirements

Windows NT/2000: Requires Windows 2000 SP1 or later
Library: Use Microsoft Commerce 2000 Default Pipeline Components Type Library (pipecomplib.tlb)

IPipelineComponentAdmin.GetConfigData Method

The **GetConfigData** method returns a **Dictionary** object that contains the configuration data for the component to be used to display these values. The **GetConfigData** method enables the user interface component to read the current value from the component and display it on the property page initially.

Syntax

object.**GetConfigData**()

Parameters

None

Return Values

This method optionally returns a **CDictionary** object from which the user interface can read the configuration data.

Error Value

If an error is raised, **Err.Number** is set to one of the values documented in Appendix A, "Error Messages."

Remarks

When a **BizTalkPort** object is first saved, this method is called to get the defaults for use in autoconfiguring the application integration component (AIC) from the **Dictionary** object provided. Components must provide defaults for all mandatory properties, whenever possible.

This method is called when the user selects the property page. It is used to supply property page defaults. It is called again when the property page is closed. The contents of the returned **Dictionary** object are not used.

Components must always return a valid dictionary pointer from **GetConfigData**.

Requirements

Windows NT/2000: Requires Windows 2000 SP1 or later
Library: Use Microsoft Commerce 2000 Default Pipeline Components Type Library (pipecomplib.tlb)

IPipelineComponentAdmin.SetConfigData Method

The **SetConfigData** method sets the configuration for a component, using the contents of a **Dictionary** object. With this method, the user interface can set or change these values. The **SetConfigData** method enables the user interface to write the updated value from the property page to the component.

Syntax

object.**SetConfigData**(_
   pConfigDictionary **As Object** _
)

Parameters

pConfigDictionary
   CDictionary object that contains the configuration information.

Return Values

None.

Error Value

If an error is raised, **Err.Number** is set to one of the values documented in Appendix A, "Error Messages."

Remarks

The server calls the **SetConfigData** method when the property page is saved. It is used to verify the values entered by the user on the property page. The contents of this provided **Dictionary** object are also stored in the database.

This method is called immediately before the **Execute** method of the **IPipelineComponent** interface at run time, when the server is ready to send a document to the component. Data stored during design time from autoconfiguration or from property-page updates is passed to the component to allow for property setup prior to calling the **Execute** method.

Components validate the properties provided in the **SetConfigData** method and raise an error if any of the properties are invalid or missing.

Requirements

Windows NT/2000: Requires Windows 2000 SP1 or later
Library: Use Microsoft Commerce 2000 Default Pipeline Components Type Library (pipecomplib.tlb)

SchemaImporter Object

Use this object to handle the importing of DTDs, XDRs, and well-formed XML documents.

The properties of the **SchemaImporter** object are shown in the following table.

Property	Description
ImportFormatDescription	Returns descriptive text about a supported import format.
ImportFormatIcon	Returns an icon for a supported import format.
NumberOfSupportedImportFormats	Returns the number of supported data formats from which a schema can be extracted.

The method of the **SchemaImporter** object is shown in the following table.

Method	Description
ExtractXMLSchema	Extracts a schema from a document.

Requirements

Windows NT/2000: Requires Windows 2000 SP1 or later
Library: Use Microsoft BizTalk Server Import Extension Module 1.0 Type Library (ExtensionMod.dll)

SchemaImporter.ExtractXMLSchema Method

The **ExtractXMLSchema** method extracts a schema from a document.

Syntax

object.**ExtractXMLSchema**(_
   lFormatIndex **As Long**, _
   bstrDocumentPath **As String** _
)

Parameters

lFormatIndex
   Index value that specifies the type of document from which to import the schema. Pass in 0 to import well-formed XML, 1 to import a document type definition (DTD), or 2 to import an XDR schema.

bstrDocumentPath
   Path to the document from which to import the schema.

Return Values

This method returns an **Object** that contains information about the extracted XML schema.

Error Value

If an error is raised, **Err.Number** is set to one of the values documented in Appendix A, "Error Messages."

Requirements

Windows NT/2000: Requires Windows 2000 SP1 or later
Library: Use Microsoft BizTalk Server Import Extension Module 1.0 Type Library (ExtensionMod.dll)

SchemaImporter.ImportFormatDescription Property

The **ImportFormatDescription** property returns descriptive text about a supported import format.

Syntax

object.**ImportFormatDescription**(_
   lFormatIndex **As Long** _
)

Parameters

lFormatIndex

Index value that specifies the type of document from which to import the schema. Pass in 0 to import well-formed XML, 1 to import a document type definition (DTD), or 2 to import an XDR schema.

Return Values

This property returns a **String** that contains a textual description of the input document format.

Error Value

If an error is raised, **Err.Number** is set to one of the values documented in Appendix A, "Error Messages."

Remarks

This is a read-only property.

Requirements

Windows NT/2000: Requires Windows 2000 SP1 or later
Library: Use Microsoft BizTalk Server Import Extension Module 1.0 Type Library
(ExtensionMod.dll)

ISchemaImporter.ImportFormatIcon Property

The **ImportFormatIcon** property returns an icon for a supported import format.

Syntax

object.**ImportFormatIcon(** _
    lFormatIndex **As Long** _
)

Parameters

lFormatIndex

Index value that specifies the type of document from which to import the schema. Pass in 0 to import well-formed XML, 1 to import a document type definition (DTD), or 2 to import an XDR schema.

Return Values

This property returns a **Long** that is the icon identifier for the input format.

Error Value

If an error is raised, **Err.Number** is set to one of the values documented in Appendix A, "Error Messages."

Remarks

This is a read only-property.

Requirements

Windows NT/2000: Requires Windows 2000 SP1 or later
Library: Use Microsoft BizTalk Server Import Extension Module 1.0 Type Library (ExtensionMod.dll)

SchemaImporter.NumberOfSupportedImportFormats Property

The **NumberOfSupportedImportFormats** property returns the number of supported data formats from which a schema can be extracted.

Syntax

object.**NumberOfSupportedImportFormats**

Parameters

None

Return Values

This property returns a **Long** that contains the number of supported import formats.

Error Value

If an error is raised, **Err.Number** is set to one of the values documented in Appendix A, "Error Messages."

Remarks

This is a read-only property.

Requirements

Windows NT/2000: Requires Windows 2000 SP1 or later
Library: Use Microsoft BizTalk Server Import Extension Module 1.0 Type Library (ExtensionMod.dll)

SchemaImporterError Object

Use this object to identify and decipher errors or warnings.

The properties of the **SchemaImporterError** object are shown in the following table.

Property	Description
IsWarning	Returns a value that identifies the object as an error or a warning.
NodePath	Returns the path to the node that generated the error or warning.
Text	Returns the error or warning message.

Requirements

Windows NT/2000: Requires Windows 2000 SP1 or later
Library: Use Microsoft BizTalk Server Import Extension Module 1.0 Type Library
(ExtensionMod.dll)

SchemaImporterError.IsWarning Property

The **IsWarning** property returns a value that identifies the object as an error or a warning.

Syntax

object.**IsWarning**

Parameters

None

Return Values

This property returns a **Boolean** value. Set to **True** if the object is a warning; otherwise, set to
False to indicate that the object is an error.

Error Value

If an error is raised, **Err.Number** is set to one of the values documented in Appendix A,
"Error Messages."

Remarks

This is a read-only property.

Requirements

Windows NT/2000: Requires Windows 2000 SP1 or later
Library: Use Microsoft BizTalk Server Import Extension Module 1.0 Type Library
(ExtensionMod.dll)

SchemaImporterError.NodePath Property

The **NodePath** property returns the path to the node that generated the error or warning.

Syntax

object.**NodePath**

Parameters

None

Return Values

This property returns a **String** that is the fully qualified name of the node that generated the error or warning.

Error Value

If an error is raised, **Err.Number** is set to one of the values documented in Appendix A,
"Error Messages."

Remarks

This is a read-only property.

Requirements

Windows NT/2000: Requires Windows 2000 SP1 or later
Library: Use Microsoft BizTalk Server Import Extension Module 1.0 Type Library
(ExtensionMod.dll)

SchemaImporterError.Text Property

The **Text** property returns the error or warning message.

Syntax

object.**Text**

Parameters

None

Return Values

This property returns a **String** that is the text associated with the error or warning.

Error Value

If an error is raised, **Err.Number** is set to one of the values documented in Appendix A, "Error Messages."

Remarks

This is a read-only property.

Requirements

Windows NT/2000: Requires Windows 2000 SP1 or later
Library: Use Microsoft BizTalk Server Import Extension Module 1.0 Type Library
(ExtensionMod.dll)

SchemaImporterErrorProvider Object

Use this object to return errors or warnings.

The properties of the **SchemaImporterErrorProvider** object are shown in the following table.

Property	Description
Error	Returns the error or warning.
NumberOfErrors	Returns the number of errors or warnings.

Requirements

Windows NT/2000: Requires Windows 2000 SP1 or later
Library: Use Microsoft BizTalk Server Import Extension Module 1.0 Type Library
(ExtensionMod.dll)

SchemaImporterErrorProvider.Error Property

The **Error** property returns the error or warning.

Syntax

object.**Error**(_
    lIndex **As Long** _
)

Parameters

lIndex
    Index of the required error or warning.

Return Values

This property returns a **SchemaImporterError** object that contains the error or warning.

Error Value

If an error is raised, **Err.Number** is set to one of the values documented in Appendix A, "Error Messages."

Remarks

This is a read-only property.

Requirements

Windows NT/2000: Requires Windows 2000 SP1 or later
Library: Use Microsoft BizTalk Server Import Extension Module 1.0 Type Library
(ExtensionMod.dll)

SchemaImporterErrorProvider.NumberOfErrors Property

The **NumberOfErrors** property returns the number of errors or warnings.

Syntax

object.**NumberOfErrors**

Parameters

None

Return Values

This property returns a **Long** that indicates the number of errors.

Error Value

If an error is raised, **Err.Number** is set to one of the values documented in Appendix A, "Error Messages."

Remarks

This is a read-only property.

Requirements

Windows NT/2000: Requires Windows 2000 SP1 or later
Library: Use Microsoft BizTalk Server Import Extension Module 1.0 Type Library
(ExtensionMod.dll)

Related Topics

"How Receipts Are Logged" in Chapter 13, "Tracking Documents"

"Understanding Receipts" in Chapter 9, "Configuring BizTalk Messaging Services"

Creating Custom Components Reference for C++

This section provides reference information about components and interfaces used by Microsoft BizTalk Server 2000 for Microsoft Visual C++ programming. Reference information is provided for all interfaces exposed for extending BizTalk Server 2000.

IBizTalkAcknowledge Interface

Use this object to process receipts sent to the server.

Use the **IBizTalkAcknowledge** interface to access the methods of the **BizTalkAcknowledge** object.

The methods of the **BizTalkAcknowledge** object are shown in the following table.

Method	Description
AckDocument	Processes receipts received for documents.
AckGroup	Processes receipts received for document groups.
AckInterchange	Processes receipts received for document interchanges.

Requirements

Windows NT/2000: Requires Windows 2000 SP1 or later
Header: Include BTSDocTracking.h

IBizTalkAcknowledge::AckDocument Method

The **AckDocument** method processes receipts for documents.

Syntax

HRESULT AckDocument(
    BSTR *bstrSyntax,*
    BSTR *bstrTrackingId,*
    DTA_ACK_STATUS *enumAckStatus*
);

Parameters

bstrSyntax
    [in] **BSTR** that contains the syntax of the outbound document to be acknowledged, for example, X12 or EDIFACT.

bstrTrackingId
    [in] **BSTR** that contains the unique tracking identifier of the document. This value is a globally unique identifier (GUID). This value can be obtained from the Tracking_ID field in the dta_outdoc_details table. For more information, see "Supporting the Tracking Database with Parser and Serializer Components" earlier in this chapter.

enumAckStatus
    [in] Enumeration value that indicates the receipt status. Valid values are from the **DTA_ACK_STATUS** enumeration.

Return Values

For a list of all error messages returned by BizTalk Server, see Appendix A, "Error Messages."

Remarks

This method is called only for receipts on individual documents. If the receipt must be mapped, a document definition that points to the CanonicalReceipt.xml file (available in the WebDAV repository) must be created for the receipt.

Requirements

Windows NT/2000: Requires Windows 2000 SP1 or later
Header: Include BTSDocTracking.h

IBizTalkAcknowledge::AckGroup Method

The **AckGroup** method processes receipts for document groups.

Syntax

HRESULT AckGroup(
    BSTR *bstrSyntax,*
    BSTR *bstrVersion,*
    BSTR *bstrRelease,*
    BSTR *bstrFunctionalGroupId,*
    BSTR *bstrControlId,*
    BSTR *bstrSrcAppName,*
    BSTR *bstrDestAppName,*
    DTA_ACK_STATUS *enumAckStatus*
);

Parameters

bstrSyntax
> [in] **BSTR** that contains the syntax of the outbound document to be acknowledged, for example, X12 or EDIFACT. You must use the exact strings for the following syntax types:

> - x12

> - edifact

> - custom xml

bstrVersion
> [in] **BSTR** that contains the version of the syntax, used primarily for EDI.

bstrRelease
> [in] **BSTR** that contains the release of the version of the syntax, used primarily for EDI.

bstrFunctionalGroupId
> [in] **BSTR** that contains the code for the type of documents in a group, used primarily for EDI.

bstrControlId
> [in] **BSTR** that contains the unique identifier for the control number, used primarily for EDI.

bstrSrcAppName
> [in] **BSTR** that contains the name of the source application.

bstrDestAppName
> [in] **BSTR** that contains the name of the destination application.

enumAckStatus
> [in] Enumeration value that indicates the receipt status. Valid values are from the **DTA_ACK_STATUS** enumeration.

Return Values

For a list of all error messages returned by BizTalk Server, see Appendix A, "Error Messages."

Remarks

This method is called only for receipts on document groups.

Requirements

Windows NT/2000: Requires Windows 2000 SP1 or later
Header: Include BTSDocTracking.h

IBizTalkAcknowledge::AckInterchange Method

The **AckInterchange** method processes receipts for document interchanges.

Syntax

HRESULT AckInterchange(
    BSTR *bstrSyntax,*
    BSTR *bstrInterchangeId,*
    BSTR *bstrVersion,*
    BSTR *bstrControlId,*
    BSTR *bstrSrcAliasQualifier,*
    BSTR *bstrSrcAliasId,*
    BSTR *bstrSrcAppName,*
    BSTR *bstrDestAliasQualifier,*
    BSTR *bstrDestAliasId,*
    BSTR *bstrDestAppName,*
    DTA_ACK_STATUS *enumAckStatus*
);

Parameters

bstrSyntax
    [in] **BSTR** that contains the syntax of the outbound document to be acknowledged, for example, X12 or EDIFACT. You must use the exact strings for the following syntax types:

- X12

- EDIFACT

- Custom XML

bstrInterchangeId
    [in] **BSTR** that contains the unique tracking identifier of the interchange. This value is a globally unique identifier (GUID).

bstrVersion

[in] **BSTR** that contains the version of the syntax, used primarily for EDI.

bstrControlId

[in] **BSTR** that contains the unique identifier for the control number, used primarily for EDI.

bstrSrcAliasQualifier

[in] **BSTR** that contains the qualifier of the source organization. This value indicates how the *bstrSrcAliasId* parameter is to be interpreted. Valid values come from the organization identifier qualifiers that are created when the user creates an alias for an organization. Common qualifiers include the DUNS number, telephone number, and BizTalk. The default qualifier for all new organizations is *Organization Name* and refers to the name of the organization in the database. If a BizTalk Framework 2.0–compliant document is submitted and a qualifier is not found during parsing, the qualifier defaults to *BizTalk*.

bstrSrcAliasId

[in] **BSTR** that contains the value of the qualifier of the source organization. For example, if the *bstrSrcAliasQualifier* parameter is Telephone, this value is the telephone number.

bstrSrcAppName

[in] **BSTR** that contains the name of the source application.

bstrDestAliasQualifier

[in] **BSTR** that contains the qualifier of the source organization. This value indicates how the *bstrDestAliasId* parameter is to be interpreted. Valid values come from the organization identifier qualifiers that are created when the user creates an alias for an organization. Common qualifiers include the DUNS number, telephone number, and BizTalk. The default qualifier for all new organizations is *Organization Name* and refers to the name of the organization in the database. If a BizTalk Framework 2.0–compliant document is submitted and a qualifier is not found during parsing, the qualifier defaults to *BizTalk*.

bstrDestAliasId

[in] **BSTR** that contains the value of the qualifier of the source organization. For example, if the *bstrDestAliasQualifier* parameter is Telephone, this value is the telephone number.

bstrDestAppName

[in] **BSTR** that contains the name of the destination application.

enumAckStatus

[in] Enumeration value that indicates the receipt status. Valid values are from the **DTA_ACK_STATUS** enumeration.

Return Values

For a list of all error messages returned by BizTalk Server, see Appendix A, "Error Messages."

Remarks

This method is called only for receipts on document interchanges.

Requirements

Windows NT/2000: Requires Windows 2000 SP1 or later
Header: Include BTSDocTracking.h

IBizTalkCorrelation Interface

Implement **IBizTalkCorrelation** to create receipt correlator components.

The method of the **BizTalkCorrelation** object is shown in the following table.

Method	Description
Correlate	Extracts all relevant information from the document, document group, or interchange.

✒ Note

- This interface is not available in Microsoft Visual Basic.

Requirements

Windows NT/2000: Requires Windows 2000 SP1 or later
Header: Include BTSParserComps.h

IBizTalkCorrelation::Correlate Method

The **Correlate** method extracts all relevant information from the document, document group, or interchange.

Syntax

HRESULT Correlate(
   IUnknown* *Acknowledge,*
   IDictionary* *Dict*
);

Parameters

Acknowledge
   [in] Pointer to the **IBizTalkAcknowledge** interface to invoke and set the receipt flag.

Dict
   [in] Pointer to an **IDictionary** interface of an object that contains the receipt information.

Return Values

For a list of all error messages returned by BizTalk Server, see Appendix A, "Error Messages."

Requirements

Windows NT/2000: Requires Windows 2000 SP1 or later
Header: Include BTSParserComps.h

IFunctoid Interface

In C++, implement the **IFunctoid** interface to create custom mapping functions. The **IFunctoid** interface defines the generic protocol for calling custom functions used by the mapping tool.

This object must register its class identifier (CLSID) under a well-known category identifier (CATID) of the function objects enumerated by the mapping tool. The CATID is {2560F3BF-DB47-11D2-B3AE-00C04F72D6C1}. Each custom object can support multiple functions and can contain icons and names for each supported function.

Function identifiers from 0 to 1000 are reserved for built-in functions in BizTalk Mapper. User-defined functions (custom functions) should use function identifiers 1001 and higher.

The properties of the **CannedFunctoid** object are shown in the following table.

Property	Description
FunctionsCount	Returns the number of functions implemented by the functoid.
Version	Returns the version of the functoid.

The methods of the **CannedFunctoid** object are shown in the following table.

Method	Description
GetFunctionParameter	Retrieves the connection-type bit flags for the specified parameter.
GetFunctionDescripter	Retrieves information about a specific functoid.
GetScriptBuffer	Retrieves the script code used to implement the functoid.

Requirements

Windows NT/2000: Requires Windows 2000 SP1 or later
Header: Include CannedFunctoid.h

IFunctoid::FunctionsCount Property

The **FunctionsCount** property returns the number of functions implemented by the functoid.

Syntax

HRESULT get_FunctionsCount(
    long* *plCount*
);

Parameters

plCount
    [out, retval] Pointer to a **long** that contains the number of functions implemented by the functoid.

Return Values

For a list of all error messages returned by BizTalk Server, see Appendix A, "Error Messages."

Remarks

This is a read-only property.

Requirements

Windows NT/2000: Requires Windows 2000 SP1 or later
Header: Include CannedFunctoid.h

IFunctoid::GetFunctionDescripter Method

The **GetFunctionDescripter** method retrieves information about a specific functoid.

Syntax

HRESULT GetFunctionDescripter(
    long *lIndex,*
    FUNC_CATEGORY* *pFuncCategory,*
    SCRIPT_CATEGORY* *pScriptCategory,*
    FUNC_TYPE* *pFuncType,*
    BSTR* *pbstrName,*
    BSTR* *pbstrToolTip,*
    long* *plBitmapID,*
    long* *plParmCount,*
    FUNCID* *pFuncId*
);

Parameters

lIndex
    [in] **Long** that specifies the index number of the function.

pFuncCategory
    [in, out] Pointer to a value that contains the **FUNC_CATEGORY** bit flags for this function.

pScriptCategory

[in, out] Pointer to a value that contains the **SCRIPT_CATEGORY** bit flags for this function. This value must be set to **SCRIPT_CATEGORY_VBSCRIPT** for this release.

pFuncType

[in, out] Pointer to a value that contains the **FUNC_TYPE** bit flags for this function.

pbstrName

[in, out] Pointer to a **BSTR** that contains the function name.

pbstrToolTip

[in, out] Pointer to a **BSTR** that contains the ToolTip that appears when the mouse pointer is paused over the custom functoid icon in the mapping tool.

plBitmapID

[in, out] Pointer to the **long** bitmap identifier of the bitmap used for the custom functoid icon displayed in the mapping tool.

plParmCount

[in, out] Pointer to a **long** that contains the number of parameters implemented by the function.

pFuncId

[out, retval] Pointer to a **long** that contains the function identifier.

Return Values

For a list of all error messages returned by BizTalk Server, see Appendix A, "Error Messages."

Requirements

Windows NT/2000: Requires Windows 2000 SP1 or later
Header: Include CannedFunctoid.h

IFunctoid::GetFunctionParameter Method

The **GetFunctionParameter** method retrieves the connection-type bit flags for the specified parameter.

Syntax

HRESULT GetFunctionParameter(
  FUNCID *funcId,*
  long *lParameter,*
  long* *plConnectionType*
);

Parameters

funcId
> [in] **Long** that contains the function identifier.

lParameter
> [in] **Long** that contains the function parameter number. For output parameters, a value of -1 is used.

plConnectionType
> [out, retval] Pointer to a **long** that contains the **CONNECTION_TYPE** bit flags for the specified parameter.

Return Values

For a list of all error messages returned by BizTalk Server, see Appendix A, "Error Messages."

Remarks

This is a read-only property.

Requirements

Windows NT/2000: Requires Windows 2000 SP1 or later
Header: Include CannedFunctoid.h

IFunctoid::GetScriptBuffer Method

The **GetScriptBuffer** method retrieves the script code used to implement the functoid.

Syntax

Get method:

HRESULT GetScriptBuffer(
> **FUNCID** *cFuncId*,
> **long** *lInputParameters*,
> **BSTR*** *pbstrScriptBuffer*
);

Parameters

cFuncId
> [in] **Long** that contains the function identifier.

lInputParameters
> [in] **Long** that indicates the number of connected input parameters for the specified function.

pbstrScriptBuffer
> [out, retval] Pointer to a **BSTR** that contains the script code used to implement the function.

Return Values

For a list of all error messages returned by BizTalk Server, see Appendix A, "Error Messages."

Remarks

This is a read-only property.

Requirements

Windows NT/2000: Requires Windows 2000 SP1 or later
Header: Include CannedFunctoid.h

IFunctoid::Version Property

The **Version** property returns the version of the functoid.

Syntax

HRESULT get_Version(
    long* *pVersion*
);

Parameters

pVersion
    [out, retval] Pointer to a **long** that contains the custom functoid version.

Return Values

For a list of all error messages returned by BizTalk Server, see Appendix A, "Error Messages."

Remarks

This is a read-only property.

If the custom functoid is modified in any way, the author should update the version number.

Requirements

Windows NT/2000: Requires Windows 2000 SP1 or later
Header: Include CannedFunctoid.h

IBizTalkParserComponent Interface

Use this object to convert a document to XML for later processing and to identify the **BizTalkChannel** objects necessary to process the documents.

Use the **IBizTalkParserComponent** interface to access the methods of the **BizTalkParserComponent** object.

The methods of the **BizTalkParserComponent** object are shown in the following table.

Method	Description
GetGroupDetails	Gets details of the group for the Tracking database. This method is called only if there are groups in the interchange.
GetGroupSize	Gets the size of the group after all documents in the group are parsed. This method is called only if there are groups in the interchange.
GetInterchangeDetails	Gets information about the organization identifiers of the source and destination **BizTalkOrganization** objects.
GetNativeDocumentOffsets	Identifies offsets from the beginning of the stream for final details about the group in the Tracking database for final logging.
GetNextDocument	Examines the data in a document and determines when to get the next document if this is not the last document.
GroupsExist	Determines if the interchange contains groups.
ProbeInterchangeFormat	Identifies the format of the interchange.

Remarks

Application integration components must be properly registered so that they are recognized by BizTalk Server 2000. Application integration components register with the category ID **CATID_BIZTALK_AIC**. The CATIDs are defined in the bts_sdk_guids.h file. For more information, see "Registering Application Integration Components" earlier in this chapter.

Note

- This interface is not available in Microsoft Visual Basic.

Requirements

Windows NT/2000: Requires Windows 2000 SP1 or later
Header: Include BTSParserComps.h

IBizTalkParserComponent::GetGroupDetails Method

The **GetGroupDetails** method gets details of the group for the Tracking database.

Syntax

HRESULT GetGroupDetails(
    IDictionary* *Dict*
);

Parameters

Dict
    [in] Pointer to an **IDictionary** interface of an object that contains details about the group. All information is returned as string types, no matter how it appears in the data.

Return Values

For a list of all error messages returned by BizTalk Server, see Appendix A, "Error Messages."

Remarks

This method is called only if groups are detected in the interchange.

Requirements

Windows NT/2000: Requires Windows 2000 SP1 or later
Header: Include BTSParserComps.h

IBizTalkParserComponent::GetGroupSize Method

The **GetGroupSize** method gets the size of the group after all documents in the group are parsed.

Syntax

HRESULT GetGroupSize(
    long* *GroupSize*,
    BOOL* *LastGroup*
);

Parameters

GroupSize
    [out] Pointer to a **long** that contains the size of the interchange.

LastGroup
> [out] Pointer to a Boolean value that indicates whether the group is the last group in the interchange. If this parameter is set to TRUE, the next method called is **GetGroupDetails** for the next group in the data. If it is set to FALSE, the component is finished. When it is released, it leaves the **IStream** interface after the last byte it has read.

Return Values

For a list of all error messages returned by BizTalk Server, see Appendix A, "Error Messages."

Remarks

After all documents in the group are called, the final details about the group are required. Both output parameters are added to the Tracking database for final logging.

This method is called only if there are groups in the interchange.

Requirements

Windows NT/2000: Requires Windows 2000 SP1 or later
Header: Include BTSParserComps.h

IBizTalkParserComponent::GetInterchangeDetails Method

The **GetInterchangeDetails** method gets information about the organization identifiers of the source and destination **BizTalkOrganization** objects.

Syntax

HRESULT GetInterchangeDetails(
    IDictionary* *Dict*
);

Parameters

Dict
> [in] Pointer to an **IDictionary** interface of an object that contains information about the organization identifiers of the source and destination **BizTalkOrganization** objects.

Return Values

For a list of all error messages returned by BizTalk Server, see Appendix A, "Error Messages."

Remarks

The minimum sets of fields are:

Field	Description
src_id_type	Source qualifier
src_id_value	Source ID
dest_id_type	Destination qualifier
dest_id_value	Destination ID

The parameters of the **Submit** method of the **IInterchange** interface override any fields set here.

Requirements

Windows NT/2000: Requires Windows 2000 SP1 or later
Header: Include BTSParserComps.h

IBizTalkParserComponent::GetNativeDocumentOffsets Method

The **GetNativeDocumentOffsets** method identifies offsets from the beginning of the stream for final details about the group in the Tracking database for final logging.

Syntax

HRESULT GetNativeDocumentOffsets(
  BOOL *SizeFromXMLDoc*,
  LARGE_INTEGER* *StartOffset*,
  long* *DocLength*
);

Parameters

SizeFromXMLDoc
  [out] Boolean value that indicates the XML document passed in from the **GetNextDocument** method was used to determine the size. If this parameter is TRUE, the server fills in the *StartOffset* and *DocLength* values for the document just parsed. If this parameter is FALSE, the server ignores the values in *StartOffset* and *DocLength*.

StartOffset
  [out] Pointer to a **LARGE_INTEGER** that contains the location of the beginning of the document. This parameter is returned if the *SizeFromXMLDoc* parameter is set to TRUE.

DocLength

[out] Pointer to a **long** that contains the length of the document. This parameter is returned if the *SizeFromXMLDoc* parameter is set to TRUE.

Return Values

For a list of all error messages returned by BizTalk Server, see Appendix A, "Error Messages."

Remarks

This method is called immediately after the **GetNextDocument** method whether or not the document is valid (as long as the parser does not return an error value). These are offsets into the **IStream** object relative to the beginning of the stream, not the beginning of the interchange.

Requirements

Windows NT/2000: Requires Windows 2000 SP1 or later
Header: Include BTSParserComps.h

IBizTalkParserComponent::GetNextDocument Method

The **GetNextDocument** method examines the data in a document and determines when to get the next document, if this is not the last document.

Syntax

HRESULT GetNextDocument(
    IDictionary* *Dict,*
    BSTR *DocSpecName,*
    BOOL* *DocIsValid,*
    BOOL* *LastDocument,*
    GeneratedReceiptLevel *ReceiptGenerated,*
    BOOL* *DocIsReceipt,*
    BSTR* *CorrelationCompProgID*
);

Parameters

Dict

[in] Pointer to an **IDictionary** interface of an object into which to set the XML instance created on parsing the current document. The parsed XML document is placed into the working_data field of the dictionary.

DocSpecName

[in] **BSTR** that contains the name of the BizTalk document specification used to generate the XML from the document's native format.

DocIsValid

[out] Pointer to a Boolean value that indicates whether the document instance is valid. If it is invalid but the parser can recover from it, set this parameter to FALSE. This parameter and the *LastDocument* parameter are independent. Therefore, if there are no more documents and the last one is invalid, both flags are set. If the document is invalid and the parser cannot continue, it might return an error value. The server then stops at the current position of the **IStream** pointer. The component places the invalid data (if the parser can recover) in the working_data field for inspection by the system administrator if the document is invalid.

LastDocument

[out] Pointer to a Boolean value that indicates whether this is the last document instance in the group or interchange. When the last document is found, the *LastDocument* flag is set to TRUE. If there are groups, this flag signals the last document in the group, and the **GetGroupSize** method is called. If there are no groups, this is the last call to get document data from the parser, and the **IStream** pointer is set appropriately.

ReceiptGenerated

Enumeration value. Valid values are from the **GeneratedReceiptLevel** enumeration.

DocIsReceipt

[out] Pointer to Boolean value that identifies whether or not this document is a receipt.

CorrelationCompProgID

[out] Pointer to a **BSTR** that contains the program ID for the correlation of documents.

Return Values

For a list of all error messages returned by BizTalk Server, see Appendix A, "Error Messages."

Requirements

Windows NT/2000: Requires Windows 2000 SP1 or later
Header: Include BTSParserComps.h

IBizTalkParserComponent::GroupsExist Method

The **GroupsExist** method determines whether the interchange contains groups.

Syntax

HRESULT GroupsExist(
    BOOL* *GrpsExist*
);

Parameters

GrpsExist

[out, retval] Pointer to a Boolean value that indicates whether the data format contains groups. If this parameter is set to FALSE, the **GetGroupDetails** and **GetGroupSize** methods are never called.

Return Values

For a list of all error messages returned by BizTalk Server, see Appendix A, "Error Messages."

Requirements

Windows NT/2000: Requires Windows 2000 SP1 or later
Header: Include BTSParserComps.h

IBizTalkParserComponent::ProbeInterchangeFormat Method

The **ProbeInterchangeFormat** method identifies the format of the interchange.

Syntax

HRESULT ProbeInterchangeFormat(
  IStream* *pData*,
  BOOL *FromFile*,
  BSTR *EnvName*,
  IStream* *pReceiptData*,
  BSTR* *Format*
);

Parameters

pData

[in] Pointer to the **IStream** object that contains the data for the document interchange. Additional information about the **IStream** object is available on the MSDN Online Library Web site (msdn.microsoft.com/library/default.asp).

FromFile

[in] Boolean value. TRUE indicates that the data came from the file referred to by the *FilePath* parameter of the **Submit** or the **SubmitSync** method of the **IInterchange** interface. FALSE indicates that the data came from the *Document* parameter of **Submit** or **SubmitSync** as a string. If the data is from a file, no conversion is made. If the data is a string, you can use UNICODE/MBCS techniques to understand it.

EnvName

[in] **BSTR** that contains the name of the envelope.

pReceiptData

[in] Pointer to the **IStream** object that contains the receipt document.

Format

[out] Pointer to a **BSTR** that contains the format. If the server recognizes the format, it must fill in this parameter with a nonempty string and hold on to (add a reference count to) the **IStream** interface because it is not given back to the component. This **IStream** object is read-only; it supports only the **Read**, **Stat**, and **Seek** methods. All other methods return E_NOTIMPL. This method should not return a failure if it does not recognize the format. It returns S_FALSE or an empty or NULL *Format* string. If you do not recognize the format, you do not need to move the **IStream** pointer back to its original position; the server resets the **IStream** pointer. Unless your format requires it, do not assume that the pointer is at the beginning. The pointer can be somewhere in the middle during the probing stage.

Return Values

For a list of all error messages returned by BizTalk Server, see Appendix A, "Error Messages."

Remarks

This is the first method that is called by the server. If **ProbeInterchangeFormat** returns an error in the middle of the document list, it blocks the server from detecting more document types, even if they could be handled by a custom parser that follows the failed parser, if there are two or more custom parsers on a server. If the first custom parser fails, any document that follows is not parsed, even if the other custom parser could handle it, because the server ends the entire parsing operation at the time of the failure.

Requirements

Windows NT/2000: Requires Windows 2000 SP1 or later
Header: Include BTSParserComps.h

IBizTalkSerializerComponent Interface

Use this object to convert a document from XML to the document's original native format.

Use the **IBizTalkSerializerComponent** interface to access the methods of the **BizTalkSerializerComponent** object.

The methods of the **BizTalkSerializerComponent** object are shown in the following table.

Method	Description
AddDocument	Adds an XML document for storage by the serializer component.
GetDocInfo	Gets details of the document.
GetGroupInfo	Gets details of the group, such as size and offset, for the Tracking database.
GetInterchangeInfo	Gets information about the interchange created.
Init	Outputs the document instance to the serializer component and indicates where it should be sent.

Remarks

Application integration components must be properly registered so that they are recognized by BizTalk Server 2000. Application integration components register with the category ID **CATID_BIZTALK_AIC**. The CATIDs are defined in the bts_sdk_guids.h file. For more information, see "Registering Application Integration Components" earlier in this chapter.

Note

- This interface is not available in Microsoft Visual Basic.

Requirements

Windows NT/2000: Requires Windows 2000 SP1 or later
Header: Include BTSSerializerComps.h

IBizTalkSerializerComponent::AddDocument Method

The **AddDocument** method adds an XML document for storage by the serializer component.

Syntax

HRESULT AddDocument(
    long *DocHandle,*
    IDictionary* *Transport,*
    BSTR *TrackID,*
    long *ChannelID*
);

Parameters

DocHandle

> [in] **Long** that contains the handle to the document that is stored by the component and later retrieved when calling the **GetDocInfo** method. This parameter supports out-of-order recreation of the interchange in case the documents need to be reordered (such as in X12).

Transport

> [in] Pointer to an **IDictionary** interface of an object that contains the XML document to be stored. It is on the working_data field. This parameter cannot be set by the component. This is an optional parameter.

TrackID

> [in] **BSTR** that contains the document tracking ID used by the server.

ChannelID

> [in] **Long** that contains the **BizTalkChannel** object associated with the current document.

Return Values

For a list of all error messages returned by BizTalk Server, see Appendix A, "Error Messages."

Remarks

This method is called only once per interchange.

Requirements

Windows NT/2000: Requires Windows 2000 SP1 or later
Header: Include BTSSerializerComps.h

IBizTalkSerializerComponent::GetDocInfo Method

The **GetDocInfo** method gets details of the document.

Syntax

HRESULT GetDocInfo(
  long* *DocHandle,*
  BOOL* *SizeFromXMLDoc,*
  LARGE_INTEGER* *DocStartOffset,*
  long* *DocLen*
);

Parameters

DocHandle

[out] Pointer to a **long** that contains the document handle. For each ID that is passed back, this address is assigned to the group record that was created when the **GetGroupInfo** method was called. This parameter also returns properties of the document, for example, size and length, unless the *SizeFromXMLDoc* parameter is set to TRUE, in which case the other parameters are ignored.

SizeFromXMLDoc

[out] Pointer to a Boolean value that indicates that the document offset and length values are retrieved from the XML document. If this parameter is TRUE, the server fills in the *DocStartOffset* and *DocLen* values for the document. If this parameter is FALSE, the server ignores the values in *DocStartOffset* and *DocLen*.

DocStartOffset

[out] Pointer to a **LARGE_INTEGER** that contains the offset to the beginning of the document. This parameter is returned if *SizeFromXMLDoc* is set to TRUE.

DocLen

[out] Pointer to a **long** that contains the length of the document. This parameter is returned if *SizeFromXMLDoc* is set to TRUE.

Return Values

For a list of all error messages returned by BizTalk Server, see Appendix A, "Error Messages."

Remarks

This method is called once for every document in a group (or interchange, if there are no groups).

Requirements

Windows NT/2000: Requires Windows 2000 SP1 or later
Header: Include BTSSerializerComps.h

IBizTalkSerializerComponent::GetGroupInfo Method

The **GetGroupInfo** method gets details of the group, such as size and offset, for the Tracking database.

Syntax

HRESULT GetGroupInfo(
  long* *NumDocs,*
  LARGE_INTEGER* *GrpStartOffset,*
  long* *GrpLen*
);

Parameters

NumDocs
> [out] Pointer to a **long** that contains the number of documents in the group.

GrpStartOffset
> [out] Pointer to a **LARGE_INTEGER** that contains the offset to the start of the group in the **IStream** interface.

GrpLen
> [out] Pointer to a **long** that contains the length of the group.

Return Values

For a list of all error messages returned by BizTalk Server, see Appendix A, "Error Messages."

Remarks

This method is called the number of times returned by the **GetInterchangeInfo** method. Call the **GetDocInfo** method for each document in the group.

Requirements

Windows NT/2000: Requires Windows 2000 SP1 or later
Header: Include BTSSerializerComps.h

IBizTalkSerializerComponent::GetInterchangeInfo Method

The **GetInterchangeInfo** method gets information about the interchange created.

Syntax

HRESULT GetInterchangeInfo(
> **BSTR*** *InterchangeID,*
> **long*** *lNumGroups*
);

Parameters

InterchangeID
> [out] Pointer to a **BSTR** that contains the interchange ID, which is placed in the Tracking database.

lNumGroups
> [out] Pointer to a **long** that contains the number of groups generated in the interchange. This can be either 0 or 1. A document can exist in only one group.

Return Values

For a list of all error messages returned by BizTalk Server, see Appendix A, "Error Messages."

Remarks

This method is called after all the documents are passed in.

Requirements

Windows NT/2000: Requires Windows 2000 SP1 or later
Header: Include BTSSerializerComps.h

IBizTalkSerializerComponent::Init Method

The **Init** method outputs the document instance to the serializer component and indicates its destination.

Syntax

HRESULT Init(
    BSTR *srcQual,*
    BSTR *srcID,*
    BSTR *destQual,*
    BSTR *destID,*
    long *EnvID,*
    IDictionary* *pDelimiters,*
    IStream* *OutputStream,*
    long *NumDocs*
);

Parameters

srcQual
    [in] **BSTR** that contains the source-organization identifier qualifier.

srcID
    [in] **BSTR** that contains the source-organization identifier value.

destQual
    [in] **BSTR** that contains the destination-organization identifier qualifier.

destID
    [in] **BSTR** that contains the destination-organization identifier value.

EnvID
    [in] **Long** that contains the envelope identifier value.

pDelimiters

> [in] Pointer to an **IDictionary** interface of an object that contains the delimiters used in the document.

OutputStream

> [in] Pointer to an **IStream** interface that contains the data of this document. This **IStream** pointer is write-only. The only methods that are supported are **Write** and **Stat**; all other methods return E_NOTIMPL. Additional information about the **IStream** object is available on the MSDN Online Library Web site (msdn.microsoft.com/library/default.asp).

NumDocs

> [in] **Long** that contains the number of documents sent as part of this interchange. For this release, this parameter is set to 1.

Return Values

For a list of all error messages returned by BizTalk Server, see Appendix A, "Error Messages."

Requirements

Windows NT/2000: Requires Windows 2000 SP1 or later
Header: Include BTSSerializerComps.h

IBTSAppIntegration Interface

Use this object to create an entry point for receiving a document.

Use the **IBTSAppIntegration** interface to access the methods of the **BTSAppIntegration** object.

The method of the **BTSAppIntegration** object is shown in the following table.

Method	Description
ProcessMessage	Processes the document.

Remarks

Application integration components must be properly registered so that they are recognized by BizTalk Server 2000. Application integration components register with the category ID **CATID_BIZTALK_AIC**. The CATIDs are defined in the bts_sdk_guids.h file. For more information, see "Registering Application Integration Components" earlier in this chapter.

Requirements

Windows NT/2000: Requires Windows 2000 SP1 or later
Header: Include btsaic.h

IBTSAppIntegration::ProcessMessage Method

The **ProcessMessage** method processes a document and returns a response document, if available. This method is called at run time when the server is sending a document to the component.

Syntax

HRESULT ProcessMessage(
  BSTR *bstrDocument*,
  BSTR* *pbstrResponseDocument*
);

Parameters

bstrDocument
  [in] **BSTR** that contains the document.

pbstrResponseDocument
  [retval, out] Pointer to a **BSTR** that contains the response document.

Return Values

For a list of all error messages returned by BizTalk Server, see Appendix A, "Error Messages."

Remarks

Components can return a response string to pass back a text-based response to an application, using the **SubmitSync** method of the **IInterchange** interface to send documents.

Components must raise an error if a problem with processing occurs so that the document can be retransmitted or sent to the Suspended queue. If no error is returned, the server assumes that the component successfully processed the data.

Requirements

Windows NT/2000: Requires Windows 2000 SP1 or later
Header: Include btsaic.h

IPipelineComponent Interface

Use this object to create custom pipeline components that can execute in Microsoft BizTalk Server 2000 to extend its functionality.

Use the **IPipelineComponent** interface to access the methods of the **PipelineComponent** object.

The methods of the **PipelineComponent** object are shown in the following table.

Method	Description
EnableDesign	Configures the component for execution in one of two modes: design mode or execution mode.
Execute	Executes the operation expected of the component, given the transport **Dictionary** object and other configuration settings.

Remarks

Application integration components must be properly registered so that they are recognized by BizTalk Server 2000. Application integration components register with the category ID **CATID_BIZTALK_AIC**. The CATIDs are defined in the bts_sdk_guids.h file. For more information, see "Registering Application Integration Components" earlier in this chapter.

Requirements

Windows NT/2000: Requires Windows 2000 SP1 or later
Header: Include pipecomp.h

IPipelineComponent::EnableDesign Method

The **EnableDesign** method configures the component for execution in one of two modes: design mode or execution mode.

Syntax

HRESULT EnableDesign(
    BOOL *fEnable*
);

Parameters

fEnable
    Boolean value that indicates the mode of the component. A value of TRUE specifies that the component runs in design mode. A value of FALSE (default) specifies execution mode.

Return Values

For a list of all error messages returned by BizTalk Server, see Appendix A, "Error Messages."

Remarks

The pipeline component runs in execution mode by default.

This method is called when the **Override messaging port defaults** page is opened in the Channel Wizard's **Advanced Configuration** page. It is also called when the property page is closed and the *fEnable* parameter is set to TRUE. Design mode is not enabled unless this method has been called with the *fEnable* parameter set to TRUE.

Design-only fields are returned only when the *fEnable* parameter is set to TRUE. Otherwise, the **Dictionary** object passed to the server contains unnecessary information.

Requirements

Windows NT/2000: Requires Windows 2000 SP1 or later
Header: Include pipecomp.h

IPipelineComponent::Execute Method

The **Execute** method executes the operation expected of the component, given the transport **Dictionary** object and other configuration settings. BizTalk Server 2000 calls this method, passing in the transport **Dictionary** object. The component can read these **Dictionary** object values, perform the necessary functions, and optionally write new values back to the transport **Dictionary** object for further processing.

Syntax

HRESULT Execute(
  IDispatch* *pDispOrder*,
  IDispatch* *pDispContext*,
  long *lFlags*,
  long* *plErrorLevel*
);

Parameters

pDispOrder
    [in] Pointer to the transport **Dictionary** object.

pDispContext
    [in] Not supported for this release.

lFlags
    [in] Reserved.

PlErrorLevel
    [out, retval] Reserved.

Return Values

For a list of all error messages returned by BizTalk Server, see Appendix A, "Error Messages."

Remarks

For a component designed to run in BizTalk Server 2000, the first parameter is a **Transport Dictionary** object. The **Transport Dictionary** values can be read by the component for processing. The string values supplied by the server for all application integration components (AICs) are as follows:

- Src_ID_Type: The type of identifier used for the source organization.

- Src_ID_Value: The value of the source organization identifier.

- Dest_ID_Type: The type of identifier used for the destination organization.

- Dest_ID_Value: The value of the destination organization identifier.

- Document_Name: The name of the input document definition.

- Tracking_ID: A key value that is based on the globally unique identifier (GUID) and used for tracking.

For a component that runs in a Commerce Server order-processing pipeline, the first parameter contains the **OrderForm** object.

This method is called at run time when the server is sending a document to the component. This method is called immediately after the **SetConfigData** method of the **IPipelineComponentAdmin** interface. The document is passed in the first parameter as a dictionary within the working_data field of the **Dictionary** object. Components can add the *ResponseField* key to the **Dictionary** object to pass back a text-based response to an application, using the **SubmitSync** method of the **IInterchange** interface.

The component must raise an error if a problem with processing occurs so that the server can retry transmission later and, after all retries, send the document to the Suspended queue. If no error is returned, the server assumes that the component successfully processed the data.

Requirements

Windows NT/2000: Requires Windows 2000 SP1 or later
Header: Include pipecomp.h

IPipelineComponentAdmin Interface

Use this object between the component and the component user interface.

Use the **IPipelineComponentAdmin** interface to access the methods of the **PipelineComponentAdmin** object.

The methods of the **PipelineComponentAdmin** object are shown in the following table.

Method	Description
GetConfigData	Returns a **Dictionary** object that contains the configuration data for the component for the user interface to display these values.
SetConfigData	Sets the configuration settings for a component, using the contents of a **Dictionary** object.

Remarks

Application integration components must be properly registered so that they are recognized by BizTalk Server 2000. Application integration components register with the category ID **CATID_BIZTALK_AIC**. The CATIDs are defined in the bts_sdk_guids.h file. For more information, see "Registering Application Integration Components" earlier in this chapter.

Requirements

Windows NT/2000: Requires Windows 2000 SP1 or later
Header: Include pipecomp.h

IPipelineComponentAdmin::GetConfigData Method

The **GetConfigData** method returns a **Dictionary** object that contains the configuration data for the component to be used to display these values. The **GetConfigData** method enables the user interface component to read the current value from the component and display it on the property page initially.

Syntax

HRESULT GetConfigData(
   IDispatch** *ppConfigDictionary*
);

Parameters

ppConfigDictionary
   [out, retval] Address of a pointer to a **Dictionary** object from which the user interface can read the configuration data.

Return Values

For a list of all error messages returned by BizTalk Server, see Appendix A, "Error Messages."

Remarks

When a **BizTalkPort** object is first saved, this method is called to get the defaults for use in autoconfiguring the application integration component (AIC) from the **Dictionary** object provided. Components must provide defaults for all mandatory properties, whenever possible.

This method is called when the user selects the property page. It is used to supply property page defaults. It is called again when the property page is closed. The contents of this returned **Dictionary** object are not used.

Components must always return a valid dictionary pointer from the **GetConfigData** method.

Requirements

Windows NT/2000: Requires Windows 2000 SP1 or later
Header: Include pipecomp.h

IPipelineComponentAdmin::SetConfigData Method

The **SetConfigData** method sets the configuration for a component, using the contents of a **Dictionary** object. With this method, the user interface can set or change these values. The **SetConfigData** method enables the user interface to write the updated value from the property page to the component.

Syntax

HRESULT SetConfigData(
   IDispatch* *pConfigDictionary*
);

Parameters

pConfigDictionary
   [in] Pointer to a **Dictionary** object that contains the configuration information.

Return Values

For a list of all error messages returned by BizTalk Server, see Appendix A, "Error Messages."

Remarks

The server calls the **SetConfigData** method when the property page is saved. It is used to verify the values entered by the user on the property page. The contents of this provided **Dictionary** object are also stored in the database.

This method is called immediately before the **Execute** method of the **IPipelineComponent** interface at run time, when the server is ready to send a document to the component. Data stored during design time from autoconfiguration or from property-page updates is passed to the component to allow for property setup prior to calling the **Execute** method.

Components validate the properties provided in the **SetConfigData** method and raise an error if any of the properties are invalid or missing.

Requirements
Windows NT/2000: Requires Windows 2000 SP1 or later
Header: Include pipecomp.h

ISchemaImporter Interface

Use this object to handle the importing of DTDs, XDRs, and well-formed XML documents.

Use the **ISchemaImporter** interface to access the properties and methods of the **SchemaImporter** object.

The properties of the **SchemaImporter** object are shown in the following table.

Property	Description
ImportFormatDescription	Returns descriptive text about a supported import format.
ImportFormatIcon	Returns an icon for a supported import format.
NumberOfSupportedImportFormats	Returns the number of supported data formats from which a schema can be extracted.

The method of the **SchemaImporter** object is shown in the following table.

Method	Description
ExtractXMLSchema	Extracts a schema from a document.

Requirements
Windows NT/2000: Requires Windows 2000 SP1 or later
Header: Include SchemaImporter.h

ISchemaImporter::ExtractXMLSchema Method

The **ExtractXMLSchema** method extracts a schema from a document.

Syntax
HRESULT ExtractXMLSchema(
   long *lFormatIndex*,
   BSTR *strDocumentPath*,
   IDispatch** *ppSchemaDOM*
);

Parameters

lFormatIndex

> [in] Index value that specifies the type of document from which to import the schema. Pass in 0 to import well-formed XML, 1 to import a document type definition (DTD), or 2 to import an XDR schema.

strDocumentPath

> [in] Path to the document from which to import the schema.

ppSchemaDOM

> [out, retval] Address of a pointer to an **IDispatch** interface that contains the extracted XML schema.

Return Values

For a list of all error messages returned by BizTalk Server, see Appendix A, "Error Messages."

Requirements

Windows NT/2000: Requires Windows 2000 SP1 or later
Header: Include SchemaImporter.h

ISchemaImporter::ImportFormatDescription Property

The **ImportFormatDescription** property returns descriptive text about a supported import format.

Syntax

HRESULT get_ImportFormatDescription(
> **long** *lFormatIndex*,
> **BSTR*** *ppbstrDescription*

);

Parameters

lFormatIndex

> [in] Index value that specifies the type of document from which to import the schema. Pass in 0 to import well-formed XML, 1 to import a document type definition (DTD), or 2 to import an XDR schema.

ppbstrDescription

> [out, retval] Pointer to a **BSTR** that contains a textual description of the input document format.

Return Values

For a list of all error messages returned by BizTalk Server, see Appendix A, "Error Messages."

Remarks

This is a read-only property.

Requirements

Windows NT/2000: Requires Windows 2000 SP1 or later
Header: Include SchemaImporter.h

ISchemaImporter::ImportFormatIcon Property

The **ImportFormatIcon** property returns an icon for a supported import format.

Syntax

HRESULT get_ImportFormatIcon(
　　long *lFormatIndex*,
　　long* *pIconID*

);

Parameters

lFormatIndex
　　[in] Index value that specifies the type of document from which to import the schema. Pass in 0 to import well-formed XML, 1 to import a document type definition (DTD), or 2 to import an XDR schema.

pIconID
　　[out, retval] Pointer to a **long** that contains the icon identifier for the input format.

Return Values

For a list of all error messages returned by BizTalk Server, see Appendix A, "Error Messages."

Remarks

This is a read only-property.

Requirements

Windows NT/2000: Requires Windows 2000 SP1 or later
Header: Include SchemaImporter.h

ISchemaImporter::NumberOfSupportedImportFormats Property

The **NumberOfSupportedImportFormats** property returns the number of supported data formats from which a schema can be extracted.

Syntax

HRESULT get_NumberOfSupportedImportFormats(
   long* *plNumber*

);

Parameters

plNumber
   [out, retval] Pointer to a **long** that indicates the number of supported import formats.

Return Values

For a list of all error messages returned by BizTalk Server, see Appendix A, "Error Messages."

Remarks

This is a read-only property.

Requirements

Windows NT/2000: Requires Windows 2000 SP1 or later
Header: Include SchemaImporter.h

ISchemaImporterError Interface

Use this object to identify and decipher errors or warnings.

Use the **ISchemaImporterError** interface to access the properties of the **SchemaImporterError** object.

The properties of the **SchemaImporterError** object are shown in the following table.

Property	Description
IsWarning	Returns a value that identifies the object as an error or a warning.
NodePath	Returns the path to the node that generated the error or warning.
Text	Returns the error or warning message.

Requirements

Windows NT/2000: Requires Windows 2000 SP1 or later
Header: Include SchemaImporter.h

ISchemaImporterError::IsWarning Property

The **IsWarning** property returns a value that identifies the object as an error or a warning.

Syntax

HRESULT get_IsWarning(
   VARIANT_BOOL* *pIsWarning*

);

Parameters

pIsWarning
   [out, retval] Set to **VARIANT_TRUE** if the object is a warning; otherwise, set to
   VARIANT_FALSE to indicate that the object is an error.

Return Values

For a list of all error messages returned by BizTalk Server, see Appendix A, "Error
Messages."

Remarks

This is a read-only property.

Requirements

Windows NT/2000: Requires Windows 2000 SP1 or later
Header: Include SchemaImporter.h

ISchemaImporterError::NodePath Property

The **NodePath** property returns the path to the node that generated the error or warning.

Syntax

HRESULT get_NodePath(
   BSTR* *pbstrNodePath*

);

Parameters

pbstrNodePath
> [out, retval] Pointer to a **BSTR** that contains the fully qualified name of the node that generated the error or warning.

Return Values

For a list of all error messages returned by BizTalk Server, see Appendix A, "Error Messages."

Remarks

This is a read-only property.

Requirements

Windows NT/2000: Requires Windows 2000 SP1 or later
Header: Include SchemaImporter.h

ISchemaImporterError::Text Property

The **Text** property returns the error or warning message.

Syntax

HRESULT get_Text(
   BSTR* *pbstrText*

);

Parameters

pbstrText
> [out, retval] Pointer to a **BSTR** that contains the text associated with the error or warning.

Return Values

For a list of all error messages returned by BizTalk Server, see Appendix A, "Error Messages."

Remarks

This is a read-only property.

Requirements

Windows NT/2000: Requires Windows 2000 SP1 or later
Header: Include SchemaImporter.h

ISchemaImporterErrorProvider Interface

Use this object to return errors or warnings.

Use the **ISchemaImporterErrorProvider** interface to access the properties of the **SchemaImporterErrorProvider** object.

The properties of the **SchemaImporterErrorProvider** object are shown in the following table.

Property	Description
Error	Returns the error or warning.
NumberOfErrors	Returns the number of errors or warnings.

Requirements

Windows NT/2000: Requires Windows 2000 SP1 or later
Header: Include SchemaImporter.h

ISchemaImporterErrorProvider::Error Property

The **Error** property returns the error or warning.

Syntax

HRESULT get_Error(
    long *lIndex*,
    ISchemaImporterError** *pdswError*

);

Parameters

lIndex
    [in] Index of the required error or warning.

pdswError
    [out, retval] Address of a pointer to an **ISchemaImporterError** interface that contains the error or warning.

Return Values

For a list of all error messages returned by BizTalk Server, see Appendix A, "Error Messages."

Remarks

This is a read-only property.

Requirements

Windows NT/2000: Requires Windows 2000 SP1 or later
Header: Include SchemaImporter.h

ISchemaImporterErrorProvider::NumberOfErrors Property

The **NumberOfErrors** property returns the number of errors or warnings.

Syntax

HRESULT get_NumberOfErrors(
    long* *plNumberOfErrors*

);

Parameters

plNumberOfErrors
    [out, retval] Pointer to a **long** that indicates the number of errors.

Return Values

For a list of all error messages returned by BizTalk Server, see Appendix A, "Error Messages."

Remarks

This is a read-only property.

Requirements

Windows NT/2000: Requires Windows 2000 SP1 or later
Header: Include SchemaImporter.h

Related Topics

"How Receipts Are Logged" in Chapter 13, "Tracking Documents"

"Identification" in Chapter 9, "Configuring BizTalk Messaging Services"

"Understanding Receipts" in Chapter 9, "Configuring BizTalk Messaging Services"

Custom Component Enumerations

The enumerations in this section provide the descriptions and possible values of properties and parameters used with extensible interfaces and objects in BizTalk Server 2000. These values are applicable when using either the Microsoft Visual Basic or Visual C++ programming languages.

Receipt Enumerations

The receipt enumerations provide possible values of properties and parameters for the **IBizTalkAcknowledge** interface.

DTA_ACK_STATUS

The **DTA_ACK_STATUS** enumeration has one of the following values.

Name	Value	Description
DTA_ACK_NONE	0	No receipt is expected.
DTA_ACK_PENDING	1	The receipt is expected but has not yet arrived.
DTA_ACK_OVERDUE	2	The receipt has timed out.
DTA_ACK_ACCEPTED	3	The receipt has arrived with a status of accepted.
DTA_ACK_PARTIALLY_ACCEPTED	4	The receipt has arrived with a status of accepted with errors.
DTA_ACK_REJECTED	5	The receipt has arrived with a status of rejected.

GeneratedReceiptLevel

The **GeneratedReceiptLevel** enumeration has one of the following values.

Name	Value	Description
NoReceiptGenerated	0	No receipt is created.
DocReceiptGenerated	1	A receipt is generated for each document.
GroupReceiptGenerated	2	A receipt is generated for each group.
InterchangeReceiptGenerated	3	A receipt is generated for each interchange.

Functoid Enumerations

The functoid enumerations provide possible values of properties and parameters for the IFunctoid interface.

CONNECTION_TYPE

The **CONNECTION_TYPE** enumeration defines the following values.

Name	Value	Description
CONNECT_TYPE_NONE	0	The connection type is none.
CONNECT_TYPE_FIELD	1	The connection type is field.
CONNECT_TYPE_RECORD	2	The connection type is record.
CONNECT_TYPE_RECORD_CONTENT	4	The connection type is record content.
CONNECT_TYPE_FUNC_STRING	8	The connection type function is string.
CONNECT_TYPE_FUNC_MATH	16	The connection type function is mathematical.
CONNECT_TYPE_FUNC_DATACONV	32	The connection type function is data conversion.
CONNECT_TYPE_FUNC_DATETIME_FMT	64	The connection type function is date/time format.
CONNECT_TYPE_FUNC_SCIENTIFIC	128	The connection type function is scientific.
CONNECT_TYPE_FUNC_BOOLEAN	256	The connection type function is Boolean.
CONNECT_TYPE_FUNC_SCRIPTER	512	The connection type function is script.
CONNECT_TYPE_FUNC_COUNT	1024	The connection type function is count.
CONNECT_TYPE_FUNC_INDEX	2048	The connection type function is index.
CONNECT_TYPE_FUNC_CUMULATIVE	4096	The connection type function is cumulative.
CONNECT_TYPE_FUNC_VALUE_MAPPING	8192	The connection type function is value mapping.
CONNECT_TYPE_FUNC_LOOPING	16384	The connection type function is looping.
CONNECT_TYPE_FUNC_ITERATION	32768	The connection type function is iteration.
CONNECT_TYPE_FUNC_DBLOOKUP	65536	The connection type function is database lookup.
CONNECT_TYPE_FUNC_DBEXTRACT	131072	The connection type function is database extraction.
CONNECT_TYPE_ALL	-1	The connection type includes all connection types.
CONNECT_TYPE_ALL_EXCEPT_RECORD	-3	The connection type includes all connection types except records.

FUNC_CATEGORY

The **FUNC_CATEGORY** enumeration defines the following values.

Name	Value	Description
FUNC_CATEGORY_STRING	3	The function category is string.
FUNC_CATEGORY_MATH	4	The function category is mathematical.
FUNC_CATEGORY_DATACONV	5	The function category is data conversion.
FUNC_CATEGORY_DATETIME_FMT	6	The function category is date/time format.
FUNC_CATEGORY_SCIENTIFIC	7	The function category is scientific.
FUNC_CATEGORY_BOOLEAN	8	The function category is Boolean.
FUNC_CATEGORY_SCRIPTER	9	The function category is script.
FUNC_CATEGORY_COUNT	10	The function category is count. This value is not supported for this release.
FUNC_CATEGORY_INDEX	11	The function category is index.
FUNC_CATEGORY_CUMULATIVE	12	The function category is cumulative.
FUNC_CATEGORY_VALUE_MAPPING	13	The function category is value mapping. This value is not supported for this release.
FUNC_CATEGORY_LOOPING	14	The function category is looping. This value is not supported for this release.
FUNC_CATEGORY_ITERATION	15	The function category is iteration. This value is not supported for this release.
FUNC_CATEGORY_DBLOOKUP	16	The function category is database lookup.
FUNC_CATEGORY_DBEXTRACT	17	The function category is database extraction.
FUNC_CATEGORY_UNKNOWN	31	The function category is unknown.

FUNC_TYPE

The **FUNC_TYPE** enumeration defines the following values.

Name	Value	Description
FUNC_TYPE_STD	1	The function type is standard.
FUNC_TYPE_VARIABLEINPUT	2	The function type is variable input.
FUNC_TYPE_SCRIPTOR	3	The function type is script.

SCRIPT_CATEGORY

The **SCRIPT_CATEGORY** enumeration defines the following values.

Name	Value	Description
SCRIPT_CATEGORY_VBSCRIPT	0	The custom functoid function is written in the Microsoft Visual Basic Scripting Edition (VBScript) language.
SCRIPT_CATEGORY_JSCRIPT	1	The custom functoid function is written in the Microsoft JScript® language. This value is not supported for this release.
SCRIPT_CATEGORY_XSLSCRIPT	2	The custom functoid function is written in the Extensible Stylesheet Language (XSL). This value is not supported for this release.

Part 6: Learning How to Use Microsoft BizTalk Server 2000

This part provides a quick overview of BizTalk Server features and detailed instructions on how to create organizations, document definitions, maps, channels, messaging ports, and XLANG schedules. By working through the tasks, you will gain a clear understanding of the flow and transformation of document data as it passes through various organizations. You can start with your own documents and data or take advantage of practice files available on the CD-ROM.

In This Part

- **BizTalk Server 2000 Tutorial.** This chapter provides step-by-step procedures to help you configure BizTalk Server to establish and run a business-to-business automated procurement process.

CHAPTER 16

Microsoft BizTalk Server 2000 Tutorial

In this tutorial you will learn how to configure Microsoft BizTalk Server 2000 to establish and run a business-to-business automated procurement process.

You will also learn how BizTalk Server components and services work together to integrate loosely coupled, long-running business processes, both within and between businesses.

In This Chapter

- Scenario

- Preliminary Setup

- Module 1: Modeling Business Processes

- Module 2: Creating Specifications and Maps

- Module 3: Configuring BizTalk Messaging Services

- Module 4: Completing the XLANG Schedule

- Tutorial Summary

- Creating Auxiliary Components

Scenario

The BizTalk Server 2000 Tutorial illustrates the core features and flexibility of BizTalk Server 2000. In each module, the Tutorial addresses topics crucial to understanding the basics of BizTalk Server and business-to-business operations. The Tutorial employs a buyer and a seller system to demonstrate the flow and transformation of document data as it passes through various organizations. ProElectron, Inc. is the name of the buyer system, and Bits, Bytes, and Chips, Inc. is the name of the seller system. These buyer and seller systems are set up by creating organizations, document definitions, maps, channels, messaging ports, and XLANG schedules in BizTalk Server 2000.

The name of the organization that represents the buyer system on the seller system is "ProElectron on Seller." In this case, the messaging port associated with "ProElectron on Seller" delivers documents through a channel from the seller system to the buyer system. Documents are routed by messaging ports, which use a selected transport service, such as HTTP, FILE, or an application integration component (AIC). Channels are used to process and transform the documents prior to being routed by the messaging ports.

In the Tutorial, the flow of data initiates when a purchase order (PO) request enters the buyer system. The buyer system places the PO request into a message queue, which triggers the XLANG schedule to begin processing. The PO request total is extracted and the order is either approved or denied, based on the amount of the request. If approved, the data is passed to a Windows Script Component that writes the data to a file. A File receive function accepts the PO request data and sends it through a channel for processing. The channel uses a map to transform the PO request into an actual PO document. The PO is routed by the messaging port associated with the channel to an ASP file that sends the document to the seller system.

On the seller system, the PO is processed by a channel and then routed by the messaging port to an application integration component (AIC) that generates an invoice document. The invoice is then processed by another channel and routed by a messaging port to an ASP file that sends the invoice to a message queue on the buyer system.

When the invoice is placed in the message queue on the buyer system, the XLANG schedule proceeds with sending the invoice data through a channel that uses a map to convert the invoice to a payment. To complete the transaction, the payment document is routed to a directory that represents the seller system by the messaging port.

The following illustration is an interaction diagram for the business-to-business automated procurement system implemented by ProElectron and Bits, Bytes, & Chips. Arrows denote the flow of data among roles and entities. For more information about interaction diagrams, see "Interaction Diagrams" in Chapter 8, "BizTalk Orchestration Services."

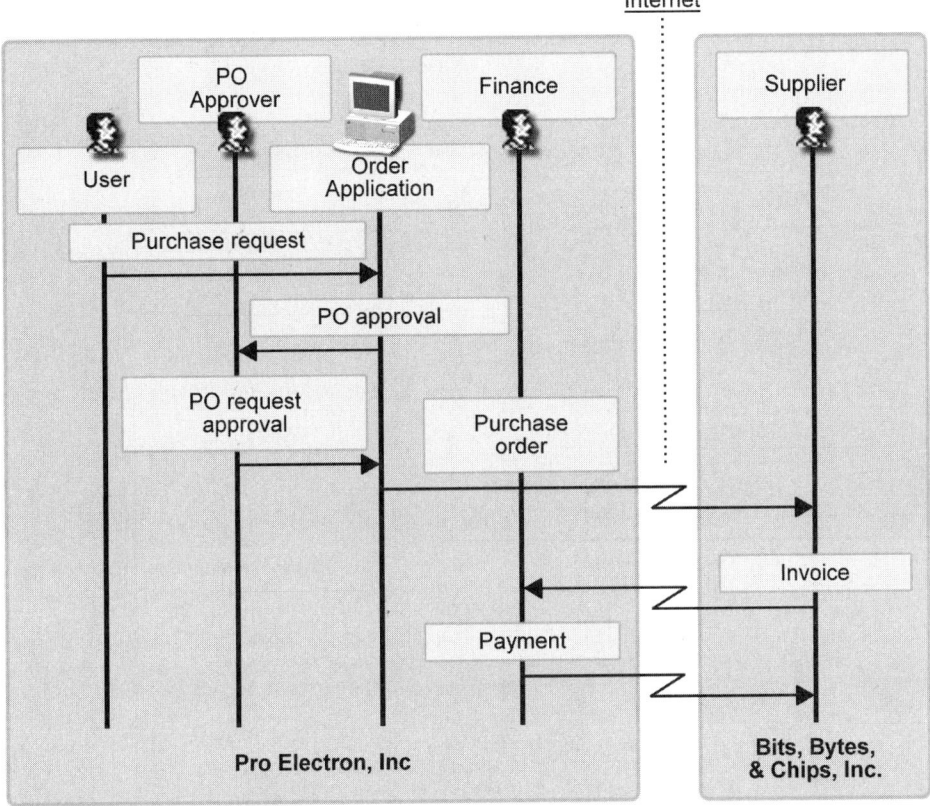

Important

- For the purposes of this scenario, both the buyer and seller systems are configured on a single installation of BizTalk Server 2000.

The following illustration shows the movement of the documents through the buyer and seller systems. It also shows the interaction between the XLANG schedule, BizTalk Messaging Services, and the auxiliary components. This illustration is a useful reference that you might want to print and have available as you work through the modules in this tutorial.

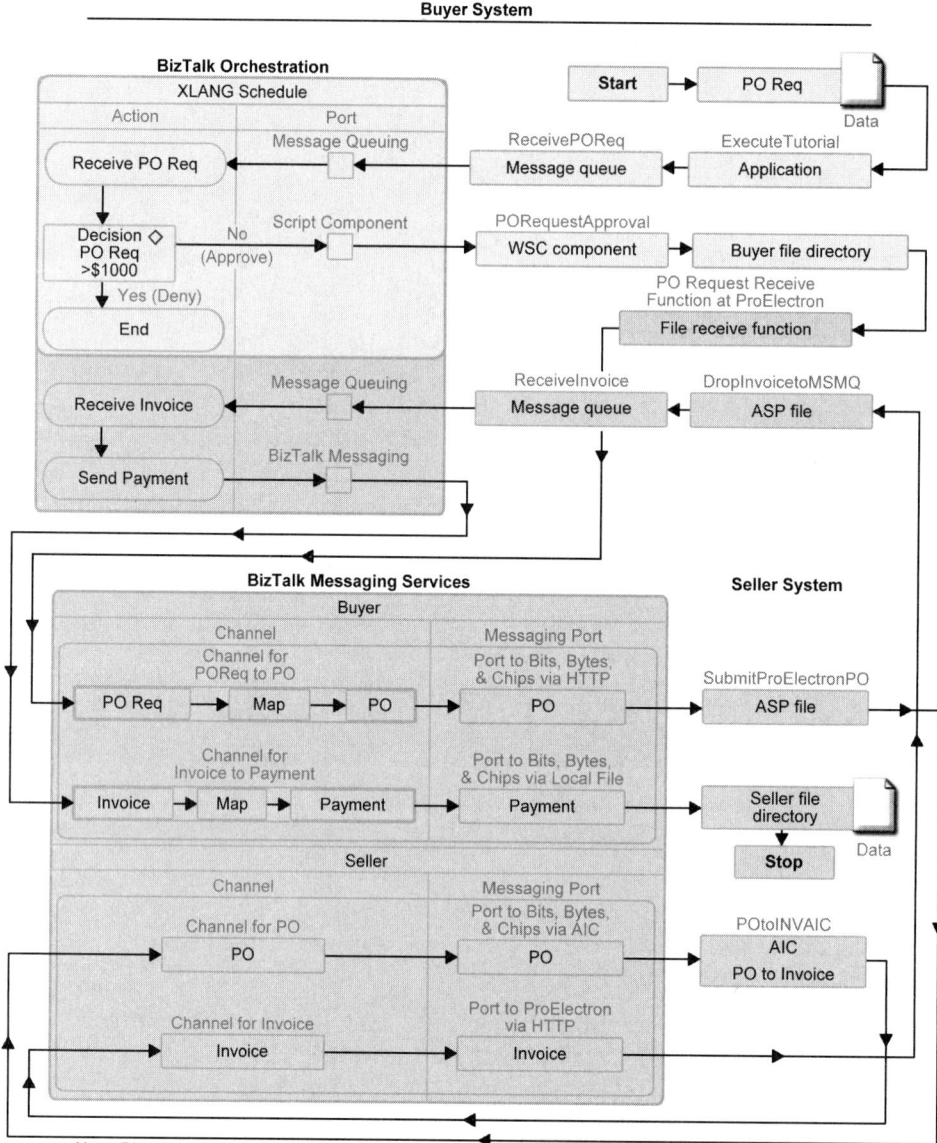

Note: Directional arrows denote flow of data.

Module Overview

Module 1: Modeling Business Processes

In this module, you learn how to:

- Use BizTalk Orchestration Designer to create an XLANG schedule drawing that models the procurement processes for ProElectron. For more information, see Chapter 8, "BizTalk Orchestration Services."
- Compile the XLANG schedule drawing into an XLANG schedule. For more information, see "To compile an XLANG schedule drawing into an XLANG schedule" in Chapter 8, "BizTalk Orchestration Services."
- Run the XLANG schedule to see how a message moves through the buyer system.

Module 2: Creating Specifications and Maps

In this module, you learn how to:

- Use BizTalk Editor to create document specifications. For more information, see Chapter 5, "Creating Specifications."
- Use BizTalk Mapper to create maps. For more information, see Chapter 6, "Mapping Data."

Module 3: Configuring BizTalk Messaging Services

In this module, you learn how to:

- Use BizTalk Messaging Manager to configure BizTalk Messaging Services for Bits, Bytes, and Chips. For more information, see "Using BizTalk Messaging Manager" in Chapter 9, "Configuring BizTalk Messaging Services."
- Use BizTalk Server Administration to create a File receive function for Bits, Bytes, and Chips. For more information, see "To add a File receive function" in Chapter 11, "Administering Servers and Applications."

Module 4: Completing the XLANG Schedule

In this module, you learn how to:

- Implement a port in the XLANG schedule drawing that you started in Module 2 by using a BizTalk Messaging implementation. For information about the differences between ports and messaging ports, see "Understanding Port Implementations" in Chapter 8, "BizTalk Orchestration Services," and "Understanding Messaging Ports" in Chapter 9, "Configuring BizTalk Messaging Services."
- Complete the XLANG schedule drawing and compile it into an XLANG schedule.
- Run the schedule to understand the complete movement of messages between the buyer and seller systems.

🔲 Shortcuts

Shortcuts enable you to save time and effort by using an existing XLANG schedule, a document specification, a map, or a configuration script. By using shortcuts, you can advance to subsequent sections of the tutorial.

To use shortcuts, the components must be installed on drive C.

Requirements

To successfully complete this tutorial, you must install BizTalk Server 2000 and all its dependencies. For a complete list of the hardware and software requirements for BizTalk Server 2000, see Chapter 1, "Installing BizTalk Server 2000."

Preliminary Setup

Before you begin the tutorial, you must create the following:

- One folder containing four subfolders.

- Two local Web site folders containing ASP files.

- Two message queues for the buyer system.

To create folders

In this procedure, you create one folder that contains four subfolders. You use two of the subfolders as locations for messages as they move into and out of the buyer and seller systems, and two as content folders for the buyer and seller Web sites.

To create the folders:

1. In Windows Explorer, browse to the root directory of your C:\ drive.

   ### ☝ Caution

   - You must create the following folders on your C:\ drive.

2. Create a new folder on the root of the C:\ drive; name the folder **TutorialFiles**.

3. Click the new folder called **TutorialFiles** and create four subfolders with the following names:

   - **Buyer**

   - **Seller**

   - **SubmitPO**

   - **InvoiceToQueue**

To copy files

In this procedure, you copy files needed to complete the tutorial.

1. On the BizTalk Server installation drive, browse to **\Program Files\Microsoft BizTalk Server\Tutorial\DocSpecsandMaps** and copy **POReqtoPO.xml**.

2. Paste the file to **\Program Files\Microsoft BizTalk Server\BizTalkServerRepository\Maps\Microsoft**.

3. Use the following table to copy and paste additional files to the **TutorialFiles** subfolders.

Copy from:	Paste to:
\Program Files\Microsoft BizTalk Server\Tutorial\Components\SubmitPO\Solution\ SubmitProElectronPO.asp	C:\TutorialFiles\SubmitPO
\Program Files\Microsoft BizTalk Server\Tutorial\Components\InvoicetoQueue\Solution\ DropInvoicetoMSMQ.asp	C:\TutorialFiles\InvoiceToQueue
\Program Files\Microsoft BizTalk Server\Tutorial\Components\InvoicetoQueue\Solution\Global.asa	C:\TutorialFiles\InvoiceToQueue

To create local Web site folders

In this procedure, you create two virtual directories. The first directory simulates the buyer Web site that receives invoices. The second directory simulates the seller Web site that receives purchase orders.

1. On the **Start** menu, point to **Settings** and click **Control Panel**.

2. Double-click **Administrative Tools**.

3. Double-click **Computer Management**.

   The Computer Management console appears.

4. In the Computer Management console tree, expand **Services and Applications**, expand **Internet Information Services**, and then click **Default Web Site**.

5. On the **Action** menu, point to **New** and click **Virtual Directory**.

   The Virtual Directory Creation Wizard opens.

6. On the **Welcome to the Virtual Directory Creation Wizard** page, click **Next**.

7. On the **Virtual Directory Alias** page, in the **Alias** box, type **SubmitPO** and click **Next**.

8. On the **Web Site Content Directory** page, click **Browse**.

9. Browse to **C:\TutorialFiles\SubmitPO**, click **OK**, and then click **Next**.

10. On the **Access Permissions** page, click **Next**.

11. Click **Finish** to close the Virtual Directory Creation Wizard.

12. In the Computer Management console tree, click **Default Web Site**.

13. To create the folder that simulates the buyer Web site, repeat steps 5 through 11, with the following variations:

    - In step 7, in the **Alias** box, type **InvoiceToQueue**.

    - In step 9, browse to **C:\TutorialFiles\InvoiceToQueue**.

    Your Computer Management console should appear similar to the following illustration.

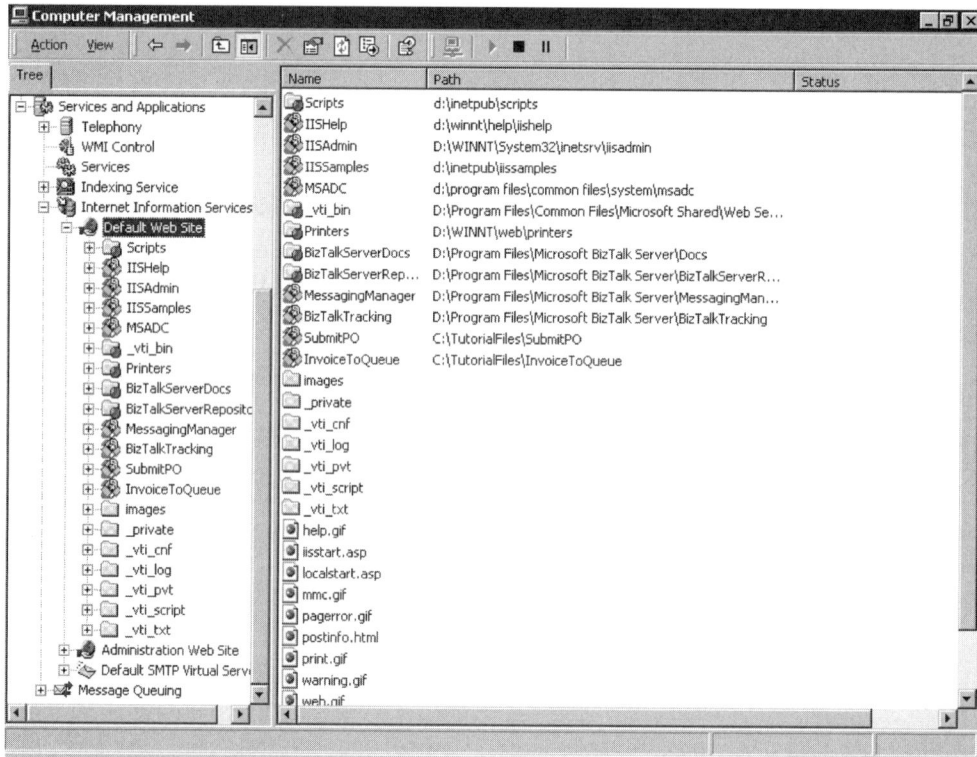

14. Close the Computer Management console.

To create message queues

In this procedure, you create two message queues to enable the buyer system to send and receive messages.

Note

- To complete this procedure, Message Queuing must be installed. For instructions about installing Message Queuing, see "To install Message Queuing" in Chapter 1, "Installing BizTalk Server 2000."

To create the message queues:

1. On the **Start** menu, point to **Settings** and click **Control Panel**.

2. Double-click **Administrative Tools**.

3. Double-click **Computer Management**.

    The Computer Management console appears.

4. In the Computer Management console, expand **Services and Applications**, expand
    Message Queuing, and then click **Private Queues**.

5. On the **Action** menu, point to **New** and click **Private Queue**.

    The **Queue Name** dialog box appears.

6. In the **Name** box, type **ReceivePOReq**.

7. Select the **Transactional** check box and click **OK**.

8. To create the second message queue, repeat steps 5 through 7, with the following variation:

    *   In step 6, in the **Name** box, type **ReceiveInvoice**.

    Your Computer Management console should appear similar to the following illustration.

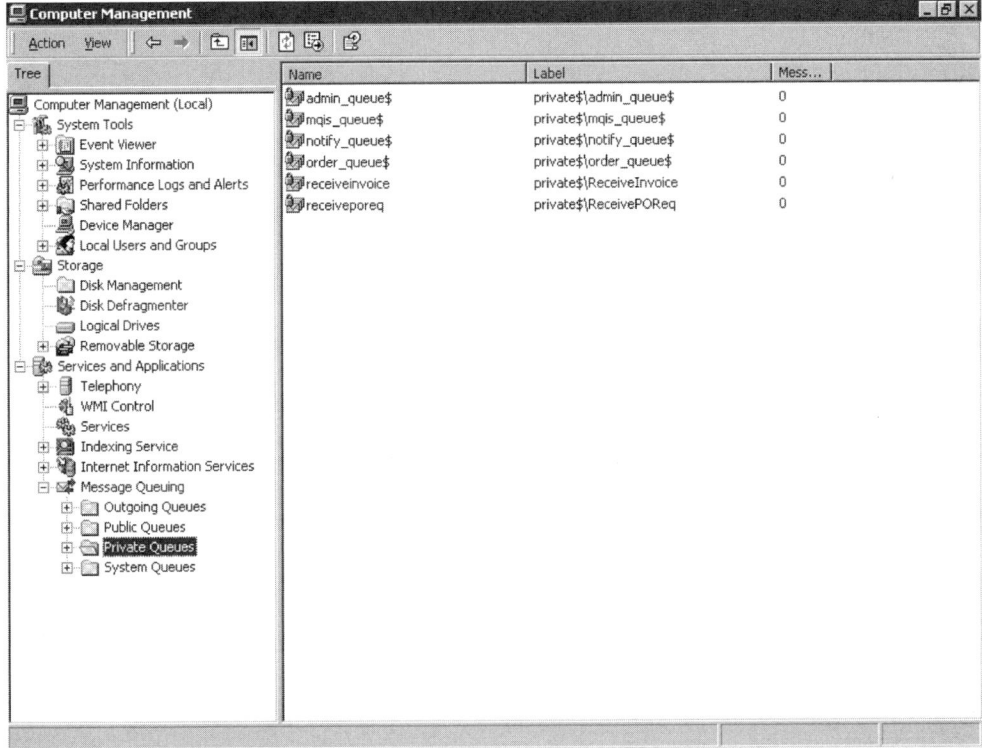

9. Close the Computer Management console.

To install the auxiliary components

In this procedure, you install the following auxiliary components:

- A Windows Script Component (WSC) on the buyer system that you use to implement a port to an XLANG schedule, and that accepts the approval or denial status for a purchase order request from the XLANG schedule.

- An application integration component (AIC) on the seller system that you use to generate an invoice that is based on the data in the purchase order from the buyer.

  ☞ **Caution**

  - If these components have been installed previously on your computer, you must first uninstall them. To uninstall the components, see the following procedure, "To uninstall the auxiliary components."

To install the auxiliary components:

1. On the BizTalk Server installation drive, browse to **\Program Files\Microsoft BizTalk Server\Tutorial\Setup**.

2. Double-click **Install_POtoInvoice.vbs**.

   A message box appears, indicating that the component was successfully installed.

3. Browse to **\Program Files\Microsoft BizTalk Server\Tutorial\Components\POReqApproval\Solution** and click **PORequestApproval.wsc**.

4. On the **File** menu, click **Register**.

   A message box appears, indicating that the component was successfully registered.

To uninstall the auxiliary components

☞ **Caution**

- Do not use this procedure unless you are removing a previous installation of the components.

1. For the POtoInvoice component, browse to **\Program Files\Microsoft BizTalk Server\Tutorial\Setup** on the BizTalk Server installation drive.

2. Double-click **Remove_POtoInvoice.vbs**.

   A message box appears, indicating that the component was successfully uninstalled.

3. For the Windows Script Component, browse to **\Program Files\Microsoft BizTalk Server\Tutorial\Components\POReqApproval\Solution** and click **PORequestApproval.wsc**.

4. On the **File** menu, click **Unregister**.

   A message box appears, indicating that the component was successfully unregistered.

To reinstall the components, see the previous procedure, "To install the auxiliary components."

Module 1: Modeling Business Processes

In this module, you use BizTalk Orchestration Designer to create an XLANG schedule drawing that describes an automated procurement process. You then compile the XLANG schedule drawing into an executable XLANG schedule, which controls the flow of messages for the buyer system.

Objectives

- **Create an XLANG schedule drawing that describes the automated procurement process.** For more information, see "Creating XLANG Schedule Drawings" in Chapter 8, "BizTalk Orchestration Services."

- **Connect the actions in a logical sequence that describes the business processes.** For more information, see "Connecting Shapes" in Chapter 8, "BizTalk Orchestration Services."

- **Implement the business processes by connecting actions to ports.** For more information, see "To establish the communication flow between an action and a port" in Chapter 8, "BizTalk Orchestration Services."

- **Add a rule to the business processes by writing a script expression.** For more information, see "Designing Rules" in Chapter 8, "BizTalk Orchestration Services."

- **Define the data flow for messages.** For more information, see "Communication Shapes" in Chapter 8, "BizTalk Orchestration Services."

- **Save the XLANG schedule drawing and compile the drawing into an XLANG schedule.** For more information, see "Compiling XLANG Schedules" in Chapter 8, "BizTalk Orchestration Services."

- **Run the XLANG schedule to process the message through BizTalk Server.** For more information, see "Running XLANG Schedules" in Chapter 8, "BizTalk Orchestration Services."

Creating the XLANG Schedule for the Buyer

In this procedure, you model the business processes for the buyer and create an XLANG schedule.

To create the XLANG schedule, see the following procedure, "To create the buyer actions."

Shortcut

To use the existing XLANG schedule, see "To run the XLANG schedule" later in this chapter.

To create the buyer actions

1. On the **Start** menu, point to **Programs**, point to **Microsoft BizTalk Server 2000**, and then click **BizTalk Orchestration Designer**.

2. On the **Business Process** page, drag the **Action** shape from the **Flowchart** stencil to the left of the **Separator** bar.

    Position the shape directly below the **Begin** shape.

3. Right-click the **Action** shape and click **Properties**.

    The **Action Properties** dialog box appears.

4. In the **Name** box, type **Receive PO Request** and click **OK**.

    ### ☞ Caution

    *   For this scenario to run correctly, you must type all names exactly as indicated. The tutorial components use these names.

5. On the **Business Process** page, drag the **Decision** shape from the **Flowchart** stencil to the left side of the **Separator** bar.

    Position this shape below the **Receive PO Request** action.

6. Right-click the **Decision** shape and click **Add Rule**.

    The **Rule Properties** dialog box appears.

7. In the **Rule name** box, type **Denied** and click **OK**.

    Later in this module, you add a script expression that implements the decision rule, after you bind the **Decision** shape to the Script Component, which provides the message and field names.

8. Repeat steps 2 through 4 to create the following three actions:

    *   Position a second **Action** shape to the right of the **Decision** shape. Name this action **Send Denial**.

    *   Position a third **Action** shape below the **Decision** shape. Name this action **Send Approval**.

    *   Position a fourth **Action** shape below the **Send Approval** action. Name this action **Write PO Request to File**.

9. On the **Business Process** page, drag the **End** shape from the **Flowchart** stencil to the left side of the **Separator** bar.

    Position the shape below the **Send Denial** action.

    If the purchase order request is not approved, the XLANG schedule displays a denial message and ends.

10. On the **Business Process** page, drag the **End** shape from the **Flowchart** stencil to the left side of the **Separator** bar.

    Position the shape below the **Write PO Request to File** action.

    If the purchase order request is approved, the XLANG schedule writes the purchase order request to a file directory, displays an approval message, and then ends.

To connect the buyer actions in a sequence

1. Click the **Begin** shape to highlight the control handles.

   Drag the bottom control handle to the top connection point of the **Receive PO Request** action.

   The **Receive PO Request** action represents the start of the business process. When a purchase order request is received, the XLANG schedule starts running.

   ### ✍ Notes

   - A green box on a highlighted shape indicates a control handle. You can drag control handles to connect to an action.

   - A blue X on a shape indicates a connection point.

   - Connection points on the side of an **Action** shape are used only to connect to ports, not to other **Action** shapes.

2. Repeat step 1 to create a connection for the following action:

   - Connect the **Receive PO Request** action to the **Decision** shape.

3. Select the **Denied** rule in the **Decision** shape and drag the right control handle of the **Denied** rule to the top connection point of the **Send Denial** action.

4. Select the **Else** rule in the **Decision** shape and drag the left control handle of the **Else** rule to the top connection point of the **Send Approval** action.

   ### ✍ Note

   - You can connect the rules in the **Decision** shape to the **Send Approval** and **Send Denial** actions from either the right or left control handle.

5. Connect the **Send Approval** action to the **Write PO Request to File** action.

6. Connect the **Write PO Request to File** action to the **End** shape positioned below it.

7. Connect the **Send Denial** action to the **End** shape positioned below it.

8. On the **File** menu, click **Save As**.

   The **Save XLANG Schedule Drawing As** dialog box appears.

9. Browse to **\Program Files\Microsoft BizTalk Server\Tutorial\Schedule\Lab** on the BizTalk Server installation drive.

10. In the **File name** box, type **Buyer1** and click **Save**.

The XLANG schedule drawing that you created and saved should appear similar to the following illustration.

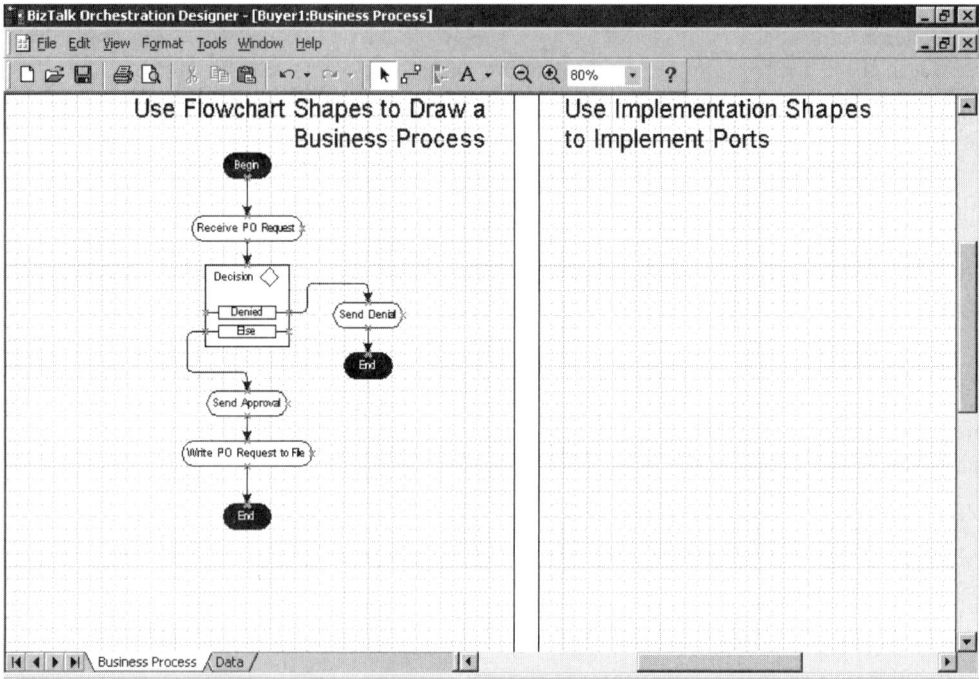

To implement a port by using Message Queuing to receive a purchase order request

The service is configured to monitor a message queue for a purchase order request. When this occurs, the XLANG schedule begins processing. For information about the usage of ports and messaging ports in this tutorial, see Chapter 14, "Orchestrating Business Processes with BizTalk Server 2000."

To implement the port:

1. On the **Business Process** page, drag the **Message Queuing** shape from the **Implementation** stencil to the right side of the **Separator** bar.

   Position the **Message Queuing** shape so that it is horizontally aligned with the **Receive PO Request** action.

   The Message Queuing Binding Wizard opens.

2. On the **Welcome to the Message Queuing Binding Wizard** page, verify that **Create a new port** is selected.

3. In the **Create a new port** box, type **ReceivePORequest** and click **Next**.

4. On the **Static or Dynamic Queue Information** page, verify that **Static queue** is selected and click **Next**.

5. On the **Queue Information** page, click **Use a known queue for all instances**.

6. In the **Enter the queue name** box, type **.\private$\ReceivePOReq** and click **Next**.

7. On the **Advanced Port Properties** page, click **Finish**.

   On the **Business Process** page, the **ReceivePORequest** port and the associated Message Queuing implementation appear.

To create the communication flow for the Receive PO Request action

1. Select the **Receive PO Request** action and drag the control handle on the right of the **Receive PO Request** action to the left connection point of the **ReceivePORequest** port.

   The XML Communication Wizard opens.

2. On the **Welcome to the XML Communication Wizard** page, click **Receive** and click **Next**.

3. On the **Message Information** page, verify that **Create a new message** is selected.

4. In the **Message name** box, type **POReq** and click **Next**.

5. On the **XML Translation Information** page, verify that **Receive XML messages from the queue** is selected and click **Next**.

6. On the **Message Type Information** page, in the **Message type** box, type **POReq** and click **Next**.

7. On the **Message Specification Information** page, click **Browse**.

   The **Browse for Specification** dialog box appears.

8. Browse to **\Program Files\Microsoft BizTalk Server\Tutorial\DocSpecsandMaps** on the BizTalk Server installation drive.

9. Click **POReq.xml** and click **Open**.

10. Click **Add**.

    The **Field Selection** dialog box appears.

11. In the **Select node** area, expand **Total**, click **POTtl**, and then click **OK**.

    In the **Message fields** area, **POTtl** should appear in the list of message fields.

12. Click **Finish**.

After you implement the port and create the communication flow, the XLANG schedule drawing should appear similar to the following illustration.

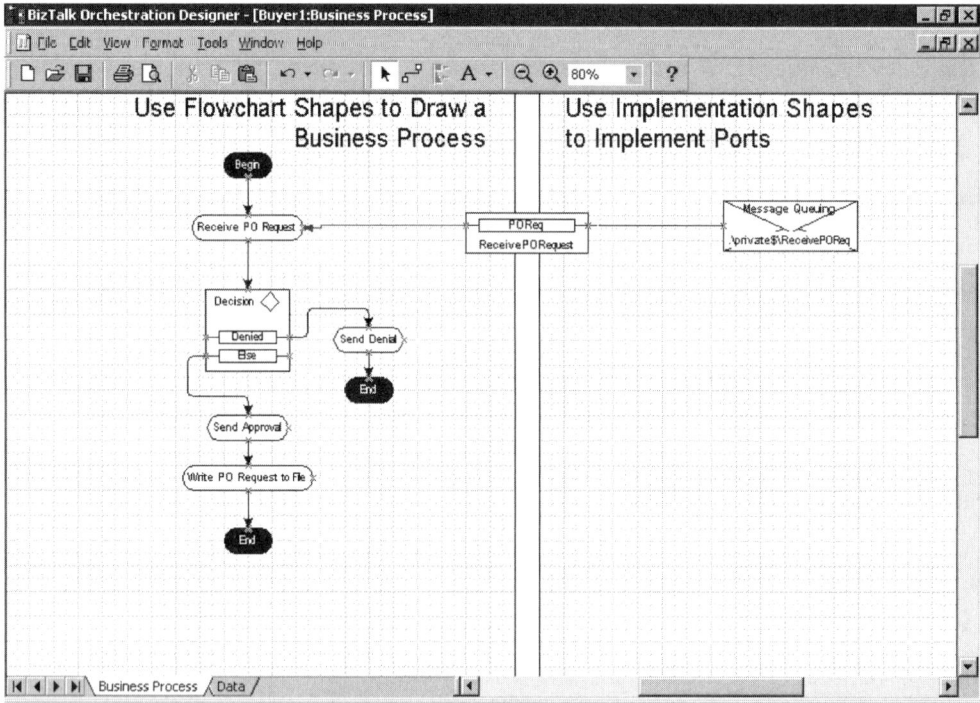

To implement a port by using a script component

The XLANG schedule passes the value in the total field of the purchase order request to the **Decision** shape. The scripting expression in the decision rule forks the path of the schedule and sends the appropriate message to the port implementation that uses a Windows Script Component, based on the total of the purchase order request.

To implement the port:

1. On the Implementation stencil, drag the **Script Component** shape to the right of the **Separator** bar that divides the two sides of the drawing.

   Position the shape so that it is horizontally aligned with the **Decision** shape.

   The Script Component Binding Wizard opens.

2. On the **Welcome to the Script Component Binding Wizard** page, in the **Create a new port** box, type **ApprovalComponent** and click **Next**.

3. On the **Static or Dynamic Communication** page, verify that **Static** is selected and click **Next**.

4. On the **Specify the Script File** page, click **Browse**.

5. Browse to **\Program Files\Microsoft BizTalk Server\Tutorial\Components\POReqApproval\Solution** on the BizTalk Server installation drive.

6. Click **PORequestApproval.wsc**, click **Open**, and then click **Next**.

7. On the **Component Instantiation Information** page, verify that **Use the Prog ID "BTSTutorial.PORequestApproval"** is selected and click **Next**.

8. On the **Method Information** page, click **Check All** and click **Next**.

9. On the **Advanced Port Properties** page, click **Finish**.

To define message properties for the script component

1. Select the **Send Denial** action and drag the control handle on the right to the **ApprovalComponent** Windows Script Component port.

   The Method Communication Wizard opens.

2. On the **Welcome to the Method Communication Wizard** page, verify that **Initiate a synchronous method call** is selected and click **Next**.

3. On the **Message Information** page, verify that **Create a new message** is selected and click **Next**.

4. On the **Message Specification Information** page, in the **Methods** list, click **SendDenial** and click **Finish**.

5. Select the **Send Approval** action and drag the control handle on the right of the **Send Approval** action to the **ApprovalComponent** port.

   The Method Communication Wizard opens.

6. On the **Welcome to the Method Communication Wizard** page, verify that **Initiate a synchronous method call** is selected and click **Next**.

7. On the **Message Information** page, verify that **Create a new message** is selected and click **Next**.

8. On the **Message Specification Information** page, in the **Methods** list, click **SendApproval** and click **Finish**.

9. Select the **Write PO Request to File** action and drag the control handle on the right of the **Write PO Request to File** action to the **ApprovalComponent** port.

   The Method Communication Wizard opens.

10. On the **Welcome to the Method Communication Wizard** page, verify that **Initiate a synchronous method call** is selected and click **Next**.

11. On the **Message Information** page, verify that **Create a new message** is selected and click **Next**.

12. On the **Message Specification Information** page, in the **Methods** list, verify that **WriteToFile** is selected and click **Finish**.

To write the script expression for the decision rule

The denial decision rule contains properties that define the shape's behavior. The scripting expression refers to data contained in messages, and evaluates to either TRUE or FALSE. The scripting expression also defines the logic and variable names that are used by the **Decision** shape.

If the total of the purchase order request exceeds $1000:

- The **Decision** shape sends a denial message to the port.

- A message box notifies the user of the denial.

- The XLANG schedule ends.

If the total of the purchase order request is $1000 or less:

- The **Decision** shape sends an approval message to the script component.

- The script component displays a message box that notifies the user of the approval.

- The script component writes the purchase order request message to a local file directory.

- The XLANG schedule ends.

To write the script expression:

1. Click the **Data** tab at the bottom of the page.

   The **Data** page appears.

2. View the **POReq** message to find the field name.

   To write the script expression, both the message name and the field name are required. In this case, the message name is POReq and the field name is POTtl.

3. Click the **Business Process** tab at the bottom of the page.

   The **Business Process** page appears.

4. Right-click the **Decision** shape and click **Properties**.

   The **Decision Properties** dialog box appears.

5. Verify that **Denied** is selected and click **Edit**.

   The **Rule Properties** dialog box appears.

6. In the **Script expression** box, type **POReq.POTtl > 1000**.

   This indicates that if the total field in the purchase order request is greater than $1000, the request is denied.

7. Click **OK** to close the **Rule Properties** dialog box, and click **OK** to close the **Decision Properties** dialog box.

The XLANG schedule drawing should appear similar to the following illustration.

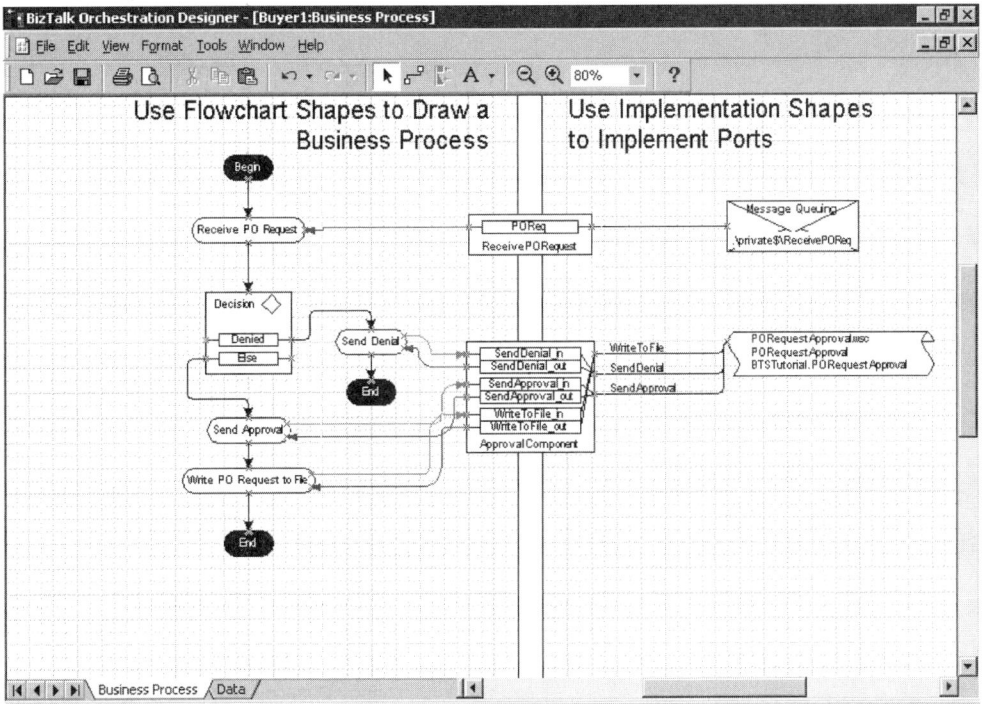

To define the data flow

To define data flow within the business process, you create connections between fields in **Message** shapes on the **Data** page.

To define the data flow:

1. Click the **Data** tab at the bottom of the page.

   The **Data** page appears.

2. In the **POReq** message, click the **Document** field and drag the control handle on the right to a connection point on the **Document** field in the **SendDenial_in** message.

3. Repeat step 2 by clicking the **Document** field and dragging the highlighted control handle on the right from the **POReq** box to a connection point on the following fields:

   - The **Document** field in the **SendApproval_in** box.

   - The **Document** field in the **WriteToFile_in** box.

✍ Note

- Click the **Document** field of the **POReq** message before trying to drag the control handle to the other fields.

The completed **Data** page should appear similar to the following illustration.

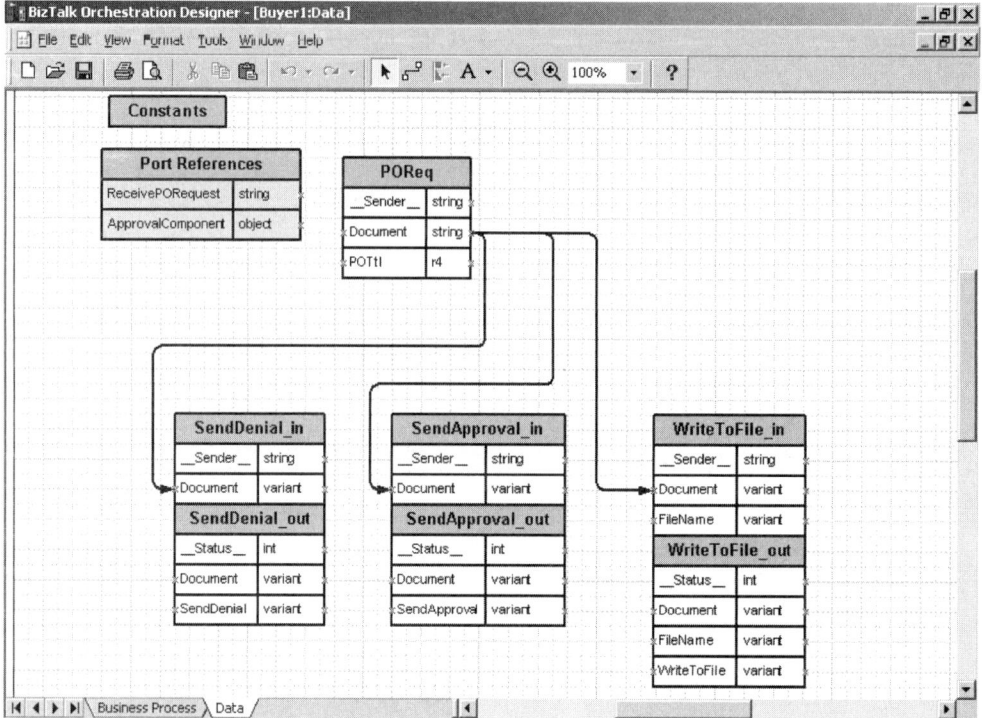

To save the XLANG schedule drawing

- On the **File** menu, click **Save Buyer1.skv**.

To compile the XLANG schedule

1. On the **File** menu, click **Make XLANG Buyer1.skx**.

   The **Save XLANG Schedule to** dialog box appears.

2. Verify that the XLANG schedule will be saved to the **\Program Files\Microsoft BizTalk Server\Tutorial\Schedule\Lab** folder on the BizTalk Server installation drive and click **Save**.

3. On the **File** menu, click **Exit** to close **BizTalk Orchestration Designer**.

To run the XLANG schedule

In this procedure, you run the XLANG schedule twice to view the approval and denial of purchase order requests.

To run the XLANG schedule:

1. Browse to **\Program Files\Microsoft BizTalk Server\Tutorial\Schedule\Solution** on the BizTalk Server installation drive.

2. Double-click **ExecuteTutorial.exe**.

   This application is used to activate the XLANG schedule by means of a moniker.

   The **ExecuteTutorial** application opens.

3. Click **Browse for Schedule**.

   Shortcut

   If you are using the existing XLANG schedule, browse to **\Program Files\Microsoft BizTalk Server\Tutorial\Schedule\Solution** and continue to step 5.

4. If you created the **Buyer1** XLANG schedule, browse to **\Program Files\Microsoft BizTalk Server\Tutorial\Schedule\Lab**.

5. Click the **Buyer1.skx** XLANG schedule file and click **Open**.

6. Click **Browse for Data File** and browse to **\Program Files\Microsoft BizTalk Server\Tutorial\Schedule\SampleData**.

7. Click **POReqAccept.xml** and click **Open**.

8. Click **Start XLANG Schedule**.

   Because its total is less than $1000, the purchase order request is approved. A message box appears, notifying you that the application passed data to the XLANG Scheduler Engine. At this point, the application is finished. A second message box notifies you that the purchase order request has been approved. Click **OK** to close the dialog boxes.

9. Click **End** to close the **ExecuteTutorial** application.

   Important

   - If you see an automation error when running this application, check to make sure that you have properly configured the private queue and that its name is correct.

10. Browse to **C:\TutorialFiles\Buyer**.

    The file name is **POReq*XXXXX*.xml**, where *XXXXX* represents a unique set of numbers. Double-click the file to open it in Microsoft Internet Explorer. This is a copy of the purchase order request file that the application posted to the message queue. After viewing this file, delete it.

11. Repeat steps 1 through 5 to run the **ExecuteTutorial** application again.

12. Click **Browse for Data File** and browse to **\Program Files\Microsoft BizTalk Server\Tutorial\Schedule\SampleData**.

13. Click **POReqDeny.xml** and click **Open**.

14. Click **Start XLANG Schedule**.

    Because its total exceeds $1000, the purchase order request is denied. A message box appears, notifying you that the application is finished. A second message box notifies you that the document denial has been received. Click **OK** to close the dialog boxes.

15. Click **End** to close the **ExecuteTutorial** application.

The following diagram illustrates the flow of data when you run the XLANG schedule.

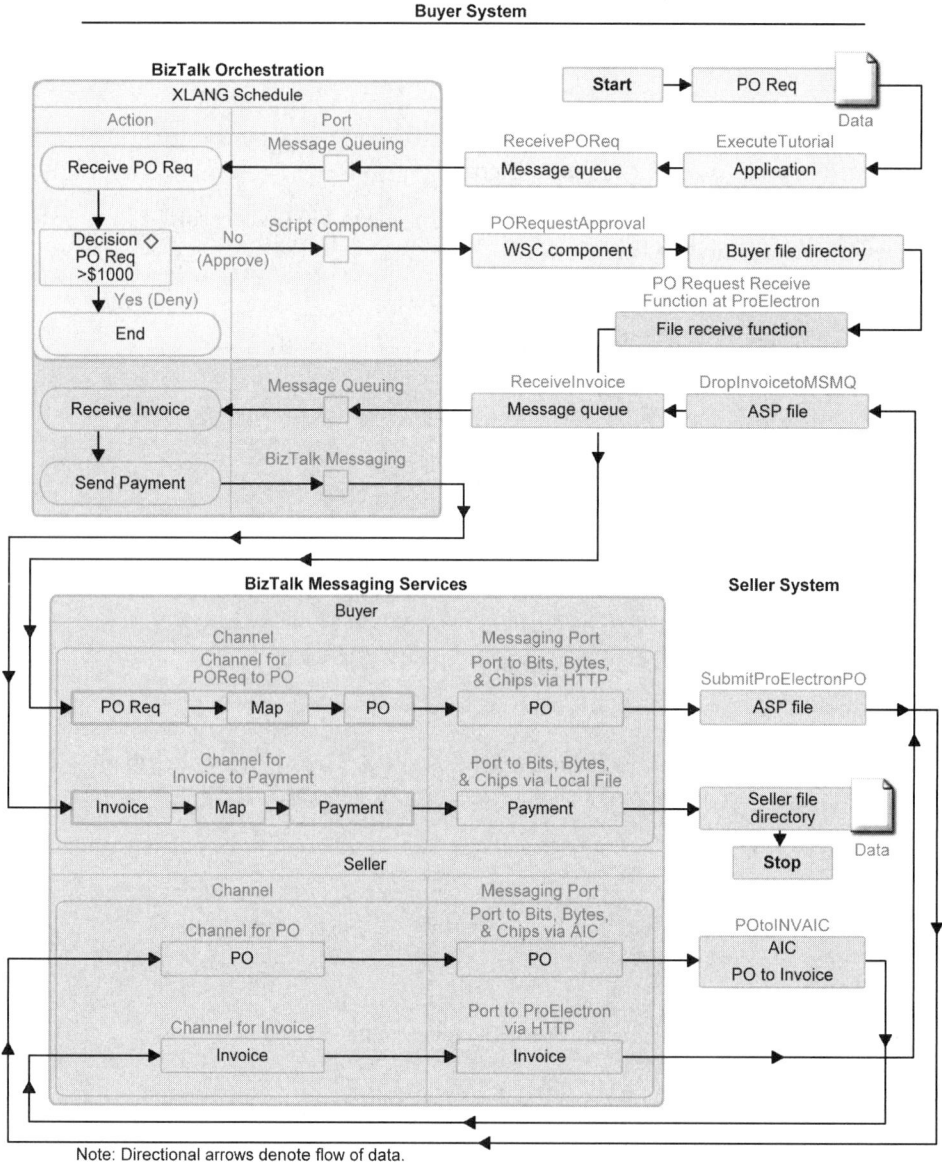

Note: Directional arrows denote flow of data.

Module 1 Summary

In this module, you accomplished the following:

- **Created the XLANG schedule drawing that described the automated procurement process.** For more information, see "Creating XLANG Schedule Drawings" in Chapter 8, "BizTalk Orchestration Services."

- **Connected the actions in a logical sequence that described the business process.** For more information, see "Connecting Shapes" in Chapter 8, "BizTalk Orchestration Services."

- **Implemented the business process by connecting actions to ports.** For more information, see "To establish the communication flow between an action and a port" in Chapter 8, "BizTalk Orchestration Services."

- **Added a rule to the business process by writing a script expression.** For more information, see "Designing Rules" in Chapter 8, "BizTalk Orchestration Services."

- **Defined the data flow for messages.** For more information, see "Communication Shapes" in Chapter 8, "BizTalk Orchestration Services."

- **Saved the XLANG schedule drawing and compiled the drawing into the XLANG schedule.** For more information, see "Compiling XLANG Schedules" in Chapter 8, "BizTalk Orchestration Services."

- **Ran the XLANG schedule twice to process the purchase order request through BizTalk Server, observing the approval and denial.** For more information, see "Running XLANG Schedules" in Chapter 8, "BizTalk Orchestration Services."

The highlighted areas of the following diagram illustrate the steps you completed in this module.

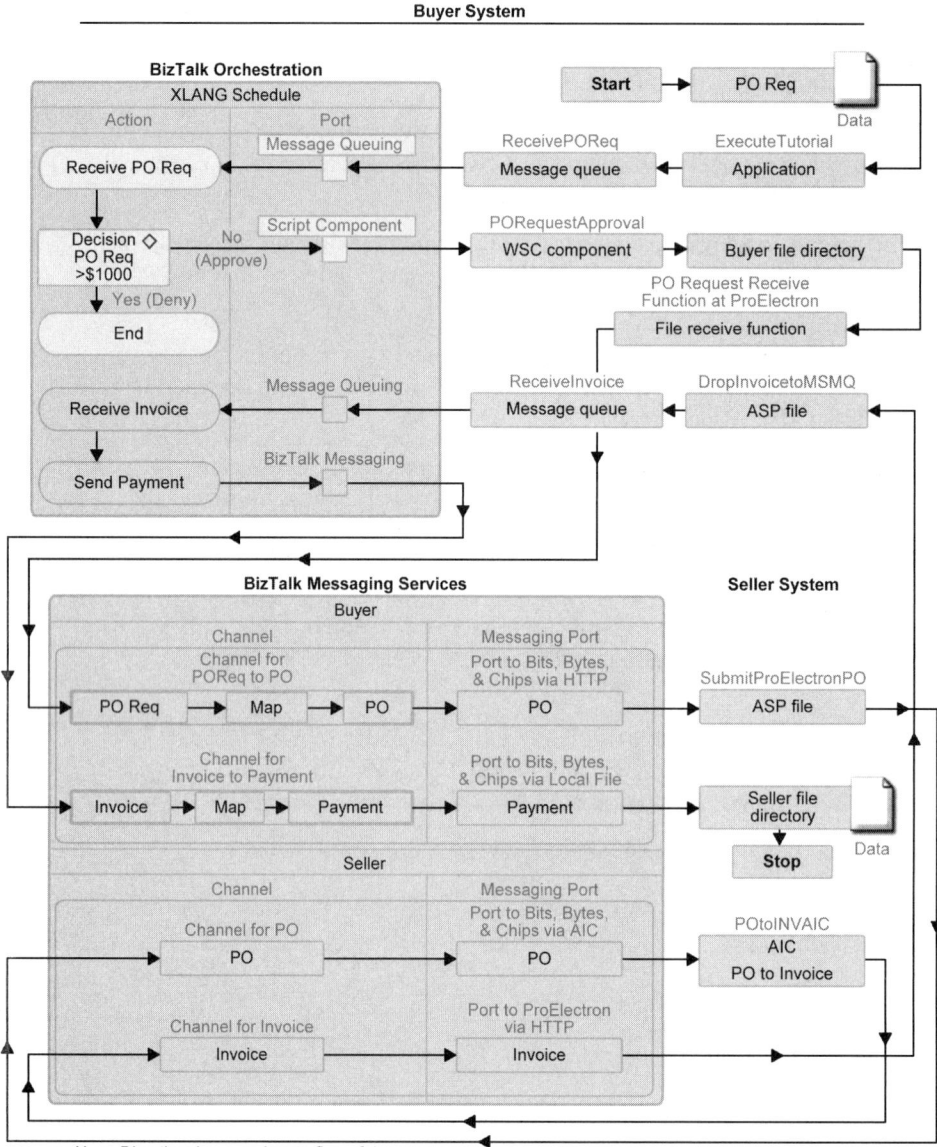

Note: Directional arrows denote flow of data.

Module 2: Creating Specifications and Maps

In this module, you use BizTalk Editor to create specifications and BizTalk Mapper to create maps.

Objectives

- **Create a specification.** For more information, see Chapter 5, "Creating Specifications."

- **Add new records and fields to a specification.** For more information, see "To add new fields to records" in Chapter 5, "Creating Specifications."

- **Create a map.** For more information, see Chapter 6, "Mapping Data."

- **Create links between fields in a map.** For more information, see "Creating Links" in Chapter 6, "Mapping Data."

- **Use functoids to mathematically manipulate values in a map.** For more information, see "Understanding Functoids" in Chapter 6, "Mapping Data."

- **Save specifications and maps to the WebDAV repository.** For more information, see "To store specifications" in Chapter 5, "Creating Specifications," and "To store maps" in Chapter 6, "Mapping Data."

Using BizTalk Editor

You can use BizTalk Editor to create, edit, and manage specifications.

To use BizTalk Editor to create the payment specification, see "To create the payment specification" later in this chapter.

Shortcut

To use the existing payment specification, see the following procedure, "To use the existing payment specification."

To use the existing payment specification

1. Copy **PaymentSpec.xml** from **\Program Files\Microsoft BizTalk Server\Tutorial\DocSpecsandMaps** on the BizTalk Server installation drive.

2. Paste the file to **\Program Files\Microsoft BizTalk Server\BizTalkServerRepository\DocSpecs\Microsoft**.

To use BizTalk Editor to create the purchase order request specification, see "To create the purchase order request specification" later in this chapter.

Shortcut

To use the existing purchase order request specification, see "To use the existing purchase order request specification" later in this chapter.

To create the payment specification

1. On the **Start** menu, point to **Programs**, point to **Microsoft BizTalk Server 2000**, and then click **BizTalk Editor**.

2. On the **File** menu, click **New**.

   The **New Document Specification** dialog box appears.

3. Click the **Blank Specification** icon and click **OK**.

4. In the root node, click **BlankSpecification**.

5. On the **Declaration** tab, double-click the Value field in the Name row, type **Payment**, and then press ENTER.

6. Double-click the Value field in the Model row, click **Open**, and then press ENTER.

To add new records to the Payment root node of the payment specification

1. Right-click the **Payment** root node and click **New Record**.

2. Name this record **PaymentHeader** and press ENTER.

3. Follow steps 1 and 2 to create and name four additional records under the **Payment** root node.

   These records are all child records of the **Payment** root node. Name the records as follows:

   - **Seller**
   - **Buyer**
   - **Item**
   - **PaymentSummary**

To add new records to existing records in the payment specification

1. Right-click the **Seller** record and click **New Record**.

2. Name the record **Address** and press ENTER.

3. Follow steps 1 and 2 to create child records for the parent records listed in the following table.

Parent record	Child record names
Seller	ContactInfo
Buyer	Address
Buyer	ContactInfo

To add new fields to existing records in the payment specification

1. Right-click the **PaymentHeader** record and click **New Field**.

2. Name this field **PONumber** and press ENTER.

3. On the **Declaration** tab, double-click the Value field in the Data Type row, click **String**, and then press ENTER.

4. On the **Declaration** tab, double-click the Value field in the Minimum Length row, type **1**, and then press ENTER.

5. On the **Declaration** tab, double-click the Value field in the Maximum Length row, type **22**, and then press ENTER.

6. Follow steps 1 through 5 to create fields for the records or child records listed in the following table.

    Each record contains multiple fields.

    You do not have to create the fields for the buyer because parallel record names exist for the buyer and seller. All records with the same name contain the same record and field information. When you add fields to the Seller/Address or Seller/ContactInfo record, the Buyer/Address or Buyer/ContactInfo record is automatically updated with the same fields.

Parent record	Field name	Data type	Minimum length	Maximum length
PaymentHeader	Date	Date	Not applicable	Not applicable
Seller/Address	Name	String	1	60
	Address1	String	1	55
	Address2	String	1	55
	City	String	2	30
	State	String	2	2
	Zip	String	3	15
	Country	String	2	3
Seller/ContactInfo	Name	String	1	60
	Number	String	1	60
Item	Quantity	Real(r4)	Not applicable	Not applicable
	Price	Real(r4)	Not applicable	Not applicable
	Description	String	1	80
	ExtendedPrice	Real(r4)	Not applicable	Not applicable
PaymentSummary	Total	Real(r4)	Not applicable	Not applicable

To store the payment specification to WebDAV

1. On the **File** menu, click **Store to WebDAV**.

   The **Store to WebDAV** dialog box appears.

2. Double-click the **Microsoft** folder.

3. In the **File name** box, type **PaymentSpec** and click **Save**.

4. On the **Tools** menu, click **Validate Instance**.

   The **Validate Document Instance** dialog box appears.

5. Browse to **\Program Files\Microsoft BizTalk Server\Tutorial\Schedule\Solution** on the BizTalk Server installation drive.

6. Click **payment_valid.xml** and click **Open**.

   Warnings or errors, if any, appear on the **Warnings** tab.

The payment specification should appear similar to the following illustration.

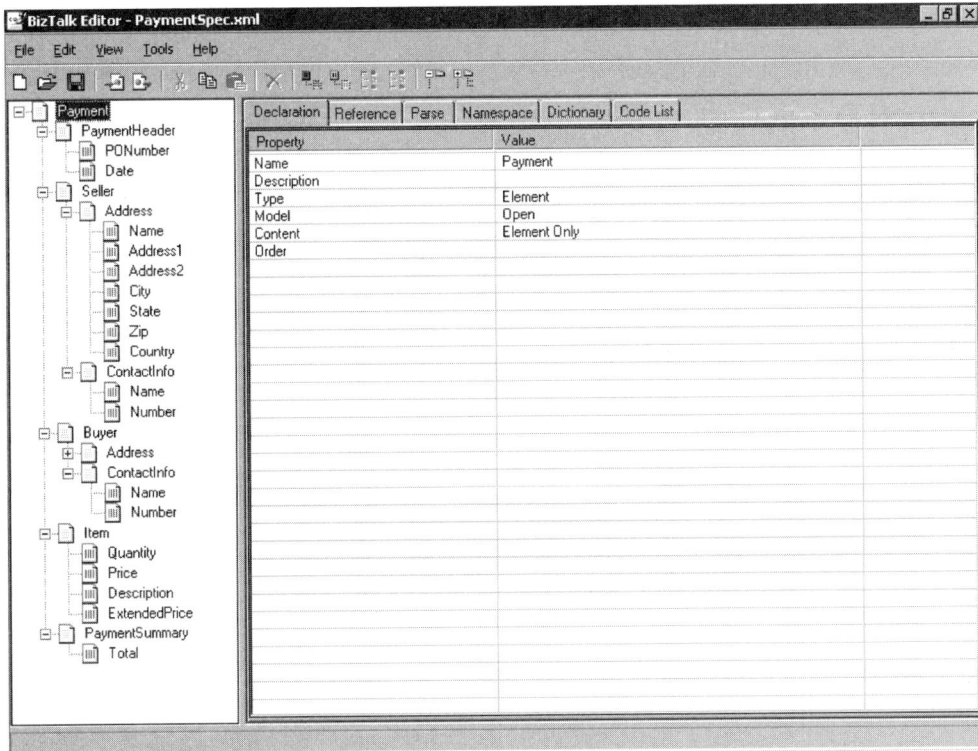

To use BizTalk Editor to create the purchase order request specification, see "To create the purchase order request specification" later in this chapter.

Shortcut

To use the existing purchase order request specification, see the following procedure, "To use the existing purchase order request specification,"

To use the existing purchase order request specification

1. Copy **POReq.xml** from **\Program Files\Microsoft BizTalk Server\Tutorial\DocSpecsandMaps** on the BizTalk Server installation drive.

2. Paste the file to **\Program Files\Microsoft BizTalk Server\BizTalkServerRepository\DocSpecs\Microsoft**.

To create the purchase order request specification

In this procedure, you create the root node of the purchase order request specification.

To create the root node:

1. On the **File** menu, click **New**.

   The **New Document Specification** dialog box appears.

2. Click the **Blank Specification** icon and click **OK**.

3. In the root node, click **BlankSpecification**.

4. On the **Declaration** tab, double-click the Value field in the Name row, type **POReq**, and then press ENTER.

5. Double-click the Value field in the Model row, click **Open**, and then press ENTER.

To add new records to the root node in the purchase order request specification

1. Right-click the **POReq** root node and click **New Record**.

2. Name this record **Header** and press ENTER.

3. Follow steps 1 and 2 to create and name five additional records under the **POReq** root node.

   These records are all child records of the **POReq** root node. Name the records as follows:

   - **EmployeeInfo**
   - **BillTo**
   - **ShipTo**
   - **Item**
   - **Total**

To add new records to existing records in the purchase order request specification

1. Right-click the **BillTo** record and click **New Record**.

2. Name the record **Address** and press ENTER.

3. Follow steps 1 and 2 to create and name a child record **Address** for the parent record called **ShipTo**.

To add new fields to existing records in the purchase order request specification

1. Right-click the **Header** record and click **New Field**.

2. Name this field **Date** and press ENTER.

3. On the **Declaration** tab, double-click the Value field in the Data Type row, click **Date**, and then press ENTER.

4. Right-click the **EmployeeInfo** record and click **New Field**.

5. Name this field **EmpID** and press ENTER.

6. On the **Declaration** tab, double-click the Value field in the Data Type row, click **String**, and then press ENTER.

7. On the **Declaration** tab, double-click the Value field in the Minimum Length row, type **1**, and then press ENTER.

8. On the **Declaration** tab, double-click the Value field in the Maximum Length row, type **60**, and then press ENTER.

9. Follow steps 4 through 8 to create fields for the records or child records listed in the following table.

   Each record contains multiple fields.

   You do not have to create the fields for ShipTo because parallel record names exist for BillTo and ShipTo. All records with the same name contain the same record and field information. When you add fields to the BillTo/Address record, the ShipTo/Address record is automatically updated with the same fields.

Parent record	Field name	Data type	Minimum length	Maximum length
EmployeeInfo	LastName	String	1	30
	FirstName	String	1	30
BillTo/Address	Name	String	1	60
	Address1	String	1	55
	Address2	String	1	55
	City	String	2	30
	State	String	2	2
	Zip	String	3	15
	Country	String	2	3
Item	Quantity	Real(r4)	Not applicable	Not applicable
	Price	Real(r4)	Not applicable	Not applicable
	Description	String	1	80
	UnitofMeasure	String	2	2
	ExtendedPrice	Real(r4)	Not applicable	Not applicable
Total	LineItemTtl	Real(r4)	Not applicable	Not applicable
	QtyTtl	Real(r4)	Not applicable	Not applicable
	POTtl	Real(r4)	Not applicable	Not applicable

To save the purchase order request specification

1. On the **File** menu, click **Store to WebDAV**.

   The **Store to WebDAV** dialog box appears.

2. Verify that the **Microsoft** folder is open.

3. In the **File name** box, type **POReq** and click **Save**.

4. On the **Tools** menu, click **Validate Instance**.

   The **Validate Document Instance** dialog box appears.

5. Browse to **\Program Files\Microsoft BizTalk Server\Tutorial\Schedule\SampleData** on the BizTalk Server installation drive.

6. Click **POReqAccept.xml** and click **Open**.

   Warnings or errors, if any, appear on the **Warnings** tab.

   The purchase order request specification should appear similar to the following illustration.

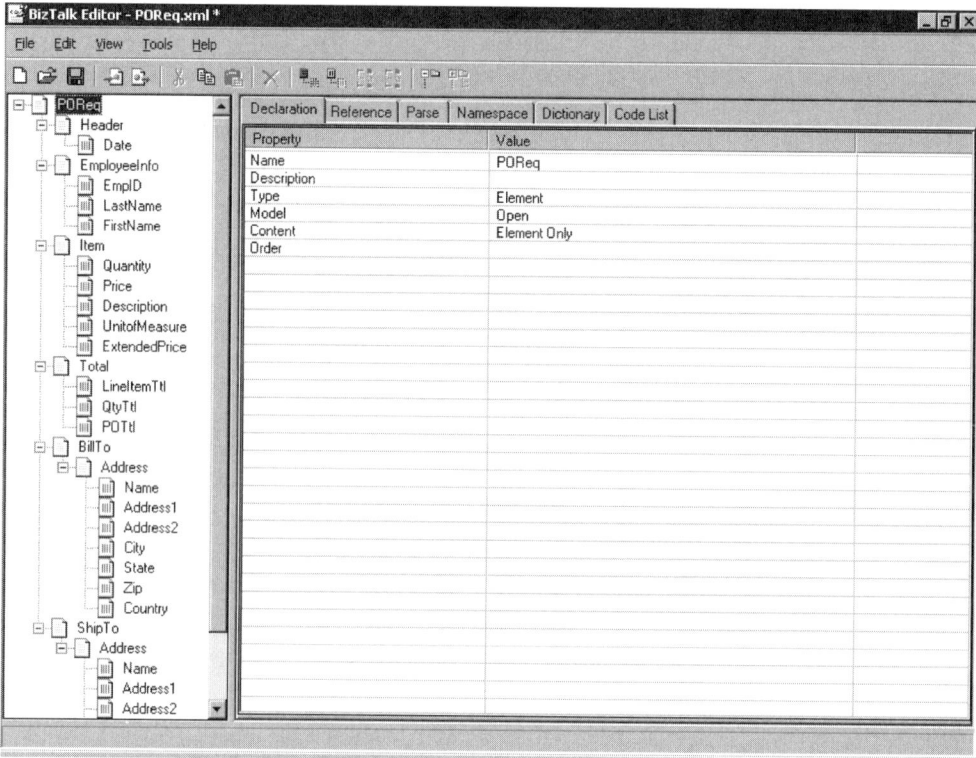

7. On the File menu, click **Exit** to close the BizTalk Editor console.

Using BizTalk Mapper

In this procedure, you use BizTalk Mapper to create a map that transforms the data from a message that conforms to the CommonInvoice specification into data in a message that conforms to the PaymentSpec specification.

BizTalk Messaging Services uses a map within a channel to specify how data in a document of one format is transformed into a document of a different format.

To use BizTalk Mapper to create the map, see "To create the InvoiceToPayment map" later in this chapter.

Shortcut

To use the existing map, see the following procedure, "To use existing InvoiceToPayment map."

To use existing InvoiceToPayment map

1. Copy **InvoiceToPayment.xml** from **\Program Files\Microsoft BizTalk Server\Tutorial\DocSpecsandMaps** on the BizTalk Server installation drive.

2. Paste the file to **\Program Files\Microsoft BizTalk Server\BizTalkServerRepository\Maps\Microsoft**.

Continue to "Module 3: Configuring BizTalk Messaging Services" later in this chapter.

To create the InvoiceToPayment map

1. On the **Start** menu, point to **Programs**, point to **Microsoft BizTalk Server 2000**, and then click **BizTalk Mapper**.

2. On the **File** menu, click **New**.

   The **Select Source Specification Type** dialog box appears.

3. Click the **WebDAV Files** icon and click **OK**.

   The **Retrieve Source Specification** dialog box appears.

4. Double-click the **Microsoft** folder.

5. Click **CommonInvoice.xml** and click **Open**.

   The **Select Destination Specification Type** dialog box appears.

6. Click the **WebDAV Files** icon and click **OK**.

7. Click **PaymentSpec.xml** and click **Open**.

To create links between fields

In the following procedure, you link fields from the source specification to fields in the destination specification.

To create links between fields:

1. In the Source Specification tree, expand the **InvoiceHeader** record to display the associated fields.

   For more information, see "Expand tree items" in Chapter 6, "Mapping Data."

2. In the Destination Specification tree, expand the **PaymentHeader** record to display the associated fields.

3. Drag the **InvoiceHeader/Date** field from the Source Specification tree to the **PaymentHeader/Date** field in the Destination Specification tree.

4. Follow steps 1 through 3 to create links between the fields listed in the following tables.

Source record/field	Destination record/field
InvoiceHeader/Number	PaymentHeader/PONumber
Seller/Address/Name	Seller/Address/Name
Seller/Address/Address1	Seller/Address/Address1
Seller/Address/Address2	Seller/Address/Address2
Seller/Address/City	Seller/Address/City
Seller/Address/State	Seller/Address/State
Seller/Address/PostalCode	Seller/Address/Zip
Seller/Address/Country	Seller/Address/Country
Seller/ContactInfo/ContactName	Seller/ContactInfo/Name
Seller/ContactInfo/ContactNumber	Seller/ContactInfo/Number
Buyer/Address/Name	Buyer/Address/Name
Buyer/Address/Address1	Buyer/Address/Address1
Buyer/Address/Address2	Buyer/Address/Address2
Buyer/Address/City	Buyer/Address/City
Buyer/Address/State	Buyer/Address/State
Buyer/Address/PostalCode	Buyer/Address/Zip
Buyer/Address/Country	Buyer/Address/Country
Buyer/ContactInfo/ContactName	Buyer/ContactInfo/Name
Buyer/ContactInfo/ContactNumber	Buyer/ContactInfo/Number
Item/ItemHeader/Quantity	Item/Quantity
Item/ItemHeader/Price	Item/Price
Item/ItemDescription/Description	Item/Description
InvoiceSummary/InvoiceTotal/Amount	PaymentSummary/Total

To use functoids to create links

In this procedure, you use a functoid to multiply the Quantity field by the Price field in the source specification, and place this value in the ExtendedPrice field in the destination specification.

To use functoids to create links:

1. On the **View** menu, click **Functoid Palette**.

    The **Functiod Palette** appears.

2. Click the **Mathematical** tab, drag the **Multiplication** functoid ▣ to the mapping grid, and then close the **Functoid Palette.**

3. In the Source Specification tree, drag the **Item/ItemHeader/Quantity** field to the functoid.

4. In the Source Specification tree, drag the **Item/ItemHeader/Price** field to the functoid.

5. Drag the **Multiplication** functoid to the **Item/ExtendedPrice** field in the Destination Specification tree.

To compile the map

1. On the **Tools** menu, click **Compile Map**.

2. In the lower pane, click the **Output** tab.

    The information on the **Output** tab indicates that an XSL map has been created. Warnings or errors, if any, appear on the **Warnings** tab.

To store the map to WebDAV

1. On the **File** menu, click **Store to WebDAV**.

    The **Store to WebDAV** dialog box appears.

2. Double-click the **Microsoft** folder.

3. In the **File name** box, type **InvoiceToPayment** and click **Save**.

    The map you create should appear similar to the following illustration.

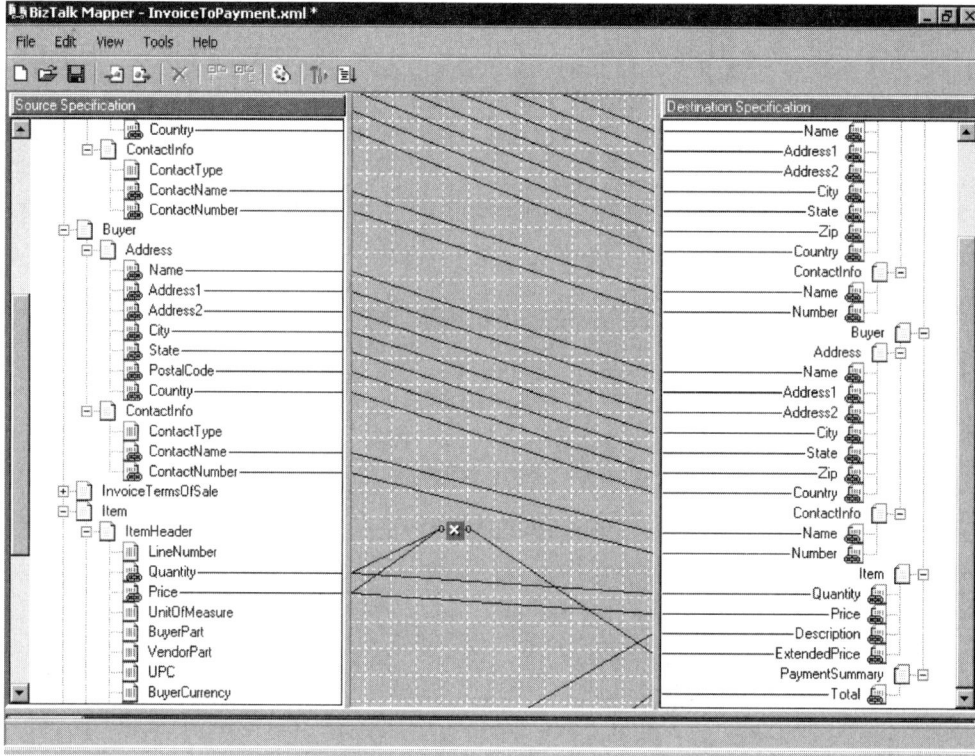

4.   On the **File** menu, click **Exit** to close the BizTalk Mapper console.

Module 2 Summary

In this module, you accomplished the following:

- **Created a specification.** For more information, see "Understanding Specifications" in Chapter 5, "Creating Specifications."

- **Added new records and fields to a specification.** For more information, see "To add new fields to records" in Chapter 5, "Creating Specifications."

- **Created a map.** For more information, see Chapter 6, "Mapping Data."

- **Created links between fields in a map.** For more information, see "Creating Links" in Chapter 6, "Mapping Data."

- **Used functoids to mathematically manipulate values in a map.** For more information, see "Understanding Functoids" in Chapter 6, "Mapping Data."

- **Saved specifications and maps to the WebDAV repository.** For more information, see "To store specifications" in Chapter 5, "Creating Specifications," and "To store maps" in Chapter 6, "Mapping Data."

The highlighted areas of the following diagram illustrate the steps you completed in this module.

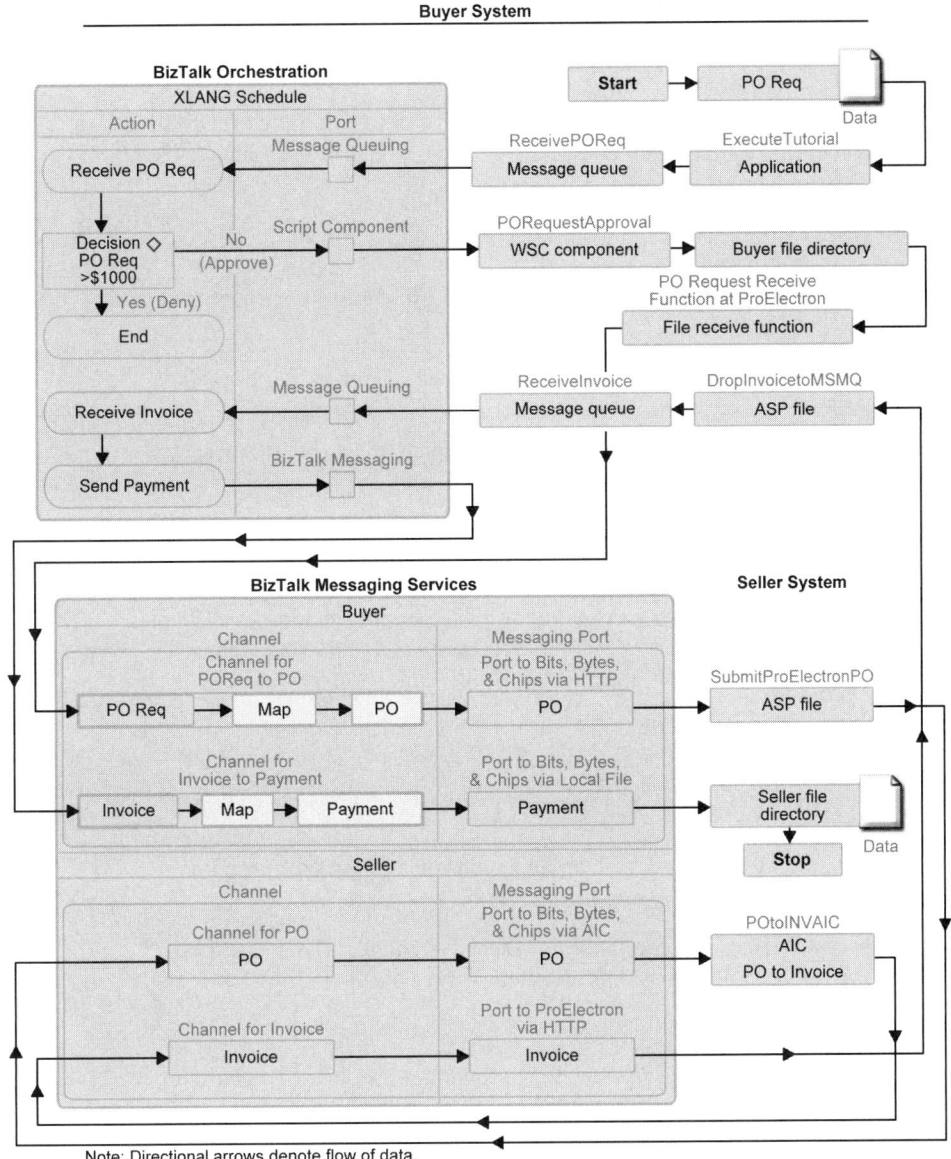

Note: Directional arrows denote flow of data.

Module 3: Configuring BizTalk Messaging Services

In this module, you learn how to use BizTalk Messaging Manager to configure organizations, channels, and messaging ports for the seller and buyer systems. You also learn how to use BizTalk Server Administration to configure a File receive function.

Objectives

- **Create document definitions.** For more information, see Chapter 9, "Configuring BizTalk Messaging Services."

- **Create organizations.** For more information, see Chapter 9, "Configuring BizTalk Messaging Services."

- **Create messaging ports.** For more information, see Chapter 9, "Configuring BizTalk Messaging Services."

- **Create channels.** For more information, see Chapter 9, "Configuring BizTalk Messaging Services."

- **Use a map in a channel to transform a document.** For more information, see Chapter 6, "Mapping Data."

- **Create a receive function.** For more information, see "Receive Functions" in Chapter 11, "Administering Servers and Applications."

Configuring the Buyer System

You use BizTalk Messaging Manager to create organizations that represent your trading partners.

To use BizTalk Messaging Manager to configure the buyer system, see "To create the organizations for the buyer system" later in this chapter.

Shortcut

To use a script to configure the buyer system, see the following procedure, "To configure the buyer system using a configuration script."

To configure the buyer system using a configuration script

This script configures the following:

- A source organization named **ProElectron on Buyer** on the buyer system.

- A destination organization named **Bits,Bytes,Chips on Buyer** on the buyer system.

- Four document definitions that reference specifications for CommonPO, CommonInvoice, PaymentSpec, and POReq.

- A messaging port and channel that define the movement of a purchase order request from the buyer system to the seller system by using an HTTP transport service to an ASP file on the seller system.

- A messaging port and channel that define the movement of an invoice that has been delivered to the buyer and transform it into a payment document on the seller system.

☞ Caution

- If you used BizTalk Messaging Manager and BizTalk Server Administration to configure the buyer system, do not run the configuration script.

To run the script that configures BizTalk Messaging Services for the buyer system:

1. Browse to **\Program Files\Microsoft BizTalk Server\Tutorial\Setup\MessagingConfigurationScript** on the BizTalk Server installation drive.

2. Double-click **ConfigureBuyer.VBS**.

   A message box appears, indicating success.

Continue to "Configuring the Seller System" later in this chapter.

To create the organizations for the buyer system

☞ Caution

- If you used the configuration script, do not use BizTalk Messaging Manager and BizTalk Server Administration to configure the buyer system. Continue to "Configuring the Seller System" later in this chapter.

1. On the **Start** menu, point to **Programs**, point to **Microsoft BizTalk Server 2000**, and then click **BizTalk Messaging Manager**.

2. If the **BizTalk Messaging Manager** dialog box appears, click **Cancel**.

3. On the **File** menu, point to **New** and click **Organization**.

   The **New Organization** dialog box appears.

4. In the **Organization name** box, type **Bits,Bytes,Chips on Buyer** and click **OK**.

5. Repeat steps 3 and 4, naming the new organization **ProElectron on Buyer**.

To create the document definitions for the buyer and seller systems

In this procedure, you create four document definitions that reference the document specifications, CommonInvoice, CommonPO, PaymentSpec, and POReq. These document definitions are shared by the buyer and seller systems.

To create the document definitions:

1. On the **File** menu, point to **New** and click **Document Definition**.

   The **New Document Definition** dialog box appears.

2. In the **Document definition name** box, type **Purchase Order**.

3. Select the **Document specification** check box and click the **Browse** button.

   The **Select a Document Specification from the WebDAV Repository** dialog box appears.

4. Double-click the **Microsoft** folder.

5. Click **CommonPO.xml** and click **Open**.

6. Click **OK** to close the **New Document Definition** dialog box.

7. Repeat steps 1 through 6 to create a new document definition with the following variations:

   • Name the new document definition **Invoice**.

   • Click the **CommonInvoice.xml** specification from WebDAV.

8. Repeat steps 1 through 6 to create a new document definition with the following variations:

   • Name the new document definition **Purchase Order Request**.

   • Click the **POReq.xml** specification from WebDAV.

9. Repeat steps 1 through 6 to create a new document definition with the following variations:

   • Name the new document definition **Payment**.

   • Click the **PaymentSpec.xml** specification from WebDAV.

To create a messaging port to Bits, Bytes, & Chips for the buyer system

In this procedure, you create a messaging port for the buyer system. A messaging port defines the destination for a document.

The messaging port that you create has as its destination organization "Bits,Bytes,Chips on Buyer." This port uses the HTTP transport service to deliver documents to Bits, Bytes, & Chips.

To create the messaging port:

1. On the **File** menu, point to **New**, point to **Messaging Port**, and then click **To an Organization**.

   The New Messaging Port Wizard opens.

2. In the **Name** box, type **Port to Bits,Bytes,Chips via HTTP** and click **Next**.

3. On the **Destination Organization** page, in the **Organization** area, click **Browse**.

   The **Select an Organization** dialog box appears.

4. Click **Bits,Bytes,Chips on Buyer** and click **OK**.

5. In the **Primary transport** area, click **Browse**.

   The **Primary Transport** dialog box appears.

6. In the **Transport type** list, click **HTTP**.

7. In the **Address** box, after the **http://** prefix, type the *name of your computer*, followed by **/SubmitPO/SubmitProElectronPO.asp**, click **OK**, and then click **Next**.

   For example, http://Computer1/SubmitPO/SubmitProElectronPO.asp.

   To find the name of your computer, complete the following steps:

   1. On the **Start** menu, point to **Settings** and click **Control Panel**.

   2. Double-click **Administrative Tools**.

   3. Double-click **Computer Management**.

      The Computer Management console appears.

   4. On the **Action** menu, click **Properties**.

      The **Computer Management (Local) Properties** dialog box appears.

   5. Click the **Network Identification** tab.

      The name of your computer appears in the **Computer name** field.

8. On the **Envelope Information** page, click **Next**.

9. On the **Security Information** page, verify that the **Create a channel for this messaging port** check box is selected.

10. In the **Channel type** list, click **From an organization** and click **Finish**.

    The New Channel Wizard opens.

To create a channel from ProElectron for the buyer system

In this procedure, you create a channel for the messaging port.

To create the channel:

1. On the **General Information** page, in the **Name** box, type **Channel for POReq to PO** and click **Next**.

2. On the **Source Organization** page, click **Browse**.

   The **Select an Organization** dialog box appears.

3. Click **ProElectron on Buyer**, click **OK**, and then click **Next**.

4. On the **Inbound Document** page, to the right of the **Inbound document definition name** box, click **Browse**.

   The **Select a Document Definition** dialog box appears.

5. Click **Purchase Order Request**, click **OK**, and then click **Next**.

6. On the **Outbound Document** page, to the right of the **Outbound document definition name** box, click **Browse**.

   The **Select a Document Definition** dialog box appears.

7. Click **Purchase Order** and click **OK**.

8. Verify that the **Map inbound document to outbound document** check box is selected.

9. To the right of the **Map reference** box, click **Browse**.

   The **Select a Map from the WebDAV Repository** dialog box appears.

10. Double-click the **Microsoft** folder.

11. Click **POReqtoPO.xml**, click **Open**, and then click **Next**.

12. On the **Document Logging** page, click **Next**.

13. On the **Advanced Configuration** page, click **Finish**.

To create a messaging port to Bits, Bytes, & Chips within the buyer system

In this procedure, the messaging port sends documents within the buyer system by using the File transport service. The documents are sent internally to the folder specified in the destination address.

To create the messaging port:

1. On the **File** menu, point to **New**, point to **Messaging Port**, and then click **To an Organization**.

   The New Messaging Port Wizard opens.

2. In the **Name** box, type **Port to Bits,Bytes,Chips via Local File** and click **Next**.

3. On the **Destination Organization** page, in the **Organization** area, click **Browse**.

   The **Select an Organization** dialog box appears.

4. Click **ProElectron on Buyer** and click **OK**.

5. In the **Primary transport** area, click **Browse**.

   The **Primary Transport** dialog box appears.

6. In the **Transport type** list, click **File**.

7. In the **Address** box, after **file://**, type **C:\TutorialFiles\Seller\payment%tracking_id%.xml**.

For example, file://C:\TutorialFiles\Seller\payment%tracking_id%.xml.

✎ Note

- For the File transport service, the default transport-component setting is to append new files to an existing file in the specified directory. To create a new file with a unique name for each document instance, you must use the following file path format:

  ```
  file://C:\dir\file%tracking_id%.xml
  ```

8. Click **OK** to close the **Primary Transport** dialog box and click **Next**.

9. On the **Envelope Information** page, click **Next**.

10. On the **Security Information** page, verify that the **Create a channel for this messaging port** check box is selected.

11. In the **Channel type** list, click **From an organization** and click **Finish**.

   The New Channel Wizard opens.

To create a channel from Bits, Bytes, & Chips for the buyer system

The channel that you create in this procedure processes invoices that are received from Bits, Bytes, & Chips and uses a map to transform the invoice into a payment.

To create the channel:

1. On the **General Information** page, in the **Name** box, type **Channel for Invoice To Payment** and click **Next**.

2. On the **Source Organization** page, in the **Organization** area, click **Browse**.

   The **Select an Organization** dialog box appears.

3. Click **Bits,Bytes,Chips on Buyer**, click **OK**, and then click **Next**.

4. On the **Inbound Document** page, to the right of the **Inbound document definition name** box, click **Browse**.

   The **Select a Document Definition** dialog box appears.

5. Click **Invoice**, click **OK**, and then click **Next**.

6. On the **Outbound Document** page, to the right of the **Outbound document definition name** box, click **Browse**.

   The **Select a Document Definition** dialog box appears.

7. Click **Payment** and click **OK**.

8. Verify that the **Map inbound document to outbound document** check box is selected.

9. To the right of the **Map reference** box, click **Browse**.

   The **Select a Map from the WebDAV Repository** dialog box appears.

10. Double-click the **Microsoft** folder.

11. Click **InvoicetoPayment.xml**, click **Open**, and then click **Next**.

12. On the **Document Logging** page, click **Next**.

13. On the **Advanced Configuration** page, click **Finish**.

14. On the **File** menu, click **Exit** to close BizTalk Messaging Manager.

To create a File receive function for the buyer system

In this procedure, you create a File receive function that retrieves the buyer's purchase order request from a local file directory and submits it to BizTalk Messaging Services.

The following illustration shows the relationship between the sending business application, the file system, and the receive function.

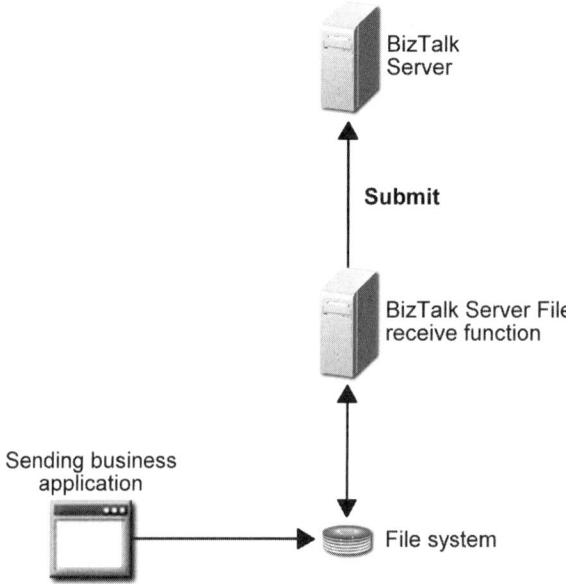

To create the File receive function:

1. On the **Start** menu, point to **Programs**, point to **Microsoft BizTalk Server 2000**, and then click **BizTalk Server Administration**.

2. Expand **Microsoft BizTalk Server 2000**, expand **BizTalk Server Group**, and then click **Receive Functions**.

3. On the **Action** menu, point to **New** and click **File Receive Function**.

   The **Add a File Receive Function** dialog box appears.

4. In the **Name** box, type **PORequest Receive Function at ProElectron**.

5. In the **Server on which the receive function will run** box, click the name of a server in the BizTalk server group.

6. In the **File types to poll for** box, type ***.xml**.

7. In the **Polling location** box, type **C:\TutorialFiles\Buyer**.

8. Click the **Advanced** button.

   The **Advanced Receive Function Options** dialog box appears.

9. In the **Channel name** list, click **Channel for POReq to PO** and click **OK**.

10. Click **OK** to close the **Add a File Receive Function** dialog box.

11. Close BizTalk Server Administration.

Configuring the Seller System

You use BizTalk Messaging Manager to create organizations that represent your trading partners.

To create the organizations for the seller system

1. On the **Start** menu, point to **Programs**, point to **Microsoft BizTalk Server 2000**, and then click **BizTalk Messaging Manager**.

2. If the **BizTalk Messaging Manager** dialog box appears, click **Cancel**.

3. On the **File** menu, point to **New** and click **Organization**.

   The **New Organization** dialog box appears.

4. On the **General** tab, in the **Organization name** box, type **Bits,Bytes,Chips on Seller** and click **OK**.

5. Repeat steps 3 and 4, naming the new organization **ProElectron on Seller**, and click **OK**.

To create a messaging port to Bits, Bytes, & Chips for the seller system

In this procedure, you create a messaging port that defines the destination for a document. This messaging port sends documents internally within the seller system using an application integration component (AIC) as the transport service.

An AIC typically serves as an integration point between BizTalk Server 2000 and a back-end application. In this scenario, the AIC functions both as the integration point and as a hypothetical back-end application. The messaging port passes the purchase order to the AIC. The AIC transforms the purchase order into an invoice and submits it to a channel in BizTalk Messaging Services on the seller system.

The purchase order could also be transformed into an invoice by using a map in the channel, but for simplicity the AIC performs this function in this scenario.

To create the messaging port:

1. On the **File** menu, point to **New**, point to **Messaging Port**, and then click **To an Organization**.

   The New Messaging Port Wizard opens.

2. In the **Name** box, type **Port to Bits,Bytes,Chips via AIC** and click **Next**.

3. On the **Destination Organization** page, in the **Organization** area, click **Browse**.

   The **Select an Organization** dialog box appears.

4. Click **Bits,Bytes,Chips on Seller** and click **OK**.

5. In the **Primary transport** area, click **Browse**.

   The **Primary Transport** dialog box appears.

6. In the **Transport type** list, verify that **Application Integration Component** is selected and click **Browse**.

   The **Select a Component** dialog box appears.

7. Click **POToINVAIC ConvertPOToInvoice** and click **OK**.

8. Click **OK** to close the **Primary Transport** dialog box and click **Next**.

9. On the **Envelope Information** page, click **Next**.

10. On the **Security Information** page, verify that the **Create a channel for this messaging port** check box is selected.

11. In the **Channel type** list, click **From an organization** and click **Finish**.

    The New Channel Wizard opens.

To create a channel from ProElectron for the seller system

In this procedure, you create a channel for the messaging port.

The channel that you create has as its source organization "ProElectron on Seller," which represents the buyer on the seller system. This channel processes purchase orders that are received from ProElectron. Because both the inbound and the outbound document definitions are identical, no map reference is required for this channel and no document transformation occurs.

To create the channel:

1. On the **General Information** page, in the **Name** box, type **Channel for PO** and click **Next**.

2. On the **Source Organization** page, in the **Organization** area, click **Browse**.

   The **Select an Organization** dialog box appears.

3. Click **ProElectron on Seller**, click **OK**, and then click **Next**.

4. On the **Inbound Document** page, to the right of the **Inbound document definition name** box, click **Browse**.

   The **Select a Document Definition** dialog box appears.

5. Click **Purchase Order**, click **OK**, and then click **Next**.

6. On the **Outbound Document** page, to the right of the **Outbound document definition name** box, click **Browse**.

   The **Select a Document Definition** dialog box appears.

7. Click **Purchase Order**, click **OK**, and then click **Next**.

8. On the **Document Logging** page, click **Next**.

9. On the **Advanced Configuration** page, click **Finish**.

To create a messaging port to ProElectron for the seller system

The destination organization that you create for the messaging port is named "ProElectron on Seller," which represents the buyer on the seller system. This messaging port sends documents from the seller system to the buyer system. This port uses the HTTP transport service to deliver documents to the specified buyer address.

When this port is used, an invoice message is sent to an ASP page on the buyer system that then posts the invoice to a message queue on the buyer system.

To create the messaging port:

1. On the **File** menu, point to **New**, point to **Messaging Port**, and then click **To an Organization**.

   The New Messaging Port Wizard opens.

2. On the **General Information** page, in the **Name** box, type **Port to ProElectron via HTTP** and click **Next**.

3. On the **Destination Organization** page, in the **Organization** area, click **Browse**.

   The **Select an Organization** dialog box appears.

4. Click **ProElectron on Seller** and click **OK**.

5. In the **Primary transport** area, click **Browse**.

   The **Primary Transport** dialog box appears.

6. In the **Transport type** list, click **HTTP**.

7. In the **Address** box, after the **http://** prefix, type the *name of your computer*, followed by **/InvoiceToQueue/DropInvoicetoMSMQ.asp**, click **OK**, and then click **Next**.

   For example, http://Computer1/InvoiceToQueue/DropInvoicetoMSMQ.asp.

To find the name of your computer, complete the following steps:

1. On the **Start** menu, point to **Settings** and click **Control Panel**.

2. Double-click **Administrative Tools**.

3. Double-click **Computer Management**.

   The Computer Management console appears.

4. On the **Action** menu, click **Properties**.

   The **Computer Management (Local) Properties** dialog box appears.

5. Click the **Network Identification** tab.

   The name of your computer appears in the **Computer name** field.

8. On the **Envelope Information** page, click **Next**.

9. On the **Security Information** page, verify that the **Create a channel for this messaging port** check box is selected.

10. In the **Channel type** list, click **From an organization** and click **Finish**.

    The New Channel Wizard opens.

To create a channel from Bits, Bytes, & Chips for the seller system

The channel that you create in this procedure has as its source organization "Bits,Bytes,Chips on Seller." This channel processes invoices that are sent to ProElectron on the seller system according to the rules of the messaging port, **Port to ProElectron via HTTP**.

To create the channel:

1. On the **General Information** page, in the **Name** box, type **Channel for Invoice** and click **Next**.

2. On the **Source Organization** page, in the **Organization** area, click **Browse**.

   The **Select an Organization** dialog box appears.

3. Click **Bits,Bytes,Chips on Seller**, click **OK**, and then click **Next**.

4. On the **Inbound Document** page, to the right of the **Inbound document definition name** box, click **Browse**.

   The **Select a Document Definition** dialog box appears.

5. Click **Invoice**, click **OK**, and then click **Next**.

6. On the **Outbound Document** page, click **Browse**.

   The **Select a Document Definition** dialog box appears.

7. Click **Invoice**, click **OK**, and then click **Next**.

8. On the **Document Logging** page, click **Next**.

9. On the **Advanced Configuration** page, click **Finish**.

10. On the **File** menu, click **Exit** to close BizTalk Messaging Manager.

Module 3 Summary

In this module, you accomplished the following:

- **Created document definitions.** For more information, see Chapter 9, "Configuring BizTalk Messaging Services."

- **Created organizations.** For more information, see Chapter 9, "Configuring BizTalk Messaging Services."

- **Created messaging ports.** For more information, see Chapter 9, "Configuring BizTalk Messaging Services."

- **Created channels.** For more information, see Chapter 9, "Configuring BizTalk Messaging Services."

- **Used a map in a channel to transform a document.** For more information, see Chapter 6, "Mapping Data."

- **Created a File receive function.** For more information, see "Receive Functions" in Chapter 11, "Administering Servers and Applications."

To view the document definitions, organizations, messaging ports, channels, and map that you created in this module, use the **Search Now** button in BizTalk Messaging Manager.

The highlighted areas of the following diagram illustrate the steps you completed in this module.

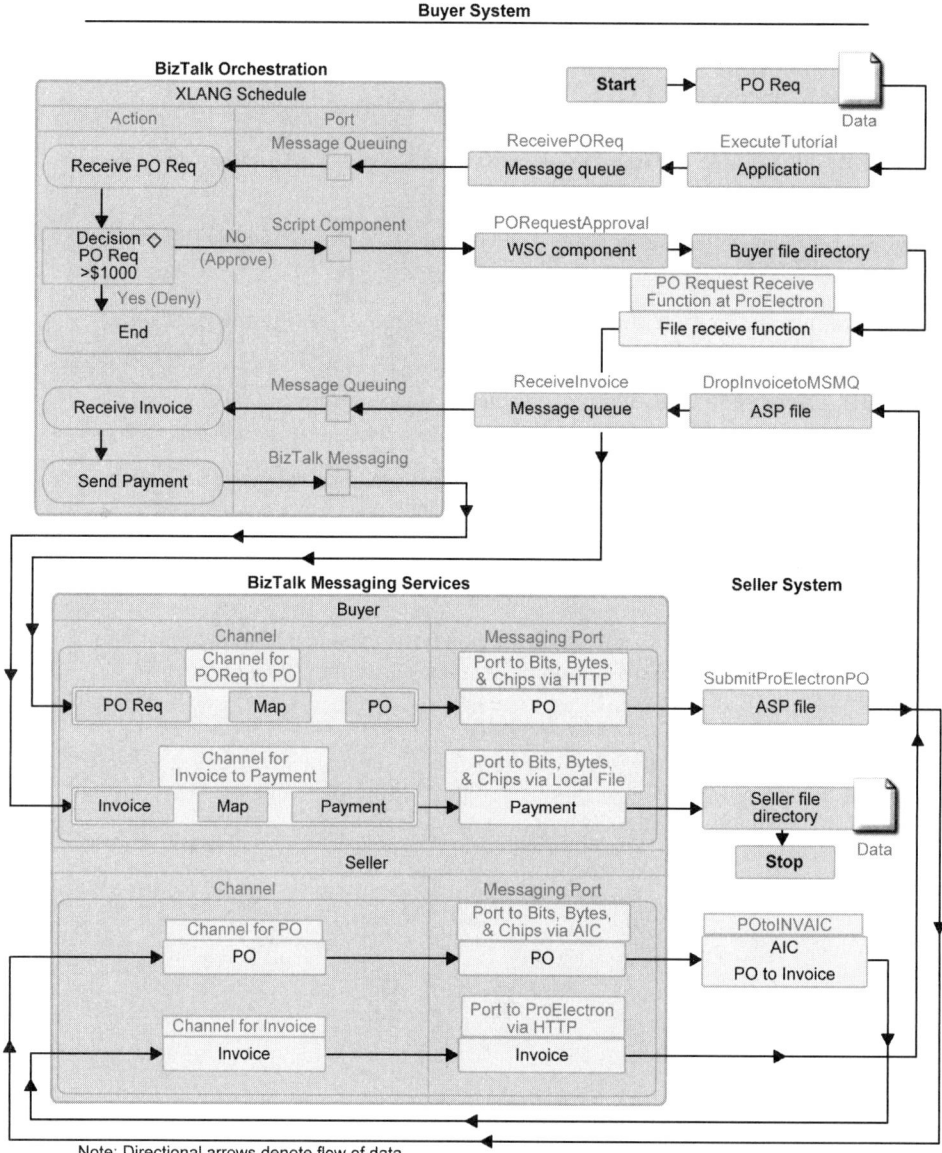

Note: Directional arrows denote flow of data.

Module 4: Completing the XLANG Schedule

In this module, you use BizTalk Orchestration Designer to implement a port by using BizTalk Messaging Services. You then compile and run the completed XLANG schedule.

Objectives

- **Add invoice and payment actions.** For more information, see "To add shapes" in Chapter 8, "BizTalk Orchestration Services."

- **Implement a port using BizTalk Messaging Services.** For more information, see "Using the BizTalk Messaging Shape" in Chapter 8, "BizTalk Orchestration Services."

- **Compile and run the completed XLANG schedule.** For more information, see "Compiling XLANG Schedules" and "Running XLANG Schedules" in Chapter 8, "BizTalk Orchestration Services."

To complete the XLANG schedule, see the following procedure, "To add invoice and payment actions."

Shortcut

To use the existing XLANG schedule, see "To run the completed XLANG schedule" later in this chapter.

To add invoice and payment actions

In this procedure, you add an action that receives the invoice from the buyer and another action that sends the payment message to the seller.

To create the actions:

1. On the **Start** menu, point to **Programs**, point to **Microsoft BizTalk Server 2000**, and then click **BizTalk Orchestration Designer**.

2. On the **File** menu, click **Open**.

   The **Open XLANG Schedule Drawing** dialog box appears.

3. If you are using the existing **Buyer1.skv** file, in the **Open XLANG Schedule Drawing** dialog box, browse to **\Program Files\Microsoft BizTalk Server\Tutorial\Schedule\Solution** on the BizTalk Server installation drive, click **Buyer1.skv**, and then click **Open.**

   If you created the **Buyer1.skv** file in Module 1, browse to **\Program Files\Microsoft BizTalk Server\Tutorial\Schedule\Lab**, click **Buyer1.skv**, and then click **Open.**

   ### Note

- There will be a blank drawing in BizTalk Orchestration Designer, which you can close.

4. Highlight the connection between the **Write PO Request to File** action and the **End** action and press DELETE.

5. Move the **End** action down to allow room for two new action shapes.

6. On the **Business Process** page, drag the **Action** shape from the **Flowchart** stencil to the left side of the **Separator** bar.

   Position the shape directly below the **Write PO Request to File** action.

7. Right-click the **Action** shape and click **Properties**.

   The **Action Properties** dialog box appears.

8. In the **Name** box, type **Receive Invoice** and click **OK**.

9. On the **Business Process** page, drag the **Action** shape from the **Flowchart** stencil to the left side of the **Separator** bar.

   Position the shape directly below the **Receive Invoice** action.

10. Right-click the **Action** shape and click **Properties**.

    The **Action Properties** dialog box appears.

11. In the **Name** box, type **Send Payment** and click **OK**.

12. Connect the **Write PO Request to File** action to the **Receive Invoice** action.

13. Connect the **Receive Invoice** action to the **Send Payment** action.

14. Connect the **Send Payment** action to the **End** shape.

To bind the Message Queuing service to receive an invoice

The **Receive Invoice** action is bound to a message queuing service. When an invoice is dropped to the invoice message queue that is defined by the service, it activates the **Receive Invoice** action.

To bind the message queuing service:

1. On the **Business Process** page, drag the **Message Queuing** shape from the **Implementation** stencil to the right side of the **Separator** bar that divides the two sides of the drawing.

   Position the **Message Queuing** shape so that it is horizontally aligned with the **Receive Invoice** action.

   The Message Queuing Binding Wizard opens.

2. On the **Welcome to the Message Queuing Binding Wizard** page, verify that **Create a new port** is selected.

3. In the **Create a new port** box, type **ReceiveInvoice** and click **Next**.

4. On the **Static or Dynamic Queue Information** page, verify that **Static queue** is selected and click **Next**.

5. On the **Queue Information** page, click **Use a known queue for all instances**.

6. In the **Enter the queue name** box, type **.\private$\ReceiveInvoice** and click **Next**.

7. On the **Advanced Port Properties** page, click **Finish**.

To define message properties for the Receive Invoice service

1. Select the **Receive Invoice** action and drag the control handle on the right of the **Receive Invoice** action to the **ReceiveInvoice** port.

   The XML Communication Wizard opens.

2. On the **Welcome to the XML Communication Wizard** page, click **Receive** and click **Next**.

3. On the **Message Information** page, verify that **Create a new message** is selected.

4. In the **Message name** box, type **CommonInvoice** and click **Next**.

5. On the **XML Translation Information** page, verify that **Receive XML messages from the queue** is selected and click **Next**.

6. On the **Message Type Information** page, in the **Message type** box, type **CommonInvoice** and click **Next**.

7. On the **Message Specification Information** page, click **Finish**.

To bind the BizTalk Messaging Services

In this procedure, you bind a BizTalk Messaging Service to the XLANG schedule drawing and name the channel that is being used.

To bind the BizTalk Messaging Services:

1. On the **Business Process** page, drag the **BizTalk Messaging** shape from the **Implementation** stencil to the right side of the **Separator** bar that divides the two sides of the drawing.

   Position the **BizTalk Messaging** shape so that it is horizontally aligned with the **Send Payment** action.

   The BizTalk Messaging Binding Wizard opens.

2. On the **Welcome to the BizTalk Messaging Binding Wizard** page, verify that **Create a new port** is selected.

3. In the **Create a new port** box, type **SendPayment** and click **Next**.

4. On the **Communication Direction** page, verify that **Send** is selected and click **Next**.

5. On the **Static or Dynamic Channel Information** page, verify that **Static channel** is selected.

6. In the **Enter the name of a known, pre-existing channel** box, type **Channel for Invoice To Payment** and click **Finish**.

Note that **Channel for Invoice To Payment** was created in Module 3.

To define message properties for the BizTalk Messaging Services

1. Drag the control handle on the right of the **Send Payment** action to the **SendPayment** port.

The XML Communication Wizard opens.

2. On the **Welcome to the XML Communication Wizard** page, click **Next**.

3. On the **Message Information** page, click **Add a reference to an existing message**, click **CommonInvoice**, and then click **Next**.

4. On the **XML Translation Information** page, verify that **Send XML messages to the queue** is selected and click **Next**.

5. On the **Message Type Information** page, click **Next**.

6. On the **Message Specification Information** page, click **Finish**.

To save the completed XLANG schedule drawing

1. On the **File** menu, click **Save As**.

The **Save XLANG Schedule Drawing As** dialog box appears.

2. Browse to **\Program Files\Microsoft BizTalk Server\Tutorial\Schedule\Lab** on the BizTalk Server installation drive.

3. In the **File name** box, type **Buyer2** and click **Save**.

To compile the completed XLANG schedule

1. On the **File** menu, click **Make XLANG Buyer2.skx**.

The **Save XLANG Schedule to** dialog box appears.

2. Browse to **\Program Files\Microsoft BizTalk Server\Tutorial\Schedule\Lab** on the BizTalk Server installation drive.

3. In the **File name** box, type **Buyer2** and click **Save**.

Your completed XLANG schedule drawing should appear similar to the following illustration.

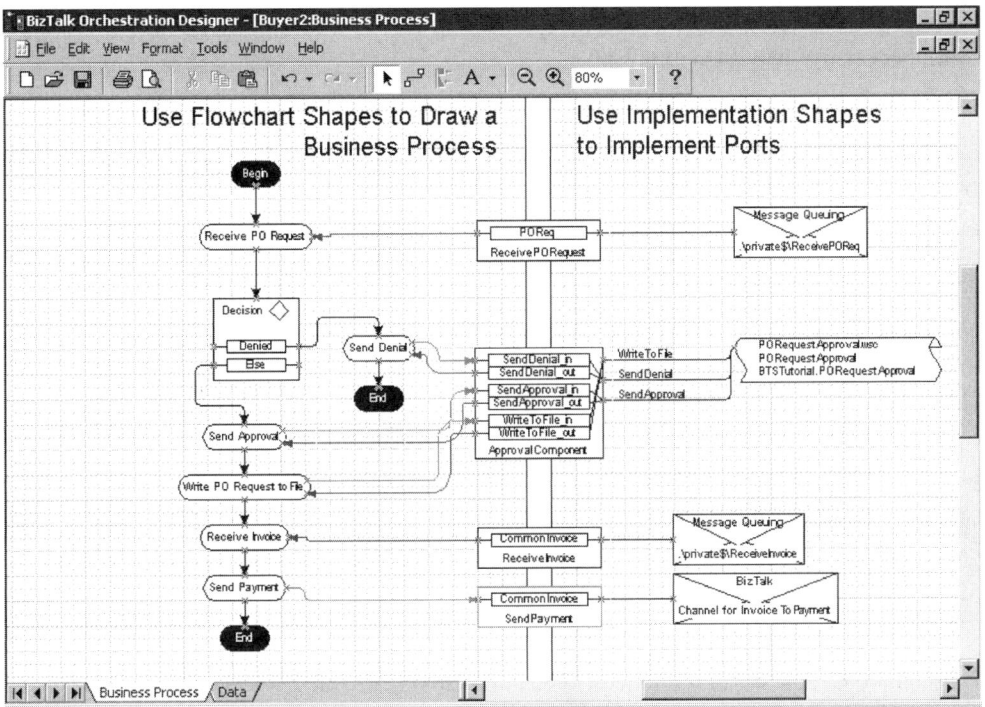

4. On the **File** menu, click **Exit**.

To run the completed XLANG schedule

You have completed the configuration of a business-to-business automated procurement solution. You can now run the application that activates the XLANG schedule.

In this procedure, you use an application that activates the XLANG schedule and delivers a purchase order request to the message queue that the schedule is monitoring.

To run the XLANG schedule:

1. Browse to **\Program Files\Microsoft BizTalk Server\Tutorial\Schedule\Solution** on the BizTalk Server installation drive.

2. Double-click **ExecuteTutorial.exe**.

    This application is used to activate the XLANG schedule by means of a moniker.

    The **ExecuteTutorial** application opens.

3. Click **Browse for Schedule**.

Shortcut

If you are using the existing XLANG schedule, browse to **\Program Files\Microsoft BizTalk Server\Tutorial\Schedule\Solution** and continue to step 5.

4. If you created the **Buyer2 XLANG** schedule, browse to **\Program Files\Microsoft BizTalk Server\Tutorial\Schedule\Lab**.

5. Click the **Buyer2.skx** XLANG schedule and click **Open**.

6. Click **Browse for Data File** and browse to **\Program Files\Microsoft BizTalk Server\Tutorial\Schedule\SampleData**.

7. Click **POReqAccept.xml** and click **Open**.

8. Click **Start XLANG Schedule**.

   Because its total is less than $1000, the purchase order request is approved. A message box appears, notifying you that the application passed data to the XLANG Scheduler Engine. At this point, the application is finished. A second message box notifies you that the purchase order request has been approved. Click **OK** to close the dialog boxes.

9. Click **End** to close the **ExecuteTutorial** application.

10. Browse to **C:\TutorialFiles\Seller**.

    You see the payment file. The file name is **Payment*XXXX*.xml**, where *XXXX* is representative of a unique set of numbers. Double-click the file to open it in Microsoft Internet Explorer.

You have submitted a purchase order request. The purchase order request was approved and ended in a payment message being posted to the seller system.

Module 4 Summary

In this module, you accomplished the following:

- **Added invoice and payment actions.** For more information, see "Connecting Shapes" in Chapter 8, "BizTalk Orchestration Services."

- **Implemented a messaging port using BizTalk Messaging Services.** For more information about implementing a messaging port using BizTalk Messaging Services, see "Using the BizTalk Messaging Shape" in Chapter 8, "BizTalk Orchestration Services."

- **Compiled and ran the completed XLANG schedule.** For more information, see "Compiling XLANG Schedules" and "Running XLANG Schedules" in Chapter 8, "BizTalk Orchestration Services."

The highlighted areas of the following diagram illustrate the steps you completed in this module.

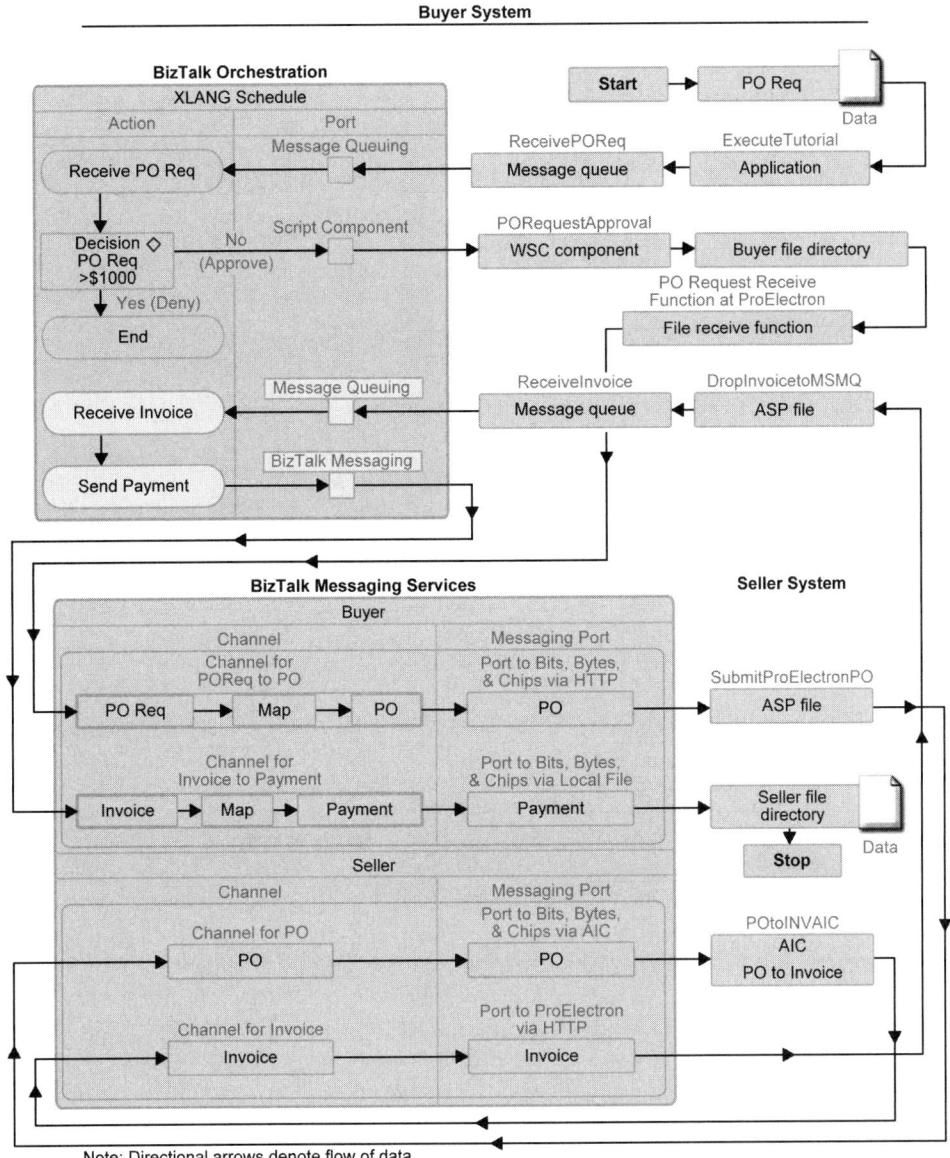

Note: Directional arrows denote flow of data.

Tutorial Summary

In this tutorial you configured Microsoft BizTalk Server 2000 to establish and run a business-to-business automated procurement process.

The following illustration shows the flow of data through BizTalk Server while running the Buyer2 XLANG schedule at the end of Module 4.

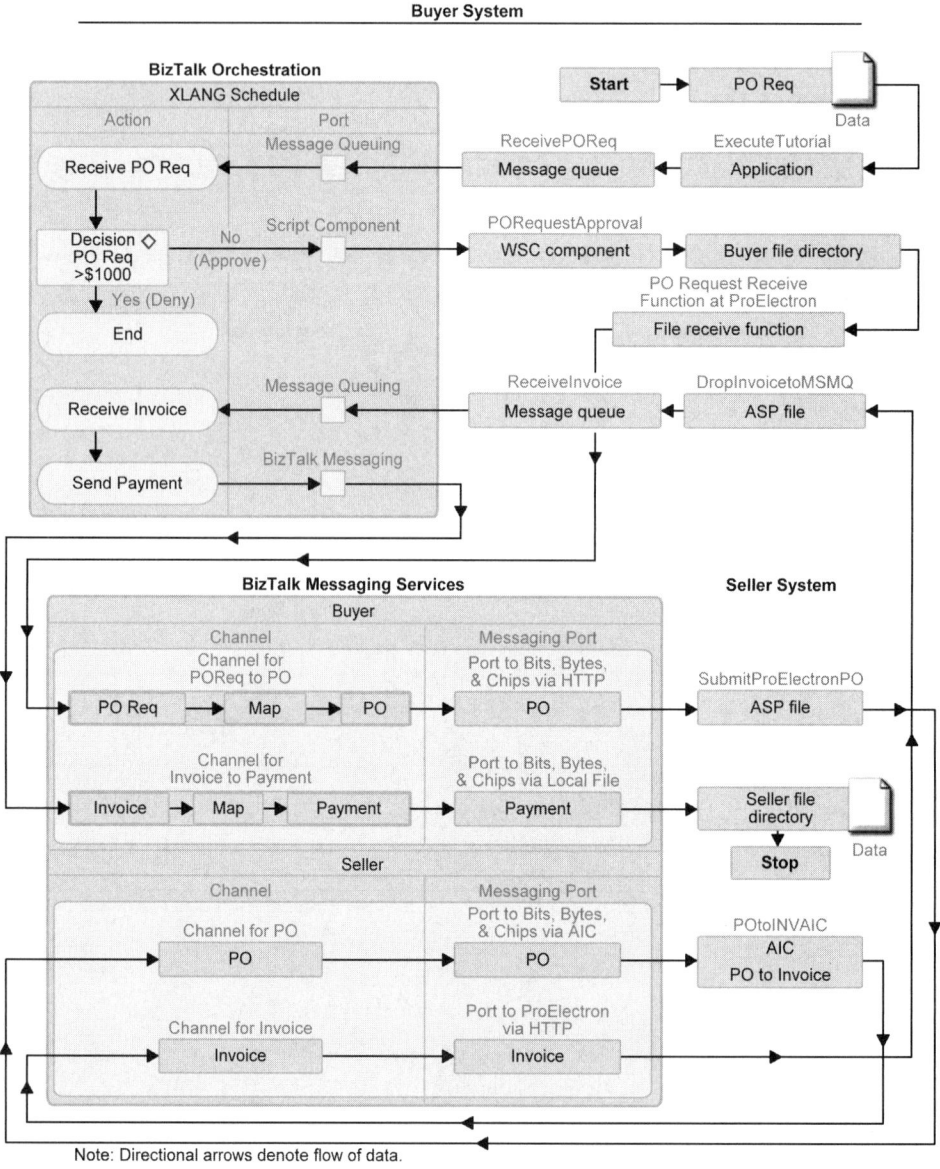

Note: Directional arrows denote flow of data.

You learned how BizTalk Server components and services work together to integrate loosely coupled, long-running business processes, both within and between businesses.

You also learned how to:

- Use BizTalk Orchestration Designer to model business processes by creating an XLANG schedule drawing.
- Use BizTalk Messaging Manager to create organizations, channels, messaging ports, and document definitions.
- Use BizTalk Editor to create specifications.
- Use BizTalk Mapper to create maps.
- Compile and run an XLANG schedule.

You have successfully completed the tutorial. For detailed information about creating the auxiliary components used in this tutorial, see the following section, "Creating Auxiliary Components."

Creating Auxiliary Components

In this section, you will learn how to create auxiliary components that work in conjunction with Microsoft BizTalk Server 2000 to process data. Each component and its role and relationship in the process are described in detail.

Specifically, you create:

- An application on the buyer system that activates an XLANG schedule and sends a purchase order (PO) request to a message queue that is bound to the XLANG schedule that controls the flow of messages through the buyer system.
- A Windows Script Component (WSC) on the buyer system that accepts the approval or denial status for a purchase order request from the XLANG schedule. If approved, the WSC displays an approval message and writes the purchase order request to a local file directory, where the BizTalk Messaging Services for the buyer system retrieves it. If denied, the WSC displays a denial message and the schedule ends.
- An application integration component (AIC) on the seller system that generates an invoice based on the data in the purchase order from the buyer.
- An ASP file on the buyer system that submits a purchase order to BizTalk Server.
- An ASP file on the seller system that delivers an invoice to a message queue.

Creating the Application

In this topic, you create an application that activates an XLANG schedule and then drops a purchase order request to a queue. You use this application to test the implementation of the XLANG schedule and the configuration of BizTalk Messaging Manager.

To complete the lab, modify the code in the sample project. You will focus on the code that is specific to activating the XLANG schedule and to dropping a message into a queue. Ancillary code is provided for you.

Each step corresponds to a segment of code. Look for comment blocks similar to the following example:

```
''''''''''''''''''''''''''''''''''''''''''''''''''''''''
'To Do: Step A
''''''''''''''''''''''''''''''''''''''''''''''''''''''''
```

Following this code are lines that have question marks (?) indicating placeholders where you must make a change. Replace the question marks with the proper code to complete the lab. For example:

```
Private g_MSMTxDisp As ?
```

should be changed to:

```
Private g_MSMTxDisp As MSMQ.MSMQTransactionDispenser
```

 **Note**

- These lines of code have been commented out. Be sure to remove the comment mark at the beginning of the lines to which you make changes. The steps are not necessarily in order in the code window.

To open the application

1. Browse to **\Program Files\Microsoft BizTalk Server\Tutorial\Schedule\Lab** on the BizTalk Server installation drive.

2. Double-click **ExecuteTutorial.vbp**.

To add the required references to the application

In this procedure, you enable the application to implement a number of dynamic-link libraries (DLLs) required to use Message Queuing, XML, and the scripting run time.

1. On the **Project** menu, click **References**.

2. Select **Microsoft Message Queue 2.0 Object Library**.

   The full path for this type library is \WINNT\System32\msxml2.dll.

3. Select **Microsoft Scripting Runtime**.

   The full path for this DLL is \WINNT\System32\Scrun.dll.

4. Select **Microsoft XML, v 3.0**.

   The full path for this DLL is \WINNT\System32\msxml3.dll.

5. Click **OK**.

To define and initialize the Message Queue objects

In this procedure, you add the code to use the chosen type libraries. The lettered steps in the following list correspond to the lettered steps in the code provided.

1. In the Project window, expand **Forms** and click **Form1 (ExecuteTutorial.frm)**.

2. On the **View** menu, click **Code**.

3. In the **General Declarations** section at step A in the code, create the **Message Queue** objects as shown in the following example:

```
Private g_MSMTxDisp As MSMQ.MSMQTransactionDispenser
Private g_MSMQQueue As MSMQ.MSMQQueue
Private g_MSMQInfo As MSMQ.MSMQQueueInfo
```

4. In the **Form_Load** event section at step B in the code, initialize the **Message Queue** objects as shown in the following example:

```
Set g_MSMQInfo = CreateObject("MSMQ.MSMQQueueInfo")
Set g_MSMTxDisp = CreateObject("MSMQ.MSMQTransactionDispenser")
```

To add code to place data on a queue

In this procedure, you add a new subroutine called ExecuteMSMQ. This routine is called by the **cmdRunSked_Click** event. You add the code to call this subroutine in the following procedure.

- Place the following code at the end of the code window in your project at step C:

```
Public Sub ExecuteMSMQ(ByVal strQueuePath As String, DataToQueue As String)
    Dim QueueMsg As New MSMQMessage

    Dim strData As String
    Dim fSend As Boolean
    Dim txt As TextStream
    Dim mybyte() As Byte

    g_MSMQInfo.FormatName = strQueuePath
    Set g_MSMQQueue = g_MSMQInfo.Open(MQ_SEND_ACCESS, MQ_DENY_NONE)
    mybyte = StrConv(DataToQueue, vbFromUnicode)
    QueueMsg.Body = DataToQueue

    Set MSMQTx = g_MSMTxDisp.BeginTransaction
    QueueMsg.send g_MSMQQueue, MSMQTx
    MSMQTx.Commit

    Set QueueMsg = Nothing
    Set MSMQTx = Nothing

End Sub
```

To add code to activate the XLANG schedule and call ExecuteMSMQ

In this procedure, you add code to the **cmdRunSked_Click** event that activates the XLANG schedule and calls code that sends a message to a queue.

1. In the **cmdRunSked_Click** event section at step D of the code, call **ExecuteMSMQ**, as shown in the following code:

```
ExecuteMSMQ "DIRECT=OS:.\private$\ReceivePOReq", objfs.OpenTextFile( _
txtData.Text, ForReading).ReadAll
```

2. In the **cmdRunSked_Click** event section at step E of the code, call **GetObject** to instantiate the XLANG schedule by moniker, as shown in the following code:

```
Set SendPAQ = GetObject(txtSked.Text)
```

To save and compile the application

In this procedure, you save and compile the application.

1. On the **File** menu, click **Save Project**.

2. On the **File** menu, click **Make ExecuteTutorial.exe**.

   The **Make Project** dialog box appears.

3. Browse to the **\Program Files\Microsoft BizTalk Server\Tutorial\Schedule\Lab** folder on the BizTalk Server installation drive and click **OK**.

You can now run the application to execute the buyer schedule in Modules 1 and 4.

Creating the Windows Script Component

In this topic, you create a Windows Script Component (WSC) that is bound to the XLANG schedule. The purpose of the WSC is to display a message box with approval or denial status of the purchase order request, and to optionally write the purchase order request to a local file if it is approved.

To add script to register the component

In this procedure, you add script that allows the component to be registered to the file.

1. On the **Start** menu, point to **Programs**, point to **Accessories**, and then click **Notepad**.

2. Add the following script:

```
<?xml version="1.0"?>
<component>
<?component error="true" debug="true"?>
<registration
    description="PORequestApproval"
    progid="BTSTutorial.PORequestApproval"
    version="1.00"
    classid="{2938621b-40fc-48e2-827c-bed74e21a538}"
>
</registration>
```

Because you are using the same class ID as the preconfigured component, the old component is overwritten in the registry.

To add script to implement the methods

This component exposes three methods. The first method sends an approval status in the form of a message box that is displayed to the user. The second method sends a denial status, also in the form of a message box that is displayed to the user. The decision as to which method is called is dictated by the decision rule in the XLANG schedule drawing. The last method writes the purchase order to a local file if the purchase order request has been approved.

1. Add the three method signatures to the end of the file:

```
<public>
    <method name="SendApproval">
        <PARAMETER name="Document"/>
    </method>
    <method name="SendDenial">
        <PARAMETER name="Document"/>
    </method>
    <method name="WriteToFile">
        <PARAMETER name="Document"/>
        <PARAMETER name="FileName"/>
    </method>
</public>
```

2. Add the script that implements the methods to the end of the file:

```
<implements type="Behavior" id="Behavior"/>

<script language="VBScript">
<![CDATA[

function SendApproval(Document)
    MsgBox "Scheduler Engine Accepted document :" + vbcrlf + + vbcrlf + Document, _
    0, "Document Approval Received"
end function

function SendDenial(Document)
    MsgBox "Scheduler Engine Denied document :" + vbcrlf + + vbcrlf + Document, _
    0, "Document Denied"
end function

function WriteToFile(Document, FileName)
    dim objFileSys, strTimeNow

    if FileName = "" then
        FileName = "c:\TutorialFiles\Buyer\POReq*.xml"
    end if

'Generate a Unique Number used to generate unique files using a mask
    strTimeNow = left(Replace(CStr(FormatDateTime(Now(), 3)),":",""), 6)

'Create File System Object
    Set objFileSys = CreateObject("Scripting.FileSystemObject")
```

```
'Create the Specified file, write the document data and close
   Set filestream = objFileSys.CreateTextFile(Replace(FileName, "*", strTimeNow), False)
   filestream.writeline Document
   filestream.close
end function

]]>
</script>

</component>
```

3. On the **File** menu, click **Save As**.

    The **Save As** dialog box appears.

4. Browse to **\Program Files\Microsoft BizTalk Server\Tutorial\Components\POReqApproval\Lab** on the BizTalk Server installation drive.

5. In the **File name** box, type **PORequestApproval.wsc**.

6. In the **Save as type** box, click **All Files** and click **Save**.

7. Close Notepad.

8. Browse to **\Program Files\Microsoft BizTalk Server\Tutorial\Components\POReqApproval\Lab**.

9. Right-click **PORequestApproval.wsc** and click **Register**.

This component can be substituted for the preconfigured WSC used in Module 1. To use this component, you must remove the existing WSC binding from the schedule and then create a new WSC binding that points to your component.

To delete the WSC component

In this procedure, you delete the WSC component from the Buyer2 XLANG schedule drawing. You can rebind the component you have created.

1. On the **Start** menu, point to **Programs**, point to **Microsoft BizTalk Server 2000**, and then click **BizTalk Orchestration Designer**.

2. To use the drawing created in Module 4, open the **Buyer2.skv** file located at **\Program Files\Microsoft BizTalk Server\Tutorial\Schedule\Lab** on the BizTalk Server installation drive.

    To use the existing Buyer2 drawing, open the **Buyer2.skv** file located at **\Program Files\Microsoft BizTalk Server\Tutorial\Schedule\Solution**.

3. Click the **Script Component** shape and press DELETE.

4. Click the **Data** tab.

5. Delete the **SendApproval**, **SendDenial**, and **WritetoFile** messages.

You are now ready to use your WSC component in the schedule. Do the following:

1. Implement a port to **Buyer2.skv** by using your WSC component.

   For an example of how to do this, see "To implement a port by using a script component" earlier in this chapter. However, use your component instead of the component in the procedure.

2. Define the method communication for the port implementation.

   For an example of how to do this, see "To define message properties for the script component" earlier in this chapter.

3. Define the data flow for the port.

   For an example of how to do this, see "To define the data flow" earlier in this chapter.

4. Save the XLANG file.

   For an example of how to do this, see "To save the XLANG schedule drawing" earlier in this chapter.

5. To test your component, run the **ExecuteTutorial** application located at **\Program Files\Microsoft BizTalk Server\Tutorial\Schedule\Solution** on the BizTalk Server installation drive.

Creating the Application Integration Component (AIC)

In this topic, you create a new application integration component called POtoINVAIC that converts a purchase order document into an invoice document using the MSXML DOM.

To create an ActiveX DLL project for the AIC

1. Start Microsoft Visual Basic 6.0.

2. In the **New Project** dialog box, click the **New** tab, click **ActiveX DLL**, and then click **Open**.

   This creates a new project for your component, called Project 1.

3. To rename both the project and the control to something more meaningful, in the project tree window, click **Project1** and, in the properties window, change the **(Name)** property to **POtoInvAIC**.

4. In the project tree window, click **Class1(Class1)** and, in the properties window, change the **(Name)** property to **ConvertPOtoInvoice**.

To add the required references for the AIC

In this procedure, you enable the component to implement a number of interfaces required by BizTalk Server 2000.

1. On the **Project** menu, click **References**.

2. Click **Microsoft BizTalk Server Application Interface Components 1.0 Type Library**.

   The full path for this type library is \Program Files\Microsoft BizTalk Server\btscomplib.tlb.

3. Select **Microsoft BizTalk Server Interchange 1.0 Type Library**.

   The full path for this type library is \Program Files\Microsoft BizTalk Server\cisapi.tlb.

4. Select **Microsoft Scripting Runtime**.

   The full path for this DLL is \WINNT\System32\Scrun.dll. Use this library to create a file system object and open a text stream that is used to write a purchase order to disk.

5. Select **Microsoft XML, v 3.0**.

   The full path for this DLL is \WINNT\System32\msxml3.dll.

6. Click **OK**.

To implement the required interface

For BizTalk Server to recognize a component as an AIC, it must implement one of two interfaces. For the purposes of this tutorial, you implement the **IBTSAppIntegration** interface.

1. In the Project window, click the **ConvertPOtoInvoice** class module.

2. On the **View** menu, click **Code**.

3. Add the following line of code at the top of the code window to ensure that all variables are explicitly declared to minimize simple errors:

```
Option Explicit
```

4. Implement the required interface by adding the following line of code after the **Option Explicit** statement:

```
Implements IBTSAppIntegration
```

To define and initialize the class objects

In this procedure, you add code to define the MSXML class objects to create the XML files using the DOM. You create a string variable that points to the project style sheet that converts a purchase order into an invoice.

1. Place the following code beneath the **Implements IBTSAppIntegration** statement:

```
'Class Object Defines
Private m_DOMCommonPO As MSXML2.DOMDocument
Private m_DOMStylesheet As MSXML2.DOMDocument
Private m_objSubmit As BTSInterchangeLib.Interchange

'Embedded Project Stylesheet to Convert CommonPO to CommonInvoice
Private m_strStylesheet As String
```

2. Add the following code to initialize the XML DOM objects that will convert the purchase order to an invoice, as well as the **Interchange** object that submits the final invoice document to BizTalk Server:

```
Private Sub Class_Initialize()
'Create DOM/Interchange Objects
    Set m_DOMCommonPO = New MSXML2.DOMDocument
    Set m_DOMStylesheet = New MSXML2.DOMDocument
    Set m_objSubmit = New BTSInterchangeLib.Interchange

'Configure DOM Objects to be Synchronous
    m_DOMCommonPO.async = False
    m_DOMStylesheet.async = False

'Fill Stylesheet Embedded String
    m_strStylesheet = m_strStylesheet + ""

End Sub
```

To implement the interface method

The **ProcessMessage** method of the **IBTSAppIntegration** interface takes an incoming XML common purchase order document transmitted from BizTalk Server and performs a translation on the data to convert it into an XML common invoice document. The common invoice document is then submitted back to BizTalk Server. The intent is to simulate a back-end system that receives purchase orders and eventually returns an invoice for those purchase orders.

1. Add the function definition and dimension variables, as in the following code:

```
Private Function IBTSAppIntegration_ProcessMessage( _
                            ByVal bstrDocument As String) As String
    Dim bstrInvoiceDocument As String
    Dim objScripting As New Scripting.FileSystemObject
'Initialize ProcessMessage to null
    IBTSAppIntegration_ProcessMessage = ""
```

2. Add the code to load the received data into a DOM object and validate that it is in the proper format by adding the following code beneath the **IBTSAppIntegration_ProcessMessage** statement:

```
m_DOMCommonPO.loadXML bstrDocument

If m_DOMCommonPO.parseError.errorCode <> 0 Then 'The data was not valid XML
'Raised errors are not caught in the component, and will be sent back to BizTalk Server
    Err.Raise m_DOMCommonPO.parseError.errorCode, _
    "AICSample.ConvertPOToInvoice Component", _
    "The provided document was not valid XML and could not be processed because:" + _
    vbCrLf + vbCrLf + m_DOMCommonPO.parseError.reason + vbCrLf + " on line: " + _
    CStr(m_DOMCommonPO.parseError.Line) + vbCrLf + "at position: " + _
    CStr(m_DOMCommonPO.parseError.linepos)
End If
```

3. Add code to use the resource file that contains XSL code that converts a purchase order to an invoice by adding the following code beneath the **End If** statement:

```
If m_strStylesheet = "" Then
    m_strStylesheet = StrConv(LoadResData(101, "CUSTOM"), vbUnicode)
End If

m_DOMStylesheet.loadXML m_strStylesheet
bstrInvoiceDocument = m_DOMCommonPO.transformNode(m_DOMStylesheet)

If bstrInvoiceDocument = "" Then ' Mapping Failed Raise an Error
    Err.Raise vbObjectError + 100, "AICSample.ConvertPOToInvoice Component", _
    "The provided CommonPO document could not be translated into a Common Invoice " + _
    "as the map produced blank output."
End If
```

4. Add code to submit the invoice document to BizTalk Messaging Services by adding the following code beneath the **End If** statement:

```
IBTSAppIntegration_ProcessMessage = m_objSubmit.Submit(BIZTALK_OPENNESS_TYPE_NOTOPEN, _
bstrInvoiceDocument, , , "Bits,Bytes,Chips on Seller", , "ProElectron on Seller")

End Function
```

The submit call returns the submission ID, which in this case is not used.

To terminate the class objects

To ensure that all objects are released from memory when the class terminates, add this code to the end of your project:

```
Private Sub Class_Terminate()
    Set m_DOMCommonPO = Nothing
    Set m_DOMStylesheet = Nothing
    Set m_objSubmit = Nothing
End Sub
```

To create the resource file

In this procedure, you add the resource file that contains the XSL for transforming a purchase order into an invoice.

1. On the **Add-Ins** menu, click **Add-In Manager**.

   The **Add-In Manager** dialog box appears.

2. Click **VB 6 Resource Editor**.

3. In the **Load Behavoir** area, click **Loaded/Unloaded** to load the resource editor, click **Load on Startup**, and then click **OK**.

4. On the **Tools** menu, click **Resource Editor**.

5. Click the **Add Custom Resource** icon on the tool bar.

   The **Open a Custom Resource** dialog box appears.

6. Browse to **\Program Files\Microsoft BizTalk Server\Tutorial\Components\POtoInvoice\Lab** on the BizTalk Server installation drive, click **POtoINVAIC.txt**, and then click **Open**.

   ### ☙ Caution

   - Make sure that the ID of your resource is 101. By default, the first resource you create has an ID of 101, but this number increments by one if you change the resource. To change the resource ID to 101, right-click the resource ID and click **Properties**. In the ID box, type 101.

7. Click the **Save** icon.

   The **Save Resource File As** dialog box appears.

8. Browse to **\Program Files\Microsoft BizTalk Server\Tutorial\Components\POtoInvoice\Lab**.

9. In the **File name** box, type **POtoInvAICLab.RES** and click **Save**.

10. Close the Resource Editor.

To build the component and set binary compatibility

Since you are creating a new component, you must build the component at this point, and then set the project properties for binary compatibility with the newly created DLL. Binary compatibility ensures that each time you compile the DLL you do not generate a new globally unique identifier (GUID) for the object.

1. On the **File** menu, click **Save Project As**.

   The **Save File As** dialog box appears.

2. Browse to **\Program Files\Microsoft BizTalk Server\Tutorial\Components\POToInvoice\Lab** on the BizTalk Server installation drive.

3.   In the **File name** box, type **ConvertPOtoInvoice.cls** and click **Save**.

The **Save Project As** dialog box appears.

4.   Browse to **\Program Files\Microsoft BizTalk Server\Tutorial\Components\POToInvoice\Lab**.

5.   In the **File name** box, type **POToInvAICLab** and click **Save**.

6.   On the **File** menu, click **Make POToInvAICLab.dll**.

The **Make Project** dialog box appears.

7.   Browse to **\Program Files\Microsoft BizTalk Server\Tutorial\Components\POtoInvoice\Lab** and click **OK**.

8.   On the **Project** menu, click **POToInvAICLab Properties**.

9.   Click the **Component** tab.

10. Click **Binary Compatibility**.

11. Click **Browse** ([...]) and browse to **\Program Files\Microsoft BizTalk Server\Tutorial\POtoInvoice\Lab**.

12. Click **POToInvAICLab.dll** and click **Open**.

13. Click **OK**.

To register the AIC

In this procedure, you register the AIC so that it can be recognized by BizTalk Server. BizTalk Server looks at the list of registered COM components and then queries those components to determine which of these implement either the **IBTSAppIntegration** interface or the **IPipelineComponent** interface. All components that meet this criteria are displayed in a list of components in BizTalk Messaging Manager.

1.   On the **Start** menu, point to **Settings** and click **Control Panel**.

2.   Double-click **Administrative Tools**.

3.   Double-click **Component Services**.

The Component Services console appears.

4.   In the console tree, expand **Component Services**, expand **Computers**, expand **My Computer**, and then click **COM+ Applications**.

5.   Right-click **COM+ Applications**, point to **New**, and then click **Application**.

The COM Application Install Wizard opens.

6.   On the **Welcome to the COM Application Install Wizard** page, click **Next**.

7.   On the **Install or Create a New Application** page, click **Create an empty application**.

8.   In the **Enter a name for the new application** box, type **POToInvAICLab**.

9. In the **Activation type** area, click **Server application** and click **Next**.

10. In the **Account** area, click **Interactive User-the current logged on user** and click **Next**.

   ### ☑ Note

   - The current logged on user must be a member of the BizTalk Server Administrators group and must remain logged on while running this scenario.

11. Click **Finish**.

12. In the console tree, expand **COM+ Applications** and expand the new package you created, called **POToInvAICLab**.

13. Click **Components**.

14. Browse to **\Program Files\Microsoft BizTalk Server\Tutorial\Components\POtoInvoice\Lab** on the BizTalk Server installation drive.

15. Drag **POToInvAICLab.dll** to the **Components** folder in **Component Services**.

16. Close **Component Services**.

You can now reconfigure the port to use the new AIC, using the following steps:

1. Open BizTalk Messaging Manager.

2. In the **Search** area, click **Messaging ports** and click **Search now**.

3. In the **Messaging port name** list, double-click **Port to Bits,Bytes,Chips via AIC**.

4. On the **General Information** page, click **Next**.

5. On the **Destination Organization** page, in the **Primary transport** area, click **Browse**.

   The **Primary Transport** dialog box appears.

6. Click **Browse**.

7. In the **Available Components** list, click **POToInvAICLab ConvertPOtoInvoice** and click **OK**.

8. Click **OK** to close the **Primary Transport** dialog box and click **Finish**.

9. Test your component by running the **ExecuteTutorial** application located at **\Program Files\Microsoft BizTalk Server\Tutorial\Schedule\Solution** on the BizTalk Server installation drive.

Error Messages

The properties and methods of the BizTalk Messaging Configuration object model use standard Component Object Model (COM) **HRESULT** return values to communicate whether the operation was successful or not.

In C++, these values are the actual return values from the methods (including property **get_** and **put_** methods). The program must explicitly perform error checking by examining these return values, or use some variation of structured error handling.

In Microsoft Visual Basic, and in Visual Basic Scripting Edition (VBS), these values are placed in the **Number** property of the global **Err** object. Error handling is either handled automatically by displaying a standard error dialog box, or by checking the value of the **Number** property of the global **Err** object. The **On Error Resume Next** command disables automatic error handling, enabling explicit error handling.

Standard COM Errors

The following table shows the most common standard COM errors returned by the properties and methods of the BizTalk Server objects.

Constant	Value (32-bit)	Description
S_OK	00000000	The standard return value used to communicate successful completion.
S_FALSE	00000001	An alternate success value, typically used to communicate successful, but non-standard completion. The precise meaning depends on the method or property in question.
E_UNEXPECTED	8000FFFF	A catastrophic failure.
E_NOTIMPL	80004001	Not implemented error.
E_OUTOFMEMORY	8007000E	Out of memory.
E_INVALIDARG	80070057	One or more arguments are not valid.
E_NOINTERFACE	80004002	The interface is not supported.
E_POINTER	80004003	The pointer is not valid.
E_HANDLE	80070006	The handle is not valid.
E_ABORT	80004004	The operation was aborted.
E_FAIL	80004005	Unspecified error.
E_ACCESSDENIED	80070005	General access denied.
MK_E_NOOBJECT	800401E5	The object identified by this moniker could not be found.

Additional information may be available by using the global **Err** object. In Visual Basic, the **Description** property of the **Err** object may contain a text description of the error.

In C++, call the OLE DB method **GetErrorInfo** on the **IErrorRecords** interface to retrieve the most recently set **IErrorInfo** pointer in the current logical thread. The **GetDescription** method of the **IErrorInfo** interface may return a text description of the error. For more information about the **GetErrorInfo** method, go to the MSDN Online Library Web site (msdn.microsoft.com/library/default.asp) and browse to OLE DB Interfaces in the Platform SDK.

BizTalk Server 2000 Error Messages

The BizTalk Messaging Configuration object model error messages defined by BizTalk Server can be used in your application by including the bts_config_errors.h file located in the BizTalk Server installation directory at \Program Files\Microsoft BizTalk Server\SDK\Include. These error messages, returned during design time by the methods and properties of the object model, contain a BTS_ prefix in the message name. All other errors occur during run time, when BizTalk Server is processing a document.

The following table contains both design time and run time errors.

Message name	Value	Description
CIS_E_OBJECT_NOT_FOUND	0x0100	The object was not found.
CIS_E_STATE_NOT_FOUND	0x0101	The state engine state was not found in the messaging port definition.
CIS_E_STATE_TRANSITION	0x0103	The state table contains a bad engine state transition.
CIS_E_BAD_ENGINE_CONFIG_FILE	0x0105	The string that describes the input state configuration is not valid.
CIS_E_CANNOT_ADD_STATE	0x0106	BizTalk Server could not add the user-defined state to the system.
CIS_E_NO_COMPONENT_FOUND	0x0107	There is no component in the state definition or the ProgID is wrong.
CIS_E_PIPECOMP_ADMIN_REQUIRED	0x0108	The required **IPipelineComponentAdmin** interface was not found on the component.
CIS_E_BAD_COMPONENT_TYPE	0x0109	The component type specified for the state engine is not recognized.
CIS_E_BAD_STATE_CONFIG	0x010A	The state configuration is not valid.
CIS_E_BAD_STATE_TYPE	0x010B	The specified state type is not recognized.
CIS_E_BAD_COMPONENT_CONFIG	0x010C	The component configuration is not valid.
CIS_E_INTERNAL_FAILURE	0x010F	An internal server failure occurred due to an unknown cause.
CIS_E_CREATE_SCHEDULER_FAILED	0x0111	The Queue Scheduler for the service could not be created.

Message name	Value	Description
CIS_E_AGREEMENT_SELECT_FAILED	0x0112	No channels matched the input criteria. Verify that a messaging port and a channel exist, and that they match the following fields: Source qualifier: "%1" Source identifier value: "%2" Source document name: "%3" Destination qualifier: "%4" Destination identifier value: "%5" Also verify that any expressions specified for the channels are compatible with this document.
CIS_E_ERROR	0x0113	An error occurred in BizTalk Server.%n %n Details:%n ----------------------------%n %1
CIS_E_SERVICE_INITIALIZATION_FAILURE	0x0114	The service failed to start. Verify that this server is enlisted in a BizTalk Server group.
CIS_E_SCHEDULER_FAILED	0x0115	The Queue Scheduler failed and has exited.
CIS_E_WORKER_THREAD_FAILED	0x0116	A worker thread failed and has exited.
CIS_E_SHARED_QUEUE_DB_EXEC_FAILED	0x0117	Execution against the Shared Queue database has failed.
CIS_E_CANT_READ_WORK_ITEM	0x0119	A work item in the Shared Queue database cannot be read.
CIS_E_CHECKPOINT_FAILED	0x011c	Checkpointing the work item failed.
CIS_E_CREATE_DEAD_WORK_ITEM_FAILED	0x011e	A new work item in the Suspended queue cannot be created.
CIS_E_GET_SNAPSHOT_FAILED	0x0122	A snapshot of the Shared Queue database cannot be taken.
CIS_E_FREE_INTERCHANGES_FAILED	0x0124	The specified interchanges cannot be freed.
CIS_E_DELETE_INTERCHANGE_FAILED	0x0125	The specified interchange cannot be deleted.
CIS_E_RECEIVING_INTERCHANGE_FAILED	0x0127	The specified interchange was not received.
CIS_E_GETTING_NEXT_SCHEDULED_WORK_ITEM_FAILED	0x0128	The next scheduled work item cannot be obtained for processing.
CIS_E_GET_COUNT_FAILED	0x0129	The count on the shared queues cannot be obtained.
CIS_E_TRANSMISSION_FAILED	0x012a	All retry transmissions failed.
CIS_W_TRANSMISSION_ATTEMPT_FAILED	0x012b	A transmission attempt failed.

Message name	Value	Description
CIS_W_TRANSMISSION_XFER_TO_ SECONDARY	0x012c	The primary transport for messaging port "%1" cannot transmit the data. The server will switch to the secondary transport.
CIS_E_RECEIPT_GENERATION_FAILED	0x012e	After creating the work item, the attempt to generate a receipt failed.
CIS_E_RECEIPT_GENERATION_FAILED_ NO_WORK_ITEM	0x012f	The attempt to generate a receipt failed before the work item was created.
CIS_E_L1_RECEIPT_CORRELATION_FAILED	0x0130	Receipt correlation failed.
CIS_E_AGREEMENT_LACKING_PARAMS	0x0133	At least one of the fields necessary to select a channel is missing. Verify that your document and envelopes extract the proper fields for the parser, or specify the necessary fields upon submission. Channel selection fields: Source identifier type: "%1" Source identifier value: "%2" Source document name: "%3" Destination identifier type: "%4" Destination identifier value: "%5"
CIS_E_AGREEMENT_FAILED	0x0134	The channel cannot be selected.
CIS_E_ORIGINAL_L1_INTERCHANGE_ MISSING	0x0135	When trying to correlate an incoming receipt, the original interchange and related document(s) are no longer present.
CIS_E_UNEXPECTED_DB_BEHAVIOR	0x0136	An unexpected return occurred. The database may need to be restarted.
CIS_E_AGREEMENT_INVALID_MAP	0x0137	The map specified by the reference "%1" is not valid. Verify that the reference points to a valid map created by BizTalk Mapper.
CIS_I_SERVICE_MSG	0x0138	1%
CIS_E_AGREEMENT_MAP_FAILED	0x0139	The XML document could not be translated. The map specified by reference "%1" failed. Verify that the map is up to date.
CIS_E_XML_ERROR	0x013A	The XML document could not be parsed on line: %2, position: %3 for the following reason: "%1"
CIS_E_AGREEMENT_PROCESSING_FAILED	0x013f	The server could not finish processing the document.

Message name	Value	Description
CIS_E_AGREEMENT_PROCESSING_ FAILED_W_NAME	0x0140	The following channel configuration setting is not valid: "%1"
CIS_E_AGREEMENT_INVALID_QUERY	0x0141	The "%2" query for the "%1" document tracking field is not a valid XSL pattern. This pattern must be removed or corrected.
CIS_I_SERVICE_START	0x0142	The service has started.
CIS_I_SERVICE_STOP	0x0143	The service has stopped.
CIS_E_ERROR_EX	0x0144	An error occurred in BizTalk Server.%n %n Details:%n -----------------------------%n %1 %2 %3 %4 %5 %6 %7 %8 %9 %n
CIS_E_ERROR_EX_HEAD	0x0145	================================ ======== ================================ ======= Date: %1 Source: BizTalk Server 2000 Time: %2 Category: BizTalk Server 2000 User: %3 Computer: %4 Description: An error occurred in BizTalk Server. Details: -------
CIS_E_ERROR_EX_FOOT	0x0146	
CIS_E_INVALID_DATA_FORMAT	0x0147	The business document that was passed in is not in a recognized format and could not be parsed or decrypted.
CIS_E_CREATE_ENGINE	0x0148	BizTalk Server was unable to create a new instance of the processing engine to process a work item. This might be due to a failure to create a new COM+ transaction.
CIS_E_MISSING_DESTINATION_ DOCUMENT_SPEC	0x0149	BizTalk Server has detected an incomplete messaging port. The destination specification is missing from the messaging port.
CIS_E_PROCESSING_THREAD_FAILED	0x014A	The processing thread failed to start. This might be due to a failure to create the state engine.
CIS_E_NOSRCORG	0x014B	No source organization that corresponds to the ID and Qualifier pair has been specified.

Message name	Value	Description
CIS_E_NODESTORG	0x014C	No destination organization that corresponds to the Identifier and Qualifier pair has been specified.
CIS_E_NODOC	0x014D	No document that corresponds to the document name has been specified.
CIS_E_NOPIPELINES	0x014E	No channel that corresponds to the parameters has been specified.
CIS_E_NOT_RESUBMITTABLE	0x014F	The state of the item in the Suspended queue does not allow resubmission.
CIS_E_PIPESELECT_POLICY_FAILED	0x0150	No channels matched the certificates that were found with the incoming data. The following certificates accompanied the submitted data: Signature certificate reference: "%1" Encryption certificate reference: "%2"
CIS_E_SUBMIT_INVALIDDOC	0x0151	The submitted document is not valid. See the following messages for more details.
CIS_E_SUBMITSYNC_TOOMANYDOCS	0x0152	The **SubmitSync** method failed because multiple documents where found within the data. Only one document is allowed per synchronous submission. If this is a structured flat-file submission, then the most common cause of failure is extra leading or trailing white space around the data.
CIS_E_SUBMITSYNC_TOOMANYPIPES	0x0153	The synchronous submission could not be completed because multiple valid channels matched the incoming document. Only one channel is allowed to match the incoming document.
CIS_E_XMIT_NOTRANSPORTCOMP	0x0154	This server could not create a component with the class ID "%1" for transport. Verify that this component is properly registered. The following error was returned:
CIS_E_XMIT_EMPTY_DOCUMENT	0x0155	Messaging port "%1" cannot transmit a zero-byte document.
CIS_E_XMIT_FAILED_W_NAME	0x0156	The server could not finish processing messaging port "%1".

Message name	Value	Description
CIS_E_XMIT_NO_INTERFACE	0x0157	The server could not obtain the "%1" interface from the transport component with CLSID "%2".
CIS_E_XMIT_NO_BTS_AIC_INTERFACES	0x0158	The server could not obtain either the "%1" or "%2" interfaces from the BizTalk Server application integration component with CLSID "%3".
CIS_E_XMIT_FAILED_W_DETAILS	0x0159	The server encountered a transport error while processing the messaging port "%1", which uses a transport component with a ProgID of "%2".
CIS_E_NOHDR_ERROR_EX	0x015A	%1 %2 %3 %4 %5 %6 %7 %8 %9 %n
CIS_W_COMP_NOACK	0x015B	The correlation component "%1" could not find a document for which to send a receipt. No action will be taken.
CIS_E_CORRELATIONCOMP_FAILED	0x015C	The correlation component "%1" returned an unexpected failure. The document will be placed in the Suspended queue.
CIS_E_CORRELATION_FAILED	0x015D	Receipt correlation processing failed.
CIS_E_XML_VALIDATE_ERROR	0x015E	The XML document has failed validation for the following reason: %1
CIS_E_CHANNEL_ACCESSDENIED	0x015F	The submitted document does not have the necessary signature or encryption required by channel "%3". The following certificates accompanied the submitted data: Signature certificate reference: "%1" Encryption certificate reference: "%2"
CIS_I_SERVICE_RESTARTING	0x0160	The service is restarting.
BTS_E_CONSTRAINT	0x1201	Constraint Error
BTS_E_NOOBJECT	0x1202	The object was not found.
BTS_E_INTERNALFAILURE	0x1203	An internal failure occurred.
BTS_E_ENVELOPE_CONTROLNUMBER	0x120C	If the envelope format is set to X12 or EDIFACT, the control number value must be set to a number greater than or equal to 1.
BTS_E_ENVELOPE_DELIMETER	0x120D	If the envelope format is set to X12, then delimiters are required and must be set.

Message name	Value	Description
BTS_E_ENCRYPTION_CUSTOM_NOCLSID	0x120E	If the encryption type is Custom, then the class identifier (CLSID) must also be specified.
BTS_E_ENCODING_CUSTOM_NOCLSID	0x120F	If the encoding type is Custom, then the class identifier (CLSID) must also be specified.
BTS_E_SIGNATURE_CUSTOM_NOCLSID	0x1210	If the signature type is Custom, then the class identifier (CLSID) must also be specified.
BTS_E_INVALIDCONTROLNUMBER	0x1212	The control number value must be set to a number greater than or equal to 1.
BTS_E_ENVELOPE_INUSE	0x1213	The format of the envelope cannot be changed because it is used in a messaging port.
BTS_E_CHANNEL_MISSINGMAPSOURCE	0x1215	The channel is missing the MapSource node.
BTS_E_INVALID_CERT_USAGE	0x1216	The certificate is not valid for the current usage. An encryption certificate cannot be used for signing; nor can a signing certificate be used for encryption. Make sure that the correct certificate is selected.
BTS_E_MISSINGSMTPHOST	0x1218	The SMTP host is missing. The SMTP host can be configured in BizTalk Server Administration.
BTS_E_INVALID_ENCRYPT_STORE	0x1219	The encryption store type is not valid. The store type must be BIZTALK.
BTS_E_INVALID_SGNTCERT_STORE	0x121A	The signature store type is not valid. The store type must be MY.
BTS_E_DATATOOLONG	0x121B	The data length is too long.
BTS_E_INVALID_VERIFY_ENCRYPTCERT_ STORE	0x121C	The encryption verification store type is not valid. The store type must be MY.
BTS_E_INVALID_VERIFY_SGNTCERT_ STORE	0x121D	The signature verification store type is not valid. The store type must be BIZTALK.
BTS_E_ORGANIZATION_UNIQUE_ID	0x121F	The organization identifier must be a unique identifier.
BTS_E_ORGANIZATION_UNIQUE_NAME	0x1220	The organization name must be a unique name.

Message name	Value	Description
BTS_E_OBJECT_ALREADY_EXISTS	0x1221	The object already exists. You cannot call the **Create**() method on a BizTalk Messaging Configuration object multiple times without also calling the **Clear**() or **Remove**() methods.
BTS_E_ALIAS_UNIQUE_ID	0x1222	The identifier must be a unique identifier.
BTS_E_ALIAS_UNIQUE_NAME	0x1223	The identifier name for this organization must be a unique name.
BTS_E_ALIAS_UNIQUE_QUALIFIERVALUE	0x1225	The identifier must have a unique qualifier-value pair.
BTS_E_ALIAS_FOREIGN_OWNERID	0x1226	The organization cannot be removed because it is referred to by an identifier.
BTS_E_XMLSHARE_UNIQUE_ID	0x1227	The primary identifier for the XML Share table in the SQL Server database must be a unique identifier.
BTS_E_XMLSHARE_UNIQUE_REFERENCE	0x1228	The reference for the XML Share table in the SQL Server database must be a unique reference.
BTS_E_DOCUMENT_UNIQUE_ID	0x1229	The document identifier must be a unique identifier.
BTS_E_DOCUMENT_UNIQUE_NAME	0x122A	The document name must be a unique name.
BTS_E_DOCUMENT_FOREIGN_SHAREID	0x122C	The XML Share table in the SQL Server database cannot be removed because it is referred to by a document.
BTS_E_ENVELOPE_UNIQUE_ID	0x122D	The envelope identifier must be a unique identifier.
BTS_E_ENVELOPE_UNIQUE_NAME	0x122E	The envelope name must be a unique name.
BTS_E_ENVELOPE_FOREIGN_SHAREID	0x1230	The XML Share table in the SQL Server database cannot be removed because it is referred to by an envelope.
BTS_E_CONTROLNUMBER_UNIQUE_ID	0x1231	The control-number identifier must be a unique identifier.
BTS_E_PORTGROUP_UNIQUE_ID	0x1232	The distribution list identifier must be a unique identifier.

Message name	Value	Description
BTS_E_PORTGROUP_UNIQUE_NAME	0x1233	The distribution list name must be a unique name.
BTS_E_MISSING_VALUE	0x1235	The identifier value property must have a value.
BTS_E_MISSING_SRCORGID	0x1236	The Channel **SourceOrganization** property must have a value.
BTS_E_APPLICATION_UNIQUE_ID	0x1237	The application identifier must be a unique identifier.
BTS_E_APPLICATION_FOREIGN_OWNERID	0x1238	The organization cannot be removed because it is referred to by an application.
BTS_E_APPLICATION_UNIQUE_NAME	0x1239	For applications within this organization, the application name must be a unique name.
BTS_E_CHANNEL_UNIQUE_ID	0x123A	The channel identifier must be a unique identifier.
BTS_E_CHANNEL_UNIQUE_NAME	0x123B	The channel name must be a unique name.
BTS_E_CHANNEL_FOREIGN_INPDOCID	0x123D	The inbound document cannot be removed because it is used by a channel.
BTS_E_CHANNEL_FOREIGN_OUTDOCID	0x123E	The output document cannot be removed because it is used by a channel.
BTS_E_CHANNEL_FOREIGN_PORTGROUPID	0x123F	The distribution list cannot be removed because it is used by a channel.
BTS_E_CHANNEL_FOREIGN_SRCORGID	0x1240	The source organization cannot be removed because it is used by a channel.
BTS_E_ENVELOPE_INVALIDFORMAT	0x1241	The only valid envelope-format strings are: Custom, Custom XML, EDIFACT, Flatfile, X12, and Reliable. The previously specified format will remain unchanged.
BTS_E_CHANNEL_FOREIGN_CONTROLNUMID	0x1242	The control number cannot be removed because it is used by an channel.
BTS_E_PORT_UNIQUE_ID	0x1243	The messaging port identifier must be a unique identifier.
BTS_E_PORT_UNIQUE_NAME	0x1244	The messaging port name must be a unique name.
BTS_E_CHANNEL_FOREIGN_SRCAPPID	0x1247	The source application cannot be removed because it is used by a channel.

Message name	Value	Description
BTS_E_PORT_FOREIGN_DSTORGID	0x1248	The destination organization cannot be removed because it is used by a messaging port.
BTS_E_PORT_FOREIGN_DSTALIASID	0x1249	The destination identifier cannot be removed because it is used by a messaging port.
BTS_E_PORT_FOREIGN_ENVID	0x124A	The envelope cannot be removed because it is used by a messaging port.
BTS_E_CHANNEL_FOREIGN_SRCALIASID	0x124B	The source identifier cannot be removed because it is used by a channel.
BTS_E_PORT_FOREIGN_DSTAPPID	0x124C	The destination application cannot be removed because it is used by a messaging port.
BTS_E_PORT_FOREIGN_CONTROLNUMID	0x124D	The control number cannot be removed because it is used by a messaging port.
BTS_E_DOCUMENT_MISSING_REFERENCE	0x124E	The Reference property must have a value if the TrackingFields or PropertySet properties are specified.
BTS_E_DOCUMENT_REFERENCE_CANT_BE_CHANGED	0x124F	A document reference cannot be modified if it is referred to by a channel.
BTS_E_PORTGROUP_NOTOPENGRP	0x1251	Messaging ports that are set to an open destination or set to an XLANG schedule (BIZTALK_OPENNESS_TYPE_EX_TOWORKFLOW) cannot be used in distribution lists.
BTS_E_PORTGROUP_DUPLICATEPORT	0x1252	A duplicate messaging port cannot be added to the distribution list.
BTS_E_OUTPUTCONFIG_UNIQUE_ID	0x1255	The output configuration identifier must be a unique identifier.
BTS_E_OUTPUTCONFIG_FOREIGN_PORTID	0x1256	The messaging port cannot be removed because it is used by a channel.
BTS_E_OUTPUTCONFIG_FOREIGN_CHANNELID	0x1257	The channel cannot be removed because it is used by a messaging port.
BTS_E_PORT_LOOPBACK_RELIABLE	0x125F	A messaging port with the transport type Loopback cannot be associated with an envelope that uses the Reliable format.

Message name	Value	Description
BTS_E_ALIAS_RESERVEDWORD	0x1262	Group is a reserved word for qualifiers and cannot be used as the qualifier for an identifier.
BTS_E_DOCUMENT_NEEDMAPREF	0x1268	A map reference is required to transform the inbound document to the outbound document if the document specifications are different.
BTS_E_PORT_DESTORGNOTSPECIFIED	0x126C	This messaging port must have a destination organization specified.
BTS_E_PORT_MISSING_PRITRANSTYPE	0x126D	You must specify a primary transport type for this messaging port. The primary transport cannot be blank, and it cannot be an open destination.
BTS_E_PORT_MISSING_PRITRANSADDRESS	0x126E	This messaging port must have a primary transport address specified.
BTS_E_PORT_INVALID_SECTRANSTYPE	0x126F	The secondary transport type cannot be set to Open, Loopback, or to BizTalk Orchestration Activation.
BTS_E_PORT_MISSING_SECTRANSADDRESS	0x1270	The secondary transport address is missing, although the transport type has been defined.
BTS_E_PORT_INVALID_ORG	0x1271	The organization specified in this messaging port does not exist.
BTS_E_PORT_INVALID_ALIAS	0x1272	The identifier specified for the organization in this messaging port either does not exist or it does not belong to the organization.
BTS_E_PORT_INVALID_APPLICATION	0x1273	The application specified for the organization in this messaging port either does not exist or it does not belong to the organization.
BTS_E_PORT_INVALID_ENVELOPE	0x1274	The envelope specified in this messaging port does not exist.
BTS_E_PORT_OPEN_DESTORG_SPECIFIED	0x127C	An open-destination messaging port cannot have a destination organization specified.
BTS_E_PORT_OPEN_DESTAPP_SPECIFIED	0x127E	An open-destination messaging port cannot have a destination application specified.

Message name	Value	Description
BTS_E_PORT_OPEN_PRITRANSTYPEOPEN	0x127F	An open-destination messaging port must specify a primary transport type as an open destination.
BTS_E_PORT_OPEN_PRITRANSADDRESS	0x1280	An open-destination messaging port cannot specify a primary transport address.
BTS_E_PORT_OPEN_PRITRANSPARAMETER	0x1281	An open-destination messaging port cannot specify a primary transport parameter.
BTS_E_PORT_OPEN_SECTRANSTYPE	0x1282	An open-destination messaging port cannot specify the secondary transport type.
BTS_E_PORT_OPEN_SECTRANSADDRESS	0x1283	An open-destination messaging port cannot specify a secondary transport address.
BTS_E_PORT_OPEN_SECTRANSPARAMETER	0x1284	An open-destination messaging port cannot specify a secondary transport parameter.
BTS_E_PORT_OPEN_ENCRYPTIONTYPE	0x1285	An open-destination messaging port cannot specify an encryption type.
BTS_E_PORT_OPEN_ENCRYPTIONREF	0x1286	An open-destination messaging port cannot specify an encryption reference.
BTS_E_PORT_SIGNATTYPEANDREFERENCE	0x1287	The signature type is specified; however, the signature reference is missing.
BTS_E_PORT_ ENCRYPTIONTYPEANDREFERENCE	0x1288	The encryption type is specified; however, the encryption reference is missing.
BTS_E_ALIAS_DEFAULT	0x128A	One and only one default identifier is required and permitted at all times. The default identifier cannot be missing, nor can it be duplicated.
BTS_E_ALIAS_AUTO	0x128B	The alias, which uses the name "Organization" and the qualifier "OrganizationName," is a system-created alias. You cannot remove this alias, create another alias that uses the same name and qualifier, or change any fields of this alias.
BTS_E_TRANSPORT_SYNTAXAPPINT	0x128E	Either the syntax of this address is incorrect for the Application Integration Component transport type property, or the component is not registered, or else the component is not a valid AIC component.

Message name	Value	Description
BTS_E_TRANSPORT_SYNTAXFILE	0x128F	The syntax of this address is incorrect for the File transport type.
BTS_E_TRANSPORT_SYNTAXHTTP	0x1291	The syntax of this address is incorrect for the HTTP transport type.
BTS_E_TRANSPORT_SYNTAXHTTPS	0x1292	The syntax of this address is incorrect for the HTTPS transport type.
BTS_E_TRANSPORT_SYNTAXSMTP	0x1293	The syntax of this address is incorrect for the SMTP transport type.
BTS_E_TRANSPORT_SYNTAXNONE	0x1294	You cannot specify a transport address or a parameter when the transport type is set to None, or when the source or destination are Open.
BTS_E_TRANSPORT_LOCALHOST	0x1295	The transport address cannot contain the word "localhost". Replace it with the computer name instead.
BTS_E_PORTGROUP_LASTPORT	0x1296	The messaging port cannot be removed if it is the last remaining messaging port in a distribution list.
BTS_E_TRANSPORT_MISSING_PRISMTPPARAMETER	0x1298	A primary transport parameter is required for the SMTP transport type.
BTS_E_TRANSPORT_MISSING_SECSMTPPARAMETER	0x1299	A secondary transport parameter is required for the SMTP transport type.
BTS_E_NAMEREQ	0x129A	The Name property must always be at least one character long.
BTS_E_INVALIDTIMEFORMAT	0x129B	The time format is not valid. Enter the time, in hours, in a 24-hour format (from 0 to 23 hours). You can enter only hours, not minutes or seconds.
BTS_E_TIMESTAMP	0x129C	This object cannot be saved or removed because the timestamp has changed.
BTS_E_PORTGROUP_MISSING_PORT	0x129D	A distribution list must contain at least one messaging port.
BTS_E_ORGANIZATION_REMOVEDEFAULT	0x129E	The home organization cannot be removed.
BTS_E_PORT_SERVICEWINDOW_EQUAL	0x129F	The start time (FromTime) and end time (ToTime) for the service window cannot be equal.

Message name	Value	Description
BTS_E_ENVELOPE_ REFERENCENOTALLOWED	0x12A2	The reference property cannot be set for this envelope format.
BTS_E_ENVELOPE_REFERRED	0x12A3	This envelope cannot be removed because it is used in a messaging port or channel.
BTS_E_TRANSPORT_LOOPBACK_ SECTYPECONFLICT	0x12A4	The secondary transport type cannot be specified for the messaging port if the primary transport type is set to Loopback.
BTS_E_TRANSPORT_LOOPBACK_ SECADDRESSCONFLICT	0x12A5	The secondary transport address cannot be specified for the messaging port if the transport type is set to Loopback.
BTS_E_PORT_LOOPBACK_ SERVICEWINDOW	0x12A6	The service window cannot be specified for the messaging port if the transport type is set to Loopback.
BTS_E_PORT_OPEN_DESTALIAS_SPECIFIED	0x12A7	An open-destination messaging port cannot have a destination identifier specified.
BTS_E_PORT_OPEN_SERVICEWINDOW	0x12A8	The service window cannot be specified for the messaging port if the messaging port is an open-destination messaging port.
BTS_E_PORT_SERVICEWINDOWTIMES	0x12AA	To use a service window, you must set both the From and To times or else, do not set either time.
BTS_E_TRANSPORT_LOOPBACK_ PRIADDRESSCONFLICT	0x12AC	A primary transport address cannot be specified for the messaging port if the transport type is Loopback.
BTS_E_PORT_ORGCHANGE	0x12AD	The destination-organization identifier cannot be changed after it is created.
BTS_E_PORT_OPENNESSCHANGE	0x12AE	The Openness property cannot be changed after it is created.
BTS_E_PORT_SIGNATURE_CHANNEL_ CERTREF	0x12AF	The signature-certification reference for a channel does not match the signature type for the port.
BTS_E_PORT_SIGNATURE_CHANNEL_OPEN	0x12B0	A messaging port that contains a signature type cannot be connected to an open-source channel. Also, a messaging port that is already connected to an open-source channel cannot have a signature type assigned to it.

Message name	Value	Description
BTS_E_CHANNEL_OPEN_SRCORG	0x12B1	An open-source channel cannot specify a source organization.
BTS_E_PORTGROUP_LOOPBACKPORT	0x12B2	A messaging port that uses the Loopback transport type cannot be added to a distribution list. Also, the transport type of a messaging port that is already included in a distribution list cannot be changed to Loopback.
BTS_E_CHANNEL_OPEN_SRCALIAS	0x12B3	An open-source channel cannot have a source identifier specified.
BTS_E_CHANNEL_OPEN_SRCAPP	0x12B4	An open-source channel cannot specify a source application.
BTS_E_CHANNEL_PORTORPORTGROUP	0x12B5	Either a messaging port or a distribution list, but not both, must be specified in a channel.
BTS_E_CHANNEL_MISSING_DOCUMENT	0x12B6	Both input and output documents are needed in a channel.
BTS_E_CHANNEL_INVALIDTYPE	0x12B7	A channel cannot be set to an open destination or set to an XLANG schedule (BIZTALK_OPENNESS_TYPE_EX_TOW ORKFLOW).
BTS_E_CHANNEL_MISSING_ OUTDOCREFERENCE	0x12B8	If the inbound document definition for a channel has a reference to a specification, the outbound document definition must also have a reference to a specification.
BTS_E_CHANNEL_ TRACKFIELDSCANTBESET	0x12B9	If the inbound document definition for a channel does not have a reference to a specification, the tracking fields cannot be set.
BTS_E_CHANNEL_EXPRESSIONCANTBESET	0x12BA	If the inbound document definition for a channel does not have a reference to a specification, the channel-filtering expressions cannot be set.
BTS_E_CHANNEL_MAPREFCANTBESET	0x12BB	If the inbound document definition for a channel does not have a reference to a specification then a reference to a map cannot be set.

Message name	Value	Description
BTS_E_CHANNEL_NOTSAME_INPDOC_ OUTDOC	0x12BC	If the inbound document definition for a channel does not have a reference to a specification then the outbound document handle should be the same of inbound document handle.
BTS_E_CHANNEL_OPEN_RECEIPTCONFLICT	0x12BD	Channels that are set from an open source or set from an XLANG schedule (BIZTALK_OPENNESS_TYPE_EX_FRO MWORKFLOW) cannot be receipt channels.
BTS_E_CHANNEL_RECEIPT_ RECEIPTTIMEOUT	0x12BE	The **Expect Receipt Timeout** property cannot be set on a receipt channel.
BTS_E_CHANNEL_RECEIPT_ CANTSETRECEIPTCHANNEL	0x12BF	An identifier cannot be set on a receipt channel.
BTS_E_CHANNEL_RECEIPT_CONFLICT	0x12C0	In a receipt channel, the source specification from the original channel must be used as the destination specification, and the destination specification from the original channel must be used as the source specification.
BTS_E_CHANNEL_SRCORGDEFAULT	0x12C1	If the channel is set from an XLANG schedule (BIZTALK_OPENNESS_TYPE_EX_FRO MWORKFLOW), the source organization must be the home organization.
BTS_E_CHANNEL_PORT_BOTHOPEN	0x12C2	Both the channel and messaging port cannot be set to Open.
BTS_E_CHANNEL_RECEIPT_INVALID	0x12C3	The Receipt Channel and Expect Receipt Timeout properties cannot be set for an open-source channel. These properties also cannot be set if the messaging port is set to an open destination, set to an XLANG schedule (BIZTALK_OPENNESS_TYPE_EX_TOW ORKFLOW), or if the messaging port uses the Loopback transport type.
BTS_E_CHANNEL_ RECEIPTMATCHNOTFOUND	0x12C4	The corresponding receipt channel for this channel could not be found.

Message name	Value	Description
BTS_E_CHANNEL_RECEIPT_OPENPORT	0x12C5	A receipt channel can be connected only to messaging ports that are not open messaging ports.
BTS_E_CHANNEL_RECEIPT_LOOPBACKPORT	0x12C6	A receipt channel cannot be connected to a messaging port that uses the Loopback transport type. Also, the transport type of a messaging port that is already connected to a receipt channel cannot be changed to Loopback.
BTS_E_CHANNEL_CANNOTUPDATE	0x12C8	After a channel is created, the following properties cannot be changed: source organization, openness designation, messaging port, distribution list, and receipt channel designation.
BTS_E_PORT_INVALIDOPENNESS	0x12C9	A messaging port cannot be set to an open source; nor can it be set from an XLANG schedule (BIZTALK_OPENNESS_TYPE_EX_FROMWORKFLOW).
BTS_E_CHANNEL_CONTROLNUMBER_ENVELOPEFORMATMISMATCH	0x12CA	If the envelope format for the messaging port is X12 or EDIFACT, the control-number value on the channel must be set.
BTS_E_PORT_ENVELOPE_SERIALIZERCLSID	0x12CB	If the envelope format for the messaging port is set to Custom, a class identifier (CLSID) for the serializer component must be specified.
BTS_E_CHANNEL_AIC_TRANSPORTCLSID	0x12CD	If the transport type associated with the channel is set to Application Integration Component, a class identifier (CLSID) must be specified for the primary transport.
BTS_E_CHANNEL_RECEIPT_PORTGROUP	0x12CE	If a channel is connected to a distribution list, a receipt channel cannot be specified.
BTS_E_COMPONENTREQUIRES2AGGREGATEFTM	0x12CF	To be a valid object in the BizTalk Object Model, this custom component must aggregate the free-threaded marshaler.
BTS_E_CERTREFNOTFOUND	0x12D1	Either the certificate reference could not be found in MY or BIZTALK stores or it is not valid.

Message name	Value	Description
BTS_E_NODOC	0x12D2	The Document Definition has been removed from the database. Avoid deleting objects when documents might exist in the queues which reference these objects.
BTS_E_NOENV	0x12D3	The envelope has been removed from the database. Avoid deleting objects when documents might exist in the queues which reference these objects.
BTS_E_NOCHANNEL	0x12D4	The channel has been removed from the database. Avoid deleting objects when documents might exist in the queues which reference these objects.
BTS_E_INVALIDREFERENCE	0x12D5	Either the WebDAV repository reference does not contain a valid HTTP address or it contains the text "localhost." Please provide either a valid HTTP address or replace the text "localhost" with the actual computer name.
BTS_E_CANNOTCONTAINSUBOBJECTS	0x12D6	The property set and delimiter objects cannot contain any subobjects.
BTS_E_INVALIDTRACKFIELDS	0x12D7	The "x_custom_search" field in the tracking field dictionary must be a simple list.
BTS_E_CHANNEL_INVALID_ORG	0x12D8	The organization specified in this channel does not exist.
BTS_E_CHANNEL_INVALID_ALIAS	0x12D9	The identifier specified for the organization in this channel either does not exist or it does not belong to the organization.
BTS_E_CHANNEL_INVALID_APPLICATION	0x12DA	The application specified for the organization in this channel either does not exist or it does not belong to the organization.
BTS_E_CHANNEL_INVALID_INPDOCID	0x12DB	The input document specified in this channel does not exist.
BTS_E_CHANNEL_INVALID_OUTDOCID	0x12DC	The output document specified in this channel does not exist.
BTS_E_CHANNEL_INVALID_PORTGROUP	0x12DD	The distribution list specified in this channel does not exist.

Message name	Value	Description
BTS_E_OBJECT_NOT_XMLSERILIZABLE	0x12DE	The given **dictionary** or **simplelist** object must implement **IPersistXML** methods.
BTS_E_CHANNEL_INVALID_PORT	0x12E0	At least one messaging port that is referenced in this channel either does not exist or it is not associated with this channel.
BTS_E_CHANNEL_RECEIPT_VERSIGN_DECRYPT	0x12E1	The **Verify Signature** or **Decrypt Encryption** properties cannot be set on a receipt channel.
BTS_E_INVALID_REQUEST_CHANNEL	0x12E2	A channel that is connected to a distribution list cannot be used as a request channel.
BTS_E_DESTINATION_NOT_FOUND	0x12E3	The destination URL is not specified, and the messaging port is an open destination. Either the destination URL or a destination for the messaging port must be specified.
BTS_E_DESTINATION_CONFLICT	0x12E4	Both a destination URL and a destination for the messaging port cannot be specified. Specify only one of these properties.
BTS_E_ASYNC_TRANSPORT	0x12E5	The transport type for the request channel is not valid. Only the HTTP, HTTPS, and Application Integration Component transport types are valid for a request channel.
BTS_E_INVALID_RESPONSE_CHANNEL	0x12E6	The response channel can be connected only to a messaging port with a transport type set to Loopback.
BTS_E_INVALID_VERSION	0x12E7	The database version is incompatible with the installed version of the server. Try running setup again.
BTS_E_INVALID_SCHEMA	0x12E8	The document or envelope specification is not valid. Open the specification in BizTalk Editor, and then on the Tools menu, click Validate Specification. Resolve any warnings to ensure that the specification is valid.
BTS_E_CHANNEL_RECEIPTCHANNEL_PORTGROUP	0x12E9	A receipt channel cannot be connected to a distribution list.

Message name	Value	Description
BTS_E_TRANSPORT_ORCHESTRATION_ OPENNESS	0x12EA	A messaging port that uses the BizTalk Orchestration Activation transport type must have the Openness Type property set to an XLANG schedule (BIZTALK_OPENNESS_TYPE_EX_TOW ORKFLOW).
BTS_E_TRANSPORT_ORCHESTRATION_ ADDRESSPARAMETER	0x12EB	Both a primary address and a parameter are required for a messaging port that uses a BizTalk Orchestration Activation transport type.
BTS_E_ORCHESTRATION_INVALIDORG	0x12EC	A messaging port that uses a BizTalk Orchestration Activation transport type must have the home organization set as the destination organization.
BTS_E_INVALID_FILTEREXPRESSION	0x12ED	The channel filtering expression is not valid. Make sure that the node-path expression is valid.
BTS_E_MULTIPLEDOCDEFSFORPROPSET	0x12EE	Multiple document definitions were found for the given property set. Only a single document definition for a given property set is expected.
BTS_E_INVALID_PROPSET	0x12EF	The PropertySet cannot contain nonstring element values.
BTS_E_DBSCHEMA_MISMATCH	0x1300	The existing Database Schema is not compatible with the current version of the product. You must delete the existing database.
BTS_E_UNEXPECTED_INSTALL	0x1301	The existing Database Schema is newer than the current version that is installed. Setup will rollback the changes.
CIS_E_DOCSCHEMA_ATTRIB_MISSING	0x1400	The "%3" attribute is missing in the "%4" element. Line: %1, Pos: %2.
CIS_E_DOCSCHEMA_INVALID_ATTRIB_ VALUE	0x1401	The "%3" attribute value "%4" is not valid. Line: %1, Pos: %2.
CIS_E_DOCSCHEMA_EMPTY_ELEMENT	0x1402	The "%3" element cannot be empty. Line: %1, Pos: %2.

Message name	Value	Description
CIS_E_DOCSCHEMA_INVALID_CHILD_ ELEMENT	0x1403	The "%3" element cannot be a child of the "%4" element. Line: %1, Pos: %2.
CIS_E_DOCSCHEMA_MULTIPLE_INFO	0x1404	Only one record description or one field description is allowed for each element declaration. One of the descriptions must be removed. Line: %1, Pos: %2.
CIS_E_DOCSCHEMA_INVALID_FIELD_DECL	0x1405	The root node cannot contain a field. The root node of the document must contain a record. Verify that the root node in your document is declared as a record. Line: %1, Pos: %2.
CIS_E_DOCSCHEMA_INVALID_LEN_DECL	0x1406	The minimum length value must be no greater than the maximum length value. Line: %1, Pos: %2.
CIS_E_DOCSCHEMA_INVALID_POSLEN_ DECL	0x1407	The value of the start position must be no greater than the value of the end position. Line: %1, Pos: %2.
CIS_E_DOCSCHEMA_NO_INFO_YET	0x1408	A field description or record description must be specified before references to other elements. Line: %1, Pos: %2.
CIS_E_DOCSCHEMA_INVALID_ SCHEMATYPE_XML	0x1409	Only non-XML document specifications are allowed for this format. The schema_type attribute has the value "xml". Verify that the specification selected is a non-XML specification. Line: %1, Pos: %2.
CIS_E_DOCSCHEMA_NO_INFO	0x140A	No record information or field information was found in the "%3" element. Line: %1, Pos: %2.
CIS_E_DOCSCHEMA_INVALID_ATTRIB	0x140B	The "%3" attribute is not allowed in the "%4" element. Line: %1, Pos: %2.
CIS_E_DOCSCHEMA_MISSING_ELEM_DECL	0x140C	There is no element with the name "%1" in the document specification.
CIS_E_DOCSCHEMA_MISSING_ATTR_DECL	0x140D	There is no attribute with the name "%1" in the document specification.
CIS_E_DOCSCHEMA_INVALID_ POSITIONAL_DECL	0x140E	The "%1" record cannot be a child of the "%2" positional record. Only fields can be children of positional records.

Message name	Value	Description
CIS_E_DOCSCHEMA_INVALID_RECORD_ CHILDREN	0x140F	The children of the "%1" delimited record must either be all records or all fields. Records with no tag identifier cannot have mixed records and fields as children.
CIS_E_DOCSCHEMA_NO_RECORD_ CHILDREN	0x1410	The "%1" delimited record must have at least one child. Records with no tag identifier must have at least one child, or else the record cannot be found in a non-XML format. Either add a child to the record, give the record a tag identifier, or remove the record from the specification.
CIS_E_DOCSCHEMA_MISSING_RECORD_ TAG	0x1411	The "%1" delimited record is marked to repeat but it does not have a tag identifier. Only the last record in a document specification is allowed to have this property. If this record appears only once in the document, then mark it as a single occurrence. Otherwise, give the record a tag identifier that tells the server where to look for the next record in the specification.
CIS_E_DOCSCHEMA_NO_ROOT_ELEMENT	0x1412	The root-node name "%3" was not found in the specification. Line: %1, Pos: %2.
CIS_E_DOCSCHEMA_INVALID_ROOT_ ELEMENT	0x1413	The "%3" element cannot be the root node of this document. Only <Schema> is allowed. Line: %1, Pos: %2.
CIS_E_DOCSCHEMA_INVALID_EMPTY_ ATTRIBUTE	0x1414	The "%3" attribute in the "%4" element cannot be empty. Either specify a nonempty value or remove the attribute. Line: %1, Pos: %2.
CIS_E_DOCSCHEMA_INVALID_REFERENCE	0x1415	The "%1" record has an illegal cyclic path through the "%2" record. The only cyclic reference allowed for a record is if the record has a tag identifier that allows the system to terminate the search. Either remove the cyclic reference or add an appropriate tag identifier to the document specification.
CIS_E_DOCSCHEMA_LOADFAILED	0x1416	The specification failed to load. See the following messages for details.

Message name	Value	Description
CIS_E_DOCSCHEMA_MISSING_NS	0x1417	Valid BizTalk Server specifications for non-XML documents must have the namespace declarations of "urn:schemas-microsoft-com:BizTalkServer", "urn:schemas-microsoft-com:datatypes", and "urn:schemas-microsoft-com:xml-data" in the root node of the specification.
CIS_E_DOCSCHEMA_INVALID_SCHEMA_USAGE	0x1418	The specification referenced in the "%1" document is not compatible with the "%2" format. Select a specification that is compatible with this format, or if this is a valid specification for the defined format, assign "%2" to the "standard" property on this specification.
CIS_E_DOCSCHEMA_MISSING_POSLEN_DECL	0x1419	The "%3" field is missing a start and end position, and is referenced in the "%4" positional record. Specify valid start and end positions for this field. Line: %1, Pos: %2.
CIS_E_DOCSCHEMA_DUPLICATE_NAMESPACE	0x141A	The duplicate namespace declaration "%3" has been found. Please remove the duplicate reference to same namespace. Line: %1, Pos: %2.
CIS_E_PARSER_EOF	0x1430	The end of the file was reached prematurely.
CIS_E_PARSER_MISSING_TAG	0x1431	The required "%1" record was not found in the inbound document.
CIS_E_PARSER_MISSING_FIELD	0x1432	The required field "%1" in the "%2" record was not found in the inbound document.
CIS_E_PARSER_FAILURE	0x1433	The parser failed to convert the document due to processing errors. See the following messages for details.
CIS_E_PARSER_INVALIDDATA	0x1434	The parser cannot match the current position of the data with the specification. Verify that the version of this specification is consistent with the version of the data and that the root parsing tags match.

Message name	Value	Description
CIS_E_PARSER_NO_DATA	0x1435	There is no data that can be parsed on the dictionary. Verify that either the "working_data" field or the "file_path" field contains nonempty data.
CIS_E_PARSER_INVALID_ENVNAME	0x1436	The envelope name "%1" does not reference a valid envelope for the BizTalk Server parser. Either the envelope name does not exist or there is an envelope specification attached that is not valid.
CIS_E_PARSER_NO_COMPONENTS_FOUND	0x1439	No parser component recognizes the data. This might be caused by an interchange specification that is missing or not valid, or it might be caused by data that is not valid. Verify that both the interchange specification (if one is specified) and the data match.
CIS_E_PARSER_COMPONENT_FAILED	0x1440	While trying to process document #%4 during submission "%1", the parser component named "%2" failed on the method "%3" with the error code "%5". Possible causes are: the component found unexpected data in the incoming stream; a document specification could not be found given the data; or an internal component failure occurred. If this problem continues, remove this component from the valid list of parser components or contact your system administrator.
CIS_E_PARSER_DOCUMENT_FAILED	0x1441	Document #%4 within submission "%1" was returned as a document that was not valid from the parser component named "%2". The most frequent cause is a document specification that is not valid or else the component was unable to determine the necessary routing fields. Verify that the proper specification is defined for this data.
CIS_E_PARSER_INVALID_DATETIME	0x1442	The "%1" date or time format does not match the format of the "%2" data extracted from the incoming data.

Message name	Value	Description
CIS_E_PARSER_INVALID_COMPONENT	0x1443	Within submission "%1", the parser component named "%2" could not be loaded. Verify that this component can be run in a stand-alone executable and that the server has sufficient permissions to start it.
CIS_W_PARSER_SKIPPED_COMPONENT	0x1444	The parser was unable to probe the specified component. This component will be skipped.
CIS_E_PARSER_UNUSEABLE_DOCNAME	0x1445	The parser cannot use the document "%1" as it has no specification. Please attach a specification to this document or specify a different one.
CIS_E_PARSER_CONTROL_NUMBER_MISMATCH	0x1446	The control number of segment "%1" (%2) does not match that of segment "%3" (%4).
CIS_E_PARSER_DOCCOUNT_INCORRECT	0x1447	The document or segment count contained in tag "%1" (%2) does not match the number of documents or segments processed (%3).
CIS_E_PARSER_X12_ISA_PARSE_FAILED	0x1448	The parser cannot parse the ISA section of the X12 document. This segment is fixed-width; if fields in this segment do not have correct length, the parsing will fail because the delimiters are picked up from the wrong offsets.
CIS_E_PARSER_MIN_LENGTH	0x1449	The data contains a field value ("%1") that doesn't meet minimum length requirement for tag "%2" (minimum length is %3).
CIS_E_PARSER_MAX_LENGTH	0x144A	The data contains a field value ("%1") that doesn't meet maximum length requirement for tag "%2" (maximum length is %3).
CIS_E_PARSER_NO_DATA_CONSUMED	0x144B	No data was read by the parser. Make sure that the code page is set correctly for the data. If the data is UNICODE, make sure that there is no byte order mark (0xFFFE or 0xFEFF) appears at the beginning of the file.
CIS_E_PARSER_UNSUPPORTED_EDIFACT_SYNTAX	0x144C	EDIFACT documents with the "UNOX" or the "UNOY" syntax identifier are not supported.

Message name	Value	Description
CIS_E_PARSER_DATA_REMAINING	0x144D	Additional data in the document instance was not parsed. Make sure that the document instance you want to validate contains only one document.
CIS_E_PARSER_MISSING_DELIMITER	0x144E	While parsing record "%1", the parser cannot find the required delimiter: "%2" (%3).
CIS_E_PARSER_MISSING_LEADING_ DELIMITER	0x144F	While parsing record "%1", the parser cannot find the required leading delimiter: "%2" (%3).
CIS_E_PARSER_MISSING_TRAILING_ DELIMITER	0x1450	While parsing record "%1", the parser cannot find the required trailing delimiter: "%2" (%3).
CIS_E_VALIDATE_GROUP_RULE	0x1451	In record "%1", if any of the following fields exist, then all must exist: %2
CIS_E_VALIDATE_GROUP_ALL	0x1452	In record "%1", all of the following fields must exist: %2
CIS_E_VALIDATE_GROUP_ONE	0x1453	In record "%1", only one of the following fields can exist: %2
CIS_E_PARSER_INVALID_WRAP_CHAR_ FOUND	0x1454	While parsing record "%1", the parser found an occurrence of a wrap character, "%2", that is not valid.
CIS_E_VALIDATE_GROUP_ANY	0x1455	In record "%1", one or more of the following fields must exist: %2
CIS_E_PARSER_EXTRA_DELIMITER	0x1456	While parsing record "%1", the parser found the following extra delimiter: "%2".
BTS_E_DOCUMENT_HAS_INVALID_ MANIFEST	0x1457	Error parsing the manifest.
CIS_E_ADMIN_CACHE_PARSERS	0x1504	The latest modification date from the administration parser table could not be loaded.
CIS_E_ADMIN_INIT_CACHE	0x1505	The configuration data in the global cache could not be initialized.
CIS_E_ADMIN_RELOAD_CACHE	0x1506	The configuration data from the database could not be reloaded.

Message name	Value	Description
CIS_E_ADMIN_PARSER_GETCLSID	0x1507	The class identifiers (CLSIDs) of the parser records could not be loaded.
CIS_E_ADMIN_CACHE_ OBJECTNOTCREATED	0x1509	The administration cache cannot be created.
CIS_E_ADMIN_CACHE_INITIALLOAD	0x150A	The configuration cache data from the database could not be loaded.
CIS_E_ADMIN_ADD_SERVER_ACCESS_ DENIED	0x150B	Server "%1" cannot be added because access to the "%2" is denied.
CIS_E_ADMIN_ADD_SERVER_NO_SERVICE	0x150C	Server "%1" cannot be added because BizTalk Server is not installed on the computer.
CIS_E_ADMIN_DELETE_SERVER_NO_ ACCESS	0x150D	The "%1" server cannot be deleted because access to the "%2" service is denied and the service cannot be stopped.
CIS_E_ADMIN_DELETE_GROUP_SERVER_ RUNNING	0x150E	This server group cannot be deleted because the "%1" server is still running.
CIS_E_ADMIN_DELETE_GROUP_SERVER_ ACCESS_DENIED	0x150F	This server group cannot be deleted because access to the "%1" service on "%2" server is denied.
CIS_E_ADMIN_NOGROUP	0x1512	The specified administration group does not exist.
CIS_E_ADMIN_NOSERVER	0x1513	The specified administration server does not exist.
CIS_E_ADMIN_NORECEIVESERVICE	0x1514	The specified administration receive function does not exist in the database.
CIS_E_ADMIN_UNEXPECTED_REMOVE_ RECEIVESERVICE	0x1515	An unexpected error occurred while trying to remove the "%1" receive function from the database.
CIS_E_ADMIN_UNEXPECTED_REMOVE_ GROUP	0x1516	An unexpected error occurred while trying to remove the "%1" group from the database.
CIS_E_ADMIN_UNEXPECTED_REMOVE_ SERVER	0x1517	An unexpected error occurred while trying to remove the "%1" server from the database.
CIS_E_ADMIN_NOTIMESTAMPS	0x151A	The specified administration timestamps object does not exist in the database.

Message name	Value	Description
CIS_E_ADMIN_REFRESH_THREAD_ERROR	0x151B	The configuration refresh thread encountered an error while loading the configuration data.
CIS_E_ADMIN_REFRESH_THREAD_EXIT	0x151C	The configuration refresh thread cannot load the configuration data because of a previous error.
CIS_E_ADMIN_RECSVC_GENERAL	0x151D	The configuration refresh thread cannot set up one or more receive functions. This might be because SQL Server is not started.
CIS_E_ADMIN_CREATE_GROUP	0x1529	The server group cannot be created because "%1".
CIS_E_ADMIN_LOAD_GROUP_PROPS	0x152A	The group properties cannot be loaded because "%1".
CIS_E_ADMIN_SAVE_GROUP_PROPS	0x152B	The group properties cannot be saved because "%1".
CIS_E_ADMIN_REMOVE_GROUP	0x152C	The server group cannot be removed from the database because "%1".
CIS_E_ADMIN_GETALLADMINGROUPS	0x152D	All server groups cannot be retrieved from the database.
CIS_E_ADMIN_GETSERVERS	0x152E	All servers for the "%1" server group cannot be retrieved from the database because "%2".
CIS_E_ADMIN_GETRECEIVESERVICES	0x152F	All receive functions for the "%1" group cannot be retrieved from database because "%2".
CIS_E_ADMIN_GETPARSERS_IN_GROUP	0x1531	All parsers for the "%1" server group cannot be retrieved from the database because "%2".
CIS_E_ADMIN_GETLOCALSMTPHOST	0x1538	The local SMTP host cannot be retrieved because "%1".
CIS_E_ADMIN_CREATE_SERVER	0x1539	The server cannot be created because "%1".
CIS_E_ADMIN_LOAD_SERVER_PROPS	0x153A	The server properties cannot be loaded because "%1".
CIS_E_ADMIN_SAVE_SERVER_PROPS	0x153B	The server properties cannot be saved because "%1".

Message name	Value	Description
CIS_E_ADMIN_REMOVE_SERVER	0x153C	The server cannot be removed from the database because "%1".
CIS_E_ADMIN_GETALLADMINSERVRES	0x153D	All servers cannot be retrieved from the database.
CIS_E_ADMIN_GETSERVERBYNAME	0x153E	The server properties for "%1" cannot be retrieved because "%2".
CIS_E_ADMIN_DECRYPT_PASSWORD	0x1540	The "%1" property cannot be retrieved.
CIS_E_ADMIN_EXEC_COMMMAND_ON_ PARSER	0x154F	The SQL command "%1" on the parser database table cannot be executed because "%2".
CIS_E_ADMIN_CREATE_RECEIVESERVICE	0x155D	The receive function cannot be created because "%1".
CIS_E_ADMIN_LOAD_RECEIVESERVICE_ PROPS	0x155E	The receive function properties cannot be loaded because "%1".
CIS_E_ADMIN_SAVE_RECEIVESERVICE_ PROPS	0x155F	The receive function properties cannot be saved because "%1".
CIS_E_ADMIN_REMOVE_RECEIVESERVICE	0x1560	The receive function cannot be removed from the database because "%1".
CIS_E_ADMIN_GETALLRECEIVESERVICES	0x1561	All receive functions cannot be retrieved from the database because "%1".
CIS_E_ADMIN_ GETALLRECEIVESERVICESINSERVER	0x1562	All receive functions cannot be retrieved for the "%1" server because "%2".
CIS_E_ADMIN_LOAD_TIMESTAMPS	0x1563	All timestamps cannot be retrieved from the database because "%1".
CIS_E_ADMIN_GETSQCONNECT	0x1570	The Shared Queue database connection string cannot be retrieved from the database.
CIS_E_ADMIN_GETCOMPUTERNAME	0x1571	The name of the local computer cannot be retrieved. Internally, BizTalk Server is using "localhost" as the computer name.
CIS_E_ADMIN_MIN_CONSTRAINT	0x1573	The size of the "%1" property is less than the minimum required length for "%2".
CIS_E_ADMIN_MAX_CONSTRAINT	0x1574	The size of the "%1" property is greater than the maximum length allowed for "%2".
CIS_E_ADMIN_GET_MGMTDB_CONNECT_ PROPS	0x1575	The BizTalk Messaging Management database properties cannot be retrieved.

Message name	Value	Description
CIS_E_ADMIN_KEY_EMPTY	0x1576	The key to the database table, property "%1", is empty.
CIS_E_ADMIN_COCREATE_IN_CREATE	0x1577	An instance of the "%1" object could not be created while creating a new "%2" object.
CIS_E_ADMIN_ADO_OPEN_CONNECTSTRING	0x1578	The connection to the BizTalk Messaging Management database could not be opened.
CIS_E_ADMIN_COCREATE_IN_LOAD	0x1579	An instance of the "%1" object could not be created while loading the "%2" properties.
CIS_E_ADMIN_COCREATE_IN_SAVE	0x1580	An instance of the "%1" object could not be created while saving the "%2" properties.
CIS_E_ADMIN_COCREATE_IN_REMOVE	0x1581	An instance of the "%1" object could not be created while trying to remove the "%2" object.
CIS_E_ADMIN_COCREATE_IN_GETALL	0x1582	An instance of the "%1" object could not be created while trying to get all instances of "%2".
CIS_E_ADMIN_COCREATE_IN_GETALL_INSERVER	0x1583	An instance of the "%1" object could not be created while trying to get all instances of the "%2" object in the "%3" server.
CIS_E_ADMIN_GET_PROP	0x1584	The "%1" property cannot be retrieved.
CIS_E_ADMIN_CLOSE_ADO_CONNECTION	0x1585	The ADO connection cannot be closed.
CIS_E_ADMIN_CLOSE_ADO_RECORDSET	0x1586	The ADO record set cannot be retrieved.
CIS_E_ADMIN_ENCRYPT_PASSWORD	0x1587	The "%1" property cannot be processed.
CIS_E_ADMIN_COCREATE_IN_GETALLNAMES	0x1588	An instance of the "%1" object could not be created while trying to get the names of all the "%2" object instances.
CIS_E_ADMIN_COCREATE_IN_GETOTHERS_OF_GROUP	0x1589	An instance of the "%1" object could not be created while trying to get all instance of the "%2" object in the "%3" group.
CIS_E_ADMIN_COCREATE_IN_GET_SMTPHOST	0x158A	An instance of the "%1" object could not be created while trying to get "%2" for the local server.
CIS_E_ADMIN_COCREATE_IN_GET_SQ_CONNECTSTRING	0x158B	An instance of the "%1" object could not be created while trying to get the Shared Queue parameters of "%2" in order to connect to the database.

Message name	Value	Description
CIS_E_ADMIN_COCREATE_SERVER_BYNAME	0x158C	An instance of the "%1" object could not be created while trying to get the properties of the "%2" server instance of the "%3" class.
CIS_E_ADMIN_GETSQCONNECT_IN_OPEN	0x158D	The Shared Queue database connection string could not be retrieved from the database because "%1".
CIS_E_ADMIN_COCREATE_EXEC_SQL_COMMAND_ON_PARSER	0x158E	An instance of the "%1" object could not be created while trying to execute a SQL command on the "%2" database table.
CIS_E_ADMIN_COCREATE_PARSER_CLSIDS_IN_GROUP	0x158F	An instance of the "%1" object could not be created while retrieving the class identifiers (CLSIDs) for the parsers that belong to the "%2" group.
CIS_E_ADMIN_INVALID_ARGUMENT	0x1590	An unexpected internal error occurred. An invalid "%1" argument was used when calling the "%2" method.
CIS_E_ADMIN_MAX_ENUM_CONSTRAINT	0x1591	The value of the "%1" property is greater than the maximum value allowed for "%2".
CIS_E_ADMIN_MIN_ENUM_CONSTRAINT	0x1592	The value of the "%1" property is smaller than the minimum value allowed for "%2".
CIS_E_ADMIN_CREATE_CHANGETYPE_TO_BSTR	0x1593	The type of the "%1" property could not be changed to a string.
CIS_E_ADMIN_CREATE_CHANGETYPE_TO_BOOL	0x1594	The type of the "%1" property could not be changed to Boolean.
CIS_E_ADMIN_COCREATE_IN_ENUMINSTANCES	0x1595	An instance of the "%1" object could not be created while enumerating instances of the "%2" object.
CIS_E_ADMIN_COCREATE_IN_PUTINSTANCE	0x1596	An instance of the "%1" object could not be created while setting an instance of the "%2" object.
CIS_E_ADMIN_COCREATE_IN_GETOBJECT	0x1597	An instance of the "%1" object could not be created while getting an instance of the "%2" object.
CIS_E_ADMIN_COCREATE_IN_DELETEINSTANCE	0x1598	An instance of the "%1" object could not be created while deleting an instance of the "%2" object.

Message name	Value	Description
CIS_E_ADMIN_COCREATE_IN_LOADPROPS	0x1599	An instance of the "%1" object could not be created while loading properties for an instance of the "%2" object.
CIS_E_ADMIN_COCREATE_IN_ LOADPARSERS	0x159B	An instance of the "%1" object could not be created while loading parsers from a database for an instance the "%2" object.
CIS_E_ADMIN_COCREATE_IN_ SETPARSERSFROM_REGISTRY	0x159C	An instance of the "%1" object could not be created while setting parsers from the registry for an instance of the "%2" object.
CIS_E_ADMIN_COCREATE_IN_ SETPARSERSFROM_CLIENT	0x159D	An instance of the "%1" object could not be created while setting parsers from the client for an instance of the "%2" object.
CIS_E_ADMIN_COCREATE_IN_ REFRESHPARSERLIST	0x159E	An instance of the "%1" object could not be created while refreshing the parser list for an instance of the "%2" object.
CIS_E_ADMIN_COCREATE_IN_ MOVETOSUSPENDED_Q	0x159F	An instance of the "%1" object could not be created while moving an instance of "%2" to the Suspended queue.
CIS_E_ADMIN_COCREATE_IN_RESUBMIT	0x15A0	An instance of the "%1" object could not be created while resubmitting an instance of "%2".
CIS_E_ADMIN_COCREATE_IN_VIEWDOC	0x15A2	An instance of the "%1" object could not be created while viewing a document instance of "%2".
CIS_E_ADMIN_COCREATE_IN_ VIEWERRORDESC	0x15A3	An instance of the "%1" object could not be created while viewing the error description of an instance of "%2".
CIS_E_ADMIN_COCREATE_IN_ VIEWINTERCHANGE	0x15A4	An instance of the "%1" object could not be created while viewing the interchanges of an instance of "%2".
CIS_E_ADMIN_COCREATE_IN_ FREEINTERCHANGES	0x15A5	An instance of the "%1" object could not be created while freeing the interchanges for an instance of a "%2".
CIS_E_ADMIN_COCREATE_IN_ STARTSERVER	0x15A6	An instance of the "%1" object could not be created while starting the server for an instance of a "%2".

Message name	Value	Description
CIS_E_ADMIN_COCREATE_IN_STOPSERVER	0x15A7	An instance of the "%1" object could not be created while stopping the server for an instance of a "%2".
CIS_E_ADMIN_NO_DELETE_SERVER_IN_RECVSERVICE	0x15A8	The "%1" server cannot be deleted because it is the processing server for at least one receive function.
CIS_E_ADMIN_UPDATE_GROUP_SERVER_RUNNING	0x15A9	The server group properties cannot be changed because the "%1" server is still running.
CIS_E_ADMIN_UPDATE_GROUP_SERVER_ACCESS_DENIED	0x15AA	The server group properties cannot be changed because access to the "%1" service on "%2" server is denied.
CIS_E_ADMIN_UPDATE_SERVER_SERVER_RUNNING	0x15AC	The server properties cannot be changed because the "%1" server is still running.
CIS_E_ADMIN_UPDATE_SERVER_SERVER_ACCESS_DENIED	0x15AD	The server properties cannot be changed because access to the "%1" service on "%2" server is denied.
CIS_E_ADMIN_UPDATE_READ_ONLY_PROP	0x15AE	The "%1" property cannot be changed. It is a read only property.
CIS_E_ADMIN_DIFFERENT_ROOT	0x15AF	The "%1" server may already belong to a different BizTalk Server installation.
CIS_E_ADMIN_NOT_RESUBMITABLE	0x15B0	This Suspended queue item cannot be submitted again.
CIS_E_ADMIN_DBCONNECT	0x15B1	BizTalk Server failed to access the "%1" database on the "%2" server with the database connection information.
CIS_E_ADMIN_PURGE_SUSPENDEDQ	0x15B2	An instance of the "%1" object could not be created while deleting documents from "%2".
CIS_E_ADMIN_REQ_PROP_MISSING	0x15B3	%1 cannot be NULL.
CIS_E_ADMIN_WMI_ERROR_HANDLING	0x15B4	The BizTalk Server WMI provider error-handling method failed. The original error description for the error that called the error-handling method is: "%1".
CIS_W_ADMIN_QUERY_FAILED	0x15B5	An attempt to get the Where clause values for a WMI Query failed.

Message name	Value	Description
CIS_E_ADMIN_INVALID_ENUM_CONSTRAINT	0x15B6	The value "%2" of the "%1" property is not valid.
CIS_E_ADMIN_OPENNESS_CONSTRAINT	0x15B7	The value "%2" of the "%1" property is not permitted when the value of the **IsPassThrough** property is set to **TRUE**.
CIS_E_ADMIN_RECEIVE_INVALID_SERVER_GROUP	0x15B8	the specified server and/or group is not valid
CIS_E_ADMIN_INVALID_INSTANCE_NAME	0x15B9	The specified instance name "%1" contains at least one of the following characters that is not valid: [` ~ ! @ # $ % ^ & * ( ) + = [ ] { }	\ ; " ' < > , . ?]
BTS_E_ADMIN_GROUP_UNIQUE_NAME	0x15BA	A BizTalk Server group with the same name already exists in the BizTalk Messaging Management database.
BTS_E_ADMIN_TIMESTAMPS_DATA_CORRUPTION	0x15BB	Internal data corruption has been detected in the adm_TimeStamps table of the BizTalk Messaging Management database.
BTS_E_ADMIN_SERVER_UNIQUE_NAME	0x15BC	A BizTalk Server with the same name already exists in the BizTalk Messaging Management database.
BTS_E_ADMIN_SERVER_FOREIGN_GROUP NAME	0x15BD	This BizTalk Server does not reference a valid BizTalk Server group in the BizTalk Messaging Management database.
BTS_E_ADMIN_RECSVC_UNIQUE_NAME	0x15BE	A BizTalk Server receive function with the same name already exists in the BizTalk Messaging Management database.
BTS_E_ADMIN_RECSVC_FOREIGN_GROUPNAME	0x15BF	This BizTalk Server receive function does not reference a valid BizTalk Server group in the BizTalk Messaging Management database.
BTS_E_ADMIN_PARSER_UNIQUE_ID	0x15C1	A BizTalk Server parser with the same CLSID and Group Name already exists in the BizTalk Messaging Management database.
BTS_E_ADMIN_PARSER_FOREIGN_GROUPNAME	0x15C2	This BizTalk Server parser does not reference a valid BizTalk Server group in the BizTalk Messaging Management database.

Message name	Value	Description
CIS_E_ADMIN_DB_SPROCVERSION	0x15C3	The "%1" database on the "%2" server does not contain the necessary database schema.
CIS_E_ADMIN_DB_VERSION	0x15C4	The "%1" database on the "%2" server is not compatible with the current version of the product.
CIS_E_DTA_LOG_INTERCHANGE_DETAILS_FAILED	0x1604	The details of an interchange could not be logged.
CIS_E_DTA_LOG_DOCUMENT_DETAILS_FAILED	0x1605	The details of a document could not be logged.
CIS_E_DTA_LOG_GROUP_DETAILS_FAILED	0x1606	The details of a group could not be logged.
CIS_E_DTA_INIT_FAILED	0x160A	The DTA object could not be initialized.
CIS_E_DTA_FAILED_TO_GET_ADMIN_PROPERTIES	0x160E	The administration properties could not be obtained.
CIS_E_DTA_DATABASE_CONNECTION	0x160F	The server could not establish connection to the Tracking database.
CIS_E_DTA_LOG_DOCUMENT_FAILED	0x1619	A copy of the document could not be logged.
CIS_E_DTA_LOG_INTERCHANGE_FAILED	0x1620	A copy of the interchange could not be logged.
CIS_E_DTA_OBJECT_IS_UNINITIALIZED	0x1623	The DTA initialization method must be explicitly invoked before any DTA method can be invoked.
CIS_E_DTA_FAILED_TO_COMMIT	0x1625	Changes could not be committed to the database.
CIS_E_DTA_FAILED_TO_LOG_SOURCE_XML	0x1626	The intermediate source XML could not be logged.
CIS_E_DTA_FAILED_TO_LOG_DEST_XML	0x1627	The intermediate destination XML could not be logged.
CIS_E_DTA_ACK_NO_ROW_FOUND	0x162B	Acknowledgment correlation failed. The correlation key(s) given did not match any record in the Tracking database.
CIS_E_DTA_ACK_MULTIPLE_ROWS_FOUND	0x162C	Acknowledgment correlation failed. The correlation key(s) given match more than one record in the Tracking database.

Message name	Value	Description
CIS_E_DTA_LOG_MIME_FAILED	0x162D	The MIME data for submission "%1" could not be logged.
CIS_W_DTA_LOG_TRACKING_FIELD_ FAILED	0x162E	The following tracking field for submission "%1" could not be logged: Tracking field: %2 Specification field name: %3 Actual value: %4 Possible causes are either a conversion error or an arithmetic overflow error. Check the tracking field settings in the document or channel configuration.
CIS_W_DTA_LOG_BINARY_TRACKING_ FIELD_FAILED	0x162F	The following tracking field for submission "%1" could not be logged: Tracking field: %2 Specification field name: %3 The submission could not be logged because the corresponding XML element or attribute is set to binary type, which can only be tracked as custom type tracking field. Correct the tracking field settings in the document or channel configuration.
CIS_E_DTA_INIT_TRANSACTIONAL_ SESSION	0x1631	The server could not create a transactional session for the Tracking object.
CIS_W_DTA_RECORD_UPDATE_FAILED	0x1632	An attempt to update a tracking record has failed. The record was probably deleted prior to the update action.
CIS_E_RESPONSE_DOM_LOAD_FAILED	0x1701	The XML-DOM could not be loaded from the response data.
CIS_E_RECEIVE_MSMQ_BYOT_CREATE_ FAILED	0x1702	A Message Queuing receive function failed to create an IInterchange object using a Bring Your Own Transaction (BYOT) object. This may have been caused by editing the BizTalk Server COM+ application or configuring the BYOT object in its own COM+ application. This BizTalk Message Queuing receive function will be stopped.
CIS_E_RECEIVE_MSMQ_ZERO_BYTE_DOC	0x1703	A Message Queuing receive function read a zero byte document. This document has been discarded.

Message name	Value	Description
CIS_E_RECEIVE_SERVICE_FAILED	0x1704	There was a failure processing the "%1" receive function. Check your receive function configuration in BizTalk Server Administration.
CIS_E_INITWORKITEM	0x1705	There was a failure creating the internal work item. Make sure that SQL Server is running.
CIS_E_NOPIPELINE	0x1706	A channel with the name "%1" cannot be located.
CIS_E_OPEN_PASSTHROUGH	0x1707	The channel and messaging port openness type are not compatible with the submit method call.
CIS_E_DLQ_DETAILS	0x1708	Details about the Suspended queue could not be retrieved.
CIS_E_INVALID_OPENDEST	0x1709	The destination specified for the following open-destination messaging port was not valid: %1
CIS_E_SQL_MISSINGROWS	0x170a	Rows were missing from the record returned by SQL OLEDB provider.
CIS_E_BTF_TIME_STAMP_EXPIRED	0x170b	The BizTalk Framework document "%1" was received with an expired "%2" timestamp. This message will be discarded.
CIS_E_ACCESS_DENIED	0x170c	The current process did not have administrative privileges and cannot access the Suspended queue.
CIS_E_BTF_ERROR_FINDING_TAG	0x170d	The parser could either not find the BizTalk Framework tag "%1", or the tag did not have a value. This document will be moved to the Suspended queue.
CIS_E_INVALID_FORMAT	0x170e	The "%1" envelope format is not recognized by the server. Specify a valid envelope format.
CIS_E_INVALID_MAP	0x170f	The server could not load the map that is referenced by this channel.
CIS_E_MALFORMED_EXPR	0x1710	The expression "%1" is malformed and cannot be interpreted by the server.

Message name	Value	Description
CIS_E_DB_SHUTDOWN	0x1711	The server is shutting down because of a database failure.
CIS_E_SUBMIT_BLOCKED	0x1712	All submit calls have been blocked due to a database failure. After correcting this problem, please go to Component Services and shut down the 'BizTalk Server Interchange Application', before attempting to call any submit method.
CIS_E_CERT_NOT_FOUND	0x1713	The required certificate cannot be found in the certificate store.
CIS_E_NODATA	0x1714	The Submit method call did not contain a document or a file path.
CIS_E_TOOMUCH_DATA	0x1715	The Submit method call contained both a document and a file path.
CIS_E_INVALID_OPENFLAG	0x1716	The Submit method call was passed an openness type that is not valid. Refer to the BizTalk Server 2000 Help documentation for the enumeration of these values.
CIS_E_PASSTHROUGH_PARAMS	0x1717	The Submit method call contained a channel along with source, destination, or document name information. Do not include source, destination, or document name information when passing the channel as a parameter within a Submit method call.
CIS_E_NOSRCID	0x1718	The Submit method call contained a source qualifier but no source identifier.
CIS_E_NODESTID	0x1719	The Submit method call contained a destination qualifier but no destination identifier.
MSG_TIMEBOMB_EXPIRED	0x171A	Thank you for evaluating Microsoft BizTalk Server 2000. The period for this evaluation version has ended. Please contact Microsoft or your software reseller to obtain a licensed version of Microsoft BizTalk Server 2000.

Message name	Value	Description
CIS_E_LOOPBACK	0x171B	An attempt was made to submit a document that uses the Loopback transport type. The Loopback transport type can only be used when calling the **SubmitSync** method.
CIS_E_DBEXECUTE	0x171C	The following stored procedure call failed: "%1".
CIS_E_MISSING_SMTPHOST	0x171D	In order to use the SMTP transport, the SMTP host must be specified. To specify an SMTP host, in BizTalk Server Administration expand Microsoft BizTalk Server 2000, right-click BizTalk Server Group, and then click Properties to open the BizTalk Server Group Properties dialog box. On the General tab, in the SMTP host box, specify the SMTP host that you want to use.
CIS_E_INVALIDHANDLE	0x171E	This method expected a submission handle or an array of submission handles, but the incoming data was not valid. Verify that the parameters are correct.
CIS_E_DBCONNECT	0x171F	BizTalk Server failed to initialize a connection to database: "%1" on server: "%2".
CIS_E_PASSTHROUGH_WITH_NOCHANNEL	0x1720	A valid channel name must be specified as a submission parameter on a Submit or **SubmitSync** method call when the pass-through flag is set to true.
CIS_W_DBFAILURE	0x1721	The database call failed and returned the following error string: "%1". If possible, we will attempt to retry this call.
CIS_E_GET_BTMPARAMS	0x1722	Unable to load connection parameters for BTM database. Please go to the Administration MMC to resolve this problem.
CIS_E_UNABLE_TO_CREATE_CUSTOM_ PRE_PROC	0x1723	The custom preprocessing component for the receive function "%1" could not be created. This document will be moved to the Suspended queue.

Message name	Value	Description
CIS_E_CUSTOM_PRE_PROC_FAILED	0x1724	The custom preprocessing component used by the receive function "%1" failed. This document will be moved to the Suspended queue.
CIS_E_CUSTOM_PRE_PROC_NO_BSTR	0x1725	The custom preprocessing component used by the File receive function "%1" failed to return a valid BSTR. A valid BSTR is required. This document will be moved to the Suspended queue.
CIS_E_CUSTOM_PRE_PROC_INVALID_DATA	0x1726	The custom preprocessing component used by the Message Queue receive function "%1" cannot be called because the message contains data that is not a BSTR or a BYTE array. This document will be moved to the Suspended queue.
CIS_E_CUSTOM_PRE_PROC_INVALID_CP	0x1727	The custom preprocessing component used by the Message Queue receive function "%1" failed to return a valid code page. This document will be moved to the Suspended queue.
CIS_E_CUSTOM_PRE_PROC_INVALID_DATA_OUT	0x1728	The custom preprocessing component used by the Message Queue receive function "%1" failed to return a valid document, the document must be either a BSTR or a BYTE array. This document will be moved to the Suspended queue.
CIS_E_CUSTOM_FILE_PRE_PROC_FAIL	0x1729	The custom preprocessing component used by the file receive function "%1" failed. The document "%2" will be moved to the Suspended queue.
CIS_E_CUSTOM_PRE_PROC_CANT_SET_CTX	0x172A	The server was unable to set the context on the custom preprocessing component used by the receive function "%1". This document will be moved to the Suspended queue.
CIS_E_FILERCV_FILE_SHARE_DOWN	0x172B	The file receive function "%1" was unable to connect to the network share "%2". This receive function will try to connect again.

Message name	Value	Description
CIS_E_FILERCV_NETWORK_DOWN	0x172C	The file receive function "%1" is experiencing network problems and was unable to connect to the network share "%2". This receive function will try to connect again.
CIS_E_RECEIVE_FUNCTION_DISABLED	0x172D	The receive function "%1" has experienced problems, it will be shut down and disabled. Once these problems have been corrected, re-enable this receive function in BizTalk Server Administration.
CIS_E_UNRECOVERABLE	0x172E	There was a serious error within the BizTalk Server scheduler component. The server is being shut down. Resolve this problem and then restart the server.
CIS_E_RELIABLE_NOACK	0x172F	The server has not received a receipt for the reliable message.
CIS_E_DLQ_ID	0x1730	Suspended Queue ID: "%1"
CIS_E_CANNOT_FIRE_EVENT	0x1731	The server cannot send a WMI event for the Suspended queue item "%1". The most likely cause is that the user configured for this submission has insufficient privileges to access WMI.
CIS_E_SERIALIZER_INVALID_DOCUMENT	0x1800	The document with the "%1" tracking identifier is invalid XML. The serializer cannot continue.
CIS_E_BTF_INVALID_ADDRESS_TYPE	0x1801	The BizTalk Framework document has an "type" specified that is not valid for the "%1" address field. This document will be moved to the Suspended queue.
CIS_E_RELIABLE_MSG_RECEIPT_REQ_BY	0x1802	The BizTalk Framework document "%1" will not be transmitted as it has an expired "receiptRequiredBy" timestamp. This message will be discarded.
CIS_E_CUSTOM_ENVELOPE_ERROR	0x1803	The custom envelope:"%1" had the property "%2" specified, but the custom envelope generator could not to locate the XML node. This document will be moved to the Suspended queue.

Message name	Value	Description
CIS_E_SERIALIZER_INVALID_DATETIME	0x1804	The "%1" date or time format is not valid. Correct the format specification.
CIS_E_SERIALIZER_INVALID_DTDATA	0x1805	The "%1" date or time field is not a valid ISO8601 format. Make sure that the XML date or time is formatted correctly.
CIS_E_SERIALIZER_INVALID_DELIMITER	0x1806	The "%1" delimiter is either missing or has a value specified that is not valid. Update the delimiter value.
CIS_E_SERIALIZER_MISSING_PROPSET	0x1807	The "%1" document is missing the entire property set that is required for this serializer to run.
CIS_E_SERIALIZER_MISSING_PROP	0x1808	The property set for the "%1" document either is missing or does not contain a valid value for the "%2" property. Add or correct this property.
CIS_E_SERIALIZER_INVALIDARG	0x1809	Both source and destination qualifiers and values are required for this serializer to run. Specify qualifiers and values in the messaging port for this transaction.
CIS_E_SERIALIZER_MISMATCH_SPEC	0x180A	The serialization produced no output. Verify that the document specification matches the outbound XML document.
CIS_E_SERIALIZER_FAILED	0x180B	The serializer could not finish processing. See the following messages for details.
CIS_E_SERIALIZER_INVALID_SRCQUAL	0x180C	The "%1" qualifier for the source identifier is too long to be placed in the outbound document header. Update the channel with a shorter qualifier.
CIS_E_SERIALIZER_INVALID_SRCID	0x180D	The "%1" value for the source identifier is too long to be placed in the output header. Update the channel with a shorter value.
CIS_E_SERIALIZER_INVALID_DESTQUAL	0x180E	The "%1" qualifier for the destination identifier is too long to be placed in the output header. Update the port with a shorter qualifier.

Message name	Value	Description
CIS_E_SERIALIZER_INVALID_DESTID	0x180F	The "%1" value for the destination identifier is too long to be placed in the output header. Update the port with a shorter identifier.
CIS_E_SERIALIZER_INVALID_POSREC	0x1810	The "%1" positional record is defined to contain a record length of zero. This happens when there is no tag, and none of the fields in this record specify start and end positions. Update the fields to have valid start and end positions for this record.
CIS_E_SERIALIZER_NODELIMS	0x1811	This serializer component requires delimiters specified in the messaging port. Specify a valid delimiter set for this component.
CIS_E_SERIALIZER_INVALID_CHAR	0x1812	The serializer component has encountered a character, "%1", that is not valid. An entry specified in the <InvalidCharacterMap> tag of the document specification states that characters between "%2" and "%3" are not valid.
CIS_E_SERIALIZER_INVALID_LENGTH	0x1813	The length of the "%1" field ("%2") is not valid; it must be between %3 and %4. This document will be rejected.
CIS_E_SERIALIZER_SELECT_SINGLE_NODE_FAILED	0x1814	The serializer component cannot find the node using the query "%1". This document will be rejected.
CIS_E_SERIALIZER_RELIABLE_URL_MISSING	0x1815	The reply-to URL required for reliable messaging was not set. This document will be rejected.
CIS_E_SERIALIZER_CONTROL_NUMBER	0x1816	The serializer component cannot find a control number for %1 %2 in the BizTalk Management database. This document will be rejected.
CIS_E_CUSTOM_ENV_PARSE_TABLE_ERROR	0x1817	The serializer component failed to build the custom envelope ID:"%1", this was due to errors in the XML Schema supplied. This document will be moved to the Suspended queue.

Message name	Value	Description
CIS_E_SUBSYNC_RELIABLE_MSG	0x1818	The BizTalk Framework document that was submitted has "reliability" information specified. This information is not permitted in a synchronous call.
CIS_E_CUSTXML_BODY_NOT_FOUND	0x1819	The parser was unable to locate the XML document node by using the query specified in the XML specification: "%1".
CIS_E_BTF_ACK_BAD_MSG_ID	0x181A	The BizTalk Framework receipt had a <prop:identity> tag that is not valid: "%1". This document will be moved to the Suspended queue.
CIS_E_BTF_MANIFEST_REF_MISSING	0x181B	The BizTalk Framework document has a <manifest> tag without the mandatory <reference> tag. This document will be moved to the Suspended queue.
CIS_E_CUSTOM_ENV_NO_DOC_NODE	0x181C	The serializer failed to create the custom envelope because the Document Container Node property was not specified in the XML specification. This document will be moved to the Suspended queue.
CIS_E_BTF_INVALID_XSI_TYPE	0x181D	The BizTalk Framework document contains an xsi:type attribute "%1" that is not valid. This attribute must not have spaces, and the first character must be alphabetical. This document will be moved to the Suspended queue.
CIS_E_SERIALIZER_INVALID_SYNTAX_IDENTIFIER	0x181E	The EDIFACT Syntax Identifier "%1" is not valid. Update the channel with a correct identifier.
CIS_E_SERIALIZER_INVALID_UNA_CONTROL	0x181F	The EDIFACT UNA Control value "%1" is not valid. Update the channel with a correct value.
CIS_E_SERIALIZER_EXPECT_BSTR_VALUE	0x1820	The configuration data for the field "%1" must be a string. Update the data for this field.
BTS_E_XMLSERIALIZER_MISSING_DEST	0x1821	The BizTalk Framework header could not be generated because no destination identifier was specified.

Message name	Value	Description
BTS_E_XMLSERIALIZER_MISSING_SRC	0x1822	The BizTalk Framework header could not be generated because no source identifier was specified.
CIS_E_BTF_IDENTITY_MISSING	0x1904	The parser could not find the mandatory BizTalk Framework tag "identity". This document will be moved to the Suspended queue.
CIS_E_BTF_EXPIRESAT_MISSING	0x1905	The parser could not find the mandatory BizTalk Framework tag "expiresAt". This document will be moved to the Suspended queue.
CIS_E_MSMQ_NOT_INSTALLED	0x1906	The Message Queuing receive function could not be started because the Message Queuing service is not installed on the server.
CIS_W_FILE_RECEIVE_RETRY_FAILURE	0x1907	There are file(s) in the "%1" directory that cannot be accessed by the file receive function. The receive service will try again to access the file(s) in "%2" seconds.
CIS_E_FILE_RECEIVE_DELETE_FAILURE	0x1909	The following file could not be deleted after processing: "%1". Make sure that the file attribute is not set to read-only.
CIS_E_LOGON_USER_FAILURE	0x190a	Unable to logon with the account %1. Make sure that %2 has been granted "logon locally" privilege on this server and that the BizTalk Server account has "act as part of the operating system" privilege.
CIS_E_MSMQ_RECEIVE_IMPERSONATION_ FAILURE	0x190b	The "%1" Message Queuing receive function could not impersonate the logged on user.
CIS_E_RECEIVE_CANNOT_CREATE_ THREAD	0x190c	A receive-function thread cannot be created due to a system error.
CIS_E_MSMQ_RECEIVE_OPENQ_FAILURE	0x190d	The following Message Queuing queue cannot be opened: "%1" (Message Queuing error code: 0x%2=%3). Verify the existence and security setting of the queue.

Message name	Value	Description
CIS_E_MSMQ_RECEIVE_PEEKQ_FAILURE	0x190e	The Message Queuing queue could not be read: "%1" (Message Queuing error code: 0x%2=%3).
CIS_E_MSMQ_RECEIVE_RETRIEVEQ_FAILURE	0x190f	A message could not be retrieved from the following Message Queuing queue: '%1' (Message Queuing error: 0x%2=%3).
CIS_E_FILE_RECEIVE_FINDCHANGE_FAILURE	0x1910	The file-change notification cannot be set up on the following directory: "%1". Make sure that the path is correct.
CIS_E_SET_CURRENT_DIR_FAILURE	0x1911	The current directory cannot be set to: "%1". Make sure that the path is correct.
CIS_W_RECEIVE_SUBMIT_FAILURE	0x1914	A submit request initiated from the "%1" receive function has failed.
CIS_E_READONLY_FILE	0x1915	The "%1" receive function picked up the following file: '%2'. This file is marked as read-only and cannot be processed.
CIS_E_BAD_RECSVC	0x1916	There was a serious failure in the receive function "%1". This receive service will be shut down, please check the event log for additional error messages.
CIS_E_FILE_RECEIVE_IMPERSONATION_FAILURE	0x1917	The "%1" file receive function could not impersonate the logged on user.
CIS_E_MSMQ_RECEIVE_UNEXPECTED_PASSTHROUGH	0x1918	The ""%1"" Message Queuing receive function is not configured for a pass-through submission, but it has encountered a document that was submitted previously as a pass-through submission. Change this receive function to accept pass-through submissions or remove the pass-through document from the queue. This receive function will be shut down.
CIS_E_BTSDOCUMENT_INVALIDNAME	0x1A00	The document named "%1" does not exist. Correct the document name or add the document to the BizTalk Messaging Management database.
CIS_E_BTSDOCUMENT_INVALIDDOC	0x1A01	The server could not load any documents with the given criteria.

Message name	Value	Description
CIS_E_BTSDOCUMENT_AMBIGUOUS_ NAMESPACE	0x1A02	The root node "%1" is ambiguous because documents "%2" and "%3" refer to different specifications with that name. Either change the specifications to remove this ambiguity or use the document name explicitly.
CIS_E_BTSDOCUMENT_AMBIGUOUS_ PROPSET	0x1A03	The property set is ambiguous because documents "%1" and "%2" refer to the same property set.
CIS_E_BTSDOCUMENT_AMBIGUOUS_ PROPSETSHAREID	0x1A04	The property set is ambiguous because documents "%1" and "%2" refer to the same property set and have reference "%3".
CIS_E_BTSDOCUMENT_ INVALIDPROPERTYSET	0x1A05	The following property set was specified: %1.
CIS_E_BTSDOCUMENT_ EMPTYPROPERTYSET	0x1A06	The property set was empty.
CIS_E_BTSDOCUMENT_LOADFAILED	0x1A07	The document "%1" could not be loaded. Possible causes are using a non-envelope specification, or incorrectly configured tracking details.
CIS_E_BTSENVELOPE_LOADFAILED	0x1A20	The envelope "%1" could not be loaded. A possible cause is that the specification is not valid. Configure a valid envelope specification.
CIS_E_FAILED_TO_JOIN_TX	0x1A21	BizTalk Server failed to join a transaction. Ensure both the DTC and the SQL Server database are running.
MSG_COM_CREATE_FAILED	0x1B01	An instance of the %1 class cannot be created: %2.
MSG_CONNECT_WMI_FAILED	0x1B02	A connection to Windows Management on "%1" cannot be established: %2.
MSG_COSETPROXY_FAILED	0x1B03	The authentication credential cannot be set for the Windows Management connection: %1.
MSG_WMI_ENUMINST_FAILED	0x1B04	Instances of the BizTalk Server WMI provider class "%1" cannot be enumerated: %2.

Message name	Value	Description
MSG_WMI_GETPROP_FAILED	0x1B05	The property value of "%1" cannot be retrieved from the BizTalk Server WMI provider because of an unexpected error: %2.
MSG_WMI_EXECQUERY_FAILED	0x1B06	An unexpected error is preventing execution of the BizTalk Server WMI provider query "%1": %2.
MSG_WMI_GETOBJ_FAILED	0x1B07	The BizTalk Server WMI provider instance of "%1" cannot be retrieved because of an unexpected error: %2.
MSG_WMI_PUTPROP_FAILED	0x1B08	The property value of "%1" cannot be changed because of an unexpected error: %2.
MSG_WMI_PUTINST_FAILED	0x1B09	The property values of the BizTalk Server WMI provider instance "%1" cannot be updated because of an unexpected error: %2.
MSG_WMI_DELINST_FAILED	0x1B0A	The BizTalk Server WMI provider instance "%1" cannot be deleted because of an unexpected error: %2.
MSG_WMI_CREATEINST_FAILED	0x1B0B	A new instance of the WMI class "%1" cannot be created in the BizTalk Server WMI provider: %2.
MSG_WMI_CREATEGETOBJ_FAILED	0x1B0C	A new instance of the BizTalk Server WMI provider class "%1" cannot be created because of an unexpected error: %2.
MSG_WMI_EXECMETHOD_GETOBJ_FAILED	0x1B0D	The method "%1" of the BizTalk Server WMI provider class "%2" cannot be executed because of a failure to retrieve the class: %3.
MSG_WMI_EXECMETHODCLASS_FAILED	0x1B0E	The method "%1" of the BizTalk Server WMI provider class "%2" cannot be executed because of a failure to retrieve the method information: %3.
MSG_WMI_EXECMETHODSPAWN_FAILED	0x1B0F	The method "%1" of the BizTalk Server WMI provider class "%2" cannot be executed because of an unexpected error: %3.

Message name	Value	Description
MSG_WMI_EXECMETHODPUTPARAM_ FAILED	0x1B10	The method "%1" of the BizTalk Server WMI provider class "%2" cannot be executed because of a failure to set the parameter value: %3.
MSG_WMI_EXECMETHOD_FAILED	0x1B11	The method "%1" of the WMI class "%2" cannot be executed by the BizTalk Server WMI provider: %3.
MSG_GET_HOSTNAME_FAILED	0x1B12	The local computer name cannot be obtained because of an unexpected error: %1.
MSG_OUT_OF_MEMORY	0x1B14	Insufficient memory.
MSG_FAIL_LOAD_BMP	0x1B17	At least one of the bitmaps cannot be loaded in the BizTalk Server Administration console: %1.
MSG_FAIL_SET_BMPSTRIP	0x1B18	At least one pair of bitmaps cannot be added to the image list of the BizTalk Server Administration console: %1.
MSG_ERROR_WMI_PATH_EMPTY	0x1B19	The requested operation cannot be completed because of a previous WMI failure. The WMI object path is empty in this case.
MSG_ERROR_BTM_GRP_ENUM_FAIL	0x1B20	Unknown problems are preventing the WMI provider from enumerating a list of server groups from the BizTalk Messaging Management database: %1.
MSG_ERROR_GRP_DTA_DB_FAIL	0x1B21	Unknown problems are preventing the WMI provider from accessing the Tracking database for the "%1" group.
MSG_ERROR_GRP_SQ_DB_FAIL	0x1B22	Unknown problems are preventing the WMI provider from accessing the Shared Queue database the "%1" group.
MSG_ERROR_GRP_BOTH_DB_FAIL	0x1B23	Unknown problems are preventing the WMI provider from accessing the Tracking and Shared Queue databases for the "%1" group.
MSG_ERROR_DECRYPT_FAIL	0x1B24	Password decryption failed: %1.

Message name	Value	Description
MSG_WARN_ENUM4ROOTUPD_FAILED	0x1B27	Unknown problems are preventing the WMI provider from retrieving following list of servers and their states to prepare for BizTalk Messaging Management database update: %1
MSG_ERROR_CHANGE_ROOTDB	0x1B28	The server "%1" cannot be updated with the new BizTalk Messaging Management database information: %2.
MSG_ERROR_CHANGE_ROOTDB_CONNECT	0x1B29	We cannot connect to the WMI namespace "%1" to update server "%2" with the new BizTalk Messaging Management database information: %3
MSG_CHANGE_ROOTDB_SUMMARY	0x1B30	The BizTalk Messaging Management database change request has been completed. %1%2 %3%4
MSG_CHANGE_ROOTDB_ON_LOCAL	0x1B3A	Because the server and server group information cannot be retrieved from the original BizTalk Messaging Management database, the BizTalk Messaging Management database information will be updated only on the local computer "%1". The update has been successful.
MSG_ERROR_UNEXPECTED_ENDOFLIST	0x1B3C	An unexpected end of list (EOL) for the "%1" class enumeration has been reached.
MSG_ERROR_ORG_QUALIFIERS_FROM_DB_FAILED	0x1B3D	The organization qualifiers cannot be retrieved from the BizTalk Messaging Management database because of an unexpected error. "%1".
MSG_ERROR_ORG_VALUES_FROM_DB_FAILED	0x1B3E	The organization values cannot be retrieved from the BizTalk Messaging Management database because of an unexpected error. "%1".
MSG_WARN_NOT_RESUBMITABLE	0x1B3F	In the selected group of multiple items, at least one item cannot be submitted again.
MSG_WARNING_PROP_VALUES_CHANGED	0x1B40	%1 "%2" specified for receive function "%3" has been removed from the BizTalk Messaging Management database.

Message name	Value	Description
MSG_WARNING_QUALIFIER_CHANGED	0x1B41	The qualifier and identifier pair "%1" and "%2" specified for receive function "%3" is not valid in the BizTalk Messaging Management database.
MSG_WARNING_ORGANIZATION_ CHANGED	0x1B42	Organization "%1" specified for receive function "%2" is not valid in the BizTalk Messaging Management database.
MSG_TIMEBOMB_DAYS_LEFT	0x1B43	Thank you for evaluating Microsoft BizTalk Server 2000. The period for this evaluation version has %1 days left. Please contact Microsoft or your software reseller to obtain a licensed version of Microsoft BizTalk Server 2000.
INTERCHANGE_EVENT	0x3005	BizTalk Server: %1

Note

- When an error occurs, the numeric variables preceded by a percent sign (%) are replaced with relevant information, such as an object name.

Code Samples

Several samples are shipped with BizTalk Server 2000. The following sections contain information about the location and description of each sample provided.

📝 Notes

- When using C++, you need to add \Program Files\Microsoft BizTalk Server\SDK\Include to the include directory list.

- Some of the samples have a dependency on the Pipecomplib.tlb file. For these samples, you need to add \Program Files\Common Files\Microsoft Shared\Enterprise Servers\Commerce to the include directory list.

BizTalk Messaging Services Code Samples

Sample files for BizTalk Messaging Services are located in the Messaging Samples folder in the Microsoft BizTalk Server installation drive. Browse to \Program Files\Microsoft BizTalk Server\SDK\Messaging Samples on the installation drive to find the sample files. This is only a relative path. Depending on your installation of BizTalk Server 2000, you might have to modify this path.

Sample folder name	Readme file	Description
BTConfigAssistant	Readme.doc	This tool enables the user to see all details of a configuration. It also provides a mechanism to easily import and export configurations.
BTFDevToolkit	ReadMe.txt	This folder contains the BizTalk Framework Developers Toolkit and XML Components.
BTSAppIntegration\VB (Visual Basic)	Readme.txt	This sample demonstrates an application integration component (AIC) that implements the **IBTSAppIntegration** interface.
BTSAppIntegration\VC (C++)	Readme.txt	This sample demonstrates an AIC that implements the **IBTSAppIntegration** interface using ATL.
CustomPreProcessor	Readme.txt	This sample demonstrates a simple implementation of a custom preprocessor to be used with either File or Message Queuing receive functions.
DirectIntegration	Readme.doc	This tool helps users submit documents to BizTalk Messaging Services and check the results of the submission. Tracking and Suspended Queue information is used to determine the results.
DistributionList	DistributionList Readme.txt	This sample configures a BizTalk distribution list (port group) and submits a document to it.
MapTest	Readme.txt	This tool enables users to create a document using an XML document instance, a compiled BizTalk Server map, and an optional schema.
Miscellaneous	No readme files are included with these samples.	This folder includes several Microsoft Visual Basic Scripting Edition (VBScript) files that perform various tasks. Descriptions are available in comment blocks at the beginning of these files. To view them, open the .vbs file in an editor.
PipelineComponent\VB (Visual Basic)	Readme.txt	This sample demonstrates an AIC that implements the **IPipelineComponent** and **IPipelineComponentAdmin** interfaces in Visual Basic.
PipelineComponent\VC (C++)	Readme.txt	This sample demonstrates an AIC that implements the **IPipelineComponent** and **IPipelineComponentAdmin** interfaces, using ATL.
ReceiveScripts	ReceiveReadme.txt	This folder contains example files for receiving data into BizTalk Messaging Services.

Sample folder name	Readme file	Description
Sample1	Sample1Readme.txt	This sample demonstrates how to configure BizTalk Messaging Services and submit a document to BizTalk Server 2000. Also included in the sample are the creation and use of open destination messaging ports, organization aliases, and custom envelopes.
Sample2	Sample2Readme.txt	This sample demonstrates how to configure BizTalk Messaging Services to generate receipts when sending documents.
Sample3	Sample3Readme.txt	This sample demonstrates how to configure a distribution list (port group) and send a document to it.
SampleFunctoid	Readme.txt	This sample demonstrates a custom functoid that performs date format conversion.
SampleImporter	Readme.txt	This sample demonstrates a custom import module, which imports a delimited flat file and displays it in BizTalk Editor.
SOC	Readme.txt	This sample demonstrates a synchronous interaction with the XLANG Scheduler Engine.
SQLServerAgentJobs	Readme.txt	This sample demonstrates SQL scripts for monitoring receipts and purging the tracking information.
VBCustPreProcessor	Readme.txt	This sample demonstrates a simple implementation of a custom preprocessor to be used with a File receive function.
XSDConverter	Readme.txt	This sample converts an XDR schema to an XSD schema.

BizTalk Orchestration Services Code Samples

Sample files for BizTalk Orchestration Services are located in the XLANG Samples folder in the Microsoft BizTalk Server installation drive. Browse to \Program Files\Microsoft BizTalk Server\SDK\XLANG Samples on the installation drive to find the sample files. This is only a relative path. Depending on your installation of BizTalk Server 2000, you might have to modify this path.

Sample folder name	Readme file	Description
ASP	ReadMe.htm	This sample demonstrates how to call a schedule from ASP script, passing in data and getting back the result.
Dispatcher	ReadMe.htm	This sample demonstrates a dispatcher application that sends and receives documents on behalf of a client application. When a document is sent, the dispatcher saves the "From Address" in a database before sending the document and uses the saved address to route the response document to the correct sender.
Dynamic Binding\COM	ReadMe.htm	This sample demonstrates how to bind dynamically to a COM component. The COM component that the schedule binds to is specified at run time.
Dynamic Binding\Queue	ReadMe.htm	This sample demonstrates how to bind dynamically to a message queue. The queue path is specified at runtime.
Integrating BizTalk Services\BTF Correlation	Readme.doc	This sample illustrates use of BizTalk Framework 2.0 and orchestration to accomplish interoperability between two applications. It allows two or more applications to engage in a potentially long-lived exchange of messages. Each exchange is capable of referring back to the data passed in previous exchanges.
Integrating BizTalk Services\http	Setting Up HTTP Sample.doc	In this sample, there are three organizations: purchaser, supplier, and inventory. The purchaser submits a purchase order to the supplier. The supplier then forwards this order to its inventory organization, and the inventory organization sends back an acknowledgement to a dynamic port set up by the supplier.

Sample folder name	Readme file	Description
Integrating BizTalk Services\non-http	Setting Up NonHTTP Sample.doc	This sample shows how to reply to a per instance queue. The contents of the reply indicate whether or not an expense was approved.
Iteration	ReadMe.htm	This application demonstrates how to iterate though a list of items and process each item independently based on some condition.
Loop	ReadMe.htm	This application demonstrates how to use the while shape to retry some business process a limited number of times. A loop counter component is used to track the number of times the loop has executed. The loop terminates when the retry count is reached or when the simulated work completes successfully.
NestedTxns	ReadMe.htm	This sample illustrates the concepts of nested transactions, aborting a transaction, and compensation. The scenario includes ordering an item, submitting payment, receiving the item, returning the item, and having the payment reversed.
Personalized Queues	ReadMe.htm	This sample shows how to use both a shared queue and a per-instance queue.
PublicInterfaces	ReadMe.htm	This sample demonstrates how to use the XLANG public interfaces to enumerate and manage running schedule instances, and their XLANG host applications.
QueueListener	ReadMe.htm	This sample demonstrates how to continuously monitor a queue for data and start another schedule when new data is available.
Transaction Abort	Abort handler Sample.htm	This sample demonstrates the usage of the Abort handler and auto return with transactions.
WorkFlowAudit	docs\readme.txt	This sample component persists detected events into the InterchangeDTA database, which is the default BizTalk Server Tracking data store.
WorkFlowAuditClient	readme.txt	This sample listens for events fired by the XLANG Scheduler Engine.
XML Translation	ReadMe.htm	This sample demonstrates how to use the **SubmitSync** method of the **IInterchange** interface to transform an XML document in a schedule.

Release Notes

This appendix contains important, late-breaking information about this release of BizTalk Server 2000.

☙ Caution

- Before you continue, several Microsoft Windows 2000 components must be updated to ensure the correct functionality of BizTalk Server 2000. An updated list of required and suggested updates is available on the Microsoft BizTalk Server 2000 Web site (www.microsoft.com/biztalk/). You can download the updates directly from the location given on the Web site.

  After you have updated the Windows 2000 components, you can continue with the BizTalk Server 2000 installation.

◈ Important

- For additional information about installing BizTalk Server 2000, see the following section, "BizTalk Server 2000 Installation."

- Prior to installing BizTalk Server, it is strongly recommended that you review this appendix as well as Chapter 1, "Installing BizTalk Server 2000." This chapter provides detailed instructions for installing BizTalk Server on a single computer.

- A comprehensive set of online documentation is provided with BizTalk Server 2000. To use the online documentation after you install BizTalk Server, click **Start**, point to **Programs**, point to **Microsoft BizTalk Server 2000**, and then click **BizTalk Server Documentation**.

BizTalk Server 2000 Installation

The following are known issues for this release of BizTalk Server 2000.

Microsoft SQL Server requirements when installing BizTalk Server 2000 on Microsoft Windows 2000 Server or Advanced Server

Issue: BizTalk Server 2000 can be installed on Microsoft Windows 2000 Server or Windows 2000 Advanced Server, with the NTFS file system. Microsoft Internet Explorer 5 (or later) and Microsoft Visio 2000 SR-1 are required. In addition, the computer installed with BizTalk Server 2000 must have read/write access to a server(s) installed with Microsoft SQL Server 7.0 (SP2 or later) or Microsoft SQL Server 2000 under one of the following conditions:

- SQL Server must be installed on the same computer as BizTalk Server 2000.

  –Or–

- The computer that runs BizTalk Server 2000 must have read/write access to a remote computer(s) running SQL Server.

Microsoft SQL Server requirements when installing BizTalk Server 2000 on Microsoft Windows 2000 Professional

Issue: BizTalk Server 2000 can be installed on Windows 2000 Professional (or later), with the NTFS file system. Internet Explorer 5 (or later) and Visio 2000 SR-1 are required. Additionally, the computer that runs BizTalk Server 2000 must have read/write access to a server(s) running Microsoft SQL Server 7.0 (SP2 or later) or SQL Server 2000.

BizTalk Messaging Services

The following are known issues for this release of BizTalk Server 2000.

Processing SMIME signed and/or encrypted messages generates errors

Issue: While processing SMIME signed and/or encrypted messages within BizTalk Messaging Services, errors such as "The parameter is incorrect" and "Decryption Failed" might appear.

The BizTalk Server service does not shut down when the server is out of memory

Problem: If the server on which BizTalk Server is installed runs out of memory, the BizTalk Server service still attempts to process documents. All documents are placed on the Suspended queue.

Solution: Restart the BizTalk Server service.

Errors that are caused by a custom script might not be displayed in Event Viewer

Issue: Some errors returned by Microsoft XML (MSXML) Parser within a custom script function might not be passed to the server. Errors associated with a document in the Suspended queue might not reflect the error returned in the script.

Large data segments in an IDOC document are not posted to an SAP system

Problem: When large data segments are used in an IDOC document that is routed to an SAP system for processing, some of the data might not be processed. This might be caused by a time-out value configured on the SAP system.

Solution: Try changing the time-out value on the SAP system.

Document specifications, envelope specifications, and maps are stored in two locations

Issue: If a specification or map is modified with BizTalk Editor or BizTalk Mapper and then saved to the repository, the specification or map must be reloaded into BizTalk Messaging Manager so the server can recognize the changes and the database content can be updated.

Encountering memory failures when running BizTalk Messaging Manager on a per-user installation of BizTalk Server 2000

Problem: If BizTalk Server 2000 is installed for an individual user (by clicking the **Only for me** option during installation), when running BizTalk Messaging Manager, you will encounter an insufficient memory error.

Solution: On the BizTalk Server 2000 CD, follow the instructions in the Support/SetupCurrentUser folder.

Message Queuing receive function does not accept a pass-through submission

Problem: Message Queuing receive functions shut down and the following error message is displayed: Change this receive function to accept pass-through submissions or remove the pass-through document from the queue.

Solution: The receive function is not configured to accept pass-through submissions; however, the receive function received a document that was sent as a pass-through submission. Write an application that examines the queue for the **AppSpecific** property of messages in the queue to determine which document came through as a pass-through submission. Remove the document and restart the receive function.

Redundant or simultaneous resubmission of documents might create duplicate instances

Problem: If multiple users, or multiple instances of BizTalk Server Administration, are resubmitting batches of the same documents at the same time, duplicate instances might be created in the Work queue.

Solution: Do not resubmit the same groups of documents from multiple instances at the same time.

BizTalk Orchestration Services

The following are known issues for this release of BizTalk Server 2000.

Visual Basic components are not available for binding in the COM Component Binding Wizard

Problem: When a Microsoft Visual Basic component is being debugged, it is not listed in the COM Component Binding Wizard in BizTalk Orchestration Designer.

Solution: You must bind the port to the COM component when Visual Basic is not in debug mode.

Testing for the outcome of a transaction

Issue: To test for transaction outcome, you should use a message created in the transaction on-failure process. You should not test for transaction outcome by testing for the existence of a message used in the transaction. In the case of failure, you should not use any messages that the transaction might have modified except in that transaction on-failure process.

Standard toolbar is not visible after starting BizTalk Orchestration Designer

Problem: When starting BizTalk Orchestration Designer, the standard toolbar might not be visible because settings from a previous session have not been saved.

Solution: You must manually select the standard toolbar in Microsoft Visio:

1. On the **File** menu, click **Exit** to close BizTalk Orchestration Designer.

2. On the **Start** menu, point to **Programs** and click **Microsoft Visio**.

3. On the **View** menu, point to **Toolbars** and click **Standard**.

4. On the **File** menu, click **Exit** to close Visio.

5. On the **Start** menu, point to **Programs**, point to **Microsoft BizTalk Server 2000**, and then click **BizTalk Orchestration Designer**.

   The toolbar appears.

XLANG schedule drawings created in the beta release of BizTalk Server 2000 are not compatible with drawings created in the released version

Issue: XLANG schedule drawings (.skv files) that are created by using BizTalk Orchestration Designer in the beta release of BizTalk Server 2000 are not compatible with the format used by the released version of BizTalk Server 2000.

Limitation in COM+ Bring Your Own Transaction (BYOT) functionality

Problem: COM+ Bring Your Own Transaction (BYOT) functionality enables a component to be created with, or to inherit, an external transaction. Due to a limitation in BYOT functionality, you will encounter unexpected behavior if COM+ hasn't been initialized in the process where BYOT is to be used.

If a BYOT component is imported into a COM+ application, it fails to launch traditional COM components. BYOT functionality is provided by a component called Byot.ByotServerEx, which is registered as a traditional COM component, not a COM+ application.

Solution: When using BYOT functionality with COM components for the XLANG Scheduler Engine, you must create a wrapper component that is written and installed into a COM+ application. All method calls to the component are forwarded from the wrapper component. Documentation in the MSDN Library offers an alternate workaround, which is to wrap Byot.ByotServerEx into a COM+ application. This, however, creates unexpected behavior when trying to reference traditional COM components.

Remove the PDC evaluation copy of Microsoft Visio 2000 prior to installing Visio 2000 Standard Edition (SR-1)

Issue: The 2000 Professional Developers Conference (PDC) CD-ROM included an evaluation copy of Microsoft Visio 2000 Standard Edition. This version of Visio 2000 must be removed. Unexpected behavior will result if you upgrade the evaluation version to Visio 2000 Standard Edition (SR-1). The Visio32.exe installed by Visio 2000 Standard Edition has a file version of 6.0.0.2072 and timestamp of February 07, 2000. The Visio32.exe installed by the evaluation copy provided at the PDC has a file version of 6.0.0.2072 and a timestamp of April 25, 2000. Other than the timestamp, there is no discernible difference between the two releases.

Visual Basic AIC components might suspend operation or generate an access violation inside MSVBVM60.DLL when called under stress from BizTalk Server

Problem: A Visual Basic AIC component might suspend operation or generate an access violation if a Visual Basic ActiveX DLL is hosted in a multithreaded environment, such as Microsoft Internet Information Services, Microsoft Transaction Services, or BizTalk Server, and the Retain In Memory project setting is not enabled.

Solution: Ensure that all Visual Basic components set the Unattended Execution and Retain in Memory project settings. For more information about this problem and how to implement this change, go to the Microsoft Knowledge Base Web site (support.microsoft.com/support/kb/articles/Q241/8/96.ASP).

Messages created in a while loop appear with empty fields after the end of the while loop

Problem: Testing for the existence of messages (by using the system field, MessageName.[__Exists__]) after a while loop always evaluates to TRUE. This problem occurs when the path taken in the while loop does not create the message because of the decision branch taken or a transaction abort.

Solution: Do not test for the existence of messages after the while loop. Instead, to check for flow control, use a stateful component to note the path taken in the while loop and use this information in the stateful component outside the loop.

All messages of the same type on the same port must match exactly

Problem: A compilation error occurs, indicating that the XLANG schedule drawing contains conflicting specification representations.

Solution: When you use the XML Communication Wizard, make sure all messages of the same type on the same port match exactly. This includes field names, message types, and XPath queries. The location of the specification must also be the same. On the **Message Specification Information** page of the XML Communication Wizard, make sure that the **Validate messages against the specification** check box is selected consistently.

BizTalk Orchestration Services Code Samples

Issue: Sample files are located in the XLANG Samples folder in the Microsoft BizTalk Server installation drive. Browse to \Program Files\Microsoft BizTalk Server\SDK\XLANG Samples on the installation drive to find the sample files. This is only a relative path. Depending on your installation of BizTalk Server 2000, you might have to modify this path.

The following samples are available in the BizTalk Server 2000 SDK.

Sample folder name	Readme file	Description
ASP	ReadMe.htm	**CreditCheck.** This sample demonstrates how to call a schedule from ASP script, passing in data and getting back the result.
Dispatcher	ReadMe.htm	**Dispatcher.** This sample demonstrates a dispatcher application that sends and receives documents on behalf of a client application.
Dynamic Binding\COM	ReadMe.htm	**Scramble.** This sample demonstrates how to bind dynamically to a COM component.
Dynamic Binding\Queue	ReadMe.htm	**QueueBind.** This sample demonstrates how to bind dynamically to a message queue.
Integrating BizTalk Services\BTF Correlation	Readme.doc	**Stateful Conversation.** This sample illustrates the use of BizTalk Framework 2.0 and BizTalk Orchestration Services to accomplish stateful interoperability between two applications.
Integrating BizTalk Services\http	Setting Up HTTP Sample.doc	**Using the HTTP Transport.** In this sample, there are three organizations: purchaser, supplier, and inventory. The purchaser submits a purchase order to the supplier. The supplier then forwards this order to its inventory organization, and the inventory organization sends back an acknowledgement to a dynamic port set up by the supplier.

Sample folder name	Readme file	Description
Integrating BizTalk Services\non-http	Setting Up Non-HTTP sample.doc	**Using a Non-HTTP Transport.** In this sample, there are three organizations: expense requestor, finance, and marketing. The expense requestor organization submits an expense request to the finance organization. The finance organization forwards this request document to the marketing organization. The marketing organization sends back an expense reply to a per-instance queue set up by the finance organization. This reply indicates whether or not the expense was approved.
Iteration	ReadMe.htm	**LineItems.** This sample demonstrates how to iterate through a list of items and process each item independently.
Loop	ReadMe.htm	**Retry.** This sample demonstrates how to use the **While** shape to retry a business process a limited number of times.
NestedTxns	ReadMe.htm	**Nested Transactions.** This sample illustrates three concepts: Nested Transactions, Aborting a Transaction, and Compensation.
Personalized Queues	ReadMe.htm	**Very Long-Lived, Per-Instance Queue.** This sample uses a shared queue and per-instance queues.
PublicInterfaces	ReadMe.htm	**XLANG Public Interfaces.** This sample demonstrates how to use the XLANG public interfaces to enumerate and manage the running schedule instances, and the XLANG host applications.
QueueListener	ReadMe.htm	**QueueListener.** This sample demonstrates how to continuously monitor a queue for data, and start another XLANG schedule when new data is available.
Transaction Abort	Abort handler sample.htm	**Abort Handler.** This sample demonstrates how to handle an exception.
WorkFlowAudit	readme.txt	**WorkFlowAudit Component.** This sample contains one interface, **IUserEvent**.
WorkFlowAudit Client	readme.txt	**WorkFlowAuditClient.** After you register the component in this sample, run the WorkflowAuditClient.exe application.
XML Translation	ReadMe.htm	**Loopback.** This sample demonstrates the use of **SubmitSync** to perform an XML transformation.

Cannot open BizTalk Orchestration Designer

Problem: One or more of the files in the VBA folder have not been properly registered or have become corrupt. This problem can result from uninstalling Microsoft Office.

Solution: If Microsoft Office 2000 is not installed:

1. Insert the Microsoft Office 2000 CD into the disk drive.
2. Open Windows Explorer and browse to **d:\Install\BIN\SP\VBA** (where 'd' is the letter of your CD drive).
3. Right-click **Vba6.msi** and click **Install**.

If Microsoft Office 2000 is installed:

1. Open Microsoft Access.
2. Create a blank database.
3. Save the database.
4. Close Microsoft Access.

Internet Explorer cannot open certain XLANG schedule files

Problem: Some XLANG schedule files (.skx files), especially schedules that use constant values, cannot be viewed using Internet Explorer 5.5 or earlier versions.

Solution: Use a text editor such as Microsoft Notepad to view the XLANG schedule file.

Non-XML string data is truncated when an XLANG schedule receives data from BizTalk Messaging Services

Issue: When non-XML text documents are received by an XLANG schedule from a port that is implemented by Message Queuing or BizTalk Messaging, carriage-return (CR) characters are removed from the document when it is received by the schedule. This is problematic when a MIME-encoded message is sent to a schedule that must later send or use the data elsewhere. In this case, the document sent out by the schedule does not contain the CR characters and does not appear to be a valid MIME-encoded document.

BizTalk Server Administration

The following are known issues for this release of BizTalk Server 2000.

File receive functions stop processing documents

Problem: If you use File receive functions, and if there are other processes that use files at the same time as BizTalk Server, it is possible that one or more File receive functions might stop processing documents and become unavailable. This occurs when BizTalk Server successfully processes a file, but cannot delete it because the file is being accessed by another application. The File receive function is disabled to ensure that the data is not processed a second time if the other application(s) stops using the file.

Solution: To prevent this problem from occurring, make sure that any files placed in folders monitored by File receive functions are not actively being used by other applications. This can include some virus protection software that monitors incoming files.

BizTalk Document Tracking

The following are known issues for this release of BizTalk Server 2000.

The cursor appears as an hourglass in the View Document Instance Data dialog box

Problem: If you have Microsoft Internet Explorer 5 installed on your computer, when you view document instance data, the pointer might appear as an hourglass instead of an arrow or a pipe. If this happens, you can still select **View native format** or **View XML format** or click the **Save As** and **Close** buttons.

Solution: If you upgrade to Microsoft Internet Explorer 5.5, the pointer appears as an arrow or a pipe.

Maintaining the Tracking database

Issue: If you configured all tracking options for a server group in BizTalk Server Administration and if you configured a channel(s) and/or document definition(s) to track fields in BizTalk Messaging Manager, the size of the Tracking database might increase rapidly. To maintain the Tracking database, you can use DTA_SampleJobs.sql, a sample SQL script that is provided to purge the Tracking database. After you install BizTalk Server 2000, you can find this sample script in \Program Files\Microsoft BizTalk Server\SDK\Messaging Samples\SQLServerAgentJobs. Review the Readme included with this sample for more information about how to tailor the script to your BizTalk Server configuration.

For more information about tracking settings, see "Using BizTalk Document Tracking" in Chapter 13, "Tracking Documents."

The sample DTA_SampleJobs.sql references a stored procedure that does not exist

Problem: The sample DTA_SampleJobs.sql references a stored procedure that does not exist. When this sample is run in SQL Server Query Analyzer, it fails. This sample is located in the \Program Files\Microsoft BizTalk Server\SDK\Messaging Samples\SQLServerAgentJobs folder.

Solution: Follow the instructions in the ReadMe.txt file that is associated with the DTA_SampleJobs.sql sample to open the sample in the SQL Server Query Analyzer that points to the Tracking database, and then complete the following:

Between the following two lines of code:

```
drop procedure [dbo].[dta_job_purge_extra_rows]
```

–and–

```
GO
```

Insert the following code:

```
--
///////////////////////////////////////////////////////////////////////////////
/////
if exists (select * from sysobjects where id = object_id(N'[dbo].[dta_getgmt_time]') and
OBJECTPROPERTY(id, N'IsProcedure') = 1)
drop procedure [dbo].[dta_getgmt_time]
GO

CREATE PROCEDURE [dbo].[dta_getgmt_time]
@gmt datetime output
AS
DECLARE @mins int
EXEC master.dbo.xp_regread N'HKEY_LOCAL_MACHINE',
N'SYSTEM\CurrentControlSet\Control\TimeZoneInformation', N'ActiveTimeBias', @param = @mins
output
SET @gmt = dateadd(mi, @mins, GETDATE())
--
///////////////////////////////////////////////////////////////////////////////
/////
```

Save DTA_SampleJobs.sql and run it in the SQL Server Query Analyzer that points to the Tracking database.

Type mismatch error in advanced queries

Problem: If you configure a nonstandard format for dates, numbers, time, currency, and so on in **Regional Options** in **Control Panel**, you might not be able to save a new query or view advanced queries that you saved.

Solution: To view existing advanced queries, only choose options available in the lists in **Regional Options**. For example, on the **Date** tab, in the **Short date format** list, choose options in the list. Do not type or cut and paste other formats in the **Short date format** list.

Working with float and real data types

Issue: The **float** and **real** data types are known as approximate data types. The behavior of **float** and **real** data types follows the IEEE 754 specification on approximate numeric data types. Approximate numeric data types do not store the exact values specified for many numbers; they store an extremely close approximation of the value. For many applications, the tiny difference between the specified value and the stored approximation is not noticeable. At times, though, the difference becomes noticeable. Because of this approximate nature of the **float** and **real** data types, do not use these data types when exact numeric behavior is required, such as in financial applications, in operations involving rounding, or in equality checks. Instead, use the **integer**, **decimal**, **money**, or **smallmoney** data type.

The Tracking database does not log an interchange parsing error if the trailer is incorrect

Issue: The Tracking database does not log an interchange parsing error if the interchange trailer is incorrect in an EDI interchange. If an interchange contains a valid document, but the interchange trailer contains incorrect information, the parser recognizes this as a nonfatal error and submits the document to BizTalk Server for processing. An error is logged in Event Viewer, but no error is logged in the Tracking database because the Tracking database does not differentiate between fatal errors and nonfatal errors.

Exceeding the size of an Integer data type when tracking the Number data type as an Integer

Problem: BizTalk Server allows the **Number** data type to be tracked as an **Integer** data type. If the value of the number in the document exceeds the size of the **Integer** data type, a warning message appears. This warning message contains the value that could not be tracked.

Solution: Do not exceed the size of the **Integer** data type when tracking a **Number** data type as an **Integer**.

The Document Type column ToolTip is labeled incorrectly

Issue: On the **Query Results** page of BizTalk Document Tracking, the ToolTip for the Document Type column is labeled incorrectly as **Document Error Description**. This label should read **Document Type**.

XPath strings are truncated at 79 characters

Problem: When tracking specification fields as an **Integer**, **Real**, **Date**, or **Text** data type, specification field names that exceed 79 characters are truncated.

Solution: Track these specification fields as a **Custom** data type. By doing this, the field names are stored together with the field values in an SQL **ntext** column, which holds a maximum length of 2^30 - 1 (1,073,741,823) characters.

Unable to locate details and receipt status for a document

Problem: In BizTalk Server Administration, the **Enable document tracking** check box might not be selected. If this check box is not selected, receipts cannot be correlated.

Solution: To enable document logging, complete the following steps:

1. On the **Start** menu, point to **Programs**, point to **Microsoft BizTalk Server 2000**, and then click **BizTalk Server Administration**.

2. In BizTalk Server Administration, expand **Microsoft BizTalk Server 2000**, right-click the BizTalk Server group for which you want to change document tracking settings, and then click **Properties**.

3. On the **Tracking** tab, select the **Enable document tracking** check box.

4. Select any other options that you want to use.

BizTalk Editor and BizTalk Mapper

The following are known issues for this release of BizTalk Server 2000.

Validating EDI instances against specifications

Issue: BizTalk Editor and BizTalk Mapper provide a subset of EDI document specifications and an associated EDI code list database. These specifications are generated directly from data obtained from officially recognized publishers of the X12 and EDIFACT standards. It is highly recommended that you validate EDI instances against specifications that are created prior to a production implementation of processes that use these specifications. For more information and updates about EDI specifications and standards, go to the Microsoft BizTalk Server 2000 Web site (www.microsoft.com/biztalk/).

Storing a file to WebDAV fails

Problem: If storing a file from BizTalk Editor or BizTalk Mapper to the WebDAV repository fails (for example, permission is denied, the file is read-only, and so on), the appropriate error message appears. However, if you close the file and retrieve it again from WebDAV, you are viewing the locally cached file rather than the one from the WebDAV repository. The file appears as if it was stored from the WebDAV repository even though the **Permission Denied** dialog box appears.

Solution: Clear the Internet Explorer cache:

1. Start Internet Explorer.

2. On the **Tools** menu, click **Internet Options**.

3. Click **Delete Files**.

Importing an XDR file fails

Problem: XDR import fails if the default value for an attribute of type IDREFS is specified in the attribute declaration, as shown in the following code:

```
<AttributeType name="Field1" d:type="idrefs" default="a1 a2"> </AttributeType>
<attribute type="Field1" required="no"></attribute>
```

Solution: Move the default value to the attribute reference in the XDR schema before importing it into BizTalk Editor, as shown in the following code:

```
<AttributeType name="Field1" d:type="idrefs"> </AttributeType>
<attribute type="Field1" required="no" default="a1 a2"></attribute>
```

Storing a file to WebDAV from BizTalk Editor or BizTalk Mapper fails

Problem: When storing a file to WebDAV, you might receive the message "No key matching the described characteristics could be found within the current range." A potential cause for this problem is the permission settings in Internet Information Services (IIS). For solutions to this problem, see, "Troubleshooting BizTalk Editor" in Chapter 5, "Creating Specifications" or "Troubleshooting BizTalk Mapper" in Chapter 6, "Mapping Data."

Solution: If the problem persists after granting necessary permissions to the user in IIS, the solution is to save the file (by selecting the **File** menu and selecting the **Save As** option) to the WebDAV repository location on the computer where it resides. If the BizTalk Server installation path on the computer that has the WebDAV repository is C:\Program Files\Microsoft BizTalk Server, note the following file paths:

- For BizTalk Editor, the WebDAV repository file path is \Program Files\Microsoft BizTalk Server\BizTalkServerRepository\DocSpecs.

- For BizTalk Mapper the WebDAV repository file path is \Program Files\Microsoft BizTalk Server\BizTalkServerRepository\Maps.

By selecting the **File** menu and selecting the **Save As** option, save the file to the appropriate location specified above. Alternatively, you can save the file to a temporary file and then use Windows Explorer to copy the temporary file to the appropriate location.

BizTalk Server Samples

The following are known issues for this release of BizTalk Server 2000.

BizTalk Messaging samples cannot be built

Problem: Cannot build the samples in the directory \Program Files\Microsoft BizTalk Server\SDK\Messaging Samples.

Solution: Install the MSXML 3.0 SDK release from the XML Developer Center Web site (msdn.microsoft.com/xml). Then implement the following changes to the Microsoft Visual Studio environment to compile the BizTalk Messaging samples:

1. On the **Tools** menu, click **Options**.

    The **Options** dialog box appears.

2. Click the **Directories** tab and add the following paths to the **Directories** area for **Include files**:

    [System Drive]\Program Files\Common Files\Microsoft Shared\Enterprise Servers\Commerce

    [Install Drive]\Program Files\Microsoft BizTalk Server\SDK\Include

    [Install Drive]\Program Files\Microsoft XML Parser SDK\inc

3. Add the following path to the **Directories** area for **Executable files**:

    [Install Drive]\Program Files\Microsoft BizTalk Server

4. Add the following path to the **Directories** area for **Library files**:

    [Install Drive]\Program Files\Microsoft XML Parser SDK\lib

Implement the following changes to the \Program Files\Microsoft BizTalk Server\SDK\Messaging Samples\CustomPreProcessor\CustomPreProcessor.dsw workspace:

1. Change properties of all files in the directory so that they are not read-only.

2. Open the CustomPreProcessor.dsw workspace.

3. Change line 32 of the PreProcessor.cpp file to **#include <Msxml2.h>**.

4. On the **Project** menu, click **Settings**.

    The **Project Settings** dialog box appears.

5. Click the **Link** tab and add **msxml2.lib** to the list of libraries in the **Object/library modules** area.

Implement the following changes to the \Program Files\Microsoft BizTalk Server\SDK\Messaging Samples\BTSAppIntegration\VC\ATL\AtlBTSComp.dsw workspace.

1. Change properties of all files in the directory so that they are not read-only.

2. Open the AtlBTSComp.dsw workspace.

3. Change line 6 of the BTSComp.cpp file to **#include <Msxml2.h>**.

4. On the **Project** menu, click **Settings**.

   The **Project Settings** dialog box appears.

5. Click the **Link** tab and add **msxml2.lib** to the list of libraries in the **Object/library modules** area.

BTConfigAssistant sample icon images cannot be loaded

Problem: The BTConfigAssistant sample fails to load icon images because the associated .FRX file is missing. The form, Form1.frm, which contains binary information but lacks the associated .FRX files, does not function correctly.

Solution: Complete the following steps:

1. Browse to **\Program Files\Microsoft BizTalk Server\SDK\Messaging Samples\BTConfigAssistant**.

2. Right-click **Form1.frm**, click **Properties**, clear the **Read-only** check box, and then click **OK**.

3. In Microsoft Visual Basic, open BTConfigAssistant.vbp.

4. In the Project - BTConfigAssistant pane, expand **Forms** and double-click **Form1.frm**.

   For any error messages that you receive when loading the form, click **OK** and continue.

5. In the Properties - Form1.frm pane, click the **Icon** property and click the **[...]** button.

6. Browse to **\Program Files\Microsoft BizTalk Server\SDK\Messaging Samples\BTConfigAssistant\FACE02.ICO**, select the icon, and then click **OK**.

DirectIntegration sample icon images cannot be loaded

Issue: The DirectIntegration sample fails to load icon images because the associated .FRX file is missing. The form, frmDirectIntegration.frm, which contains binary information but lacks the associated .FRX files, does not function correctly.

Solution: Complete the following steps:

1. Browse to **\Program Files\Microsoft BizTalk Server\SDK\Messaging Samples\DirectIntegration**.

2. Right-click **frmDirectIntegration.frm**, click **Properties**, clear the **Read-only** check box, and then click **OK**.

3. In Microsoft Visual Basic, open DirectIntegration.vbp.

4. In the Project - DirectIntegration pane, expand **Forms** and double-click **frmDirectIntegration.frm**.

   For any error messages that you receive when loading the form, click **OK** and continue.

5. In the Properties - frmDirectIntegration pane, click the **Icon** property and click the **[...]** button.

6. Browse to **\Program Files\Microsoft BizTalk Server\SDK\Messaging Samples\DirectIntegration\MISC05.ICO**, select the icon, and then click **OK**.

BizTalk Server 2000 International Issues

The following are known issues for this release of BizTalk Server 2000.

Connecting to Microsoft SQL Server fails on a computer that does not have SQL Server installed

Problem: Installing BizTalk Server on a computer without Microsoft SQL Server installed and trying to set up a BizTalk Server database on a remote SQL Server machine that is running a different default language version of SQL Server might result in an error. The message "Cannot open database requested in login, Database Name. Login fails" might appear while running the BizTalk Server Database Wizard.

Solution: To prevent this problem, create a sample user DSN before installing BizTalk Server:

1. On the **Start** menu, point to **Settings** and click **Control Panel**.

2. Double-click **Administrative Tools**.

3. Double-click **Data Sources (ODBC)**.

   The ODBC Data Source Administrator console appears.

4. Select the **User DSN** tab.

5. Click **Add**.

   The **Create New Data Source** dialog box opens.

6. Select **SQL Server** in the **Name** list and click **Finish**.

7. Complete the Create a New Data Source to SQL Server Wizard and create a sample user DSN.

Incorrect behavior in BizTalk Editor when using Korean IME

Problem: If you are using the IME to enter Korean characters for record or field names in BizTalk Editor, BizTalk Editor enables duplicate names even though the correct error message box appears when you try to rename a record or field to an existing name. BizTalk Editor also enables entering invalid record or field names when using the Korean IME that would otherwise not be allowed.

Solution: Delete the invalid record or field before continuing.

Math functoids do not work when using a comma to express a decimal number

Problem: Many locales use a comma (,) as the decimal symbol. A number that uses a comma as the decimal symbol fails validation using Microsoft XML (MSXML) Parser because MSXML expects a period (.) to be used as the decimal symbol.

Solution: Change the decimal symbol from a comma to a period in the system locale settings:

1. On the **Start** menu, point to **Settings** and click **Control Panel**.
2. Double-click **Regional Options**.

   The **Regional Options** dialog box appears.
3. Click the **Numbers** tab.
4. In the **Decimal symbol** list box, type a period (.).
5. Click **Apply** and click **Ok**.

Connecting to databases created by a different language version of BizTalk Server

Issue: BizTalk Server cannot connect to databases created by a different language version of BizTalk Server 2000.

XML elements and/or attributes of Number data type might not be tracked correctly in some foreign locales

Problem: Depending on the system locale, a numeric value in XML data might be misinterpreted by BizTalk Server when logged as an integer tracking field in the Tracking database. For example, in a German locale an XML Number data type value of 4.0 is logged as 40 in the Tracking database because the decimal point (.) is misinterpreted as the digit grouping symbol.

Solution: There are two workarounds for this problem. First, if you know in advance that the element/attribute value stores a decimal number, you can change the XML element/attribute data type to **Real (r4)** or **Double Real (r8)**. Second, you can configure the document definition or channel to log an element/attribute with a Number data type as **Real** instead of **Integer**.

Unable to export XLANG schedule drawing correctly

Problem: XLANG schedule drawings that use non-ASCII characters in the name of ports, messages, and/or fields might not export correctly in a different system locale setting from the one in which the XLANG schedule drawing was created.

Solution: Install the locale in which the XLANG drawing was created as the system default, and then make the .skx file from the XLANG schedule drawing.

Using the keyboard to convert Korean characters to Chinese characters causes BizTalk Editor to fail

Problem: Converting Korean characters to Chinese characters by using the CHINESE key on a Korean keyboard causes BizTalk Editor to fail.

Solution: You can enter Chinese characters directly (for example, copying a Chinese character from Notepad) into BizTalk Editor.

Using non-ASCII data in the BizTalk Server 2000 Tutorial

Problem: The BizTalk Server 2000 Tutorial does not work with non-ASCII data.

Solution: Change the code for the scripting component (PORequestApproval.wsc) to use the XML DOM to write data.

BizTalk Servers in a group of servers must operate in the same language

Issue: BizTalk Servers that operate in different languages cannot belong to one server group. BizTalk Server groups are language-specific.

Message names and field names with non-ASCII characters will not work in script expressions

Issue: In BizTalk Orchestration Designer, message names and field names defined in the XML Communication Wizard and the Method Communication Wizard can contain only ASCII characters if the names are used in rules. The VBScript engine that processes the rules fails to process non-ASCII characters.

Working with long date and time formats

Problem: Using long date and time formats might introduce truncations in BizTalk Document Tracking because the date and time selection control only supports short formats.

Solution: If you encounter any problem with date and time format, you can change the formats used by your computer by clicking **Regional Options** in **Control Panel**.

Instance validation fails when using a comma to express a decimal number

Problem: If a comma (,) is used instead of a period (.) when expressing a decimal number in a document instance, instance validation might fail. This happens because the parser converts the document instance into an XML document and then uses the XML Document Object Model (DOM) to validate the XML document against the document specification. The XML DOM does not allow a comma to be used as a decimal point. For more information, go to the MSDN Online Library Web site (msdn.microsoft.com/library/default.asp) and search for XML Data Types Reference.

Solution: Use a period when expressing decimal numbers in a document instance.

Unicode limitation of the ActiveX Controls used in BizTalk Document Tracking

Issue: The date and time selection control, the list view, and the tree view cannot display Unicode characters. Therefore, mixed-language support is limited. For example, if an English computer accesses BizTalk Server with BizTalk Document Tracking Web pages and data that includes a double-byte character set (DBCS), the characters are displayed as question marks (?) in the English client.

Channel names with non-ASCII characters do not work in URL query strings

Issue: In BizTalk Orchestration Designer, if non-ASCII characters are included in the channel names defined in the BizTalk Messaging Binding Wizard for nonactivation receive, submitting documents with HTTP might not succeed. The channel names are being passed in the query string part of the URLs, and non-ASCII characters are not supported in the query strings.

Unicode WebDAV limitations

Problem: Files can only be saved in Unicode encodings in the WebDAV repository. However, the WebDAV repository cannot store files with names in different code pages, and WebDAV does not support Unicode characters in file names.

Solution: Make sure that your system locale is set to your language. For example, international users who install this release of BizTalk Server 2000 on an English Windows 2000 computer and want to name files with characters that are not supported in the Latin I code page (Windows 1252) must change the system locale to their user locale.

Yen symbol or Won symbol appears as backslash in Output pane after instance validation

Problem: If you create a document instance containing a Japanese Yen symbol or Korean Won symbol while your system locale is set to Japanese or Korean, when that document instance is successfully validated against the corresponding specification, the Yen symbol or Won symbol appears as a backslash in the Output pane of BizTalk Editor.

Solution: To view the Yen symbol or Won symbol rather than a backslash, you can view the source of the Output pane:

1. In the Output pane that displays a backslash rather than the Yen symbol or Won symbol, right-click anywhere within the pane and click **View Source**.

2. In the Notepad instance, on the **Format** menu, click **Font**.

   The **Font** dialog box appears.

3. In the **Font** area, click **Tahoma** and click **OK**.

   The monetary symbols should appear as expected.

Miscellaneous

The following are known issues for this release of BizTalk Server 2000.

No scripts available to manage the persistence database used by BizTalk Orchestration Services

Issue: There are no scripts available to manage old XLANG schedule instances along with other utilities to manage the persistence database used by BizTalk Orchestration Services.

Microsoft SQL Server set to use Binary Sort Order

Issue: If SQL Server is set to use Binary Sort Order, case sensitivity is respected in channel names, EDI property sets, and so on.

Failed to connect to a second named instance of Microsoft SQL Server

Problem: During BizTalk Server 2000 setup, there is a failure to connect to a second named instance of SQL Server. BizTalk Messaging Management database administrative objects do not work with NamedPipes for a second instance of SQL Server; therefore, TCP/IP is required.

Solution: Run SQL Server setup and select "Connectivity Only." After SQL Server components are installed, complete the following steps:

1. On the **Start** menu, point to **Programs**, point to **Microsoft SQL Server**, and then click **Client Network Utility**.

   The SQL Server Client Network Utility console appears.

2. Select TCP/IP as the first enabled protocol in the **Enabled protocols by order** area.

3. Click **OK**.

BizTalk Server 2000 beta upgrade

Problem: It is not possible to upgrade an existing installation of BizTalk Server 2000 Beta to an installation of the released version.

Solution: Before you can install the BizTalk Server 2000 released version, you must remove the BizTalk Server 2000 beta and remove the Microsoft SQL Server databases that were created during the installation of the beta. To remove existing databases:

1. On the **Start** menu, point to **Programs**, point to **Microsoft SQL Server**, and then click **Enterprise Manager**.

2. Expand **Microsoft SQL Servers**, expand **SQL Server Group**, and then expand the server that contains the databases that you want to delete.

3. Expand the **Databases** folder.

4. Right-click each of the databases that were created during the installation of BizTalk Server 2000 beta and click **Delete**.

Local file transport appends to existing file

Issue: For the File transport type, the default transport-component setting is to append new files to an existing file in the specified directory. In the case of reliable messaging, if an acknowledgment is not received the document is resent, based on the number of retries. The repeated document is appended to the existing document.

EDI interchanges containing multiple groups cause BizTalk Server to stop responding

Problem: For EDI, both X12 and EDIFACT, submitting interchanges to BizTalk Server that contain more than a single functional group causes the server to stop responding, if "generate receipt" is checked for the affected channels in the BizTalk Messaging configuration.

Solution: Submit single group interchanges.

Cancellation of the setup wizard displays an erroneous error message

Problem: Cancellation of setup during the database creation stage of the database creation wizard causes a setup error.

Solution: Click **OK** to close the error message box. The cancellation process proceeds as expected.

SAP DCOM compatibility requirements

Issue: To use the SAP application integration component (AIC) shipped with the released version of BizTalk Server 2000, you must have version 4.6B of the SAP BAPI DCOM connector on your system.

WebDAV does not work after installing prerelease versions of Microsoft Office 10

Issue: Using prerelease versions of Microsoft Office on the same computer as BizTalk Server 2000 is not recommended.

Uninstalling the application proxy for the BizTalk Server Interchange Application on a remote client displays an error

Problem: To submit a document from a remote client, you must install the application proxy using the export from a COM+ application. When uninstalling the application proxy on a remote computer, the error message "Error registering COM+ application. Contact your system personal or administrator" appears.

Solution: Before uninstalling the application proxy, complete the following steps:

1. On the **Start** menu, point to **Settings**, click **Control Panel**, double-click **Administrative Tools**, and then double-click **Component Services**.

   The Component Services console opens.

2. Expand **Computers**, expand **My Computer**, expand **COM+ Applications**, right-click **BizTalk Server Interchange Application**, and then click **Properties**.

   The **BizTalk Server Interchange Application Properties** dialog box appears.

3. Click the **Advanced** tab.

4. In the **Permission** area, clear the **Disable deletion** and **Disable changes** check boxes.

5. Click **OK**.

Server clustering and BizTalk Server 2000

Issue: For information about server clustering and BizTalk Server 2000, go to the Microsoft BizTalk Server Web site (microsoft.com/biztalk/) and search for "clustering".

Update to Setting Up HTTP Sample.doc for Using the HTTP Transport Sample

Problem: The XLANG HTTP transport sample readme file, Setting Up HTTP Sample.doc, should specify how to enable anonymous access for the resource.

Solution: In the section "Creating the Purchaser Web Site" in Setting Up HTTP Sample.doc, do the following after the BizTalkSample virtual directory is created:

• View the properties of the newly created virtual directory.

• Click the **Directory Security** tab.

• Enable anonymous access for the virtual directory.

Unsupported SAP AIC sample

Issue: AIComp.dll is an unsupported sample that provides a guideline for BizTalk Server integration with SAP by means of AICs (application integration components). AIComp.dll is a sample SAP AIC that implements the **IPipelineComponent** and **IPipelineComponentAdmin** interfaces. AIComp.dll wraps the SAP DCOM connector, which provides input access to SAP by allowing the delivery of SAP iDoc messages. IDOC.dll is the DLL that is created from the SAP DCOM connector. iDoc.dll and AIComp.dll are build compatible; therefore, AIComp.dll must be recompiled with every new build/version of IDoc.dll.

Permission denied errors occur when accessing the BizTalk Server Administration Microsoft Management Console (MMC), BizTalk Messaging Manager, or the BizTalk Messaging Configuration object model

Problem: BizTalk Server 2000 Setup adds the local group BUILTIN\Administrators to the BizTalk Server Administrators group. However, a user that belongs to the Administrators group but does not belong explicitly to the BizTalk Server Administrators group will encounter permission denied errors when accessing the BizTalk Server Administration MMC, BizTalk Messaging Manager, or the BizTalk Messaging Configuration object model.

Solution: Use the Computer Management console to add individual users explicitly to the BizTalk Server Administrators group.

Upgrading from the Evaluation or Standard Edition to the Enterprise Edition of BizTalk Server

Issue: To upgrade to the Enterprise Edition of BizTalk Server, complete the following steps:

1. Uninstall the Evaluation or Standard Edition of BizTalk Server.

   Note that any receive functions that are configured will be lost; in addition, any configuration changes made to the BizTalk Server COM+ packages will be lost during the uninstallation. Do not delete the BizTalk Messaging Management, Shared Queue, and Tracking SQL Server databases.

2. Install the Enterprise Edition of BizTalk Server.

   During BizTalk Server setup, select the previously created BizTalk Messaging Management, Shared Queue, and Tracking SQL Server databases.

3. Recreate the receive functions and make any changes to the BizTalk Server COM+ packages, if required.

Installing or uninstalling BizTalk Server fails to add or remove BizTalk Server COM+ applications

Problem: When the Microsoft Distributed Transaction Coordinator (MSDTC) is stopped, installing or uninstalling BizTalk Server fails to add or remove BizTalk Server COM+ applications.

Solution: Ensure that the MSDTC service is running before installing or uninstalling BizTalk Server COM+ applications.

BizTalk Server parsers do not recognize Julian dates

Problem: BizTalk Server parsers do not recognize the Julian date format in an incoming document instance. A Julian date format includes three digits that indicate the day (DDD). Although it is possible to create specifications in BizTalk Editor that use the Julian date format, this capability is provided for use only with custom parsers that can recognize document instances using the Julian date format.

Solution: Do not use the Julian date format in a specification or a document instance unless you are employing a custom parser that recognizes the Julian date format.

How to Use Help

How to Use Help

The Microsoft BizTalk Server 2000 Help system uses HTML to format and display information. The Help Viewer provides an integrated table of contents, an index, and a full-text search feature so that you can find information easily. Book icons open to reveal sub-books and topics. To expand the table of contents and view topics within a book, click the expand indicator (+) next to a book title. When you click the collapse indicator (-), the topics are hidden. The Help Viewer has the added benefit of enabling you to see the table of contents, index, or search results at the same time you are viewing a Help topic.

The Help Viewer also includes the **Favorites** tab, which you can use to bookmark topics. This enables you to quickly display topics that you refer to often.

To learn more about BizTalk Server 2000, you can use the table of contents to browse through the documentation. When you click a topic in the table of contents, information is displayed in the content pane of the Help window.

The table of contents is organized in books according to the major features and functions that BizTalk Server 2000 provides. Within each book, you can find chapters that contain the following information:

- How To
- Concepts
- Troubleshooting
- Resources

For procedural and task-based information, start with the How To chapters. For more general information about BizTalk Server 2000, its features, and other information, start with the Concepts and Resources chapters.

For programming information in the BizTalk Server 2000 Interface Reference, you can use a language-filtering tool to view information specific to Microsoft Visual Basic, Visual C++, or both.

Finding a Help Topic

In the Help Viewer, the following browse and search options are available:

- **Contents tab**

  1. To browse through the table of contents, click the **Contents** tab.

  2. Double-click the book icons to reveal topic entries and sub-books.

  3. Click a table-of-contents entry to display the corresponding topic.

- **Index tab**

  1. To see a list of index entries, click the **Index** tab and then either type a word or scroll through the list.

     Topics are often indexed under more than one entry.

  2. Double-click an index entry to display the corresponding topic.

- **Search tab**

  1. To locate every occurrence of a word or phrase, click the **Search** tab, type the word or phrase for which you want to search, and then click **List Topics**.

     To improve the search results, combine multiple words or phrases with AND, OR, NEAR, or NOT.

  2. Double-click a search results entry to display the corresponding topic.

- **Favorites tab**

  1. To bookmark a topic, use the **Contents**, **Index**, or **Search** tab to locate and then display a topic.

  2. Click the **Favorites** tab and click **Add** to save the topic title to the **Topics** list.

  3. Double-click a bookmark in the **Topics** list to quickly display the topic.

Bookmarking a Help Topic

1. Use the **Contents**, **Index**, or **Search** tab to locate and then display the topic you want to bookmark.

2. Click the **Favorites** tab and click **Add**.

The Help Viewer adds the topic title to the **Topics** list. Later, you can return to this list and double-click the bookmark to quickly display the topic.

Notes

- You can create a list of favorite/frequently visited Help topics.

- To remove a bookmark from the **Topics** list, click the bookmark and click **Remove**.

Copying a Help Topic

1. In the topic pane of the Help Viewer, right-click inside the topic you want to copy and click **Select All**.

2. Inside the topic, right-click again and click **Copy**.

   This copies the topic to the Clipboard.

3. Open the document to which you want to copy the topic.

4. Click the place in your document where you want the information to appear.

5. On the **Edit** menu, click **Paste**.

✒ Notes

- If you want to copy only part of a topic, select the part you want to copy, right-click the selection, and then click **Copy**.

- Step numbers are not copied to the Clipboard.

Printing a Help Topic

To print a single topic

1. Right-click the topic you want to print and click **Print**.

2. In the **Print** dialog box, click **Print**.

   –Or–

1. On the **Contents** tab, select a topic.

2. On the toolbar, click **Print**, click **Print the selected topic**, and then click **OK**.

3. In the **Print** dialog box, click **Print**.

To print all topics within a book

1. On the **Contents** tab, select a book.

2. On the toolbar, click **Print**, click **Print the selected heading and all subtopics**, and then click **OK**.

3. In the **Print** dialog box, click **Print**.

◆ Important

- It is recommended that the page orientation be set to **Landscape**; however, printing code samples, large illustrations, and significant text might result in incomplete printing.

Changing the Font Size

You can increase the font size of text for easier viewing, or you can decrease the font size to see a representation of the layout of a page.

- On the toolbar, click the **Font** (⃝) button to increase or decrease the text size.

Using Language Filtering

To provide only the information that is relevant to your programming environment, BizTalk Server 2000 Help implements a language-filtering tool. On the title bar of topics in the BizTalk Server 2000 Interface Reference, you will find a filter button that provides a language menu. This menu gives you the choice of viewing documentation tailored either to Visual C++ or to Visual Basic. If you choose **Show All**, you will see information for both languages. Regardless of your language selection, you will always see information (such as general concepts) that is relevant to both languages.

- To view the language-filtering options, click the filter (⃝) button on the title bar and click one of the following options:
- **C++**
- **Visual Basic**
- **Show All**

🖉 Note

- When you select a language-filtering option, that selection remains in effect for all other pages that you view until you change the option again.

Help Viewer Shortcut Keys

You can use shortcut keys to accomplish tasks in the BizTalk Server 2000 Help Viewer. The following table is a quick reference to the shortcut keys available in Help Viewer.

🖉 Note

- Functionality that is not included in this list can be obtained by using the numeric keypad to move the mouse pointer with MouseKeys. For more information about MouseKeys in Windows 2000 Server Help, see "Using the keyboard to move the mouse pointer." In Windows 2000 Professional Help, see "To move the mouse pointer by using MouseKeys."

Help Viewer shortcut keys

Press	To
ALT+SPACEBAR	Display the system menu.
SHIFT+F10	Display the Help Viewer shortcut menu.
	📝 **Note**
	• Use this shortcut when the focus is in the topic pane.
ALT+TAB	Switch between the Help Viewer and other open windows.
ALT+O	Display the **Options** menu.
ALT+O, and then press T	Hide or show the navigation pane.
CTRL+TAB	Switch to the next tab in the navigation pane.
CTRL+SHIFT+TAB	Switch to the previous tab in the navigation pane.
UP ARROW	Move up one topic in the table of contents, index, or search results list.
DOWN ARROW	Move down one topic in the table of contents, index, or search results list.
PAGE UP	Move up one page in the table of contents, index, or search results list.
PAGE DOWN	Move down one page in the table of contents, index, or search results list.
F6	Switch focus between the navigation pane and the topic pane.
ALT+O, and then press R	Refresh the topic that appears in the topic pane.
UP ARROW or DOWN ARROW	Scroll through a topic.
CTRL+HOME	Move to the beginning of a topic.
CTRL+END	Move to the end of a topic.
CTRL+A	Highlight all text in the topic pane.
ALT+O, and then press P	Print a topic.
ALT+O, and then press B	Move back to the previously viewed topic.
ALT+O, and then press F	Move forward to the next (previously viewed) topic.
TAB	Move between related topics.
	📝 **Note**
	• Use this shortcut when the focus is in the topic pane.
ALT+F4	Close the Help Viewer.

Contents tab shortcut keys

Press	To
ALT+C	Display the **Contents** tab.
RIGHT ARROW	Open a book.
LEFT ARROW	Close a book.
BACKSPACE	Return to the previous open book.
UP ARROW or DOWN ARROW	Select a topic.
ENTER	Display the selected topic.

Index tab shortcut keys

Press	To
ALT+N	Display the **Index** tab.
UP ARROW or DOWN ARROW	Select a keyword in the list.
ALT+D or ENTER	Display the associated topic.

Search tab shortcut keys

Press	To
ALT+S	Display the **Search** tab.
ALT+L	Start a search.
ALT+D or ENTER	Display the selected topic.

Favorites tab shortcut keys

Press	To
ALT+I	Display the **Favorites** tab.
ALT+A	Add a topic to the **Topics** list.
ALT+P	Select a topic in the **Topics** list.
	☑ Note
	• Use this shortcut when the focus is in the topic pane and you want to move to the **Topics** list.
ALT+R	Remove a topic from the **Topics** list.
ALT+D	Display a topic from the **Topics** list.

Accessibility for People with Disabilities

Microsoft is committed to making its products easier for everyone to use. For information about features that make Microsoft BizTalk Server 2000 more accessible, see the following:

- "Help Viewer Shortcut Keys" earlier in this chapter.

- "BizTalk Editor Shortcut Keys" in Chapter 5, "Creating Specifications."

- "BizTalk Mapper Shortcut Keys" in Chapter 6, "Mapping Data."

- "BizTalk Orchestration Designer Shortcut Keys" in Chapter 8, "BizTalk Orchestration Services."

- "BizTalk Messaging Manager Shortcut Keys" in Chapter 9, "Configuring BizTalk Messaging Services."

- "BizTalk Server Administration Shortcut Keys" in Chapter 11, "Administering Servers and Applications."

- "BizTalk Document Tracking Shortcut Keys" in Chapter 13, "Tracking Documents."

Note

- For further information about accessibility options, in Windows 2000 Server online Help, in the Getting Started with Windows 2000 book, see "Accessibility for People with Disabilities." In Windows 2000 Professional online Help, see "Accessibility for Special Needs."

Contacting Microsoft Product Support Services

Product name: Microsoft BizTalk Server 2000

Support options: To get the latest information on your support options, go to the Microsoft Product Support Services Web site (support.microsoft.com/directory/productsupportoption.asp).

- **Worldwide support:** Options, hours, and cost in your country may differ from the United States; check with your local office for details.

- **Conditions:** Microsoft product support services are subject to then-current prices, terms, and conditions, which are subject to change without notice.

Online Support and Information

- Microsoft BizTalk Server 2000 Web site (www.microsoft.com/biztalkserver)

- Microsoft Product Support Services Web site (support.microsoft.com/directory/productsupportoption.asp)

- Microsoft COM Web site (www.microsoft.com/com/)

- Microsoft Message Queuing Web site (www.microsoft.com/msmq/)

- Microsoft SQL Server Web site (www.microsoft.com/sql/)

- Microsoft Windows Script Technologies Web site (msdn.microsoft.com/scripting/)

- Microsoft XML Developer Center Web site (msdn.microsoft.com/xml/default.asp)

- MSDN Online Web site (msdn.microsoft.com/default.asp)

- MSDN Online Library Web site (msdn.microsoft.com/library/default.asp)

- Microsoft Accessibility Web site (www.microsoft.com/enable/)

Glossary

A

abort

To cancel a transaction that is in progress, and to run an alternate business process instead.

action

To send or receive a message. Send or receive actions can be synchronous or asynchronous, depending upon which application services are implemented in an XLANG schedule.

ANSI X12

EDI standards set by Accredited Standards Committee X12, whose work is approved by the American National Standards Institute.

asynchronous communication

A single message that is either sent or received within the context of a single communication action.

See also: synchronous communication

B

binding

A process by which the technology used to implement a port is specified.

See also: port

BizTalk Document Tracking

A Web-based user interface (UI) that is used to access all BizTalk Messaging Services tracking information. It can also track XLANG schedule status for BizTalk Orchestration Services.

BizTalk Editor

A tool with which you can create, edit, and manage specifications. With BizTalk Editor you can create a specification based on a specification template, an existing schema, certain types of document instances, or a blank specification.

BizTalk Framework

A platform-neutral e-commerce framework that is based on Extensible Markup Language (XML) schemas and industry standards. The framework enables integration across industries and between business systems, regardless of platform, operating system, or underlying technology. Specifically, it is composed of three things: schema, products, and services. For more information about the BizTalk Framework, go to the BizTalk Web site (www.microsoft.com/biztalk/).

BizTalk Mapper

A tool with which you can create maps that define the correspondence between the records and fields in one specification and the records and fields in another specification. A map contains an Extensible Stylesheet Language (XSL) style sheet that is used by BizTalk Server to perform the transformation described in the map.

BizTalk Messaging Management database

A Microsoft SQL Server database that stores the information related to all server configurations, including group and server settings, receive functions, and all messaging configuration information for the objects that are created by using BizTalk Messaging Manager, or by accessing the BizTalk Messaging Configuration object model.

BizTalk Messaging Manager

A graphical user interface (UI) that can be used to configure BizTalk Messaging Services to exchange documents between trading partners and applications of the home organization.

See also: BizTalk Messaging Services

BizTalk Messaging Services

Services that include sending, receiving, parsing, and tracking documents; receipt generation and correlation; and data mapping, integrity, and security.

See also: BizTalk Messaging Manager

BizTalk Orchestration Designer

A design tool used to create drawings that describe long-running, loosely coupled, executable business processes. The XLANG schedule drawing is compiled into an XLANG schedule that is used to execute the automated business process.

BizTalk Orchestration Services

Services that include designing, compiling, and running XLANG schedules. Additional services include the ability to create custom COM+ applications to host dedicated XLANG schedule instances, and the persistence of XLANG schedules.

BizTalk Server 2000

A new Microsoft product for business-process automation and application-integration both within and between businesses. BizTalk Server 2000 provides a powerful Web-based development and execution environment that integrates loosely coupled, long-running business processes, both within and between companies.

BizTalk Server 2000 features include the composition of new and existing XLANG schedules; integration among existing applications; the definition of document specifications and specification transformations; and the monitoring and logging of run-time activity.

The server provides a standard gateway for sending and receiving documents across the Internet, as well as providing a range of services that ensure data integrity, delivery, security, and support for the BizTalk Framework and other key document formats.

BizTalk Server Administration

A Microsoft Management Console (MMC) interface that is used to administer the BizTalk Server 2000 group of servers and their properties, to monitor receive functions, and to monitor work items in the Microsoft SQL Server queues that the server group uses.

C

channel

A set of properties that designates the source of documents and defines specific processing steps that are performed by BizTalk Messaging Services before a document is delivered to the destination designated by the messaging port or distribution list with which the channel is associated.

See also: open channel, open messaging port, pass-through submission, receipt channel, source application, source organization, trading partner

channel filtering

To compare the value of fields within a document instance to values in expressions designated within a channel. This comparison filters the selection of which channel or channels the server invokes to process a document.

checkpoint

A storage location in the Shared Queue database in which the current state of a work item is stored. In case of a server failure, documents that were queued to the failed server can be retrieved from the Shared Queue database and redistributed to other servers within the server group, based on the information provided by the checkpoint.

code list

A list of code values used as abbreviations for a variety of textual information. For example, ST is the code list value for Ship To and is most commonly used to qualify an address.

commit

To implement all changes requested by a pending transaction. This action occurs when all actions within a transaction are successfully completed.

Communication shapes

Shapes that are used to identify the exact content of a message and type of application service that is implemented within an XLANG schedule drawing. This category of shapes includes **Constants**, **Message**, **Port**, and **Port References**.

See also: Flowchart shapes, Implementation shapes, XLANG schedule drawing

compensation

A process by which reparation is made for a completed transaction. For example, if payment has been made for an order that then cannot be fulfilled, the payment is returned to the purchaser.

compile

In BizTalk Mapper, to create an Extensible Stylesheet Language Transformations (XSLT) version of a map that can be used by BizTalk Server. The map is stored in the WebDAV repository and used by BizTalk Server to translate one document format into another document format.

See also: data mapping, data translation, Extensible Markup Language (XML), map

concurrency

Two or more actions that are carried out at the same time.

D

data mapping

In BizTalk Mapper, to create a correspondence between the records and fields of a source specification and the records and fields of a destination specification.

See also: compile, data translation

data translation

A process that converts data from one format to another format. Data translation occurs within BizTalk Server at run time. The rules that are specified in a map are used to convert data from a source specification format to a destination specification format, as well as to perform any operations or calculations that are required on the data.

See also: compile, data mapping, Extensible Markup Language (XML), map

decision

A process that evaluates one or more rules sequentially. In BizTalk Orchestration Designer, a decision is represented by the **Decision** shape. Rules are Microsoft Visual Basic Scripting Edition (VBScript) expressions that are used by **Decision** and **While** shapes.

dehydrate

To store all state information for an XLANG schedule instance in a Microsoft SQL Server database while the XLANG Scheduler Engine is waiting to receive a message before executing the next action in the business process.

See also: XLANG Scheduler Engine

dehydrated schedule

A schedule that is stored in a database temporarily while waiting for receipt of a message before continuing to the next action in the sequence. All state information about the schedule is stored in the database until the message is received. Dehydrating schedules reduces the load on the computer that is hosting the schedule.

delimited flat file

A file that contains one or more records that are represented as a group of fields separated by a delimiter character. The records themselves are also separated by delimiter characters.

destination application

A home-organization application that has been designated in a messaging port as the destination for documents.

See also: home organization

destination organization

A trading partner organization that has been designated in a messaging port as the destination for documents.

See also: openness, organization, source organization

destination specification

The specification in a map that represents the outgoing document. BizTalk Mapper maps from a source specification to a destination specification.

See also: source specification

dictionary

A collection of properties associated with each item of work processed by BizTalk Server. These properties are exposed in BizTalk Editor so that users can tell BizTalk Server how to find values within document instances for properties that are used to locate a messaging port.

distribution list

A group of messaging ports that can be used to send the same document to several different trading partner organizations or applications of the home organization. In the BizTalk Messaging Configuration object model, this is referred to as a port group.

See also: home organization, messaging port, trading partner

document definition

A set of properties that represents a specific document. Document definition properties include a pointer to a document specification and can include global tracking fields and selection criteria.

See also: global tracking fields, selection criteria

document instance

A representation of the actual data that is sent to BizTalk Server. A document instance differs from a specification in that the specification defines the structure of the data, while a document instance is a representation of the specific data contained in a structure.

See also: global tracking fields, pass-through submission

document standard

The structure that defines a transaction set, such as an X12 850 standard. An implementation guideline can be created from a document standard.

document type

A designation for the type of document on which a specification is based. For example, if a specification is based on 850Schema.xml from the X12 standard, when that specification is opened in BizTalk Editor, 850 appears in the document type field on the **Reference** tab for the root node.

document type definition (DTD)

A standard definition that specifies which elements and attributes might be present in other elements and attributes and that specifies any constraints on their ordering, frequency, and content.

dynamic port

A port that requires that specific location information be provided for an XLANG schedule at run time. The location for a dynamic port is provided by a message that passes the location information to the reference for the port at run time.

See also: port, static port

dynamic queue

A queue that has an unknown address. Ports that use a Message Queuing implementation can use a dynamic queue when the location of the queue is not known. The address of this queue must be provided by a message that passes the queue address to the reference for the port at run time.

See also: per-instance queue, static queue

E

EDIFACT

Electronic Data Interchange For Administration, Commerce, and Transport. The international EDI standard as developed through the United Nations. This standard is commonly used in Europe, as well as Japan and other Asian countries and regions. Also known as UN/EDIFACT.

electronic data interchange (EDI)

A set of standards used to control the transfer of documents, such as purchase orders and invoices, between computers.

See also: selection criteria

envelope

1. A set of properties that defines an envelope. Envelope properties include an envelope format and can include a pointer to an envelope specification.

2. Header and footer information, or header information only, that encapsulates or precedes document data for transport.

envelope format

The format of documents that an envelope can contain; for example, XML or X12.

Extensible Markup Language (XML)

A specification developed by the World Wide Web Consortium (W3C) that enables designers to create customized tags beyond the capabilities of standard HTML. While HTML uses only predefined tags to describe elements within the page, XML enables the developer of the page to define tags. Tags for virtually any data item, such as a product or an amount due, can be used for specific applications. This enables Web pages to function as database records.

See also: compile, data translation, map, XML-Data Reduced (XDR), XPath

Extensible Stylesheet Language (XSL)

A style sheet format for Extensible Markup Language (XML) documents. XSL is used to define the display of XML in the same way that cascading style sheets (CSS) are used to define the display of Hypertext Markup Language (HTML). BizTalk Server uses XSL as the translation language between two specifications.

F

Flowchart shapes

Shapes that represent the routing logic in an XLANG schedule drawing. This category of shapes includes **Abort**, **Action**, **Begin**, **Decision**, **End**, **Fork**, **Join**, **Transaction**, and **While**.

See also: Communication shapes, Flowchart stencil, Implementation shapes, XLANG schedule drawing

Flowchart stencil

A drawing stencil provided by BizTalk Orchestration Designer. The **Flowchart** stencil provides all the shapes that can be used to design the process flow of a business process that can be executed by a running XLANG schedule.

See also: Flowchart shapes, Implementation stencil

functoid

Built-in reusable function that enables complex structural manipulation operations between source specification elements, destination specification elements, and other functoids.

See also: link

Functoid Palette

A toolbox that contains all functoids that can be used to create relationships between source specification elements and destination specification elements.

G

global tracking fields

Document specification fields, designated in a document definition, that are logged to a tracking database for each instance of an actual document processed by BizTalk Messaging Services.

See also: document definition, document instance

H

home organization

An object that represents your business in BizTalk Messaging Manager. The home organization is created for you when BizTalk Server 2000 is installed. Only the home organization can have applications.

See also: destination application, distribution list, organization, source application, trading partner

I

Implementation shapes

Shapes that represent the technologies that the XLANG Scheduler Engine supports. This category of shapes includes **BizTalk Messaging**, **COM Component**, **Message Queuing**, and **Script Component**.

See also: Communication shapes, Flowchart shapes, Implementation stencil

Implementation stencil

A drawing stencil provided by BizTalk Orchestration Designer. The **Implementation** stencil provides all the shapes that can be used to bind a port to an implementation technology.

See also: Flowchart stencil, Implementation shapes

implementation technologies

Technologies used to implement a port in an XLANG schedule. The technologies supported by the XLANG Scheduler Engine include COM components, Windows Script Components, Message Queuing Services, and BizTalk Messaging Services.

industry standard

A defined standard that is used for the exchange of information. Standards are extensible, and they follow a well-defined set of rules, or syntax.

inner transaction

A transaction that is contained within the process flow of another transaction.

See also: long-running transaction, nested transaction, outer transaction, transaction

interchange

A collection of one or more document instances that comprises a single transmission and is exchanged from application to application within an organization or from one trading partner to another.

L

line-of-business (LOB) application

An organization's primary business application. BizTalk Server 2000 supports numerous communication protocols that enable line-of-business applications to reliably send and receive information.

link

In Microsoft BizTalk Mapper, a simple value-copy (or name-copy) operation from a field in the source specification to a field in the destination specification, or to a functoid.

See also: functoid

long-running transaction

A collection of actions that sends and receives messages over an indefinite period of time. Typically, long-running transactions contain several nested short-lived transactions.

See also: inner transaction, nested transaction, outer transaction, short-lived transaction, transaction

Loopback

A specific type of transport service that enables the return of current state data to the application from which the state data originated. Loopback uses the **SubmitSync** method call to restore the state data to the original application.

See also: transport services

M

map

An XML file that defines the correspondence between the records and fields in one specification and the records and fields in another specification. A map contains an Extensible Stylesheet Language (XSL) style sheet that is used by BizTalk Server to perform the transformation described in the map. Maps are created in BizTalk Mapper.

See also: compile, data translation, Extensible Markup Language (XML)

mapping

The process of specifying the way in which data in one structure is transformed into another structure.

message

1. A packet of data that is sent or received by an XLANG schedule.

2. In BizTalk Orchestration Designer, a shape on the **Data** page that corresponds to the messages in an XLANG schedule. **Message** shapes are composed of uniquely named fields, each containing a single data item of a specified data type.

messaging port

A set of properties that directs how documents are enveloped, secured, and transported to a designated destination organization or application.

See also: distribution list

moniker

A name that represents an object and that can include the complete path or address that identifies the location of the object.

See also: port

N

nested transaction

One or more transactions that are contained within the process flow of a larger transaction.

See also: inner transaction, long-running transaction, outer transaction, transaction

node path

An expression used to obtain XML element and attribute information, select data that matches specific criteria, and perform comparisons on the data retrieved. More formally known as XPath.

See also: XPath

non-self-routing document

A document that is missing one or more of the following pieces of routing information: source organization identifier, destination organization identifier, or document definition.

O

open channel

A channel that is explicitly declared as open to any source organization. The source data for an open channel is passed to BizTalk Messaging Services either within the document or in a parameter submitted with the document.

See also: channel, openness, source organization

open messaging port

A messaging port that is explicitly declared as open to any destination organization. The destination data for an open messaging port is passed to BizTalk Messaging Services either within the document or in a parameter submitted with the document.

See also: channel, openness, source organization

openness

A lack of explicit information about a source in a channel or destination in a messaging port. Channels contain information that identifies the source. Messaging ports contain information that identifies the destination. If a channel is designated as an *open source,* the source information is not explicitly declared in the channel and is provided by other means. Usually this information is contained in the instance of the document that is sent, or it is set as parameters in a **Submit** method call. Similarly, if a messaging port is designated as an *open destination,* the destination information is not explicitly declared in the messaging port and is instead provided in the document instance or in the parameters of a **Submit** method call.

See also: destination organization, open channel, open messaging port, source organization

organization

A trading partner or a business unit within a trading partner, or, in the case of the home organization, your own business.

See also: destination organization, home organization, organization identifier, source organization, trading partner

organization identifier

A set of properties that uniquely identifies an organization. An organization can have multiple organization identifiers. Organization identifiers consist of the following properties: a name, a qualifier, and a value.

See also: organization

outer transaction

A transaction that contains one or more transactions within its process flow.

See also: inner transaction, long-running transaction, nested transaction, transaction

P

parser

A component of BizTalk Server that translates non-XML files (for example, X12, EDIFACT, and flat file) into XML files.

pass-through submission

A submission that bypasses the parsing, decoding, decryption, transformation, and signature verification stages of processing. The document instance is passed directly to the channel that is specified in the submission parameters. This type of submission can be used to transmit binary files without data corruption, or to use only the server transport and global tracking features.

See also: channel, document instance

per-instance queue
A queue that is created for use with each new instance of an XLANG schedule.

See also: dynamic queue, static queue

persistence database
A database that is used to store XLANG schedule state when an XLANG schedule is dehydrated. A default database called the Orchestration Persistence database is provided during installation of BizTalk Server 2000.

pipeline component
A component created to integrate applications with BizTalk Server 2000. Developers can use either the **IPipelineComponent** or the **IPipelineComponentAdmin** interface, or the lighter-weight **IBTSAppIntegration** interface, to develop these components.

port
A named location that uses a specific implementation. In BizTalk Orchestration Designer, a port is defined by the location to which messages are sent or from which messages are received, and the technology that is used to implement the communication action. The location is uniquely identified by the name of the port.

See also: binding, dynamic port, moniker, port implementation, port location, port name, port reference, static port

port group
A group of messaging ports that can be used to send the same document to several different trading partner organizations or applications. In BizTalk Messaging Manager, this is referred to as a distribution list.

port implementation
A specific technology used by a port to implement a communication action.

See also: port, port location, port name, port reference

port location
The location associated with a specific port. The location is also dependent on the port implementation that is used. Each implementation provides a different type of location for the port.

See also: port, port implementation, port name, port reference

port name
A unique identification for a port. This identification is used to correlate the port location with a specific port.

See also: port, port implementation, port location, port reference

port reference
A unique message that contains the port location for every port in an XLANG schedule. The **Port References** shape is located on the **Data** page. Any data flow into or out of this message contains the port location for a port.

See also: port, port implementation, port location, port name

positional flat file

A file that contains fields that are the same fixed length, and that contains records that have a common end-of-record terminator.

Q

quiescent state

A state that represents processing activity that is inactive or at rest, or when a process is in standby mode.

R

receipt channel

A channel that contains the information necessary to process a receipt that can be returned to the sender of a document.

See also: channel

receive functions

Functionality that enables any BizTalk server(s) to monitor directories and submit documents to BizTalk Server for processing. BizTalk Server 2000 supports File and Message Queuing receive functions.

rehydrate

To retrieve all state information for an XLANG schedule instance from a Microsoft SQL Server database after a message is received by the XLANG Scheduler Engine.

See also: XLANG Scheduler Engine

reliable messaging

A feature of BizTalk Framework 2.0 protocol that supports guaranteed, once-only delivery of documents in heterogeneous environments across the Internet.

resubmit

A procedure that submits interchanges or documents to BizTalk Server from the Suspended queue. The document is processed from the point of failure.

Retry queue

A table within the Shared Queue database in Microsoft SQL Server. The Retry queue is associated with a server group that contains items of work scheduled for transmission after an initial transmission has been attempted.

See also: Scheduled queue, Shared Queue database, Suspended queue, transport services, Work queue

routing logic

The set of rules that determines the sequence of execution within an XLANG schedule. Routing logic is implemented by the **Decision** shape in BizTalk Application Designer.

S

Scheduled queue

A table within the Shared Queue database in Microsoft SQL Server. The Scheduled queue is associated with a server group that contains interchanges that have been received but not yet processed by BizTalk Server.

See also: Retry queue, Shared Queue database, Suspended queue, Work queue

schema

The definition of the structure of an XML file. A schema contains property information as it pertains to the records and fields within the structure.

selection criteria

A name-value pair designated in a document definition. The name-value pairs are used to uniquely identify a document definition for inbound EDI interchanges, based on values found in the functional group header, and to insert values in the functional group header for outbound EDI interchanges.

See also: document definition, electronic data interchange (EDI)

self-routing document

A document that contains all the necessary routing information, such as source and destination organization identifiers and a document definition, in the routing tags or within the document.

serializer

A component of BizTalk Server that translates XML files into non-XML files (for example, X12, EDIFACT, and flat files).

server group

A collection of individual servers that is centrally managed, configured, and monitored.

Shared Queue database

A Microsoft SQL Server database that is shared by all servers within a server group. The Shared Queue database stores all checkpoint information related to documents processed by BizTalk Server. If a server fails, other computers that use the same Shared Queue database can continue to retrieve messages from and post messages to the Work queue. This provides redundancy and process load balancing. The Shared Queue database is graphically presented in BizTalk Server Administration as a series of distinct queues.

See also: Retry queue, Scheduled queue, Suspended queue, Work queue

short-lived transaction

A collection of grouped actions that are performed as a single logical unit of work.

See also: long-running transaction, transaction

source application

A home-organization application that has been designated in a channel as the source of documents.

See also: channel, home organization

source organization

A trading partner organization that has been designated in a channel as the source of documents.

See also: channel, destination organization, open channel, open messaging port, openness, organization, trading partner

source specification

The specification in a map that represents the incoming document. BizTalk Mapper maps from a source specification to a destination specification.

See also: destination specification

specification

A BizTalk Server-specific XML schema. Specifications are created in BizTalk Editor and can be based on industry standards (such as EDIFACT, X12, and XML) or on flat files (delimited, positional, or delimited and positional). BizTalk Mapper uses specifications, opened as source specifications and destination specifications, to create maps.

state

The condition at a particular time of any of numerous elements of computing.

See also: XLANG schedule state

static port

A port that requires that all necessary information be provided for an XLANG schedule at design time. The designer who creates the XLANG schedule must know the location to which messages are sent or from which messages are received, as well as the technology chosen to implement the communication action.

See also: dynamic port, port

static queue

A queue that has a well-known address. Ports that use a Message Queuing implementation can use a static queue when the location of the queue is known and does not change.

See also: dynamic queue, per-instance queue

Suspended queue

A table within the Shared Queue database in Microsoft SQL Server. The Suspended queue is associated with a server group. The queue contains work items for which any error or failure was encountered during processing. The queue stores the documents until they can be corrected and reprocessed, or simply deleted.

See also: Retry queue, Scheduled queue, Shared Queue database, Work queue

synchronous communication

Messages that are sent or received in pairs and that occur within the context of a single communication action.

See also: asynchronous communication

T

Tracking database

A Microsoft SQL Server database associated with a server group that enables the tracking of documents that are processed by the server either individually or in batches. You can also track XLANG schedule status.

trading partner

An external organization with which your home organization exchanges electronic data. The messaging ports, distribution lists, channels, and XLANG schedules that you create govern the exchange of documents among trading partners.

See also: channel, distribution list, home organization, organization, source organization

transaction

A discrete activity within a computer system, such as an entry of a customer order or an update of an inventory item. Transactions are usually associated with database management, order-entry, and other online systems. In BizTalk Orchestration Designer, transactions are represented as a collection of actions that are grouped within a **Transaction** shape.

See also: inner transaction, long-running transaction, nested transaction, outer transaction, short-lived transaction

transaction set

A collection of segments in an EDI schema that has a specific order and a particular meaning for a particular business transaction.

transport services

A set of services that includes network protocols and application integration components (AICs).

BizTalk Server 2000 supports a core set of transport services. This enables the server to send documents to organizations or applications whether or not the applications are capable of communicating directly with the server by using a COM interface. BizTalk Server 2000 supports the File, HTTP, HTTPS, and SMTP network protocols and Message Queuing. Transport services are also referred to as transport components.

See also: Loopback, Retry queue

V

version

In BizTalk Server 2000, either a specific release number for a specification or the industry-standard version number from which a specification is created.

W

Web Distributed Authoring and Versioning (WebDAV)

An extension to the HTTP 1.1 standard that exposes a hierarchical file storage media, such as a file system, over an HTTP connection. WebDAV locks documents to prevent users from accidentally overwriting each other's changes. It also enables users to share and work with server-based documents, regardless of their authoring tools, platforms, or the type of Web servers on which the files are stored.

well-formed XML

A standard that dictates that an XML document that has a single root and elements must nest completely or not at all.

Work queue

A table within the Shared Queue database in Microsoft SQL Server. The Work queue is associated with a server group. It contains interchanges that are currently being processed by BizTalk Server 2000.

See also: Retry queue, Scheduled queue, Shared Queue database, Suspended queue

X

XLANG identity

A globally unique ID that is used to distinguish version instances of an XLANG schedule drawing. This property is read-only and cannot be changed. Every time an XLANG schedule drawing is updated, this identity is also updated. The XLANG identity can be used to correlate an XLANG schedule with the specific version of an XLANG schedule drawing from which the schedule was compiled.

XLANG language

A language that describes the logical sequencing of business processes, as well as the implementation of the business process by using various implementation technologies. The XLANG language is expressed in XML.

XLANG schedule

Specific business processes expressed in the XLANG language. An XLANG schedule is saved with the file extension .skx.

See also: XLANG schedule drawing, XLANG schedule instance, XLANG Scheduler Engine

XLANG schedule drawing

A drawing that represents a business process. In BizTalk Orchestration Designer, once a drawing is complete, it can be compiled and run as an XLANG schedule. An XLANG schedule drawing is saved with the file extension .skv.

See also: Communication shapes, Flowchart shapes, XLANG schedule, XLANG Scheduler Engine

XLANG schedule instance

An evocation of a schedule. An XLANG schedule represents only the business process and implementation services. A single instance, or multiple instances, of an XLANG schedule can be run by the XLANG Scheduler Engine. Different instances of the same XLANG schedule contain different messages, but all instances follow the same business-process rules.

See also: XLANG schedule, XLANG Scheduler Engine

XLANG schedule state

The information contained in an XLANG schedule instance. This information includes messages that have been sent or received by that instance, any COM objects used by that instance, and the progress of that instance toward the completion of the business process.

See also: state

XLANG Scheduler

The default COM+ application that is installed when you install BizTalk Server 2000. This application is used to host running instances of XLANG schedules.

XLANG Scheduler Engine

A service that runs XLANG schedule instances and controls the activation, execution, dehydration, and rehydration of an XLANG schedule.

See also: dehydrate, rehydrate, XLANG schedule, XLANG schedule drawing, XLANG schedule instance

XML-Data Reduced (XDR)

An XML Schema dialect proposed by Microsoft and submitted to the World Wide Web Consortium (W3C) in 1998. Like XML-Data, XDR is a syntax for Extensible Markup Language (XML) schemas that define the characteristics of an XML document. XDR is a subset of XML-Data.

See also: Extensible Markup Language (XML)

XPath

A comprehensive language used for navigating through the hierarchy of an XML document. XPath expressions can obtain XML element and attribute information, select data that matches specific criteria, and perform comparisons on the data retrieved. Also called a node path.

See also: Extensible Markup Language (XML), node path

Index

Ready solutions for the IT administrator

Keep your IT systems up and running with the ADMINISTRATOR'S COMPANION series from Microsoft. These expert guides serve as both tutorials and references for critical deployment and maintenance of Microsoft products and technologies. Packed with real-world expertise, hands-on numbered procedures, and handy workarounds, ADMINISTRATOR'S COMPANIONS deliver ready answers for on-the-job results.

Practical, *portable* guides for IT administrators

For immediate answers that will help you administer Microsoft products efficiently, get ADMINISTRATOR'S POCKET CONSULTANTS. Ideal at the desk or on the go from workstation to workstation, these hands-on, fast-answers reference guides focus on what needs to be done in specific scenarios to support and manage mission-critical products.

Microsoft® Windows NT® Server 4.0 Administrator's Pocket Consultant

U.S.A.	$29.99
U.K.	£20.99
Canada	$44.99

ISBN 0-7356-0574-2

Microsoft SQL Server™ 7.0 Administrator's Pocket Consultant

U.S.A.	$29.99
U.K.	£20.99
Canada	$44.99

ISBN 0-7356-0596-3

Microsoft Windows® 2000 Administrator's Pocket Consultant

U.S.A.	$29.99
U.K.	£20.99
Canada	$44.99

ISBN 0-7356-0831-8

Microsoft Press® products are available worldwide wherever quality computer books are sold. For more information, contact your book or computer retailer, software reseller, or local Microsoft Sales Office, or visit our Web site at mspress.microsoft.com. To locate your nearest source for Microsoft Press products, or to order directly, call 1-800-MSPRESS in the U.S. (in Canada, call 1-800-268-2222).

Prices and availability dates are subject to change.

mspress.microsoft.com

Microsoft® Resource Kits— powerhouse resources to minimize costs while maximizing performance

Deploy and support your enterprise business systems using the expertise and tools of those who know the technology best—the Microsoft product groups. Each RESOURCE KIT packs precise technical reference, installation and rollout tactics, planning guides, upgrade strategies, and essential utilities on CD-ROM. They're everything you need to help maximize system performance as you reduce ownership and support costs!

Microsoft® Windows® 2000 Server Resource Kit
ISBN   1-57231-805-8
U.S.A. $299.99
U.K.   £189.99 [V.A.T. included]
Canada $460.99

Microsoft Windows 2000 Professional Resource Kit
ISBN   1-57231-808-2
U.S.A. $69.99
U.K.   £45.99 [V.A.T. included]
Canada $107.99

Microsoft BackOffice® 4.5 Resource Kit
ISBN   0-7356-0583-1
U.S.A. $249.99
U.K.   £161.99 [V.A.T. included]
Canada $374.99

Microsoft Internet Explorer 5 Resource Kit
ISBN   0-7356-0587-4
U.S.A. $59.99
U.K.   £38.99 [V.A.T. included]
Canada $89.99

Microsoft Office 2000 Resource Kit
ISBN   0-7356-0555-6
U.S.A. $59.99
U.K.   £38.99 [V.A.T. included]
Canada $89.99

Microsoft Windows NT® Server 4.0 Resource Kit
ISBN   1-57231-344-7
U.S.A. $149.95
U.K.   £96.99 [V.A.T. included]
Canada $199.95

Microsoft Windows NT Workstation 4.0 Resource Kit
ISBN   1-57231-343-9
U.S.A. $69.95
U.K.   £45.99 [V.A.T. included]
Canada $94.95

mspress.microsoft.com

MICROSOFT LICENSE AGREEMENT

Book Companion CD

IMPORTANT—READ CAREFULLY: This Microsoft End-User License Agreement ("EULA") is a legal agreement between you (either an individual or an entity) and Microsoft Corporation for the Microsoft product identified above, which includes computer software and may include associated media, printed materials, and "on-line" or electronic documentation ("SOFTWARE PRODUCT"). Any component included within the SOFTWARE PRODUCT that is accompanied by a separate End-User License Agreement shall be governed by such agreement and not the terms set forth below. By installing, copying, or otherwise using the SOFTWARE PRODUCT, you agree to be bound by the terms of this EULA. If you do not agree to the terms of this EULA, you are not authorized to install, copy, or otherwise use the SOFTWARE PRODUCT; you may, however, return the SOFTWARE PRODUCT, along with all printed materials and other items that form a part of the Microsoft product that includes the SOFTWARE PRODUCT, to the place you obtained them for a full refund.

SOFTWARE PRODUCT LICENSE

The SOFTWARE PRODUCT is protected by United States copyright laws and international copyright treaties, as well as other intellectual property laws and treaties. The SOFTWARE PRODUCT is licensed, not sold.

1. GRANT OF LICENSE. This EULA grants you the following rights:

    a. Software Product. You may install and use one copy of the SOFTWARE PRODUCT on a single computer. The primary user of the computer on which the SOFTWARE PRODUCT is installed may make a second copy for his or her exclusive use on a portable computer.

    b. Storage/Network Use. You may also store or install a copy of the SOFTWARE PRODUCT on a storage device, such as a network server, used only to install or run the SOFTWARE PRODUCT on your other computers over an internal network; however, you must acquire and dedicate a license for each separate computer on which the SOFTWARE PRODUCT is installed or run from the storage device. A license for the SOFTWARE PRODUCT may not be shared or used concurrently on different computers.

    c. License Pak. If you have acquired this EULA in a Microsoft License Pak, you may make the number of additional copies of the computer software portion of the SOFTWARE PRODUCT authorized on the printed copy of this EULA, and you may use each copy in the manner specified above. You are also entitled to make a corresponding number of secondary copies for portable computer use as specified above.

    d. Sample Code. Solely with respect to portions, if any, of the SOFTWARE PRODUCT that are identified within the SOFTWARE PRODUCT as sample code (the "SAMPLE CODE"):

        i. Use and Modification. Microsoft grants you the right to use and modify the source code version of the SAMPLE CODE, *provided* you comply with subsection (d)(iii) below. You may not distribute the SAMPLE CODE, or any modified version of the SAMPLE CODE, in source code form.

        ii. Redistributable Files. Provided you comply with subsection (d)(iii) below, Microsoft grants you a nonexclusive, royalty-free right to reproduce and distribute the object code version of the SAMPLE CODE and of any modified SAMPLE CODE, other than SAMPLE CODE (or any modified version thereof) designated as not redistributable in the Readme file that forms a part of the SOFTWARE PRODUCT (the "Non-Redistributable Sample Code"). All SAMPLE CODE other than the Non-Redistributable Sample Code is collectively referred to as the "REDISTRIBUTABLES."

        iii. Redistribution Requirements. If you redistribute the REDISTRIBUTABLES, you agree to: (i) distribute the REDISTRIBUTABLES in object code form only in conjunction with and as a part of your software application product; (ii) not use Microsoft's name, logo, or trademarks to market your software application product; (iii) include a valid copyright notice on your software application product; (iv) indemnify, hold harmless, and defend Microsoft from and against any claims or lawsuits, including attorney's fees, that arise or result from the use or distribution of your software application product; and (v) not permit further distribution of the REDISTRIBUTABLES by your end user. Contact Microsoft for the applicable royalties due and other licensing terms for all other uses and/or distribution of the REDISTRIBUTABLES.

2. DESCRIPTION OF OTHER RIGHTS AND LIMITATIONS.

    • **Limitations on Reverse Engineering, Decompilation, and Disassembly.** You may not reverse engineer, decompile, or disassemble the SOFTWARE PRODUCT, except and only to the extent that such activity is expressly permitted by applicable law notwithstanding this limitation.

    • **Separation of Components.** The SOFTWARE PRODUCT is licensed as a single product. Its component parts may not be separated for use on more than one computer.

    • **Rental.** You may not rent, lease, or lend the SOFTWARE PRODUCT.

    • **Support Services.** Microsoft may, but is not obligated to, provide you with support services related to the SOFTWARE PRODUCT ("Support Services"). Use of Support Services is governed by the Microsoft policies and programs described in the user manual, in "on-line" documentation, and/or in other Microsoft-provided materials. Any supplemental software code provided to you as part of the Support Services shall be considered part of the SOFTWARE PRODUCT and subject to the terms and conditions of this EULA. With respect to technical information you provide to Microsoft as part of the Support Services, Microsoft may use such information for its business purposes, including for product support and development. Microsoft will not utilize such technical information in a form that personally identifies you.

    • **Software Transfer.** You may permanently transfer all of your rights under this EULA, provided you retain no copies, you transfer all of the SOFTWARE PRODUCT (including all component parts, the media and printed materials, any upgrades, this EULA, and, if applicable, the Certificate of Authenticity), **and** the recipient agrees to the terms of this EULA.

- **Termination.** Without prejudice to any other rights, Microsoft may terminate this EULA if you fail to comply with the terms and conditions of this EULA. In such event, you must destroy all copies of the SOFTWARE PRODUCT and all of its component parts.

3. **COPYRIGHT.** All title and copyrights in and to the SOFTWARE PRODUCT (including but not limited to any images, photographs, animations, video, audio, music, text, SAMPLE CODE, REDISTRIBUTABLES, and "applets" incorporated into the SOFTWARE PRODUCT) and any copies of the SOFTWARE PRODUCT are owned by Microsoft or its suppliers. The SOFTWARE PRODUCT is protected by copyright laws and international treaty provisions. Therefore, you must treat the SOFTWARE PRODUCT like any other copyrighted material **except** that you may install the SOFTWARE PRODUCT on a single computer provided you keep the original solely for backup or archival purposes. You may not copy the printed materials accompanying the SOFTWARE PRODUCT.

4. **U.S. GOVERNMENT RESTRICTED RIGHTS.** The SOFTWARE PRODUCT and documentation are provided with RE-STRICTED RIGHTS. Use, duplication, or disclosure by the Government is subject to restrictions as set forth in subparagraph (c)(1)(ii) of the Rights in Technical Data and Computer Software clause at DFARS 252.227-7013 or subparagraphs (c)(1) and (2) of the Commercial Computer Software—Restricted Rights at 48 CFR 52.227-19, as applicable. Manufacturer is Microsoft Corporation/One Microsoft Way/Redmond, WA 98052-6399.

5. **EXPORT RESTRICTIONS.** You agree that you will not export or re-export the SOFTWARE PRODUCT, any part thereof, or any process or service that is the direct product of the SOFTWARE PRODUCT (the foregoing collectively referred to as the "Restricted Components"), to any country, person, entity, or end user subject to U.S. export restrictions. You specifically agree not to export or re-export any of the Restricted Components (i) to any country to which the U.S. has embargoed or restricted the export of goods or services, which currently include, but are not necessarily limited to, Cuba, Iran, Iraq, Libya, North Korea, Sudan, and Syria, or to any national of any such country, wherever located, who intends to transmit or transport the Restricted Components back to such country; (ii) to any end user who you know or have reason to know will utilize the Restricted Components in the design, development, or production of nuclear, chemical, or biological weapons; or (iii) to any end user who has been prohibited from participating in U.S. export transactions by any federal agency of the U.S. government. You warrant and represent that neither the BXA nor any other U.S. federal agency has suspended, revoked, or denied your export privileges.

6. **NOTE ON JAVA SUPPORT.** THE SOFTWARE PRODUCT MAY CONTAIN SUPPORT FOR PROGRAMS WRITTEN IN JAVA. JAVA TECHNOLOGY IS NOT FAULT TOLERANT AND IS NOT DESIGNED, MANUFACTURED, OR INTENDED FOR USE OR RESALE AS ON-LINE CONTROL EQUIPMENT IN HAZARDOUS ENVIRONMENTS REQUIRING FAIL-SAFE PERFOR-MANCE, SUCH AS IN THE OPERATION OF NUCLEAR FACILITIES, AIRCRAFT NAVIGATION OR COMMUNICATION SYSTEMS, AIR TRAFFIC CONTROL, DIRECT LIFE SUPPORT MACHINES, OR WEAPONS SYSTEMS, IN WHICH THE FAILURE OF JAVA TECHNOLOGY COULD LEAD DIRECTLY TO DEATH, PERSONAL INJURY, OR SEVERE PHYSICAL OR ENVIRONMENTAL DAMAGE. SUN MICROSYSTEMS, INC. HAS CONTRACTUALLY OBLIGATED MICROSOFT TO MAKE THIS DISCLAIMER.

DISCLAIMER OF WARRANTY

NO WARRANTIES OR CONDITIONS. MICROSOFT EXPRESSLY DISCLAIMS ANY WARRANTY OR CONDITION FOR THE SOFTWARE PRODUCT. THE SOFTWARE PRODUCT AND ANY RELATED DOCUMENTATION ARE PROVIDED "AS IS" WITHOUT WARRANTY OR CONDITION OF ANY KIND, EITHER EXPRESS OR IMPLIED, INCLUDING, WITHOUT LIMITATION, THE IMPLIED WARRANTIES OF MERCHANTABILITY, FITNESS FOR A PARTICULAR PURPOSE, OR NONINFRINGEMENT. THE ENTIRE RISK ARISING OUT OF USE OR PERFORMANCE OF THE SOFTWARE PRODUCT REMAINS WITH YOU.

LIMITATION OF LIABILITY. TO THE MAXIMUM EXTENT PERMITTED BY APPLICABLE LAW, IN NO EVENT SHALL MICROSOFT OR ITS SUPPLIERS BE LIABLE FOR ANY SPECIAL, INCIDENTAL, INDIRECT, OR CONSEQUENTIAL DAMAGES WHATSOEVER (INCLUDING, WITHOUT LIMITATION, DAMAGES FOR LOSS OF BUSINESS PROFITS, BUSINESS INTERRUP-TION, LOSS OF BUSINESS INFORMATION, OR ANY OTHER PECUNIARY LOSS) ARISING OUT OF THE USE OF OR INABILITY TO USE THE SOFTWARE PRODUCT OR THE PROVISION OF OR FAILURE TO PROVIDE SUPPORT SERVICES, EVEN IF MICROSOFT HAS BEEN ADVISED OF THE POSSIBILITY OF SUCH DAMAGES. IN ANY CASE, MICROSOFT'S ENTIRE LIABIL-ITY UNDER ANY PROVISION OF THIS EULA SHALL BE LIMITED TO THE GREATER OF THE AMOUNT ACTUALLY PAID BY YOU FOR THE SOFTWARE PRODUCT OR US$5.00; PROVIDED, HOWEVER, IF YOU HAVE ENTERED INTO A MICROSOFT SUPPORT SERVICES AGREEMENT, MICROSOFT'S ENTIRE LIABILITY REGARDING SUPPORT SERVICES SHALL BE GOV-ERNED BY THE TERMS OF THAT AGREEMENT. BECAUSE SOME STATES AND JURISDICTIONS DO NOT ALLOW THE EXCLUSION OR LIMITATION OF LIABILITY, THE ABOVE LIMITATION MAY NOT APPLY TO YOU.

MISCELLANEOUS

This EULA is governed by the laws of the State of Washington USA, except and only to the extent that applicable law mandates governing law of a different jurisdiction.

Should you have any questions concerning this EULA, or if you desire to contact Microsoft for any reason, please contact the Microsoft subsidiary serving your country, or write: Microsoft Sales Information Center/One Microsoft Way/Redmond, WA 98052-6399.

System Requirements

The evaluation software included with this book has a 120-day limit on use; the software will automatically be disabled four months after installation. The 120-day evaluation editions of BizTalk Server 2000 and SQL Server 2000 can be upgraded on your system to full versions. The 120-day evaluation edition of Visio 2000 should be uninstalled from your system prior to upgrading to a full version.

The 120-day evaluation editions provided with this book are not the full retail product and are provided only for the purpose of evaluation. Microsoft Technical Support does not support these evaluation editions. For additional support information regarding this book and the CD-ROMs (including answers to commonly asked questions about installation and use), visit the Microsoft Press Technical Support Web site at *http://mspress.microsoft.com/support/*. You can also email *mspinput@microsoft.com*, or send a letter to Microsoft Press, Attn: Microsoft Press Technical Support, One Microsoft Way, Redmond, WA 98502-6399.

Evaluation Edition of Microsoft BizTalk Server 2000 Enterprise Edition

To use the BizTalk Evaluation Edition software, you need a computer equipped with the following minimum configuration:

- PC with a Pentium-compatible 300-MHz or higher processor.

- Microsoft Windows 2000 Server with Service Pack 1 or later, Windows 2000 Advanced Server with Service Pack 1 or later, or Windows 2000 Professional with Service Pack 1 or later operating system.

- Minimum of 128 MB of RAM. Additional memory may be required, depending on operating system requirements.

- 6 GB of available hard-disk space. Actual requirements will vary based on your system configuration and the applications and features you choose to install.

- Microsoft Internet Explorer 5.0 or later.

- Microsoft Visio 2000 Standard Edition SR-1 or 120-day evaluation edition of Visio 2000 Standard Edition SR-1 (included) required to use BizTalk Server Orchestration Designer.

- Microsoft SQL Server 7.0 with Service Pack 2, SQL Server 2000, or 120-day evaluation edition of SQL Server 2000 Enterprise Edition (included); must be installed before installing BizTalk Server.

- CD-ROM drive.

- VGA or higher-resolution monitor; Super VGA recommended.

- Microsoft Mouse or compatible pointing device.

Evaluation Edition of Microsoft Visio 2000 Standard Edition SR-1

To use the Visio Evaluation Edition software, you need a computer equipped with the following minimum configuration:

- PC with a Pentium-compatible 166-MHz or higher processor.

- Microsoft Windows 95 or later operating system, or Microsoft Windows NT operating system version 4.0 with Service Pack 3 or later.

- Minimum of 16 MB of RAM. Additional memory may be required, depending on operating system requirements.

- 80 MB of available hard-disk space.

Evaluation Edition of Microsoft SQL Server 2000 Enterprise Edition

To use the SQL Evaluation Edition software, you need a computer equipped with the following minimum configuration:

- PC with Pentium-compatible 166-MHz or higher processor.

- Microsoft Windows NT Server 4.0 or Windows NT Server 4.0 Enterprise Edition with Service Pack 5 or later, Windows 2000 Server, Windows 2000 Advanced Server, or Windows 2000 Datacenter Server operating system.

- Minimum of 64 MB of RAM (128 MB or more recommended). Additional memory may be required, depending on operating system requirements.

- Hard-disk space required:

  - 95–270 MB for database server; approximately 250 MB for typical installation

  - 50 MB minimum for Analysis Services: 130 MB for typical installation

  - 80 MB for Microsoft English Query (supported on Windows 2000 operating system but not logo certified)

- Microsoft Internet Explorer 5.0 or later.

Networking support for SQL Server: Microsoft Windows 95, Windows 98, Windows Millennium Edition, Windows NT 4.0, or Windows 2000 built-in network software (additional network software is not required unless you are using Banyan VINES or AppleTalk ADSP; Novell NetWare IPX/SPX client support is provided by the NWLink protocol of Windows networking.

Clients supported by SQL Server: Windows 95 (supported for client connectivity only; does not include graphical tools support), Windows 98, Windows Me, Windows NT Workstation 4.0, Windows 2000 Professional, UNIX (requires ODBC client software from a third-party vendor), Apple Macintosh (requires ODBC client software from a third-party vendor), and OS/2 (requires ODBC client software from a third-party vendor).

OWNER REGISTRATION CARD   *Register Today!*   0-7356-1384-2

Return the bottom portion of this card to register today.

Microsoft® BizTalk™ Server 2000 Documented

FIRST NAME   MIDDLE INITIAL   LAST NAME

INSTITUTION OR COMPANY NAME

ADDRESS

CITY   STATE   ZIP

(   )

E-MAIL ADDRESS   PHONE NUMBER

U.S. and Canada addresses only. Fill in information above and mail postage-free.
Please mail only the bottom half of this page.

**For information about Microsoft Press®
products, visit our Web site at
mspress.microsoft.com**

Microsoft®